ELECTIONS

4TH EDITION

A to Z

CQ PRESS | AMERICAN GOVERNMENT A TO Z SERIES

ELECTIONS

FOURTH EDITION

A TO Z

DAVE TARR
BOB BENENSON

⑤SAGE | **CQPRESS**

Los Angeles | London | New Delhi
Singapore | Washington DC

Los Angeles | London | New Delhi
Singapore | Washington DC

FOR INFORMATION:

CQ Press
An Imprint of SAGE Publications, Inc.
2455 Teller Road
Thousand Oaks, California 91320
E-mail: order@sagepub.com

SAGE Publications Ltd.
1 Oliver's Yard
55 City Road
London EC1Y 1SP
United Kingdom

SAGE Publications India Pvt. Ltd.
B 1/I 1 Mohan Cooperative Industrial Area
Mathura Road, New Delhi 110 044
India

SAGE Publications Asia-Pacific Pte. Ltd.
3 Church Street
#10-04 Samsung Hub
Singapore 049483

Acquisitions Editor: Doug Goldenberg-Hart
Developmental Editor: John Martino
Production Editor: Astrid Virding
Copy Editors: Mark Bast and Dan Gordon
Typesetter: C&M Digitals (P) Ltd.
Proofreader: Dennis Webb
Indexer: Kathy Paparchontis
Cover Designer: Auburn Associates, Inc., Baltimore, Maryland
Marketing Manager: Ben Krasney

Printed in the United States of America

Library of Congress Cataloging-in-Publication Data

Tarr, Dave.

Elections A to Z / Dave Tarr and Bob Benenson.—4th ed.

p. cm.
Includes bibliographical references and index.

ISBN 978-0-87289-769-4 (cloth)

1. Elections—United States—Encyclopedias. I. Benenson, Bob. II. Moore, John Leo, 1927-Elections A to Z. III. Title.

JK1976.T37 2012
324.60973′03—dc23   2012008921

This book is printed on acid-free paper.

12 13 14 15 16 10 9 8 7 6 5 4 3 2 1

CQ PRESS
AMERICAN GOVERNMENT A TO Z SERIES

With more than 1,000 easy-to-read alphabetical entries, the CQ Press American Government A to Z Series provides concise information on the institutions of American democracy. Available in print and online, these A to Z reference works are the best sources for any American government curriculum. They are ideal for high school coursework and for undergraduate survey courses.

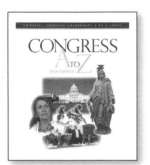

Congress
A to Z, **5th Edition**
No other volume so clearly and concisely explains the inner workings of the national legislature.

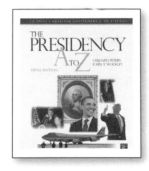

The Presidency
A to Z, **5th Edition**
This is an invaluable quick-information guide to the executive branch and its responses to the challenges facing the nation over time.

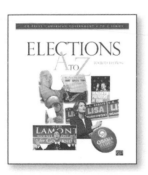

Elections
A to Z, **4th Edition**
This single, convenient volume explores vital aspects of campaigns and elections, from voting rights to the current state of House, Senate, and presidential elections.

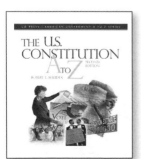

The U.S. Constitution
A to Z, **2nd Edition**
This is an ideal resource for anyone who wants reliable information on the U.S. Constitution and its impact on U.S. government and politics.

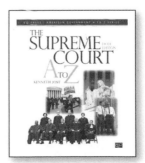

The Supreme Court
A to Z, **5th Edition**
This is the definitive source for information on the Court, its justices, and its impact on American democracy.

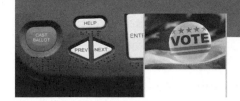

Contents

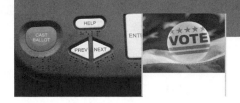

About the Authors

The original edition of *Elections A to Z* was written largely by John L. Moore with assistance from a number of Congressional Quarterly writers and CQ Press sponsoring editor Shana Wagger. Mr. Moore, who died in 2010, had a long journalistic career with Congressional Quarterly including service in the news department of the *CQ Weekly* magazine and, later, as assistant director in the book publishing division that today is known as CQ Press. Mr. Moore was the author of *Speaking of Washington,* published by CQ Press, and was involved in numerous other reference works on Congress and the federal government, including as volume editor of *CQ's Guide to U.S. Elections.*

The second edition was revised by Mr. Moore working with other seasoned CQ writers including David Hosansky, Patricia Ann O'Connor, Ron de Paolo, Kenneth Jost, and Bruce Maxwell. The third edition was revised by Bob Benenson, a thirty-year veteran of political reporting and CQ political editor from 1998 until 2010, and staff writer Gregory Giroux.

The new edition was revised by Bob Benenson, currently a freelance author based in Chicago, and David R. Tarr, former executive editor of CQ Press and editor of numerous CQ Press reference volumes. The editors are grateful to Doug Goldenberg-Hart, Senior Acquisitions Editor, January Layman-Wood, Reference Development Supervisor, and Sarah Walker, Associate Editor, for their excellent support.

About this Book

Elections A to Z is part of CQ Press's five-volume American Government A to Z series, which provides essential information about the history, powers, and operations of the three branches of government; the election of members of Congress and the president; and the nation's most important document, the Constitution. In these volumes, CQ Press's writers and editors present engaging insight and analysis about U.S. government in a comprehensive, ready-reference encyclopedia format. The series is useful to anyone who has an interest in national government and politics.

Elections A to Z offers accessible information about the historical foundations of U.S. elections, including the constitutional amendments that expanded the franchise to minorities, women, and youth; qualifications for office; pivotal events and groundbreaking candidates; campaign regulations and strategies; and the roles of political consultants, the media, and political parties. It also covers recent trends in House, Senate, presidential, and some state-level elections.

The fourth edition of *Elections A to Z* has been thoroughly updated to incorporate important contemporary events, such as the 2010 midterm elections that shifted party control in the House back to Republicans and brought into that chamber a new collection of deeply conservative members who, in 2011, used their influence to push the GOP even further to the right and in the process thwarted efforts at bipartisan agreement on major financial issues. The new edition discusses the emergence of the Tea Party movement that helped boost Republican candidates in 2010 elections and controversies over legislation in some states to require voters to show picture identifications to vote and to reduce opportunities for early voting. Editors have extensively updated developments in primary scheduling, campaign finance reform—including the important *Citizens United v. Federal Election Commission* decision in 2010—voting technology, and political participation. Also updated are discussions on reapportionment and redistricting for the next decade following the 2010 census. Also examined in more detail in this volume is the growing impact of social networking and new media, such as Twitter and Facebook, on the electoral scene.

The extensive appendix contains updated material on election topics including historical election returns, political party leadership and conventions, state government, and women, blacks, and Hispanics in Congress.

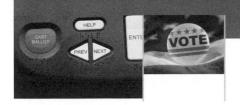

Preface

The first decade of the twenty-first century, as observed by those who participate in and chronicle elections as well as ordinary election buffs, was remarkable: tumultuous, volatile, angry, and unpredictable. And yet, as the nation headed into a national election in 2012 that promised to be one of the more important votes of recent times, the patterns and customs of the American system of choosing leaders—and in the process casting judgment on the leaders and their actions—was as recognizable as it was from the beginning of the nation.

As always, there is an accepted and peaceful transfer of power when the voters decide it is time for that to occur. The election process since the nation's early days has been defined largely by two dominant political parties, Republicans and Democrats or their predecessors—albeit with the periodic rise of third-party movements whose policies and ideas often find their way into the platforms of the dominant parties. Also, as has been frequently seen, elections may encompass significant differences of opinions among voters about the nature, the purpose, and the goals that should be pursued by the office holders elected by the voters.

The 2000s decade—if not a fundamental break from the past—stood out for the strains the nation encountered during the period. The election outcomes reflected those strains. Some traumatic events were unexpected, principally the terrorist attacks by Islamic extremists on September 11, 2001, even though similar—if far less serious—assaults on American interests had preceded it outside U.S. borders. Some were from decisions in the aftermath of September 11 to engage the nation in two lengthy and grinding wars from which the United States was still trying to find ways to extract itself as the 2012 voting approached. And others were self-inflicted, most notably the great economic recession that began in 2007 following the collapse of a vast housing bubble in which value seemed to go only up, until it burst.

The volatile political landscape to the decade was reflected in the mirror of elections beginning in 2000, almost a year before the September 11 attacks, when Republican George W. Bush won a disputed and extraordinarily narrow victory in the presidential Electoral College when contested vote counts in one state, Florida, were awarded to him by a 5–4 ruling of the Supreme Court, even though the national popular vote was won by his opponent, Democrat Al Gore.

The Bush administration then embarked on controversial actions that became the foundation for increasing national discord for the decade, most notably a military invasion of Iraq to topple dictator Saddam Hussein on grounds that his regime was developing weapons of mass destruction, a presumed threat that turned out to be false. Bush, and the Congress that was controlled by Republicans for more than half the decade, stated a commitment to conservative fiscal principles but oversaw a rapid expansion of the national debt by enacting significant cuts in taxes, even while military spending was rapidly escalating, and creating expensive new programs in education ("No Child Left Behind") and health care (the Medicare prescription drug benefit).

Initially, Americans of both parties rallied behind Bush in his self-proclaimed "war on terror," and election judgments reflected that support. With the exception of a short time in the Senate, Republicans retained a congressional majority won first in 1994 and the president won reelection in 2004, this time by a small but clear majority.

It was after his reelection that the nation's voters began to shift, first as the Iraq war and a lesser conflict in nearby Afghanistan, which had provided a safe haven for the al Qaeda terrorists who committed the September 11 attacks, dragged on without an end in sight, then in 2005 when the federal government stumbled in providing relief to the human misery in New Orleans and elsewhere on the Gulf Coast caused by Hurricane Katrina, and especially by 2008 when the housing bubble burst and the economy—nationally and globally—all but collapsed. The first judgment by voters was rendered in 2006 when Democrats recaptured control of Congress for the first time since 1994. The second, and more decisive judgment, came in 2008 when Barack Obama won the presidency for the Democrats and his party significantly increased its congressional majorities.

Fully in control of two of the federal government branches for the first time in more than a decade and a half, Democrats undertook an aggressive and largely progressive agenda in a variety of areas but most notably in economic stimulus involving billions of federal dollars, financial support for banks and the troubled domestic auto industry that also totaled in the billions, tough financial regulation in the wake of economic collapse, and—most controversially—complex and far-reaching changes in the nation's health care system.

For their efforts, Democrats were punished two years later, in 2010 midterm elections, by the iron law of retrospective voting in which a deeply disaffected group of angry voters went to the polls and tossed out fifty-four House incumbents, all but two Democrats, thereby returning control of that chamber to the GOP. It was the largest number of incumbents sacked in one election since at least 1952. Voters also dismissed a bevy of Senate Democrats allowing a Republican pickup of six seats—not enough for majority control but ample to block Democratic initiatives and appointments.

The world of pundits concluded that the volatility came from the absence of devoted Democrats who backed Obama two years earlier, an energized Republican base that had moved more dramatically conservative, the continuing economic troubles with unemployment still at or above 9 percent, and a less quantifiable but nevertheless perceptible anxiety among some voters that a distant national government was intruding on their lives as never before.

Still, as the preface to this volume noted in 2007, much about American government at the beginning of a new century had not changed even with the roller coaster of voter sentiment of the 2000s. The tripartite government structure—executive, legislative, and judicial branches—was unchanged. The fundamental principal of federalism that defined America's political structure—federal and state governments dividing powers while sharing loyalty from citizens—was as vibrant as ever. And the nation remained a basically market-oriented society that eschewed other social and economic systems tried elsewhere. All this and more was still true in 2012.

Indeed, the 2000s elections provided many instances of the continually evolving strengths of deciding matters at the ballot box, albeit not always neatly and without ambiguity.

Two events in 2008 built on the long, sometimes painfully slow, march of broadening participation in the electoral process, from an early understanding of "the people" to mean propertied white men to the modern concept that also includes women, minorities, and young adults. One of those events was the election of Obama, the first African American chosen for the highest office in the land. The second was the success of his principal opponent for the Democratic nomination, Hillary Rodham Clinton, a New York senator at the time and former first lady during the presidency of her husband Bill Clinton. Although she eventually came up short in the nomination contest with Obama, she became the first female in American history with a legitimate chance of being elected president, and ended up being chosen by Obama to serve as his secretary of state.

Making sense of these ever-changing electoral trends is a primary purpose of *Elections A to Z*. The user will find in the more than 225 entries an approachable but definitive explanation of the nation's electoral process, from the historical developments leading to today's headlines to examinations of events behind those headlines.

The vast majority of the articles have been updated to reflect new information and more than half have been extensively revised. Campaign financing, for example, is discussed in multiple entries, including a description of the much discussed—and highly controversial—Supreme Court decision in 2010 (*Citizens United v. Federal Election Commission*) giving new free speech rights to corporations and unions that may—or may not—result in vast new political advocacy spending that could markedly alter campaign strategies and the flow of money into elections. New to the book is a separate entry on the Tea Party movement that emerged in 2009 and played a big role in Republican activism in 2010. Whether the Tea Party proves to be a limited-time event or a model of a future and much more conservative Republican Party may be seen in 2012 voting.

Among the dozens of articles that *Elections A to Z* editors have revised to account for changing issues in elections are the following: the impact of the decennial census in 2010 on reapportionment of House seats between states and redistricting within states that may alter political power balances for the next decade; changes in the political makeup of both major political parties and the growing role of independent voters; the rapidly expanding influence and use of the Internet and new media in politics; controversies over voter identification at the ballot box and early voting before the normal election day; the huge role of money in politics; and the increasing stampede among states to hold early presidential primaries.

The first decade of the twenty-first century was unlike any other since the 1930s and 1940s swept away an old global order and made possible more than a half century of social, economic, and political changes. Historians are not likely to credit the 2000s with that outsized role in the years that follow, but the decade has illuminated both the change and the continuity in the American electoral system. The volatility of the period leading up to the important 2012 national election may also prove to have cast a bright light on the American voters' attitude toward the never fully answered—or answerable—question of the fundamental nature and purpose of government and the government's proper role in society.

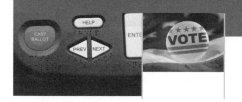

Historic Milestones in U.S. Elections

Few aspects of the American democratic system have changed so much as the elections process. Because the Constitution has little to say on the subject, the rules for choosing government leaders have developed gradually through events, legislation, and court opinions. Following are some major milestones in the course of that development.

1787

The "Great Compromise" at the Constitutional Convention in Philadelphia pacifies less-populous states by giving each state two senators and a House delegation based on population, assuring even the smallest state at least three votes in Congress (and in the Electoral College). Senators are to be elected by the state legislatures (changed to popular vote election in 1913 by the Seventeenth Amendment) for six-year terms. Representatives are to be popularly elected to two-year terms.

1789

George Washington wins the first U.S. presidential election, held on February 4. The election is tantamount to unanimous as Washington receives the maximum possible number of electoral votes, sixty-nine. (New

George Washington set many precedents during his two terms, often consciously so. Here, he delivers his inaugural address, in April 1789.

Source: Library of Congress

York's sixteen electoral votes are not cast because of a dispute in the state legislature; North Carolina, fourteen votes, and Rhode Island, six votes, also are not eligible because they have not yet ratified the Constitution.) John Adams, second with thirty-four votes, wins the vice presidency. Washington is inaugurated on April 30 in New York City, then the nation's capital. He is reelected in 1792.

1796

In the first competitive presidential election and the first to feature opposing political parties, Federalist candidate John Adams wins the first two-party presidential election. Democratic-Republican nominee Thomas Jefferson is second and therefore is elected vice president.

1800

Thomas Jefferson and Aaron Burr tie in electoral votes for the presidency. The election devolves to the House of Representatives, which elects Jefferson. The unforeseen possibility of a tie vote leads to adoption of the Twelfth Amendment to the Constitution (1804), requiring separate Electoral College voting for president and vice president.

1807

Jefferson formalizes Washington's two-term precedent for presidents, which until 1951 appears nowhere in law. Jefferson sets forth his reasons in a December 10 letter to the Vermont state legislature, which had asked him to run for a third term. Seven other states sent similar letters.

1824

The decades-long system of presidential candidate selection by congressional party caucuses, known as "King Caucus," comes to an end. State legislatures nominate four candidates representing different factions of the Democratic-Republican Party, which had dominated in a virtual single-party system for nearly a quarter-century. Andrew Jackson of Tennessee wins the popular vote but falls short of the required electoral vote majority, throwing the election to the House for the second time in U.S. history. The House elects John Quincy Adams of Massachusetts, who placed second in both the electoral and popular vote. Jackson's loss leads to his election in 1828 and formation of the present-day Democratic Party.

1831

The first national party conventions are held in Baltimore. The Anti-Masons nominate William Wirt in September, and the National Republicans nominate Henry Clay in December. Both lose to President Andrew Jackson, the Democratic nominee, in 1832.

1832

The Democrats hold their first national convention, also in Baltimore, and adopt a two-thirds rule for presidential nomination. Jackson is nominated for reelection by the required two-thirds majority vote.

1837

For the first and only time, the Senate decides a vice presidential election as the Constitution provides. Democrat Martin Van Buren's chosen running mate, Richard M. Johnson, falls one vote short of the required majority because Virginia's Democratic electors object to his moral character. The Senate nevertheless votes along party lines (33 to 16) to elect Johnson.

1840

Van Buren and Johnson become the first sitting president and vice president defeated for reelection. They lose to William Henry Harrison and John Tyler, candidates of the Whig Party, which was founded in 1834.

1841

Harrison dies April 4, 1841, just one month after his inauguration, becoming the first president to die in office. Tyler establishes the precedent for the vice president's becoming president rather than just the "acting president."

1844

Democrat James K. Polk, who was not expected to compete for the presidency, becomes the first dark-horse presidential candidate nominated by a major party. Polk goes on to win the election.

1850

Zachary Taylor, the second and last Whig to win the presidency, dies in office of natural causes. Vice President Millard Fillmore succeeds him but does not win the party's nomination for the 1852 election.

1854

Political activists opposed to the expansion of slavery into the western territories gather at Ripon, Wisconsin, and form the Republican Party. With the Whigs torn over the slavery issue, the Republicans soon emerge as the Democrats' counterpart in the nation's two-party system.

1856

Democrat Franklin Pierce becomes the only elected president denied renomination by his own party. He had alienated fellow northerners by signing legislation that made the Kansas territory a bloody battleground over the slavery issue. James Buchanan wins the Democratic nomination and the presidency.

1860

The new Republican Party elects its first president, Abraham Lincoln, and the divided nation advances toward Civil War. The election is the last in which at least one state (South Carolina) has no popular voting for president; instead, South Carolina's electors are chosen by the legislature.

(South Carolina allows popular voting after the war, when it and other former Confederate states resume participation in presidential elections.)

1865

Abraham Lincoln is assassinated six weeks after beginning his second term and just days after the surrender of the Confederacy brings an end to the Civil War and southern secession. While attending the theater in Washington, D.C., on the evening of April 14, he is shot by well-known actor John Wilkes Booth, a southern sympathizer. Lincoln dies the next day. Vice President Andrew Johnson succeeds to the presidency and immediately comes into conflict with the radical northern Republicans who plan harsh postwar treatment of the rebel states. The Radical Republicans gain control of Congress in the 1866 midterm elections and later impeach Johnson, who narrowly escapes conviction.

1870

The Fifteenth Amendment, enfranchising newly freed slaves, is ratified on February 3. The first blacks are elected to Congress: Republican Hiram R. Revels of Mississippi serves in the Senate from 1870 to 1871. Mississippi Republican Blanche K. Bruce is elected to the Senate in 1874 and is the first black member to serve a full term in that chamber.

1874

The donkey and elephant emerge as symbols of the Democratic and Republican parties after drawings by cartoonist Thomas Nast. Though initially intended by Nast as jabs at the parties, they are adopted by both and become important as guides to illiterate and semiliterate voters and as a boon to editorial cartoonists.

1876

A special commission decides a contested presidential election for the first and only time. Democrat Samuel J. Tilden wins the popular vote against Republican Rutherford B. Hayes, but the electoral vote outcome hangs on the disputed votes of three southern states. Congress appoints a commission that reaches a compromise on

Cartoonist Thomas Nast created enduring symbols of the two major parties: the Democratic donkey and Republican elephant.

Source: Library of Congress

March 2, 1877, and awards the votes to Hayes in return for his pledge to remove federal troops from the South. He wins by a bare Electoral College majority of 185–184.

1880

The Republican Party, stalemated over its choice of presidential nominee, drafts Rep. James A. Garfield of Ohio. His general election victory makes him the first—and, through 2008, only—president elected directly from the House of Representatives.

1881

On July 2, only four months after taking office, Garfield is shot in Washington, D.C., by Charles J. Guiteau, a deranged federal job seeker. The bullet lodges near Garfield's spine, and he dies on September 19. He is succeeded by Vice President Chester A. Arthur, who fails to win the Republican nomination in 1884.

1887

Congress enacts the Electoral Count Act, which charges states with resolving future electoral vote disputes similar to the one that followed the Tilden-Hayes contest in 1876.

1890

Wyoming enters the Union as the first state to enfranchise women. As a territory, Wyoming had given the vote to women in 1869.

1892

A mechanical voting machine built by Jacob H. Myers is used for the first time at Lockport, New York. Inventor Thomas A. Edison had received his first patent for a similar machine twenty-three years earlier.

Democrat Grover Cleveland becomes the first and still only president elected to two nonconsecutive terms. Cleveland first won in 1884; he was defeated in 1888 by Republican Benjamin Harrison, but then defeated Harrison in 1892. Cleveland, although eligible to seek reelection in 1896, declined to do so.

1901

The first presidential primary law is passed in Florida. The primary gets its biggest impetus when the 1904 Republican convention refuses seating to backers of Wisconsin governor Robert M. La Follette, leader of the GOP's Progressive wing. In 1905 La Follette successfully promotes legislation in his state that provides for primary election of delegates to national party conventions.

President William McKinley, a Republican first elected in 1896 and reelected in 1900, dies on September 14 in Buffalo, New York, of gunshot wounds inflicted by Leon Czolgosz, an anarchist who said he was acting in the name of victims of social injustice. McKinley is succeeded by Vice President Theodore Roosevelt. In 1904 Roosevelt is elected to a full four-year term, the first presidential successor ever to be so elected. Roosevelt's ebullient personality and support for the Progressive movement that was then a force in American politics made him so popular that he is later included, along with Washington, Jefferson, and Lincoln, as one of the four faces carved into South Dakota's Mount Rushmore.

1912

Roosevelt, disappointed in the turn toward traditional conservatism by his successor and former vice president William Howard Taft, deserts the Republican Party to run on his own Progressive "Bull Moose" ticket. He attains the highest third-party vote in history, but the split in the GOP helps to elect Democrat Woodrow Wilson.

1913

Popular election of senators becomes the norm when the Seventeenth Amendment is ratified, replacing election by state legislatures. Some states institute popular election of senators before it becomes mandatory, beginning with the 1914 midterm elections.

1916

Jeannette Rankin, a Montana Republican, becomes the first woman elected to the U.S. House, four years before the Nineteenth Amendment ensures women's suffrage in all states. During her two terms (1917–1919; 1941–1943) Rankin, an isolationist on foreign policy, becomes the only member of Congress to vote against both world wars.

1918

Socialist Party leader and perennial presidential candidate Eugene V. Debs is sentenced to ten years in prison for his statements against U.S. intervention in World War I, which began in 1917. He nevertheless receives almost a million votes (3.4 percent of the vote) in 1920, his last election. President Warren G. Harding, a Republican elected in 1920, frees Debs in 1921.

1920

The Nineteenth Amendment, giving full voting rights to women, is ratified on August 26. Some states allowed women to vote earlier. By 1918 fifteen states had enfranchised women.

1923

Harding dies in office August 2. Vice President Calvin Coolidge becomes president.

1924

The first female governors are elected: Miriam "Ma" Ferguson in Texas and Nellie Tayloe Ross in Wyoming. Ross succeeded her husband, who had died; Ferguson's husband had been impeached and removed from office.

1928

New York governor Alfred E. Smith, a Democrat, becomes the first Roman Catholic nominated for president on a major-party ticket. The urbanite Smith favors repeal of Prohibition, opposes the Ku Klux Klan, and is an unabashed liberal—all considered "alien traits" by much of the still rural, dry United States. He loses to Republican Herbert C. Hoover.

Oscar S. DePriest, a Republican from Chicago, is the first black elected to Congress in thirty years. The affinity for the Republican Party—the party of Abraham Lincoln—among those blacks who were allowed to vote later shifts dramatically to the Democrats, beginning with President Franklin D. Roosevelt's Depression-era New Deal economic programs and culminating in President Lyndon B. Johnson's efforts to enact civil rights legislation in the 1960s.

Franklin D. Roosevelt, center, surrounded by members of his cabinet. Roosevelt made an indelible mark on the United States in winning four successive presidential elections.
Source: Library of Congress

A stock market crash in October 1929 sets off an economic downturn that spirals into the Great Depression, ending nearly a decade of prosperity that had benefited the Republican Party. Hoover's reluctance to employ federal government resources to alleviate suffering caused by the Depression dooms his chances for reelection in 1932.

1932

At the Democratic National Convention in Chicago, Franklin D. Roosevelt becomes the first major-party candidate to accept a presidential nomination in person. In his acceptance speech, he promises a "new deal" for the American people; the term becomes the motto of his presidency and the driving force behind a vast expansion of the federal government. The Democrats win control of the White House and Congress as the nation battles the Great Depression, the worst in U.S. history. Roosevelt's first three-and-a-half months in office produce an unprecedented flood of economic legislation and establish the "hundred-day" yardstick for measuring the initial success of future presidents.

1934

The second session of the Seventy-third Congress meets for the first time on January 3 in accordance with the Twentieth Amendment (the so-called Lame Duck Amendment) to the Constitution. The amendment, ratified in 1933, also fixes January 20 as the beginning of each four-year presidential term, effective in 1937. Previously it had been March 4, by statute.

At their convention, Democrats abolish the two-thirds majority rule for presidential or vice presidential nomination, which previously resulted in protracted balloting. The South objects because the rule had assured the region virtual veto power over any nominee. To make up for the loss, the South is given more votes at later conventions.

1940

FDR becomes the only president to break the traditional two-term limit when he is elected for a third time. He benefits from public concerns about changing the nation's leadership at a time when aggression by Nazi Germany and Japan were drawing the United States closer to active involvement in World War II. His popular margin of victory narrows from four years earlier, however, in part because some voters object to his disregard of the unwritten "no-third-term" rule.

The Republicans hold the first televised national convention, in Philadelphia. With few Americans yet owning sets, the viewing audience is quite small.

1944

The Supreme Court in *Smith v. Allwright* outlaws white primaries. Previously, political parties as "private" organizations, particularly in the South, were permitted to exclude blacks from membership and participation.

1945

Roosevelt dies in office April 12, less than three months into the fourth term to which he was elected in 1944, and less than a month before the United States and its allies defeat Nazi Germany. He is succeeded by Vice President Harry S. Truman.

Truman's authorization of the use of atomic bombs at Hiroshima and Nagasaki forces Japan's surrender in August, bringing World War II to an end.

1946

Postwar economic problems, including inflation and management-labor conflicts that had been constrained during the war, contribute to the Republicans' first congressional majorities since before the Depression.

1948

Beset by continued economic adjustments and conflict with the Republican-controlled Congress, and lacking his predecessor's charisma, Truman begins his bid for a full term as president as an underdog—a situation seemingly made worse when party factions break away to form the States' Rights Party and the Progressive Party. But Truman shocks the pollsters and defeats his Republican challenger, Thomas E. Dewey. The upset produces a historic photo of Truman gleefully holding up the erroneous *Chicago Daily Tribune* banner headline, "Dewey Defeats Truman." Democrats regain control of both chambers of Congress.

1950

With the advent of the Cold War with the Soviet Union spurring a strong anticommunist move-ment in the United States, Sen. Joseph McCarthy, a Wisconsin Republican, muscles his way to the forefront with a speech alleging he had a list in his briefcase of names of numerous communists who had infiltrated the federal government.

1951

The Twenty-second Amendment, setting a two-term limit for presidents, is ratified February 27. Truman, who became president in 1945 on Roosevelt's death and was elected in his own right in 1948, was exempted from the law. He chose not to run again in 1952.

1952

Former general Dwight D. Eisenhower, who led Allied armies in Europe during World War II, enters politics as the Republican nominee and defeats Democrat Adlai E. Stevenson. (Eisenhower beats Stevenson again in 1956.) His running mate, Richard M. Nixon, survives a political controversy over whether political allies kept a secret financial account for him by giving an emotional address to the nation September 23. Nixon claims the only gift he received from a political associate was a little dog his young daughter named "Checkers"; the address is subsequently known as the "Checkers Speech."

1954

Strom Thurmond of South Carolina, then a Democrat, becomes the only senator ever elected by a write-in vote.

Democrats, who lost both the House and Senate in 1952, win both back and settle in for a long period of control. Republicans will not reclaim the majority in the Senate for twenty-six years and in the House for forty years.

1960

The first debate between presidential candidates, Democrat John F. Kennedy and Republican Richard M. Nixon, is televised from Chicago, Illinois, on September 26. The 1960 general election is the first in which television plays a major role in media coverage of the candidates and issues. With a narrow victory over Nixon, Kennedy becomes the first Roman Catholic president.

1962

The Supreme Court in *Baker v. Carr* permits federal court suits to require reapportionment and redistricting of state

John F. Kennedy used the relatively new medium of television to defeat Richard Nixon in the 1960 presidential election.

Source: National Archives

legislative districts that violate the principle of one person, one vote. The Court later extends the requirement to congressional districts.

1963

Gray v. Sanders, the first major one-person, one-vote Supreme Court decision, is handed down on March 18. The Court rules that Georgia's "county unit" system of electing officers to state posts violates the equal protection guarantee of the Fourteenth Amendment by giving more weight to the votes of persons in rural counties than in urban counties.

Civil rights leader Martin Luther King Jr. in August makes his "I have a dream" speech at the Lincoln Memorial in Washington, D.C.

President Kennedy is assassinated November 22 in Dallas, Texas; two days later Lee Harvey Oswald, a political malcontent arrested for the crime, is ambushed by nightclub owner Jack Ruby and shot dead while in police custody. Kennedy is succeeded by Vice President Lyndon B. Johnson, a former Senate majority leader who wins approval of much of Kennedy's "New Frontier" legislative program and uses his clout in the Democratic-controlled Congress to push historic civil rights legislation that ends officially sanctioned discrimination against blacks.

1964

The Twenty-fourth Amendment is ratified on February 4, abolishing the poll tax as a requisite to voting in primary or general elections for president and other federal officials. The controversial tax had often been a bar to voting, especially among poor blacks.

The Supreme Court hands down a decision in *Wesberry v. Sanders* February 17, extending the one-person, one-vote doctrine to congressional districts. The Court rules that substantial disparity in a state's district populations results in unequal representation in the U.S. House. Congressional districts should be as nearly equal in population "as is practicable."

Congress passes the Civil Rights Act of 1964, which prohibits discrimination in employment, public accommodations, and federally funded programs.

Lyndon B. Johnson scores the largest popular vote landslide in history, taking 61.1 percent of the vote against conservative Arizona Republican Barry Goldwater. LBJ's percentage surpasses FDR's 60.8 percent against Alfred M. Landon in 1936.

The stage is set for Johnson's Vietnam policy in 1964 when Congress, by an overwhelming margin, approves the Gulf of Tonkin resolution authorizing the president to take any action he deemed necessary to combat alleged aggression by North Vietnam.

1965

Passage of the Civil Rights Act of 1964 helps pave the way for the Voting Rights Act of 1965, which provides protections for African Americans wishing to vote.

1966

Edward Brooke, a Massachusetts Republican, becomes the first African American popularly elected to the Senate.

1967

The Twenty-fifth Amendment, ratified February 10, sets procedure in case of presidential disability or vacancy in the office of vice president.

1968

Urban riots break out in response to the April 4 assassination of Martin Luther King Jr. in Memphis, Tennessee.

Widespread opposition to the Vietnam War prompts Johnson to decline to seek renomination. Robert F. Kennedy, brother of the late President Kennedy and a leading candidate for the nomination, is assassinated on June 6 in Los Angeles by Sirhan Sirhan, a Palestinian immigrant whose diaries referred to Kennedy's support for Israel in a war with Arab nations in 1967. Protests by antiwar activists and leftist radicals against the candidacy of Johnson's handpicked successor, Vice President Hubert H. Humphrey, draw a violent response from police, marring the Democratic convention at Chicago. The party split helps Republican Richard M. Nixon to win a narrow comeback victory over Humphrey.

In the general election, former Democratic governor George C. Wallace of Alabama, an outspoken segregationist, runs on the American Independent Party ticket and draws conservative support. Wallace wins five southern states and 13.5 percent of the vote.

In congressional elections, New York Democrat Shirley Chisholm becomes the first black woman elected to the U.S. House.

1969

Powell v. McCormack, the landmark Supreme Court decision handed down on June 16, prohibits the House of Representatives from adding to the constitutional qualifications for House membership. The Court rules that the House lacked the authority to exclude a duly elected representative who met the constitutional qualifications of age, residence, and citizenship. The decision reinstates Adam Clayton Powell, a New York Democrat, who was excluded for misconduct and misuse of public funds.

1971

The Twenty-sixth Amendment lowers the voting age to eighteen nationally. Ratification takes only 107 days, less than half the time required for any other constitutional amendment. It is spurred by an unusually large number of young people in the population, together with the Vietnam War and conscription into the army for eighteen-year-olds.

Congress passes the Federal Election Campaign Act of 1971, which creates the Federal Election Commission, limits spending for political advertising by candidates for federal office, and requires full disclosure of campaign contributions and expenditures. Major amendments are enacted in 1974 and 1976. The spending limits are later (in 1976) found unconstitutional except for presidential candidates who accept public financing of their campaigns. An overhaul is enacted in 2002 as the Bipartisan Campaign Reform Act.

1972

George Wallace, who returned to a second tenure as Alabama governor in 1970, is shot May 15 at a Laurel, Maryland, shopping center while campaigning for the Democratic presidential nomination. Partially paralyzed, he withdraws as a candidate.

The Democrats adopt McGovern-Fraser Commission proposals opening the party to more participation by rank-and-file voters. The commission's guidelines are designed to counteract rules and practices that inhibited access to the states' delegate selection process or diluted the influence of those who had access. The presidential selection reforms bring about a proliferation of primaries in subsequent presidential election years.

The former head of the commission, Sen. George S. McGovern of South Dakota, wins the Democratic presidential nomination. His running mate, Sen. Thomas F. Eagleton of Missouri, withdraws after the convention after revelations that he had past psychiatric treatment and is replaced on the ticket by R. Sargent Shriver of Maryland, an in-law of the late John F. Kennedy and Robert F. Kennedy.

President Nixon easily defeats McGovern to win the election, but his victory culminates less than two years later in the first and still only presidential resignation. A preelection burglary at the Democratic National Committee headquarters in Washington's Watergate Hotel is traced to Republican operatives. Investigation discloses Nixon's active role in the subsequent attempted cover-up.

1973

Vice President Spiro T. Agnew resigns on October 10 as part of a plea bargain with federal prosecutors. Agnew faced trial on corruption charges from his years as governor of Maryland. In the first use of the Twenty-fifth Amendment (1967) to fill a vacancy in the vice presidency, Nixon nominates House Minority Leader Gerald R. Ford, who wins confirmation by Congress.

1974

Facing near-certain impeachment in the Watergate scandal, President Nixon resigns August 9 and is succeeded by Ford, who remains the only president to serve in the office without being elected on a national ticket.

Ford pardons Nixon of any crimes he might have committed in the Watergate scandal, causing a political backlash that contributes to big gains by the Democratic majorities in the Senate and the House in the 1974 midterm elections and Ford's defeat by Democrat Jimmy Carter in the 1976 election.

1976

Buckley v. Valeo, a major Supreme Court campaign finance decision, is handed down January 31. It sanctions public financing of presidential elections but bars spending limits for candidates who reject federal funding. The decision also removes ceilings on contributions to one's own campaign.

The first debate of vice presidential candidates, Democrat Walter F. Mondale and Republican Bob Dole, is televised October 15 from Houston, Texas.

1979

Beset by economic problems and energy shortages, President Carter is dealt a serious political blow in November when Islamic radicals in Iran, shielded by that nation's new theocratic government, take over the U.S. embassy and hold fifty-two Americans hostage for more than a year.

1980

Carter loses the presidential election to Republican Ronald Reagan, a former actor and former California governor who runs on a strongly conservative agenda and a promise to restore America's strength and confidence. Reagan's win, with George H. W. Bush as his vice presidential nominee, spurs a big gain for the Republicans in the Senate contests, giving the party its first majority in twenty-six years.

Richard Nixon leaving the White House. His resignation in 1974 was unprecedented.

Source: Nixon Project, National Archives

1981

In his inaugural address on January 20, Reagan signals a major ideological shift by stating, "Government is not the solution to our problem; government is the problem." The Iranian hostage crisis ends; the Americans held for 444 days are freed as the inauguration takes place.

Congress passes much of the tax and budget ideas dubbed as "Reaganomics," which included reductions in taxes and spending on many federal programs.

Reagan survives an assassination attempt March 30 outside a Washington hotel. He is shot by John Hinckley, who was trying to get the attention of an actress on whom he had developed a crush.

> **"Government is not the solution to our problem; government is the problem."**
>
> **—Ronald Reagan,** in his 1981 inaugural address

1984

Democratic presidential nominee Walter Mondale, Carter's vice president, chooses Geraldine Ferraro of New York as his running mate. Ferraro, a three-term House member, becomes the first woman nominated on a major-party presidential ticket. But a growing economy and a charisma gap between Reagan and Mondale help the Republican president win a landslide reelection victory: Reagan takes all of the electoral votes except those in Mondale's native Minnesota and the District of Columbia.

1986

Democrats rebound to take control of the Senate after a six-year Republican majority.

1988

Republican George H. W. Bush defeats Democrat Michael S. Dukakis, then governor of Massachusetts, to become the first sitting vice president since Martin Van Buren (in 1836) to win the presidency.

1989

Virginia elects the first African American governor, L. Douglas Wilder, a Democrat who serves one term. The next black governor, Democrat Deval Patrick of Massachusetts, will be elected in 2006.

1990

Kansas elects Joan Finney, Democrat, as governor. Kansas is the first state to have women as governor, senator (Nancy Landon Kassebaum, Republican), and House member (Jan Meyers, Republican) at the same time.

1991

Bush organizes a sizable international alliance and launches a military offensive to end Iraq's occupation of neighboring Kuwait, which began in August 1990. The quick success of the U.S.-led effort leads to a big jump in Bush's job approval rating, but he sinks to political vulnerability by the end of the year as voters refocus on a recessionary economy.

1992

Bush, also like Van Buren, is defeated after a single term in office, losing to Democrat Bill Clinton, the governor of Arkansas. Texas billionaire H. Ross Perot mounts the strongest-ever individual presidential campaign and receives 18.9 percent of the popular vote as an independent.

1994

In a midterm setback to Clinton's Democratic administration, the Republican Party takes control of Congress, winning the House for the first time in forty years and the Senate for the first time in eight years. The House GOP strategy engineered by Rep. Newt Gingrich of Georgia centers on his proposed conservative agenda, the "Contract with America." The House elects Gingrich as Speaker, and gains in the South cement his party's position as predominant in the region.

1995

Ruling in an Arkansas case, *U.S. Term Limits Inc. v. Thornton*, the Supreme Court on May 22 strikes down state attempts to impose term limits on House and Senate members. Only a constitutional amendment can change the qualifications for service in Congress, the Court says. The Republican majority in Congress puts such a constitutional amendment to a vote, but it fails, and the issue soon fades.

1996

Clinton is the first Democrat elected to a second full term since Franklin Roosevelt in 1936. Republicans stave off a Democratic effort to reclaim the House; this makes Gingrich the first Republican reelected as Speaker of the House in sixty-eight years.

The election also clearly establishes the South as the GOP's new bastion. With the Plains and Rocky Mountain states, half the country is strongly Republican. The other half, made up of the Northeast, Midwest, and Pacific Coast states, is strongly Democratic.

Some states, notably Oregon, conduct the first experiments with elections by mail, other than those associated with absentee voting.

1998

The nation is stunned in January by revelation of a sex scandal that threatens the Clinton presidency. Clinton is accused of having an affair from 1995 to 1997 with Monica S. Lewinsky, who was a twenty-one-year-old White House intern when the relationship began. Clinton at first denies the allegations, both to the news media and under oath in court depositions, then later admits to having a sexual relationship with Lewinsky.

Clinton's policies nevertheless remain popular—thanks to a growing economic boom and a period of relative peace around the world—and voters rebuke the Republicans for focusing on impeaching Clinton by giving the Democrats a small gain of seats in the House, a rarity in midterm elections. Gingrich resigns as House Speaker and leaves Congress. His heir apparent, Robert Livingston of Louisiana, confesses to marital infidelity and declines to run for Speaker, ceding the position to J. Dennis Hastert of Illinois. Livingston, too, announces his intention to resign, as the House prepares to vote on impeachment of Clinton.

After considering Independent Counsel Kenneth W. Starr's report to Congress, the House impeaches Clinton December 19 on charges of perjury and obstruction of justice.

1999

The Senate on February 12 acquits Clinton on both impeachment charges. With a two-thirds majority (67 votes) needed for conviction, neither article receives even a simple majority (51 votes). The extreme partisanship engendered by the impeachment adds to bad blood entering the 2000 elections.

2000

The presidential contest of 2000 is among the closest in history. The Republican candidate, Texas governor George W. Bush, wins twenty-nine states and 246 electoral votes to Vice President Al Gore's twenty states (plus the District of Columbia) and 267 electoral votes. The 25 electoral votes that will decide the presidency are in Florida, where Bush is certified the winner by 537 popular votes, but the outcome is tied up in the courts for weeks. Litigation over recounts of problematic punch-card ballots ends in the U.S. Supreme Court on December 12, when the Court by a 5–4 vote in *Bush v. Gore* ends the recounts. Nationwide, Gore outpolls Bush by 539,898 votes (a margin of 0.51 percent of all ballots cast).

In 2000 Hillary Rodham Clinton became the first former first lady to win election to public office when she became senator for New York.

Source: CQ Photo/Scott J. Ferrell

Bush becomes only the fourth president in history to receive fewer popular votes than his opponent. He takes the office formerly held by his father, George H. W. Bush; the only other father and son to have served as president were John Adams (1797–1801) and John Quincy Adams (1825–1829).

Democrats, however, gain four seats in the Senate, leaving them in a 50–50 tie with the Republicans. Among the newly elected senators is outgoing first lady Hillary Rodham Clinton. She is the only first lady to seek elective office, and she is successful in her first run for office against Republican Rick Lazio in New York. Her win leads to speculation about a possible future bid for the White House.

In the House, Democrats also gain seats, to narrow the already razor-thin Republican majority to 221–212 (with 2 independents). Several of the congressional races are decided by less than one thousand votes, which is indicative of how closely divided the electorate is nationwide.

2001

George W. Bush's inauguration gives Republicans control of the White House and both chambers of Congress simultaneously for the first time since 1953–1955; Vice President Dick Cheney's role as president of the Senate breaks the chamber's 50–50 tie and enables the Republicans to organize as the controlling party. In June, however, Sen. James Jeffords of Vermont quits the GOP to become an independent and gives the Democrats the majority by aligning with them for organizational purposes.

Terrorists affiliated with Osama bin Laden's al Qaeda movement hijack passenger aircraft on September 11 and crash them into the twin towers of New York City's World Trade Center and the Pentagon outside Washington, D.C. Heroic efforts by passengers cause hijackers to crash a fourth plane, apparently heading for another target in the nation's capital, in an open field in Pennsylvania. This attack on U.S. soil spurs Bush, who had mainly focused on cutting taxes and other domestic issues in the first months of his presidency, to reorient his central efforts toward national security and foreign policy issues.

Bush deploys the U.S. military to assist local forces in Afghanistan, who quickly rout the radical Taliban government and its al Qaeda allies. Bin Laden eludes attempts to capture him.

2002

Congress enacts campaign finance legislation banning most unregulated "soft money" from federal elections and restricting use of issue ads to disguise illegal corporate and union support for candidates. Congress also passes the Help America Vote Act, aimed at assisting states in improving their voting procedures.

In the first election since the September 11, 2001, terrorist attacks on the United States, Republicans regain control of the Senate and strengthen their House majority. As a popular wartime president, Bush duplicates the Roosevelt and Clinton feat of gaining House seats at midterm.

California elects the first sisters to serve together in Congress. Linda Sanchez of Los Angeles joins older sister Loretta Sanchez of Orange County, a House member since 1997. Another Californian, Nancy Pelosi, is elected House minority leader, making her the first woman to serve as a party leader in Congress.

The Bush administration shifts its focus to Iraq, declaring dictator Saddam Hussein a threat to national security and accusing him of stockpiling weapons of mass destruction. Both chambers of Congress review intelligence provided by the administration—much of which turns out to be flawed—and approve a resolution in October permitting Bush to use military force against Iraq.

Speaker of the House Nancy Pelosi, a Democrat from California, was the first woman in American history to lead a major party in the U.S. Congress.

Source: CQ Photo/Scott J. Ferrell

Former vice president Al Gore, who won the popular vote for president in 2000, announces he will not run again in 2004.

2003

Declaring Iraq's cooperation with international arms inspectors insufficient, Bush leads a small coalition that invades Iraq and rapidly deposes Saddam Hussein's regime.

In May Bush dons a flight suit and lands in a Navy jet on the deck of an aircraft carrier off California. He declares major combat operations in Iraq ended while standing before a banner reading "Mission Accomplished." This event haunts Bush politically; the extended American intervention in Iraq proves to be far more costly in lives and money than the administration had predicted. Intensive searches fail to turn up the stockpiled weapons of mass destruction that were key justifications for going to war.

2004

Despite tepid job approval ratings caused largely by the war in Iraq, Bush is reelected to a second term with 51 percent of the popular vote and 286 electoral votes. Democratic nominee and Massachusetts senator John Kerry's diffident political image and failure to respond effectively to negative characterization of his combat record during the Vietnam War and his role as a war protester following his service hobble his campaign.

The Republicans gain four seats in the Senate, boosting them to fifty-five seats in the chamber.

2005

Bush faces a domestic political calamity caused by his administration's belated and ineffective response to catastrophic damage to the Gulf Coast caused by Hurricane Katrina in late August. Meanwhile, public dissent grows over the war in Iraq. Together, the issues send the political fortunes of Bush and the Republicans into a downward spiral.

2006

Republicans attempt to focus voters' attention toward local issues and to brand Democrats as too liberal to be trusted with national security. They are undermined by a series of corruption scandals that force resignations of four GOP members and cast a cloud over several others. Democrats take control of both houses of Congress, gaining thirty House seats—fifteen more than they need for a majority—and six Senate seats.

2008

Democrats complete their full return to power when Illinois Sen. Barack Obama is elected president with an overwhelming majority in the Electoral College margin of 365 votes to 173 for his challenger and fellow senator, John McCain of Arizona. Obama also wins a comfortable margin in the popular vote, 52.9 percent to 45.7 percent. Obama's victory is a landmark in American elections as he becomes the first African American to win the highest office in the land. Congressional Democrats take even more firm control in both chambers as well, with a majority in the House of 257 to 178 and in the Senate of fifty-seven to forty-one with two Independents who caucus with Democrats. With full control of both ends of Pennsylvania, Democrats launch an aggressive progressive agenda that includes a multibillion economic stimulus bill, a far-reaching overhaul of the nation's health care system, and much tougher regulation of the financial sector.

The year also is notable as a woman, Hillary Rodham Clinton, becomes the first female candidate with a legitimate chance to be the nominee of a major political party, even though in the end she loses to Obama.

2010

The Democratic hegemony lasts just two years as Republicans stage a huge comeback in midterm elections, recapturing the House majority with a net gain of sixty-three seats—many of which are won by exceptionally conservative candidates. The GOP also gains six Senate seats, which is not enough to achieve a majority but ample to hamper, and usually block, Democratic initiatives. The nation is thus returned to divided government that, in 2011 in the 112th Congress, is repeatedly displayed to voters as the parties find themselves unable to compromise on even the most vital legislative activities, driving the nation at one point to within hours of defaulting on its financial obligations in an imbroglio over the usually routine act of increasing the national debt limit.

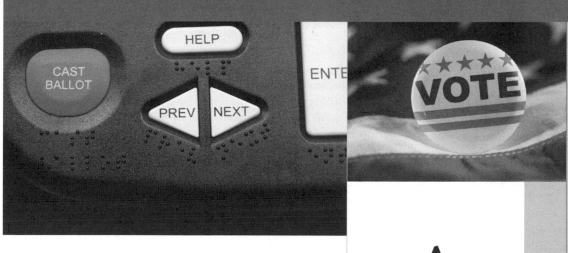

Absentee Voting

Absentee voting is the term that describes casting a ballot by some means other than in the polling booth on election day. The procedure is increasingly referred to as early voting, which involves two main types of voter choice: early in-person (EIP) and voting by mail (VBM). Both are intended to allow a voter who cannot be at a voting booth on election day to cast a ballot that can be verified as legitimate.

Absentee voting began during the Civil War when Union soldiers were caught up in the political struggle and, with President Abraham Lincoln's encouragement, wanted to participate in the elections back home. But until quite recently, the practice of absentee voting was quite limited in the United States.

Seeking in many cases to maintain the tradition of a single voting day, and concerned about the possibility of fraud in ballots marked without oversight by election officials, many states required voters to explain why they would be unable to get to the polls on election day—excuses could include business travel, illness, military duty, and vacation—and some even required voters to sign affidavits.

Such requirements no longer exist in most states. With many states and voting participation advocates seeking ways to reverse a long-term decline in turnout, there has been a major expansion and liberalization of absentee voting, in which voters mail in their marked ballots or drop them off with state election officials by a designated date, and early voting, in which states and localities set up designated sites where voters can cast their votes in the weeks before election day.

Airmen at the Grand Forks Air Force Base request absentee ballots on September 7, 2006.

Source: Courtesy photo, Grand Forks Air Force Base website

Absentee voting in the United States began during the Civil War, when President Abraham Lincoln supported Union soldiers in their desire to participate in elections. Absentee voting procedures for active-duty military personnel were essentially ad hoc until World War II, which ended the nation's isolationist foreign policy tendencies and led—at the time and in the following decades—to the stationing of large numbers of American troops overseas. This led to legislation to protect the absentee voting rights of military personnel under the Federal Voting Assistance Act of 1955 and the Uniformed and Overseas Citizens Absentee Voting Act. In 2009 Congress passed the Military and Overseas Voter Empowerment Act following reports of lost or late ballots and burdensome procedures to register and obtain ballots.

However, by 2011 some states were changing their election laws to restrict voting outside the polling booths on election day. In legislative sessions in 2011 some states approved or were debating shortening the time period in which absentee voting could occur. The changes were aimed principally at early voting procedures by allowing fewer days before the regularly scheduled election. Florida, for example, reduced early voting days to seven from fourteen and Georgia to twenty-one from forty-five.

Advocates of the changes said tighter restrictions were needed to protect against voting fraud, but critics charged they were designed largely to limit ballot access by certain voter groups, especially ones who typically voted Democratic. The critics, primarily Democrats, said the changes were initiated largely by Republican-controlled legislatures with support from GOP governors to make voting more difficult for Democratic constituencies.

But there is no dispute that absentee voting, whether early or by mail, has become increasingly popular. In 2008, an estimated 38 million early votes were cast in states allowing voting other than on the official election day. A Census Bureau survey for the 2008 national elections found that 70 percent of voters reporting they voted on election day, down from 80 percent four years earlier, and 30 percent voted earlier, up from 20 percent in 2004. Of voters who cast ballots early, 52 percent reported doing so by mail.

By the 2010 elections, according to the National Conference of State Legislators, thirty-two states and the District of Columbia offered early voting in some form. All states offered some form of absentee voting, allowing a mail-in paper ballot, while thirty states and the District of Columbia offered "no excuse" absentee balloting in which a voter could obtain a ballot without stating a reason. Other states allowed absentee balloting only under specific circumstances. Eight states and the District of Columbia allowed permanent no-excuse absentee balloting.

The state of Oregon has taken absentee voting as far as it can go. Since 2000 its elections have been wholly conducted on a vote-by-mail basis. Ballots are mailed to all registered voters about a month before the deadline, which coincides with the traditional election day. Voters mark the ballots and return them either by mailing them or dropping them off at designated collection sites.

Early voting practices have become accepted and popular in many places. In Texas, a state that has strongly promoted early voting, the secretary of state's office reported that during the 2006 general elections, about 1.1 million votes, roughly one-quarter of all statewide ballots, were cast early or absentee, the vast majority of those in person.

This trend has greatly built upon the availability of absentee voting, which has long been helpful to Americans living outside the United States. Both major political parties have overseas organizations of absentee voters, Democrats Abroad and Republicans Abroad.

The VOTING RIGHTS ACT OF 1965 and later amendments interpreted the RIGHT TO VOTE broadly, encompassing the polling place, voters' physical disabilities, language handicaps, and other aspects of the elections process that might deny a person or groups of people access to the ballot box or voting booth. The act also directed the Justice Department to determine if state election laws were depriving military personnel of voting rights. There are some politicians and election watchdog groups who are concerned about this trend. The following are among their stated qualms:

- Early and absentee balloting raises the risk of fraud. Critics say these practices offer those seeking to corrupt the election process more opportunities to "stuff the ballot box" or coerce individual voters into voting for candidates they would not have backed otherwise. Advocates say this risk is greatly exaggerated.
- Large numbers of absentee ballots can complicate vote counting and delay the outcome of very close elections. Critics point out that disputes over counting of absentee ballots were involved in two of the most controversial elections of recent times—the 2000 presidential vote in Florida that Republican George W. Bush eventually won, giving him the electoral votes needed to defeat Democrat Al Gore, and the 2004 election for governor in the state of Washington, in which Democrat Christine Gregoire was declared the winner over Republican Dino Rossi weeks after election day.
- Early voting skews the candidates' campaigns. Candidates traditionally have planned their strategies to build momentum and make a big final push just before election day. In early voting states, candidates must allocate resources to reach voters who might be casting ballots days or even weeks before election day. Some observers also worry that voters casting early ballots might regret their votes if the closing days and weeks of the campaigns bring new information or revelations that change their minds about the candidates.
- Early voting does not have a significantly positive impact on voter turnout. Curtis Gans, an influential academic analyst of voter turnout, strongly contends that his data analysis shows little gain in overall participation in states that have introduced early voting.
- Early voting cheapens the voting experience. Veteran political analyst Norman Ornstein of the American Enterprise Institute, a Washington, D.C.–based think tank, voiced this point of view in a November 2004 column published in the Capitol Hill paper *Roll Call*. "In America, individuals join their neighbors at a local polling place, underscoring their role as a part of a collective society, then go into a curtained booth to make their choices as free individuals," Ornstein wrote. "Every conceivable step should be taken to make the votes cast on election day easy to do—longer hours, ample poll workers and voting machines, easier registration, and so on. But we should not make voting the equivalent of sending in a Publishers Clearing House contest form."

> **"We should not make voting the equivalent of sending in a Publishers Clearing House contest form."**
>
> **—Norman Ornstein,** American Enterprise Institute political analyst

Yet supporters of absentee and early voting say these concerns are greatly overstated. And with most officials in states where early voting is widely practiced maintaining support, and with no major movement against the practice among voters in general, it appears likely to grow in use.

Vote by Mail

Given the success of absentee voting and the dependability of the postal service, various groups have advocated vote-by-mail plans to encourage wider participation in the electoral process, which in the United States has been characterized by a VOTER TURNOUT much lower than in many other industrialized countries. In 1995 and 1996 the vote-by-mail concept was put to the test in two states, Nevada and Oregon, which conducted several elections entirely by mail.

The largest test took place in Oregon, which used mail-in votes to choose a successor to Republican senator Bob Packwood, who had resigned under allegations of sexual harassment. The winner was Democrat Ron Wyden, the first senator elected by mail.

Supporters of the opposing candidates in the Washington State governor's race hold a demonstration over the recount that included hundreds of uncounted absentee ballots.

Source: AP Images/Ted S. Warren

Both critics and advocates of expanded voting options cite developments in the Pacific Northwest states to make their arguments. Proponents of Oregon's transition to a universal vote-by-mail system cite reviews that show strong voter participation and little evidence that the process is tainted by attempts at vote fraud. Opponents point to the neighboring state of Washington, which has experienced complications resulting from processing thousands of absentee ballots. After an initial canvass of the 2004 election for governor showed Republican Dino Rossi with a razor-thin lead over Democrat Christine Gregoire, 573 uncounted absentee ballots turned up in King County, which includes Seattle and is the state's premier Democratic Party stronghold. The inclusion of these votes in a protracted recount process helped Gregoire claim a victory by 129 votes out of about 2.75 million cast.

For the SPECIAL ELECTION, both the primaries in 1995 and the general election in early 1996 were conducted by mail. Oregon officials were pleased with the "turnout"—about 57 percent of the eligible 1.8 million voters. The primaries to select contenders for the House seat vacated by Wyden also were conducted by mail, but the special election itself was a conventional voting-booth affair held in conjunction with the Oregon presidential primaries.

Oregon subsequently became the first state to decide to hold all elections by mail. In the 1998 MIDTERM ELECTIONS, Oregon voters approved Ballot Measure 60 requiring vote by mail in biennial primary and general elections. The measure eliminated polling places, but it did not affect current law allowing absentee ballots or voting at the elections office. The rate of voter participation in Oregon in 2000 was reported to be in the neighborhood of 80 percent, which is significantly higher than the national average.

A potential for abuse of the vote-by-mail system surfaced in Oregon when candidates were able to obtain from election officials the names of voters who had not yet returned their ballots. Critics said this information left voters open to undue solicitation or even harassment by candidates.

An argument against use of the mail to provide a longer voting period is that it could invite fraud, and indeed, there have been instances where the number of votes cast in an election, including absentee ballots, exceeded the number of people living in the community. Another problem with mail-in votes is that the wrong persons could cast duplicate or undelivered ballots. But the chances of this particular fraud's being successful are reduced by the standard requirement that the voter's signature be on the envelope.

Changes in the status of candidates' campaigns may also cause complications. In Nevada, the 1996 Republican presidential primary was held by mail-in vote. The party's eventual nominee, Bob Dole, won, but many votes had been mailed in before another leading candidate, Malcolm S. "Steve" Forbes Jr., dropped out of the race on March 14.

Proponents argue that the benefits of voting by mail—including convenience, speed, and lower costs—outweigh the disadvantages, which include the lost sociability of gathering at the polls, the easing of the procedure to accommodate less civic-minded voters, and the possible abuse of the system or delay in the certification of a winner.

In an Oregon survey, 76.5 percent of those polled said they preferred voting by mail over going to a polling place. Women and older voters were strongest in favor of mail voting.

Mail elections are estimated to cost one-third to one-half less than conventional elections. The U.S. Postal Service in promotional advertising has estimated that the cost of postal voting "can be as much as $1 million lower, because there are no polling personnel to pay, no space to rent, no polling equipment to transport and set up."

Although mail voting may be cheaper than a regular election, absentee voting in conjunction with a voting-booth election is more expensive per vote than the polling place balloting. Election officials estimate that absentee ballots require three to four times more labor to process.

Because absentee ballots are assumed to be ripe for fraud, election workers devote considerable time to ensuring that they are legitimate. When the ballot is received, a worker usually checks the name on the envelope to verify that the person is a qualified absentee voter and that the signatures match those on file from the voters' registration records. The worker also must verify that the person has not already voted.

In many states the ballot may then be entered into a computer that counts it, but by law the ballot cannot actually be tabulated until after the polls close on ELECTION DAY. In contrast, the ballots marked in a voting booth are presumed

More on this topic:
Election Day, p. 173
Motor Voter Act, p. 340
Special Elections, p. 603
Voter Turnout, p. 656
Voting Rights Act, p. 663

to be authentic and are counted at the polling place or a central election station when the polls close. Mechanical or computerized voting machines provide an immediate tally at each polling place.

Because many absentee voters mail or drop off their ballots at the last minute, election workers already may be swamped with regular returns when the last batches of time-consuming absentee ballots come in. The absentee ballots are usually set aside, sometimes by law, to be dealt with the day after the election—or as long as it takes to verify that they are not fraudulent. If the election is close, it may be days, weeks, or even months before the winner is known.

Postal voting is part of a larger trend since the 1980s toward easier voting, including steps to increase voter registration, such as the federal MOTOR VOTER ACT of 1993, which allows voters to sign up when they obtain or renew their driver's license. Most states, however, have simply made absentee ballots available to all, creating a hybrid system that proponents of postal voting decry as "the worst of both worlds," combining the labor-intensive costs of absentee voting with the equipment and location costs of voting-booth elections.

Absolute Majority

In electoral or legislative voting, an *absolute majority* is more than 50 percent of all those eligible to vote, regardless of how many actually voted. A *simple majority,* by contrast, consists of a majority of those voting, not of the whole eligible pool. Nearly all electoral politics and legislative procedures in the United States are based on the principle of a simple majority.

The U.S. Senate is often used as an example to illustrate these terms because it has exactly 100 members. Therefore, an absolute majority of the Senate is fifty-one or more votes. But not all senators vote on every motion or bill, and most bills or motions carry if they receive most of the votes that were cast—even if this is short of the absolute majority of fifty-one.

For instance, if only sixty-six senators vote on a bill, it passes if there are at least thirty-four "ayes," because that is more than half of the total vote. But it would be only 34 percent of the Senate membership and therefore a simple majority, not an absolute majority.

The same principle applies to most American elections. Even in states, districts, and other jurisdictions typically marked by high turnout, the number of actual participants always falls well short of 100 percent; therefore, in almost any election, the winner—even if he or she takes a majority of votes cast— will receive votes from less than a majority of all eligible voters. In jurisdictions marked by low voter turnout, winners of elections are typically chosen by smaller fractions of the total electorate.

There is, however, a huge exception to this rule: the election for president of the United States, in which the winner is determined not by the nationwide popular vote, but by the sum of electoral votes won by the candidates on a state-by-state basis.

To be elected president or vice president, a candidate must receive an absolute majority of the 538 votes in the ELECTORAL COLLEGE, or at least 270 votes. A presidential candidate with an electoral vote majority is deemed elected even if that candidate receives less than a majority of the votes cast—something that has happened eighteen times—or even fewer popular votes than an opponent. (See ELECTORAL ANOMALIES.)

The latter has happened four times in U.S. history, most recently in 2000. Republican George W. Bush trailed Democrat Al Gore by one-half of one percentage point in the national popular vote, but he was elected president with a bare majority of 271 electoral votes after a Supreme Court ruling in the case of BUSH V. GORE effectively decided a controversial vote-counting dispute in Florida in his favor.

That 271 majority was the smallest for a presidential winner in all the elections since 1964, the first in which the total number of electoral votes reached 538 (equal to the 535 members of Congress plus three votes for the DISTRICT OF COLUMBIA). Although Bush was reelected with a 51 percent popular vote majority in his 2004 race with Democrat John Kerry, his 286 electoral vote majority ranks as the second smallest of that era. Democrat Jimmy Carter's 297 electoral votes in his 1976 victory over Gerald R. Ford, the Republican incumbent, is the third smallest.

President Ronald Reagan, a Republican, scored the most lopsided electoral vote victory in the same period, with 525 votes or 97.6 percent to Democratic challenger Walter Mondale's thirteen votes or 2.4 percent in the 1984 election.

> **More on this topic:**
>
> Contested Elections,
> p. 125
>
> Electoral Anomalies,
> p. 179
>
> Electoral College and
> Votes, p. 186

There have been three instances when no presidential candidate received the required electoral vote majority. In 1800 and 1824 the presidents—Thomas Jefferson and John Quincy Adams, respectively—were elected by the House of Representatives as provided by the Constitution. In 1876, when the electoral vote total was in dispute, a fifteen-member commission, consisting of five senators, five representatives, and five Supreme Court justices, decided the outcome in favor of Republican Rutherford B. Hayes. (See CONTESTED ELECTIONS; ELECTORAL COLLEGE AND VOTES)

While many critics of the electoral vote system advocate converting to a system in which the candidate with the most popular votes wins, there is little support for requiring the winning candidate to receive votes from an absolute majority of the entire voting-age population of U.S. citizens. That is because such an absolute majority would be nearly impossible to achieve under current U.S. voting practices.

The hard-fought 2004 presidential election spurred an uptick in voter turnout, which had gone through a period of general decline. Even so, only about 55 percent of the voting-age population and roughly 60 percent of the voting-eligible population participated in the election, according to the United States Election Project at George Mason University in Virginia.

Using those figures, Bush's 51 percent popular vote victory in 2004 represented votes cast by slightly more than one-quarter of the voting-age population and less than one-third of the voting-eligible population (which excludes noncitizens and felons who are not eligible to vote).

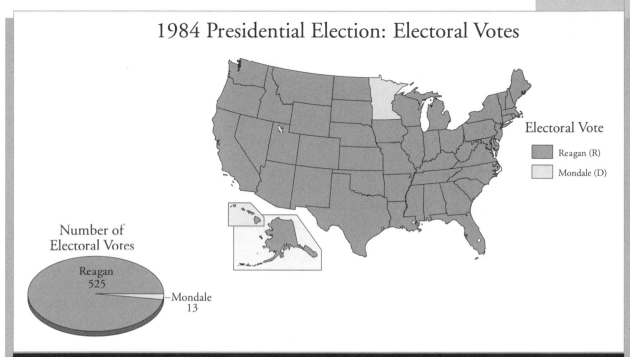

1984 Presidential Election: Electoral Votes

Electoral Vote

Reagan (R)

Mondale (D)

Number of Electoral Votes

Reagan 525

Mondale 13

In 1984 President Ronald Reagan, a Republican, won 525 electoral college votes or 97.6 percent to Democratic challenger Walter Mondale's thirteen votes or 2.4 percent. This was the most lopsided electoral vote victory since 1964, the first in which the total number of electoral votes reached 538.

Source: J. Clark Archer, Stephen J. Lavin, Kenneth C. Martis, and Fred M. Shelley, *Historical Atlas of U.S. Presidential Elections 1788–2004* (Washington, D.C.: CQ Press, 2006).

American Independent Party (1968–) and American Party (1972–)

Both the American Party and the American Independent Party descended from the original American Independent Party that served as the vehicle for George C. Wallace's third-party presidential candidacy in 1968.

Wallace, the governor of Alabama from 1963 to 1967 and from 1971 to 1979, emerged in the early 1960s as a fiery defender of the racial segregation then common in the South. He burst onto the national scene in 1964 as a Democratic presidential candidate opposed to the Civil Rights Act that would be enacted that year.

Expected to make an impact largely in the South, Wallace entered three primaries in northern states—Wisconsin, Indiana, and Maryland—and surprised political observers by winning between 30 percent and 43 percent of the popular vote in these contests. His unexpectedly strong showing brought the term "white backlash" into the political vocabulary as a description of the racial undertone of the Wallace vote, even as Lyndon B. Johnson, the incumbent president, brushed aside the challenge to claim the Democratic nomination.

In 1968 Wallace broke with the Democrats and launched his second presidential bid under the label of the newly established American Independent Party. His candidacy capitalized on the bitter

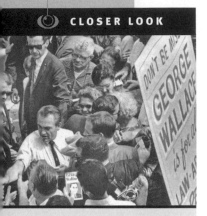

CLOSER LOOK

George Wallace campaigns in Glen Burnie, Maryland, on July 13, 1968.

Source: AP Images

George Wallace, as the American Independent Party candidate, was the last third-party presidential contender to win electoral votes: he carried five southern states and 46 electoral votes. But the party was centered almost entirely on Wallace himself, and it quickly faded from influence when he returned to the Democratic Party fold.

reactions of millions of voters, especially whites and blue-collar workers, to the upheavals of the mid-1960s, including civil rights activism, urban riots, demonstrations against the Vietnam War, and the heavy federal spending on "Great Society" programs by Johnson's administration and the Democratic-controlled Congress. With the help of volunteer groups, Wallace was able to get on the ballot in all fifty states.

Wallace did not hold a convention for his party, but in October he announced his vice presidential running mate—Curtis LeMay, a retired Air Force general—and released an issues platform. That November, the Wallace-LeMay ticket made one of the strongest third-party showings of the twentieth century: 9,906,473 votes or 13.5 percent of the popular vote. Wallace and LeMay carried five southern states and won forty-six electoral votes, the last time, through the 2008 election, that an alternative-party candidate carried any states.

Wallace, however, did not sustain an interest in building the American Independent Party. He entered the 1972 Democratic presidential nominating contest and had some strong early showings, but his campaign was cut short when he was severely wounded in an assassination attempt. Wallace also entered the 1976 primary field but made less of an impact.

The American Independent Party remained active in the 1972 race—appearing in many states as the American Party—and united behind John G. Schmitz, a Republican U.S. representative from California (1970–1973), as its presidential nominee. Thomas J. Anderson, a farm magazine and syndicated news features publisher from Tennessee, was the party's vice presidential candidate. In the November election, the Schmitz-Anderson ticket won 1,099,482 votes (1.4 percent of the popular vote) but failed to win any electoral votes.

An internal split subsequently ended the party's national influence. By 1976 there were two distinct entities: the American Party, headed by Anderson, and the American Independent Party, headed by William K. Shearer, who had been chairman of the party's California affiliate.

The American Party, with Anderson as its 1976 nominee, stressed "permanent principles" of the party, including opposition to foreign aid, U.S. withdrawal from the United Nations, and an end to trade with or recognition of communist nations. The platform included planks opposing abortion, gun control, the Equal Rights Amendment, and government-sponsored health care and welfare programs.

But the party was on the ballot in only eighteen states, including eight where the American Independent Party—which had a similar issues agenda—also appeared. The American Independent Party nominated former Georgia governor Lester Maddox (1967–1971), a Democrat known for his segregationist views, as its presidential nominee and former Madison, Wisconsin, mayor William Dyke, a Republican, as its vice presidential candidate.

At the party's convention in Chicago, a group of nationally prominent conservatives made a bid to take over the party and use it as a vehicle to build a new conservative coalition. Richard Viguerie, a fund-raiser for Wallace and a nationally known direct mail expert, was the leader of the group. He was joined at the convention by two leading conservatives—William Rusher, publisher of the *National Review,* and Howard Phillips, the former head of the Office of Economic Opportunity (1973) and leader of the Conservative Caucus, an activist group.

Viguerie, Phillips, and Rusher all argued that the American Independent Party should be overhauled, changed from a fringe group to a philosophical home for believers in free enterprise and traditional moral values. They also hoped they could attract North Carolina senator Jesse Helms,

New Hampshire governor Meldrim Thomson, or Illinois representative Philip M. Crane—all Republican conservative stalwarts—to run for president. The gambit failed; Phillips went on to found the Constitution Party, which later claimed a remnant of the American Independent Party as its California affiliate.

Neither fragment of Wallace's original party made much of a ripple in 1976, with Maddox receiving only 170,531 votes (0.2 percent of the national total) and Anderson slightly behind with 160,773 votes.

The parties fielded candidates in several subsequent elections but received minuscule vote totals. The American Party last appeared on a presidential ballot in 1996, with candidate Diane Beall Templin receiving 1,847 total votes.

American National Election Studies (ANES) *See* NATIONAL ELECTION STUDIES

American Party—Know Nothings (1856) *See* KNOW NOTHING (AMERICAN) PARTY

Anti-Federalists (1789–1796)

Never a formal party, the Anti-Federalists were a loosely organized group opposed to ratification of the Constitution. Thwarted in that goal, they nonetheless played a significant role in the history of the nation by pressing for what became known as the Bill of Rights. With the adoption of the Constitution in 1788, the Anti-Federalists served as the opposition to the Federalists in the early years of Congress.

Anti-Federalists were primarily rural, agrarian men from inland regions who favored individual freedom and states' rights, which they felt would be jeopardized by the new Constitution. After ratification, the efforts of the Anti-Federalists led to adoption of the first ten amendments, the Bill of Rights, which spelled out the major limitations of federal power.

As the opposition faction in Congress during the formative years of the Republic, the Anti-Federalists basically held to a strict interpretation of the Constitution, particularly in regard to the various economic proposals of Treasury Secretary Alexander Hamilton to centralize more power in the federal government.

Although never the majority faction in Congress, the Anti-Federalists were a forerunner of Thomas Jefferson's Democratic-Republican Party, which came into existence in the 1790s and dominated American politics for the first quarter of the nineteenth century.

> **More on this topic:**
>
> *Democratic-Republican Party, p. 155*

Anti-Masonic Party (1832–1836)

Born in the late 1820s in upstate New York, the Anti-Masonic Party focused the strong, antielitist mood of the period on a conspicuous symbol of privilege, the Masons. The Masons were a secret

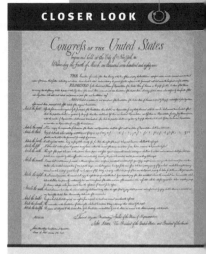

The Anti-Federalist Party played a role in the drafting of the Bill of Rights.
Source: National Archives and Records Administration

The Anti-Federalist Party had a short life in the earliest days of the nation, but it played a big role in two major historical developments: the drafting of the first ten amendments to the Constitution, known as the Bill of Rights, and the emergence of the Democratic-Republican Party, which dominated U.S. politics for a quarter-century after the election of Thomas Jefferson as president in 1800.

William Wirt
Source: Library of Congress

fraternal organization with membership drawn largely from the upper class. Conversely, the appeal of the Anti-Masonic movement was to the common man—poor farmers and laborers especially—who resented the secrecy and privilege of the Masons.

The spark that created the party came in 1826. William Morgan, a dissident Mason from Batavia, New York, was allegedly on the verge of exposing the inner workings of the order when he mysteriously disappeared and never was seen again. Masonic leaders' refusal to cooperate in the inconclusive investigation of Morgan's disappearance led to suspicions that Masons had kidnapped and murdered him and were suppressing the inquiry.

From 1828 through 1831, the new Anti-Masonic Party spread through New England and the Middle Atlantic states, in many places establishing itself as the primary opposition to the Democrats. In addition to its appeal to the working classes, particularly in northern rural areas, and its opposition to Masonry, the Anti-Masons displayed a fervor against immorality, as seen not only in secret societies but also in slavery, intemperance, and urban life.

In September 1831 the party held the first national nominating convention of any party in American history. One hundred and sixteen delegates from thirteen states gathered in Baltimore, Maryland, and nominated former attorney general William Wirt of Maryland for the presidency. While Wirt received only 100,715 votes (7.8 percent of the popular vote) and carried only Vermont, the Anti-Masons did reasonably well at other levels, winning two governorships and fifty-three House seats.

But the 1832 election was the high point for the Anti-Masons as a national party. The decline of the Masons, especially in New York, where the number of lodges dropped from 507 in 1826 to forty-eight six years later, robbed the Anti-Masons of an emotional issue and hastened their decline. In the 1836 campaign, the party endorsed Whig candidate William Henry Harrison. Subsequently, the bulk of the Anti-Masonic constituency moved into the WHIG PARTY.

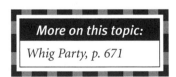

More on this topic:

Whig Party, p. 671

Apportionment *See* REAPPORTIONMENT AND REDISTRICTING

At-Large

An official elected by an entire jurisdiction rather than a subdivision of it is said to be elected *at-large.* United States senators, two for each state, run statewide and therefore are elected at-large. So are the governors and other constitutional officers in each of the fifty states.

Nearly all U.S. representatives, however, are elected from CONGRESSIONAL DISTRICTS that are smaller than an entire state; they generally do not run at-large. The only current exceptions are the representatives from the seven states—Alaska, Delaware, Montana, North Dakota, South Dakota, Vermont, and Wyoming—that have the constitutional minimum of one House seat because of their small populations. In these cases the entire state is the district, and the House member effectively is a statewide officeholder.

States also are divided into districts for the purpose of electing members of their own legislatures. These state legislative districts are similar to congressional districts, only smaller in most cases.

The major exception is the California Senate, which has forty members. A population boom since World War II has earned California its current apportionment of fifty-three U.S. House seats. As a result, the forty state senate seats are larger than the fifty-three congressional districts.

Under the Supreme Court's BAKER V. CARR ruling in 1962, both houses of a state legislature must be apportioned according to population. In many states the house is twice as large as the senate, and a senate district may comprise two house districts. Unlike Congress, some state legislatures still have MULTIMEMBER DISTRICTS.

City council districts are often known as wards. Frequently a city council will be made up of some members elected at-large and others elected by the ward he or she represents.

Racial and ethnic minorities tend to oppose at-large election because it makes them less likely to gain representation in the legislative body in question. Many have favored the creation of MINORITY-MAJORITY DISTRICTS, in which minority-group voters make up most of the local population and thus have a stronger opportunity to elect one of their group to office. At-large elections place minority-group candidates in competition with members of the majority group, making it more difficult for them to win elections, especially in areas where voting tends to be racially or ethnically polarized.

CLOSER LOOK

The seven states with the smallest populations currently have just the one member of the U.S. House of Representatives guaranteed them under the Constitution. These states are Alaska, Delaware, Montana, North Dakota, South Dakota, Vermont, and Wyoming.

Australian Ballot *See* BALLOT TYPES

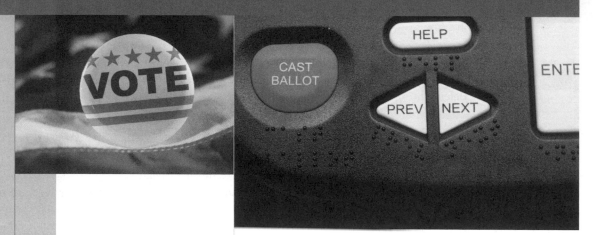

B

Baker v. Carr

The Supreme Court's decision in *Baker v. Carr* (1962) began a historic overhaul of the process for apportioning seats in the state legislatures throughout the country and presaged the similar move toward population balance among congressional districts that followed soon after.

The ruling, which dealt with a Tennessee case, established only the narrow principle that federal courts have jurisdiction to review claims of unconstitutional apportionment of legislative districts. Within two years, however, the Court laid down a sweeping constitutional rule—the ONE-PERSON, ONE-VOTE doctrine—that forced every state legislature in the country except one (Oregon) to redraw legislative districts and give urban and suburban dwellers a proportional voice in legislatures that had been dominated by rural interests because of improper REAPPORTIONMENT AND REDISTRICTING.

Tennessee's legislature had not reapportioned itself in sixty years despite a provision in the state constitution requiring that it be done every ten years. As in many states where the population was becoming more urban, the effort to evade reapportionment was spurred by entrenched rural interests that feared losing clout to the cities.

By the 1950s, the population shift from the farms to the cities had produced dramatic disparities in the pattern of representation for seats in the Tennessee house and senate. Underrepresented urban dwellers tried but failed to get state courts to enforce the provision. They then filed suit in federal district court in 1959, alleging that the legislature's failure to reapportion itself violated their right to equal protection of the laws under the Fourteenth Amendment. Charles W. Baker,

chairman of the Shelby County (Memphis) legislative body, was the lead plaintiff; Joe Carr, the Tennessee secretary of state, was the first-named defendant.

> ## "The mere fact that the suit seeks protection of a political right does not mean it presents a political question."
>
> —*Supreme Court Justice William J. Brennan Jr.,* writing in *Baker v. Carr* (1962)

The Supreme Court had ruled in a similar case in 1946 that federal courts had no jurisdiction over the "political question" of legislative reapportionment. Following the precedent in *Colegrove v. Green,* the federal district court in Nashville unanimously dismissed the suit. The Tennessee plaintiffs asked the Supreme Court to review the case and reconsider the precedent. The Justice Department, in a brief written by Solicitor General Archibald Cox, supported their plea.

The Court moved cautiously in scrapping the precedent. By a 6–2 vote it held that the plaintiffs' constitutional claims were "justiciable" despite the political-question doctrine. "The mere fact that the suit seeks protection of a political right does not mean it presents a political question," Justice William J. Brennan Jr. wrote in the March 26, 1962, decision. Brennan said the holding did not require the Court to address the merits of the plaintiffs' claim. Three justices—William O. Douglas, Tom C. Clark, and Potter Stewart—wrote concurring opinions. Clark said he would have granted relief to the plaintiffs but also said he would allow some "rational" departures from equal-population districts.

More on this topic:
One Person, One Vote, p. 373
Reapportionment and Redistricting, p. 517

In a dissenting opinion, Justice Felix Frankfurter, who had written the opinion in *Colegrove,* decried the new decision. "There is not under our Constitution a judicial remedy for every political mischief," he wrote. Justice John Marshall Harlan II, the second dissenter, called the ruling "an adventure in judicial experimentation."

Within a year, similar reapportionment suits were filed in thirty-six states. Years later, Chief Justice Earl Warren listed *Baker v. Carr* as the most important case decided by the Warren Court.

Ballot Access

Being listed on the ballot is almost always the basic first step in winning an election, but for alternative candidates running under the banner of THIRD PARTIES or as independents, getting on the ballot is not easy. Controversies over ballot access erupt frequently in the United States.

Under the U.S. TWO-PARTY SYSTEM, the Democratic and Republican parties are ensured a place on the ballot in every partisan election for office. They also control the election bureaucracy in most jurisdictions and frequently resist the listing of splinter groups that could siphon votes from their candidates.

Since the advent of the BALLOT TYPE known as the secret or Australian ballot in the late 1800s, states rather than parties have compiled the official election ballots. This task is one of the major functions of the states in the elections process shared with the federal government. (See STATE AND FEDERAL ELECTION RESPONSIBILITIES.)

The drastic differences in states' willingness to facilitate candidacies outside the two major parties are illustrated by the requirements in Tennessee and Texas. Tennessee requires candidates for any office to collect petition signatures from only twenty-five eligible voters to get on the ballot. Texas, on the other hand, requires third-party and independent candidates to produce signatures equal to 1 percent of the vote in the most recent governor's election. Based on turnout in the 2006 election for governor, non-major-party candidates for statewide office in 2008 were required to collect about 44,000 signatures to qualify—and they had to do so within only sixty days after the parties with automatic ballot status picked their general election nominees in that year's primary election.

North Carolina at one time had one of the most restrictive ballot access standards, requiring roughly 85,000 signatures for a new party to make the statewide ballot. The standard essentially blocked new parties from forming and getting ballot access. However, in mid-2011 the state legislature was nearing completion of legislation—with bipartisan support—that would lower the number of signatures needed to as little as 15,000.

The ballot access issue received unusual attention during the 2004 presidential election campaign of Ralph Nader, a well-known consumer activist running on a strongly liberal agenda. Nader had run for president in 2000 as the nominee of the Green Party, which had received enough votes in previous elections to qualify for automatic ballot status in many states. Nader was on the ballot that year in forty-seven states and the District of Columbia; he was excluded only in North Carolina, Oregon, and South Dakota. Although he only received 2.7 percent of the national POPULAR VOTE, his vote total exceeded the margin between Republican George W. Bush and Democrat Al Gore in Florida and New Hampshire, two states that were crucial to Bush's narrow electoral vote victory margin—leading to a long-lasting debate about whether Nader had spoiled Gore's chances for victory.

In 2004, however, Nader took a very different route, running as an independent rather than seeking the Green Party's nomination, and had a minuscule impact. Nader faced formidable obstacles to getting on the ballot in many places and was listed in only thirty-four states. He ended up with 463,653 votes nationally, 0.4 percent of the national total and less than one-sixth of the nearly 2.9 million votes he had received just four years earlier.

Some experts and activists on the ballot access issue say it can take as many as 1 million petition signatures collected nationwide for an independent presidential candidate to obtain ballot status in all fifty states and the District of Columbia. Given the need to establish organizations and set up a campaign infrastructure in each state where ballot access is sought, the process is prohibitive for all but the best-funded candidates. The only independent presidential candidate in recent years to make the ballots in all fifty states and Washington, D.C., was self-financed billionaire Ross Perot in 1992.

Those who find the major-party nominees wanting consider the ballot access obstacle course unfair, and many of them say it is undemocratic. "In order to keep our political system healthy, we must once again allow people the freedom to vote for the qualified candidate of their choice. Such freedom is not only essential to the health of our government but also our right as citizens of the United States," wrote Richard Winger, a tireless advocate of easing ballot restrictions, in 1994, the year after he founded *Ballot Access News*. More than a dozen years later, the publication maintained an extensive repository of information and news developments about the issue on its website.

Third parties also complain that many states force them to file too early to try to secure a place on the general election ballot, weeks or months before they know who their candidates will be. Some states require all parties to hold PRIMARIES to nominate candidates, which small third parties often are not prepared to do, especially early in the election year when the major parties have clustered their primaries. (See FRONT-LOADING.)

One way that most states limit potentially strong competition to the major-party candidates is with the imposition of "sore loser" laws that prevent candidates who have lost a party primary for an office from running in the general election as an independent candidate. And even the few states that do not have such laws hardly make it easy for primary losers to jump into the general election contest. This "sore loser" barricade played out twice in Senate elections in the 2000s, first in 2006 in Connecticut and again in 2010 in Alaska.

In Connecticut Independent candidates who wish to be on the ballot must file the required petition signatures by the end of business the day after the primary, which gives a primary loser virtually no latitude in gaining a place on the November ballot. It is not impossible, though, as Sen. Joseph I. Lieberman proved in his trouble-fraught but ultimately successful bid for a fourth term in 2006.

Lieberman, the 2000 Democratic vice presidential nominee, had been expected to win another in a series of easy reelection victories. But his high-profile support for President George W. Bush's decision to go to war in Iraq and to extend the U.S. military commitment there drew him fierce opposition from liberal activists in his own party. Many of them rallied around the upstart candidacy of Ned Lamont, a wealthy businessman who opposed the war. As the August 2006 primary approached, it became clear that Lieberman was at serious risk of losing the Democratic nomination.

Recognizing that he would have no time to launch a petition drive for an independent candidacy if he waited for the primary results, Lieberman announced he would collect signatures in advance of the primary and would run as an independent if he were denied the Democratic nomination. The move was a gamble, as it further alienated Democratic loyalists and may have even contributed to his narrow primary defeat by Lamont. But he easily qualified the next day to run as an independent, asked voters to judge him by his overall record and not just on Iraq, and won reelection. He received 50 percent of the vote to 40 percent for Lamont and 10 percent for Alan Schlesinger, the politically weak candidate nominated by the Republican Party.

As he had promised during the campaign, Lieberman caucused with the Democrats, although he changed his party label from Democrat to independent and provided them with a crucial vote that enabled them to take control of the Senate following the election of 2006. In return he received committee assignments that included the chairmanship of the Homeland Security and Governmental Affairs Committee.

In Alaska in 2010 the incumbent senator, Lisa Murkowski, a Republican, unexpectedly lost the primary to a candidate that her campaign never took seriously. He was Jeff Miller, a former U.S. magistrate judge and a favorite of TEA PARTY activists who brought a surge of energy to many candidates nationwide in 2010 that significantly helped Republicans recapture control of the House of Representatives. He also was supported by former governor Sarah Palin, who was the GOP nominee for vice president in 2008 and a controversial and polarizing figure in U.S. politics after her party lost that contest. News reports also noted that Murkowski and Palin had long been rivals in Alaskan GOP circles.

Murkowski's loss was a major surprise to political observers who concluded that she overlooked the strength of voter discontent represented by the Tea Party movement and did not take the challenge seriously.

When she lost to Miller she—unlike Lieberman—was unprepared to run as an independent. Instead she elected to wage a write-in campaign to win reelection, a long-shot effort that not only required voters to take the extra step of penning in her name but to get the spelling correct. The last successful Senate write-in campaign came fifty years earlier when Strom Thurmond won a Senate seat in South Carolina in 1954. But Murkowski prevailed, beating Miller by more than 10,000 votes; however, her winning total was only 39 percent of total votes cast because of the presence of five other candidates in the race, including Miller.

In the congressional elections of 2010, incumbent Alaska senator, Lisa Murkowski, a Republican, won reelection with a write-in campaign, the first time a U.S. senator was elected this way since 1954. Murkowski had lost the GOP primary to a lightly regarded challenger who had the energetic backing of Tea Party conservatives. Blocked by state law from running as an independent, she elected to wage a write-in campaign to win reelection, a long-shot effort that not only required voters to take the extra step of penning in her name but to get the spelling correct. She prevailed by more than 10,000 votes.

Source: AP Images/Chris Miller

The states' right to require petitions for ballot access was upheld by the Supreme Court in *Jenness v. Fortson* (1971). The Court ruled that a state could require separate petitions for each candidate of a new party, with a maximum of signatures from 5 percent of the number of voters registered in the previous election for the office.

States also may specify how the signatures are gathered. Requirements may include one or more of the following:

- A minimum percentage must be obtained from each congressional district to show state-wide support.
- Signatures from persons who voted in the major-party primaries are unacceptable.
- No solicitation of signatures may be conducted by persons who live outside the district.
- Signers are required to pledge that they intend to vote for the new party's candidate.
- A limited time period is allowed for the collection of signatures.
- Signers are required to provide information they are not likely to know, such as their voter registration number or voting precinct designation.

Defenders of ballot access rules state that the requirements are not aimed at stifling alternative voices but, rather, at keeping ballots from becoming unwieldy, avoiding confusing voters with too many choices, and discouraging frivolous candidacies. They point out that states with low ballot access requirements can end up with laundry lists of candidates. One example they cite is the 1996 special election primary in Maryland's Seventh Congressional District following Democratic representative Kweisi Mfume's resignation to become president of the national NAACP. Twenty-seven Democratic candidates piled onto the ballot. Elijah E. Cummings, then a veteran state legislator, won the primary with 37 percent. He went on to win the general election before settling in to dominate the Baltimore-based district's politics for many years.

Advocates of restrictions also call attention to California's free-for-all gubernatorial recall election in 2003. While California has relatively steep ballot access rules for regular elections, the state has only minimal requirements in the exceedingly rare circumstance of an election to recall, or remove, a governor from office. This occurred in 2003 when a sufficient number of voters signed petitions, circulated mainly by Republican activists, to recall Democrat Gray Davis, who had been elected to a second term in 2002.

When California voters went to the polls on October 7, 2003, they had to vote on two matters. First they faced a simple yes-or-no question on whether to remove Davis from office; 55 percent of the voters favored recalling Davis. But on the second question—who should replace Davis should he be recalled—voters were confronted with a daunting list of 135 candidates (though few hopefuls had run visible and active campaigns). The list included former child television star Gary Coleman; comedian Leo Gallagher, best known for smashing watermelons with a mallet as part of his stage act; and two people associated with the pornography industry, *Hustler* magazine publisher Larry Flynt and actress Mary Carey. Emerging as the clear victor was Republican Arnold Schwarzenegger, the action film icon who was making his political debut (and would go on to easily win a full term in the regularly scheduled election of 2006) and

More on this topic:

Ballot Types, p. 17

Removal from Office, p. 530

State and Federal Election Responsibilities, p. 606

Third Parties, p. 627

Two-Party System, p. 636

who outran such established political figures as Democratic lieutenant governor Cruz Bustamante and Republican state senator Tom McClintock.

Ballot Types

The search for the perfectly designed ballot, the one that will make the candidate choices and procedure for casting a vote clear and obvious to all voters, has been a quest since the earliest days of American democracy—and, despite great advances in voting technology and education among the American electorate, has remained elusive well into the first decade of the twenty-first century.

That decade began with many states and localities employing punch-card ballots, which had supplanted traditional mechanical voting devices and paper ballots as a means of facilitating computerized vote counting. But an electoral crisis over the results of the 2000 presidential voting in Florida—the state with the electoral votes that ultimately decided the outcome in favor of Republican George W. Bush—provoked a national phase-out of punch-card ballots.

An official canvass gave Bush a 537-vote lead in Florida in 2000, but Democratic nominee Al Gore's campaign protested that he had been cost many votes because of flaws in the punch-card balloting process.

One of the problems cited by the Gore camp was the so-called butterfly ballot employed that year in Palm Beach County. Most punch-card ballots in use elsewhere listed candidates in a single column, with a single file of boxes or circles from which a voter could punch out the tab for his or her favored candidate. But the butterfly ballot listed candidates on both sides of a single column of punch-out boxes, with small arrows indicating which box belonged to which candidate. The confusing design of the ballot resulted in a number of complaints from voters who believed they had accidentally cast votes for Reform Party candidate Pat Buchanan when they meant to vote for Gore.

The more widespread issue with the ballots introduced the word *chad* into the nation's political vocabulary.

The Gore campaign challenged Bush's lead in Florida, arguing that poorly functioning hole-punch machines had failed to completely dislodge the tiny paper rectangles, known as chads, that enable the computerized ballot readers to recognize that a vote has been cast for a candidate. Citing a sizable number of undervotes—meaning ballots on which votes were recorded in contests for other offices but not in the race

Source: Cagle Cartoons, Inc.

for president—Gore demanded a hand recount of ballots in several counties. Before the process was effectively terminated more than a month after the election by the Supreme Court in its *BUSH V. GORE* decision, Americans were transfixed by the televised spectacle of local election officials examining individual ballots, in some cases holding them up to the light, to see if they could determine a voter's intent to cast a vote for a particular candidate.

The mess spurred many states to replace their punch-card balloting systems. This process was greatly accelerated by a provision in the HELP AMERICA VOTE ACT OF 2002 that provided federal funding for states to replace punch-card machines prior to the 2004 presidential election. The law did, however, include a provision allowing states to apply for an extension to 2006.

Yet the new touch-screen electronic voting machines—technology that many states chose to replace the punch cards—turned out to have their own problems in the 2006 elections. Prior to the elections, widespread concerns were voiced that the machines could be programmed or "hacked" by persons attempting vote fraud, but these appear to have been overstated. There were complaints in numerous localities, though, that the machines had incorrectly recorded votes, failed to register votes, or had a faulty ballot design that caused voters to overlook a contest.

Florida, somewhat ironically, was the site of the biggest controversy over this new technology during the 2006 election. The House election in Florida's Thirteenth District produced the only race that year that was contested past the swearing-in of the 110th Congress in January 2007. Protesting the certified victory of Republican Vern Buchanan by a 369-vote margin, Democratic candidate Christine Jennings cited a disproportionate undervote in Sarasota County, which was also where she ran strongest in the official vote count. Jennings argued that the electronic machines had failed to record many votes intended for her. Some voters in the district complained that the ballot design caused them to overlook the House contest altogether.

Coincidentally, the Thirteenth District seat had been left open by an unsuccessful Senate bid by Republican representative Katherine Harris, who, as the state's chief election official in 2000, was at the center of the controversy over the Bush-Gore presidential vote count.

Three Centuries of Change

When the first elections were held in Britain's North American colonies, English balloting customs prevailed. In some elections, the colonists cast written ballots. But because many voters could not read, the election official sometimes called for a voice vote or a show of hands. In other elections, voters would make their choice on an issue or candidate by throwing an object symbolic of their choice, for example, a kernel of corn for a yea, a dried bean for a nay, into a receptacle.

During the colonial period, the most commonly used methods of voting appear to have been the voice vote or the show of hands. Although there is a record of another kind of ballot—the secret ballot—being used in 1634 by freemen to oust an unpopular English governor, its widespread use in American elections did not happen until more than two centuries later.

From the beginning of the revolutionary period to the early part of the nineteenth century, another method of balloting came into favor. In this system, an eligible voter would write the name of his choice or choices on a slip of paper and then pass it to an election judge who would then drop it in the ballot box.

The increasing growth and subsequent domination of political parties over the political process in the early and middle nineteenth century soon spelled changes in this style of balloting, however. Political operatives have been nothing if not clever over the years about using voting procedures to further their own and their party's interests. Illiteracy or the barest traces of literacy were commonplace in the early United States, and party leaders decided to make it easier for uneducated voters, whose ability to write was likely confined to their signature, and exceptionally useful for themselves. Party representatives would hand out preprinted lists of their party's nominees, which the individual voter could then turn over to the election judge for deposit in the ballot box. The illiterate voter was spared the laborious task of reading or writing out a long list of names (indeed, of reading or writing anything), and the party leader greatly aided his entire slate of nominees, enhancing the party's unity and political power.

Because the list of offices to be voted upon steadily increased through the nineteenth century, getting all the names printed entailed using long strips of paper that resembled the railroad tickets of the day. The list of a party's candidates for a specific election came to be called—and remains—the *ticket*.

The ticket system of voting was tailor-made for corruption and was soon riddled with it. Those who dispensed the ballots outside polling places, it was charged, could easily ensure that their chosen voters voted the way the leaders wanted. Because a voter had to choose a particular ticket before entering the polling place, the leaders or their operatives at the polling place made sure the voter entered with their ticket and no one else's. Intimidation of voters became rife, making a mockery of the democratic voting process. Choices, in short, could not be freely made and expressed; many voters were told how to vote, some were bribed, and others were intimidated, often by the threat or actual use of physical violence.

Any voting system that encouraged the growth of one party's domination of a state's or city's political life was guaranteed efforts by that party to preserve it. Abuses, many in the election process, spawned widespread demands for reform down to the most fundamental element of an election—the ballot.

The most important innovation introduced by this reform movement was the adoption in the United States of the so-called Australian ballot, which had first been used in South Australia in 1856. Joseph P. Harris, author of a definitive study of the American electoral system, defines the Australian ballot as "an official ballot, printed at public expense, by public officers, containing the names of all candidates duly nominated, and distributed at the polls by the election officers."

Besides ostensibly removing the elements that unduly favored one party over another in the preparation and distribution of earlier ballots, the Australian ballot carried the essential ingredient of secrecy; the voter would cast his ballot in secret, and it would be counted in such a way that it was impossible to determine how the voter voted. With this kind of ballot came the shielded voting booth, followed by the VOTING MACHINE, so that the individual voter was free from prying eyes.

After the exceptionally close 1884 presidential election, replete with charges of vote fraud and fears of a deadlocked election, the winner, Democrat Grover Cleveland, campaigned hard for the reform measure that eventually became the Electoral Count Act. This measure gave each state final authority in determining the legality of its choice of electors. After its passage, the secret ballot movement gained momentum across the country. The Australian ballot was first adopted by Kentucky in 1888 and soon was in place in all the states except South Carolina, which did not adopt it until 1950.

The Australian ballot form is used in all elections in all states now; and although the actual forms of the ballot may change considerably from state to state, they must by law fit into one of five major categories. Even with the advent of computerized voting, the electronic ballot form still must conform to these basic types:

- Party Column. In this form, all the candidates of a particular political party are listed in a vertical column. The party lists are arranged side by side, and a single vertical column at the left margin displays the office being contested. In this way, the names of all candidates for any particular office are next to each other in a horizontal line that runs across the ballot. This form of ballot, some critics say, encourages "straight-ticket" voting. (See SPLIT- AND STRAIGHT-TICKET VOTING.)

- **Office Group.** The candidates of all parties running for a particular office are listed in a vertical column with the office being contested listed at the top of the column. This form of ballot was adopted to discourage straight-ticket voting by forcing the voter to read each name for each office and, it was hoped, reflect further on a candidate's individual merit before marking the ballot.
- **Party Circle.** A political party, on this kind of ballot, will have a circle or box printed at the top of its list of candidates, and the voter, by making a mark in the box, signifies that he or she is voting for the party's ticket. In a variation, voters must make a mark next to the name of every individual candidate of his or her chosen party to vote a straight ticket. Yet another version was called the Massachusetts Plan: In this type, all the names of candidates of all parties for each office are placed in alphabetical order under a heading bearing the name of the office. The voter must then make a mark next to each of his or her choices.
- **Party Emblem.** Several states allow the printing of some kind of party emblem (the Democrats' donkey, the Republicans' elephant, for example) at either the head of a party's column of candidates or next to the name of each of its candidates. This makes identification of a nominee's party affiliation more obvious to the less-literate voter. Many states do not allow emblems, but some will permit a candidate's party affiliation to be printed under his or her name, particularly when a large number of parties contest a given election.
- **Write In.** Every state now offers the *WRITE-IN VOTE*—a means of voting for a candidate not listed on the ballot. Some candidates are left off because they decided to run after the deadline for inclusion on the ballot had passed. In most voting jurisdictions, the ballot has a blank space at the bottom of the list of candidates for a particular office where the voter can write in a name. Some states allow the pasting on of a preprinted label bearing the candidate's name in this space, but this is less common. States that did not permit write-ins or paste-ons were referred to as having "no-Johnny-come-lately" ballots.

Many ballots today also include *INITIATIVES AND REFERENDUMS*, *REMOVAL FROM OFFICE*, and bond issue questions that require voter approval by a simple yes or no. Given the complexity of some of these questions, which are usually couched in formal, legislative language, most initiative or referendum ballots add an "explanatory or interpretive statement" to aid voters in making a fully informed choice.

The style of any state's ballot is set by that state's election laws, those statutes agreed upon by its legislators to impose upon all those involved in the actual election process a firm set of rules and procedures that will leave virtually no room for deviation, whether through chance or an individual election official's discretionary choice—though this, as illustrated by the varying standards for ballot design and recount procedures in Florida counties during the 2000 presidential vote controversy, is hardly universal. The implementation and oversight of the state's election laws are delegated to a state board of elections, the state's GOVERNOR, or, the most common arrangement, the secretary of state, who also serves as the chief election officer.

In voting analyst Harris's definition, the chief election officer "publishes the election laws, receives the official returns and usually tabulates the results for the official CANVASSING BOARD, certifies to the county officers in charge of printing the ballots the names of candidates for state office, certifies the form of the ballot and the working of referendum propositions, and attends to various other clerical details in connection with state elections."

At the next level down, most states' election laws require local officials, such as the county clerk, board of supervisors, or the mayor and city council, to supervise officials of a specific voting district, be it a county or a city. At the lowest level are the only election officials most voters ever see—those present at their particular voting place on ELECTION DAY. Here is where the voter lists and district registers are used to ascertain their eligibility and where the ballots, in whatever form, are cast, counted, and certified. In case of a RECOUNT or CONTESTED ELECTION, further counting and certification takes place later at the election board headquarters, where ABSENTEE VOTING ballots, in most locations, are also counted.

Even though most state laws require these voting-district boards to be nonpartisan, in most jurisdictions the party in the majority gets the majority of positions on the board, which can lead, in some cases, to partisanship or to somewhat less benign treatment of voters from the minority parties. Therefore, the officials that run the actual voting districts, writes Harris, "determine the character of elections."

Bandwagon Effect

The term *bandwagon effect* is used to describe the attraction that successful campaigns have for voters, particularly those who may be undecided as ELECTION DAY nears. If a popular candidate seems to be rolling along to victory, people may "hop on the bandwagon" to be on the winning side.

The term derives from the spectacle of the old-time circus bandwagon coming down Main Street, blaring joyous music and tempting young boys to climb aboard. Indeed, the word *bandwagon* still conjures up visions of bright colors, balloons, and celebration.

POLITICAL CONSULTANTS and campaign managers try to cultivate an image of a confident and happy campaign, even if POLLING shows that their candidate is headed for defeat. They play on voter psychology, knowing that people hesitate to waste votes on a losing cause.

For that reason, the bandwagon effect is a serious element in the controversy over the news media's FORECASTING ELECTION RESULTS while the polls are still open in some parts of the country or in parts of a state where a close statewide race is being decided. Some voters, hearing that their candidate is winning, may rush to the polls to be on the bandwagon. Others may stay home thinking the race is over.

This concern ties in with controversies over the use of EXIT POLLS by the television networks to try to quickly call outcomes after each state's polling places close. The first big flap of this kind occurred in 1980. Exit polls indicated that Ronald Reagan would defeat incumbent president Jimmy Carter—a prediction that was confirmed when actual returns starting coming in from states in the East—prompting Carter to concede while the polls were still open in the West. Some Democrats complained afterward that the bandwagon effect had caused some western Democratic voters to stay home.

Candidates and their campaign managers try to orchestrate public appearances that will put the candidate in a favorable light. Richard Nixon appears the hero in this 1968 campaign photo.

Source: National Archives and Record Administration

Democratic presidential hopeful Sen. Hillary Rodham Clinton, D-N.Y., speaks to supporters at her Montana and South Dakota primary night event in New York Tuesday, June 3, 2008. Though Clinton did not concede defeat to her rival, Barack Obama, she spoke about the vice presidential spot on his fall ticket. (AP Photo/Elise Amendola)

The limitations of the bandwagon effect were evident in the Democratic contest for the 2008 presidential nomination. Hillary Clinton, the wife of former president Bill Clinton and the nation's first lady during his two terms in the White House and later a New York senator, was widely considered the front runner to be the party's nominee that year. Her campaign openly encouraged party stalwarts to join her early—get on the bandwagon—to be with the winner. In the early handicapping, most observers believed she would have an easy road to the nomination.

But Illinois Sen. Barack Obama disagreed. Without broad backing in the party, except for the warm endorsement of Sen. Ted Kennedy, D-Mass., a party icon, Obama announced on February 10, 2007, he was running, less than a month after Clinton announced. Although Clinton continued to be seen as the favorite, Obama laid out a systematic nationwide campaign to contest not only the smaller states with primaries but also most of the caucus states; Clinton relied more on big-state primaries. As a result, the Democratic contest continued, formally, until June, but with hindsight it became clear that Obama had all but locked up the nomination by victories in February primaries. From then on it became increasingly clear that Clinton, in spite of her early bandwagon notoriety, could never assemble enough delegates to the Democratic convention to top Obama.

The exit poll issue again flared up in the 2000 presidential race, during the controversial contest between Republican George W. Bush and Democrat Al Gore for Florida's crucial electoral votes. Republicans attempted to counter Gore's claim of widespread vote-counting irregularities by arguing that voter turnout in the strongly conservative Panhandle region had been suppressed by the networks' use of exit poll data to make early (and erroneous) projections of a Gore victory in Florida. While the polls in most of Florida closed at 7:00 p.m. Eastern time, the Panhandle is in the central time zone so its polls closed an hour later.

Perhaps the most consistent illustration of the bandwagon effect in recent campaigns, however, has occurred in the major parties' presidential nominating process. Since the early 1970s when primaries became the main instrument of determining voters' presidential preferences, each party's front-running candidate has tended to gain momentum from victories in the early primaries, with the bandwagon effect quickly forcing other contenders from the race.

Beauty Contest

A *beauty contest* presidential preference primary is a sort of popularity straw vote. It does not affect the allocation of delegates to the Democratic or Republican NATIONAL PARTY CONVENTIONS. (See PRIMARY TYPES.)

The concept of the beauty contest primary had adherents during the rise of presidential primaries in the twentieth century. The format addressed voters' interests in having a say in the presidential contest without eroding the party bosses' ability to determine which candidate their states' delegates would back.

More on this topic:

National Party Conventions, p. 347

New Hampshire Primary, p. 369

Proportional Representation, p. 493

But voters' demands for the ultimate power to choose the presidential delegates led both parties to replace beauty contest primaries with actual delegate selection primaries. In the 2004 campaign to choose a Democratic challenger to President George W. Bush, only Idaho held a beauty contest primary. Caucuses determined the actual allocation of delegates.

Oregon originated the beauty contest primary in 1910, nine years after Florida passed the first presidential primary law. Oregon's was the first in which voters expressed preference for the candidates themselves, rather than for the delegates. The delegates, however, were legally bound to vote for the candidates in accordance with the beauty contest results.

The first-in-the-nation NEW HAMPSHIRE PRIMARY, then a beauty contest–type vote, attracted national attention in 1952 when World War II general Dwight D. Eisenhower outpolled the leading candidate for the Republican nomination, Sen. Robert Taft of Ohio. Eisenhower's name had been placed on the ballot by Sen. Henry Cabot Lodge of Massachusetts, leader of the "Draft Eisenhower" movement. "Ike" went on to win the nomination and the presidency.

The same year in New Hampshire's Democratic beauty contest, Sen. Estes Kefauver of Tennessee scored a surprise victory over President Harry S. Truman, who later said he had decided before the primary not to seek reelection. The Democratic convention ultimately nominated former Illinois governor Adlai E. Stevenson, who lost to Eisenhower in the November election.

Since 1952 the New Hampshire primary, no longer a beauty contest, has grown in importance as a crucial first step for presidential aspirants. New Hampshire delegates of both parties are now divided among the candidates by PROPORTIONAL REPRESENTATION, with each receiving the number reflecting his or her share of the primary vote.

Bill Bradley, seeking the Democratic party's nomination in 2000, targeted the beauty contest in the state of Washington in an attempt to claim some political momentum. Here, Bradley celebrates after catching a five-pound king salmon at Seattle's Public Market, February 11, 2000.

Source: AP Images/Charles Rex Arbogast

Beauty contests still have some symbolic importance. Bill Bradley, a Democratic presidential contender in 2000, targeted the beauty contest in the state of Washington in a bid to try to claim some political momentum, but he failed to upset FRONT-RUNNER Al Gore.

Bellwether

In politics a *bellwether* is a candidate or place that indicates the likely outcome of an election. It takes its name from shepherds' practice of putting a bell on the lead male sheep to signal which way the flock is heading.

For years, Maine enjoyed a reputation as the bellwether in presidential elections. From 1860 to 1932 it voted for the winning candidate in all but three of the nineteen elections, prompting the saying, "As Maine goes, so goes the nation."

Rep. John Hostettler waves to supporters in Evansville, Indiana, after his defeat on November 7, 2006.

Source: AP Images/Daniel R. Patmore

While the term *bellwether* is most often applied to the voting behavior of states and localities, it also is applied to individual candidates whose prospects of victory are seen as indicators for the national outcome of an election. During the 2006 midterm congressional elections, for example, television networks and political publications such as Congressional Quarterly's CQPolitics.com previewed the "races to watch" early on election night that would provide indications of whether the Democrats would succeed in their effort to end the Republicans' twelve-year control of the U.S. House of Representatives. When the states with the earliest poll closing times produced defeats for Republican incumbents such as Kentucky's Anne M. Northup and Indiana's Chris Chocola, John Hostettler, and Mike Sodrel, it became clear that it would be a good night for the Democrats. They went on to gain thirty House seats in the election, fifteen more than they needed for a majority.

But that reputation was built on a flawed premise. The reason Maine had such a consistent record was that it was a Republican Party stronghold during an era of Republican dominance in presidential politics. Its reputation came crashing down during the Great Depression, when the repudiation of Republican president Herbert Hoover and the rise of Franklin D. Roosevelt heralded a new era of Democratic Party preeminence. In 1936, when Roosevelt was elected to a second term in a LANDSLIDE, Maine and Vermont were the only states that favored Republican nominee Alfred M. Landon—spurring Democratic National Committee chairman James A. Farley to quip, "As Maine goes, so goes Vermont."

Other states and even local jurisdictions have emerged at times as bellwethers. Missouri, home of 1948 presidential winner Harry S. Truman, has a rather sturdy reputation. An amalgam of large industrial cities with sizable minority populations, growing suburbs, and rural areas—including many that have a southern orientation—Missouri is perhaps the epitome of an electoral "swing" state.

The last time—before 2008—Missouri voted for the losing presidential candidate was in 1956, when Democratic challenger Adlai E. Stevenson outpolled Republican incumbent president Dwight D. Eisenhower by a margin of just two-tenths of one percentage point. Between then and 2004, the state voted Republican in all seven races won by that party and Democratic in that party's five White House victories. However, the record was broken in 2008 when the state went for Sen. John McCain, R-Ariz., who lost the presidential contest to Illinois Sen. Barack Obama. But Missouri nearly retained its record: McCain bested Obama by only 3,903 votes out of nearly 3 million cast.

In the first years of the twenty-first century, it appeared the conservative strain in Missouri politics might be taking precedence over its bellwether characteristic by turning the state dependably Republican. Republican Jim Talent narrowly ousted interim Democratic senator Jean Carnahan in a 2002 special election; Republican George W. Bush, who carried Missouri by just three points in his 2000 presidential win, boosted his margin to seven points in 2004; and Republican Matt Blunt won a close race for governor in 2004 to end a twelve-year Democratic hold on the office. But in 2008 Democrat Jeremiah W. "Jay" Nixon won the governorship with 58 percent of the vote.

Missouri's bellwether reputation had been burnished in 2006, a strong year for Democrats nationally, when voters in its Senate election ousted the well-regarded Talent in favor of Democrat Claire McCaskill, who had narrowly lost the 2004 governor's election to Blunt.

Bicameral

The U.S. Congress, like the legislatures of every state except Nebraska, is *bicameral*. It consists of two chambers, the Senate and the House of Representatives. A UNICAMERAL legislature has but one house.

When the Constitution was being drafted at Philadelphia in 1787, the founders agreed from the outset that Congress, which they designed to be the heart of the Republic, would be bicameral. They disagreed, however, on how the members of each chamber would be elected.

Their debate on the question helps to explain why they favored a two-house lawmaking body rather than a single-house body. Precedence was one factor. The founders were familiar with bicameralism in the British Parliament, most of the colonial governments, and ten of the thirteen states. (The remaining three original states eventually converted to bicameral legislatures.)

As Virginia delegate George Mason put it during the Constitutional Convention, the minds of Americans were settled on two points: "an attachment to republican government [and] an attachment to more than one branch in the Legislature." (See REPUBLICAN GOVERNMENT.) With two branches or houses to the legislature, the delegates were able to resolve a dispute that threatened to break up the convention and the effort to frame a new government. It concerned the fears of small states that they would be dominated by the larger states if seats in both chambers were apportioned according to population, as proposed for the House. The solution, known as the Great Compromise or Connecticut Compromise, was to give each state two senators regardless of population. Even the smallest state was also assured at least one representative.

Convention delegates who were suspicious of a national government preferred election to the House of Representatives by the state legislatures. "The people immediately should have as little to do" with electing the government as possible, said Roger Sherman of Connecticut, because "they want [lack] information and are constantly liable to be misled."

The majority, however, twice defeated election by the legislatures. Popular election for the House was agreed to with only one state dissenting. The government "ought to possess . . . the mind or sense of the people at large," said Pennsylvania delegate James Wilson.

There was little support for the view that the people also should elect the Senate. Nor did the delegates think that the House should choose members of the Senate from among persons nominated by the state legislatures. Election of the Senate by the state legislatures was agreed to with only two states dissenting. DIRECT ELECTION of senators did not become the rule in every state until ratification of the Seventeenth Amendment in 1913.

The lower houses of the state legislatures served as models for the U.S. House. At the time, all the states had at least one chamber elected by popular vote. The three unicameral legislatures— in Georgia, Pennsylvania, and Vermont—also were popularly elected.

More on this topic:
Direct Election, p. 161
Republican Government, p. 535
Unicameral, p. 640

Roger Sherman was the most prominent of Connecticut's representatives to the Constitutional Convention of 1787. His delegation presented the outline of "the Great Compromise," which broke the deadlock over representation between large and small states.

Source: Library of Congress

The founders intended the Senate to be a restraining influence on the House, and the Senate still claims to be the more deliberative body. George Washington is said to have called the Senate "the saucer where the political passions of the nation are cooled."

Bilingual Voters

The federal VOTING RIGHTS ACT of 1965, which guaranteed the vote to racial minorities, also required states and localities to provide voting and other election-related information to millions of Americans whose primary language is not English.

The nation's Hispanic population as recorded in the 2010 census was 50.5 million, or 16.3 percent of the total. The increase in Hispanic population in the United States since 2000, 15.2 million persons, accounted for more than half of the total population increase during the ten-year period. Moreover, the 2010 increase followed a 63 percent jump in the 2000 census over the figure in 1990. The increases were concentrated in the South and West. Political analysts said this gave Hispanics—which traditionally had voted Democratic—the necessary votes to control elections in Texas, California, and less populous southwestern states, if larger numbers of their group could be brought into the voting booth.

Nevertheless, Hispanics voted in smaller proportional numbers than members of other groups. For example, exit polls showed that Hispanics made up only 5 percent of the nation's electorate in the 2006 midterm congressional elections. There are a variety of reasons for this disproportion, including substantial numbers of recent immigrants who were not citizens, many of whom had entered and were residing in the United States illegally. In addition, the percentage of Hispanic residents younger than the voting age of eighteen was somewhat higher than that of the nation as a whole. Further, Hispanics' lower rate of political participation may also be attributed to the language barrier.

In the late twentieth and early twenty-first centuries, the United States experienced the largest wave of immigration in nearly a century. The majority of the new immigrants came from Mexico and Spanish-speaking nations in Latin America. It is immigrants such as these that the Voting Rights Act is meant to serve. More than forty years after its enactment, however, the act's provisions remain subject to contention. An English-only movement believes that providing bilingual voter information discourages assimilation, while supporters of bilingual voting assistance see it as an inclusive measure that allows all citizens to be engaged in their government.

"For language minorities, the expiring provisions certainly enhance political inclusion. English-only voting materials bar non-English speaking citizens from voting by effectively imposing a literacy test as a condition of exercising the franchise."

—**Debo P. Adegbile** of the NAACP Legal Defense and Educational Fund, testifying in support of renewal of the bilingual voting assistance provisions of the Voting Rights Act before the Senate Judiciary Committee on June 21, 2006

"This long tradition of assimilation has always included the adoption of English as the common means of communication. Unfortunately, the proliferation of multilingual government sends the opposite message to non-English speakers: it is not necessary to learn English because the government will accommodate them in other languages."

—Advocacy group U.S. English, explaining on its website the rationale behind the "English-only" movement in early 2007

With portions of the Voting Rights Act set to expire in 2007, Congress in 2006 debated the bilingual provisions, but lawmakers were reluctant to risk alienating Hispanic voters. In a near-unanimous vote across both chambers, Congress approved a twenty-five-year extension of the temporary provisions of the act, including the bilingual voting requirements. President George W. Bush signed the bill on July 27, 2006.

Yet in November 2006, Arizona voters approved a state constitutional amendment making English the state's official language and requiring the government to provide services—with the exception of voting procedures proscribed by the Voting Rights Act—in English only. That made Arizona the twenty-eighth state to make English its official language and suggested that the issue of bilingual voting remained open for debate. By 2011 more than half the states had some type of official-English requirements in place.

Even as debate continues over whether bilingual election services benefit or hold back Hispanic Americans, politicians of both parties—including Republican George W. Bush in his successful 1994 and 1998 campaigns for governor of heavily Hispanic Texas and his victorious 2000 and 2004 bids for president—have adjusted to the realities of this fast-growing constituency by addressing Hispanic audiences at least partially in Spanish and by advertising in Spanish-language media. Doing so is particularly important in states such as California, Texas, New York, Florida, and Arizona, where Hispanics make up such substantial portions of the overall population that they can tip the balance in a close statewide contest.

Democrats, long seen as the major party that is more sympathetic to minority groups and lower-income Americans, generally have enjoyed an overall advantage over Republicans among Hispanic voters. This has been true among such large segments of the Hispanic population as Mexican Americans and Puerto Ricans; the latter are U.S. citizens with automatic voting rights as residents of a U.S. commonwealth. The Republican leanings among Cuban Americans stem largely from the GOP's overall anticommunist attitude and specific opposition to the communist regime of Cuban president Fidel Castro.

The Republicans' efforts to wean a substantial number of Hispanics away from the Democratic Party have been hindered in recent years by a deep split within the GOP over immigration, particularly how to deal with the millions of Hispanics who entered and are living in the United States illegally. Bush and many other business-oriented Republicans long advocated a position that the U.S. economy needs immigrant laborers to take the low-wage jobs that Americans do not want. But when Bush pressed the Republican-controlled 109th Congress (2005–2007) to pass legislation creating a guest-worker program that would include a possible path to citizenship for many illegal immigrants, there was a populist backlash among many conservative Republicans who viewed the proposal as providing a form of amnesty to those who broke immigration laws.

While the Senate passed a bill that was close to Bush's preference, the House passed an alternative that was more punitive toward illegal immigrants and contained no guest-worker option. This created a legislative stalemate and reinforced a view held by many Hispanics that the Republican Party was "anti-immigrant."

Effect of Federal Laws

The 1965 Voting Rights Act banned LITERACY TESTS for voting. It also stipulated that a citizen could not be denied the vote because of an inability to read or write English, if he or she had

CLOSER LOOK

One side effect of immigration and the federal legislation was a quadrupling of the number of Hispanic members of Congress. From 1877 to 1967 there had been no more than four Hispanic members at any one time, and for most Congresses in that period there were none or one or two. After 1967 the number increased gradually, reaching thirty-one in the 112th Congress, which began in January 2011.

That Congress included twenty-nine Hispanic House members and two senators. Twenty-one House members were Democrats, eight were Republicans; each party had one senator.

In spite of Hispanic gains in recent years, their numbers in Congress were far short of the national Hispanic population. The 2010 census showed a population of 50.5 million Hispanics. If Hispanics were represented proportionally in Congress, they would hold eighty-seven seats.

successfully completed the sixth grade (or the equivalent depending on state requirements) in a school under the American flag conducted in a language other than English.

In *Katzenbach v. Morgan* (1966) the Supreme Court upheld the provision on accredited American flag schools. It was intended to enfranchise Puerto Ricans educated in such schools, living in the United States but unable to demonstrate literacy in English.

In 1975 Congress extended the act for seven years and expanded the bilingual provisions. Additional protection was given to persons of Spanish heritage, Asian Americans, and Alaska natives. Federal preclearance of state election law changes was required in any jurisdiction where the Census Bureau had determined the following: more than 5 percent of the voting-age citizens were of a single language minority; election materials had been printed only in English for the 1972 presidential election; or fewer than 50 percent of the voting age citizens had registered or voted in the 1972 presidential election.

In 1982 Congress extended the bilingual election provisions to 1992 and the rest of the act to 2007. Ten years later, the bilingual requirements also were renewed to 2007. The amendment required that bilingual services be provided in jurisdictions with ten thousand or more non-English speakers, even if they did not make up 5 percent of the population. Among the first to be affected were several counties in the Los Angeles, San Francisco, Chicago, and Philadelphia areas.

The 1993 MOTOR VOTER ACT, enabling citizens to register to vote while obtaining a driver's license, greatly expanded the VOTER REGISTRATION rolls all across the country, including sections where many voters had limited proficiency in English. Affected communities had to recruit and train bilingual poll workers. In some jurisdictions outmoded voting systems proved to be inadequate to handle the added requirements.

Santa Clara County, California, for example, had to provide ballots in Vietnamese and Chinese. It also had to seek a replacement for its aged punch-hole system "because the length of the ballot and the use of bilingual ballots has made the continued use of Votomatic impossible."

Bipartisan Campaign Reform Act (BCRA) of 2002 *See* CAMPAIGN FINANCE

Black Suffrage

The struggle of blacks for full voting rights in the United States is almost as old as the country itself. For the most part, the struggle ended in 1965 with passage of the historic VOTING RIGHTS ACT. Yet there are still instances where impediments are placed in the way of African Americans' RIGHT TO VOTE.

In the early days of the Republic, voting was restricted to adult white males, but only about half of them were eligible to vote. States required ownership of property or payment of taxes, which excluded poor white men. Slaves, Indians, and women could not vote. By the early twentieth century, most of the ineligible groups had broken down their barriers to the franchise. But voting discrimination against African Americans was the last to be rectified. (See DIRECT ELECTION; WOMEN'S SUFFRAGE.)

The U.S. Constitution sanctioned slavery. The constitutional provision that declared a black person to be three-fifths a person for CENSUS considerations was the ugly codification of what many early Americans considered blacks to be: property. In *Scott v. Sandford* (1857), popularly known as the *Dred Scott Case,* the Supreme Court confirmed this notion, holding that slaves were property, not included under the word *citizen* in the Constitution, and therefore unable to claim any of the rights and privileges of many white Americans.

Although a tiny fraction of free blacks in the northern states had some voting rights at the beginning of the nineteenth century, they were the exception. In 1861, when the Civil War broke out, twenty-seven of the thirty-three states prohibited blacks from voting. Before World War II began in the 1940s for the United States, only about 150,000 blacks in the South, or about 3 percent of the estimated population of 5 million blacks of voting age in that region, were registered to vote.

Slavery and the Civil War

The Civil War was not fought only about slavery, as many popular versions of American history suggest, but also over the issues of states' rights and the North-South balance of power in national politics. When President Abraham Lincoln issued the Emancipation Proclamation on January 1, 1863, it granted freedom to slaves in states fighting against the Union. Although the proclamation was questionable legally, and was motivated partly by a hope to enlist blacks as Union soldiers, it led to the extension of the long-denied vote to blacks. Lincoln had openly expressed the desire to move slowly and cautiously on the inclusion of blacks in the democratic process, however, saying he wished to give priority to "very intelligent" blacks and to blacks who had fought on the Union side.

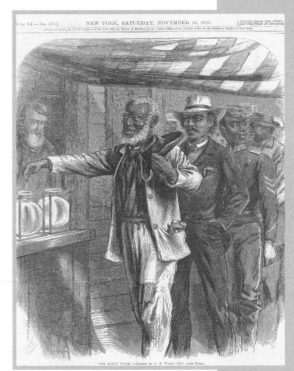

Black suffrage after the Civil War was seen primarily as a system for the Radical Republicans to control Congress by permanently negating the disproportionate political power of the southern planters. In many southern states, "black codes" had been passed that effectively prohibited blacks from voting and holding office. The Radical Republicans in Congress after the war's end responded to these codes by passing a number of measures to bring blacks into political life, the most important of which was the Reconstruction Act of 1867. The act set up military governments in the states of the Confederacy and tied their readmission to the Union to passage of the Fourteenth Amendment.

Many scholars believe that after the Bill of Rights, the Fourteenth Amendment is the most important addition to the Constitution. The amendment, particularly after expanded interpretations by the Supreme Court in the twentieth century, bans *states* from limiting the "privileges

Blacks, including a Union soldier, are depicted casting their first ballots in an image published November 16, 1867. In fact, it would take about a hundred years to secure voting rights for African Americans.

Source: Library of Congress

and immunities" of American citizens and orders *states* to respect all citizens' rights to "due process" and "equal protection of the laws." The provisions contained in the Bill of Rights deal with the relationship between a citizen and the federal government, and it took many years before these provisions were made applicable to the states. The Fourteenth Amendment, ratified in 1868, reduces the representation in Congress of states that deny the franchise to any male over twenty-one, a punishment that has never been carried out. The Fifteenth Amendment, which grants the franchise to all adult males regardless of race or "previous condition of servitude," was ratified the following year.

The addition of blacks to the American electorate was a crucial factor in Republican Ulysses S. Grant's slim 300,000-vote margin of victory in the 1868 presidential election—a year in which blacks first won election to state and federal offices, as federal troops with ties to the Republican Party enforced their voting rights in the former Confederate states. Between 1870 and 1900, twenty-two southern blacks won election to Congress, and two black Republicans from Mississippi served in the U.S. Senate. (See HOUSE OF REPRESENTATIVES, QUALIFICATIONS; SENATE, QUALIFICATION.)

"Jim Crow" Laws

Between 1858 and 1876, the Republican congressional majority had grown substantially with the addition of seven new northern states. The party also twice benefited from congressional REAPPORTIONMENT AND REDISTRICTING. No longer fearful that the "King Cotton" planters would obstruct them, the Republicans abandoned Reconstruction; as part of the political deal that gave the disputed 1876 presidential election to Republican Rutherford B. Hayes, the Republicans agreed to remove federal troops from the South and to allow southern states—where the long-dominant Democrats were quickly restored to power—to enact measures that restricted blacks' ability to participate in politics and the full life of the community. Without federal protection, the vast majority of blacks were essentially disenfranchised.

The states of the old Confederacy kept blacks from voting with an arsenal of racially discriminatory measures known as "Jim Crow" laws. Among these were POLL TAXES, LITERACY TESTS, property requirements, tests of morality, and GRANDFATHER CLAUSES, which exempted poor whites from the measures by guaranteeing the vote to citizens whose ancestors had voted or had served in the state militia.

Another device was the WHITE PRIMARY, which allowed the politically dominant Democratic Party to exclude blacks with the twisted legal argument that the party was a private organization and therefore not covered by the Fourteenth Amendment. While most blacks who had voted counted themselves as Republicans, most southern whites were Democrats. Given the measures that kept blacks from the polls and the growing threat of violence for those few who could overcome the various barriers and dare to vote, the Democratic SOUTHERN PRIMARY became the region's important election.

In the 1944 Supreme Court case *Smith v. Allwright,* white primaries were struck down in an interpretation that seemed sufficiently broad to forestall any evasion. The marginally increased black participation in southern Democratic primaries, however, did not seriously challenge white political control for another twenty years. Political scientist V. O. Key Jr. estimated that between 400,000 and 600,000 blacks in eleven southern states voted in 1946, only 10 percent to 12 percent of the total population of adult blacks in the region.

In response to the wide range of VOTER REGISTRATION requirements that restricted ballot access to blacks and vulnerable whites, such as illiterates, the total vote in southern states dropped by as much as 60 percent between 1884 and 1904.

Assault on Voting Discrimination

In the twentieth century, Congress and the federal courts mounted a sustained assault against voting discrimination against blacks. In 1915 the Supreme Court, in *Guinn v. United States,* ruled the grandfather clause unconstitutional. The white primary fell in 1944, and the Court, in the 1966 decision *Harper v. Virginia Board of Elections*, declared state poll tax requirements for voting in state elections unconstitutional.

The CIVIL RIGHTS ACT of 1957 established the Civil Rights Commission, which was empowered to study voter discrimination. The act also greatly expanded the attorney general's power to bring federal lawsuits against anyone restricting blacks' right to vote. A 1960 law gave the Justice Department the power to bring further legal action in cases that disclosed patterns of discrimination. It also authorized the appointment of federal officials to monitor elections.

Even these efforts to enhance voter rights for blacks provided insufficient protections. During the early 1960s, state legal barriers remained in place, and extreme opponents of the civil rights movement committed acts of violence against some blacks who tried to register to vote and the whites who were trying to assist them.

The big breakthroughs for blacks occurred in the mid-1960s, during the presidency of Democrat Lyndon B. Johnson. The 1964 Civil Rights Act required states to adopt uniform election procedures for all citizens, mandated that states show sufficient cause for rejecting voters who had completed the sixth grade or demonstrated an equivalent level of intellectual competence, and made the procedures for federal consideration of voting rights cases easier. Also in 1964, the ratification of the Twenty-fourth Amendment banned the use of the poll tax in federal elections.

Efforts to expand the franchise for blacks gained major momentum in early 1965, after Alabama troopers in the city of Selma used tear gas and clubs to break up a planned voting rights march from that city to the state capital of Montgomery. Among those injured was civil rights activist John Lewis, who later would go on to a long career in the U.S. House representing Atlanta, Georgia.

Later in 1965, passage of the sweeping Voting Rights Act suspended literacy tests. The act also required federal supervision of voter registration in all states and counties that on November 1, 1964, still had literacy tests or other qualifying examinations and where less than 50 percent of all voting-age citizens had voted in the 1964 presidential election. Jurisdictions under federal supervision henceforth needed Washington's approval for any changes in election procedures. This act alone added an estimated 1 million blacks to the voting rolls.

A 1970 amendment to the Voting Rights Act suspended all literacy tests for five years, regardless of whether they were discriminatory. Later that year, the Supreme Court upheld the law's constitutionality, and the tests were abolished permanently in 1975. Further, the "trigger" for federal involvement was applied to additional states and jurisdictions by amendments passed in 1970, 1975, and 1982. The 1982 law extended for an additional twenty-five years the provisions requiring nine states and parts of thirteen others to seek Washington's approval for election law changes.

The 1982 amendments to the 1965 Voting Rights Act also allowed states to create MINORITY-MAJORITY legislative districts by concentrating black and Hispanic voters.

The Republican Party was initially wary of this development as minority voters at the time leaned strongly toward the Democratic Party; they worried that the creation of more minority-dominated districts would enable the Democrats to expand their strength. But a conservative swing in the nation, especially among white voters in the former Democratic stronghold of the South, benefited the Republican Party. Further, by the early 1990s, leading Republican strategists allied with some supporters of increased minority representation. While promoting expanded minority representation helped improve the party's image among black and Hispanic voters, redistricting plans that concentrated minority voters in a handful of districts also boosted the dominance of conservative white voters in surrounding districts.

More on this topic:

Civil Rights Act, p. 102

Grandfather Clause, p. 241

Literacy Tests, p. 309

Poll Taxes, p. 426

Reapportionment and Redistricting, p. 317

Right to Vote, p. 549

Voting Rights Act, p. 663

White Primary, p. 674

As a result, while the number of minority-represented districts grew as a result of redistricting plans enacted in the early 1990s, so did the number of suburban and outlying districts in which white Republicans supplanted traditionally conservative southern Democrats. This phenomenon greatly abetted the Republicans' successful efforts in 1994 to gain a House majority that would last twelve years.

Not all white conservative voters were enamored of this strategy, known as "stacking of voters," though. In the 1993 SHAW V. RENO decision, the Supreme Court ruled that districts drawn to improve chances of minority representation could be so "bizarre" in shape that they could be considered unconstitutional racial redistricting or gerrymandering. Striking down three districts in Texas and one in North Carolina as unconstitutional, the Court ruled in Bush v. Vera (1996) that the districts were drawn with race as the overwhelming factor.

There has been no revival of formal legal obstacles to minority voting. While Democrats in the early twenty-first century maintained large advantages in support from blacks and Hispanics, both major parties openly competed for their backing. But minority advocates nonetheless contend there are instances in which minority voters are impeded in exercising their right to vote.

For example, during the contested 2000 presidential election, there were allegations of efforts to intimidate or mislead blacks to keep them from voting in Florida. In 2004 some Democrats and black activists accused Republican officials in Ohio of subterfuges that blocked blacks from voting in another close presidential vote. The votes in both states clinched Republican George W. Bush's presidential victories.

Additionally, several states have imposed or sought to impose voter identification requirements. Proponents say these are aimed at limiting voter fraud, but opponents describe them as backdoor methods of preventing many minorities from voting.

With the federal Voting Rights Act amendments enacted in 1982 set to expire in 2007, a twenty-five-year extension of the nonpermanent provisions was passed by the Republican-controlled Congress in 2006 and signed into law by Bush that July. The measure was enacted over the objections of some lawmakers and officials from states covered by the preclearance provisions requiring them to get approval from the U.S. Justice Department or the federal district court in Washington, D.C., prior to making any changes to election procedures and district maps. The affected states argued unsuccessfully that the provisions were unnecessarily time-consuming and expensive, given the removal of strictures against minority voting, the vast increase in black voter registration and participation, and the sizable roster of black elected officials in those states.

Blanket Primary   See PRIMARY TYPES

Blue Dog Democrats

The Blue Dog Coalition of conservative and centrist House Democrats was formed in the wake of the party's sweeping losses in the 1994 midterm elections, in which the Republican Party took control of both the House of Representatives—for the first time in forty years—and the Senate.

The 1994 elections took a particular toll on Democrats from conservative-voting areas, especially in the South, a region where the Republicans had already eroded the Democrats' longstanding dominance. Republicans widely targeted Democrats in these areas by seeking to tie them to a national Democratic Party that the GOP described as too liberal.

The Blue Dogs emerged as part of an effort to stem that trend. They attempted to impress upon voters that there was a viable conservative wing of the congressional Democratic Party and persuade the more liberal party leadership that conservatives needed to play a bigger role in Democratic agenda setting.

The coalition took its name from a series of quirky paintings by New Orleans artist George Rodrigue featuring a wide-eyed blue dog; a piece showing the blue dog in front of the U.S. Capitol became the group's logo. But the name also was a play on "yellow dog Democrat," an old expression from the days of the Democratic "Solid South." The label referred to a party loyalist who would vote for a yellow dog rather than a Republican, whose party was reviled for decades in the South because of its association with Abraham Lincoln and the Civil War.

The Blue Dog Coalition faced an almost immediate setback, as five of its initial twenty-one members switched parties in 1995 to join the new House Republican majority. The Blue Dogs also struggled to achieve the bipartisan outreach on issues such as a balanced federal budget that they had hoped would temper some of the more hard-line conservative objectives of the congressional Republican leadership.

Republican gains in the South played a major role in the party's takeovers of the U.S. House and Senate in the 1994 election and subsequent dominance over the next dozen years. The diminished numbers of southern Democrats in Congress also dramatically altered the once-formidable conservative coalition they had formed with Republicans. The GOP determined it could achieve most of its goals without the votes of the Blue Dogs and other conservative Democrats and focused its efforts on maintaining party unity rather than reaching out to potentially sympathetic Democrats. That marginalization led some political scientists to dismiss the conservative coalition as a remnant of the era when the South was largely a one-party Democratic monolith.

Yet rather than fading away, the Blue Dog Coalition grew to more than forty members as its leaders, focusing on the group's central theme of fiscal responsibility, reached out from the most conservative wing of the Democratic Party to those holding more centrist views. Democratic leaders—frustrated by failed attempts in a series of election cycles to overturn the GOP's dominance of Congress—also became more accommodating to the input of Blue Dogs and other center-right Democrats in shaping the party's electoral strategy.

CLOSER LOOK

The Blue Dog Coalition of Democrats, founded in 1995, had a strongly southern cast in its early years. But as members reached out to other Democratic colleagues who shared their core value of fiscal responsibility, the coalition's roster took on a more national perspective. Its lineup of forty-three members in mid-2007—shortly after the Democrats took control of the House following their victory in the 2006 elections—included just eighteen members from southern states. The group increased to more than fifty with the next election but suffered catastrophic losses in 2010 when Republicans, winning a net of sixty-three seats and House control, reduced its membership to twenty-six.

Democratic whip Steny Hoyer and the Blue Dog Coalition denounce the ballooning federal deficit on March 18, 2004.

Source: Office of the Majority Leader, Steny Hoyer

The Blue Dogs were rewarded in 2006, when Democrats gained thirty seats, ending the Republicans' twelve-year House majority. A number of the Democrats who won Republican seats ran as centrists and were elected from "swing" or even Republican-leaning districts. The gains were reinforced in 2008 but then all but wiped out when the GOP gained a net of sixty-three seats in a rout of Democrats in 2010. The Blue Dogs lost twenty-nine members in that election, twenty-three by defeat and the rest to retirement or runs for other offices. Their caucus was cut almost in half.

Boll Weevil

In the 1980s, conservative southern Democrats in the House of Representatives called themselves *Boll Weevils*. Although the boll weevil is a destructive pest in cotton fields, the House Boll Weevils adopted the name because of the insect's southern habitat and resistance to eradication. They often voted with House Republicans to help enact President Ronald Reagan's economic programs, which included reducing tax rates and limiting "big government" spending programs.

The Boll Weevils' opposite number called themselves *Gypsy Moths*, after another destructive and persistent insect. The moderate Republican Gypsy Moths represented mostly northeastern and midwestern districts where gypsy moth infestations had damaged forest areas. House Gypsy Moths often opposed "Reaganomics," which included cutbacks in domestic programs. As a group, they had become extinct in the 2000s as Democrats captured all northeastern seats, until 2010, and the House Republican Party became solidly conservative.

More on this topic:

*Blue Dog Democrats,
p. 32*

With Republicans controlling both chambers of Congress in the 1990s, a new breed of conservative Democrats emerged in the House under the name BLUE DOG DEMOCRATS. The almost two-dozen Blue Dogs were mostly southern Democrats, but about a third were from northern states. Some of the Blue Dogs had been Boll Weevils.

The *Boll Weevil* term originated in the House during the Eisenhower administration, but it had fallen into disuse until it was revived during the Reagan presidency.

Border States

The term *border state* has various definitions based on its context. For example, in international affairs, such as trade, immigration, and border security, a border state would be one that abuts Canada, Mexico, or, under some definitions, one of the nation's coastlines.

In a political sense, though, "border state" has been mainly used to characterize states located on the cusp between the northern and southern regions of the United States.

As defined in the midnineteenth century, there were four border states: Delaware, Kentucky, Maryland, and Missouri. Although these states allowed slavery, they did not secede from the Union, and they fought on the Northern side in the Civil War. When the western counties of Virginia split off and became the state of West Virginia in 1863, a fifth border state was created.

All five technically were Southern states because they were below the Mason-Dixon Line, the generally accepted demarcation between the North and the South. Surveyors Charles Mason and Jeremiah Dixon established the line in the 1760s as the border between Pennsylvania and Maryland.

But the five states came to be called border states rather than southern states because of their proximity to the Confederate border and their loyalty to the Union.

Over the years, political scientists, geographers, and statisticians have altered the list of what they consider to be "border states." The U.S. Bureau of the CENSUS, however, does not use the border state classification. It divides the fifty states into four regions (Northeast, Midwest, South, and West) and further divides each of those into two subregions, except for the South, which has three subregions. Under the Census Bureau grouping, four of the five original border states are listed under the South except for Missouri, which is under Midwest.

But other organizations use different criteria for organizing the states. Congressional Quarterly, for instance, includes Kentucky and West Virginia in its definition of southern states. But Maryland and Delaware, which long had quite conservative voting tendencies, have moved to the left politically and now have voting tendencies that place them with the states of the Northeast region.

While some question whether Maryland and Delaware still fit the political definition of border states, other political and demographic changes over time could shift states into that category. Virginia, for example, was long a bastion of southern conservatism; the state's capital of Richmond was the capital of the Confederacy. That once made Virginia solidly Democratic and in the latter part of the twentieth century shifted the state dependably into the Republican column. But the vast population growth of the Northern Virginia suburbs of Washington, D.C.—which have more in common with the Northeast Corridor than the Deep South—has given that region a Democratic edge, making Virginia more of a swing state, and perhaps a traditional border state, in the early twenty-first century. In fact, Virginia in 2008 voted for Barack Obama, a black Democrat, who comfortably carried the state with 52.6 percent of the total vote. It was only the third time since 1948, and the first since 1964, that the state went Democratic for president.

Brass Collar Democrat

Brass collar Democrat refers to a Democrat who votes a straight party ticket, though the term has fallen into general disuse in recent years. It is related to the also increasingly archaic term "yellow dog Democrat," a staunch party loyalist who supposedly would vote for a yellow dog rather than a Republican.

Both are mainly southern expressions that generally applied to conservative Democrats in the days when the so-called Solid South was a Democratic Party stronghold. Republicans, reviled as the "party of Lincoln" after the Civil War, made inroads in the twentieth century and now dominate politics in much of the South. Brass collar or yellow dog Democrats are therefore scarce today. (See REALIGNMENTS AND DEALIGNMENTS.)

The derivation of *brass collar Democrat* is unclear, but some language experts believe it, too, may have a canine connection. They surmise that it may refer to the heavy brass collars that made it easier to control strong-willed dogs.

In the mid-1990s moderate to conservative Democrats in the U.S. House of Representatives formed what they called the Blue Dog Coalition. The member BLUE DOG DEMOCRATS, mostly from the South, pledged to form a working relationship with the majority House Republicans in an effort to achieve common goals, but they met with limited success.

More on this topic:

Blue Dog Democrats, p. 32

Realignments and Dealignments, p. 513

Brokered Convention

Now a thing of the past, brokered NATIONAL PARTY CONVENTIONS were not unusual after conventions came into general use as presidential nominating devices in the midnineteenth century. They were so called because power brokers—influential party leaders, financiers, and FAVORITE SONS—"wheeled and dealed" to steer the nomination to the candidate of their choice, who was not necessarily the first choice of the DELEGATES in the hall.

The nomination of William McKinley (center) as the 1896 Republican candidate was orchestrated well in advance of the convention by power broker Mark Hanna (right).

Source: Library of Congress

Two controversial rules, since abolished by the Democrats and never used by the Republicans, made DEMOCRATIC PARTY conventions especially susceptible to manipulation by power brokers. They were the TWO-THIRDS RULE, which required a two-thirds majority vote for nomination, and the UNIT RULE, which enabled the majority of a state delegation to cast all the delegation's votes as a bloc.

The need for a two-thirds majority helped to make multiple balloting a characteristic of Democratic conventions for many years until the party dropped the rule in 1936. The record was 103 roll calls taken in 1924 before the convention settled on John W. Davis of New York as the party's nominee to oppose the Republican incumbent, Calvin Coolidge.

By contrast, only one GOP convention took more than ten roll calls to nominate a presidential candidate. That was in 1880, when James A. Garfield won on the thirty-sixth ballot.

Many of the Democrats' multiple ballots were used to dispense with favorite-son candidates, whose names were placed in nomination by various state delegations. Like brokered conventions, favorite-son candidates are now largely relics of a bygone era. Both were outmoded by the rise of primaries, which diminished the role of the conventions, and by PRESIDENTIAL SELECTION REFORMS that democratized the nominating process. (See PRIMARY TYPES.) Since 1952 neither of the major parties has taken more than one ballot to nominate a standard bearer.

Although the Democrats' rules made their conventions more vulnerable to domination by party bosses, one of the most famous of brokered conventions was a Republican event—the 1912 convention that pitted the forces of President William Howard Taft against those of former president Theodore Roosevelt.

Because the permanent convention chair would not be filled until the many credentials disputes were settled, the temporary chair was unusually powerful at the divided convention. The post was won by Sen. Elihu Root of New York, whose rulings helped Taft to win the credentials fight and eventually the nomination. Accusing Root of steamroller tactics, Roosevelt supporters rubbed sandpaper and blew horns to imitate the sound of a steamroller. Roosevelt's own candidacy as nominee of the Progressive, or "Bull Moose," Party split the GOP vote and helped Democrat Woodrow Wilson to win the presidency.

Wilson's own nomination in 1912 required forty-six roll calls and provided an example of a convention that party leaders were unable to broker in favor of the first ballot leader, House Speaker Champ Clark of Missouri. Clark received a majority on the tenth ballot, but he was never able to win the 730 votes needed for nomination under the two-thirds rule. It was the first time since 1844 that a majority vote-getter on an earlier ballot ultimately lost the Democratic nomination.

Normally, the absence of a clear FRONT-RUNNER at the outset is the hallmark of a brokered convention. Jockeying for the lead position takes place among the favorite son and other candidates, their supporters, and the power brokers. The Republican convention of 1896, however, was in a sense brokered in advance by industrialist Mark Hanna, who engineered the first-ballot nomination of Ohio governor William McKinley. Hanna, McKinley's mentor and campaign manager, wooed delegates for his candidate for more than a year before the convention. When the opening gavel sounded, McKinley's nomination was almost a foregone conclusion.

More on this topic:

Delegates, p. 142

Favorite Son, p. 202

National Party Conventions, p. 347

Presidential Selection Reforms, p. 476

Primary Types, p. 485

Progressive Party–Bull Moose, p. 489

Two-thirds Rule, p. 638

Unit Rule, p. 642

Buckley v. Valeo

The Supreme Court's ruling in *Buckley v. Valeo* (1976) limited, on First Amendment grounds, the ability of Congress or other legislative bodies to control campaign spending. But the Court upheld limits on individual contributions, disclosure requirements for expenditures and contributions, and the new system of PUBLIC FINANCING OF CAMPAIGNS for major presidential candidates. The guidelines laid down by the Court in this case largely governed the provisions on what constituted an "issue ad" and what constituted an overt effort to promote the election of a candidate for federal office.

Critics of the decision spent the next quarter century or so attempting to find limits on campaign spending that would withstand Court scrutiny. In the meantime, loopholes left by the decision were discovered and money flowed through the CAMPAIGN FINANCE system at an ever-increasing rate.

Buckley stemmed from a challenge to a 1974 campaign finance law. The plaintiffs included James L. Buckley, who had been elected to the Senate from New York on the Conservative Party ticket but then joined the Republican Party ranks in Congress; Eugene J. McCarthy, the antiwar former Democratic senator from Minnesota; the New York Civil Liberties Union; and *Human Events*, a conservative publication. They claimed that the restrictions on individual contributions and on overall campaign spending violated freedom of speech and political association. Francis Valeo, the secretary of the Senate, was named as the lead defendant.

The Court announced its decision in an unsigned, 137-page opinion on January 30, 1976. In its most important ruling, the Court held, 7–1, that proposed spending limits for congressional candidates violated the First Amendment's protections for freedom of speech. "A restriction on the amount of money a person or group can spend on political communication during a campaign necessarily reduces the quantity of expression," the Court stated. Only Justice Byron R. White dissented on that point.

The Court left other important parts of the law standing. The justices upheld, 6–2, the limits on individual contributions to candidates as a permissible means of preventing the risk of corruption. By a different 6–2 vote, they also rejected First Amendment and equal protection challenges to public financing for presidential candidates. The ruling allowed spending limits on candidates

*Sen. James L. Buckley,
Conservative-Republican
from New York, was the
lead plaintiff in the lawsuit
that set the ground rules of
campaign finance for more
than two decades.*

Source: CQ Photo

who accepted public financing, but it barred ceilings on "independent expenditures" by individuals in connection with federal elections. Finally, the Court unanimously held that the composition of the FEDERAL ELECTION COMMISSION (FEC) violated separation-of-power principles because the law provided for Congress to appoint some of the commission's members.

Congress moved quickly to reestablish the FEC by providing for the president to appoint all of its voting members, with Senate confirmation. But the other gaps left by the Court's ruling could not be closed.

The decision torpedoed the goal of reducing campaign spending. Instead, it allowed unlimited spending by candidates from their own pockets, paving the way for lavish spending by millionaire candidates. Among them were several presidential candidates who financed their own campaigns after refusing public funding, including Ross Perot in 1992 and Malcolm S. "Steve" Forbes Jr. in 1996 and 2000. Perot ran again in 1996, but this time his new REFORM PARTY accepted public financing. Wealthy candidates for Congress also occasionally finance their own campaigns to avoid the time-consuming task of fund-raising and to free themselves from federal limitations on contributions. For example, in 2000 Democrat Jon S. Corzine of New Jersey, a Wall Street businessman, loaned his successful Senate campaign more than $60 million.

In addition, *Buckley* made it possible for individuals and groups to spend as much as they wanted provided they kept their electioneering separate from the candidates' official campaigns. The ruling established the controversial "magic words" test: a communication would be regarded as an issue ad and not a regulated campaign communication if the wording did not urge voters directly to vote for or against a particular candidate. (A footnote in the ruling defined express terms to include such phrases as "vote for," "elect," "support," or "defeat.") Critics said this was naïve, as it allowed outside political parties and outside groups to use independent expenditures to laud a favored candidate or savage an opponent as long as the magic words were never uttered. But efforts to overturn that ruling were unavailing over the course of more than three decades.

Some individuals and groups disagreed with the Court's reasoning that the First Amendment extended to campaign spending. But the Court reaffirmed the premise in later campaign finance regulation cases.

More on this topic:
Campaign Finance, p. 53
Political Advertising, p. 394

The Bipartisan Campaign Reform Act of 2002 placed some restrictions on issue ads, specifically barring those commercials within the final weeks before an election that mention a candidate by name. The law, however, did not attempt to alter the "magic words" test established by the *Buckley v. Valeo* decision.

Bull Moose   *See* PROGRESSIVE PARTY–BULL MOOSE (1912)

Bullet Vote   *See* MULTIMEMBER DISTRICTS

Bundling

The gathering together of individual campaign contributions is known as *bundling*. The technique enables a POLITICAL ACTION COMMITTEE (PAC) or party committee to stay within the CAMPAIGN FINANCE laws and still present a candidate with a gift large enough to gain his or her attention and possibly ensure access to the officeholder.

Bundling is just one of several methods developed by businesses, INTEREST GROUPS, and others to circumvent the contribution limits imposed by Congress since the 1970s to lessen the influence of big money in campaigns for federal office. In the wake of the passage of the campaign finance law known as the Bipartisan Campaign Reform Act (BRCA) of 2002, the most common of these other avenues has been the practice known as *independent expenditure*, in which political parties and interest groups may use regulated HARD MONEY contributions to abet a candidate's election as long as those expenditures are made without the candidate's prior knowledge or cooperation.

Another common practice over the years has been the use of SOFT MONEY or unregulated donations to parties for use on campaign activities. Provisions of BCRA barred the use of soft money in campaigns for federal offices (it is still permitted in some state-level campaigns). In response, there was a major expansion in the use of political action committees exempt from Federal Election Committee regulation because they are set up under Section 527 of the Internal Revenue Code and thus could accept soft-money contributions from interest groups and individuals who previously poured those funds into the national party organizations. (See 527 POLITICAL ORGANIZATIONS.)

The use of bundling predated the current federal limits on campaign contributions. The liberal-oriented Council for a Livable World (CLW) originated the technique in 1962 by soliciting checks payable to George S. McGovern's Senate campaign in South Dakota.

A variation on the bundling system is the "political donor network," pioneered in 1985 as EMILY's List—its name an acronym from the phrase "Early Money Is Like Yeast—it makes dough rise." The group was formed to provide financial resources to abet the election chances of Democratic female candidates who favored abortion rights. EMILY's List has been the largest single PAC in terms of receipts over the past several election cycles, including 2005–2006, when the group reported more than $34 million in contributions. In February 2007 the organization indicated that it had raised more than $240 million since its founding.

Corporate executives use bundling to aggregate their political contributions into larger sums. Like other individuals, they face strict limits on how much money they may give to an individual candidate. This was set for many years at $1,000 per candidate per election—with the primary and general election contests in each election cycle deemed separate elections—but the limit was raised to $2,000 with the enactment of BCRA. An inflation-adjustment clause boosted the figure to $2,500 for the 2011–2012 cycle. (See table, page 56.)

Even with the increase, an individual contribution would not necessarily draw the candidate's attention. But if ten executives each gave $2,300, the $23,000 bundle would make more of an impression. In fact, that amount is more than double the maximum amount ($10,000) that a political action committee may contribute to any one candidate over two years, even under BCRA.

From time to time, the news media have published allegations that some bundled contributions were actually illegal gifts that corporations paid to their executives or employees as "bonuses," with the understanding that they were to be passed on to the candidate the company wished to help.

The practice of bundling came under unusual scrutiny after the Democrats gained control of both chambers of Congress following the 2006 campaign in which the party's candidates cited several highly publicized ethics controversies to accuse Republicans of a "culture of corruption." A package of rules changes aimed at tightening regulations on members' contacts with lobbyists produced by the Senate in the early days of the 110th Congress included an unexpected provision: a requirement that lobbyists file quarterly reports listing all of their contributions to candidates, including those that they collected from other individuals and then bundled before transmitting them to the candidates' treasuries. A parallel House measure, passed in May 2007, contained a provision that also would require lobbyists to report bundled contributions.

The bundling provisions were part of larger lobbying reform bills that required a House-Senate conference committee to resolve differences between each chamber's version. The final bill, which cleared and was signed into law in September 2007, required campaign committees—including a candidate's campaign committee, a party committee, or a leadership political action committee (PAC)—to provide reports to the Federal Election Commission two times a year on the bundled campaign contributions they received from a lobbyist or a committee established or controlled by a lobbyist in excess of $15,000 over six months. The reports had to include the names, address, and employer of each lobbyist "reasonably known" to have provided two or more bundled contributions, as well as the total amount of contributions provided by that lobbyist.

Bush v. Gore

By a 5–4 vote divided along conservative-liberal lines, the Supreme Court on December 12, 2000, resolved the five-week dispute over the presidential election results in Florida and effectively elected Republican George W. Bush as the nation's forty-third president. The decision stopped the manual count of several thousand contested ballots that had been ordered by the Florida Supreme Court, leaving Bush the certified winner by 537 votes of the state's twenty-five electoral votes, enough to give him the presidency.

Although the U.S. Supreme Court sent the case back to the Florida court for further consideration, the decision left Vice President Al Gore's attorneys little maneuvering room to pursue his challenge, and the Democratic nominee conceded the election to Bush on December 13. It was a painful decision for Gore, who outran Bush in the nationwide POPULAR VOTE by approximately 537,000 votes. (See PRESIDENTIAL ELECTIONS CHRONOLOGY: ELECTION OF 2000.)

Protesting the Count

The Court's decision capped the most extraordinary period in U.S. presidential politics in more than a century. The November 7 CONTESTED ELECTION left Gore with 267 electoral votes—just three short of the 270 needed under the Constitution for election as president. (A Washington, D.C., elector later withheld her vote from Gore to protest the District of Columbia's lack of congressional representation, reducing his total to 266.) Bush had 246 electoral votes. In doubt were Florida's 25 electoral votes, which would provide the margin of victory.

The uncertainty over the outcome was magnified by serious reporting blunders committed on election night by the major television networks. Almost immediately after polls closed in most of Florida, most networks projected based on exit polling that Gore had carried Florida; this sent Democrats' hopes soaring that Gore had clinched a national victory, as Florida—the nation's fourth-most populous state—had, like most of the South, been trending Republican and was regarded as crucial to Bush, whose brother Jeb was the state's governor.

But as the precinct returns came in, it became clear that the exit polls had included flawed data and that the race was too close to call. As the evening wore on, Bush pushed ahead to a razor-thin but steady lead, prompting the networks to call the state—and the election—for the Republican candidate. Early on November 8, Gore called Bush to congratulate him but later called back to withdraw his concession as the margin of victory shrank and allegations were made of voting irregularities across the state. Gore's second call set the tone for what would emerge as one of the most baldly partisan election disputes in the nation's history.

For five weeks lawyers and partisans for the two sides clashed in the courts, at local elections headquarters, and even in the streets. Bush sought to preserve his slim lead by erecting legal roadblocks to the recounting of thousands of ballots that were in dispute. Needing every vote he could get, Gore demanded that all disputed votes in several specific localities be counted again. However, he did not demand a statewide RECOUNT, a tactical error that enabled Bush forces to argue successfully that a partial recount would deny some Florida voters equal protection of the laws.

Throughout the ordeal, the nation and the world watched as election workers peered at ballots looking for signs of voter intent, and as judges struggled with Florida's sometimes conflicting laws to determine the state legislature's intent. It was the closest the United States had come to a constitutional crisis over a presidential election since the dispute over the 1876 election between Republican Rutherford B. Hayes and Democrat Samuel J. Tilden, which dragged on for months and was finally resolved in Hayes's favor by a bipartisan commission.

In the end Bush won because he had two important allies working in tandem: the calendar and the Supreme Court. Under a federal law enacted in 1887, a state's electors had to be selected by December 12 if they were to be free from challenge in the U.S. Congress. Although nothing in the law prevented electors from being selected after December 12—after the 1960 election, Hawaii did not select its electors until January 4—the Bush team argued that the Florida legislature had intended December 12 to be the deadline for selecting electors.

Bush's attorneys then used every legal maneuver they could muster to prevent or delay voter recounts until this deadline had passed and it was too late to overturn the Bush lead. As the December 12 date approached, the final arbiter of whether additional votes would be counted was the Supreme Court, which for the first time found itself in a position to determine who would become president. On the key decision in the case of *Bush v. Gore,* the Court's five most conservative justices sided with Bush, the conservative candidate, and the four most liberal justices sided with Gore, the liberal candidate.

The coincidence of this split did not go unnoticed. Editorial writers and legal experts said that the Court should have refused to review the dispute and left it for Congress to resolve. By injecting the Supreme Court into a political issue, the Court had weakened its own legitimacy as well as Bush's claim to the White House, those critics said. John Paul Stevens, one of the dissenting justices, said the Court's ruling "can only lend credence to the most cynical appraisal of the work of judges throughout the land." Another dissenter, Justice Stephen G. Breyer, referred to the Court action as "this self-inflicted wound."

Nor did it escape public notice that the Republican nominee who had campaigned on states' rights had turned to the federal judiciary to overrule the Florida state courts

CLOSER LOOK

Rep. Katherine Harris, R.-Fla., concedes the Senate race to Sen. Bill Nelson, D.-Fla., the incumbent, as her husband looks on, November 7, 2006.

Source: AP Images/Steve Nesius

It took them six years, but Democrats exacted political revenge against one of the principal players in the 2000 presidential vote controversy: Republican Katherine Harris, who then held the position of Florida secretary of state under an appointment by Governor Jeb Bush, one of George W. Bush's brothers. Harris, an acknowledged George W. Bush supporter and the state's top election official, certified the Republican presidential victory in Florida—and was accused by Democrats of helping thwart the ensuing recounts. Although she won the first of two terms in the U.S. House from a Republican-leaning Florida district in 2002, she ran a stumbling and controversy-plagued campaign in 2006 when she challenged Democratic senator Bill Nelson. Democrats watched as Nelson trounced Harris by 60 percent to 38 percent.

or that his promises of inclusion did not seem to extend to disputed ballots cast primarily by African Americans, the urban poor, and the elderly.

On December 14 Florida governor Jeb Bush announced that he was creating a special task force to investigate the integrity of Florida's election process. He also said he would welcome an investigation by the U.S. Commission on Civil Rights into allegations of voting irregularities, including incidents of intimidation directed at African American voters. Across the country, politicians and election officials promised to review election laws and procedures to prevent similar situations in the future.

Most Americans accepted the Court's decision and Gore's concession calmly. The fact that the transition of power between the outgoing Clinton and incoming George W. Bush administrations was accomplished peaceably, even under these extremely strained circumstances, was widely seen as symbolic of both the strength and resilience of the American democracy.

There were, however, long-lasting political consequences. Many Democrats and liberal activists continued to believe Bush's first victory was illegitimate: one of their major slogans opposing his reelection in 2004 was "Re-Defeat Bush." The 2004 election fell sharply along partisan battle lines. Major contributing factors to Bush's victory were his image of leadership in the wake of the September 11, 2001, attacks and the public's indifference toward the Democratic nominee, Massachusetts senator John Kerry. Bush's approval ratings dropped precipitously following the election, as the war in Iraq that he had launched in March 2003 grew more unpopular and his administration responded ineffectively in 2005 to the Gulf Coast devastation wrought by Hurricane Katrina. This galvanized the Democratic opposition and led to the Democrats' big gains in the 2006 elections that gave them majorities in the U.S. Senate and House.

The Contest and the Decision: Equal Protection Under a Deadline

The contest phase of the dispute began November 26, when Florida secretary of state and top election official Katherine Harris, a Republican activist and Jeb Bush appointee, certified Bush the winner by 537 votes. The following day Gore filed suit in state court, contesting the results of the certification on the grounds that there were still enough uncounted votes to change the outcome of the election. Throughout this phase the Gore attorneys argued that the will of the people could not be fully known until all the ballots were counted; the Bush attorneys argued that recounts in individual counties using different standards were unfair and a violation of the Constitution's equal protection clause.

On December 1 the U.S. Supreme Court heard arguments in the suit brought by Bush challenging the extended certification deadline. Three days later, on December 4, the Court issued an unsigned opinion setting aside the Florida Supreme Court's decision extending the deadline for manual recounts and asked the Florida court to clarify two issues regarding its original decision. On the same day, Florida judge N. Sanders Sauls rejected Gore's suit contesting the election results.

Gore appealed Sauls's ruling to the state supreme court. By a 4–3 decision on December 8 the state court ordered an immediate manual recount of all the "undervotes"—some 45,000 ballots statewide that had not been counted because machines had not detected a vote for president. The ruling revived Gore's flagging hopes for the White House and sent Bush's lawyers back to the Supreme Court, where they sought a stay of the recount while they appealed the state supreme court ruling. On December 9 the Court granted the stay and agreed to hear the appeal. On December 11 the Court heard oral arguments, and on December 12, at about 10:00 p.m., it handed down its historic ruling.

The majority opinion was unsigned, but it was obvious from the four dissents that the main opinion had been supported by the five most conservative justices—Chief Justice William H.

Rehnquist and justices Sandra Day O'Connor, Anthony M. Kennedy, Antonin Scalia, and Clarence Thomas. Rehnquist wrote a concurring opinion that was joined by Scalia and Thomas. Justices Stevens, Breyer, David H. Souter, and Ruth Bader Ginsburg each wrote dissents that were joined in part by the other dissenters. Court reporters said the unsigned or "per curiam" Court opinion appeared to be largely the work of O'Connor and Kennedy, neither of whose name appeared on any of the signed opinions. O'Connor and Kennedy were the most moderate justices on the Court and often were the decisive votes in close cases.

The majority opinion itself appeared to be a failed effort at finding a compromise that would draw the support of liberal and conservative justices. In its main finding, the majority ruled that the state supreme court's failure to establish uniform standards for manually counting the undervotes denied Florida voters their constitutionally guaranteed right to equal protection of the laws.

Breyer and Souter indicated in their dissents that they, too, were troubled by the equal protection problems associated with standards that varied from county to county and even among teams of counters. Breyer and Souter would have sent the case back to the state supreme court with instructions to establish uniform standards and proceed with the recount, but the majority said there was no time for that to happen before December 12, the deadline for the state to obtain the so-called safe harbor for its electors protecting them from challenge in Congress. Because the Florida Supreme Court held that the state legislature had intended to obtain that safe harbor, the majority said, the dissenters' proposed remedy to extend the count beyond that deadline "contemplates action in violation of the Florida election code" and was therefore inappropriate.

In their separate opinions, the four dissenters argued that the federal questions involved were insubstantial and the Court should never have agreed to review the case in the first place. "Of course, the selection of the President is of fundamental national importance," Breyer wrote. "But that importance is political, not legal. And this Court should resist the temptation unnecessarily to resolve tangential legal disputes, where doing so threatens to determine the outcome of the election." Stevens was blunter in his criticism: "What must underlie petitioners' entire federal assault on the Florida election procedures is an unstated lack of

> **"None are more conscious of the vital limits on judicial authority than are the members of this Court, and none stand more in admiration of the Constitution's design to leave the selection of the President to the People, through their legislatures, and to the political sphere. When contending parties invoke the process of the courts, however, it becomes our unsought responsibility to resolve the federal and constitutional issues the judicial system has been forced to confront."**
>
> —Excerpt from the U.S. Supreme Court's majority opinion in *Bush v. Gore,* which effectively decided the 2000 presidential election in favor of Republican candidate George W. Bush

> **"Of course, the selection of the President is of fundamental national importance. But that importance is political, not legal. And this Court should resist the temptation unnecessarily to resolve tangential legal disputes, where doing so threatens to determine the outcome of the election."**
>
> —*Justice Stephen Breyer,* writing in his dissent in the 2000 Supreme Court decision of *Bush v. Gore*

More on this topic:

Contested Elections, p. 125

Popular Vote, p. 431

Recount, p. 526

confidence in the impartiality and capacity of the state judges who would make the critical decision if the vote count were to proceed. Otherwise their position is without merit," Stevens wrote.

In their concurring opinion, Rehnquist, Scalia, and Thomas acknowledged that "in most cases, comity and respect for federalism compel us to defer" to state courts on interpretations of state law. But the three justices said there were a "few exceptional cases in which the Constitution imposes a duty or confers a power on a particular branch of a state's government" and thus presented a "federal question" that was appropriate for the Supreme Court to address. *Bush v. Gore* was one of those exceptional cases, Rehnquist wrote, because it involved a presidential election and because the Constitution specifically delegated authority to oversee presidential elections to state legislatures. Having justified their intervention in the case, the three then found the state supreme court's interpretation of the Florida election law to be "absurd."

Both Stevens and Ginsburg rejected the equal protection argument advanced by the majority. "We live in an imperfect world, one in which thousands of votes have not been counted," Ginsburg said. "I cannot agree that the recount adopted by the Florida court, flawed as it may be, would yield a result any less fair or precise than the certification that preceded that recount." All four dissenters lambasted the majority for hinging the outcome of the case on the December 12 safe-harbor deadline. No state was required to meet that deadline, Souter said. The only penalty for failing to meet it was loss of the safe harbor and "even that determination is to be made, if made anywhere, in the Congress."

◉ CLOSER LOOK   **Chronology of 2000 Recount in Florida**

November 7, 2000	Florida election deemed too close to call, with Republican George W. Bush holding a narrow lead. TV networks retract premature reports declaring first that Democrat Al Gore had won the state's twenty-five electoral votes and later that Bush had carried the state—and as a result had been elected president.
November 8–10	Gore telephones Bush to concede early November 8, then calls back to withdraw his concession. Gore seeks Florida hand recounts in four largely Democratic counties. Bush has unofficial 1,784-vote lead November 9. All but one of Florida's sixty-seven counties complete machine recount required by state law; Bush lead falls to 327 votes.
November 11–14	Broward, Miami-Dade, Palm Beach, and Volusia counties undertake manual recounts requested by Gore; federal court rejects Bush bid to block hand counts November 13; Volusia finishes recount November 14.
November 13	Florida secretary of state Katherine Harris, a Republican appointee, says she will enforce state law deadline of November 14 for counties to submit returns and will not include manual recounts; election boards in Volusia and Palm Beach counties ask state court judge to overturn deadline.
November 14–16	Leon County circuit judge Terry P. Lewis, sitting in the state capital of Tallahassee, says Harris must justify her position on deadline; Harris reaffirms decision November 15; Lewis hears new round of arguments November 16.
November 17	Lewis upholds Harris's decision to disregard manual recounts, but Florida Supreme Court bars certification of state results pending oral arguments on November 20; federal appeals court rejects Bush suit over manual recounts.

November 18	Bush lead grows to 930 votes with absentee ballots; Bush campaign criticizes Democrats for challenging absentee ballots from military voters.
November 21	Florida Supreme Court rules manual recounts must be included in presidential race if submitted to Harris by 5:00 p.m. on Sunday, November 26.
November 22–24	Shouting, fist-waving crowd, including Republican congressional aides, tries to enter private room where Miami-Dade County officials have resumed recounts. County stops recount, pleading too little time and denying intimidation by the demonstrators. State supreme court rejects November 23 Gore suit to force Miami-Dade to resume counting. U.S. Supreme Court agrees to hear Bush appeal of Florida Supreme Court action allowing extended deadline for certifying presidential race.
November 25–26	Manual recounts: Broward finishes November 25; Palm Beach falls just short of completion.
November 26	Harris announces November 26 that state elections canvassing board certifies Bush as winner by 537-vote margin; Bush claims victory, says he and Cheney are "honored and humbled" to have won Florida's electoral votes.
November 27–29	Gore formally contests the Florida election November 27. He sues in Leon County Circuit Court claiming the number of legal votes "improperly rejected" and illegal votes counted in Nassau, Palm Beach, and Miami-Dade counties is enough to change outcome. Judge N. Sanders Sauls orders ballots brought to Tallahassee for possible counting. More than one million ballots are trucked with police escort to the state capital.
December 1	U.S. Supreme Court hears Bush appeal of deadline extension. Florida justices refuse to order revote requested in Palm Beach County because of controversial "butterfly ballot" used there, which Democrats claimed misled some voters to cast ballots for conservative third-party candidate Pat Buchanan instead of the liberal Gore.
December 2–3	Judge Sauls hears testimony on whether 13,000 ballots from Miami-Dade and Palm Beach counties should be manually counted. Both sides call witnesses on reliability of punch-card voting systems.
December 4	Sauls rejects Gore's request for manual recount and refuses to decertify Bush as winner. U.S. Supreme Court asks state high court to explain its November 21 action allowing manual recounting and extending deadlines.
December 8–9	Florida justices order hand count of ballots on which machines found no vote for president. U.S. Supreme Court halts the hand counts the next day.
December 10–11	U.S. Supreme Court receives briefs and hears arguments in *Bush v. Gore*.
December 12	U.S. Supreme Court splits 5–4 in ruling for Bush against further hand counts, hours after the Republican-controlled Florida legislature convenes a special session to meet the federal deadline for designating presidential electors. (Twenty states miss the deadline by a few days, without penalty.)
December 13	Gore concedes election, congratulates Bush, and jokingly adds, "And I promised him that this time I wouldn't call him back."
December 18	Presidential electors meet in state capitals to cast votes. One District of Columbia elector, Barbara Lett-Simmons, withholds her vote from Gore in protest of the national capital's lack of representation in Congress. Final electoral vote tally is 271 for Bush, 266 for Gore with one abstention.

January 6, 2001	Congress meets in joint session to count electoral votes. As Senate president, Vice President Gore presides over his own defeat. Twenty Gore supporters, mostly Congressional Black Caucus members, try to block Florida's votes, but Gore rejects each representative's written objection because none has also been signed by a senator as the 1887 Electoral Vote Count Act requires.
January 20	Bush is inaugurated as president and Cheney as vice president. Protests, largely nonviolent, mar—but do not disrupt—the inaugural parade.

By-Election *See* SPECIAL ELECTIONS

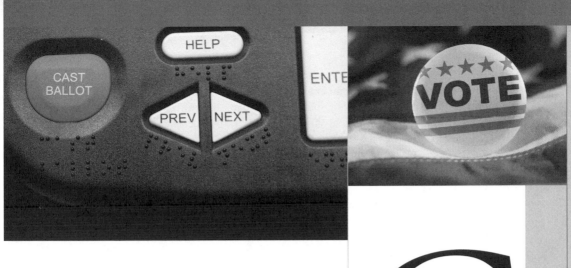

C

Campaign, Basic Stages of

All political campaigns go through the same basic stages. The goal is to get elected, and that requires a candidate—whether at the ward or national level—to follow a progression of steps over a period of months or even years.

In the end, "All politics is local," as was often said by Rep. Thomas P. "Tip" O'Neill Jr., a Democrat from Massachusetts, who served in the House from 1953 to 1987 and was Speaker for the final eight years of his tenure. Whether the issue is as parochial as a bike trail or a new stoplight or as freighted with national urgency as matters of war and peace, all campaigns ultimately boil down to an effort to win the heart and mind of the individual voter.

The only major difference between running for alderman and running for president is the degree of elaboration. The higher the office, the larger and more complex the organization required to conduct the campaign. And running for national or statewide office requires many more campaign tools and much more money than running for local office. Perhaps what all elections have most in common is that candidates must campaign hard right to the finish in order to ensure victory. Studies show that in most cases the average voter already has his or her mind made up long before ELECTION DAY. Yet the candidate who takes for granted the allegiance of past supporters, or who writes off a certain bloc as committed to the opposition, does so at considerable peril. Political history is littered with cases of upset victories or defeats.

The Exploratory Stage

Many candidates start their campaigns with an exploratory stage, though not all "exploratory" campaigns are created equal.

Sometimes a candidate who has made an inalterable decision to run will nonetheless go through the motion of creating an exploratory committee for a variety of reasons, from wanting to milk public attention by making multiple candidacy announcements, to deferring full scrutiny from the media and opponents, to skirting campaign finance rules that apply to candidates who have officially entered a race.

But other would-be candidates are truly uncertain whether to commit to running, and for them, an exploratory period provides an opportunity to study the political landscape and assess his or her chances of winning. The decision is especially difficult for would-be presidential candidates. (See PRESIDENT, NOMINATING AND ELECTING.)

Voters are little involved in the exploratory stages. They may not even be aware of the potential candidate, let alone considering which person to support. But the prospective candidate is much aware of the voters at this point.

Rather than guess at the kind of reception to expect from the media and the public, the candidate may send up a trial balloon by letting it be known that he or she is contemplating a run for the office. Or the candidate may hire a POLLING organization to test the market more scientifically.

The prospective candidate may also use family, friends, associates, elected officials, and POLITICAL CONSULTANTS as sounding boards on the advisability of entering the race. Not the least of considerations is money. Even the most modest campaigns entail some expense, and the costs of staging a successful bid for Congress or even the state legislature can often require budgets exceeding $1 million; presidential campaigns cost far more, now regularly clocking in at hundreds of millions of dollars. The candidate must also take the requirements of CAMPAIGN FINANCE laws into account.

Once the decision to run is made, the candidate needs to address the formalities of filing with the state or local elections board, CANVASSING BOARD, or other appropriate authorities. Sometimes a filing fee is charged, or petitions must be submitted with the signatures of a specified number of registered voters. Care must be taken with the latter, as many candidates have found the validity of their petition signatures challenged by opposing candidates or their supporters.

Candidates for federal office (president, vice president, or Congress) must also register with the FEDERAL ELECTION COMMISSION (FEC) and report periodically on campaign receipts and spending. Almost all states also regulate campaign financing, requiring financial disclosure and, in some cases, limiting contributions by individuals and groups.

Building an Organization

Election to most offices today is a two-step process. Candidates must first run in PRIMARY or CAUCUS elections to obtain the party's nomination to run in the general election. Under the TWO-PARTY SYSTEM, most primaries and caucuses are held by the DEMOCRATIC and REPUBLICAN parties. But some alternative parties, long lumped together under the label of THIRD PARTIES, also use primaries to select their nominees.

Not all primaries are partisan events, however. Many U.S. elections, especially at the local level, are nonpartisan, with no party designation shown on the ballot. Nonpartisan elections often are held in off (odd-numbered) years, rather than on the general election day in November of even-numbered years. And even within the two-party system, primaries in some states are open to voters who are not members of the party holding the primary. (See PRIMARY TYPES.)

The widespread use of the primary system means that campaigns begin earlier than in the past, and candidates must start well before the primary to build a political organization of paid and voluntary workers. Recruiting these individuals is one of the major tasks in the early phases of a campaign.

People are needed to compile lists of potential supporters, make and receive phone calls, operate computers and office machines, distribute campaign paraphernalia such as lawn signs and bumper stickers, coordinate the candidate's appearances, devise CAMPAIGN STRATEGIES, plan use of the media through advertising, seek favorable MEDIA COVERAGE of the campaign, and handle fund-raising and myriad other electioneering chores. Increasingly, the proliferation of "new media" platforms has prompted campaigns to bring in staffers who have a feel for reaching out to voters via e-mail, text messaging, and social networking.

Most campaign workers are volunteers. In a large campaign the candidate may hire a campaign manager, a fund-raiser, a publicist, and a treasurer but rely on friends and supporters to do all the rest of the necessary work.

The campaign may open a temporary storefront headquarters or a number of strategically located offices to centralize the various operations. Or the campaign headquarters may be the candidate's home.

Getting Started

To many, if not all, candidates, asking for money is distasteful. But unless they are personally wealthy they have to do it, early and often. PUBLIC FINANCING OF CAMPAIGNS is available to presidential candidates, but only if they raise enough money and meet other qualifications for matching grants; in addition, this money comes with restrictions, including spending caps, that the best-funded candidates often find disagreeable, leading more and more of them to opt out of the system (as Democrat Barack Obama notably did during his successful 2008 presidential campaign). Several states also provide some financial assistance to qualifying candidates.

Essentially, fund-raising is an inescapable aspect of political campaigns. From the outset, candidates spend much of their time sending letters or making phone calls to request contributions or loans. Compliance with federal or state financial disclosure laws may require setting up a special bank account to receive and disburse the funds.

Less tangible than money but helpful to a candidate are endorsements from community leaders, organizations, current officeholders, and other influential persons. Experienced candidates rank the gathering of endorsements as a high priority for fledgling campaigns.

Another early priority of a campaign is learning as much as possible about the DISTRICT or other jurisdiction where the candidate is running. State and local elections boards often sell lists of voters to assist in canvassing. Some candidates begin by touring the entire district to become familiar with its boundaries and characteristics, even if they have lived there all their lives. At the same time they may be looking for strategic locations for campaign signs and posters.

A corollary of knowing the district is defining the issues. The candidate needs to keep abreast of current affairs and address the concerns of his or her particular electorate. Many candidates use PUBLIC OPINION polls to help define the issues and indicate positions to take on them.

Campaigning Techniques

One of the first things a candidate might do is come up with a catchy CAMPAIGN SLOGAN. Such slogans have been a part of electioneering since the earliest days of the Republic and, since the 1896 presidential election, often appear on CAMPAIGN BUTTONS.

Stump speeches and "pressing the flesh" by shaking the hands of voters outside factory gates or shopping malls are still staples of the campaign art. Door-to-door canvassing may be feasible in a compact district, and even presidential candidates use local supporters to engage in this kind of "retail" campaigning; some candidates have gone so far as to walk across their states to gain attention and meet voters.

Radio played a major role in Republican Calvin Coolidge's victory in the 1924 presidential race.
Library of Congress

An alternative way to reach large numbers of voters is a "live" phone bank of callers asking for voters' support, or an automated phone bank that can play the candidate's recorded appeal if the person called is willing to listen.

The extensive travel expected of presidential candidates today was once a rarity. William Jennings Bryan started the WHISTLE-STOP tradition in his bid as the Democratic presidential nominee in 1896 but still lost to Republican William McKinley, who in keeping with tradition staged a "front-porch" campaign from his home in Canton, Ohio.

Today, candidates reach many more voters by television and radio than in person. Ads on television are the largest single expense in many campaigns, and candidates welcome free guest spots on TV and radio news and talk shows. In 1992 Texas billionaire Ross Perot launched his INDEPENDENT bid for the presidency, the strongest ever by an individual, with an "I'm available" remark on CNN's *Larry King Live* TV show; actor Arnold Schwarzenegger announced his intention to run for governor of California as a Republican in a 2003 recall election during an appearance on NBC's *Tonight Show with Jay Leno,* and other candidates have sought bookings on popular programs to launch their bids for office.

Televised DEBATES and forums enable voters to compare the IDEOLOGIES, knowledge, personalities, and speaking skills of competing candidates. Presidential nominees have debated in every election since 1976, and similar forums have become common in congressional and state elections as well.

Direct mail is another technique of grassroots campaigning. Some political consultants have developed sophisticated methods of targeting mass mailings to voters who share the candidate's political philosophy or are likely to be persuaded by his or her arguments.

The most important recent development in campaigning is that communications with voters are increasingly high-tech. The 1996 presidential election year was the first in which candidates started to use the Internet extensively as a campaign medium. Within a decade, it was common for virtually every serious candidate and most long shots to have websites. Former Vermont governor Howard Dean became a trailblazer during his unsuccessful bid for the 2004 Democratic presidential nomination with his aggressive use of the Internet to raise campaign funds.

In early 2007, as candidates started lining up to run in the 2008 presidential campaign, several contenders—including the early front-runner for the Democratic nomination, New York senator Hillary Rodham Clinton—announced their intentions to run or supplemented their official candidacy announcements by posting videos on their campaign websites. But Clinton, the wife of former president Bill Clinton, ended up losing the nomination to Obama, then a senator from Illinois, who broke new ground in using new media as a communications and fundraising tool.

Yet in politics, everything old can be new again. In the early years of the twenty-first century, the proliferation of media outlets and Internet sites raised questions among candidates and political professionals about the efficacy of mobilizing targeted audiences through paid advertising alone. So they returned to the time-tested technique of door-to-door campaigning and other grassroots methods of direct voter contact in efforts to motivate voters to go to the polls.

The Final Hours

The closing days of political campaigns are the most frantic, with candidates desperately trying to reach as many voters as possible before they go to the polls. For primary losers, the campaign is effectively over, but some remain in the race as independents or third-party candidates, and in some states there are RUNOFF elections if no one wins a majority in the primary.

For presidential primary winners the next major events are the NATIONAL PARTY CONVENTIONS, where their nominations are made official by thousands of DELEGATES from all over the country.

For the general election the presidential and vice presidential nominees, as well as survivors of primaries for other offices, must repeat many of the same steps they completed for the primaries. A major difference is that they may be starting with an existing organization, which the candidate may decide needs to be enlarged or overhauled. In modern presidential politics, the nominee's primary organization is often kept intact, usually taking the place once held by the national party committees in running the campaign.

The traditional time to begin general election campaigns is the Labor Day holiday, but many candidates no longer wait until then. The campaign may start right after the primaries or party conventions and end on election day in the candidate's hometown. In 1996 Republican nominee Bob Dole, to dispel the notion that at seventy-three he was too old to be president, finished his campaign with a grueling ninety-six-hour marathon that took him through twenty states and wound up in Russell, Kansas, where he voted looking none the worse for wear. He nevertheless lost the election by a sizable margin to Democratic incumbent Bill Clinton.

Staging campaigns has been complicated in recent years, however, by the vast expansion in most states of options allowing voters to cast their ballots early—either in person, in the growing number of states where that option exists, or by ABSENTEE VOTING, which once was strictly limited to emergency situations in most states but today is much more readily available. With voters in some states allowed to cast their ballots as early as a month before election day, candidates cannot afford to reserve their resources for one last big push at the end.

Still, most voters in most states continue to go to polling places on election day, and parties and candidates concentrate on GET OUT THE VOTE activities, making last-minute phone bank calls to urge people to vote. They may offer transportation to the polls to those voters, especially the elderly or disabled, who need it. Other campaign workers may be assigned as poll watchers—where this is permitted—to look out for irregularities.

Once the results are in, the winners claim victory and the losers concede defeat. But if it is a close or CONTESTED ELECTION, the speeches might have to wait for a RECOUNT and a tally of the absentee votes.

For the candidates, the end of the campaign is less glamorous than the earlier stages. The headquarters must be emptied, the bills paid, and the organization disbanded. Finally, many communities require the prompt removal of campaign signs and posters.

More on this topic:
Campaign Finance, p. 53
Political Consultants, p. 399
President, Nominating and Electing, p. 437
Primary Types, p. 485
Two-Party System, p. 636

Campaign Buttons

The modern political campaign button was born in 1896 when supporters of Republican presidential candidate William McKinley wore his portrait on buttons promising a "full dinner pail." Today official campaign buttons are mostly collectors' items, as the emphasis of most campaigns has shifted to mass media and POLITICAL ADVERTISING as means of reaching voters and building recognition of candidates' names.

As this pastiche of buttons shows, even prior to the media age campaigns were conducted through simple images and slogans.

Source: Courtesy of Christopher Schardt

Voters continue to expect buttons, bumper stickers, and other campaign paraphernalia, however, and private vendors help to supply that demand when it is not met by parties and candidates, because of cost or because they do not see these extras as priorities.

Americans since George Washington's time have decorated their lapels with printed political statements. But in the early days the items were made of cloth, and most commemorated sitting presidents or events such as the inauguration rather than political campaigns. A forerunner of the McKinley-type button appeared in 1840, when the ticket of William Henry Harrison and John Tyler won the White House with the CAMPAIGN SLOGAN "Tippecanoe and Tyler Too." Harrison had obtained his nickname during the frontier wars with American Indians in the early 1800s; as a general, he led U.S. troops to victory in the Battle of Tippecanoe.

Harrison's buttons were coin-like tokens that could be worn in a buttonhole. By the 1860s, with the invention of photography, black-and-white portraits were added to these metal plate tokens, which were then called "ferrotypes." Within a few elections, photos were commonly being mounted on cardboard or paper that could be pinned to the wearer's clothing.

In 1893 the first patent was granted for a process that wrapped celluloid, a tough plastic, over a metal disk that could be fastened to the lapel by a pin on an attached metal ring. This was the campaign button as it is known today. In the 1920s portrait reproduction was enhanced through the use of lithographs on the buttons. Some new, high-tech buttons feature pop-up or moving parts, blinking lights, holograms, or even tape-recorded messages.

Campaign buttons reveal much about America's past, and not all of it is flattering. When New York governor Alfred E. Smith was nominated by the Democratic Party in 1928 as the first major-party Roman Catholic candidate

"Washington Wouldn't. Lincoln Couldn't. Roosevelt Shouldn't."

—Slogan from 1940 campaign button opposing Franklin Delano Roosevelt's bid for a third term as president

More on this topic:

Campaign Slogans,
p. 67

Political Advertising,
p. 394

to run for president, anti-Catholic elements put out an anti-Smith button that called for "A Christian in the White House." Opponents of Democrat Franklin D. Roosevelt's groundbreaking bid for a third presidential term in 1940 produced buttons that read, "Washington Wouldn't. Lincoln Couldn't. Roosevelt Shouldn't."

There is an avid community of political memorabilia collectors in the United States. American Political Items Collectors (APIC), a nonprofit group established in 1945, offers a website and print publications, runs a museum, and organizes trading conventions. The group claims more than 2,000 members and suggests that there are many potential areas of specialization for collectors, such as "pinback buttons only," "focus on a single candidate," and "Prohibition movement."

Campaign Finance

The cost of political campaigns in the United States has risen sharply since the 1950s, fueling intense controversies about the ways candidates for office at all levels of government raise and spend money. Congress, state legislatures, and local lawmaking bodies have responded by  adopting laws requiring disclosure of campaign contributions and expenditures and limiting contributions by individuals and organizations.

Some facets of campaign finance regulation, such as requirements that campaigns and organizations that seek to influence election outcomes must publicly report the sources of the financial donations they receive, have achieved widespread (though hardly unanimous) support.

But if the goal of campaign finance reformers was to rein in the rate of increase in overall and individual campaign spending—and thereby reduce the impact of money in politics—then the campaign finance laws enacted in recent years have not met that standard.

The Center for Responsive Politics (CRP), based in Washington, D.C., estimated a total of $5.3 billion in combined spending by candidates, political parties, and outside groups during the 2008 election cycle, the year in which the nation elected Democrat Barack Obama as president and expanded existing Democratic Party majorities in both the U.S. Senate and House. That was up by 27 percent in just the four years since the 2004 presidential election year, in which Republican incumbent George W. Bush narrowly defeated Democrat John Kerry.

> **"Campaign finance reform means that your votes should not be stifled by cash register politics. A lot of problems will move towards solution if we can get the boulders called political action committees and private money [removed] and get public elections financed publicly."**
>
> **—Liberal activist Ralph Nader,** a longtime advocate of limiting the influence of money in politics, speaking during his 2000 campaign as the Green Party nominee for president in an interview on PBS's *News Hour with Jim Lehrer* on June 30, 2000

CRP subsequently estimated that total spending of about $4 billion during the 2010 midterm election cycle—a comeback year for Republicans, who regained control of the U.S. House, cut deeply into the Democrats' Senate majority, and made big gains at the state level. That was a big jump up from the $2.8 billion in total spending during the 2006 cycle, when Democrats had the upper hand.

These overall increases have been fueled by increasingly sophisticated and successful efforts by individual candidates to raise large amounts of campaign money, with the emergence of the

Internet as a fund-raising tool proving immensely helpful to them. Obama's campaign, which broke new ground in its innovative use of web-based fund-raising, spent $741 million, obliterating the previous record of $345 million set by Bush in 2004. In fact, Obama's campaign spending exceeded, by more than $80 million, the *combined* spending by Bush and Kerry four years earlier.

Obama's fund-raising prowess also enabled him to become the first major-party presidential nominee to decline public financing and the spending limits that come with it under laws enacted during the 1970s in the wake of the Watergate corruption scandal that forced Richard M. Nixon to become the first and still only president to resign his office. Obama's decision to eschew public funding for the entirety of the campaign culminated a trend, which had gained momentum in both parties earlier in the past decade, of candidates declining public financing during presidential nominating campaigns in lieu of raising unlimited amounts of campaign cash.

The implications of the 2008 campaign were expected to be felt during the 2012 presidential contest, in which Obama was seeking reelection against a Republican Party that drew multiple candidates into its primary and caucus field. The fact that Obama had a total spending advantage of more than three dollars to one over 2008 Republican nominee John McCain—who spent $228 million, including $81 million in public funds that he accepted for the general election campaign—was not lost on either party.

Meanwhile, the system of campaign finance regulation has faced consistent attacks from opponents who view limitations on donations and spending, by individuals and by corporate interests, as violating the protections of free speech under the First Amendment of the U.S. Constitution. Most of those holding this position were on the conservative side of the political spectrum, which tends to be supportive of the interests of wealthier Americans and businesses, though it also was shared by some liberals of libertarian persuasions, such as the American Civil Liberties Union.

This backlash intensified following the enactment in 2002 of the Bipartisan Campaign Reform Act, or BCRA, which was sponsored in the Senate by McCain of Arizona and Russ Feingold, a Democrat of Wisconsin. The overall law was upheld by the Supreme Court in 2003, including its provisions that bar "soft money"—unlimited donations to the national political parties—allowed under previous campaign finance laws, that were supposed to be used for "party-building" activities but were often channeled into election-related activities in support of individual candidates.

But a subsequent decision by the Supreme Court, issued in January 2010, had an immediate impact in creating new avenues for campaign spending outside the conventional (and heavily regulated) channels and created the potential for an even greater torrent of money to flood into the political system.

BCRA had barred corporate interests (including businesses and labor unions) from using independent expenditures to pay for broadcast issue ads—which often are cleverly crafted messages aimed at influencing the outcomes of elections—within sixty days of a general election or within thirty days of a primary. But in the case of *Citizens United v. Federal Election Commission*, decided by a vote of 5–4, the Supreme Court struck down that provision and in doing so established as a matter of constitutional law that corporate interests have free speech rights equivalent to those of individuals in regard to campaign finance matters.

"There is no basis for the proposition that, in the political speech context, the government may impose restrictions on certain disfavored speakers," wrote Justice Anthony M. Kennedy in the majority opinion.

Activist groups in both parties, in some cases led by prominent political consultants, responded quickly to this ruling by establishing political action committees, dubbed SuperPACs, which cumulatively spent hundreds of millions of dollars right up through Election Day to advance their political goals. Conservative groups, many of them pursuing pro-business agendas, dominated this form of spending during the 2010 election cycle, though it was not immediately clear whether that will be a permanent situation or if it reflected the fact that the conservative-oriented Republican Party was having an especially strong year in 2010.

There is nothing new about judicial skepticism about legislative efforts to rein in "big money" in politics. The big push during the 1970s to control the costs of campaigns was thwarted by a Supreme Court decision that barred mandatory spending limits for candidates or independent groups. In addition, contribution limits, aimed at reducing the influence of wealthy individuals or organizations, have always proved difficult to enforce and easy to circumvent.

And while advocates of campaign finance reform cite poll numbers showing strong public opinion in favor of limiting campaign spending, their efforts have been hindered by a lack of intensity on the issue among voters. Campaign finance reform—like other political process issues, such as redistricting, the Senate filibuster, and the process for confirming appointees to the federal judiciary—ranks low on the average voter's list of priorities below "kitchen table" issues such as jobs, health care, and education.

System's Half-Century Evolution

The earliest campaign finance laws date from the late 1800s and early 1900s, but the current wave of reform efforts began in the 1960s and gained strength in the 1970s. The sharp rise in presidential campaign spending led Congress to enact a system of PUBLIC FINANCING of campaigns by major-party candidates for president. Then the Watergate scandal during President Richard Nixon's administration resulted in enactment of a federal law that placed limits on individual contributions to federal candidates. The law also established the FEDERAL ELECTION COMMISSION (FEC) as an independent regulatory agency to enforce its provisions.

The 1974 law, which sought to bar individuals from bestowing suitcases full of cash on the campaigns of favored candidates, nonetheless left the door open for an explosive increase in campaign giving by POLITICAL ACTION COMMITTEES (PACs). These organizations are formed by corporations, labor unions, or INTEREST GROUPS to raise money from their employees or members and funnel contributions to candidates. The growth in PACs raised fears about the influence of special interests on congressional candidates.

At the federal level, a second source of controversy surrounded the skyrocketing use of so-called SOFT MONEY—virtually unlimited campaign funds raised by national political parties from individuals and groups ostensibly to help finance party organizational efforts and voting drives at the state and local level but widely deployed in traditional campaign activities carefully crafted by party strategists to avoid violating the letter of the campaign finance law. Congress exempted these funds from federal contribution limits in 1979. Many advocates and experts believe that the growth in soft-money spending by both the Republican and the Democratic parties undercut attempts to reduce the influence of campaign contributions in presidential campaigns.

A seven-year effort to tighten regulation on these money sources—led by McCain and Feingold in the Senate and by Republican Christopher Shays of Connecticut and Democrat Martin T. Meehan of Massachusetts in the House—led to the enactment of the Bipartisan Campaign Reform Act of 2002, a law known by its acronym BCRA (pronounced "bick-rah") or simply as "McCain-Feingold." The measure, with its ban on the use of soft money in federal campaigns, first took effect for the 2004 campaign cycle.

Almost immediately, it became evident that party fund-raisers would prove more than adept at stepping up their efforts to raise hard money and fill the void left by the ban on soft money. Meanwhile, the law had no mechanism to prevent big donors from taking their soft money and

CONTRIBUTION LIMITS FOR THE 2011–2012 ELECTION CYCLE

Donors	To Candidate Committees	To PACs[1]	To State, District, and Local Party Committees[2]	To National Party Committees[3]	Special Limits
Individual	$2,500* per election[4]	$5,000 per year	$10,000 per year combined limit	$30,800* per year	Biennial limit of $117,000* ($46,200 to all candidates and $70,800 to all PACs and parties)[5]
State, District, and Local Party Committee	$5,000 per election combined limit	$5,000 per year	Unlimited transfers to other party committees	Unlimited	None
National Party Committee[2]	$5,000 per election	$5,000 per year	Unlimited transfers to other party committees	Unlimited	$43,100* to Senate candidate per campaign[6]
PAC Multicandidate[7]	$5,000 per election	$5,000 per year	$5,000 per year combined limit	$15,000 per year	None
PAC Not Multicandidate[7]	$2,500* per election	$5,000 per year	$10,000 per year combined limit	$30,800* per year	None

Source: Federal Election Commission

*The limits are indexed for inflation.

[1] These limits apply to both separate segregated funds (SSFs) and political action committees (PACs). Affiliated committees share the same set of limits on contributions made and received.

[2] A state party committee shares its limits with local and district party committees in that state unless a local or district committee's independence can be demonstrated. These limits apply to multicandidate committees only.

[3] A party's national committee, Senate campaign committee, and House campaign committee are each considered national party committees, and each have separate limits, except with respect to Senate candidates—see Special Limits column.

[4] Each of the following is considered a separate election with a separate limit: primary election, caucus or convention with the authority to nominate, general election, runoff election, and special election.

[5] No more than $46,200 of this amount may be contributed to state and local parties and PACs.

[6] This limit is shared by the national committee and the Senate campaign committee.

[7] A multicandidate committee is a political committee that has been registered for at least six months, has received contributions from more than fifty contributors, and—with the exception of a state party committee—has made contributions to at least five federal candidates.

pouring it into loosely regulated PACs known as 527 groups for the section of the tax code under which they are regulated by the Internal Revenue Service (rather than the FEC, which oversees campaign finance activities by candidates and traditional PACs that have to adhere to hard-money rules).

The intention of BCRA was to lessen the influence of money on politics, but in practice the measure got off to a rocky start. In the 2004 presidential cycle, the first election campaign under the new law, both President George W. Bush, the Republican incumbent, and Massachusetts senator John Kerry, his Democratic challenger, chose during the primary portion of the presidential campaign to opt out of the public financing system that provides a set amount of funding to presidential candidates but also places strict limits on candidate spending.

Although both candidates did take public funding for the general election campaign, the overall spending by the major-party nominees for 2004 shattered all previous records. According to the Center for Public Integrity, a nonpartisan watchdog group, Bush spent $345.2 million on his 2004 campaign, close to double his 2000 spending of $185.9 million (which was then an all-time record for a presidential campaign). Kerry spent $310 million, nearly two-and-a-half times the

$120 million spent on the 2000 campaign by the narrowly defeated Democratic candidate, Vice President Al Gore.

The 2004 presidential campaign spending figures were matched apace by congressional candidates. Overall candidate spending on the 2004 House elections amounted to roughly $1.2 billion, exceeding that in the 2001–2002 election cycle by 24 percent, according to the Center for Public Integrity. Data from the 2005–2006 cycle, in which the Democrats staged a successful push to take control of the U.S. Senate and House, showed that this record, too, was smashed. Yet these figures would again be dwarfed by the spending on the 2008 and 2010 campaigns, with no end to the escalation in sight.

Critics of current campaign finance practices have continued to advocate measures to further limit contributions and to close other gaps in the existing laws. They have also sought to control congressional campaign spending by proposing public campaign financing or other subsidies for candidates for the House and the Senate. From the opposite perspective, some lawmakers, advocates, and experts have criticized the current laws as complex and counterproductive and have dismissed the concerns about the cost of political campaigns as overstated. Along with First Amendment arguments, they point out that the population of the United States has grown enormously just during the period in which campaign finance has been the subject of ongoing national debate—from 203 million in 1970 to 308 million in 2010—raising the cost for candidates, parties, and interest groups to reach their target audiences. These opponents of the current system have pushed for raising or repealing contribution limits, reducing other regulations, and blocking any expansion of public campaign financing.

> *"Reformers desperate to resuscitate taxpayer funding [of elections] cite the supposedly scandalous fact that each party's 2008 presidential campaign may spend $500 million. If so, Americans volunteering to fund the dissemination of speech about candidates for the nation's most consequential office will contribute $1 billion, which is about half the sum they spend annually on Easter candy. Some scandal."*
>
> **—George Will,** a well-known conservative commentator and critic of efforts to restrict campaign donations and spending, in a column published in the *Washington Post,* September 28, 2006

Early Reforms

Money—once famously described as "the mother's milk of politics" — has been important to American politics since the early days of the Republic. In those days, some candidates (including George Washington) gave rather than received by rewarding their supporters with whiskey. The spread of popular democracy in the nineteenth century brought with it greater demands for campaign money that were met first by the patronage-based "spoils system" and then after the Civil War by fund-raising from corporations and wealthy industrialists.

These practices spawned the first efforts to regulate campaign finance. As part of the country's first federal civil service law in 1883, Congress prohibited the solicitation of political contributions from FEDERAL WORKERS covered by the law. In 1907 Congress followed the lead of several states by passing a law, the Tillman Act, that prohibited banks and corporations from making political contributions to candidates for federal office.

In 1910 Congress passed the Publicity Act, the first federal campaign disclosure law, but the measure required reporting of campaign spending only after elections. Amendments a year later added campaign spending limits for House and Senate candidates. But the ceilings were unrealistically low—$5,000 for House candidates and $10,000 for Senate candidates—and went largely unenforced.

The Supreme Court dealt a blow to congressional efforts to regulate campaign fund-raising in 1921 by ruling in *Newberry v. United States* that Congress had no power over party primaries. Twenty years later, however, the Court reversed itself and allowed regulation of primary elections. (See WHITE PRIMARY.)

In 1925—in the wake of "Teapot Dome," a scandal in which high-ranking government officials enriched themselves and associates through manipulation of western oil leases—Congress passed the Corrupt Practices Act, which reinforced the campaign spending disclosure requirements and attempted to cap spending at $25,000 for Senate campaigns. But again the provisions were not enforced. A new provision added in 1940 that limited individual contributions to $5,000 also proved to be ineffective; contributors evaded the ceilings by making multiple donations to separate campaign committees for the same candidates, as permitted by the law. In 1943, however, Congress closed one gap by prohibiting labor unions from making direct contributions to candidates for federal office. Three years later, the Congress of Industrial Organizations (CIO) responded by creating a separate political arm—the first PAC—to raise money from union members to contribute to federal candidates.

Rising Costs

Political campaign spending, relatively low as late as 1948, began rising with the advent of television advertising in the 1950s. In presidential campaigns, for example, victorious Republican Dwight D. Eisenhower spent $6.6 million in his 1952 race—more than three times the amount spent by Republican nominee Thomas E. Dewey during his unsuccessful challenge to Democratic incumbent Harry S. Truman four years earlier. In 1960 Republican Richard M. Nixon and winning Democrat John F. Kennedy each spent roughly $10 million. In his next two presidential campaigns, which he won, Nixon set new records for presidential campaign spending: $25.4 million in 1968 and $61.4 million in 1972. Democrats did not keep pace with Republican fund-raising, but their spending rose too: Hubert H. Humphrey spent $11.6 million in 1968; four years later George McGovern spent $30 million.

Albert B. Fall, secretary of the interior under President Warren Harding, was the first cabinet member ever convicted of a felony; he secretly leased federal oil reserves to oil magnates Henry Sinclair and Edward Doheny. Fall received $400,000, which he argued was a loan and not a bribe. The Corrupt Practices Act was passed in 1925, but its provisions were not enforced.

Source: Library of Congress

Congressional campaign spending also rose despite the low ceilings prescribed by law. Moreover, the law's disclosure provisions proved to be ineffective. Congress had given the job of maintaining campaign contributions and spending reports to its own officers, the House clerk and Senate secretary. Experts said the reports were of little use, but the lawmakers failed to approve various proposals to create an independent agency to take over the job.

The rising costs, along with discontent with the weak federal legislation, brought calls for reform in the 1950s and 1960s. In 1962 a presidential commission on campaign costs called for raising spending limits, establishing an independent agency to implement the law, and providing matching public funds to presidential candidates. President Kennedy showed little interest in the issue, but in 1966 his Democratic successor, President Lyndon B. Johnson, submitted a campaign finance bill that called for strengthening disclosure requirements and contribution limits and repealing spending limits. The House passed the bill, but it was bottled up in the Senate.

Meanwhile, Sen. Russell Long, a Democrat from Louisiana, managed to get a public financing provision for presidential campaigns enacted into law late in 1966 by attaching it to an unrelated, end-of-session measure. A year later, however, opponents from both parties succeeded in suspending the provision before it could take effect for the 1968 campaign.

Watergate Scandals

The pressure to strengthen federal campaign finance laws continued after Nixon's election to the presidency in 1968. In 1971 the Democratic-controlled Congress passed two reform measures. The Federal Election Campaign Act strengthened disclosure provisions by requiring reports from political committees, not just candidates, and by requiring identifying information from political contributors. It also limited federal candidates to spending 10 cents per voter on "communications media." Nixon signed the bill into law on February 7, 1972.

Meanwhile, the Revenue Act of 1971 resuscitated public campaign financing for presidential candidates, with funds to come from a $1 checkoff on income tax returns. The bill also provided for a tax credit or deduction to encourage political contributions. Nixon signed the measure but only after forcing Democrats to agree that public financing was not to take effect until after the 1972 campaign. (The $1 checkoff was subsequently raised to $3.)

The Watergate scandals that forced Nixon to resign in 1974 exposed a host of fund-raising abuses during Nixon's 1972 reelection campaign. The president's campaign committee used

The front page of the **New York Times** *on May 1, 1973, announced the resignation of four of President Richard Nixon's key aides.*

Source: The Granger Collection, New York

a secret fund—consisting of illegal, laundered corporate contributions and some legal but undisclosed contributions—to finance the break-in at the DEMOCRATIC NATIONAL COMMITTEE headquarters in the Watergate complex in Washington, D.C., on June 17, 1972. In addition, investigations by the special prosecutor and the Senate Watergate Committee after Nixon's reelection showed that campaign funds were also used to pay hush money to the Watergate burglars. (See SCANDALS.)

The political convulsions from these disclosures resulted in a fortified federal campaign finance law signed by President Gerald R. Ford two months after Nixon's resignation on August 9, 1974. The new law—titled the Federal Election Campaign Act Amendments—limited individuals to giving $1,000 per candidate per election or a total of $25,000 to all candidates, federal party committees, or federally registered PACs. It also sought to cap overall spending by limiting spending on congressional races: $140,000 for House races and ceilings for Senate races tied to each state's population, ranging upward from $250,000 for the smallest states. The act also set up public financing for presidential—but not congressional—campaigns, with matching funds for candidates during party primaries and full public funding for the general election. Finally, the act created the six-member Federal Election Commission to administer the law; it specified that the FEC would have no more than three members from any one party, which has resulted in a permanent split of three Republicans and three Democratic members.

Some states followed Congress's lead in enacting similar campaign spending and contribution limits for state campaigns. California voters, for example, approved a ballot INITIATIVE along those lines in 1974.

Limits of Reform

Just two years after its enactment, the Supreme Court ruled major parts of the new federal law unconstitutional. The Court's ruling in *BUCKLEY V. VALEO* struck down mandatory candidate spending limits and allowed individuals to make unlimited "independent expenditures" if they had no connection with official campaign organizations. The Court also ruled the composition of the FEC unconstitutional because the law provided for Congress to appoint some of the commission's members.

Congress reestablished the FEC in the spring of 1976 by amending the law to provide for the president to appoint all of its voting members, subject to Senate confirmation. But the Court's ruling left the lawmakers with no evident means of controlling overall campaign spending except by public financing, which was politically unpopular. It also resulted in invalidation of state-enacted campaign spending limits.

Some of the changes and decisions made in the 1970s had significant unanticipated consequences. One of these was the explosive growth in the number of PACs and their influence. In 1971 Congress had sanctioned the use of regular corporate and union funds to pay the overhead costs of PACs. The 1974 law placed more stringent limits on individual contributions ($1,000 per election) than on those of PACs ($5,000 per election). The 1974 law also lifted restrictions on the formation of PACs by federal government contractors. Further impetus came the following year when the FEC ruled that a corporation, Sun Oil Co., could establish a PAC and solicit contributions to it from stockholders and employees. Corporate PACs jumped from 139 in late 1975 at the time of the Sun Oil ruling to 433 by the end of 1976. Overall, the number of PACs went from 608 at the end of 1974 to 3,907 by the end of 2000. But the more telling statistics on PAC growth were those on PAC giving. In the 1979–1980 election cycle, PACs contributed $55 million to congressional candidates. A decade later they contributed nearly $150 million, and by the 2000 election the total had reached more than $245 million.

The dramatic growth in soft money was another example of a development no one had seen coming. In response to protests that the 1974 law was too strict, the FEC in 1978 decided to relax some of the rules covering the separation of federal campaign funds from state and local parties' nonfederal money, allowing the parties to use the latter for a portion of their administrative costs as well as voter drives and generic party activities. Similarly, Congress in 1979 exempted from federal contribution limits any sums given to state and local party committees for general voter registration or mobilization activities as long as they were not aimed at influencing federal elections. These actions by the FEC and Congress, intended to encourage volunteer and grassroots party activity, triggered a surge in soft money.

Once the national parties determined that they, too, could use soft money for certain expenses, they began raising millions of dollars for their nonfederal accounts. The use of soft money was pioneered by Ronald Reagan in his 1980 campaign and grew in importance with each succeeding election, amounting to almost $500 million in spending by the national party committees in the 2000 election and raising renewed demands for stricter campaign finance laws.

Soon soft money was being spent not only for certain party expenses but also for major POLITICAL ADVERTISING campaigns said to promote party issues, not candidates. The line between the two types of advertising, however, often was very thin and nearly impossible to discern. The Supreme Court in its 1976 *Buckley* ruling had ruled that limits on campaign contributions applied only to "advocacy ads" containing so-called magic words, such as "vote for," "elect," or "support." Many took the position that if "issue ads" did not include such terms, they were not subject to any reporting requirements or spending limits.

The use of issue ads by the parties and outside groups grew dramatically in the 1990s, and by the 1996 election many of them were being purchased with soft money. Federal regulations barred the national parties from using soft money for more than 40 percent of the costs of such ads, while limits on state parties varied. Interest groups and individuals, however, had no restrictions on how much unregulated money they could spend on the ads.

The parties' enthusiasm in the 1996 election for soft money and the issue ads it could buy helped produce the most significant campaign finance scandal since Watergate. In 1998 an FEC staff audit determined that many issue ads for President Bill Clinton and Republican challenger Bob Dole contained a clear "electioneering message" and that their campaigns should return a total of $24 million from their 1996 public funding grants. Overruling its staff, the commission unanimously voted against return of the ad money and upheld the unregulated use of issue ads.

Parties gained additional clout in 1996 when the Supreme Court ruled that they could spend as much hard money as they wanted on independent expenditures—spending that was not coordinated with a campaign—on behalf of federal candidates.

Partisan Stalemates

After the reforms of the 1970s, Congress proved less amenable to making major changes in the system. Indeed, it would be more than two decades before a new campaign finance law was enacted.

The House in 1979 passed a bill to reduce PAC contributions, but the bill died in the Senate the following year under threat of a filibuster. Campaign finance reform fell off the congressional agenda in the 1980s with Republicans in control of the White House and the Senate. Democrats recaptured the Senate in the 1986 election and in the next Congress put forward a comprehensive bill calling for public financing for Senate candidates who accepted spending limits. Republicans countered with proposals to eliminate or restrict PACs, which were proving to be a more important source of funds for the Democrats than for the GOP. The competing partisan interests produced deadlock. Democrats brought a bill to the Senate floor in 1988 but failed to break a Republican filibuster.

In 1990 the House and the Senate passed somewhat similar Democratic-backed bills late in the session; however, lawmakers never met to try to resolve the differences. Two years later, Democrats succeeded in getting legislation through both chambers of Congress, but President George H. W. Bush—objecting to its spending limits, public financing, and creation of separate systems for House and Senate campaigns—vetoed the measure. The effort to override the veto fell nine votes short in the Senate.

Reformers' hopes for breaking the deadlock were raised with the election of a Democrat, Bill Clinton, as president in 1992. Other factors also added to the pressure for reworking the federal law. Campaign costs were continuing to rise, and many members of Congress were finding that fund-raising took up more and more of their time. A variety of public interest groups complained that the high cost of campaigning created advantages for incumbents, who enjoyed fund-raising advantages over challengers, and for wealthy candidates, who could spend unlimited amounts of their personal funds.

Concerns about the influence of special interest groups were rising with the growth in contributions from PACs. Critics said the tendency of PACs to favor incumbents bolstered their fund-raising edge over challengers.

Despite these factors, the Democratic-controlled Congress failed to give final approval to campaign finance legislation in 1993 or 1994. Both the House and the Senate approved Democratic-sponsored bills in 1993, but House leaders waited until August 1994 to appoint conferees to work out differences between the two bills. With adjournment nearing, Republicans in the Senate then used parliamentary tactics to block a conference. Some critics blamed the Democrats for waiting until the eleventh hour to work on a compromise version of the legislation and even questioned how sincere they were in their pursuit of campaign reform.

Buddhist nuns and their representatives testify under immunity in September 1997 before the Senate Governmental Affairs Committee investigating Vice President Al Gore's fund-raising activities during the 1996 election cycle.

Source: AP Images/Joe Marquette

The Republican takeover in the next Congress made little difference in campaign finance legislation. Hopes were raised briefly in June 1995 when Clinton and House Speaker Newt Gingrich, a Georgia Republican, agreed in a "town hall" meeting in New Hampshire to create a bipartisan commission to recommend an overhaul of campaign finance laws. The commission was never created, and Clinton and Gingrich blamed each other for the failure.

In Congress, though, senators McCain and Feingold joined in sponsoring a reform measure that called for voluntary spending limits in return for certain incentives and would have banned PAC and soft-money contributions. The effort was stopped once again by a filibuster. Meanwhile, the House in 1996 rejected competing Republican- and Democratic-sponsored campaign finance bills.

Public attention was riveted on the flaws of the campaign finance system by actions taken during the 1996 presidential election campaign. At the root of the scandal that erupted were allegations that foreign money—particularly Chinese—had made it into the campaign in violation of federal law and that the national parties' pursuit and use of soft money may have crossed the line into illegal activity. The national party committees raised a total of $262 million in soft money in the 1996 election cycle—$124 million by the Democrats and $138 million by the Republicans. Critics said the funds were raised and spent in close coordination with the respective presidential campaigns, undercutting the goal of insulating candidates for the White House from private fund-raising.

Much of the focus was on the Democrats. As the scandal unfolded, it was revealed that the Democratic National Committee (DNC) had accepted nearly $3 million in illegal or suspect contributions, money the DNC said it would return. The fund-raising tactics of President Clinton and Vice President Al Gore were also central to the scandal. The news media provided accounts of the Clintons entertaining large donors at private White House coffees and inviting some contributors for overnight stays in the Lincoln bedroom or to go along on government foreign trade missions, and of Gore making fund-raising calls from his office and attending a controversial fund-raiser at a Buddhist temple in California.

The Republican-led Congress launched investigations in both chambers, which seemed to do little more than embarrass the Democrats for their fund-raising excesses. Investigators came up with no proof of allegations that the Chinese government had conspired to influence U.S. elections through large campaign contributions or that the White House had knowingly accepted illegal foreign contributions or that the Clinton administration ever changed policy in exchange for campaign contributions. During the investigation, Republicans were embarrassed as well when it was revealed that a Republican National Committee (RNC) think tank also accepted foreign money that might have been passed on to the RNC. There were calls for an independent counsel to look into allegations of fund-raising abuses by Clinton and Gore, but Attorney General Janet Reno found that the allegations did not meet the standard for such an appointment. A Justice Department campaign finance task force did obtain guilty pleas and convictions in some of the cases it brought against individuals and corporations for activities in the 1996 election. The FEC also levied civil penalties.

In the wake of the scandal, McCain and Feingold renewed the drive for their bill, and more than fifty other proposals were also introduced in the early days of the 105th Congress (1997–1999). The House in 1998 passed a sweeping measure after its backers, led by Republican Christopher Shays of Connecticut and Democrat Martin T. Meehan of Massachusetts, surmounted attempts by the GOP leadership to block its consideration on the House floor. A Senate bill succumbed once again to a filibuster. But what was interesting this time around was how much the focus of the debate had changed. PAC contributions, spending limits, and public funding were no longer the dominant issues. In fact, the House bill included no provisions in those areas, and Senate sponsors dropped those provisions in an attempt to broaden GOP support for their bill. The House and Senate bills focused instead on banning soft money and redefining issue advocacy advertising, reflecting the dramatic growth of both in the 1990s and the enormous controversy surrounding them.

In the 106th Congress (1999–2001), the House passed a bill that was substantively the same as the legislation it had approved the previous year. Senate sponsors put aside—at least for the time being—their proposal to regulate issue ads more closely and opted instead for a narrow bill that focused on banning soft money. They hoped this move would neutralize GOP opponents' argument that the bill was a violation of free speech rights at least enough to pick up the votes to overcome a filibuster. But the new strategy, like the old ones, failed.

Bipartisan Campaign Reform Act of 2002

Three events served to break the logjam in the early 2000s. McCain made campaign finance reform a central issue in his populist-toned bid for the 2000 Republican presidential nomination. After his defeat by George W. Bush in the primaries, McCain—who had been targeted by "527" groups that favored Bush—achieved an incremental step during the 106th Congress with the enactment of a bill placing reporting and spending requirements on those previously secret political organizations. In the 107th Congress (2001–2003), Democrats' gains in the Senate and the support of Republican senator Thad Cochran of Mississippi gave reformers enough votes to shut down the perennial filibuster against campaign finance legislation. The Senate passed the McCain-Feingold bill in early 2001, but the legislation stalled in the House, where there were competing proposals. Finally, the collapse of the giant energy company Enron in December 2001 highlighted the campaign spending habits of the grossly mismanaged corporation and embarrassed both parties. The scandal put the legislation over the top.

Republican senator John McCain of Arizona (left) and Democratic senator Russ Feingold of Wisconsin (center) discuss their campaign finance bill in March 2001.

Source: CQ Photo/Scott J. Ferrell

The new law—the Bipartisan Campaign Reform Act of 2002—that was cleared for President Bush's signature on March 20, 2002, completely banned federal campaign organizations from raising and spending soft money.

State and local party organizations were allowed to raise up to $10,000 per contributor per year to pay for party organizing and get-out-the-vote efforts. But outside organizations, particularly 527s, continued to be eligible to receive unlimited soft-money contributions as long as they were not used specifically on federal campaigns—a provision that many observers came to see as a giant loophole.

In what would remain a persistently controversial provision years after its enactment, the bill also barred the use of soft money on political communications—issue ads—that refer to a specific federal candidate within thirty days of a primary election and within sixty days of a general election.

A Supreme Court ruling in June 2007, in the case of *Federal Election Commission v. Wisconsin Right to Life,* loosened these restrictions in a precursor of the more sweeping *Citizens United* decision less than three years later. The Court ruled that the limits on "electioneering communications" by outside groups could not be enforced as long as there could be a reasonable interpretation that the issue ads were aimed at another purpose besides influencing voters to support or oppose a specific candidate.

Meanwhile, strictly limited HARD MONEY contributions, which had never been adjusted for inflation following passage of the 1974 FECA law, got what many participants said was a long-overdue increase, from $1,000 per candidate per election to $2,000. An inflation escalator clause, which raised allowable contributions by $100 per candidate per election in each subsequent cycle, set the limit at $2,500 for the 2011–2012 campaign cycle.

Bush was not an advocate of the legislation, saying that he favored fuller disclosure of the sources of political contributions over the limitations included in the bill. He signed the measure on March 27 without enthusiasm, eschewing a public ceremony and calling the legislation "flawed." Within days of its enactment, the law was the subject of lawsuits filed by Sen. Mitch McConnell of Kentucky and interest groups such as the National Rifle Association, the American Civil Liberties Union, and the Christian Coalition, which charged that their First Amendment freedoms were abridged by both the soft-money and electioneering communications limits.

The issue was not resolved until December 10, 2003, when the Supreme Court resolved a protracted legal fight by upholding all of the central provisions of the bill by a 5–4 margin.

Although some of the measure's opponents had warned that the soft-money ban would virtually cripple the effectiveness of the national parties, both the Republicans and Democrats proved extremely capable of supplanting the prohibited unlimited donations with thousands of new

hard-money donations. Presidential candidates George W. Bush and Kerry in 2004 and congressional candidates in 2004 and 2006 raised more money than candidates had before BCRA was enacted. And, most frustrating of all for the advocates of reform, soft money did not go away but rather found a hearty welcome from 527 organizations, which were the fastest-growing sector in campaign fund-raising and spending.

Numerous Democratic-allied groups, including many with ties to organized labor, raised millions of dollars for 527s that attacked Bush's policies, and these appeared to gain the initiative early in the 2004 campaign. But the 527 organization that ultimately would have the most impact was the Swift Boat Veterans for Truth, which sought to discredit Kerry's reputation as a Vietnam War hero and highlight his antiwar activities after he had left the service. The groups' members were veterans who opposed the Democratic nominee, but they were largely financed by Republican businessmen.

Following the 2004 and 2006 elections, many people seeking to limit the money spent on influencing campaigns quickly came to the conclusion that they would need to "reform the reforms." However, those who were skeptical about the McCain-Feingold law, including a "strange bedfellows" coalition of civil libertarians and interest groups across the ideological spectrum, said that efforts to rein in campaign spending were futile and constituted undemocratic limits on the freedom of speech and association. These groups argued that the cure for what ailed the political system was not a limit on fund-raising and spending but, rather, full and instant electronic disclosure of from whom candidates, parties, and interest groups were getting their money and to whom they were giving it.

> **"Just as troubling to a functioning democracy as classic quid pro quo corruption is the danger that officeholders will decide issues not on the merits or the desires of their constituencies but according to the wishes of those who have made large financial contributions. . . . The evidence set forth . . . convincingly demonstrates that soft-money contributions to political parties carry with them just such a temptation."**
>
> —Excerpts of the five-Justice majority opinion in December 2003 that upheld the major provisions of the 2002 Bipartisan Campaign Reform Act

> **"The dangers posed by speech regulations have led the Court to insist upon principled constitutional lines and a rigorous standard of review. The majority now abandons those distinctions and limitations."**
>
> —Justice Anthony M. Kennedy, joining three other justices in the minority on the December 2003 Supreme Court ruling upholding the 2002 Bipartisan Campaign Reform Act

The Citizens United Case

Opponents of BCRA scored a major victory with the Court's narrowly approved decision in the *Citizens United* case.

The case was not necessarily sweeping in nature, and the Court could have decided it on narrow grounds had it chosen to do so. *Citizens United*, a conservative group headed by veteran activist David Bossie, sought to air a documentary that was strongly critical of Democratic senator Hillary Rodham Clinton of New York, the former first lady to President Bill Clinton, during the primary season in which she was seeking her party's 2008 nomination for president. The Supreme Court was considering an appeal by *Citizens United* of a decision by the U.S. District Court for the District of Columbia that defined *Hillary: The Movie* as a campaign ad that therefore was barred under BCRA's electioneering communications provisions.

But rather than simply overruling the lower court's interpretation of the documentary as a campaign ad, five of the nine justices ruled that the electioneering communications provisions amounted to an unconstitutional infringement on the First Amendment rights of corporate interests.

"If the First Amendment has any force, it prohibits Congress from fining or jailing citizens, or associations of citizens, for simply engaging in political speech," Justice Kennedy wrote in the majority opinion.

The decision drew a strong dissent that was written by Justice John Paul Stevens. "At bottom, the Court's opinion is thus a rejection of the common sense of the American people, who have recognized a need to prevent corporations from undermining self government since the founding, and who have fought against the distinctive corrupting potential of corporate electioneering since the days of Theodore Roosevelt," Stevens wrote. "It is a strange time to repudiate that common sense. While American democracy is imperfect, few outside the majority of this Court would have thought its flaws included a dearth of corporate money in politics."

Most of the criticism of the decision came from Democrats who worried that wealthy individuals and business corporate interests would unleash a torrent of money to elect conservative candidates, most of them Republicans. These critics included President Obama, leading to an unusually public conflict between the executive and judicial branches.

During his 2010 State of the Union address, which took place in the week following the *Citizens United* decision, Obama said, "With all due deference to separation of powers, last week the Supreme Court reversed a century of law that, I believe, will open the floodgates for special interests, including foreign corporations, to spend without limit in our elections." He added, "I don't think American elections should be bankrolled by America's most powerful interests or, worse, by foreign entities. They should be decided by the American people. And I urge Democrats and Republicans to pass a bill that helps correct some of these problems."

Justice Samuel Alito, a conservative member of the Court who was seated with other justices in the U.S. House chamber for the speech, reacted to the remarks by wincing and could be seen on television mouthing the words, "Not true."

Congressional Democrats did attempt to follow Obama's lead and pass legislation that would have placed strict disclosure requirements on outside groups that would seek to take advantage of the electioneering opportunities afforded them under the *Citizens United* decision. The House did pass what was called the DISCLOSE Act (an acronym for Democracy Is Strengthened by Casting Light on Spending in Elections) in June 2010. But solid Republican opposition in the Senate, which then had a wide Democratic majority, left the bill one vote shy of the sixty needed to break a GOP filibuster and allow a floor vote that almost certainly would have resulted in the measure's passage.

A report by the Center for Responsive Politics following the 2010 midterm elections, in which the Republican Party made major gains nationally, found that the Democrats' concerns were borne out, at least for that election cycle. The CRP study found that $191 million in political spending was laid out by Republican-allied groups, a figure that exceeded spending by similar groups in any previous cycle by roughly $70 million. Outside groups allied with the Democrats spent $92 million in the 2010 cycle, according to the study.

Campaign Slogans

Campaign slogans are the products of efforts by political candidates and their advisers to reduce the central themes of their campaigns to a few memorable words.

As *New York Times* language columnist William Safire observed in his *New Political Dictionary* (1993), "Good slogans have rhyme, rhythm, or alliteration to make them memorable; great slogans may have none of these, but touch a chord of memory, release pent-up hatreds, or stir men's better natures." Another requirement of a campaign slogan is brevity. Modern slogans must be short enough to fit on a campaign button, bumper sticker, placard, or brief television spot—all standard fixtures of present-day electioneering. (See CAMPAIGN, BASIC STAGES OF.)

A slogan can be designed to emphasize a personal rapport between candidate and voter. For example, the dominant political mantra of the 1950s was the catchy "I Like Ike," a play on the nickname of World War II general Dwight D. Eisenhower, the Republican who easily won the 1952 and 1956 presidential elections.

A campaign may adopt a slogan that reminds voters of a candidate's signal achievement. The victorious 1840 national ticket of William Henry Harrison and John Tyler urged voters to support "Tippecanoe and Tyler Too," a reference to Harrison's victory as commander in an 1811 battle with Indian tribes at a place called Tippecanoe in a frontier area that later became Indiana. In 1916 Democrat Woodrow Wilson was reelected as president on the slogan "He Kept Us Out of War." In April 1917, however, just a month after he was sworn in to a second term, Wilson persuaded Congress that the United States should enter World War I in response to provocations by Germany.

A slogan may apply to a candidate's entire policy agenda, such as Democrat Franklin D. Roosevelt's New Deal in 1932 and Democrat John F. Kennedy's New Frontier in 1960. Such a policy-related slogan may become superseded by a more populist phrase that emerges from the campaign trail: Democrat Harry S. Truman's 1948 pledge of a Fair Deal is less known than the slogan that encapsulated his feistiness and determination, "Give 'Em Hell, Harry!"

Candidates, particularly incumbents seeking reelection, may choose a slogan that focuses on the most positive portrayal of the state of the nation. "It's Morning Again in America," proclaimed Republican Ronald Reagan's successful 1984 reelection campaign.

A slogan may attempt to appeal to both intellect and emotion. In an effort to offset characterizations that he was a conservative extremist—which ultimately would doom him to a landslide defeat by Democratic incumbent Lyndon B. Johnson—1964 Republican nominee Barry Goldwater used the slogan "In Your Heart, You Know He's Right."

But a slogan may also encapsulate the most bitter rhetoric of a campaign. Some Democrats in 1964 circulated a sarcastic rejoinder to Goldwater's slogan: "In Your Guts, You Know He's Nuts." Some Republicans, in an unsuccessful effort to stave off Democrat Grover Cleveland in 1884, portrayed the Democrats as the party of "Rum, Romanism, and Rebellion"—references to the general Democratic opposition to prohibition of alcoholic beverages, the party's support base among mainly immigrant Roman Catholics, and the party's strong ties to the South, which just two decades earlier had sparked the Civil War by attempting to secede from the Union.

There are some slogans that are golden oldies, returning when the occasion fits and sometimes used by either major party. When a party in power becomes unpopular, it is not uncommon for the challenging party to ask voters, "Had Enough?" In 2006 many Democratic candidates wielded that slogan in their party's successful effort to overturn the Republicans' majorities in the Senate and the House.

THE SACRILEGIOUS CANDIDATE.

William Jennings Bryan warned against crucifying U.S. agricultural producers on a "cross of gold," earning him the Democratic presidential nomination in 1896. Republican William McKinley prevailed in the election.

Source: Library of Congress

Economic issues figure in several other memorable slogans or speech phrases. For instance, William Jennings Bryan's famed "Cross of Gold" speech at the 1896 Democratic convention condemned opposition to expansion of the money supply through free coinage of silver. "You shall not press down upon the brow of labor this crown of thorns," Bryan roared. "You shall not crucify mankind upon a cross of gold."

The speech won Bryan the presidential nomination, making him at thirty-six the youngest standard bearer of a major party. Despite a strenuous campaign—the first one involving extensive travel—Bryan lost to Republican William McKinley, who campaigned from his front porch with the slogans "McKinley and the Full Dinner Pail" and "Stop Bryan, Save America."

In the 1932 election—which took place among the devastating effects of the Great Depression—the Democrats, led by Franklin Roosevelt, attacked the economic policies of Republican incumbent Herbert Hoover with slogans such as "Sweeping Depression Out" and "Kick Out Depression with a Democratic Vote." For his part, Hoover denied ever making the promise attributed to him: "A Chicken in Every Pot, a Car in Every Garage." In 1960, as the heir to a sluggish economy at the end of Eisenhower's tenure, Vice President Richard M. Nixon, the GOP nominee for president, was vulnerable to Kennedy's promise to "Get the Country Moving Again."

Twenty years later, Ronald Reagan turned the tables on Democrat Jimmy Carter by asking the voters, "Are you better off than you were four years ago?" Saddled with double-digit inflation, most voters agreed they were not.

Other notable economic slogans include the 1930s "We Share Our Wealth: Every Man a King" movement of Louisiana's Huey P. Long and George H. W. Bush's 1988 pledge, "Read My Lips. No New Taxes." Like many slogans, Bush's words came back to haunt him after he agreed to a tax increase.

Alliteration, as in the nineteenth-century cases of "Tippecanoe and Tyler Too" and "Rum, Romanism, and Rebellion," is a favorite of sloganeers, and catch phrases that repeat letters or sounds are among the hardest to forget.

Democrat Grover Cleveland won the 1884 election even though he was the object of the derisive "Ma, Ma, Where's My Pa?" rhyme because he had fathered an illegitimate child. After he won, his supporters added the line, "Gone to the White House, Ha, Ha, Ha."

The "Win with Willkie" slogan evolved from "We Want Willkie," a phrase chanted repeatedly at the 1940

Candidates have long depended on catchy phrases in their campaigns.

Source: Dwight D. Eisenhower Library

Republican National Convention by supporters of Wendell L. Willkie for president. Willkie, an Indiana public utilities executive, won the nomination but failed to deny Roosevelt a historic third term.

Similarly, "Dump the Hump" was the rallying cry of Vietnam War protesters who wanted the 1968 Democratic convention to nominate Minnesota senator Eugene J. McCarthy for president instead of Vice President Hubert H. Humphrey. President Lyndon B. Johnson had dropped out of the race after McCarthy made an impressive second-place finish against him in the NEW HAMPSHIRE PRIMARY.

As the first president to seek more than two full terms, FDR was the target of several negative slogans, including 1940's "No Third Term," "Don't Be a Third Termite," and "No Man Is Good Three Times."

Some slogans have been alliterative and combative. For example, in the 1840s American expansionists urged warfare unless Britain gave up the whole Pacific Northwest as far north as the parallel at fifty-four degrees, forty minutes; hence the slogan, "Fifty-four Forty or Fight." But President James K. Polk compromised with the British, limiting the Northwest Territory to the forty-ninth parallel, now the major boundary between the United States and Canada.

The themes of change or stability underlie numerous slogans, particularly regarding war. During the Civil War in 1864, Republicans urged the reelection of Abraham Lincoln. Their rallying cry

Democratic presidential hopeful Sen. Barack Obama, D-Ill., speaks at a rally in front of a sign that says "Change we can believe in," on Friday, February 8, 2008, at Key Arena in Seattle. Behind him are, from left, U.S. Rep. Adam Smith, D-Wash., Washington governor Chris Gregoire, and Seattle mayor Greg Nickels.

Source: AP Photo/Ted S. Warren

was, "Don't Change Horses in the Middle of the Stream." Almost a century later, Democrats used the same words to support FDR's wartime reelection in 1944. Other stay-the-course slogans include "Let Us Continue" and "All the Way with LBJ" (after the assassination of President Kennedy), as well as "Four More Years" and "Reelect the President" (for Richard Nixon in 1972).

On the other hand, "It's Time for a Change" worked for Eisenhower, who pledged "I Shall Go to Korea" if elected in 1952 in an effort to end the Korean War, and for Democrats Kennedy in 1960 and Bill Clinton in 1992, who promised new beginnings after years of Republican administrations. Similarly, Republican George W. Bush in his 2000 speech accepting the presidential nomination raised what he portrayed as deficiencies in the administration of Clinton and Vice President Al Gore—who was that year's Democratic nominee—with the mantra, "Help Is on the Way," although that never caught on as a campaign slogan.

Almost sixty years after Eisenhower's successful campaign, the idea of "change" worked for Democrat Barack Obama, who was elected president in 2008. He introduced the idea of change to emphasize his argument that he would bring new ideas and politics to a nation weary of eight years of Republican President George W. Bush. Obama used "change" in at least a half dozen slogans, the most memorable of which was "Change We Can Believe In."

Campaign Strategies

All political candidates need a game plan for winning election. As contestants for the biggest electoral prize in the United States, presidential candidates require the most developed and comprehensive campaign strategies. Most of the strategic components used by contenders for the nation's highest office are, however, much the same as those for election to other major offices, such as GOVERNOR, house member, or senator.

The strategy chosen by a presidential candidate and his or her advisers must cover all campaign stages, including the earliest, or "exploratory," phase when the situation must be assessed and a decision made whether to run. If there is sufficient evidence—or even a gut feeling—that there will be significant voter support and a reasonable chance to win some DELEGATES to the NATIONAL PARTY CONVENTION, then candidacy may be announced and other aspects of the strategy carried forward.

The strategy must be dynamic and adaptable, with a mechanism to let the candidate know if he or she is faltering and what corrective action is needed, or when an unexpected opportunity exists that the candidate can use to gain the initiative if he or she moves quickly and adeptly.

Political scientists have identified the common types of strategies as *insider, outsider, early knockout, trench warfare, slow buildup,* and *wait and see.* Most of these strategies, or combinations of them, are employed in the prenomination period, when the target is not a single rival from the opposing party but often a host of them within the same party.

- Insider. The insider strategy, one of the oldest, depends heavily on the endorsements and resources of major-party and government figures. This approach was dominant in the period before the PRESIDENTIAL SELECTION REFORMS made by the DEMOCRATIC PARTY beginning in 1968 and subsequently adopted in part by the REPUBLICAN PARTY. Today, even an insider strategy requires entering and winning most of the primaries.
- Established insiders enjoy benefits, including name identification, expansive fund-raising networks, and access to the political mobilization and get-out-the-vote networks of their fellow insider supporters. Such assets usually—but not always—result in the strongest insider candidate gaining FRONT-RUNNER status in the campaign.
- Establishment support helped both of the major-party nominees in 2000 fend off challengers who cast themselves as outsiders. Texas governor George W. Bush, son of former president George H. W. Bush, held off Arizona Sen. John McCain, who had cast himself as a Republican Party "maverick." Democrat Al Gore, the incumbent vice president, easily defeated former New Jersey senator Bill Bradley, who sought to portray himself as a voice for political reform. Similarly, in 2004, former Vermont governor Howard Dean, who ran on the core issue of his opposition to the war in Iraq and gained much of his support from younger voters, raced to the top of polls measuring voter sentiment in the contest for the Democratic nomination, but he was quickly felled in the primaries by Massachusetts Sen. John Kerry, who had more establishment support.
- Successful campaigns by candidates who enter a race without much of an insider support base—such as those of Democrats Jimmy Carter in 1976 and Bill Clinton in 1992—most often occur when there is no single rallying figure for the political establishment.
- Outsider. Insider strategies are most successful, however, when the voting public is generally satisfied with the direction that the nation is headed and generally thinks well of their

government. Since the middle of the 2000s decade, though, the electorate has been roiled by dissatisfaction with the political establishment—first largely because of dissent over a protracted military intervention in Iraq and government failures in responding to Hurricane Katrina in 2005, and then greatly exacerbated by a financial crisis, beginning in 2008, that caused serious economic dislocation. This, in turn, has prompted many presidential hopefuls to try to distance themselves from the government (even, in some cases, when they were longtime officeholders) and to run as "outsiders."

- In the outsider strategy, the candidate runs against the entrenched political establishment, offering a fresh face to disenchanted voters. Barack Obama was a notable success story for the outsider strategy. Obama—whose February 2007 candidacy announcement came just more than two years after he moved directly from the state Senate in Illinois to the U.S. Senate—based his campaign on inspirational rhetoric of change and hope that struck a nerve with many voters, and his bid to become the nation's first African American president enhanced his outsider appeal. He first won the Democratic presidential nomination in an upset over early front-runner Hillary Rodham Clinton, a New York senator whose status as former President Bill Clinton's first lady gave her ultimate insider status. Obama then won by a comfortable margin over Republican nominee McCain, in part by blunting his efforts to maximize the maverick image he had sought to cultivate over many years.

- Like the insider approach, the outsider stance over the years has had a mixed record of success. It worked for Carter in 1976, Ronald Reagan in the 1980, and Barry Goldwater in the 1964 GOP primaries, but not for Eugene J. McCarthy in the 1968 Democratic nominating contest or Reagan in 1976 when he lost the GOP nomination to President Gerald R. Ford. Robert F. Kennedy's outsider attempt in 1968 was cut short by his assassination. Jesse L. Jackson in 1984 and 1988, Edmund G. "Jerry" Brown Jr. and Patrick J. Buchanan in 1992, and Democrat Dean in 2004 gave voice to disaffected outsiders but never posed a real threat to the front-runners.

- Early knockout. Using the early knockout strategy, front-runners seek a string of early PRIMARY and CAUCUS victories in hopes that the competition will quickly drop out. The phenomenon of states scheduling their primaries and caucuses earlier and earlier and clustering their contests in each successive presidential election year, known as FRONT-LOADING, has helped abet that strategy. Candidates who produce strong showings in the earliest contests have tended over the past few decades to build unstoppable momentum. That happened for Kerry in the 2004 Democratic contest and both Bush and Gore in 2000. Bob Dole, the front-runner for the Republican nomination to oppose President Clinton in 1996, survived some early setbacks at the hands of hard-line conservative commentator Patrick Buchanan; he turned the tide by winning a key early primary in South Carolina and sweeping all of the remaining contests. But while McCain in 2008 knocked his rivals—including former governors Mitt Romney of Massachusetts and Mike Huckabee of Arkansas—out of the running early in the nominating campaign, Obama had to contend with a determined effort by Hillary Clinton that lasted through the end of the primary and caucus season before she conceded the Democratic nomination to him.

- Trench warfare. The unpopular trench-warfare approach pits two or more strong rivals against each other in the political equivalent of hand-to-hand combat. The objective is to outlast opponents the candidate cannot hope to outdistance. The bitter, debilitating contests often handicap the party nominee in the ensuing general election. The races between Humphrey, McCarthy, and Kennedy (until his death) in 1968; Humphrey, George

S. McGovern, and George C. Wallace in 1972; Ford and Reagan in 1976; Carter and Massachusetts Sen. Edward M. Kennedy in 1980; and Walter F. Mondale, vice president to Carter, and Colorado Sen. Gary Hart in 1984 were examples of trench warfare. The impact of the front-loading of the nominating contests over more recent election cycles has reduced the prospect of two or more heavyweight candidates staging a sustained and politically debilitating battle, with the prolonged Obama-Clinton battle an exception.

- Slow buildup. The slow-buildup goal is to avoid early traps and criticism and gain the aura of party savior when other candidates look weak. Had he not been killed, Robert Kennedy might have won the 1968 Democratic nomination using this strategy. He delayed his entry and won the important California primary, then held late in the season. Similarly, Sen. Henry Jackson of Washington tried unsuccessfully to win the 1976 nomination with victories in the late primaries. Today, however, the slow-buildup strategy is obsolete. The necessity of raising tens of millions of dollars and building nationwide organizations had become so pressing by the run-up to the 2008 election that close to twenty hopefuls between the two parties had either officially announced their candidacies or had stated publicly that they were considering bids by early March 2007.

- Rudolph Giuliani, the former mayor of New York City who sought the 2008 Republican nomination, tried a variation on this theme, skipping the Iowa caucuses and New Hampshire primary that for years have kicked off the nominating campaigns and bidding for a game-changing breakthrough in Florida, which has a large population of transplanted New Yorkers. The strategy failed badly, though, and Giuliani quit the race after a mediocre showing in the Florida primary.

- Wait and see. The wait-and-see strategy is also largely obsolete. Presidential nominations no longer are decided at party conventions. Since 1960 all but one have been sewn up beforehand in the primaries and caucuses. Humphrey, the incumbent vice president, won the 1968 Democratic nomination after a divisive primary season without entering a single contest. The ensuing resentment within the party, however, led to the reforms that have made a repeat of the 1968 situation unlikely.

In 1980 President Carter entered the Democratic convention with more than enough delegates committed to him to clinch the nomination over his challenger, Massachusetts Sen. Edward M. Kennedy, but with lagging national job approval ratings that put his reelection chances at great risk. Some Democratic officials, worried about Carter's ability to fend off charismatic conservative Reagan, sought to free delegates from obligations to vote for a particular candidate with the hope that another candidate might emerge in a deadlocked convention, but the effort failed. In 1988 New York governor Mario M. Cuomo refused to enter the primaries but said he would accept a convention draft, which never materialized. Massachusetts governor Michael S. Dukakis locked up enough delegates prior to the convention to ensure his nomination on the first ballot, though he would lose to the elder George Bush that November.

Strategies in Action

As a nonincumbent, a candidate may favor an outsider strategy. But if it succeeds, and he or she is elected, the candidate may seek reelection as an insider. Jimmy Carter's campaigns in 1976 and 1980 provide classic examples of both strategies in action at separate times.

As a former Georgia governor looking to the presidency in 1976, Carter followed an outsider script outlined in 1972 by an aide, Hamilton Jordan. Jordan advised Carter to travel abroad to gain exposure to foreign policy problems and to become involved in national politics because, he wrote, Carter would "have to convince the press, public, and politicians that he knows how to run a government."

Although not well known nationally at first, Carter gained publicity and credibility with his anti-Washington campaign. He ran as a "New South" leader, who eschewed the politics of racial division that had marked previous presidential contenders from the region and who could help heal the wounds of the Watergate scandal and the Vietnam War. By the time MEDIA COVERAGE of Carter's campaign began, including examination of his record in Georgia, Carter had become a strong front-runner.

In contrast, Carter followed an insider strategy to fend off the 1980 nomination challenge from Edward M. Kennedy, a brother of the late president John F. Ken-

Jimmy Carter's 1976 and 1980 presidential campaigns exemplify outsider and insider strategies, respectively. Here, Carter disembarks from the airplane Peanut One for a campaign stop in Pennsylvania in September 1976.

Source: Library of Congress

nedy and the late senator Robert F. Kennedy. Besides using his INCUMBENCY to line up support from party and business leaders, Carter manipulated the primary and caucus calendar to his advantage. Aides persuaded three southern states—Alabama, Florida, and Georgia—to hold their primaries together on March 11, then unusually early on the primary calendar, ensuring a big sweep for Carter. They also managed to avoid a Kennedy sweep on Massachusetts's primary day, March 4, by having neighboring Connecticut switch its primary to March 25. At the Democratic convention, Carter delegates voted down the proposed rules change that would have benefited Kennedy on the first ballot, which Carter won to gain renomination.

In the general election, however, insider Carter was no match for outsider Reagan. Plagued by the Iran hostage crisis, high inflation, and a national malaise (which he described in a speech without actually using the word), Carter became a one-term president.

On the other hand, the past two presidents who won reelection—Bill Clinton in 1996 and George W. Bush in 2004—each benefited from a strong economy and were able to win second terms running as insiders and urging voters to maintain continuity in Washington.

Deciding on a Strategy

With so many strategies to choose from, a candidate must size up himself or herself as well as the number and strengths of the competition, the fund-raising situation, the issues to address, the degree of public acceptance, and the mood of the district, state, or nation.

The strategy chosen for the primary and caucus season may differ from the one used for the general election, when most contests are one-on-one. For presidential candidates, success in the early primaries is crucial. Victories in the IOWA CAUCUSES and NEW HAMPSHIRE PRIMARY can quickly transform a candidate from dark horse to front-runner in terms of improved POLLING results, delegate counts, endorsements, financial and volunteer backing, and media coverage. Conversely, failure in these contests has caused many candidates to drop out before they have had a chance to demonstrate their vote-getting ability in home territory. For example, in 2011 Tim Pawlenty, a former Minnesota governor, dropped out of the race for the 2012 Republican presidential nomination on August 14 after a poor showing in an Iowa straw poll, even though he had officially announced his candidacy less than three months earlier, on May 23.

Pawlenty, however, was just the latest is a long succession of would-be presidential candidates who never got past the starting gate. Poor showings in the 1999 Iowa straw poll prompted Sen. Lamar Alexander of Tennessee and Dan Quayle, the vice president under George H. W. Bush, to immediately leave the Republican race. They were soon followed by Elizabeth Dole, later a North Carolina senator, and Pat Buchanan, who had challenged incumbent Bush for the 1992 Republican presidential nomination (and would later run as the Reform Party candidate in 2000). In 2007, Tommy Thompson, the former governor of neighboring Wisconsin, finished sixth with 7 percent (behind others who never went far in the race, such as Sen. Sam Brownback of Kansas and Rep. Tom Tancredo of Colorado) and took that as his cue that it was time for him to leave the competition.

Because primaries tend to draw mainly the most motivated voters, and because the most motivated voters tend to be activists associated with the parties' ideological wings—liberals for the Democrats and conservatives for the Republicans—many candidates tailor their messages for the nominating campaign to "play to the base." But they have to make sure they do not alienate more moderate "swing" voters who often make up the decisive factor in national elections, and it is not unusual to see a candidate, upon clinching the nomination, pivot quickly to "move to the middle."

Yet the polarization of politics in recent years, from at least the mid-1990s, may make that pivot difficult to finesse for candidates unless ideological and partisan tensions abate. Ideological activists—including the conservatives who fomented the Tea Party movement during the 2010 midterm election cycle—have become more demanding that candidates stick to what they view as their party's principles instead of moderating their views for the general election campaigns.

Once the primaries have winnowed out most candidates, the survivors concentrate on the delegate count. The delegate-selection process is shorter than it used to be, however, because of the FRONT-LOADING trend. Large states such as California, New Jersey, Ohio, and Pennsylvania formerly held their primaries late in the season, which required the candidates to campaign for months to obtain enough delegates to assure nomination.

Front-loading has changed the dynamics of strategic planning for presidential aspirants. Survivors of the early knockout strategy cannot realistically hope to dislodge the front-runner with a slow-buildup strategy. Especially in an age of PROPORTIONAL REPRESENTATION, late surges of support are unlikely to undo the mathematics of delegate counts.

Fund-raising ability is a must for all candidates. Presidential candidates can obtain PUBLIC FINANCING of their campaigns, but only if they meet a threshold of fund-raising in the primaries and if their party did well enough in the previous general election's popular vote to qualify for funding in the next election. The public financing also comes with spending limitations, and candidates in recent primary campaigns have taken to eschewing public money and relying on their own fund-raising prowess.

This opting-out of the public financing system applied to only the primary campaign through the 2004 election, as both Bush and Kerry accepted public financing and the accompanying restrictions for the general election. By 2008, several candidates bypassed the public financing system in order to raise larger sums than they would have qualified to receive under the public financing formulas—most prominently Obama, who set a precedent by eschewing public funds for the general election and shattered previous presidential fund-raising records.

Congressional elections are not publicly funded, but they are subject to federal contribution limits. Most states regulate campaign funding; some provide partial public financing.

To avoid federal spending limits and disclosure requirements, some wealthy individuals have financed presidential campaigns without accepting public funds. Former Texas governor John B. Connally in 1980 and publishing magnate Malcolm S. "Steve" Forbes Jr. in 1996 spent heavily in the primaries, trying unsuccessfully to win the Republican nomination.

Texas billionaire Ross Perot also passed up federal financing to run as an INDEPENDENT in 1992. His third-place finish with almost 19 percent of the vote was more than enough to qualify his new Reform Party for public funding in the 1996 election, though Perot soon lost interest and the Reform Party became an ephemeral factor in national politics. New York City mayor Michael Bloomberg, a wealthy media magnate, was rumored to be considering a similar independent bid for president in 2008, especially after he split with the Republican Party—on whose line he had been elected mayor in 2001 and 2005 (and would again in 2009)—and declared himself unaffiliated with either major party, but he declined to make that race and later denied he was even thinking of an independent bid for president in 2012.

Most other recent presidential candidates have relied on public funding, and their choice of strategy has been dictated largely by the need to risk resources early in hopes of scoring an electoral breakthrough and attracting more contributions. An exception was Jerry Brown, a former California governor who freed himself from fund-raising pressures in 1992 with a "shoe-string" campaign for the Democratic nomination. He set a contribution limit of $100 and asked voters to give by calling a toll-free telephone number. The strategy proved somewhat effective, although it left him well short of competing seriously with Clinton for the nomination. Brown placed next to Clinton with 20.1 percent of the total Democratic primary vote but would later continue in public life as mayor of Oakland and California attorney general before his 2010 election to begin a second tenure as governor.

Another strategy consideration is electability. Although in life "looks aren't everything," in political campaigns appearances are important. In the media age, a candidate's visage must be camera friendly. It need not be Hollywood idol beautiful or handsome (although that quality was an asset to actor Ronald Reagan), but it must at least not be a distraction from the candidate's other strengths, such as intelligence, speaking ability, competence, and experience.

Some analysts believed that John F. Kennedy, then a senator from Massachusetts, prevailed over Vice President Richard Nixon in 1960 in large part because of his appearance in the first

In political campaigns, appearances are important. Here, youthful and attractive Massachusetts senator John F. Kennedy (left) campaigns with running mate Sen. Lyndon B. Johnson (center) and Sen. Ralph Yarborough in Wichita Falls, Texas, on November 3, 1960.

Source: LBJ Library photo by Frank Muto

presidential DEBATE. On the black-and-white television screens of the time, Nixon appeared pale and ill at ease, while Kennedy looked tan and calm. Polls showed that many people who heard the debate on radio, however, thought that Nixon had "won."

Numerous studies have indicated that some voters are so concerned about "wasting" a vote that electability is a major aspect of their decision making. The candidates, too, are concerned about their electability, especially toward the end of the primary season. Then they try even harder to show the public, the media, and political professionals that they would do best against the likely nominee of the other party.

In the general election presidential nominees tailor their strategies to undermine the electability of their opponents and draw as many votes as possible from all regions of the country. They especially want to win the most populous states because these states have the most electoral votes, which go to the popular vote winner in each state. To be elected president or vice president, a nominee needs an ABSOLUTE MAJORITY, or at least 270 of the 538 votes in the ELECTORAL COLLEGE.

California with its fifty-five electoral votes is the biggest prize. With changes caused by congressional reapportionment that resulted from the 2010 population census, Texas will remain in second place with thirty-eight electoral votes, followed by New York and Florida tied at twenty-nine, and Pennsylvania and Illinois with twenty each.

Sometimes, however, a candidate finds it advantageous to try to assemble a winning combination of smaller states. In 2000 George W. Bush won one of the closest presidential elections ever, losing the popular vote to Al Gore but winning 271 electoral votes—just one more than the majority needed to claim victory. Gore focused his campaign on a big-state strategy and won big prizes such as California, New York, Pennsylvania, Illinois, and Michigan. But Bush, who took his home state of Texas and a crucial contested victory in Florida, succeeded by gathering the electoral votes of numerous smaller states. In the end, Bush won thirty states, while Gore won twenty plus the District of Columbia. Had Gore managed to win just one more state—including his home state of Tennessee, where Bush instead claimed the eleven electoral votes—he would have had enough to win the presidency.

The 2004 campaign followed a similar profile, although Bush won a narrow majority of the popular vote and expanded his electoral vote majority to a total of 286 (fifteen more than he had accrued in 2004). With Kerry, a New Englander with a liberal image, heading the Democratic ticket, the party had little hope of a breakthrough in the conservative South and the less populous and conservative-leaning states of the Midwest and Mountain West; thus, Kerry had to try to maximize his appeal in the larger states. His strategy fell short, as Bush clinched his reelection with a narrow victory in Ohio that gave him the twenty electoral votes that the state held at the time.

Bush this time won thirty-one states, one more than in his first White House victory. The incumbent president took close contests in Iowa and New Mexico, states where Gore had prevailed in 2000, while losing New Hampshire, a state Bush had won in 2000.

Obama, benefitting throughout his 2008 general election campaign from dissatisfaction with outgoing president Bush in particular and the Republican Party in general, pledged to compete broadly in states across the nation, and his strategy paid off grandly. His win with 53 percent of the popular vote to 46 percent for McCain translated into a 365–173 electoral vote victory, with Obama carrying twenty-eight states plus the District of Columbia. His victories in Indiana and Virginia were the first for a Democratic presidential nominee since incumbent Lyndon B. Johnson carried those states in a 1964 landslide.

Campaigning

A political candidate's success in winning election depends largely on his or her effectiveness in campaigning—the process of seeking votes through a wide variety of means. These may range from door-to-door neighborhood visits to gigantic outdoor rallies; from simple lawn signs to elaborate and costly television barrages; and increasingly, strategic use of new-media platforms, such as e-mail, text messaging, and social networking, to provide—or at least simulate—direct contact between the candidate and voters.

Whether for local office, such as the city council, or national office, such as Congress or even the presidency, all political campaigns go through the same stages. First is the exploratory stage, in which the candidate sizes up the competition and assesses the chances of winning. Sometimes the candidate will form an exploratory committee or hire a POLLING organization to help make the decision.

If the decision is to run, the candidate must file with the appropriate elections authority and perhaps pay a filing fee. To get on the ballot, many jurisdictions require the submission of petitions signed by a specified number of qualified voters. Candidates for the presidency and Congress must file with the FEDERAL ELECTION COMMISSION (FEC) and report regularly on receipts and spending; candidates for state and local office in many places also must report campaign finance activity to the appropriate authorities.

Another campaign stage is the formation of an organization, usually made up mostly of volunteers. For all but the least competitive races, a candidate seeking to win nomination and then election needs help—to raise money, devise strategy, gain media attention, operate phone banks, initiate personal contact with voters, and do everything necessary to persuade supporters to come out to the polls. Today most nominations are made in PRIMARY elections or CAUCUSES. Candidates who clear that first hurdle are likely to keep and augment the same organization for the general election campaign.

Modern elections are expensive, particularly with respect to television advertising. The major-party candidates in the 1996 presidential election, Democratic incumbent Bill Clinton and Republican challenger Bob Dole, spent what then appeared a stunningly high combined amount of $113 million on television ads. Just eight years later, Republican incumbent George W. Bush and Democratic challenger John Kerry each easily surpassed that amount en route to combined TV ad spending of nearly $350 million. The 2008 major-party contenders, victorious Democrat Barack Obama and Republican John McCain, took it up another notch, combining for $445 million in ad spending, according to the Campaign Media Analysis Group.

Even for candidates below the presidential level, television advertising is the largest expense. Even with the rapid expansion of new-media tools, most candidates for major offices in the early twenty-first century continued to build their media strategies around television.

In 2002 candidates, parties, and INTEREST GROUPS spent more than $1 billion on television advertising, according to the Alliance for Better Campaigns, a nonpartisan group advocating free air time for political discussion. Estimates of spending for the 2006 midterm elections, in which the Democrats ended a dozen years of Republican dominance, pegged overall spending at roughly $2 billion. In 2010, a year in which the political pendulum swung back strongly in the Republicans' favor, TV campaign ad spending from all sources hit $2.3 billion, according to estimates by Moody's Investors Service.

This rapid inflation in campaign spending occurred despite the enactment of the Bipartisan Campaign Reform Act (BCRA) of 2002, which supplemented and in some cases supplanted the provisions of the Federal Election Campaign Act (FECA) that was first enacted in 1971 and significantly amended in 1974. BCRA is more widely known as "McCain-Feingold" after its lead Senate sponsors: John McCain, the Arizona Republican who ran against Obama in the 2008 presidential contest, and Russ Feingold, a Wisconsin Democrat who continued to serve in the Senate until his defeat by Republican Ron Johnson during the 2010 GOP resurgence.

The legislation, which aimed to address concerns about the growing influence of money in politics, took effect for the 2004 elections and did bar national parties and candidates for federal office from accepting large, unregulated SOFT MONEY contributions from interest groups and individuals. But candidates and their national party organizations proved highly adept at substituting greater amounts of smaller and strictly regulated HARD MONEY donations—while the unregulated soft-money contributions flowed to outside groups that used them to influence the outcomes of elections. (See CAMPAIGN FINANCE.)

The ability of outside groups, some with close ties to each of the major political parties, to spend freely on advertising aimed at influencing elections received an additional boost from the January 2010 ruling by the Supreme Court in the case of *Citizens United v. Federal Election Commission.* The decision, approved on a 5–4 vote, struck a major provision of the McCain-Feingold law that had barred corporations and unions from using broadcast media for "electioneering communications" within sixty days of a general election and within thirty days of a primary. The controversial decision equated the free speech rights of corporate entities with those of individuals.

The rush of money into the elections process and the increasingly sophisticated efforts by candidates to tap all available sources for campaign cash—including the Internet—has eroded the system of public financing for presidential candidates that was established under the FECA amendments of 1974. Candidates who accept public funding must abide by spending limits, and major candidates' ability to raise huge campaign treasuries on their own has spurred several in recent campaigns to eschew public funding and its limits.

Congressional campaigns are not publicly funded and therefore are not subject to spending limits under the Supreme Court's *Buckley v. Valeo* decision (1976), which in effect said that such limits inhibit free speech.

Evolution of Campaigning

The use (or misuse) of money has been a hallmark of campaigns since the earliest days of the Republic. Some candidates, including George Washington, reportedly rewarded their supporters with free whiskey. With the growth of government and the "spoils system" of political patronage, politicians held out the promise of jobs as an enticement for votes. Later reforms in campaign finance and the civil service system outlawed some of the more blatant vote-inducing practices, but one of the most prevalent—NEGATIVE CAMPAIGNING—remains a characteristic of many U.S. political contests.

Despite the drumbeat of criticism that negative campaigning attracts in each modern election cycle, the "attack ads" common these days seem mild compared to some nineteenth-century campaign rhetoric, much of which was laceratingly personal.

Supporters of President John Quincy Adams in 1828 dredged up thirty-five-year-old allegations that challenger Andrew Jackson and Rachel Robards had married before her divorce became final (they had remarried in 1794). Jackson won, but Rachel died of a heart attack before his inauguration, a death Jackson attributed partly to her distress over the attacks on her morality. In their famed 1858 debates over the national issue of slavery, Senate candidates Stephen Douglas and Abraham Lincoln pandered to racial fears and assailed each other with insults. But instead of being "turned off" by the slurs, the large crowds cheered and jeered in delight.

Sometimes a derogatory political taunt can backfire, as happened to opponents of Grover Cleveland's presidential candidacy in 1884. They chanted, "Ma! Ma! Where's my pa?" because Cleveland had fathered a son out of wedlock, whom he continued to support financially. After Cleveland won, his supporters gloated, "Gone to the White House, ha, ha, ha!" (See CAMPAIGN SLOGANS.)

The use of the term *campaign* in U.S. politics dates to the early nineteenth century. John Quincy Adams used it in 1816, referring to one of his political efforts. But early presidential candidates, including Adams in his 1824 and 1828 campaigns, considered it unseemly to solicit votes directly from the people. Believing the office should seek the candidate, they left it largely to their supporters to publicize their qualifications and positions on issues, in hopes of obtaining the electoral vote majority needed for election.

The POPULAR VOTE was less important in early U.S. elections than it is today. State legislatures chose electors in many cases; South Carolina in 1868 became the last state to initiate the selection of presidential electors by popular vote. In addition, the right to vote was restricted to propertied white men during the early days of the Republic and was extended only gradually to all adult citizens.

African American men, for instance, gained the constitutional right to vote in all states with the ratification of the Fifteenth Amendment in 1870, but by 1900 southern states had passed laws effectively disfranchising most blacks. Blacks did not regain the vote in substantial numbers until passage of the VOTING

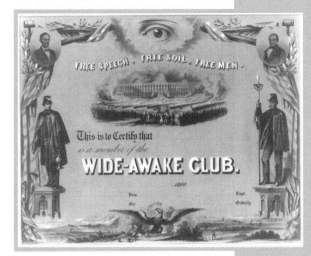

In 1860 members of a Republican marching club, the Wide-Awakes, marched for presidential candidate Abraham Lincoln. This membership certificate reflects the club's dedication to the Union and the nonextension of slavery.

Source: Library of Congress

RIGHTS ACT of 1965. Women did not gain voting rights in all states until ratification of the Nineteenth Amendment in 1920. Popular election of U.S. senators became mandatory with the Seventeenth Amendment in 1913.

Nonetheless, as the nation inched closer to universal suffrage (at least for men) during the nineteenth century, it became essential for candidates to gain exposure to large numbers of voters, a major challenge in the era prior to national mass communication. To that end, supporters held parades and rallies to whip up enthusiasm for their causes and leaders. Among the most colorful paraders were cape-wearing young men belonging to the Wide-Awake Club, a Republican march-

ing club. The "Wide-Awakes" carried lanterns, sang songs, and performed intricate maneuvers as they marched for Abraham Lincoln in 1860. Almost half a million "Wide-Awakes" helped make Lincoln the first Republican president.

In the late nineteenth century large barbecues or picnics became common as events where politicians could mingle with the voters, "pressing the flesh" (shaking hands) and perhaps addressing the crowd from the bandstand. In the twenty-first century, such gatherings remain popular at the local level.

*The term **whistle stop** came into popular usage in 1948. In September 1992 President George H. W. Bush and Barbara Bush campaigned in Ohio on the train Spirit of America.*

Source: George Bush Presidential Library

It was not until 120 years after the declaration of the United States of America that presidential aspirants began traveling extensively to appeal for votes. William Jennings Bryan, the Democratic Party nominee in 1896, covered 18,000 miles by train to make 600 speeches. Nevertheless, Republican William McKinley defeated Bryan with a "front-porch" campaign in which he remained at his home in Canton, Ohio.

The term *whistle stop*, however, did not come into popular usage until President Harry S. Truman popularized it with his cross-country train treks in 1948. Truman scored an upset victory that year over New York governor Thomas E. Dewey.

Truman's fiery speeches also gave rise to a slogan—"Give 'Em Hell, Harry!"—that became permanently identified with his campaign. Other candidates have tried to find catchy phrases to use on campaign buttons, which first appeared in 1896, and on more recent inventions such as bumper stickers and television ads. The first buttons featured McKinley's likeness and his "Full Dinner Pail" slogan.

Most slogans are positive, such as "I Like Ike" for Republican Dwight D. Eisenhower in the 1950s, or "Tippecanoe and Tyler, Too," for the 1840 Whig ticket of William Henry Harrison, hero of the 1811 Battle of Tippecanoe, in an area that later became Indiana, and John Tyler. But others are negative, such as "Dump the Hump," used against Democratic presidential nominee Hubert H. Humphrey in 1968.

Although President Herbert Hoover, a Republican whose presidency (1929–1933) coincided with the onset of the Great Depression, denied that he ever promised Americans "a chicken in every pot, a car in every garage," food has long been associated with appeals for votes, especially from ethnic groups. In New York City, with its large Jewish population, candidates pose for pictures while eating kosher Coney Island hot dogs. In a Polish community, the favored sausage may be kielbasa. In Chinatown, candidates may opt for chopsticks and egg rolls. As African Americans and Hispanics have grown in number, so have the pictures of politicians devouring ribs or tortillas.

But ethnic campaigning is not confined to food. To court the Irish vote, candidates don green and strut in St. Patrick's Day parades on March 17. In October they try to be seen at Columbus Day festivities in Italian areas. The wise candidate tailors his or her campaign to the characteristics of the constituency at stake.

The high cost of political advertising on television leaves candidates little money to spend on campaign buttons, billboards, and other traditional artifacts of campaigning. Nevertheless, candidates and their supporters usually manage to buy relatively inexpensive printed material such as bumper stickers, posters, and lawn signs on stakes. When several competitive races are being fought, suburban lawns may sprout a forest of cardboard messages vying for the voters' eyes and attention. The objective is to build support for the candidates through name recognition that may translate into votes on ELECTION DAY.

Music, too, may be important to a campaign. That chant taunting Grover Cleveland's paternity situation in 1884 was set to music and widely distributed as a ditty. During the Great Depression, "Happy Days Are Here Again!" became the theme song of Democrats and their victorious 1932 presidential candidate, Franklin D. Roosevelt. Republicans happily sang Irving Berlin's "I Like Ike" for their nominee, World War II hero Eisenhower, in the 1950s. And after the nomination in 1992 of Clinton, who became the first "baby boomer" president, the Democratic convention hall rocked to Fleetwood Mac's "Don't Stop Thinking About Tomorrow."

In recent years, though, musical performers have gotten their backs up over the use of their songs, without permission, in political campaigns. One of the first was Bruce Springsteen, a rock star with well-known progressive political leanings, who objected to the use of his song "Born in the U.S.A." in the 1984 reelection campaign of President Ronald Reagan, a Republican and conservative icon. Many commentators noted that despite the anthem-like refrain of "born in the U.S.A.," the song's lyrics amounted to an indictment of the nation's treatment of working-class Americans in general and Vietnam War veterans in particular.

Campaigning takes many other forms of electioneering. There is no one sure way to campaign. What works for one candidate may do nothing for another; or it might do the candidate more harm than good.

Most candidates make promises to the voters, sometimes effectively. Eisenhower kept his 1952 pledge to go to Korea to seek an end to the war there. But Democrat Walter Mondale's statement that the president elected in 1984—whether it was he or Republican incumbent Reagan—would have to raise taxes proved detrimental to the challenger's already weak campaign.

Even successful campaign techniques can cause problems in the long run if the members of the voting public come to feel that a winning candidate has not lived up to expectations. For example, Obama's victory in the 2008 presidential contest was abetted greatly by his charismatic evocation of his central themes of hope and change, which had great appeal to an electorate that had grown largely dispirited over the prolonged U.S. military involvement in Iraq, an economy that spiraled into a deep recession just in the year before the November election, and other national setbacks. But when Obama struggled during his first two years in office to turn the economy around and to gain approval of key parts of his policy agenda despite Democratic control of both chambers of Congress, disgruntled voters swung to the Republicans in large numbers in the 2010 midterm elections and boosted the GOP back into control of the U.S. House.

Televised candidate debates now are regarded as required rituals in presidential campaigns and contests for many other offices. But that is a rather recent tradition. The first face-to-face DEBATE between presidential nominees took place in 1960 between John F. Kennedy and Richard M. Nixon and only became a regular part of presidential campaigning sixteen years later with the contest between Republican Gerald Ford and Jimmy Carter, the Democrat who ousted him from the White House. (See Appendix, General Election Debates, 1960–2008; pages 708–709.)

Besides debates, standard forms of modern electioneering include stump speeches, greeting voters at factory gates, direct mail, obtaining endorsements from newspapers and community leaders, operating phone banks, and appearing on radio and television talk shows. Use of the Internet also has become a standard campaign procedure.

Decline of Party Influence

Far-reaching changes in election procedures and communications technology since the early twentieth century have freed candidates from much of their former dependency on political party organizations for money and other necessities of an effective campaign. Through telephones, radio, television, and the Internet, candidates may now pitch their appeals directly to the electorate. (See CANDIDATE-CENTERED CAMPAIGNS.)

Today's candidates gain nomination by winning party primaries and caucuses, rather than by being handpicked by the leaders of the Democratic or Republican parties, which have dominated the American TWO-PARTY SYSTEM since the midnineteenth century. In a primary or caucus the candidates compete, in effect, for the party's endorsement. Only a few states permit a formal preprimary PARTY ENDORSEMENT, which indicates on the ballot the candidate favored by the party leadership.

Although the primary system has empowered rank-and-file voters, it has also contributed to the long duration and skyrocketing cost of political campaigns. The successful candidate must campaign extensively to win the nomination and then campaign again to defeat the opposing party's nominee in the general election. Both campaigns can be expensive.

A decline in PARTY IDENTIFICATION among voters also has contributed to the trend toward candidate-centered campaigns. Since the 1970s, when the major parties (especially the Democrats) changed their rules to strengthen the primary system and give more representation to women and racial minorities, more voters began to think of themselves as INDEPENDENTS rather than as Democrats or Republicans. (See SPLIT- AND STRAIGHT-TICKET VOTING.)

Faced with this situation, candidates try to focus the campaign on their positive attributes, including personality, physical appearance, education, experience, and views on issues of concern to the constituencies they want to represent.

In most cases the candidate will not run away from the party but will merely say little about it in campaign speeches or advertising. Where the party or its philosophy is deemed a liability, the candidate may try to disassociate the campaign from the national party or some of its most prominent members. In the 1980s, for example, when the term *liberal* was widely shunned as "the L-word," Democratic candidates in some states preferred not to be linked with Sen. Edward M. Kennedy of Massachusetts or others closely associated with liberal causes. And while voters in most elections pay little attention to efforts to tie members of Congress to their party's leadership, the Republicans appeared to have unusual success in linking Democratic incumbents to the liberal views associated with Nancy Pelosi of California who was House Speaker from 2007 until 2011.

Similarly, Republican candidates for Congress and other offices were much more zealous about associating themselves with President George W. Bush in 2002—when his assertive response to the al-Qaeda attacks of September 11, 2001, had earned him high job approval ratings—than in 2006, as dissent over the war in Iraq caused a sharp decline in Bush's popularity and contributed to his party's loss of control of both the U.S. Senate and House, or in 2008, when Democrats ran a Bush-bashing campaign and captured the White House while expanding their majorities in both chambers of Congress.

For offices where candidates run as a pair, as for president and vice president, or governor and lieutenant governor in some states, the top candidate may try to find a running mate who balances the ticket geographically, philosophically, or in some other way. Although most nominees strive for a geographic balance, Clinton of Arkansas chose Gore of Tennessee as vice president in 1992, making it the first successful all-southern ticket since Andrew Jackson of Tennessee and John C. Calhoun of South Carolina won in 1828. Along with Gore, Clinton won with a largely candidate-centered campaign. In 2000 Bush chose veteran public servant Dick Cheney to compensate for Bush's lack of experience in foreign affairs while Gore, a Protestant, chose as his running mate Joseph Lieberman, a Connecticut senator who was the first Jew to appear on a major-party presidential ticket.

Bush retained Cheney on his ticket when he ran for reelection in 2004. Democratic presidential nominee John Kerry went for geographic balance by picking as his running mate North Carolina senator John Edwards, who had made a strong showing during the primaries as a rival to Kerry for the top spot. However, the Kerry-Edwards ticket, though competitive nationwide, failed to meet the hopes of Democrats for a breakthrough in the South, where Republicans had dominated over several election cycles. Bush swept the southern states en route to a relatively narrow electoral vote victory.

The major-party presidential candidates took dramatically different approaches in choosing their running mates in 2008. Obama selected an old political pro, Delaware Sen. Joseph R. Biden Jr. who had served thirty-six years in the Senate and was considered to have expertise in foreign policy—an area in which Obama, a senator of Illinois for just four years, was considered relatively inexperienced. McCain, by contrast, tried a bold move to shake up a race in which he consistently trailed in the polls and in which his longtime efforts to promote himself as an independent-minded "maverick" had given him limited appeal among the Republicans' conservative base. McCain selected Sarah Palin, then a first-term governor who was virtually unknown outside her home state of Alaska, who energized conservative activists with her personal charisma and hard-line rhetoric but alienated many independent swing voters.

George W. Bush chose Dick Cheney as his running mate in 2000 to compensate for his own lack of foreign affairs experience, thereby balancing the ticket. Here, Cheney reviews U.S. Military Honor Guard units in Ceremonial Hall, Ft. Myer, Virginia, on January 12, 1993, while serving as secretary of defense, a position he held from 1989 to 1993.
Source: U.S. Department of Defense

Candidate-centered campaigns rely more on the news and advertising media than on the party to get their messages to the voters. And with the rise of the Internet they are even becoming less dependent on the print and broadcast media. Campaign websites, besides disseminating the candidate's position on issues, help collect the e-mail addresses of swing voters as well as likely supporters. These addresses may be used in turn for candidate appeals for money or volunteers to make phone calls or do other work for the campaign. The collected names and addresses can be stored for future campaigns as well as the one at hand. In this way, said political scientist Michael Cornfield, a specialist in political Internet usage, the candidates are "building digital political machines" with a potential for continuous two-way correspondence between the politician and the voters.

Candidate-centered campaigning is more personal than party-centered campaigning and therefore is more likely to be negative, attacking the opponent's character and qualifications instead of emphasizing the attacker's own fitness for the office being sought. Consequently, it is not surprising that recent elections have seen a rise in negative campaigning, despite the public's distaste for it as shown in numerous polls. In the 1990s a new type of attack ad became prevalent, partly through the use of unlimited SOFT MONEY contributions given to parties supposedly for party-building activities. Such ads circumvented federal and state contribution limits because they did not use the candidate's name even though clearly targeted at a particular candidate, a campaign stratagem that has its roots in the so-called "magic words" test that defines a political communication as "issue advertising" as long as it does not expressly call for the election or defeat of a candidate. Congress in 2002 outlawed most soft money in federal elections, effective after that year's

More on this topic:
Campaign Finance, p. 53
Candidate-Centered Campaigns, p. 84
Negative Campaigning, p. 365
Party Identification by Voters, p. 377
Polling, p. 427
Two-Party System, p. 636

November 5 *MIDTERM ELECTION*. There were indications almost immediately, however, that interest groups already had found ways to get around the ban, in part by channeling their soft-money donations to political organizations known as 527s, which are organized under Section 527 of the Internal Revenue Code.

Candidate-Centered Campaigns

Political candidates, through much of the nation's history, were highly dependent on their parties' organizations for the resources needed to run and promote their campaigns. In fact, most candidates for public office were handpicked by party leaders or caucuses closed to all but party officials. This, however, is no longer the case. Political "machines" began to decline in the 1960s as parties, responding to voter demands for more say in the selection of candidates, increasingly turned to primary elections as an alternative to controlled caucuses. This, along with factors such as greater individual access to the media and decentralized campaign fund-raising, has essentially turned candidates into free agents who are no longer dependent on the parties' organizational resources.

Their CAMPAIGN STRATEGIES are candidate centered and media oriented. Through television, and increasingly through new-media platforms, candidates can reach voters without party advertising. They can create their own campaign organizations by hiring POLITICAL CONSULTANTS who specialize in all the techniques of modern campaigning—POLLING, direct mail, creation and placement of TV commercials, and targeted appeals to various voter groups that today often include e-mail appeals, text messaging, and social networking.

Candidates can even deemphasize their party ties when doing so is advantageous, such as when the party's leadership or policy agenda is widely considered to be unpopular or controversial. Such candidate-centered campaigning shapes attitudes about the candidates, but it does little to reinforce partisan commitments among the electors and can render PARTY IDENTIFICATION a less powerful influence, as underscored by the growing numbers of voters who in recent years have declared themselves to be independents rather than a member of a party. Although voters see differences between the DEMOCRATIC and REPUBLICAN parties, issues and evaluations of the candidates themselves are looming larger in their decisions.

That does not mean, however, that parties no longer play a serious and integral role in shaping campaigns, especially for the higher-level offices such as president, U.S. representative or senator, and governor.

The decline of the iron-handed party "bosses" and the commensurate rise of self-starting candidates mean that party officials no longer dominate the electoral process by handpicking slates of candidates for all offices.

Yet the national party organizations—including the Democratic National Committee and Republican National Committee; their Senate campaign units, the Democratic Senatorial Campaign Committee and the National Republican Senatorial Committee; and the House campaign organizations, the Democratic Congressional Campaign Committee and the National Republican Congressional Committee—maintain significant influence by using their strategic expertise to decide to target those states and districts that look potentially winnable, working to recruit the strongest candidates for those races, urging partisan activists to contribute money to their high-priority candidates, and raising tens of millions of dollars in their own right, much of which is deployed in independent expenditures aimed at influencing the outcomes of races.

Federalism, the dispersal of authority to a wide array of government units and elected officials, has contributed to the decentralization of power in American politics. Parties must organize not only to win the presidency but also to win offices in the thousands of constituencies found in the fifty states. Each of these election DISTRICTS has its own party organization, elected officials, and candidate organizations.

Frequently, their interests and priorities are quite different from those of their party's national leadership. For example, when the Democratic leader in New York City's borough of the Bronx was asked whether he was concerned about the outcome of the 1996 presidential election, he responded, "It doesn't affect our life one bit. National politics—president and such—are too far removed from the bread-and-butter things that matter to local leaders and mayors and governors. The local leader cares about a senior citizen center, a local concern." By creating thousands of distinct party organizations and separately electing state and local officials, the American brand of federalism has made centralized control of the parties virtually impossible.

The decentralizing effects are reinforced by the manner in which nominations are made and elections are conducted. Party nominations for state, local, and congressional offices are made through a system of primaries and CAUCUSES. Because today the voters, not the party leaders, control the nominating process, the candidates build personal—not party—organizations to compete in the primaries. Knowing that it is their personal campaign efforts and organizations that win primary elections, officeholders do not necessarily feel a strong sense of obligation to their party organization.

Indeed, electoral survival requires building a personal organization and not depending on popular presidents or a party organization to carry one to victory. Individual candidates are responsible for most of their own CAMPAIGN FINANCE needs. Armed with adequate financing, a candidate can then secure the other resources essential to a campaign—media experts, pollsters, computer specialists, direct-mail specialists, accountants, lawyers, campaign managers, and consultants.

INCUMBENCY lends itself to candidate-centered campaigning, particularly for members of Congress. Members of Congress—unlike the president, most GOVERNORS, and many STATE LEGISLATORS—are not subject to TERM LIMITS. Half the states have at certain points tried to limit congressional terms, especially during the early 1990s when public interest in term limits peaked, but their efforts were struck down by the Supreme Court, leaving Congress as a refuge for career politicians.

Campaigning for reelection to Congress has become almost a full-time job. For example, the Democratic Congressional Campaign Committee in 2004 developed a program known as "Front-line Democrats," made up of incumbents who appeared potentially vulnerable to Republican challenges in that election year and to whom the party targeted additional financial and logistical assistance. The first crop of twenty-nine Frontline Democrats for the 2008 elections was announced by mid-February 2007, just a month after the 110th Congress had been sworn in, and included twenty-four freshmen members of the big class of 2006 that boosted the Democrats to a House majority.

Success frequently breeds imitation in Congress, and the National Republican Congressional Committee initiated its "Young Guns" program—a counterpart to the Frontline Democrats—early in a 2010 midterm election cycle that would see the GOP surge back to seize control of the House.

Senators or representatives who win reelection term after term become better known than their challengers, and they have an easier time raising money and obtaining endorsements from other officeholders. They also establish records on which they can run, while the challengers can only promise to do as well or better.

As a campaign strategy, use of incumbency has historically been effective. In nearly all recent election years prior to 2010, the reelection rates of U.S. House incumbents seeking reelection greatly exceeded 90 percent. But the rise of the conservative Tea Party movement that helped the Republican Party build momentum during the 2010 campaign, and an overall public dissatisfaction with Congress caused primarily by enduring national economic problems, resulted in a sharp drop in the incumbent reelection rate that year, to 86.3 percent, the lowest in forty years.

A similar phenomenon has prevailed in the Senate, with reelection rates during the "swing" years from 2006 through 2010 well below the 96.2 percent recorded as recently as 2004. The success rates for Senate incumbents seeking reelection was 79.3 percent in 2006, 83.3 percent in 2008, and 84 percent in 2010.

The Effect of Image

With the campaign focused on the candidate, his or her image—personality, physical appearance, style, and background—takes on special importance. Nowhere is this more true than in presidential politics, where the candidates are known to the public mostly from the MEDIA COVERAGE of their campaigns.

As in state and local elections, presidential candidates are more independent of their parties than they were in the past. Most nominees go into the general election part of the campaign with the same organization that helped them win the primaries. Beginning in 1976, presidential candidates have been eligible for PUBLIC FINANCING, further relieving their dependence on the parties' national committees, although the vast expense of modern campaigning has spurred an increasing number of candidates in recent contests—including Barack Obama during his successful 2008 campaign for president—to eschew the system to avoid the spending restrictions that come with the public money.

Today the parties rely more on the candidates than the other way around. Candidates with a favorable public image can contribute significantly to their party's vote on ELECTION DAY.

Dwight D. Eisenhower, whose personal appeal transcended partisanship, was a classic example of a candidate whose image added substantially to his total vote in his successful bids as the Republican presidential nominee in 1952 and 1956. His status as a World War II hero and his perceived personal qualities—sincerity, sense of duty, commitment to family, religious devotion, and sheer likeability, all of which were captured in the CAMPAIGN SLOGAN "I Like Ike"—caused heavy Democratic defections to the Republican Party in both of his successful campaigns for the White House.

In both 1984 and 1988 Democratic nominees were hurt by voters' negative perceptions of them. President Ronald Reagan—a former actor and California governor with an image of virility, conservative principles, and confidence—benefited in 1984 from public perceptions of his Democratic opponent, former vice president Walter Mondale, as "a weak leader," "a big spender," and "tied to special interests." In 1988, exit polls showed that voters for Republican presidential nominee George H. W. Bush, Reagan's two-term vice president, considered Democratic nominee and Massachusetts governor Michael S. Dukakis "too liberal," indicating that the Bush campaign succeeded in defining Dukakis in terms of his IDEOLOGY. Dukakis supporters, on the other hand, said that Bush's NEGATIVE CAMPAIGNING was what they liked least about him.

Candidate images also played a role in the 1992 and 1996 elections. Despite allegations of marital infidelity while he was governor of Arkansas, Democratic challenger Bill Clinton successfully played on public worries in 1992 over the state of the economy. EXIT POLLS showed that the candidate's qualities that mattered most to voters were "will bring about change" (favored Clinton over President Bush 67 percent to 5 percent) and "cares about people like me" (favored Clinton, whose campaign slogan was "Putting People First," over Bush 64 percent to 11 percent). To voters, Bush's most positive qualities were his experience and his ability to handle a crisis.

With the economy healthy in 1996, President Clinton, still fighting off the effects of real estate and sexual harassment SCANDALS from his days as governor, again overcame the character issue to win reelection. His Republican challenger, Bob Dole, had image problems of his own, including a sharp tongue that had given him an enduring reputation for meanness. Some voters also perceived Dole as too old for the job. At seventy-three, Dole would have been the oldest president at the time of his election.

In 2000 Clinton's would-be Democratic successor, Al Gore, found himself saddled with an image of being stiff and was frequently accused of stretching the truth. He confused voters by alternating between campaigning as a populist and a moderate, and he fueled late-night jokes by hiring a gender theorist to provide him with wardrobe advice. Similarly, Republican nominee George W. Bush, a son of President George H. W. Bush, faced doubts: some voters saw him as an intellectual lightweight who was seeking to build a family political dynasty. Yet Bush, who appealed to the middle by campaigning on a platform of "compassionate conservatism," held a pair of trump cards. Many voters considered him both more likeable and more

In the 1988 presidential election, voters considered Michael S. Dukakis too liberal, but they disliked George H. W. Bush's negative campaigning. Here, Dukakis and Bush debate each other in October 1988.

Source: George Bush Presidential Library

consistent in his views on issues than either of the Democrats he ended up defeating: Gore in 2000, an election marked by the controversial and decisive vote count in Florida, and Massachusetts senator John Kerry in 2004.

Obama's message of hope and change, reinforced by his charismatic speaking style, resonated in a 2008 campaign that focused on voters' growing concerns over the economy (which nearly collapsed just before election day that year), anger over the protracted U.S. military involvement in Iraq that was initiated by the younger Bush, and the repercussions of the botched government efforts to address the human hardships caused by Hurricane Katrina in New Orleans and other areas of the Gulf Coast in 2005.

John McCain, the longtime senator of Arizona who was Obama's Republican opponent that year, had considerable political assets of his own, including his history as a Vietnam prisoner of war and his reputation as an independent-minded maverick. But age and temperament concerns, as with Dole twelve years earlier, worked against McCain. And while his choice of Alaska governor Sarah Palin, a combative conservative, as his vice presidential nominee helped him energize the Republican voting base, it also alienated moderate voters he needed to win over if he was to defeat Obama.

Running for Congress

Congressional candidates are largely on their own. They can normally count on only moderate levels of support from their party organizations. They assemble their own campaign staffs, collect their own financial contributions, and emphasize their own records.

Most have been able, through highly personalized campaigning, to insulate themselves from national swings of electoral sentiment. As a result, presidential COATTAILS (the ability of popular presidential candidates to carry their party's House and Senate candidates into office) have been extremely short in most recent elections.

In 2000, for example, the presidential candidates had little influence over congressional elections, in part because their own race was so close. Even though George W. Bush narrowly won the White House, Democrats won a handful of seats in both chambers, achieving a 50–50 split in the Senate. In a sign of the weak reach of the parties, moderate Vermont senator James Jeffords tipped the balance to the Democrats several months later when he quit the Republican Party.

In 2002 a then highly popular President Bush broke with recent tradition and campaigned aggressively for Republican candidates. Partly because of his influence, Republicans gained seats in both chambers of Congress—the first time that a president's party had picked up seats in both the House and Senate in midterm elections since 1934.

In 2004 Bush took 51 percent of the vote to defeat Kerry, making him the first "majority" president since his father's victory in 1988. The Republicans achieved a net gain of four Senate seats but gained only three House seats; the House seats were picked up as the result of the partisan mid-decade redistricting of Texas.

The tide turned in the 2006 midterm elections, when Democrats gained control of both the House and Senate for the first time in twelve years. And those Democratic majorities were expanded by further significant gains made in 2008, suggesting that Obama might have had some coattails in that campaign.

But any Democratic hopes that Obama would provide a lasting boost to their party were resoundingly crushed in 2010, when the GOP rebounded to wrest away control of the House and cut deeply into the Democrats' Senate majority. The high unemployment that lingered well after the statistical end of the deep recession that Obama inherited from Bush increased voter anger, which in turn was inflamed by controversial measures, such as an expensive economic stimulus bill and a complex overhaul of the nation's health insurance system, that were lauded by Obama and approved by the Democratic-controlled Congress.

The members of Congress who emerge from this new kind of decentralized and highly personalized electoral atmosphere owe less to their party organizations than did the candidates of old. Most House and Senate members consider themselves loyal party members and generally vote with the party leadership on roll-call votes. But they also recognize that it was their own efforts and the image they conveyed to their constituents—not the party's—that got them elected.

Today's Congress is actually 535 separate political enterprises, all being run simultaneously. It is an institution in which individuals with diverse objectives—reelection, power in the chamber, policy leadership, service to constituents, and even presidential aspirations—pursue their goals, sometimes in conflict with colleagues and sometimes with their assistance and cooperation. It is a far cry from the days when party leaders handpicked the nominees, and Congress was made up of two large camps—Democratic members and Republican members—all beholden to the local parties that put them there.

Candidate Image *See* ELECTORAL BEHAVIOR;

PARTY IDENTIFICATION BY VOTERS

Canvassing Board

A board of canvassers is an official body, usually bipartisan, that has a wide range of responsibilities for the conduct of elections at the state, county, or local level.

The name of the board may vary from state to state. Maryland's, for example, is called the Maryland State Administrative Board of Election Laws, or SABEL. The bipartisan board is made up of five members appointed by the governor for four-year terms. Each city or county elections board in Maryland is called the Board of Supervisors of Elections.

Counties in some New England states have no government functions outside of the JUDICIAL SYSTEM. In these states the elections or canvassing boards operate at the state, city, and town levels.

Functions of the canvassing board may include VOTER REGISTRATION, establishing precincts and voting sites, approving and training precinct officials, preparation and distribution of ballots and voting equipment, collection of precinct vote counts, certifying the election results, forwarding certificates of election to the winners, investigating any voting irregularities, and maintaining elections records. (See CONTESTED ELECTIONS; DISTRICTS, WARDS, AND PRECINCTS.)

State elections boards are also responsible for administration of voter registration in compliance with the National Voter Registration Act of 1993, popularly known as the *MOTOR VOTER ACT*. Other aspects of elections are shared with the federal government, including administration of the Help America Vote Act of 2002, enacted in an effort to improve voting technology in the wake of balloting problems—particularly in Florida—that caused controversy in the 2000 presidential election between Republican George W. Bush and Democrat Al Gore. (See *STATE AND FEDERAL ELECTION RESPONSIBILITIES.*)

More on this topic:
Bush v. Gore, p. 40
Motor Voter Act, p. 340
State and Federal Election Responsibilities, p. 606
Voter Registration, p. 653

Caucus

A political caucus is a meeting of party members to act on official business, chiefly the nomination of candidates. In the PRIMARY-dominated era of presidential politics, however, caucuses have survived almost as an anachronism in the nominating process. As the number of primaries has grown, caucuses have lost much of their former significance.

As late as 1968, candidates sought to run well in primary states mainly to gain a bargaining chip with which to deal with powerful leaders in the caucus states. Republicans Barry M. Goldwater in 1964 and Richard M. Nixon in 1968 and Democrat Hubert H. Humphrey in 1968 all built up solid majorities among caucus-state delegates that carried them to their parties' nominations. Humphrey did not even enter a primary in 1968.

In subsequent presidential elections, reforms aimed at opening up the nominating process to rank-and-file voters spurred a proliferation of primaries, and candidates in turn placed their principal emphasis on these popular-vote contests. Beginning with Democratic candidate George S. McGovern in 1972 and President Gerald R. Ford and Democratic challenger Jimmy Carter in 1976, all victorious candidates in recent presidential nominating contests have won by securing large majorities of the primary-state DELEGATES.

Despite the growing primacy of primary voting in the process, Carter's victory in Iowa transformed the state's "first in the nation" caucus into the means of attracting national publicity. Going into the 2012 elections, more than three decades later, the Iowa caucus maintains its status as the campaign's kickoff event.

Complex Method

Compared with a primary, the caucus system is complicated. Instead of focusing on a single primary election ballot, the caucus presents a multitiered system that involves meetings scheduled over several weeks, sometimes even months. There is mass participation only at the first level (the so-called first-round caucuses), with meetings often lasting several hours and attracting only the most enthusiastic and dedicated party members.

Operation of the caucus varies from state to state, and each party has its own set of rules. Most begin with PRECINCT caucuses or some other type of local mass meeting open to all party voters. Participants, often publicly declaring their votes, elect delegates to the next stage in the process. In smaller states, such as Delaware and Hawaii, delegates are elected directly to a state convention, where the NATIONAL PARTY CONVENTION delegates are chosen. In larger states, such as Iowa, there is at least one intermediate step. Most frequently, precinct caucuses elect delegates to county conventions, which then choose the national convention delegates.

Voter participation, even at the first level of the caucus process, is much lower than in primaries. Caucus participants usually are local party leaders and activists. Many rank-and-file voters find a caucus complex, confusing, time-consuming—even intimidating.

In a caucus state the focus is on one-on-one campaigning. Time, not money, is the most valuable resource. Because organization and personal campaigning are so important, an early start is far more crucial in a caucus state than in a primary state. And because only a small segment of the electorate is targeted in most caucus states, candidates tend to use POLITICAL ADVERTISING sparingly.

Although the basic steps in the caucus process are the same for both parties, the rules that govern them are vastly different. Democratic rules have been revamped substantially since 1968, establishing national standards for grassroots participation. Republican rules have remained largely unchanged, with the states given wide latitude in drawing up their delegate-selection plans.

In some states, one party holds caucuses while the other holds primaries. Even if both parties hold caucuses, they might not be on the same date.

Caucuses 1980–2008

For both the Republican and Democratic parties, the percentage of delegates elected from caucus states declined sharply throughout the 1970s. But the Democrats temporarily broke the downward trend and elected more delegates by the caucus process in 1980 than in 1976. Between 1980 and 1984 six states switched from a primary to a caucus system; none went the other way.

Since 1984 the trend has turned back toward primaries. In 1996 primaries were held by one or both parties in forty-four states, the District of Columbia, and Puerto Rico, a pattern that has held up with only slight variations since.

IOWA, NEW HAMPSHIRE, AND BEYOND

Following is a list of the Iowa and New Hampshire winners since 1980 and the eventual nominee. In most cases, that nominee has been the winner in New Hampshire, not Iowa, although for the Democrats in 1992 it was neither.

Year	Party	Iowa Winner	N.H. Winner	Nominee
2008	Democrats	Obama	Clinton	Obama
	Republicans	Huckabee	McCain	McCain
2004	Democrats	Kerry	Kerry	Kerry
	Republicans	No vote	Bush, G. W.	Bush, G. W.
2000	Democrats	Gore	Gore	Gore
	Republicans	Bush, G. W.	McCain	Bush, G. W.
1996	Democrats	Clinton	Clinton	Clinton
	Republicans	Dole	Buchanan	Dole
1992	Democrats	Harkin	Tsongas	Clinton
	Republicans	No vote	Bush, G.	Bush, G.
1988	Democrats	Gephardt	Dukakis	Dukakis
	Republicans	Dole	Bush, G.	Bush, G.
1984	Democrats	Mondale	Hart	Mondale
	Republicans	No vote	Reagan	Reagan
1980	Democrats	Carter	Carter	Carter
	Republicans	Bush, G.	Reagan	Reagan

Source: Various issues of *CQ Weekly*

Events in 1984 and 1988 pointed up weaknesses in the caucus system. A strong caucus-states showing by Walter F. Mondale in 1984 led many Democrats to conclude that caucuses are inherently unfair. More than primaries, the complicated, low-visibility world of caucuses is open to takeover by insiders. In Mondale's case, a mainstream Democratic coalition of party activists, labor union members, and teachers had dominated the caucuses in his behalf.

In 1988 the Iowa Democratic caucus was seen as an unrepresentative test dominated by liberal INTEREST GROUPS. And the credibility of the caucus was shaken by the withdrawal from the race of the two winners—Democrat Richard Gephardt, a member of Congress from Missouri, and Republican Bob Dole, a senator from Kansas—within a month after the caucus was held. Furthermore, several other state caucuses were marked by vicious infighting between supporters of various candidates.

In 1992 the presence of a FAVORITE SON candidate, Sen. Tom Harkin of Iowa, among the leading Democratic candidates for president further diminished the Iowa caucus's significance as a rival to the NEW HAMPSHIRE PRIMARY in predicting the parties' eventual nominees. Harkin easily won the caucus, but he soon dropped out after fading in the primaries in which Bill Clinton, then the governor of Arkansas, emerged as the dominant candidate.

With the field for the GOP nomination wide open in 1996 for the first time since 1980, Dole again prevailed in Iowa, winning 26.3 percent of the vote. He subsequently lost the New Hampshire primary to his chief Iowa opponent, conservative commentator Patrick J. Buchanan, but rebounded strongly to clinch the nomination within a few weeks.

The importance of parochial issues in a caucus setting was brought to light in the 2000 Republican caucuses. To Iowa voters, a candidate's support for maintaining federal incentives for production of ethanol, a corn-based alternative fuel, was a virtual litmus test. Therefore, Arizona senator John McCain—who opposed such subsidies at the time and would later emerge as the most serious threat to FRONT-RUNNER George W. Bush in the Republican nominating process—skipped the Iowa caucuses altogether. Bush won the caucuses easily, as did eventual Democratic nominee Al Gore.

In 2004 Iowa launched Massachusetts senator John Kerry's drive to the Democratic nomination and dealt what turned out to be a devastating blow to the outsider candidacy of former Vermont governor Howard Dean. Briefly leading in preference polls of Democratic voters on the strength of his opposition to the war in Iraq, Dean slipped to third in the Iowa caucus vote. Shouting over the noise of a crowd of supporters at a caucus night rally, Dean grew red-faced as he exhorted supporters to keep up the fight—then let out a strange scream. The video, played incessantly on television and circulated on the Internet, made Dean look foolish and undermined his campaign.

The Democratic presidential contest in 2008 provided a different twist on the role of caucuses. The two principal contenders for the nomination were former first lady, and New York senator, Hillary Rodham Clinton, who was the front-runner and widely considered presumptive nominee. Her primary challenger was Illinois junior senator Barack Obama. Clinton's campaign focused on the large states holding primaries in which she hoped the BANDWAGON EFFECT would push her to easy victory. Obama, by contrast, ran a national campaign that focused on smaller caucus and primary states as well as the large battleground states. With this strategy he piled up committed delegates through February and March, collecting so many that Clinton faced a nearly impossible job of overtaking him, even though she won 300,000 more votes in the primary elections than Obama. Although the contest lasted until June, when Obama's nomination was secure, political observers concluded that he won the nomination in the winter months with his focus on caucus and smaller primary states.

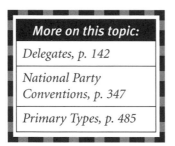

More on this topic:

Delegates, p. 142

National Party Conventions, p. 347

Primary Types, p. 485

Caucus Pros and Cons

Besides its complexity and tendency toward domination by party professionals, a major complaint about the caucus process is that it does not involve enough voters. The low turnouts are thought to be less representative of voter sentiment than a higher-turnout primary.

Staunch defenders, however, believe a caucus has party-building attributes a primary cannot match. They note that several hours at a caucus can involve voters in a way that quickly casting a primary ballot does not. The state party comes away from caucus meetings with lists of thousands of voters who can be tapped to volunteer time or money, or even to run for local office. And while the multitiered caucus process is often a chore for the state party to organize, a primary is substantially more expensive.

Census

A census of the U.S. population has been taken every ten years since 1790. The process turns up much valuable information about the demographics of American society, but its constitutional purpose is to determine how many members each state will have in the House of Representatives. The size of the House has been fixed at 435 seats since Arizona and New Mexico joined the Union as the forty-seventh and forty-eighth states in 1912 (except for a temporary addition of two seats in 1959 when Alaska and Hawaii became the last of the fifty states; the House reverted to 435 in the reapportionment of seats that followed the 1960 census and preceded the 1962 elections).

The most-discussed proposal to expand the size of the House beyond 435 arose during the middle of the 2000s. After years of frustration in their efforts to gain a full-voting representative for the District of Columbia, some leading officials in the nation's capital signed on to a proposal by Republican Thomas M. Davis III, then a representative of Virginia's suburbs of Washington. Davis's measure would have added a full seat for strongly Democratic D.C., offset by a new seat for overwhelmingly Republican Utah (to address complaints about counting procedures that state officials said unfairly cost Utah an additional House seat following the 2000 census).

The bill, which would have permanently increased the number of House seats to 437, passed the House in April 2007. But the proposal ran into opposition mainly from four sources: those who believe the U.S. Constitution precludes full congressional representation for the District of Columbia; those who opposed any increase in the size of the House; those who thought the inclusion of a seat for Utah was a superfluous partisan sop for Republicans, especially since it was predicted (accurately, it turned out) that Utah's fast-growing population would earn it an additional seat after the 2010 census; and some in D.C. who supported either statehood or the provision of two U.S. senators to the District as well and saw the proposal for House representation only as less than half a loaf.

The proposal's last gasp came in 2009, at the start of the 111th Congress, in which Democrats controlled both chambers of Congress. Utah Republican Sen. Orrin Hatch took the lead this time and his bill to institute the Utah-D.C. plan passed the Senate on a 61–37 vote. But Davis's decision not to seek reelection in 2008 had deprived the proposal of its leading advocate in the House, where the bill ultimately was shelved.

After each census Congress uses the process of REAPPORTIONMENT to determine the allocation of all House seats among the states for the next decade, according to population. Though every state is guaranteed a minimum of one representative, some states gain representatives at the expense of others as the country's population shifts. Then the affected state legislatures use the census data for REDISTRICTING—redrawing CONGRESSIONAL DISTRICTS as well as state legislative DISTRICTS to make their populations as nearly equal as possible.

Equality among districts within a state is required by the Supreme Court's ONE-PERSON, ONE-VOTE decision handed down in the *Gray v. Sanders* ruling of 1963. Until then, some rural-dominated legislatures had drawn the lines to make farm districts much smaller in population than urban districts, in effect giving city dwellers less representation in the legislature. In 1964 the Court applied the same one-person, one-vote standard to Congress in *Wesberry v. Sanders*.

In recent years, particularly since computer technology advances have permitted exacting precision in drawing district lines, the courts have come to demand nearly perfect population equality among districts—a standard that some critics state has been taken to an illogical extreme. Coupled with legislation requiring more equitable representation of minority groups, this technology has greatly affected the redistricting process. Some congressional districts have become so weirdly contorted that they give new meaning to the term GERRYMANDER, the shaping of districts to benefit a particular politician, party, or minority group.

Efforts to get an accurate census count of African Americans and other minorities, and then link their neighborhoods through RACIAL REDISTRICTING, have proven to be particularly difficult and controversial. For example, the Twelfth Congressional District in North Carolina, as first drawn in the early 1990s, included nearly every black neighborhood in the 175 miles between Durham and Charlotte and at times was no more than a strip along Interstate 85.

Conventional census methods usually undercount minorities and the poor. Many in those groups do not receive or respond to the forms mailed out by the U.S. Bureau of the Census. Almost immediately after the results of the 2010 census were released in December of that year, officials in California—by far the nation's most populous state with an official census population of more than 37 million—complained that there had been a 1.5 million person undercount there. New York City officials contended that about 50,000 people lived in occupied properties that had been listed as vacant by the Census Bureau and therefore went uncounted.

Officials in Detroit—already suffering from a long-term decline tied to shrinkage in its economically crucial auto industry that had sent its population plummeting from more than 2 million in 1950 to less than 1 million in 2000—said that the additional 25 percent loss (to 713,777) reported in the 2010 census was exaggerated by an undercount.

Prior to the 2000 census, which missed an estimated 3.3 million people, the Census Bureau proposed to use statistical sampling techniques—like those used in POLLING—to address the undercount problem. Ninety percent of households would be covered by questionnaire, telephone, or census visit. Enumerators would visit one in ten of the remaining households, and the additional data would be extrapolated from those surveys. Such sampling, the bureau said, could reduce the undercount from 2.1 percent to one-tenth of 1 percent.

The Democratic administration of President Bill Clinton supported the plan, but the Congress then controlled by Republicans acted to block it. Republicans believed that sampling would benefit Democrats because minorities, the homeless, and young people away from home tend to vote for Democratic candidates. They contended that the Constitution requires an actual head count. Some members of Congress sued to stop the sampling and largely succeeded. The Court ruled 5–4 in January 1999 that sampling estimates could not be used for reapportionment. The Court, however, did not foreclose using sampling numbers for redistricting within states.

The Census Bureau initially said it would release both the actual and estimated numbers, but the Bush administration in 2001 decided against releasing estimates, contending that the actual head count was more accurate. The decision angered minorities who felt they were disadvantaged by the actual count, as well as some city leaders who faced the prospect of losing funding under federal formulas for social programs such as Medicaid if urban populations were underrepresented in the census numbers.

Nonetheless, the Census Bureau has used sampling techniques to try to develop estimates—down to the census block level—of detailed population demographics, including how many members of the nation's rapidly growing Hispanic constituency were citizens or noncitizens. This information, which previously had been gathered as part of the "long form" distributed to some census participants, was derived during the 2010 census cycle from five-year estimates calculated from the Census Bureau's Annual Community Survey.

The controversy was not the first one caused by the census. After the 1920 census, Congress, for the first time, could not agree on a reapportionment plan for the House. The 1910 allocation of seats remained the same until after the 1930 census, when farm states lost the seats they should have lost earlier because of the U.S. population shift to the cities.

Constitutional Mandate

The Constitution made the first apportionment of the House because no reliable figures on the population were available at the time. The constitutional formula produced a House of sixty-five members divided among the thirteen original states. This apportionment was in effect for the First

and Second Congresses, 1789–1793. (See HOUSE OF REPRESENTATIVES, ELECTING; HOUSE OF REPRESENTATIVES, QUALIFICATIONS.)

Article I, section 2, clause 3 of the Constitution called for a decennial census beginning in 1790 on which to base future apportionments of House seats. It states: "The actual Enumeration shall be made within three years after the first Meeting of the Congress of the United States, and within every subsequent Term of Ten years, in such manner as they shall by Law direct." Each state was guaranteed at least one representative.

Federal marshals, going from house to house on foot or horseback, took the early national censuses. The first census in 1790 took nine months and counted 3,929,214 people. By comparison, the 2010 census counted the U.S. population at 308,745,538, up a bit less than 10 percent from 281,421,906 in 2000. The Census Bureau first estimated that the nation's population broke the 300 million mark in October 2006.

> *"The actual Enumeration shall be made within three years after the first Meeting of the Congress of the United States, and within every subsequent Term of Ten years, in such manner as they shall by Law direct."*
>
> —Article I, section 2, clause 3 of the Constitution

In the early years of the Republic, a slave was counted as three-fifths of a person for House apportionment purposes. Slaves, women, and many white men who did not pay taxes or own property could not vote. Although they were counted for purposes of representation, they lacked true representation in Congress for many years until they gained the FRANCHISE. Gradually all religious, property, race, sex, and other adult voting restrictions fell. (See BLACK SUFFRAGE; NATURE OF REPRESENTATION; RIGHT TO VOTE; WOMEN'S SUFFRAGE; YOUTH SUFFRAGE.)

In 1850, census takers began recording every inhabitant by name, classified for the first time by age, sex, race, place of birth, and other categories. Thirty years later a census office in Washington, D.C., took over the marshals' duties as enumerators. In 1902 Congress created the Bureau of the Census in what is now the Department of Commerce.

With every census, the bureau has expanded its coverage and analyses of the U.S. population, economy, and other facets of American life. Besides the national census, the bureau makes special interim censuses of regions, states, and cities. It also gathers all manner of statistics on agriculture, education, elections and voter turnout, law enforcement, manufacturing, and other areas that affect the nation as a whole. The bureau publishes the information in numerous reports, notably its annual and historical versions of the *Statistical Abstract of the United States*.

Much of the updated information is available on the Census Bureau's website: www.census.gov.

Count and Consequences

The seemingly straightforward task of counting heads is more complex and subject to dispute than are most activities of government agencies. So much depends on the census findings that the losers seldom give up without a fight and the winners are only too willing to claim their rewards.

Prized above all in the fallout from the census is full representation in Congress and the state legislatures. Many battles over U.S. House or state legislative seats have been fought in the capitals or courts, usually with the underrepresented gaining some ground in their struggle for equal rights.

A case in point is the prolonged dispute over the landmark census of 1920. Although the rural states managed to stave off the consequences for a full decade, California and other states with large urban populations ultimately gained the seats to which they were entitled according to the census figures.

ANIMAL FARM

SOME ARE MORE EQUAL THAN OTHERS

1 RURAL AREA VOTE =100 CITY VOTES

HERBLOCK
©1961 THE WASHINGTON POST Co.

From **Herblock: A Cartoonist's Life** *(Times Books, 1998), courtesy of the Prints and Photographs Division, Library of Congress, LC-DIG-ppmsc-03534*

In the 1960s a number of lawsuits pointed up the great disparities of apportionment in the state legislatures and the U.S. House, culminating in decisions that nudged the legislatures closer to the Supreme Court's one-person, one-vote standard.

The lopsidedness was worst in the state capitals. By 1960 no state legislative body had less than a 2-to-1 population disparity between the most and least heavily populated districts. In some it was far greater. The disparity was 242–1 in the Connecticut house, 223–1 in the Nevada senate, 141–1 in the Rhode Island senate, and 9–1 in the Georgia senate.

In congressional districts the census showed that one Texas district had one-fourth as many inhabitants as the largest district. Arizona, Maryland, and Ohio each had at least one district with three times as many inhabitants as the least populated. But in contrast to the 1920s situation, it was the suburbs—not the cities—that were most underrepresented. After World War II the population shifted away from the central cities, but again the legislatures were slow to make apportionment mirror reality.

They were no longer able, however, to ignore the problem of malapportionment. As a result of the 1960s Court decisions in cases such as *Gray v. Sanders* and BAKER V. CARR, nearly every state was forced to redraw its district lines. By the 1990s the effects were obvious. Most states came close to population equality among districts. After the 1990 census all thirty congressional districts in Texas, for example, had the same population: 566,217. This degree of accuracy, seen as remarkable at the time, quickly became the standard as computer databases enabled surgically accurate calculations of district populations.

Most census-related disputes in the 1990s arose from questions of who to count and how to do it. With the United States' growing racial diversity, legal and illegal immigration, and unsolved gaps between the rich and the poor, it was not easy for the Census Bureau to avoid controversy over methodology.

In addition to its role in congressional reapportionment, the census supplies the data for drawing state and local district boundaries and for distributing certain federal funds. If that distribution favors one group over another, the Census Bureau endures criticism from those who think they have gotten the short end of the stick. Some public officials complain that the bureau's effort to count all people living in the United States has unfair political ramifications.

The inclusion of illegal aliens in the population figures is one area of dispute. The Fourteenth Amendment, ratified in 1868, changed the Constitution's original census wording to require apportionment based on a count of "the whole number of persons in each State, excluding Indians not taxed." To the Census Bureau this phrase means including undocumented aliens, a number of whom are residing illegally within the United States, a policy troubling to states that fear losing House seats to states such as California and Texas that have high rates of illegal immigration. Defenders of the policy say that any questions used to separate out illegal aliens could discourage others from responding and undermine the accuracy of the census. Many supporters also say that illegal immigration is a national problem and that states that bear the brunt of the resulting additional social costs should receive appropriate representation and federal assistance.

Census Bureau efforts to address the undercounting of minorities has produced even more heated debate. In 1991, during the administration of Republican George H. W. Bush, the Commerce Department refused to adjust the 1990 census despite the apparent 2.1 percent undercount. In 1996 the Supreme Court upheld a lower court's ruling against New York City and others in support of Commerce's decision to make no adjustment.

A postcensus survey by the National Research Council, an affiliate of the National Academy of Sciences, found that more than 9 million people had not been counted, while several million had been counted erroneously, for an estimated net undercount of about 5.3 million people. According to the survey, blacks were undercounted by 4.8 percent, American Indians by 5 percent, and Hispanics by 5.2 percent. The 5.3 million undercount estimate was later revised to 4.7 million.

A related problem arose from the difficulty of racial identification. With the multiplicity of races in the United States, many people do not fit neatly into any one category such as "white," "black," Asian, or Latino. They may be a blend of several such categories, making it difficult for them to find the right block to check on the census form.

To make it easier for them, and make the census more accurate, the Clinton administration announced that the 2000 census, for the first time, would allow Americans to check off as many categories as they like to describe their race. The administration rejected, however, the creation of a single "multiracial" category, as proposed by some multiracial advocacy groups. In the 2000 census, about 6.8 million people (2.4 percent) reported belonging to more than one race. By the 2010 census, when respondents were given fifty-seven multiple-race options from which to choose, 9 million people, or 2.9 percent of the nation's total population, reported belong to more than one race.

More on this topic:
Gerrymander, p. 226
One Person, One Vote, p. 373
Reapportionment and Redistricting, p. 517
Right to Vote, p. 549

Another long-standing question, whether to count overseas military personnel and dependents, was decided in their favor for the 1990 census. Reversing policy, the Census Bureau included them in 1990 and counted 923,000, who, for purposes of reapportionment, were assigned to the state each individual considered home. Americans stationed abroad had also been counted once before, in the 1970 census during the Vietnam War.

But even this aspect of head counting has sparked some controversy. In the 2000 reapportionment, conducted under a complicated formula, North Carolina narrowly edged out Utah for the last of the 435 seats. North Carolina, which has several major military bases, was credited with a number of military service members whose last address was in the state, even if they would normally regard another state as their home. Utah officials complained this was unfair, especially as their state was not given full credit for the large number of Mormons temporarily living out of state. Utah lost the case in court, although the issue was revived in the legislative proposal that aimed to pair a first-ever seat for the District of Columbia with an additional seat for Utah.

The Census Bureau addressed this issue for the 2010 census by attributing overseas military personnel to the states they regarded as their home. This led to some irony: This time it was North Carolina officials who complained that their state was robbed out of an additional seat, because many members of the military who had been based in the state had been relocated to participate in the major U.S. military commitments to Iraq, Afghanistan, and elsewhere that had developed over the previous decade.

Challenger *See* INCUMBENCY

Citizens Party (1979–1984)

Organized in 1979 as a coalition of dissident liberals and populists, the first Citizens Party convention chose author and environmental scientist Barry Commoner as its 1980 presidential candidate and La Donna Harris, wife of former Democratic senator Fred R. Harris of Oklahoma, as its candidate for vice president.

The Citizens Party ticket ran on the central theme that major decisions in America were made to benefit corporations and not the average citizen. The party proposed public control of energy industries and multinational corporations, a halt to the use of nuclear power, a sharp cut in military spending, and price controls on food, fuel, housing, and health care.

The Commoner-Harris ticket was on the ballot in twenty-nine states and the District of Columbia in 1980. Party leaders asserted that it was the largest number of ballot positions attained by any alternative party in its first campaign. Commoner ran in all of the large electoral vote states except Florida and Texas. He made his biggest push in California, Illinois, Michigan, New York, and Pennsylvania, where party leaders believed they could tap a "sophisticated working-class population" and appeal to political activists who had been involved in the environmental and antinuclear movements that had arisen in the late 1970s.

There was little return on the party's efforts, though. The Citizens Party won just 234,294 votes, or 0.3 percent of the 1980 vote in an election in which President Jimmy Carter, a Democrat, was unseated by Republican Ronald Reagan, a conservative whose philosophy on most issues was a polar opposite to that of the Citizens Party activists.

In its second and final presidential campaign in 1984, the Citizens Party chose outspoken feminist Sonia Johnson of Virginia. Johnson first attracted national attention in 1979, when the Mormon Church excommunicated her for supporting the proposed Equal Rights Amendment (ERA). In 1982 she staged a thirty-seven-day hunger strike in an unsuccessful effort to pressure the Illinois legislature to approve the ERA. The Citizens Party selected party activist Richard J. Walton of Rhode Island to accompany Johnson on the ticket. Winning 72,200 votes in 1984, the ticket garnered 0.1 percent of the vote and subsequently faded from the political scene.

Citizens United vs. Federal Election Commission *See* CAMPAIGN FINANCING

Citizenship and Voting

A primary right of every American citizen age eighteen and over is the RIGHT TO VOTE, the "first liberty," as historians and political scientists have called it. But what defines the nature of citizenship? What exactly is a citizen?

The first four articles of the Constitution mention the words *citizen* and *natural born citizen*. Article I requires that members of both houses of Congress be U.S. citizens. Article II says the president must either be a U.S. citizen "at the time of Adoption of this Constitution" or be a "natural born citizen." Articles III and IV concern questions of federal courts' jurisdiction over citizens and the extension of rights from all states to citizens of any particular one. But nowhere does the Constitution define the word *citizen*.

Constitutional scholars and historians agree that the phrase "natural born citizen" represents the framers' intent to impose an ancient doctrine called *jus soli* or "right of land or ground," meaning that citizenship arises from place of birth. An opposing concept, *jus sanguinis*, "right of blood," implies that citizenship derives from one's parents.

Jus soli, or birthright citizenship as it has come to be called, represented, beyond the concept of citizenship alone, several utilitarian ideas to the framers: It helped to clarify property rights in the new land and to mitigate or eliminate jurisdictional disputes between citizens of different states. Perhaps most important, it helped to lessen the very real fear of massive expatriation during wartime, a phenomenon that many of the framers had witnessed firsthand during the War of Independence as crown loyalists fled to Canada or back to England, there to oppose the Revolution.

Although they were deprived of many of their civil rights during World War II, Japanese Americans could still vote. In November 1942 citizens of Japanese descent wait to have their absentee ballots notarized at the Tule Lake Relocation Center in Newell, California.

Source: National Archives and Records Administration

Despite the adoption of the "right of land or ground" concept in deciding citizenship, several groups of native-born Americans were excluded from citizenship and hence from the political processes of the new nation: women; second-generation slaves born on American soil; and Native Americans, who, under the "right of land" concept, should have been the first citizens of the young country.

The *Dred Scott* decision of 1857 (*Scott v. Sandford*), the most famous (or infamous) attempt to define citizenship before the onset of the Civil War, ruled that a black person could not be a citizen. According to Chief Justice Roger B. Taney, who wrote the opinion for the 7–2 majority, the Constitution did not intend blacks to be included under the term *citizen* and therefore no black could claim any of the rights and privileges held by U.S. citizens. Slaves or their descendants, Taney wrote, "are not included, and were not intended to be included, under the word 'citizen' in the Constitution."

Constitutional Amendments

In its very first phrase the Fourteenth Amendment, ratified eleven years later after the slavery crisis had convulsed the nation in civil war, reversed the *Scott* decision with the ringing declaration that

All persons born or naturalized in the United States and subject to the jurisdiction thereof, are citizens of the United States and of the State wherein they reside. No State shall make or enforce any law which shall abridge the privileges or immunities of citizens of the United

States; nor shall any State deprive any person of life, liberty, or property, without due process of law; nor deny to any person within its jurisdiction the equal protection of the laws.

For Native Americans, even with the passage of the Fourteenth Amendment, the road to full citizenship, which blacks had seemingly won with the amendment's ratification, proved more difficult. In an 1884 case, *Elk v. Wilkins,* the Court ruled that even though Native Americans were indeed born in the United States, they as members of tribes or Indian nations were not wholly "subject to the jurisdiction" of the U.S. government. Under the decision, Native Americans living in tribes remained an exception to the Fourteenth Amendment until 1925, when Congress enacted a law saying they are subject to U.S. jurisdiction and therefore entitled to citizenship.

The jurisdiction question was raised in the 1898 decision in *United States v. Wong Kim Ark,* which concerned a person born in the United States to resident-alien Chinese parents. The case arose when Wong Kim Ark was denied readmission after a visit to China.

The decision came at a time when anti-Chinese sentiment was running high. Waves of immigrants from the Far East had raised fears of economic dislocation among many working-class Americans, most of them white Europeans. Congress in 1882 had specifically barred Chinese from becoming citizens through the naturalization process, and Congress's right to discriminate in this fashion had been upheld by the Court. The authorities therefore said that Wong Kim Ark could not be a citizen because his parents could not become citizens.

In deciding that Wong Kim Ark was indeed a citizen, the Court applied an English common law principle—allegiance to the king. Under that principle, children of aliens born in England were natural-born subjects, as were children of England's ambassadors and diplomats born abroad because they owed obedience to the king, the opinion said. The law had been applied to all English colonies before the Declaration of Independence and would apply now. *Jus sanguinis,* which said the child's citizenship was that of his parents, did not.

After the Fourteenth Amendment was ratified, the issues of citizenship and voting were addressed in several other amendments:

- The Fifteenth Amendment, ratified in 1870 in the middle of the Reconstruction Era, provided for BLACK SUFFRAGE: "The right of citizens of the United States to vote shall not be denied or abridged by the United States or by any State on account of race, color, or previous condition of servitude."
- The Nineteenth Amendment, ratified in 1920, finally guaranteed WOMEN'S SUFFRAGE.
- The Twenty-third Amendment, ratified in 1961, extended the right to vote for president to the citizens of Washington, D.C., the nation's capital.
- The Twenty-fourth Amendment, ratified in 1964, abolished the POLL TAX, one of the more noxious and lingering legal devices (known as the "Jim Crow" laws) that had been enacted by the southern states after Reconstruction to deprive blacks of the vote.
- The TWENTY-SIXTH AMENDMENT, ratified in 1971 after a campaign that featured the slogan "Old enough to fight and die, old enough to vote," lowered the voting age for American citizens to eighteen. (See YOUTH SUFFRAGE.)

The Supreme Court has ruled, in *Schneiderman v. United States* (1944) and in *Trop v. Dulles* (1958), that U.S. citizenship is so prized and valuable an asset that the federal government would be guilty of "cruel and unusual punishment" in depriving even those citizens who espouse antithetical political views or, as in the *Trop* case, desert in wartime of what the Court recognized as their "status in organized society." Another 1958 decision, *Perez v. Brownell,* said that Congress had the power to remove the citizenship of a person who had voted in a foreign election. But in a 1967 case, *Afroyim v. Rusk,* the Court overruled the *Perez* decision, holding that citizenship could be relinquished only voluntarily.

However, not all citizens—be they native-born, black, female, Native American, eighteen-year-olds, or naturalized citizens—are allowed to vote: convicted felons and persons ruled legally insane are barred from voting. In recent years, though, there has been a growing movement to relax barriers to voting for those persons previously convicted of felonies but regarded as having paid their debts to society. Some activists view felon nonvoting laws as hitting the African American population especially hard because of the disproportionate incarceration rate of young black males.

Naturalization Process

The United States was founded by immigrants and their descendants and has remained a refuge for many from other countries. American citizenship, with all its implicit and explicit rights, is available to those new arrivals who enter into the naturalization process. To qualify, an applicant must be eighteen or older and have been a lawful resident of the United States for a continuous period of five years. For spouses of U.S. citizens, the period is three years. During the five-year period, the applicant must have been physically present in the United States for at least half the required residence period.

An applicant for naturalization must demonstrate an understanding of the English language, including an ability to read, write, and speak words in ordinary usage (although exceptions are made for applicants over fifty-five who have been lawful residents for at least fifteen years). Applicants must have demonstrated "good moral character, attached to the principles of the Constitution and well disposed to the good order and happiness of the United States" for five years prior to making their applications. They must also demonstrate, in a personal interview with an examiner from the U.S. Citizenship and Immigration Services, that they have a "knowledge and understanding of the fundamentals of the history, and the principles and form of government, of the United States." If, at the conclusion of the process, a favorable decision to grant citizenship is made, an applicant becomes a citizen after swearing an oath of allegiance to the United States. The new citizen is then eligible to vote as soon as he or she registers to do so.

One legal scholar writes that the Supreme Court's actions on citizenship are notable in their "remarkably limited scope. This is so since, while one must be a citizen to vote or to hold federal office, most of the Constitution's key rights and liberties do not extend to citizens only. No less than the entire Bill of Rights applies to 'the people'—citizen and the noncitizen alike."

More on this topic:
Black Suffrage, p. 28
Poll Taxes, p. 426
Right to Vote, p. 549
Women's Suffrage, p. 678
Youth Suffrage, p. 687

The Supreme Court has steadfastly defined citizenship by the *jus soli* or birthright citizenship doctrine and made it exceptionally difficult for the government to wrest citizenship away from individuals. It is on the issues of voting and of holding elected office that the Court's predominating concern with the Constitution's provisions for equal protection has tended to focus on citizenship questions.

Civil Rights Acts

During the ten-year Reconstruction period immediately following the Civil War, white Americans sympathetic to black Americans in the reunified United States tried to secure voting and other civil rights for the freed slaves. But the determination of many whites in southern states to block BLACK SUFFRAGE, together with restrictive interpretations by the U.S. Supreme Court, held African American voting to a trickle.

Among the Reconstruction-era remedies approved by Congress and the states were three amendments to the U.S. Constitution and seven pieces of implementing legislation. None, however, brought about significant permanent change in the racial composition of southern voting. Not until 1965 did a sweeping VOTING RIGHTS ACT finally provide the means and security for large numbers of African Americans to go to the polls in southern states.

The first of the three Civil War amendments, the Thirteenth, ratified in 1865, simply abolished slavery. The next two extended civil rights to the former slaves and proved to be more difficult to carry out.

Historians have asserted that the Supreme Court's narrow interpretation of the Fourteenth and Fifteenth Amendments provided an environment that made possible the long denial of full voting rights to African Americans. The Fourteenth Amendment, ratified in 1868, made blacks citizens and prohibited states from denying citizens due process and equal protection of the laws; the Fifteenth Amendment, ratified two years later, prohibited the federal and state governments from denying the right to vote to citizens on the basis of race, color, or previous condition of servitude. The voting rights provisions of both amendments applied only to men at that time. (See WOMEN'S SUFFRAGE.)

By 1875, when the Reconstruction period was drawing to a close, Congress had passed seven statutes, each entitled "Civil Rights Act," to implement and enforce the three amendments. Most of the seven acts did not deal directly with voting rights but rather conferred rights and protections already enjoyed by white citizens. Taken as a whole, however, the acts made it clear that the Reconstruction Congress, controlled by the so-called Radical Republicans, intended the Fourteenth and Fifteenth Amendments to provide the RIGHT TO VOTE to black citizens. The Radical Republicans, who disagreed with the lenient policy toward the defeated South promulgated by President Abraham Lincoln prior to his death in 1865, saw the black vote as a way to thwart the return to political power of white southerners who had strongly backed the Confederate cause.

The Civil Rights Act of 1870, known as the Enforcement Act, set criminal penalties for interfering with suffrage under the Fifteenth Amendment or the Civil Rights Act of April 9, 1866. The latter, passed over President Andrew Johnson's veto, gave blacks full equality under the law "as is enjoyed by white citizens." Debate over the constitutionality of the 1866 law, which provided for enforcement by federal troops if necessary, led to the Fourteenth Amendment.

The Civil Rights Act of 1871, an amendment to the Enforcement Act, called for the appointment of election supervisors and deputy marshals in cities with populations over twenty thousand if two citizens requested them in writing to a federal judge. The supervisors were to watch for abuses of voting rights.

All or parts of the post–Civil War civil rights acts were nullified by state or federal courts. The last of the seven, the Civil Rights Act of 1875, outlawed racial discrimination in hotels, theaters, transportation, or jury selection. The Supreme Court nullified it in 1883 (*Civil Rights Cases*).

As time went on, the southern states were able, with increasingly greater effectiveness, to evade those parts of the laws that the courts did not invalidate. The states used so-called exclusionary devices such as LITERACY TESTS, the GRANDFATHER CLAUSE, the WHITE PRIMARY, and POLL TAXES to keep blacks from voting. Outside the law, white groups, including the Ku Klux Klan, kept blacks from voting by terrorizing them, sometimes through violence. Thus, the voting rights guarantees of the Fourteenth and Fifteenth Amendments represented an unkept promise to African Americans in the southern states until the second half of the twentieth century when, in the environment of a massive civil rights movement, Congress moved decisively to fulfill the old guarantees.

On the heels of the Civil Rights Act of 1957, which created the Civil Rights Commission, and the wide-ranging Civil Rights Act of 1964, which bars discrimination in public accommodations and employment, Congress enacted the Voting Rights Act of 1965. In upholding the Voting Rights Act and later amendments, the Supreme Court invoked the Fourteenth and Fifteenth Amendments that the Court of the previous century had so narrowly construed.

The Court's New Attitude

Two rulings, both issued on March 27, 1876, had pointed the direction in which the Supreme Court would take the voting rights issue for decades into the future. In *United States v. Reese*, the Court held that the Fifteenth Amendment did not give anyone the right to vote. It simply guaranteed the right to be free from racial discrimination in the exercise of the right to vote, a right granted under state laws. Therefore, Congress exceeded its power to enforce the Fifteenth Amendment when it enacted laws that penalized state officials who denied blacks the right to vote, refused to count votes, or obstructed citizens from voting.

In the second ruling, *United States v. Cruikshank,* the Court dismissed indictments brought against Louisiana citizens accused of using violence and fraud to prevent blacks from voting. Because the indictments did not charge that the actions were motivated by racial discrimination, they were not federal offenses.

In the two rulings, the Court laid down the doctrine that the amendments did not authorize the federal government to protect citizens from each other but only from discriminatory state legislation and that they gave protection only where such legislation discriminated because of race and color.

From the end of Reconstruction until well into the twentieth century, Congress took virtually no action that might have fostered black suffrage. Moreover, the courts generally avoided taking an activist role in interpreting the Fifteenth Amendment or in applying Reconstruction laws pertaining to voting rights.

According to the U.S. Civil Rights Commission, by 1910 every state of the former Confederacy had either disenfranchised African Americans or had otherwise deprived them of political effectiveness through the use of exclusionary devices. In the case of literacy tests, a prospective voter was required to read, and sometimes to explain, a passage from a state constitution. Grandfather clauses exempted a voter from the literacy test if his ancestor had voted in or before 1866, which included hardly any former slaves or their ancestors. Finally, in allowing the Democratic Party to restrict primaries to whites, many states argued that political parties were private clubs or associations and that primary elections were functions of the parties, not the states.

In a precedent-setting literacy test case, *Williams v. Mississippi,* which the Supreme Court decided in 1898, Henry Williams, a black man, had been indicted for murder by an all-white jury. The jurors were selected from a list of registered voters who had, among other qualifications, passed a literacy test. Williams challenged the test as unconstitutional. His attorneys argued that

CLOSER LOOK

The civil rights laws enacted in the 1960s had a major impact on partisan politics. Over the objections of their southern conservative wing, Democratic Party leaders—most prominently President Lyndon B. Johnson, a Texan—adopted the cause of civil rights. For many years, blacks were affiliated with the Republicans— "the party of Lincoln"—rather than the Democrats, who dominated politics in the South, where they instituted "Jim Crow" laws following Reconstruction. Blacks began to shift parties as Democrat Franklin D. Roosevelt introduced New Deal social programs in the 1930s. In the 1960s they migrated in large numbers to the Democratic Party, which built an overwhelming and lasting advantage among black voters. But a backlash among southern whites, who opposed the Democrats' shift toward liberalism and embrace of the civil rights movement, helped the Republican Party make unprecedented inroads in the South. Yet by the end of the century, the civil rights advances of the 1960s promoted by the Democrats had become an accepted part of life in the South even as the Republicans had become the region's dominant party.

his conviction was invalid because the laws under which the grand jury was selected allowed discrimination in voter registration, violating the Equal Protection Clause of the Fourteenth Amendment. Writing for the Court's majority, Justice Joseph McKenna refused to find the Mississippi statutes in violation of the Equal Protection Clause. The "evil" was not in the laws themselves, he wrote, because they did not on their face discriminate against blacks. The only evil resulted from the effect of their discriminatory administration.

In the 1915 case of *Guinn v. United States,* the Supreme Court began to move toward a broader interpretation of the Fifteenth Amendment. In a unanimous ruling, the Court struck down Oklahoma's voting system, which combined a literacy test with a grandfather clause, as an unconstitutional violation of the Fifteenth Amendment. The decision was the first voting rights case in which the Court looked beyond the nondiscriminatory form of a law to scrutinize its discriminatory intent.

A 1921 Court decision involving CAMPAIGN FINANCE in *Newberry v. United States* seemed to say that Congress lacked the power to regulate primaries. Twenty years later, however, in *United States v. Classic,* the Court overruled *Newberry* and said that the white primary was an integral part of the election process and therefore subject to federal regulation. But it was only in 1953, in *Terry v. Adams,* that the Court ended a resourceful effort by Texas Democrats to maintain the white primary in that state. Because the DEMOCRATIC PARTY for many decades was dominant in southern states, voting in primary elections was more important than voting in the general election.

The last exclusionary device to fall was the poll tax. Early in the country's history, poll taxes had been levied as a less burdensome requirement for voting than landholding. But, for the most part, those poll taxes had been eliminated by the time of the Civil War. The tax was revived in the 1890s as an additional way to restrict suffrage in the southern states to whites. Officials, however, usually described poll taxes as merely a means to "cleanse" the rolls of ineligible voters and prevent ELECTION FRAUD.

In 1937 the Supreme Court upheld the constitutionality of the poll tax against a challenge that it violated the equal protection guarantee of the Fourteenth Amendment. Proposals to abolish the tax were introduced in every Congress from 1939 to 1962. In August 1962 Congress approved a constitutional amendment outlawing poll taxes in federal elections. The states completed ratification of the Twenty-fourth Amendment on January 23, 1964. Two years later, the Supreme Court held that the poll tax also was an unconstitutional requirement for voting in state and local elections.

Voting Rights Act of 1965

Congress passed the comprehensive Voting Rights Act of 1965 against a disturbing backdrop of attacks by southern whites on peaceful marches by blacks demonstrating for voting rights. The law was designed to close all the legal loopholes that had for so long allowed state and local officials to block VOTER REGISTRATION of blacks. Earlier, President Lyndon B. Johnson had asked a joint session of Congress to pass the sweeping measure. He said, "No law that we now have on the books . . . can ensure the right to vote when local officials are determined to deny it."

The law suspended all literacy tests and provided for appointment of federal voting registrars in states that had such tests together with low voting rates. The provisions applied to six southern states and part of a seventh state. The act also required covered states or counties to obtain federal approval before changing their voting laws or procedures.

Enactment of the Voting Rights Act of 1965 resulted in a marked increase in the number of blacks registering, voting, and running for office in southern states. The Civil Rights Commission in 1968 reported that registration of African Americans had climbed to above 50 percent of the black voting-age population in every southern state. In the first ten years the act was in force, an estimated 2 million African Americans were added to voting rolls in the South.

The Voting Rights Act was immediately challenged as infringing upon state power to oversee elections. In *South Carolina v. Katzenbach,* the Supreme Court in 1966 upheld the power of Congress to pass the law and also upheld all of its major provisions, including the suspension of literacy tests. Delivering the opinion for the Court, Chief Justice Earl Warren wrote that the provision suspending the tests "was clearly a legitimate response to the problem, for which there is ample precedent in Fifteenth Amendment cases."

With a single exception, the Court in all challenges upheld the law and interpreted it broadly. The exception was *Mobile v. Bolden* (1980). In that case, the Court ruled that the act did not reach a voting system that had a discriminatory effect unless there was also evidence of a discriminating intent. The ruling upheld an at-large system of electing city commissioners in Mobile, Alabama. African Americans said the system diluted their right to vote by effectively preventing the election of blacks. In a 1982 revision of the law, Congress responded by deleting any requirement of discriminatory intent.

President Lyndon B. Johnson, who hailed from the southern state of Texas, proposed and was an avid backer of the Voting Rights Act of 1965 that became the key to a voting revolution throughout most states in the South.

Source: LBJ Library photo by Frank Muto

The first extension of the law, for five years, was approved by Congress in 1970. States and local governments were forbidden to use literacy tests or voter qualifying devices through 1975. When the act was again renewed and amended, in 1975, supporters won a seven-year extension. They also gained two major provisions designed to give greater protection to certain "language minorities," defined as persons of Spanish heritage, American Indians, Asian Americans, and Alaska Natives. (See BILINGUAL VOTERS.)

A third extension of the act was approved in 1982. The amended law that year was given strong backing from members of both the House and Senate, including legislators from southern states. More than twice as many southern Democrats in both chambers of Congress voted for passage in 1982 than when the law was initially approved in 1965. Observers said the change reflected, among other things, the addition of many new black voters in southern constituencies.

The 1982 legislation extended for twenty-five years provisions of the law requiring nine states and portions of thirteen others to obtain Justice Department approval for alterations in their election laws and procedures.

With the federal Voting Rights Act amendments enacted in 1982 set to expire in 2007, a twenty-five-year extension of the nonpermanent provisions was cleared by the Republican-controlled Congress in 2006 and signed into law by Republican president George W. Bush. Some lawmakers and officials objected to the extension because their states were covered by the act's preclearance provisions that required them to obtain approval from the U.S. Justice Department or the federal district court in Washington, D.C., prior to making any changes to their election procedures and district maps. The affected states argued unsuccessfully that the preclearance provisions were unnecessarily time-consuming and expensive, given the removal of strictures against minority voting, the vast increase in black voter registration and participation, and the sizable roster of black elected officials in those states.

Club for Growth

Founded in 1999 by a group headed by well-known, business-oriented conservatives, the political action organization known as the Club for Growth has distinguished itself not so much by its agenda—its advocacy of tax reductions and government fiscal discipline is shared by many conservative groups—but by the aggressive tactics with which it pursues its goals.

Before the Democratic caucuses in Iowa that led off the 2004 presidential nominating process, the group set its sights on former Vermont governor Howard Dean, whose populist-themed campaign had pushed him into serious contention. In a Club for Growth ad run in Iowa, an actor playing a farmer said, "Howard Dean should take his tax-hiking, government-expanding, latte-drinking, sushi-eating, Volvo-driving, *New York Times*-reading, Hollywood-loving, left-wing freak show back to Vermont, where it belongs."

What is unusual about the Club for Growth is that it does not limit itself to criticism of Democrats; it also targets Republicans deemed by the group's leaders to be insufficiently conservative. The group's political action committee has financially backed conservative opponents to candidates, including some moderate Republican congressional incumbents, whom it labels as RINOs ("Republican in Name Only"); has encouraged its members to donate money to these conservative candidates; and has intervened in a number of races by airing hard-hitting "independent expenditure" ads in their states and districts.

The Club for Growth made its first big splash in the 2004 Republican Senate primary in Pennsylvania. The group attacked moderate incumbent Arlen Specter and backed conservative challenger Patrick J. Toomey. Specter, who received visible support from President George W. Bush, hung on, but just barely, defeating Toomey by 51 percent to 49 percent before winning more easily in the November general election.

Toomey, who left open his U.S. House seat to challenge Specter, became president of the Club for Growth after the election, replacing founding president Steven Moore. Toomey was in office until 2009; in 2010 he ran a successful campaign for a Pennsylvania Senate seat. Once in the Senate in 2011 he surprised some political observers by moderating slightly his adamant opposition to any tax increases.

In 2011 the Club for Growth president was Chris Chocola. He served two terms in the U.S. House from Indiana, from 2003 to 2007. While the group made a more visible effort during the 2006 congressional primaries to back like-minded conservatives running for open seats that were safely Republican, it did not stray from its controversial policy of criticizing moderate Republicans.

The group brought down its first incumbent RINO in the August 2006 primary in Michigan's Seventh District, in which its favored candidate, conservative Tim Walberg, defeated one-term GOP representative Joe Schwarz. The Club for Growth also played a prominent role in the unsuccessful challenge to Rhode Island Republican senator Lincoln Chafee by conservative Cranston mayor Steve Laffey in the party's September primary.

Many Republicans have strongly criticized the Club for Growth for divisive tactics that they say hurt the party's chances to hold its seats. Many were enraged by the organization's Rhode Island campaign; Chafee's defeat in November 2006 by Democrat Sheldon Whitehouse was crucial to the Democrats' Senate takeover for the 110th Congress. Some critics argued that Laffey's bruising challenge had fatally damaged the liberal Chafee's chances of maintaining GOP control of the seat in the strongly Democratic-leaning state.

But officials of the Club for Growth said they were not backing down from their efforts to hold the Republican Party to what they viewed as its conservative principles. "At the end of the day, we're not a subsidiary of the Republican Party," Toomey told Congressional Quarterly's CQPolitics.com during the 2006 campaign. "Our mission is not to worry so much about the number of Republicans in office at any point in time. It's to make sure that the right people are getting elected."

Coalition

A coming together of distinct parties or people of different IDEOLOGIES is called a *coalition*. In a TWO-PARTY SYSTEM, formation of a coalition is often required to elect candidates or enact legislation.

One of the oldest and best known such groupings in U.S. political history was the conservative coalition of southern Democrats and Republicans in Congress. The coalition was in decline for years and extinct by the end of the 1990s because conservative southern Democrats switched to the Republican Party and GOP candidates began winning regularly in their own right. But earlier the coalition operated for more than half a century as a formidable obstacle to enactment of progressive initiatives including CIVIL RIGHTS ACTS, the VOTING RIGHTS ACT, and other legislation on the liberal agenda.

The conservative coalition first appeared in the late 1930s in opposition to another famous alliance, President Franklin D. Roosevelt's Democratic coalition of southern Protestants, Jews, blacks, blue-collar workers, farmers, and urban Catholics. The South then, and for several decades, tended to view the Republican Party negatively because of its historic association with Abraham Lincoln, the Civil War, and the policies of the Reconstruction-era policies. Yet despite the Democrats' reliance on the "Solid South," some powerful southern committee chairmen joined with Republicans to fight Roosevelt's New Deal policies that significantly expanded the size and role of the federal government.

The conservative coalition was an ad-hoc grouping formed automatically in Congress whenever a majority of southern Democrats joined with a majority of Republicans to oppose a majority of northern Democrats. Analysis of the conservative coalition was one of several voting studies compiled regularly by Congressional Quarterly.

Today, the South is so solidly Republican that the conservative coalition has disappeared. When Republicans captured the House in the 1994 elections, the coalition seemed to fade into near irrelevance. In 1995–1996 the venerable conservative voting bloc appeared on only about 12 percent of roll-call votes, compared with 30 percent twenty-five years earlier. When the conservative coalition did come together, it was unstoppable: it was

CLOSER LOOK ◉

While some congressional coalitions have broad agendas, others are very esoteric in their interests. Among those in existence in 2007 were the following:

- The Interstate 69 Caucus
- Congressional Ski and Snowboard Caucus
- Congressional Friends of Denmark
- U.S.-Mongolia Friendship Caucus
- Qatari-American Economic Strategic Defense, Cultural, and Educational Partnership Caucus
- Congressional Bike Caucus

More on this topic:

Blue Dog Democrats, p. 32

Civil Rights Acts, p. 102

Ideology, p. 259

Two-Party System, p. 636

Voting Rights Act, p. 665

on the winning side of 100 percent of the votes. By 2000 it made its appearance on just 4 percent of roll-call votes, but its success rate dropped to 41 percent.

Ultimately, *Congressional Quarterly* eliminated the conservative coalition from its catalog of vote studies. Yet just because the conservative coalition now appears a historical artifact does not mean that political coalition-making is dead. There actually are dozens of congressional coalitions and caucuses, many of which are bipartisan and focus on specific demographic, regional, industrial, or other interests.

One of them, the BLUE DOG Coalition, was created in 1995 by moderate-to-conservative Democrats, mostly from the South, who hoped to maintain a working relationship with the Republican majority that resulted from the 1994 House elections. This effort at outreach was blunted, though, by the hard-edged partisanship practiced at the time by Republican leaders, and the Blue Dogs have since mainly oriented their efforts toward gaining a stronger voice for less liberal members in House Democratic Party affairs. The Blue Dog group was further damaged by the 2010 elections when more than half of its members lost their seats to Republicans.

Other congressional coalitions formed along ideological lines are groups such as the Progressive Caucus, made up of liberal Democrats; the centrist New Democrat Coalition and Republican Main Street Partnership; and the conservative Republican Study Group in the House.

Regional groupings include the Appalachian Caucus, Chesapeake Bay Watershed Task Force, and the Northeast-Midwest Congressional Coalition.

Coattails

Candidates who seek to benefit from the popularity of a president, senator, governor, or other prominent figure of their party are said to be grabbing for that person's coattails, referring back to the days when many men wore long frock coats. For example, congressional and state-level candidates might ride the coattails of a strong presidential candidate. A candidate for governor might gain votes for the party's candidates for state and local offices.

Abraham Lincoln, then a U.S. representative from Illinois, is credited with popularizing the

Zachary Taylor
Source: Library of Congress (engraved by John Sartain).

coattails metaphor in 1848. Responding on the House floor to an accusation that he and others were taking shelter under Mexican War hero and Whig presidential candidate Zachary Taylor's "military coat tail," Lincoln noted that the Democrats were still running under the coattails of another war hero, former president Andrew Jackson.

The coattails effect was a major factor in American politics during the long period in which parties' candidates for all offices ran as a "slate" or "ticket," and candidates were mainly handpicked by party leaders. Many states in those days allowed straight-ticket voting by providing a checkoff or lever that allowed voters to choose all of a party's candidates at once, and party "machines" in urban and other areas urged voters to exercise that option.

The result was that candidates for the U.S. House of Representatives, state legislatures, and local offices often won or lost based on the strength of their parties' candidates for statewide or national office. A popular candidate at the top of the ticket could have coattails that would sweep large numbers of the party's members into office. An unpopular candidate could bring electoral disaster to the party, a phenomenon known as "reverse" coattails.

A prominent example of reverse coattails occurred in 1932, a presidential election year in the midst of the Great Depression. A seismic political swing—more the result of the unpopularity of incumbent Republican president Herbert Hoover than the popularity of Democratic challenger Franklin D. Roosevelt—resulted in the Democrats' scoring net gains of ninety-seven seats in the House and twelve seats in the Senate, along with major gains in state and local offices across the country.

The coattails effect has weakened in recent decades, however. Party machines and their grip on the nominating process have greatly diminished because of demographic changes and the emergence of popular primaries as the means for choosing candidates since the 1960s. Many candidates therefore have their own political organizations and loose ties to the party, and they have more freedom to choose when they will associate themselves with or distance themselves from the top of the ticket.

Many voters have also become more inclined to vote for the candidates they prefer, regardless of party, a practice known as split-ticket voting. Many states have even eliminated the option of the straight-ticket lever or checkoff. (See SPLIT- AND STRAIGHT-TICKET VOTING.)

Andrew Jackson

In response to the accusation that he was taking shelter under Zachary Taylor's "military coat tail," Lincoln noted that the Democrats were still running under the coattails of war hero and former president Andrew Jackson.

Source: Library of Congress

Despite these developments, the coattails factor is not completely extinct. For example, in 2004 President George W. Bush's strength at the top of the ticket in conservative southern states helped his party's Senate nominees win key open-seat races in that region, helping the party to a net gain of four seats.

But there is debate over the cause-and-effect relationship between the top of the ticket and overall party success. Landslide 2006 victories in New York by Democratic senator Hillary Rodham Clinton and gubernatorial nominee Eliot Spitzer may have helped three fellow New York Democrats win U.S. House seats that had been held by Republicans. Those three also were aided, however, by a national downturn in public approval of President Bush, based largely on dissent over the war in Iraq and the Republican Party in general.

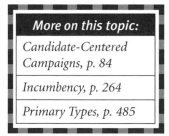

More on this topic:

Candidate-Centered Campaigns, p. 84

Incumbency, p. 264

Primary Types, p. 485

In 2008, the nomination of an African American, Barack Obama, as the Democrat's presidential candidate helped his party win such traditionally Republican southern states as Virginia and North Carolina that had sizeable black populations. Obama's overall popularity also gave a lift to Democratic candidates in numerous congressional races. But in 2010 any coattail effect Obama may have had two years earlier had disappeared entirely as Republicans won a net of sixty-three House seats, and control of the chamber, and significantly cut into the Democratic majority in the Senate.

The unpopularity of incumbent Herbert Hoover (pictured) resulted in net Democratic gains of ninety-seven seats in the House and twelve seats in the Senate in 1932, an example of the phenomenon called "reverse" coattails.

Source: Library of Congress

Other factors play a key role in voting decisions. INCUMBENCY is frequently a stronger factor in elections than the popularity of the candidate heading the ticket. Incumbents usually win and challengers usually lose.

Most states elect their governors and other state officials in nonpresidential election years to minimize the effect of national politics on state and local elections.

Communist Party U.S.A. (1924–)

In 1919, shortly after the Russian Revolution, Soviet communists encouraged American left-wing groups to withdraw from the Socialist Party and to form a communist party in the United States. After several years of internal dissension, a new political organization named the Workers' Party of America was established in 1921 at the insistence of Moscow. The goal of the new party was revolutionary—to overthrow capitalism and to create a communist state ruled by the working classes.

William Z. Foster, a labor organizer, was the party's first presidential candidate, in 1924. National tickets were run every four years through 1940. The party sat out the presidential elections from 1944 through 1964, due to World War II and escalating Cold War tensions, but ran presidential tickets from 1968 through 1984.

The party never had more than a relative handful of adherents, however. Its peak year at the polls was 1932, when the desperation of the Great Depression led a number of Americans to examine politically extreme alternatives. Even then, Foster received just 103,253 votes, or 0.3 percent of the POPULAR VOTE.

The communists have a distinctive place in American political history as the only party to have had international ties. In 1929 a party split brought the formal creation of the Communist Party of the United States, with acknowledged status as a part of the worldwide communist movement (the Communist International).

The Communist International terminated during World War II—in part because the United States had entered into an alliance with the Soviet Union to defeat the armies of Germany and Japan—and in 1944 the party's leader in America, Earl Browder, dissolved the party and committed the movement to operate within the two-party system. In the 1944 campaign the communists endorsed President Franklin D. Roosevelt, though he repudiated their support.

With the breakup of the U.S.-Soviet alliance after World War II, the Communists reconstituted themselves as a political party. But they did not field their own candidate in 1948; instead they supported the left-wing Progressive Party candidacy of Henry Wallace, who had served as vice president during Roosevelt's third term (1941–1945). Communist Party activity then was limited in the Cold War period of the 1950s by restrictive federal and state legislation that virtually outlawed the party.

With the gradual easing of restrictive measures, the Communist Party resumed electoral activities in the late 1960s. In a policy statement written in 1966, the party described itself as "a revolutionary party whose aim is the fundamental transformation of society."

The party's appeal at the polls, however, continued to be minimal. Its presidential candidates in 1968, 1972, 1976, 1980, and 1984—the last year that they appeared on the ballot—each received less than one-tenth of 1 percent of the vote.

Compulsory Voting   *See* INTERNATIONAL AND U.S. ELECTIONS COMPARED

Congressional District

The 435 congressional DISTRICTS in the United States resemble a gigantic jigsaw puzzle. In fact, the dual processes of REAPPORTIONMENT AND REDISTRICTING—adjusting the districts after each ten-year CENSUS—have aptly been described as "jigsaw politics."

The districts come in all shapes and sizes. Some are rich, some are poor. Some are crowded, some are sparsely settled. Some in one area have little in common with those in another area, except that they are all the foundation blocks of the American system of representative DEMOCRACY.

Congressional districts have physical shapes, yet they are not about geography but about people. As such, the districts have been the subject of some of the most fiercely fought political battles in U.S. history. In politics, people mean votes, and votes mean power. And power is at the heart of more than two centuries of haggling over where the district lines are drawn to benefit this or that party, this or that rural or urban area, this or that racial group, and even this or that individual member of Congress.

Under the Constitution as interpreted since 1964 by the Supreme Court, each congressional district must be as nearly equal as possible in population to every other district in that state, based on the census population figures. This requirement ensures adherence to the principle of ONE PERSON, ONE VOTE. Computer technology has helped the states draw districts that meet the Court's rigid mathematical guidelines, which have become increasingly stringent.

This is something that state lawmakers in Pennsylvania learned the hard way after they redrew their congressional district map following the 2000 census. A federal district court ordered the map adjusted because of a population deviation that amounted to just nineteen people between the most and least populated districts—or an average of one person for each of the state's nineteen districts. Yet equality of population does not come close to telling the full story, here or elsewhere.

Debate still rages about the legality of political GERRYMANDERING, the artful drawing of district lines to benefit a particular party or candidate. Until 1986 the Supreme Court completely avoided this particular "political thicket," as famed Justice Felix Frankfurter referred to all judicial intervention in redistricting in a 1946 opinion. Jurists considered the use of redistricting for partisan purposes to be a matter for the elected branches, not the courts. And as the most recent decisions on this subject indicate, most still do.

In its 1986 ruling in the case of *Davis v. Bandemer,* which involved a highly partisan state legislative district map drawn by Indiana Republicans, the Court found that political gerrymandering is subject to constitutional review. The decision left the door ajar for the Court to determine in the future that a partisan gerrymander is so patently unfair that it constitutes an assault of the rights of voters to equal protection under the law.

But even as it made its ruling, the Court let stand the districting plan at issue in the case. Further, in the more than two decades since, the judiciary has resisted overruling legislative district maps on strictly partisan grounds, or setting standards for when an egregious gerrymander might exist.

In 1989 the Supreme Court refused to overturn what was widely regarded as a textbook example of political gerrymandering by Democrats in California. The district map, based on the 1980 census, "carefully stretched districts from one Democratic enclave to another—sometimes joining them with nothing but a bridge, a stretch of harbor, or a spit of land . . . avoiding Republicans block for block and household for household," according to one writer. By a 6–3 vote, the Court found that California Republicans had not proven a general pattern of exclusion from the political process.

In a more recent decision, involving the Pennsylvania congressional district map drawn by the Republican-controlled legislature following the 2000 census, a Court majority in *Vieth v. Jubeliler* (2004) let stand the principle expressed in *Davis v. Bandemer* that gerrymandering in principle could be a justiciable issue. At the same time, the Court rejected the claims by Democratic plaintiffs that the Pennsylvania map involved a violation of the Constitution.

The same reasoning was applied in a case brought by a variety of Texas plaintiffs, including Democratic activists, against a partisan Republican mid-decade redistricting enacted prior to the 2004 elections. The Supreme Court, ruling in the 2006 case of *League of United Latin American Citizens v. Perry,* denied the plaintiffs' effort to overturn the entire map as an egregious gerrymander.

The Court, however, did uphold the lead plaintiff's claim that the lines drawn for the Twenty-third Congressional District impeded the right of Hispanic voters to elect the candidate of their choice and ordered the district redrawn. The decision underscored the fact that there have been only two issues on which the Court has been willing to strike down redistricting plans: population inequality and discrimination based on race or ethnicity. (See RACIAL REDISTRICTING.)

District Characteristics

Equality of population within a state's districts has not erased the diversity of congressional districts in other respects or across state lines. The reapportionment of the 435 House seats based on state population according to the 2000 and 2010 census left seven states—Alaska, Delaware, Montana, North Dakota, South Dakota, Vermont, and Wyoming—with only the one seat they are guaranteed under the Constitution. The lone House member from Montana, the most populous of these single-district states, represented more than 989,000 people, more than any other member of Congress, based on the 2010 numbers. The Wyoming representative, though, had just over 563,000 constituents, fewer than any congressional district in any other state.

The state of Alaska is the largest congressional district, covering 570,374 square miles or just slightly more than one square mile for every one of the 710,231 Alaskans counted in the 2010 census. By contrast, urban districts in many states had much high density. Although the U.S. House is sometimes referred to as the "lower" chamber of Congress (erroneously because the House and Senate have equal legislative power), a representative in one state may have more constituents than a U.S. senator in another. Maine's two House members, for example, each represented about 664,000 people following the 2010 count—more than the entire population of Vermont or Wyoming.

Legislatures in mid-2011 were still drawing new district lines for the next decade but the results were expected to mirror the 2000 results, when the average district had about 650,000 residents, making congressional districts among the world's largest electoral units. To maintain a semblance of personal contact with so many constituents, virtually all House members maintain one or more district offices in addition to their Washington, D.C., offices. Most visit their district offices frequently and also keep in touch with their staff and constituents by telephone, radio and television, press releases, direct mail, and the Internet.

Shifts in 2000 and 2010

The reapportionment after the 2000 census continued a decades-long trend in which states of the South and the West with fast-growing populations gained seats at the expense of slower-growing states in the Northeast and upper Midwest. This trend continued after the 2010 census but at a slightly reduced pace.

There were no massive one-state gains in the 2000 or 2010 reapportionments, however, as there were after the 1990 census, when a population boom in California netted the nation's most populous state seven new seats. California in 2010 retained its fifty-three seats while Texas picked up four seats and Florida two. Ohio and New York each lost two seats, and a number of other states gained or lost one seat each. As a region, the West and Southwest picked up four seats and the South a net of seven seats. The Midwest and Northeast lost eleven seats. This continued a pattern evident since the end of World War II in the mid-1940s. Seven of the most populous northern states—New York, Pennsylvania, Illinois, Ohio, Michigan, New Jersey, and Massachusetts—went from 167 seats in the 1950 reapportionment to 114 following the 2010 census, a reduction of about a third.

Congressional Elections

Congressional elections are the world's oldest broadly popular elections. The House of Representatives was elected by POPULAR VOTE in 1788, forty years before most presidential electors were chosen that way. House elections have come to be considered a close second behind presidential elections in determining national political trends and in conferring legitimacy upon those who exercise political power in the United States. (See HOUSE OF REPRESENTATIVES, ELECTING; REALIGNMENTS AND DEALIGNMENTS.)

Although popular election of the Senate did not come until early in the twentieth century, the biennial House elections alone justify the claim that modern democratic popular elections originated with congressional elections. The American vote for House candidates in 1832 was higher than Britain's vote the same year in that country's parliamentary election, even though Britain had five times the U.S. population.

The first two congressional elections, in 1788 and 1790, confirmed popular willingness to give the new Constitution and national government a chance to function. The FEDERALISTS, supporters of President George Washington, won majorities in the House.

But 1792 was a premature modern election fought along party lines. Thomas Jefferson's DEMOCRATIC-REPUBLICANS (forerunners of today's Democrats), having organized on a national basis, were able to capture the House while Washington was reelected. The rise of the Democratic-Republicans to overwhelming majority power after 1800 caused popular interest to focus on factional contests for the presidency.

Nineteenth Century

Congressional elections were comparatively undramatic for the next three decades. The Federalists declined, and Democratic-Republicans held the presidency and both chambers of Congress from 1800 to 1840.

In 1824 the presidential election went to the House because no candidate won an electoral vote majority. The House elected John Quincy Adams, even though Andrew Jackson had led a four-way

The 1858 Illinois Senate race was the most important congressional race in U.S. history. The campaign debates between Democrat Stephen A. Douglas and Republican Abraham Lincoln became a national dialogue on slavery. These landmark debates have been reenacted over the years, as in Du Page County, Illinois, during the New Deal.

Source: Library of Congress

race. Jackson and his allies organized the modern DEMOCRATIC PARTY and made the 1826 MIDTERM ELECTION a referendum on the legitimacy of the Adams administration. The Jacksonians won. Jackson defeated Adams in 1828, and all future midterm congressional elections became in large part a referendum on the incumbent presidential administration.

In 1848 the WHIG PARTY—successors to Adams's NATIONAL REPUBLICAN PARTY as the leading opposition to the Democrats—lost Congress while succeeding for their second and last time in electing a war hero president, Zachary Taylor. (The first was William Henry Harrison, who was elected in 1840 but lived just a month after his inauguration in March 1841.) It was the only time between 1792 and 1956 that a president-elect's party failed to capture the House. The setback preordained the Whigs' disintegration over the slavery issue.

Although Democrats elected presidents in 1852 and 1856 on platforms of preserving the Union by attempting to compromise on the slavery issue, anti-Democratic "Free Soil" COALITIONS won the 1854 and 1858 midterm elections, choosing a Free Soil Speaker of the House both times after many ballots.

The Senate, elected for staggered terms by state legislatures, tended to be isolated from popular turmoil. It was more Democratic than the House from 1800 to 1860 and later tended to be more Republican than the House from 1860 to 1914, when popular election of senators began. (See DIRECT ELECTION and SENATE, ELECTING.)

But the 1858 Senate race in Illinois between Stephen A. Douglas, a Democratic leader of the Senate, and former representative Abraham Lincoln of the newly organized REPUBLICAN PARTY, became the single most important congressional race in American political history. The Lincoln-Douglas DEBATES turned into a national debate on the people's right to prevent the expansion of slavery into new territories. Lincoln won the popular vote, but Democrats gained a majority in the Illinois legislature, which reelected Douglas.

Civil War and Aftermath

In 1860 the Republicans, led by Lincoln, gained complete control of the national government and held it for fourteen years through the Civil War, Lincoln's assassination, and postwar Reconstruction. But from 1874 through 1890 the Democrats won every midterm House election on issues such as ending Reconstruction without guarantees of civil rights for newly freed blacks, civil service reform, low tariffs, and farm relief.

The Democrats took the presidency and Congress in 1892 for the first time since 1856, but they proved completely unable to handle an ensuing financial panic and farmers' revolt. The Republicans gained more House seats in 1894 than in any election until that time, and they held control of the government from 1896 to 1910.

But when the Progressive spirit of the age faltered within the Republican Party, it found a new home with the Democrats, who controlled the presidency and Congress from 1912 to 1918 and had the most successful reform administration (Woodrow Wilson's) since Lincoln's first term. The Progressive Era ended in bitterness and disillusionment after the United States' 1917–1918 participation in World War I. The Republicans regained control of Congress in 1918 and the White House with the election of Warren G. Harding in 1920, and the party's pro-business agenda suited the national mood during the "Roaring Twenties."

The nation's political balance then shifted dramatically, with long-term consequences. The Republicans were slow to respond to the stock market crash of 1929 that sparked an economic downturn and spiraled into the Great Depression. This enabled the Democrats, who in 1930 ran on a platform of relief, recovery, and reform, to win an overwhelming majority in the House

Democrat Franklin D. Roosevelt's presidential victory in 1932 helped the Democrats gain a majority in the Senate, which they held for fifty-two of the next sixty-two years. Here, Roosevelt addresses Congress in 1945.

Source: Library of Congress

that they would maintain—with two brief lapses (1947–1949, 1953–1955)—over the next sixty-four years. Democrat Franklin D. Roosevelt's 1932 presidential victory—the first of his unparalleled four White House wins—helped the Democrats gain an astounding ninety-seven seats and a majority in the Senate (which they held for fifty-two of the next sixty-two years). This ushered in a period of unprecedented federal intervention in the economy and growth of the federal bureaucracy.

The Postwar Years

After World War II the two parties became more competitive in presidential elections, but the Democrats remained dominant in Congress. In 1956 Republican Dwight D. Eisenhower was reelected president, but he also became the first presidential victor since 1848 to fail to carry his party to control of Congress.

In the postwar period the ideological conflicts of the 1930s, focused on the expansion of the federal government, were softened, and it was possible for the two major parties to argue more about means and less about basic national aims. The Republican Party essentially acquiesced to the continuation of much of Roosevelt's New Deal agenda that included welfare programs, Social Security, farm subsidies, and public housing. Both parties generally agreed on the policy of containing the expansionist tendencies of the communist Soviet Union during a period that became known as the Cold War. And for much of the 1950s, Democrats declined to object to Republican-led efforts to "root out" communist sympathizers in the United States.

Although they were more liberal as a whole, especially on economic issues, than the Republicans, the Democrats' strong hold on the House was predicated largely on a tenuous coalition that included not only liberals, ethnic and religious minorities, and organized labor, but also white southern conservatives whose continued solid support was based on historic antipathy toward the

Republican Party dating back to the Civil War. The fault lines that would ultimately reshape congressional politics by returning the Republican Party to competition were already evident. As Democrats embraced more liberal policies toward civil rights and continued to expand government, southern Democrats in the House became more inclined to align with Republicans in what for many years was known as the conservative coalition.

It was during the postwar era that both parties became truly national. Democrats extended their power and influence into the Midwest and northern New England, territory that had been unwaveringly Republican. Republicans made significant new breakthroughs in the growing industrial South and won the votes of millions of Americans who had never voted Republican before.

The 1964 elections, in which the Democrats captured most of the power centers from the presidency to the state legislatures, were such a huge success for the Democratic Party that some observers speculated that the Republican Party was doomed. Lyndon B. Johnson, who stepped up from the vice presidency upon John F. Kennedy's death in 1963, portrayed Republican challenger Barry Goldwater as an extremist and was elected with 61 percent of the vote; his coattails produced a thirty-eight-seat Democratic gain in the House for a total of 295 seats and a two-seat Senate gain for sixty-eight seats. The Democrats at this point were more dominant in Congress than they had been since the early years of the Franklin Roosevelt era.

Many Republicans, noting the somber outcome of an election in which their party had moved far to the right and by implication had repudiated the national stance on most matters, began to work to return the party to a centrist course. In addition, the party began to make inroads into the South as southern white conservatives began to leave the Democratic Party over Johnson's adoption of the civil rights movement and the national party's increasingly liberal trend. The seeds of change planted in 1964, although they took years to germinate fully, served as the basis for a Republican revival in the late twentieth century.

Protests against the Vietnam War, such as this one in 1967, contributed to the weakening of the Democratic Party.
Source: LBJ Library photo by Frank Wolfe

The Vietnam War Years

The 1960s and 1970s were among the most turbulent decades in the nation's history. With the Vietnam War, urban riots, and the rise of the baby boom generation, the seeds of great upheavals already were sprouting before President John F. Kennedy's assassination in November 1963.

The year 1965 saw the last major burst of legislative accomplishments and national optimism for some time.

With the large majorities created by the Johnson landslide, the Democratic Congress enacted federal aid to education, a national health insurance program for the elderly (Medicare) and for the poor (Medicaid), and the VOTING RIGHTS ACT. But the Johnson administration's fortunes soon changed. The decision to commit massive American ground forces to Vietnam resulted in increased opposition to the war, stimulating student and racial unrest. Blacks, unsatisfied with their progress in American society, burst forth in anger and rioted in American cities. The Rev. Martin Luther King Jr., the civil rights leader, and New York senator Robert F. Kennedy, brother of the slain president, were assassinated in 1968.

The Democratic Party coalition broke apart under these strains, and Republican Richard Nixon was elected president. The Democrats kept control of Congress, however, and Nixon, like Johnson, had to deal with antiwar demonstrations. His gradual withdrawal of American troops, climaxing with the peace settlement of January 1973, finally removed the war from the top of the American political agenda.

But the nation was promptly hit by a fresh series of calamities, including an oil crisis and steep inflation. Throughout 1973 and 1974 the Watergate SCANDAL implicated several top public officials, including the president, in illegal activities. The immediate result was Nixon's resignation, the first presidential resignation in U.S. history. This was followed by a forty-three-seat gain for the House Democrats (to a total of 291) in the 1974 midterm elections. Deeper ramifications could be found in the American people's weakening of confidence in their government and leaders, which ultimately would benefit an increasingly conservative Republican Party that identified "big government" as the source of many of the nation's difficulties.

After Nixon's resignation, Vice President Gerald R. Ford became president. With his low-key personality and image of personal integrity, Ford helped calm the country after these misfortunes. But he was not seen by many as a strong leader, and by 1977 the Democrats again had control of the White House as well as both chambers of Congress.

Years of Uneasy Peace

In large part the 1976 presidential victory of Democratic political outsider Jimmy Carter, a former governor of Georgia, stemmed from the voters' weariness with the usual political leadership of the country and their search for a new start. But however great the hopes, Carter soon became embroiled in national problems and Washington politics. Even with a Congress controlled by his own Democratic Party, Carter was unable to push through much of his legislative program.

By mid-1979 few were optimistic that the energy shortages and double-digit inflation would be resolved any time soon. In November 1979 the nation's confidence was shaken further when Iranian militants seized the U.S. Embassy in Tehran, taking Americans hostage. The crisis cast a pall over the remainder of Carter's term, ending when the hostages were released just minutes after conservative Republican Ronald Reagan was inaugurated in 1981 to replace Carter.

In 1984 Ronald Reagan was reelected in a landslide, but two years later the GOP lost control of the Senate as the president's conservative agenda lost momentum. Here, Reagan delivers his acceptance speech at the national convention in August 1984.

Source: Ronald Reagan Library

Besides sweeping Carter from office in 1980, Reagan provided COATTAILS for a Republican takeover of the Senate and became the first GOP president since Eisenhower to have his party in the majority in either chamber of Congress. Democrats remained in control of the House, although a thirty-three-seat Republican gain winnowed their majority to 243 seats. The Democrats gained twenty-six seats back in the 1982 midterm elections, abetted by recession, and continued to make small gains through 1990, spurring talk that they had achieved a permanent majority in the House.

By 1984 the economy had rebounded, and Reagan was reelected in a landslide. Nevertheless, the GOP lost control of the Senate in the 1986 midterm elections. The party's prospects that year were damaged by the waning momentum of Reagan's conservative agenda, combined with economic problems in the farm economy that hurt Republican candidates in some states where they usually prospered. Just after the elections, a major White House scandal came to light, involving the sale of arms to Iran in an attempt to free American hostages in Lebanon and the illegal siphoning of the sale proceeds to help the contra guerrillas in Nicaragua.

While in office, Reagan took a hard-line approach to the Cold War with the Soviet Union and the nuclear arms race. By the time he left, he had become a strong supporter of superpower disarmament, welcoming the U.S.-Soviet summitry he had once disdained. The general popularity he maintained through the end of his presidency carried over to his vice president, George H. W. Bush, who was elected to the Oval Office with a comfortable margin in 1988.

The End of the Cold War

In the early 1990s the world watched as, one by one, the countries of the Warsaw Pact broke away from the Soviet Union to turn toward democracy and market economies and then as the Soviet Union itself broke apart. Seemingly overnight, the superpower rivalry that had dominated U.S. defense and foreign policy—and influenced presidential and congressional elections—for nearly half a century was over.

During the Cold War, the electorate as a whole seemed more comfortable putting Republicans in the White House to handle the defense and foreign policy issues of the nation. At the same time, the voters consistently elected Democratic majorities in Congress who could be counted on to create and sustain popular domestic programs.

When the Cold War ended in 1991, national security seemed less salient as an issue—as George H. W. Bush was to learn when he lost his bid for reelection to former Vietnam War protester Bill Clinton in 1992.

End of an Era in the House

The Democrats' confidence—or overconfidence—in their decades of congressional dominance made their fall from power in 1994, just two years after Clinton had ended the twelve-year Reagan-Bush Republican hold on the White House, all the more stunning.

There were several major ingredients to the stew the Democrats found themselves in as the 1994 midterm elections approached. Although Clinton was elected in 1992 with just 43 percent of the popular vote and a 5 percentage-point margin over Bush in an election marked by the strong independent candidacy of businessman H. Ross Perot, he declared a mandate for an activist agenda. He was not able to push most of his proposed reforms, including an overhaul of the nation's health care system, through the Democratic-controlled Congress.

Meanwhile, Republicans, particularly in 1992, had picked up House seats in the South, where the party had been excelling for years in presidential elections, abetted by favorable redistricting plans and the retirement of many southern Democrats that provided the GOP with opportunities in districts with conservative-leaning constituencies. A series of corruption scandals in the late 1980s and early 1990s tarnished the Democratic-controlled Congress's image and handed a political bludgeon to a new generation of aggressively conservative and partisan Republican leaders, including Newt Gingrich of Georgia, a future House Speaker, and Tom DeLay of Texas, a future majority leader.

Running on a conservative campaign platform called the "Contract with America," Republicans in 1994 gained eight seats in the Senate to take control of that chamber and, perhaps more significantly, added fifty-two seats in the House to break the Democrats' forty-year lock on that chamber.

With Clinton and the Democrats on the defensive, the Gingrich-led Republicans pursued an agenda of reductions in taxes, federal program spending, and government regulation and gave social-issue conservatives more prominence than had the Democrats. But the combative nature of the relationship between GOP House leaders and the White House sparked partisan confrontations, including one that resulted in a brief shutdown of much of the federal government.

In the 1994 midterm elections, Republicans gained eight seats in the Senate and fifty-two seats in the House, taking control of both chambers. Here, future House Speaker Newt Gingrich of Georgia, left, and incoming Senate Majority Leader Bob Dole meet reporters on December 2, 1994.

Source: AP Images/John Duricka

Clinton won reelection in 1996, though his short coattails limited Democrats to a three-seat House gain, leaving Republicans in control of both houses of Congress in what seemed to be a deliberate affirmation by voters of divided government. As a result, Clinton became the first Democratic president reelected without carrying either chamber of Congress for his party.

The more surprising results came in 1998, when Clinton was embroiled in the humiliating and career-threatening scandal stemming from his extramarital sexual relationship with a former White House intern, Monica Lewinsky. Even under less difficult circumstances, second midterm elections tend to be difficult for the party holding the White House; the scandal appeared to have the Democrats heading into a political abyss. House Republicans doggedly pursued Clinton for lying under oath to a federal jury about his affair and impeached the president (who was acquitted in his Senate trial). (See REMOVAL FROM OFFICE.) However, in their zeal, House Republicans managed mainly to alienate voters, who disapproved of Clinton's personal behavior but still gave him strongly positive job approval ratings during a period of economic growth and relative peace around the world. These voters provided the Democrats with a token five-seat gain that November—a poor result for the Republicans that prompted Gingrich to resign his seat.

George W. Bush's narrow and controversial presidential victory in 2000 and the Republicans' maintenance of their majorities in Congress gave the GOP lawmakers a Republican White House to work with for the first time. Bush was able to achieve quick enactment of some major policy priorities, including an education policy overhaul and the largest tax cuts seen in years. Matters were complicated, however, in June 2001 when longtime Republican senator James Jeffords of Vermont became an independent and threw his support to the Democrats, giving them a 51–49 advantage that they would maintain for eighteen months.

The political landscape changed dramatically after the September 11, 2001, terrorist attacks, initially to the advantage of Bush, who received strong public approval ratings for his assertive declaration of a "war on terror." During Bush's first term, Congress helped him enact the antiterrorism surveillance law known as the USA PATRIOT Act, a prescription drug benefit package under Medicare shaped to Bush's specifications, and a fateful resolution passed in October 2002 that authorized the president to employ military force to oust Saddam Hussein's dictatorial regime in Iraq.

Republicans in Congress saw their standing rise because most voters saw them as the more stalwart party on national security issues. In the 2002 elections, Democratic candidates tried to blame Republicans for the sluggish economy, but the public focused on terrorist threats and a possible war with Iraq. Republicans picked up six seats in the House and captured two Senate seats, taking control of that chamber by a narrow 51–49 margin.

Bush was reelected in 2004, and the Republicans again made small gains in the House. House majority leader Tom DeLay was quoted discussing the dawn of a permanent Republican majority— which quickly turned into a prediction as flawed as the Democrats' when they were in charge in the early 1990s. Ethics controversies and corruption scandals erupted in the lead-up to the 2006 midterm elections. Hardest hit were House Republicans, many of whom had built close relationships with business lobbyists during their decade in power. One of the first victims was DeLay, whose eroded political standing spurred him to resign from the House in 2006. Meanwhile, Bush's approval ratings plummeted following his 2004 victory, largely because of the devolution of the war in Iraq into a long-term commitment that was far deadlier and more expensive than the public initially had been led to expect.

Democrats Surge in 2006 and 2008; Republicans in 2010

The conditions in 2006 were ripe for a Democratic comeback: the once-dominant party returned to power with a thirty-seat House gain for a total of 233 seats (and a six-seat Senate gain that also gave the Democrats a narrow majority in that chamber).

The January 4, 2007, convening of the 110th Congress brought an event of historic significance: Rep. Nancy Pelosi of California was elected by her Democratic colleagues as the first woman to serve as Speaker of the House. It was the best showing for Democrats since the 1974 elections.

In 2008, with the liberal base energized over the presidential candidacy of Barack Obama, Democrats padded their majorities by adding twenty-four House seats and eight Senate seats. This gave them majorities of 257–178 in the House and, with the support of two independents, 59–41 in the Senate. The Democratic triumphs were especially impressive in New England, where they held every House seat, and in southern states such as Virginia and North Carolina, where an influx of northern residents helped provide winning margins to moderate Democratic Senate candidates. Democrats also ran strongly in several western states such as Colorado and New Mexico, where they picked up both House and Senate seats. With Obama winning the presidential race, Democrats controlled the White House and both chambers of Congress for the first time since 1994.

Nevertheless, incumbents in 2008 won reelection at a high rate. In the House 94.3 percent seeking reelection won; in the Senate 83.3 percent won after five of thirty incumbents were defeated. The 111th Congress began with nine new senators and fifty-five new representatives. With several appointments following resignations of senators who joined Obama's cabinet, plus Obama and his running mate Sen. Joseph R. Biden Jr., of Delaware, the 111th Congress got underway with fourteen new senators.

But two years later, voters in the 2010 midterm elections turned against Democrats with a vengeance. In the House, Republicans had a net gain of sixty-three seats and regained control of the chamber by a margin of 242 to 193. In the Senate the GOP gained six seats, shy of the number needed to regain the majority.

Between the two chambers, the 2010 elections brought in 100 freshmen who had never before served in Congress: ninety-one in the House and nine in the Senate. Twelve other victors had served in earlier Congresses or were in the House in 2010 when they won Senate seats starting in 2011.

Most of the influx came in the House: ninety-six new House members (about one-fifth of the membership) were elected in 2010, including five who had served in earlier congresses before losing their seats.

As a result, the reelection rate in 2010 for House members seeking to stay in office plummeted to 86.3 percent, from 94.3 percent two years earlier. This election was the first since 1992 in which the rate dropped below 90 percent and only the eighth time in the sixty-five years since the 1946 elections after World War II. The influx of new members brought down the average length of representatives at the beginning of the 112th Congress to 9.8 years, a little below the 10.3 years of the previous Congress, according to an examination of the 112th Congress by the Congressional Research Service.

The GOP's less dramatic gains in the Senate brought the Democratic majority to 53–47, down from 59–41 before the election. That was a reelection rate of 84 percent, about the same as two years earlier. The average length of service in that chamber in 2011 was 11.4 years; in the previous Congress it was 13.4 years, according to the CRS study.

The 2010 outcome continued a volatile period in American politics that dated, some observers thought, to 1992 when an independent candidate for president, H. Ross Perot, garnered nearly 20 percent of the vote, the largest share since 1912 when Republican Teddy Roosevelt, estranged from his party, ran on a separate ticket known as the Bull Moose Party.

The latter years of the 2000s were especially volatile as the economy—both within the United States and globally—all but crashed, producing the worst recession since the Great Depression in the 1930s. The result was a soaring unemployment rate—still about 9 percent in 2011—and the expenditure of substantial sums of money by the federal government to keep the economy from getting worse and trying to get it moving again.

Federal actions, started under Republican George W. Bush and expanded under Democrat Barack Obama, included significant financial support for banks and Wall Street investment houses, financial rescue of the auto industry, enactment of multibillion dollar stimulus programs, passage of new financial regulation reforms, and efforts to revitalize the collapsed national housing market. To these crises was added voter fatigue over two continuing wars throughout the decade, in Iraq and Afghanistan.

After Obama's election, Democrats, over nearly unwavering Republican opposition, enacted a sweeping and deeply controversial overhaul of the nation's health system, including a requirement that all citizens purchase health insurance.

All of this coalesced into ever more volatile anger among increasing numbers of voters. The anger was captured most prominently by the emergence of a movement that became known as the Tea Party. Not really a political party, it was rather a movement of largely conservative voters, many of them in retirement years and relatively financially comfortable, who informally aligned with Republicans but in their forceful denunciation of the federal government and its controlling Democratic majority brought to the 2010 elections an energy that resembled, at the other end of the political spectrum, the energy of Democrats who carried Obama into the White House two years earlier.

The anger propelling Tea Party adherents, prompted in particular by passage of the health care legislation, reinforced other widespread voter discontent over the continual bad economic news that kept unemployment high and the housing market in the ditch.

The electoral result was the sweeping Republican gains in 2010 and particularly the about-face done by voters who considered themselves independent rather than aligned with either major party. Strongly supportive of Obama and fellow Democrats in 2008, the independent vote flipped in 2010 and backed Republicans over Democrats by a 56 percent to 38 percent margin.

Conservative *See* IDEOLOGY

Conservative Party of New York *See* THIRD PARTIES

Constituency

The people who elect a government official make up his or her constituency. They may be all the people of the United States, in the case of the president; or they may be the residents of a small community, in the case of a town council member.

Constituency service is an important aspect of elective office, especially in lawmaking bodies such as Congress or a state legislature. Most constituents are voters, and legislators who ignore the voters do so at their own peril.

The high reelection rates of incumbents indicate that few officeholders neglect the needs of their constituents. Well over 90 percent of U.S. representatives typically win reelection, many with more than 60 percent of the vote. Senators and other incumbents also usually win if they seek reelection. (See INCUMBENCY.)

Caseworkers make up a large part of congressional staffs. They help constituents obtain Social Security and veterans' benefits, navigate through the bureaucratic maze for various problems, appeal decisions of executive agencies, and do all manner of other favors for the people they serve.

Keeping in touch with their constituents is something many lawmakers feel is too important to be left entirely to their staffs. All members of Congress have offices in their state or DISTRICT, as well as in Washington. Many return home every weekend and frequently schedule "town meetings" to hear what is on constituents' minds.

Political scientist Richard F. Fenno Jr. observed that the "home styles" of House members in their districts often differ from their styles at work in Washington. The differences stem from the contrast in the lawmakers' minds between their geographic constituency and their personal constituency of loyalists, supporters, and intimates. To deal successfully with the different constituencies, House members devise styles suited for each one.

Although civil service and other restrictions on FEDERAL WORKERS have limited the government jobs that members of Congress can dispense, patronage remains an important service they can provide. But today the jobs are less likely to be on the government payroll than they are to be supplied indirectly through a large defense contract or public works project in the state or district.

Congress's ability to award so-called pork barrel projects to favored regions was jeopardized for a time in the 1990s by a law giving President Bill Clinton the authority to veto individual items in appropriations bills. But the Supreme Court invalidated the line-item veto as an unwarranted delegation of Congress's own powers under the Constitution. In 2006 billions of dollars of earmarks—or designated spending for specific local projects, often in the districts and states of senior or otherwise well-placed lawmakers—became a key issue in the Democrats' successful efforts to wrest control of both chambers of Congress from the Republicans.

The results of the 2006 elections also proved the limitations of the "all politics is local" philosophy, which is treated as political gospel by some party strategists. While reminding voters of the government funds and other benefits that they have been able to obtain for their constituents is usually a winning strategy for incumbents, 2006 was one of those years in which broader national and international concerns—including the war in Iraq, economic distress, dismay over the fumbled federal response to the devastation inflicted on the Gulf Coast by Hurricane Katrina in 2005, and concerns over a series of embarrassing ethics scandals involving Republican members of Congress—had a stronger influence over voters' decisions. The same pattern was seen in 2008, when the nation—and the world—had plunged into the most serious economic slump in half a century. It continued into 2010 with continued high unemployment, an economy still in the doldrums, a continuing housing crisis with thousands of homes going into foreclosure, and stark political controversies over the Obama administration's legislative program that included large and complex health care and financial regulation reforms.

Constitutional Union Party (1860)

The short-lived Constitutional Union Party was formed in 1859 in the hope of heading off a Civil War over slavery. The party's founders sought compromise positions to promote national conciliation in the face of rampant sectionalism, which included southern states' threats of secession.

The party appealed to conservative remnants of the American (Know-Nothing) and Whig parties, who viewed preservation of the Union as their primary goal and secondary to other concerns, including the divisive issue of slavery.

The Constitutional Union Party held its first and only national convention in Baltimore in May 1860. For president the party nominated John Bell of Tennessee, a former senator and Speaker of the House of Representatives, who previously had been both a Democrat and a Whig. The convention adopted a short platform, which intentionally avoided controversial subjects, most notably slavery. Instead, the platform simply urged support for "the Constitution, the Union and the Laws."

In the fall election, Bell received 590,901 votes (12.6 percent of the popular vote) and won Kentucky, Tennessee, and Virginia, known then and now as southern BORDER STATES. The Bell ticket finished last in the four-way presidential race, however; together with the sectional split in the Democratic Party, it was a prominent factor in the victory of Republican Abraham Lincoln. In the

More on this topic:

Border States, p. 34

months after the 1860 election, the Constitutional Union Party continued to urge national conciliation, but with the outbreak of the Civil War the party disappeared.

Constitution Party (U.S. Taxpayers Party) (1992–)

The Constitution Party, founded in 1992 as the U.S. Taxpayers Party, is most closely identified with the organizing efforts of Howard Phillips, a former Republican who served in the administration of President Richard M. Nixon but quit the party in the early 1970s because he believed it had failed to adhere to strict conservative principles.

Phillips was director of the Office of Economic Opportunity in the Nixon White House, but he did not share the agenda of expanded federal intervention voiced by Democrats who previously held the position. He quit the position, according to the Conservative Caucus website, because "Nixon reneged on his commitment to veto further funding for 'Great Society' programs" put in place in the 1960s by Democratic President Lyndon B. Johnson.

> **"The mission of the Constitution Party is to secure the blessings of liberty to ourselves and our posterity through the election, at all levels of government, of Constitution Party candidates who will uphold the principles of the Declaration of Independence and the Constitution of the United States. It is our goal to limit the federal government to its delegated, enumerated, Constitutional functions and to restore American jurisprudence to its original Biblical common-law foundations."**
>
> —Constitution Party mission statement as published on the party's website, February 2007

Phillips was part of a group of prominent conservatives that tried but failed in 1972 to take control of the American Independent Party, which conservative firebrand George Wallace of Alabama had created as the vehicle for his 1968 third-party presidential bid. Phillips subsequently founded in 1974 the Conservative Caucus, which took a hard-line conservative approach to the major debates of the ensuing decades. As of early 2007, he continued to serve as the organization's chairman.

Ronald Reagan's election to two terms in the White House on a conservative platform quelled some activist dissent toward the direction of the Republican Party, but it revived when George H. W. Bush, never a favorite of "movement" conservatives, succeeded Reagan. Fueled by anger over a broken "no new taxes" pledge Bush made in his 1988 speech accepting the Republican presidential nomination, Phillips and his allies founded the U.S. Taxpayers Party. After failing to persuade a big-name conservative icon such as Patrick J. Buchanan, Oliver North, or Jesse Helms to run on the party line, Phillips became the party's 1992 presidential nominee. Appearing on the ballot in twenty-two states and receiving at least a scattering of write-in votes from seven others, Phillips took 43,434 votes out of the more than 104 million cast as Democrat Bill Clinton unseated Bush.

Running again as the nominee in 1996, Phillips was listed on ballots in forty-two states and received votes in all but two. His total improved to 184,658 votes of more than 96 million cast as Clinton won reelection.

Phillips was the party's nominee once more in 2000—the first election under the new Constitution Party banner—but took roughly half the votes (98,020) that he had four years earlier. Republican George W. Bush, running on a more strongly conservative agenda than did his father, the former president, won a narrow and controversial electoral vote victory to claim the Oval Office.

In 2004 the Constitution Party nominated a new candidate, Michael Peroutka. Peroutka still received only a fraction of the national vote, but he bumped the party's total up to 143,630 despite failing to meet ballot access requirements in seven states.

Despite its distinctly minority status in national politics, the Constitution Party has made some local advances in areas of the nation with strongly conservative constituencies. Rick Jore's election to the Montana house in 2006 made him the first Constitution Party candidate to win a state legislative seat.

Contested Elections

"Every Vote Counts" is a slogan repeated over the years by those trying to persuade reluctant or unmotivated voters to go to the polls. These voters often believe that an individual's vote does not make a difference. Yet once in a while elections are so close that a few votes one way or the other could change the outcomes, and these instances are the ones that voter mobilization activists highlight in their campaigns to GET OUT THE VOTE. (See VOTER TURNOUT.)

In such tight races, the results are frequently contested by the candidate initially declared the loser. Most—but not all—such challenges fail.

Challenges may be based on allegations that elections officials or VOTING MACHINES mistabulated the ballots or on charges of election fraud, which could result in a change in the result if enough ballots were invalidated. Absentee voting may be the deciding factor in a close vote, and the counting of those ballots may take days or weeks as the disputants and their lawyers pore over each vote.

The most spectacular example of a contested election in recent years was the 2000 presidential vote in Florida that decided the national election in favor of Republican candidate George W. Bush. Democratic nominee Al Gore's allegations of irregularities and undercounts of votes cast on paper punch-card ballots resulted in a series of recounts, rulings by state officials, and court cases that ended five weeks after election day with a 5–4 Supreme Court ruling in BUSH V. GORE that effectively decided the election in Bush's favor.

The 2004 governor's race in the state of Washington produced a dramatic contested election and a rare example of the initial election result in a major race being reversed. After a protracted series of recounts, Democratic nominee Christine Gregoire, who trailed Republican candidate Dino Rossi by a razor-thin margin in the initial count, ended up winning by a similarly thin margin.

Before calling for a recount, candidates must consider the consequences of pursuing a challenge to the election results—and failing—on their future political careers. In 2000 Republicans mocked the Democratic ticket of Gore and Sen. Joseph I. Lieberman of Connecticut as "Sore Loserman" during the Florida recount battle.

In 2006 Republican senator George Allen of Virginia had the legal right under state law to demand a recount: Democratic challenger Jim Webb's victory margin was just less than 9,000 votes of the more than 2.3 million cast. Allen declined to contest the results, even though Webb's upset win clinched the Democrats' takeover of the Senate in the ensuing Congress. Many observers speculated that Allen's decision to forgo a recount was influenced by his hopes for a future comeback in a race for the Senate or for governor.

Although the two-party system and the ELECTORAL COLLEGE almost guarantee that every president and vice president can claim an electoral vote majority, eighteen presidents have been elected with less than 50 percent of the POPULAR VOTE, including Democrat Bill Clinton in both 1992 and 1996. Four of those eighteen presidents actually lost the popular vote, including Bush in 2000.

Other presidents attained a slight majority, including Democrat John F. Kennedy in 1960, but won by such slim margins that a few thousand votes' difference in four or five pivotal states could have changed the result. The 1968 and 1976 elections also were in that category.

To resolve the disputed returns in the presidential election of 1876, Congress created an electoral commission, shown here deliberating by candlelight. Made up of five senators, five House members, and five Supreme Court justices, the commission voted 8–7 to give Republican candidate Rutherford B. Hayes the disputed electoral votes.

Source: Library of Congress

In 1960 the vote was 34.2 million for Kennedy and 34.1 million for Richard Nixon, a margin of about one-tenth of 1 percentage point or 115,000 votes. It was so close that Nixon delayed his concession until the afternoon of the next day. But after considering the option during a vacation, Nixon decided against demanding a recount, saying it would take "at least a year and a half" and would throw the federal government into turmoil. Some Republicans in 2000 contrasted Nixon's actions with those of Gore in demanding that the Democrat, likewise, concede to Bush.

Below the presidential level, contested elections are commonplace. The House and Senate, invoking their constitutional authority to judge the qualifications and elections of their own members, have settled hundreds of contested elections—usually in favor of the candidate of the party in power. In recent years, however, such actions, which have the inherent potential to exacerbate partisan tensions, have been few and far between.

The House, with 435 elections every two years, is governed in elections disputes by the Federal Contested Election Act of 1969. The act defines candidates as those listed on the ballot or as bona fide WRITE-IN candidates, thereby eliminating challenges from most candidates denied BALLOT ACCESS by their state. PRIMARY elections are not covered by the act. The Senate, which elects one-third of its one hundred members every two years, has no comparable legislation.

Tightened federal and state laws have reduced the likelihood of vote fraud as a factor in close elections. More recent cases of contested elections have centered on racial and ethnic bias rather than outright fraud as a possible distorting factor.

President

Only twice in U.S. history have popular vote irregularities been at the heart of a contested presidential election. The first time was in the race between Republican Rutherford B. Hayes of Ohio and Democrat Samuel J. Tilden of New York in 1876. The dispute centered on rival sets of electoral votes that resulted from popular vote controversies in three southern states.

Tilden won the popular vote, 4.3 million or 51 percent to Hayes's 4.0 million or 49 percent. By the following morning, however, it became apparent that if the Republicans could hold South Carolina, Florida, and Louisiana, Hayes would be elected with 185 electoral votes to 184 for Tilden. But if a single elector in any of these states voted for Tilden, the vote would throw the election to the Democrats. Passions on both sides were so high some feared a new civil war.

Popular vote tallies in all three states—where Reconstruction-era policies imposed after the South's surrender in 1865 were still in effect—were called into question, intensifying the situation. As historian Eugene H. Roseboom described the circumstances, with references to the "carpetbagger" Republicans who came from the North,

> The Republicans controlled the state governments and the election machinery, had relied upon the Negro masses for votes, and had practiced frauds as in the past. The Democrats used threats, intimidation, and even violence when necessary, to keep Negroes from the polls; and where they were in a position to do so they resorted to fraud also. The firm determination of the whites to overthrow carpetbag rule contributed to make a full and fair vote impossible; carpetbag hold on the state governments made a fair count impossible. Radical reconstruction was reaping its final harvest.

Both parties pursued the votes of the three states with little regard for propriety or legality, and in the end all three states sent double sets of elector returns to Congress. The Constitution gives no guidance on what to do in such cases.

Between 1865 and 1876 Congress had a Republican-sponsored rule—the Twenty-second Joint Rule—that might have helped resolve the Hayes-Tilden dispute. It provided that when Congress met in joint session to count electoral votes, no votes objected to could be counted except by the concurrent votes of both the Senate and House. The rule had lapsed at the beginning of 1876, however, when the Senate refused to readopt it because the House was in Democratic control. Had the Twenty-second Joint Rule remained in effect, the Democratic House could have objected to any of Hayes's disputed votes. Instead, Congress had to find some new method of resolving electoral disputes.

It created a joint committee to work out a plan, resulting in the Electoral Commission Law of 1877, which applied only to the 1876 electoral vote count. The law established a fifteen-member commission made up of five senators (three majority-party Republicans and two minority Democrats), five representatives (three majority, two minority), and five Supreme Court justices (two from each party and one independent). Because the independent justice was appointed to a Senate seat, he disqualified himself, and the Democrats accepted a Republican they regarded as somewhat independent. He voted with the Republicans on every dispute, however, ensuring Hayes's victory.

A Democratic threat to block the month-long count until after Inauguration Day, then March 4, was not carried out because of an agreement reached between the Hayes forces and southern Democrats. The southerners agreed to let the electoral count continue without obstruction. In return Hayes agreed that, as president, he would withdraw federal troops from the South, end Reconstruction, and make other concessions. The southerners, for their part, pledged to respect black rights, a pledge they did not carry out.

The compromise enabled the Senate president to announce at 4:00 a.m. on March 2, 1877, that Hayes had been elected president with 185 electoral votes, as against 184 for Tilden. Because March 4 fell on a Sunday, Hayes was sworn in privately at the White House. His formal inauguration followed on Monday. The country acquiesced, ending the crisis that brought the nation to the brink of domestic upheaval.

In 1887 Congress enacted permanent legislation on the handling of disputed electoral votes. The Electoral Count Act of that year gave each state final authority in determining the legality of its choice of electors and required a concurrent majority of both the Senate and House to reject any electoral votes. It also established procedures for counting electoral votes in Congress.

A Florida newspaper, the Orlando Sentinel, *put out four election editions on Wednesday, November 8, 2000, the day after the presidential election. The headlines reflect the confusion as to who had won the state's crucial twenty-five electoral votes.*

Source: AP Images/Peter Cosgrove

That 1887 law came into play for the first time in the election of 2000. Neither Republican George W. Bush nor Democrat Gore could reach 270 electoral votes without Florida's 25. Bush stood at 246 without Florida, and Gore at 267. When the polls closed on November 7, Bush enjoyed a 1,725-vote margin in Florida. An initial recount cut the lead to 930 votes, and subsequent recounts narrowed the difference to 537.

In early December the vote count was still the subject of litigation. Democrats filed a number of suits in a variety of venues to dispute various aspects of the vote tabulation. Successful in requesting hand recounting of ballots in some Florida counties, Democrats filed suit to force populous Miami-Dade and Palm Beach counties to recount theirs and also filed suit to force Florida's secretary of state, the state's top elections official, to extend the deadline for certifying the results beyond December 12, in order to allow more time for recounts. Another suit, brought by a pro-Democratic private citizen, sought to have absentee ballots thrown out in two Florida counties because applications for many of the absentee ballots had lacked voter identification numbers, and Republican Party operatives had added the numbers, in violation of the law. The crux of that case was whether disfranchisement of all absentee voters in those counties was a fair and legal remedy.

Fearing that all of this time-consuming litigation would deny Florida its vote in the Electoral College, and fearing that its outcome might deny the election to Bush, the Republican-dominated Florida legislature called a special session for the express purpose of certifying a pro-Bush slate of electors. Congress, meanwhile, began researching its options for dealing with the crisis.

The Gore campaign won a major victory when the Florida Supreme Court on December 8 ordered a statewide recount of contested ballots. But the Bush campaign appealed to the U.S. Supreme Court, which on December 9 ordered a temporary halt to the recount pending a full hearing of the appeal. On December 12 the Court issued a 5–4 ruling in *Bush v. Gore* that effectively ended the recounts in Florida, thus handing the state's twenty-five electoral votes and the election to Bush.

Nationwide, the vote was almost as close as in Florida: Gore led Bush by approximately 540,000 votes out of the roughly 105 million cast.

Senate

The closest Senate election since 1913, when DIRECT ELECTION of senators began, was the 1974 New Hampshire contest between Republican Louis C. Wyman and Democrat John A. Durkin. In the initial tally Wyman held a slight lead over Durkin, who contested the result.

After two recounts the state's final tally showed Wyman the winner by only two votes, 110,926 to 110,924 for Durkin, who had led the first recount by ten votes. Durkin then challenged Wyman's right to the seat that had been left open by retiring Republican Norris H. Cotton. After seven months of wrangling and forty-one roll-call votes, the Senate for the first time declared itself unable to decide an election contest. It declared the seat vacant and Durkin asked for a new election, which was held September 16, 1975.

Durkin easily won the rerun with 140,788 votes to Wyman's 113,007. Meanwhile, retired senator Cotton had returned briefly (August 8–September 18, 1975) to his old seat as an interim appointee pending the results of the special election.

An even longer dispute over a Senate election ended in October 1997 when the Senate Rules and Administration Committee concluded it had no grounds to overturn the election of Louisiana Democrat Mary L. Landrieu. Her Republican opponent, Louis "Woody" Jenkins, had contested the election held eleven months earlier.

Jenkins asked the Senate to unseat Landrieu and order a new election because of what he called widespread vote fraud, including vote buying and multiple voting. But by a bipartisan 16–0 vote, the Republican-controlled committee said it had "not found a cumulative body of evidence of fraud, irregularities or other errors." No further Senate action was needed to end the investigation.

The action was consistent with most of the approximately 100 contested elections judged by the Senate in its history. In only nine cases, including Wyman-Durkin, had the Senate denied a seat to the state-certified winner. Louisiana's Republican governor Mike Foster had certified Landrieu the winner by a 5,788-vote margin out of 1.5 million votes cast.

The Supreme Court has ruled only once on whether a state law can interfere with Congress's constitutional right to judge the election returns of its own members. *Roudebush v. Hartke* (1972) concerned a Senate election dispute between Republican challenger Richard L. Roudebush and Democratic incumbent Vance Hartke of Indiana. Hartke won but tried to block a recount sought by Roudebush. The Court ruled that the state recount, which did not change the result, "does not prevent the Senate from independently evaluating the election any more than the initial count does. The Senate is free to accept or reject the apparent winner in either count, and, if it chooses, to conduct its own recount."

House

In 1965 the House settled an unusual challenge to the election of the so-called Mississippi Five, four Democrats and one Republican certified as winners in 1964. The Democrats were Thomas G. Abernethy, William M. Colmer, Jamie L. Whitten, and John Bell Williams. The Republican was Prentiss Walker.

Their right to be seated was contested by a biracial group, the Mississippi Freedom Democratic Party, originally formed to challenge the seating of the state's all-white delegation to the Democrats' 1964 NATIONAL PARTY CONVENTION. Unsuccessful in getting its candidates on that year's congressional ballot, the group conducted a rump election in which Annie Devine, Virginia Gray, and Fannie L. Hamer were the winners.

When the three women tried to enter the House floor, they were barred. Because of the dispute, however, Speaker John W. McCormack, a Massachusetts Democrat, asked the regular Mississippi delegation to stand aside while the other House members were sworn in.

William F. Ryan, a New York Democrat, contended that the official congressional election in Mississippi had been invalid because of interference with BLACK SUFFRAGE. African Americans had been systematically prevented from voting, Ryan said.

The House, however, adopted on January 4, 1965, by voice vote a resolution to seat the white men of the regular Mississippi delegation. Later that year, Congress enacted the VOTING RIGHTS ACT of 1965, which contained strict sanctions against states that practiced discrimination against minority voters. In 1969 Representative Ryan objected to passage of the Federal Contested

Rep. Loretta Sanchez, D-Calif., second from right, and other House members climb the steps of the U.S. Capitol on November 5, 1997, after calling for an end to the investigation into the results of the congressional race between Sanchez and Republican Robert K. Dornan. From left are Rep. Ellen Tauscher, D-Calif., Rep. Karen McCarthy, D-Mo., Rep. Carolyn Maloney, D-N.Y., Sanchez, and Rep. Debbie Stabenow, D-Mich.

Source: AP Images/Brian K. Diggs

Elections Act, noting that under it the three women in the Mississippi Five case would have been ineligible to challenge the election because their names were not on the official ballot.

Losers in three close House races in 1984 contested the results. One of the three races, in Indiana, became what appeared to be the closest House contest in the twentieth century. It led to four months of acrimony between Democrats and Republicans. Debate on the election took up far more time than almost any other issue the House considered in 1985.

Incumbent Frank McCloskey, a Democrat, apparently had won reelection to his District 8 seat by seventy-two votes. But correction of an arithmetical error (ballots in two precincts had been counted twice) gave Republican challenger Richard D. McIntyre an apparent thirty-four-vote victory. On that basis, the Indiana secretary of state certified McIntyre the winner.

But when Congress convened on January 3, 1985, the Democratic-controlled House refused to seat McIntyre pending an investigation of alleged vote fraud. Three times after that, Republicans pushed the seating of McIntyre to a vote, losing each time while picking up no more than a handful of votes from the Democrats.

A recount showed McIntyre's lead had increased to 418 votes, after more than 4,800 ballots were thrown out for technical reasons. But a task force of the Committee on House Administration, with auditors from the congressional General Accounting Office, conducted its own recount and, on a two-to-one partisan split, found McCloskey the winner by four votes. Republicans then tried to get a new election by declaring the seat vacant. They lost, 229–200; nineteen Democrats joined with 181 Republicans in voting for a new election.

After Republicans tried unsuccessfully to have the majority reverse itself and count thirty-two absentee ballots, the House voted 236–190 (ten Democrats sided with the Republicans) to seat McCloskey. GOP members walked out of the House in protest, accusing the Democrats of stealing the election.

The Supreme Court subsequently refused to get involved in the dispute. It let stand a lower court's ruling against McIntyre that the House had a constitutional right to judge its own membership. In a 1986 rematch, McCloskey handily defeated McIntyre. (See HOUSE OF REPRESENTATIVES, QUALIFICATIONS.) The Democrat ultimately lost his seat in the election of 1994, a year in which the Republicans took control of both the House and Senate.

In February 1998 thirteen months of acrimonious debate with ethnic overtones ended when the Republican-led House refused to overturn the defeat of California Republican Robert K. Dornan by Democrat Loretta Sanchez, a Hispanic woman. Dornan charged the election was stolen by the illegal votes of noncitizens, mostly Hispanics.

A special three-member task force said it found evidence of 748 noncitizen votes, not enough to offset Sanchez's 984-vote victory in 1996. Rep. Steny H. Hoyer of Maryland, the lone Democrat on the task force, supported the dismissal of the case but criticized the process as contrary to the Federal Contested Elections Act and "an unprecedented intrusion into the privacy of hundreds of thousands of persons who did no wrong." He said the 748 included naturalized citizens and persons who may have inadvertently violated California's absentee voting law.

Dornan, an outspoken conservative who often clashed with Democrats during his twelve years in the House, accused Sanchez and her supporters of impeding the investigation by not cooperating. Dornan's former Orange County district, once a Republican stronghold, had become a swing district through legal and illegal immigration. In the 1998 election, Sanchez kept her seat by fighting off a challenge from Dornan.

> *In March 1998 a tie vote for mayor in Estancia, New Mexico, was broken by a poker game. The winning hand was an ace-high flush.*

State and Local

Numerous elections for governor have been contested since the nation was founded, with rival governments existing in several southern states during the Civil War. In modern times one of the most celebrated disputes took place in Georgia after the death in 1946 of Governor-elect Eugene Talmadge. The courts invalidated the legislature's attempt to name Talmadge's son Herman as the replacement, which elevated the lieutenant governor to the vacancy. (See GOVERNOR.)

More on this topic:
Bush v. Gore, *p. 40*
Direct Election, p. 161
Election Fraud, p. 175
Electoral College and Votes, p. 186
Popular Vote, p. 431
Voter Turnout, p. 656

Courts have reversed or invalidated several gubernatorial elections. In 1956, after weeks of vote counting, Rhode Island Democratic governor Dennis J. Roberts appealed his defeat by Republican Christopher Del Sesto. The state supreme court threw out some 5,000 absentee ballots on a technicality, making Roberts the winner by 711 votes. Complaining that the election was stolen, Republicans got their revenge two years later when Del Sesto decisively defeated Roberts.

Minnesota governor Elmer L. Anderson, a Republican, had to relinquish his title after three months in office when the state supreme court reversed his 1962 election. Democrat Karl F. Rolvaag became the winner by ninety-one votes out of almost 1.25 million cast.

In one of the most bitterly contested gubernatorial elections in recent history, Republican Ellen R. Sauerbrey refused for months to concede her 1994 defeat in Maryland to Democrat Parris N. Glendening. After the official canvass announced Thanksgiving Eve showed her losing by 5,993 votes out of 1.4 million cast, Sauerbrey snapped, "Everybody knows that turkeys weren't the only thing that was being stuffed in Baltimore city this month."

She charged fraud, including votes by thirty-seven dead people. But *Washington Post* reporters quickly found most of them alive, and a county court concluded that Sauerbrey had not proven that fraud or procedural errors changed the election result.

The bitterness continued in 1998 with a Glendening-Sauerbrey rematch marked by massive NEGATIVE CAMPAIGNING on both sides. Media analysts ranked the attack ads as among the most negative in a MIDTERM ELECTION year characterized by "carpet bombing" of harsh ads in many contests coast to coast. Sauerbrey lost again and this time conceded defeat on election night.

At the municipal level, Florida courts reinstated Joe Carollo as mayor of Miami in March 1998 because of alleged fraud. Carollo had been narrowly defeated in a runoff election with Xavier L. Suarez. (See ELECTION FRAUD.)

The same month in the much smaller community of Estancia, New Mexico (population 792), a tie vote for mayor was broken in novel fashion—by a poker game. With an ace-high flush, incumbent James Farrington defeated JoAnn Carlson, who had tied with him at sixty-eight votes in a field of five candidates. New Mexico law requires municipal election ties to be settled by a game of chance.

> **More on this topic:**
>
> *Party Identification by Voters, p. 377*
>
> *Primary Types, p. 485*
>
> *Sophisticated Voting, p. 595*

Crossover Voting

Voting in the PRIMARY of an opposing political party is called crossover voting. It is permitted in states with open primaries and is possible in closed primaries provided the voter changes his or her party registration before the specified deadline. (See PRIMARY TYPES.)

Most crossover voting takes place when the other party's primary is more interesting than one's own, or when the voter genuinely wants to support a candidate of the party to which he or she does not belong. There have been instances, however, of a practice known as "raiding"—partisans crossing over to try to help nominate the weakest opponent. Political scientists agree that raiding, a nefarious type of SOPHISTICATED VOTING, is not very prevalent.

A larger factor in the rise of crossover voting and the trend to open primaries is the decline of PARTY IDENTIFICATION BY VOTERS. With voters less attached to one party or the other, there is more demand for the opportunity to choose among candidates regardless of party labels. About two dozen states have open primaries or CAUCUSES for one or both parties.

Advocates of open primaries argue that they bring the large pool of INDEPENDENT voters into the nominating process. The independents are a moderating influence, they contend, because partisan voters tend to nominate candidates whose IDEOLOGY is more extreme than that of a party's average member.

The political parties understandably dislike crossover voting. They feel that it weakens party allegiance and makes it more difficult to discipline errant members elected to office by denying them renomination. The parties also resent the intrusion of outsiders into their affairs.

Cumulative Voting

An alternative election system that improves minority groups' chances of obtaining a greater share of seats in a legislative body is called cumulative voting. The system works only in MULTIMEMBER DISTRICTS where each voter has more than one vote.

In conventional voting, a nine-member county council, for example, may have six seats elected by district and three seats elected AT-LARGE by all the county voters. If a minority group makes up one-third of the county population but is clustered in one district, it usually has little chance of electing any of the council candidates running countywide. Assuming the group succeeds in electing one of its own in the district where it is a majority, it would still be two seats shy of the three seats needed to equal its one-third proportion of the county population.

In cumulative voting, however, all nine seats might be filled at-large. Each voter would have nine votes to distribute among the candidates or to concentrate on one or a few. The nine top vote getters would be the winners. If the minority group put up several candidates and concentrated its votes on them it would have a good chance of electing two or more, thereby gaining partial or full PROPORTIONAL REPRESENTATION on the council.

Under federal law, cumulative voting is not possible for CONGRESSIONAL ELECTIONS. Each member of the House of Representatives is elected from a single district. The only at-large voting for House members takes place in the states—Alaska, Delaware, Montana, North Dakota, South Dakota, Vermont, and Wyoming as of 2012—that are entitled to only one seat because of their low populations. Even in those states, each voter may vote for only one candidate for representative. (See HOUSE OF REPRESENTATIVES, ELECTING.)

Cumulative voting has been used in state and local elections, however, and some reformers advocate a law change to permit its use in congressional elections. A 1993 RACIAL REDISTRICTING case in North Carolina drew renewed attention to the cumulative voting concept as an alternative to the drawing of MINORITY-MAJORITY DISTRICTS to ensure minority representation. The Supreme Court ruling in SHAW V. RENO reinstated a challenge to the two North Carolina districts, but the dispute was resolved without any effort in Congress to allow cumulative voting.

Also in 1993 the writings of law professor Lani Guinier in favor of cumulative voting helped to kill her nomination by President Bill Clinton to head the Justice Department Civil Rights Division. The incident demonstrated that the idea of cumulative voting has the potential to be explosively controversial. Opponents contend that it violates the Supreme Court's ONE-PERSON, ONE-VOTE standard and in effect imposes quotas for membership in legislatures.

In April 1994 a federal judge ordered Worcester County, Maryland, to institute cumulative voting in electing its commissioners to correct racial discrimination perpetuated by the county's district-based elections. Although African Americans made up 21 percent of the county population, none had ever sat on the five-member commission. Four seats were elected by districts and one was elected countywide. The five commissioners, all white, appealed the federal judge's order and won a partial victory. Instead of cumulative voting, the county redrew the five districts, making each one as nearly equal in population as practicable, including one where African Americans were in the majority. The new minority-majority district elected the county's first African American commissioner.

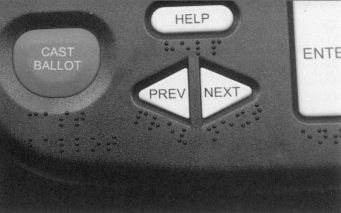

D

Dark Horse

James K. Polk is generally considered the first dark-horse candidate in American history to win the presidency.

Source: Library of Congress

A political dark horse is a candidate who comes out of nowhere to receive serious consideration as a compromise recipient of a party's nomination.

The first dark-horse candidate actually elected president was James K. Polk of Tennessee, who won the Democratic nomination in 1844 and went on to defeat the Whig candidate, Henry Clay of Kentucky. Polk was also the first and only former House Speaker ever elected president. Newt Gingrich, a former Georgia representative (1979–1999) who was House Speaker from 1995 to 1999, announced in May 2011 that he would seek the Republican presidential nomination in 2012, but his campaign initially collapsed soon after the announcement when nearly all his staff resigned over differences on strategy and questions about Gingrich's commitment. However, by the end of the year his campaign had taken on a new life as large numbers of the GOP conservative base found new things to like in the former Speaker's comments. As the election year began Gingrich was essentially tied with former Massachusetts governor Mitt Romney in preference polls taken by media outlets and others. Political observers noted, however, that no votes had yet been cast in any Republican primary or caucus.

Early NATIONAL PARTY CONVENTIONS were open and deliberative. Party leaders often arrived with no idea who would eventually head the ticket, a situation that allowed dark-horse candidates to emerge with some frequency. What happened at the Democrats' 1844 convention was a little different. Former president Martin Van Buren of New York was the FRONT-RUNNER for the nomination, and Lewis Cass of Michigan was the second leading contender. But Van Buren opposed the extension of slavery and the annexation of Texas, and his view cost him his front-runner status. It was also Clay's position and an unpopular one with the Democrats, who needed southern support to defeat Clay.

In the convention voting, delegates soon deadlocked between Van Buren and Cass. Neither could muster the votes required under the Democrats' now-abandoned TWO-THIRDS RULE, which required a candidate to receive support from at least two-thirds of the delegates to win the nomination. On the eighth ballot Polk was suggested as a compromise, and on the next ballot he won the nomination.

Other presidents who began as dark horses were Franklin Pierce in 1852, Rutherford B. Hayes in 1876, Warren G. Harding in 1920, and Jimmy Carter in 1976. Carter owed his dark-horse success to the PRIMARY system's replacement of the national conventions as the way presidential nominations have been decided since the 1960s.

More on this topic:
Front-Runner, p. 222
National Party Conventions, p. 347
Primary Types, p. 485
Two-Thirds Rule, p. 638

Origins of the term *dark horse* are as obscure as some of the dark horse candidates were before they gained celebrity. *New York Times* language columnist William Safire cites a source for the first printed use of the term as a political label as a reference to Abraham Lincoln in 1860. The term was first used in an 1831 book by future British prime minister Benjamin Disraeli to describe an unknown horse winning a race.

Debates

Debates between presidential contenders have become a mainstay of political campaigns, both in the PRIMARY season and in the fall campaigns after the parties have chosen their nominees. Now almost taken for granted, the debates are a relatively recent phenomenon. Until the second half of the twentieth century, White House aspirants did not debate face-to-face. There is no legal requirement for presidential candidates to participate in debates, and it is not that unusual for candidates to opt out of one or more of the debates held during the nominating process. However, the expectations of the public and the media concerning the general election debates make it unlikely that any major-party candidate would dare the political risk of dodging these showdowns.

The first debate between major-party nominees, Republican Richard M. Nixon and Democrat John F. Kennedy, took place on September 26, 1960. It is often referred to as the first "televised" debate, as if there were earlier presidential debates, just not on television. There were none. When Republican Abraham Lincoln and Democrat Stephen Douglas held their famed debates, they were Senate candidates; they did not face off in debates as presidential opponents in 1860.

When the first presidential debate took place a hundred years later, television did play an important role. Nixon was widely considered by viewers to have "lost" the debate to Kennedy, in part because of his poor makeup and haggard appearance. Those listening on the radio largely considered Nixon the winner.

Unlike formal, academic debates, the presidential confrontations have been loosely structured, with a panel of journalists or audience members asking the questions in the early years. Since 1992 debate sponsors have experimented with various formats, with the moderator questioning the candidates and the audience sometimes allowed to participate. Throughout, there have been no judges to award points and therefore no way to determine who "won" or "lost" except by samplings of PUBLIC OPINION through POLLING. Media commentators make immediate assessments of winners and losers, however, and their judgments undoubtedly influence the public's opinion about which candidate won the debate.

American-style debates generally have not been copied among candidates for high office in INTERNATIONAL ELECTIONS. In Britain's 1997 parliamentary elections it had been announced that Prime Minister John Major, the Conservative leader, would debate his Labour Party opponent, Tony Blair. The debate never took place, however, and with Labour's victory Blair succeeded Major as head of the government.

In the United States the debate tradition is not confined to presidential candidates. Candidates for GOVERNOR, the U.S. Senate, and at least the most competitive U.S. House races typically debate one or more times during a campaign, with most such sessions televised. C-SPAN (the Cable-Satellite Public Affairs Network) reported that in 2006 it had carried 161 debates from gubernatorial and congressional races, up from 142 in 2004; most of these were rebroadcasts of debates that had earlier been carried on state and local television outlets in the candidates' home locations.

Incumbents' Reluctance

Incumbent presidents and FRONT-RUNNERS—before 1960 but more so afterward—resisted agreeing to debates because they feared giving their opponents a boost in stature by appearing on the same stage with them. They also feared that a less-than-perfect performance might undermine their advantages in the polls or give opponents ammunition for the campaign trail.

In 1976, however, President Gerald R. Ford decided to challenge Jimmy Carter to a series of televised debates. Far behind in the polls, Ford was generally perceived to be a poor stump performer but well prepared for debates. Ford and his advisers calculated that he had little to lose and much to gain by debating.

The outcome was mixed. Surveys taken immediately after the second debate indicated that viewers, by almost a two-to-one margin, thought that Ford had won. However, subsequent media attention to Ford's misstatement that Eastern Europe was not then dominated by the Soviet Union dramatically reversed that opinion within three days.

In recent years front-runners have been obliged to take part in debates to avoid the charge that they were "hiding" from their opponents. President Ronald Reagan agreed to debate Democrat Walter F. Mondale in 1984 despite Reagan's huge leads in the polls. For the next election the chairmen of the Democratic and Republican national committees secured their candidates' commitments a year in advance to participate in debates.

Although debates are a vehicle for transmitting policy positions, viewers often seem to be more impressed by the style of the debaters than by their stands on the issues. Nixon's appearance in 1960 is a case in point. People who heard the debate on radio thought that Nixon had won, but television viewers were impressed with Kennedy's manner and his healthier appearance. Likewise, Reagan won against Jimmy Carter in 1980 largely because of his style. He conveyed a warm image through his use of folksy anecdotes, his rejoinders to the president ("There you go again . . ."), and his answers, which were structured in easy-to-understand terms.

The importance of style was again illustrated by the 1992 debates in which Republican incumbent George H. W. Bush, Democrat Bill Clinton, and INDEPENDENT candidate Ross Perot participated.

There were three debates, each with different rules and format—each favoring one of the candidates' speaking styles. Clinton, for example, was most effective in the format that allowed the candidates to stroll around the platform and speak directly to audience members. Although Bush held his own in the discussion of issues, his most memorable moment came when cameras caught him glancing at his watch in what many commentators took as an effort to determine how much time was left in the debate.

In 1996 Perot, this time running as the nominee of his new REFORM PARTY, was closed out of the debates by a presidential debates commission. Clinton and his Republican challenger, Bob Dole, debated twice without generating much excitement. With Clinton far ahead in the polls, Dole partisans urged him to use the debates to assail Clinton on what they perceived as his weakest point: character. But Dole refrained from mentioning the scandals

Democratic candidate Sen. John Kerry gestures toward President George W. Bush during the second of three debates held during the 2004 presidential campaign.
Source: AP Images/M. Spencer Green

swirling around Clinton's administration, such as an independent counsel's investigation of the Whitewater land deal in Arkansas while Clinton was governor, allegations against him of adultery and sexual harassment, and newly disclosed campaign contributions from foreign nationals in apparent violation of CAMPAIGN FINANCE laws.

Part of Dole's reticence may be attributed to his campaign's awareness that the *Washington Post* had interviewed a woman who claimed to have had an affair with Dole while he was still married to his first wife. According to accounts published afterward, the Dole camp feared that the *Post* would reveal the story before the election, delivering what one aide said would be a "mortal threat" to Dole's candidacy. But the *Post* did not publish the story, and against strong criticism its editors defended the decision to withhold the information from the voters. (See MEDIA COVERAGE OF CAMPAIGNS.)

But cleaner debates also meant duller debates, and it showed in the ratings. Television viewership for the debates was down sharply. An estimated 28.4 million households tuned in for the first 1996 debate, as compared with 43.1 million households for the second 1992 debate.

In the neck and-neck 2000 presidential contest, the debates appeared to offer Vice President Al Gore an excellent opening to outshine his less experienced opponent, Texas governor George W. Bush. Democrat Gore did win the first debate, according to snap polls of viewers taken just after the event, partly because he was more specific about policy details. But in the following days, pundits criticized him for being too aggressive and overbearing, noting that he had interrupted Bush and sometimes sighed during the governor's responses. By the second debate, the normally aggressive Gore had taken these criticisms to heart so much that he appeared wooden. In contrast, Republican Bush came across in the debates as relaxed and focused. Because he was expected to lose the debates, Bush prevailed simply by holding his own, especially when the discussion turned to his perceived weak suit: foreign policy.

Gore appeared to get back on track in the final debate, but by then fewer people were tuning in. Although the television audience for the first debate was estimated at close to 47 million, about 10 million fewer people watched the third. The 2000 debates overall marked a continuing trend of declining viewership for presidential debates, which had risen to as high as 70 million for debates in 1976 and 1992.

The effect of debates is hard to measure, especially because—as in the 1976 Ford-Carter match—they are quickly followed by a barrage of media commentary and speculation over who won, and energetic efforts by the candidates' campaigns and supporters to "spin" the perceptions to their candidates' favor.

The media's role is often a point of controversy, especially when there is an implication that news organizations have set thresholds prior to the debates by which they will judge candidates' performances. Democrats, for example, complained loudly in 2000 that the media had "set the bar low" for Republican George W. Bush.

Vice Presidential Debates

Except for 1980, vice presidential nominees have debated since 1976 when Republican Dole faced Democrat Mondale. Both men were highly partisan, but some experts thought that Dole's acerbic style damaged the Ford-Dole ticket, perhaps enough to have caused its defeat in the close election. At one point in the debate, Dole caused a stir by describing the wars fought during the twentieth century—including World War II, in which Dole served and was badly wounded—as "Democrat wars."

The 1984 vice presidential debate featured Democrat Geraldine Ferraro, the first woman nominated by a major party, and Republican George H. W. Bush. Bush boasted afterward that he had "kicked ass" and won, but polls showed the public was evenly divided about the victor.

Republican senator Dan Quayle, Bush's RUNNING MATE in 1988, did not fare well against the rhetoric of Democratic senator Lloyd M. Bentsen Jr. of Texas. When the youthful Quayle sought to compare his experience in Congress with that of John F. Kennedy, Bentsen uttered one of the most famous of all debate quotes. "Senator, I served with Jack Kennedy," he said. "I knew Jack Kennedy. Jack Kennedy was a friend of mine. Senator, you're no Jack Kennedy."

James Stockdale, independent candidate Perot's running mate, was included in the 1992 vice presidential debate but was often reduced to the role of bystander as Quayle and Democrat Al Gore bickered. Hampered by a balky hearing aid, Stockdale seemed confused and out of his element.

"Senator, I served with Jack Kennedy. I knew Jack Kennedy. Jack Kennedy was a friend of mine. Senator, you're no Jack Kennedy."

—Democratic vice presidential nominee Lloyd M. Bentsen Jr. to Republican nominee Dan Quayle during their 1988 debate

Prenomination Debates

Debates in the primary and CAUCUS season, when candidates are trying to win their party's nomination, have become common since the number of primaries increased in the 1970s. These debates may be the most useful in helping voters and political pundits sort out and get to know the candidates of each party. Especially in the early stages of a campaign, debates are important because they offer the only large event at which candidates can be judged.

Debates among party contenders have been prominent parts of every presidential campaign since 1980. Debates in Iowa and New Hampshire that year were considered crucial turning points in the Republican nominating process. Ronald Reagan became vulnerable in Iowa when he refused to debate his opponents; he fell from 50 percent to 26 percent in the public opinion polls between December and the day after the January 5 debate.

Just weeks later, Reagan's bluntness in the Nashua, New Hampshire, debate gave his campaign an important lift. Reagan invited other Republican candidates to join a one-on-one debate he had scheduled with George Bush. When Bush resisted the inclusion of the others and debate moderator Jon Breen ordered Reagan's microphone cut off, Reagan, misstating Breen's name, declared angrily, "I paid for this microphone, Mr. Green." The self-righteous declaration won applause for Reagan and made Bush appear stiff and uncompromising.

The 1984 Democratic debates first chipped away at former vice president Mondale's status as front-runner and then dealt a devastating blow to Gary Hart's candidacy. Mondale's mocking of Hart's "new ideas" campaign with an allusion to a popular television commercial for the Wendy's fast-food chain ("Where's the beef?") left the Colorado senator on the defensive in a major Atlanta debate.

The more crowded the candidate field, however, the less useful the role that debates play in helping voters define their views of the candidates. Media outlets that sponsor debates are reluctant to exclude any significant candidate to avoid the appearance of making their own determinations of candidates' legitimacy. As a result, some nominating campaign debates include so many candidates that they barely fit on the stage, and none gets more than a few minutes to express his or her views.

Presidential Debate Commission

Beginning in 1976, most of the broadcast debates were sponsored by the television networks and/or the nonpartisan League of Women Voters. The league was a pioneer in sponsoring debates as voter education in congressional and state elections of the 1920s. There were no presidential debates in the elections of 1964, 1968, or 1972 because of incumbents' or front runners' reluctance to help publicize their opponents' campaigns.

As debates among nominees became the norm after the Carter-Ford appearances, the formats basically were similar in the next three elections: a moderator, journalists as questioners, a time limit on candidates' responses, and opportunities for rebuttal by candidates and follow-up questions by the reporters.

Increasingly, however, squabbles arose over who should sponsor debates and who should decide on the ground rules. In 1980 the League of Women Voters tried to arrange a debate that would include Democratic president Carter, Republican challenger Reagan, and independent candidate John B. Anderson. The White House objected, and Reagan debated Anderson alone. The second debate featured Carter and Reagan, without Anderson.

After the 1984 debates, which again pointed up the league's difficulties in coping with White House efforts to dictate debate terms, two formal studies were undertaken—in 1985 by the Commission on National Elections in Washington and in 1986 by the Twentieth Century Fund at Harvard. Both recommended a change to a permanent, independent debate sponsor.

As an outgrowth of the studies, the two major parties cooperated in creating the Commission on Presidential Debates (CPD) in 1987 under leadership of the national party chairmen, Frank J. Fahrenkopf Jr., Republican, and Paul G. Kirk Jr., Democrat. Both continued to chair the CPD long after leaving their party posts. They and ten other men and women make up the CPD board of directors.

The commission retained the moderator/reporters format for the 1988 debates. A question asked at the second of those debates, however, may have contributed to the commission's subsequent decision to use a single-moderator format for the 1992 and 1996 debates.

The controversial question was asked at the opening of the October 13, 1988, debate between incumbent vice president George H. W. Bush and Democrat Michael S. Dukakis. The reporter, Bernard Shaw of Cable News Network (CNN), who was also the moderator, addressed the first question to Dukakis, who was widely regarded as the winner of the first debate. Shaw asked

Dukakis if he would favor the death penalty if his wife, Kitty Dukakis, were raped and killed. Dukakis said no. His unemotional explanation did little to counteract the Bush campaign's efforts to portray Dukakis as soft on crime. Largely because of Dukakis's impassive answer, most commentators rated Bush as the winner.

After the first 1992 debate the commission dropped the panel of reporters, with all questions asked by the moderator or, in some cases, audience members in a town hall format. The commission settled on Jim Lehrer of public television's *Newshour with Jim Lehrer* as moderator of all the 1996 debates.

As with the League of Women Voters, the White House did not always cooperate with the commission. The first Clinton-Dole debate, scheduled for September 25, 1996, in St. Louis, had to be canceled because Clinton was speaking to the United Nations the day before and at a fund-raiser the night of the debate. Similarly, George H. W. Bush rejected the first scheduled debate of 1992.

In 1996 the CPD sponsored DebateWatch '96, a focus group effort to assess the debates and improve their effectiveness. Several corporations provided financial support. The CPD site on the Internet provided transcripts and other information about the debates.

There were three debates between George W. Bush and Gore in 2000. All three were moderated by Lehrer of PBS, though the formats differed. Bush and Gore interacted only with Lehrer in the first two debates; in the first, the candidates stood at lecterns, and in the second, they sat at a table for a less formal discussion. The third was a town hall event in which audience members asked the questions.

Bush again agreed to three debates when he sought reelection in 2004 against Democrat John Kerry. Lehrer moderated the first debate, in which the candidates stood at lecterns. The second debate, a town hall affair, was moderated by Charles Gibson of ABC News. The third, with the candidates again at lecterns, was moderated by Bob Schieffer of CBS News.

In the 2008 presidential race in which there was no incumbent, Democrat Barack Obama and Republican John McCain had three debates and their vice presidential running mates one. The first was moderated again by Lehrer; the other two by Tom Brokaw of NBC and Bob Schieffer of CBS. All events were sponsored by the Commission on Presidential Debates. Two of the presidential debates were divided into segments on different topics in which the candidates discussed their views, responded to questions from the moderator, and were able to address each other. The third debate was a town meeting format in which candidates responded to questions from the public, either present at the session or over the Internet.

The debates were carried out with relatively little controversy. Unlike some earlier debates, no major gaffes were committed by any of the candidates.

One of the few controversies occurred off-scene when McCain proposed postponing the first session so he and Obama could return to Washington, D.C., to participate in ongoing talks about a financial package to stem the economic collapse that faced the nation. Obama rejected the idea, arguing that voters needed to hear candidate views more than ever. McCain later backed down and the debate went ahead as scheduled on September 26.

Third-party Participation

In 1996 the CPD made its most controversial decision to date by barring Ross Perot from the Clinton-Dole debates, even though he took part in the 1992 debates, won 19 percent of the vote, and had qualified for nearly $30 million in PUBLIC FINANCING for his second candidacy. As an independent in 1992, Perot had avoided federal limits on campaign spending by not taking public money.

Memorable Moments in Presidential Debates

For all of the candidates' high-flown rhetoric during presidential and vice presidential debates over the years, the best-remembered moments have tended to be the gaffes, flashes of humor, or out-of-the-ordinary demeanor of the candidates. The following are other moments that caught attention in these debates.

1976. A technical problem at the Philadelphia site of the first presidential debate between Republican incumbent Gerald R. Ford and Democrat Jimmy Carter results in a twenty-seven-minute delay, during which the candidates stand awkwardly at their lecterns. In the second debate, Ford undermines an otherwise solid performance when he states that Poland was not dominated by the Soviet Union.

Republican Bob Dole, in his vice presidential debate with Democrat Walter F. Mondale, stumbles by attributing the deaths of 1.6 million members of the American military to the "Democrat wars" of the twentieth century, a description that includes World War II.

1980. Responding to an attack by Carter on his views about Medicare, Republican challenger Ronald Reagan tells the incumbent, "There you go again." The assertive response to Carter's criticisms, delivered in Reagan's trademark genial manner, stings the increasingly unpopular president and wins the challenger new fans.

1984. Reagan, seeking reelection at age seventy-three and already the oldest president in history, raises questions about his strong front-runner status over Democratic nominee Mondale when he delivers his closing statement that includes a rambling anecdote about traveling on California's Pacific Coast Highway that he fails to complete. Reagan rebounds in the second debate with a witty remark dismissing age as an issue in the campaign: he pledges not to try to exploit the "youth and inexperience" of his opponent, a fifty-six-year-old former vice president.

1988. Democratic presidential nominee Michael S. Dukakis, a Massachusetts governor branded by the campaign of Republican nominee George H. W. Bush as weak on crime, is asked a barbed question by the moderator about whether he would favor the death penalty if his own wife were raped and murdered. Dukakis's passionless iteration of his position opposing the death penalty plays into Bush's hands.

During the vice presidential debate, forty-one-year-old Republican nominee Sen. Dan Quayle, seeking to rebut criticism that he was too green for the job, compares his experience in public office with that of Democrat John F. Kennedy before he became the youngest man elected president in 1960. The much-senior Democratic nominee, Sen. Lloyd Bentsen, skewers Quayle by responding, "Senator, I served with Jack Kennedy. I knew Jack Kennedy. Jack Kennedy was a friend of mine. Senator, you are no Jack Kennedy."

1992. Bush, whose political problems stem in part from a failure to build a personal rapport with voters, is caught by television cameras checking his watch during a town hall–style debate with Democratic challenger Bill Clinton and independent candidate H. Ross Perot.

2000. Democratic vice president Al Gore has particular problems finding the right personal approach in his three debates with Republican nominee George W. Bush. In their first debate, Gore is criticized for audibly sighing as if to show disdain for some of Bush's comments. He is portrayed by some as overcompensating in the second debate. Gore then takes an aggressive posture in the third, town hall debate; there is a strange moment in which Gore stands within inches of Bush while the Republican candidate makes a statement.

2004. Bush, running for a second term, gives an uneven performance in his first debate with Democrat John Kerry.

Kerry stirs up controversy during the third debate when, during a discussion on whether homosexuality is an inherent trait or a lifestyle choice, he bluntly refers to one of Vice President Dick Cheney's daughters—whose sexual orientation is well known—as a lesbian.

2008. Memorable moments are largely missing from 2008 debates. Both candidates seek to project competence and trust, with each sticking closely to campaign talking points. The third debate brings in Joe Wurzelbacher, who becomes known as Joe the Plumber after speaking with Obama during an Ohio campaign stop and claims Obama's tax plans would hamper expanding a plumbing business with new hires. Republicans pick up on this and Joe becomes a brief icon for the campaign. Polls after each debate give Obama modest margins over McCain.

The CPD accepted the recommendation of its advisory board, which said Perot should be excluded because he lacked a "realistic chance" to win. That was the only criterion applied, the board said. Critics said the decision proved what some had claimed all along, that sponsorship by a bipartisan commission biased the debate system against THIRD PARTIES. Some recommended restructuring to make the commission more nonpartisan than bipartisan.

Rebuffed, Perot fell back on talk show appearances and paid *infomercials* (part providing information, part selling his candidacy) to get his message across. The networks were reluctant to sell him the airtime, however, because the infomercials drew relatively few viewers. In the end, Perot fell far short of his 1992 mark, winning only 8.4 percent of the 1996 vote.

Perot and Ralph Nader of the GREEN PARTY declined to take part in a debate on C-SPAN with three other third party candidates—Harry Browne, LIBERTARIAN; John Hagelin, NATURAL LAW; and Howard Phillips, CONSTITUTION.

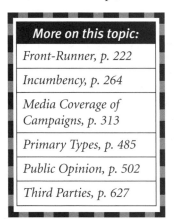

More on this topic:

Front-Runner, p. 222

Incumbency, p. 264

Media Coverage of Campaigns, p. 313

Primary Types, p. 485

Public Opinion, p. 502

Third Parties, p. 627

In a decision affecting third-party candidates' future access to televised debates, in 1998 the Supreme Court, 6–3, agreed that networks have discretion to exclude independent or minor-party candidates from debates they sponsor. The case arose from a suit brought by Ralph P. Forbes, an independent candidate for Congress in Arkansas, who was barred from a 1996 debate sponsored by the state's Educational Television Network. The editors concluded that Forbes was not a serious candidate and therefore not eligible to participate with the Democratic and Republican candidates. A federal appeals court upheld Forbes's position. The FEDERAL ELECTION COMMISSION sided with the Arkansas network, contending that public television licensees would likely abandon their sponsorship of political debates if the lower-court ruling were upheld. Writing for the Court, Justice Anthony M. Kennedy said that the decision to exclude Forbes was a "reasonable, viewpoint-neutral exercise of journalistic discretion" because the exclusion was based on the candidate's "objective lack of support" and not on his political views.

The third-party participation issue came up again in 2000, when the CPD decided to exclude Green Party nominee Nader from the debates, despite some indication from polling that he could have an influence on the outcome of the very close race between George W. Bush and Gore. Nader sued the CPD after he was barred from attending the first debate, even as a spectator. The suit was settled out of court, with the CPD agreeing to issue an apology and pay an undisclosed amount of money.

Delegates

The process of selecting delegates to the NATIONAL PARTY CONVENTIONS has changed dramatically since 1968. Most delegates of both major parties now win their seats through PRESIDENTIAL PRIMARY elections—a development that has vastly enhanced the influence of rank-and-file voters in choosing the party's nominee and greatly diminished the influence of party leaders.

Although the DEMOCRATIC PARTY spearheaded the transformation with formal rules changes requiring broader representation of women   and minorities, the proliferation of primaries also has affected the REPUBLICAN PARTY's delegate selection process.

Only 116 delegates from thirteen states attended the first national nominating convention held by the ANTI-MASONIC PARTY in 1831, but with the addition of more states and the adoption of increasingly complex voting-allocation formulas by the major parties, the size of conventions

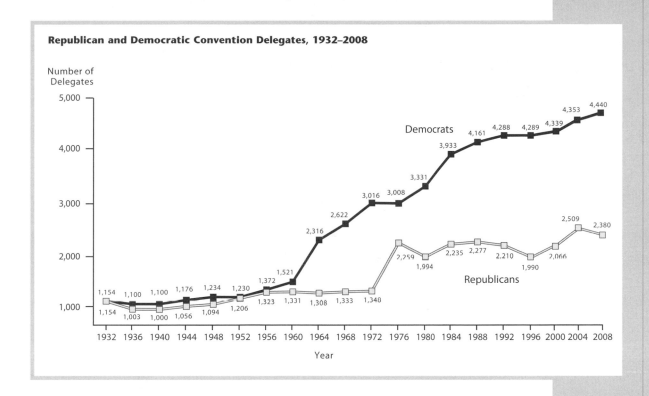

Republican and Democratic Convention Delegates, 1932–2008

spiraled, especially since the 1960s. The expanded size reflected the democratization of modern conventions, with less command by a few party leaders and dramatic growth among youth, women, and minority delegations. (See Republican and Democratic Convention Delegates, 1932–2008, this page.)

With the larger size of conventions has come a formalization in the method of delegate selection, which at first was often haphazard. At the Democratic convention in 1835, for example, Maryland had 188 delegates to cast the state's ten votes. In contrast, Tennessee's fifteen votes were cast by a traveling businessman who happened to be in the convention city at the time.

In those days delegates were handpicked by party leaders, and nomination deals often were made in so-called smoke-filled rooms off the convention floor. More recently, under the CAUCUS system, delegates were named at state party conventions. Some states, notably Iowa, still hold caucuses, but since the early twentieth century the trend has been toward the use of primaries to choose delegates and allow party members to vote their presidential preference. (See IOWA CAUCUS.) Nevertheless, the continued dominance of conventions by party bosses prompted calls for changes in the way delegations were formed.

Democratic Rules Changes

The PRESIDENTIAL SELECTION REFORMS were an aftermath of the violence-marred 1968 Democratic convention in Chicago. That convention nominated Vice President Hubert H. Humphrey over antiwar activist Sen. Eugene J. McCarthy of Minnesota even though Humphrey had not participated in a single primary. State delegations that opposed Humphrey felt excluded. They

Party conventions were once wide-open affairs at which almost anything could happen, including the nomination of dark-horse candidates. Over time, changes in the nominating system have turned national conventions into rubber stamps. Pictured is the 1868 Republican convention in Chicago at which delegates unanimously nominated Civil War hero Ulysses S. Grant.

Source: Library of Congress

complained that the delegate-selection process was unfair and that party leaders had manipulated the outcome of the convention.

As a result, in February 1969 the party established the Commission on Party Structure and Delegate Selection, chaired by Sen. George S. McGovern of South Dakota and later by Rep. Donald M. Fraser of Minnesota. (The commission came to be known as the McGovern-Fraser Commission.) A little more than a year later, the commission issued eighteen detailed guidelines to be followed in the state delegate-selection process.

The mandatory guidelines condemned discrimination due to race, color, creed, sex, or age and required that affirmative steps be taken to give delegate slots to women, minorities, and young people in proportion to their population in each state. They also barred restrictive fees and petition requirements for delegate candidates. The guidelines banned the UNIT RULE, followed by the party since its inception, under which all delegates representing a state had to vote as the majority of their delegation voted. They also limited the influence of party committees in the selection of convention delegates.

In addition, the guidelines urged a move toward PROPORTIONAL REPRESENTATION. Under this system, delegates are assigned in proportion to the percentage of the total that each presidential candidate receives in the primary. The major alternative is a WINNER-TAKE-ALL system, in which the candidate who wins the plurality of the popular vote receives all of the delegate votes.

By democratizing the process substantially, these delegate-selection reforms had a considerable impact. At the same time, they greatly reduced the power of party leaders, prompting some to complain that the party had been dismantled.

Although states were largely in compliance with the guidelines by 1972, there was considerable resistance to the reforms. To address these concerns, the Democrats created commissions in 1972 (when McGovern was the party's presidential nominee) and again in 1976. But neither the commission headed by Barbara A. Mikulski of Maryland (1972) or by Morley Winograd of Michigan (1976) changed the McGovern-Fraser rules significantly, and the notion of fair representation became generally accepted.

Concern that the reforms had gone too far in reducing the influence of party leaders still ran high. So in 1980 the party created yet another commission, this one chaired by North Carolina governor James B. Hunt Jr. The main recommendation made by the Hunt Commission was to increase the number of delegate slots reserved at the national convention for party leaders and elected officials—or SUPERDELEGATES, as they have come to be called. Every state is now guaranteed enough slots to accommodate its "core" Democratic officials, defined as the governor, members of Congress, and mayors of cities with populations of more than 250,000.

Effect on Primaries

As a result of the reforms, the number of primaries ballooned. Most state party leaders thought that the adoption of a presidential primary was the easiest and surest way to conform to the rules and prevent challenges to their convention delegations.

Primaries almost tripled between 1968 and 2000, while the number of caucuses shrank. Of the 2,066 delegates to the 2000 Republican convention in Philadelphia, almost 84 percent were selected in primaries. The much larger Democratic convention in Los Angeles saw 2,815 (64.8 percent) of the 4,339 delegates selected in primaries, against 791 (18 percent) from caucus states. Of the rest, 802 Democratic delegates (18 percent) were superdelegates, and the remainder were a delegation from South Dakota picked by that state's party leaders. One or both parties held primaries in forty-one states and the District of Columbia.

In 2008 primaries were held in forty-one states and the District of Columbia.

The reforms also transformed the presidential nominating convention itself. Many thought that the use of proportional representation would enhance the role of the convention by creating a situation in which there were many candidates but no FRONT-RUNNERS. Instead, the crowding of primaries and caucuses earlier and earlier in the presidential election year of each succeeding cycle typically enabled the candidate who prevailed in the earliest events to build unstoppable momentum. The convention, as a result, has become a rubber stamp, formally adopting a decision that has already been made by the popular vote of the rank and file.

The proliferation of primaries that accompanied the Democratic reforms also affected the Republicans. The Republican Party, however, did not experience the same sort of wrenching pressures to reform as did the Democratic Party, mostly because the Republicans were a smaller, more ideologically cohesive party than the Democrats. The Republican Party also had far fewer minority members, which meant there was less demand for equal representation of minorities within its ranks. Furthermore, the Republicans had already instituted several of the reforms sought by the

Democrats. For instance, use of the unit rule had been banned at Republican conventions since the midnineteenth century.

Allocating the Seats

When the convention system began in the nineteenth century, the Democrats and the Republicans distributed delegate seats based on each state's ELECTORAL COLLEGE strength, which is equal to the state's representation in Congress—two senators for each state plus the number of representatives in the House.

Under this method, the South was overrepresented at GOP conventions in relation to the number of Republican voters in that region. After the divisive 1912 convention at which President William Howard Taft defeated former president Theodore Roosevelt for the nomination, the party made the first major deviation from the Electoral College ratio. Taft's almost solid support from the South pointed up the disparity in representation, prompting the party to reduce the allocation for southern states at the 1916 convention.

At their 1924 convention the Republicans applied the first bonus system, by which states were awarded extra votes for supporting the Republican presidential candidate in the previous election. The Democrats first used a bonus system in 1944, completing a compromise arrangement with southern states for abolishing the party's controversial two-thirds nominating rule. Since then both parties have used various delegate allocation formulas.

From 1932 through 1960 the Democratic and Republican conventions were about the same size, roughly 1,200 to 1,300 delegates. But in 1964 the Democrats added about a thousand delegates, and the total number at their convention climbed steadily until the 1992 and 1996 elections, when it leveled off at about 4,290.

At their 1972 convention the Republicans added more than 900 new delegate slots, bringing the total to 2,259 for 1976. The Ripon Society, an organization of liberal Republicans, sued to have the new rules overturned. They argued that because of the extra delegates awarded to states that voted Republican in the previous presidential election, less populous southern and western states were favored at the expense of the more populous but less Republican eastern states. The challenge failed when the Supreme Court in February 1976 refused to hear the case and let stand a U.S. court of appeals decision upholding the rules.

The numbers of delegates for the parties in 2008 stood at 2,380 for the Republicans' convention in Minneapolis-St. Paul and 4,440 for the Democrats' gathering in Denver.

Credentials Disputes

Selection as a delegate does not automatically guarantee admittance to the convention floor as a voting participant. The parties examine the credentials of each delegate to make sure he or she has a right to be there. In the past, the credentials process often was used to exclude certain delegations in favor of others, producing some historic political disputes.

Before the opening of a convention the national committee compiles a temporary roll of delegates. The roll is referred to the convention's credentials committee, which holds hearings on the challenges and makes recommendations to the convention, the final arbiter of all disputes.

In the twentieth century most of the heated credentials fights concerned delegations from the South. In the Republican Party the challenges focused on the power of the Republican state organizations to dictate the selection of delegates. The issue was hottest in 1912 and 1952, when the party throughout most of the South was a skeletal structure whose power was restricted largely to selecting convention delegates.

The furious 1912 struggle centered on Roosevelt's effort to wrest the Republican nomination from President Taft. The Roosevelt forces brought seventy-two delegate challenges to the floor, but the test of strength between the two candidates came on a procedural motion. By a vote of 567 to 507, the convention tabled a motion by the Roosevelt forces to bar the delegates under challenge from voting on any of the credentials contests. All the credentials challenges were settled in favor of the delegates for Taft, who won the nomination. Roosevelt went on to run as an independent, and the split cost the Republicans the election.

The 1952 GOP dispute arose over the seating of delegations from Georgia, Louisiana, and Texas as retired general Dwight D. Eisenhower and Sen. Robert A. Taft of Ohio contested for the nomination. The national committee, controlled by Taft forces, had voted to seat delegations from the three states that were friendly to Taft. But the convention voted 607 to 531 to seat a Georgia delegation favorable to Eisenhower. It then seated Eisenhower delegates from Louisiana and Texas without roll calls. Eisenhower won the nomination on the first ballot.

After the 1952 dispute, the Republicans established a subcommittee of the national committee to review credentials challenges in advance of the convention. Within the Democratic Party, the question of southern credentials emerged after World War II on the volatile issues of civil rights and party loyalty. Important credentials challenges on these issues occurred at the 1948, 1952, 1964, and 1968 Democratic conventions.

There were numerous credentials challenges at the 1972 Democratic convention, but unlike those at its immediate predecessors, the challenges involved delegations from across the nation and focused on violations of the party's newly adopted guidelines. After their divisive 1968 convention, the Democrats also created a formal credentials procedure to review all challenges before the opening of the convention.

Equally important to the settlement of credentials challenges are the rules under which the convention operates. The Republican Party adopts a new set of rules at every convention. Although large portions of the existing rules are enacted each time, general revision is always possible. The Democratic Party's first set of formal rules was the set adopted at the 1972 convention on recommendation of the McGovern-Fraser Commission.

More on this topic:
Anti-Masonic Party, p. 9
Caucus, p. 89
Democratic Party, p. 155
National Party Conventions, p. 347
Presidential Primaries, p. 468
Presidential Selection Reforms, p. 476
Proportional Representation, p. 493
Republican Party, p. 541
Superdelegate, p. 617
Unit Rule, p. 642
Winner Take All, p. 675

Results

By the end of the 1990s, the Democrats' tinkering with delegate selection had produced a set of nominating rules characterized by the following: primaries and caucuses restricted to a three-month "window" in election years (basically March through May, exempting the earlier NEW HAMPSHIRE PRIMARY and Iowa caucus); participation restricted to party members; proportional representation required, with bans on all types of contests where primary victors win all or extra delegates; candidates entitled to approve delegates loyal to their candidacy; delegations allowed to have both pledged and uncommitted superdelegates; delegations divided equally between men and women; and representation by youth and minorities encouraged.

Through tradition rather than formal rules, the Republicans likewise made their nominating process more open and representative of the party as a whole. At its 1996 convention in San Diego, the GOP changed its rules to lock in some of those guarantees, beginning with the 2000 presidential election. The changes required states to submit delegate-selection plans by July 1, 1999, to avoid last-minute jockeying for early primary positions; set a primary and caucus period in 2000, from the first Monday in February to the third Tuesday of June, with extra delegates awarded states voting later in that period, beginning March 15; and took steps to minimize chances of non-Republicans dominating GOP primaries in states where all parties appear on a single ballot.

Efforts to create a more orderly system for scheduling primaries were thwarted in the first decade of the twenty-first century. The national parties could only try to set rules for when the primary and caucus events should be held, provide incentives to states to hold their contests later in the primary season, and threaten sanctions (including the loss of convention delegates) against states that attempt to schedule their events outside the established "window." But under this anarchic state-option system, the parties were powerless to brake the "front-loading" frenzy.

Democracy

The term *democracy* means rule by the people. It is derived from two Greek words, *demos* (people) and *krato* (rule or power). Democratic government basically has two forms: *direct* or *pure* democracy and *representative* or *indirect* democracy. The United States is a representative democracy.

In a pure democracy, such as those of ancient Greece and today's New England town meetings, citizens participate directly in making government decisions. In many states, citizens also can make or review laws through INITIATIVES AND REFERENDUMS. But for the most part, government decisions in the United States and most Western nations are made by men and women elected by the people to represent them.

> *"Many forms of government have been tried, and will be tried in this world of sin and woe. No one pretends that democracy is perfect or all-wise. Indeed, it has been said that democracy is the worst form of government except all those other forms that have been tried from time to time."*
>
> **—Prime Minister Winston Churchill**
> **addressing the House of Commons in November 1947**

The American type of representative democracy features a presidential system in which a chief executive is elected independently of the national legislature. In the parliamentary systems of most European nations, the majority party or coalition of parties in the national legislature selects the chief executive, who is called a prime minister, premier, or chancellor.

Democracies also differ in how they divide power between the national government and regional governments. Australia, Canada, Germany, and the United States are organized on a federal basis—that is, they divide power between the national government and states or provinces. But in Britain and France all government authority resides with the national government.

Whatever its form, democracy is not perfect. "Indeed," Prime Minister Winston Churchill told the House of Commons in 1947, "it has been said that democracy is the worst form of government, except all those other forms that have been tried from time to time."

Control of Leadership

Despite their significant differences, the Western democracies all meet a basic test of a democracy: their citizens have a relatively high degree of control over what their leaders do. Citizens' efforts to influence political leaders are expected, accepted, and frequently successful. This sets Western democracies in stark contrast to regimes such as the People's Republic of China, where open opposition to government policies is virtually prohibited.

Achieving an orderly succession—the transfer of government authority without serious disruptions—has been a long-standing problem of governance. The conventional democratic solution to this problem is routine elections, ensuring that leadership positions will become vacant at periodic intervals without beheadings or revolutions.

In the United States, succession is accomplished without elections in case of death in the most powerful offices. In such cases, a president of the United States is succeeded by the VICE PRESIDENT, while a state governor would be succeeded by the officeholder first in line of succession, who in most states is the LIEUTENANT GOVERNOR.

Democratic procedures operate best when there is an expectation that policy changes in the short run will be modest and relatively narrow, and there will be no wholesale changes in the economic order or the system of government. Losers of an election need not fear being liquidated or deprived of their liberty without due process of law. They know that all concerned will be able to continue the struggle in the next election. There is, in other words, a societal consensus on the limits of the political struggle.

Lyndon B. Johnson takes the oath of office, as Jacqueline Kennedy watches, aboard Air Force One after the assassination of John F. Kennedy. The smooth transition from president to president, whether through election or succession, is a hallmark of democracy.

Source: LBJ Library photo by Cecil Stoughton

Americans, for example, operate on the assumption that politics will continue to function within the existing constitutional order. They further assume that the economic system will be primarily a free-enterprise one. But within these areas of fundamental agreement, Americans dispute narrower issues such as the level of the minimum wage, the need to take military action in various parts of the world, appropriate sentences for those convicted of crimes, and the amounts to be spent on defense, health care, and education.

In a democracy, there is not only the freedom to dissent, but also the expectation that peaceful protests will be heard and considered, though not necessarily heeded, and that no reprisals will be taken against the protesters. The freedom to dissent is accompanied by the right to join with others to seek redress of grievances by ousting officeholders through the electoral process.

No single set of institutions is required for a democratic order. All Western-style democracies, however, supplement the executives, courts, and councils found in any government—nondemocratic as well as democratic—with institutions and processes that link the ruled with the rulers, permit

Anti–Iraq war protesters march toward the Pentagon on March 17, 2007. Democracy ensures the right to protest without fear of reprisal.

Source: AP Images/Evan Vucci

consultation with the governed, manage succession of authority, and reconcile competing interests within society. Although the exact nature of the institutions and processes that carry out these functions varies from one representative democracy to another, most democratic orders have the following elements in common:

- Political parties to contest elections, mobilize public support for or opposition to the government's policies, and handle the succession of power
- An elected legislature to serve as the agent and advocate of the representatives' constituents, to symbolize consultation with the governed, and to act as a conduit to communicate approval of and dissent from official policy
- Electoral procedures to express mass approval or disapproval of government policy, to set limits on the course of government policy, and to renew leaders' terms of office or dismiss them
- Nonparty associations and groups, widely known as INTEREST GROUPS, to supplement the formal system of representation in the legislature, to communicate their members' views to government officials, and to act as a means of consultation between the governed and the governors
- Additional linkages between the government and its citizens to provide supplementary means of communications through guarantees of freedom of the press, the right to petition the government for redress of grievances, and protection against official reprisals for dissent against government actions

Constitutional Framework

American politics always functions within the shadow of the Constitution, which sets the legal framework for the government. The Constitution obliges the national government to guarantee to the states a REPUBLICAN GOVERNMENT, a term the framers used to distinguish the American system from either a monarchy or a direct democracy.

The educated men who wrote the Constitution in 1787 (twenty-six of the fifty-five delegates had college degrees) were well acquainted with the IDEOLOGY of democracy, the British and French political philosophers who espoused it, and the efforts to achieve it abroad, notably in France. As delegates they were intent on drafting a written constitution because the unwritten British constitution had not protected the colonists' basic rights.

The delegates also were wary of pure democracy, which they equated with mob rule. They were aware that historically many pure democracies had disintegrated as tyrannies. Although not a delegate himself, John Adams of Massachusetts voiced the sentiments of the times when he wrote, "Remember, democracy never lasts long. It soon wastes, exhausts, and murders itself. There was never a democracy yet that did not commit suicide." Instead, the delegates created a *republic* in which liberty and representative government were combined.

But by itself the founders' handiwork, the Constitution, does not explain America's unique brand of representative democracy or its stability. Other nations, especially in Latin America, have copied the U.S. constitutional system, but they have not developed stable democratic political orders. Rather, some of these countries may enjoy occasional periods of free elections and civilian rule, but they then suffer military coups, authoritarian rule, and instability. The difficulty of instituting democratic forms of government in nations inured to totalitarian rule was underscored recently by the difficulties faced in Iraq following the March 2003 U.S.-led invasion that ended the rule of dictator Saddam Hussein.

At the time the United States was founded, circumstances were favorable to the development of democracy. The vast American subcontinent, with its abundant natural resources and fertile land, had no history of feudalism, no titled aristocracy, and no monopoly of landownership by a privileged few.

In the early years of settlement and nationhood, governments imposed few limitations on those seeking to improve their lots in life. For those for whom opportunities seemed limited, the vast western frontier was available for starting a new life.

But the frontier and the prospect of free land and a new life in the West did not last forever. By 1900 the western frontier was largely closed, and the United States was becoming an industrialized nation whose people were increasingly crowded into teeming cities. The nation has also absorbed many millions of immigrants from other nations. It has undergone economic booms and busts, and it has engaged in a number of foreign wars, some of which became unpopular with the American public. Parties have risen to long periods of dominance and fallen out of favor, seemingly overnight.

Yet such challenges and changes are viewed almost universally as symbolic of the adaptability, resilience, and durability of American democracy.

More on this topic:
Ideology, p. 259
Initiatives and Referendums, p. 270
Interest Group, p. 273
Political Culture in America, p. 407
Republican Government, p. 535

Democratic Leadership Council

Founded in 1985 by a group of centrist Democrats seeking to counter what they perceived as an overly liberal trend in the party, the Democratic Leadership Council (DLC) played a visible and sometimes controversial role in debates over the party's leadership and agenda. In early 2011, however, it closed down in the face of continuing financial problems and the resignation of its leader, Bruce Reed, who joined the staff of Vice President Joseph R. Biden Jr. The organization's future had been in doubt since the 2010 midterm elections in which House Republicans gained a net of sixty-three seats and took control of the chamber. Many moderate Democrats—the type of party member associated with the DLC—lost in the rout.

The DLC was founded in the wake of the 1984 presidential election. Republican incumbent Ronald Reagan won forty-nine states in a landslide victory over Democrat Walter F. Mondale, Jimmy Carter's vice president (1977–1981). The DLC, headed for more than two decades by former congressional and White House aide Al From, contended that the Democratic Party would not regain the primacy it had held for years following the 1932 presidential election of Franklin D. Roosevelt if it did not shed the public perception that it was beholden to liberal interest groups, antibusiness, and weak on defense. The DLC hoped to pull the party to the political center.

From and other DLC leaders have long accorded themselves credit for playing a major role in the 1992 and 1996 presidential election victories of Democrat Bill Clinton, the Arkansas governor who was a founding DLC member and served as the group's chairman in the early 1990s. Clinton, who campaigned as a "different kind of Democrat," declared in a State of the Union address that the "era of big government" was over. He worked with the Republican-controlled Congress to overhaul federal welfare programs and to enact trade liberalization measures such as the North American Free Trade agreement; the latter was opposed by many Democrats, with their long-standing ties to organized labor.

But liberal activists contended that the DLC had less clout in the 1992 and 1996 elections than it claimed, attributing Clinton's successes more to his personal charisma and his overall adherence to most of the traditional Democratic Party agenda than his centrist views on some issues. The DLC was outspoken in its support for Bush's decision to launch the war in Iraq in 2003, and this support became a sore spot for many Democrats. Liberal criticism intensified when Connecticut senator Joseph I. Lieberman—a longtime DLC chairman, Gore's vice presidential running mate in 2000, and a supporter of the war in Iraq—lost the Democratic Senate primary in 2006 to antiwar candidate Ned Lamont but ran as an independent and won reelection. Many liberals said that Lieberman and the DLC were out of sync with the majority of party activists.

Democratic National Committee

The chief administrative body of the DEMOCRATIC PARTY is the Democratic National Committee (DNC). With almost 450 members, the DNC is well more than twice the size of its major-party counterpart, the REPUBLICAN NATIONAL COMMITTEE.

In both parties, the NATIONAL PARTY CONVENTION is the highest governing authority. But between the four-year conventions the national committees and their staffs carry out the parties' day-to-day business—not the least of which is raising millions of dollars to support party efforts to win the presidency, governorships, and control of Congress and state legislatures.

Formed in 1848, the DNC is the oldest national party committee. Since 1984 it has operated from its first permanent home, a $6.5 million office building on Capitol Hill at 430 South Capitol Street, S.E., in Washington, D.C. Previous locations in New York and Washington (including the Watergate offices famously burglarized by Republican operatives in 1972, an act that led to the resignation of President Richard M. Nixon in 1974) were rented.

The core traditional responsibility of the national committee is issuing the *Call for the National Convention,* which sets forth the method of allocating delegates to each state. The *Call* establishes the convention's standing committees and temporary rules. (See PRESIDENT, NOMINATING AND ELECTING.)

The DNC assists in conducting the party's presidential campaign, works to elect Democrats to state and local offices, and plays a major role in formulating and disseminating party policy. Sub-units of the DNC are the executive committee and four standing committees: credentials, rules and bylaws, resolutions, and budget and finance. The DNC normally meets twice a year, in the winter and summer. In presidential election years, it also meets after the national convention.

Through its rules and PRESIDENTIAL SELECTION REFORMS, the Democratic Party has pioneered in expanding participation by women and minorities. It requires national convention delegations to be equally divided between men and women. It was the first major party to have a chairwoman, Jean Westwood of Utah in 1972, and to nominate a woman as its vice presidential candidate, Geraldine Ferraro in 1984. In addition, it was the first party to have an African American national chairman, Ronald H. Brown (1989–1993). Brown, credited with helping to put Bill Clinton in the White House, was killed in an airplane crash while on a European mission as secretary of commerce in 1996.

In both major parties the position of chair was originally part time, often filled by a member of Congress. Now it is a full-time, salaried position. The chair is selected by vote of the committee members, although the DNC has generally ratified the candidates handpicked by Democratic presidents when the party wins the White House. The visibility and approach of the chair depends on the personality and agenda of the individual holding the job.

Jean Westwood was the first woman to serve as the chair of a major party. Here, she is interviewed on election night, November 11, 1972.

Source: Library of Congress

Ron Brown, the first African American to head a major party committee, held the post from 1989 to 1993.

Source: Library of Congress

Brown's successor as chairman, Chicago political consultant David Wilhelm, resigned after enduring two years of heavy criticism, especially after the Republican takeover of Congress in the 1994 MIDTERM ELECTION. Wilhelm was succeeded by a dual chairmanship of Donald L. Fowler of South Carolina, who had chaired a DNC reform study group, the Fairness Commission, and Sen. Christopher J. Dodd of Connecticut, who held the title of general chairman.

Fowler and Dodd led a highly effective fund-raising operation that helped Clinton win reelection in 1996. Their success, however, was marred by SCANDALS. Shortly before the election it was disclosed that the DNC had accepted large contributions from Asian and other foreign business interests, which by law are barred from participation in U.S. elections. Some major contributors, including foreigners, were invited to White House coffees with President Clinton. In all, the Democrats raised $122.3 million in so-called SOFT MONEY from corporations and individuals for party building, advertising, and other activities that indirectly benefited Clinton's reelection campaign. Although the DNC denied any illegality, it later returned almost $3 million in suspect contributions and wound up heavily in debt. The scandal brought attention to the issues surrounding soft money and political reformers' attempts to cut back or eliminate the use of such funds. (See CAMPAIGN FINANCE.)

A Clinton ally, Terry McAuliffe, became the chairman of the DNC in 2001. McAuliffe, a veteran fund-raiser, provided critical support to Clinton's 1996 reelection campaign (although McAuliffe's role in that year's campaign finance abuses came under examination). Vice President Al Gore went so far as to hail McAuliffe as "the greatest fund-raiser in the history of the universe." But many Democrats blasted McAuliffe after the 2002 MIDTERM ELECTIONS, when the party lost seats in both chambers of Congress.

In 2005, shortly after the Republicans held on to the White House with President George W. Bush's narrow win over Democrat John Kerry in 2004, the DNC made the somewhat surprising choice of appointing former Vermont governor Howard Dean as chairman to replace the retiring McAuliffe.

Supporters of Dean—who rose from obscurity to become an early contender for the 2004 Democratic presidential nomination based on his fierce denunciations of Bush, especially over the war in Iraq—hoped he would be a more effective spokesman for the party than had McAuliffe. Others worried that Dean would present too liberal an image for a party struggling to broaden its appeal, and that he might be too volatile a presence. (Most Americans knew Dean best from the frequently aired footage of the strange scream he emitted while exhorting his supporters not to give up after he finished in third place in the 2004 Iowa caucuses.)

But in 2006 Dean's efforts during his first election cycle as chairman, during which the Democrats took advantage of Bush's declining popularity to gain control of both chambers of Congress, provided some additional surprises. Dean continued to attack Bush for what the Democrats claimed were policy failures, but he kept a relatively low profile. Further, rather than concentrating on campaigning in the "blue" states of the Northeast, Midwest, and West Coast, Dean announced a fifty-state strategy to rebuild withered Democratic organizations and restore the party to competition in the South, the rural Midwest, and the interior West, where it had performed poorly over a number of years. (See Reference Material, National Party Chairs, 1848–2011, page 702.)

The DNC chair in 2011 was Rep. Debbie Wasserman Schultz, a House member from Florida.

National party chairs traditionally subordinate their own political ambitions to that of the president when the party is in power. Democratic chairman James A. Farley, however, broke with that tradition in 1940 after a falling out with President Franklin D. Roosevelt. Farley unsuccessfully challenged Roosevelt's bid for a third-term nomination. During Roosevelt's first two terms Farley also served as postmaster general, a practice now prohibited by the Hatch Act's restrictions on FEDERAL WORKERS' POLITICAL ACTIVITY.

Other Democratic aspirants have gained the party chairmanship after their own national office candidacies failed. In 1960 nominee John F. Kennedy considered two senators, Lyndon B. Johnson of Texas and Henry M. Jackson of Washington, as potential RUNNING MATES. After his first choice, Johnson, accepted the offer, Kennedy named Jackson to head the DNC. In office himself after Kennedy was assassinated, Johnson became the only modern president who never appointed a party chairman.

In 1968 Hubert H. Humphrey chose Edmund S. Muskie of Maine over Sen. Fred Harris of Oklahoma as his running mate. Harris then lost out briefly as party chairman to Lawrence F. O'Brien, who both preceded and followed Harris in the DNC job in the 1968–1972 period. In 1992 national chairman Ronald Brown was mentioned as a possible running mate to Clinton, who settled instead on Sen. Al Gore of Tennessee.

More on this topic:

Campaign Finance, p. 53

National Party Conventions, p. 347

Republican National Committee, p. 539

Scandals, p. 560

Soft Money, p. 592

Party rules empower the DNC to fill the vacancy if a nominee resigns or dies before the election. This situation arose in 1972 when vice presidential nominee Thomas Eagleton withdrew as George S. McGovern's running mate after it was disclosed that Eagleton had a past history of clinical depression. The DNC then ratified McGovern's choice of a successor, R. Sargent Shriver of Maryland.

Democratic National Convention *See* NATIONAL PARTY CONVENTION

Democratic Party (1832–)

The modern Democratic Party is the oldest political organization in the United States. It is a direct descendant of the political movement surrounding Andrew Jackson's rise to the presidency in the 1820s, with a lineage that reaches back to Thomas Jefferson and the nation's earliest days. There remain some threads that connect the Democratic Party of the early twenty-first century to that of the party's founders long ago, such as a shared advocacy of the laboring classes. In many ways, however, today's party is so different from its forebears that they might as well be different parties altogether.

The party founded as the voice of agrarian Americans shifted its base to the nation's urban centers. The party born as a reaction by states' rights advocates against the strong central government advocated by the Federalist Party shifted profoundly, especially since President Franklin D. Roosevelt's New Deal era of the 1930s, to embrace an activist federal government. The party willing to secede and go to war in the South to defend slavery in the nineteenth century—and which for many years after the Civil War carried the banner of segregation in the South—adopted the cause of minority rights in the midtwentieth century and today receives strong support from black voters. Meanwhile, the party's overall shift to liberalism at the national leadership level turned the Democrats' "Solid South" into the party's weakest region, as an increasingly conservative Republican Party attracted southern voters.

The South's withdrawal from the historically powerful but tenuous Democratic coalition caused setbacks for the party beginning in the late 1960s. From the 1968 through 2008 elections, Republicans won seven of eleven presidential races, and they broke the Democrats' lock on Congress by winning control of both chambers in 1994 and holding on for most of the next dozen years. A series of debates over the "soul" of the Democratic Party pitted the party's mainly liberal base—including (to varying degrees) blacks, Hispanics, Jews, and other ethnic minorities, as well as feminists and gay rights advocates, who wanted the party to express a clear "progressive" agenda—against Democratic centrists, represented by groups such as the now-defunct DEMOCRATIC LEADERSHIP COUNCIL, who argued that the party's liberal image was costing it elections. The Democratic congressional and presidential victories in 2006 and 2008 shifted the party toward a more vigorous progressive agenda, especially in the House under the leadership of Speaker Nancy Pelosi of California, an unapologetic liberal voice. However, the party suffered massive losses in the 2010 midterm elections, especially in the House, which returned control to the GOP. The size of the losses, and President Barack Obama's generally centrist positions, raised new questions about the party's political path in the near-term future.

"I don't belong to any organized political party. I'm a Democrat."

—Cowboy humorist Will Rogers (1879–1935)

Yet the party's losses in the South and other conservative regions have been largely offset by a counter realignment. Even with losses in the 2010 election, the party's dominance is growing in New England, the one-time bastion of Yankee Republicanism, and it has gained majority status in populous states such as New York, California, and Illinois, where Republicans until not long ago were highly competitive. Further, the Democrats have made incursions into affluent suburban areas, where the Republicans' attachment to the social conservative movement has worn down the GOP's traditional appeal.

Although the party remains a "big tent" for some of the most liberal representatives and senators, and even some members representing conservative districts and states, and is still subject to internal schisms, the Democrats responded with unusual discipline during the 2006 midterm elections to the opportunity presented by the sharp drop in public support for the Republican administration of George W. Bush and the Republican-controlled Congress. In doing so, the Democrats gained thirty House and six Senate seats to regain control of both chambers. The party built on this success in 2008 before stumbling badly in 2010 as the voters showed their anger and frustration over continuing economic problems—unemployment stuck at about 9 percent, home foreclosures, huge federal financial aid to banks and others perceived to have caused the recession, and more—and at least some of the Democrats' signature legislative enactments, especially a far-reaching health care bill.

Nineteenth Century

There is no precise birth date for the Democratic Party. It developed as an outgrowth of Thomas Jefferson's DEMOCRATIC-REPUBLICAN PARTY, which began in opposition to FEDERALIST policies and splintered into factions in the 1820s.

The party led by War of 1812 hero Andrew Jackson, who won the first of two terms as president in 1828, after 1830 became simply the Democratic Party, the name by which it has since been known. The new party encouraged and benefited from the increasing democratization of American politics that began in the 1820s. Andrew Jackson became a symbol of this mass democracy, and his presidency ushered in a period of Democratic dominance that lasted until the Civil War.

The Democrats were a national party, with a particular appeal among workers, immigrants, and settlers west of the Alleghenies. The success of the party in the pre–Civil War period was due in part to a national organization stronger than that of its rivals. In 1832 the Democrats were the first major party to hold a national nominating convention, and in 1848 they became the first party to establish an ongoing national committee. (See DEMOCRATIC NATIONAL COMMITTEE.)

Between 1828 and 1860 the party held the White House for twenty-four years, controlled the Senate for twenty-six years, and controlled the House of Representatives for twenty-four years. Leadership in the party generally resided in Congress. The Democrats' two-thirds nominating rule, adopted at the 1832 convention and retained for a century, gave the South veto power over the choice of a national ticket. The result, not only in the pre–Civil War years but until the rule was eliminated in 1936, was the frequent selection of conservative candidates for president.

The Democratic Party traces its lineage back to President Andrew Jackson.

Source: Library of Congress

The early philosophy of the Democratic Party stressed a belief in a strict interpretation of the Constitution, states' rights, and limited spending by the federal government. While party members throughout the nation accepted these basic tenets, there was no national consensus on the volatile slavery issue, which strained the party in the midnineteenth century and finally divided it geographically in 1860. Two separate Democratic tickets were run in the 1860 election—one northern, one southern. The party division aided the election of the candidate of the new antislavery Republican Party, Abraham Lincoln, who won a sizable electoral vote majority even though he received less than 40 percent of the popular vote.

During the Civil War the northern wing of the party—the only part functioning as part of the United States' governing system, as southern Democrats had joined the secessionist Confederate States of America—was factionalized. One group, the Copperheads, was hostile to the Union war effort and favored a negotiated peace with the Confederacy. The stance of the Copperheads, coupled with the involvement of many southern Democrats in the Confederate government, enabled the Republicans for a generation after the Civil War to denounce the reunified Democratic Party as the "party of treason."

Displaced as the majority party by the Republicans in most of the North, the strength of the Democrats was in the South, which voted in large majorities for Democratic candidates. Party strength outside the South was scattered, being most noticeable among ethnic populations in urban areas and voters in the border states. The period of Republican dominance lasted for nearly three-quarters of a century, 1860 to 1932. The Democrats occupied the White House for sixteen of these seventy-two years, controlled the House of Representatives for twenty-six years, and controlled the Senate for ten years.

Twentieth and Twenty-first Centuries

The Great Depression, which began in 1929, dramatically altered American politics and provided the opportunity for the Democrats to reemerge as the majority party. The Democrats swept to victory behind Franklin D. Roosevelt in 1932, and, with widespread popular acceptance of his New Deal programs, a new coalition was formed. The new majority coalition combined the bulk of the African American electorate, the academic community, and organized labor with the party's core strength among urban ethnic and southern voters.

Between 1932 and 1980 the Democrats occupied the presidency thirty-two of forty-eight years and controlled both houses of Congress for forty-four years. The acceptance of Roosevelt's New Deal, coupled with the elimination of the two-thirds rule for nominating the party's presidential candidates and the decline of southern power in the party's ranks, resulted in more liberal party leadership. The liberal stance of most party leaders included belief in a broad interpretation of the Constitution and increased use of federal power and government spending to combat the problems of society.

But the party's unity was never wholly unchallenged even at the peak of its power. As a party of diverse elements, its strength traditionally was undermined by southern Democrats' loose alliance with Republicans. At the national level the Democrats were split by explosive issues such as the Vietnam War, which prompted violent protest demonstrations at the 1968 Democratic convention in Chicago.

In the 1970s the party began revising its delegate-selection rules to give minorities and women more representation in the party's national nominating convention. The effect of the rules changes was largely negated, however, by the growth of primaries and the resultant evolution of the convention into an event where nominations are merely formalized. (See Reference Material, Changes in Democrats' Nominating Rules, p. 697.)

The Democrats remained the majority party during the 1970s, despite the impact of divisive issues and conservative members' defections to the Republicans, particularly in presidential elections. The 1980 election brought signs of a power shift, however, as the Republicans regained the presidency and won control of the Senate for the first time in twenty-eight years. The 1982 midterm elections swept twenty-six new Democrats into the House and strengthened the Democrats' control of that chamber. According to a Gallup poll taken in the spring of 1983, when the nation was beginning to recover from the most serious recession since the depression of the 1930s, more than twice as many people described themselves as Democrats (46 percent) than as Republicans (23 percent).

As the economy rebounded under the leadership of Republican president Ronald Reagan, the Democratic Party lost ground, according to a Gallup poll taken in August 1984. By this time the percentage of people who identified themselves as Democrats had dropped to 42 percent, while the Republican share increased to 28 percent. In the 1984 election Democratic presidential nominee Walter F. Mondale won 40.6 percent of the popular vote and only 13 of the 538 electoral votes—overshadowing the history made by Mondale's running mate, Rep. Geraldine A. Ferraro of New York, the first (and, until 2008, the only) woman to receive a major-party nomination for national office. Republicans in 2008 nominated Sarah Palin, Alaska's governor, to be their vice presidential nominee.

By late 1986 the Democratic Party rejuvenated. Congressional elections gave the Senate back to the Democrats with a 55–45 majority. Some experts speculated that the "forgotten middle class" and other groups that suffered from federal budget cuts voted Democratic in hope of finding a voice there. A Democratic Congress paired with a Republican president limited the GOP's power.

Yet the Democrats were not able to rally enough support in 1988 to elect their candidates—Massachusetts governor Michael S. Dukakis for president and Texas senator Lloyd Bentsen for vice president. The Democratic ticket received 45.6 percent of the popular vote and 111 electoral votes. In Congress, meanwhile, the Democrats held on to their majority. In the midterm elections of 1990, they even picked up eight seats in the House and one seat in the Senate.

In 1992 the Democrats paired for the first time two southern moderates, Gov. Bill Clinton of Arkansas and Sen. Albert Gore Jr. of Tennessee, on the presidential ticket. Widespread dissatisfaction with government and the lingering effects of the recession of 1990 and 1991 helped the Democrats regain the presidency after twelve years. Clinton campaigned as a "new Democrat" who declared that "the era of big government is over." The presence of a strong independent candidate, Ross Perot, although not substantially affecting the outcome, resulted in Clinton's being elected without a majority. The Clinton-Gore ticket took 43.0 percent of the popular vote and received 370 electoral votes.

President Bill Clinton welcomes South African president Nelson Mandela to the White House in 1994. Even after leaving office, Clinton remains actively involved in the modern Democratic Party and in international affairs.

Source: William J. Clinton Presidential Library

The flush of victory was short-lived, however. While the Democrats were winning back the White House they were losing ten seats in the House. Party strength in the Senate remained unchanged. Two years later the midterm elections were even more disastrous for the party. Undermined by Clinton's failure to gain enactment of many of his highest priorities—including an overhaul of the nation's health care system—and a series of congressional corruption scandals that amplified voters' sentiment for change, the Democrats lost control of Congress, ending forty years of Democratic rule in the House and eight in the Senate. From 1995 to 1996, as the Republican Congress led by Speaker Newt Gingrich tried to dismantle decades-old social programs, Clinton adopted more moderate positions and fought successfully to maintain his budget priorities.

Boosted by his budget stand against the Republican Congress and buoyed by continued good economic news, Clinton defeated his Republican challenger, former Senate majority leader Bob Dole, in the 1996 presidential race. Clinton won reelection with 49.2 percent of the popular vote and 379 electoral votes. Although Perot was again a candidate, he won only 8.4 percent of the popular vote—less than half of what he won four years earlier. Despite holding on to the White House, the Democrats did not regain control of Congress. In the congressional elections, the Democratic Party lost two seats in the Senate while picking up nine seats in the House.

In the 1998 midterm elections, with Clinton under threat of impeachment, the Republicans hoped to make substantial gains in Congress and the statehouses. But it was not to be. In the Senate the Republicans made no gains, while in the House the Democrats picked up five seats.

Congressional Democrats fared well in 2000 despite the narrow defeat of Vice President Al Gore by Republican George W. Bush in the presidential contest. The party pulled even with the Republicans in the Senate and narrowed the House margin to 221–212 (with two independents). With the Democrats' loss of the White House, however, Republicans controlled both houses of Congress and the presidency simultaneously for the first time since 1953–1955, the first two years of Dwight D. Eisenhower's first administration.

The Democrats briefly regained the Senate in June 2001 when Vermont Republican James Jeffords, declaring the GOP had shifted too far to the right, became an independent who caucused with the Democrats and gave the party a narrow majority. Divided government was short-lived, however. In the wake of September 11, 2001, and Bush's declaration of a global war on terrorism, Republicans swept the 2002 elections, regaining the Senate and making Bush the third president since 1934 to gain House seats at midterm.

In 2004 Republicans had to settle for a relatively narrow majority in the House as Bush won a narrow reelection victory over Democratic senator John Kerry of Massachusetts. In the Senate, the GOP picked up several seats, boosting the party to 55 seats and a seemingly solid hold on the Senate.

Democrats rebounded in the 2006 midterm elections, in the wake of Bush's plummeting popularity and congressional Republicans' series of political and personal scandals, and took control of both the House and Senate.

Democrats built on this success two years later in an historic election in which an African American, Barack Obama, won the nomination and the presidency with a comfortable 52.9 percent of the popular vote and an even more lopsided 365-to-173 Electoral College margin. Democrats scored impressively in Congress as well, increasing their House margin from 236 to 199 before the election to 247 to 178 after. They increased their Senate margin to fifty-seven Democrats plus two independents that voted with them, providing a nearly filibuster-proof majority of fifty-nine votes. The results were widely attributed to national fatigue with eight years of controversial Republican control, especially with continuing major military actions in Iraq and Afghanistan. A major global recession that began in 2008, which included failure of huge Wall Street investment banks and the near-destruction of America's auto industry, helped Democrats argue it was time for a change. Lastly, the excitement surrounding nomination of a black candidate for president energized the Democratic Party faithful, who turned out in substantial numbers—as well as opening their wallets for campaign donations—to allow Obama to gain a relatively easy victory.

But the cheers and prediction of Democratic hegemony into the distant future proved as ill-considered as GOP predictions for their own party during the better years of Bush's two terms. Obama and congressional Democrats used their majorities in 2009 and 2010 to push a variety of legislative and administrative actions that for different reasons caused a major negative reaction by many voters who became the 2010 political activists comparable to Obama's troops two years earlier. The result was a sixty-three-seat GOP gain in the House that gave the party control of the chamber, and a six-seat gain in the Senate that fell short of control but gave Republicans the needed votes to block major Obama initiatives.

Perhaps most ominously for Democrats was the about face done by voters in 2010 who considered themselves independent rather than aligned with either major party. Strongly supportive of Obama and fellow Democrats in 2008, the independent vote flipped in 2010 and backed Republicans over Democrats by a 56-percent-to-38-percent margin.

Democratic-Republican Party (1796–1828)

The Democratic-Republican Party dominated national politics from Thomas Jefferson's election in 1800 until 1828.

Source: Library of Congress

The Democratic-Republican Party developed in the early 1790s as the organized opposition to the incumbent Federalists and successor to the Anti-Federalists. The Anti-Federalists, who emphasized their support of states' rights, were a loose alliance of elements initially opposed to the ratification of the Constitution and subsequently to the policies of the George Washington administration, which were designed to centralize power in the federal government.

Thomas Jefferson was the leader of the new party, whose members as early as 1792 referred to themselves as Republicans. (Today's Republican Party, founded in 1854, has no historical relationship with Jefferson's Republicans.) The Jeffersonian party gradually picked up the Democratic-Republican label in some states. During the presidency of Tennessee populist Andrew Jackson (1829–1837), party adherents referred to themselves more frequently as Democrats. The party held its first national convention in Baltimore in 1832 and became known simply as the Democratic Party in 1844. Party members in many states continue to honor their founders with Jefferson-Jackson events.

The Democratic-Republicans favored states' rights, a literal interpretation of the Constitution (a view that became known as *constructionism*), and expanded democracy through extension of suffrage and popular control of the government. The party was dominated by rural, agrarian interests, intent on maintaining their dominance over the growing commercial and industrial interests of the Northeast. The principal strength of the party came from the southern and mid-Atlantic states.

The Democratic-Republicans first gained control of the federal government in 1800, when Jefferson was elected president and the party won majorities in both chambers of Congress. For the next twenty-four years, the young nation gave the superficial appearance of a one-party system: the Democratic-Republicans controlled both the White House and Congress, the last eight years virtually without opposition.

For all but four years during this period, there was a Virginia–New York alliance controlling the executive branch; the three presidents—Jefferson, James Madison, and James Monroe—were from Virginia, and three of the four vice presidents came from New York.

But a party encompassing sharply differing regional and philosophical viewpoints was fated to suffer from deep factionalism, which came to a head in the presidential election of 1824. That year four Democratic-Republican Party leaders ran for

> **More on this topic:**
>
> *Democratic Party, p. 155*
>
> *Presidential Elections Chronology, p. 451*
>
> *Republican Party, p. 535*

president. None won the necessary majority of electoral votes, so the election was sent to the House of Representatives as set out in the Constitution. John Quincy Adams won the election in the House, although Jackson had received more popular votes.

The two-party system revived shortly thereafter. The Jackson faction maintained control of the Democratic-Republican Party, while the Adams faction formed the National Republican Party (also not a linear antecedent of the modern Republican Party). The first presidential election under this new partisan system came in 1828, when Jackson unseated Adams.

Direct Election

Almost all political offices in the United States are filled by direct election. More specifically, holders of these offices are chosen by direct *popular* election. That is, the people make their choices at the polls, and the winners are elected then and there.

Not so with the highest offices in the land. The president and vice president are indirectly elected through the mechanism known as the ELECTORAL COLLEGE. When they vote for those two offices, the voters are actually choosing electors who will later assemble in each state and elect the president and vice president.

Until the early twentieth century, U.S. senators also were indirectly elected, although in a different manner. Before the Seventeenth Amendment to the Constitution won final approval in 1913, the legislature in each state elected the state's two senators. Some states, however, began direct election of senators in the years just before the amendment made it mandatory. (See SENATE, ELECTING.)

In the early years of the country, presidential elections were even more indirect than they are today. The Constitution left it to the states to decide the method of choosing presidential electors, and most states chose to have their legislature name the electors.

That method was in keeping with the intent of the framers of the Constitution, who were wary of the general public's ability to select a president having the right qualities of leadership, character, and intelligence. It was thought that the electors should be the wisest and most educated men in each state, who would in turn be capable of selecting the man most qualified to be president or vice president. (Until the system was changed by the Twelfth Amendment in 1804, the electors did not ballot separately for vice president. The runner-up for president became the vice president. See PRESIDENT, NOMINATING AND ELECTING.)

At the time, virtually all voters were adult white males who owned property. States could have permitted women to vote, but none did so. All thirteen original states limited the FRANCHISE to property owners and taxpayers, which meant that less than half the adult, white-male population was eligible to vote in federal elections. Gradually the barriers to voting fell, and today almost all American citizens over age eighteen who have not been convicted of a felony are eligible to vote. (See POPULAR VOTE; RIGHT TO VOTE; WOMEN'S SUFFRAGE; YOUTH SUFFRAGE.)

Gradually, too, the selection of presidential electors moved from state legislatures to the voters. Even in the first presidential election, in 1789, four states chose electors by direct popular election: Delaware, Maryland, Pennsylvania, and Virginia. Two others, New Hampshire and Massachusetts, used a combination of legislative and popular election. Legislatures made the choices in four states: Connecticut, Georgia, New Jersey, and South Carolina. A dispute prevented the New York legislature from choosing electors in 1789. And two states, North Carolina and Rhode Island, had not yet ratified the Constitution and so could not participate in the first election.

The rise of political parties after 1800 accelerated the trend toward popular election of presidential electors. Several states switched back temporarily to legislative election, but all finally settled for popular election. By 1836 only the South Carolina legislature was still choosing electors. Not until after the Civil War did South Carolina institute popular voting for presidential electors.

Awarding of each state's Electoral College votes (now totaling 538: equal to the size of the House of Representatives, 435; the size of the Senate, 100; and 3 for the DISTRICT OF COLUMBIA) has evolved into a WINNER-TAKE-ALL system. In all but two states, the presidential ticket that wins the largest share of the popular vote in a state (not necessarily a majority) receives all of the state's electoral votes.

The exceptions are Maine and Nebraska, which distribute electoral votes on the basis of special presidential election DISTRICTS. The districts coincide with the congressional districts (two in Maine and three in Nebraska), and the plurality winner in each district wins that electoral vote. The other two votes in each state go to the statewide plurality winner. Although it is conceivable for the electoral vote to be split under such a system, Maine and Nebraska, until 2009, consistently cast all their electoral votes for a single candidate. In 2008, however, Democrat Barack Obama won Nebraska's second congressional district, which includes Omaha, by 3,000 votes, giving him one of the state's five electoral votes. Obama easily carried both of Maine's congressional districts.

Electors pledged to the presidential ticket on which they were elected cast their votes for that ticket. There have been cases of so-called faithless electors who vote for another candidate or even abstain altogether (as was the case in 2000, when a District of Columbia elector for Democrat Al Gore left her ballot blank to protest the District's lack of congressional representation). But in recent years there have been no true cases of a state's electoral votes being split between two candidates, other than in Nebraska in 2008. Before that, the most recent instance of a state's electoral vote being split, other than by the action of a single faithless elector, was in 1960 when six "unpledged Democrats" in Alabama voted for Sen. Harry F. Byrd of Virginia, a traditional Southern conservative, rather than for the state's popular-vote winner, Massachusetts senator John F. Kennedy. (See box, "Faithless Electors," p. 189.)

From time to time, efforts have been made to eliminate the Electoral College or at least revise the presidential selection system to ensure that the person elected is indeed "the people's choice" and not a candidate who happened to win because of a splintered vote. The disputed 2000 presidential election, in which Republican George W. Bush won a majority of the Electoral College even though he trailed Democrat Al Gore by about a half-million votes, sparked several proposals in Congress to change the system to one of direct voting. Bush was the fourth candidate to win the White House despite losing the popular vote. (See ELECTORAL ANOMALIES; ELECTORAL COLLEGE AND VOTES.)

Proposed changes generally fall into two categories. One would eliminate the Electoral College altogether and create a direct voting system in which the candidate who wins the most votes becomes president. In cases in which the vote is split between three or more candidates and no one wins an outright majority (or a strong plurality, such as 40 percent), the general election could be followed by a runoff between the two top vote getters. The other approach would retain the Electoral College but reform it in a number of ways, such as doing away with electors and guaranteeing that a candidate who wins the majority of votes in a state automatically gets the state's electoral votes. Another approach is in a movement gaining strength by 2011 that pledges a state—through enactment of legislation—to cast all their electoral votes for the winner of the national popular vote. Eight states, with seventy-seven electoral votes, had enacted such legislation by July 2011. The legislation would take effect only when enacted in identical form by states with a majority of electoral votes—270.

More on this topic:

Electoral Anomalies, p. 179

Electoral College and Votes, p. 186

Popular Vote, p. 431

President, Nominating and Electing, p. 437

Right to Vote, p. 549

Senate, Electing, p. 576

District of Columbia

Throughout most of the history of the District of Columbia, residents have been deprived of voting rights enjoyed by citizens of all the states of the Union. In the post–World War II era, largely as a result of unrelenting political pressure, District residents regained the RIGHT TO VOTE for president and vice president and for mayor and other local officials. They also won the right once again to send a nonvoting delegate to the U.S. House of Representatives.

In the same period, however, District residents failed in their push to achieve the right to elect a full congressional delegation. A constitutional amendment providing for that advance in suffrage, although approved by Congress, failed when presented to the states for ratification.

The unique status of the District of Columbia with respect to both voting and governance was established under Article I, section 8, clause 17 of the U.S. Constitution. The clause says it is in the power of Congress "to exercise exclusive Legislation in all Cases whatsoever, over such District . . . as may, by Cession of particular States, and the Acceptance of Congress, become the Seat of Government of the United States."

Moreover, after the Civil War issues of race and partisan politics were impediments to the enlargement of suffrage. African American residents constituted about one-third of the District's population in 1870, and that proportion increased in coming decades. In the latter part of the twentieth century, there were far more Democrats registered to vote in the District than Republicans, leading to a well-founded belief that if residents could vote they would elect only Democratic candidates.

Nineteenth Century

In the very early years of the nineteenth century, voters in the area now covered by the District of Columbia had the right to vote in many elections. For example, they voted in the presidential election of 1800 but had no votes in the ELECTORAL COLLEGE. Also in the early years, although the mayor was appointed by the president, voters in the City of Washington (at the heart of the District of Columbia) cast ballots for a twelve-member council and an eight-member board of aldermen. In 1820 Congress permitted them to elect the mayor.

BLACK SUFFRAGE was established in the District of Columbia in 1867, three years before ratification of the Fifteenth Amendment, which prohibits voting discrimination on the basis of race.

Congress granted suffrage at that time "without any distinction on account of color or race" to male citizens twenty-one years of age and older who had resided in the District of Columbia for at least one year. President Andrew Johnson vetoed the legislation, but both chambers of Congress overrode his veto.

Blacks quickly became influential in local politics, and in a short time they controlled both the city council and the board of aldermen. With the support of black voters, the Republican candidate for mayor won a narrow victory in 1868. When projects initiated by the mayor resulted in heavy debt and when his successor as mayor of Washington also ran into difficulties, Congress looked for another way to govern the federal city.

The plan Congress chose was a modified territorial form. It provided for the appointment of a GOVERNOR by the president and for the election of a nonvoting delegate to the U.S. House of Representatives. It called for a territorial assembly consisting of an eleven-member council appointed by the president and a twenty-two-member house of delegates elected by the voters. Finally, it established a five-member board of public works, its members appointed by the president. The act of Congress setting up the territorial system also stipulated that the entire District would be considered a single entity for political purposes.

Actions by the powerful board of public works led in four years to the end of the territorial experiment. The board put in water mains and a sewerage system, paved the streets, and developed parks. But the cost was high. When in 1873 President Ulysses S. Grant appointed the board's executive officer, Alexander Shepherd, as governor, Congress was alarmed. A joint congressional committee reported that the government was weakened by graft and mismanagement. Abolishing the board of public works, the assembly, and the nonvoting delegate to the House, Congress established a three-member commission to administer the city. Congress also took on the District's legislative functions itself. Made permanent by Congress on July 1, 1878, the three-commissioner system stayed in place until 1967. Historians have pointed to hostility to black suffrage as a major reason the three-commissioner form was prolonged.

Post–World War II

A step toward restoration of voting rights in the District was taken in 1955, when Congress approved legislation setting up the federal city's first election machinery in eighty-one years. The measure, signed into law on August 12 by President Dwight D. Eisenhower, a Republican, authorized the election of members of the national committees of both political parties along with delegates to the NATIONAL PARTY CONVENTIONS. A year earlier, Eisenhower had vetoed a somewhat similar bill because it would have allowed FEDERAL WORKERS in the District to engage in partisan political activity, a violation of the Hatch Act. That provision was omitted in the bill that became law.

The admission of Alaska and Hawaii to the Union as the forty-ninth and fiftieth states was seen as a catalyst for approval by Congress in 1960 of a proposed amendment to the U.S. Constitution permitting District residents to vote in presidential elections. That action was a major milestone in the long effort District residents made to obtain the voting rights taken for granted by residents of the states. The proposed amendment gave the District of Columbia three electors in the ELECTORAL COLLEGE—equivalent to a state with two senators and the minimum one member of the House of Representatives. As introduced, the amendment also would have given residents a nonvoting delegate in the House. District advocates later dropped that provision to clinch congressional approval and to increase the likelihood that the amendment would be ratified.

Submitted to the states in June 1960, the Twenty-third Amendment was ratified in less than a year, on March 29, 1961. Most of the opposition to the amendment came from the South, and it was motivated, historians have said, by the issue of race. (The District of Columbia at the time was more than 50 percent black.)

In the 1960s the civil rights movement provided another spur to the enlargement of suffrage in the District of Columbia. The District was in effect governed by members of Congress, many of whom were from the South. Responding to those pressures, and to controversies over local school programs, Congress in 1968 authorized the election of an eleven-member board of education. District residents cast their votes for members of the board in November 1968. For sixty-two years, under a 1906 act of Congress, the board had been chosen by judges of the U.S. District Court of the District of Columbia.

Two years later, in 1970, Congress approved legislation providing for the election of a nonvoting delegate to the U.S. House. District residents had not been represented by such a delegate since 1875. While bills providing for a nonvoting delegate had been introduced repeatedly after the demise of the territorial form in 1884, up until the 1950s they had made little headway in Congress.

The nonvoting delegate plan had received a boost in 1969 when President Richard M. Nixon, a Republican, advocated the delegate as a temporary measure until ratification of an amendment providing for full congressional representation in Congress could be completed. Nixon signed the nonvoting delegate measure into law on September 22, 1970.

District voters on March 23, 1971, elected Walter E. Fauntroy, a Democrat, as the first nonvoting delegate from the District of Columbia since Norton P. Chipman, a Republican, left the House at the final adjournment of the Forty-third Congress on March 4, 1875. Fauntroy held the position through 1990, when he was succeeded by fellow Democrat Eleanor Holmes Norton, who held the delegate's seat as of June 2011.

Established in 1874, the three-commissioner government in the District lasted for ninety-three years. In 1967 President Lyndon B. Johnson, a Democrat, replaced the three commissioners with a single commissioner and a city council. The president appointed the commissioner and council members. Three years later, President Nixon raised hopes of home-rule advocates when he sent a message to Congress calling for partial self-government. The right to vote for local officials would greatly extend suffrage in the District.

Many bills calling for home rule had been introduced in Congress over the years. One reached the floor of the House in 1948, but it was killed by southern Democrats. For the next twenty-four years, the House District of Columbia Committee kept similar legislation bottled up in committee. Congressional elections in 1972, however, freed up the process as the committee chairman and five other committee members, all southerners, either retired or were defeated for reelection.

Partial Home Rule

Legislation providing for partial home rule was approved by the House District Committee on July 31, 1973, by a 20–4 vote. The legislation provided for an elected mayor and an elected thirteen-member council. The Senate cleared the bill on December 19, 1973, and President Nixon signed it into law December 24. Under the law, Congress reserved the right to legislate for the District of Columbia at any time and established a procedure by which it could veto any action taken by the city council. Still, despite the restrictions on the city government, District voters at last were able to elect their political leaders.

All of the first five elected mayors were African Americans, beginning with Walter E. Washington in 1975. He was succeeded in 1978 by Marion S. Barry Jr., a civil rights activist whose long tenure as mayor was marred by the city's financial problems and a national SCANDAL surrounding Barry's 1990 arrest and subsequent conviction for cocaine possession. After a four-year hiatus, including six months in jail, Barry was reelected mayor in 1994, succeeding Sharon Pratt Kelly. When Barry decided against seeking another term in 1998, Anthony A. Williams resigned as the city's financial officer and was elected mayor. When Williams declined to seek a third term in 2006, Democrat Adrian Fenty, a member of the city council, was elected to succeed him. He was defeated in his 2010 reelection bid by Vincent C. Gray, a member of the city council.

In 1995, with the District of Columbia heading toward bankruptcy, Congress passed nonpartisan legislation creating a powerful financial control board to oversee the elected government. The passage of this measure was abetted by concerns about Barry's return to the mayor's office. The control board would continue to function until the District government produced four consecutive balanced budgets. President Clinton signed the legislation into law on April 17, 1995.

In 1997 Congress enabled the control board to strip power from the District's elected officials and to reorganize the city bureaucracy. As a vote of confidence for Mayor-elect Williams, the control board in December 1998 restored most of the powers it had stripped from Barry.

Proposed Amendment

District of Columbia advocates in the 1970s continued to press for a full congressional delegation of two senators and one or two representatives, depending on population. It was a goal residents had formally sought twenty-three times without success. Full congressional representation could be achieved only by amending the Constitution. That was so because the Constitution provided that the House was to be composed of "Members chosen . . . by the People of the several States" and that the Senate was to be composed of "two Senators from each State." Furthermore, Supreme Court decisions beginning in 1805 made it clear that the District of Columbia was not a state.

Congress in 1978 narrowly approved such an amendment. In the Senate the vote was 67–32, just one more than the required two-thirds. As proposed, the amendment treated the District as a state for purposes of congressional and Electoral College representation, for representation in presidential elections, and for ratification of proposed constitutional amendments.

District of Columbia Delegate Eleanor Holmes Norton, left, greets DC Vote executive director Ilir Zherka, after the Senate passed the District of Columbia House Voting Right Acts, 61–37, at the U.S. Capitol in Washington, on Thursday, Feb. 26, 2009.

(AP Images/Jaqueline Martin)

Sent to the states for ratification, the proposed amendment died seven years later, on August 22, 1985, when the statutory deadline for ratification expired. Only sixteen states had ratified it, well short of the thirty-eight required. Barry's well-publicized problems as mayor were widely cited as a major factor in the District's failure to win equal status with the fifty states.

The issue of congressional representation did not go away, however. During the 1990s, the District adopted a protest message on its license plate, proclaiming "Taxation Without Representation," which crystallized the complaints of D.C. activists that District residents paid federal taxes but had no voting representatives in Congress.

A new concept for providing at least partial representation emerged in 2003. Rep. Thomas M. Davis III, a Republican from the Northern Virginia suburbs of Washington, D.C., proposed to expand the size of the House from 435 to 437 seats. He advocated giving the strongly Democratic District of Columbia a permanent seat that would be balanced by granting an additional seat—presumably—to heavily Republican Utah, where officials complained that they had been unfairly deprived of a seat following the 2000 census because of flawed procedures for counting the state's many Mormon missionaries. Under Davis's bill, the District of Columbia would receive one seat in subsequent decennial reapportionments.

D.C. delegate Norton, despite her initial concern that the proposal would not provide full representation for District residents, signed on and advocated for the legislation. Davis and Norton pushed unsuccessfully to get the Republican-controlled Congress to bring it to a vote in 2006 and then joined forces again to push the measure in the newly Democratic-controlled Congress in 2007. The House passed the bill, 241–177, in April 2007, but the measure faced a veto threat from the Bush administration and languished before Congress adjourned. Renewed in the next Congress, the bill was caught up in a separate dispute over gun controls in the District and did not advance. Republican control of the House after the 2010 elections precluded serious consideration of the proposal for at least two more years.

Districts, Wards, and Precincts

For purposes of voting and representation, the United States is made up of many jurisdictions of various sizes. They range from whole states to compact neighborhoods. Each is important in its own way to the political structure of the country.

The nation as a whole votes only for two offices: president and vice president. Although they appear on state ballots as a team, the two top officers are elected separately in the ELECTORAL COLLEGE.

All other federal, state, and local officials are elected in subunits of the United States. In Congress, each state is entitled to two senators regardless of population, and they are elected statewide in all cases. The House of Representatives is based on population, and each member is elected by his or her CONGRESSIONAL DISTRICT. Other types of districts serve as representational areas for state, city, and county legislatures.

District

A congressional district is the geographical area represented by a single member of the House of Representatives. For states with one representative, the entire state is the congressional district. As a result of the 2000 census, seven states have only one representative through the first decade of the twenty-first century: Alaska, Delaware, Montana, North Dakota, South Dakota, Vermont, and Wyoming. These members are elected AT LARGE by voters of the whole state.

The 435 seats in the House are allocated on the basis of population after each ten-year CENSUS. In the forty-three states with two or more representatives, the state legislature divides the state into congressional districts, depending on the number of House members the state is entitled to. Under the Supreme Court's ONE-PERSON, ONE-VOTE rulings, all districts must be as nearly equal in population as possible. (See REAPPORTIONMENT AND REDISTRICTING.)

Computer technology enables redistricters to make congressional districts almost exactly equal in population. After the 1990 census, for example, each of Colorado's six congressional districts had roughly 549,000 residents, with a variance of only sixteen persons from the largest district to the smallest. By the redistricting cycle following the 2000 census, several states were able to create districts of exactly equal populations or districts in which the population differentials were no more than one or two people.

Because of the technology available, courts have come to demand nearly perfect population equality among districts. The degree to which this principle has become enshrined was evident in 2002, when a federal district court ruled that officials in Pennsylvania (population 12,291,054, according to the 2000 census) had violated the one-person, one-vote principle, even though the differential between the most populous and least populous among the state's nineteen congressional districts was just nineteen people.

Under court order, the Pennsylvania legislature redrew its district map prior to the 2004 elections so that the districts were equal in population, based on census data. Several other states had avoided litigation by producing maps in which the districts were either perfectly equal or within a person or two.

Critics believe such court rulings have taken the principle of one person, one vote too far by demanding zero deviation in population across districts. Some point out that census data can only be presumed accurate at the time the population is enumerated by the Census Bureau; in this case, spring 2000. By the next day or the next year, the total state population has almost certainly changed because of deaths, births, and migration.

Although the Supreme Court requirements for population equality have made redistricting much less arbitrary than it used to be, the process is still largely political. Parties try to win the state governorships and legislative majorities so that they can control the redrawing of district lines following the decennial census. Even within the confines of the Court rulings, it is possible to draw district lines to benefit the political party in power. This practice is known as GERRYMANDERING.

In recent years legislatures also have used a type of gerrymandering, called RACIAL REDISTRICTING, to achieve a racial balance in the state's representation in the House. In such cases, lines are drawn to create districts where the racial minority is in the majority and therefore more likely to elect someone from that group to represent them in Washington. Several of these districts have been created to satisfy Justice Department mandates. The Supreme Court, however, has rejected some oddly shaped minority-majority districts, requiring the lines to be redrawn.

States also are divided into districts for the election of state legislators. Only one state, Nebraska, has a unicameral (one chamber) legislature. All the others are bicameral, with one body usually known as a senate and another body called a house or assembly. Unlike the U.S. Senate, where both senators represent the entire state, state senates are elected from senatorial districts much like house districts, but larger. Some state legislatures still have MULTIMEMBER DISTRICTS, which have been banned from U.S. House elections since the 1840s.

State legislatures use U.S. Census Bureau data in drawing their own district lines. Those districts, too, must conform to the Supreme Court's one-person, one-vote doctrine if the seats are apportioned on the basis of population.

Districts, congressional or state legislative, are often part of the political party organizational framework within a state. The Democratic and Republican parties, for example, may have a state central committee and a separate, smaller committee for each congressional district.

Ward

A ward is a form of district usually associated with city council and other municipal elections. A large city may be divided into numerous wards, each with its own political party committee. Some wards are multimember districts, with two or more city or county council members elected to represent that ward.

The term *ward heeler* is a somewhat derogatory name for rank-and-file party workers. It is derived from the practice of training a dog to follow obediently at the heels of its master. In the past more than today, ward heelers unquestioningly did the bidding of big-city political bosses. Many cities now hold nonpartisan elections for local offices, which diminishes the influence of party organizations or leaders as has the use of primaries to determine nominees for local as well as state and federal elections.

Most city councils are elected at large, or by wards with some members elected at large. Minority groups favor the ward system because they seldom can gain adequate representation in citywide elections. A disadvantage is that wards tend to emphasize the interests of neighborhoods rather than the community as a whole.

Precinct

The precinct is the smallest unit of the American electoral system. It is where grassroots political activity is practiced and nurtured. Districts and wards are divided into precincts for voting purposes. As of 2004, there were about 186,000 voting precincts in the United States, each with a polling place serving 200 to 1,000 or more voters.

Precincts serve as the basic building block for political organization. Each party normally appoints a precinct captain as party leader in the neighborhood and as its representative on the larger city or county party committee. Precincts may also elect delegates to city or county party conventions.

In the IOWA CAUCUS, for many years the first of its kind in presidential election years, party members vote in precinct caucuses for the candidates they want to receive their party's nomination. The same system is used in other states that use the CAUCUS rather than the PRIMARY system.

Before the development of the welfare system, the needy often looked to the political parties for help in obtaining food, clothing, and shelter, and the precinct captain was the person to see for such requests. Today the precinct captain's job is mostly one of education and organization: to explain the benefits of party membership, register voters, and lead GET OUT THE VOTE efforts on ELECTION DAY.

Dixiecrats *See* STATES' RIGHTS DEMOCRATIC PARTY

Election Cycle in America

The basic election cycle in the United States is keyed to the length of the terms the Constitution set for the president and members of Congress and to the election schedules for those offices set in statute by Congress. The election cycles for specific offices differ based on the lengths of terms for those offices. All U.S. House seats are up for election every two years, the president is elected to a term of four years, and U.S. senators are elected to six-year terms.

But in modern political parlance, an election cycle is defined as a two-year period in which the focal point is the latest round of U.S. House elections, held in November of the second (and even-numbered) year. Those House elections coincide in each election cycle with contests for a third of the Senate seats and in every other cycle with the presidential election.

The Federal Election Commission (FEC), the independent regulatory agency that enforces federal election laws and discloses campaign finance information, works on this cycle as well. In organizing its data collection and reporting deadlines for candidates seeking federal offices, the FEC sets a two-year cycle that starts with January 1 of the odd-numbered (or "off-election") year and ends December 31 of the following even-numbered (or "election") year.

Though most of the nation's election contests are held in even-numbered years, the term *off-election year* is a bit of a misnomer. For example, five states—Kentucky, Louisiana, Mississippi, New Jersey, and Virginia—elect their governors in odd-numbered years, and elections are held for state- and local-level offices in many jurisdictions. And for many of the "election year" races, the increasing demands for early fund-raising, candidate recruiting, and other logistical elements of campaigns have pushed political activity earlier and earlier into the election cycle, creating what some observers refer to as the "permanent campaign."

The staggered terms of varying lengths for the House, the Senate, and the presidency are a central feature of American elections. The framers of the Constitution wanted to ensure that it would be virtually impossible for the entire government to be turned out in any single election. The election cycle therefore serves as part of the system of checks and balances that prevents any one branch of the federal government from assuming tyrannical powers.

Article I, section 2, states that the House of Representatives "shall be composed of Members chosen every second year by the people of the several States." Section 3 says, "The Senate of the United States shall be composed of two Senators from each State for six years." Senators, the article provides, are to be divided into three classes, with one class being elected every second year. Article II, section 1, says, "The executive Power shall be invested in a President of the United States of America. He shall hold his Office during the Term of four Years," as would, the article says, the vice president.

Requiring House members to face the electorate every two years made them more answerable to their constituents than a longer term would and presumably made them more responsive to the people's needs and wishes.

The Senate's longer term of service, constitutional scholars have noted, gave its members a certain distance from the day-to-day concerns that House members must confront in their biennial worries about reelection. The lessening of reelection requirements would allow senators the time and freedom to deliberate longer-range concerns; and the staggering of the Senate's classes ensured continuity of experience, expertise, and, it was hoped, statesmanship. As has become obvious over the years, the Senate serves as a brake on its sister house, on the president, and even on the judiciary, not least because its members are insulated from the urgent press of reelection.

Although the Supreme Court has struck down efforts in a number of states to impose TERM LIMITS on their members of Congress, the Twenty-second Amendment to the Constitution (1951) limits the president to election to two four-year terms. Only Franklin D. Roosevelt, who died in 1945 at the start of his fourth term, served more than eight years as president.

It is still possible, though, for a president who moves up from the vice presidency to serve more than eight years, even under the Twenty-second Amendment, if he or she fills a presidential vacancy with two years or less remaining in the term. For example, Democrat Lyndon B. Johnson became president in November 1963 upon the assassination of President John F. Kennedy and then won a full term in 1964. He was eligible to run in for reelection in 1968, even though he had served more than a year of Kennedy's unexpired term. He chose not to, mainly because of the unpopularity of his Vietnam War policy.

More on this topic:

House of Representatives, Electing, p. 250

President, Nominating and Electing, p. 437

Senate, Electing, p. 576

CLOSER LOOK

The staging of U.S. election cycles is illustrated by this chart showing which elections for high office were held in consecutive years.

2007	2008	2009	2010
	President		
	Senate: 35 seats		Senate: 37 seats
	House: 435 seats		House: 435 seats
Governor: 3 seats	Governor: 11 seats	Governor: 2 seats	Governor: 37 seats

Republican representative Darrell Issa receives his ballot for the 2003 California gubernatorial recall election. Issa played a key role in the campaign to oust Governor Gray Davis.

Source: AP Images/Lenny Ignelzi

The most dramatic example of the recall process in the nation's history occurred in 2003 in California. Although Democratic governor Gray Davis had been reelected just the previous November, his mismanagement of the state's finances—and its $38 billion budget deficit—led to weak job approval ratings and enabled a recall movement to quickly blossom. After amassing enough petition signatures to force a recall election in October 2003, Californians, in simultaneous votes, opted to remove Davis from office and replace him with Republican Arnold Schwarzenegger, a movie star making his first bid for public office. Schwarzenegger got off to a rocky start marked by confrontations with the Democratic-controlled legislature, but he projected a more conciliatory profile during his 2006 reelection campaign and won with ease.

Republican Gerald R. Ford moved up from the vice presidency in August 1974 after President Richard M. Nixon resigned because of his involvement in the Watergate scandal. Because Ford served more than two years of Nixon's unexpired term, he would have been ineligible to run for reelection in 1980 had he won the 1976 election. The point became moot, however, as Ford lost to Democrat Jimmy Carter in 1976.

By law, federal elections are held on the first Tuesday after the first Monday in November of even-numbered years. The Supreme Court has ruled that states may not deviate from this date for presidential and congressional elections. (See ELECTION DAY.)

In the name of economy and efficiency, most states also hold their elections for state and local officials in November along with the balloting for federal offices. Some states, however, elect their governor and other state officials in odd-numbered years to prevent national issues and candidacies from influencing the outcome of state contests.

PRIMARY or CAUCUS elections to nominate candidates for congressional, state, and local offices are usually held anywhere from two to eight months before the general election. State legislatures set the dates for these elections, as well as those for the PRESIDENTIAL PRIMARIES held in about forty states. The scheduling of primaries has altered the election cycle in recent years as states jockey for an earlier primary position to exert greater influence on the presidential selection process, a process that accelerated markedly in the run-up to the 2008 contest. (See DELEGATES; FRONT-LOADING; NEW HAMPSHIRE PRIMARY; PRESIDENTIAL PRIMARIES.)

Special elections to fill a vacated Senate or House seat can be called by a state GOVERNOR, who, if empowered by the state legislature or constitution, may make a temporary appointment of a senator until an election is held. In some states a special RUNOFF PRIMARY is held outside the normal election cycle if no candidate receives a majority of the vote.

Another type of election outside the normal cycle is one allowed under the provisions of the recall laws effective in several states. Under these laws, if a specified percentage of voters sign a recall petition, a special election must be held to decide whether that particular incumbent can complete the term or must leave office immediately.

At the federal level, the impeachment process allows the removal of the president or other officials impeached by the House and convicted by the Senate. Only two presidents have been impeached by the House: Andrew Johnson, who was accused of overstepping his authority in 1867, and Bill Clinton, who was accused of lying under oath concerning a sex scandal in 1998. Both were subsequently acquitted in their Senate trials. Richard M. Nixon almost certainly would have been impeached by the House and convicted by the Senate over his actions in the Watergate scandal, but he resigned in 1974 before charges were brought against him in Congress. (See REMOVAL FROM OFFICE.)

Election Day

For more than a century, the day for federal and most state elections has been the first Tuesday after the first Monday in November in even-numbered years. Most states have also chosen to hold their primary elections on Tuesdays, though on various dates across the election-year calendar.

This is not one of the most universally popular aspects of the American democracy. Because of the increasingly busy weekday lives of most Americans, many find Tuesday less than convenient, and some scholars think elections should be held on a weekend day, as in many European countries, to encourage higher VOTER TURNOUT.

A simple act of Congress could move the date. No constitutional amendment would be required, because the election day is not fixed in the Constitution. Article I, section 4, allows the states to set the "Times, Places and Manner of holding Elections for Senators and Representatives," but it adds that "the Congress may at any time by Law make or alter such Regulations."

For presidential elections, Article II, section 1, provides that Congress may determine the time of choosing electors and the day on which they give their votes, "which Day shall be the same throughout the United States."

But Congress has not taken steps to change the national election day, and a few states have even experimented with Saturday primary elections. Delaware long held Saturday primaries, but state lawmakers abandoned the practice after the 2004 election based on complaints that it effectively disenfranchised voters who observe the Jewish Sabbath. The state moved its primary election to the more traditional Tuesday beginning in 2006. Instead of changing the day set for election day, many states have addressed concerns about convenience and turnout by easing rules for ABSENTEE VOTING and adopting early voting procedures.

CLOSER LOOK

Congressional voting events not on Tuesdays in 2006
Tennessee primary: Thursday, August 3
Hawaii primary: Saturday, September 23
Louisiana's 2nd Congressional District runoff: Saturday, December 9

Legislative History

In 1792 Congress set the meeting date for presidential electors—the participants in the ELECTORAL COLLEGE, which decides presidential elections based on the candidates' state-by-state success rather than the national popular vote—but it left some leeway in the time period for appointing electors. The act designated the first Wednesday in December of election years for electors to meet and cast their votes for president and vice president. But the act permitted states to appoint the electors any day within thirty-four days before the December date on which the electors were to convene and vote.

Problems arose because of the lack of a specific day for choosing electors. States selected electors on different dates, sometimes influencing the choices in neighboring states that had not yet made their appointments.

Congress moved to rectify the situation with an act in January 1845 that said electors must be selected on the "Tuesday next after the first Monday in the month of November of the year in which they are to be appointed." The same Tuesday in November of even-numbered years became the national election day for the House of Representatives under an act of Congress in 1872. After the Seventeenth Amendment mandated popular election of senators in 1913, Congress amended the act to include Senate elections.

The sponsor of the 1872 Uniform Federal Election Day Act, Rep. Benjamin Franklin Butler, Massachusetts Republican, argued during floor debate that Indiana, Ohio, and Pennsylvania held an "undue advantage" because those states elected their representatives in October. He recalled that in 1840 the news about the outcomes of House elections in Pennsylvania and other states had influenced voters' decisions about the presidential election that November, deciding the result of that election "as effectively as it was afterward done."

The legislative history of the 1845 and 1872 acts indicates that Congress weighed several factors in choosing the month and day for all federal elections. November was agreed upon because weather is temperate then, and, with the harvest in, farmers are more likely to vote. The first and last days of the month met objections because they might complicate the closing out of business accounting books. As to the day, religious objections ruled out Sunday and possibly Monday as well, because Monday voting might require Sunday travel to the polls in large states. Tuesday and Wednesday were acceptable. Thursday was dismissed because it was Britain's election day. Friday was the end of the work week, and Saturday was a shopping day.

Why Tuesday was chosen is unclear. One theory is that it was the day when people were likely to be in town for court sessions or farmers' markets. But the first Tuesday was rejected because it might fall on the first of the month. Therefore the first Tuesday after the first Monday emerged as Congress's choice.

The Supreme Court has upheld Congress's power to override state attempts to hold federal elections at other times. In *Foster v. Love* (1997), the Court nullified Louisiana's unique open PRIMARY as it applied to federal elections. Under the law invalidated by the Court, Louisiana had held its congressional primary in October, with all candidates running on the same ballot, regardless of party. The legal point of contention was that a candidate could win the election outright in October if he or she won a majority of the primary vote. A runoff—coinciding with the November national election day—would be held between the two top vote-getters (regardless of party) only if no candidate had won a majority in October.

The Court ruled that this system conflicted with Congress's intention of preventing early elections from influencing the vote of later elections. (See PRIMARY TYPES). Determined to maintain its election system, Louisiana officials moved the state's all-candidate primary to coincide with the national election day, with December runoffs to be held for those contests in which no candidate received a majority. But this system ultimately proved awkward, and the state later adopted procedures, effective with the 2008 elections, to create a more conventional primary system in which parties would hold their own primaries to nominate candidates for the November general elections.

Proposals for Change

Some argue that an election day geared to the mostly rural pace of nineteenth-century America is an anachronism that no longer meets the needs of the fast-paced, high-tech country of the twenty-first century. They contend that bold change is needed to reverse the decline in voter participation and the widespread disenchantment with the U.S. electoral process. (See zzz.)

Proponents of change note that some foreign countries make election day a holiday or hold weekend elections to make it easier for people to vote without losing work time. Some also make voting mandatory by imposing small fines on nonvoters. (See INTERNATIONAL AND U.S. ELECTIONS COMPARED.)

Some critics say that polling hours (thirteen to fourteen hours in most states) leave too small a "window" for voting when many Americans are working longer hours or on unconventional schedules. Longtime NBC television newscaster Tom Brokaw suggested that polls be open twenty-four hours on a rolling basis across the country, so that all close at the same time. His plan, however, would increase expenses for poll workers and for their security in some areas.

Congress has considered but not enacted uniform poll-closing bills to alleviate the problem of western voters' being influenced by the networks' early calling of election results based on EXIT POLLS and vote returns in eastern states, where polls close earlier because of time-zone differences. Broadcasters have eased the problem in recent years by voluntarily holding back on their election calls until most polls have closed across the country.

> **More on this topic:**
>
> *Absentee Voting, p. 1*
>
> *Electoral College and Votes, p. 186*
>
> *International and U.S. Elections Compared, p. 280*
>
> *Primary Types, p. 485*
>
> *Voter Turnout, p. 656*

Voting by telephone or the Internet has been suggested as another way to make election day more convenient, but as of 2011, concerns about potential fraud and manipulation of such remotely cast votes have not been resolved to the satisfaction of most election officials and many independent election analysts.

Election Fraud

Fraud is an ever-present danger in elections. Authorities go to great lengths to prevent it through VOTER REGISTRATION and other restrictions, yet allegations of vote fraud arise in virtually every election cycle. State and community efforts to regulate and observe elections more closely have largely eliminated the blatant attempts to "stuff the ballot box" and to intimidate or bribe voters that often were alleged in the not-too-distant past, especially during the long era in which iron-fisted partisan "machines" dominated the electoral process.

But accusations of fraud have hardly disappeared. Concerns have been raised that the electronic voting machines in widespread use by the 2004 presidential election could be the targets of fraud committed by clever partisan programmers or outside "hackers." As a result, by 2011, there seemed to be a strengthening movement to ensure that electronic voting machines include a paper record of each vote to provide election officials with documentary evidence should a recount or investigation of the outcome be necessary. Also by 2011 increasing controversy surrounded efforts in a number of states to require a voter to present proof of his or her identity—often a photo identification card—to obtain a ballot.

Voting fraud allegations often focus on minorities such as African Americans and Hispanics, groups that tend to heavily favor Democratic candidates. In the aftermath of the close presidential outcomes in Florida in 2000 and in Ohio in 2004—both of which clinched electoral vote victories for Republican George W. Bush—Democrats accused local Republican operatives of using intimidation, misleading information, or other ruses to dissuade or delay minority group members from voting. Republicans, on the other hand, accused Democrats in such locations of purposely overlooking eligibility problems among voters inclined to vote Democratic.

The sensitivity of applying antifraud measures that could result in the disqualification of a number of black voters—most of whom were prevented from exercising their franchise prior to the civil rights era of the 1960s—has rendered many such efforts controversial.

For example, the Republican-controlled Georgia legislature and Republican governor Sonny Perdue enacted a law in 2005, to take effect with the 2006 elections, requiring all voters to present a state-issued photo identification card to prove their identities when they go to the polls. The measure was predicated on a rising concern that illegal immigrants were participating in elections illegally. But minority rights advocates, backed by Democrats, successfully sued to block implementation of the law that year: They argued that minorities, who were disproportionately represented among the state's poor, would be the voters least likely to already have an official ID, such as a driver's license, and that requiring these voters to pay to obtain a special ID for voting purposes was the equivalent of the discriminatory poll taxes that were barred by a constitutional amendment in 1964.

> **"The election procedures implemented . . . do not necessarily result in the turning away of qualified, registered voters by election officials for lack of proper identification. A voter who arrives at the polls on election day without identification may cast a conditional provisional ballot [and] is allowed five business days to return . . . and present proper identification."**
>
> —The majority opinion in *Purcell v. Gonzalez*, a 2006 Supreme Court case that upheld an Arizona law requiring voters to present a state-issued photo identification card when they go to the polls

The state judge who invalidated the law found it would have unconstitutionally barred wholly eligible voters if they showed up at the polls without the required ID.

Yet the same October, the Supreme Court allowed a new voter ID law to stand in Arizona, a state with large populations of both Hispanics and illegal immigrants. The measure had been approved by Arizona voters as a ballot proposition in 2004. The Court in 2008 turned down a challenge to an Indiana law requiring a photo ID to vote. These cases gave support to advocates of tighter ID requirements in other states. By 2011 voter ID had become the most contentious issues of several about access to the polling booth. In nearly all cases, the battle split neatly along partisan lines, with Democrats accusing Republicans of imposing requirements to keep thousands of voters from the polls, particularly in areas and with constituencies that tended to vote Democratic. By May 2011 eleven states required a photo ID, such as a driver's license. Another eighteen required some type of identification that did not have to include a photo.

ABSENTEE VOTING is seen by a number of elections officials as particularly vulnerable to abuse, despite stringent requirements in all the states to ensure that the ballots are mailed to the proper voter, signed on the outside of the envelope to protect the privacy of the vote, and returned by the specified deadline. Absentee ballots have been central to the settling of numerous CONTESTED ELECTIONS.

If the Supreme Court had not intervened to settle the exceedingly close 2000 Florida race between Republican George W. Bush and Democrat Al Gore, several hundred disputed absentee ballots might have been the deciding factor in that election as well. But the Court's 5–4 decision in BUSH V. GORE halted the recounts and effectively certified Bush as the winner.

Four days before the Court announced its decision on December 12, 2000, lower courts ruled against Gore in his suits charging absentee ballot illegalities in Florida's Seminole and Martin counties. There, officials had allowed Republican operatives to correct flaws on absentee ballot applications that had been printed without voter identification numbers. Gore's lawyers argued that the mistake invalidated the ballots. But on December 8 both judges handling the separate cases agreed that although "irregularities" happened, the voters were not at fault and that the ballots fairly reflected their will.

An earlier example of litigation over absentee voting in Florida was Miami's 1997 mayoral race, in which a Florida grand jury found "outright fraud" in absentee voting. Ballots allegedly were tampered with or sold, voted in the names of dead persons or nonresidents, cast for confused elderly voters, or given to persons who were paid to vote.

Overturning a lower court that ordered a new election, an appeals court invalidated all 4,000 absentee ballots and reinstated Miami mayor Joe Carollo, who had lost a close RUNOFF election to Xavier L. Suarez. To do otherwise, the court said, "would be sending out the wrong message that the worst that would happen in the face of voter fraud would be another election."

A different kind of absentee ballot controversy was central to the protracted recount in the 2004 election for governor in the state of Washington. After an initial canvass showed Republican Dino Rossi with a razor-thin lead over Democrat Christine Gregoire, 573 uncounted absentee ballots turned up in King County, which includes Seattle and is the state's premier Democratic Party stronghold. Despite Republicans' protests about the authenticity and eligibility of these ballots, their inclusion in the recount helped Gregoire claim a victory by 129 votes out of about 2.75 million cast. She easily won reelection four years later.

BALLOT ACCESS rules pose another opportunity for election fraud. In a notable case, the 2002 reelection campaign of Washington, D.C., mayor Anthony A. Williams was fined $277,700 for massive fraud and forgery in his nominating petitions to get on the Democratic primary ballot. Ruled off the ballot, Williams won the primary as a WRITE-IN candidate and later won reelection. City officials said there were "5,465 obvious forgeries" on Williams's petitions, including names of actor Kelsey Grammer, singer Billy Joel, and United Nations secretary-general Kofi Annan. Fraudulent signatures included those of persons who circulated the petitions and were supposed to witness every voter's signature.

Reforms and Technology

Fraud in conventional voting at the polling place is less common than it was in the late nineteenth and early twentieth centuries during the heyday of big-city political bosses such as William M. "Boss" Tweed in New York, James M. Curley in Boston, and Frank Hague in Jersey City. In those days, tales were told of underlings instructed to "vote early and often," of jobless men paid a dollar or two for each vote, obituary pages used as voting lists, and wardens entering voting booths in the guise of giving assistance and pulling the straight-ticket lever for the party in power.

With the waning of the urban political machines, reforms reduced the chances of overt fraud. Tighter regulation, screening of polling place officials, bipartisan verification of voters' identification, opening of

The late nineteenth century was rife with big-city political bosses whose stock in trade was election fraud. Thomas Nast's 1871 cartoon depicts "Boss" Tweed and his cronies.

Source: American Antiquarian Society

Though predictions of widespread irregularities involving electronic machines in the 2006 elections turned out to be overstated, the controversy was at the heart of the biggest congressional election dispute that year. Republican Vern Buchanan was declared the winner by a narrow 369-vote margin over Democrat Christine Jennings in the open-seat race in Florida's Thirteenth District. But Jennings staged a long effort to overturn that result based on the unusually high number of 18,000 "undervotes"—ballots on which votes were cast electronically for other offices but not in the House race—in the county where Jennings had run best in the official count. Jennings argued that a computer flaw had resulted in the machines' failure to register votes that had been cast in the House contests; others contended that a poorly designed ballot had caused many people to overlook the House race.

the polls to election watchers, and other monitoring activities have made fraudulent voting at the polling place more difficult than in the past. But it is still not impossible. The widespread replacement of paper ballots by mechanical VOTING MACHINES also reduced the opportunities for tampering with votes or spoiling them with a surreptitious mark. The machines had a vote counter that wardens could read as soon as the polls closed, and that could be impounded for later verification in case of a RECOUNT.

In the late 1990s, however, many communities replaced the old lever-operated machines with electronic systems that conspiracy theorists viewed with suspicion. Both conservatives and liberals worried that modems in the machines for transmission of electronic data could be rigged by the opposing party in favor of their candidates. Although no hard evidence of such fraud was produced, the skeptics campaigned on the Internet and in newsletters for the return of paper ballots, which they contended were more difficult to falsify and easier to verify and recount. Computers, they argued, left no tamper-proof physical record of how many votes were cast for each candidate. But in the aftermath of the 2000 Florida election, modern computerized systems were generally recognized as more reliable than the obsolete punch-card voting machines that had caused much of the confusion in Florida.

Almost two years after the 2000 election, Congress passed an election standards bill containing antifraud protections, including a requirement that voters who registered by mail produce proof of identity and residency when they voted for the first time. Exceptions were granted for Oregon and Washington, where much voting was by mail, allowing voters to submit driver's licenses or partial Social Security numbers as proof of identity. President George W. Bush signed the law, known as the Help America Vote Act, on October 29, 2002, and its provisions gradually took effect over the next four years.

Watchdog Activities

Besides electronic voting machines, another target of vote watchers is the Clinton administration's MOTOR VOTER ACT of 1993, which allows motorists to register to vote while obtaining a driver's license. The *Wall Street Journal*, in a March 1998 editorial, said the law "created lax registration and voting procedures" because "forty-seven states don't require proof of legal U.S. residence much less citizenship for such a license."

In the DISTRICT OF COLUMBIA, the editorial noted, voter registration went from 58 percent to 86 percent even though the city had lost 100,000 residents since 1980. "Felons, dead people, non-residents and fictitious registrations clog the rolls in Washington, where anyone can walk up and vote without showing I.D."

On the other hand, the *Washington Post* reported that stricter procedures instituted in compliance with the Motor Voter Act had helped Maryland to avoid a repetition of its disputed 1994 gubernatorial election, when the loser alleged fraud caused by inaccurate voting lists. The 1998 contest between the same candidates produced the same winner but no claims of fraud.

In Maryland and elsewhere, however, allegations of old-fashioned, "low-tech" election fraud arose in the 2002 midterm elections. Baltimore Democrats cried foul over a pamphlet distributed anonymously in mostly African American precincts giving the wrong election date and falsely warning residents that they could not vote if they had unpaid rent, parking tickets, or "most important, any warrants." A similar pamphlet was circulated in heavily African American

Louisiana districts in an apparent attempt to mislead supporters of Sen. Mary L. Landrieu. It wrongly said they could vote on December 10 if it rained on the runoff election day, December 7. The fraud failed. Landrieu won reelection with the help of a large African American turnout.

South Dakota Republicans questioned the 524-vote victory of Sen. Tim Johnson over challenger John Thune, who had held a narrow lead until the last votes were counted, from a Native American reservation in Shannon County. Democrats attributed the victory to an aggressive GET-OUT-THE-VOTE drive among Native Americans. The party fired one of the drive workers, a woman suspected of trying to falsify hundreds of absentee ballot applications. State authorities charged her with forgery.

Electoral Anomalies

The American political system sometimes produces a result that deviates from what normally would be expected. One such anomaly is the phenomenon of "minority" presidents—the eighteen presidents elected through 2008 without receiving a majority of the POPULAR VOTE.

Four of those candidates actually lost the popular vote to their opponents and still won the presidency: John Quincy Adams in 1824, Rutherford B. Hayes in 1876, Benjamin Harrison in 1888, and George W. Bush in 2000.

In Adams's case, the election was thrown to the House of Representatives after he and three other candidates failed to gain the required majority of ELECTORAL COLLEGE votes. Under the Twelfth Amendment, the House had to choose from among the three highest vote-getters. It chose Adams, who had run second to Andrew Jackson in both popular and electoral votes. The third contender, Treasury Secretary William H. Crawford, was paralyzed from a recent stroke. Speaker Henry Clay, who ran fourth and was therefore out of the running, helped swing the House vote to Adams.

Only four candidates have lost the popular vote but still won the presidency (clockwise from top left): John Quincy Adams, Rutherford B. Hayes, Benjamin Harrison, and George W. Bush.
Sources: Library of Congress; bottom left, White House

Only one other presidential election was decided by the House. That was in 1800 when Thomas Jefferson and his intended vice president, Aaron Burr, tied in the electoral vote before the Twelfth Amendment required separate voting for president and vice president. The House chose Jefferson on the thirty-sixth ballot to succeed John Adams, father of John Quincy Adams, and Burr became vice president.

In 1876 Democrat Samuel J. Tilden outpolled Republican Hayes, but his electoral vote total was one short of a majority, with the votes of three southern states in dispute. To resolve the crisis, Congress set up a special fifteen-member commission, which decided the disputed votes in Hayes's favor, giving him a bare majority victory of 185 votes to Tilden's 184. Under a compromise that broke the impasse, Hayes agreed to remove federal troops from the South after he took office, ending the Reconstruction era that had bitterly divided the nation. Southern white Democrats gained domination of Congress, and Republican industrial interests solidified a hold on presidential politics that lasted until Democrat Franklin D. Roosevelt was elected in 1932.

"I have ever considered the constitutional mode of election . . . as the most dangerous blot on our Constitution, and one which some unlucky chance will some day hit."

—Thomas Jefferson to George Hay, after surviving the first contingent election, 1823

Electoral Vote Effect

All other instances of presidential elections with less than a majority of the popular vote (including Harrison in 1888 and George W. Bush in 2000) were attributable to the Electoral College system, which tends to exaggerate narrow victories and permit a minority president to claim something of a mandate to enact the administration's legislative agenda.

In 1888 Republican Harrison trailed Democratic president Grover Cleveland in the popular vote, 48.6 percent to 47.8 percent, with other

---

"MINORITY" PRESIDENTS

Under the U.S. electoral system, there have been eighteen presidential elections (decided by either the Electoral College itself or by the House of Representatives) where the victor did not receive a majority of the popular votes cast in the election. Four of these future presidents—John Quincy Adams in 1824, Rutherford B. Hayes in 1876, Benjamin Harrison in 1888, and George W. Bush in 2000—actually trailed their opponents in the popular vote.

The table shows the percentage of the popular vote received by candidates in the eighteen elections in which a "minority" president (designated by boldface type) was elected.

Year Elected	Candidate	Percentage of Popular Vote	Candidate	Percentage of Popular Vote	Candidate	Percentage of Popular Vote	Candidate	Percentage of Popular Vote
1824	Jackson	41.34	**Adams**	30.92	Clay	12.99	Crawford	11.17
1844	**Polk**	49.54	Clay	48.08	Birney	2.30		
1848	**Taylor**	47.28	Cass	42.49	Van Buren	10.12		
1856	**Buchanan**	45.28	Fremont	33.11	Fillmore	21.53		
1860	**Lincoln**	39.82	Douglas	29.46	Breckenridge	18.09	Bell	12.61
1876	Tilden	50.97	**Hayes**	47.95	Cooper	.97		
1880	**Garfield**	48.27	Hancock	48.25	Weaver	3.32	Others	.15
1884	**Cleveland**	48.50	Blaine	48.25	Butler	1.74	St. John	1.47
1888	Cleveland	48.62	**Harrison**	47.82	Fisk	2.19	Streeter	1.29
1892	**Cleveland**	46.05	Harrison	42.96	Weaver	8.50	Others	2.25
1912	**Wilson**	41.84	T. Roosevelt	27.39	Taft	23.18	Debs	5.99
1916	**Wilson**	49.24	Hughes	46.11	Benson	3.18	Others	1.46
1948	**Truman**	49.52	Dewey	45.12	Thurmond	2.40	Wallace	2.38
1960	**Kennedy**	49.72	Nixon	49.55	Others	.72		
1968	**Nixon**	43.42	Humphrey	42.72	Wallace	13.53	Others	.33
1992	**Clinton**	43.01	G. Bush	37.45	Perot	18.91	Others	.64
1996	**Clinton**	49.24	Dole	40.71	Perot	8.40	Others	1.65
2000	Gore	48.40	**G. W. Bush**	47.90	Nader	2.70	Others	1.00

candidates sharing the 3.6 percent remainder. But by winning New York and other populous states of the North and West, Harrison took 58.1 percent of the electoral vote, a clear majority. Four years later, the ousted Cleveland defeated Harrison to become the only president to serve two nonconsecutive terms.

In the election of 2000, Vice President Al Gore, the Democratic candidate, outpolled Republican George W. Bush, then governor of Texas, by approximately 540,000 votes out of more than 105 million cast nationwide. But that earned him just 267 electoral votes, three short of the absolute majority (270 of the 538 votes) needed to win the election. The final outcome hinged on the contested popular-vote outcome in Florida, which would decide the disposition of that state's twenty-five electoral votes. Gore, had he won Florida, would have won the election with 291 electoral votes. But after a series of protracted recounts effectively

> **CLOSER LOOK**
>
> To many observers of modern American politics, the most out-of-the ordinary result occurred in the 2000 Missouri race that resulted in the only election of a deceased candidate to the U.S. Senate. Popular Democrat Mel Carnahan, who was ending a two-term tenure as governor, was staging a serious challenge to unseat Republican senator John Ashcroft when his plane crashed on October 16 on the way to a campaign event. Carnahan, his son Randy (the plane's pilot), and a campaign aide were killed. The tragedy appeared at first to ensure Ashcroft's reelection. But Democrat Roger Wilson, who moved up from lieutenant governor to fill out the remaining weeks of Carnahan's unexpired term, announced that if voters gave the late governor a posthumous victory, he would appoint his widow, Jean Carnahan, as interim senator until the 2002 special election that would then take place for the final four years of the term. A combination of sympathy for the Carnahan family and some voters' qualms about Ashcroft's staunchly conservative views led to Carnahan's victory by about 49,000 votes and a 2 percentage-point margin. Jean Carnahan served for two years but lost the 2002 special election, by a margin of 1 percentage point, to Republican Jim Talent.

ended by a 5–4 ruling by the Supreme Court more than a month after the election, Bush was accorded Florida's twenty-five electoral votes by a 537-vote margin, giving him a national total of 271 votes. (Gore was officially credited with 266 electoral votes because of another anomaly—a so-called faithless elector in the District of Columbia withheld her vote from Gore to protest the District's lack of voting representation in Congress.)

Bush's predecessor, Democrat Bill Clinton, had his own voting anomaly. With his 49.2 percent popular-vote reelection victory in 1996, Bill Clinton became only the third president in history to win two terms with less than half of the vote each time. (He won in 1992 with 43.0 percent.) The other two also were Democrats: Cleveland, in 1884 and 1892, and Woodrow Wilson, in 1912 and 1916.

An electoral vote anomaly of another sort arose in 1872 when famed newspaper editor Horace Greeley, the Democratic/Liberal Republican presidential candidate, died after losing the election to Ulysses S. Grant but before the electoral votes were counted in early January 1873. Electors from the six states he won divided their votes among other candidates. Three of the electors voted for Greeley anyway, but Congress did not recognize their votes.

In another unusual circumstance, Vice President James S. Sherman died shortly before the 1912 election that he and President William Howard Taft lost to Woodrow Wilson and Thomas R. Marshall. It was too late for Sherman's name to be changed on the ballots in every state, so his electoral votes went to his replacement, Nicholas Murray Butler. (See RUNNING MATE.)

Oddities in Congressional Elections

CONGRESSIONAL ELECTIONS have produced a number of anomalies, particularly in the South, where slavery, the Civil War, Reconstruction, and racial antagonisms created special problems in the electoral process. The counting of slaves for the apportionment of House seats posed an especially difficult problem.

Under a compromise adopted in the Constitution (Article I, section 2), every five slaves would be counted as three persons. After the Civil War and the emancipation of slaves, the Fourteenth

It is rare for a candidate whose name is not on the official ballot to win via a write-in campaign, but it does happen. Strom Thurmond of South Carolina did just that during the 1954 Senate elections. He is the only senator so elected between 1913 and 1954. But fifty-six years later, in 2010, Republican Lisa Murkowski, the incumbent Alaskan senator, won with a write-in campaign.

Thurmond succeeded because he was unusually well-placed. He had served as governor from 1947 to 1951. When Democratic senator Burnet R. Maybank died in September 1954, the state Democratic Party picked state senator Edgar A. Brown to run in his stead in November; the move might have been tantamount to victory, as the state's then-weak Republican Party did not field a candidate. But Thurmond, protesting the party's decision to not hold a primary, staged a write-in campaign. Better known and enjoying the endorsements of most state newspapers, Thurmond received 63.1 percent of the vote.

In another anomaly, Thurmond resigned in 1956 to fulfill a promise to present himself in a special election primary, but he was returned to the Senate without opposition. He retired in January 2003, at age 100, after serving more than forty-eight total years in the Senate, a tenure punctuated by his switch in 1964 to the Republican Party that would presage a dramatic shift in regional partisan alignment.

In Alaska in 2010 Murkowski unexpectedly lost the primary to a candidate that her campaign never took seriously, Jeff Miller, a former U.S. magistrate judge. He was supported by former governor Sarah Palin, who was the GOP nominee for vice president in 2008.

Murkowski's surprise loss was attributed to overlooking the strength of voter discontent represented by the Tea Party movement.

When she lost to Miller she was unable, under Alaskan law, to run as an independent. Instead she elected to wage a write-in campaign, a long-shot effort that not only required voters to take the extra step of penning in her name but to get the spelling correct. But Murkowski prevailed, beating Miller by more than 10,000 votes; however, her winning total was only 39 percent of total votes cast because of the presence of five other candidates in the race, including Miller.

Amendment required that blacks be fully counted for apportionment purposes. On this basis, several southern states tried to claim additional representation on readmission to the Union. Tennessee, for example, elected an extra U.S. representative in 1868, claiming that adding the full slave population entitled the state to nine instead of eight House members. Virginia and South Carolina followed suit. But the House refused to seat the additional representatives, requiring the states to wait for the regular reapportionment after the 1870 census for any changes in their representation.

A formula in the Fourteenth Amendment, designed to coerce southern states to accept black voting participation by reducing House seats wherever voting rights were abridged, never was implemented because of its complexity. Instead, the Republican-controlled House unseated Democrats from districts in former Confederate states where abuses of the RIGHT TO VOTE were charged. Between 1881 and 1897, the House unseated eighteen Democrats on this basis.

Another anomaly, of a different sort, arose from the 1930 MIDTERM ELECTION, when the beginning of the Great Depression threatened to end the Republicans' long-standing domination of the House. On election night in November, it appeared that the Republicans had nevertheless retained the House by a narrow margin. The tally showed 218 Republicans elected, against 216 Democrats and one independent. But in those days, before the Twentieth Amendment moved up the convening date, thirteen months elapsed between the election and the convening of the new Congress. During that interval, an unusually large number of deaths (fourteen) occurred among the newly elected representatives.

In SPECIAL ELECTIONS to fill the vacancies, several had no effect on the political balance because the same party retained the seat. But in three cases Republicans who died were replaced by Democrats, tipping the balance to the Democrats' favor in time for them to organize the new Congress in December 1931. A fourth Republican vacancy went to the Democrats in early 1932.

When the Seventy-second Congress convened on December 7, 1931, House Democrats held the edge, 219 to 215, with one independent. As the majority, they were able to elect Democrat John Nance Garner of Texas as Speaker.

Even without the special-election gains, control of the House likely would have passed to the Democrats in 1931. Immediately after the 1930 general election, a group of Farm Belt Republicans announced that they would withhold their votes from veteran Speaker Nicholas Longworth of Ohio and allow the Democrats to organize the House, which they did. The vote for Garner as Speaker was 218 to 207, a margin greater than the three seats the Democrats gained during the preceding thirteen months.

In 1932 Garner was elected as Franklin D. Roosevelt's first vice president in a partisan landslide that gave the Democrats a sizable majority in the House.

Democrats also took control of the Senate in 2001 under unusual circumstances. The 2000 elections left the Senate divided 50–50 between the parties, with Republican vice president Dick Cheney representing the tie-breaking vote that enabled his party to run the chamber. But a few months into the session, Sen. James Jeffords of Vermont announced that he would leave the Republican Party, become an INDEPENDENT, and support Democratic leader Tom Daschle. This gave the Democrats an effective 51–49 edge. Jeffords, a moderate voice in the increasingly conservative Republican Party, said his switch was because of disagreements with party leaders over issues such as defense and the environment.

Sen. James Jeffords of Vermont left the Republican Party in 2001 to become an independent and caucus with the Democrats, effectively shifting the balance of power in the Senate.

Source: CQ Photo / Scott J. Ferrell

A 1972 House election oddity resulted from the preelection disappearance of two House Democrats, Majority Leader Hale Boggs of Louisiana and Nick Begich of Alaska, during an Alaskan airplane trip. Despite their absence, both were reelected. Boggs's wife, Lindy, was elected to succeed him after he was declared legally dead in 1973. Begich was declared legally dead after the 1972 election, and a special election to replace him was held in 1973.

In 2000 Gov. Mel Carnahan of Missouri was locked in a tight race for Senate with the Republican incumbent, John Ashcroft, when he died in a plane crash a few weeks before ELECTION DAY. Carnahan's name remained on the ballot, however, and voters elected him posthumously to the Senate. Missouri's new governor appointed Carnahan's widow, Jean, to the seat.

Similarly, Hawaii elected Democrat Patsy Mink posthumously to the House of Representatives in 2002. The twelve-term incumbent died five weeks before election, but her name remained on the ballot. Her overwhelmingly Democratic district gave her 52 percent of the vote on November 5, in part to keep the seat open for a special election. Democrat Ed Case won a special election in January 2003 to complete her term.

Another 2002 anomaly occurred when Sen. Paul D. Wellstone of Minnesota died in a plane crash two weeks before he was up for reelection. Minnesota law allowed parties to make a late substitution on the ballot. The state's Democratic Party found an unusual replacement for Wellstone, former vice president Walter F. Mondale. Campaigning for only one week, the seventy-four-year-old Mondale lost in a close vote to Republican Norm Coleman.

In 2006 Rep. Mark Foley of Florida resigned from the House just six weeks before the November general election, after it was revealed that he had had improper communications with young male House pages. Republicans selected state representative Joe Negron as their new nominee, but under Florida law Foley's resignation came too late to remove his name from the ballot. However, the law also provided that votes cast for Foley would be automatically transferred to Negron, but the election was won by Democrat Tim Mahoney.

Some anomalies involve a state that votes strongly for one party in most elections but favors the other party in some smaller subset. The largely rural and conservative-leaning state of North Dakota has been a Republican stronghold in presidential races for much of its history and has elected mostly Republican governors and sizable Republican majorities in the state legislature. Yet from the 1986 through 2006 elections, the state elected only Democrats to its two U.S. Senate and one U.S. House seat. Massachusetts, on the other hand, is such a Democratic stronghold that voters elected only Democrats to its congressional delegation (two senators, ten House members) from the 1996 through 2006 elections. But from 1990 through 2002, state voters elected Republicans as governor, a streak that ended with the victory of Democrat Deval Patrick in 2006.

Electoral Behavior

Many factors shape the choices a voter makes on ELECTION DAY. Collectively, the voters' decisions constitute the electorate's political behavior, which may vary from one election to another.

Political scientists generally agree that PARTY IDENTIFICATION exerts the strongest influence on the voter's choice among candidates. Although the proportion of INDEPENDENTS is substantial, most Americans still identify themselves as Democrats or Republicans. As a rule, when they step into the voting booth, they support their party's nominee for the office at stake.

Other factors, however, may outweigh party affiliation under certain circumstances. This is particularly true in PRIMARY elections, when the candidates are all of the same party and vying for a group's nomination. In such cases, the candidate's public image—looks, personality, background, grasp of the issues, inspirational qualities, and the like—may be the chief determinant.

In the television age, candidates usually run independently of the parties, making image all the more important. In such CANDIDATE-CENTERED CAMPAIGNS, especially for the presidency, the voter is unlikely to be personally acquainted with those who are running. All he or she is likely to know about the candidate comes from MEDIA COVERAGE of the campaign or MEDIA USE by the campaign through interviews, talk-show appearances, and POLITICAL ADVERTISING. This information in turn helps to shape the voter's perception of the candidate's image as negative or positive.

POLLING measures the public's attitude toward the candidates leading up to the election. Often the approval ratings fluctuate. Both major-party nominees for president usually receive a POST-CONVENTION BOUNCE in the ratings.

In the 1996 election, for example, President Bill Clinton was consistently ahead in the polls, even though he was under investigation by an independent counsel for his role in the Arkansas Whitewater real estate deal before he became president. He was also facing an unprecedented sexual harassment trial in a civil suit brought by Paula Jones, a former Arkansas state employee.

CLOSER LOOK

The Ups and Downs of George W. Bush

The following are the job approval ratings for President George W. Bush, as recorded by the New York Times/CBS News polls, soon after his first inauguration in 2001, at his high point following his assertive response to the attacks of September 11, 2001, after his close reelection victory in 2004, and at his low point shortly before leaving office following the 2008 elections.

Poll Dates	Approve	Disapprove	Don't Know
February 10–12, 2001	53%	21%	26%
September 20–23, 2001	89	7	5
November 18–21, 2004	51	44	5
June 26–28, 2007	27	65	8
January 11–14, 2009	22	73	5

Yet Republican challenger Bob Dole could not match Clinton's overall approval ratings from the American public.

The public's view of a president, measured by personal and job approval ratings in opinion polls, can change sharply and sometimes over relatively short periods of time. This was the experience of Republican president George H. W. Bush, who was elected in 1988, and his son, George W. Bush, who won presidential elections in 2000 and 2004.

The elder Bush saw his approval ratings soar to record heights in early 1991 after a U.S.-led coalition forced a quick end to the occupation of Kuwait by Iraq, which had invaded its smaller neighbor the previous August. For a time, it appeared Bush was a shoo-in to win a second term in 1992. But economic problems and a broken promise not to raise taxes sent his approval ratings plummeting as fast as they had risen. Bush lost the 1992 election to Democrat Clinton.

In part, Bush was a victim of RETROSPECTIVE VOT-ING, another major aspect of electoral behavior. The voters looked back on Bush as vice president and then successor to the popular Ronald Reagan, and they found Bush wanting in comparison with Clinton. INCUMBENCY and previous service did more harm than good to Bush's reelection chances. Voters apparently doubted Bush's ability to handle the worsening economy.

To an unusually strong degree, ISSUE VOTING also helped Clinton, particularly in the 1996 campaign. His stands on abortion rights, health care, child care, edu-

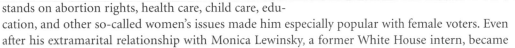

President George W. Bush comforts a firefighter while touring the World Trade Center site in September 2001. Bush's approval rating approached 90 percent following his assertive response to the terrorist attacks but fell to less than 30 percent in 2007 as a result of the unpopular war in Iraq.

Source: AP Images/Doug Mills

cation, and other so-called women's issues made him especially popular with female voters. Even after his extramarital relationship with Monica Lewinsky, a former White House intern, became public in 1998, Clinton continued to draw strong support in the polls from women.

A decade after the elder Bush left the White House, the younger Bush's approval ratings broke his father's previous records less than a year into his presidency, as the public rallied behind his assertive efforts to punish the al-Qaeda terrorists who masterminded the September 11, 2001, attacks on the United States and the radical Taliban government of Afghanistan that had sheltered them. Bush's popularity helped him push a resolution through Congress in October 2002 authorizing him to use military force against the regime of Iraqi dictator Saddam Hussein, which had repeatedly failed to cooperate with UN weapons inspectors and the administration said was hoarding weapons of mass destruction. His approval ratings also abetted the Republican Party's successful effort to win control of the Senate.

But it became clear that the Iraq war, which was launched in March 2003 and quickly succeeded at felling Saddam Hussein, had spawned an insurgency opposed to the U.S. presence and a cycle of vicious sectarian violence, leading to an American commitment that was far more expensive, deadly, and long-term than the public had anticipated. Despite tepid job approval numbers during his 2004 reelection campaign, Bush managed a narrow victory over his Democratic challenger John Kerry. However, deepening problems in Iraq, combined with a weak response by the Bush administration to the destruction along the Gulf Coast wreaked by Hurricane Katrina in August 2005, sent the president's job approval ratings toppling from their post-9/11 highs of about 90 percent into the low 30 percent range. The president's low popularity in turn contributed to a 2006 midterm election that saw his Republican Party lose control of both chambers of Congress. His ratings got no better in the last two years in office as the Iraq war dragged on and the economy in 2008 plunged into the worst recession in more than half a century. Voter fatigue with the Bush years, and the consequences of the recession, helped boost Barack Obama's successful quest for the White House in 2008.

Electoral behavior is also affected by the age of the voters. Older people have higher VOTER TURNOUT rates than young people, particularly those in the eighteen-to-twenty-one age group. ABSENTEE VOTING makes it possible for people who are away from home or have difficulty getting to the polls to participate in elections. Some states are experimenting with elections conducted entirely by mail.

The public's POLITICAL SOCIALIZATION remains one of the most enduring factors in determining how people vote. Lessons learned in childhood, or remarks overheard from parents, help to shape the IDEOLOGY that will likely guide the voter for a lifetime.

Electoral College and Votes

The election of a president and vice president is accomplished through the Electoral College system, which the framers of the Constitution conceived as a compromise between selection by Congress and DIRECT ELECTION by popular vote. Each state has as many members in the college as it does in Congress, and it is those 538 electors—equal to the 435 House members and 100 senators, plus three votes added for the District of Columbia under the Twenty-third Amendment to the Constitution, ratified in 1961—who actually elect the government's two top officers.

Few of the framers' actions have been more criticized. Thomas Jefferson decried the indirect election system as "the most dangerous blot on our Constitution," and people have been calling for reform ever since.

The compromise made a great concession to the less-populous states because it assured them of three electoral votes (two for their two senators and at least one for their representative) no matter how small their populations might be. The plan also left important powers with the states by giving complete discretion to state legislatures to determine the method of choosing electors.

The system finally agreed upon (Article II, section 1, clause 2) grew out of problems arising from diverse state voting requirements, the slavery problem, big-state versus small-state rivalries, and the complexities of the balance of power among different branches of the government. Moreover, it was probably as close to a direct popular election as the men who wrote the Constitution thought possible and appropriate at the time.

Direct election was opposed because it was believed generally that the people lacked sufficient knowledge of the character and qualifications of possible candidates to make an intelligent choice. Many delegates also feared that the people of the various states would be unlikely to agree on a single person, usually casting their votes for FAVORITE SON candidates well known to them.

The term *Electoral College* itself does not appear in the Constitution. It was first used unofficially in the early 1800s and became the official designation for the electoral body in 1845.

How the System Works

When Americans vote for a particular presidential candidate, they are in fact voting for a slate of electors pledged to that candidate. The winning electors in each state then meet in their state capital on the first Monday after the second Wednesday in December to cast their votes for president and vice president. A statement of the vote is sent to Washington, D.C., where Congress counts the votes on January 6.

An ABSOLUTE MAJORITY of electoral votes (270 out of a total of 538 in recent years) is needed to elect. This normally is not a problem under the nation's long-standing TWO-PARTY SYSTEM; in most elections, only the major-party candidates have qualified for electoral votes, and the statistical likelihood that the sums of the candidates' state electoral vote victories will add up to an exact 269–269 tie under today's alignment is low (though the 271 votes that gave Republican George W. Bush the White House in 2000 came perilously close).

Yet the possibility exists for a tie, or for an unusually strong third-party candidate to win enough electoral votes to deprive any major-party candidate of an electoral majority. In such an instance, the House of Representatives must choose the president, which has occurred twice in U.S. history: in the 1800 election won by Thomas Jefferson and the 1824 election won by John Quincy Adams. (The 1876 presidential election, in which there was a schismatic dispute over which candidate had secured an electoral vote majority, was resolved by a bipartisan commission in favor of Republican Rutherford B. Hayes.) In the case of a House election of a president, each state's delegation has one vote—which almost certainly would go to the candidate of the party holding the most seats in that delegation—and a candidate must receive the votes of a majority of states for election. (The Senate chooses the vice president if no candidate wins a majority of the Electoral College vote for that office.)

Originally, no distinction was made between Electoral College ballots for president and vice president. That caused confusion when the two-party system developed and parties began to nominate party tickets for the two offices. All the electors of one party tended to vote for their party's two nominees. But with no distinction between the presidential and vice presidential nominees, there was danger of a tie vote. That actually happened in the election of 1800. The election was thrown into the House of Representatives, which was forced to choose between running mates Thomas Jefferson and Aaron Burr.

In 1804 the Twelfth Amendment was added to the Constitution, requiring separate votes for the two offices. The amendment kept the constitutional requirement that the electors vote for at least one candidate who "shall not be an inhabitant of the same state with themselves," which in effect ensured that the president and vice president would be from different states. (See PRESIDENTIAL ELECTIONS CHRONOLOGY.)

The only unanimously elected president was the first one, George Washington. In 1789, before the system was changed and each elector had two votes, Washington received 100 percent of the electoral votes it was possible for one candidate to receive. Under the system as revised by the Twelfth Amendment, two candidates came close to unanimous election: James Monroe in 1820 received 98.3 percent of the electoral vote, and Franklin D. Roosevelt in 1936 received 98.5 percent.

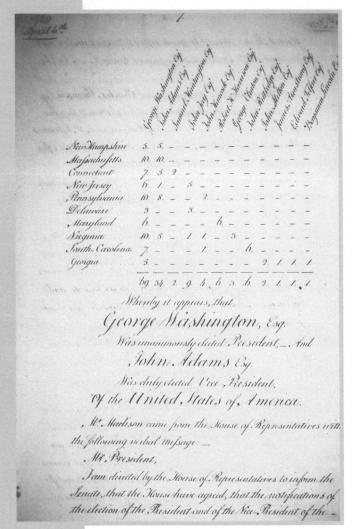

Page 7 of the Senate Journal, April 6, 1789, showing the electoral vote in the first presidential election, which awarded George Washington a unanimous vote.

Source: National Archives and Records Administration

Until the Twentieth Amendment was adopted in 1933, there were no rules for parceling out electoral votes of a candidate who died after the election. This ELECTORAL ANOMALY happened in 1872 when the Democratic/Liberal Republican candidate, Horace Greeley, died after losing the popular vote to Ulysses S. Grant. Left to their own judgment, the sixty-six Democratic electors divided their votes among four candidates. Three Georgia electors insisted on casting their votes for the deceased Greeley, but Congress refused to count them.

Presumably the Twentieth Amendment (the so-called Lame Duck Amendment) would apply if a future candidate should die after winning electoral votes. The amendment states that the vice president-elect becomes president if the president-elect dies before taking office. It also empowers Congress to decide what to do if the president-elect and the vice president-elect both fail to qualify by the date prescribed for commencement of their terms, and it gives Congress authority to settle problems arising from the death of candidates in cases in which the election is thrown to the House (president) or Senate (vice president).

If a presidential or vice presidential nominee resigns or dies after the NATIONAL PARTY CONVENTION but before ELECTION DAY, the vacancy on the ticket is filled by the DEMOCRATIC NATIONAL COMMITTEE or the REPUBLICAN NATIONAL COMMITTEE. Both major parties have had to replace vice presidential nominees. (See RUNNING MATE; VICE PRESIDENT.)

Method of Choosing Electors

The Constitution stipulates that each state shall specify how its electors are to be chosen. Initially, the norm was for state legislatures to appoint electors, although a handful of states used direct popular election. After the first three presidential elections, popular vote increasingly became the preferred method for choosing electors. Since 1860, the only state to use legislative appointment was Colorado in 1876.

After 1832 electors came to be chosen by what is known as the *general ticket*. Electors for each party are grouped together on a general party ticket and are elected as a bloc. In all but a few states, electors' names do not even appear on the ballot. Instead, voters cast their ballot for a particular party's presidential ticket, and the winner of the popular vote wins all of the state's electors, in what is known as WINNER TAKE ALL.

FAITHLESS ELECTORS

One cause for splits in a state's electoral vote is the so-called faithless elector. By 2008, according to the Congressional Research Service, twenty-seven states and the District of Columbia had laws requiring electors to vote for the state's popular winner. These states were Alabama, Alaska, California, Colorado, Connecticut, Florida, Hawaii, Maine, Maryland, Massachusetts, Michigan, Mississippi, Montana, Nebraska, Nevada, New Mexico, North Carolina, Ohio, Oklahoma, Oregon, South Carolina, Vermont, Virginia, Washington, Wisconsin, and Wyoming.

In Michigan and North Carolina, a "faithless elector" was not to be counted, with the remaining electors filling the vacancy. New Mexico, North Carolina, Oklahoma, South Carolina, and Washington provided criminal penalties or fines for violations. However, no faithless elector has ever been punished, and experts doubt that it would be constitutionally possible to do so.

In reality, electors are almost always faithful to the candidate of the party with which they are affiliated, law or no law. But at times in U.S. political history, electors have broken ranks to vote for candidates not supported by their parties. In 1796 a Pennsylvania Federalist elector voted for Democratic-Republican Thomas Jefferson instead of Federalist John Adams. Some historians and political scientists claim that three Democratic-Republican electors voted for Adams. However, the fluidity of political party lines at that early date and the well-known personal friendship between Adams and at least one of the electors make the claim of their being faithless electors one of continuing controversy. In 1820 a New Hampshire Democratic-Republican elector voted for John Quincy Adams instead of the party nominee, James Monroe.

There was no further occurrence until 1948, when Preston Parks, a Harry S. Truman elector in Tennessee, voted for Gov. J. Strom Thurmond of South Carolina, the States Rights Democratic Party (Dixiecrat) presidential nominee. Since then, there have been the following instances:

- In 1956 W. F. Turner, an Adlai Stevenson elector in Alabama, voted for Walter B. Jones, a local judge.
- In 1960 Henry D. Irwin, a Richard Nixon elector in Oklahoma, voted for Sen. Harry F. Byrd, Democrat of Virginia.
- In 1968, Lloyd W. Bailey, a Nixon elector in North Carolina, voted for George C. Wallace, the American Independent Party candidate.
- In 1972 Roger L. MacBride, a Nixon elector in Virginia, voted for John Hospers, the Libertarian Party candidate.
- In 1976 Mike Padden, a Gerald R. Ford elector in Washington State, voted for former governor Ronald Reagan of California.
- In 1988 Margaret Leach, a Michael Dukakis elector in West Virginia, voted for Dukakis's running mate, Sen. Lloyd Bentsen of Texas.
- In 2000 Barbara Lett Simmons, an Al Gore elector in Washington, D.C., withheld her vote from Gore.
- In 2004 an anonymous Kerry elector in Minnesota voted for Kerry's running mate, Sen. John Edwards of North Carolina.

Source: *Guide to U.S. Elections*, 6th ed. (Washington, DC: CQ Press, 2009), 819b.

Maine and Nebraska are exceptions. They allocate their electors by presidential-election districts that match their CONGRESSIONAL DISTRICTS (two in Maine and three in Nebraska). Though the winner of the statewide popular vote is guaranteed two electoral votes (equal to the two senators in each state), the remaining votes are individually allocated to the leading candidate in each of the state's congressional districts. Until 2008, the two states always cast their votes for one candidate. But in that election, Democrat Barack Obama won one Nebraska congressional district and thus one electoral vote from the state. Maine continued its history of casting votes for one candidate.

Under the Constitution, electors are free to vote as they please, but electors who do so are rare and are known as *faithless electors*. Some states prohibit faithless voting, but the constitutionality of such laws has not been tested. The most recent instance of a faithless elector was in 2000, when an elector from the District of Columbia pledged to Democrat Al Gore abstained from voting to protest the District's lack of voting representation in Congress. Gore thus received 266 electoral votes, instead of 267.

The Constitution did not say what to do if there were disputes about electors' ballots. That issue became a critical concern following the 1876 election when, for the first time, the outcome had to be determined by decisions on disputed electoral votes. The 1876 campaign pitted Republican Hayes against Democrat Samuel J. Tilden. Tilden led in the popular vote by more than 250,000 votes but fell one vote short of a majority in the Electoral College; the votes of three southern states were in dispute. After Republicans agreed to withdraw federal troops from the South, effectively ending the post–Civil War Reconstruction era, a special commission awarded all the disputed electoral votes to Hayes.

In 1887 Congress passed permanent legislation for the handling of disputed electoral votes. The 1887 law, still in force, authorized each state to determine the legality of the choice of electors. Majorities of both the House and Senate are needed to reject any disputed electoral votes. If the two chambers cannot agree, the electors certified by the governor are accepted.

These measures, which sat untested for more than a century, were suddenly being discussed in 2000. Four weeks after the November 7 election, Vice President Al Gore had 267 electoral votes to Texas governor George W. Bush's 246; Florida's twenty-five electoral votes, which would push either candidate over the 270-vote threshold needed for election, were in dispute. Bush led in the statewide popular vote by 1,725 votes when the polls closed. A machine recount cut Bush's lead to 930, and subsequent hand recounts, conducted primarily in Democratic-leaning counties, cut his lead to 537 votes.

A number of court cases at the state and federal level relating to the recounts and to the legality of how absentee ballots were handled put Florida's slate of electors in doubt. As Democratic challengers worked their way through the courts, the Republican-dominated Florida legislature (House, 77–43; Senate, 25–15) convened a special session to pass legislation consistent with the 1887 law and the Constitution. On December 12, by a 79–41 vote, the state house of representatives named a slate of Bush electors to the Electoral College. Before the Florida Senate acted on the resolution, the U.S. Supreme Court ended all recount procedures, and Bush prevailed in Florida, clinching the presidency. The 1887 law remains untested.

Bush, who trailed Gore in the national popular vote in 2000, won a close but clear-cut victory in 2004. He took 51 percent of the national popular vote and 286 electoral votes to defeat Democrat John Kerry, a senator from Massachusetts.

Other Anomalies

The complicated and indirect system of presidential selection has led to anomalies other than the Horace Greeley situation. In 1836, for example, the Whigs sought to take advantage of the electoral system by running different presidential candidates in different parts of the country. William Henry Harrison ran in most of New England, the mid-Atlantic states, and the Midwest; Daniel Webster ran in Massachusetts; Hugh White of Tennessee ran in the South. The theory was that each candidate would capture electoral votes for the Whig Party in the region where he was strongest. Then the Whig electors could combine on one candidate or, alternatively, throw the election into the House, whichever seemed to their advantage. The scheme did not work, however, because Martin Van Buren, the Democratic nominee, captured a majority of the electoral votes.

Critics of the Electoral College system point out several possible sources of an electoral crisis. First, a candidate who loses the popular vote may still be elected president. That has happened four times in the nation's history. Adams in 1824, Hayes in 1876, Benjamin Harrison in 1888, and George W. Bush in 2000 won the presidency with a smaller popular vote than their opponents received.

In the 1824 election, Andrew Jackson, hero of the War of 1812, ran ahead of Adams in both the popular and electoral voting, but he fell short of the necessary majority, throwing the election to the House, which chose Adams.

In 1888 Republican Harrison won about 100,000 fewer votes (of almost 12 million cast) than Democratic incumbent Grover Cleveland, but he won the electoral college vote by 233 to 168 because he won in larger states that had more electoral votes.

In 2000, Bush trailed Gore in the national popular vote by approximately 540,000 votes out of more than 105 million cast. In percentage terms, Gore outpolled Bush 48.38 to 47.87, a margin of 0.51 percent, yet he won only twenty states and the District of Columbia to Bush's thirty states. Despite winning ten fewer states, Gore lost in the electoral count by only four votes.

Only once has the Senate elected a vice president because no candidate won an electoral vote majority. Richard M. Johnson, Martin Van Buren's running mate on the Democratic ticket, fell one vote short in 1837 after Van Buren won the presidency. Objecting to Johnson's alleged sexual relationships with female slaves, Virginia's electors gave their votes to another candidate. Limited by the Twelfth Amendment to a choice between the two top contenders, the Senate voted along party lines for Johnson over Francis Granger, a Whig.

Richard M. Johnson is the only vice president to have been elected by the Senate. He was chosen in 1837, when no candidate won an electoral vote majority.

Source: Library of Congress

Because a presidential ticket takes a state's electoral votes by winning most of the popular vote (a PLURALITY) and not necessarily a majority (more than 50 percent), the system permits lopsided electoral vote victories and the election of so-called minority presidents. Since 1824 there have been eighteen minority presidents, including three elected twice with less than a majority of the popular vote: Grover Cleveland (1884 and 1892), Woodrow Wilson (1912 and 1916), and Bill Clinton (1992 and 1996).

Clinton's 1996 win provided a vivid example of how the electoral system can exaggerate the margin of victory. Although Clinton won only 49 percent of the popular vote, he gained 70 percent of the electoral vote (379), against 30 percent (159) for Republican challenger Bob Dole. Dole won 41 percent of the popular vote, and Reform Party candidate Ross Perot won 8 percent, with no electoral votes.

Clinton targeted the largest states and the strategy paid off. He took California (54 votes), New York (33 votes), and six of the other states in the top-ten electoral vote category. Of the top ten he lost only Texas (32 votes) and North Carolina (14 votes).

Reform Efforts

Although the Electoral College system prevents the smaller states from being completely left out, it has not stopped the megastates from dominating the presidential election process. To correct the imbalance, numerous reforms have been proposed, including elimination of the Electoral College altogether.

Concern also has been expressed about a possible deadlock in the Electoral College if the election involves more than two candidates. If a third-party candidate won one or two states in a close race, he or she could try to play an important "broker" role either in the Electoral College or, if one candidate did not receive a majority in the Electoral College, in the House.

George Wallace's candidacy on the American Independent Party ticket in 1968 presented such a contingency. Republican Richard M. Nixon, a former vice president, and Democrat Hubert H. Humphrey, the incumbent vice president, ran one of the closest races in history. Yet Wallace, despite earlier hopes of winning the whole South, won only five states and forty-six electoral votes. If Nixon had lost just California or two or three smaller states that were close, he would have been denied an electoral majority.

Proposals to change or do away with some of the obsolete and odd features of the Electoral College system have included direct election of the president, bonus electors for the winner of the national popular vote, and proportional allocation of a state's electoral vote, which would lead to more frequent congressional selection of the president. Another proposal that gained interest by 2011 involved an interstate compact in which signatory states pledged to cast their electoral votes for the winner of the national popular vote. The proposal required state legislatures to adopt enacting bills in identical form and specified that it would not go into effect until enough states had joined to constitute a winning majority—270 votes—in the Electoral College. Eleven states had approved legislation by 2011; the proposal was under active consideration in other states.

More on this topic:
Direct Election, p. 161
Favorite Son, p. 202
Plurality, p. 386
Popular Vote, p. 431
Third Parties, p. 627
Two-Party System, p. 636
Vice President, p. 644
Winner Take All, p. 675

None of the reforms has been adopted. Each, except possibly the last one, would need a constitutional amendment, requiring a two-thirds vote of Congress. During the Ninety-fifth Congress (1977–1979), a majority in the Senate voted to abolish the Electoral College as proposed by President Jimmy Carter, but the proposed amendment did not receive the necessary two-thirds vote.

For all its supposed faults, the Electoral College system has withstood repeated assaults for several reasons. Some states, large or small, fear that they would lose out if the president were elected directly by the people. And despite its potential for failure, the system has defenders who hold to the adage, "If it ain't broke, don't fix it." They point out that, for the most part, the system has worked for more than 200 years, with scant evidence that it will not continue to work just as well in the twenty-first century.

Entrance Polls *See* EXIT POLLS

Equal Time and Rebuttal Rules

The First Amendment's protection of press freedom extends to all forms of news media. Unlike print media, however, the electronic media are subject to some government regulation, including a few rules that affect elections. The most important of these are the *equal time* and related *right of rebuttal* rules, ensuring balance in airtime given to political candidates.

Access to the airwaves, television especially, has become vital to campaigns for major elective offices in the United States. Television is the dominant medium by which candidates try to "sell" themselves to the voters and convey their positions on issues. Television advertising expenditures on presidential races, by the candidates' campaigns alone, have measured in the hundreds of millions of dollars since the mid-1990s. Moody's Investors Service, in a June 2011 analysis, estimated that there had been $2.3 billion in spending on political TV ads in 2010, a midterm election year in which there was no presidential contest.

Thus, free airtime can be crucial to candidates, particularly those who are less well-known than the FRONT-RUNNER candidates.

Under the equal-time rule, a station that gives time to one candidate for a specific office must make the same opportunity available to other candidates for the same office. But the rule does not apply to regular news programs, most talk shows, or DEBATES between candidates. The right-of-rebuttal rule requires stations to make their facilities available to any person to respond after he or she has been assailed on radio or television.

In practice, though, the impact is more limited than the law suggests. Commercial radio and television stations rarely give free airtime because it opens them to equal-time demands from numerous INDEPENDENT and third-party candidates.

If one candidate buys airtime on a broadcasting outlet, the only legal requirement is that other candidates for the same office be given the opportunity to buy their own ad time at comparable rates. But the law does not require broadcasters to give an opposing candidate free airtime if he or she cannot afford to buy. If a candidate buys time to attack an opponent, the broadcaster is obliged to try to schedule rebuttal time if the opponent wishes to buy it.

With the increase in NEGATIVE CAMPAIGNING since the 1980s, "attack ads" have become commonplace, resulting in expensive barrages and counterbarrages of political commercials.

Public radio and television stations, which sometimes give airtime to candidates, won the right in 1998 to exclude certain candidates from their broadcast debates. Ruling in *Arkansas Educational Television v. Forbes,* the Supreme Court voted 6–3 to affirm public TV's right to limit debate participants to those it believes have sufficient public support.

Debates are considered under the law to be news events that are exempt from equal-time provisions. Spot news coverage of officeholders in their official capacities, including news conferences, is also exempt from equal-time rules, even though this kind of visibility is one of the biggest advantages accruing to incumbents when they run for reelection or another office.

First Amendment Considerations

Newspapers, magazines, and other publications also play critical roles in MEDIA USE BY CAMPAIGNS and MEDIA COVERAGE OF CAMPAIGNS. For the most part they, too, try to provide balanced coverage of political campaigns. Unlike the electronic media, however, newspapers and magazines are not required by law or government regulation to provide equal news or advertising space to opposing viewpoints. The Supreme Court has upheld the print media's exemption from such regulation under the free press and free speech protections of the First Amendment. In *Miami Herald Publishing Co. v. Tornillo* (1974), the Court unanimously struck down a Florida law that required newspapers to grant political candidates equal space to reply to criticism of their public records.

The Court on the other hand has upheld the government's authority to regulate the broadcast industry. Citing the limited number of radio and television frequencies available, the Court in 1943 sustained the power of the Federal Communications Commission (FCC) to determine who receives licenses to use the airwaves. It emphasized, however, that the FCC must award licenses on the basis of neutral principles that do not favor one applicant over another because of an applicant's particular views.

FCC regulations fall into three categories: (1) rules limiting the number of stations controlled by a single organization; (2) rules calling for examination of the goals and performances of stations as part of their periodic licensing; and (3) rules guaranteeing fair treatment of individuals.

Under the Communications Act of 1934, the FCC for years sharply limited the number of radio and television stations a single organization could own in the same media market or nationally. In a comprehensive rewriting of the telephone and broadcast laws, however, Congress in 1996 relaxed the limits on ownership of multiple radio and television stations. The new law also made it easier for broadcasters to renew their licenses. The Telecommunications Act of 1996 (PL 104–104) extended the license period to eight years, with no consideration of competing applications required unless the owner had not served the public or had violated laws or FCC regulations.

A company could own unlimited AM (amplitude modulation) or FM (frequency modulation) radio stations nationally so long as they did not exceed the multiple ownership limits that apply in individual markets; these limits vary, depending on the size of the market. A network or other company also could own an unlimited number of TV stations, provided their signals did not reach more than 35 percent of the nation's households. The new law also removed a prohibition against cross-ownership of cable systems and TV stations in the same market.

Regulation Controversies

Federal law requires broadcasters to "serve the public interest, convenience, and necessity." This rather vague standard gives the FCC little guidance to determine whether to renew a station's license other than to review the mix of programs presented, the proportion of public service offerings, and the inclusion of programs for selected groups. But the agency does not try to scrutinize program content in any detail. With its limited staff, the FCC has been neither inclined nor able to rigorously define and enforce rules on programming for the public interest.

In principle, the equal-time and rebuttal rules are related to—but different from—the now-abandoned *fairness doctrine* that caused almost four decades of controversy in broadcast and political circles. The FCC developed the fairness doctrine in the late 1940s to require licensees to devote a reasonable percentage of time to coverage of public issues and to provide an opportunity for presentation of contrasting points of view on those issues. Broadcasters challenged the doctrine, however, as a violation of their right to determine program content free from government interference.

In 1969 the Court in *Red Lion Broadcasting Co. v. Federal Communications Commission* upheld the government's authority to impose such regulations. Again citing the scarcity of broadcast frequencies, the Court said that a broadcaster "has no constitutional right to be the one who holds the license or to monopolize a radio frequency to the exclusion of his fellow citizens."

Broadcasters continued to fight the fairness doctrine. They contended that it actually worked against presentation of different viewpoints on public policy issues. Instead, they pointed out, the fairness doctrine encouraged stations to avoid controversial programming. The proliferation of third parties made compliance even more difficult.

There also was evidence that the broadcast media, wishing to comply with the fairness doctrine and not risk losing their licenses, assumed that every political issue has two sides and only two sides, when in fact many issues are more complex than that. As CBS correspondent Bill Plante put it during the 1980 campaign, "If you have somebody who's calling the president an idiot, you then almost have to have somebody who's saying, 'Well, no, he's not, he's a great statesman.'"

In 1987, however, broadcasters finally won their battle. They gained a sympathetic hearing from President Ronald Reagan, who vetoed a congressional attempt to convert the fairness doctrine from FCC policy into statutory law. After the veto, the FCC promptly voted 4–0 to abolish the thirty-eight-year-old doctrine. The commission emphasized, however, that the action did not affect its enforcement of the equal-time or right-of-rebuttal requirements.

After the fairness doctrine was repealed, congressional oversight and potential litigation still maintained pressure on broadcasters to continue airing opposing viewpoints. For example, the broadcast of rebuttals after presidential, gubernatorial, and mayoral addresses dealing with major public issues is now commonplace.

In the 1990s *issue advertising* emerged as a controversial form of political debate. Keyed to ISSUE VOTING, issue ads provided a means to circumvent contribution limits of CAMPAIGN FINANCE laws. Instead of contributing directly to an antiabortion candidate, for example, the candidate's supporters could spend without limit on antiabortion ads as long as the ads did not violate the so-called "magic words" test, established by the Supreme Court in 1976 in the campaign finance case of *Buckley v. Valeo,* that deems issue advertising as subject to spending and fund-raising limitations only if it expressly advocated for or against the election of a specific candidate.

> ## "If you have somebody who's calling the president an idiot, you then almost have to have somebody who's saying, 'Well, no, he's not, he's a great statesman.'"
>
> **—CBS correspondent Bill Plante,** during the 1980 presidential campaign

The Supreme Court ruled in *Columbia Broadcasting System v. Democratic National Committee* (1973) that broadcasters could refuse to sell commercial time for issue-related advertising. In *CBS, Inc. v. Federal Communications Commission* (1981) it upheld a law that required broadcasters to provide candidates for federal office with "reasonable access" to buying commercial time.

Although cable systems transmit signals by wire rather than the airwaves, the FCC began regulating cable television in the 1960s, in part to protect broadcasters from unfair competition and to require cable operators to serve local community needs. In 1986 the Court for the first time held that the First Amendment applies to the cable franchising process. The ruling in *City of Los Angeles v. Preferred Communications Inc.* allowed an unsuccessful applicant for a franchise to pursue a claim that the city violated his press freedom rights and antitrust law by granting only one franchise in the area to be served.

Generally the FCC regulates the electronic media with a light hand. With its vague statutory mandate and small staff, as well as its constant buffeting by conflicting industry, congressional, and administration pressures, the agency has earned the reputation of a benign regulator. Even so, the broadcasting industry is vulnerable to government pressures in a way that the print industry is not.

In 1998, for example, FCC chairman William Kennard—reportedly with President Clinton's backing—proposed that commercial broadcasters be compelled to provide free airtime to political candidates. The rule, he said, would be "minimally intrusive and doesn't trample anyone's First Amendment rights."

Broadcasters and their allies insisted such a rule could come only from Congress, where they were prepared to lobby against the potential loss of revenue. They argued that owners pay heavy fees for their licenses and candidates already receive discounts and special access to broadcast advertising under federal law. With key lawmakers voicing their opposition, the initiative quickly lost momentum.

Exit Polls

Few aspects of modern American politics are as inherently useful to political scientists, party strategists, and the news media as exit polls—surveys taken of voters as they leave polling places around the country. The polls not only provide an election day hint of the outcomes of the major contests before the actual voting concludes, but they also offer a wealth of information about the demographics of the electorate and the issues and attitudes that shaped their voting decisions.

Yet few aspects of modern American politics have been more prone to controversy. A sampling error in Florida prompted networks to declare early on Election Night 2000 that Democratic presidential nominee Al Gore had won a crucial victory in that state; the subsequent retraction of that projection and the networks' call later in the evening that Republican George W Bush had won the state and the election helped create the atmosphere of confusion that prevailed over the five weeks during which Gore contested the result in Florida, which ultimately was resolved in Bush's favor.

In a subsequent internal investigation, the Voter News Service (VNS), which had conducted exit polls for a combine of TV networks and the Associated Press wire service, identified a number of errors in its exit polling model and practices that contributed to the erroneous data. Among them was a failure to recognize the growing importance of early voting, resulting in a miscalculation of Florida's ABSENTEE VOTING.

The low point for national exit polling came in 2002, when early counts, or "runs," of survey results on election day turned up percentages for competing candidates that appeared (and in many cases turned out to be) so inaccurate that the TV networks' polling combine withheld and never published them.

These problems prompted the National Election Pool, as the network combine is known, to scrap its old system and hire two companies, Edison Media Research and Mitofsky International, to jointly produce the exit polls beginning with the 2004 elections. The latter company was owned by Warren Mitofsky, who originated modern exit polling in 1967 while working for CBS News; Mitofsky died in 2006 at age 71.

The 2004 presidential exit polls did not cause the kind of controversy the 2000 polls did, but they were not free from criticism. Early runs in key states such as Florida and Ohio showed Democratic challenger John Kerry leading President Bush. When these numbers were leaked, primarily by political Web log or "blog" sites on the Internet, they caused an optimistic buzz among Democratic activists, consternation among Republicans, and a skewed perspective among reporters preparing for the election night coverage. Bush won both of those battleground states to clinch his reelection.

> **"Doing an early poll is like reporting the results of the game at halftime."**
>
> **—Pollster Joe Lenski,**
> speaking to the Associated Press
> after the 2004 presidential election

Exit polling experts blamed those who leaked the early information, not the polls themselves. "Doing an early poll is like reporting the results of the game at halftime," said Joe Lenski, Mitofsky's polling partner, in 2004, during a postelection interview with the Associated Press. "You only have about a third of the information. No other survey research is held to that level of accuracy." Lenski said that exit poll runs done later in the day more accurately reflected the final outcomes.

The exit polling combine sought to address this situation during the 2006 midterm elections by requiring reporters seeking access to early exit poll data to spend most of election day with the polling researchers in a closed room—labeled "The Vault"—without outside communication. The procedure prevented leaks of information based on the early runs. As it turned out, the poll results on the candidate matchups—the benchmark for the accuracy of the demographic and other data in the poll—proved to be extremely close to the mark.

Exit polls are a relatively new technique in the science of POLLING, which has become an indispensable tool in modern American politics. They have been widely used in presidential elections only since 1984.

In the early years of such polling, the major television networks set up their own competing operations. The expense, redundancy, and potential for producing conflicting results drove the networks to pool their resources beginning with the 1990 MIDTERM ELECTIONS, first with the Voter News Service (VNS), then with its Edison-Mitofsky successor. The cooperatives included the Associated Press and the ABC, CBS, CNN, Fox, and NBC networks.

Entrance polls are a parallel but far less common practice conducted for the same purposes as exit polls. Entrance polling is more practicable when it is easier to interview people going into a voting place than leaving it. This is generally the case with presidential CAUCUSES, where the voters trickle in but leave all at once when the caucus ends, making it difficult for reporters to interview a representative sampling of the participants.

Brief History

The origins of exit polls are somewhat obscure, but by most accounts they are the brainchild of Warren Mitofsky, a former CENSUS statistician. NBC had used a form of exit poll in the 1964 California primaries, but it was less scientific than today's version.

Mitofsky organized the first full-fledged exit poll in Kentucky's gubernatorial contest in 1967, the same year CBS hired him to set up the first polling operation within a news organization.

Previously, the networks, sometimes working with professional pollsters, had relied solely on precinct voting and past voting patterns to project the winners on election night. Though these data remain fundamental to the media's efforts to make calls, especially in the closest races, exit polls added a key new element to the coverage of results.

Under Mitofsky's direction, the CBS team devised a systematic sampling technique of interviewing voters at specific intervals, such as every third voter, as they left the voting place. The interviewers were stationed in precincts selected to provide a cross-section of the electorate. These early exit polls were mostly for internal use by the reporters and forecasters. The results were not made public as a general rule.

Hubert H. Humphrey accepts the Democratic Party's nomination in 1968. Exit polls were first used in the presidential election between Humphrey and Richard M. Nixon, one of the closest races in American history.
Source: AP Images

Having tested it in the Kentucky race, CBS used the exit poll in the 1968 presidential contest between Hubert H. Humphrey and Richard M. Nixon, again only as a check against actual vote counts. Exit polls were conducted in twenty states, with voters asked some demographic information as well as how they voted.

By 1980 other networks were using exit polls, and some were more aggressive than CBS in basing projections on them. CBS was still using exit polls mostly for analysis and verification of the early vote counts.

As a result, NBC and ABC beat CBS in projecting Ronald Reagan's LANDSLIDE victory over Jimmy Carter in 1980. Exit polls by all three networks showed that Reagan would be the big winner in what had been expected to be a close race. But the CBS unit, still led by Mitofsky, did not project the winner until after Carter conceded.

Carter's decision to concede at about 10:00 p.m. eastern standard time, while polls were still open in California, aroused controversy about exit polls and the networks' decisions to "declare" winners early. Many argued that these results discouraged voters who had not yet cast their ballots because they believed their votes would not make a difference.

Some states subsequently tried to ban exit polls by creating so-called no–First Amendment zones near voting places, making it difficult if not impossible for poll takers to identify and interview people who had just voted. But the courts ruled that First Amendment free speech and free press rights cannot be excluded from certain areas.

On Capitol Hill, the House and Senate held hearings on exit polls but made no attempt to prohibit their use. Congress did adopt resolutions before the 1982 and 1984 elections, however, asking the networks to refrain from projecting results until all polls had closed, except those in Alaska and Hawaii.

The competitive instinct to be first caused most network news directors to set aside such concerns and widely use exit surveys to call races, sometimes within seconds of the polls closing in a state. But the serious controversies that evolved in the elections of 2000, 2002, and 2004 spurred a new cautiousness, and the networks generally withheld calls on close races and managed to avoid any egregious mistakes in their election night coverage in the three election cycles that followed.

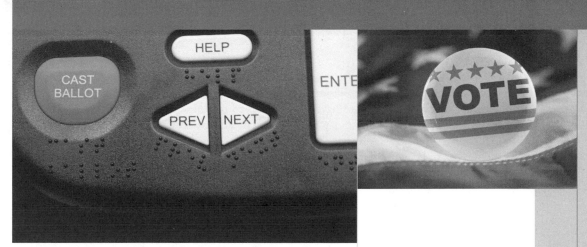

"527" Political Organizations

Tax-exempt organizations established under Section 527 of the Internal Revenue Code, widely known as "527" groups, have been a significant factor in U.S. politics for just more than a decade. The aggressive and often controversial manner in which political activists used these groups made a rapid impact on political campaigns and almost certainly played a key role in the outcome of the close 2004 presidential contest between Republican incumbent George W. Bush and Democratic challenger John Kerry.

But in the early years of the second decade of the twenty-first century, it was not clear if these 527 groups would continue their meteoric rise—or be eclipsed by a new political fund-raising vehicle known as the SuperPAC.

The emergence of SuperPACs was spurred by the January 2010 ruling by the U.S. Supreme Court, in the case of *Citizens United v. Federal Election Commission*, that struck down a provision in the Bipartisan Campaign Reform Act (BCRA) of 2002 that barred corporate entities (including businesses and labor unions) from "electioneering communications"—broadcast ads that were fashioned as issue advertising but were aimed at influencing election outcomes—within sixty days of a general election and thirty days of a primary. In ruling by a 5–4 majority that these restrictions violated the free-speech rights of corporate entities, the Court essentially established as a matter of law that corporations have free-speech rights equivalent to those of individuals.

Still, 527s set the pattern that SuperPACs followed. They were used by Republicans and Democrats and across the ideological spectrum, were allowed to accept unlimited contributions, and put the money raised to use in independent-expenditure advertising campaigns that often contained thinly veiled attacks on the opposite party or individual candidates.

The biggest issue involving 527s concerns those expensive independent-expenditure campaigns. Under a long-debated provision in the Supreme Court ruling in BUCKLEY V. VALEO (1976), political parties and other groups have been permitted to run "issue advertising" that praises or more often criticizes candidates for public office. The ads avoid the decision's "magic words" of "vote for" or "vote against" so they will not be regarded as campaign contributions—even though candidates might benefit politically from the ads.

Ads such as these have been a point of contention for advocates of CAMPAIGN FINANCE reform who contend that the "magic words" rule is too easy to circumvent. They say that the message in an ad attacking a candidate is unmistakable, even if the ad urges voters to call the candidate to express their opposition to his or her views but stops short of telling them to vote against the candidate.

Critics of issue ads have accused some of the most prominent 527s organizations, which are not generally regulated by the Federal Election Commission (FEC), of being especially blatant in their efforts to electioneer without running afoul of the "magic words" requirement. The advent of SuperPACs, some of which were even more overt in their negative advertising, exacerbated such concerns.

Activists have also expressed concern that 527 groups are eligible to accept and use unlimited and often sizable SOFT MONEY contributions, from interests such as businesses or unions or from wealthy individuals, to try to influence campaigns for president and Congress. Cumulative contributions to 527s skyrocketed after national party committees were barred from accepting soft money under BCRA.

According to data from Congressional Quarterly's MoneyLine, total spending by 527 groups leapt from $103 million during the 2000 presidential campaign year (pre-BCRA) to $595.6 million in 2004. Similarly, in midterm campaigns dominated by congressional elections, 527 spending in 2006 was $423.6 million compared with $229.5 million in 2002. Spending levels for 527s persisted in the hundreds of millions of dollars in ensuing elections.

These groups had their first big impact on the outcome of a national election in 2004. Initially it appeared that the rise of 527s would be of greatest benefit to Democrats: groups such as America Coming Together and the Media Fund, which ultimately joined forces as the Joint Victory Campaign 2004, began running ads that harshly criticized George W. Bush and his Republican administration in the 2003 run-up to the campaign.

Republicans had planned to rely on the massive treasuries of the Bush reelection campaign and the Republican National Committee to carry their messages to voters; they had not anticipated a significant effort by Republican-allied 527s (which, under federal campaign law, could not coordinate their efforts with candidates or political party officials). National Republican Party officials initially called on the FEC to police 527s more strictly to ensure that they were not violating electioneering rules for independent expenditures.

But by March 2004, the leaders of the Republican National Committee adopted an "if you can't beat them, join them" approach and signaled to sympathetic 527s that they were free to engage in the presidential campaign as much as they wished. Two such groups ended up having an outsized impact with ads that benefited Bush. One praised the president and the other attacked his Democratic general election opponent, Massachusetts senator Kerry.

The positive ad, titled "Ashley's Story," was run by the Progress for America Voter Fund and featured a girl whose mother died in the September 11, 2001, attacks on the World Trade Center in New York. Footage of Ashley being hugged and encouraged by Bush during a campaign stop in Ohio and her statement that Bush had made her feel safe not only were emotionally resonant, but also played to the president's theme that he was uniquely qualified to protect Americans from the threat of international terrorism.

The negative ads were run by the Swift Boat Veterans for Truth, a group composed largely of conservative and Republican-allied veterans of the Vietnam War and funded substantially by a small number of conservative businessmen who favored Bush's reelection.

The group took two tacks: One was to attempt to raise questions about the credibility of Kerry's much-touted record of heroism when he served as captain of a Navy swift boat on river patrols during the Vietnam War. The other, and likely the more damaging effort, focused on Kerry's activities as a Vietnam War protester after he returned to the United States and left the service. These ads, which contended that Kerry's actions had emboldened enemy forces and endangered U.S. prisoners of war, reopened political wounds from that tumultuous era.

Kerry's failure to respond quickly and effectively to the Swift Boat ads is viewed by many political analysts as having contributed greatly to his defeat at Bush's hands.

The influence that these largely unregulated and unaccountable groups have wielded led to rising demands by campaign watchdogs and some leaders in

A Republican state legislator, Sen. Damon Thayer of Kentucky, is seen shown on the chamber's floor in 2010 defending a bill he introduced to strengthen disclosure rules on so-called 527 organizations.

Source: AP Photo/Ed Reinke

both parties for the FEC to take stronger action to ensure that 527s are not violating the law. There were signs that the FEC was shedding its traditional reluctance to do so. In February 2007, the commission announced a settlement under which the Progress for America Voter Fund would pay a $750,000 fine for openly advocating the election of Bush and defeat of Kerry, which FEC officials said required the group to file as a federal political action committee and accept only strictly limited HARD MONEY donations rather than soft money.

> **More on this topic:**
>
> *Buckley v. Valeo, p. 37*
>
> *Campaign Finance, p. 53*
>
> *Hard Money, p. 245*
>
> *Soft Money, p. 592*

But the FEC did not restrain the overall flow of money to 527s. In addition, the commission responded to the unexpected advent of SuperPACs mainly by passing judgment on whether the groups fit the requirements of federal campaign finance law or were disallowed because they would have permitted the parties and candidates for federal office to circumvent contribution limits, and did not take an aggressive stand in addressing the amounts of money SuperPACs could raise nor how they spent it.

Fairness Doctrine   *See* EQUAL TIME AND REBUTTAL RULES.

Faithless Electors   *See* ELECTORAL COLLEGE AND VOTES.

Favorite Son

A favorite-son candidate is not usually a serious candidate for political office. The term is a vestige of the long era of American politics in which NATIONAL PARTY CONVENTIONS played the crucial role in selecting presidential nominees, and in which virtually all candidates for office were men.

The term *favorite son* applied to political figures nominated by allies in their home states. Although some of these candidates emerged as serious contenders at conventions, most did not; their names were submitted mainly to give them and their states bargaining leverage in the competition among the serious contenders at so-called BROKERED CONVENTIONS. In the age of the PRIMARY, which has dramatically diminished the role of the nominating convention since the 1960s, the favorite son is almost an anachronism.

Brokered conventions were more likely in the DEMOCRATIC PARTY before 1936 because the old TWO-THIRDS RULE often necessitated numerous ballots until a candidate obtained the two-thirds majority vote required for nomination. Republican nominations have always been made by a simple majority.

PRESIDENTIAL SELECTION REFORMS have made brokered conventions and favorite-son candidacies unlikely but not impossible. Since 1972 the Democrats have required names placed in nomination to have the written support of at least fifty delegates from three or more states, with no more than twenty signatures from any one delegation.

By rule or practice, the parties have also limited the number and length of seconding speeches for nominations. As the role of conventions in choosing nominees diminished, so did the voting public's interest in the events. Party strategies have sought to employ faster-paced television production values to try to hold a viewing audience—to the extent that some critics have described recent conventions as nothing more than four-day "infomercials." And one of the surest ways to lose that audience is to allow boring, long-winded oratory in support of favorite sons to go unchecked.

The framers of the U.S. Constitution saw the favorite-son concept as basic to the *PRESIDENTIAL NOMINATING AND ELECTING* system. Eschewing election of the president by national popular vote, they expected that the states would put forth their most qualified candidates as favorite sons, and that the wise and learned ELECTORAL COLLEGE members would choose the two best candidates, with the winner becoming president and the second-place finisher becoming vice president.

> **More on this topic:**
>
> *Brokered Convention, p. 36*
>
> *National Party Conventions, p. 347*
>
> *President, Nominating and Electing, p. 437*
>
> *Presidential Selection Reforms, p. 476*

But with adoption of the Twelfth Amendment, requiring separate balloting for president and vice president, and with the trend toward popular election of electors rather than appointment by state legislatures, the role of favorite son changed. Instead of creating a pool of likely presidents, it became more of an honorary position with some potential for influencing the final outcome of the nominating process.

Federal Election Commission

The Federal Election Commission (FEC), an independent agency created by Congress in 1975, administers and enforces the CAMPAIGN FINANCE laws affecting candidates for federal office.

The FEC keeps a comprehensive database of receipts and spending reported by candidates for federal offices—the presidency, the U.S. Senate, and the U.S. House—which in recent years has been accessible at the commission's website, www.fec.gov. It also investigates alleged violations of campaign finance laws and can levy sanctions, including heavy fines, if a majority of the six commissioners concur that rules have been broken.

Yet the structure of the FEC makes it difficult for the commissioners to agree on many cases, especially those that involve presidential candidates and other high-profile campaigns. The commission operates under a rule, aimed at barring one party from using the FEC as a tool for penalizing its opposition, that limits any party to no more than three of the six seats—a standard that has given the commission a split of three Democrats and three Republicans since its inception.

And the FEC in recent years has reflected the high levels of political polarization in society in general, with the Democratic members strongly favoring stricter regulation, and the Republican members, many of them holding libertarian leanings, pulling in the other direction.

The FEC also has been constrained by court rulings over the years that have tended to side with those who believe that campaign spending should be covered by the free-speech protections guaranteed by the First Amendment of the U.S. Constitution.

The two basic laws for which the FEC is responsible are the Federal Election Campaign Act of 1971 (FECA), as amended, and the Bipartisan Campaign Reform Act (BCRA) of 2002, widely known as "McCain-Feingold" after its lead Senate sponsors, Republican John McCain of Arizona and Democrat Russ Feingold of Wisconsin. FECA requires disclosure of sources and uses of funds for presidential and congressional campaigns, limits the size of contributions, and provides for partial PUBLIC FINANCING OF CAMPAIGNS for the presidency. The 2002 law bans the use of unregulated SOFT MONEY by the national parties and federal candidates and places restrictions on a certain kind of POLITICAL ADVERTISING, known as issue advocacy.

But the reach of these laws, and the latitude of the FEC to tighten regulation of campaign finance under the statute, has been consistently challenged by critics—many of them from the conservative side of the political spectrum who view limits on campaign spending as constricting free speech. Those opponents won key victories in a pair of lawsuits that have limited the FEC's ability to regulate the escalation of political spending, which in turn has led many who favor stricter regulation to describe the FEC as "toothless."

The Supreme Court, in its 1976 ruling in the case of *Buckley v. Valeo,* established the "magic words" test to determine whether an ad qualified as an independent expenditure rather than a regulated contribution to a candidate's campaign. The court ruled that a message qualified as issue advertising, and not direct electioneering subject to campaign finance restrictions under FECA, as long it did not expressly call for the election or defeat of a candidate.

While the Supreme Court, in 2003, initially upheld the constitutionality of virtually all major provisions of BCRA, the nation's next major campaign finance law, it dealt a major blow to the statute and to pro-regulation forces in its January 2010 ruling in the case of *Citizens United v. Federal Election Commission.* The ruling, approved by a 5–4 vote, struck a provision in BCRA that barred corporate entities from directly spending unlimited amounts to influence the outcomes of elections. The controversial ruling effectively certified that corporations and unions have free-speech rights under the Constitution that are equivalent to those of individuals, and opened a new conduit for outside interests to spend freely on political advertising.

The FEC found itself in the middle of heated debate over BCRA from the time the law was passed. Supporters of the 2002 statute were unhappy with the FEC's regulations implementing the new law and launched a legal challenge of their own. Subsequent rule making placated these

Citizens United President David Bossie, right, meets with reporters outside the Supreme Court in Washington, Thursday, Jan. 21, 2010, after the Supreme Court ruled on a campaign finance reform case.

Source: AP Photo/Lauren Victoria Burke

critics to some degree, but there continued to be considerable dispute about the FEC's response to the vast growth of independent campaign expenditures by so-called 527 POLITICAL ORGANIZATIONS seeking to influence the outcomes of federal elections.

These tax-exempt groups, so named because they are established under Section 527 of the Internal Revenue Code, rose to prominence during the 2004 presidential campaign. Democratic-allied groups spent millions of dollars on television ads attacking the record of President George W. Bush, while Republican-leaning groups did the same to the record of the Democratic presidential nominee, Massachusetts senator John Kerry.

Carefully crafted to avoid telling voters to "vote for" or "vote against" a candidate—the "magic words" test—the ads were denounced by critics for their unmistakable intent to persuade people to vote for or against Bush or Kerry.

Concerns were also raised by the flood of unregulated and often sizable soft-money contributions from wealthy individuals and interest groups that flowed to 527 groups after the national political parties were barred by BCRA from accepting such donations.

Critics pressured the FEC to scrutinize and crack down on the activities of 527s, and there were signs that the FEC was shedding its reluctance to do so. In February 2007, for example, the commission announced that the pro-Republican Progress for America Voter Fund would pay a $750,000 fine for openly advocating in television ads the election of Bush and defeat of Kerry in the 2004 election. Such advocacy, FEC officials said, required the group to file as a federal political action committee and accept only strictly limited HARD MONEY donations rather than soft money. But the FEC maintained its position that it would judge 527 group activities on a case-by-case basis rather than writing specific regulations governing their behavior.

The gap of more than two years between the 2004 election and that ruling underscored a frequent complaint from critics of the FEC about the amount of time it takes the commission to issue a penalty even when it does muster the votes to act. Defenders of the commission say, however, that it needs more financial resources than have been provided by Congress. The FEC also faces workload issues caused by a proliferation of complaints, issued by candidates or their partisan supporters against their rivals, alleging campaign finance irregularities. Although many of these claims prove spurious and are intended to cast opponents in a negative light, the FEC must still investigate them.

There is nothing new about the FEC catching heat from all sides of the political spectrum. The FEC has faced fierce criticism over the years from political partisans and watchdog groups for what they perceive as its inability or unwillingness to aggressively pursue and punish campaign finance law transgressors. Yet on the other side of the spectrum are the libertarian critics, who are primarily conservatives but include some liberals, who say that much campaign finance law represents an imposition on the First Amendment's guarantee of freedom of speech. Among those holding this view is Bradley Smith, a law professor and critic of much of the nation's campaign finance law, who served on the FEC from 2000 to 2006. "Campaign finance reform is creating an intrusive regulatory regime that's steadily eroding Americans' political freedoms," Smith wrote in 2007.

Candidates and their campaign committees, party committees, and POLITICAL ACTION COMMITTEES (PACs) formed to support one or more candidates must register with the FEC once they cross a certain threshold of financial activity. They then must report periodically to the FEC on their campaign receipts and expenditures. Individuals or committees making independent expenditures for or against a candidate also must file reports. The FEC makes the reports available to the public.

FEC staff members review the reports for omissions. If any are found, the commission may request additional information from the candidate or committee. If the FEC finds an apparent law violation, it has the authority to seek a conciliation agreement including a civil penalty. If a conciliation agreement cannot be reached, the FEC may sue for enforcement in U.S. District Court. The commission may refer to the Justice Department any matter that involves a willful violation.

The FEC also administers the Presidential Election Campaign Fund, which makes possible the public funding of PRESIDENTIAL PRIMARIES, NATIONAL PARTY CONVENTIONS, and presidential general elections. (See PRESIDENT, NOMINATING AND ELECTING.) Each year the fund receives money from the optional $3 checkoff on individual income tax returns ($6 on a joint return), which does not increase taxpayers' liability. But declining levels of taxpayer participation in the program—and the growing tendency of top-tier presidential candidates to eschew the public financing system in order to raise unlimited sums of money for their campaign—underscore the widespread skepticism of public financing of political campaigns. According to Internal Revenue Service figures, fewer than 10 percent of tax filers chose to participate in the program in the early twenty-first century, as compared with 25 percent or better in the early years of the program in the late 1970s.

Background

There had been several attempts to reform campaign financing before the 1971 statute was enacted. Several provisions in laws enacted in the 1800s aimed at protecting federal employees from being pressured to make campaign contributions. With the backing of President Theodore Roosevelt, Congress in 1907 passed the Tillman Act, making contributions by corporations and national banks unlawful.

In 1910 the first Federal Corrupt Practices Act was passed, establishing disclosure requirements for committees involved in House races. The following year a new law extended disclosure requirements to committees influencing Senate elections as well as to House and Senate candidates. The 1911 law also set limits on how much congressional candidates could spend. The system was next overhauled by the Corrupt Practices Act of 1925, which served as the basic campaign finance law until the 1970s. The 1925 statute revised candidates' spending limits and incorporated existing provisions that banned contributions by corporations and banks, prohibited solicitation of contributions from federal employees, and required disclosure reports. But the new law was riddled with loopholes and contained no provisions for enforcement.

There were some changes over the years, including the addition in 1943 of a ban on direct contributions by labor unions, but no major overhaul occurred until the 1971 act. Soon after came the Watergate SCANDAL of the Richard Nixon administration, stemming from a burglary at the DEMOCRATIC NATIONAL COMMITTEE headquarters in the Watergate hotel and office building complex in Washington, D.C., and the subsequent attempted cover-up that drove President Nixon from office. The scandal involved the role of money in politics and spurred further reforms. Congress in 1974 passed the most significant overhaul of campaign finance legislation in the nation's history. Creation of the FEC was a part of the overhaul.

The Supreme Court in 1976 in *Buckley v. Valeo* declared unconstitutional several parts of the 1974 amendments, including the method for selecting members of the FEC. The Court said the method violated the separation of powers and appointments clauses of the Constitution because four commissioners were appointed by congressional officials but exercised executive powers. Amendments passed in 1976 reconstituted the FEC as a six-member commission appointed by the president and confirmed by the Senate.

The clerk of the House and secretary of the Senate served as nonvoting ex officio members until 1993 when a federal court ruled the practice unconstitutional. The FEC then reconstituted itself without the ex officio members.

Operations

The FEC offices are located at 999 E Street, N.W., in Washington, D.C., 20463. Many of the commission's reports and compilations are available on the FEC's website: *www.fec.gov.* (See Reference Material, Political and Election Websites, pages 700–701.)

The commissioners serve staggered six-year terms, and as of 1998, new commissioners are limited by law to one term. But as Republicans and Democrats in Congress began, during the first decade of the twenty-first century, to leave no stone unturned in search of new partisan battles to fight, the rancor over the confirmation of some appointees to the FEC made party leaders increasingly reluctant to nominate candidates to replace incumbent members who were scheduled to cycle off the commission. As a result, five of the six commissioners holding seats as of January 2012 were serving extended tenures—including Ellen L. Weintraub, whose appointed term had actually expired almost five years earlier, in April 2007.

Along with the rule requiring that no more than three commissioners may be members of the same political party, the chairman and vice chairman, elected annually, must be from different political parties.

Senior FEC staff members include a staff director, deputy staff directors, general counsel, commission secretary, and assistant staff directors for audit, reports analysis, public disclosure, information, and administration.

The limit of no more than three commissioners from the same party has resulted in a three Democrat–three Republican commission, making it nearly impossible to take serious action against either party. The likelihood of frequent stalemates increased when Congress subsequently required that four commissioners must vote in favor before any action can be taken. Many complaints of campaign finance violations end up being dropped after long delays because the commissioners are split along party lines and cannot reach a decision.

The FEC found itself at the center of controversy in the 1996 presidential election and aftermath because of its inaction at the time in the face of numerous allegations of campaign funding irregularities. The parties' frenzied fund-raising turned into a full-blown CAMPAIGN FINANCE scandal, with the focus primarily on the Democrats who were working to ensure the reelection of President Bill Clinton. The allegations and counterallegations touched off investigations on

Capitol Hill and within the Justice Department. But although the FEC had indirectly exposed some of the 1996 irregularities through its required disclosure reports, the agency remained mostly silent during those investigations. Then-chairman John Warren McCarry described the FEC as "underfunded and overworked," while its critics dismissed the agency as an ineffective overseer of elections laws.

Part of the scandal stemmed from the millions of dollars in so-called soft money raised by the national political parties. Meant to be used for party-building activities, much of the soft money reportedly was used to support the candidacies of Clinton and his Republican challenger, Bob Dole, even though each received $61.8 million from the public fund and was limited by law to spending only that amount. An FEC staff audit found that both campaigns had benefited from millions of dollars in Democratic and Republican national committee expenditures for "issue ads" that amounted to spending in excess of the federal grants. The FEC, however, rejected the staff recommendation that the campaigns be required to return the excess to the federal Treasury.

The scandal also involved allegations of foreign money, especially from Chinese donors, playing a role in the campaign in violation of federal law. In September 2002, nearly six years after the election, the FEC announced civil fines totaling $719,500 and other financial penalties against Democratic political committees, as well as individuals and corporations involved in fund-raising for the Democrats. Charges included soliciting, making, and/or accepting prohibited foreign national contributions, contributions in the name of another, corporate contributions, and excessive personal contributions. Some of those involved had already pled guilty or been convicted in federal court for the same abuses. Again, some critics faulted the FEC for not exacting tougher penalties.

In the aftermath of the 1996 election scandal, both parties had pledged to support reforms to strengthen the FEC and tighten the campaign finance system. The new law targeting key problems in the system was finally enacted in 2002. But the euphoria of its principal congressional sponsors was short-lived. A court challenge of the new law came as no surprise to them, but they were outraged by the FEC regulations implementing the new law. They accused the agency of creating loopholes that would allow federal candidates to continue raising soft money. The House sponsors filed suit in federal court to overturn the regulations, and the Senate sponsors vowed to challenge the FEC regulations through legislation in 2003. The lawmakers said they also would consider pushing legislation to abolish or restructure the FEC, though this turned out to be an idle threat, and the FEC'S methods for carrying out its responsibilities remained fundamentally unchanged.

More on this topic:
Buckley v. Valeo, p. 37
Campaign Finance, p. 53
Hard Money, p. 245
Political Action Committees, p. 389
Public Financing of Campaigns, p. 496
Soft Money, p. 592

Federal Matching Funds See PUBLIC FINANCING OF CAMPAIGNS.

Federal Workers' Political Activity

Limitations on political activity by federal government employees, put in place by the Hatch Act of 1939, were eased in 1993 when President Bill Clinton signed into law a revision of that statute. The legislation affected the nearly three million federal and postal workers as well as state and local government employees in jobs largely funded by federal grants.

Although the Hatch Act originally was intended to protect government workers from being fired or demoted for declining to donate to political campaigns, many chafed under provisions seen as too restrictive. Passage of the new law climaxed a two-decade effort by congressional Democrats, whose alliance with organized labor had gained them strong support from unions representing federal workers, to grant the requested relief.

The loosening of restrictions did not prevent Clinton and the Democrats from losing control of both chambers of Congress in the MIDTERM ELECTION of 1994, the result of widespread public dissatisfaction with the Democrats' longtime dominance of Congress. But with the revision enacted into law, "un-Hatched" federal workers of both parties were able for the first time to serve as DELEGATES to the 1996 NATIONAL PARTY CONVENTIONS. They also were able in some instances to run for local office and take part in other long prohibited political activities.

The act named for Sen. Carl A. Hatch, New Mexico Democrat, is actually two statutes. The second Hatch Act, enacted in 1940, contained the provisions that apply to federally financed state and local workers.

Hatch proposed restrictions on federal workers after a Senate committee found that political appointees in the Works Progress Administration had coerced employees into contributing to political campaigns. At the time, fewer than 32 percent of the 950,000 federal workers were career public servants. The rest were political appointees.

As of 2000 about 43 percent of 3.2 million employees were in the civil service system. The total did not include the Central Intelligence Agency or the National Security Agency, whose employment figures are secret. The CIA, NSA, and several other agencies, including the FEDERAL ELECTION COMMISSION, remained subject to the pre-1993 restrictions.

Under the original law, federal workers could not actively participate in partisan campaigns. They could, however, take part in nonpartisan elections such as those for school boards or city councils. They could give money to candidates but not stuff envelopes or work on GET-OUT-THE-VOTE drives for a particular candidate or party. They could wear campaign buttons and have bumper stickers on their cars.

Loosening the Reins

Critics argued that the Hatch Act denied federal workers the right of political expression guaranteed to other citizens, that it was outdated because the federal workforce was made up mostly of career professionals, and that the jumble of rules and regulations was contradictory and confusing. Opponents to revising the act argued that doing so would politicize the workforce. They noted that the Supreme Court had twice, in 1947 and 1972, upheld the constitutionality of the Hatch Act.

Republican presidents Gerald R. Ford, Ronald Reagan, and George H. W. Bush had used the veto or veto threats to block earlier Democratic-sponsored efforts in Congress to soften the act. They and others feared that liberalization would enhance the ability of employee unions to help elect Democrats. Public-sector unions have consistently directed 90 percent or more of their campaign contributions to Democratic candidates. In 1996 federal workers contributed $312,000 to Clinton's reelection campaign but only $80,000 to Republican challenger Bob Dole, according to the Center for Responsive Politics.

The Hatch Act does not apply to employees of the Executive Office of the President, to individuals appointed by the president and confirmed by the Senate, or to members of the armed forces, whose conduct is governed by separate Defense Department rules. The act covers most DISTRICT OF COLUMBIA employees, but not the mayor or city council. The 1993 revision permitted more political activity by covered D.C. government employees.

Under the revised rules, according to the independent U.S. Office of Special Counsel (OSC), covered federal employees are permitted to

- be candidates for public office in nonpartisan elections;
- register and vote as they choose;
- assist in *VOTER REGISTRATION* drives;
- express opinions about candidates and issues;
- contribute money to political organizations;
- attend political fund-raising functions;
- attend and be active at political rallies and meetings;
- join and be an active member of a political party or club;
- sign nominating petitions;
- campaign for or against *INITIATIVE AND REFERENDUM* questions, constitutional amendments, and municipal ordinances;
- campaign for or against candidates in partisan elections;
- make campaign speeches for or against candidates in partisan elections;
- distribute campaign literature in partisan elections; and
- hold office in political parties or clubs.

According to the same OSC advisory, federal employees are *not* permitted to

- use official authority or influence to interfere with an election;
- solicit or discourage political activity of anyone having business before their agency;
- solicit or receive political contributions (which may be done in limited situations by federal labor or other employee organizations);
- be candidates for public office in any partisan elections;
- engage in political activity while on duty, in a government office, wearing an official uniform, or using a government vehicle; or
- wear political buttons on duty.

Permitted activities for covered state and local employees include running for public office in nonpartisan elections; campaigning for and holding office in political organizations; actively campaigning for candidates in partisan and nonpartisan elections; and contributing money to political organizations and attending fund-raising functions.

Covered state and local employees are not permitted to be a candidate for public office in a partisan election; use official authority or influence to interfere with or affect the results of an election or nomination; or directly or indirectly coerce contributions from subordinates in support of a political party or candidate.

Penalties for Hatch Act violations are dismissal or (for federal employees) a minimum thirty-day suspension without pay or (for state or local employees) forfeiture by the affected government of the federal assistance equal to two years of the charged employee's salary.

Earlier Acts

The Civil Service Act of 1883, known as the Pendleton Act for its sponsor, Sen. George H. Pendleton, Ohio Democrat, barred government employees from soliciting political contributions and protected them from coerced assessments for campaigns. The act marked the first significant

President James A. Garfield was elected in 1880. His assassination by a job seeker less than eight months into his administration led his successor, Chester A. Arthur, to sign into law the Pendleton Civil Service Reform Act.

Source: Library of Congress

effort by Congress to control the so-called spoils system of substantial turnover in patronage jobs with each new administration.

The assassination of President James A. Garfield in 1881 by a deranged federal job seeker, Charles J. Guiteau, stimulated popular support for reforming the civil service and taming the spoils system. Chester Alan Arthur, the vice president who was sworn in upon Garfield's death, was a Republican civil service reform advocate. As president, Arthur signed the Pendleton Act, creating the bipartisan Civil Service Commission and a merit employment system that gradually covered most career federal employees.

The arrival of Franklin D. Roosevelt's New Deal in 1933 brought to Washington many new federal workers who owed their jobs to Roosevelt and the Democratic Party. To forestall abuses by the grateful officeholders, a COALITION of Republicans and conservative Democrats passed the Hatch Act (officially the Political Activities Act) in 1938.

By 1948 nearly 84 percent of federal workers were in classified civil service positions and therefore subject to the Hatch Act restrictions. But enforcement of the act fell under the same agency that administered the civil service system, a situation unacceptable to President Jimmy Carter when he took office in 1977.

At Carter's behest Congress enacted the most sweeping reform of the civil service system since the Pendleton Act. The Civil Service Reform Act of 1978 abolished the Civil Service Commission and split its functions among the Office of Personnel Management (OPM), the Merit Systems Protection Board (MSPB), and the Federal Labor Relations Authority.

The independent Office of Special Counsel was created in 1979 to investigate and prosecute personnel practices, including Hatch Act violations, before the MSPB. Under the Whistleblower Protection Act of 1989 the OSC and MSPB are charged with protecting employees from reprisals for reporting suspected violations.

The approximately 45 percent of federal employees who are not under the OPM's competitive merit system fall under the excepted service, which includes the FBI, or the Senior Executive Service of officials who have less job security than employees in the OPM system.

In addition to the CIA, NSA, and FEC, the Office of Special Counsel listed itself, the MSPB, and several other agencies as those whose employees are prohibited from political activity under the pre-1993 restrictions. Several of the agencies listed were transferred to the new Department of Homeland Security enacted in November 2002. Others affected by the legislation were moved elsewhere and renamed, including the Bureau of Alcohol, Tobacco, and Firearms, which went from Treasury to the Justice Department with the word *Explosives* added to its name.

Federalist Party (1789–1816)

John Adams (left) and Alexander Hamilton were the driving forces behind the Federalist Party, which failed to win the presidency or either house of Congress after 1800.

Source: Library of Congress

The Federalist Party grew out of the movement that drafted and worked for the ratification of the Constitution of 1787, which established a stronger national government than that in operation under the existing Articles of Confederation. Supporters of the new constitutional government were known as Federalists, and in the formative first decade of the Republic they controlled the national government. With President George Washington staying aloof from the development of political parties, Alexander Hamilton of New York and John Adams of Massachusetts exercised the leadership of the Federalists. The party's basic strength was among urban, commercial interests, who were particularly drawn to the Federalists because of the party's belief in a strong federal economic policy and the maintenance of domestic order—viewpoints based on a broad interpretation of the Constitution.

The Federalists were perceived widely as a party of the aristocracy, a decided liability in the late eighteenth and early nineteenth centuries, when the right to vote was being widely extended to members of the middle and lower classes. Never so well organized as the rival Democratic-Republicans (the forerunner of the modern Democratic Party), the Federalists were unable to compete for support of the important rural, agrarian elements that then made up the majority of the electorate.

The election of Thomas Jefferson in 1800 spurred the rise of his Democratic-Republicans to a quarter-century of thorough dominance of national politics and ended Federalist control of the White House and Congress. After 1800 the Federalists did not elect a president or win a majority

More on this topic:

Democratic-Republican Party, p. 160

in either chamber of Congress. The party's strength was limited for the most part to largely commercial New England, where Federalists advocated states' rights and were involved in threats of regional secession in 1808 and again during the War of 1812.

The party soon began to lose its energy, and in 1812 the Federalists held their last meeting of party leaders to field a presidential ticket. Four years later there were no nominations, but Federalist electors were chosen in three states. Although this marked the last appearance of the party at the national level, the Federalists remained active in a few states until the mid-1820s.

Fifteenth Amendment   *See* VOTING RIGHTS ACT.

Forecasting Election Results

American statistician George Gallup pioneered methods for measuring public opinion and forecasting election results.

Source: AP Images

In the highly competitive news industry, timely reporting is essential. Nowhere is this more evident than in the predicting of electoral outcomes.

At intervals before an election, the news media use various POLLING techniques to help them determine who is ahead in the race and report that information to their readers, viewers, or listeners. Candidates and their parties, INTEREST GROUPS, POLITICAL CONSULTANTS, as well as large segments of the general public, follow the poll reports closely—sometimes out of curiosity and sometimes because they have a vested interest in how the election turns out.

The scientific sampling methods used today are far more sophisticated than those once used by newspapers, but complete accuracy remains an elusive goal.

Participants in the lively segment of the news media known as election handicapping—performed by such outlets as *National Journal's* The Cook Political Report, as well as veteran analysts such as Stuart Rothenberg and Larry Sabato—take polls into consideration but integrate their own knowledge of demographics, voting history, and the issues of the day in making their election predictions.

Evolution of Polling

Old-time reporters relied on their instincts and "seat-of-the-pants journalism" to help them identify the likely winners. They were assisted at times by their newspapers, which early in the nineteenth century began taking what came to be known as a STRAW VOTE before elections. The straw vote or poll began simply, with reporters asking train or steamship passengers about their candidate preferences. By the 1930s some straw votes had become elaborate affairs, involving extensive mailings of returnable ballots.

At about the same time an Agriculture Department analyst named Jerzy Heyman developed the systematic sampling techniques that are at the heart of modern polling. The Survey Research Center of the Inter-university Consortium for Political and Social Research at the University of Michigan is an outgrowth of the agriculture program. (See NATIONAL ELECTION STUDIES.)

Pioneer pollsters George Gallup, Elmo Roper, and Archibald Crossley soon adopted the sampling methodology and used it successfully to predict Franklin D. Roosevelt's LANDSLIDE victory over Alfred M. Landon in 1936. Twelve years later the still-young polling industry received a black eye with its almost unanimous prediction that Thomas E. Dewey would unseat President Harry S. Truman in the 1948 election.

Harry S. Truman gleefully holds up a newspaper announcing, incorrectly, his defeat in the 1948 presidential election. Since then, election forecasting has improved tremendously in methodology and accuracy.
Source: St. Louis Mercantile Library at the University of Missouri, St. Louis

The setback was only temporary; pollsters learned from their mistakes, and the activity grew into a respected and valued profession. It would be another two decades, however, before the news media began taking full advantage of the professional pollsters' generally successful methods of forecasting election results. *Washington Post* political reporter David S. Broder recalls in his 1987 book *Behind the Front Page* that in 1960 he camped out for a week in Beckley, West Virginia, to try to sense PUBLIC OPINION in the crucial presidential PRIMARY between Democrats John F. Kennedy and Hubert H. Humphrey. Although Humphrey was expected to defeat Kennedy in the state, which had only a 5 percent Catholic population, Broder found considerable support for Kennedy, and he reported it in the paper he was then working for, the *Washington Star*.

Although Kennedy's "surprise" defeat of Humphrey vindicated his reporting, Broder wrote, "I wish now I had used 'newspaper interviews' rather than 'polling' to describe what I did, for there was nothing scientifically random about the selection of those 112 people [I interviewed]."

Broder had used methods pioneered by Samuel Lubell, a journalist who knocked on doors in selected precincts to sample public opinion in an election. At that time the major pollsters such as Gallup and Roper were still developing their highly accurate methods of political polling, and few newspapers used their services.

Today the television networks and most large newspapers have their own polling operations, sometimes in association with another media company or a professional polling organization. The *Washington Post* began systematic polling in 1977.

Scientific polling has not entirely replaced informal means of gauging how people feel about candidates. The print and electronic media still use straw polls or *man-on-the-street* interviews for that purpose, even though they have little validity as genuine polls.

A *preference poll*, also known as a *trial heat* or a *horserace poll*, is another unscientific type of opinion sampling. It usually takes the form of a mock election in which people are asked who they would vote for if the election were held tomorrow. As commonly used today, "trial heat" usually refers to a contest between candidates of opposing parties. Preference polls measure public attitudes toward candidates of the same party, as in a primary.

The notorious PUSH POLL is not a poll at all but rather a form of NEGATIVE CAMPAIGNING. Candidates or their consultants may employ the technique to discredit opponents. They use computer technology to dial hundreds or thousands of voters in the guise of a poll and ask the respondents if they would vote for the opponent if they knew he or she was a communist, a child abuser, or some other disreputable type of person, whether or not that characterization has any basis in fact.

Most of the legitimate types of polls are used to forecast results weeks or months in advance of an election. Two other types, EXIT POLLS and more rarely used entrance polls, do not come into play until ELECTION DAY. Then the news media send representatives to ask people leaving the polls how they voted, or people approaching the voting station or caucus auditorium how they plan to vote.

Exit polls, the more common of the two, came into widespread use in the 1980s. Through 2002 exit polling was a joint effort of the Associated Press and the broadcast networks through an organization called the Voter News Service and using the logo *VNS*.

Because they are based on responses from people who have actually voted, or are on their way to vote, exit and entrance polls gained a reputation for high accuracy and were controversial for that very reason. There were complaints that they influenced the outcome of elections if they were broadcast while some polls were still open. In 1984 and 1996 presidents Ronald Reagan and Bill Clinton, respectively, were declared the winners by the media just minutes after polls closed in the East.

At times, however, exit polls have proven to be as misleading as the early polls that predicted Truman's defeat. In the 2000 presidential election, networks that relied on VNS polls twice called Florida wrong—the first time placing it in Democrat Al Gore's column, the second time declaring that it went for Republican George W. Bush. Finally the networks said the state was too close to call. (After a recount and a series of court battles, Bush was declared the winner in Florida by a scant 537 votes out of almost six million cast. See CONTESTED ELECTIONS.) The polling errors were caused by several factors, including incorrect information from Jacksonville that was fed into computers and exit polls conducted in heavily Democratic precincts in the Tampa area that were not representative of the state.

VNS overhauled its computer system to prevent a recurrence of the problem. But it suffered another embarrassment in the 2002 midterm elections, when it pulled the plug on exit poll data because of concerns that the new system was not yet reliable. Instead, it provided just raw vote totals. News services were forced to report the votes as they came in, which prevented them from calling close races until late in the evening—a reminder of the long election nights that were common before exit polls.

Two months later, VNS closed its doors. It was quickly replaced, though: the television networks and the Associated Press wire service, which make up the National Election Pool, hired Edison Media Research and Mitofsky International to jointly produce the exit polls beginning with the 2004 elections. The latter company was owned by Warren Mitofsky, who originated modern exit polling in 1967 while working for CBS News.

The 2004 presidential exit polls did not cause the kind of controversy that the 2000 polls had, but they were not free from criticism. Early runs in key states such as Florida and Ohio showed Democratic challenger John Kerry leading President

More on this topic:

Exit Polls, p. 196

Polling, p. 427

Public Opinion, p. 502

Push Poll, p. 507

Straw Vote, p. 614

George W. Bush; when these numbers were leaked prematurely, primarily by political web log or "blog" sites on the Internet, they caused an optimistic buzz among Democratic activists, consternation among Republicans, and a skewed perspective among reporters preparing for the election night coverage. Bush ultimately won both of those battleground states to clinch his reelection.

During the 2006 midterm elections, the exit polling combine sought to address the "leak" problem by requiring reporters seeking access to early exit poll data to spend most of election day with the polling researchers in a closed room, labeled "The Vault," without outside communication. When the poll results were reported after voting had concluded across the country, the data on head-to-head matchups between Democratic and Republican candidates—the benchmark for the accuracy of the demographic and other data in the poll—turned out to be extremely close to the mark.

Fourteenth Amendment *See* BLACK SUFFRAGE.

Franchise

The American electorate has changed markedly over the years as it has grown in size. Since the early days of the nation, when the franchise—eligibility to vote—was limited to the property-owning class of white men, one voting barrier after another has fallen to pressures for wider suffrage.

First unpropertied white men, then black men, all women, and finally young people pushed for the franchise. By the early 1970s almost every restriction on voting had been removed, and virtually every adult citizen eighteen years of age and older had won the RIGHT TO VOTE. (See BLACK SUFFRAGE; WOMEN'S SUFFRAGE; YOUTH SUFFRAGE.)

During the first few decades of the Republic, all thirteen of the original states limited the franchise to property holders and taxpayers. Seven states required ownership of land, or a life estate as opposed to a leased estate, as a qualification for voting. The other six states permitted persons to qualify by substituting either evidence of ownership of certain amounts of personal property or payment of taxes. (See FREEHOLDER.)

The framers of the Constitution apparently were content to have the states limit the right to vote to adult males whom they viewed as having a real stake in good government. This meant, in most cases, persons in the upper economic levels. Not wishing to discriminate against any particular type of property owner (uniform federal voting standards inevitably would have conflicted with some of the state standards), the Constitutional Convention of 1787 adopted without dissent the recommendation of its Committee of Detail that the states be allowed to set their own qualifications for voting. As embodied in the Constitution, this provision (Article I, section 2) states that persons eligible to elect the House of Representatives "shall have the Qualifications requisite for Electors of the most numerous Branch of the State Legislature."

Under this provision, with states controlling the qualifications, fewer than half of the adult white men in the United States were eligible to vote in federal elections. Because no state made women eligible (although states were not forbidden to do so), only one white adult in four qualified to go to the polls. Slaves—black or American Indian—were ineligible, and they formed almost one-fifth of the American population as enumerated in the CENSUS of 1790. Also ineligible were white indentured servants, whose status during their period of service was little better than that of the slaves.

A print commemorating a celebration held in Baltimore on May 19, 1870, in honor of the Fifteenth Amendment, which had been ratified on February 3. The intent of the constitutional amendment was subverted for nearly a century, especially in the South, through poll taxes, literacy tests, and intimidation.

Source: Library of Congress

Actually, these early state practices represented a liberalization of restrictions on voting that had prevailed at one time in the colonial period. Roman Catholics had been disfranchised in almost every colony, Jews in most colonies, Quakers and Baptists in some. In Rhode Island, Jews remained legally ineligible to vote until 1842.

For half a century before the Civil War there was a steady broadening of the electorate, which was energized by the rise to the presidency in 1828 of populist Tennessee Democrat Andrew Jackson. The new western settlements supplied a stimulus to the principle of universal male suffrage for whites, and Jacksonian democracy encouraged its acceptance. Gradually, the seven states making property ownership a condition for voting substituted a taxpaying requirement: Delaware in 1792, Maryland in 1810, Connecticut in 1818, Massachusetts in 1821, New York in 1821, Rhode Island in 1842, and Virginia in 1850. By the middle of the nineteenth century most states had removed even the taxpaying qualifications, but some retained LITERACY TESTS and the POLL TAX well into the twentieth century.

On the federal level the Constitution has been amended five times to override state qualifications denying the franchise to certain categories of people. The Fourteenth Amendment, ratified in 1868, directed Congress to reduce the number of representatives from any state that disfranchised adult male citizens for any reason other than commission of a crime. No such reduction was ever made, even though a number of states effectively prevented African American men from voting by literacy tests, intimidation, and other means.

The Fifteenth Amendment, ratified in 1870, prohibited denial of the right to vote "on account of race, color or previous condition of servitude," though discriminatory laws enacted mainly in the South created legal obstacles that effectively prevented most blacks from voting over most of the ensuing century. The Nineteenth Amendment in 1920, which prohibited denial of that right "on account of sex," had a more immediate impact on integrating women into the electoral system.

The Twenty-fourth Amendment, which came into effect in 1964, barred denial of the right to vote in any federal election "by reason of failure to pay any poll tax or other tax." The poll tax, especially in the South, posed a significant barrier to voting by the poor, both black and white. The amendment reflected the growing movement to provide minorities, especially blacks, with the civil rights of which they had long been deprived.

Finally, in 1971 the Twenty-sixth Amendment lowered the voting age to eighteen in federal, state, and local elections.

Congress moved toward the goals of the latter two amendments both prior and subsequent to their ratification. In the 1950s and 1960s, lawmakers enacted a series of statutes to enforce the Fifteenth Amendment's guarantee against racial discrimination in voting. The most significant was the VOTING RIGHTS ACT of 1965, which resulted in a sharp increase in VOTER REGISTRATION and VOTER TURNOUT among African Americans.

A federal law passed in 1970 nullified state residence requirements of longer than thirty days for voting in presidential elections, suspended literacy tests for a five-year period (the suspension was made permanent in 1975), and lowered the minimum voting age to eighteen years from twenty-one, the requirement then in effect in all but a few states.

A 1970 Supreme Court ruling upheld the voting-age change for federal elections but invalidated it for state and local elections. In the same decision the Court upheld the provision on residence requirements and sustained the suspension of literacy tests with respect to both state and local elections. The Twenty-sixth Amendment was ratified six months after the Court's decision, ensuring the same minimum age for all elections.

The right to vote in presidential elections was extended to citizens of the DISTRICT OF COLUMBIA by the Twenty-third Amendment, ratified in 1961. Residents of the nation's capital had been disfranchised from national elections except for a brief period in the 1870s when they elected a nonvoting delegate to the House of Representatives.

In general, by the turn of the twenty-first century, the only remaining restrictions prevented voting by the insane, convicted felons, and otherwise eligible voters who were unable to meet short residence requirements. A nascent movement after about 2000 pressed for loosening restrictions on felons who had paid their debts to society. By 1992 the American electorate, as measured by the 104 million people who voted for president, had exceeded 100 million for the first time. Voter turnout shot up for the contentious 2004 presidential election between Republican incumbent George W. Bush and Democrat John Kerry, producing 122.3 million voters. Four years

CLOSER LOOK

In 1848 the Free Soil Party nominated former Democratic president Martin Van Buren as its presidential candidate. Van Buren had been elected president in 1836, after serving as secretary of state and vice president under President Andrew Jackson. But an economic crisis hit early in his presidency, and Van Buren never recovered politically. He was decisively defeated for reelection in 1840 by William Henry Harrison, the nominee of the Whig Party. Van Buren was rebuffed by the Democrats in 1844 when he sought the nomination, in part because of his opposition to expanding slavery into new western territories. There was some irony in his decision to run as a Free Soiler, in that some historians regard his efforts to build the Democratic Party as a precursor to the modern political party organization.

Legend has it that Van Buren may be responsible for the adoption of "OK" as an everyday synonym for "good" or "all right." Van Buren hailed from Kinderhook, an old Dutch-founded town in the Hudson Valley of New York. He was given the nickname "Old Kinderhook," which was subsequently shortened to "O.K." Some of Van Buren's political supporters formed "O.K. Clubs" to promote his political campaigns.

later, with no incumbent in the presidential race, it increased again, to 131.3 million. The total was driven, in part, by enthusiasm among Democrats for Barack Obama, who became the first African American ever to be nominated for the nation's highest office. (See table, Growing Franchise in the United States, 1930–2008, page 658.)

Free Soil Party (1848–1852)

Born as a result of opposition to the extension of slavery into the newly acquired Southwest territories, the Free Soil Party was launched formally at a convention in Buffalo, New York, in August

*In 1848 the Free Soil Party nominated for-
mer Democratic president Martin Van Buren
for the presidency.*

Source: Library of Congress

1848. The Free Soilers were composed of antislavery elements from the DEMOCRATIC and WHIG PARTIES. Representatives from all the northern states and three BORDER STATES attended the Buffalo convention, where the slogan "free soil, free speech, free labor and free men" was adopted. This slogan expressed the antislavery sentiment of the Free Soilers as well as the desire for cheap western land.

The convention selected former Democratic president Martin Van Buren (1837–1841) as the party's presidential candidate and Charles Francis Adams, the son of President John Quincy Adams (1825–1829), as his vice presidential RUNNING MATE.

In the 1848 election the Free Soil ticket received 291,501 votes (10.1 percent of the POPULAR VOTE) but was unable to carry a single state. The party did better at the congressional level, winning nine House seats and holding the balance of power in the organization of the closely divided new Congress.

The 1848 election marked the peak of the party's influence. With the passage of legislation in 1850 that aimed for a compromise on the expansion of slavery, the Free Soilers lost their basic issue and began a rapid decline. The party ran its second and last national ticket in 1852, headed by John Hale, who received 155,210 votes (4.9 percent of the popular vote). As in 1848, the Free Soil national ticket failed to carry a single state.

Although the party went out of existence shortly thereafter, its program and constituency were absorbed by the nascent REPUBLICAN PARTY, the birth and growth of which dramatically paralleled the resurgence of the slavery issue in the mid-1850s.

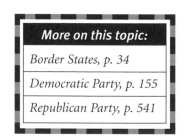

More on this topic:

Border States, p. 34

Democratic Party, p. 155

Republican Party, p. 541

Freeholder

Possession of property was a common requisite for the RIGHT TO VOTE in the formative years of the United States. The Constitution left it to the states to determine who could vote, and all states at first restricted that right to white men. Many states also limited the vote to men of property or freeholders.

Property qualifications had existed in all the colonies and endured afterward, although they varied from state to state. Colonial restrictions tended to be harsher than those adopted by the states and often were based on a measure of real estate ownership. It was widely thought that only a man with a "stake in society" would vote responsibly, and property was tangible evidence that he held such a stake.

Actual ownership of real estate was not always required. Lifetime tenure as a leaseholder sometimes sufficed. In Virginia—the home of some of the most important members of the 1787 Constitutional Convention and four of the first five presidents—property possession had been a prerequisite for voting since 1677. From 1705 until 1736 the laws were quite liberal: any male tenant who held land for life (his own or that of another person such as his wife or child) was considered a freeholder and could vote. Leasing property for the duration of one's own lifetime or for that of a family member was the equivalent of owning property.

From 1736 onward, the Virginia definition of freeholder was more restrictive. To vote, a man living in the countryside had to hold twenty-five acres of cultivated land with a house, or one hundred acres (changed to fifty in 1762) of uncleared land. A man living in town had to hold a house with a lot. By the standards of the time, those requirements were not excessive.

The American Revolution brought no suffrage reform to Virginia, although it did to other states. The Virginia Constitution of 1776 stated that voting requirements "shall remain as exercised at present." Even those who paid taxes or fought in the militia could not vote unless they held the requisite amount of land. By 1800 Virginia was one of five states that retained real estate property qualifications. (At the other extreme, four states had established universal suffrage for white men by 1800.) While various other states allowed the ownership of personal property, such as a horse-drawn carriage, or the payment of taxes to substitute for holding real estate, Virginia held on to its old property qualifications until 1830.

Property requirements of one kind or another were not abandoned by all the states until 1856. But because the United States was predominantly a middle-class society with fairly widespread ownership of property, such qualifications were not so significant a limit to voting as they may first have appeared.

More on this topic:
Franchise, p. 215
Right to Vote, p. 549

Front-Loading

The clustering of PRIMARY and CAUCUS elections early in the presidential election year has come to be known as *front-loading*. Largely the result of competition among the states to gain influence over the parties' choices of presidential nominees by scheduling their voting events before those of most other states, the phenomenon began in earnest with the 1988 presidential election and continued into the 2008 election cycle. As the 2012 cycle got underway, states continued to jostle for early advantage. However, party leaders by 2011 managed to impose a more orderly sequence of caucuses and primary voting that avoided many of the difficulties of 2008. Republican leaders had some success in persuading several states to hold primaries and caucuses later in the season and accept rules changes to restrict the importance of early voting. One change barred states from holding winner-take-all delegate primaries before April 1. They also set "Super Tuesday," the name long applied to the busiest day on the primary calendar, for March 6 rather than February 5 that was used four years earlier. One result of these moves was that ten states scheduled their Republican primaries or caucuses for Super Tuesday in 2012, half as many as in 2008. Democrats did not have to deal with these issues in 2012 because President Barack Obama had no challenges to seeking reelection.

In 1984 the traditional first-in-the-nation New Hampshire primary was held on February 28, and there were just eight state primaries in the month of March. With the establishment of a primary-cluttered SUPER TUESDAY on the second Tuesday of March in 1988, the New Hampshire contest shifted up to February 16, and twenty-one other states held primaries by the end of March.

In 2008, when the New Hampshire primary was on January 8, three other states held January primaries (two of them in violation of party restrictions) and twenty-two states held February primaries; only five held primaries in March. In total forty-one states held presidential primaries in 2008, a new record exceeding the previous record of thirty-eight four year earlier. (See maps, pages 221–222.)

In 2012 New Hampshire held its first-in-the-nation presidential primary on January 10, one week after Iowa held its caucuses. Two other January primaries followed: South Carolina on January 21 and Florida on January 31, both sanctioned by the parties.

Many observers both inside and outside of partisan circles are worried about this phenomenon. From a months-long process that culminated with often-crucial big-state contests in June, the front-loaded primary calendar since the early 1990s has consistently enabled front-running candidates to gain unstoppable momentum and clinch the parties' nominations by early March. This, say critics, leads to general election campaigns that are too long, too expensive, and often too negative. Further, the accelerated calendar penalizes states that decline to participate in the front-loading, as the nominations are typically decided before they vote.

But some strategists argue that it is best for the interests of the parties and the nominees to determine the winners early so they can avoid a serious bruising from their fellow contenders for the nomination and also save money for the fall campaign. Their views, although widely held, proved totally wrong for Democrats in 2008. The two principal contenders, Barack Obama, the eventual winner, and Hillary Rodham Clinton, the early front-runner, battled through primaries into June, when Clinton conceded. The long battle did not hurt the Democratic ticket, which went on to win the White House.

> **"I am concerned that our nominating process has become so compressed that it does not serve the party or the voters very well."**
>
> —RNC chairman Haley Barbour in January 1996

The process of front-loading has continued with little serious effort by the parties to rein it in. Even before the 1996 primary season was over, the REPUBLICAN NATIONAL COMMITTEE created a task force to consider changes in the nominating process, including a less compressed primary schedule. Haley Barbour, who was chairman of the Republican National Committee (RNC) from 1993 to 1997 (and in 2003 was elected governor of Mississippi), said in January 1996, "I am concerned that our nominating process has become so compressed that it does not serve the party or the voters very well."

The task force recommended, and the RNC adopted, a plan to award "bonus" convention delegates to states that held their primaries or caucuses later in the process. But the plan was not successful—more states continued to advance the dates of their nomination contests because the additional delegates were too meager a reward to justify forgoing the added attention associated with holding an early nomination contest.

In 1999 RNC Chairman Jim Nicholson appointed former Tennessee senator Bill Brock to head a commission to examine changes to the nomination process. It held numerous hearings and developed a plan to group states into four blocks, based on population, that would hold primaries on dates spread across several months, with smaller states voting first and the largest states voting last. The plan received initial backing from the RNC. But Bush campaign officials, preparing for the 2000 convention in Philadelphia that would showcase their candidate, blocked the proposal from floor consideration out of concern that a fight over an internal issue would mar the carefully planned schedule of convention festivities.

Democrats after 2000 showed signs of giving in to the front-loading phenomenon. The change was engendered partly by state parties wanting to play a bigger role in the process and partly by the desire of Democratic officials to coalesce early behind a candidate. In 2002 the Democratic National Committee (DNC) adopted rules allowing states to hold their nomination contests as early as the first Tuesday in February, matching the Republican schedule, with exceptions for Iowa and New Hampshire to hold their contests earlier. In 2005 the DNC's Commission on Presidential Nomination Timing and Scheduling held hearings and issued a report that recommended allowing one or two additional caucuses and one or two primaries before the first Tuesday in February 2008. Nevada received a berth to hold a 2008 caucus in mid-January, and Democratic officials allowed South Carolina to schedule a 2008 primary in late January. On their own initiative, however, two other states—Michigan and Florida, both eager to increase their clout in the nominating drama—scheduled January primaries. Party officials threatened to deny convention seats to delegates from those states, but the issue was resolved before the conventions.

As late as the 1984 campaign, the primary and caucus events were spread from late February until mid-June; front-runner Walter F. Mondale, though a former vice president and the Democratic establishment favorite, faced a tough challenge from Colorado senator Gary Hart and did not win the delegates he needed for the nomination until June 5.

That election influenced the move to front-load the 1988 campaign. Some Democratic officials believed the prolonged Mondale-Hart fight had hurt the party's chances, setting the stage for President Ronald Reagan's sweeping landslide in November 1984. Meanwhile, the strongly liberal tone of the unsuccessful ticket of Minnesotan Mondale for president and New York representative Geraldine A. Ferraro for vice president stirred the more conservative wing of the party, mainly in the South, to seek a greater voice in the process.

The major upshot of this was Super Tuesday, which fell on March 8 and included twelve southern states among the sixteen Democratic primaries held that day. Though Sen. Al Gore of Tennessee did win Super Tuesday primaries in his home state and in Oklahoma, North Carolina, Kentucky, and Arkansas, the strongest overall showings were turned in by two more liberal candidates: Massachusetts governor Michael S. Dukakis, who went on to win the nomination but lost the election to Republican George H. W. Bush in November 1988, and Rev. Jesse Jackson, an African American civil rights activist who benefited from the large percentage of blacks in the Democratic primary electorate in most southern states.

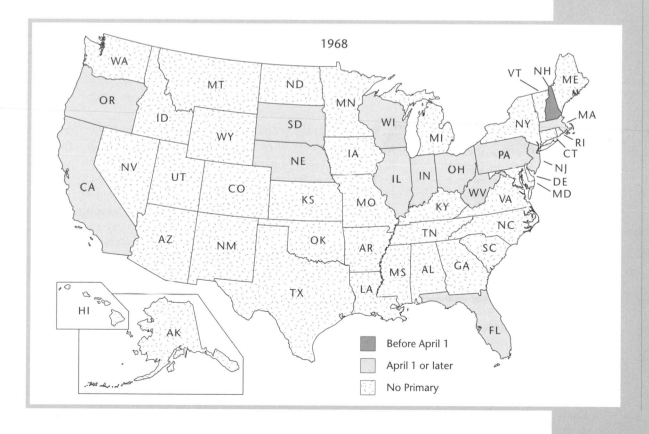

1968

Before April 1
April 1 or later
No Primary

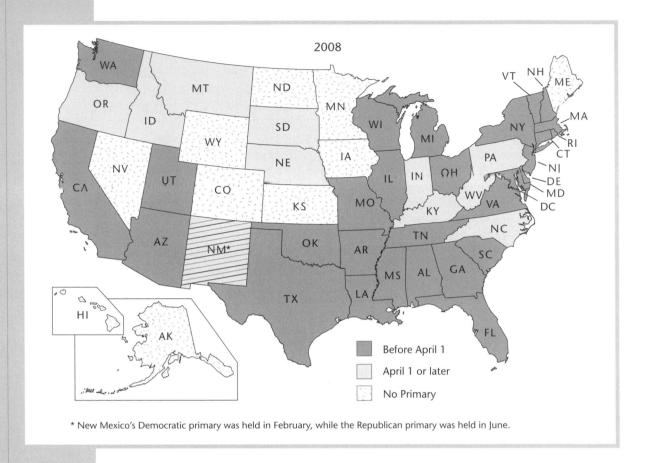

2008

Before April 1

April 1 or later

No Primary

* New Mexico's Democratic primary was held in February, while the Republican primary was held in June.

More on this topic:
Caucus, p. 89
Iowa Caucus, p. 284
New Hampshire Primary, p. 369
Primary Types, p. 485
Super Tuesday, p. 615

Over the years, the front-loading process has helped some early front-runners restart campaign BANDWAGONS that initially failed to gather momentum. In 1996, for example, former Kansas senator Bob Dole, the favorite for the Republican nomination to challenge Democratic incumbent Bill Clinton, stumbled in early contests but swept the next round in early March. George W. Bush in 2000 lost early contests in New Hampshire, Arizona, and Michigan to Arizona senator John McCain, but his strong showing in a cluster of primaries held March 7 and 14 effectively earned him the Republican nomination.

Front-Runner

The leading candidate in a political race is called the *front-runner.* Front-runner status is often achieved by establishing a sizable lead over competing candidates in public opinion polls, though other factors, such as a more recognized name, superior political experience, or a big fund-raising advantage, can also earn a candidate that mantle.

Being dubbed the front-runner has some real advantages. It can attract other politicians and voters to join forces with the leading candidate, a phenomenon known by the old-fashioned but common phrase "jumping on the bandwagon." This in turn helps the front-runner build upon his or her existing advantages and sometimes creates unstoppable momentum for that candidate.

The networks of supporters that front-runners tend to build also help them rebound if they face some adversity. For example, George W. Bush's status as the front-runner for the Republican presidential nomination in 2000 appeared threatened briefly by the unexpectedly strong showing by Sen. John McCain of Arizona in early primaries. But Bush regrouped, drawing on his formidable campaign organization in key states. He scored crucial victories over McCain and coasted to the nomination that would ultimately send him to the White House.

Thomas E. Dewey was a perennial front-runner for the Republican presidential nomination and for the presidency. In May 1948, while campaigning in Grants Pass, Oregon, he was escorted by members of the Oregon Cavemen Club

There is a downside to being declared the front-runner. In multicandidate contests, especially primaries, other candidates often will "gang up" on the perceived front-runner to try to bring him or her back to the pack. Additionally, the front-runner often ends up competing against expectations set by the media and others in the political community. If the front-runner's lead in the polls diminishes, it is often said that the candidate is slipping or that the competition is gaining ground.

In presidential politics a perennial front-runner was Thomas E. Dewey, the crime-busting district attorney who was elected the Republican governor of New York in 1942. Two years earlier Dewey, then thirty-eight years old, was a prime contender for the GOP nomination to oppose Franklin D. Roosevelt's unprecedented bid for a third term as president. At the NATIONAL PARTY CONVENTION, Dewey ran ahead of his competition on the first ballot but lost his lead on the second and steadily weakened after that. His candidacy for the 1940 nomination ultimately was overwhelmed by the DARK-HORSE popularity of Indiana businessman Wendell L. Willkie, who would ultimately lose the general election to Roosevelt that November.

As governor in 1944, Dewey was the clear front-runner for his party's presidential nomination, which he won with only one dissenting convention vote. But Roosevelt defeated Dewey to gain a fourth term, which he did not live to complete.

In 1948 Dewey was again the front-runner for the nomination, and he won it after his opponents withdrew following the second ballot. Although Dewey was widely favored to win the November election, President Harry S. Truman embarrassed the forecasters with a surprise victory. Dewey was never again a front-runner for national office.

Democrat Jimmy Carter's campaign for president in 1976 is a case in which a candidate used front-runner status as an asset. An obscure former governor of Georgia, Carter pursued an outsider CAMPAIGN STRATEGY to attract public attention and establish his credentials as a potential national leader. After

More on this topic:

Bandwagon Effect, p. 21

Campaigning, p. 76

Dark Horse, p. 134

CLOSER LOOK

The 2008 Democratic presidential contest proved that although well-known front-runners have many advantages, it does not always work to his (or in the case of 2008, her) advantage. Hillary Rodham Clinton, the former first lady during her husband's presidency in the 1990s and later New York's junior senator, was widely perceived in early handicapping as the front-runner and likely nominee. However, junior Illinois Sen. Barack Obama did not agree. Formally entering the race about the same as Clinton, Obama waged a forceful nationwide campaign in caucus and primary states of all sizes. In doing so he assembled a collection of committed delegates, and later SUPERDELEGATES who saw where the wind was blowing, that made Clinton's effort to catch up an uphill battle. Although the battle continued through the spring, she conceded, and enthusiastically endorsed Obama, in early June.

winning early primaries and caucuses in New Hampshire and other states, Carter arrived at the Democratic convention with the nomination locked up. He then entered the general election campaign with a big lead in the polls, which helped him withstand a late surge by the incumbent president, Republican Gerald R. Ford.

Similarly, in 1992 another relatively unknown southern governor, Bill Clinton of Arkansas, dubbed himself the "comeback kid" after he lost the important NEW HAMPSHIRE PRIMARY and still managed to become the front-runner for the Democratic presidential nomination. He went to the convention with enough delegates for a first-ballot victory.

But sixteen years later, in 2008, his wife, Hillary Rodham Clinton, could not repeat her husband's feat. In that year Clinton was considered the front-runner and an early safe bet to win the nomination. Eight Democrats with some name recognition entered the race, but only two—Clinton and her main competitor, Barack Obama—denominated the primary season. Clinton focused on the large battleground states and had by the end won more primary votes than Obama. But Obama ran a nationwide campaign that went into not only the big states but most of the smaller ones holding primaries and caucuses. This strategy allowed him to gather enough delegates, mainly before winter was over, to all put preclude Clinton every catching up.

Fund-Raising   *See* CAMPAIGN FINANCE; HARD MONEY; SOFT MONEY.

Fusionism

In modern American politics the term *fusionism*—meaning candidates running under several party labels at the same time—is associated chiefly with New York. State law there permitted multiple-party nominations after other states prohibited them.

For most of the twentieth century the Democratic machine known as Tammany Hall so dominated New York City politics that reform candidates had little chance of election unless they formed a COALITION with other parties. Between 1901 and 1933 New Yorkers elected three fusion mayors, in addition to two elected in the late 1800s.

The most famous of the five was Fiorello La Guardia, a Republican who won in 1933 with 446,833 votes in the Republican column and 421,689 in the City Fusion Party column; under New York's recognition of fusion candidates, his votes on those separate lines were tallied together. La Guardia was reelected in 1937 and 1941, but in those elections the City Fusion Party votes added insignificantly to his victory margin.

Though the last Fusion Party candidate appeared on New York mayoral ballots in 1957, the state has maintained a tradition of active alternative parties by continuing to allow votes cast for major-party nominees endorsed by those third parties to be included in their vote totals. For example, the state's Conservative Party gives its line on the ballot for most offices to the nominee of the Republican Party.

It is unclear whether those codesignations add a significant number of votes to the candidate's bottom line, or if they mainly provide another symbolic option for voters who would have supported that major-party candidate anyway.

As in New York, THIRD PARTIES find it advantageous to ally themselves with another party in nominating a candidate. But because cross-filing and fusionism tend to weaken PARTY IDENTIFICATION BY VOTERS, the political parties that dominate the American TWO-PARTY SYSTEM often exert pressure to have state legislatures prohibit such practices.

The Supreme Court, however, has upheld an antifusion statute similar to those on the books in most states. The Court ruled in a 1997 Minnesota case, *McKenna v. Twin Cities Area New Party,* that the state's ban on fusionism does not interfere with the free association rights of third-party members. A federal district court had held that the prohibition on multiple-party nominations violated the First Amendment.

Fusionism is related to the practices of cross-filing (seeking the nomination of more than one party) and cross-endorsing (a party's endorsing of another party's candidate). (See PARTY ENDORSEMENT OF CANDIDATES.)

California permitted cross-filing until 1959. In 1946, for example, Republican governor Earl Warren also won the Democratic nomination and easily won reelection.

Fusionism has made some rare appearances in presidential politics. In 1900 the Democratic nominee for president, William Jennings Bryan, was also the candidate of the Populist (People's) Party's Fusionist Faction. The Populists' Anti-Fusionist Faction opposed joining with the Democrats in 1896 and ran its own candidate, Wharton Barker, in 1900. Republican William McKinley defeated Bryan in both elections.

Fusion Party candidate Fiorello La Guardia, right, served as mayor of New York City from 1934 to 1945.

Source: AP Images

More on this topic:

Coalition, p. 107
Party Endorsement of Candidates, p. 376
Populist (People's) Party, p. 434
Third Parties, p. 627

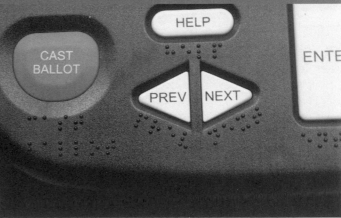

G

Gerrymander

Before the Massachusetts election of 1812, Gov. Elbridge Gerry signed a bill redrawing the state senatorial districts so that his party, the Democratic-Republicans, would be likely to win more seats than their actual numbers warranted. One of the new districts looked like a salamander and was quickly dubbed a "gerrymander," a term that continues to be used to describe a redistricting plan designed to benefit one party.

Source: Library of Congress

Redistricting, the process for redrawing legislative districts every decade to reflect population changes, goes back to the nation's earliest days. So do the efforts by major political parties to use redistricting to improve their chances to make political gains. That point is underscored by the fact that the term *gerrymander*—used to describe the practice of manipulating election DISTRICT boundaries to benefit a certain incumbent or political party—originated in 1812.

Gov. Elbridge Gerry of Massachusetts, a former vice president of the United States and signer of the Declaration of Independence, inadvertently gave the practice his name. When his DEMOCRATIC-REPUBLICAN PARTY carved out a misshapen Essex County state legislative district, artist Gilbert Stuart (better known to history for painting portraits of George Washington) penciled a head, wings, and claws onto the district map and exclaimed, "That will do for a salamander!" Whereupon editor Benjamin Russell replied, "Better say a Gerrymander!"

In the ensuing 1812 election the opposing FEDERALISTS, packed largely into the outlying district, won 51 percent of the total vote in the state Senate races but gained only eleven of forty seats. Politicians ever since have tried to emulate Gerry's success with the mapping process.

Whether gerrymandering is a legitimate exercise of political power or an effort to fix the results of elections in advance has been a subject of unending debate in U.S. political circles. Not all gerrymandering over the years has been strictly partisan. Strategic redistricting was often used in the past to perpetuate the interests of rural residents even as America became an urbanized society. This often led to *malapportionment,* or the creation in individual states of districts that had great population disparities, an issue that was ultimately addressed and eliminated by the ONE PERSON, ONE VOTE Supreme Court rulings of the 1960s.

There also have been different kinds of RACIAL REDISTRICTING, none of which were without controversy. Some states divided large concentrations of African American or other minority voters among several districts, hindering their opportunity to elect members of their constituency groups to Congress or other governmental bodies, a practice that received the label of "cracking." In the 1960s, the passage of civil rights laws, particularly the VOTING RIGHTS ACT, created pressure to end this practice. In the 1990s, those laws were interpreted to establish a practical mandate that states create, whenever practicable, many more MINORITY-MAJORITY DISTRICTS that could and often did elect African Americans, Hispanics, and other minorities to office.

But this, in turn, created occasional backlash among some white voters who argued that the practice of "packing" minority voters into such districts had been taken too far, a point on which the courts agreed in a few cases. Some of the most oddly shaped districts in recent decades were drawn to pull together widely separated pockets of black or Hispanic voters and improve their chances of electing minority candidates to public office.

Partisan gerrymandering takes a variety of forms. The better known examples are those in which a dominant party in a state—one that holds the governorship and control of the legislature, the key levers in most states' redistricting processes—uses its power to redraw district maps to its benefit and the detriment of the other.

Another kind of gerrymandering, known as *incumbent protection,* receives less attention, in part because it has the patina of bipartisanship, but tends to occur more frequently. Most states are not completely controlled by a single party at the time of redistricting, and it is not always in the interests even of a dominant party to make drastic changes to the district *status quo.* Under incumbent-protection plans, the districts are designed to improve the chances of most or all of each party's incumbents to win reelection. Although this practice pleases the incumbents, it appalls those who view such protection as an obstacle to more competitive elections.

The existence of incumbent protection plans may be a hindrance to voters and party officials who have sought, with little success over the years, to overturn partisan gerrymanders. Defenders of the partisan gerrymanders reason that if it is fair to draw rambling, irregularly shaped districts for the purposes of protecting incumbents, it should not then be illegitimate to draw oddly shaped districts to defeat them.

The courts, long resistant to getting involved in redistricting cases, have been reluctant to define what might constitute a political gerrymander so "egregious" that it needs to be ruled unconstitutional. For example, the Supreme Court in *Davis v. Bandemer* (1986) declined to overturn a state legislative redistricting plan in Indiana on partisan grounds, stating that no judicial standard existed for measuring when, if ever, a partisan gerrymander violated the constitutional

The legal proceedings over the map of Pennsylvania congressional districts enacted prior to the 2002 elections—based on redistricting using population statistics from the 2000 census—highlight three of the central aspects of the debates over legislative gerrymandering.

Population equality. The one aspect of redistricting on which the judicial system has demanded rigid adherence since the one-person, one-vote rulings of the 1960s is a near-perfect balance of population among all districts. The rapid advances in computer technology used to draw district lines have prompted jurists in the most recent cases to demand nearly zero population deviation. In the Pennsylvania case of *Vieth v. Pennsylvania*, decided in 2003, a federal district court required a redistricted map to be slightly altered prior to the 2004 election because of a difference of nineteen people between the state's most and least populous districts—an average of just one person for each of the state's nineteen districts.

Partisan gerrymandering. The courts have maintained their long-standing reluctance to intervene in the intensely political partisan aspects of redistricting. The district court that in *Vieth v. Pennsylvania* threw out the Pennsylvania map because of population deviation also threw out the claims made by Democratic plaintiffs that the district map drawn by the Republicans who then controlled the state's government had violated their constitutional rights by drawing an egregiously one-sided map. Following the remapping, the state's delegation went from eleven Democrats and ten Republicans to seven Democrats and twelve Republicans. (Pennsylvania lost two seats in the reapportionment following the 2000 census because of slow population growth.)

Redistricting determinism. One of the justifications that courts have often used in upholding partisan gerrymanders is that there is no way to prove that all of the districts designed to favor one party will continue to do so over the entirety of the ten-year redistricting cycle. This, as it turned out, became a cogent point in Pennsylvania during the 2006 midterm congressional elections. Aided by the national downturn in the fortunes of the Republican Party, caused in large part by low approval ratings for President George W. Bush and the unpopularity of the war in Iraq, four Democratic candidates won House seats that had been held by Republican incumbents. As a result, the Pennsylvania delegation at the start of the 110th Congress in 2007 was made up of eleven Democrats and eight Republicans—more of an edge than the Democrats had before the Republicans redrew the map.

rights of voters. But the ruling left open a small window of opportunity for plaintiffs to sue by saying it was not out of the question that jurists could develop such a standard.

It was under this ruling that the Court issued its 2004 decision in the case of *Vieth v. Jubeliler,* in which Pennsylvania Democrats sued to overturn a highly partisan congressional district map that was drawn by the Republicans then dominant in the state. The Court, by a 5–4 vote, rejected the Democrats' complaint, though a majority of justices again said it was not impossible for an unconstitutional partisan gerrymander to exist.

The issue came up once again in the Court's 2006 decision in the case of *League of United Latin American Citizens v. Perry,* a consolidation of several cases seeking to overturn a highly unusual and highly partisan mid-decade redistricting map in Texas implemented by the state's dominant Republican Party. The Supreme Court again rejected claims that the new map, which in its first use in the 2004 elections produced a five-seat net gain of U.S. House seats for Republicans in Texas, was unconstitutional on partisan grounds.

The aftermaths of both the Pennsylvania and Texas cases of the past decade showed both the strengths and limitations of gerrymandering as a tool for partisan domination.

In Texas, a state that has long had strong overall Republican leanings, the gains that party made in the election after enactment of its gerrymandered map proved sturdy, withstanding serious damage even in the 2006 and 2008 election cycles that favored Democrats nationally. After the midterm elections in 2010, a strong comeback year for Republicans nationally, the GOP held a 23–9 lead over the Democrats in the state's U.S. House delegation.

But Pennsylvania is much more of a swing state that gives Democrats more opportunities to compete, and both major parties—the Republicans who drew the redistricting map prior to the 2002 elections and the Democrats who sued to overturn it—overestimated how solid the GOP's advantages would be if the political pendulum swung to the Democrats' favor. Combined Democratic gains in 2006 and 2008 swung the state's congressional delegation from the 12–7 edge intended by the Republican mapmakers to a 12–7 Democratic advantage. The big Republican upsurge in 2010 again exactly flipped the split to 12–7 in favor of the GOP, but the gyrations showed that the gerrymandering attempt there was flawed.

Court actions in each recent ruling also underscored the two principal facets of redistricting that judges have consistently found to be justiciable over the past few decades: population equality and impact on racial and ethnic minorities.

Before the Pennsylvania case reached the Supreme Court, a lower federal court had required the state legislature to adjust the lines in the congressional district map because the districts were of unequal size, even though the differential between the largest and smallest of the nineteen districts was just nineteen people.

In Texas, the one portion of that mid-decade redistricting map that the Supreme Court overruled and required to be redrawn was the design of the Twenty-third Congressional District. A majority of the justices agreed with the Democratic plaintiffs that the district as designed by the Republican lawmakers disadvantaged Hispanic voters, violating the VOTING RIGHTS ACT of 1965. The Court ruled that a reduction in the size of the district's Hispanic population violated the right of members of that group to elect the candidate of their choice— rejecting Republicans' contention that Hispanics had been shifted to other districts not because they were Hispanics but, rather, because they strongly favored Democratic candidates and therefore threatened the continued incumbency of the district's Republican representative, Henry Bonilla. After the district was redrawn under the Court's order to include more Hispanic voters, Bonilla indeed lost his seat that fall to Democratic challenger Ciro D. Rodriguez, though Rodriguez subsequently was unseated in 2010 by Francisco Canseco, like Bonilla a Hispanic Republican.

Slowly Entering the "Political Thicket"

Until the 1960s, the Court avoided all types of REAPPORTIONMENT AND REDISTRICTING cases. In *Colegrove v. Green* (1946), Justice Felix Frankfurter wrote, "It is hostile to a democratic system to involve the judiciary in the politics of the people. . . . Courts ought not to enter this political thicket."

But by 1962 the Court had changed its collective mind. In BAKER V. CARR, it ruled that malapportionment is a matter for judicial review, while leaving open the standards to be applied in such cases. A year later, in *Gray v. Sanders,* the Court began spelling out the most basic of those standards: ONE PERSON, ONE VOTE. Different-sized populations in a state's legislative districts violate the principle of equal protection of the laws under the Fourteenth Amendment and therefore are unconstitutional, the Court said. In 1964 it extended the one-person, one-vote test to congressional elections, and the federal Voting Rights Act of 1965 further reinforced the notion of equality in districting.

It was not until *Davis v. Bandemer,* the 1986 Indiana case, however, that the Supreme Court even suggested that gerrymandering was subject to constitutional challenges where neither race nor the one-person, one-vote standard had been met, or at least was not at issue. The Court ruled that gerrymanders may be challenged for unfairly discriminating against political parties. In this case, the Court ruled, the Indiana plan would stand because it takes more than one election to prove that such a plan is discriminatory.

The *Davis* case arose from the redistricting plan adopted by the Indiana General Assembly in 1981. The Republican Party, in control of the governorship and both chambers of the legislature, redrew election districts based on 1980 CENSUS data. Acting in secret with computerized data on the political makeup of each region, the Republicans offered a plan two days before the end of the legislative session and passed it by a party-line vote. No public hearings were held, and Democratic legislators had no opportunity to participate in the design process. They were given only forty hours to come up with their own plan for the state's 4,000 precincts.

Republicans were frank about what they had done. "The name of the game is to keep us in power," one member said. The legislators announced that the plan was designed to yield fifty-six "safe" Republican seats and thirty Democratic seats in the lower house, with the remainder being "toss-ups." In the state senate the Republicans expected the plan to give them thirty seats to the Democrats' eight to ten.

"The name of the game is to keep us in power."

—A Republican legislator in Indiana, referring to the redistricting plan that led to **Davis v. Bandemer**

On appeal by the Democrats, the federal district court examined the extent of the plan's manipulations. New election districts dissected counties and townships into strange shapes lacking common political bonds, "with no concern for any adherence to principles of community interest," the court said. Nor did the new boundaries for senate districts necessarily coincide with the districts for house seats, adding to potential voter confusion. The MULTIMEMBER DISTRICTS established for some house seats stacked Democrats into districts where their majority would be overwhelming, while fragmenting other traditionally Democratic districts, so Republicans would stand a better chance in WINNER-TAKE-ALL contests among multiple candidates.

The 1982 elections demonstrated the success of the plan, with all one hundred house seats up for election. Although Democratic candidates received about 53 percent of the popular vote, Democratic candidates took only forty-three seats compared with fifty-seven for the Republicans.

The special three-judge district court panel invalidated the 1981 reapportionment on grounds that it violated the principle of equal protection of the laws and presented a controversy that courts could settle. The court ordered the legislature to prepare a new plan for future elections.

Because the jurisdiction of federal courts does not extend to political questions, the first issue addressed by the Supreme Court in *Davis* was whether the Court could decide the case. By a 6–3 vote, the Court found "such political gerrymandering to be justiciable," but it reversed the district court ruling as having applied "an insufficiently demanding standard in finding unconstitutional vote dilution."

The opinion by Justice Byron R. White reviewed *Baker v. Carr* and other one-person, one-vote rulings to establish that it had previously indicated that reapportionment cases could present justiciable issues. "Our past decisions also make clear that even where there is no population deviation among the districts, racial gerrymandering presents a justiciable equal protection claim," the Court added. Acknowledging that it had often upheld lower courts when they dismissed political cases as nonjusticiable, the Court said that "we are not bound by those decisions."

The decision resolved the apparent inconsistency in favor of justiciability, whether the violation of the equal protection claim is made by a political or by a racial group.

Justice Sandra Day O'Connor dissented in part. She argued that judicial review of purely political redistricting cases will "lead to political instability and judicial malaise. If members of the major political parties are protected by the Equal Protection Clause from dilution of their voting strength, then members of every identifiable group that possesses distinctive interests should be able to bring similar claims."

By a separate 7–2 vote the Court decided against invalidating the Indiana reapportionment scheme. It disagreed with the district court finding of an equal protection violation based on the results of a single election. Indiana is a swing state, White noted. "Voters sometimes prefer Democratic candidates, and sometimes Republicans." The district court did not rule out the possibility that in the next few elections the Democrats could win control of the assembly. "Nor was there any finding that the 1981

"[In a swing state v]oters sometimes prefer Democratic candidates, and sometimes Republicans."

—*Justice Byron R. White*, in Davis v. Bandemer (1986)

reapportionment plan would consign the Democrats to a minority status throughout the 1980's. . . . Without findings of this nature, the District Court erred in concluding that the 1981 Act violated the Equal Protection Clause," the Court said.

Although *Davis v. Bandemer* was expected to open the door to other challenges to political gerrymandering plans, the Court declined to become involved in 1989 when it reaffirmed without comment a lower court's decision to uphold California's congressional map, widely recognized as a classic example of a partisan gerrymander—with Democratic congressman Phil Burton, who masterminded the plan prior to the 1982 elections, describing it at the time as his "contribution to modern art." Unlike malapportionment, nonracial gerrymandering, by early in the second decade of the twenty-first century, had not been definitively prohibited by law.

Get Out the Vote

Efforts by political parties and candidates to get sympathetic voters to actually participate in elections are as old as American democracy itself. But the methods for generating VOTER TURNOUT have changed significantly over the years.

Virtually gone are the torchlight marches, the bandwagon-led parades, the fiery hours-long stump speeches, and the whistle-stop train tours that made political participation not only a civic duty, but a form of entertainment that brought color into the lives of what then was a mainly working-class electorate. With greater overall affluence and ubiquitous electronic communications providing a myriad of distractions, a relative few Americans today view politics as "entertaining."

Those events have been replaced by increasingly sophisticated, computer database–driven methods of voter contact, often targeting the "party base" voters already deemed most likely to turn out. As a result, individuals may be bombarded by personal visits, live and recorded phone calls, postal and electronic mail, text messages, outreach through social media, and other forms of communication aimed at getting them to go vote (without, the campaigners hope, driving them into a frustrated rage over the intrusiveness of these efforts).

Each election cycle seems to bring a new wrinkle in *GOTV*, the acronym that political insiders commonly use for *Get Out the Vote*. And success quickly breeds imitation.

Following the 2004 presidential election, won by Republican incumbent George W. Bush, much fuss was made about the Republican National Committee's effective "72-Hour Plan"—developed by longtime Bush political adviser Karl Rove and his associates—that deployed large numbers of party staffers and activists to key "battleground" states during the last three days of the campaign to ensure that voters inclined to support Bush and other Republican candidates went to the polls. The GOP's army of GOTV workers came equipped with computer-generated lists of registered party members and other voters identified as sympathetic to Bush and the Republican Party in general.

Analysts wondered whether this strategy would be as successful in the 2006 elections, in which Republicans were faced with the possibility of losing seats, largely because of a sharp decline in Bush's approval ratings that resulted in important part from the growing unpopularity of the war in Iraq and unease caused by the government's delayed response to human suffering inflicted by Hurricane Katrina in 2005.

In fact, voter dissatisfaction created a disparity in voter intensity that may have doomed the Republicans' hopes of maintaining the control of both chambers of Congress that they held going into that year's elections: Polls consistently indicated that voters who favored Democratic candidates were more likely to vote, and many Republicans expressed discouragement over the state of their party. But the Democrats clinched their resurgence to capture both the Senate and the House by catching up with the Republicans, with unexpected speed, in the development of sophisticated databases that they used to ensure that their base voters turned out.

The Democrats also made innovative use of small, portable digital electronic devices that provided access to voter information that earlier was available only on bigger laptop machines or even desktop computers. These approaches helped the party stay on its roll through the 2008 elections. Barack Obama, whose campaign also broke new ground in using e-mail, text messaging, and social media as campaign organizing and fund-raising tools, won as the Democratic candidate for president, and his party expanded its majorities in the Senate and the House.

But the political pendulum swung back in 2010, when deepening voter dissatisfaction—mainly over an economy that had not strongly rebounded from the financial crisis and a deep recession that began in December 2007 and worsened through 2008—boosted the GOP back into a share of power. With voter intensity working to their benefit as it had for the Democrats in the previous two election cycles, Republican campaign strategists (and conservative activists allied with the nascent TEA PARTY movement) used voter databases and electronic tools to ensure that their voters turned out in greater numbers than those of the Democrats.

Yet these elections also proved the limitations of sophisticated technology in getting voters out to the polls. The Democrats tried vigorously to repeat the success that these techniques had brought them in 2006 and 2008, but a good part of their political base in 2010 was dispirited by the nation's setbacks and was not receptive to the messages the party was sending. The Republicans ended up scoring a huge gain to recapture control of the House and cut deeply into the Democrats' Senate majority.

One of the reasons that parties, candidates, and the interest groups that support them must go to such lengths to generate voter turnout is that demographic changes have made it somewhat harder to do.

After the nation shifted in the late nineteenth and early twentieth century from a mainly rural to an urbanized society, much of the population was packed into densely populated cities in which party political machines had easy access. The suburbanization of America in the mid to late twentieth century created a more diffuse population that is harder to organize politically.

The reduction of the minimum voting age from twenty-one to eighteen in 1971 under the Twenty-sixth Amendment added many new potential voters to the system, but this youngest cohort of the voting-age population has consistently participated at much lower levels than the rest of the electorate. Generating youth voter turnout is made more difficult by states' varying laws for where college students can register to vote—where they go to school or in their hometowns? Part of the Democrats' big success in 2008 was turning out the youngest voters in higher than average numbers, with many driven by dissent with Bush's policies and the historic nature of Obama's bid to become the nation's first African American president. But the party's failure to repeat this success two years later in the midterm elections cost it dearly.

Additionally, the surge of Hispanic immigrants has given this constituency great potential political clout. But it is largely unrealized to date because so much of the Hispanic population is made up of noncitizens who are not eligible to vote, and even the Hispanic citizen population has

A bus provided by the Sixth Avenue Baptist Church of Birmingham, Alabama, gets African American voters to the polls on primary election day in 1972. Low voter turnout prompts widespread efforts, such as free rides, to get more people to the polls.

Source: National Archives and Records Administration

an above-average percentage of children under age eighteen who are not eligible to vote. This greatly complicates voter contact and outreach efforts in places that have large concentrations of Hispanic residents.

These are among the factors that have contributed to VOTER TURNOUT rates in U.S. elections that are relatively low in comparison to those of other nations with democratic forms of government. (See INTERNATIONAL AND U.S. ELECTIONS COMPARED.)

Political scientists cite voter apathy and lack of interest as the major causes of persistent low turnout rates. PUBLIC OPINION polls show that many Americans find politics boring. (See zzz.)

To combat the trend, political parties and organizations such as the League of Women Voters appeal to the public's sense of civic duty with a wide array of advertising campaigns in the print and electronic media. Readers and viewers are bombarded with messages urging, "Vote for the Candidate of Your Choice. But Vote!" Young voters in particular have long been targeted by such GOTV efforts as the nonpartisan "Rock the Vote" campaign.

With their large numbers of officials and members, labor unions have been able to operate phone banks that blanket areas with calls asking people to vote and sometimes offering transportation to the polls. The AFL-CIO, as part of its COALITION with the Democratic Party, has for years conducted drives to get out the vote, almost exclusively for Democratic candidates.

With the rise of POLITICAL ADVERTISING on television, large-scale campaign parades and rallies, once major components of get-out-the-vote efforts, have become largely things of the past. The televised NATIONAL PARTY CONVENTIONS are among the few remaining collective events used to whip up enthusiasm for candidates and voting.

> **More on this topic:**
>
> *National Party Conventions, p. 347*
>
> *Public Opinion, p. 502*
>
> *Voter Turnout, p. 656*

Individual candidates, sometimes with party assistance, tailor get-out-the-vote activities to their own needs, concentrating their resources in areas where their supporters are most numerous. Such drives are generally thought of as patriotic, public service endeavors because nonvoting is considered undemocratic and unhealthy for the electoral process. But that view is not universally accepted. Some authorities on government feel that uninterested persons should not be cajoled into voting because they are apt to make poor choices if they have not taken the time to study the issues and the candidates' qualifications. Others, though, reject this thinking as "elitist."

Governor

The role of governors as their states' chief executives makes them the most powerful elected officials in the United States other than the president of the United States. Four of the six presidents from 1976 to 2008—Democrat Jimmy Carter of Georgia (elected president in 1976), Republican

The governor's office has been the springboard to the Oval Office for four of the past six presidents, from 1976 to 2008. Yet even some political activists without presidential aspirations see the governor's office, especially in the nation's more populous states, as a place where they can both effect change and reach for national prominence. Examples include Arnold Schwarzenegger, former Republican governor of California, and Jennifer A. Granholm, former Democratic governor of Michigan. Both might have been attractive candidates for their parties' presidential tickets had they not been born in Austria and Canada, respectively. Under the Constitution only persons born in the United States may serve as president. And yet these two examples also show how prominent governors can fall from political popularity swiftly. Both, on leaving office at the beginning of 2011, were among the most unpopular governors holding office—Schwarzenegger in large part due to endless California budget crises, and Granholm due to the crumbling Michigan economy that accompanied the near collapse of the auto industry in the deep recession that began in 2008.

Ronald Reagan of California (1980 and 1984), Democrat Bill Clinton of Arkansas (1992 and 1996), and Republican George W. Bush of Texas (2000 and 2004)—trumpeted their "executive experience" as governors as key evidence that they were capable of running the nation. In all, seventeen U.S. presidents have been state governors.

Like the president, a governor must depend on political skills to achieve a record of accomplishment in office. Many have served in their state legislatures or as members of Congress before running for governor and are thus well acquainted with the legislative process. Even U.S. senators, despite their potential for national prominence, sometimes chafe at the limitation of being one of one hundred lawmakers and jump at the opportunity to actually run things as governor.

As political scientist Larry Sabato has observed, today's governors are a far cry from the glad-handing "good-time Charlies" of the past. He described the new breed as being, for the most part, "vigorous, incisive, and thoroughly trained leaders."

Governors' duties vary in detail from state to state, but basically they are the same. Most state constitutions today have the "strong governor, weak legislature" system, which is the reverse of the situation that prevailed in the "good-time Charlie" era, the first half of the twentieth century.

The governor's chief responsibility is to enforce the laws of the state. Other duties include reporting to the legislature on the "state of the state"; preparing the state's operating and capital budgets, along with a tax budget to provide the revenue; appointing department heads and other officials, often subject to legislative confirmation; signing or vetoing new laws; participating in the federal grant-in-aid system; issuing pardons of criminals, sometimes in conjunction with a pardoning board; and commanding the state militia (known today in virtually all states as the National Guard).

Most governors have long had a power that the president gained only recently (and temporarily)—the line-item veto, which is the authority to disapprove individual items in an appropriations bill without vetoing the whole bill. As president, Reagan was denied the line-item veto by a Democratic-controlled Congress. But the Republicans who controlled Congress in the mid-1990s, and who had described controlling federal spending as a top priority in their rise to power in the 1994 elections, granted it to Democratic president Clinton. The U.S. Supreme Court, however, ruled in 1998 that the presidential line-item veto was an unconstitutional intrusion on the lawmaking prerogatives of Congress.

Unlike the U.S. Constitution, most state constitutions require governors to sign a balanced budget. Reagan, whose "supply-side economics" resulted in record-high federal deficits, often called for a balanced budget amendment for the United States, as did the congressional Republicans' "Contract with America" in 1994. Proposals for such an amendment did not receive the required two-thirds approval of Congress, however, and both Republicans and Democrats, when in control of the White House and/or Congress, have often countenanced high levels of deficit spending. The balanced budget amendment rose once again in 2011 when House

"Today's governors are a far cry from the glad-handing 'good-time Charlies' of the past."

—political scientist Larry Sabato

Republicans, and some Senate GOP members, insisted on sending the proposal to the states as part of a legislative package to increase the national debt limit. The House approved the proposal, but the Senate did not.

Governors' salaries in 2008 ranged from a high of $212,179 in California, which Republican governor Arnold Schwarzenegger, a famous and wealthy movie star before entering politics, did not accept, to a low of $70,000 in Maine. The average salary for a governor that year was approximately $128,000, about $46,000 below the salary for a member of Congress.

Campaigns for governor seats are expensive, with combined spending in many states running into the tens of millions of dollars. Candidates for the California governorship spent a combined $128 million in the primary and general elections in 2006. Republican incumbent Arnold Schwarzenegger spent $46 million, while losing Democratic candidate Phil Angelides spent $39 million.

As of 2011, there were forty-five states that had a LIEUTENANT GOVERNOR, who is the next in line should a vacancy occur in the governor's office; two of the forty-five were elected members of the legislature who served as lieutenant governor. In twenty-five of those states, the governor and lieutenant governor are elected on a party ticket. In eighteen, the governor and lieutenant governor run separately, making it possible for a governor of one party and a lieutenant governor of another to serve together, which also could occur in the two states where a legislative member fills the position.

Governorship History

In the formative years of the United States, Americans looked with suspicion on the office of governor. To them, these officials were reminders of the British-appointed governors who symbolized the mother country's control and tyranny during the colonial era.

Colonial legislatures, on the other hand, had been able to assert control over appropriations and in this way became champions of colonial rights against the governors. After the Revolutionary War, when drawing up their constitutions, states gave most of the power to the legislative bodies and placed restrictions on the governors, including the term of office and the method of election.

For all their power today, governors still are on a tighter leash from the people than most other officials elected under our federal system of government. Presidents have been limited to two terms since 1951 by constitutional amendment, but the Supreme Court has nullified state efforts to impose TERM

PARTY LINEUP OF GOVERNORS

The figures that follow show the number of governorships held by the two major parties after each election since 1950. They do not reflect midterm changes or the results of elections in odd-numbered years.

Year	Democrat	Republican	Independent
1950	23	25	0
1952	18	30	0
1954	27	21	0
1956	29	19	0
1958	35	14	0
1960	34	16	0
1962	34	16	0
1964	33	17	0
1966	25	25	0
1968	19	31	0
1970	29	21	0
1972	31	19	0
1974	36	13	1
1976	37	12	1
1978	32	18	0
1980	26	24	0
1982	34	16	0
1984	34	16	0
1986	26	24	0
1988	28	22	0
1990	27	21	2
1992	30	18	2
1994	19	30	1
1996	18	31	1
1998	17	31	2
2000	19	29	2
2002	24	26	0
2004	22	28	0
2006	28	22	0
2008	29	21	0
2010	20	29	1

Source: *Guide to U.S. Elections*, 6th ed. (Washington, DC: CQ Press, 2010); *The Rhodes Cook Letter*, December 2010; *American Votes 28, 2007–2008* (Washington, DC: CQ Press, 2009).

Nellie Tayloe Ross, right, director of the Bureau of the Mint, is all smiles as Vice President and Mrs. Alben Barkley present President Harry S. Truman with the gold medal for distinguished service in Congress. Ross was one of the first two female governors elected in the United States, both in 1924.

Source: Harry S. Truman Library

LIMITS on their members of Congress. By contrast, thirty-six states limited tenure of governors in some fashion as of 2011. Most had limits of two four-year terms, but Virginia prohibited its governor from seeking reelection after just one four-year term. (Former Virginia governors are permitted, however, to run for another term in later elections.)

There is near conformity on the length of terms, with forty-eight states installing governors for four years. Two-year terms, once common, are now in effect only in the neighboring New England states of New Hampshire and Vermont. One-year terms, also not unusual in the nation's early days, have been relegated to history.

Gubernatorial politics tend to reflect national trends. For years, especially from the New Deal era of President Franklin D. Roosevelt in the 1930s on, Democrats held most governorships. But the Republican upsurge in 1994 that enabled the party to establish a dozen years of dominance in Congress also had an impact in the states: after the 1998 election, thirty-one governors were Republicans, seventeen were Democrats, and two (in Maine and Minnesota) were independents. The Democrats in 2006 made a six-seat net gain in governorships, for a total of twenty-eight, that was in line with the party's takeover of both chambers of Congress. Democrats improved on that slightly in 2008 with a gain of one additional seat. But in 2010, the strongest Republican year since 1994, the GOP came charging back to hold twenty-nine seats compared to twenty for the Democrats. (See table, Party Lineup of Governors, p. 235.)

The first female governors were elected in 1924, four years after the Nineteenth Amendment granted WOMEN'S SUFFRAGE in every state. Elected that year to succeed their husbands were Nellie Tayloe Ross of Wyoming and Miriam "Ma" Ferguson of Texas, both Democrats. According to the Center for American Women in Politics, twenty-nine women have served as governor in twenty-two states as of early 2007, with nine female governors—an all-time high—in office at that time.

The first popularly elected African American governor was Democrat L. Douglas Wilder of Virginia, who served from 1990 to 1994. Democrat Deval Patrick's win in Massachusetts in 2006 made him the second. The first two Hispanic governors were elected in 1974: Jerry Apodaca in New Mexico and Raul Castro in Arizona, both Democrats; New Mexico Democrat Bill Richardson was the only Hispanic governor in office in early 2007. Gary Locke, a Democrat of Chinese descent, became the first Asian American governor with his election in Washington in 1996.

Length of Terms

As of 1789, the four New England states—Connecticut, Massachusetts, New Hampshire, and Rhode Island (Vermont was admitted to the Union in 1791 and Maine in 1820)—held gubernatorial elections every year. Some of the Middle Atlantic states favored somewhat longer terms: New York and Pennsylvania had three-year terms for their governors, although New Jersey instituted a one-year term. The BORDER and southern states had a mix: Maryland and North Carolina governors served a one-year term, South Carolina had a two-year term, and Delaware, Virginia, and Georgia had three-year terms. No state had a four-year term.

Over the years, states have changed the length of gubernatorial terms. With some occasional back and forth movement, the general trend has been toward longer terms. New York, for example, has changed the governor's term of office four times. Beginning in 1777 with a three-year term, the state switched to a two-year term in 1820, back to a three-year term in 1876, back to a two-year term in 1894, and to a four-year term beginning in 1938.

Maryland provides another example of a state that has changed its gubernatorial term several times. Beginning with one year in 1776, the state extended the term to three years in 1838, then to four years in 1851. Regular gubernatorial elections were held every second odd year from then through 1923, when the state had one three-year term so that future elections would be held in even-numbered years, beginning in 1926. Thus, the state held gubernatorial elections in 1919, 1923, and 1926, and then every four years after that.

The trend toward longer gubernatorial terms shows up clearly by comparing the length of terms in 1900 and 2011. Of the forty-five states in the Union in 1900, twenty-two, almost half, had

LENGTH OF GOVERNOR TERMS

State	1900	2010	Year of Change to Longer Term	State	1900	2010	Year of Change to Longer Term
Alabama	2	4	1902	Montana	4	4	—
Alaska[1]	—	4	—	Nebraska	2	4	1966
Arizona[1]	—	4	1970	Nevada	4	4	—
Arkansas	2	4	1986	New Hampshire	2	2	—
California	4	4	—	New Jersey	3	4	1949
Colorado	2	4	1958	New Mexico[1]	—	4	1970
Connecticut	2	4	1950	New York	2	4	1938
Delaware	4	4	—	North Carolina	4	4	—
Florida	4	4	—	North Dakota	2	4	1964
Georgia	2	4	1942	Ohio	2	4	1958
Hawaii[1]	—	4	—	Oklahoma[1]	—	4	—
Idaho	2	4	1946	Oregon	4	4	—
Illinois	4	4	—	Pennsylvania	4	4	—
Indiana	4	4	—	Rhode Island[3]	1	4	1912, 1994
Iowa	2	4	1974	South Carolina	2	4	1926
Kansas	2	4	1974	South Dakota	2	4	1974
Kentucky	4	4	—	Tennessee	2	4	1954
Louisiana	4	4	—	Texas	2	4	1974
Maine	2	4	1958	Utah	4	4	—
Maryland	4	4	—	Vermont	2	2	—
Massachusetts[2]	1	4	1920, 1966	Virginia	4	4	—
Michigan	2	4	1966	Washington	4	4	—
Minnesota	2	4	1962	West Virginia	4	4	—
Mississippi	4	4	—	Wisconsin	2	4	1970
Missouri	4	4	—	Wyoming	4	4	—

Sources: *Book of the States, 2002*, vol. 34 (Lexington, KY: Council of State Governments, 2002); *CQ Weekly*, various issues.

1. Oklahoma was admitted to the Union in 1907, Arizona and New Mexico in 1912, and Alaska and Hawaii in 1959. Oklahoma, Alaska, and Hawaii have always had four-year gubernatorial terms; Arizona began with a two-year term and switched to four years in 1970. New Mexico (1912) began with a four-year term, changed to two years in 1916, and went back to four years in 1970.

2. Massachusetts switched from a one-year term to a two-year term in 1920 and to a four-year term in 1966.

3. Rhode Island switched from a one- to a two-year term in 1912 and to a four-year term in 1994.

two-year terms. One (New Jersey) had a three-year term, while Rhode Island and Massachusetts were the only states left with one-year terms. The remaining twenty states had four-year gubernatorial terms.

By 2011 forty-three of those same forty-five states had four-year terms, as did the five states admitted to the Union after 1900—Oklahoma (1907), Arizona and New Mexico (1912), and Alaska and Hawaii (1959). This left only two states with two-year terms: New Hampshire and Vermont. Arkansas, one of the last holdouts, voted in 1984 to switch to a four-year term, effective in 1986. Rhode Island voters in 1992 approved a constitutional change to a four-year term beginning with the 1994 election. (See table, Length of Governor Terms, page 237.)

Elections in Nonpresidential Years

Along with the change to longer terms for governors came another trend—away from holding gubernatorial elections in presidential election years. The separation reduces the likelihood that presidential politics will influence the choice of state officials.

Except for North Dakota, every state that switched in the twentieth century to four-year gubernatorial terms scheduled its elections in nonpresidential election years. That left only eleven states holding their gubernatorial elections at the same time as the presidential election—Delaware, Indiana, Missouri, Montana, North Carolina, North Dakota, Utah, Washington, and West Virginia with four-year terms, and New Hampshire and Vermont, the remaining states with two-year terms.

Five states elect governors in odd-numbered years. Kentucky, Louisiana, and Mississippi hold their contests the year before the presidential election year, while New Jersey and Virginia hold theirs the year after.

Methods of Election

Yet another way in which Americans of the early federal period restricted their governors was by the method of election. In 1789 the only states in which the people directly chose their governors by popular vote were New York and the four New England states. In the remaining eight states, state legislatures chose the governors, which enhanced the power of the legislatures in their dealings with the governors.

But several factors—including the democratic trend to DIRECT ELECTION, the increasing trust in the office of governor, and the need for a stronger and more independent chief executive—led to the gradual introduction of popular votes in all the states. By the 1860s, the remaining eight original states all had switched to popular ballots. Pennsylvania was first, in 1790, followed by Delaware in 1792, Georgia in 1824, North Carolina in 1835, Maryland in 1838, New Jersey in 1844, Virginia in 1851, and South Carolina in 1865, after the Civil War.

All the states admitted to the Union after the original thirteen, with one exception, made provision from the very beginning for popular election of their governors. The exception was Louisiana, which from its admission in 1812 until a change in the state constitution in 1845 had a unique system of gubernatorial elections. The people participated by voting in a first-step popular election. In a second step, the legislature was to select the governor from the two candidates receiving the highest popular vote.

Because of the domination of the Democratic Party in the South for many years after the Civil War, the Democrats' SOUTHERN PRIMARY was more important than the general election in the selection of governors and other officials in some southern states. Victory in the party's primary often was tantamount to election, with the winner facing weak or token Republican opposition in the November election.

Although the so-called Solid South trended toward a two-party region in the latter decades of the twentieth century before becoming largely a Republican stronghold, the South continued to produce some anomalies in the election of governors. Louisiana, for example, holds an open primary for governor every four years, in the odd-numbered year preceding the presidential election year. Candidates from all parties run on the same ballot. Any candidate who receives a majority is elected. If no candidate receives 50 percent, a RUNOFF is held in November between the two top finishers.

Number of Terms

Another limitation placed on governors is a restriction on the number of terms they are allowed to serve. In the early years at least three states had such limitations. Governors of Maryland were eligible to serve three consecutive one-year terms and then were required to retire for at least one year. Pennsylvania allowed its governors three consecutive three-year terms and then forced retirement for at least one term. In New Jersey, according to the state constitution of 1844, a governor could serve only one three-year term before retiring for at least one term.

LIMITATIONS ON GOVERNOR TERMS

In most states with limits of one or two consecutive terms, governors may serve again after a one-term hiatus. Thus, in a state with a two-term limitation, the governor must retire after two consecutive terms. After a one-term interim, he or she may serve again.

State	Maximum Number of Consecutive Terms (as of 2011)	State	Maximum Number of Consecutive Terms (as of 2011)	State	Maximum Number of Consecutive Terms (as of 2011)
Alabama	2	Louisiana	2	Ohio	2
Alaska	2	Maine	2	Oklahoma	2
Arizona	2	Maryland	2	Oregon[2]	2
Arkansas	2	Massachusetts	No limit	Pennsylvania	2
California	2	Michigan	2	Rhode Island	2
Colorado	2	Minnesota	No limit	South Carolina	2
Connecticut	No limit	Mississippi[1]	2	South Dakota	2
Delaware[1]	2	Missouri[1]	2	Tennessee	2
Florida	2	Montana[3]	2	Texas	No limit
Georgia	2	Nebraska	2	Utah	3
Hawaii	2	Nevada	2	Vermont	No limit
Idaho	No limit	New Hampshire	No limit	Virginia	1
Illinois	No limit	New Jersey	2	Washington	No limit
Indiana[2]	2	New Mexico	2	West Virginia	2
Iowa	No limit	New York	No limit	Wisconsin	No limit
Kansas	2	North Carolina	2	Wyoming[3]	No limit
Kentucky	2	North Dakota	No limit		

Source: Book of the States, 2002, vol. 34 (Lexington, KY: Council of State Governments, 2002), Table 4.9; corroborated with more recent sources.

1. Delaware, Mississippi, and Missouri have absolute two-term limits. That is, no person may serve more than two gubernatorial terms in his or her lifetime.

2. Indiana and Oregon prohibit a person from serving more than eight years in any twelve-year period.

3. Montana and Wyoming prohibit a person from serving more than eight years in any sixteen-year period.

In 2011 most states—thirty-six—placed some sort of limitation on the number of consecutive terms the governor could serve. In all but two of those states, the limit was two four-year terms. Only Virginia limited its governor to one term, while Utah had a three-term limit. Twenty of the states allowed governors to seek a return to the office after some period of time, typically four years. (See table, Limitations on Governor Terms, page 239.)

Majority-Vote Requirement

A peculiarity of gubernatorial voting that has almost—but not completely—disappeared from the American political scene is the requirement that the winning candidate receive a majority of the popular vote. Otherwise, the choice devolves upon the state legislature, or, in one case, a runoff between the two highest-polling candidates is required.

The only recent example of this occurred in the 1999 gubernatorial election in Mississippi. Democrat Ronnie Musgrove took 49.6 percent of the vote to Republican Mike Parker's 48.5 percent, leaving him just short of the majority he needed to win outright. The legislature was dominated by Democrats, and Musgrove was easily elected by the state house of representatives.

Centered in New England, this practice was used mainly in the nineteenth century. All six New England states, plus Georgia, had such a provision in their state constitutions at one time. New Hampshire, Vermont, Massachusetts, and Connecticut already had the provision when they entered the Union between 1789 and 1791. Rhode Island required a majority election but did not adopt a provision for legislative election until 1842. Maine adopted a majority provision when it split off from Massachusetts to form a separate state in 1820. Georgia put the majority provision into its constitution when it switched from legislative to popular election of governors in 1825.

The purpose of the majority provision appears to have been to safeguard against a candidate's winning with a small fraction of the popular vote in a multiple field. In most of New England, the provision was part of the early state constitutions, formed largely in the 1780s, before the development of the TWO-PARTY SYSTEM.

Ron Heitz of Waukesha, Wis., attends the state Democratic Party's annual convention in Milwaukee on Friday, June 3, 2011, where he signs a pledge to support an eventual recall of Wisconsin Gov. Scott Walker.

Source: AP Photo/Dinesh Ramde. Removal from Office

The emergence of two major political parties diminished the prospects of multiple candidates for the same office. Nevertheless, each of these states had occasion to use the majority provision at least once. Sometimes, in an extremely close election, minor-party candidates received enough of a vote to keep the winner from getting a majority of the total vote. And at other times strong THIRD-PARTY movements or disintegration of the old party structure resulted in the election being thrown into the state legislature.

Vermont is the only state besides Mississippi that retains the majority-vote provision. In 1986 and 2002 no Vermont candidate received a majority, and the legislature chose the governor: Democrat Madeleine M. Kunin in January 1987 and Republican Jim Douglas in January 2003.

Term limits ensure a steady turnover of governors in most states. Elections every four years also enable the voters to replace an unpopular governor. In addition, governors deemed guilty of unethical conduct, failure to carry out the requirements of their office, or crimes and misdemeanors may be removed from office through impeachment or recall.

This happens rarely, but California provided a spectacular example in 2003 when it removed Democratic governor Gray Davis and replaced him with Republican Arnold Schwarzenegger, a movie star who ran well ahead of the runners-up in a field that included 135 candidates.

Davis committed no crimes, but he struggled to maintain public support because of his rather colorless personality, his implementation of unpopular tax increases, and his poor handling of a state energy crisis. He was recalled from office just eleven months after he had won a second term.

The only previous recall of a governor occurred in 1921, when North Dakota voters ousted Gov. Lynn J. Frazier, Republican and National Prohibition Party member, who had been forced into a special election with Ragnvald A. Nestos, Independent Republican. Frazier was in his third two-year term when he was removed, along with two cabinet members. The following year Frazier was elected to the U.S. Senate, where he served until 1941.

A gubernatorial recall effort was brewing in Wisconsin in 2011 against Scott Walker, a Republican. Walker, facing significant budget issues, aggressively attacked a variety of spending issues, but the most controversial effort was directed at public employee unions. His proposal, which became law, rescinded collective bargaining for state public employee workers. Walker said the changes were needed to allow local governments the flexibility to meet expenses without raising taxes, but organized labor, and most Democrats, charged that Walker and Republican allies were using the state's financial problems to break unions. The controversy went on for weeks and brought hundreds of protesters, from within the state and elsewhere, to the legislative chambers. Although Walker succeeded, opponents immediately began organizing a recall effort, which under state law could not occur until early 2012. However, nine Wisconsin state legislators faced recall votes in summer 2011. (See REMOVAL FROM OFFICE.)

Impeachment by the state legislature, similar to the federal system in which the House impeaches (charges) and the Senate acquits or convicts, was used five times in the twentieth century to remove governors. The most recent case was that of Arizona governor Evan Mecham, Republican, who was impeached and convicted in January 1988. He was found guilty of obstructing an investigation and improperly using official funds. Mecham's removal through impeachment ended a recall movement against him.

Other governors have resigned after being convicted in the JUDICIAL SYSTEM. Among such cases is that of Maryland governor Marvin Mandel, Democrat, who served time in prison while suspended from office after his 1977 conviction on federal mail fraud charges. After his conviction was reversed, he served the remaining few hours of his term.

Alabama governor Guy Hunt, Republican, was removed from office in 1993 after he was convicted of diverting inaugural funds to personal use. Democrat Jim Guy Tucker, who as lieutenant governor succeeded President Bill Clinton as governor of Arkansas, resigned in 1996 after being convicted of bank fraud conspiracy in connection with the Whitewater real estate SCANDAL. In September 1997 Arizona governor J. Fife Symington III, Republican, resigned after being convicted of making false statements to obtain loans for his real estate business.

Grandfather Clause

In the parlance of politics and elections, the term *grandfather clause* has two principal meanings. One deals with voting rights, the other with campaign funds.

The older use of the term refers to the laws passed in seven southern states after the Civil War that exempted illiterate whites from LITERACY TESTS, which had been instituted as a legal means of preventing African Americans, many of them former slaves, from voting. Though the uneducated whites were not capable of passing the tests, they were "grandfathered" under a waiver for individuals whose ancestors had voted before 1867. Few blacks could meet that test because they or their forebears had been slaves who were not regarded as citizens under the law and therefore had not been eligible to vote.

The Supreme Court ruled in 1915 that these grandfather clauses violated the Fifteenth Amendment to the Constitution, which prohibited denial of the RIGHT TO VOTE on account of race.

The other reference to a grandfather clause came much more recently and concerned a loophole in the 1979 CAMPAIGN FINANCE law that permitted House members to pocket leftover campaign funds for their personal use. The law barred personal use of excess campaign funds except by grandfathered members—those who were in office on January 8, 1980. The funds became taxable as income, but once the members disclosed the conversion of the money to personal use their reporting obligations ended. There was no comparable rule in the Senate, which prohibited personal use of excess campaign money by members past or present.

The House practice, though it would have disappeared by attrition as members elected before 1980 left the House, remained controversial. Some senior members who never faced a competitive challenge because of their popularity, seniority, "safe" districts, or other factors continued to raise and pile up large amounts of money in their campaign accounts, which they could cash out upon retirement.

Between 1980 and the beginning of 1989, grandfathered members converted to personal use at least $862,000, including more than $710,000 in cash. Another $115,000 was borrowed or used to retire personal loans unconnected with their former campaigns. At least $37,000 went for cars, furniture, travel, and other services.

More on this topic:
Literacy Tests, p. 309
Right to Vote, p. 549
Voting Rights Act, p. 663

But the ethical questions raised by the practice led Congress to close the grandfather clause loophole with a provision in a 1989 ethics and pay law. House members were made ineligible to convert excess campaign funds if they stayed in the House past the beginning of the 103rd Congress in January 1993, so eligible members seeking to take the money had to retire before then.

Green Party (1996–)

With famed consumer activist Ralph Nader heading its ticket, the liberal Green Party made an impressive debut in U.S. presidential politics in 1996. Nader received 685,040 votes (0.7 percent of the popular vote), to finish fourth, albeit a distant fourth, behind the Reform Party's Ross Perot.

Just four years after its formal founding, the party made its first significant impact on American politics. Declaiming both the Republican and Democratic parties as too closely tied to corporations and big campaign donors, Nader ran as the Green Party nominee for the second time, claiming a modest 2,882,738 votes, or 2.7 percent of the national vote,

Consumer advocate Ralph Nader was the Green Party's candidate for president in 1996 and 2000.

Source: CQ Photo/Scott J. Ferrell

and no electoral votes in a contest that Republican George W. Bush won by a razor-thin electoral-vote majority. But Nader's vote totals in Florida and New Hampshire exceeded Bush's victory margins over Democratic nominee Al Gore, leading to a lasting debate over whether Nader played the role of a "spoiler" who helped elect Bush.

The Greens were far less prominent in the 2004 election, when Nader opted to run as an independent. While Nader collected 465,650 votes (0.4 percent) nationally in the 2004 election that Bush won over Democrat John Kerry, the Green Party ticket headed by lawyer and party activist David Cobb took just 119,630 votes (0.1 percent). In 2008 the party sank even lower. Its presidential candidate was Cynthia A. McKinney, a former House member. Under her flag, the party garnered 161,797 votes, just 0.1 percent of the total vote. Nader ran as an independent, getting 739,034 votes, or 0.6 percent.

Although Nader declined to play an ongoing party-building role, Green Party officials have focused more of their efforts in recent years on candidates for local offices in order to build a party base from the bottom up. The party's website in early March 2007 claimed at least 220 Green Party officeholders in twenty-eight states and the District of Columbia; most were small-city mayors, city council members, school board members, and neighborhood advisory commissioners.

Although new to the United States, the Green Party was part of a decentralized worldwide movement for peace, social justice, and the environment. In the 1990s the Greens established a significant political presence in Europe, especially in Germany where they joined the governing Social Democratic Party coalition after the 1998 elections.

Nader spoke at the Green Party convention in Los Angeles in August 1996 and agreed to be its candidate. He refused campaign contributions, however, and left the organizational work to the party.

Nader was the Green Party nominee again in 2000, but ran a much more active campaign than four years earlier. He took his populist, anticorporate campaign to a variety of venues, ranging from television studios to union meetings, in a bid to put together what he described as a "blue-green" coalition of disaffected voters. Nationwide polls in the summer of 2000 showed Nader drawing roughly 5 percent of the vote and even more than that in several battleground states, including California. His poll standing was strong enough to make Nader a factor in the race, and of particular concern to Democrats, whose liberal wing was especially vulnerable to raiding by the Nader forces.

Democrats responded by urging voters who might be inclined to support Nader to vote for Gore to avoid allowing Bush to win what was accurately viewed as a very close election. Some Nader supporters, worried about the possibility that their candidate could indeed become a spoiler, circulated proposals for "vote trading," under which Nader voters would pledge to vote for Gore in the crucial battleground states in exchange for Gore voters' promise to favor Nader in a state where their votes would not have a material impact, because a landslide outcome (in favor of either Gore or Bush) was expected. There is no evidence that this idea gained significant appeal.

Greenback Party (1876–1884)

The National Independent or Greenback-Labor Party, commonly known as the Greenback Party, was launched in Indianapolis, Indiana, in November 1874 at a meeting organized by the Indiana Grange. The party grew out of the Panic of 1873, a post–Civil War economic depression, that hit farmers and industrial workers particularly hard. Currency was the basic issue of the new party, which opposed return to the gold standard and favored retention of the inflationary paper money (known as greenbacks), first introduced as an emergency measure during the Civil War.

The party in 1876 ran Peter Cooper, a New York philanthropist, for president and drafted a platform that focused entirely on the currency issue. Cooper, though, received just 75,973 votes (0.9 percent of the popular vote), mainly from agrarian voters.

Spurred by the continuing depression, a Greenback national convention in 1878 effected the merger of the party with various labor reform groups and adopted a platform that addressed labor and currency issues. Showing voting strength in the industrial East as well as in the agrarian South and Midwest, the Greenbacks polled more than 1 million votes in the 1878 congressional races and won fourteen seats in the U.S. House of Representatives. This marked the high point of the party's strength.

A return of national prosperity undermined the party's appeal, however, and its ability to grow was hindered by an ongoing prospect that it would merge with one of the existing major parties and by a split between the agrarian and labor wings of the party. In the 1880 election, the party elected only eight representatives, and its presidential candidate, Rep. James B. Weaver of Iowa, received 305,997 votes (3.3 percent of the popular vote), far less than party leaders expected.

The party slipped further four years later, when the Greenbacks' candidate for president, former Massachusetts governor Benjamin F. Butler, a longtime Republican, received 175,096 votes (1.7 percent of the popular vote). With the demise of the Greenbacks, most of the party's constituency moved into the Populist Party, the agrarian reform movement that gained strength in the South and Midwest in the 1890s.

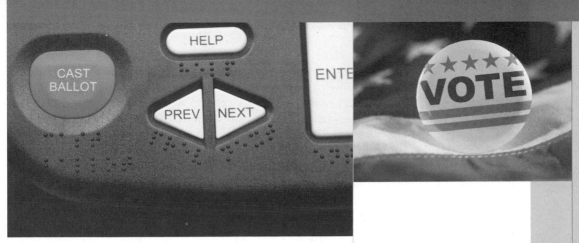

Hard Money

Campaign spending at all levels of government escalated despite the enactment of laws in the 1970s aimed at limiting the flood of money in politics. This led in the mid-1990s to renewed reform efforts, which ultimately culminated in the enactment of the Bipartisan Campaign Reform Act (BCRA) of 2002.

The key provision of this often-stalled and heavily debated statute barred unlimited donations, known as SOFT MONEY, to the national political parties for use in campaigns for federal offices—thus limiting those campaigns to the use of limited and strictly regulated *hard-money* donations. (For details about those legal limits, see CAMPAIGN FINANCE.)

Supporters of the law predicted that the soft-money ban would at least serve as a brake to the escalating costs of campaigning. Opponents warned, though, that national parties would be weakened by the loss of access to soft money, which both the Republicans and Democrats relied on heavily.

Yet the continued growth of campaign spending in the election cycles immediately following the enactment of BCRA would frustrate those who had advocated for the measure and provide new avenues for unlimited spending, outside the formal structures of the national parties, for those opposed to stricter campaign finance regulation.

Both sides were quickly proved wrong about the impact of the soft-money ban on the health of the parties during the 2004 presidential and 2006 midterm election campaigns, the first after the law took effect. The national parties proved extremely agile in shifting their fund-raising efforts to chasing down many thousands of smaller hard-money donations to replace the fewer but much more sizable soft-money contributions. The Democratic National Committee during the 2004 presidential election cycle raised $404.4 million, in hard dollars, compared with $158.1 million in 2000, when soft-money contributions were still legal; the Republican National Committee's hard-money receipts jumped to $392.4 million in 2004 from $225.4 million in 2000.

The accelerating impact of the Internet as a means to connect with political supporters—and persuade them to make hard-money donations—made those initial concerns look even more exaggerated. The innovative use of new media by Democrat Barack Obama's successful 2008 campaign for president enabled him to become the first major-party nominee to eschew public funds for both the primary and general elections since such funds were first made available to candidates during the 1976 campaign. Obama ended up raising a record-shattering $779 million during his 2008 run.

Even some candidates who were unsuccessful at the polls that year were unexpectedly proficient at using the web as a conduit for hard-money donations. One of these was Texas representative Ron Paul, a longtime House member who long had a reputation as a quirky crusader for conservative libertarianism but was little known nationally before he launched a long-shot bid for the Republican presidential nomination in 2008. Paul used several web-based fund-raising pushes, which his campaign labeled as "money bombs," to raise a total of nearly $32 million for that campaign, even though he never was remotely a competitive candidate for the nomination that went to Arizona senator John McCain (who was a coauthor of the 2002 campaign finance reform law).

Meanwhile, hundreds of millions of dollars in soft money, which previously might have gone directly into Republican and Democratic party coffers, instead flowed into POLITICAL ACTION COMMITTEES (PACs) that were formed under Section 527 of the tax code and known as "527s." These groups were eligible to receive such unlimited funding and used much of the money on independent expenditures to influence a wide range of campaigns—including many for federal offices, such as president of the United States.

SuperPACs, a new outside political force that emerged following a landmark Supreme Court ruling in January 2010, quickly appeared to have the potential to be an even bigger pipeline for unlimited spending than the 527 groups. SuperPACs sprung up almost immediately after the Court, by a 5–4 vote, struck down a provision that had barred corporate entities, including business and labor unions, from using broadcast ads as "electioneering communications" within sixty days of a general election and within thirty days of a primary election. The ruling established as a matter of law that corporate entities have free-speech rights that are essentially equivalent to those of individuals, a controversial concept that appeared certain to be the subject of continued debate. (See CAMPAIGN FINANCE)

Compared with soft-money contributions, hard money has produced relatively few headlines since the FEDERAL ELECTION COMMISSION (FEC) in 1976 began administering and enforcing the Federal

Rep. Ron Paul, R-Texas, was a prominent candidate for the GOP presidential nomination in 2012, appealing especially to libertarian voters. Even before this 2012 run, Paul in a long-short 2008 effort to get the GOP nomination used several web-based fund-raising pushes, which his campaign called "money bombs," to collect nearly $32 million for his campaign.

Election Campaign Act of 1971 (the 1970s campaign finance law that established the FEC) and its amendments. The bipartisan commission relies mostly on voluntary compliance with the campaign law's contribution and spending limits, although the FEC has the authority to investigate suspected violations and, if necessary, to impose fines and order repayment of public funds.

BCRA requires disclosure of receipts and expenditures by candidates for federal office. Whereas the 1971 law set contribution limits for individuals and political committees that were fixed and remained unchanged for three decades, the provisions of the 2002 law allowed the FEC to make adjustments for inflation at the start of each two-year election cycle.

In fact, the FEC did so in each of the first five election cycles covered by BCRA. For the 2011–2012 cycle, individuals could give $2,500 per election per candidate, with primary and general elections deemed separate elections; they also could give up to $30,800 to a national party committee per election cycle and $5,000 to individual political action committees, for a biennial limit of $117,000 in all contributions over the two-year cycle. Except for the limit on donations to PACs, which remained constant, all of these figures were higher than those in effect when BCRA was first implemented in the 2003–2004 cycle.

Presidential candidates who accept PUBLIC FINANCING must abide by overall spending limits in their campaigns. Front-running candidates, with their growing capacity to raise vast amounts of money on their own without the spending limitations that come with federal financing, started a trend, though, that has since greatly weakened the public financing system. Since Republican George W. Bush's campaign in 2000, many such candidates have opted out of the public financing system in the primary election, and Obama's decision to take that up a notch by eschewing public financing and the spending limits that come with it for the 2008 general election as well appeared certain to influence the financial planning of presidential candidates in subsequent campaigns. Because House and Senate campaigns are not publicly funded, congressional candidates are subject to contribution but not spending limits.

More on this topic:
Buckley v. Valeo, p. 37
Bundling, p. 39
Campaign Finance, p. 53
Political Action Committees, p. 389
Public Financing of Campaigns, p. 496
Soft Money, p. 592

Confronted with the ban on giving unlimited soft money to parties, interest groups and wealthy individuals have used other means to get around the hard-money contribution limits. One is BUNDLING—the collection of a number of checks, each within the legal gift limit, that are sent as a single package to a candidate under the auspices of a PAC, lobbyist, or party committee. The group gets the credit, and presumably access to the candidate, and because the bundle is made up of individual legal-sized donations, it is within the law.

Another technique that skirts the limits is the so-called independent expenditure—money spent by another person, a group, or a party organization to benefit a candidate's campaign but without coordination or collusion with the candidate. The Supreme Court ruled in BUCKLEY V. VALEO (1976) that such spending is a form of free speech protected by the First Amendment to the Constitution. If it is truly independent, the Court said, it may not be restricted.

Hatch Act *See* FEDERAL WORKERS' POLITICAL ACTIVITY.

Help America Vote Act of 2002

The 2000 national election, which featured Republican presidential candidate George W. Bush's razor-thin victory over Democrat Al Gore, was burdened with some of the biggest controversies over the nation's voting systems in modern times.

"The vitality of America's democracy depends on the fairness and accuracy of America's elections. When problems arise in the administration of elections, we have a responsibility to fix them."

—President George W. Bush at the signing ceremony for the Help America Vote Act of 2002, which arose from the need to overhaul the nation's voting procedures in light of disputes over the 2000 presidential election

The counting of paper punch-card ballots, a subject of numerous disputes in many localities over many years, reached a crescendo in 2000 in Florida, which had the twenty-five electoral votes that would decide the Bush-Gore contest. Voters across the nation watched as Florida election officials gazed at individual paper ballots trying to determine whether a voter had attempted but failed to completely dislodge the tiny paper rectangle known as a "chad" that would enable their intended vote to be counted. The election was not officially decided until the Supreme Court's decision in *BUSH V. GORE* ended the recounts five weeks after election day.

Meanwhile, a number of eligible voters, many of them minorities, claimed that they had been thwarted in their efforts to vote by problems that mainly involved voter registration rolls. Some alleged that they had been purposely disenfranchised in an effort to influence the election's outcome.

Such problems threatened the integrity of the nation's election system and the citizens' confidence that their votes would be counted accurately. Congress took action, in the form of the Help America Vote Act (HAVA) of 2002.

The law set broad standards for the conduct of federal elections, putting the federal government's imprint on a process traditionally handled by state and local governments, and authorized nearly $3.9 billion in federal aid over the ensuing three years to assist states and localities in meeting those standards.

HAVA authorized the federal government to provide up to $650 million in grants to states to help them rapidly improve their voting technology. Half of that money was to be dedicated to enabling states and localities to replace punch-card and mechanical-lever voting machines; most states using the aid to replace their old machines were required to do so prior to the 2004 presidential election, though a number of states requested and received extensions to 2006. The other half of the money was to be used to improve election administration, including the recruiting and training of poll workers.

Electronic touch-screen voting machines are gradually replacing traditional paper ballots.

Source: AP Images/Don *Wright*

The measure authorized another $3 million over three years to help states meet the requirements of the law and improve election administration. In addition, $100 million over three years was authorized to fund efforts to make polls accessible to disabled voters.

To provide greater assurance that eligible citizens are not deprived of their RIGHT TO VOTE, the bill required each state to institute a uniform, centralized, and computerized statewide voter registration list; to allow a provisional ballot to be cast by anyone whose eligibility to vote is challenged at a polling place; and to provide a means for each voter to check and if necessary correct his or her voting decisions before irrevocably casting a ballot.

To address concerns about voter fraud, the law requires those seeking to register to vote to present a government-issued driver's license or the last four digits of their Social Security numbers. First-time voters must produce identification at the polls, such as a valid photo ID, a bank statement, or a government document with the voter's name and address.

As with many political "reform" efforts, the changes wrought by HAVA were far from trouble-free. Many states rushed to replace their outmoded, low-tech machines with electronic touch-screen devices; unfortunately, many of these were new to the market and had not been thoroughly "test-driven" in actual elections. Moreover, voters expressed concern that the machines could be programmed by manufacturers or technicians, or infiltrated by outside "hackers," to produce a desired partisan result.

These fears proved unfounded. But there were thousands of reports across the nation of problems involving electronic voting machines. Many were caused by the lack of familiarity of voters and poll workers (most of whom were volunteers and many of whom were elderly) with the new technology.

The biggest voting controversy of 2006 centered on touch-screen voting machines. Florida officials declared Republican Vern Buchanan the winner by 369 votes over Democrat Christine Jennings in an open-seat race in the state's Thirteenth Congressional District. Jennings, however, sued and called for a revote, citing a disproportionate number of "undervotes"—ballots on which votes were cast in other contests but not in the House race—in the district's most-populous county. Jennings's camp argued that a programming problem caused the machines not to count votes that had been cast in the House race; other critics said poor design of the electronic ballots had caused many voters to overlook the House contest. Buchanan was sworn in as a member of the 110th Congress.

In light of this and other such disputes, some members of Congress in 2007 made an effort to amend HAVA to require states to institute a "paper trail," by retaining a hard-copy record of each vote cast, to ensure the integrity of the vote counts and enhance the ability of officials to conduct recounts if necessary. But many states and localities decried the cost of such a requirement, with some saying they might have to scrap the expensive voting machines they had purchased in the wake of HAVA's enactment because they lacked a paper-trail capability.

Home Rule

The power of a local government, usually a city, to write its own charter and manage its own affairs is called *home rule*. The term derives from British usage in the long controversy over self-government for Ireland.

In U.S. national politics, the issue of home rule pertains mostly to the question of self-government for the DISTRICT OF COLUMBIA. As the nation's capital, the District has unique status as a federal enclave carved out of Maryland and controlled by Congress.

The framers of the Constitution kept the District separate so that the policymakers of the national government would not be subordinate to the legislators of the state where the capital happened to be located. Although the District has had a nonvoting delegate to Congress since 1971, its efforts to gain statehood have been thwarted. A constitutional amendment to give the District full representation in Congress failed because too few states ratified it by the 1985 deadline.

Congress granted limited home rule to the District in 1973 but retained the power to overrule actions of the city government. The city subsequently elected its first mayor and city council. In 1995, however, Congress installed a powerful control board to oversee the District's near-bankrupt financial affairs. The move was spurred in part by ethics controversies surrounding longtime Democratic mayor Marion Barry, who had been returned to the office despite having served time in jail for possession of crack cocaine. Congress increased the board's authority in 1997, further weakening the District's already limited home rule. In December 1998, as the District was preparing to swear in Democrat Anthony Williams as its new mayor, the control board restored most of the powers of the mayor's office.

Congress nonetheless maintains considerable control over the District's affairs, including approval of the budget set by its elected officials. Though this oversight is justified by its defenders on grounds that the federal government provides the financing that subsidizes much of the District's budget, many local officials view it as an objectionable imposition on home rule.

The Twenty-third Amendment to the Constitution, ratified in 1961, gave District residents the RIGHT TO VOTE in presidential elections with the District accorded three electoral votes in every contest since 1964. That makes the District stand out from the fifty states, which are accorded electoral votes equaling the size of their congressional delegations (two senators plus the state's apportionment of House members). Because the District's population is made up mostly of Democratic-leaning constituencies such as African Americans, Hispanics, and white liberals, Democratic presidential nominees have won those three electoral votes easily in every election.

Outside the District of Columbia, states may confer home rule on their cities and counties under the method specified by the individual state constitution. Once home rule is granted, the affected jurisdiction appoints a commission to draft a charter that is subject to approval by the voters. American cities may enjoy a degree of freedom from interference by the state legislature, but as creatures of the state they ultimately are subject to the state's control.

> **More on this topic:**
>
> *District of Columbia, p. 163*

House of Representatives, Electing

The framers of the U.S. Constitution intended the House of Representatives to be the branch of government closest to the people. The members would be popularly elected; the terms of office would be two years so that the representatives would not lose touch with their homes; and the House would be a numerous branch, with members having relatively small constituencies.

Today, more than two hundred years later, the House is still the people's branch, with members elected much as the framers intended. Unlike SENATE ELECTIONS, which were fundamentally changed by the Seventeenth Amendment, House elections remain basically the same, except that the legislature itself has grown along with the population, bringing added expense and complexity to the electoral process.

The Senate, fixed at two senators for each state regardless of population, has grown from the original twenty-six members to 100. From sixty-five seats in the First Congress, the House has swelled to its current size of 435 seats, beginning in 2011. Some critics—in what appears a distinctly minority opinion at this juncture of American history—say that this number has become insufficient, noting the vast growth of the nation's population over the past century: whereas House members represented an average of 212,000 people following the 1910 census, their average constituency had more than tripled to over 700,000 people after the 2010 census.

The Constitution set few qualifications for House membership. To be eligible, one must be at least twenty-five years old, a U.S. citizen for at least seven years, and a resident of the state from which elected. From time to time the states, and even the House itself, have tried to add to those requirements, but the Supreme Court has invalidated such efforts as unconstitutional. (See HOUSE OF REPRESENTATIVES, QUALIFICATIONS.)

Future president James Madison argued that representatives should serve three-year terms, while others thought they should be elected annually. The delegates to the Constitutional Convention in 1787 compromised on two-year terms.

Source: Library of Congress

Term Length and Limits

The two-year term for House members was a compromise at the Constitutional Convention in 1787. Many delegates wanted annual elections, believing they would make the House more responsive to the wishes of the people. James Madison, however, had argued for a three-year term, to allow representatives time to gain knowledge and experience in national and local affairs before they had to stand for reelection.

Proposals have been made to extend the term to four years; the last time was in 1966 when President Lyndon B. Johnson urged it in his State of the Union message. With House members making up the largest part of the House chamber audience, Johnson's proposal received loud applause. Afterward, however, critics argued that making the terms coincide with the president's four-year term would create a House of "coattail riders" and end the minority party's tendency to make gains in MIDTERM ELECTIONS. The proposed constitutional amendment never emerged from committee.

During the 1990s another concern arose—that House members serve too long, despite having to run for reelection every two years. INCUMBENCY, in the view of many observers, leads to stagnation of ideas, concentration of power among a few individuals, and a shift from party-centered campaigns to CANDIDATE-CENTERED CAMPAIGNS where the challenger is at a disadvantage. Turnover in the modern House elections in most years is low, unlike in the pre–Civil War era when about half the members were newcomers after each election.

To offset the advantages of incumbency, twenty-three states voted in the 1990s to impose TERM LIMITS on their members of Congress. The Supreme Court, however, struck down such limits, ruling on May 22, 1995, in an Arkansas case that states may not add to the qualifications for Congress spelled out in the Constitution. The landmark 5–4 decision in *U.S. Term Limits Inc. v. Thornton* effectively nullified congressional term limit statutes enacted by these states.

Term limits, however, had already affected an election. In 1994 the congressional Republicans' "Contract with America" pledged "a first-ever vote on term limits to replace career politicians with citizen legislators." In the elections that fall, voters in the state of Washington ousted the Democratic House Speaker, Thomas S. Foley, a fifteen-term veteran. Over Foley's strong opposition, his state had approved term limits in 1992. When the GOP-controlled Congress was seated in January 1995, Rep. Newt Gingrich of Georgia, architect of the Contract with America, replaced Foley as

Speaker. But the House voted down a constitutional amendment to overturn the Supreme Court's term limits decision. The proposal would have limited House members to three two-year terms.

Opponents of term limits argue that the proper vehicle for bringing new members into Congress is the election booth where voters can decide if they want a change in the people they send to Washington. This argument has proven more potent in the years closing out the twentieth century and through the first decade of the new century. Substantial voter discontent sent many incumbents back home in the early 1990s, especially in 1992 and even more in 1994 when Republicans gained fifty-two House seats and control of the chamber. Continued voter discontent, along with other strains of running for office—such as constant fund-raising and almost constant campaigning, and an increasingly shrill political environment fed by talk radio, Internet sites, and attack advertising on television—produced more office-holder turnover in following years. The 2006 and 2008 elections produced significant Democratic gains, which were reversed in 2010 when Republicans came charging back with a net gain of sixty-three House seats and chamber control and a six-seat gain in the Senate, although not a majority. The GOP Senate gain was not enough to win control but more than enough to bring the party back from irrelevance to be a meaningful player; in the previous Congress, Democrats—with help from independents who caucused with them—had an almost filibuster-proof majority.

Ninety-six new House members, about a fifth of the membership, were elected in 2010, although five had served in earlier congresses before losing their seats.

Size of the House

The Constitution specified (Article I, section 2) that the original House would have sixty-five representatives, with each state entitled to at least one. It also directed that the House be apportioned according to population after the first CENSUS in 1790.

Until then the thirteen states were to have the following numbers of representatives: Connecticut, five; Delaware, one; Georgia, three; Maryland, six; Massachusetts, eight; New Hampshire, three; New Jersey, four; New York, six; North Carolina, five; Pennsylvania, eight; Rhode Island, one; South Carolina, five; and Virginia, ten. This apportionment of sixty-five seats remained in effect during the First and Second Congresses (1789–1793). (Seats allotted to North Carolina and Rhode Island were not filled until 1790, after those states had ratified the Constitution.)

Originally the Constitution limited the House to one representative for every 30,000 inhabitants, with three-fifths of a state's slave population added to the whole number of free citizens in the state. This concession to the South, where slavery was prevalent, helped to produce anomalies in House elections that continued through the emancipation of slaves and into the Reconstruction era after the Civil War. The House refused to seat some southern representatives because of disputes over the apportionment of seats after former slaves were fully counted as part of the population. (See ELECTORAL ANOMALIES.)

In its apportionment measure after the first census, Congress in April 1792 set the ratio at one member for every 33,000 inhabitants and fixed the exact number of representatives to which each state was entitled. Thereafter, Congress enacted a new apportionment measure, including the mathematical formula to be used, every ten years (except 1920, when Congress could not agree on a plan) until a permanent apportionment method became effective in 1929. If the Constitution's original allotment of one representative for every 30,000 persons were still in use, the House would have had more than 10,000 members after the 2010 census.

The size of the House has been fixed at a maximum of 435 since Arizona and New Mexico joined the Union in 1912. (Two seats temporarily were added from 1959 to 1963 after Alaska and Hawaii became states.) (See REAPPORTIONMENT AND REDISTRICTING.)

House members are elected from CONGRESSIONAL DISTRICTS. State legislatures redraw the district lines after each census. Under the Supreme Court's ONE-PERSON, ONE-VOTE doctrine, the legislators are obligated to make the districts as equal in population size as possible.

Majority Elections

Nearly all House members today are elected by plurality, with victory going to the candidate winning the largest share of the votes. But at one time or another five New England states required a majority share—more than 50 percent—to win a seat in the U.S. House. If no candidate gained a majority, new elections were held until one contender succeeded.

The provision was last invoked in Maine in 1844, in New Hampshire in 1845, in Massachusetts in 1848, in Vermont in 1866, and in Rhode Island in 1892. Sometimes, multiple races were necessary because none of the candidates could achieve the required majority. In the Fourth District of Massachusetts in 1848 and 1849, for example, twelve successive elections were held to try to choose a representative. None of them was successful, and the district remained unrepresented in the House during the Thirty-first Congress (1849–1851).

The only state that has required its House members to achieve a majority vote in recent times was Louisiana. Under a unique system put in place in the 1970s, candidates for offices, including the House, all ran on the same ballot, regardless of party, in a first-round election. If a candidate won a majority vote in that contest, he or she was deemed elected. If a winner was not declared, the top two vote-getters, regardless of party, would move on to a runoff. But Louisiana enacted a law in 2006 that converted the state to a more conventional system as of the 2008 elections. Under the new system, voters in party primaries selected the nominees for the general election in which the leading candidate, even if short of a majority, becomes the winner.

House elections sometimes are decided by very small margins, with the apparent loser or losers calling for a RECOUNT. In such cases, the final results may not be known for weeks. (See CONTESTED ELECTIONS.)

Districts in some states formerly elected more than one representative. Congress abolished these MULTIMEMBER DISTRICTS in 1842.

Seven states have populations so small they are entitled to only one representative, who is elected AT-LARGE to represent the entire state. Following the 2010 census, the single-member states were Alaska, Delaware, Montana, North Dakota, South Dakota, Vermont, and Wyoming. Despite being the smallest state geographically, Rhode Island had a population that entitled it to two House members.

Rep. Dean Heller of Nevada, left, and Rep. Heath Shuler of North Carolina, right, were both freshmen members of the 110th Congress.
Source: CQ Photo/Scott J. Ferrell

Elections in Odd-Numbered Years

Like multimember districts, House elections in odd-numbered years have faded from general usage. Before ratification of the Twentieth ("Lame Duck") Amendment in 1933, which, among other things, specified January 3 as the end of one congressional term and the beginning of the next, regular sessions of Congress began in December of odd-numbered years. There were, therefore, eleven months in the odd-numbered years to elect members before the beginning of the congressional session.

In 1841, for example, twelve states held general elections for representatives for the Twenty-seventh Congress, convening that year: Alabama, Connecticut, Illinois, Indiana, Kentucky, Maryland, Mississippi, New Hampshire, North Carolina, Rhode Island, Tennessee, and Virginia.

Although it faded well before the Twentieth Amendment took effect, the practice of odd-year elections continued until late in the nineteenth century. In 1875 four states still chose their representatives in regular odd-year elections: California, Connecticut, Mississippi, and New Hampshire. But by 1880 all members of the House were being chosen in even-numbered years (except for special elections to fill vacancies).

One major problem encountered by states choosing their representatives in odd-numbered years was the possibility of a special session of the new Congress being called before the states' elections were held. Depending on the date of the election, a state could be unrepresented in the House. For example, California elected its House delegation to the Fortieth Congress (1867–1869) on September 4, 1867, in plenty of time for the first regular session scheduled for December 2. But Congress already had met in two special sessions—March 4–20 and July 3–20—without any representation from California.

Special Elections

When a vacancy occurs in the House, the usual procedure is for the governor of the affected state to call a special election. Such elections may be held at any time throughout the year, and there are usually several during each two-year Congress. Senate vacancies often are filled by gubernatorial appointment, sometimes followed by a special election. (See SENATE, ELECTING.)

At times there are delays in the calling of House special elections. One of the longest periods in which a congressional district went unrepresented occurred in 1959 and 1960, following the death on April 28, 1959, of Rep. James G. Polk, Democrat, of Ohio's Sixth District.

The election to replace Polk did not take place until November 1960. It was held simultaneously with the general election for the same seat, and the winner, Ward M. Miller, a Republican, served only the two months remaining in the term. For the full term, the Republican and Democratic parties nominated candidates different from those who ran for the short term.

Some states still have special-election procedures that result in lengthy delays, though not as extreme as in the case just mentioned. One of these is New Jersey. In January 2006 longtime Democratic representative Bob Menendez was selected by Democratic governor Jon Corzine to fill the Senate seat Corzine vacated after his election as governor in 2005. According to state law, the special election to fill the vacant seat for the Thirteenth District had to be timed to the regular election schedule, with a primary in June and a general election in November. As a result, the seat sat vacant for ten months until Democrat Albio Sires won the special election for the remaining few weeks of Menendez's unexpired term—on the same day that Sires also won the election for the subsequent full term.

Even in states without such laws, the expense of staging elections sometimes prompts state officials to time special elections to coincide with already scheduled elections. But most states move expeditiously to fill vacancies and restore full representation to the district of a prematurely departed member.

Campaign Costs

Unlike presidential campaigns, congressional election campaigns receive no PUBLIC FINANCING and therefore are not subject to spending limits. House and Senate campaigns are, however, restricted by contribution limits and disclosure requirements administered by the FEDERAL ELECTION COMMISSION (FEC).

The costs of campaigning for the House have soared in recent years despite legislative efforts—the Federal Election Campaign Act (FECA) of 1971 and the Bipartisan Campaign Reform Act (BCRA) of 2002—to rein in the influence of money in politics. In the election cycle of 2009–2010, which saw Republicans take back House control, candidates for that chamber spent $1.1 billion, according to figures from the Federal Election Commission compiled by the Center for Responsive Politics, a nonpartisan political watchdog group, compared to $938 million two years earlier and $855 million in 2006. Democratic candidates in 2009–2010 spent $541.6 million and Republicans $535.1 million. Spending by individual candidates of more than $1 million has become commonplace.

In the original 1971 version of FECA, Congress tried to limit spending on congressional races. But the Supreme Court ruled in *BUCKLEY V. VALEO* (1976) that such limits are unconstitutional without public funding of campaigns. In the revised law, contribution limits were kept, but spending limits were dropped, except for presidential candidates who accept the public grants.

Party Shifts in the House

The founders set House terms at two years in part to make the chamber responsive to changes in the public's mood. Yet incumbents' ability to raise large sums of campaign money, along with their high visibility and intense focus on their constituents' parochial issues, has for many years made partisan control of the House remarkably stable. Big swings, those that result in a partisan shift, occur infrequently.

Such a swing occurred in 2006, when declining public support for President George W. Bush and the Republican-controlled Congress led to a thirty-seat gain for the Democrats. That gave them 233 seats at the start of the 110th Congress, fifteen more than they needed for a majority.

But that was the first turnover in power in a dozen years. The Republicans had gained control with a fifty-two-seat gain in the 1994 midterm elections, ending a forty-year period of unbroken Democratic dominance in the House. For twenty-six of those years (1955–1981), the Democrats also held the Senate majority for a record of thirteen consecutive Congresses controlled by the same party.

But only four more years after 2006 were required for another shift when Republicans gained a net of sixty-three House seats to regain control.

The twentieth century began with a long period of GOP dominance of American politics. In the thirty-two years from 1901 to 1933, the Republicans controlled the House for all but eight years (1911–1919). But the economic calamity of the Great Depression, which in 1932 swept Democrat Franklin D. Roosevelt into the White House with the first of his four presidential victories, caused one of the greatest reversals of fortune in congressional history as well. Over the sixty-two years from 1933 to 1995, the Republicans controlled the House for only four years, 1947–1949 and 1953–1955. Throughout the twentieth century Republican control of the House mostly coincided with Republican presidencies.

Regionally, the makeup of the House majority strength shifted dramatically in the latter half of the twentieth century. The South, once called the "Solid South" because of its solidarity with the Democratic Party, now forms the core of Republican electoral strength in presidential and congressional elections. The Northeast, once a GOP stronghold, now provides much of the Democratic base of support.

House of Representatives, Qualifications

Article I, section 2, of the Constitution set few requirements for election to the U.S. House of Representatives: a member had to be at least twenty-five years of age, have been a U.S. citizen for seven years, and be an inhabitant of the state from which elected. Qualifications for Senate membership are similar. (See SENATE, ELECTING; SENATE, QUALIFICATIONS.)

Besides age, citizenship, and residency, there were other de facto requirements for House election in the early days of the Republic. They included race, sex, and property. Since the Constitution left it to the states to determine who could vote, this in effect limited House membership to propertied white males.

At first, most states had some kind of property requirement for voting. But the democratic trend of the early nineteenth century swept away most property qualifications, producing practically universal white male suffrage by the 1830s. It would be about forty more years, however, before anyone other than a white male citizen could gain membership in the House.

Gradually, several changes in the Constitution broadened the FRANCHISE (the RIGHT TO VOTE) in ways that affected House elections. The Fifteenth Amendment (1870) extended the franchise to newly freed slaves; the Nineteenth Amendment (1920) granted WOMEN'S SUFFRAGE; the Twenty-fourth Amendment (1964) abolished the POLL TAX; and the Twenty-sixth Amendment (1971) broadened YOUTH SUFFRAGE, lowering the voting age to eighteen from twenty-one. In 1965 Congress passed the VOTING RIGHTS ACT to remove barriers several states and localities had erected to keep blacks and other minorities from voting. Other laws and Supreme Court decisions affected BLACK SUFFRAGE and RACIAL REDISTRICTING.

House Characteristics

The average age of House members in the 112th Congress when it began in January 2011 was 56.7 years.

The first black representative, South Carolina Republican Joseph H. Rainey, served from 1870 to 1879.

Source: Library of Congress

There are no legal limits on the number of terms House members can serve—intermittent efforts to impose such limits have failed—and some lawmakers have built prodigious careers. Mississippi Democrat Jamie L. Whitten held the record tenure of fifty-three years for more than a decade after his retirement in January 1995 at age 84. (He died nine months later.) But Michigan Democrat John D. Dingell, who was first elected in a December 1955 special election and was eighty years old when reelected in 2006, set a new tenure record in 2009.

The first black representative was Joseph H. Rainey, a South Carolina Republican, who served from 1870 to 1879. Another African American, John W. Menard of Louisiana, had won a seat in 1868, but the House excluded him because of an election dispute.

Jeannette Rankin, a Montana Republican, was the first woman elected to Congress. She served in the House twice, 1917–1919 and 1941–1943, and was the only member of Congress to vote against U.S. entry into both World Wars.

The first black woman in the House was Shirley Chisholm, a New York Democrat, who served from 1969 to 1983. The first Jewish woman in the House was Bella S. Abzug, a New York Democrat, who served three terms after being elected in 1970.

At the beginning of the 112th Congress seventy-two representatives were women, including a number of African Americans. In addition, three women were elected as nonvoting delegates from the District of Columbia and U.S. territories.

African Americans held forty-two House seats at the start of the 112th Congress. Hispanic Americans, whose numbers expanded greatly in recent decades, held twenty-nine House seats.

Qualification Disputes

One of the most important Supreme Court decisions regarding qualifications for House membership concerned a black representative, New York Democrat Adam Clayton Powell Jr., but his race ostensibly was not the issue. It was Powell's flamboyant conduct and apparent disregard for the law that led to his being excluded from the House on March 1, 1967.

Jeannette Rankin, a Montana Republican, was the first woman elected to Congress. She served two terms in the House, 1917–1919 and 1941–1943.

Source: Library of Congress

A House member since 1945, Powell had risen to the chairmanship of the Education and Labor Committee. But as his power grew, Powell came under increasing criticism for absenteeism, income tax evasion, libel, contempt of court, and other offenses alleged or proven.

After his reelection in 1966, Powell was stripped of his chairmanship and recommended for censure and a fine for "gross misconduct." Instead, the full House voted 307–166 to deny Powell his seat.

Powell sued, arguing that he met the constitutional qualifications of age, citizenship, and residency. The Supreme Court agreed and on June 16, 1969, ruled 7–1 in *Powell v. McCormack* that Powell had been improperly excluded. Powell, who meanwhile had been reelected in 1968, lost interest in Congress and rarely attended sessions. He lost the 1970 Democratic primary for his seat and died in April 1972.

Another type of effort to add to the qualifications for Congress swept the nation in the 1990s in the form of TERM LIMITS. These, too, were struck down by the Supreme Court as unconstitutional.

Twenty-three of the fifty states had enacted some form of limitation on the number of terms their senators and representatives could serve. Advocates viewed long INCUMBENCY as dangerous to democratic government. Opponents argued that experience makes better lawmakers and that, besides, the voters are entitled to choose their own representatives so long as they meet the constitutional requirements.

The Court ruling against state-imposed term limits for Congress came in a May 1995 decision in *Term Limits Inc. v. Thornton.* By a 5–4 majority the Court declared that Arkansas may not add to the qualifications for Congress enumerated in the Constitution. (See HOUSE OF REPRESENTATIVES,

Adam Clayton Powell Jr. was at the center of a Supreme Court ruling, Powell v. McCormack (1969),that prevented the House from adding qualifications for membership in Congress to those enumerated in the Constitution.

Source: AP Images

ELECTING; TERM LIMITS.) Congressional efforts to enact term limits by law or by constitutional amendment in the mid-1990s failed, and national efforts to promote term limits subsequently stalled and now attract scant if any attention. Members of Congress who had promised to limit their tenures during the movement's heyday later reneged on their pledges, usually without political repercussions.

Basically, the Constitution makes clear that Congress has exclusive authority to judge the qualifications of its members. Article I, section 5, states in part, "Each House shall be the Judge of the Election, Returns and Qualifications of its own members."

From time to time, this authority conflicts with the right of the people to decide who will represent them. But in the thirty-five cases involving qualifications for House membership since 1789, the House admitted the challenged representative in twenty-two cases.

Only twelve of the thirty-five cases involved the three qualifications set by the Constitution: age, citizenship, or residency. The only person excluded for one of those reasons was John Bailey, independent, unseated in 1823 as not being a resident of the Massachusetts district that elected him, even though the Constitution requires only that the person elected reside in the state. He subsequently was elected to the same seat and served until 1831.

Four exclusions were for disloyalty during the Civil War. The Fourteenth Amendment to the Constitution, ratified in 1868, barred from Congress anyone who "engaged in insurrection or rebellion" against the United States. The four men denied seats had been elected from southern states in 1867. Other exclusions from the House have been for malfeasance, polygamy, and sedition.

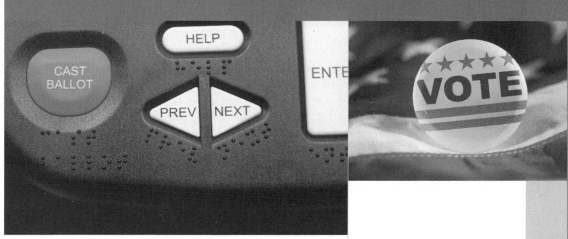

Ideology

An organized and coherent set of attitudes about government and public policy is known as a political ideology. The word *ideology,* or science of ideas, originated in eighteenth-century France during the intellectual Age of Enlightenment that produced the American form of DEMOCRACY.

The strongly liberal opinions of Ohio's Rep. Dennis Kucinich mirrored the views of the left-wing of the Democratic Party. However, in 2012 he lost a primary contest with a fellow Democrat in a new House district created by redistricting, ending his long career in Congress.

Source: CQ Photo/Scott J. Ferrell

In contemporary America people with a liberal ideology traditionally have supported a strong national government that actively promotes social welfare and equality and intervenes to regulate the economy. Holders of a conservative ideology, by contrast, have believed that government should have a limited role in regulating the economy and providing social services. They have stressed that people are primarily responsible for their own welfare.

There are variations within these broad definitions, however. This is widely seen in present-day America in debates over so-called social issues, such as whether abortion should be legal. Most liberals, who are supportive of many other forms of government intervention, oppose efforts to pass laws that would restrict or bar women from exercising the right to choose to have an abortion. Many conservatives, on the other hand, who normally tout a "small government" philosophy, have no qualms advocating government intervention to bar the procedure on grounds that they believe it is immoral. The abortion issue, although still an important concern of many Americans, had faded somewhat by the end of the 2000s. It was replaced in the last several years of the decade with an increasingly vitriolic debate about the proper role of the government in individual affairs, focusing most noticeably on a health care reform requirement that all Americans purchase insurance, and in regulating business and financial activity.

Shifts can occur over time even within the boundaries of an ideology. For example, stringent advocacy of balanced federal budgets long was a trademark of American conservatism. But since the emergence of "supply-side economics" during the presidency of Republican Ronald Reagan in the 1980s, many conservatives have put a priority on keeping tax rates as low as possible even if that causes sizable budget deficits, at least in the short term; this was underscored by the fact that Republican-controlled Congresses in the early years of the twenty-first century—during the presidency of Republican George W. Bush—signed off on spending and taxing policies that resulted in large deficits even as many members continued to decry overspending by the federal government. These two strains began to merge by 2010 and 2011 when most Republicans became adamant about both cutting national debt and balancing the federal budget but at the same time doing it through program cuts, including entitlements, and not by raising any new revenue through taxes. Many liberals for years advocated proposals for redistributing wealth from the affluent to the needy and providing federal financial assistance for underprivileged individuals and communities; these ideals were embodied in programs such as President Franklin D. Roosevelt's New Deal in the 1930s and President Lyndon B. Johnson's Great Society in the 1960s. However, some of their ambitions were scaled back by the 1990s and later in the face of questions about the efficacy and cost of the programs, and sharp criticism from conservatives. But underlying progressive beliefs of Democrats remained strong and were evident at the end of the 2000s in increasingly bitter struggles with Republicans over such issues as health care, embodied in a far-reaching reform plan passed by Democrats in 2010, much stronger oversight of financial institutions, and—perhaps most potent of all—the ongoing debate in mid-2011 about requiring America's most wealthy citizens to pay higher taxes, mainly through allowing tax reductions for this group enacted during the George W. Bush administration to lapse.

People who fall between the liberal and conservative viewpoints are considered moderates. Most analysts believe that the majority of Americans actually are in the political center, rather than adhering wholeheartedly on all issues with either the liberal or conservative worldview.

Other, more extreme ideologies have gained adherents and controlled governments in other countries, such as the Nazi movement in Germany during the World War II era and communism in the former Soviet Union and current-day North Korea and Cuba. In the United States, though, only the SOCIALISTS, who advocated collective ownership of production and distribution, had any measurable and sustained popularity as a THIRD PARTY, and their strength in the first third of the twentieth century faded as economic prosperity reached more Americans. Adherents to extreme political movements have never made up more than a sliver of the U.S. population, as illustrated by the minuscule vote totals received by the Communist Party even during the desperate economic circumstances of the Great Depression.

Americans generally find a home in the two major political parties, liberals in the DEMOCRATIC PARTY and conservatives in the REPUBLICAN PARTY, though neither party excludes members who stray from party orthodoxy. For most of the twentieth century, highly conservative voters in southern states held major sway in the Democratic Party—a vestige of southerners' resentment toward the Republican Party dating to the Civil War—even as the party as a whole shifted toward a more liberal viewpoint.

Sharp differences within party ranks, however, can lead to breaches that cause political realignments. This has been seen in the mass movement of many white southern voters from the Democratic to the Republican Party since the 1960s, but also in the shift of many liberal Republicans—in regions such as New England and the rest of the Northeast—to the Democratic Party.

Extent of Ideological Thinking

Although students of PUBLIC OPINION have engaged in a lively debate about the extent of the ideological thinking of the American public, the evidence indicates that it is not high. Surveys have shown that few voters use terms such as *liberal* or *conservative* in evaluating candidates.

When the Republican Party scored big gains to take control of both chambers of Congress in the 1994 midterm elections, ending forty consecutive years of Democratic Party rule in the House in the process, conservatives attributed the GOP's success largely to the conservative campaign platform known as the Contract with America developed by Rep. Newt Gingrich of Georgia, who then served as Speaker from 1995 to 1999. Nevertheless, many political analysts believe that the 1994 Republican upsurge was related more to dissatisfaction with the Democrats than a ratification of the Republicans' conservative agenda.

Rep. Newt Gingrich, a Georgia Republican, was the standard-bearer for conservative principles in the 1980s and 1990s. He served as Speaker of the House for four years and coauthored the conservative campaign platform known as the Contract with America.

Source: CQ Photo/Scott J. Ferrell

The limits to strict adherence to ideology were evident when the Democrats staged their own comeback in the 2006 congressional elections. Needing to take over a number of Republican-held seats in districts whose voters were evenly divided between the parties or Republican-leaning, the Democrats eschewed a comprehensive platform based on liberal policy ideas, instead emphasizing some broad principles on which almost all their candidates could agree—such as criticism of President George W. Bush's handling of the war in Iraq—while letting their nominees shape their campaigns to fit the views of the voters in their states and districts. The tactic succeeded, with the Democrats gaining control of both the Senate and the House.

Democrats built on this momentum in 2008 to win the presidency and increase congressional majorities to the point where they could pass their health care reform legislation and other bills that, in the eyes of conservatives, improperly expanded the reach of the federal government into the lives of citizens.

The divergence between these views was pushed along by the increasingly rarified—some observers said distilled—makeup of each party. Democrats, freed of an uncomfortable alliance with conservative members from the South, became a party more dominated by liberals, many of whom were from the east and west coasts. Republicans, of contrast, gradually shed members who were centrists or even moderately liberal, through election defeats, retirements, and in a few cases voluntary departure from the party because of the perceived direction it was taking. The changes in the GOP were most dramatically seen in the emergence of what came to be known as the TEA PARTY movement late in the decade. Not really a political party, the movement was a loose coalition of like-minded conservatives nationwide that demanded Republican candidates adhere to exceptionally conservative views on social, political, and economic issues—especially on not raising taxes to balance federal expenses with additional revenues.

The increase in vitriol between conservative and liberal politicians, and the gradual departure of moderates from both parties, has hindered centrist efforts to achieve compromises on many major issues.

The reasons for the rise in ideological thinking are not altogether clear, but it is likely that the high-voltage political environment of the 1960s and 1970s had an impact. The 1964, 1968, and 1972 elections took place in the supercharged and often polarizing atmosphere of civil rights demonstrations, urban riots, and the Vietnam War. Moreover, these elections were characterized by sharp policy differences between the presidential candidates.

For example, the 1964 Republican nominee, conservative senator Barry Goldwater of Arizona, offered Americans "a choice, not an echo" as he campaigned against a committed liberal Democrat, President Lyndon B. Johnson. Goldwater even sought to capitalize on criticism that his brand of conservatism was too extreme. "I would remind you that extremism in the defense of liberty is no vice," he said in accepting his nomination. "And let me remind you also that moderation in the pursuit of liberty is no virtue."

Two decades later, under the cheery conservatism of Ronald Reagan, it was the liberals who were on the defensive. Even the most committed liberals avoided the label, and comedians joked that they were afraid to use "the L word." The percentage of self-described liberals plunged from approximately 25 percent in 1976 to around 15 percent in 1981, about where it remained in the 1990s.

Yet even though Reagan's victory for president in 1980 was widely seen by conservatives as vindication, the activist wing on the Republican right, represented by such figures as Gingrich and Rep. Tom DeLay of Texas, continued to feel stifled in the legislative process, not only by liberal Democrats but by a centrist GOP leadership they believed was too conciliatory with the Democrats. These activists' aggressive ideological edge helped galvanize the party's efforts to gain control of Congress and, that accomplished, to use parliamentary means and hardball politics to limit the Democrats' influence over legislation.

That was an effective tactic while most voters viewed matters as going generally well for the nation. But Americans' limited tolerance for ideologically based politics again was on display in 2006. The growing unpopularity of the war in Iraq, controversies over the government's response to the devastating impact of Hurricane Katrina on New Orleans and other Gulf Coast locales in 2005, and other issues led to a steep decline in the public's job approval ratings for Congress. These issues, with the probable exception of Iraq, paled when the nation, beginning in mid-2007, headed into what became the most serious economic downturn since the 1930s Great Depression. A housing bubble burst, Wall Street banks failed, auto companies nearly went bankrupt, and unemployment soared to over 10 percent and still remained at 8.6 percent in November 2011, just a year before the next national election. In the face of these conflagrations, the time-tested Republican tactic of branding Democrats as liberals who were out of the political mainstream failed.

Some analysts claim that ideological thinking has been on the rise, but the thrust of political science research is that most Americans do not view politics from an ideological perspective.

"I would remind you that extremism in the defense of liberty is no vice. And let me remind you also that moderation in the pursuit of liberty is no virtue."

—**Conservative senator Barry Goldwater** of Arizona, accepting his party's nomination for president at the 1964 Republican National Convention

Although Americans are more likely to consider an issue from the perspective of individual or group self-interest, it is important to make a distinction between the mass public and the political elites—individuals active and influential in political decision making. Candidates, for example, are more likely than the average citizen to have coherent views on current political affairs. They are also more likely to rely on ideological criteria in evaluating issues and political events.

Analysts have discovered as well that, in their ideologies, political activists are less moderate than average voters. This difference is shown by a comparison of the ideologies of the DELE-GATES to the NATIONAL PARTY CONVENTIONS, held every four years, and those of the rank-and-file voters. Not only is there regularly a major "ideology gap" between Republican and Democratic national convention delegates, but Republican delegates are considerably more conservative than rank-and-file Republicans, and Democratic delegates are more liberal than their party's voters.

This situation has implications for presidential nominating politics. Republican presidential aspirants must demonstrate their conservative credentials to have a chance of being nominated. Even George H.W. Bush, an incumbent president, was forced to stress conservative themes in 1992 while fending off the right-wing challenge of media commentator Patrick Buchanan. By the same token, Democratic candidates for presidential nominations must certify their liberal bona fides. Bill Clinton, who proclaimed himself to be a "new kind of Democrat," also made it a point in 1992 and 1996 to cultivate support among liberal constituencies (such as organized labor, feminists, African Americans, and gays and lesbians) with substantial influence over the nominating process. Similarly, the presidential candidates in 2000 each tended to their constituencies, with Democrat Al Gore sounding a populist note and Bush striking a more conservative theme on many issues than his leading opponent, John McCain.

This increasing use of political litmus tests continued and expanded through the end of the decade and was seen most dramatically in 2010 when conservative Republican activists, pushed aggressively by Tea Party adherents, managed to defeat in primary elections several GOP incumbents with solid conservative credentials. In their place the GOP nominated candidates, virtually all of them Tea Party favorites, that the voting public in the general elections rejected. This resulted, most political observers later concluded, in the Republicans sacrificing a number of Senate races, which—had they won with less extreme candidates—could have given the party control of the Senate along with the House.

Ideology in Operation

The functioning of American politics is profoundly influenced by the scant attention most people pay to ideological concerns and their failure to divide themselves neatly into distinct liberal or conservative groups. Instead of a situation in which liberals and conservatives stand united against each other, people tend to fall into either the liberal or conservative camp depending on the domestic or foreign policy issue at stake.

Economically liberal auto workers, for example, may fight business interests on issues such as raising the minimum wage or requiring health insurance for workers. Later, however, they may find themselves arm-in-arm with the major auto makers in jointly opposing tougher government clean air standards for auto emissions, because they believe these standards pose an economic threat to American auto manufacturers. Similarly, people who are on the far left or the far right of the political spectrum may find themselves comrades-in-arms in opposing free trade or other international agreements. In the late 1990s, for example, independent Vermont representative

Bernard Sanders, a one-time socialist, and Texas representative Ron Paul, a libertarian, joined forces to oppose increased U.S. support of the International Monetary Fund.

So people who are at odds on one issue today may find themselves allied on another issue tomorrow, making it difficult for cumulative antagonisms to build up through a series of confrontations. The overlapping and inconsistent belief systems that characterize the American public, therefore, reduce the intensity of political conflict. At the same time, however, these overlapping belief systems make it hard to form political alliances based on common attitudes. This in turn contributes to the government's frequent difficulty in reaching policy decisions.

The public's lack of ideological perspectives on many issues also has meant that voters often settle for the easier route of simple PARTY IDENTIFICATION. Party allegiance is an important component of the political thought process for many voters and a basis for their ELECTION DAY decisions.

Impeachment *See* REMOVAL FROM OFFICE.

Incumbency

For a political candidate, nothing succeeds like success. Once in office, the incumbent usually has a far better-than-average chance of being reelected. For presidents, the reelection rate has been about 66 percent. Though the incumbents in the U.S. House of Representatives were vulnerable to frequent swings in public mood during the nation's early years, the vast improvements in their ability to communicate and stay in touch with constituents, build huge campaign treasuries, and use computer technology to craft districts that provide them with political security have given most members something akin to lifetime job security. House incumbent reelection rates in all election years from 1946 until 2010 were over 90 percent in all but eight contests. That changed abruptly in 2010 when fifty-four incumbents were defeated, all but two Democrats, and the reelection rate dropped to 86.3 percent. The last time it dropped below 90 percent was nearly twenty years earlier, in 1992.

The Senate return rate is also high, if somewhat less consistent. That is because the much smaller number of Senate incumbents subject to reelection in each cycle magnifies the impact if any one of them is defeated. The unusually poor reelection rate for Republican incumbents in 2006—eight of fourteen, or 57 percent—dragged the overall reelection rate down to 79.3 percent. It improved to 83.3 percent in 2008 and 84.0 percent in 2010. But in those thirty-one contests from 1946 through 2010 the rate exceeded 90 percent just seven times. (See Incumbents Reelected, Defeated, or Retired table, p. 723)

Presidency

The best indication that incumbency gives an advantage to the sitting president is the success rate of those who sought reelection or election in their own right if they had succeeded to the presidency. Of the thirty-one attempts (including Franklin D. Roosevelt's in 1936, 1940, and 1944) twenty-one were successful, through and including George W. Bush's in 2004.

Other recent history, however, has shown that renomination is not inevitable. Lyndon B. Johnson, Gerald R. Ford, Jimmy Carter, and George H. W. Bush all faced strong challenges when they sought to run again. Johnson in 1968 ultimately decided against seeking renomination, and he is not included in the thirty-one presidential reelection efforts. Since 1951, when the Twenty-second Amendment was ratified, the second-term incumbent president has been barred from running again. The amendment exempted Harry S. Truman in 1952, but he chose not to seek a second full term.

If the incumbent appears at all vulnerable, another candidate likely will emerge to contend for the nomination. The decline of PARTY IDENTIFICATION and the rise of CANDIDATE-CENTERED CAMPAIGNS and INTEREST GROUP can make an incumbent appear vulnerable if economic or foreign policy crises develop.

Nevertheless, incumbency offers advantages. The president can dominate MEDIA COVERAGE, divert attention from domestic problems with foreign policy initiatives, and make use of budgetary and regulatory powers. So great is the prestige of the office that most party members are reluctant to reject an incumbent. No president since Chester A. Arthur in 1884 has lost a renomination effort at a NATIONAL PARTY CONVENTION.

Republican Chester A. Arthur was the last incumbent president not renominated by his party.

Source: Library of Congress

When it appeared in 1980 that he might become the first president since Arthur to lose the convention vote, Carter embarked on a CAMPAIGN STRATEGY that overwhelmed challenges by Massachusetts senator Edward M. Kennedy and California governor Edmund G. "Jerry" Brown Jr. Carter won renomination by using the powers of incumbency. He stayed at the White House occupied with the Iranian hostage crisis, trying to appear above the partisan fray. At the same time he was deeply engaged in the primary strategy— persuading southern states, where support for the former Georgia governor was strongest, to push their primaries to the early part of the schedule.

Incumbents play to the natural reluctance of voters to exchange a known commodity for a newcomer. Their CAMPAIGN SLOGANS stress stability rather than change. The Carter-Mondale slogan in 1980 was "A Tested and Trustworthy Team." Similarly, pointing to a healthy economy and peace abroad, Clinton and Vice President Al Gore campaigned on a "Don't Rock the Boat" theme in 1996.

President George W. Bush, running for reelection in 2004 while the nation was at war in Iraq and fighting a war on terrorism sparked by the September 11, 2001, attacks, tried to focus attention on national security issues and invoked the nation's tradition of not "switching horses in midstream."

Even in an era in which much of the public has become jaded and cynical about politics, the incumbent alone has the undoubted advantage of being introduced before campaign audiences as "the president of the United States."

Deciding whether and how to participate in televised DEBATES with their challengers is an important tactical decision for an incumbent president. As a rule, challengers have more to gain in debates because they are put on an equal footing with the president and have a chance to demonstrate that they can deal with substantive issues.

In 1976 President Ford's strategy included challenging his opponent, Carter, to a series of televised debates. With their man behind in the polls—because of the aftermath of the Watergate

Although incumbency has its advantages, it is not a guarantor of victory. President George H. W. Bush's handling of the 1991 Gulf War caused his approval ratings to soar. Within months, however, they had tumbled to 59 percent, and Bush ultimately lost the 1992 election to Democratic candidate Bill Clinton.

Source: George H. W. Bush Presidential Library

scandal that had forced Ford's Republican predecessor, Richard M. Nixon, to resign—Ford's advisers calculated that he had little to lose and much to gain. There had been no such debates since 1960, and they were bound to be a decisive element in the campaign. They were, but not to Ford's advantage. Ford's gaffe in saying that the Soviet Union did not dominate Eastern Europe hurt him and helped Carter. Nevertheless, presidents since Ford have consented, sometimes reluctantly, to debates with their opponents. The negotiations about format, moderators, and the inclusion of THIRD-PARTY candidates can sometimes be almost as interesting as the debates.

In debates and other venues, incumbents are easily placed on the defensive because they are tied to their records and their policies. They may become the victims—or beneficiaries—of RETROSPECTIVE VOTING as citizens judge from their records whether they should be kept in office or replaced. Presidents are blamed for failures as well as remembered for successes. They are even saddled with events beyond their control. Oil shortages, regional conflicts abroad, and adverse economic conditions may arise through no particular fault of the incumbent president.

In other ways the two major-party nominees are on equal footing in the general election campaign. Since 1976 these nominees have been eligible for identical PUBLIC FINANCING grants to underwrite their campaigns. The news media cover the two candidates on a roughly equal basis. Even when vigorous third-party or INDEPENDENT candidates—such as George Wallace in 1968, John Anderson in 1980, Ross Perot in 1992 and 1996, and Ralph Nader in 2000—run for the presidency, the spotlight usually stays trained on the Democratic and Republican nominees.

The president benefits from the public's reluctance to reject a tested national leader for an unknown quantity. This is especially true if the nation faces a possible threat from overseas, as was the case when Roosevelt ran for an unprecedented third term during the early days of World War II. The people's emotional bond with the president is an important, if unquantifiable, factor in the equation. Perhaps the outstanding examples in recent years are Lyndon Johnson's 1964 reelection, which benefited from the nation's deep desire for continuity in the wake of President John F. Kennedy's assassination, and President Ronald Reagan's evocation of patriotic themes in his 1984 campaign for reelection.

The defeats of presidents Ford, Carter, and George H. W. Bush demonstrate that incumbency does not guarantee victory. Negative perceptions of actions or abilities—such as Ford's pardon of the disgraced president Nixon and Carter's handling of economic and foreign policy crises—can doom an incumbent. Both Ford and Carter suffered from bitter struggles for their party nominations.

Congress, Governors, and State Legislators

A seat in the House or Senate carries with it advantages that help the occupants gain reelection, sometimes for many terms. Incumbents have the franking privilege, which allows them to send supposedly nonpolitical mailings to constituents without paying postage. They have the use of video and audio recording studios for taping news releases for the hometown radio and television stations. They have a work schedule that allows for campaigning and a travel allowance that permits them to be back in their home districts nearly every weekend.

The result of these and other perquisites of office is that turnover is low in most years, although the entire House and one-third of the Senate come up for election every two years. Most House elections since 1949 have brought fewer than eighty new members to that 435-member body. The 2002 election produced an exceptionally low turnover, with only fifty-five freshmen in the House in 2003. The 2006 election also produced fifty-five House freshmen in 2007, including three former members who had been defeated in 2004. The 100-member Senate also has relatively low turnover. The 2006 election produced 10 new senators, which is about the historical norm. But as a result of the 2010 election, an unusual election year, ninety-seven freshman came into the House at the beginning of the 112th Congress in 2011—ninety-one of them for the first time; five has served terms in earlier congresses. The Senate had sixteen freshmen as the 112th Congress began, although seven of them had been members of the House previously.

The preponderance of congressional districts are drawn to be *safe* for the incumbent party through the process known as GERRYMANDERING. This usually takes one of two forms. In states where one party completely controls the redistricting process (in most states, by holding the governorship and majorities in the state house and state senate in the year following the decennial census), that party may lock in its advantage by drawing districts to pack some with Republican voters and some with Democratic voters, making the incumbents of those parties more certain of reelection. Similarly, if control over redistricting is divided between the parties, they often will compromise on an incumbent protection plan that ends up having the same effect.

Almost half the states tried to ensure more rotation in their congressional delegations by imposing TERM LIMITS on the members. But in 1995 the Supreme Court ruled that the Constitution does not permit states to impose such limits on qualifications for Congress.

Congressional incumbents also enjoy a significant advantage in CAMPAIGN FINANCE. POLITICAL ACTION COMMITTEES overwhelmingly favor incumbents over challengers because if reelected they can help the special interests in committee and on the floor. Challengers represent a risk because they likely will not win. Most noninstitutional donors are likely to stick with the incumbent they know over the challenger who, in most cases, is new to them.

The partisan turnover of seats is proportionately higher in state contests for governor, but this is not because incumbents are more susceptible to defeat when they seek reelection. The big difference is that most states impose term limits on governors.

For example, the Democratic upswing in 2006 carried over into the elections for governor, as that party captured seats in six states that had been held by Republicans. Five of those wins, however, were for seats left open by retiring incumbents.

More on this topic:

Candidate-Centered Campaigns, p. 84

Gerrymander, p. 226

Interest Group, p. 273

Media Coverage of Campaigns, p. 313

National Party Conventions, p. 347

Party Identification by Voters, p. 377

Retrospective Voting, p. 547

Of the twenty-seven incumbents who sought reelection that year, just two lost, for a reelection rate of 93 percent. Only Maryland Republican governor Robert L. Ehrlich Jr. was defeated by a challenger of the other party (Democrat Martin O'Malley). Alaska Republican governor Frank Murkowski lost in the primary to Sarah Palin, who went on to keep the seat in Republican hands that November.

Similarly, in 2010 there were seventeen open gubernatorial seats, either from term limits or because an incumbent chose not to run again. Of the open seats Republicans picked up nine and Democrats five. One went to an independent who previously was a Republican. Of incumbents seeking reelection that year just two lost, in Ohio and Iowa.

Unlike members of Congress, exempted from term limits by the Constitution, legislators in many states are subject to some form of term limits, often eight years in one state legislative chamber. Most of the legislature term limits were enacted after 1990 and only recently started to have an effect on incumbency. Although they do not affect the percentage of incumbents winning reelection if they are eligible, they increase turnover and reduce the percentage of the legislature returning after each election. It has been reported that some state legislatures are already feeling the effects of term limits—the members lack expertise and institutional memory.

Independent

The most recent independent to become a governor occurred in 2010 when Lincoln Chafee, formerly a Republican, won the state house in Rhode Island. Chafee in 2006 lost his bid for reelection to the Senate as a Republican.

It is not impossible for an independent—a candidate running on his or her own, without the structure of a major-party or even THIRD-PARTY nomination—to win a partisan election in the United States: it happened in two cases in the 2006 Senate elections and again in 2010. Yet these contests were exceptions that proved how dominant the DEMOCRATIC PARTY and the REPUBLICAN PARTY continue to be.

One of the independents elected in 2006 was longtime Democratic senator Joseph I. Lieberman of Connecticut, who lost the Democratic primary in August but petitioned his way onto the November ballot and won the general election.

The other was Vermont's Bernard Sanders, a liberal iconoclast who called himself a democratic socialist and had developed a strong popular following while serving as an independent over eight terms as the state's only House member. Sanders won easily to succeed the retiring James Jeffords, who had declared himself an independent in 2001 during his final Senate term but had won his three terms running as a Republican.

The 2010 race occurred in Alaska with incumbent Lisa Murkowski, a Republican, winning reelection after losing the GOP primary to a relatively obscure challenger that her campaign never took seriously until too late. The general election race made modern history because Murkowski won with a write-in campaign, the first such successful victory since 1954 when Strom Thurmond, then a Democrat, won a Senate seat in South Carolina. Murkowski's challenger was a favorite of Tea Party activists who brought an energy and devotion to an array of campaigns in 2010, helping some and hurting others.

Murkowski, not expecting to lose the primary, had not taken steps earlier that would have allowed her to run formally as an independent candidate and have had her name printed on the ballot. Rather, she had to persuade voters to write her name exactly as required on ballots. She said she continued to consider herself a Republican and would continue to caucus with the GOP.

Even Lieberman and Sanders were not independents in the purest sense of the word. Both had pledged to caucus with Senate Democrats, a pledge that when kept following the election gave the Democrats the 51 votes they needed to take control of the Senate in 2007 (which in turn enabled both senators to obtain committee assignments from the Democratic leaders).

Six independents have been elected as governors since 1951. Two of them were in Maine, a state where voters are especially proud of their independent voting tradition: James B. Longley held the office as an independent from 1975 to 1979, and Angus King did the same from 1995 to 2003. The others were Lowell P. Weicker Jr. of Connecticut (1991–1995), Walter J. Hickel of Alaska (1990–1994), and Jesse Ventura of Minnesota (1999–2003). The election of Ventura, a flamboyant former professional wrestler, caused a particular sensation on the national political scene, but he had difficulty dealing with the state legislature—in part because he had no partisan ties to any of its members—and chose not to seek a second term.

The most recent independent to become a governor occurred in 2010 when Lincoln Chafee, formerly a Republican, won the statehouse in Rhode Island. Chafee in 2006 lost his bed for reelection to the Senate as a Republican.

No independent candidate has ever won the presidency or even come close. The strongest such bid was made in 1912 by former president Theodore Roosevelt, who ran on the ticket of the new PROGRESSIVE, or BULL MOOSE, PARTY, which only existed for that election. Roosevelt took 27 percent of the vote, behind victorious Democrat Woodrow Wilson (41 percent) but ahead of his Republican successor and former vice president, William Howard Taft (23 percent).

In more recent times, the strongest independent candidate showings were by billionaire businessman H. Ross Perot, who in 1992 took 19 percent in the election won by Democrat Bill Clinton (43 percent) over Republican George H. W. Bush (37 percent), and staunchly conservative former Alabama governor George Wallace, who created the AMERICAN INDEPENDENT PARTY as the vehicle for the 1968 campaign in which he took 13.5 percent to victorious Republican Richard M. Nixon's 43.4 percent and Democrat Hubert H. Humphrey's 42.7 percent. Wallace did carry five southern states and received 46 electoral votes, making him the most recent presidential candidate not affiliated with a major party to win any electoral votes.

Independent candidates have not gained much traction even though a general decline in PARTY IDENTIFICATION has resulted in many more voters declaring themselves as independents than have in the past. For a number of years, polls have shown a basically trisected electorate: one-third Democratic, one-third Republican, and one-third independent. But some public opinion researchers say that most of the unaffiliated voters actually lean strongly toward one or the other major parties and will vote for its candidates under most circumstances. Only a small fraction, say these researchers, are completely unattached to either the Democrats or Republicans.

Another and even bigger obstacle to many would-be independent candidates comes in the form of BALLOT ACCESS requirements, usually consisting of petition signatures, filing fees, or both; these vary dramatically from state to state but can be quite steep in some places.

This problem is greatly multiplied for independent presidential candidates seeking ballot access in all fifty states. The degree of difficulty for an independent candidate compared to one running even on a third-party line was illustrated by liberal activist Ralph Nader. Running as the Green Party nominee in 2000, Nader was on the ballots in forty-seven states and the District of Columbia and received 2.9 million votes or 2.7 percent of the total vote. He arguably had an influence on the outcomes in at least a pair of states where the margin between victorious Republican George W. Bush and Democrat Al Gore was quite small. But in 2004 Nader chose to run as an independent and was on ballots in only thirty-four states and the District of Columbia. He ended up with just 466,000 votes nationwide, or 0.3 percent of the total.

Independent Expenditures *See* HARD MONEY.

Infomercials *See* MEDIA USE BY CAMPAIGNS;
POLITICAL ADVERTISING.

Initiatives and Referendums

A ballot initiative is a form of direct DEMOCRACY in which the people propose new laws subject to approval by all the state's voters. A referendum is similar, except that it usually originates with the legislature.

Ballot initiatives have become increasingly important, especially in California, where they are called propositions. California has permitted such questions to be on the ballot since 1912. The state's ballot measures on issues such as tax limitation (Proposition 13 in 1978), barring state-funded social services to illegal immigrants (Proposition 187 in 1994), and "English-only" education (Proposition 227 in 1998) have attracted national attention and often are copied in other states. In 2002, for example, Massachusetts voters approved an English immersion initiative similar to California's. With much at stake, INTEREST GROUPS frequently spend millions of dollars for POLITICAL ADVERTISING in initiative campaigns, which are professionally managed by POLITICAL CONSULTANTS.

One of the more recent evolutions of the initiative process has been its use by conservative political strategists allied with the Republican Party and liberal strategists allied with the Democratic Party to try to stimulate voter turnout. They attempt to use initiatives on issues on which voters have passionate views to get them to the polls—where they also will almost certainly vote for like-minded candidates for public office.

This tactic was used in 2004, when conservatives placed initiatives to ban same-sex marriage on ballots in a number of states, in part to boost the reelection chances of Republican president George W. Bush. Liberal groups, abetted in their organizational efforts by the Ballot Initiative Strategy Center in Washington, D.C., used the same tactic in 2006 when they placed popular initiatives to raise the minimum wage on ballots in several states, which aided efforts to turn out Democratic voters in that party's successful campaign to gain control of the U.S. Senate and House.

According to the Initiative and Referendum Institute at the University of Southern California, as of mid-2011, twenty-three states allowed citizens to place initiatives on their election ballots that, if approved by voters, would have the force of law. Another two states allowed voters to use the initiative process to place state constitutional amendments on the ballot, an option also available in sixteen of the legislative initiative states.

There also is a version of citizen legislating known as *popular referendum*, under which measures that have been passed by the state's legislature and enacted into law can be placed on the ballot so voters can pass judgment on them. A law is considered revoked if a majority of voters disapprove of it in a popular referendum. This option is available in twenty-four states, twenty-one of which also have initiatives.

These voter-activated ballot measures are separate from *legislative referendums*, the term for measures that state legislatures put before voters for their approval. All states have some form of legislative referendum.

Because the U.S. Constitution does not permit Congress to delegate its responsibilities, there are no initiatives or referendums on federal laws.

A plebiscite is a type of referendum on a political entity's boundaries or form of government. In 1998, for example, the U.S. House of Representatives approved the holding of a plebiscite in the Commonwealth of Puerto Rico on whether it should remain a commonwealth, become independent, or become a Spanish-speaking state of the United States. (The voters in effect chose to remain a commonwealth.)

States vary widely in the number of signatures needed to place an initiative on the ballot. Generally it ranges from 5 percent to 15 percent of the number of votes for governor in the previous election. Amendments to the state constitution require more signatures than proposals for state laws. Often the petitioning is a two-step procedure: first, the sponsors must petition for permission to circulate a ballot question; then, if enough signatures for certification are obtained, they must circulate a petition to place the initiative on the ballot.

Nine states (Alaska, Maine, Massachusetts, Michigan, Nevada, Ohio, Utah, Washington, and Wyoming) use the indirect initiative, which sends the proposed law to the legislature for its consideration. If it is not passed, the initiative can then be put before the voters. Two of those states, Utah and Washington, under certain circumstances also allow direct initiatives, which are placed on the ballot without first going through the legislature. Two states, Massachusetts and Mississippi, use indirect initiatives for constitutional amendments.

CLOSER LOOK

Ballot Proposals by State

All states allow state lawmakers to place referendums on the ballot to ask voters whether they approve of a law passed by legislators. Twenty-seven states have some time of procedure that allows voters an opportunity to place proposals on the ballot that have the force of law if they are approved.

There are three main types of these measures. Legislative or statutory initiatives allow voters to place on the ballot proposals for new laws, usually by meeting thresholds of petition signatures. Constitutional initiatives allow voters to gain ballot placement for proposed new amendments to state constitutions. Popular referendums allow voters to put a proposition on the ballot asking whether a law passed by the state legislature should be allowed to stand.

Not all twenty-seven states allow the same kinds of ballot propositions; only fifteen offer all three options. Following is a breakdown of which states offer which kinds of ballot propositions:

Allow legislative initiative, constitutional initiative, and popular referendum (fifteen): Arizona, Arkansas, California, Colorado, Massachusetts, Michigan, Missouri, Montana, Nebraska, Nevada, North Dakota, Ohio, Oklahoma, Oregon, South Dakota

Allow legislative initiative and popular referendum (six): Alaska, Idaho, Maine, Utah, Washington, Wyoming

Allow legislative initiative and constitutional initiative: (three): Florida, Illinois, Mississippi

Allow popular referendum only (three): Kentucky, Maryland, New Mexico

Source: Initiative and Referendum Institute at the University of Southern California

California Example

The most famous initiative, California's Proposition 13 in 1978, rolled back property taxes to 1 percent of 1975–1976 home values and capped further increases at 2 percent a year until the house was sold. The measure won 65 percent approval.

Sponsored by antitax activists Howard Jarvis and Paul Gann, Prop 13, as it came to be known, had far-reaching consequences. Although it gave homeowners a tax break, it forced cutbacks in government services and led to a complex fee system to make up for the lost revenue. Other states followed suit, with some of the same results.

Above all, Prop 13 reinvigorated the initiative process. Between 1912 and 1978, Californians had voted on 153 ballot measures. In the twenty-four years after Prop 13, they faced decisions on 126 measures. Only 98 of the 279 total measures, or 35.7 percent, won approval.

Movie actor Arnold Schwarzenegger spearheaded a much-publicized drive in 2002 for increased funding of afterschool activities in California. Proposition 49, intended to cut juvenile crime and drug use, won by a comfortable margin. Schwarzenegger reportedly contributed $1 million of the $8.5 million Prop 49 campaign fund.

Schwarzenegger had less success with his aggressive use of initiatives following his unusual October 2003 election as governor that coincided with a voter RECALL of Democratic incumbent Gray Davis. When Schwarzenegger, a Republican, first entered office, he took a confrontational approach to the Democratic-dominated state legislature. This culminated in his calling of a special election in November 2005 for eight state ballot propositions, four of which he promoted and for which he actively campaigned. But voters, by wide margins, defeated the Schwarzenegger-backed measures designed to raise the requirements for public school teachers to gain tenure, require the express permission of union members for their dues to be used for political purposes, create new state spending limitations, and take control of congressional and state legislative redistricting from the state legislature and turn it over to a panel of retired judges.

After his setbacks on these initiatives, Schwarzenegger pivoted and took a more conciliatory approach. This bipartisan outreach helped him enormously in the Democratic-leaning state, and he easily won reelection in November 2006.

Initiatives Industry

A corps of advertising, political, POLLING, public relations, and other types of consultants has grown up around the business of persuading voters to approve or disapprove ballot questions. Even the gathering of signature petitions can be contracted out to firms specializing in that activity.

For example, as of 2007 California law gave initiative sponsors 150 days in which to gather 433,971 valid signatures of registered voters to put a statute proposal on the ballot; 694,354 signatures are needed for a constitutional amendment. Faced with such numbers, based on a percentage of the gubernatorial vote, sponsors must turn to signature companies for help. Estimated costs in California, by far the most popular initiative state, have been placed by some sources as in the $2 million to $3 million range; petition signature collectors in many states are also paid a "bounty" per name.

Overall costs of an initiative campaign can rival those for governor or Congress. California's insurance industry reportedly spent $80 million in a futile effort to prevent a rollback of auto insurance prices. In the 1998 fight over Native American casinos, the tribes spent $66.3 million to counter a $25.8 million Nevada gambling industry offensive against the measure.

Other multimillion-dollar campaigns have been waged by tobacco companies against anti-smoking initiatives, technology companies against a law making it easier to sue for securities fraud, and organized labor against curtailment of union dues for political purposes.

In these and other initiative contests, special interests were on one or both sides of the issue. In Washington State in 1997, the National Rifle Association spent $3 million, much of it raised out of state, to defeat a handgun safety initiative. Supporters spent $800,000. The same year in Oregon, a consortium of Christian groups spent $4 million in an unsuccessful campaign for an initiative to repeal Oregon's assisted suicide law, the first such state law in the nation.

Controversial ballot issues also affect races for elective office. Candidates often take a stand for or against the question, and the candidate's position in turn helps to influence voters' choices of candidates. Arkansas voters in 1996 approved a law to label candidate ballots with their stances on TERM LIMITS, but the state supreme court invalidated the law as unconstitutional. The U.S. Supreme Court let the ruling stand.

California's Republican governor Pete Wilson staked his prestige on passage in 1998 of Proposition 226, the so-called paycheck protection initiative requiring annual, written permission to use union members' dues for political purposes. Although Wilson was leaving office, the proposition's defeat may have hurt his presidential ambitions.

Growing Popularity

The number of statewide initiatives that reached the ballot rose from 67 in 1992 to 202 in forty states in 2002, of which 62 percent won approval, according to ballotwatch.com, website of the Initiative and Referendum Institute. After slipping to 162 in November 2004, the number of qualified ballot measures in 2006 shot back up to 204; in both years, the success rate was 67 percent. But in 2010 the number dropped again, to 159 propositions in thirty-six states, with an approval rate of 64 percent.

California's Republican governor Pete Wilson supported Proposition 226, which required employers to obtain annual, written permission to use union members' dues for political purposes. The initiative was defeated in the 1998 primary election.

Source: CQ Photo/Scott J. Ferrell

Among the reasons put forth for such growth are public frustration with inaction and partisan bickering in legislatures, the imitation of successful initiatives, and interests groups' bypassing of legislatures to go directly to the people.

An additional reason is that initiative campaigns have become lucrative businesses. In 1998 there were a half-dozen signature-gathering firms in California and Nevada, operating as far away as Florida and Massachusetts. By one estimate those companies accounted for 90 percent of the initiatives that reached the ballot. Typically, a company will be circulating petitions for several initiatives at the same time.

In a January 1999 case, *Buckley v. American Constitutional Law Reform*, the Supreme Court struck down as "excessively restrictive of political speech" three Colorado limits on petition circulators. A badge requirement was struck down 8–1. Nullified 6–3 were rules that the signature collectors be registered voters and that sponsors disclose their names and pay.

> ### "The best weapon against the ineffective, the weak and the corrupt is in our hands each election day."
>
> **—David Broder,**
> Democracy Derailed: Initiative Campaigns and the Power of Money

Despite its growing popularity, the ballot initiative movement has its detractors, notably veteran *Washington Post* political reporter David S. Broder, author of *Democracy Derailed: Initiative Campaigns and the Power of Money*. Acknowledging its popular appeal and reformist roots, Broder argues that "this method of lawmaking is alien to the spirit of the Constitution and its carefully crafted set of checks and balances. Left unchecked the initiative could challenge or even subvert the system that has served the nation so well for more than two hundred years." Instead of avoiding elected representatives, he concludes, "The best weapon against the ineffective, the weak and the corrupt is in our hands each election day."

Interest Group

Whether cherished as a special way that citizens can have their say in government—or vilified as a "special interest" that seeks disproportionate clout—the interest group is an integral part of the American political process.

An interest group is an organized body of individuals who share goals and try to influence public policy. The operative elements of this definition are "organized" and "influence public policy." African Americans, farmers, manufacturers, and workers are not interest groups in and of themselves. Unless they become organized, they have individual interests and are *potential* interest groups. But the National Association for the Advancement of Colored People (NAACP), the American Farm Bureau Federation (AFBF), the National Association of Manufacturers (NAM), and the AFL-CIO *are* organized groups, made up of such individuals, that seek to influence government policy.

Not all interest group activity is carried on by huge entities such as the AFL-CIO or the Farm Bureau. Some organizations consist only of a small staff backed by financial patrons. For example, the Media Access Project is a public interest law firm concerned about the public's access to government information that, in January 2012, listed four full-time staff members on its website.

Interest groups can wax and wane as the relevance of the issues they pursue changes. The American Temperance Union and other groups committed to the prohibition of alcoholic beverage consumption made up a powerful political force from the early nineteenth through the early twentieth centuries. Their influence diminished dramatically after the unpopularity of Prohibition, imposed in 1919 by the Eighteenth Amendment to the Constitution, resulted in its repeal by the Twenty-first Amendment in 1933. The emergence of the abortion issue during the 1960s spawned major new interest groups such as the abortion rights advocacy organization NARAL (formerly the National Abortion and Reproductive Rights Action League) and the antiabortion National Right to Life organization.

Most interest groups have lobbyists on their staffs, or at least on a retainer to represent the group in the halls of government. The latter category includes the so-called hired guns—Washington lawyers, public relations consultants, and other professionals, who, for a fee, try to influence government policy for their clients. The most prominent lobbyists tend to have close ties to policymakers because they used to work for the government. The many dozens of former prominent and rank-and-file members of Congress who have gone through the "revolving door" include powerful lawmakers, such as former Senate majority leader Howard Baker, former House Speaker Thomas Foley, and former House Appropriations chairman Robert Livingston, as well as former executive branch and congressional staffers.

Interest groups receive a lot of bad press, especially when there are well-publicized controversies involving allegations of excessive coziness between current members of Congress and particular groups, or suggestions that lawmakers have given interest groups a seat at the table when legislation affecting their agenda is being drafted.

Yet they perform an essential function in American DEMOCRACY: They are one way in which people who share the same attitudes or interests can be represented informally before Congress, executive

The power of interest groups in the political process has long been observed. In this nineteenth-century cartoon by Joseph Keppler, the Senate is watched over by fat-cat "monopolists" who crowd through an open door while the "people's entrance" is locked shut.

Source: Library of Congress

agencies, and state and local legislative or regulatory bodies. This informal system of group representation supplements the formal system of geographic area representation used in Congress—states in the Senate and districts in the House of Representatives.

In their representational roles, interest groups provide policymakers with specialized information that otherwise might not be readily available. Interest groups also provide an avenue for more effective political participation than is likely to be achieved by a lone person picketing in front of the White House.

Composition and Growth

Since the 1960s there has been a virtual explosion in the number and diversity of interest groups operating in Washington. As the scope of government activities has grown, more and more groups have recognized the benefits of having a presence in the nation's capital.

The composition of the interest group system has changed as well. The traditional farm, union, professional, and business groups must now compete with a vast array of citizens' groups organized around an idea or cause and having no occupational basis for membership. In addition, individual corporations, states, cities, counties, and universities have gravitated toward Washington to advance or protect interests that can be dramatically affected by government policy.

Not surprisingly, business-oriented and socially conservative lobbying groups tend to gain somewhat in stature when Republicans control the White House and Congress; labor unions and other liberal organizations fare better when Democrats are in charge.

Business-oriented groups are among the strongest of the Washington lobbies. The largest of these are the so-called peak business organizations that seek to represent general business interests. These include the U.S. Chamber of Commerce, the National Association of Manufacturers (NAM), the Business Roundtable, and the National Federation of Independent Business (NFIB). NAM is made up of large manufacturing concerns; the Business Roundtable includes approximately two hundred of the nation's largest companies such as IBM, General Motors, AT&T, and Shell Oil; and NFIB represents hundreds of thousands of small businesses.

The more specialized business groups, called trade associations, are composed of companies in the same line of business. Trade associations range from the American Bankers Association with its thousands of member banks to the much smaller International Association of Refrigerated Warehouses and the Pet Food Institute.

Individual corporations also try to influence policymaking. Many maintain Washington offices, and those without an office frequently hire a law firm or lobbyist to look out for their interests. They also take advantage of the resources of groups such as the U.S. Chamber of Commerce and the trade associations to which they belong.

Labor unions have a larger base of individual members than do business organizations, though their membership as a percentage of the nation's workforce has declined since its peak in the decades immediately following World War II. The largest and most influential union is the AFL-CIO, a confederation of dozens of operating unions such as the United Steel Workers, United Auto Workers, and United Brotherhood of Carpenters and Joiners of America, though not all unions are affiliated with the AFL-CIO.

As the industrial sector of the economy has declined since the 1950s so have the memberships of the longtime AFL-CIO unions representing industrial and building trades workers. The auto workers, steel workers, and carpenters unions are no longer the largest. They have been replaced by white-collar and service sector unions such as the Teamsters and the American Federation of State, County, and Municipal Employees.

Agriculture, another economic sector, is organized to reflect general farm interests as well as those of specific commodity producers. The largest of the general farm interest groups is the American Farm Bureau Federation (AFBF), which tends to represent the larger, more efficient producers and to support a relatively conservative political agenda.

On many issues the AFBF is opposed by the politically weaker National Farmers Organization and National Farmers Union, which represent the dwindling number of small producers. Among the major powers in agricultural policymaking are the organizations that promote the interests of specific commodity growers and processors—for example, the National Peanut Council, Tobacco Institute, National Association of Wheat Growers, and agribusiness corporations such as Ralston Purina, Cargill, and Archer-Daniels-Midland.

Finally, professional associations represent many of the individuals whose occupations demand technical training and expertise. Political involvement is greatest among those professional groups heavily regulated by government or dependent on government for financing. Examples are the American Bar Association and the American Medical Association.

Nonprofit organizations represent the interests of people as citizens, consumers, and taxpayers, or as the elderly, disadvantaged, handicapped, and minorities. Many of these organizations—particularly those for consumers, the environment, minorities, and the poor—are commonly called public interest groups, although their "public interest" label has stirred the resentment of those who oppose them and have a different conception of the public interest. The National Rifle Association, for example, has frustrated those who would impose new regulations on gun ownership.

One of the most prominent and influential of the public interest groups is Common Cause. It has called for government reforms in areas such as CAMPAIGN FINANCE, lobbying, government ethics, congressional organization, and VOTER REGISTRATION. Persons linked by IDEOLOGY have found outlets in the interest group system as well. For liberals, there are the long-lived Americans for Democratic Action and more recently established activist groups such as Moveon.org. For conservatives, the well-established American Conservative Union has been joined just since 2009 by groups aligned with the TEA PARTY movement, such as Tea Party Patriots and Tea Party Express.

Some of the most influential organizations in Washington are lobbying firms that represent a number of clients. For example, Cassidy & Associates lobbies for the interests of universities, medical centers, and private businesses. It may receive several hundred thousand dollars for its services from a single client.

Religious and government organizations also maintain a strong presence in Washington. Religious groups were in the forefront of the CIVIL RIGHTS and anti–Vietnam War movements, while others have played a major role on both sides of social issues such as abortion and homosexual rights.

In the public sector, nearly all of the states have federal liaison offices, and many cities, counties, and state universities as well have their own Washington offices or law firms or lobbyists representing them. Major associations representing the government sector include the National Governors' Association, the National Association of Counties, and the U.S. Conference of Mayors.

Foreign Lobbying

Foreign governments also try to influence U.S. public policy. Some of this activity is carried out by foreign ambassadors and their staffs, but, increasingly, high-priced Washington lobbyists and law firms are representing foreign government and corporate clients.

Such practice is highly controversial, however, because the foreign interests may run counter to those of the United States. Representatives of a "foreign principal" are required to register with the Justice Department under the Foreign Agents Registration Act, but the act relies more on disclosure than on penalties and enforcement. Originally enacted in 1938 to guard against Nazi propaganda, the law was revised in 1966 to place more emphasis on protecting "the integrity of the decision-making process of our government."

Federal law prohibits foreign nationals from making campaign contributions in U.S. elections. Alleged violations of those laws produced a major SCANDAL regarding fund-raising for the 1996 presidential election. Both parties had to return foreign contributions, but the DEMOCRATIC NATIONAL COMMITTEE returned the larger amount.

Not all interest group activity on behalf of foreign countries is initiated by their governments or hired agents in Washington. Some nations have home-grown support organizations. For example, Israel has benefited from having an organization of Americans, the American Israel Public Affairs Committee, devoted to protecting its interests.

Interest Groups and Elections

Candidates cannot wage credible election campaigns without money, and interest groups are often willing to provide campaign cash. The chosen vehicle for these financial contributions has long been the POLITICAL ACTION COMMITTEE (PAC). The Federal Election Campaign Act (FECA) amendments of 1971 and 1974 allow a political committee created by an interest group to solicit funds for distribution to candidates. The act allows corporations and unions, which cannot legally give from their treasuries to candidates, to set up PACs that may solicit funds from stockholders or members. These provisions also apply to the proliferating number of PACs dedicated to the pursuit of esoteric issues.

The provisions were sustained by the campaign finance law overhaul titled the Bipartisan Campaign Reform Act (BCRA) of 2002—better known as McCain-Feingold after its lead sponsors, Arizona Republican senator John McCain and Wisconsin Democratic senator Russ Feingold, although with one major change. The law, which took effect following the 2002 midterm congressional elections, barred individuals and organizations, including PACs, from making unlimited SOFT MONEY donations to national political party organizations in their efforts to influence the outcomes of elections for federal offices. PACs and other interest groups may make only HARD MONEY donations that are limited by law.

The new law spurred the growth of PACs organized under Section 527 of the Internal Revenue Code, known as 527s, which are free under the existing rules to take soft-money contributions. Many corporate, union, and activist organizations established 527s as did ad hoc groups set up to promote or impede particular candidates. The activities of some of these groups, particularly their independent expenditure campaigns usually centered on television advertising, led to controversies over whether they crossed the legal line in their efforts, prompting increased calls for the Federal Election Commission to provide stricter regulation of 527 group activities. (See CAMPAIGN FINANCE.)

Nonetheless, interest groups gained even more latitude to spend money on political advertising to advance their interests as a result of the Supreme Court's January 2010 ruling in the case of CITIZENS UNITED V. FEDERAL ELECTION COMMISSION. The decision, approved by a 5–4 vote, struck provisions of McCain-Feingold that barred corporations and unions from directly engaging in "electioneering communications" within sixty days of a general election and within thirty days of a primary. The controversial ruling established, as a point of law, that corporate entities have free speech rights equivalent to those of individuals.

Campaign funds are not the only kind of campaign assistance interest groups make available to candidates. Mass membership organizations can mobilize their members to vote for and work on behalf of preferred candidates. Organized labor, for example, operates phone banks during election campaigns, contacting union households to get out the vote for union-endorsed candidates (almost exclusively Democrats).

But group members often have other commitments and beliefs that conflict with those of the group, and they may not vote in accordance with the official position of their leaders. Indeed, despite organized labor's vigorous support of Democratic presidential nominee Clinton in 1992, 45 percent of voters in union households cast their ballots instead for either his Republican opponent, incumbent George H. W. Bush, or independent Ross Perot. Exit polls taken during the 1996 election indicated that among union households 50 percent supported Clinton, 30 percent supported the Republican candidate, Robert Dole, and 9 percent voted for Perot. Strong labor and Democratic opposition helped to defeat ballot INITIATIVES in California in 1998 and 2005 that would have restricted the withholding of wages or union dues for political contributions without written, annual permission from the employee or union member.

Many major interest groups attempt to reach beyond their membership by publicizing the records—often in a negative manner—of public officials. Frequently this takes the form of a "scorecard" that measures how often lawmakers supported the organization's position on selected pieces of legislation. Some groups use these scorecards to portray the lawmakers they oppose in a highly negative light.

The League of Conservation Voters, for example, periodically announces its "Dirty Dozen," incumbent members of Congress who, in its view, had the worst records on environmental issues. And interest groups, particularly large and well-financed organizations, have made independent expenditures to bolster the campaigns of supportive members of Congress or to defeat those who have opposed them. Such expenditures, if truly independent, are exempt from the contribution limits to federal candidates.

Corporations, unions, and nonprofit sector groups often supplement their lobbying and PAC activities with POLITICAL ADVERTISING. This technique is especially evident when an interest group believes its political influence as well as its public image could benefit from a little polishing.

In the 1996 elections, "issue ads" emerged as a controversial way for groups or individuals to spend lavishly for or against candidates for Congress without running afoul of the FECA contribution limits. Ostensibly a discussion of the issues rather than the candidates, issue ads can be none-too-subtle boosts for a specific candidate if his or her views on the issue differ sharply from those of the opposing candidate. Court rulings have consistently legitimized issue advertising as long as the ads do not contain the so-called "magic words" calling directly for the election or defeat of a particular candidate, even though numerous ads over the years have contained thinly veiled attacks on candidates who were seeking election or reelection to public office.

Direct marketing by mail and telephone—targeting past and potential supporters with an appeal to join a group, contact public officials, and contribute money to an organization—is another means of mobilizing mass support for a cause or a candidate.

Regulation

The term LOBBYIST goes back to the early 1800s when favor seekers jammed the lobbies, cloakrooms, and hallways of legislatures. Initially, these hallway denizens were called "lobby agents," a designation that was shortened to lobbyists in the 1830s.

Although the term lobbying was not yet in vogue when the Constitution was written, the right to lobby was made explicit by its First Amendment, which provides that "Congress shall make no law . . . abridging . . . the right of the people . . . to petition the Government for a redress of grievances."

Such humble beginnings notwithstanding, lobbyists cumulatively—and, in some cases, individually—constitute a powerful force in politics. The profession has drawn a growing number of practitioners to its ranks, and, in recent years, the amount of money spent on lobbying activities has escalated rapidly.

According to an August 2011 posting on the Center for Responsive Politics' website, spending by Washington lobbyists to try to influence federal policy increased by almost two and a half times over twelve years, from $1.5 billion in 1998 to $3.5 billion in 2010.

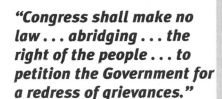

The actual number of lobbyists is difficult to pin down. In testimony on lobbying reform before the House Rules Committee in March 2006, James Thurber, the director of the Center for Congressional and Presidential Studies at American University in Washington, D.C., indicated that an estimated 32,980 lobbyists were registered by Congress; he noted, however, that various studies showed the number of active lobbyists ranged between 11,500 and 38,103. The Center for Responsive Politics pegged the number at the lower end of that spectrum, counting just less than 13,000 "unique, registered lobbyists who have actively lobbied" as of 2010.

> **"Congress shall make no law . . . abridging . . . the right of the people . . . to petition the Government for a redress of grievances."**
>
> —First Amendment to the Constitution

Many lobbyists work for firms dedicated to lobbying or for the "lobby shops" in major law firms. The latter tend to be especially attractive to former members of Congress who decide to ply the lobbying trade. Most trade associations and other major interest groups employ their own lobbyists.

So permanent has lobbying become in the fabric of American politics that it has consistently survived even serious scandals involving lobbyists exposed as having conducted illegal "influence peddling." One recent example is Jack Abramoff, a lobbyist with close ties to leading Republicans, whose downfall played a role in the Republicans' loss of control of both chambers of Congress in 2006. Abramoff was convicted of defrauding American Indian tribes that were his clients of millions of dollars, and using that money to enrich himself and associates; to provide illegal gifts to at least one House member, Ohio Republican Bob Ney, who was himself convicted on corruption charges; to arrange overseas trips for members of Congress, including high-ranking Texas Republican Tom DeLay, who resigned from the House in June 2006; and to make campaign contributions that became a damaging issue for some Republican incumbents in the 2006 campaign.

Concern about the undue influence of the growing number of special interest groups has led Congress to enact regulatory legislation. Under the Federal Regulation of Lobbying Act passed in 1946, groups and individuals seeking to influence legislation are required to register with the clerk of the House and the secretary of the Senate and to file quarterly financial statements. As it has been interpreted, however, the act has little practical impact. The Supreme Court has held that the law applies only to groups or individuals involved in direct lobbying and whose "principal purpose" is lobbying. As a result, not all groups register, and grassroots lobbying is not covered by the law. In addition, it does not apply to attempts to influence the executive branch.

There is broad support for the notion that the public is entitled to more information than the current law permits about the activities of interest groups. But proposals to strengthen the reporting and

High-ranking Republican Tom DeLay of Texas was forced to resign in 2006 in the wake of the Jack Abramoff lobbying scandal.

Source: CQ Photo/Scott J. Ferrell

More on this topic:

Campaign Finance, p. 53

Democracy, p. 148

Ideology, p. 259

Political Action Committees, p. 389

disclosure provisions of the law have raised serious issues of privacy, burdensome red tape, and the constitutional rights of free speech and petition to redress grievances.

International and U.S. Elections Compared

Any comparison of U.S. elections with those of other nations must take into account the differences in both the rights and privileges of the citizens and in the structure and function of government. What passes for an "election" in a totalitarian regime might be a mere sham in the sense of an election in the United States and in other democracies.

In 1995, for example, Iraq held a referendum on whether its dictator, President Saddam Hussein, was performing up to his people's expectations. When the results were announced, Hussein had won 99.96 percent of the vote. (He actually increased his margin of victory in 2002, winning 100 percent of the vote in a referendum on his rule.) In the old Soviet Union and in its then-satellite countries, similar high percentages were routinely chalked up for the candidates put forth by the ruling COMMUNIST PARTY. In both the Iraqi and Soviet situations, virtually every eligible voter turned up at the polls to cast a ballot.

These elections clearly were not meaningful in any sense of expressing the people's will by offering them alternatives and the freedom of choice. And the remarkably high VOTER TURNOUTS, while on their face admirable and useful for propaganda purposes, meant nothing, given the nature of political and economic coercion that these monolithic states brought to bear on their citizens to ensure high percentages.

Among the democratic countries, the United States ranks poorly in voter participation. Only 51.2 percent of voting-age Americans took part in the 2000 presidential election, under a widely used calculation. An alternative calculation using only voting-eligible persons, excluding those not legally allowed to cast ballots, showed a 54.2 percent turnout. In other similar years, with no incumbent and a vigorous campaign, rates are higher. In 2008 the measure using all voting-age persons showed a turnout rate of 56.8 percent while the one counting only eligible persons showed a 61.6 percent rate.

Turnout in MIDTERM ELECTIONS is always lower, around 40 percent.

In other democracies participation is traditionally higher in nearly all forms of elections held—from national to local. A study conducted during the 1980s found that the average turnout in eighteen of twenty countries was well above 75 percent, ranging as high as 91 percent in Australia (it rose to 96 percent in 1996). Only Switzerland ranked behind the United States.

Although some political scientists see dire omens in the U.S. turnout percentages, others point out that there are

Iraqi Prime Minister Nouri al-Maliki, center, shakes hands after addressing the U.S. Congress in 2006.

Source: CQ Photo/Scott J. Ferrell

differences that make direct comparisons difficult. When those factors are considered, the American voter participation rate compares more favorably with those of other free nations.

In sixteen of the twenty countries in the 1980s study, for example, VOTER REGISTRATION is automatic, done for the voter by the state. In Australia and New Zealand, registration is mandatory. Only in the United States, which has no national registration system, and France is the initiative to register placed entirely on the individual voter. Any American who wants to vote must make the effort to register (except in North Dakota, which has no formal registration).

Studies have indicated that voter turnout in U.S. presidential elections could rise as much as 15 percent if registration were made simpler. But the MOTOR VOTER ACT of 1993, which made voter registration forms readily available at many government offices and resulted in the registration of ten million new voters in time for the 1996 presidential election, did not increase voter turnout.

Elections in fourteen of the countries studied are held on "rest" days, not work days, making it easier for most voters to find time to go to the polls. Hold-ing elections on weekends or holidays may also help better focus the collective attention of prospective voters. In addition, most of these countries schedule as many elections as they can, from the national to the local level, on the same day, again reinforcing the idea that the citizen's vote is an institution vital to all levels of government. Some American states have experimented with weekend elections, but by law the federal ELEC-TION DAY is on a Tuesday. Many states schedule state and local elections to coincide with federal elections.

In many democracies the ballot choices are far more limited than in the United States. In Great Britain, for example, a voter must cast only one vote for a candidate to Parliament, and in Germany one vote is cast for a representative to the Bundestag and one for a political party. Researchers have found, however, that the existence of a large number of political parties depresses voter turnout. Besides being confusing, the array of names indicates to voters that the real struggle for political power will take place in the legislature as parties jockey to form major-ity coalitions.

Another finding by researchers is that democracies with a UNICAMERAL legislature have higher voter turnouts than those with a BICAMERAL system that includes a strong upper house, as in the U.S. Congress. Voters apparently believe that elections in a single-chamber system are likely to produce significant results. In the United States, only Nebraska has a unicameral legislature.

Mandatory Voting

Some democracies make voting compulsory—a coercion that likely would not find favor in the United States, with its strong traditions of individualism and independent action. In countries

---

CLOSER LOOK

There is little argument that voter participation in the United States, for many years measured at well more than 60 percent of the voting-age population, started its sharp decline in the early 1970s. But there is considerable debate over how deeply it has declined and the drop's implications for the strength of the nation's democratic institutions.

Several researchers, including Michael P. McDonald at Virginia's George Mason University, say the apparent downturn can be attributed largely to two phenomena:

1. Ratification of the Twenty-sixth Amendment in 1971, lowering the voting age nationally from 21 to 18. A surge of young voters was expected, but their participation lagged well behind that of the oldest age brackets.

2. An upsurge in immigration, especially from the 1980s on. Immigrants must become naturalized citizens to be eligible to vote, and many were slow to participate in elections after they were eligible, creating an artificial lowering of the overall turnout rate.

Rather than calculating turnout by the standard measure of its percentage of the voting-age population, McDonald advocates using the "voting eligible population" as the yardstick—a measure that typically produces turnout rates that are about 5 percentage points higher.

where voting is mandatory, nonvoters are fined. Rigorous enforcement is difficult and expensive, however, and the fines are small—about equal to a parking ticket. Nevertheless, compulsory voting has produced exceptionally large voter turnouts in all the countries that have made it the law.

But even though a government can mandate that a citizen show up at a polling place and accept a ballot, and even drop it into a ballot box, it cannot compel a voter to mark the ballot. As the political scientist Arend Lijphart writes, "Secret ballots mean that nobody can be prevented from casting an invalid or blank one."

Despite his recognition of its shortcomings, Lijphart became a strong advocate of compulsory voting. He argued that it reduces the costs of holding elections because parties do not have to spend as much to get voters to the polls. It might also reduce so-called "attack ads" and other forms of NEGATIVE CAMPAIGNING, which polls show depress voter participation. With compulsory voting, Lijphart wrote, attack ads might prove to be "no longer worth the effort."

Compulsory voting in the United States, other scholars contend, might violate individual freedom. Such a finding led the Netherlands to abolish it in 1970, resulting in a drop of nearly 40 percentage points in voter turnout. Conservative parties generally have opposed compulsion, according to Lijphart, because "high turnout is not in their partisan self-interest, . . . unequal turnout favors privileged voters, who tend to be conservative."

In the United States, the better educated are far more likely to vote than the less educated; in a matching corollary, higher-income Americans are more likely to vote than those with lower incomes. In other democracies, the better educated are only slightly more likely to vote than the less educated, perhaps because registration and voting are easier or required.

Money and Elections

Despite the laws governing CAMPAIGN FINANCE, irregularities in fund-raising have been a major problem in U.S. elections. The situation apparently worsened in the 1996 presidential election. Other major democracies, such as Great Britain and Japan, appear to have fewer such problems, even though they have looser regulations that allow much higher contributions to candidates. Unlike the United States, where corporations and unions, until 2010, could contribute to candidates only through their POLITICAL ACTION COMMITTEES, unions and companies in Canada can give directly to parties and candidates. There are regulations, however, on how much candidates and parties can spend. In 2010 the Supreme Court in CITIZENS UNITED VS. FEDERAL ELECTION COMMISSION ruled unconstitutional provisions of a campaign finance reform law that barred corporations and unions from directly engaging in "electioneering communications" within sixty days of a general election and within thirty days of a primary. The controversial ruling established, as a point of law, that corporate entities have free speech rights equivalent to those of individuals. In Russia, legal spending limits are barely enforced. In Mexico, which has higher contribution limits than the United States, the long-dominant ruling party still manages to spend above the limits by illegally giving secret government funds to its nominees.

Political candidates in Britain, Germany, and Mexico get free television time during the campaign. Advocates of free airtime in U.S. elections argue that it would result in cleaner elections because candidates would be less pressed for money to buy TV time, the largest single expense of modern U.S. campaigns. But proposals have been raised in Congress a number of times and have failed, in part because of strong opposition from the broadcasters who would be required to provide the time without compensation for the advertising revenues they would sacrifice in the process. The U.S. Federal Communications Commission has EQUAL TIME AND REBUTTAL RULES that require broadcasters to let candidates reply to attacks on them, but candidates must pay for POLITICAL ADVERTISING on television and radio.

Internet Politics

Just a few years ago, at the turn of the twenty-first century, the Internet was still a bit of a side-show in a political world still dominated by traditional print and broadcast media. Not every candidate bothered to even have a website. Among those who did, the sites rarely were more elaborate than a home page identifying the candidate along with a photo or two, a bio page providing the candidate's background, and maybe an issues page presenting the candidate's views on some key issues.

But over the next decade, the power and reach of the Internet expanded monumentally, with technological advances such as personal digital assistants (PDAs, such as the BlackBerry), smart-phones (such as the iPhone), and tablets (such as the iPad) giving high-speed e-mail and Internet access to millions of Americans not only at home, but wherever they went. Moreover, candidates, parties, and other groups were quick to adjust, rapidly making online communication a ubiqui-tous element of political strategy.

Almost all top-tier candidates for major offices, and even many running for local posts, have elaborate websites that provide basic candidate information, multimedia presentations, photo galleries, and links to positive stories about the candidate (or negative stories about his or her opponent).

Candidates also have become increasingly sophisticated and aggressive about using the web to raise campaign money. New ground broken by Democrat Barack Obama during his success-ful 2008 campaign for president helped him shatter all previous candidate fund-raising records with nearly $779 million in receipts. Even Ron Paul, a U.S. representative from Texas, raised nearly $32 million during his quixotic bid for the 2008 Republican presidential nomination, much of that col-lected in a series of one-day online fund-raising pushes that his cam-paign labeled "money bombs."

The Internet—particularly platforms such as electronic mail, text messaging, and social media networks such as Facebook and Twitter— also rapidly became an important means for outreach to established or potential supporters, both as a campaign-organizing and a get-out-the-vote tool.

While the web hardly replaced traditional media as an advertising vehicle, with candidates continuing to spend billions of dollars combined on broadcast and print ads, it certainly became an important supplemen-tary avenue for getting the word out. Many candidates today produce videos, many of them with hard-hitting negative content, that are posted only on their websites and then are publicized in hopes that the main-stream media will report on and draw attention to them.

"The effect of the Internet on politics will be every bit as transforma-tional as television was," Ken Mehlman, a former chairman of the Repub-lican National Committee, told the *New York Times* in 2006. "If you want

> **"The effect of the Internet on politics will be every bit as transformational as television was. If you want to get your message out, the old way of paying someone to make a TV ad is insufficient: You need your message out through the Internet, through e-mail, through talk radio."**
>
> **—Ken Mehlman,** a former chairman of the Republican National Committee, as quoted by the *New York Times* in 2006

to get your message out, the old way of paying someone to make a TV ad is insufficient: You need your message out through the Internet, through e-mail, through talk radio."

That effect can be positive, but it can also be hazardous to political careers, especially to those politicians who don't fully comprehend the pervasiveness of online media. The upset defeat of Virginia Republican senator George Allen in 2006 was keyed when a video showing Allen using the word "macaca" to describe a young man of Indian American descent (who had been videotaping Allen on behalf of Democratic challenger Jim Webb's campaign) went "viral" on the Internet and then was shown repeatedly by the traditional media.

Embarrassing revelations of sexually oriented online communications that were intended to be private resulted in the resignations of two members of Congress from New York in 2011: Republican Christopher Lee of an upstate district and New York City representative Anthony Weiner, a Democrat who had to endure the extra humiliation of having the media give his scandal the double-entendre label of "Weinergate."

Though it is difficult to pinpoint a specific time when the Internet came of age in political campaigns, it surely was a major force in the 2004 presidential election, when former Vermont governor Howard Dean was adept at raising contributions online for his campaign for the Democratic presidential nomination. His campaign also made skilled use of Meetup.com, an online social networking portal that allows individuals with common interests to "meet up" at certain times and locales.

The ubiquity of the Internet also transformed the formal political debates between political candidates, which normally are staid affairs. During debates, candidates may draw attention to their campaign websites. The questions asked of them increasingly include those that voters submit by e-mail. In 2007 CNN aired Democratic and Republican presidential debates that the cable network cosponsored with YouTube, the online video-sharing service that allowed users to submit their own video questions for the candidates to answer.

Iowa Caucus

From the 1970s well into the first decade of the twenty-first century, the Iowa precinct CAUCUS shared with the NEW HAMPSHIRE primary special status as the first major delegate selection events in presidential election years.

For many years, these two relatively lightly populated states were the only ones given permission by the two major national parties to hold their contests before the "window" that existed for all other states. But this led to widespread complaints from officials and political activists, particularly Democrats, in other states, who said Iowa and New Hampshire were too small to rate the primacy they held and were not representative of the diversity of the nation as a whole. For example, according to the 2000 census, Hispanics made up 13 percent of the nation's population but just 3 percent of Iowa's and 2 percent of New Hampshire's. Blacks, representing 12 percent of the nation's population, were at 2 percent in Iowa and 1 percent in New Hampshire.

Defenders of Iowa's first-in-the-nation status argue, however, that the state's relatively small and accessible population tests candidates' "retail" political skills and is therefore a better early trial of their personal appeal than the media-heavy campaigns necessary to reach voters in the more populous states.

Even though the Democratic National Committee (DNC) added two new states to the earliest part of the nominating contest schedule for the 2008 presidential elections, it did so without

nudging Iowa from its place at the top. The Iowa caucuses were held January 3, with one of the added events,
the Nevada caucuses, on January 19. New Hampshire
held its primary on January 8, less than a week after
Iowa. A primary in South Carolina was added for
January 26.

The Democratic caucuses in Iowa played an especially significant role in 2004 in shaping the campaign
to choose the challenger to President George W. Bush,
who was unopposed for the Republican nomination.
Massachusetts senator John Kerry's victory in Iowa
installed him as the solid front-runner for the Democratic nomination. On the other hand, a poor performance by longtime representative Richard A. Gephardt
of neighboring Missouri prompted him to leave the
race. In 2008 Barack Obama beat his principal opponent, Hillary Rodham Clinton, in Iowa, a victory that
foretold his success in many later caucuses that helped
pile up delegates in his eventual successful capture of
the nomination.

*A poor showing in the Iowa caucuses severely
hurt Howard Dean's chances of securing the
Democratic nomination in 2004.*
Source: CQ Photo/Scott J. Ferrell

Today, the Iowa caucuses are routinely seen as an early maker or breaker of presidential aspirations. But the event is a relative newcomer to the important place it now holds in the nominating
process.

The New Hampshire primary has been around since 1913, but the Iowa caucus event as it
evolved sprang from the new politics that captured the DEMOCRATIC PARTY in the late 1960s and
early 1970s. The grassroots activism of Iowa's precinct caucuses provided fertile ground for that
new breed of politics.

For decades Iowans held precinct caucuses in January every four years to begin the process
of selecting DELEGATES to the Democratic and Republican national conventions. But in the old
days the process was firmly in the hands of party regulars, pragmatic politicians who selected
delegates to county conventions and therefore controlled eligibility for national convention
delegates.

Sometimes these decisions would be made in the context of broader political deals between
important state bosses and particular candidates. But often they would not have anything to do
with a delegate's preference for the presidential nomination. The county convention delegates
were expected to represent their localities; the job of choosing the nominee could be left to later
convention delegates.

Rank-and-file voters were not involved. Typically, the county chair of a party would meet with
a few political cronies to choose delegates to the county convention. Sometimes the local bosses
did not even meet in caucus, because few party members were interested enough to attend. The
leaders would simply run the requisite advance notice in the local newspaper and then meet
amongst themselves to select county convention delegates.

All that changed with the Vietnam War. Angered and politically energized by the war, ordinary
voters in 1968 showed up in droves at precinct caucuses across the state. They overwhelmed the
political bosses and sent their own antiwar delegates to the county conventions. Their champion
was the antiwar insurgent candidate, Sen. Eugene J. McCarthy of Minnesota.

How the Iowa Caucuses Measured Up as a Predictor of the Party Nominees

	Iowa Winner	Nominee
Democrats		
1976	Jimmy Carter[*]	Jimmy Carter
1980	Jimmy Carter	Jimmy Carter
1984	Walter F. Mondale	Walter F. Mondale
1988	Richard A. Gephardt	Michael S. Dukakis
1992	Tom Harkin	Bill Clinton
1996	Bill Clinton[**]	Bill Clinton
2000	Al Gore	Al Gore
2004	John Kerry	John Kerry
2008	Barack Obama	Barack Obama
Republicans		
1976	Gerald R. Ford	Gerald R. Ford
1980	George H.W. Bush	Ronald Reagan
1984	Ronald Reagan[**]	Ronald Reagan
1988	Bob Dole	George H. W. Bush
1992	George H. W. Bush[**]	George H. W. Bush
1996	Bob Dole	Bob Dole
2000	George W. Bush	George W. Bush
2004	George W. Bush[**]	George W. Bush
2008	Mike Huckabee	John McCain

[*] Carter finished behind "uncommitted" but ahead of all other candidates

[**] Ran unopposed

The politicians fought back at the county conventions and reclaimed the levers of power and decision making. But the die was cast. When Sen. George S. McGovern of South Dakota, another antiwar Democrat, headed up a commission to transform party rules for the 1972 campaign, he ensured that the bosses would never again dominate the process. The ensuing PRESIDENTIAL SELECTION REFORMS forced the regulars into retreat; the activists came into their own.

Thus was born the present-day Iowa caucus. What began as an outlet for Democratic Party activism soon became a testing ground for Republican presidential aspirants as well.

Only the Democrats, however, have protected the Iowa caucus's first-in-the-nation status by party rule. The REPUBLICAN PARTY, with fewer restrictive rules generally, permits other states to hold earlier party caucuses. But in recent years, few have done so; those that did found they were unable to compete with the media and candidate attention lavished on Iowa.

Interest in the Iowa caucuses blossomed following the successful strategy employed by former Georgia governor Jimmy Carter. A long shot when he began his presidential bid, Carter recognized the publicity value of a strong showing in the campaign's kickoff event. Though Carter, with support from 28 percent of caucus voters, finished behind "uncommitted" (37 percent), he finished ahead of all other candidates and was able to claim a victory that helped him soar from underdog to front-runner in a matter of weeks.

In the years since, the Iowa caucuses have a checkered record as a BELLWETHER of the ultimate outcome of the nominating campaign. Five Democrats who went on to win the party's nomination—Carter in 1980, Walter F. Mondale in 1984, Bill Clinton in 1996, Al Gore in 2000, Kerry in 2004, and Barack Obama in 2008—finished first in Iowa. But Michael S. Dukakis in 1988 and Clinton in 1992—when Iowa senator Tom Harkin, who briefly staged a presidential bid, dominated in his home state—finished well off the pace in Iowa.

The caucuses have been even less predictive on the Republican side. Nomination winners who won in Iowa were Gerald R. Ford in 1976, Bob Dole in 1996, and George W. Bush in 2000. Incumbents seeking reelection—Ronald Reagan in 1984, George H. W. Bush in 1992, and George W. Bush in 2004—ran without intraparty opposition. John McCain, the eventual GOP nominee in 2008, lost the Iowa caucuses that year to Mike Huckabee, a former governor of Arkansas. The elder Bush edged eventual nominee Reagan in the 1980 caucuses; in 1988, when Bush would go on to win the nomination, he finished a stunning third in Iowa behind Dole and television evangelist Pat Robertson.

Issue Ads *See* MEDIA USE BY CAMPAIGNS; POLITICAL ADVERTISING.

More on this topic:

Bellwether, p. 23

Caucus, p. 89

New Hampshire Primary, p. 369

Presidential Selection Reforms, p. 476

Issue Voting

Americans are constantly urged to acquaint themselves with the issues in an election and vote accordingly. And while studies of ELECTORAL BEHAVIOR show that voters often choose among candidates largely on the basis of PARTY IDENTIFICATION and candidate image, this is not always the case.

Issues, not surprisingly, rise in importance during periods of increased public concerns about key policy debates, such as during wars and economic instability.

The several elections starting the new century, beginning with 2000, provide interesting contrasts. In 2000, at the end of Democrat Bill Clinton's two-term presidency, the nation appeared to be facing no critical foreign policy problems and was in the midst of an economic boom. Many voters focused on the personality traits of the candidates, a comparison that favored Republican George W. Bush, then governor of Texas, over Democrat Al Gore, the incumbent vice president, who was often described as "rigid" and "wooden" in his campaign style.

By the time Bush stood for reelection in 2004, much had changed for the nation. The September 11, 2001, attacks had prompted Bush to launch what he called a war against terror, and the political capital he earned with this assertive response enabled him to gain initial public approval to launch a war in Iraq in March 2003 that nonetheless was growing increasingly unpopular as the 2004 election neared. Bush again held a personality advantage over his Democratic opponent, Massachusetts senator John Kerry, who was viewed by many voters as a wealthy liberal "elitist." But many voters focused on personality traits that were closely related to the big issues of the day, such as the candidates' relative leadership abilities and constancy at a time of war.

By the 2006 midterm congressional elections, though, issues played the predominant role in the outcome. What was widely referred to as a "perfect storm" of issues hit the Republicans: growing dissent over the war in Iraq, negative views of the Bush administration's handling of the aftermath of Hurricane Katrina in 2005, economic pressures including spikes in gasoline prices, and a series of scandals involving Republican members of Congress. While GOP candidates and officials used the traditional mantra of "all politics is local" to get voters to focus on what Republican incumbents had been able to "deliver" for their local constituencies, many voters saw the election as a referendum on Bush and the Republican-controlled Congress. The outcome was a net gain for the Democrats of six seats in the Senate and thirty in the House, enough to give the party control of both chambers of Congress.

Issue voting loomed even larger in the next two election cycles. By November 2008 the nation, and the world, were deep into the worst recession in more than half a century. In the United States, a long-running housing bubble had burst, two major Wall Street investment houses disappeared, unemployment climbed to 10 percent, major financial firms and companies, including America's auto industry, were nearly collapsed, and the federal government was struggling to prevent the economy from falling into a full depression.

In this crisis atmosphere, Democrats—and their nominee Barack Obama—rode economic issues to win the White House and pad their congressional margins.

Together the Democratic successes sowed the seeds of the huge voter turnaround two years later. Democrats, firmly in control of Congress as well as the White House, launched an ambitious agenda in the 111th Congress that began in 2009. Some of the activity grew out of the economic collapse, including expensive stimulus legislation and financial regulation. But other initiatives carried forward long-standing objectives of the liberal wing of the Democratic Party. None fit this category better than a far-reaching health care reform bill, enacted over virtually unwavering Republican opposition, that sought to rein in costs, set up insurance options for customers, prevent insurance companies from long-controversial practices of excluding coverage and payments, greatly expand coverage to tens of millions of uninsured persons, and—in its most controversial portion—require every person to obtain health insurance.

These initiatives set off a furious push-back from segments of voters, particularly the most conservative ones, that in turn ignited opposition to Democratic candidates in 2010. It also spawned a new conservative movement that took the name TEA PARTY, from the American Revolutionary era. Large amounts of voter anger over what was seen as overreaching national government played out through the Tea Party movement. The issues growing out of the 111th Congress, combined with continuing voter frustration over high unemployment and a slow recovery from the recession, gave the GOP an energy and purpose it lacked in the two previous elections. The result was Republican gains of sixty-three seats in the House and six in the Senate in 2010, enough to control the former although not the latter. Moreover, many of the House freshmen were ardently supported by Tea Party advocates, which meant—in the next Congress in 2011—they would become a group unalterably opposed by President Obama and much of the activities and spending of the national government.

Although voters largely ignore foreign policy issues, unless there is a pressing crisis such as the war in Iraq, they pay attention to domestic issues. Voters care, for example, about taxes, jobs, and other hot-button issues, such as abortion, and these issues can influence their choice of candidates.

So-called issue voting, though, can be affected by some voters' tendency to project their personal issue positions onto their preferred candidates, regardless of the candidates' actual positions.

In 1968, for example, people on both sides of the debate over U.S. military involvement in the Vietnam War (hawks and doves) were found among the supporters of Richard M. Nixon and his Democratic opponent Hubert H. Humphrey. Because the candidates were less than explicit about their Vietnam policies, voters who saw a difference in their positions were responding to their own wishes and not engaging in issue voting. It is also possible for voters to adopt issue positions because their preferred candidate has taken that position.

An issue determines voter choice only when (1) voters are informed and concerned about the issue; (2) candidates take distinguishable stands on it; and (3) voters perceive how the candidate stands in relation to their own concerns. In the 1972 presidential contest between President Nixon

For some voters a candidate's stand on abortion may be the most important factor in an election decision.
Source: CQ Photo/R. Michael Jenkins

and Democratic challenger George McGovern, issues clearly had an effect. On eleven of fourteen issues studied the voters felt closer to Nixon than to McGovern, and there was a close correlation between people's perceptions of where the candidates stood and the candidate for whom they voted. Only on issues related to the environment and urban unrest did McGovern appear to be closer to citizens' positions. Nixon was viewed as closer on issues such as Vietnam, marijuana, desegregation, and campus unrest.

With most voters tending to be moderate or centrist in their orientations, and with each party made up of people with diverse viewpoints, there may be little incentive for candidates to take strongly opposing stands. They may instead straddle issues, making issue-based voting difficult for the average citizen. This tendency, normal in many if not most years, held less true in 2010 when voters deeply angered by their perceived view of Democratic actions, coalesced around candidates with outspoken views about government intrusion and overreaching. This energy, excitement, and anger brought their voters to the polls in large numbers while the corresponding enthusiastic backers of Obama two years earlier stayed home.

But in less volatile times, in the 2002 MIDTERM ELECTIONS, for example, candidates in both parties sought to blur their differences on certain issues. Many Democrats, worried about appearing too dovish on foreign policy matters, stressed their support for President George W. Bush's hard line against Iraq; many Republicans, concerned about appearing insensitive, supported such social initiatives as expanding health care benefits for the elderly. This tendency is less true in PRIMARY elections, where competing candidates within the same party need to take clear-cut positions to differentiate themselves from their opponents. It was exceptionally true in the 2010 primaries when Tea Party candidates defeated a number of more moderate Republicans, including several who most likely would have won in the general elections but were turned out in the primaries.

Voters' decisions are made easier when an incumbent is seeking reelection. Having had an opportunity to judge the candidate's performance, voters can render a verdict on his or her behavior in office. This process of electoral decision making is called RETROSPECTIVE VOTING. But it does not always hold, as again was seen in 2010 when the record of even conservative Republican incumbents was not good enough for the increasingly exceptionally conservative core of the party. As a result, a number of these incumbents (called RINOs, Republicans in Name Only, by their detractors) were defeated in primary voting.

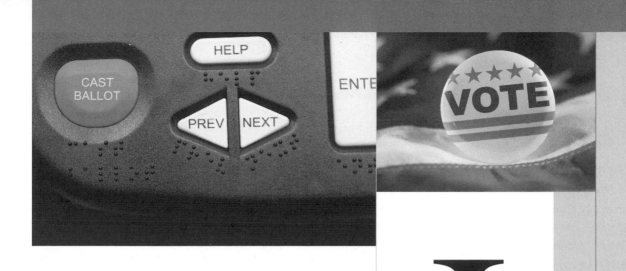

Judicial System

On December 13, 2000, the Supreme Court issued perhaps its most momentous ruling that directly affected the nation's electoral process. On a narrow 5–4 vote in the case of BUSH V. GORE, the justices effectively terminated a protracted recount of the presidential vote in Florida, where Republican George W. Bush held a tenuous 537-vote edge over Democrat Al Gore. Bush received Florida's 25 electoral votes, giving him a bare majority of 271 electoral votes and therefore the White House.

In overruling a state supreme court ruling requiring election officials to proceed with a recount of certain ballots, the U.S. Supreme Court found that the recount violated the Equal Protection Clause of the Fourteenth Amendment on grounds that the state court had failed to establish uniform standards for the manual recount of the ballots for which counters were attempting to establish voter intent.

That the Court took the case at all was unusual. Historically, the Court has been reluctant to hear cases involving executive or legislative branch elections. This was evident when the Court in 1946 considered a case of congressional redistricting in Illinois. Ruling in *Colegrove v. Green*, the Supreme Court determined that drawing district maps was a legislative prerogative and that any changes would have to come through the political rather than the judicial process. "Courts ought not to enter this political thicket," wrote Justice Felix Frankfurter at the time. In the 1960s, however, the Court's resistance broke down on this issue in its historic ONE PERSON, ONE VOTE rulings.

Yet as the ultimate authority on interpretation of the Constitution, the Supreme Court is a crucial power center in the American political system. At several points in U.S. history, the Court's decisions have helped to produce historic milestones in U.S. elections.

Using the power of judicial review, federal and state courts also have had a significant effect on the nation's electoral process. Acts of Congress, orders of the executive branch, or state laws cannot be put into effect if the courts declare them unconstitutional. But it is when the Supreme Court takes a case for review that the outcome can have the broadest and most lasting repercussions. Its decisions about the meaning of the Constitution can be changed only through its own later reinterpretation or through the difficult and time-consuming process of constitutional amendment.

The Constitution created a federal system of government in which both the national and state governments exercise significant legislative, executive, and judicial powers. Fifty state judicial systems, therefore, operate side by side with the federal court system. Each system has its own personnel and jurisdiction, and each interprets and enforces its own constitution and laws. Although the two court systems are separate and distinct, they do overlap: the constitutional principle of federal supremacy enables the federal courts to throw out state actions they deem to be in violation of the U.S. Constitution or acts of Congress.

Both the federal and state systems have trial courts and appellate courts. Trial courts are the tribunals in which a case is first heard—that is, they are courts of original jurisdiction. Cases in trial courts may be heard before a jury, or a judge may render the verdict. Appellate courts hear cases on appeal from lower courts. But appellate courts have no juries; all cases are decided by a panel of judges. These courts are concerned primarily with whether the lower courts correctly interpreted the applicable laws and followed the proper judicial procedures in deciding a case. Appellate courts normally do not consider new factual evidence because the record of the lower court constitutes the basis for judgment.

> **"None are more conscious of the vital limits on judicial authority than are the members of this Court, and none stand more in admiration of the Constitution's design to leave the selection of the President to the People, through their legislatures, and to the political sphere. When contending parties invoke the process of the courts, however, it becomes our unsought responsibility to resolve the federal and constitutional issues the judicial system has been forced to confront."**
>
> **—Excerpt from the majority opinion in the 2000 case of Bush v. Gore,** which effectively decided that year's presidential election in favor of Republican nominee George W. Bush

In contrast to the federal government's process, in which all judges are appointed by the president and confirmed by the Senate, the states use a variety of selection procedures, depending on their constitutions and statutes. Both appointment and election are used. Almost half the states follow a mixed appointment and election process, such as the Missouri plan, in which the GOVERNOR appoints judges from a list of candidates approved by a judicial commission, and a REFERENDUM is held on each appointee's performance at the next general election.

> **"Courts ought not to enter this political thicket."**
>
> **—Justice Felix Frankfurter,** referring to the Court's rejection in the 1946 case of *Colegrove v. Green* of a complaint alleging that unequal populations among district lines was unconstitutional

Origins of Judicial Review

Basic though it is to the U.S. system of government, judicial review is not mentioned in the Constitution. Rather, it was asserted by the Supreme Court in the case of *Marbury v. Madison* (1803), which arose following the election of 1800.

After losing the election, President John Adams appointed a number of federal judges in an effort to control the judiciary once his successor, Thomas Jefferson, took office. One of these appointees, William Marbury, was designated a justice of the peace for the District of Columbia.

Chief Justice John Marshall (left) set a crucial precedent in 1803 when he claimed for the Court the right to review federal legislation. The case, Marbury v. Madison, was brought by William Marbury (right), a federal appointee.

Sources: Library of Congress and the Maryland Historical Society

The outgoing Adams administration neglected to give Marbury his commission to office, however, and the new secretary of state, James Madison, refused to do so. Marbury then brought suit in the Supreme Court asking that Madison be required to give him his commission. Marbury took his case directly to the Supreme Court because an act of Congress, the Judiciary Act of 1789, had made such an issue part of the Court's original jurisdiction. The act authorized the Court to issue writs of mandamus, which compelled a federal officer to carry out his duty.

Chief Justice John Marshall's opinion for the Court stated that Marbury was indeed entitled to his commission and that Madison had erred in denying it to him. The Court ruled, however, that it lacked the power to order Madison to give Marbury his commission because the Court did *not* have jurisdiction over the case. It added that the provisions in the Judiciary Act of 1789 giving the Court jurisdiction over such cases were an unconstitutional extension by Congress of the Court's original jurisdiction, which had already been provided for in Article III, section 2.

Sparing Use

Judicial review is a power the Court has used sparingly in cases involving federal law. After *Marbury v. Madison* it was fifty-four years before another act of Congress was declared unconstitutional. This occurred in *Scott v. Sandford* (1857), a case that had later implications in the fight for BLACK SUFFRAGE.

Dred Scott, a slave, claimed to be free when his master took him to a territory where slavery was banned. The Court ruled, however, that the Missouri Compromise of 1820, which outlawed slavery in the northern territories, was unconstitutional because it took the slave owner's property without due process of law. In declaring that free Negroes were not citizens and without constitutional rights, the Court in the *Scott* case created a public furor and helped to precipitate the Civil War.

Since it asserted its power of judicial review, the Supreme Court has declared state laws or provisions of state constitutions unconstitutional more than a thousand times.

The Court and Equality of Vote

Many of the Supreme Court's farthest-reaching decisions have dealt with inequities in civil rights and voting rights through discriminatory practices such as malapportionment of legislative seats, RACIAL REDISTRICTING or GERRYMANDERING, or LITERACY TESTS that excluded African Americans from SOUTHERN PRIMARIES or the now-outlawed WHITE PRIMARIES.

In addressing the REAPPORTIONMENT AND REDISTRICTING issue, the Supreme Court announced in BAKER V. CARR (1962) that henceforth the judiciary would interject itself into the redistricting process to ensure that DISTRICTS were equal in size and adhered to the Court's ONE-PERSON, ONE-VOTE principle. This decision dramatically changed how Americans were represented in their state legislatures and Congress.

"The mere fact that the suit seeks protection of a political right does not mean it presents a political question."

—*Justice William J. Brennan Jr.,* in the majority opinion in the 1962 case of *Baker v. Carr,* which established the principle that federal courts have jurisdiction to review claims of unconstitutional apportionment of state legislative districts—a decision that a dissenter, Justice John Marshall Harlan, called "an adventure in judicial experimentation"

In 1986 the Court took a step further into this politically charged area when it stated that it would review instances of partisan gerrymandering to determine whether a political minority had suffered substantial and long-standing harm in violation of the Fourteenth Amendment's Equal Protection Clause. The Court's controversial role in redistricting policy was expanded again in 1993 when it ruled in *SHAW V. RENO* that it would consider whether minority-majority congressional districts created under the VOTING RIGHTS ACT of 1965 could deprive white voters of the equal protection of the laws.

The case involved a North Carolina plan that created two districts, one of them severely contorted, with black majorities. Both elected black representatives in 1992, and white voters challenged the plan as discriminatory. In a second opinion, *Shaw v. Hunt,* the Court ruled in 1996 that the state could not justify the plan on the basis of either possible past discrimination against a minority or compliance with the 1965 act.

The Court in recent years has continued to confine its intervention in redistricting to cases involving claims of racial discrimination and population inequality—while generally steering clear of trying to define what, if anything, constitutes a gerrymander that is egregious only on partisan grounds.

The Court and Elections

Supreme Court decisions are not self-enforcing; rather the Court must rely on others—notably the attorney general—to implement its decisions. When the issue is clear-cut and the order is directed at one person, compliance is prompt. This was the case in 1974 when the Court ordered President Richard M. Nixon to turn over to a lower federal court taped Oval Office conversations about the Watergate cover-up.

The Watergate SCANDAL arose from a June 1972 burglary at the DEMOCRATIC NATIONAL COMMITTEE headquarters in Washington's Watergate Hotel complex. Although the purpose of the break-in was never determined, the burglars and others involved were quickly linked to the Republican Party and the Nixon reelection committee. Investigators speculated that the burglars may have been attempting to plant listening devices in the DNC office or find information that would be detrimental to Nixon's opposition in the November election. Although Nixon denied any complicity in the burglary or the cover-up, the tapes proved otherwise. On July 24, 1974, the Court in *United States v. Nixon* dismissed the president's claim of executive privilege and ordered him to turn over the tapes, which revealed that Nixon was aware of plans to pay "hush money" to the burglars. Facing impeachment by the House, Nixon resigned on August 9, 1974.

The resignation resulted in the first turnover of the presidency without either a death or an election. Nixon's successor, Gerald R. Ford, had been nominated by Nixon and approved by both houses of Congress under the terms of the Twenty-fifth Amendment following the 1973 resignation of Vice President Spiro T. Agnew over tax fraud, bribery, and other changes while in public office in Maryland. With the similar election of former New York governor Nelson A. Rockefeller to succeed Ford, the nation for the first time had a president and vice president not elected by the ELECTORAL COLLEGE.

In the wake of the Watergate affair, Congress passed the Federal Election Campaign Act (FECA) amendments of 1974. These revised older CAMPAIGN FINANCE restrictions and established a PUBLIC FINANCING system for presidential elections.

Ruling on a challenge to the new law, the Court in BUCKLEY V. VALEO (1976) invalidated the spending limits as infringing on political speech, but it upheld the limits on contributions to federal candidates. Congress subsequently amended the FECA to conform to the decision.

Two years later, the Court struck down a Massachusetts law that forbade corporations to spend money to influence voters' decisions on referendum issues. In the case, *First National Bank of Boston v. Bellotti*, the Court said that laws barring corporate gifts to candidates might be justified in preventing corruption. On that basis, it ruled in *Austin v. Michigan Chamber of Commerce* (1990) that states can bar corporations from giving to political campaigns without setting up a POLITICAL ACTION COMMITTEE for that purpose.

Earlier, in *Williams v. Rhodes* (1968), the Court struck down an Ohio law that limited BALLOT ACCESS to THIRD-PARTY candidates. The Court held that the law denied equal protection of the laws to candidates and voters. Since then the Court has treated other state laws in similar fashion. In 1992, for example, it invalidated an Illinois law that required a new political party in Chicago to obtain 25,000 signatures in both the city and the suburbs to place candidates' names on a countywide ballot.

In two other 1992 cases, however, the Court rejected First Amendment challenges to election laws. It upheld a Hawaii law that blocked WRITE-IN VOTES in state elections. And it affirmed a Tennessee law that prohibited electioneering within 100 feet of the entrance to a polling place.

One of the Court's most controversial decisions tied to elections came in January 2010. That case, *Citizens United v. Federal Elections Commission*, involved provisions of a campaign finance reform bill that was enacted in 2002 that had barred corporate interests (including businesses and labor unions) from using independent expenditures to pay for broadcast issue ads—which often are cleverly crafted messages aimed at influencing the outcomes of elections—within sixty days of a general election or within thirty days of a primary. But in *Citizens United*, decided by a vote of 5–4, the Supreme Court struck down that provision, and in doing so established as a matter of constitutional law that corporate interests have free speech rights equivalent to those of individuals in regard to campaign finance matters. (See CAMPAIGN FINANCE.)

The Court and Political Parties

Early in the twentieth century, as the PRIMARY system came into widespread use, the courts regarded such elections as internal political party affairs not subject to government interference. But in a 1941 Louisiana case, *United States v. Classic,* the Supreme Court reversed the precedent and ruled that Congress may regulate primaries for federal elections. Although it was not a racial discrimination case, *Classic* led to the abolition of primaries that excluded blacks under the pretext that the parties running them were private organizations.

Several rulings in the 1970s and 1980s dealt with the states' power to protect the parties' membership rolls and nominating procedures. The decisions reflected an effort to balance the rights of political parties to run their own affairs and the rights of voters to participate in party nominating elections.

In a significant decision, *Cousins v. Wigoda* (1975), the Court ruled that parties, like individuals, have a constitutional right to political association. The case stemmed from a dispute between rival Illinois delegations to the 1972 Democratic NATIONAL PARTY CONVENTION, one pledged to the candidacy of South Dakota senator George S. McGovern and the other led by Chicago mayor Richard J. Daley. The losing Daley delegation appealed, but the Supreme Court ruled that the state courts would have had no jurisdiction because in such instances the parties settle their own claims.

Several decisions in 1973 and 1974 set out the Court's view of the permissible restrictions a state might place on persons wishing to change political parties as voters or candidates. In *Rosario v. Rockefeller* (1973), the Court upheld a state requirement that voters who wished to vote in a party's primary have enrolled in that party at least thirty days before the previous general election.

To protect voters' rights, the Court ruled, also in 1973, that states cannot impose unreasonable deadlines for party registration to vote in a primary. The case, *Kusper v. Pontikes*, involved a law that forbade voting in a party primary if the voter had participated in a primary of another party within the previous twenty-three months. But the next year, the Court upheld in *Storer v. Brown* and *Frommhagen v. Brown* a state law that barred people from running as INDEPENDENTS or candidates of new parties unless they had disqualified themselves from any other party at least one year before the election.

The Court also respected the autonomy of the political parties in two decisions involving open and closed primaries. In open primaries any registered voter may participate, but closed primaries accept only registered party members. (See PRIMARY TYPES.)

A 1981 decision, *Democratic Party of the United States v. La Follette*, allowed Wisconsin to require an open primary but said the state could not require the national party organization to recognize the results. A year later, the Court struck down Ohio's law requiring candidates to disclose the names and addresses of campaign contributors. By a 6–3 vote, the Court held in *Brown v. Socialist Workers '74 Campaign Committee* that such disclosure, particularly of contributors to minor parties, might subject the donors to harassment, violating their freedom of association.

In 1986, in *Tashjian v. Republican Party of Connecticut*, the Court held that states could not compel parties to hold closed primaries; parties could make those decisions themselves.

By unanimous vote in *Foster v. Love* (1997), the Court struck down a type of open primary used only in Louisiana. Under it, a congressional candidate was elected if he or she received a majority of votes in the primary held prior to the national election. That shortcut, the Court said, undermined Congress's intent in setting a uniform ELECTION DAY for federal elections.

Louisiana officials, determined to maintain the unique features of their primary system, adjusted to the Court's ruling by moving the state's primary to November to coincide with the national election day; that way, a congressional candidate elected outright by winning a majority in the primary would not violate the ruling barring early elections. Any contests that did not result in an outright win were resolved in December runoffs. But in 2006, the state enacted a law to bring its primary system into conformity with those in other states.

More on this topic:
Baker v. Carr, p. 12
Bush v. Gore, p. 40
Campaign Finance, p. 53
Gerrymander, p. 226
Literacy Tests, p. 309
One Person, One Vote, p. 373
Primary Types, p. 485
Racial Redistricting, p. 509
Reapportionment and Redistricting, p. 517
Voting Rights Act, p. 663
White Primary, p. 674

Jungle Primary   *See* PRIMARY TYPES.

K

Know Nothing (American) Party (1856)

The Know Nothing (American) Party of the 1850s was the most formidable nativist political organization in American history; for two years in mid-decade it was the nation's second-largest party. Nativism involved the fear of immigrants and opposition to an internal minority believed to be un-American. Members of the American Party would be called Know Nothings because when asked about their organization they were instructed to say, "I know nothing." For them, fear and hatred of Catholics, particularly "papist conspirators," created this need for secrecy.

The Know Nothings emerged from one of the many nativist secret societies proliferating in the pre–Civil War period. The migration of millions of Catholics from Ireland and Germany stimulated an intense anti-immigrant activism in the United States. Key leaders of the Order of the Star Spangled Banner saw their group as a useful instrument for shaping a new political party in 1853. Like nativists of earlier decades, leaders of the Know Nothings accused Catholics of

A sheet music cover for a quickstep dedicated to the "Know Nothings," dated 1854

Source: Library of Congress

undermining the public school system and of being responsible for a host of social problems accompanying the influx of so many poverty-stricken newcomers into the great port cities. Know Nothings advocated nominating only native-born American Protestants for political office and requiring a twenty-one-year waiting period before naturalization.

The party emerged at a critical moment in American political history. The slavery controversy was ripping apart the WHIG PARTY, and the DEMOCRATIC PARTY was suffering fissures in different states and sections. Out of this turmoil came a flood of members to the new nativist movement. For many people, a party organized around nativist themes—one that advanced "American" interests and stood for stability and union—offered a way out of the conflict between northerner and southerner, abolitionist and slaveholder. A common crusade against foreigners, they thought, could cement broken institutions and warring people.

The political divisions of the day meant the Know Nothing membership varied from section to section. In New York, where the party was born and had its strongest support, the leadership was composed of conservative Whig refugees, men who opposed antislavery elements in their former party. These included James Barker and Daniel Ullmann, the party candidate in the New York gubernatorial race in 1855. In New England, the antislavery wing of the former Whig Party, "Conscience Whigs," played the key role. Leaders in Massachusetts included Henry Wilson, president of the state senate who was a U.S. senator in 1855, and Henry J. Gardner, elected state governor in the Know Nothing landslide that year. Also swelling the party rolls in New England were abolitionists from the other major party, anti–Nebraska Act Democrats.

In the West, where Know Nothings struggled to find support, nativists sought fusion with FREE SOIL activists in Indiana and Illinois, but in Wisconsin two factions (the Same and the Jonathans) shared anti-immigrant attitudes yet split over slavery.

In the South, which contained a small immigrant population, nativism appealed to those who viewed immigrants in the Northwest and West as threatening to the southern way of life because it was assumed that newcomers would be opposed to slavery. The nativist party in the South represented an escape from the divisive struggle that threatened civil strife, but it had only limited impact.

In its peak years of 1854 and 1855, the party elected five U.S. senators, forty-three members of the House, and governors in California, Connecticut, Delaware, Kentucky, Massachusetts, New Hampshire, and Rhode Island. Despite its political success, the national Know Nothing Party could not survive the antislavery controversy. At the party gathering in Philadelphia in June 1855, a proslavery resolution led to wild debate and a massive defection led by antislavery Massachusetts nativists. Further divisions in the party, including personal rivalries between New York leaders Barker and Ullmann, created more problems.

The Know Nothings held their first and only NATIONAL PARTY CONVENTION in February 1856 and selected as their candidate former Whig president Millard Fillmore. The antislavery wing of the party convened separately and endorsed the Republican nominee, John C. Fremont. Fillmore—who had joined a Know Nothing lodge as a political maneuver and had never been a real nativist—failed at the polls, trailing in a three-way race with 21.5 percent of the POPULAR VOTE and taking only Maryland's eight ELECTORAL COLLEGE votes. Republican Fremont finished second to the Democratic Party's James Buchanan. The Know Nothings did not recover, losing members rapidly in subsequent months. Within a year, the bulk of the northern Know Nothings had joined the REPUBLICAN PARTY. By the end of the decade, the party existed only in the BORDER STATES, where it formed the basis for the unsuccessful, antiwar CONSTITUTIONAL UNION PARTY.

CLOSER LOOK

Vice President Millard Fillmore, a Whig from New York, became the nation's thirteenth president upon the death of President Zachary Taylor in 1850. He is held in low esteem by many historians who view him as the first of three presidents in the 1850s to fail to grasp the immensity of the national schism that led to the Civil War. In 1852 he was in fact denied the Whig nomination because of opposition from antislavery factions.

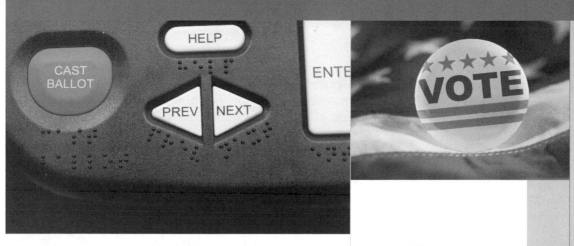

Lame Duck

The term *lame duck* refers in general to an officeholder facing the impending expiration of his or her tenure—and more specifically, one who has lost political influence because he or she will soon be leaving office. INCUMBENTS defeated, not seeking reelection, or barred by TERM LIMIT laws from succeeding themselves fall into this category.

In most congressional election years, leaders of both parties seek to wrap up all business prior to the election, usually in October, and adjourn until the next Congress is sworn in the following January. But sometimes they fail to do so; when lawmakers do reconvene after the election, it is known as a "lame-duck Congress." In such sessions, there always are members voting on legislation who will not return in the next Congress because they have been defeated or left office voluntarily.

The term originated with the British as an uncharitable description of bankrupt business owners. By the early nineteenth century it was being applied in the United States to "politically bankrupt" elected officials. Patronage jobs they hand out shortly before leaving office are called "lame-duck" appointments.

The Twentieth Amendment to the Constitution, ratified in 1933, was named the "Lame Duck amendment." It sought to reduce the time federal officeholders spent as lame ducks by shortening the intervals after presidents and members of Congress are elected and actually take office. (See PRESIDENT, NOMINATING AND ELECTING; SENATE, ELECTING; VICE PRESIDENT.)

Formerly, presidents and vice presidents had to wait about four months, from ELECTION DAY in November until inauguration on March 4, before they were sworn in. The Twentieth Amendment moved up the swearing-in to January 20, beginning in 1937.

CLOSER LOOK

The Twentieth, or "lame duck," Amendment to the Constitution provides some flexibility to congressional leaders on the exact date for Congress to convene. Section 2 of the Amendment states that Congress must meet at least once each year with the session starting at noon on January 3, "unless they shall by law appoint a different day." In reality, recent Congresses have often convened on January 3 for swearing-in ceremonies and election of the House and Senate leaders and then dispersed again until late January, when the real legislative activity began. But that was not the case in 2007. Following the Democrats' takeover of Congress in the 2006 midterm elections, both parties' leaders agreed to commence the 100th Congress on January 4.

The waiting period for newly elected members of Congress was even longer—thirteen months, from election day to the first Monday in December of the following year. The Twentieth Amendment specified that both sessions of each two-year Congress would begin on January 3, greatly reducing the postelection lame-duck period.

Prior to the implementation of a two-term limit for presidents under the Twenty-second Amendment, ratified in 1951, a president would be a lame duck only if he was defeated for reelection or announced in advance of the election that he would not seek another term.

Since the amendment went into effect, five presidents—Dwight D. Eisenhower (1952 and 1956), Richard M. Nixon (1968 and 1972), Ronald Reagan (1980 and 1984), Bill Clinton (1992 and 1996), and George W. Bush (2000 and 2004), all of whom were Republicans except Clinton—won twice and effectively became lame ducks as soon as they were sworn in for their second terms. That seldom stops presidents from declaring that their second victory is a mandate for their policy agenda, however.

All of the presidents elected twice since the Twenty-second Amendment have found their political influence weakened by second-term events. Eisenhower faced an economic recession; Nixon was forced to resign in 1974 because of his involvement in the Watergate scandal; Reagan's final two years in office were clouded by the "Iran-contra" affair; Clinton was impeached by the House in 1999 but acquitted by the Senate in a trial resulting from a sex scandal investigation that led to charges that he had lied under oath; and George W. Bush faced criticism of his handling of the war in Iraq, his administration's response to Hurricane Katrina in 2005, and controversial actions taken to counter the massive economic recession that hit during his final year in office.

Even if reelected in a LANDSLIDE, the president must deal with a Congress that is aware the president cannot run again and therefore is hampered in building popular support for initiatives and programs that many in Congress oppose. The situation is even more difficult for the second-term president if the opposing party controls Congress, as happened to Clinton beginning with the MIDTERM ELECTION of 1994 and continuing after his reelection in 1996. George W. Bush, too, was consigned to finish out the last two years of his presidency with the Democratic opposition in control of Congress following the midterm election of 2006.

> *"When you win, there is a feeling that people have spoken and embraced your point of view. And that's what I intend to tell the Congress: that I made it clear what I intend to do as the president and the people have made it clear what they wanted."*
>
> **—President George W. Bush** at a news conference on November 4, 2004, two days after he won election to a second term

Landslide

A lopsided election victory that buries the defeated candidate under the winner's votes is called a *landslide*. There is no perfect consensus on what constitutes a landslide, but in presidential politics it generally means 60 percent or more of the POPULAR VOTE.

By that measure only four presidents can claim landslide victories: Republican Warren G. Harding in 1920, Democrat Franklin D. Roosevelt in 1936, Democrat Lyndon B. Johnson in 1964, and Republican Richard Nixon in 1972.

Johnson's landslide was the largest. He polled 61.1 percent of the vote to Republican Barry Goldwater's 38.5 percent and won by about 15.9 million votes. Johnson's margin surpassed the previous record set in 1936 when Franklin Roosevelt defeated Republican challenger Alfred M. Landon, 60.8 percent to 36.5 percent for an 11.1 million-vote margin.

Harding received 60.3 percent of the popular vote for a margin of 7.0 million over Democrat James M. Cox. Nixon took 60.7 percent for a 17.9 million-vote margin over Democrat George S. McGovern. Nixon's popular-vote margin was the largest ever.

Roosevelt's 523 ELECTORAL COLLEGE vote total in 1936 (out of the total 531 at the time, when there were only forty-eight states) remains the largest electoral vote percentage (98.5) after George Washington's 100 percent in 1789.

Republican Ronald Reagan won 525 electoral votes in his 1984 defeat of Democrat Walter F. Mondale, but Reagan's 97.6 percent of the 538 electoral vote total still ranked behind Roosevelt's record share.

Reagan's two presidential victories are often called landslides, but both fell short of the 60 percent benchmark. Reagan defeated incumbent Democrat Jimmy Carter with 50.7 percent or a margin of 8.4 million in 1980, and he was reelected with 58.8 percent in 1984, for a margin of 16.8 million votes over Mondale.

The Electoral College system, which requires an ABSOLUTE MAJORITY for presidential election, tends to exaggerate the margin of success. The right combination of large-state victories can turn a popular vote plurality into an electoral vote landslide. For

Lyndon B. Johnson's 61.1 percent of the popular vote in 1964 is the record for the highest margin in U.S. presidential elections.

Source: LBJ Library photo by Yoichi R. Okamoto

More on this topic:

Mandate, p. 310

---

example, in 1996 Democrat Bill Clinton won reelection over Republican Bob Dole with only 49.2 percent of the popular vote. But Clinton won 379 of the 538 electoral votes, or 70.4 percent. (See table, "Minority" Presidents, page 180.)

Landslide presidents sometimes claim a MANDATE from the voters to carry out whatever program they promised during the campaign. Frequently, however, the mandate is not clear or the victory turns sour for some reason, cutting short the president's tenure. This was the case with Johnson, who decided against seeking another term in 1968, largely because of widespread dissent over his escalation of U.S. military involvement in Vietnam following his 1964 win, and with Nixon, who resigned less than two years after being reelected in 1972, because of his personal involvement in the Watergate SCANDAL cover-up. Corruption scandals affecting close political associates also likely would have prevented Harding from winning reelection, had he not died in office in 1923.

◉ CLOSER LOOK

Watershed Elections

The term *watershed election* is heard from time to time in discussions of election outcomes that change—or appear to change—the direction of American politics. In some cases, these watersheds occur as the result of overwhelming landslide victories by one party. But the terms *watershed* and *landslide* are not necessarily synonymous: some close elections end up having long-lasting and sweeping consequences, while some landslides end up having relatively ephemeral impacts on larger political trends.

Democrat Franklin D. Roosevelt's lopsided 1932 victory was a landslide that made lasting changes to the nation's political landscape. Spurred by the Great Depression, which created a public backlash against the administration of Republican Herbert Hoover and a Congress long controlled by the Republicans, Roosevelt's first in a series of four presidential election victories—a feat without parallel in U.S. history—ushered in an era of Democratic Party dominance that lasted, with a few relatively brief interruptions, for more than a half century.

A 1964 landslide victory by Democratic incumbent Lyndon B. Johnson over Republican Barry Goldwater appeared to be a watershed, strengthening a new era of government intervention on behalf of the poor and minorities. Johnson trounced Goldwater by 61 percent to 38 percent and 486 electoral votes to 52. Yet within four years, rancorous national divisions over Johnson's escalation of the U.S. military presence in Vietnam and a conservative backlash against his "big government" program forced the president to forgo a bid for reelection and enabled Republican Richard M. Nixon to capture the White House.

Nixon in turn appeared to win a potential watershed reelection victory in 1972. En route to taking 60 percent of the popular vote and winning a 49-state electoral rout—Democrat George McGovern won only Massachusetts and the District of Columbia—Nixon employed a "southern strategy" of appealing to white conservatives in the South that enabled him to win all eleven states of the Old Confederacy. No Republican since the post–Civil War Reconstruction era had won even a majority of those states. But Nixon's downfall in the Watergate scandal, which forced him to resign from office in August 1974—and the Democrats' nomination of former Georgia governor Jimmy Carter for president in 1976—delayed the lasting shift of the South from a solid Democratic bastion to a Republican stronghold, something that did not take root until 1980.

Republican Ronald Reagan's 1980 victory over Democratic incumbent Jimmy Carter was more of an electoral-vote landslide (489 to 49) than a popular-vote landslide (51 percent to 41 percent). But Reagan's win was consequential, marking the rise of a more ideological form of conservatism than had previously been seen in the Republican Party and effectively checking the era of federal government activism that began with Roosevelt in the 1930s.

One of the greatest watershed elections of all time—Republican Abraham Lincoln's 1860 victory that immediately preceded and to a great extent precipitated the Civil War—can hardly be described as a popular-vote landslide. Lincoln, the first Republican to win the White House, took 39.9 percent of the national popular vote in an unusual four-way race. Democrat Stephen A. Douglas ran second with 29.9 percent. Lincoln's sweep of the northern and far western states, however, did give him a substantial electoral-vote margin. Lincoln won 180 electoral votes, well above the 152 needed to win an absolute majority. Douglas, despite finishing second to Lincoln in the popular-vote tally, won just 12 electoral votes. That was fourth overall, behind Southern Democratic candidate John C. Breckinridge (72) and Constitutional Union candidate John Bell (39), whose sectional appeal enabled them to outpoll Douglas in the Electoral College.

Liberal   *See* IDEOLOGY.

Liberal Party of New York   *See* THIRD PARTIES.

LaRouche Movement (U.S. Labor Party, 1973–   )

Lyndon LaRouche, a self-taught economist who worked in the management and computer fields, first came to public attention in 1968 as a founder of the National Caucus of Labor Committees (NCLC), a Marxist group organized by splinters of the radical movements of the 1960s. After a series of efforts to dominate the NCLC, in which he and his followers were accused of acts of intimidation, LaRouche split off in 1973 to found the U.S. Labor Party. Running for president in 1976 on the U.S. Labor ticket, New Yorker LaRouche picked Wayne Evans, a Detroit steelworker, as his vice presidential RUNNING MATE.

The party directed much of its fire at the Rockefellers, one of the nation's wealthiest families. It charged that banks controlled by the Rockefellers were strangling the U.S. and world economies. In an apocalyptic vein, the party predicted a world monetary collapse by election day and the destruction of the country by thermonuclear war by the summer of 1977.

LaRouche's party developed a reputation for harassment because of its shouted interruptions and demonstrations against its political foes, including the COMMUNIST PARTY and the United Auto Workers. It accused some left-wing organizations and individuals, such as linguist Noam Chomsky and Marcus Raskin and his Institute for Policy Studies, of conspiring with the Rockefellers and the Central Intelligence Agency.

During the 1976 presidential campaign, LaRouche was more critical of Democratic challenger Jimmy Carter than of Republican incumbent Gerald R. Ford. He depicted Ford as a well-meaning man out of his depth in the presidency, but Carter as a pawn of nuclear war advocates and a disgracefully unqualified presidential candidate. LaRouche captured only 40,043 votes, less than 0.1 percent of the national vote. He was on the ballot in twenty-three states and the District of Columbia.

Lyndon LaRouche ran for president eight times between 1976 and 2004, primarily as a Democrat but also in the 1970s under the U.S. Labor Party banner.

Source: AP Images/Charles Dharapak

Although the U.S. Labor Party did not run a presidential candidate in the 1980 election, LaRouche ran a strident campaign—as a Democrat. By this time, LaRouche's politics had shifted to the right, and his speeches were fraught with warnings of conspiracy.

He continued his crusade in 1984 but as an "independent Democrat," dismissing Democratic presidential nominee Walter F. Mondale as an "agent of Soviet influence." LaRouche received 78,807 votes, or 0.1 percent of the vote.

In 1988 LaRouche again attempted to run for president as a Democrat but, failing to gain serious attention in the nominating process, garnered 25,562 votes in the general election under the banner of the National Economic Recovery Party. On December 16, 1988, LaRouche and six of his associates were convicted on forty-seven counts of mail fraud and conspiracy to commit mail fraud related to fund-raising activities. LaRouche, who declared himself a political prisoner, was sentenced to fifteen years in prison, of which he ultimately served less than six.

In 1992 the unflagging LaRouche ran again for president from his jail cell. As a convicted felon, he no longer had the right to vote himself. LaRouche ran as an independent, although his name appeared on several state ballots under various party names, including Economic Recovery. His supporters, experienced in winning ballot access, placed him on the ballot in seventeen states and the District of Columbia. He received 26,333 votes nationwide.

Since then, LaRouche has focused his efforts as a presidential candidate on the Democratic primaries. Though never competitive, he has received more votes in this venue that he ever did as a general election candidate. In 2004, for example, he received 104,793 votes, which still was a minuscule fraction of the 16.2 million votes cast in the primaries. He did not appear on 2008 ballots.

Liberal Republican Party (1872)

When Republican Ulysses S. Grant decided to run for a second term as president in 1872, it was certain that he would be renominated. But a faction of the REPUBLICAN PARTY, dissatisfied with corruption scandals and other issues in Grant's first term, split off to form a new party, the Liberal Republicans, which did not last past that year's elections.

Composed of party reformers, anti-Grant politicians, and newspaper editors, the new party focused on the corruption of the Grant administration and demanded an overhaul of the civil service system and an end to the post–Civil War Reconstruction policy in the South.

Newspaper editor Horace Greeley was the only presidential nominee of the short-lived Liberal Republican Party.

Source: Library of Congress

The call for the Liberal Republican NATIONAL PARTY CONVENTION came from the state party in Missouri, known as the birthplace of the reform movement. The convention, meeting in Cincinnati, Ohio, in May 1872, nominated Horace Greeley, editor of the *New York Tribune*, for president and Missouri governor B. Gratz Brown as his RUNNING MATE.

Greeley was a prominent figure in American public life in the mid-1800s, most famed for admonishing those seeking opportunity to "Go West, young man, go West." But Greeley, the choice of anti-Grant politicians but suspect among reformers, was not popular among many Democrats either, who recalled his longtime criticism of the DEMOCRATIC PARTY.

Yet the Democrats, still struggling in the aftermath of the Civil War that had decimated their party's strong political base in the South, eschewed nominating their own candidate. In July the Democratic National Convention endorsed the Liberal Republican ticket and platform. The COALITION was an unsuccessful one, as many Democrats refused to vote for Greeley. He received 2,834,761 votes (43.8 percent of the POPULAR VOTE) but carried only six states and lost to Grant by more than 750,000 votes out of nearly 6.5 million cast. Greeley died shortly after the election.

Underfinanced, poorly organized, and dependent on the Democrats for their success, the Liberal Republicans went out of existence after the 1872 election.

Libertarian Party (1971–)

The Libertarian Party emerged in the early 1970s as a manifestation of a growing sense among many Americans that government had grown too big and had overreached its authority, stifling the individual freedoms that these citizens professed were responsible for the nation's greatness.

This philosophy has enabled the Libertarians to maintain a presence in American politics for more than three decades. But the party's influence on elections has been limited in an era in which the nation's politics have been dominated by liberals associated mainly with the Democratic Party and conservatives tied to the Republican Party. Some of the Libertarian Party's positions on social and foreign policy issues might appeal to liberal activists, while some conservatives might find much to agree with in the party's positions against government spending and regulation. But the sharp divisions between these two factions leave little room for common ground under the Libertarian umbrella.

By the end of the 2000s, however, the emergence of the Tea Party movement suggested that much of the Libertarians' philosophy remained vigorous among some segments of voters. The Tea Party was not actually a political party but rather a confluence of distrust of the federal government and antitax fervor that energized the 2010 midterm elections and contributed to a Republican resurgence that allowed the GOP to recapture control of the House. Although often identified as exceptionally conservative voters largely sympathetic to the Republican Party, many of the views voiced by Tea Party advocates put them in the same political corner as Libertarians.

Individual responsibility and minimal government interference are the hallmarks of the Libertarian philosophy. The party, though not all of its members, has favored repeal of laws against so-called victimless crimes—such as pornography, drug use, and homosexual activity—as well as the abolition of all federal police agencies and the elimination of all government subsidies to private enterprise. In foreign and military affairs, the Libertarians have advocated removing U.S. troops from abroad, cutting the defense budget, and positioning the United States as a "giant Switzerland," with no international treaty obligations. Many of these propositions go beyond the views held even in the liberal wing of the Democratic Party and are anathema to many conservatives.

Much more appealing to those on the right are the Libertarians' views in favor of repealing legislation that they believe hinders individual or corporate action. The party, though again not all of its members, has opposed gun control, certain civil rights laws, price controls on oil and gas, labor protection laws, federal welfare and poverty programs, forced busing, compulsory education, Social Security, government-run health care, and federal land-use restrictions. Most of these stands are nonstarters for liberals and even many centrist voters.

Former Libertarian presidential candidate Ron Paul, a House member from Texas, was one of four principal candidates for the Republican presidential nomination in early-2012.

Source: CQ Photo/Scott J. Ferrell

The Libertarian Party's inability to peel away many votes from the Democratic and Republican parties is underscored by the vote numbers achieved by the party in the nine presidential elections in which it participated through 2008.

Formed in Colorado in 1971, the party nominated John Hospers of California for president in 1972. On the ballot only in Colorado and Washington, Hospers garnered 3,673 votes (including WRITE-IN votes from other states). But he received a measure of national attention when a Republican presidential elector from Virginia, Roger MacBride, cast his electoral vote for the Libertarian presidential nominee.

MacBride's action made him a hero in Libertarian circles, and the party nominated him for president in 1976. Although he appeared on the ballot in 32 states, MacBride received just 173,011 votes, or 0.2 percent of the national vote. His RUNNING MATE was David P. Bergland, a California lawyer.

The 1980 election was the high point to date, albeit a modest one, for the Libertarian Party, which appeared on the ballot in all fifty states and the District of Columbia for the first time. The party nominees, Edward E. Clark of California for president and David Koch of New York for vice president, garnered 921,299 votes or 1.1 percent of the vote nationwide. As in past elections, the major support for the Libertarians came from western states.

Since then, however, Libertarian presidential nominees have not even come close to breaking 1 percent of the total vote, although in the four national elections from 1996 through 2008 the party drew an increasing following, reaching a high total of 523,715 votes in 2008.

In 1988 the Libertarian presidential and vice presidential nominees—former Texas Republican representative Ron Paul and Andre V. Marrou, respectively—were on the ballot in forty-seven jurisdictions and received 432,179 votes, or just less than one-half of 1 percent. When Paul, a physician, decided to try to return to Congress, which he did successfully in 1996, it was as a Republican, though he maintained much of his libertarian approach: Paul's consistent and often lonely opposition to federal spending bills earned him the nickname "Dr. No." Paul also campaigned for the 2008 and 2012 Republican nominations for president, though his contrarian views harkened back to his libertarian past.

The 2004 Libertarian presidential candidate, Michael Badnarik, received 397,367 popular votes, or 0.34 percent of the total. Badnarik, a software engineer from Austin, Texas, ran on a ticket with Richard Campagna, an Iowa businessman and lawyer.

Libertarian candidates have won some state- and local-level races, and occasionally they influence the outcome of congressional elections, even when they win a relatively small percentage of the vote. For example, in a 2006 Senate race in Montana, Democratic challenger Jon Tester took 49.2 percent of the total vote to unseat Republican incumbent Conrad Burns, who received 48.3 percent. The 2.3 percent of the vote taken by Libertarian candidate Stan Jones exceeded the 0.9 percentage point difference between Tester and Burns.

Liberty Party (1839–1848)

Established in 1839, the Liberty Party was the product of a split in the antislavery movement between a faction led by William Lloyd Garrison that favored action outside the political process and a second led by James G. Birney that proposed action within the political system through the establishment of an independent antislavery party. The Birney faction launched the Liberty Party in November 1839. The following April a NATIONAL PARTY CONVENTION with DELEGATES from six states nominated Birney for president.

Although the Liberty Party was the first political party to take an antislavery position, most abolitionist voters in the 1840 election supported the Democratic or Whig presidential candidates. Birney received only 6,797 votes (0.3 percent of the popular vote).

Aided by the controversy over the U.S. annexation of slaveholding Texas, the Liberty Party's popularity increased in 1844. Birney, again the party's presidential nominee, received 62,103 votes (2.3 percent of the popular vote) but, as in 1840, carried no states. The peak strength of the party was reached two years later in 1846, when in various state elections Liberty Party candidates received 74,017 votes.

In October 1847 the party nominated New Hampshire senator John P. Hale for president, but his candidacy was withdrawn the following year when the Liberty Party joined the broader-based FREE SOIL PARTY.

James G. Birney, twice the nominee of the Liberty Party, failed to carry a state in 1840 or 1844 on an antislavery platform.

Source: Library of Congress

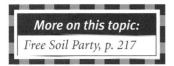

More on this topic:

Free Soil Party, p. 217

Lieutenant Governor

The lieutenant governor of a state is roughly the equivalent of the U.S. VICE PRESIDENT. His or her most important duty is to be prepared to take over as chief executive should the governorship become vacant.

As the "standby" GOVERNOR, the lieutenant governor has been the butt of jokes about the job's lack of substance. "I'm the lieutenant governor," Calvin Coolidge once told a Massachusetts woman who asked his occupation. When she excitedly asked him to tell her all about it, Coolidge replied, "I just did."

But the job in most states today is more rewarding and challenging than it was in Coolidge's day. States have added to the lieutenant governor's duties and responsibilities, just as modern presidents have found more meaningful tasks for their vice presidents than flying to funerals of foreign dignitaries. In many states, governors are empowered to assign executive tasks to the lieutenant governor.

In contrast to the past when lieutenant governor was a part-time job in the legislative branch, it is now a full-time job in most of the states that have the position. Twelve states have placed the lieutenant governor entirely in the executive branch. Like the vice president, who is president of the U.S. Senate, the lieutenant governor in most states presides over the state senate and votes only to break a tie.

Yet despite these increased responsibilities in many states, the lieutenant governor often is consigned to a relatively low-profile role. So while some lieutenant governors have later moved up to the governor's office, they are in the minority. Only a special few start their gubernatorial bids with "heir apparent" status.

For example, there were thirty-eight races for governor in 2006. The winners in only four of the races were former lieutenant governors, and three of them—Republicans M. Jodi Rell of

C. L. "Butch" Otter, the Republican governor of Idaho, was one of only four former lieutenant governors elected in 2006, when thirty-eight gubernatorial races were held.

Source: CQ Photo/Scott J. Ferrell

Connecticut, Dave Heineman of Nebraska, and Rick Perry of Texas—had filled vacancies in the governor's office prior to their first gubernatorial contests. The other former lieutenant governor to win a 2006 race for governor, Idaho Republican C. L. "Butch" Otter, served six years in the U.S. House between his tenure in the lower office and his election to the higher office.

The four major-party nominees who sought to move up directly from lieutenant governor—Republican Kerry Healey of Massachusetts and Democrats Lucy Baxley of Alabama, Mark Taylor of Georgia, and Charlie Fogarty of Rhode Island—all were defeated. Each of the three Democrats who lost were from SPLIT-TICKET states and lost to the incumbent Republican governors: Bob Riley in Alabama, Sonny Perdue in Georgia, and Donald Carcieri in Rhode Island.

As of mid-2011, forty-three states had an office of lieutenant governor, who in each case was the next in line should a vacancy occur in the governor's office. In twenty-four states, the governor and lieutenant governor are elected on a party ticket. In the other eighteen, though, the governor and lieutenant governor run separately, making it possible for a governor of one party and a lieutenant governor of another party to serve together. In addition, other states had the equivalent of a lieutenant governor. In Arizona, Oregon, and Wyoming, the secretary of state serves the function. In Maine, New Hampshire, Tennessee, and West Virginia, the president of the senate does.

Feuds between the governor and lieutenant governor are not unusual. Some state constitutions provide that the lieutenant governor becomes acting governor when the governor is outside the state, which can lead to mischief or worse if the two leaders are not on good terms.

When Edmund G. "Jerry" Brown Jr. was the Democratic governor of California in the early 1980s, he had a Republican lieutenant governor, Mike Curb, who would embarrass Brown by making appointments or issuing executive orders while the governor was absent. Other governors have had the same experience.

After Lt. Gov. Jim Guy Tucker succeeded Bill Clinton as Arkansas governor in 1992, he was invited to Clinton's inauguration as president of the United States. While Tucker was in Washington, the acting governor, senate president pro tem and fellow Democrat Jerry Jewell, pardoned two prison inmates. Later, while Tucker was in Minnesota, his Republican lieutenant governor, Mike Huckabee, signed a heritage week proclamation that Tucker had declined to sign. Tucker himself was forced from office by his conviction in connection with the Whitewater SCANDAL; Huckabee became governor by succession and went on to hold the office for more than ten years, twice winning election in his own right.

The first woman elected lieutenant governor was Democrat Mary Anne Krupsak of New York, in 1974. Another woman had earlier served as lieutenant governor, but she had been appointed to fill an unexpired term.

More on this topic:

Governor, p. 233

Literacy Tests

In the South during much of the twentieth century, literacy tests were among methods used to limit the FRANCHISE, or right to vote, to whites. Other such devices included the POLL TAX, complex VOTER REGISTRATION laws, and supposedly private WHITE PRIMARIES.

Under the literacy test method, voters were required to read aloud and/or write a passage correctly—usually a section of the state or federal Constitution. Sometimes, voters who could not pass the test could have the material read to them, to see if they could "understand" or "interpret" it correctly. This allowed local voting officials, inevitably whites, to judge whether voters passed the tests and usually resulted in whites passing and blacks failing.

As descendants of former slaves, many African Americans also had difficulty answering questions about family background, age, and birthplace. Their often-illiterate forebears may not have had access to such information or kept records. Some southern states passed so-called GRANDFATHER CLAUSES that exempted most whites from the literacy test because they—unlike many blacks—could show that their ancestors were eligible to vote in 1866. The Supreme Court ruled in *Guinn v. United States* (1915) that grandfather clauses violated the Fifteenth Amendment, ratified in 1870, that forbade denial of the RIGHT TO VOTE on account of "race, color, or previous condition of servitude." It was the first voting rights decision based on a law's discriminatory aspects.

Earlier, in *Williams v. Mississippi* (1898), the Court had upheld literacy tests as a qualification. Henry Williams was an African American indicted for murder by an all-white grand jury chosen from the pool of registered voters. All had passed a literacy test, which Williams contended was an unconstitutional requirement because it allowed discrimination in voting registration and therefore violated his equal protection rights under the Fourteenth Amendment. The Court, however, ruled that the Mississippi voting laws did not on their face discriminate but rather were used administratively for a discriminatory result.

For decades afterward the literacy tests went unchallenged. But as more blacks became educated and able to pass the tests, some southern states supplemented the "understanding and interpretation" requirements for registration. Voters had to meet standards of good citizenship, good character, and other subjective qualifications.

In 1959 in a North Carolina case, *Lassiter v. Northampton County Board of Elections*, the Supreme Court upheld the state's right to ensure an independent and intelligent electorate. How the state achieved that objective was outside its purview, the Court said.

More on this topic:
Franchise, p. 215
Grandfather Clause, p. 241
Poll Taxes, p. 426
Right to Vote, p. 549
Voter Registration, p. 653
Voting Rights Act, p. 663
White Primary, p. 674

Gradually, however, literacy tests and other formal and informal bars to voting in the South began to fall. In *Louisiana v. United States* (1965) the Court struck down Louisiana's understanding and interpretation test, calling it "not a test but a trap." The same year Congress in the VOTING RIGHTS ACT banned literacy tests and other interference with the right to vote.

Within five years, two-thirds of all southern blacks were registered, and the number of black elected officials began to climb. By 1993 there were almost eight thousand African American officials in the United States, more than half of them in the eleven states of the Old Confederacy: Alabama, Arkansas, Florida, Georgia, Louisiana, Mississippi, North Carolina, South Carolina, Tennessee, Texas, and Virginia.

M

Mandate

Mandates are usually associated with LANDSLIDE victories, particularly in presidential elections. A candidate who wins big is said to have a mandate to carry out the will of the people as expressed in the election results. In some elections, weaker candidates on the same party ticket also win, riding into office on the winner's COATTAILS.

Democratic incumbent Lyndon B. Johnson's overwhelming defeat of Republican Barry Goldwater in the 1964 presidential election, for example, was interpreted by the president and his supporters in the Democratic-controlled Congress as a go-ahead for Johnson to pursue his ambitious domestic-spending agenda that was labeled the Great Society. Although Johnson was largely successful with his legislative program, his coinciding pursuit of unpopular Vietnam War policies eventually undercut whatever mandate he may have had. He declined to seek reelection in 1968.

It is not clear, in any case, what margin of victory constitutes a mandate, or what exactly the mandate was if there was one. Democrat John F. Kennedy did not hesitate to claim a mandate for his campaign agenda after his 1960 election as president, even though his margin of victory over Republican Richard M. Nixon in 1960 was razor thin. The very fact that he won—even if it had been by one vote—was taken by Kennedy as a mandate, according to his aide, Theodore Sorensen.

Similarly, George W. Bush interpreted his 2000 victory as a mandate for conservative priorities, such as tax cuts, even though he lost the POPULAR VOTE to Al Gore and Democrats picked up seats in Congress. Bush again claimed a mandate in 2002, but this time with more justification: he helped steer his party in the MIDTERM ELECTION to gains in the House and Senate.

Presidents who win without landslide margins take a political risk in assuming a mandate. There may be no better example of that than Bush himself, following his 2004 election to a second term as president.

Despite defeating Democratic challenger John Kerry, a senator from Massachusetts, by just 2.4 percentage points, Bush declared a broad mandate for his policies. "When you win, there is a feeling that people have spoken and embraced your point of view," Bush said at a news conference two days after he won the contest. "And that's what I intend to tell Congress: that I made it clear what I intend to do as the president and the people made it clear what they wanted."

But the election may not have been as much of a ratification as Bush suggested; his victory was at least in part the result of Kerry's diffident image and stumbles as a challenger. The continuing war in Iraq, launched in March 2003 and already becoming unpopular by November 2004, deeply eroded Bush's popularity and the "political capital" he assumed he had after his reelection. His top domestic agenda priority during his reelection campaign, a controversial proposal to make major changes to the Social Security system, went nowhere in Congress in the face of strong Democratic opposition and tepid Republican support.

Exacerbated by his administration's mishandling of the crisis on the Gulf Coast following the devastation

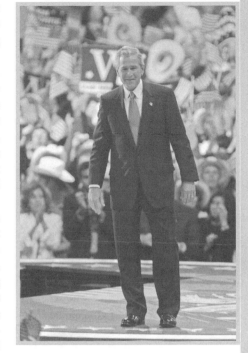

President George W. Bush at the 2004 Republican National Convention. Bush declared a broad mandate for his policies after modest victories in the 2000, 2002, and 2004 elections.

Source: CQ Photo/Scott J. Ferrell

wreaked by Hurricane Katrina in August 2005, Bush's job approval numbers plummeted and never recovered by the time of the 2006 midterm elections—contributing to the Republican Party's loss of its majorities in both the Senate and the House. Bush's continuing decline in popular support helped boost Democrats in 2008, allowing them to enlarge congressional margins and win the White House under Barack Obama.

What the real or imagined mandate implied can be difficult to interpret. Campaign promises nevertheless offer some indication of what the mandate was about, if indeed there was one. Although the public dismisses such promises as so much campaign oratory, successful candidates do try to act on them. Political scientist Jeff Fishel found that presidents from Kennedy through Republican Ronald Reagan's first term twenty years later tried through bills or executive orders to make good on about two-thirds of their campaign pledges.

But candidates do not always indicate clearly what their policies will be once elected. Kennedy's promise to "get this country moving again," for example, was vague enough to cover a wide range of voters' hopes but gave little indication of the policies he intended to follow to achieve economic growth.

Even when candidates are clear about their intentions, the voters may base their decisions on other grounds. In 1980 Reagan was forthcoming with specific proposals on taxation, government expenditures, and national security policy. PUBLIC OPINION surveys, however, indicated that the voters did not base their decisions on Reagan's conservative policies. Rather, the election was primarily a case of RETROSPECTIVE VOTING—a referendum on the performance of Democrat Jimmy Carter's unpopular administration, particularly its handling of the economy.

Much the same dynamic was in play in 2008 when Obama was elected. Although as the first African American ever nominated with a legitimate chance to win the presidency he generated great excitement among his supporters, the voters were looking back on the record of the Bush administration and—especially—the economic crises into which the nation and the world had fallen. When a huge housing bubble burst starting about mid 2007, it nearly took down the economy with it. Major Wall Street investment banks failed, America's premier auto companies nearly went bankrupt, the economy plunged into a deep recession, and unemployment soared to over 10 percent. Obama and his fellow Democrats took every opportunity to remind the voters of the grief that had occurred on the watch of the Republican president, even if the actual events had many other causes and Bush, against his basically conservative instincts, took aggressive steps to offset the economic crash.

The meaning of signals the voters send in congressional elections is even harder to discern. With so many issues and so many different voter groups involved, parties and candidates tend to collect votes for different, and even conflicting, reasons.

In the MIDTERM ELECTION of 1994, the voters seemed to be giving a mandate to the Republicans and their conservative "Contract with America" agenda. Although the president's party almost always loses seats at midterm, the Democrats' loss of fifty-two House seats was the greatest in five decades. But some political analysts then, and others looking at the election in retrospect, have played down the impact of the Contract with America. They view the 1994 Republican upsurge as a rebuke to Democrat Bill Clinton, then midway through the first of his two terms as president, and a long-standing Democratic congressional majority that had endured numerous ethics controversies.

The Republican-controlled Congress was able to enact some of the Contract with America over the next two years. Parts of the contract were passed on a bipartisan basis with Clinton's help, but others were not, notably constitutional amendment proposals for congressional TERM LIMITS and a mandatory balanced budget.

The Republicans' conservative congressional leaders' pursuit of their "small government" fiscal agenda led to a brief shutdown of the federal government at the end of the first year of the GOP majority. In that showdown with Clinton, the president came out ahead in public opinion. The GOP's aggressive effort to relax some federal health, safety, and environmental regulations—proposed as an effort to undo overly costly burdens to the economy—spurred a voter backlash that played into Clinton's hands and also eroded the GOP majority's claim of a mandate. By the end of Clinton's first term both sides could claim successes. Clinton was reelected, but the Republicans retained control of Congress.

The electorate in 1994, 1996, and 1998 appeared to be endorsing the concept of divided government rather than any specific legislative agenda. Although many had decried the twelve years of deadlock between Republican presidents and a Democratic Congress, the voters ordered a return to divided government (albeit with the parties reversed) to have the White House and Congress serve as a check on one another. That in itself may have been a form of mandate.

Voters appeared to change course in the 2002 election, bucking a long-term trend of voting against the president's party in the midterm elections. Instead, they gave clear control of both chambers of Congress to Republicans, who were perceived as more effective in dealing with threats such as terrorism.

It did not take long for the nation to return to divided government, however. Democrats staged a political comeback in 2006 and took control of both chambers of Congress, presenting President Bush a hostile legislature to deal with during the final two years of his presidency. Yet during their successful 2006 effort, Democratic Party leaders—though challenged by Republicans to come up with their own version of the Contract with America—eschewed a document of specific legislative proposals. When the Democrats won, they claimed a more limited mandate to clean up corruption in Congress and enact some of the party's more popular goals, such as increasing the minimum wage.

But in the next two elections, 2008 and 2010, the nation experienced another upheaval with some echoes of the 1990s. Democrats won full and solid control of the federal government in 2008 by enlarging a congressional majority to a nearly iron grasp and took the White House as well. Much of the outcome was driven by the economic recession and soaring unemployment that dominated political debate in the months before the election. But whether the results on election day were a mandate for Obama and his allies was not clear even though his administration chose to consider it one.

Democrats in the 111th Congress, which began in January 2009, put forth an aggressive program of legislation, some in direct response to the recession (such as a multibillion stimulus spending program and tighter regulation of financial institutions) and some to fulfill long-standing agenda items of the party's progressive wing. None was more dramatic than a two-year battle over sweeping reforms of the nation's health care system. Its provisions wonderfully pleased some segments of voters and deeply angered others. Perhaps the single most controversial part was a mandate requiring all Americans to purchase health insurance from private companies or pay a fine. Many voters, generally conservative and largely Republican, considered this a vast overreaching by the government. The anger over the health care legislation, combined with continuing discontent in various voter circles over government spending, immigration, the ongoing wars in the Middle East, perceived bailouts of banks and auto companies, a tepid economic recovery, and other issues, laid the foundation for a backlash in the 2010 midterm elections that allowed Republicans to gain sixty-three House seats and control of the chamber. Many of the freshmen who came to Washington were identified with the Tea Party movement that supplied the same energy in 2010 that the legions of Obama supporters supplied in 2008. Depending on an observer's political perspective, the 2010 election was a repudiation, or not, of the claimed mandate that the Democrats took into the 111th Congress.

More on this topic:

Landslide, p. 301

Midterm Election, p. 333

Public Opinion, p. 502

Retrospective Voting, p. 547

Mandatory Voting *See* INTERNATIONAL AND U.S. ELECTIONS COMPARED.

Media Coverage of Campaigns

There is much about elections that is exciting, at least if you are a politically engaged citizen. The opportunity to do volunteer work in a campaign that you believe in. The chance to shake hands with a well-known candidate. The color and hoopla of the nominating conventions. And, finally, the suspense on election night as the names of the winners and losers are revealed.

On the other hand, there is much about elections that the public finds boring. The long speeches. The NEGATIVE CAMPAIGNING that seems to get nastier and more prevalent with every election. The constant appeals for money for this or that campaign. And, finally, the sheer duration of the campaign seasons, which are longer in the United States than in almost any other democratic country and perhaps much longer than they need to be to ensure that the voters have sufficient information to make intelligent choices. (See INTERNATIONAL AND U.S. ELECTIONS COMPARED; ZZZ.)

What separates the exciting from the boring is chiefly the presence or absence of drama, and that in turn helps to determine the amount of attention a campaign receives from the news media, especially television and the online media that in recent years have grown to compete with traditional print and broadcast outlets as the public's primary sources of political news. In the highly competitive news business, the media are looking for a larger audience share or greater readership.

Yet what the producers and editors and bloggers think will gain the most viewers or readers may have little to do with what the individual voters find exciting about politics and elections, or what they think they need to know about the candidates and their views on issues.

Because drama thrives on conflict, the news coverage often emphasizes the "horse race" aspects of an election, rather than the candidate's qualifications or positions on issues. Much of media coverage is driven by perceptions about "momentum" and about who is up and who is down, rather than by deep (and often complicated) analyses of the positions the candidates are taking on major public policy issues. Those perceptions are often based on the latest polls from a proliferating number of public opinion researcher companies, even though those firms have varied records of accuracy.

CAMPAIGN STRATEGY, competition, and error are emphasized at the expense of candidates' records and policy pronouncements. And few things become more damaging to a candidate's chances than media recycling of their campaign gaffes.

For example, John Kerry—the 2004 Democratic presidential challenger to Republican incumbent George W. Bush—was hindered by repeated references to his awkwardly phrased comment that he voted for legislation to fund the U.S. military engagements in Iraq and Afghanistan before he voted against it. What Kerry meant was that he voted against a Republican-sponsored bill that provided $87 billion for the wars without strings attached after voting for a Democratic-backed version of the measure that would have required that some of the spending be offset by rolling back tax cuts for wealthy Americans that had been enacted with Bush's strong backing. But his phrasing branded him with an image as a vacillator.

Kerry also was hurt by another media tendency in covering elections: its reporting of controversial and often-inflammatory campaign advertisements as news in and of themselves. A group called Swift Boat Veterans for Truth, made up mostly of conservative Vietnam War veterans and financed by wealthy conservative individuals and interest groups, initially ran a small and low-budget ad campaign questioning Kerry's touted record for heroism while serving in the Navy and attacking his actions as a high-profile war protester after his return from Vietnam. It was not until the media reported on the ads as news and broadcast the claims made that the Swift Boat campaign began to seriously tarnish Kerry's image, which in turn prompted the ad hoc political action committee to intensify the ad campaign, to which Kerry was very slow to respond.

Even Democrat Barack Obama, on his way to winning the 2008 presidential race, had to deal with political firestorms caused by the media's focus on his ties (which proved to be minimal) with a Chicago college professor who once was a member of the Vietnam-era leftist radical group Weather Underground and the former longtime minister of the church to which Obama belonged, who had issued a number of strongly worded statements critical of the nation's treatment of minorities and its foreign policy. And Obama's ultimately successful push to defeat New York senator Hillary Rodham Clinton for that year's Democratic nomination was slowed when the media gave major play to leaked comments he had made at a private event that economically struggling working-class people in rural Pennsylvania "cling to guns or religion or antipathy to people who aren't like them" to deal with their frustrations.

Yet Obama also benefited from the media's tendency to try to create a dramatic context for election contests by appearing to cast the candidates in roles, as though the campaign was a theatrical production.

Critics, including some from the camps of opposing candidates, said the national media was too credulous about the inspirational—some said messianic—image that the rhetorically gifted Obama projected with his themes of "hope" and "change" (and the historic nature of his bid to become the nation's first African American president).

But this "casting" tendency can hurt candidates too. While John McCain, the senator of Arizona who won the 2008 Republican presidential nomination, enjoyed positive press for his experiences as a Vietnam prisoner of war and his image as an independent-minded political maverick, he also had difficulty overcoming his media-shaped casting as a hot-tempered old man. Similarly, early in a 2000 presidential election that ended with a controversially narrow victory for Bush, Democratic candidate Al Gore, then the incumbent vice president, was labeled early on as a prevaricator who exaggerated his accomplishments and credentials (including the often-repeated but inaccurate suggestion that he had claimed to have invented the Internet). Bush, too, suffered from his casting in the role of an intellectual lightweight, but his profile as a more affable and engaging politician than the reputedly stiff Gore made many voters see Bush as the more appealing candidate.

This stereotyping of candidates often reaches its peak during media coverage of presidential DEBATES. Journalists covering debates are more concerned with who "won" than with the issues articulated. Issues are subordinated to personalities, and electoral outcomes focus on the individual's personal victory or defeat rather than on the process and its implications for the country, state, or region. Thus the media can impinge on the ability of candidates to set the policy agenda and articulate their positions.

The media's role in setting the terms for "victory" in a debate can be controversial. In 2000 Gore was regarded as much better versed on issues than Bush, so the media set up an expectation that Gore would dominate the debates. As a result, following the debates, Bush was viewed as having done better than expected by making a credible showing and avoiding major mistakes. Much of the discussion of Gore's performance focused on personal quirks, from his sighing and eye-rolling at some of Bush's statements during the first debate, to his strangely muted performance in the second debate, to his decision to stand and loom over Bush as the Republican candidate was answering a question during the third and final debate, staged in a "town hall" setting.

By exposing a flaw in the person's history the media can derail a candidacy long before the election. In 1972 Thomas Eagleton was forced to give up the Democratic vice presidential nomination after his past treatment for depression was disclosed. Democrats Gary Hart and Joseph Biden abandoned fledgling presidential bids in 1987 after receiving adverse publicity. Hart was caught in an extramarital relationship, and Biden had engaged in plagiarism.

More recently, in the early stages of the 2012 Republican presidential nominating campaign, the unexpected rise of businessman Herman Cain as a serious contender was halted as the result of heavily reported allegations (which he denied) that he had a long extramarital affair and had sexually harassed female co-workers in the past.

SCANDAL, however, is not necessarily the kiss of death to a campaign. In 1992 Arkansas governor Bill Clinton, with his wife Hillary at his side, weathered assertions by a woman named Gennifer Flowers that she had been Clinton's mistress for twelve years. And in 1996, on the day Clinton accepted the Democratic presidential nomination for the second time, the media disclosed that one of his chief POLITICAL CONSULTANTS, Dick Morris, had a long-term relationship with a prostitute.

At the same time, Clinton himself was still under investigation by an independent counsel for the Whitewater real estate scandal in Arkansas, was fending off a sexual assault civil suit by former Arkansas state employee Paula Jones, and was under fire for receiving illicit campaign contributions from foreign nationals. Yet he defeated Republican challenger Bob Dole by a wide margin, though his second term was disrupted by an even bigger scandal, stemming from his extramarital relationship with White House intern Monica Lewinsky, which ultimately led a Senate impeachment trial in which he was acquitted.

Scandals still make headlines, but their effect on elections is perhaps less predictable than in the past. One reason is that modern paid media advertising—and the campaign funds to use this means of communication—provide candidates with ways to bypass reporters and take their message directly to the people. Television, in particular, transformed electoral politics. Cutting across all socio-economic divisions, television reaches about 99 percent of all U.S. households. One study shows that as recently as 1982 more American homes had televisions than refrigerators or indoor plumbing.

Computers, too, especially since the rapid expansion of high-speed Internet access, became major communications conduits for political information. The pervasiveness of online information provides open-minded voters with the entire universe of political information and can offset the filtering, role-casting, and horse race tendencies of mainstream media coverage of elections. News services dedicated to analyzing whether statements by candidates and political groups were truthful, such as Politifact and Factcheck.org, also emerged to help voters cut through campaign rhetoric and information overload.

But the Internet also allows voters with already strong partisan and ideological leanings to target only those information sources that confirm and reinforce their views.

Internet news sites, at least in their bare-bones version, are relatively inexpensive to set up and operate, though many have blossomed into full-scale major media players themselves. One of these is Politico, a start-up based in the Washington, D.C., suburb of Arlington, Virginia, which was launched in January 2007. Its free website quickly emerged—in part because of an aggressive marketing and publicity strategy—as an online news source that, on the national media scene, quickly eclipsed traditional subscription-based political news outlets such as Congressional Quarterly and Roll Call (which merged in 2009 to become CQ-Roll Call), National Journal (home to well-known election forecaster Charlie Cook and his Cook Political Report), and The Hill.

These news organizations have been joined by numerous, small online organizations and even individual commentators, who operate web logs, or "blogs." This proliferation has helped set the tone of political news coverage.

The power of such websites was dramatically demonstrated early on, shortly after the 2002 elections, when Senate Republican leader Trent Lott made a remark that appeared to endorse segregationist policies. Neither television nor print organizations paid much attention to the remark at first, but several online commentators assailed Lott, helping set off a firestorm of criticism that culminated with the senator eventually resigning his leadership post.

Similarly, during the 2004 presidential campaign, a conservative blog site first raised serious questions about the authenticity of documents used in a CBS News report that purported to prove that President George W. Bush, as a young man in the early 1970s, had shirked the Air National Guard duty for which he had signed up during the time of the Vietnam War. Several experts said that the documents almost certainly were forgeries, and CBS retracted its report about two weeks after it was originally aired. The imbroglio also led to the firing or resignation of some senior CBS employees and hastened anchor Dan Rather's departure from the network.

The increasing influence of web-based media extended to incorporate video with the birth and rapid growth of sites such as YouTube. Probably the most outstanding case of a web-posted video influencing an election outcome in 2006 occurred in the Senate race in Virginia. Republican senator George Allen appeared to be holding off a serious challenge from Democrat Jim Webb until, at a Republican rally, he referred to a Webb campaign volunteer of Indian ancestry as "macaca," a French-derived slang for "monkey." The Webb backer posted the footage he recorded on You-Tube, from which it was picked up and heavily reported by the traditional media and other Internet sites. Allen later denied knowing this definition of the word and apologized. The incident sharply shifted the race's momentum toward Webb, whose narrow victory helped the Democrats take over the Senate. (See Reference Material, Political and Election-Related Websites, page 700.)

Video footage of the "macaca" incident was widely circulated on Internet sites such as YouTube and is thought to have been the downfall of Virginia senator George Allen's 2006 reelection campaign. Here, Allen speaks at a news conference in 2004.
Source: CQ Photo/Scott J. Ferrell

Types of Messages

There are times when candidate messages must be filtered, in whole or in part, through the journalistic media. Political scientists David Paletz and Robert Entman have identified three types of media content: unmediated messages, partially mediated messages, and mostly mediated messages. *Unmediated messages* are those, usually paid advertising, over which the candidates exercise total control. *Partially mediated messages* are those delivered in televised press conferences, debates, talk shows, interviews, and other formats where candidates cannot totally control the content. They may air their views but are constrained by the questioning of journalists or, in debates, the responses of opposing candidates. *Mostly mediated messages* are those that the candidates control the least, such as news stories that are constructed by the media about the candidate. (For discussion of unmediated messages, see POLITICAL ADVERTISING; for partially mediated messages, see DEBATES; MEDIA USE BY CAMPAIGNS.)

Paletz and Entman contend that mostly mediated messages have the greatest effect on PUBLIC OPINION precisely because the candidates do not appear to control their content. Candidates' campaign staffs therefore use a wide variety of techniques to try to influence such coverage, including timing and staging events, restricting reporters' access to the candidate, and controlling the flow of information from the campaign organization.

INCUMBENCY particularly lends itself to efforts to attract coverage through such activities. Only an incumbent president, for example, can schedule an event in the Rose Garden or the East Room of the White House or participate in foreign "summit meetings" as Richard Nixon did in 1972.

These "visuals" are often criticized for lack of substance and avoidance of issues. But journalists' efforts to expose their shallowness can backfire, as CBS's Lesley Stahl discovered in 1984. Ronald Reagan's strategists relied on emotional, visual advertising with lots of American flags flapping in the breeze, which gave rise to a famous episode in the continuing clash between political handlers and the press. In 1984 Stahl broadcast a hard-hitting report on alleged hypocrisy in the Reagan campaign. Her spot juxtaposed footage of a Reagan speech on mental disabilities

> ## "When the pictures are powerful and emotional, they override if not completely drown out the sound."
>
> —*White House aide Richard Darman,* commenting on a news report in 1984

given at a Special Olympics event with a voice-over pointing out that Reagan had cut funding for mental health. According to Stahl, White House aide Richard Darman subsequently called her to praise her work. The puzzled reporter replied, "Did you hear what I said? I killed you."

"You people in Televisionland haven't figured it out yet, have you?" Darman countered. "When the pictures are powerful and emotional, they override if not completely drown out the sound. Lesley, I mean it. Nobody heard you."

Later, when Stahl replayed the tapes with the sound turned off, she realized that she had prepared a "magnificent montage of Reagan in a series of wonderful, upbeat scenes, with flags, balloons, children, and adoring supporters—virtually an unpaid commercial."

The visual aspect of media coverage has greatly upped the ante for candidates. The Democratic Party and Obama's campaign organization turned the last night of the 2008 Democratic National Convention, at which the nominee gave his acceptance speech, into a highly telegenic outdoor spectacular held at the stadium that is the home field for the National Football League's Denver Broncos.

But there is hardly anything new about candidates using visual media to amplify their messages. Both as a challenger and as the incumbent, Bill Clinton proved adept at using visuals to obtain free publicity. He played the saxophone on the late-night *Arsenio Hall Show* while running for the 1992 Democratic presidential nomination. After he won it, he and RUNNING MATE Al Gore boarded buses for a much-photographed tour of several states, forsaking the traditional postconvention campaign break until Labor Day. In 1996 Clinton WHISTLE-STOPPED again, this time by train to the convention, evoking images of Harry S. Truman.

As president, Clinton gave new meaning to the term *photo op.* He tried to ensure that each time he faced the cameras, he would appear on the front page or the nightly news. Throughout his reelection campaign, the hands of pollsters and other consultants were evident in the Clinton strategy. Taking his cues from a 1995 Mark Penn poll, Clinton reportedly tailored remarks, gestures, and even his bearing to suit the public taste. Instead of strolling off Air Force One, he began striding off in a military manner.

In the emotional aftermath of the September 11, 2001, terrorist attacks, George W. Bush used symbolism adroitly to win favorable media coverage. Despite concerns about security, he made a powerful statement to the nation a few weeks after the attacks by standing on the pitcher's mound in Yankee Stadium and becoming the first president since Dwight D. Eisenhower in 1956 to throw the first ball of the World Series (a good athlete, Bush fired a strike). Amid mounting patriotic sentiment, Bush often appeared at events that featured American flags; one of his first appearances to drum up support for a tax proposal in 2003 was at a northern Virginia flag company.

Bill Clinton was skilled at obtaining free publicity, giving new meaning to the term "photo op" during his eight-year presidency.
Source: William J. Clinton Presidential Library

But too much stagecraft can at times backfire badly. In May 2003 Bush cut a heroic pose by copiloting a Navy jet to a landing on an aircraft carrier anchored off the California coast. After changing out of his flight suit, the president pronounced that "major combat operations" in the war in Iraq, which he launched two months earlier, had concluded; in the background was a banner that read, "Mission Accomplished." The event was initially seen as a brilliant photo op staged by the Bush political team, capturing footage that seemed destined to be highlighted in Bush's 2004 campaign ads. But the incident instead caused a political backlash; an unexpectedly strong anti-American insurgency and brutal sectarian violence following the removal of Iraqi dictator Saddam Hussein resulted in a U.S. commitment to Iraq that was much longer, deadlier, and more expensive than Bush had projected.

In May 2003 President George W. Bush announced the end of major combat operations in Iraq in a photo op that soon backfired.
Source: AP Images/J. Scott Applewhite

Along with the categories described by Paletz and Entman, there is another element that causes controversy in each election cycle: independent advertising expenditures by party organizations aimed at boosting a candidate's campaign that nonetheless, by law, cannot be coordinated with the candidate's campaign. While such expenditures are often highly beneficial to the candidate, outside ads can clash with the strategy and issues that the candidate has established for his or her own campaign—sometimes to the candidate's detriment.

For example, in October 2006 during the home stretch of a highly competitive Senate race in Tennessee, the Republican National Committee aired a television ad that sought to lampoon Democratic candidate Harold E. Ford Jr., a black member of Congress from Memphis. The ad included a young white actress who appears to direct a sexual advance toward Ford by suggestively whispering, "Harold, call me," and by winking into the camera. Democrats and other critics said that the ad had offensive racial overtones; Republican candidate Bob Corker agreed the ad was "tacky" and had "no place in this race." Despite the negative publicity that attended the ad's airing, it did not create much of a voter backlash against Corker, who narrowly defeated Ford in the November election.

Emphasis on the "Horse Race"

News stories about candidates and campaigns—the "mostly mediated" category—have become even more mediated in the past four decades. Instead of merely reporting the "who" and "what" of elections, today's reporters feel obliged to analyze events for their readers and viewers. They focus more than in the past on the "why" aspect, and in so doing they not only outline the competitors' agendas but also help to set them.

Political scientist Thomas E. Patterson discerned the changed pattern by comparing random *New York Times* front-page stories about presidential races from 1960 through 1992. He found that coverage of the Kennedy-Nixon race in 1960 was about equally balanced between stories on policy or issues and those on the horse race or strategic aspects of the contest. By 1972 as PRIMARIES began lengthening the nominating process, the emphasis had shifted heavily away from policy to strategy. Twenty years later, in coverage of the 1992 race between Democrat Clinton, Republican incumbent George H. W. Bush, and independent H. Ross Perot, more than 80 percent of the stories were about what the candidates were doing to move up in the race. While almost all the 1960 stories were descriptive, most of those in 1992 were attempts to analyze the campaign strategies, devoting little space to the candidates' statements (their unmediated messages).

Nor was the *New York Times* alone in its concentration on strategy in 1992. Another media scholar, Matthew Robert Kerbel, found that more than half the political stories on CNN and more than a third on ABC were strategy-based. "Collectively, the 1992 coverage amounted to a personalized, politicized, self-interested account of the election, running like a narrative through the campaign," Kerbel wrote.

In an informal study of five news sources, Kerbel found more of the same in 1996. After quoting at length a *Washington Post* account of a Dole trip to California, Kerbel said that it was "analysis with a vengeance . . . seen through the eyes of an observer intent on finding thematic significance in mundane political acts."

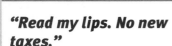

"Read my lips. No new taxes."

— Vice President George H. W. Bush's catchphrase in the 1988 presidential campaign

But Kerbel also found some self-conscious awareness in the media of too much strategy-based coverage. He noted that CBS News anchor Dan Rather went through a period where he tried to work the word "substance" into every election story. "But he said 'substance' when he really meant 'horse race,'" Kerbel commented.

Reporters usually do not find candidates' policy statements particularly newsworthy. They prefer pithy, slogan-like statements on issues that are clear-cut rather than complex and difficult to summarize. It has been argued, for example, that the 1988 presidential campaign reached a turning point when President George H.W. Bush (or his handlers) came up with the catchphrase, "Read my lips. No new taxes."

In that campaign between Bush, then the vice president, and Democrat Michael S. Dukakis, the governor of Massachusetts, strategists dealt with the "issues" by having their candidates visit a flag factory or ride in an army tank, or by raising racial fears in highlighting the case of Willie Horton, the black prisoner furloughed from a Massachusetts jail who fled to Maryland and raped a white woman, an incident that occurred during Dukakis's tenure as governor but with which he had no direct personal involvement.

It was then that substance hit an all-time low, according to veteran journalist Marvin Kalb, director of the Joan Shorenstein Center on the Press, Politics and Public Policy at Harvard University. The unfortunate "new fact of campaign life," he said, is that reporters are always looking for "small, behind-the-scenes issues of who's doing what to whom."

Dukakis recalled a time during the campaign when he gave a major environmental speech at Rutgers University, only to see the evening news focus instead on the flat tire one of his Secret Service cars got. "You can't blame consultants," Dukakis said. "It's the craziness of an election, and the media's incessant search for the new and the visual."

In 1996 Dole tumbled off a platform when a railing gave way as he was reaching down to shake hands with voters. He was not hurt, but it was the fall—not what he said that day—that made the evening TV news.

A different type of visual dominated news coverage of the 2000 presidential campaign for several days: a passionate kiss between Al Gore and his wife, Tipper, at the Democratic National Convention. Gore was widely perceived as stiff and distant, and commentators speculated whether the televised kiss would help humanize him in the eyes of voters.

(Gore did get a bounce in the polls, although it was not clear how much of that was a result of the kiss as opposed to the convention in general. The incident was recalled, with some irony, in 2010 when the Gores, long perceived as the almost-perfect political couple, announced that they were divorcing after forty years of marriage.)

So blasé are many in the media about what the candidate has to say—especially members of the traveling press corps, who hear the candidate's stock stump speech over and over—that it sometimes falls to outside observers to pick up on out-of-the-ordinary events. It was during Kerry's campaign for the May 2004 West Virginia primary that he attempted to simplify the highly nuanced matter about why he had voted for a Democratic version of a bill to fund military operations in Iraq and Afghanistan while opposing the successful Republican-drafted version. He did so by telling an audience that he had voted for the bill before voting against it. While the major media did not make an issue of the comment, a Republican campaign operative monitoring Kerry's speech did, and the party received substantial media coverage for its claim that the incident proved their argument that Kerry was a flip-flopper on important issues.

Media "Bias"

Candidates from all points on the IDEOLOGY spectrum have complained about the media's so-called bias. In complaining about liberal bias, Republicans cite surveys showing that reporters regularly vote for Democrats. Democrats though have complained about the subtle—and some-times not-so-subtle—pressure from conservative editorial boards and media owners on reporters in the field. The emergence of Fox News Channel—which uses "fair and balanced" as its slogan but has tended to strongly emphasize conservative viewpoints—has enabled Democrats to offset, to at least some extent, the claims that the media is overwhelmingly biased in their favor.

In fact, the media have been subject to increasing criticism in recent years from across the political spectrum that, out of fear of appearing biased, many media outlets give both sides equal time rather than seek to determine whether one side is more correct.

For much of the past few decades, the harshest media criticism has come from the right. GOP candidates repeatedly make derogatory references to the "liberal media." Long-time CBS news-man Bernard Goldberg scaled the top of the best-seller list with his 2001 book, *Bias*, detailing instances in which the television networks appeared to favor liberal causes. Following the 2000 and 2002 elections, however, Democrats grew increasingly alarmed over what they saw as the media's tilt toward the right. They worried that conservative commentators such as Rush Limbaugh and the perceived conservative leanings of Fox News Network were undercutting their party's message.

Media bias depends on the circumstances of the race. In 1980, for example, reporters appeared to treat Republican Ronald Reagan more favorably than Jimmy Carter, whose Democratic administration was plagued by the Iranian hostage crisis, high inflation, and other problems (although Republicans complained about frequent media references to Reagan's advanced age and concerns among some voters that his staunchly conservative rhetoric would lead to conflict with the Soviet Union, then a communist superpower). In 1992 the media produced more negative reports about Republican George H. W. Bush than Democrat Bill Clinton. The nonpartisan Center for Media and Public Affairs reported that 78 percent of Bush's preconvention coverage on the evening news was negative, compared with 59 percent of Clinton's. Bush, in fact, endured twenty-three consecutive weeks of negative coverage.

Dole in 1996 railed against the "liberal" media, declaring, "We're not going to let the media steal this election." And although a Freedom Forum–Roper Center survey of 139 reporters showed that 89 percent had voted for Clinton, most journalists, asserting their professionalism, defended their coverage as unbiased. The same press that Dole complained about, they noted, had disclosed the Clinton-Gore campaign's zealous pursuit of SOFT MONEY campaign contributions.

The situation was somewhat reversed in 2000, when Gore appeared to find himself on the losing end of media coverage. The Center for Media and Public Affairs, in a study of television coverage of the presidential primaries and the Republican convention, found that Bush consistently received more positive coverage. These findings were echoed by an unusual collaborative study by the nonpartisan Pew Research Center and Project for Excellence in Journalism, which was conducted during the campaign. The study found that 76 percent of news stories about Gore had a negative tone, whereas Bush had almost three times as much positive coverage.

Throughout the 2000 campaign, the media repeatedly portrayed Gore as someone who chronically stretched the truth or even lied. Gore, to a large degree, created his own credibility problems—most famously when he boasted in a television interview, "I took the initiative in creating the Internet." Late-night comedians jumped on the remark, which was widely retold as the vice president claiming to have "invented" the Internet. Gore, although hardly a creator of the Internet, was in fact an early supporter of the so-called information superhighway, but that fact received relatively little media coverage. Instead, reporters subsequently raised questions about Gore's truthfulness on a variety of other issues.

Overall, the networks have greatly reduced their campaign coverage. A 1998 study by Zachary Karabell for Harvard University's Joan Shorenstein Center on the Press, Politics, and Public Policy found that in 1952 over-the-air networks provided broadcast coverage of about sixty hours of each party convention, and 80 percent of U.S. households tuned in for ten to thirteen hours. But by 1996 live network coverage averaged eight hours (it would shrink further in 2000), and only 10 percent of households watched any of it. Other studies showed that between 1968 and 1992 the average length of a statement made by a presidential candidate on the evening network news broadcasts fell from forty-two seconds to less than nine seconds. In campaigns for state and congressional offices, local stations also severely restricted the air time devoted to the statements of candidates.

This downturn has been offset to some degree by the frequency of discussion of political topics on the "24/7" cable news stations such as CNN, Fox News Channel, and MSNBC. But these networks' tendency to focus on controversies, gaffes, and the "horse race" means voters still may have to take the initiative themselves to learn more about the candidates' views on issues.

Media Influence on Voters

In the 1940s, before the introduction of television into political campaigning, the media apparently had little influence on voters' decisions. Researchers believed that the media mainly *reinforced* the voters' partisan loyalties.

But partisan considerations today are less important in guiding voter choices than they were in the 1940s and 1950s. PARTY IDENTIFICATION OF VOTERS is down, which seemingly would make the media more influential in voter choices. Research has found, however, that regular viewing of network news has little or no effect on voters' awareness of candidates; yet viewing of political commercials is associated with higher voter awareness of candidates' issue stances. The simple explanation for the difference is that political commercials contain more information about the issues than do nightly news stories.

The tendency of approximately two-thirds of voters to decide on their choice for president before the general election campaign officially begins further limits the media coverage's effect on voter choice. In close elections, however, media coverage that sways even a small percentage of voters can be crucial.

Although the media may not directly affect voter choice to any great degree, they do play a significant role in setting the agenda for an election. This was demonstrated in 1990 and early 1991 during the Persian Gulf War. The prominent play the media gave to defense and foreign policy concerns meant that for this period the most important criterion for evaluating the president was his performance in foreign affairs.

In this context of military success, the first President Bush was accorded high marks. But after the war, when media coverage emphasized economic adversity at home and policy gridlock in Washington, the evaluation criteria shifted to domestic concerns, and the president received poor grades. The content and emphasis of news reporting therefore are significant because they help to create the context within which voters' choices are made. This was demonstrated again in 2002, when Republicans became the first party in almost seventy years to make gains in both chambers of Congress in the MIDTERM ELECTIONS while controlling the White House. Democrats wanted to focus their campaigns on the sluggish economy, an issue they felt favored them. But media coverage was dominated by foreign policy and terrorism, especially by the prospect of war with Iraq—and on those issues, voters seemed more comfortable with Republicans.

> **"A public that has accepted the belief that officials are acting in their own self-interest rather than in the interests of the common weal can be easily primed to see self-promotion in every political act. When journalists frame political events strategically they activate existing beliefs and understandings; they do not need to create them."**
>
> **—Joseph A. Cappella and Kathleen Hall Jamieson,** writing in *Spiral of Cynicism: The Press and the Public Good,* 1997

The media's role in setting the tone for political campaigns also was evident in the 2008 and 2010 cycles, which produced strongly contrasting results.

During the 2008 election campaign, which resulted in Obama's victory for president and gains for his Democratic Party in Congress, media coverage strongly focused on the steep decline in public support for outgoing President George W. Bush and his Republican Party—largely the result of the nation's prolonged military involvement in Iraq, the government's faulty response to human suffering caused in 2005 by Hurricane Katrina, and a slowing economy that would plunge into a deep recession after a financial industry crisis set in that fall.

But during 2010, a midterm election year that delivered a major rebound for the Republicans, media coverage focused strongly on public dissatisfaction with Obama's handling of the economy, which remained plagued by high unemployment; the unpopularity of legislative initiatives pushed through a Congress then controlled by Democrats, including an economic stimulus measure and an overhaul of the nation's health insurance system; and the rise of the TEA PARTY, a conservative backlash movement.

Voter attitudes and moods are part of that context. If voters are turned off by negative advertising, CAMPAIGN FINANCE abuses, too little emphasis on substance, and other unsavory aspects of U.S. elections, they become cynical and disinterested. VOTER REGISTRATION and VOTER TURNOUT drop, leading to more lamentations about public apathy and the decline of our electoral system.

Thus begins what Joseph A. Cappella and Kathleen Hall Jamieson of the Annenberg School of Communications call "the spiral of cynicism." Their in-depth study of news coverage included

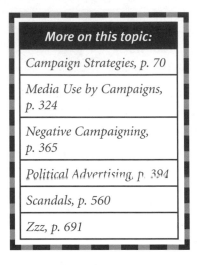

experiments with different versions of the same print or broadcast stories about a Philadelphia mayoral race and the national health care reform debate—one version was strategy based and the other, issue based.

The responses led Cappella and Jamieson to conclude in their 1997 book, *Spiral of Cynicism: The Press and the Public Good*, that the media's near-obsession with strategy coverage initiates citizen dissatisfaction that in turn breeds still more disinterest and lack of confidence in the electoral process.

They wrote: "A public that has accepted the belief that officials are acting in their own self-interest rather than in the interests of the common weal can be easily primed to see self-promotion in every political act. When journalists frame political events strategically they activate existing beliefs and understandings; they do not need to create them."

Media Use by Campaigns

The news and advertising media long ago became the primary sources of information about candidates and elections for most Americans. As a result, television, radio, newspapers, and magazines helped to determine the type of candidate who is likely to succeed. For many years, the emphasis has been on style, image, and an ability to communicate well on television.

These efforts to use mass communication platforms to reach voters have been supplemented in recent years, to a rapidly increasing extent, by technological innovations, including Internet websites, electronic mail, text messaging, and social networking sites that together comprise what is widely known as *new media.*

These very personalized means of communications have several advantages to candidates. They can reach out to simultaneously mobilize many established supporters and to try to persuade potential supporters. They can shape and present their ideas and campaign messages without having them go through the so-called media "filter."

They can even use new-media tactics to attract greater attention from traditional media sources: One frequent tactic developed during the first decade of the twenty-first century was for a campaign to produce a hard-hitting negative ad against an opposing candidate but post it only on its website (or to make a small and inexpensive media buy), while hoping that print and broadcast news outlets will "bite," deeming the ad powerful (or controversial) enough to treat as a news story in and of itself.

Still, even with the technological changes that continue to alter how campaigns communicate, these new-media platforms—going into the 2012 presidential cycle—continued to be used in addition to traditional media strategies, rather than as replacements for them.

A good example of this was Democrat Barack Obama's successful run for president in 2008. Obama's campaign broke new ground in using the Internet to boost its record-setting fund-raising and its direct outreach to voters. But Obama also put his campaign treasury to work by running an extensive advertising effort on television and radio and in newspapers, which helped him implant his themes of "hope" and "change" in the national consciousness. The closing night of the 2008 Democratic National Convention was held in the Denver Broncos' football stadium—the first time a major-party convention had moved outdoors since Democrat John F. Kennedy gave his 1960 acceptance speech in the Los Angeles Coliseum—and was staged for visual impact on television.

This stadium spectacular was just a rather grandiose extension of the media strategy that campaigns of all stripes had been employing for years. To take advantage of news coverage, daily campaign activities are geared to getting impressive "visuals" or sound bites on national and local news programs. Strategists try to adapt the day's "news" events to reinforce the campaign's overall themes and POLITICAL ADVERTISING appeals.

The candidates use television and radio throughout the PRIMARY season and again in the fall to publicize their campaigns. The pace quickens at the end of October, when many voters first begin to pay close attention to the election.

Depending on their standing in the POLLS, and on whether they are running for or against the party in power, the candidates switch back and forth between appeals to bolster their own image and ads to undermine their opponent's credibility. In 1984 President Ronald Reagan's reelection campaign used "feel good" commercials—with a theme of "It's Morning Again in America"—containing vague but heartwarming images of Americana because it wanted to reinforce a positive mood in the nation.

In this June 3, 2010, file photo, President Barack Obama uses his BlackBerry e-mail device as he walks at Sidwell Friends School in Bethesda, Md. Preparing for his 2012 reelection effort, Obama urged supporters to use Facebook to declare "I'm in" for his campaign and began using Twitter to communicate with his nearly 9 million followers. Obama broke new ground using e-mail, text messages, and the web to reach voters in 2008.

Source: AP Photo/Charles Dharapak File

In 1988 George H. W. Bush built and maintained an advantage over his Democratic challenger, Massachusetts governor Michael S. Dukakis, throughout the fall campaign by emphasizing his conservative IDEOLOGY and portraying the Democrat as a liberal out of step with the mainstream. Many criticized the vice president for his tactics, but few questioned their effectiveness. For example, Bush targeted Dukakis's veto of a state law requiring teachers to lead their pupils in reciting the Pledge of Allegiance. "What's his problem with the Pledge?" Bush asked again and again, implying that Dukakis was unpatriotic.

Although congressional campaigns have been less studied and analyzed, they also provide examples of adroit media strategies. In 1990 Minnesota Democratic Senate candidate Paul Wellstone turned his lack of funding into an asset, driving a rickety green campaign bus across the state and creating a series of humorous commercials in which he portrayed himself as hardworking and underfunded. The strategy paid off when he upset Republican incumbent Rudy Boschwitz. In 2002 Republican Saxby Chambliss won a Senate election in Georgia after running ads that portrayed Democratic incumbent Max Cleland as soft on defense; one ad appeared to associate Cleland with Osama bin Laden, the mastermind of the September 11, 2001, attacks, and Iraqi dictator Saddam Hussein. The devastating ads worked even though Cleland was a decorated veteran who lost three limbs in Vietnam.

Peaks and Valleys

Ideally, a candidate would like to keep his or her name before the voters in a favorable light throughout the campaign period. But realistically that is not always possible. Voters' interest surges and wanes at several points during the election year. Candidates and their advisers conserve their advertising budgets for periods when circumstances justify the purchase of time for expensive television spots.

The Federal Communications Commission's EQUAL TIME AND REBUTTAL RULES ensure that all candidates have equal opportunities for use of broadcast or cable television. These rules, however, do not require the broadcasters to offset the advantage that a better-funded candidate may have in the number of campaign ads that he or she is able to run.

During the nominating season, presidential candidates typically spend heavily for commercial spots in New England in an effort to win the first-in-the-nation NEW HAMPSHIRE PRIMARY. That contest and the early IOWA CAUCUS developed a culling function, forcing candidates who failed to develop early support to quit the race and, in almost all presidential election years, establishing a clear front-runner who developed inexorable momentum in subsequent PRESIDENTIAL PRIMARIES.

Candidates in recent campaigns have had to alter this widely used strategy somewhat in recent presidential election years, however, because of the practice of FRONT-LOADING, in which states compete for influence in the nominating process by moving their primaries earlier and earlier in the year. The process accelerated during the 2008 campaign, when "Super Tuesday"—the label applied since the 1980s for the date with the biggest cluster of primaries and caucuses—was set for February 5, which in turn prompted Iowa and New Hampshire to move their campaign-kickoff events to early January.

New rules instituted by the Republican Party for its 2012 nominating campaign, which the Democratic Party signaled it would follow as well, were aimed at putting the brakes on this trend. The rules barred any state from holding a contest in January, limited contests in February to four states (Iowa, New Hampshire, Nevada, and South Carolina), and set March 6 as the earliest possible date for Super Tuesday.

This new strategy appeared at risk of falling apart in the run-up to the campaign, as South Carolina and Florida moved their primaries to late January and Iowa and New Hampshire responded by shifting their events to January 3 and January 10, respectively. Yet concerns that other states would rush to move their primaries and caucuses up in yet another front-loading frenzy were allayed, as most chose to follow the new rules. For example, the March date for Super Tuesday held, and only ten states—half as many as four years earlier—crowded their events onto that date. In another big development, California, the nation's most populous and delegate-rich state, switched its primary back to its long-traditional date in early June after joining the Super Tuesday scrum in February 2008.

The front-loading phenomenon contributed to the fact that the recent major-party nominees have in effect been chosen well ahead of the NATIONAL PARTY CONVENTIONS where the nominations are formalized. Unlike the sort of conventions that took place in the first half of the twentieth century or earlier, which sometimes featured major political brawls and repeated rounds of balloting, the 2000, 2004, and 2008 Republican and Democratic conventions were carefully scripted, made-for-television affairs that included video presentations and prerecorded musical numbers. Especially in 2000, the Republicans, wary of being portrayed as out of touch with mainstream Americans, stressed their multicultural membership by having a diversity of people appear on stage, including African, Hispanic, and Asian Americans.

Both major-party nominees usually (though not always) receive a POSTCONVENTION BOUNCE from the MEDIA COVERAGE, emerging from the conventions with higher poll ratings than when they went in.

After Labor Day, the traditional start of the campaign, the polls become the most important part of the "horse race" aspect of the election. Usually, the leader in the polls after the conventions wins in November if the lead is maintained until then.

Chances are that last-minute changes will not affect the outcome. Most voters make up their minds well before ELECTION DAY. In the presidential elections from 1960 to 1996, more than 60 percent of the voters, on average, made up their minds before or during the conventions. The major expansion of ABSENTEE VOTING and early voting options, which enable millions of Americans to cast their votes in the weeks before election day, further limit the potential for dramatic late swings in support for candidates. Yet late deciders can swing the ELECTORAL COLLEGE votes of pivotal states, which are often won by margins of less than 5 percentage points. The 2000 race was especially close, with key states being decided by a few thousand (or even, in the case of Florida, a few hundred) votes. Democrat Al Gore spent the last night of the campaign in Florida in a desperate attempt to sway voters there.

Clinton's 1996 Republican opponent, former Senate majority leader Bob Dole, counted on a late surge of support that never came. In the final ninety-six hours before the election, he waged a nonstop, twenty-state campaign. Exit polls showed that Dole defeated Clinton 41 percent to 35 percent among those who decided during the last week of the campaign. But that group accounted for only 17 percent of the voters.

President George W. Bush's political operation, in concert with the Republican National Committee, gained major attention following the 2004 elections for the "72-Hour Plan," under which Republican strategists flooded key states and districts with party staffers and volunteers over the campaign's final three days to get out the GOP vote. This tactic was credited by the party and many in the media for ensuring Bush's 51 percent to 48 percent victory over Democrat John Kerry and abetting a four-seat Republican gain in the Senate.

But the party's use of the same plan in the 2006 midterm elections—though much promoted through the media to create doubt about significant Democratic gains that year—was much less effective. The sharp drop-off in public support, as revealed through polls, for Bush and the Republican-controlled Congress resulted in many voters making up their minds about the elections early on. Independent voters swung sharply Democratic, and even some Republican voters were dispirited and did not vote. While the Republicans' big get-out-the-vote push may have salvaged a few seats and limited GOP losses, the Democrats gained thirty House seats and six Senate seats to gain control of both chambers.

The Republicans' failure to recapture their 2004 voter mobilization magic resulted in part by the Democrats' own success at playing catch-up in voter turnout strategy. The Democrats appeared to gain a huge edge over the GOP in their get-out-the-vote efforts in 2008, in which Obama was elected president and the Democrats increased their majorities in the U.S. Senate and House and made significant gains in state and local offices in many areas of the nation.

But the results of the 2010 midterm elections, in which Republicans scored a major comeback, made three things clear. Each major party learns from the other's successes, each party's ability to turn out supporters depends strongly on its standing in public opinion, and there is little a party can do to alter the situation when a downturn in its popularity becomes the dominant theme of media coverage of a campaign. Persistent high unemployment following a deep economic recession, and controversies over

CLOSER LOOK

Though national conventions have become "four-day infomercials" that are almost certain to provide the parties' nominees with a temporary boost (a "postconvention bounce"), they do not guarantee lasting benefits. Candidates must be careful to build on any momentum coming out of their conventions, lest it quickly evaporate.

In 2004 the Democrats held their convention in late July, five weeks before the Republicans', an unusually long gap. Massachusetts senator John Kerry, the Democratic nominee, enjoyed mainly positive media coverage even though his postconvention bounce in the polls was small to nonexistent. Seeking to conserve campaign energy and financial resources—and apparently thinking the Republicans would take a summer hiatus as well—Kerry scaled down his campaign and took a vacation. But President George W. Bush spent the rest of August rebutting what was said and done at the Democratic convention, an active response magnified by the efforts of an outside group, not coordinated with the Bush campaign, that ran ads impugning Kerry's reputation as a Vietnam War hero.

Combined with a relentless assault on Kerry during the Republican convention, the August campaign mismatch boosted Bush to a big lead in the polls that he never fully surrendered, even though the vote results in the end were very close.

policy initiatives such as the overhaul of the nation's health insurance laws that was enacted with almost exclusively Democratic support in Congress, spurred a backlash and the rise of the conservative TEA PARTY movement, boosting the Republicans to recapture control of the House, cut into the Democrats' Senate majority, and reversed many of the state and local gains that Democrats had made in the previous two election cycles.

Getting the Message Across

As the challenger in 1992 Clinton provided an example of skillful use of the media to overcome the advantages enjoyed by the INCUMBENT, the first President Bush. The Clinton team was cohesive and disciplined, with a competitive edge that had been honed during the presidential primaries. Many of its leaders (top strategist James Carville and media consultants Frank Greer and Mandy Grunwald) had sharpened their skills in southern elections and, unlike the 1988 Dukakis campaign, had mastered the art of rebutting conservative attacks. Clinton's staff also included experienced Washington hands, such as campaign chairman Mickey Kantor and communications director George Stephanopoulos. Carville's "war room" personnel reveled in their reputations as "tough Democrats" as they scanned the news wire services and satellite feeds for attacks on their candidate, priding themselves on the speed of their responses while at the same time firing off their own first strikes.

In 1988 the Bush campaign had shown the same awareness of the need to coordinate PUBLIC OPINION polling, media advertising, candidate appearances, and use of the free media. Polls were taken every night with the results available for campaign chairman James A. Baker's daily 7:30 a.m. senior staff meeting.

At these meetings campaign activities were carefully planned to stress the campaign message of the day or week. Media consultants even inserted snappy lines into Bush's speeches—tested in advance—to ensure that they were picked up as sound bites on TV news programs.

To complete the media package, television commercials were designed to back up the chosen message. The Bush campaign also sought to limit news conferences with reporters, lest the freewheeling and often adversarial nature of these sessions resulted in the wrong messages being communicated to the voters. The campaign was thus designed to exert maximum control over what the voters would see and hear about the candidate on television, the people's most important and trusted source of news.

In 2000, however, Gore's campaign appeared to take that approach too far, limiting access to the candidate to such a degree that it may have been a factor in spawning negative coverage (see MEDIA COVERAGE OF CAMPAIGNS). Republican George W. Bush, in contrast, worked to cultivate reporters, joking with them and giving them nicknames. He also exhibited mastery in the art of staying "on message"—repeatedly focusing on the same themes day after day. He consistently accused Gore of engaging in "fuzzy math," thereby taking advantage of Gore's reputation for distorting the truth, such as when the Democrat claimed to have played a key role in creating the Internet.

When Gore questioned the underlying numbers in Bush's proposed tax cut, the Republican retorted that Gore "not only thought he invented the Internet, but he came up with a new calculator. It's a calculator that you put real numbers into, and out come political numbers." Although Gore was widely admired for his grasp of complex policy issues, he was unable to focus the campaign on weaknesses in the Bush plan.

Two Decades of Refinement and Innovation

In 1992, the campaigns by Clinton and billionaire businessman H. Ross Perot (running as an independent candidate) used many of the same time-tested techniques plus innovative ones to get their messages across. In seeking favorable free coverage, the Clinton organization took full advantage of the news media's alleged distaste for the NEGATIVE CAMPAIGNING that they said had excessively dominated the 1988 campaign. With the national press corps continually looking for distortions in the charges leveled by one candidate against another, the Clinton campaign adopted a strategy of reacting quickly to Republican attacks. If a staff response promptly faxed to the media did not do the job, Clinton frequently responded in person, in the process gaining extensive media coverage and blunting the GOP charges.

The Clinton campaign also tried to use the local television news more fully by providing local reporters in pivotal media markets with access to the candidate through satellite feeds. From one location Clinton often did five to six interviews for local evening news programs.

Using the local media had the added advantage of bypassing the national press corps with its often critical "gotcha" style of journalism. Local reporters, because they were less familiar with the details of national policy and in many cases more awed by the fact that they were participating in the discussion of the presidential campaign, were more likely to allow the candidate to get his message out without journalistic tinkering or mediation. Going one step further, the Democratic organization filmed Clinton campaign appearances and then sent the footage via satellite feeds to local stations for use on news programs.

One of the most distinctive features of 1992 was the "talk show campaign." Ross Perot was the first to discover this format as an effective way to bypass national political reporters and speak directly to the public. His campaign quite literally began on CNN's *Larry King Live*, where Perot said that, after the New Hampshire primary, he would run if "volunteers" put his name on the ballot.

Perot, financing his own campaign, also revived the use of paid half-hour infomercials to promote his candidacy and explain his policy proposals with the help of charts, graphs, and other visual props. These marathon campaign commercials had been used frequently in the 1950s and 1960s. (Obama would also use this device in the final week of the 2008 campaign by buying thirty minutes of time on the national TV networks and presenting a highly polished film that featured the personal stories of people of varying regions, races, and backgrounds striving to succeed in America.)

Clinton was the first of the major-party candidates to follow the Perot example and exploit the talk shows with appearances on nontraditional candidate venues such as the MTV and ESPN networks, as well as the *Phil Donahue*, *Arsenio Hall*, and *Larry King* shows. The early morning network broadcasts such as *Today* and *Good Morning America* even brought the candidates to the nation's breakfast tables. President Bush at first resisted participating in what he characterized as these "weird talk shows," but he too eventually followed the trend.

Unlike the tough questions posed by national political reporters about campaign tactics, polls, and inconsistencies in policy positions, the less-confrontational questions posed on talk shows concerned how the candidates would solve the problems on the minds of callers or members of the studio audience. This kind of platform, on which Clinton was highly effective, gave him an opportunity to reach voters on subjects

---

they cared about without having his message mediated by reporters. Information (and some misinformation) was also disseminated over the Internet, a development that had an increasingly important influence as more and more Americans went online.

What once made candidates look hip has now become a regular rite of passage for even the most mainstream candidates. Regular stops for candidates before the 2008 presidential election included NBC's *The Tonight Show* with Jay Leno (on which movie star Arnold Schwarzenegger had announced his bid for governor as a Republican in California's 2003 RECALL election), CBS's *Late Show with David Letterman*, and Comedy Central's *The Daily Show* with Jon Stewart.

Participation in Candidate Forums

Televised DEBATES now go hand in hand with presidential and other American elections. For nonincumbent and underdog candidates, such debates are potentially advantageous because they place these candidates on an equal footing with a president, governor, or front-running candidate for any office. On an unadorned stage, the candidates stand alone as equals. Not only are incumbents robbed of the aura of the White House or statehouse, but also their claims of superior experience can be quickly eroded during the debate by challengers who are credible and clever, which most are.

Because the news media give prime-time coverage to debates, candidates tend to see them as make-or-break events. In fact, extended negotiations among campaign managers over debate formats are usually the rule—all aimed at preventing the opposition from gaining any procedural advantage.

Wrangling over the number, timing, and format of the presidential debates in 1992 lasted until late September, with incumbent president Bush unenthusiastic about debating Clinton, who was generally considered more articulate and practiced in the debate format. The final agreement resulted in the first three-way presidential debates, with Bush, Clinton, and Perot taking part.

Similarly, the younger Bush in 2000 raised objections about the proposed debates, seeking instead to make them less informal. He was widely expected to lose the debates to the more-experienced Gore. But Bush dropped his objections when polls showed voters thought he was trying to duck the debates. In the end, he held his own against Gore, thereby preserving some momentum going into election day.

Mid-decade Redistricting

All states that have more than the minimum of one CONGRESSIONAL DISTRICT—meaning forty-three under the apportionment of seats following the 2010 census—must conduct congressional redistricting once each decade, based on the population statistics that emerge from the CENSUS conducted every ten years in the year ending in 0. Under a series of Supreme Court decisions dating back to the ONE-PERSON, ONE-VOTE rulings of the 1960s, districts within each state must be redrawn so their populations are as near to zero deviation as possible. State lawmakers often use redistricting to address political goals; these include providing opportunities for their party to gain seats or increasing political security for incumbents of one or both major parties.

The district maps in almost all circumstances are completed prior to the first congressional elections in each decade, held in the year ending in 2 (though Maine regularly performs its remap in the year ending in 3). Until recently, at least from the late 1800s forward, the only times states revised already implemented redistricting plans in the middle of a decade were when they were under court orders to do so, almost always because of population inequality among districts or because the existing map was deemed to violate the rights of voters on the basis of race. (See RACIAL REDISTRICTING.)

Nothing in the Constitution or federal law barred mid-decade redistricting, but an unspoken compact between the parties prevailed until the first decade of the twenty-first century, when Republicans used their control of the state legislatures in Colorado, Georgia, and Texas to enact partisan, mid-decade redistricting plans.

The Colorado plan failed. In early 2003 Republicans, having just taken full control of the Colorado legislature, redrew the district map to supersede a map implemented by a state court ruling prior to the 2002 elections following a stalemate in the legislature. The new map mainly sought to boost Republican strength in suburban Denver's Seventh District, which Republican Bob Beauprez won by just 121 votes in 2002. Prior to the 2004 elections, a state court struck down the plan on grounds that the state constitution barred redistricting from taking place more than once per decade.

Texas state senator Rodney Ellis meets reporters at the National Press Club in Washington, D.C., to discuss Texas redistricting in 2003.

Source: AP Images/Tyler Mallory

The mid-decade redistricting in Georgia succeeded, though with limited immediate impact. In a major breakthrough in a state where Democrats had dominated state government for more than a century, Republicans in 2004 won control of the state house of representatives to go with their already existing majority in the state senate. They used that advantage almost immediately to revoke a Democratic-drawn congressional map and replace it with one of their own. The thrust was to make the reelection prospects of two Democratic incumbents marginally more difficult: John Barrow's home political base was removed from his district, and Jim Marshall saw his district extended to include the home base of former Republican representative Mac Collins, who challenged Marshall in the 2006 election. Barrow and Marshall both survived their 2006 contests, however, albeit by narrow margins.

The mid-decade redistricting in Texas had a sweeping impact, though—one that initially was highly positive for Republicans but soon proved to have a negative side as well.

This was especially true for Tom DeLay, the powerful Texas Republican member of Congress who engineered the mid-decade redistricting. When Republicans scored a net gain of five House seats in Texas in 2004, the first election under the GOP-drawn map, the victory burnished the partisan DeLay's reputation as a strategic mastermind. But his aggressive efforts to achieve his goal ultimately caused a serious ethics controversy that first forced DeLay to surrender his position as House majority leader and later to resign from the House—setting the stage for an ironic outcome. A Democrat took over DeLay's vacated House seat in the strongly conservative suburbs of Houston.

The first time congressional redistricting came up in Texas prior to the 2002 election, the state legislature was split between a Republican-controlled Senate and a Democratic-controlled House, and they deadlocked over the remap. A state court stepped in and instituted a plan that DeLay and other Republicans complained was too generous to the Democrats, citing the strong overall Republican-voting trend in a state that had sent both George H. W. Bush and George W. Bush to the White House.

Republicans gained control of the state house in the 2002 elections, setting in motion a mid-decade redistricting effort that was sure to meet with the approval of Republican governor Rick Perry. The proposed map was an attempt to produce as much as a seven-seat gain for the Republicans, who held fifteen of the state's thirty-two seats after the 2002 House elections.

Democrats, who portrayed the unprecedented mid-decade redistricting as an unnecessary power grab by DeLay and his fellow Republicans, tried mightily to block its passage. During summer 2003, a group of Democratic state senators left the state and camped in a hotel in Oklahoma to try to block the chamber from achieving the needed quorum to move the redistricting legislation. Some state house Democrats went to New Mexico later that summer for the same purpose. But they eventually ceded to the Republicans' determination and strength in numbers.

The Republicans ended up achieving nearly all their goals. They picked up a seat almost immediately when Ralph Hall, one of the most conservative House Democrats, switched to the Republican Party. Jim Turner, whose district was split up among several districts, decided to retire. Democrats Nick Lampson, Charles W. Stenholm, Martin Frost, and Max Sandlin were defeated by Republicans. The only targeted Democratic incumbent who survived was Chet Edwards. When the dust settled after the 2004 elections, the Republicans held twenty-one of the state's thirty-two congressional seats, up six from 2002.

But Democrats' efforts to prove a partisan overreach by DeLay soon bore fruit. In September 2004 the House Ethics Committee reprimanded DeLay for prevailing on the Federal Aviation Administration to help Texas Republicans trying to track a plane used by Democratic state lawmakers in 2003 as they fled the state during the redistricting fight. Then, almost exactly a year later, a grand jury in Travis County, which includes the state capital of Austin, indicted DeLay on a charge of conspiracy in an alleged scheme to launder illegal business contributions to Republican state house candidates during the party's big push to take control of that chamber in the 2002 elections. Shortly thereafter another grand jury in Austin indicted DeLay on conspiracy and money laundering charges. A Texas judge dismissed one of the conspiracy charges in December 2005.

But a Texas jury in November 2010 convicted him on other charges, which carried prison sentences of five to twenty years. Following the decision, DeLay told reporters, "This is an abuse of power. It's a miscarriage of justice, and I still maintain that I am innocent. The criminalization of politics undermines our very system, and I'm very disappointed in the outcome." In January 2011 the presiding judge in the case sentenced DeLay to three years in prison on conspiracy changes. DeLay was given a five-year prison term on money laundering charges, but that was altered to a ten-year term on probation. He promised to appeal the conviction.

A House Republican rule prohibiting members who are under indictment from holding leadership positions forced DeLay to step down as majority leader, first temporarily in September 2005 and then permanently in January 2006. In April 2006 DeLay, whose political security at home was waning under the weight of these controversies and his close ties to corrupt lobbyist Jack Abramoff, announced he would resign from Congress, which he did that June.

DeLay also announced he was shifting his residency to Virginia in a move that he thought would make him ineligible to run in Texas, thus allowing Republican officials to remove his name from the ballot and replace him with a hand-picked candidate. But Democrats argued successfully in court that neither DeLay nor his fellow Republicans could prove beyond doubt that DeLay would not actually be living in Texas on election day. The result was that the Republican line on the November 2006 ballot was blank, forcing the GOP replacement candidate, Shelley Sekula-Gibbs, to run a nearly impossible campaign to win on WRITE-IN votes.

Despite the controversy over the Republican mid-decade redistricting, the Supreme Court—historically reluctant to get involved in partisan redistricting disputes—in July 2006 rejected most of a complaint by Democrats seeking to strike down the map. But the Court did require adjustments to the Twenty-third District, represented by Republican Henry Bonilla, on grounds that its lines hindered the ability of Hispanic voters, most of them Democrats, to elect a candidate of their choosing.

That November, Democrats won two formerly Republican House seats in Texas: in DeLay's Twenty-second District, where Nick Lampson—undermined in 2004 by the remap of an adjacent district—won the seat, and the Twenty-third, where Bonilla was defeated by Democrat Ciro D. Rodriguez.

Although Democrats had threatened to retaliate for the Texas mid-decade redistricting by following suit in states where they had recently gained full control of the legislature, such as Illinois and New Mexico, the fundamentally disruptive and divisive nature of this strategy caused them to back off—suggesting that mid decade redistricting would likely remain an exception to the rule in years to come.

More on this topic:
Census, p. 92
Congressional District, p. 111
Judicial System, p. 291
One Person, One Vote, p. 373
Racial Redistricting, p. 509
Reapportionment and Redistricting, p. 517
Scandals, p. 560

Midterm Election

The election that falls at the halfway mark of a four-year presidential term is known as the *midterm* or, less precisely, *off-year* election. Every seat in the House of Representatives and one-third of the Senate seats are at stake in this election.

The midterm election is often referred to as a referendum on the president and the president's party. If the economy is poor, if lives are being lost in an unpopular war, or if the president has a low approval rating in the PUBLIC OPINION polls for any of a variety of reasons, it is likely that the president's party will lose congressional seats—perhaps enough to change control of one or both chambers. The biggest swings in party strength in Congress over the past quarter-century have, in fact, occurred during midterm elections.

In 1982, with first-term Republican president Ronald Reagan hindered by a deep recession, Democrats made a twenty-six-seat gain in the House, nearly wiping out a thirty-three-seat gain the Republicans enjoyed as Reagan easily defeated Democratic incumbent Jimmy Carter in 1980.

In 1994 dissatisfaction with first-term president Bill Clinton's failed attempt at a sweeping overhaul of the health care system and his advocacy of tax increases to close the federal budget deficit contributed to Republicans' fifty-two-seat gain of historic significance: it ended a forty-year Democratic hold on the House. The Republicans also picked up eight Senate seats to take control of that chamber for the first time in eight years.

And in 2006, a perfect storm of problems in the first two years of Republican George W. Bush's second term—most prominent among them the plunge in public approval of the president's handling of the war in Iraq—gave the Democrats a thirty-seat gain in the House and a six-seat gain in the Senate, giving them control of both chambers of Congress.

Then, in 2010, the same thing happened to Democratic president Barack Obama after he too in 2009 pushed through into law a far-reaching health care reform bill: Republicans picked up a net of sixty-three seats in the House, returning control to the GOP after four years, and six seats in the Senate, which was not enough for chamber control but sufficient to allow the party to thwart Democratic initiatives.

The situation in 2006 underscores how unfortunate SECOND MIDTERM ELECTIONS tend to be for the party of a president who is fortunate enough to win a second term. In every election but one held in the sixth year of a two-term presidency since the beginning of the twentieth century, the party in the White House has lost House seats, often dozens, and often has faced setbacks in the Senate as well.

There is nothing predetermined about this pattern, however. Most midterm elections that ended badly for the president's party were influenced by economic problems for which voters tend to blame the president, outright missteps by the president, corruption scandals touching on the president or members of his party, or other circumstances that could have either been prevented or at least ameliorated. In the case of the 2010 elections, the recession that started in late 2007 and still depressed the economy in 2010 and the deep divisions over Democratic legislation, particularly health care reform, were the most significant influences on voter behavior.

One interesting aspect of the phenomenon is that members of Congress of the president's party often suffer more in these midterm "referendums" on a president than does a president eligible to seek reelection. Several presidents have successfully rebounded from problems that caused losses for their parties and adjusted to the verdict of voters in the midterm elections. For example, Reagan won a LANDSLIDE reelection victory in 1984, and Clinton won a second term by a comfortable margin in 1996.

Even the exceptions to the rule do not undermine the midterm election's role as a referendum on the president. In 1998 the Democrats gained five House seats despite widespread predictions of disaster stemming from Clinton's extramarital affair with former White House intern Monica Lewinsky; the electorate was more influenced that year by a strong economy and the fact that the nation was not then facing any major military conflicts abroad.

In 2002 Republicans picked up two Senate seats—enough to gain narrow control of the chamber—and six House seats. They benefited that year from strong public approval at the time for George W. Bush, based on his assertive military response to the September 11, 2001, attacks on the United States.

Part of the reason the White House party tends to do worse in midterm election years is that the president is not out on the campaign trail justifying the administration's policies—and spending hundreds of millions of dollars in campaign funds to do so. In midterm elections, members of Congress find themselves having to act as surrogates for the president, and some are placed in the awkward position of having to distance themselves from the president's less popular policies.

Another factor is that voter turnout tends to be considerably lower for midterm elections than for presidential elections. Therefore, it takes a smaller numerical swing in voting behavior to effect major changes in Congress than it does during a presidential election year. That also tends to give an advantage to groups, and political organizations, that believe deeply about certain issues and work energetically to get out voters who are their constituency.

Return to the Past

There was a time in U.S. history when the president's congressional strength ebbed and flowed dramatically. Eight times between the end of the Civil War and the end of World War II the party occupying the White House lost more than fifty House seats in the midterm election. But until 1994 it had been twenty years since the president's party lost more than forty seats at midterm.

In 1946 postwar voters were ready for a change. Democrats under Franklin D. Roosevelt and Harry S. Truman had held control of the White House and Congress for fourteen years. Republicans

Midterm Election Results, 1901–2010

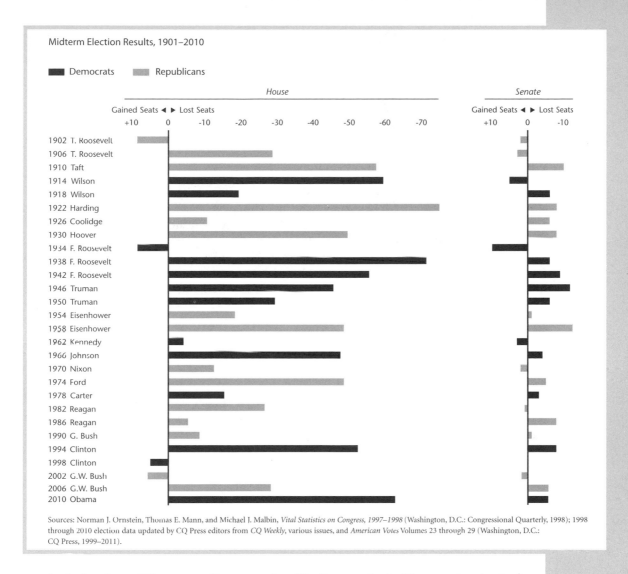

Sources: Norman J. Ornstein, Thomas E. Mann, and Michael J. Malbin, *Vital Statistics on Congress, 1997–1998* (Washington, D.C.: Congressional Quarterly, 1998); 1998 through 2010 election data updated by CQ Press editors from *CQ Weekly*, various issues, and *American Votes* Volumes 23 through 29 (Washington, D.C.: CQ Press, 1999–2011).

won both chambers of Congress as Democrats lost fifty-five seats in the House and twelve in the Senate. But the GOP domination was short-lived. Truman waged a feisty campaign against the "Do-Nothing" Eightieth Congress and a feeble Republican response. The Democrats not only retained the White House—in a surprise victory for Truman against Thomas E. Dewey—but also regained control of both chambers in 1948.

In 1958, economic recession, low farm prices, and labor agitation against right-to-work laws partly offset President Dwight D. Eisenhower's personal popularity. Against Democratic gains in the Midwest and blue-collar regions, Eisenhower's Republicans lost forty-eight House and thirteen Senate seats. Two years later they lost the White House to Democrat John F. Kennedy.

The election of 1966, two years after President Lyndon B. Johnson's LANDSLIDE election and the launching of his "Great Society" programs, dealt Democrats their worst midterm losses in twenty years. Amid mounting dissension over the Vietnam War, Johnson scaled back his

Rep. J. Dennis Hastert, an Illinois Republican, lost his position as Speaker of the House as a result of the 2006 midterm election.

Source: CQ Photo/Scott J. Ferrell

campaigning for Democrats in Congress. Although it retained control, his party lost forty-seven House seats and four Senate seats. Two years later, Johnson declined to seek renomination, and Republican Richard M. Nixon won the presidency.

Reelected in a landslide in 1972, Nixon—or more accurately, his party—encountered the midterm-losses phenomenon in 1974. By then he had suffered precipitous drops in public standing because of the damaging revelations of the Watergate scandal. Voters also were disgruntled by an economic downturn, and Republicans had trouble raising money and persuading strong candidates to run for office. Democrats were roused to action by Watergate, in part because the offenses had been directed against Democratic Party leaders: their offices in the Watergate Hotel were burglarized before the 1972 election, and the White House was implicated in the subsequent cover-up. As a result, Democrats at all levels were motivated to run for office, donate money, and work to defeat Republicans.

At the same time, an unusually large number of legislators, most of them Republican, decided to retire in 1974, opening up more seats and enhancing the Democratic challengers' chances. Facing impeachment by the House because of Watergate, Nixon resigned on August 9, 1974, further damaging the Republicans' campaigns for the congressional election three months later. The problem was compounded that September when Nixon's Republican successor, Gerald R. Ford, issued a blanket pardon to Nixon for any crimes he may have committed. The net result for the Democrats was a gain of forty-nine seats in the House and four in the Senate, solidifying their hold on Congress.

Second-term losses by the president's party tend to be more severe than first-term losses. But Clinton and his party defied the seemingly inevitable in 1998. Instead of losing more House seats, the Democrats had a net gain of five seats. The House in the 106th Congress had 228 Republicans, 206 Democrats, and 1 independent. The Senate division remained unchanged at fifty-five Republicans and forty-five Democrats.

Facing the loss of his speakership over the unexpected setback, Georgia Republican Newt Gingrich—the strategic mastermind of the Republicans' 1994 upsurge that included the conservative campaign platform known as the Contract with America—stepped down and left the House. In a surprising development, his apparent successor, Louisiana Republican Robert L. Livingston, also declined the post and resigned his seat. Livingston confessed to marital infidelity as the House prepared to impeach Clinton for perjury and obstruction of justice in connection with his illicit affair with Lewinsky. The House subsequently elected Illinois Republican J. Dennis Hastert as the new Speaker, a position that he would keep until the Republicans' twelve-year hold on the House slipped away in the 2006 elections.

Clinton's popularity apparently was a factor in the Democrats' gains and the ripple effect in the GOP House leadership. The rebuff to the Republicans was widely interpreted as an anti-impeachment signal from the voters. Even after the House impeached Clinton and his trial began in the Senate, his job approval rating in the polls remained high. (See POLLING; REMOVAL FROM OFFICE.)

Effect on Turnout

Compared with presidential contests, the midterm congressional election lacks interest for many voters. The relative apathy is reflected in the lower VOTER TURNOUT figures for election years not having a presidential election.

The turnout for the 1994 midterm election, based on the nation's voting-age population, was 36.0 percent—significantly lower than the 55.2 percent turnout in 1992 when President George H. W. Bush and challengers Clinton and Ross Perot were at the top of their respective tickets. Even with the heated competition for control of Congress inherent in the 2006 elections, only about 36 percent of the voting-age population participated, a turnout rate that was little changed in 2010.

Some political scientists and other analysts argue that the voting-age population is an inaccurate gauge of voter turnout, as it includes many U.S. residents, including noncitizens and felons, who are ineligible to vote. Many of these critics favor instead measuring voter turnout as a ratio of the voting-eligible population, which typically raises the turnout percentage by roughly 3 to 5 points each election year. Yet the mismatch between midterm and presidential election year turnout persists under this scale: according to the United States Election Project at Virginia's George Mason University, estimated voting-eligible turnout for 2006 was 40.5 percent, compared with 60.3 percent in the 2004 presidential election year; in 2010 it was 40.9 percent compared to 61.6 percent in 2008.

Put another way, roughly one-third fewer voters take part in midterm elections than in presidential elections. The total turnout for 2008 was 131.2 million, while 86.5 million Americans voted in 2010.

Factors that help explain the difference in participation between the two types of elections include the greater MEDIA COVERAGE of presidential campaigns, the lower significance that voters attach to congressional offices, the relative importance of the issues raised in the campaigns, and the attractiveness of the candidates.

Presidential Involvement

It is often to the president's advantage to campaign vigorously in the midterm election for congressional candidates of the president's party. The stronger the president is in Congress the easier it is for the White House to carry out its legislative program. But in practice the level of presidential enthusiasm for midterm campaigning varies widely. President Eisenhower said in 1954 that a president should try to provide an "umbrella of accomplishment" under which party members can run, rather than participate "too intensively and directly in off-year congressional elections."

Because it is all but inevitable that the president's party will lose House seats in the midterm election, there is almost no way for the president to look good by getting closely involved. The most he can hope to do is minimize losses. If the president is under siege within his own party, as Lyndon Johnson was in 1966, there is even more incentive for the president to keep a low profile at midterm, as Johnson did.

Midterm campaigning that inflames partisan opposition may make it harder for the president to work with the new Congress, especially if the opposition party controls it. Some presidents have also found members of the opposition party to be more supportive than their own partisans. As a result, they have naturally been reluctant to campaign against those members.

President Eisenhower said in 1954 that a president should try to provide an "umbrella of accomplishment" under which party members can run, rather than participate "too intensively and directly in off-year congressional elections."

Effect on State Elections

Like House elections, gubernatorial elections are affected by national issues and conditions. For that reason, most states elect their GOVERNORS in the middle of presidential terms, rather than at the same time as the president, when the White House race is likely to overshadow battles for the statehouses. (The term *off-year,* as used by Eisenhower, has been largely replaced in usage by MIDTERM ELECTION. This helps to avoid confusion with some state and many local elections that are held in odd-numbered years to further insulate them from being influenced by debates over national issues or candidates.)

But the move to midterm elections has not prevented state contests from being caught up in national partisan politics. The president's party loses governorships in midterm elections as consistently, and sometimes in larger percentages, than it loses House seats.

The president's party has lost governors in most midterm elections since the middle of the twentieth century.

An exception occurred in 1986, midway in President Ronald Reagan's second term, when the Republicans made a net gain of eight governors. A relatively strong economy and stable international scene kept voters focused on close-to-home issues, with Reagan's personal popularity giving an edge to GOP candidates. Also, Democrats in 1986 were defending more state house seats than the Republicans. The Democrats, however, regained control of the Senate that year. Their heavy losses in Congress in 1994 were matched by their loss of twelve governorships in those midterm elections. In 1998 the number of Democratic governors was unchanged, but Republicans lost a seat to an independent. In 2002, despite George W. Bush's popularity, the Democrats picked up three governorships. In 2006 the Republicans suffered a net loss of six governors' seats, flipping a 28–22 Republican edge to a 28–22 Democratic edge. In 2010 Republicans came back in gubernatorial races as well, picking up a net of five seats; GOP candidates won eleven seats previously held by Democrats while the latter picked up five seats. One governorship, in Rhode Island, went to an independent candidate.

Midterm elections of state legislators also consistently result in losses for the president's party. The losses of seats in these elections are more likely to result in change of party control of one or both chambers than in presidential election years.

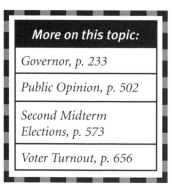

More on this topic:

Governor, p. 233

Public Opinion, p. 502

Second Midterm Elections, p. 573

Voter Turnout, p. 656

Minority-Majority District

The term *minority-majority district,* also seen as *majority-minority district,* is relatively new to American politics. Until the passage of the civil rights laws of the 1960s, including the VOTING RIGHTS ACT of 1965, Americans of African descent—the predominant minority group through most of the nation's history—were effectively prevented from exercising their RIGHT TO VOTE through nearly all of the South. Even in areas elsewhere, where blacks more readily exercised the FRANCHISE, only a small handful of legislative districts were drawn with concentrations of black populations large enough to ensure the election of minority representatives to Congress.

But over the past four decades, the federal government's enforcement and the judicial system's interpretation of the Voting Rights Act first encouraged—and by the 1990s, virtually required where at all practicable—states to draw districts in which minority groups comprised the majority of the population, a practice known as RACIAL REDISTRICTING.

Racial redistricting is one of the two major reasons that courts may set aside their traditional reluctance to get involved in the intensely political practice of legislative redistricting; the other is population imbalance among a state's districts.

The creation of minority-majority districts greatly abetted an upsurge in the number of minority-group members in the U.S. House and in state legislatures. The number of black members in the House, just five in 1967, stood at forty-two in 2011. From 1877 to 1967, there were no more than four Hispanic members at any one time, and for most Congresses in that period there were two or fewer. After 1967 their ranks increased gradually, reaching twenty-six in the 112th Congress that began in January 2011. (See Reference Material tables, pages 725–726.)

Reflecting the Democratic Party's advantage among black voters and somewhat less overwhelming but consistent advantage among Hispanics, all but two of the blacks and all but seven of the Hispanics in the House in 2011 were Democrats. There were two Hispanics in the Senate, one a Republican and one a Democrat.

The greatest number of new minority-majority districts were created during the 1990s. Some white voters and candidates, particularly in the South, challenged some of the oddly shaped districts as illegal forms of racial GERRYMANDERING and reverse discrimination. In several decisions in the 1990s, the Supreme Court agreed with the challengers and ordered the districts redrawn. In 2001, however, the justices upheld a heavily black district in North Carolina, contending that it had been drawn for the political purpose of creating a Democratic district rather than for a racial purpose. (See JUDICIAL SYSTEM and RACIAL REDISTRICTING.)

On the other hand, some critics from within the minority constituencies say that the big one-time jump in minority representation came with a political price. During the decade following the 1990 census, leading Republican strategists entered an unusual alliance with supporters of increased minority representation. While promoting expanded minority representation was seen as giving the party a better image among black and Hispanic voters by advancing their goals, redistricting plans that concentrated minority voters in particular districts also had the effect of boosting the dominance of conservative white voters in surrounding districts.

As a result, while the number of minority-represented districts grew as a result of redistricting plans enacted in the early 1990s, so did the number of suburban and outlying districts in which white Republicans supplanted traditionally conservative southern Democrats— a phenomenon that greatly abetted the Republicans' successful efforts in 1994 to gain a House majority that would last twelve years.

The dominance during those twelve years of a conservative agenda that many blacks opposed and the marginalization of the Congressional Black Caucus in policymaking provoked some second thoughts among a number of black activists. Very few suggested that existing minority-majority

The creation of minority-majority districts helped increase the number of minority-group members in the U.S. House. Rep. James Clyburn, a South Carolina Democrat, is one of forty-two African American members serving in the 112th Congress, all in the House.

Source: CQ Photo/Scott J. Ferrell

districts be dismantled, which would be legally tenuous under provisions of the Voting Rights Act barring "retrogression" of minority candidates' chances to win elections. But there was some sentiment for encouraging black and Hispanic incumbents, who are almost exclusively Democrats, to agree to the reduction of minority-group "supermajorities" in their districts in subsequent redrawings of congressional district lines. Most minority-group members represent districts that are so "packed" to their demographic and partisan advantage that they can go through a very long tenure in Congress without ever facing even mild competition in their general election campaigns. Moving some black and Hispanic voters to more politically competitive districts, this theory holds, would benefit Democrats.

Minority Presidents *See* ELECTORAL ANOMALIES; ELECTORAL

COLLEGE AND VOTES.

MotorVoter Act

Registering to vote in the United States became easier beginning May 20, 1993, when President Bill Clinton signed into law the so-called Motor Voter Act. The law required most states to provide eligible citizens the opportunity to register when they applied for or renewed a driver's license. It also required states to allow mail-in registration and to provide VOTER REGISTRATION forms at agencies that supplied public assistance, such as welfare checks or help for the disabled. Compliance with the federally mandated program was required by 1995. Costs were to be borne by the states.

The act exempted six states (Idaho, Minnesota, New Hampshire, North Dakota, Wisconsin, and Wyoming) that had no voter registration or that permitted residents to register on ELECTION DAY.

Partly as a result of the legislation, a record number of new voters, some 10 million, signed up in the first three years following implementation of the act. The FEDERAL ELECTION COMMISSION (FEC) reported to Congress in 1996—the first presidential election year after the law took effect—that the United States had 143 million registered voters, or 72.8 percent of the voting-age population. The percentage was the highest since 1960, when national registration figures first became available. In its 2001 report, the FEC noted that national registration dropped marginally, to 72.6 percent. However, registration increased among states covered by the Motor Voter Act to 73.8 percent.

The state of Maryland uses this signage to remind citizens of its motor voter program. State officials credit motor voter registration for cleaner voter rolls.

Source: Maryland Department of Transportation

For years, political activists had tried both to simplify the process of registering to vote and to shorten the length of time (the residency requirement) that many states mandated before deeming that citizens had the right to register to vote. Efforts to increase voter registration had begun in a handful of states by the mid-1980s, with state legislatures ordering motor vehicle departments to provide voter registration forms. By 1992 twenty-seven states had some type of motor voter practices in place. But state programs varied in their degree of sophistication and their effect on VOTER TURNOUT.

In most Western nations, government agencies sign up voters, but the United States places the burden for qualifying for electoral participation on the citizen. Although the procedure is still somewhat cumbersome, the Motor Voter Act along with other federal legislation has made voter registration more convenient.

The motor vehicle itself helped to create one of the obstacles to registration. As American society became more mobile, some potential voters encountered difficulty with residency requirements. Many states had required residency for as long as two years before a citizen could register to vote. The 1970 Voting Rights Act Amendment guaranteed the vote in presidential elections if the citizen had lived in the voting district for at least thirty days prior to the election. This measure, analysts have estimated, made approximately 5 million people eligible to vote in the 1972 presidential election.

In 1973 the Supreme Court ruled in *Marston v. Lewis* that states could not deny the full franchise to people who had not lived in a state for a year and in a county for three months. By 1980 seventeen states had no residency requirement, and all but one had requirements of thirty or fewer days.

President Jimmy Carter, the Democrat who held the office from 1977 to 1981, proposed several bills that would have allowed voters to register on ELECTION DAY, but they were not enacted. By the late 1980s, however, most Americans lived in states that allowed registration by postcard.

The Motor Voter Act (technically the National Voter Registration Act of 1993) was passed shortly after President Clinton took office and while his party, the Democrats, still controlled both chambers of Congress. Many congressional Republicans had opposed the legislation, with some citing a potential for ELECTION FRAUD and a cheapening of the voting process by making registration an almost casual act. But many Republicans also had an underlying partisan concern: that the measure would allow citizens of traditional Democratic constituencies—the urban poor and minorities, among others—easier access to the voting booth and therefore provide a new source of votes for the Democrats.

Opponents included Republican George H. W. Bush, the president from 1989 to 1993, who had vetoed a motor voter bill in 1992, citing possible fraud as one of his reasons.

Clinton's signing of the 1993 Motor Voter Act initially did not benefit him or his party as Republicans swept to victory in the 1994 MIDTERM ELECTIONS, taking control of both chambers of Congress for the first time in forty years. By 1996 it became clear that the increase in voter registration affected by the Motor Voter law would not necessarily be matched by an increase in actual voting participation. Although Clinton was reelected in 1996, only 49 percent of the voting-age population voted, a decrease of 6 percentage points from 1992. The 1998 turnout, although somewhat higher than expected, was only 30 percent, the lowest since 1942; the Democrats in that election gained five House seats, making Clinton the first president since Democrat Franklin D. Roosevelt in 1934 whose party won seats at midterm instead of losing them.

Whether the Motor Voter Act has reduced or increased fraud is a matter of debate. The 1998 election provided some indication that the act was helping antifraud efforts. In Maryland, for example, aides to defeated Republican gubernatorial candidate Ellen R. Sauerbrey said that the act helped to solve the problem of nonvoters clogging the rolls. In her previous loss to Democrat Parris N. Glendening in 1994, Sauerbrey charged in court that some fifty thousand votes were cast illegally—some in the name of persons who should have been purged from the voting rolls because they had not voted in years. A state judge ruled in Sauerbrey's CONTESTED ELECTION case that although he found some questionable votes, there were not enough to have changed the result.

Maryland election officials said the voting rolls were cleaner as a result of the Motor Voter Act procedures. They said the changes require them to contact voters by mail and place their names on an inactive list if they fail to respond to two mailings. If those on the inactive list do not vote in the next four years their names are removed from the rolls.

In the 2000 elections, however, complaints about motor voter procedures tripled compared with 1998, according to an FEC report. The report found problems in twenty-three of the forty-four states subject to the law, with complaints ranging from forms being filled out incorrectly to motor vehicle departments failing to forward registration data before elections. As a result, some voters were turned away from the polls.

While there still are critics of the law, it has generally come to be accepted as part of the political process. Although it has not met the high expectations of its advocates for generating higher turnout, it has defied skeptics' predictions of widespread voter fraud.

Mugwump

House Speaker James G. Blaine's ethics problems, and the rift they caused in the Republican Party, helped coin the term "mugwump" in 1884.

Source: Library of Congress

One of the more colorful epithets of American politics—*mugwump*—has survived its rather narrow meaning. It originally referred to a Republican who refused to support the presidential candidacy of James G. Blaine in 1884. Now seldom used, it means someone who bolted his or her political party in favor of another candidate.

Blaine endured ethics controversies that offended some GOP stalwarts, including allegations that he had accepted bribes from Crédit Mobilier, the Union Pacific subsidiary involved in building the transcontinental railroad. Blaine, a representative from Maine who was then Speaker of the House, avoided censure, but the stain of SCANDAL hurt his later candidacy. Supporters of Democrat Grover Cleveland, his opponent in the 1884 presidential election, chanted: "Blaine, Blaine, James G. Blaine! Continental liar from the state of Maine!" Cleveland won, despite his admission that he was supporting an illegitimate son.

Mugwump comes from the Algonquin word for chief. A more facetious derivation is attributed to a Princeton

University president, Harold Willis Dodds, who said, "A mugwump is a fellow with his mug on one side of the fence and his wump on the other." Given wide circulation by the media, Dodds's definition has endured as a secondary meaning of mugwump: a person who cannot make up his or her mind.

Multimember Districts

In the early days of the House of Representatives, several states had at least one CONGRESSIONAL DISTRICT that elected more than one member. The multimember system permitted multiple representatives to be allotted to the more populous area of a state—or perhaps the one with the most political clout—without drawing the district lines to achieve that result.

> **"A mugwump is a fellow with his mug on one side of the fence and his wump on the other."**
>
> **—Harold Willis Dodds,** Princeton University president, in the 1930s

For example, in 1824 Maryland's Fifth District, which included the city of Baltimore and areas to the north and west, chose two representatives, while the remaining seven districts chose one each. In Pennsylvania two districts (the Fourth and Ninth) elected three representatives each, and four districts (the Seventh, Eighth, Eleventh, and Seventeenth) chose two representatives each.

As late as 1840, New York still had as many as five multimember congressional districts: one (the Third), which covered the island of Manhattan, electing four members and four (the Eighth, Seventeenth, Twenty-second, and Twenty-third) choosing two each. But the practice ended in 1842 when Congress enacted a law that said "no one district may elect more than one Representative." The SINGLE-MEMBER DISTRICT provision was a part of the REAPPORTIONMENT legislation following the CENSUS of 1840.

At the state and local levels, though, multimember districts remained commonplace into modern times. Until the 1970s about a third of state house members and a sixth of state senators were elected from multimember jurisdictions. Voters in many city council districts could vote for as many seats as were up for election. Seats in multimember districts are almost always filled by AT-LARGE elections in which voters of the whole city, county, or other jurisdiction are eligible to participate.

But this led to protests from racial and other minorities that ultimately have diminished the use of multimember districts. Minority candidates who have to run in at-large elections find themselves submerged into the majority population, and their ability to win depends strongly on how willing voters in the majority are to vote for a minority. On the other hand, dividing a jurisdiction into smaller units such as districts or wards includes the possibility of designing one or more districts in which minority group members make up most of the population, enhancing the opportunity for a minority candidate to win. (See MINORITY-MAJORITY DISTRICT.)

Multimember districts were particularly prevalent and controversial in the South until those found discriminatory were struck down as unconstitutional by the Supreme Court in *White v. Regester*, a Texas case, in 1973.

Earlier, in the VOTING RIGHTS ACT of 1965, Congress had acted against multimember districts and other discriminatory practices by requiring federal preclearance of election law changes in several states, most of them in the South. In 1975 the provision was extended to states outside the South.

In a 1986 case, *Davis v. Bandemer*, the Supreme Court struck down Indiana's multimember state legislative districting plan as an illegal form of political GERRYMANDERING. Democrats

CLOSER LOOK

The National Conference of State Legislatures summarized the legal standing of multimember districts as follows in a study published in 2003:

"The U.S. Supreme Court has held that the use of multi-member legislative districts is not unconstitutional *per se*. However, the Court has invalidated the use of multi-member legislative districts where their use impedes the ability of minority voters to elect representatives of their choice. Multi-member districts that discriminate against a racial group will most likely be challenged under Section 2 of the Voting Rights Act, which requires only showing that an election practice results in discrimination.

"Challenges to multi-member legislative districts on the ground that the districts discriminate against members of a political party will continue to be raised under the Equal Protection Clause of the Fourteenth Amendment. In these cases, a discriminatory purpose and discriminatory results are necessary elements of a successful challenge.

"The Supreme Court has made clear its preference for single-member legislative districts by discouraging the use of multi-member districts in court-drawn plans absent extraordinary circumstances."

protested that the Republican-controlled legislature had drawn the district lines to dilute the Democrats' voting strength, especially in urban areas.

These laws and rulings had a significant impact on the number of multimember districts maintained by states and localities. A study by the National Conference of State Legislatures showed that by the 1990s, just four states (Nevada, North Carolina, Vermont, and West Virginia) had any multimember state senate districts; Alaska, Idaho, North Dakota, and Wyoming had eliminated theirs since the 1980s. At the same time, there were twelve states with multimember state House districts (Arizona, Arkansas, Idaho, Maryland, New Hampshire, New Jersey, North Carolina, North Dakota, South Dakota, Vermont, Washington, and West Virginia); Alaska, Georgia, Indiana, and Wyoming had eliminated theirs since the 1980s.

A form of at-large voting, called CUMULATIVE VOTING, has gained some adherents as a means for minorities to achieve proportional representation by concentrating their votes on candidates from their minority group. Cumulative voting, however, has not been widely adopted in the United States.

In some multimember districts that have at-large elections, candidates have urged voters to practice what is known as "bullet voting." Under this procedure, a candidate's supporters—who are eligible to vote for as many candidates as there are seats to be filled—are asked to vote only for him or her and withhold the other votes they may be entitled to cast.

In a 1986 Supreme Court case, *Thornburg v. Gingles*, African Americans argued that they were forced to resort to bullet voting in some multimember districts to elect members of the North Carolina legislature. The necessity of surrendering some of the votes they were entitled to cast in order to have any chance of electing the candidate of their choice deprived them of their full rights under section 2 of the 1965 VOTING RIGHTS ACT, they argued.

In its decision the Court did not prohibit multimember districts, but it spelled out in detail the steps needed to prove discrimination under section 2. The complainants must be able to show a consistent pattern of being defeated by the majority, the Court said. (See BLACK SUFFRAGE; RACIAL REDISTRICTING; VOTING RIGHTS ACT.)

More on this topic:

At-Large, p. 10

Black Suffrage, p. 28

Cumulative Voting, p. 132

Gerrymander, p. 226

Minority-Majority District, p. 338

Racial Redistricting, p. 509

Single-Member Districts, p. 589

Voting Rights Act, p. 663

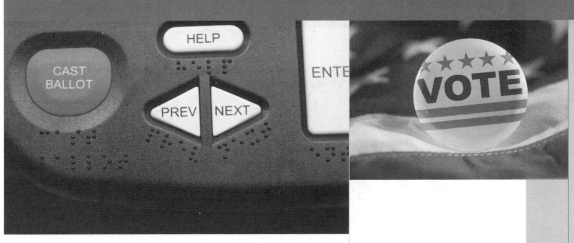

National Democratic Party (1896)

With the nation in the midst of a depression and populists in the agrarian Midwest and South demanding monetary reform, currency was the dominant issue of the 1896 campaign. This produced a brief realignment in American politics.

One aspect of this was a split in the ranks of the established Democratic Party. A conservative faction that favored the gold standard for U.S. currency—which called itself the National Democrats—bolted from the Democratic Party after its 1896 convention adopted a pro-silver platform and nominated William Jennings Bryan, a vocal advocate of that position.

The Republican Party was controlled by leaders who favored maintenance of the gold standard; gold, because of its rarity compared with silver, was a noninflationary currency. Agrarian midwestern and southern Democrats, reflecting a populist philosophy, gained control of the Democratic Party in 1896 and committed it to the free coinage of silver, an inflationary currency demanded by rural elements threatened by debts. The Democrats attracted pro-silver bolters from the Republican Party, while some gold-standard Democrats crossed over to the Republican side. Other gold-standard Democrats opposed the Republicans' protectionist position on tariffs and established an independent party.

Meeting in Indianapolis in September 1896, the National Democrats adopted a platform favoring maintenance of the gold standard and selected a ticket headed by seventy-nine-year-old Illinois senator John M. Palmer.

Democratic president Grover Cleveland and leading members of his administration, repudiated by the convention that chose Bryan, supported the National Democrats. The National

The nomination of William Jennings Bryan in 1896 splintered the Democratic Party, leading conservative party members to form the National Democratic Party.

Source: Library of Congress

Democrats made no pretense that their party would win, but rather promoted opposition to Bryan: During the campaign the National Democrats encouraged conservative Democrats to vote either for the National Democratic ticket or for the Republican candidate, William McKinley. The Palmer ticket received 133,435 votes (1 percent of the popular vote), while McKinley defeated Bryan.

Returning prosperity as the decade wore on and the Spanish-American War overshadowed the currency issue, and the intense Democratic Party factionalism that produced the National Democratic Party ended.

National Election Studies

In the last quarter of the twentieth century, social scientists in the United States and around the world benefited from a systematic examination of U.S. elections by the National Election Studies (NES). The work of the NES is highly regarded by political scientists and other scholars who need objective, factual information on American political behavior.

Founded by the U.S. National Science Foundation in 1977 as a national resource for data on voting, public opinion, and political participation, and now fully titled as the American National Election Studies (ANES), the organization is a joint project of Stanford University and the University of Michigan. Prior to Science Foundation backing, data for the time-series in elections were gathered from 1947 and after by social scientists at Michigan.

ANES describes its mission as follows: "To inform explanations of election outcomes by providing data that support rich hypothesis testing, maximize methodological excellence, measure many variables, and promote comparisons across people, contexts, and time. The ANES serves this mission by providing researchers with a view of the political world through the eyes of ordinary citizens. Such data are critical, because these citizens' actions determine election outcomes."

To that end, ANES conducts national surveys of the U.S. electorate in presidential and MID-TERM ELECTION years. During odd-numbered years it carries out research and development work through pilot studies.

The NES "time series" are made up of preelection and postelection studies in presidential election years and postelection studies in midterm election years. The lengthy time span covered helps scholars to spot and understand long-term trends and changes in PUBLIC OPINION, political values and behavior, and the political and social composition of the electorate.

The ANES website includes its Guide to Public Opinion and Electoral Behavior, which offers data ranging from 1948 through 2008 and is divided into the following categories:

- Social and Religious Characteristics of the Electorate, such as age, race, gender, education, and religion
- Ideological Self-Identification

- Public Opinion on Public Policy Issues, such as health care, affirmative action, abortion, the military, and the economy
- Support for the Political System, such as trust in government and government responsiveness
- Political Involvement and Participation in Politics, such as voter turnout, campaign contributions and other activities, attention to the campaign in the media, and interest in politics
- Evaluation of the Presidential Candidates
- Evaluation of Congressional Candidates
- Vote Choice, for president, for the U.S. House of Representatives, and split-ticket voting

The address for the ANES Web site is www.electionstudies.org.

Through 1973 the organization's collection at the University of Michigan Institute for Social Research and its Inter-university Consortium for Political and Social Research included 25,000 individual elections and the names of almost 115,000 candidates.

These data provide the basis for the first edition of *CQ Press's Guide to U.S. Elections,* published in 1975. Popular returns in the book began in 1824 for presidential, gubernatorial, and U.S. House elections and in 1913 for Senate elections. For the five subsequent editions of the book, the latest published in 2010 and updated through voting in 2008, election information was derived from Congressional Quarterly election coverage, CQ Press's *America Votes* biennial series, and election officials in many state governments.

National Party Conventions

National conventions remain major public relations and mobilizing events for the political parties. They conclude the presidential nominating process with extravaganzas of color, socializing, and occasional—though increasingly rare—drama, sometimes centering on the nominees' selection of their vice presidential RUNNING MATE.

What the conventions have not had for more than four decades is a consequential role in choosing the major parties' presidential nominees—which was the major role of these gatherings from their emergence in the 1830s through the 1960s.

PRESIDENTIAL SELECTION REFORMS that emerged from the political ferment of the 1960s aimed at shifting the power to select nominees from party bosses to rank-and-file voters by making primaries and open caucuses the main modes of allocating DELEGATES among the candidates seeking the nomination. While it remains technically possible for candidates to split the delegate votes evenly enough to deprive any one candidate of a sure majority—thus sending the contest to the convention for the final decision—it has yet to happen. The increasing practice of crowding primaries and caucuses into the earliest weeks of the nominating process, known as FRONT-LOADING, has consistently provided huge advantages to the best-known and best-funded candidates. Winning in the early contests usually tends to give the FRONT-RUNNER momentum, or a BANDWAGON effect, that quickly becomes unstoppable.

In 2000, when the nomination was up for grabs in both parties, Republican George W. Bush and Democrat Al Gore each had enough delegates to win their nominations by early March. The same was true of Democrat John Kerry in 2004, a year in which Bush, seeking a second term, had no competition for the Republican nod.

In 2008—when the nomination for both parties was open—Republicans settled early on their nominee, Arizona senator John McCain. Democrats, however, went through the full primary and caucus season, from January to June, before the selection of Barack Obama as nominee was fully settled. Obama was engaged in a spirited competition was former first lady and New York senator Hillary Rodham Clinton throughout the period. Although the contest ran into June, analysts noted that by late winter Obama had gathered enough convention delegates—in both primaries and caucuses—that he had all but locked up the nomination because not enough delegates remained in the later contests to give Clinton a realistic chance to catch up.

Obama then was nominated on the first ballot when Clinton asked the convention to suspend voting by state and name him by acclamation. In fact, since 1952 every Democratic and Republican nominee for president has been nominated on the first ballot.

The delegates to the modern conventions do perform some substantive business—such as ratifying the presidential nominee's vice presidential choice, agreeing upon a statement of party principles and issue stances or PLATFORM, and voting on various changes to national party rules.

Barack Obama, then a candidate for the U.S. Senate, delivers the keynote address to delegates during the 2004 Democratic National Convention in Boston.

Source: AP Images/Kevork Djansezian

Occasionally a new political star will emerge from the dozens of speeches that pack each convention's schedule. A recent example of this was Obama, who gave the keynote address to the 2004 Democratic National Convention in Boston. Then a state senator and the Democratic nominee for an open U.S. Senate seat, Obama delivered a dynamic and moving speech that electrified television audiences; that November, he won a landslide victory in his Senate race. Still riding the wave of popularity and publicity that his convention speech generated, he entered and eventually won the 2008 contest for the party's presidential nomination even though at the start he was considered an underdog to Clinton.

For the most part, however, the conventions have converted from once-vital forums of debate and competition to carefully programmed multimedia spectacles—often referred to as four-day "infomercials"—that are aimed at drawing and holding the attention of an increasingly disinterested voting public. The convention gives the presidential and vice presidential nominees a forum to kick off the general election campaign and to demonstrate their leadership qualities to the party and the public.

Multiple Functions

Yet despite considerable grumbling over whether the quadrennial affairs are worth the time, effort and, in recent years, significantly increased security costs, neither party has seriously contemplated doing away with the conventions.

For about 175 years, the convention has been the nominating body that the Democrats, Republicans, and most of the principal alternative, or third, parties have used to choose—or at least ratify—their candidates for president and vice president. Besides being platform writers, delegates

form the organization's supreme governing body and as such they make major decisions on party affairs. Between conventions, such decisions are made by the national committee with the guidance of the party chairman or chairwoman.

The convention is an outgrowth of the American political experience. Nowhere is it mentioned in the Constitution, nor has the convention's authority ever been a subject of congressional legislation. Rather, the convention has evolved along with the rest of the presidential selection process. It replaced the so-called King Caucus, the partisan congressional groupings that controlled nominations until they began to dissipate in the 1820s as state legislatures, state conventions, and mass meetings challenged the caucuses' power. The 1828 election of Democrat Andrew Jackson, nominated by the Tennessee legislature, signaled the death of King Caucus.

Its successor, the convention, has been the accepted nominating method of the major political parties since the election of 1832, but internal changes within the convention system have been massive since the early, formative years.

Locations and Financing

Choosing a location is the first major step in convention planning. The national committees of the two parties used to select the sites about a year before the conventions are to take place, but the increased logistical complications involved in staging the conventions has spurred earlier decisions in recent years. For example, the Republicans announced in September 2006 that they would hold their September 2008 convention in St. Paul, Minnesota. The Democrats in January 2007 selected Denver, Colorado, as the site for their August 2008 convention. By early 2010, Democrats had selected Charlotte, North Carolina, for their 2012 convention (announced in February) and Republicans had selected Tampa, Florida (announced in May).

Before the Civil War, conventions frequently were held in small buildings, even churches, and attracted only several hundred delegates and a minimum of spectators. Transportation and communications were slow, so most conventions were held in the late spring in a centrally located city. Baltimore, Maryland, was the most popular convention city in this period, playing host to the first six Democratic conventions (1832 through 1852), two Whig conventions, one NATIONAL REPUBLICAN convention, and the 1831 ANTI-MASONIC PARTY gathering—America's first national nominating convention. With the nation's westward expansion, the heartland city of Chicago became the most frequent convention center, a distinction it continued to hold into the scheduled 2012 conventions. Since its first one in 1860, Chicago has been the site of twenty-five major-party conventions (fourteen Republican, eleven Democratic), with the most recent being the 1996 Democratic convention that nominated President Bill Clinton for a second term. (See table, Sites of Major-Party Conventions, p. 350.)

> **"I pledge you, I pledge myself, to a new deal for the American people."**
>
> **—Democrat Franklin D. Roosevelt** in his 1932 speech accepting his party's presidential nomination; he was the first nominee to address a convention personally. The phrase "new deal," just a passing mention in the speech, would become the motto for his dramatic economic recovery program as he took office in the midst of the Great Depression.

> **"Only in America can a fifteen-year-old boy arrive on our shores alone, not speaking the language—with a suitcase and the hope of a brighter future—and . . . stand one step away from making history as the first Cuban-American to serve in the United States Senate."**
>
> **—Sen. Mel Martinez** of Florida, speaking at the 2004 Republican convention

SITES OF MAJOR-PARTY CONVENTIONS, 1832–2012

The chart lists the twenty-four cities selected as the sites of major-party conventions and the number of conventions they have hosted from the first national gathering for the Democrats (1832) and the Republicans (1856) through the 2012 conventions. The Democrats have hosted a total of forty-seven conventions; the Republicans forty.

	Total Conventions	Democratic Conventions		Republican Conventions	
		Number	Last Hosted	Number	Last Hosted
Chicago, Ill.	25	11	1996	14	1960
Baltimore, Md.	10	9	1912	1	1864
Philadelphia, Pa.	8	2	1948	6	2000
St. Louis, Mo.	5	4	1916	1	1896
New York, N.Y.	5	5	1992	1	2004
San Francisco, Calif.	4	2	1984	2	1964
Cincinnati, Ohio	3	2	1880	1	1876
Kansas City, Mo.	3	1	1900	2	1976
Miami Beach, Fla.	3	1	1972	2	1972
Los Angeles, Calif.	2	2	2000	0	—
Cleveland, Ohio	2	0	—	2	1936
Houston, Texas	2	1	1928	1	1992
Atlanta, Ga.	1	1	1988	0	—
Atlantic City, N.J.	1	1	1964	0	—
Boston, Mass.	1	1	2004	0	—
Charleston, S.C.	1	1	1860	0	—
Dallas, Texas	1	0	—	1	1984
Denver, Colo.	2	2	2008	0	—
Detroit, Mich.	1	0	—	1	1980
Minneapolis- St. Paul, Minn.	2	0	—	2	2008
New Orleans, La.	1	0	—	1	1988
San Diego, Calif.	1	0	—	1	1996
Tampa, Fla.	1	0	—	1	2012
Charlotte, N.C.	1	1	2012	0	—

Advances in transportation, particularly jet aircraft, have affected the scheduling and placement of conventions. In the nineteenth century, conventions were sometimes held a year or more before the election and at the latest were completed by late spring of the election year. With the ability of people to assemble quickly, conventions now are held in late summer (or early September) of the election year.

Geographic centrality is no longer the primary consideration in site selection. With the conventions drawing throngs of delegates (about 2,500 for the Republicans' 2004 convention in New York City and just more than 4,300 for the Democratic gathering in Boston) and tens of thousands more of alternate delegates, reporters and news media technicians, party officials, guests, vendors, and others, the choice of a site is limited to the relatively few cities capable of handling such a large temporary population.

In addition to adequate hotel and convention hall facilities, the safety of the delegates and other attendees is a major consideration in selection of a national party convention site. This is hardly a new concern: the island location of Miami Beach, for example, made it easier to contain Vietnam War protest demonstrators and reportedly was a factor in its selection by the Republicans in 1968—a year in which, by contrast, the Democratic convention in Chicago was marred by huge protests against the Vietnam War that turned into violent confrontations with police—and by both parties in 1972.

The security issue, though, has drawn increased attention in recent years. As late as the 1996 conventions, participants and passersby could walk up to the perimeter of the convention site before reaching a security checkpoint. By 2000, following protests against the International Monetary Fund in Seattle that turned riotous, both the Republicans in Philadelphia and the Democrats in Los Angeles greatly extended the perimeter and controlled movement with mazes of security barriers and fencing. And in 2004, the first presidential election year after the September 11, 2001, attacks, the convention cities of New York and Boston bristled with security obstacles and heavily armed police and military personnel.

Since 1976, presidential elections have received PUBLIC FINANCING, and parties have depended on host cities to supplement the amount they could legally spend on their conventions. In 2008, that amount was $16.8 million per party, which each major party received from the optional checkoff on federal income taxes for presidential campaigns. The Republicans ended their convention one day short of the planned time and returned some of the money, which brought their subsidy to $13 million. In addition, each convention was allotted $50 million for security; that money went to state and local governments providing the protection rather than to the parties.

That funding, though, pays for just a small percentage of the costs of staging the convention and housing, feeding, entertaining, and providing transportation, security, and other amenities to participants. Much of that money comes from the host committees in the convention city. In fact, the driving factor behind the site selections of recent conventions has had little to do with the preferences of the candidates or political calculations of the parties; rather it has been which cities offer the best financial package to the party in question. The Center for Responsive Politics estimated that the host committees for Boston and New York spent a combined total of $139 million on the 2004 conventions—up from the $96 million provided by Los Angeles and Philadelphia in 2000.

Much of the money raised by these host committees comes from local and some national corporate interests, creating a persistent controversy about the ethical propriety of these financial arrangements.

Call of the Convention

The second major step in the quadrennial convention process follows several months after the site selection with announcement of the convention call, the establishment of the three major convention committees—credentials, rules, and platform (resolutions)—the appointment of convention officers, and finally the holding of the convention itself. While these basic steps have undergone little change over the years, there have been major alterations within the nominating convention system.

HIGHLIGHTS OF NATIONAL PARTY CONVENTIONS, 1831–2008

1831 First national political convention held in Baltimore by Anti-Masonic Party.

1832 Democratic Party met in Baltimore for its first national convention.

1839 Whig Party held its first national convention.

1840 Democrats set up committee to select vice presidential nominees, subject to approval of convention.

1844 Democrats nominated James K. Polk—first "dark horse" candidate—after nine ballots. Silas Wright declined the vice presidential nomination. First time a convention nominee refused nomination.

1848 Democrats established continuing committee, known as "Democratic National Committee."

1852 Democrats and Whigs both adopted platforms before nominating candidates for president, setting precedent followed almost uniformly ever since.

1856 First Republican national convention held in Philadelphia.

1860 Democrats met in Charleston, S.C. After ten days and deadlocked on a presidential nominee, delegates adjourned and reconvened in Baltimore. Benjamin Fitzpatrick, the Democrats' choice for vice president, became the first candidate to withdraw after convention adjournment and be replaced by a selection of the national committee.

First Republican credentials dispute took place over seating delegates from slave states and voting strength of delegates from states where party was comparatively weak.

1864 In attempt to close ranks during Civil War, Republicans used the name "Union Party" at convention.

1868 For the first time, Republicans gave a candidate (Ulysses S. Grant) 100 percent of vote on first ballot.

A letter from Susan B. Anthony was read before the Democratic convention urging support of women's suffrage

1872 Victoria Claflin Woodhull, nominated by the Equal Rights Party, was the first female presidential candidate. African American leader Frederick Douglass was her running mate.

1880 Republicans nominated James A. Garfield for president on 36th ballot—party's all-time record number of ballots.

1884 Republican representative John Roy Lynch of Mississippi became first African American elected temporary chairman of national nominating convention.

1888 Frederick Douglass was first African American to receive a vote in presidential balloting at a major party political convention (Republican).

1900 Each party had one female delegate.

1904 Florida Democrats selected delegates in first-ever presidential primary election.

1920 For first time, women attended conventions in significant numbers.

1924 Republicans adopted bonus votes for states that went Republican in previous election. GOP convention was first to be broadcast on radio.

John W. Davis was nominated by Democrats on record 103rd ballot.

1932 Republicans began tradition of appointing party leader from House of Representatives as permanent convention chairman.

Democrat Franklin D. Roosevelt became first major-party candidate to accept presidential nomination in person.

1936 Democratic Party voted to end requirement of two-thirds delegate majority for nomination.

1940 Republican convention was first to be televised.

1944 Democrats adopted bonus votes for states that went Democratic in previous election.

Thomas E. Dewey became first Republican candidate to accept nomination in person.

1948 Democrats began appointing Speaker of the House as permanent chairman.

Republicans renominated Thomas E. Dewey—first time GOP renominated a defeated presidential candidate.

1952 Adlai E. Stevenson was chosen as Democratic nominee in one of few genuine "drafts" in history.

1956 Democrats used party loyalty provision in selecting delegates for first time.

1960 Democrats adopted civil rights plank that was strongest in party history.

Republican nominee Richard Nixon was party's first vice president nominated for president at completion of his term.

1964 Sen. Margaret Chase Smith was nominated for presidency at Republican convention—first time a woman placed in nomination by a major party.

1968 Democratic Party voted to end unit rule. Outside the Chicago convention, antiwar protests erupted in violence.

1980 Democratic delegates were composed of an equal number of men and women.

1984 Democrats nominated Rep. Geraldine A. Ferraro of New York for vice president—the first woman placed on national ticket by a major party.

1996 The Reform Party conducted its first convention in a two-stage process that allowed balloting by mail, electronic mail, or phone.

2000 Democrats nominated Sen. Joseph I. Lieberman of Connecticut for vice president—the first Jew placed on a national ticket by a major party.

2004 Security was greatly increased for the Democratic convention in Boston and the Republican convention in New York City, the first conventions after the September 11, 2001, al-Qaeda attacks and the outbreak of the war in Iraq.

2008 In a historic first, Democrats in Denver nominated Barack Obama, an African American. In another first his primary opponent was a woman, Hillary Rodham Clinton, who enthusiastically endorsed him once he had the nomination locked up. Republicans, meeting in Minneapolis-St. Paul but with less drama, nominated Sen. John McCain of Arizona, who also made history by selecting the GOP's first female candidate for vice president, Alaska's governor, Sarah Palin. The party's opening ceremonies were curtailed when a sizeable hurricane in the Gulf of Mexico threatened to remind voters of the much-criticized federal response to the devastating Gulf hurricane Katrina in 2005.

The call to the convention sets the date and site of the meeting and is issued early in each election year, if not before. The call to the first Democratic convention, held in 1832, was issued by the New Hampshire legislature. Early Whig conventions were called by party members in Congress. With the establishment of national committees later in the nineteenth century, the function of issuing the convention call fell to these new party organizations. Each national committee currently has the responsibility for allocating delegates to each state. (See DELEGATE; PRESIDENTIAL PRIMARIES; PRESIDENTIAL SELECTION REFORMS.)

Controversial Rules

Although it did not have a formal set of rules before 1972, the Democratic Party operated from its inception with two controversial practices never used by the Republicans: the UNIT RULE and the TWO-THIRDS RULE. The unit rule, which enabled the majority of a delegation to cast the delegation's entire vote for one candidate or position, even if there were dissenters, lasted the longest. The Democrats did not abolish it until their 1968 convention.

The two-thirds nominating rule required any candidate for president or vice president to win not just a simple majority but a two-thirds majority. Because the "Solid South" was heavily Democratic at the time, the rule gave the region a virtual veto over any possible nominee. Nevertheless, after trying unsuccessfully in 1932, supporters of President Franklin D. Roosevelt won abolition of the rule in 1936. In return, the South received more delegate votes at later conventions.

In its century of use, the two-thirds rule frequently produced protracted, multiballot conventions, often giving the Democrats a degree of turbulence that the Republicans, requiring only a simple majority, did not have. Between 1832 and 1932, seven Democratic conventions took more

than ten ballots to select a presidential candidate. In contrast, in their entire convention history, the Republicans have had just one convention that required more than ten ballots to select a presidential candidate. That was in 1880, when James A. Garfield was nominated on the thirty-sixth ballot over former president Ulysses S. Grant and other candidates.

A number of presidential nominations, particularly of Democratic candidates under the two-thirds rule, were made at so-called BROKERED CONVENTIONS dominated by party bosses who controlled the proceedings and selected the nominees behind closed doors. Much of the protracted balloting on the convention floor dealt with the elimination of FAVORITE SON candidates put forth by state delegations even though they had no realistic chance of being nominated. PRESIDENTIAL SELECTION REFORMS by the major political parties have made brokered conventions and favorite son candidacies largely obsolete.

One such reform survived a controversial vote at the 1980 Democratic convention. The vote concerned a new rule that bound delegates to vote on the first ballot for the candidates under whose banner they had been elected. Most of these delegates were obliged to vote for President Jimmy Carter because of his primary and caucus victories. Supporters of Sen. Edward M. Kennedy of Massachusetts, however, wanted to open the convention and pry the nomination away from Carter. They tried but failed to defeat the binding rule and improve Kennedy's first-ballot

> *"Having behind us the commercial interests and the laboring interests and all the toiling masses, we shall answer their demands for a gold standard by saying to them, you shall not press down upon the brow of labor this crown of thorns. You shall not crucify mankind upon a cross of gold."*
>
> **—Democrat William Jennings Bryan** at the 1896 Democratic convention in Chicago, at which his evocation of a populist economic program centered on the free coinage of silver helped him win the presidential nomination. Viewed as too radical by most voters, Bryan was defeated that year by Republican William McKinley.

standing. The rule won approval, 1,936.42 to 1,390.58. Passage ensured Carter's renomination. Shortly afterward, Kennedy announced that his name would not be placed in nomination.

Convention Officers

Credentials, rules, and platform are the three major convention committees, but each party has additional committees, including one in charge of convention arrangements. Within the Republican Party, the arrangements committee recommends a slate of convention officers to the national committee, which in turn refers the names to the committee on permanent organization. The officers chosen by the committee are then subject to approval by the convention. In the Democratic Party, this function is performed by the rules committee.

In both parties, the presiding officer during the bulk of the convention is the permanent chairman, usually the party's leader in the House of Representatives. However, this loose precedent was broken in the Democratic Party by a rule adopted at the 1972 convention requiring that the presiding officer position alternate every four years between the sexes. In 1976 Rep. Lindy Boggs of Louisiana became the first female convention chairman.

"For me, a few hours ago, this campaign came to an end. For all those whose cares have been our concern, the work goes on, the cause endures, the hope still lives, and the dream shall never die."

—Sen. Edward M. Kennedy of Massachusetts at the 1980 Democratic convention in New York. Though Kennedy's challenge to incumbent president Jimmy Carter for the Democratic nomination failed, he moved the audience with his evocation of the spirit of his brothers, President John F. Kennedy and New York senator Robert F. Kennedy, who were assassinated during the 1960s.

Platform Writing

The job of writing a document of party principles falls to the platform committee. Although the major-party philosophies usually do not change drastically in four years, the platform committee begins anew with each convention, and its product lasts until the party's next national convention.

Sometimes there are bitter convention fights over a particular plank, even though the platform is not binding on the party's presidential candidate, and the document is often viewed as inconsequential rhetoric. In 1948, for example, Mississippi and Alabama delegates walked out after the Democratic convention adopted a strong civil rights plank. Several days later dissidents from thirteen southern states nominated Gov. Strom Thurmond of South Carolina for president under the STATES' RIGHTS (Dixiecrat) banner. In 1964 Thurmond switched to the Republican Party.

At the 1968 Democratic convention, platform dissension spilled into the convention hall, with angry debates over controversial issues such as opposition to the Vietnam War. The divisive image this created put pressure on party leaders in ensuing years to make sure that issues that could reveal schisms within party ranks were vetted before the convention. So symbolic has the effort become that the platform, which is typically written at a series of sessions in the convention city the week before the main event, now is more likely to be produced as the result of a round of public "platform committee" hearings that are held in locations around the nation in the weeks before the convention. (See Reference Material, Major Platform Fights, p. 703; PLATFORM.)

Filling Vacancies

An important convention function that rarely has to be used is to anticipate possible vacancies at the top of the ticket. The Republicans faced this problem in June 1912 when they renominated President William Howard Taft and Vice President James S. Sherman. Because Sherman was in failing health, the convention authorized the national committee to fill any vacancy that might occur. When Sherman died October 30, just before election day, the GOP national committee selected Nicholas Murray Butler, president of Columbia University, as Taft's running mate. Sherman's name remained on the ballot, but the GOP lost to the Democratic ticket of Woodrow Wilson and Thomas R. Marshall in an election marked by a strong showing by former president Theodore Roosevelt running as a Progressive.

Today, standing rules of both major parties call for the national party committee to fill the vacancy if a nominee dies or resigns after the convention but before election day, or after the election but before Congress counts the electoral votes.

The Democratic Party was faced with this situation in 1972 when Sen. Thomas F. Eagleton of Missouri resigned as the vice presidential nominee after it was disclosed that years earlier he had undergone electroshock therapy for depression. Sen. George S. McGovern of South Dakota then chose R. Sargent Shriver of Maryland as his running mate, and the national party committee confirmed the substitute nomination.

Oratory and Coverage

The invention of new means of communication, particularly television, has significantly affected the nominating convention system. No longer are the thousands of people in the hall the primary concern of party leaders. Now their challenge is to attract and hold the attention of viewers nationally and around the world—many of whom, in the early twenty-first century, prefer to obtain information about the conventions through the Internet rather than television or radio.

Radio coverage of conventions began in 1924 and television coverage sixteen years later. One of the first changes inspired by the media age was the termination of the custom that a presidential candidate did not appear at the convention but accepted his nomination in a ceremony several weeks later. Franklin D. Roosevelt was the first major-party candidate to break this tradition when in 1932 he delivered his acceptance speech in person before the Democratic convention in Chicago. His offer of a "new deal" for the American people coined the unofficial name for his record-long presidency. Twelve years later, FDR's final rival, Thomas E. Dewey, became the first Republican nominee to give his acceptance speech to the convention, also in Chicago. Since then the final activity of both the Democratic and Republican conventions has been the delivery of the acceptance speeches by the vice presidential and presidential nominees.

With an eye on the viewing public, party leaders in recent years have streamlined the convention schedule. The result has been shorter speeches and generally fewer roll calls than at pretelevision conventions. An exception to the short-speech rule was the thirty-five-minute nominating speech Bill Clinton gave for the Democratic presidential candidate, Massachusetts governor Michael S. Dukakis, at the 1988 Democratic convention in Atlanta. In 1992, as the nominee himself, Clinton began his acceptance speech by joking that he wanted "to finish that speech I started four years ago." He went on to speak even longer: sixty-six minutes.

> **"When the Soviet Union walked out of arms control negotiations, and refused even to discuss the issues, the San Francisco Democrats didn't blame Soviet intransigence. They blamed the United States. But then, they always blame America first."**
>
> —*Jeane Kirkpatrick,* United Nations ambassador under President Ronald Reagan, in a speech to the 1984 Republican convention in Dallas that nominated Reagan to a second term. The Democrats, who held their 1984 convention in San Francisco, alleged that Kirkpatrick was trying to associate their party with that city's reputation for social liberalism and its large gay population.

Convention leaders try to put the party's major selling points—the highly partisan keynote speech, the nominating ballots, and the candidates' acceptance speeches—on in television's prime evening viewing time. (The effort to put acceptance speeches on in prime time has been especially strong since 1972, when Democratic nominee McGovern was forced to wait until 3 a.m. EDT to make his speech.)

Barbara Jordan, a Democratic representative from Texas, was the first black woman to deliver the keynote address at a major-party convention.

Source: CQ Photo/Michael Jenkins

Clare Boothe Luce, a representative from Connecticut, coined the term "G.I. Joe" at the 1944 Republican convention.

Source: Library of Congress

H. L. Mencken once wrote that convention speakers are "plainly on furlough from some home for extinct volcanoes." And indeed most convention oratory is quickly forgotten, but there are exceptions.

William Jennings Bryan, for example, electrified the 1896 Democratic convention with his "Cross of Gold" speech condemning Republican and Gold Democrat opposition to expansion of the money supply by free coinage of silver. The gold plank was defeated, and Bryan won the nomination on the fifth ballot. He lost the election but later recorded his famed speech on Thomas Edison's invention, the phonograph.

Keynoters, public figures known for their oratorical skills, are expected to whip up enthusiasm early in the convention. Until the 1950s the temporary chairman gave the keynote address, but Democrats abolished the position, and Republicans began dividing the two jobs. In recent years military or space heroes, and current or former governors or members of Congress, including women, have been popular choices, sometimes with more than one keynoter at the same convention. (See Reference Material, pp. 706, 707.)

Rep. Barbara C. Jordan, a Texas Democrat, the first black woman to keynote a convention, did it twice, in 1976 and, after she left the House, in 1992. In 1988, Texas treasurer Ann Richards poked keynote fun at the wealthy Republican candidate, fellow Texan George H. W. Bush, as having "been born with a silver foot in his mouth." She was elected governor in 1990, but Bush had the last laugh; his son George W. Bush defeated Richards in 1994. Six years later, the younger Bush accepted his first nomination as standard bearer of the Republican Party.

Although not a keynote speaker, playwright Clare Boothe Luce, then a member of Congress from Connecticut, made history at the 1944 Republican convention by coining the term "G.I. Joe."

Other convention "firsts":

- Civil War general Ulysses S. Grant won the 1868 Republican nomination on the first ballot with 100 percent of the vote.
- The first woman nominated for president at a convention was Victoria Claflin Woodhull, in 1872. Her running mate on the Equal Rights Party ticket was African American leader Frederick Douglass. At the 1888 GOP convention, Douglass became the first African American to receive a vote for presidential nomination.
- Republican Rutherford B. Hayes of Ohio and Democrat Samuel J. Tilden of New York were the first sitting governors nominated for president, in 1876.
- The first conventions to have female delegates were in 1900, when each party had one.
- The 1904 Republican convention nominated Theodore Roosevelt, the first former vice president nominated in his own right after succeeding a deceased president.
- Democrats held the longest national party convention—seventeen days in New York in 1924. It took a record 103 roll calls to nominate Wall Street lawyer John W. Davis over another New Yorker, Gov. Alfred E. Smith. Four years later Smith became the first Roman Catholic nominated for president by a major party.
- The first woman nominated for vice president was Geraldine Ferraro of New York, Democrat, in 1984. The first woman nominated for vice president on the Republican ticket was Alaska governor Sarah Palin, in 2008.
- Connecticut senator Joseph I. Lieberman became the first Jewish American nominated to a national party ticket when he was picked to run for vice president on the 2000 Democratic ticket headed by Al Gore.
- In 2008, Democrats nominated the first African American, Barack Obama, to run for president on a major party ticket.

At the 1924 Democratic convention, it took delegates 103 roll calls to nominate John W. Davis as the presidential candidate. The convention lasted seventeen days, making it the longest in U.S. history.

Source: Library of Congress

Just as they try to put their candidate's best foot forward during prime time, party leaders try to keep evidence of bitter party factionalism confined to the daytime hours when fewer people are watching. The aim is to make the party look unified and enhance the candidate's POSTCONVENTION BOUNCE in the public opinion polls. Sometimes this bounce is enough to reverse the nominees' standings, but usually the one who was ahead in ratings before the convention goes on to win the general election.

The determination to avoid debate and manage a convention with precise timing may have reached its height at the 2000 Republican convention. Concerns about the accelerating front-loading of the presidential nominating process had spurred Republican officials to empanel a party commission to consider changing the primary schedule; after extensive meetings, the commission was prepared to offer a plan to the convention that would have grouped state primaries into four blocks spread out over several weeks of the spring of the presidential election year. But plans to bring the matter to the convention floor were quashed by George W. Bush's campaign, which was preparing for his nomination at the convention. Bush planners did not want to risk that the debate would interfere with their intricately planned timeline for the convention's events.

In the media age the appearance of fairness is important, and in a sense the need to look fair and open has assisted the movement for party reform. Some influential party leaders, skeptical of reform of the convention, have found resistance difficult in the glare of television.

Before the revolution in the means of transportation and communication, conventions met in relative anonymity. Today, they are held in all the privacy of a fishbowl, with every action and every rumor closely scrutinized. They have become media events and as such are targets for incidents and demonstrations that can embarrass the party or cause security problems.

On the eve of President Clinton's 1996 acceptance speech, for example, Dick Morris, one of his top POLITICAL CONSULTANTS, was exposed as having an affair with a prostitute. News of the SCANDAL somewhat overshadowed the president's speech.

Most recent conventions, however, have had more problems with boredom than with excitement. In 1996 ABC News anchor Ted Koppel made news himself halfway through the Republican convention by declaring there was so little news that he was pulling his *Nightline* show out of San Diego. Later, at the Democratic convention, veteran ABC newsman David Brinkley called Clinton "a bore" and said his speech was "one of the worst things I've ever heard. . . . Everything in there he's already said." Brinkley, covering his last convention before retirement, thought his intemperate farewell remarks were off the air.

Since 1996, none of the major broadcast networks have offered gavel-to-gavel coverage of the conventions, requiring hardcore political fans to rely on cable news stations, C-SPAN, and the Internet in order to follow routine proceedings.

More on this topic:

Bandwagon Effect, p. 21

Brokered Convention, p. 36

Delegates, p. 142

Front-Loading, p. 219

Platform, p. 383

Postconvention Bounce, p. 435

President, Nominating and Election, p. 437

Presidential Primaries, p. 468

Presidential Selection Reforms, p. 476

Primary Types, p. 485

National Republican Party (1828–1832)

The DEMOCRATIC-REPUBLICAN PARTY, which had thoroughly dominated U.S. politics since the election of party leader Thomas Jefferson in 1800, splintered after the 1824 election into two factions. One group, led by Tennessee populist Andrew Jackson, retained the name Democratic-Republicans, which eventually was shortened to Democrats; the other faction, headed by incumbent president John Quincy Adams, assumed the name National Republicans.

Factionalism within the ranks of the Democratic-Republican Party produced four candidates in 1824, none of whom received the absolute majority of electoral votes needed to claim the presidency. Under the Constitution, the election was decided by the House of Representatives, which chose Adams, even though Jackson had received more POPULAR VOTES.

Reflecting the belief of President Adams in the establishment of a national policy by the federal government, the new party supported a protective tariff, the Bank of the United States, federal overview of public lands, and federally financed national programs of internal improvements. But Adams's belief in a strong central government contrasted with the prevailing mood of populism and states' rights.

The Adams forces controlled Congress for two years, 1825 to 1827. But as party structures formalized, the National Republicans became a minority in Congress and suffered a decisive loss in the 1828 presidential election when Adams, running for reelection, was beaten by Jackson. Adams received 43.6 percent of the popular vote and carried eight states, none in the South.

Henry Clay, the National Republican Party's nominee against Jackson in 1832, had even less success. He received only 37.4 percent of the popular vote and carried just six states, none of which, again, were in the South.

More on this topic:

Whig Party, p. 671

Poorly organized, with dwindling support and a heritage of defeat, the National Republicans went out of existence after the 1832 election, but their members provided the base for the anti-Jackson WHIG PARTY, which came into being in 1834.

CLOSER LOOK

The prevalence of the word *Republican* in party names from the early days of the United States can create some confusion over the antecedents of the modern Republican Party, which was established in the 1850s and grew to prominence in the politics of the Civil War era and beyond. The Democratic-Republicans had little to do with the modern Republicans: founded by Thomas Jefferson and later led by Andrew Jackson, the Democratic-Republican Party was actually the direct ancestor of the modern Democratic Party. The National Republican Party, a short-lived breakaway faction of the Democratic-Republicans founded in 1828, is indirectly linked to the modern Republicans. A number of National Republicans realigned with the Whig Party when it came into being in the 1830s. When the Whig Party fell apart in the 1850s, mainly because of divisions over slavery, antislavery Whigs gravitated to the new Republican Party—which also attracted adherents of minor parties, such as the Free Soil Party and the American (Know Nothing) Party, as well as some dissident Democrats.

National Unity Party (1980–1988)

Republican representative John B. Anderson of Illinois formed the National Unity Campaign as the vehicle for his INDEPENDENT presidential campaign in 1980. Anderson began his quest for the presidency that year by trying to win the REPUBLICAN PARTY nomination. But, as a relatively liberal candidate in a party coming under conservative control, he won no primaries and could claim only fifty-seven convention delegates by April 1980. Anderson withdrew from the Republican race and declared his independent candidacy.

Anderson focused his campaign on what he described as the need to establish a viable THIRD PARTY as an alternative to domination of the political scene by the Republicans, whom he said had shifted too far to the right, and Democrats, whom he viewed as too liberal. The National Unity Campaign platform touted the Anderson program as a "new public philosophy"—more innovative than that of the Democrats, described as clinging to the policies of President Franklin D. Roosevelt's New Deal agenda of the 1930s, and more enlightened than that of the Republicans, depicted as talking "incessantly about freedom, but hardly ever about justice."

John B. Anderson, an independent presidential candidate in 1980, formally established the National Unity Party in 1983. The party dissolved without ever nominating a candidate.

Source: CQ Photo

In general, the group took positions that were fiscally conservative and socially liberal. Anderson and his running mate, former Democratic Wisconsin governor Patrick J. Lucey, tried to appeal to Republican and DEMOCRATIC PARTY voters disenchanted with their parties and to the growing bloc of voters who classified themselves as independents.

The National Unity Campaign ticket was on the ballot in all fifty states in 1980, although Anderson had to wage costly legal battles in some states to ensure that result. In the end, the party won 6.6 percent of the presidential vote—far short of Republican Ronald Reagan, who unseated Democratic incumbent Jimmy Carter, but well above the 5 percent necessary to qualify for retroactive federal campaign funding.

But the party that Anderson started quickly lost momentum. In April 1984 Anderson announced that he would not seek the presidency in that year. He said that instead he would focus his energies on building the National Unity Party, which he established officially in December 1983. He planned to concentrate initially on running candidates at the local level. That August 28, Anderson reinforced his dislike of Reagan's conservative policies by endorsing Walter F. Mondale, the Democratic nominee for president, and his running mate, Geraldine A. Ferraro. Reagan nonetheless won that election in a landslide.

The National Unity Party did not run a presidential candidate in the 1988 race and by 1992 was no longer a political party.

Natural Law Party (1992–2004)

The Natural Law Party was established to promote the principles of transcendental meditation advocate Maharishi Mahesh Yogi, a well-known mystic from India. Advocating prevention-oriented government and meditative, tension-relieving programs "designed to bring national life into harmony with natural law," the party ran presidential tickets from 1992 through 2000, headed by party founder John Hagelin.

But in 2004, on the eve of the next presidential election, Hagelin abruptly changed course, closing the national party headquarters and becoming president of the U.S. Peace Government. Also associated with the Maharishi's world peace movement, the organization is described on the Natural Law Party's website as a "new, complementary government, whose purpose is to prevent social violence, terrorism, and war and to promote harmony and peace in the U.S. and throughout the world."

Hagelin, a Harvard-trained quantum physicist, was born in Pittsburgh in 1954 and grew up in Connecticut. He became associated with Maharishi International University in Fairfield, Iowa, in 1983. His running mate in 1992 was fellow Maharishi scientist Mike Tompkins, a Harvard graduate and specialist in crime prevention programs; the ticket received 39,179 votes, the eighth highest total among all candidates.

The Hagelin-Tompkins ticket, though still drawing a tiny fraction of the electorate, almost tripled its vote numbers in 1996, taking 113,659 votes and jumping to fifth in the overall rankings.

In 2000, though, the Natural Law Party slipped back to 83,525 votes, with Hagelin joined on the ticket by vice presidential nominee Nat Goldhaber, a wealthy Internet entrepreneur and long-time Maharishi follower.

Despite its title, the party seemed to have little connection with the philosophic concept of natural law, which holds that some rules of society—such as the prohibition against murder—are so basic and inherent that they must be obeyed whether or not they are legislated.

Nature of Representation

The word *representation* has come to mean "to present again by standing in the place of another." The British political philosopher John Stuart Mill described *representative government* as what "the whole people, or some numerous portion of them, exercise through deputies [representatives] periodically elected by themselves, the ultimate controlling power."

Although the concept of representation is ancient and was considered a common political mechanism by the Middle Ages, historians have noted that it was INTEREST GROUPS, not individuals, that were being represented. Three groups, called estates—the church, the nobles, and the commoners—were the bases of the medieval community. Representative assemblies of the three estates existed in, among other countries, France and Anglo-Saxon England.

The concept of the individual as the fundamental building block of the community—and therefore the element that should be represented—first emerged in seventeenth-century Britain. The theorists who evolved it were considered the proselytizers of a dangerous political heresy that had the potential to destroy the established order.

Political thinkers such as Mill, John Locke, and Jean Jacques Rousseau had already moved beyond the concept of pure DEMOCRACY (embodied in the town-meeting idealization of direct rule arising from face-to-face meetings of all citizens) to the awareness that the emerging nation-states were too large, too scattered, and too diverse to allow for this sort of participatory government.

Disregarding undemocratic alternatives (the rule of a benign despot, for example), these philosophers and others reluctantly came to the conclusion that some form of representation was called for if there was to be democracy. But while the people's will remained the paramount concern of these theorists, they agonized over how best it could be realized. Was satisfactory representation even possible?

To these theorists, the individual is the basic element of the community, not the estates or corporate interests, and the individual members of the community must be given equal representation in any political body empowered to make that community's laws. Each elected representative should express the will of the group (the constituency) that sent him to the political body, and all the members of that body should, in theory, express the will of all the constituencies in the nation-state—that is, all the people. In the words of the French political writer Honoré Mirabeau, the assembly of representatives should be "a map to scale . . . an exact working model of the mass of people in action."

If, for example, a majority of the people desired that a particular course of action be taken on behalf of the entire community, a like proportion of the representatives also should want it. The democratic theory of representation therefore rested on the beliefs that an election is a more or less trustworthy expression of public opinion; that while the persons chosen may not hold precisely the same views as their constituents on all the questions that arise, they will reflect the

Edmund Burke (1729–1797), English writer and member of Parliament, conceived of representatives as delegates of their constituents.

Source: Library of Congress

general tone of thought of the electorate and its party complexion with some degree of accuracy.

Delegate or Agent?

The most perplexing of the questions involving representation involves the rights, duties, and obligations of the elected representative to the electors and the constituency. In his *Social Contract,* Rousseau argued that any kind of representation is basically incompatible with the ideal of democracy. But when he had to get down to practicalities, Rousseau could not escape the existence and function of representatives in the emerging nation-state, and he grudgingly acquiesced to it as almost a necessary evil.

Accepted reluctantly then, the argument about the nature of representation has, over the centuries, distilled itself into two basic camps: Should the representative serve as the *delegate* of the people or as the *agent* of the people?

In the United States and in most constitutional democracies, the former position seems to be the norm—that the people, once they have elected a representative, should consider that they have delegated their sovereign rights and allow the delegate to function in the assembly as he or she sees fit.

The most eloquent and persuasive of the proponents of the delegate theory was the English political theorist Edmund Burke, who, when first elected to the House of Commons in 1774, wrote a pamphlet to his constituents about what they could expect of him:

It ought to be the happiness and glory of a representative to live in the strictest union, the closest correspondence, and the most unreserved communication with his constituents. Their wishes ought to have great weight with him; their opinion high respect, their business unremitted attention. It is his duty to sacrifice his repose, his pleasure, his satisfaction to theirs—and above all, ever, and in all cases, to prefer their interests to his own. But his unbiased opinion, his mature judgment, his enlightened conscience, he ought not to sacrifice to you, to any man, to any set of men living. . . . Your representative owes you, not his industry only, but his judgment; and he betrays instead of serving you if he sacrifices it to your opinion.

Burke reasoned that making government decisions was not merely the tallying up of constituents' sentiments for and against something, then voting for the majority viewpoint. Rather, in his view, the making of public policy requires intelligent, enlightened discussion of the best available evidence about the subject at hand, then the application of reasoning and judgment in determining a solution or course of action.

According to Burke, the representative, along with his colleagues sitting in the national assembly, was in a better position than his constituents to arrive at these decisions. He was chosen by them to think about and act on such questions presumably because he had demonstrated a high degree of wisdom, judgment, patriotism, or public spiritedness and would continue to do so. He would be acting in the company of others of similar abilities and in a place where the best available evidence on and the widest array of opinions and ideas about a public issue would be available.

Then, acting on his experience and on what he knows and has learned about an issue, the representative as delegate must vote as he thinks best even if such a decision runs counter to his constituents' views. At the next election, the voters can pass judgment on whether the representative's judgments and actions have been truly put to work in their best interests. If the majority answers no and the representative loses the election, the constituents' will has been served and their ultimate sovereignty preserved.

In the opposite view, that of representative as agent, the elected representative should serve, in the words of one political theorist, "as a communications device," acting on the direct instructions of his constituents as to how to vote on any given issue. He exists as their instrument to register their beliefs and opinions at the public forum; if these run counter to his own, he must either disregard his own beliefs and vote as his electors want, or resign his post. Should a matter arise about which there is no sign of how his constituents want him to vote, he should go home and find out their desire before voting.

In the modern era, the agent representative may base his voting decisions on the outcome of POLLS, which can, when desired, provide the answers their designer wants to see, not necessarily an accurate picture of what voters actually want.

Also, today it is unlikely that there are many issues on which the constituents' views are not known, even if imperfectly. Members of Congress, for example, spend much of their time at home trying to get the pulse of the district. And the voters have ample opportunity to let their views be known by telephone, regular and electronic mail, letters to the editor, calls to talk shows, and so forth.

Rousseau, unable to find a practical way to achieve modern democracy without representatives, designed a scheme in which those chosen to serve would be agents of citizen assemblies, each representing a given territorial constituency. The assemblies would meet, elect the representative, and, after discussion of the issues facing the national assembly, would send their representative off to vote with a highly specific list of "yeas" and "nays." He would be judged later by the local assembly by how faithfully he had executed his orders.

Left undefined in Rousseau's ideal paradigm was the question of how the delegates to the local assemblies would be chosen and how it would be ascertained that they truly represented their own constituencies.

While some studies have found that the average American voter subscribes to the "representative as agent" belief, and that the voting record of an INCUMBENT is invariably the initial point of attack of his electoral opponents, the representatives themselves, not surprisingly, see their roles differently. On the eve of World War II, nearly a hundred House members were asked to weigh the factors that influenced their vote on the tangled and emotional issue of repeal of the arms-embargo provisions of the Neutrality Act. The first choice by a wide margin was their own independent judgment of what action should be taken; the second was consideration of what their vote would mean to the fortunes of their political party. The third factor, registering only about

> *"Your representative owes you, not his industry only, but his judgment; and he betrays instead of serving you if he sacrifices it to your opinion."*
>
> —From English political theorist Edmund Burke's 1774 pamphlet to his constituents about what they could expect of him in the House of Commons

30 percent as many responses as "independent judgment," was the views of their constituents. In another study of state legislators' perceptions of their roles, independent judgment also emerged as the primary consideration in determining how a given issue should be voted upon.

Representation in Practice

Both the delegate and agent theories operate in the rarefied air of idealism, and their eighteenth-century advocates might be hard-pressed to evolve a theory that truly reflects American democracy at the outset of the twenty-first century. For example, federal legislation mostly originates in House and Senate committees, the chairmen of which exercise great discretionary power in deciding whether a proposal should even be brought up for discussion or a vote. The chairmen are chosen, in the Senate now and until recently in the House, on the basis of seniority, giving enormous power to those individuals who have been in office longest.

Until the mid-1960s, senators and representatives from southern states—individuals who by and large favored segregation, which the majority of the nation's electorate opposed—were kept in office by their constituents who also favored segregation. By dint of long service, these members rose to the chairmanships of the most important Senate and House committees and, in essence, controlled the country's legislative agenda. Yet their constituencies made up perhaps 10 percent of the entire American electorate, illustrating the "tyranny of the minority," in one view, or, in another view, the prime example of the system of checks and balances at work in preventing a tyranny of the majority.

While internal consensus governed by pragmatism must eventually prevail over what truly must and will be accomplished by legislators and the ultimate "yea" or "nay" still remains with the electorate in the voting booth, there is growing concern that many Americans are becoming alienated from their elected representatives and, by extension, from government itself. If that is the case, their voices remain mute and their desires essentially unknown, or, rightly or wrongly, extrapolated from polls.

In the 1996 presidential election, for example, fewer than 50 percent of eligible voters participated, the lowest turnout in nearly three-quarters of a century, and the winner, Bill Clinton, garnered less than half of that total. He was elected, therefore, by approximately 25 percent of the American public who was eligible to vote.

Even in the hard-fought 2004 election, which spurred an uptick in voter turnout, only about 55 percent of the voting-age population and roughly 60 percent of the voting-eligible population participated in the election, according to some estimates. Using those figures, Bush's 51 percent win amounted to the votes cast by just more than a quarter of the voting-age population and less than a third of the voting-eligible population (which excludes noncitizens and felons who are not eligible to vote).

Two years later—with no incumbent running for president—voters turned out in larger numbers (as high as 61 percent by one count) to cast their ballots. The winner, Democrat Barack Obama, garnered just under 53 percent of the total vote cast, which was widely viewed as a sound if not overwhelming endorsement from the public. Nevertheless, his vote total was only about one-third of the nation's voter-eligible population, which is all people of voting age but excluding persons—such as illegal immigrants—who cannot legally cast ballots. It meant that Obama became—in a common political cliché—president of all Americans even though about 28 percent of eligible voters would have preferred to see his opponent, Sen. John McCain, in the White House.

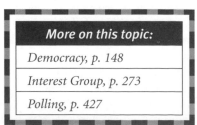

More on this topic:

Democracy, p. 148

Interest Group, p. 273

Polling, p. 427

Negative Campaigning

The practice of negative campaigning is not new. Candidates took the low road before the American TWO-PARTY SYSTEM was born. Even George Washington was not immune from personal attacks. During the Revolutionary War, the British circulated a phony letter from him "confessing" an affair with a washerwoman's daughter. Ben Franklin's grandson and namesake, Benjamin F. Bache, wrote that "the American nation has been debauched by Washington."

Other presidents, including Bill Clinton, have been the targets of character attacks, as have candidates at all levels. Political SCANDAL is an American tradition—and the grist for editorial cartoonists, comedians, and POLITICAL CONSULTANTS, as well as opposing candidates. And even when political figures are careful not to carry personal "baggage" into their campaigns, they may well see their voting records and policy views put under attack or held up for ridicule.

The public dissatisfaction with government that led to a series of wild pendulum swings in the public's support for each of the major political parties was reflected in the tenor of negative campaigning during those election cycles.

When the extended U.S. war in Iraq, the stumbling government response in 2005 to Hurricane Katrina, and the onset of a national economic downturn caused public approval of President George W. Bush to plummet, the Democrats fueled a political surge by tying Republicans in Congress and other offices to the unpopular incumbent.

But when Democrat Barack Obama, elected in 2008 to succeed Bush, presided over a period of high unemployment despite passage by the Democratic-controlled Congress of an expensive economic stimulus plan and also pushed into law a controversial overhaul of the nation's health insurance laws, his public support dropped and Republicans turned the tables, associating Democratic candidates across the country with the president in staging a big rebound in the 2010 midterm elections.

But if negative campaigning is not new, it has flourished in the age of television and the attack ad. POLITICAL ADVERTISING on television, much of it negative, has become the largest single expense of presidential campaigns and a sizable cost for other campaigns of any consequence.

The impact and pervasiveness of negative advertising has been amplified over the past decade as political action committees—many of them organized under Section 527 of the Internal Revenue Code and thus known as "527s"—raised contributions that were unlimited by federal campaign finance laws (because these groups were generally outside the purview of the Federal Election Commission) and used those funds to run extensive "independent expenditure" political ad campaigns.

These messages technically fit within the definition of "issue advertising" because they did not expressly call for the election or defeat of a specific candidate—the so-called "magic words" laid in a 1976 Supreme Court decision defining what constituted a campaign ad that fell within federal contribution limits. Yet this kind of advertising often consisted of thinly veiled efforts to influence one or more election outcomes, and also often sought to cast individual candidates in a negative light.

As technology advances, candidates and their supporters increasingly are also using the Internet as a medium for negative campaigning against opponents. One tactic that has gained currency over recent years is the production of hard-hitting negative videos aimed at opposing candidates that are posted on the websites of campaigns or political action groups rather than being aired on traditional media.

There has been much discussion over the years as to what fits the label of "negative campaigning," a phrase that itself has developed a negative connotation among many American voters.

Sen. Max Cleland of Georgia was the subject of a negative campaign ad during the 2002 elections.

Source: CQ Photo/Scott J. Ferrell

One of the sharpest debates over fair versus unfair campaign attacks occurred during the 2002 U.S. Senate race in Georgia. Congress debated the creation of a Department of Homeland Security (DHS) in the aftermath of the September 11, 2001, attacks, and Sen. Max Cleland, a Georgia Democrat, had voted for a Democratic-sponsored bill to create the department while maintaining collective bargaining rights favored by organized labor. But Cleland voted against the legislation, promoted by President Bush and ultimately enacted into law, that weakened collective bargaining in DHS. As part of a broad Republican effort to use the latter vote to portray Cleland as weak on defense, GOP challenger and House incumbent Saxby Chambliss ran an ad attacking Cleland that included a photo of al-Qaida leader Osama bin Laden, the mastermind behind the 9/11 attacks.

Chambliss, who went on to unseat Cleland, and other Republicans were adamant that the ad was fair, as it made their case that Cleland had voted against legislation implementing a federal agency aimed at protecting Americans from people such as bin Laden. But enraged Democrats described the ad as a vicious smear—especially since Cleland had lost both legs and part of an arm while serving in combat during the Vietnam War.

Nearly all who follow politics would agree that unfair or untrue aspersions about a candidate's personal life and egregious mischaracterizations of a candidate's political views and voting record should be out of bounds.

For example, in a mailed campaign piece that stunned even many veteran political observers, Bill Conrad, a candidate in the 2006 Republican primary for a California assembly seat, attacked opponent Tom Berryhill, using Berryhill's heart transplant as fodder. "Tom Berryhill doesn't have the HEART for state Assembly," the headline announced, and the piece went on to detail health problems faced by transplant recipients. Berryhill trounced Conrad in the primary and went on to an easy election victory in November.

In the strongly Democratic political year of 2008, North Carolina Republican senator Elizabeth Dole found herself trailing in polls to Democrat Kay Hagan, who began the campaign as an underdog. Late in the contest, Dole's campaign ran an ad that sought to play up Hagan's attendance at a political event staged by an activist atheist, implying that the challenger was "godless." But Hagan was actually not only a church-goer but heavily involved in her church's activities, and the attack backfired on Dole, who lost the election.

But criticisms of a candidate's political views or known facts about his or her personal life are often the subject of lively debate. While the attacked candidate often will portray an opponent as engaging in negative campaigning or "mudslinging," the opponent often will defend the tactic as simply an effort to provide voters with the background information they need to make an informed decision.

There also are divisions over the impact of negative campaigning on voters and their enthusiasm for participating in the political process. Many critics say the overtly negative tone of much of modern American politics has depressed turnout and turned voters off to politics in general; some political consultants have admitted that their campaign efforts were largely aimed at depressing turnout of voters inclined to support an opponent. But others say negative advertising is such an ingrained part of the nation's politics that it does not have much of an impact on turnout. Some even say that negative ads have the potential to increase participation by energizing voters who had only mildly opposed the candidate who was the subject of the attack ads.

"Negative TV advertising increased in the mid-1980s, but turnout has not gone down correspondingly," wrote Michael McDonald of George Mason University in Fairfax, Virginia, in an October 2006 opinion piece published by the *Washington Post*.

Political use of television began in the 1950s during the Dwight D. Eisenhower administrations, and the first negative TV spots are attributed to Adlai E. Stevenson II, Eisenhower's Democratic opponent in 1952 and 1956. In his second run against the popular "Ike," Stevenson used footage from a 1952 commercial in which Eisenhower pledged a fight against political corruption. Because the White House had experienced some corruption problems during Eisenhower's first term, the Stevenson ads sought to highlight the contrast between promise and reality.

As political television became more commonplace, so did negative ads, and controversy was never far behind. One of the most legendary political ads is the "daisy" commercial that President Lyndon B. Johnson's campaign used against Republican challenger Barry Goldwater in the 1964 contest that resulted in a landslide victory for the incumbent. Goldwater was an outspoken conservative at a time when more liberal views were ascendant in American public life, and the ad was part of a largely successful effort by Democrats to discredit him as a dangerous extremist. It showed a little girl plucking petals from a daisy, then cut to an atomic explosion in the final scene. The scare sequence, implying Goldwater would be reckless with nuclear warfare, caused an immediate storm of criticism and controversy, and the Johnson camp withdrew it after one showing.

Television news programs, however, showed the controversial commercial several times afterward—something that today has become so habitual that campaigns today often court "free media" coverage of their attack ads to try to get more bang for their advertising bucks.

Fast Forward

Not until 1988 was there another negative presidential campaign ad with the impact of the daisy commercial. The new "dubious achievement winner" was the "Willie Horton" ad. Sponsored by Republican supporters of Vice President George H. W. Bush's campaign for president, the ad was intended to portray the Democratic nominee, Massachusetts governor Michael S. Dukakis, as soft on crime because he had signed a bill permitting furloughs from prison. The ad focused on William Robert Horton Jr., an African American convicted murderer better known as Willy Horton who had raped a woman in Maryland while on leave from a Massachusetts prison, and featured a threatening-looking mug shot of Horton.

The furlough issue had first been raised during the campaign for the Democratic presidential nomination by one of Dukakis's rivals, Sen. Al Gore of Tennessee. (Gore would later serve two terms as vice president under President Bill Clinton and then lose the controversial 2000 election to Bush's son, George W. Bush.)

Gore did not emphasize the Willie Horton angle, however. That occurred when Lee Atwater, political strategist for the elder Bush, picked up the lead, and a California group paid $92,000 to run the Horton ad in the South as an independent expenditure. Although the paid ad appeared only a few times, it—like the anti-Goldwater daisy ad—was shown later on news programs because of the controversy it created, especially after Democrats complained loudly that the ad was aimed at fueling racial fears among whites. Though the Bush campaign did not pay for or air the Horton ad, it ran a complementary ad portraying the Massachusetts prison system as a revolving door.

Atwater, then a political consultant, masterminded Bush's negative campaign. As president, Bush named Atwater chairman of the REPUBLICAN NATIONAL COMMITTEE. Before he died of a brain tumor in 1991, Atwater publicly apologized for any harm his tactics had caused to Dukakis or other opponents.

Other TV spots in Atwater's 1988 strategy attacked Dukakis's patriotism (because he had vetoed a bill requiring school children to pledge allegiance to the flag), his lack of military experience (by showing him looking ludicrous while test driving an army tank in a campaign photo opportunity that backfired), and his record on pollution (by showing debris in Boston harbor).

Some media scholars, including former television reporter Marvin Kalb of Harvard's Joan Shorenstein Center on the Press, Politics, and Public Policy, regard the 1988 use of negative campaigning as the "all-time low" in presidential elections. But despite the backlash against Willie Horton–type spots, attack ads have become a mainstay of modern campaigning.

Attack Ads and Dirty Tricks

Political consultants reject suggestions that they are to blame for thirty-second attack ads. "It's the fault of a lot of people," said Republican consultant Douglas Bailey. "Consultants have contributed mightily to the mess politics is in, but on the other hand we have dealt with the world as we found it. Prime-time TV is where the numbers [of viewers] are, and they want things in thirty seconds."

Bailey and John Deardourff were pioneers in campaign advertising in the 1960s. Their negative spots against Ohio Democratic governor John Gilligan in 1974 helped return Republican Jim Rhodes to the statehouse in one of the year's few GOP victories. In the 1976 presidential campaign, Bailey-Deardourff crafted a media strategy that was praised as effective, even though it could not prevent Republican incumbent Gerald R. Ford's narrow loss to Democrat Jimmy Carter.

> "It is much easier to run a negative ad to get the voter to go against your opponent than it is to run a positive ad and get the voter to vote for you."
>
> —Political consultant Douglas Bailey in a 1996 interview, commenting on negative advertising

A big change from the 1970s, Bailey said in a 1996 interview, is that there is less risk of turning people off by running negative ads; indeed, the failure to respond to an opponent's negative ad will accord it credibility. "It is much easier," he said, "to run a negative ad to get the voter to go against your opponent than it is to run a positive ad and get the voter to vote for you."

This was underscored dramatically in the heat of the 2004 presidential contest, when Massachusetts senator John Kerry, the Democratic nominee, never fully recovered from his slow response to damaging attack ads.

On the campaign trail, Kerry hoped to overcome the longstanding public perception of the Republican Party as stronger on national defense, particularly during a time of war. Therefore, he emphasized his background as a decorated Navy combat veteran who piloted river craft known as swift boats during the Vietnam War. However, Kerry had become a leading anti–Vietnam War activist after he left the military and had long drawn resentment from conservatives, including some Vietnam veterans.

Some Kerry critics, financed by Republicans who favored the reelection of President George W. Bush, came together to form a group called the Swift Boat Veterans for Truth, which produced ads attacking Kerry. The first, which included sound bites of veterans accusing Kerry of exaggerating his war heroism, was widely portrayed by media analysts as a distortion of the record.

But the second ad, which likely did more political damage, focused on his post-military antiwar activism, including his highly publicized testimony in 1971 before a Senate committee. Kerry's testimony included accounts of atrocities committed by stressed-out U.S. military personnel; these had been related to Kerry by some veterans who said they had participated in or witnessed such events. The second Swift Boat ad included statements from a former Vietnam prisoner of war who charged that Kerry's testimony resulted in additional torments being heaped on American prisoners by their North Vietnamese captors.

The Swift Boat Veterans took advantage of the unusually long gap between the Democratic and Republican conventions—most of August—to air the ads, first with small local buys and then nationally after media coverage created widespread public discussion of the group's charges against Kerry. Kerry exacerbated his problem by taking a vacation after accepting his nomination in early August and then initially dismissing the possibility that voters would take the Swift Boat ads seriously.

Although President Bill Clinton often was the object of negative advertising during his successful 1992 and 1996 campaigns, there were also times when he and his handlers were the attackers. Law professor Bradley A. Smith, writing in the *Wall Street Journal* before the 1996 election, said that "Clinton has run one of the most relentlessly negative campaigns in recent memory" against his Republican challenger, former Kansas senator Bob Dole.

That is not necessarily bad, however, Smith wrote. "Americans love a negative campaign; always have, always will. . . . To suggest that a candidate for office should not point out his opponent's shortcomings is preposterous. The question is not whether an ad is negative, but whether it is truthful and relevant."

> **"Americans love a negative campaign; always have, always will. . . . To suggest that a candidate for office should not point out his opponent's shortcomings is preposterous. The question is not whether an ad is negative, but whether it is truthful and relevant."**
>
> **—Law professor Bradley A. Smith,** writing in the *Wall Street Journal* before the 1996 election

Truth in Advertising

The apparent disregard for truth in some political advertising is bothersome to many people. Burt Manning, chairman of the American Association of Advertising Agencies, noted with alarm a PUBLIC OPINION poll showing that the percentage of Americans who want more government regulation on truth in advertising rose from 49 percent in 1993 to 63 percent in 1995. Manning urged political consultants to emulate commercial advertisers by setting up their own self-regulating process to monitor accuracy and fairness.

Others suggest volunteer "truth squads" of ad watchers to expose advertising dishonesty. Beginning in the mid-1990s, many newspapers and electronic media outlets began running "ad watch" features that analyzed the accuracy of the content of political ads. This eventually spawned the development of Internet-based national news services, such as PolitiFact and FactCheck.org, that analyze the truthfulness of statements made by public officials and political activists.

Brown University political scientist Darrell M. West, author of *Air Wars: Television Advertising in Election Campaigns, 1952–1996,* recommended MEDIA COVERAGE as the best antidote to false and misleading campaign ads. An outright ban on campaign ads is unlikely because of free speech protections, West noted, and "government regulation clearly would be inadequate without direct and effective media oversight."

With the proliferation in recent years of media websites dedicated to election politics and of political blogs, there are more watchdogs than ever dissecting political ads and bringing perceived inaccuracies and unfair charges to light.

New Hampshire Primary

The ritual of presidential candidates trooping to New Hampshire to campaign in the state's first-in-the-nation PRIMARY has become such an accepted feature of U.S. political culture that there are few people who remember it any other way. New Hampshire established itself during the early part of the twentieth century as one of the first states to reject the traditional system of having party leaders choose presidential nominees; by the early 1950s, its primary had emerged as a key first test of popular support among the often crowded field of White House contenders.

From the 1970s into the first decade of the twenty-first century, New Hampshire's pace-setting role was challenged only by the major parties' precinct CAUCUSES in Iowa. As late as 1980, these events were held five weeks apart, but by 1996, the gap had been reduced to eight days, which became customary. For many years, the New Hampshire primary was held in mid-March, launching a relatively small round of primaries that culminated in June primaries in more populous states such as California.

But PRESIDENTIAL SELECTION REFORMS aimed at empowering rank-and-file voters over party bosses, instituted as a result of the political turmoil of the 1960s, spurred a proliferation of primaries and open caucuses, which in turn kicked off a competition among states to hold their events earlier and earlier in hope of gaining influence over the parties' candidate choice. This practice, known as FRONT-LOADING, has had two major and not necessarily positive impacts on the New Hampshire primary.

First, in order to keep ahead of the front-loading frenzy, New Hampshire has in successive elections moved the date of its primary from the cusp of spring to the dead of New England winter. By state law, New Hampshire must hold its primary ahead of other states. In 2008 New Hampshire held its primary on January 9. But then two states—in violation of national party rules—moved their primaries into January (Michigan on January 15 and Florida on January 29) in order to increase their influence on the candidate selection. Both were threatened with loss of seating at the summer conventions, but most delegates were later allowed to participate.

One other primary, in South Carolina, was moved into January with party approval. That was held on January 29. All other primaries were held in the following months, starting with Alabama on February 5 and ending with several states on June 3.

Second, and even more serious for defenders of New Hampshire's spot at the top of the calendar, there have been longstanding complaints from other states that New Hampshire's clout in the nominating process is excessive. To address criticisms that New Hampshire is too small (as the forty-second most populous state) and too homogenous (95 percent white, 1 percent African American) to reflect the diversity of the U.S. electorate, the Democratic National Committee in 2006 decided to add to the calendar two events that would compete for attention with New Hampshire: one was the South Carolina primary and the other was a January caucus in Nevada.

In an unusual turn of events, Sen. John McCain won the 2000 New Hampshire presidential primary but lost the Republican nomination to George W. Bush.

Source: CQ Photo/Scott J. Ferrell

Just as threatening was the looming rush of states to hold events early, with the actions by Michigan and Florida as the two most striking examples. Even beyond those states, however, many other states moved their primaries into February. In 2008, twenty-two states held primary elections in February compared with just nine four years earlier.

Nonetheless, a combination of tradition and fear of offending New Hampshire voters, whose state continues to be regarded a key trend-setter, sent many of the 2008 presidential hopefuls to New Hampshire to court voter support.

The legendary status of the New Hampshire primary was abetted for many years by its seemingly perfect record as a BELLWETHER: Beginning in 1952 and continuing through the end of the 1980s, each man elected president—Dwight D. Eisenhower, John F. Kennedy, Lyndon B. Johnson, Richard M. Nixon, Jimmy Carter, Ronald Reagan, and George

H. W. Bush—had first won the New Hampshire primary. The primary at times also served as a flare warning of a failing candidacy. The most prominent occasion was in 1968, as the controversy over the Vietnam War reached its peak: President Johnson, though he won the primary, saw a sizable portion of the vote go to Minnesota senator Eugene McCarthy, who was running as an antiwar activist. Johnson soon stunned the nation by announcing on national television that he would not seek reelection that year.

The primary's record has been a bit spottier in recent elections, though. In 1992 Democrat Bill Clinton broke the primary's winning streak when he was elected president despite losing the New Hampshire primary. A shocking upset of Republican front-runner George W. Bush by Arizona senator John McCain in the 2000 primary briefly added some suspense to that nominating race, but Bush ultimately cruised to the nomination and won the general election.

But the 2004 election again proved that New Hampshire could still be a key test, as two Democratic candidates from neighboring New England states staged a crucial showdown. Massachusetts senator John Kerry's status as the early front-runner for the Democratic nomination was threatened by the meteoric rise of former Vermont governor Howard Dean, whose campaign was fueled by dissent among liberal activists over the war in Iraq that Bush had launched in March 2003. Kerry's victory in the Iowa caucuses made the New Hampshire primary a do-or-die event for Dean, who had finished third in the previous contest. Kerry won the Granite State vote, sending him on his way to the nomination and effectively crushing Dean's chances. Bush defeated Kerry in November.

The 2008 contests also were not perfect. Hillary Rodham Clinton captured the New Hampshire primary but lost the nomination to Barack Obama. On the Republican side, Sen. John McCain won the primary and the nomination.

Established in 1913, New Hampshire's primary was one of the first created as part of the Progressive movement to reform political parties. But as in other parts of the country the primary did not catch on until after World War II, when many of the presidential preference primaries, like New Hampshire's, were of the BEAUTY CONTEST type that did not affect DELEGATE selection. (See PRIMARY TYPES.)

Today's New Hampshire primary is more than a mere beauty contest. National convention delegates bound or committed to particular candidates are awarded in proportion to the candidate's share of the vote, with each party setting a minimum vote percentage candidates must reach to qualify for delegates.

Both parties' primaries are of the "modified closed" type. While registered Republicans cannot vote in the Democratic primary and registered Democrats may not vote in the Republican contest, voters undeclared to a party may vote in either primary. This rule can, on occasion, have a serious impact on the primary results. For example, polling showed that McCain, whose mainly conservative record was punctuated by some differences with Republican Party orthodoxy that gave him a "maverick" image, won the state's 2000 primary, beating Bush with the help of thousands of independent voters.

Despite its ability to turn unknowns into front-runners—notably Jimmy Carter in 1976—the New Hampshire primary can sink promising campaigns. Like Lyndon Johnson in 1968, President Harry S. Truman dropped out after a relatively poor showing against Tennessee senator Estes Kefauver in 1952, though the incumbent insisted he already had decided not to run. (The Democratic Party, as the result of decisions made by party leaders at their 1952 convention, nominated Illinois governor Adlai Stevenson, who lost that November to Republican Eisenhower.)

◎ CLOSER LOOK

Democrat Bill Clinton's largely successful effort to claim victory despite losing the 1992 New Hampshire primary stands as a classic example of political "spin." Though Clinton, then the governor of Arkansas, was regarded as the most charismatic candidate in the Democratic field, his campaign was facing collapse heading into New Hampshire: foreshadowing personal controversies that would ultimately taint Clinton's two-term presidency, a woman named Gennifer Flowers had publicly claimed that she had a long-running sexual relationship with the married Clinton. With his wife, Hillary, at his side, Clinton salvaged his campaign by conducting an interview with CBS's *60 Minutes* news program in which he conceded to have "caused pain" in his marriage and asked voters to overlook that. Though former Massachusetts senator Paul S. Tsongas actually won the Democratic primary, many pundits wrote off his victory as a regional "favorite son" outcome—enabling Clinton, the runner-up in that primary, to declare himself on primary night as the "Comeback Kid" and gain enough momentum for his once-troubled bid to become the front-runner for the nomination.

Perhaps the most famous candidate flameout in New Hampshire occurred in the 1972 Democratic campaign. Edmund S. Muskie of neighboring Maine, the vice presidential nominee on the party's narrowly unsuccessful 1968 ticket headed by Hubert H. Humphrey, went to New Hampshire as the front-runner to win the nomination to challenge Republican President Nixon. But in an appearance on a snowy day outside the offices of the *Manchester Union-Leader*—a newspaper with a well-known conservative orientation—Muskie protested a pair of critical articles published by the newspaper. One piece claimed that Muskie had used a slur against French Canadians, an insult to the state's sizable Franco-American population; it later turned out to have been a rumor planted by aides to Nixon's campaign. The other attacked Muskie's wife. During his emotional statement, Muskie appeared to break into tears, though he later insisted that the moisture on his face was from melting snow. Although Muskie won the primary, the incident cost him votes and South Dakota senator George McGovern, the strong second-place finisher, went on to win the Democratic nomination before losing to Nixon in a landslide.

At the time the *Union-Leader,* under conservative publisher William Loeb, wielded powerful influence in New Hampshire politics. After Loeb's death in 1981, and with the influx of more liberal voters from the Boston area, the newspaper lost some of its power to persuade.

Nineteenth Amendment *See* WOMEN'S SUFFRAGE.

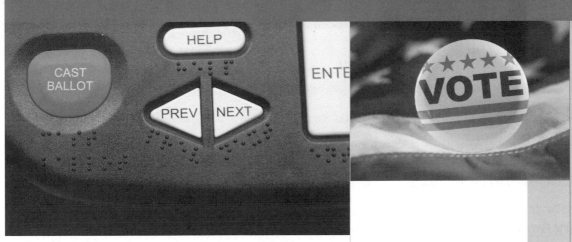

One Person, One Vote

State legislatures had no constitutional obligation before 1960 to aim at equal populations in drawing legislative and congressional districts. In a series of rulings in the 1960s, however, the Supreme Court held that "substantially equal legislative representation" was a "fundamental principle" under the Constitution. The doctrine, at first known as "one man, one vote" even though the opinion says "one person, one vote," forced legislatures and federal courts to be precise in adjusting the populations of legislative and congressional districts.

The rulings answered the question left open in the Court's first modern REAPPORTIONMENT decision, *BAKER V. CARR,* in 1962: What standard do federal courts apply in judging the constitutionality of legislative districts? A year later, the Court articulated the one-person, one-vote doctrine in a Georgia case, *Gray v. Sanders,* that challenged the state's county-unit primary system for electing statewide officials.

A voter leaves a schoolhouse in rural North Dakota after voting in 1940. Prior to the one person, one vote rulings of the 1960s, state legislatures were not required to draw election districts based on population, and certain districting systems afforded more weight to a rural vote than its counterpart in the city.

Source: Library of Congress

373

Georgia officials insisted that the system—which weighted votes to give advantage to rural districts—was analogous to the Electoral College system for choosing the president. But the Court rejected the argument.

In 1964, the Court applied the same principle to congressional and legislative districting. The first of the decisions came in another Georgia case, *Wesberry v. Sanders.* Voters in the congressional district that included Atlanta claimed in the suit that the population of their district was more than twice the ideal state average. Writing for a 6–3 majority, Justice Hugo L. Black said that the provision in Article I of the Constitution that members of the House of Representatives be chosen "by the People of the several States" implicitly established the principle of "equal representation for equal numbers."

> **"The conception of political equality from the Declaration of Independence, to Lincoln's Gettysburg Address, to the Fifteenth, Seventeenth, and Nineteenth Amendments can mean only one thing—one person, one vote."**
>
> **—Justice William O. Douglas,** in Gray v. Sanders (1963)

Four months later, on June 15, 1964, the Court held that the same principle also applied, under the Equal Protection Clause, to both chambers of bicameral state legislatures. The ruling in *Reynolds v. Sims* rejected the argument that a state, by analogy to the federal system, could constitute one house of its legislature on the basis of population and the other on an area basis. "Legislators represent people, not trees or acres," Chief Justice Earl Warren wrote. Harlan was the lone dissenter.

Over the next few years, the Court interpreted the principle to require legislatures to be "as nearly as practicable" equal. In 1969, for example, the Court rejected a Missouri congressional districting plan with a 3.1 percent population variance between districts.

In recent years, particularly since computer technology advances have permitted exacting precision in drawing district lines, the courts have come to demand nearly perfect population equality among congressional districts. The degree to which this principle has become enshrined was evident in 2002, when a federal district court ruled that officials in Pennsylvania—a state that had a population of 12,291,054 according to the 2000 census—had violated the one person, one vote principle, even though the differential between the most populous and least populous among the state's nineteen congressional districts was just nineteen people.

The state legislature, under a federal court order, redrew the map prior to the 2004 elections so that the districts were equal in population based on census data. Several other states avoided litigation by producing maps in which the districts were either perfectly equal or within a person or two of exact population equality.

There are critics, however, who believe court rulings such as this have taken the principle of one person, one vote too far. Some point out that census data can only be presumed accurate for the time in the spring of the first year of a decade—in this case the year 2000—when the state populations are enumerated by the Census Bureau; the population is not static and changes daily due to deaths, births, in-migration, and out-migration. So, these critics say, the courts hold states to a standard that is too stringent in its demand for zero population deviation between districts.

The Court, in fact, has tolerated somewhat greater variance for state and local-level political districts. In *Hadley v. Junior College District of Metropolitan Kansas City, Mo.* (1970) the Court also applied the equal population principle to all elections—state or local—of persons performing government functions. But

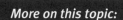

More on this topic:

Census, p. 92

Reapportionment and Redistricting, p. 517

in 1973, the Court said the rule did not apply to some special purpose electoral districts, such as those used to regulate water supplies in the West.

Open Primary *See* PRIMARY TYPES.

Oregon v. Mitchell

In a 1970 decision, *Oregon v. Mitchell,* the Supreme Court largely backed Congress's effort to override various state-imposed limits on voting. While the justices did invalidate, by a 5–4 vote, one important provision of the law that required states to allow eighteen-year-olds to vote in state and local elections, that ruling was quickly nullified by the ratification of the TWENTY-SIXTH AMENDMENT to the Constitution.

Congress included the minimum voting-age provision for federal, state, and local elections as part of the VOTING RIGHTS ACT Amendments of 1970. The law also suspended LITERACY TESTS nationwide, prohibited states from imposing residency requirements in presidential elections, and provided uniform national rules for ABSENTEE VOTING in presidential elections. Oregon led a number of states in challenging the law as an infringement of state prerogatives over voting procedures.

The justices produced five separate opinions to resolve the various issues. The Court unanimously upheld the suspension of literacy tests. Justice Hugo L. Black explained in the pivotal opinion that the provision fell within Congress's power under the FIFTEENTH AMENDMENT to outlaw racial discrimination in voting. The Court also upheld, 8–1, the residency and absentee voting provisions for presidential elections. Justice John Marshall Harlan was the lone dissenter. Three other justices who took a narrow view of Congress's power nonetheless found that lawmakers had reason to believe the restriction on residency requirements was necessary to prevent interference with an individual's privilege to take up residency in a state.

On the voting-age provision, four justices voted to uphold Congress's enactment in its entirety, while four others voted to strike the provision down completely. Black determined the outcome of the case by voting that the Constitution gave Congress power to prescribe a minimum voting age for federal elections, but not for state and local balloting.

The split decision meant that the states would have had to maintain separate voting rolls for federal and state elections. To avert that possibility, Congress proposed and the states quickly ratified the Twenty-sixth Amendment, setting a uniform minimum voting age of eighteen in all elections. (See YOUTH SUFFRAGE.) The 1972 presidential election, in which Republican incumbent Richard M. Nixon defeated Democrat George McGovern, was the first held following ratification of the amendment.

More on this topic:

Absentee Voting, p. 1

Literacy Tests, p. 309

Twenty-sixth Amendment, p. 635

Voting Rights Act, p. 663

Youth Suffrage, p. 687

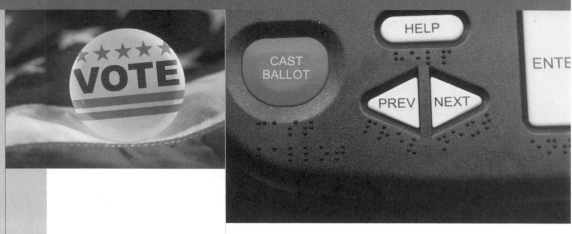

Party Endorsement of Candidates

P

In a bottom-line sense, the only party endorsement that matters for a candidate is the party's nomination to run in the general election. In nearly all states, the "endorsement" is provided by voters in a primary or caucus. In the days of political yesteryear, party leaders essentially hand-picked nominees for public office in the legendary "smoke-filled rooms." But several states still allow party officials, or at least delegates to a state or district convention, to place their imprimatur on a favored candidate. Some of these states create thresholds for other contenders that can make it difficult or impossible for them to attain BALLOT ACCESS.

For example, in the 2006 contest for the Colorado governor's seat, the state Republican convention that May endorsed Rep. Bob Beauprez, a former state GOP chairman. Marc Holtzman, a former president of the University of Denver, received 28 percent support of the delegates, short of what he needed to qualify for the August primary ballot. Holtzman then tried to petition his way onto the primary ballot but was eliminated from contention when state election officials deemed a number of signatures invalid, leaving him short of the qualifying requirement.

The endorsement system does not necessarily preclude a serious contest. One occurred in Utah's Third District, where conservative Republican conventioneers, unhappy with Rep. Chris Cannon's moderate views on how to deal with illegal immigration, provided more than enough votes at the 2006 state convention in May to qualify immigration hardliner John Jacob for the June primary. Cannon managed to hold off Jacob in the primary by 56 percent to 44 percent.

Even under Utah's system, though, the endorsement process keeps challenges to party-favored candidates from getting too freewheeling. Only two candidates can be sent on to the primary; if more than two candidates put their names into contention, balloting is held, and the lowest-ranking candidate is eliminated on each ballot until the field is winnowed to two.

Minnesota, which has endorsing conventions, allows nonendorsed candidates to petition their way on to the ballot. But the overall sensibility in the state's major parties is to avoid expensive and potentially divisive primary fights. As a result, competitors sometimes pledge in advance to accede to the endorsement decision made at the convention.

Even in states where a preprimary endorsement is mainly symbolic, it can still carry weight. When the state Republican convention in California endorsed GOP governor Arnold Schwarzenegger prior to his 2006 reelection bid, it signaled to conservative activists, unhappy with the famed movie actor's moderate views on social issues, that there would be no widespread support for a primary challenge. Schwarzenegger went on to an easy victory that November.

Sometimes, however, a party endorsement—or at least a well-known preference for a candidate—does not work, as was seen in several Senate races in 2010. One occurred in Delaware, where both parties coveted the open seat of Sen. Joe Biden who resigned when selected as Barack Obama's vice presidential candidate. Republicans got solidly behind Rep. Mike Castle, a long-serving and popular House member who was known and respected in the state. He was challenged and defeated in the primary by a Tea Party favorite, Christine O'Donnell, with support from GOP vice presidential candidate Sarah Palin. O'Donnell's exceptionally conservative views and sometimes unusual statements immediately catapulted the Democratic candidate, Chris Coons, into the lead and on election day to an easy 17 percentage point victory.

A similar drama played out in Nevada where Democratic incumbent senator Harry Reid, the Senate majority leader, was unpopular and faced an exceptionally difficult reelection effort in November until Republicans in their primary nominated another Tea Party favorite, Sharron Angle. She voiced support for various ultraconservative ideas that went against the grain of mainstream politicians in both parties such as ending Medicare and Social Security and eliminating the federal Education and Energy departments. Reid won with 50 percent of the vote to 45 percent for Angle.

Two other Senate races also showed the impact of a vigorous outside force, the Tea Party in 2010, that can defy usual party preferences. In Utah, Tea Party favorite Mike Lee, an attorney, defeated incumbent Robert R. Bennett, even though Bennett had one of the most conservative voting records in Congress. Similarly, in Alaska the Republican incumbent, Lisa Murkowski, lost the party primary to Tea Party challenger Joe Miller. But Murkowski retained her seat in the general election by winning as a write-in candidate. Neither race made a difference in Senate control, but the Delaware and Nevada races where Tea Party challengers beat back preferred Republican candidates and went down to defeat, were widely seen as lost opportunities that would have helped Republicans win control of the Senate.

The race for an open U.S. Senate seat in Delaware in 2010 illustrated the limits of party endorsements that sometimes occur. The GOP establishment got behind a popular incumbent House member who was seen as a likely winner in November. But Christine O'Donnell, right, won the Republican primary with strong support from Tea Party advocates. Her exceptionally conservative views and sometimes unusual statements immediately catapulted the Democratic candidate, Chris Coons, left, shown in a televised debate with his opponent, into the lead and on election day to an easy 17 percentage point victory.

Source: AP Photo/Jacquelyn Martin, File

The last major party realignment resulted from the effects of the Great Depression. Above, New Yorkers affected by the Great Depression wait in a bread line beside the Brooklyn Bridge.

Source: Library of Congress

Party Identification by Voters

Most Americans think of themselves as Democrats, Republicans, or independents, with a small percentage declaring themselves members of a variety of alternative organizations known as THIRD PARTIES. That allegiance is called *party identification,* a long-term and generally stable influence on voter choice that is not usually subject to sudden shifts from one election to the next.

Political scientists measure voters' party identification through POLLING studies that also gauge the strength of party members' allegiance and the party leanings of independents. The resulting scale of partisanship ranges from strong Democrat through independent to strong Republican. (See NATIONAL ELECTION STUDIES.)

According to this scale, from 1952 to 1995 between two-thirds and three-fourths of the electorate identified with the DEMOCRATIC or REPUBLICAN parties—a tendency reinforced by the strong party organizations, or machines, that still held sway in much of the nation. Democrats long held the advantage; however, the margin narrowed in the 1980s. By the early 1990s, the Democrats' advantage was gone, partly because of the public's increasing weariness with the party's dominance of government over most of the previous sixty years and partly because of the growing tendency of conservative southerners to abandon their traditional Democratic ties and identify themselves with the Republicans. A 1995 cross-section Gallup poll showed Democrats and Republicans tied nationally at 32 percent and independents ahead with 36 percent.

That split of roughly one-third Democratic, one-third Republican, and one-third independent continued to prevail for many years, through election cycles of Republican dominance and Democratic revival. A series of polls conducted by the Pew Research Center for the People and the Press showed that in 2002, 34.5 percent of respondents identified themselves as Democrats, compared with the 33.2 percent who said they were Republicans. Even in 2006, a strong year at the polls for Democrats whose gains enabled them to take control of the Senate and the House, the polling gap between the parties was just 34.9 percent Democratic to 31.6 Republican.

These figures are national means. In some regions, states, and districts, one party is more dominant and more certain to succeed in elections. But in many places, and especially in presidential elections, independents and loosely affiliated partisan identifiers, often labeled "swing voters," typically play the decisive role in determining the outcome. That does not mean that all elections will reflect the closeness in overall party identification. The popularity of one candidate, the weakness of the other, or often the combination of the two can lead to a huge shift to the stronger side, resulting in a LANDSLIDE.

The first two presidential elections of the 2000s, both won narrowly by Republican George W. Bush, certainly suggested a nation closely divided along partisan lines. In 2000 Bush won a bare majority in the Electoral College, even though he was the fourth president in history to claim the White House while losing the popular vote (Democrat Al Gore's popular vote total exceeded Bush's by just more than a half-million). Bush did better in 2004, but his 50.7 percent to 48.3 percent win over Democrat John Kerry was hardly a landslide.

The 2008 elections, in which Democrats captured the presidency, showed a move toward Democrats that was more prominent but by no means overwhelming. Barack Obama, the Democratic candidate, won just under 53 percent of the votes cast, although his victory in the ELECTORAL COLLEGE was more decisive.

Staunch partisans seldom defect to the opposition. Strong Republicans in particular show a high level of party loyalty in presidential elections. For those with weaker partisan commitments, short-term influences such as issues and candidate appeal take on greater importance and can cause substantial defections on ELECTION DAY.

Trend to Independence

One of the most notable changes in the electorate's partisanship has been the increase in the proportion of voters labeling themselves independents. This trend was especially strong from the 1960s through the mid-1970s and was most noticeable among young voters who did not align themselves with a party as quickly as older generations had. The trend became even more prominent in the latter elections of the 2000s decade.

The trend stemmed mainly from a large influx of new voters, the so-called baby boomers who came of voting age in the 1960s and 1970s, and not from partisans adopting the independent label. The tendency of voters to declare themselves independents leveled off after the mid-1970s, and in the 1980s and 1990s, partisanship showed a modest resurgence. Even so, the current number of independents is high compared with the number found in the 1950s.

Some political observers have suggested that the growing number of independents has caused a high level of volatility in elections, an argument that gained creditability in elections from 2006 to 2010. Independents, however, are not a homogeneous bloc. Scholars break them into three distinct groups: Republican leaners, Democratic leaners, and pure independents—with the latter the smallest group by far.

Moreover, the three groups behave differently in the voting booth. Most self-proclaimed independents are not uncommitted but are in fact closet Democrats and Republicans who generally are more loyal to their party than are weak partisans. Only the pure independents exhibit substantial volatility from one election to the next. Indeed, they vote in a manner that tends to reflect the election outcome in an exaggerated way. For example, in 1980 Ronald Reagan had a modest five-to-four advantage over President Jimmy Carter in the total POPULAR VOTE, but Reagan's advantage was higher (three to one) among pure independents.

In 2010, one of the most volatile elections in the past several decades, voter surveys showed a significant swing by independents toward Republicans. Exit polling on election day showed a significant preference for the GOP: 55 percent of independents favored Republicans to 40 percent for Democrats. Two years earlier 34 percent of voters described themselves as Democrats, 26 percent as Republicans, and 39 percent as independents. However, the two elections were quite different, with 2008 a national election with the presidency at stake and the 2010 voting a midterm event for congressional seats only. That made comparing the two elections tricky, but the number of persons in 2010 identifying themselves as independents was so large that it did suggest an important swing, even if it turned out to be short-lived, in voter sentiment.

Ticket Splitting and Candidate-Centered Politics

Although studies of ELECTORAL BEHAVIOR consistently demonstrate that party identification is the single most important determinant of voter choice, evidence indicates that the influence of partisanship has lessened. The incidence of SPLIT-TICKET VOTING for candidates of different parties, instead of voting a straight party ticket, has increased.

Split-ticket voting is encouraged further by the trend in the twentieth and early twenty-first centuries away from party-centered campaigns in which the party organizations controlled nominations, ran campaigns, and appealed to the voters on the basis of partisanship. Today CANDIDATE-CENTERED CAMPAIGNS predominate, especially for the presidency. With a personal organization and through extensive use of the media, particularly television, candidates sell themselves, not their parties, to the voters.

Partisan Realignments

Party identification of voters is stable but not static. Over time, the partisan alignment of the electorate may shift, producing a *realignment* or a *dealignment*.

Political scientists have discerned five different party systems in American history, beginning with the first (1789–1824), during which there was basically only one party, the DEMOCRATIC-REPUBLICAN (although the Federalists dominated in 1790), and ending with the current system (1932 to the present). Since the demise of the WHIGS in the mid-1800s, the Democratic and Republican parties have alternated dominance during the third through fifth systems. (See table, American Party Systems, p. 381.)

Party identification of voters is stable but not static.

The weakening of the New Deal Democratic coalition and Republican domination of the presidency during the 1970s and 1980s fueled speculation that the United States was on the verge of another of its periodic electoral realignments and that the fifth party system was coming to an end.

The evidence as of 2010 suggests, however, that a major realignment has not yet occurred. In the last national voting, in 2008, there continued to be modestly more Democratic than Republican identifiers among voters, despite the decline of the Democratic margin in the 1980s and early 1990s. Although the Democrats in 1992 broke the Republicans' twelve-year lock on the presidency, the Republicans broke the Democrats' even longer hold on Congress in 1994. In 2000, the Republicans captured the White House, and—after temporarily losing their Senate majority because of the defection of Vermont's James Jeffords—cemented their control of Congress with the 2002 elections. Democrats advanced by winning control of Congress in 2006 and the presidency in 2008. But the GOP regrouped dramatically in 2010, gaining a net of sixty-three House seats to win back control of the chamber, although the party fell short in the Senate.

AMERICAN PARTY SYSTEMS

Party System	Years	Major Parties	Characteristics and Major Events
First	1789–1824	Federalist Democratic- Republican	Political parties emerge in 1790s. War of 1812. Democratic-Republicans dominate, 1800–1824.
Second	1828–1854	Democratic Whig	Factional conflicts develop within Democratic Party, 1828–1836. Whigs emerge as opposition to Democrats in 1830s. Two-party competition results, with the Democrats stronger electorally. Sectional conflicts between North and South intensify and create schisms within Democratic and Whig parties.
Third	1856–1896	Democratic Republican	Republican Party emerges as major opposition to Democrats in 1850s. Lincoln elected in 1860; Civil War and Reconstruction follow. Republicans dominate, 1864–1874; two-party competition characterizes 1874–1896. Agrarian unrest surfaces; Populist Party contests 1892 election.
Fourth	1896–1932	Democratic Republican	Republicans dominate, 1896–1910. Progressive movement develops; Progressives split away from GOP and run Theodore Roosevelt for president, but Democrat Woodrow Wilson is elected. South becomes solidly Democratic. World War I and normalcy of 1920s. Republicans dominate nationally, 1920–1928.
Fifth	1932–	Democratic Republican	Great Depression of 1930s, World War II. New Deal Democratic coalition forms; Democrats dominate electorally in 1930s and 1940s. Korean and Vietnam wars. After 1950s, Democratic electoral coalition is weakened, especially among southern whites; the rise of candidate-centered politics and split-ticket voting; Republican domination of the presidency and Democratic control of Congress create an era of divided government; Democrats regain presidency in 1992. Republicans regain the presidency in 2000 and control both houses of Congress as a result of the 2002 elections, ending divided government—but only temporarily. Public dissatisfaction with President George W. Bush and the Republican-controlled Congress enables Democrats to take over the House and the Senate in the 2006 elections and the White House in 2008. But Republicans regain House control two years later with a pickup of sixty-three seats.

Source: John F. Bibby, Governing by Consent, 2nd ed. (Washington, DC: CQ Press, 1995), 189; updated by author. Also, CQ's Guide to U.S. Elections, *6th ed.* (*Washington, D.C.: CQ Press/ Sage, 2011*).

No realignment has occurred comparable to those of the 1860s and 1930s, when the compelling issues of slavery and the Great Depression tore at the fabric of American politics and caused wholesale shifts in voter partisanship. Nevertheless, striking partisan realignments have occurred on the regional level. Republicans now control most elected offices in the once solidly Democratic South, whereas the majority of northeastern states, many of which leaned Republican in the middle of the twentieth century, have now become strong Democratic bastions.

Electoral dealignment has taken place as many voters, viewing parties as less relevant, have opted to become independents. The trends toward candidate-centered campaigns and split-ticket voting also indicate more of a dealignment than a realignment at the beginning of the twenty-first century.

Peace and Freedom Party (1967–)

Although founded in Michigan, the radical Peace and Freedom Party has been active largely in California. At its outset in the political turmoil of the 1960s, the party worked with the California Black Panther Party to oppose U.S. involvement in the Vietnam War and espouse black nationalism and other so-called New Left causes.

The first Peace and Freedom nominee for president, in 1968, was Black Panther leader Eldridge Cleaver. Running with various vice presidential candidates, Cleaver received 36,563 votes. Before the 1968 election, black activist and comedian Dick Gregory broke with the Peace and Freedom Party and set up the similarly named Freedom and Peace Party with himself as the presidential nominee. He received 47,133 votes.

The party's strongest showing came in 1972, when it backed noted pacifist and pediatrician Benjamin Spock, who elsewhere in the nation ran as the PEOPLE'S PARTY nominee. Spock received 55,167 votes, about 2 percent of the state's total, under the Peace and Freedom banner in California, as Republican Richard M. Nixon easily carried the state en route to his reelection.

Much more typical was the total of 27,607 votes received by the party's 2004 ticket, headed by Leonard Peltier, an American Indian activist who has been imprisoned since his conviction in the 1975 murders of two FBI agents on the Pine Ridge Reservation in South Dakota. Peltier has long been a cause célèbre for some activists on the left who argue that he was wrongly convicted.

Despite its limited appeal to voters, the Peace and Freedom Party has remained active. It ran nominees for eight statewide offices in California in 2006, with the strongest showing by Tom Condit, who took 2.2 percent of the vote and finished fifth of six candidates in the race for insurance commissioner. The party also fielded candidates in eight congressional districts; none of its candidates garnered more than 3 percent of the total vote.

The party's platform, adopted in 2003, includes planks promoting "social ownership and democratic control of industry, financial institutions, and natural resources," conversion "from a military to a peace-oriented economy, with jobs for displaced workers," and abolition "of the CIA, NSA, AID and other agencies for interference in other countries' internal affairs."

People's Party (1970s)

One of several splinter parties that emerged from the political turmoil of the 1960s, the People's Party was founded by liberal activists and peace groups at a November 1971 convention held in Dallas, Texas. The initial cochairmen were well-known figures in American culture, pediatrician Benjamin Spock—author of a much-read book on baby care—and author Gore Vidal.

But the party's impact was limited and its existence ephemeral. The People's Party ran a presidential candidate in 1972, choosing Spock for president and black activist Julius Hobson of

Washington, D.C., for vice president. Despite hopes for widespread backing from the poor and social activists, the ticket received only 78,756 votes (0.1 percent of the national total). A total of 55,167 of those votes came from California, where its efforts were combined with those of the leftist PEACE AND FREEDOM PARTY.

At its convention, held in St. Louis, Missouri, August 31, 1975, the People's Party chose black civil rights activist Margaret Wright of California for president and Maggie Kuhn of Pennsylvania, a leader in the Gray Panthers movement for rights for the elderly, for vice president. Kuhn, however, declined the nomination and was replaced on the ticket by Spock.

The party platform focused on cutting the defense budget, closing tax loopholes, and making that money available for social programs. Other planks included redistribution of land and wealth, unconditional amnesty for war objectors, and free health care. In her campaign, Wright stressed a need for active participation by citizens in the process of government, so that institutions and programs could be run from the grass-roots rather than from the top down.

As in 1972 the party's main backing came in California, where it was again supported by the state Peace and Freedom Party. Wright's total national vote in 1976 was 49,024, and 85.1 percent (41,731 votes) of those votes came from California. The party ceased to be a functional political organization shortly thereafter.

Platform

The Democratic and Republican parties formally adopt their party platforms, or statements of party principles, at their NATIONAL PARTY CONVENTIONS, held every four years to nominate the parties' general election candidates for president and vice president.

The importance of the platform in setting an election-year agenda has diminished sharply, especially in recent years. The switch to a primary-oriented presidential nominating system, decades ago, means that the conventions now serve only to formalize selection of the nominees and adoption of the party platforms.

The parties' nominees now play a major role in shaping the documents to reflect their views. Nevertheless, nominees have often accepted some provisions they do not strongly favor in order to assuage an electorally important constituency. Similarly, most of a party's candidates for other offices will find much to like in the party's platform, even if they disagree with some of its provisions, especially on volatile social issues that can create dissension within both major parties.

To prevent any discouraging words about divisive issues from interfering with the festivities, both the

One of the major functions of national party conventions is the adoption of the party platform. Republicans held their 1920 convention in Chicago. It was the first year in which women, on the verge of obtaining suffrage, attended in significant numbers.

Source: Library of Congress

Democrats and Republicans have even dispensed with the long-standing practice of gathering their platform committees in the convention city the week before the convention to hammer out the document. Instead, they hold field hearings around the nation and, in most cases, meet at the convention only to give pro forma approval to a document that already has met the approval of the nominee-in-waiting.

Long gone are the fierce fights, played out in full view of the voting public, on matters such as civil rights (at the 1948 Democratic convention in Philadelphia) and the Vietnam War (at the 1968 Democratic convention in Chicago). These disputes aired the great issues of the day but also exposed schisms that threatened the party's hopes of winning in November.

As of the 2008 presidential election, the last time a platform plank even came to a roll-call vote by a convention was at the 1992 Democratic meeting in New York City. At this convention, Bill Clinton was nominated for what would be his first term in the White House. The specific proposal, defeated overwhelmingly, called for a delay in a middle-class tax cut, on which Clinton was campaigning, until after the federal deficit had been brought under control.

As a result of the pro forma nature of platform adoption, platforms have become most useful for the perspective they provide on where the parties stood on issues at certain points in time, and on which issues appeared repeatedly over the years and which ones were more ephemeral.

Change in the thrust of platforms, as in the philosophies of the parties themselves, is almost always evolutionary rather than revolutionary. Throughout American history, the major parties have embraced THIRD-PARTY ideas they initially rejected as too radical. After winning popular acceptance and finding their way onto the major-party platforms, some controversial proposals became law. Ideas such as the graduated income tax, popular election of senators, WOMEN'S SUFFRAGE, YOUTH SUFFRAGE, minimum wages, and Social Security were advocated by POPULISTS, PROGRESSIVES,

and other INDEPENDENTS long before they were accepted by the nation as a whole.

In contrast, Democrats and Republicans traditionally have been much more wary of adopting platform planks regarded at the time as extreme. Trying to appeal to a broad range of voters, the two major parties have tended to compromise on differences or to reject controversial planks.

The Democrats have been more ready than the Republicans to adopt once-radical ideas, but a considerable time lag usually exists between the origin of such ideas in

"This right of equal opportunity to work and to advance in life should never be limited in any individual because of race, religion, color or country of origin. We favor the enactment of and just enforcement of such Federal legislation as may be necessary to maintain this right at all times in every part of this Republic."

—Wording of the civil rights platform plank approved by the 1948 Democratic Party convention, which prompted a walkout by southern delegates determined to preserve their region's white supremacist policies. The plank also called for laws to end lynching and mob violence, abolition of the poll tax as a requisite for voting, and an end to racial segregation in the armed forces.

third parties and their eventual adoption in Democratic platforms. For example, although the Democrats by 1912 had adopted many of the Populist planks of the 1890s, the Bull Moose Progressives of that year already were way ahead of them in proposals for social legislation. Not until 1932 did the Democrats adopt many of the 1912 Progressive planks. Similarly, not until the 1960s did Democratic platforms incorporate many of the antiwar and civil rights proposals put forward in 1948 by the party's liberal wing and Henry Wallace's PROGRESSIVE PARTY.

The passage of a strong civil rights plank in the 1948 Democratic platform provoked opposition from southern states and prompted the walkout of the entire Mississippi delegation and thirteen members of the Alabama delegation. Some of the disgruntled southerners then formed their own STATES' RIGHTS DEMOCRATIC PARTY (the Dixiecrats), which held its own convention in Birmingham, Alabama, and nominated South Carolina governor J. Strom Thurmond for president and Mississippi governor Fielding L. Wright for vice president.

Interest Group Participation

Party platforms offer interest groups a welcome opportunity to influence the direction of the parties. Rather than appeal only to the party that they think will win, many groups hedge their bets and ask for a hearing before both parties.

Since 1852, most conventions have adopted their platforms before nominating their candidates. Platform fights, during the long period in which conventions actually played the key role in selecting the presidential ticket, often served as an indicator of the relative strength of rival candidates, especially when those candidates held different ideological positions. (See Reference Material, Major Platform Fights, page 703.)

The issue of abortion rights—which arose in the late 1960s and intensified in 1973, when the Supreme Court in *Roe v. Wade* established women's constitutional right to abortion—was a particularly difficult one for platform writers. Both parties had problems finding consensus positions on various aspects of the abortion issue, including a proposed constitutional amendment to overturn the Court decision.

In 1992, Republicans faced one such fight that was over before it began. Abortion rights advocates needed six delegations to challenge the platform committee's conservative right-to-life plank, but they could muster only four. Besides supporting an antiabortion amendment, the platform as adopted stated, "We oppose using public revenues for abortion and will not fund organizations that advocate it." The platform overall was even more conservative than the 1988 version. Its tone, reflected in the rhetoric of several speakers, including television evangelist Pat Robertson, led to widespread journalistic speculation that the 1992 platform was the work of the religious right. But political scientists concluded after analysis that President George H. W. Bush's advisers drafted the platform and that they had more influence on its final form than the speakers from the party's right wing.

In 1996 both parties adopted their platforms with little rancor and few headlines. Social conservatives at the GOP convention were again pleased with the antiabortion plank, but they were not showcased as prominently as they had been four years earlier. Few hard-liners were invited to speak in television prime time, and the moderates who gained the choice speaking slots made no mention of the platform.

Abortion rights advocates tried to have "tolerance language" inserted to acknowledge the right of Republicans to disagree with the party's call for a constitutional ban on abortion. Despite the support of Bob Dole, the party's nominee that year, the tolerance move was beaten down.

By contrast, the Democratic platform adopted later the same month in Chicago contained language recognizing that not everyone agrees with the plank supporting women's right to choose abortion. The new clause said, "The Democratic Party is a party of inclusion. We respect the individual conscience of each American on this difficult issue, and we welcome all our members to participate at every level of our party."

Both parties again moved to the center in 2000, avoiding platform battles. The Democrats repeated their abortion language of 1996. Republicans quickly rejected two amendments to the platform offered by abortion rights advocates. One would have altered the platform language to accept the views of those who disagree with the majority's antiabortion sentiment; the other would have deleted the platform's opposition to abortion in cases of rape and incest, or when a woman's life was in danger from a resulting pregnancy.

> **More on this topic:**
>
> *President, Nominating and Electing, p. 437*
>
> *Presidential Selection Reforms, p. 476*

The 2004 Democratic platform backed abortion rights but revised the document's wording, saying that "we stand proudly for a woman's right to choose" and that the procedure should be "safe, legal and rare." The 2004 Republican platform reaffirmed the party's antiabortion position, again supporting what it called a "human life" constitutional amendment to overturn *Roe v. Wade.* These positions were largely repeated in the 2008 platforms.

Plurality

A plurality is the margin by which most U.S. elections must be won. In a race of two or more candidates, the one who gets the most votes wins. The number of additional votes received by the winner is his or her plurality.

The plurality may amount to a majority (more than 50 percent of the total vote), but a majority is usually not required in American elections. An exception is the RUNOFF system used in some states, where a second or runoff election is held between the two top finishers if no candidate received a majority in the initial primary election. Such a contest received national attention in 2002, when Louisiana senator Mary Landrieu was forced into a December runoff after receiving 46 percent of the vote on ELECTION DAY out of a nine-person field that included candidates from both parties. In the weeks leading up to the runoff, President George W. Bush and other top GOP officials urged Louisianans to vote for Landrieu's Republican challenger because they wanted to pad their fragile Senate majority. But Landrieu captured 52 percent of the vote in the runoff.

The 2002 Louisiana senatorial race drew national attention when incumbent Mary Landrieu, above, narrowly won a runoff election against her Republican challenger.

Source: CQ Photo/Scott J. Ferrell

Another exception to the plurality requirement is the ELECTORAL COLLEGE system used for presidential elections. To be elected president, a candidate must receive a majority of the 538 electoral votes—equal to the total number of U.S. senators and representatives, plus three votes that the DISTRICT OF COLUMBIA would have if it were a state. Presidential election actually requires winning an ABSOLUTE MAJORITY of the electoral vote, because presidential electors must cast all 538 votes. The winner therefore must receive at least 270 electoral votes—one-half of 538 plus one. If no candidate receives an absolute majority, the House of Representatives must choose the president. This has happened twice in U.S. history, in 1800, when the House chose Thomas Jefferson, and in 1824, when the winner was John Quincy Adams. (See PRESIDENT, NOMINATING AND ELECTING.)

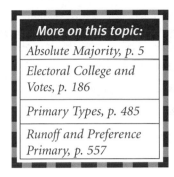

More on this topic:

Absolute Majority, p. 5

Electoral College and Votes, p. 186

Primary Types, p. 485

Runoff and Preference Primary, p. 557

Pocketbook Voting

Pocketbook voting means making electoral choices according to one's perceived economic interest. In the United States, the class conflict that pocketbook voting often implies has been tempered by many other voter concerns and by the political process itself. Nevertheless, public concerns about issues such as taxation and government spending have been evident since the founding of the country.

At times, class differences clearly affected U.S. elections. In the early years of the nineteenth century, the Jeffersonians, many from lower economic strata, successfully challenged the economic power of supporters of the FEDERALIST PARTY. Later in the century Andrew Jackson won the presidency with the broad support of poorer members of the electorate.

After the Civil War, many workers became affiliated with the Knights of Labor, which entered slates of candidates in numerous state and local elections in the 1880s. But workers' political parties never found a secure footing in American politics.

A 1928 campaign ad for Herbert Hoover appealed to voters' pocketbooks, promising "a chicken for every pot. And a car in every backyard, to boot."

Source: National Archives and Records Administration

Role of the Economy

In the twentieth century, pocketbook voting reached a high-water mark with President Franklin D. Roosevelt's New Deal. In the midst of the Great Depression, Roosevelt's economic proposals had strong appeal to the jobless and working poor.

Similarly, in 1960 John F. Kennedy promised to "get the country moving again," and in 1980 Ronald Reagan, citing double-digit inflation, asked, "Are you better off today than you were four years ago?" In 1992 the phrase "It's the economy, stupid," originally meant as a reminder to Bill Clinton's campaign staffers, became his de facto CAMPAIGN SLOGAN. But the prosperous economy of 2000 failed to help Clinton's vice president, Al Gore, who lost the White House to Republican George W. Bush in a campaign in which Republicans focused on such issues as strong leadership and trustworthiness.

In the national election of 2008 and the midterm voting two years later economic issues were significant. By November 2008 the United States and most of the world had plunged into the steepest economic decline since the Great Depression of the 1930s as major and smaller banks

failed, housing values collapsed and foreclosures mounted, auto companies faced bankruptcy, and unemployment soared to more than 10 percent. Republicans were hurt far more than Democrats because the GOP had controlled the White House since 2000 and Congress for most of that time.

> ### *"Are you better off today than you were four years ago?"*
>
> —**Ronald Reagan,** campaigning in 1980

Taxes tend to be a particularly volatile issue. The Republicans' ability to appeal to anti-tax attitudes of middle-income voters has frequently been an obstacle to Democrats who favor using tax dollars to ameliorate social ills. This was evident in the first decade of the twenty-first century, when President George W. Bush pushed several large tax cuts through a Republican-controlled Congress. When Democrats sought to portray the cuts as a boon for the wealthiest Americans, Bush and his allies accused them of practicing "class warfare." Yet even tax-related issues are not always clear cut, but the controversy in 2011 over raising new revenue through tax increases to help reduce the federal deficit proved a defining line between the two parties. By the time the issue was settled, temporarily, in mid-2011 no new taxes had been approved.

Closer to home, in state and local elections, people repeatedly vote their pocketbooks on issues such as income and property taxes, bond issues for highway and other public works projects, and land-use and zoning plans. The issue of the annual property tax on automobiles dominated POLITICAL ADVERTISING in the 1997 Virginia gubernatorial race, which was won by Republican Jim Gilmore, the candidate promising repeal. But Gilmore's insistence on pursuing the car-tax

> ### *"It's the economy, stupid!"*
>
> —**Bill Clinton's** 1992 de facto campaign slogan

cuts in the face of an economic downturn caused a state fiscal crisis that left him highly unpopular by the end of his term. His Democratic successor, Mark Warner, took political risks to address the budget problems, including raising some taxes, but the state's return to fiscal solvency on his watch earned him strong job approval ratings.

Most states, California especially, regularly put pocketbook issues before the voters by means of ballot measures known as INITIATIVES AND REFERENDUMS.

POLLING has shown consistently that in PUBLIC OPINION the REPUBLICAN PARTY, at least to some extent, favors the rich over the poor. The DEMOCRATIC PARTY generally wins the support of Americans on the lowest rungs of the economic ladder. Political beliefs and opinions, however, are associated with a number of variables besides income. They include education, occupation, race, gender, ethnicity, age, religion, and region. (See PARTY IDENTIFICATION BY VOTERS.)

Little Cohesion

Wide divergences of opinion among income classes seldom translate into unified action at the polls by one group or the other. Although theoretically the more numerous low-income voters could overwhelm opposition in elections and bring about ever-larger social programs and ever-greater costs to the government, results rarely are that simple. One reason, according to social and political scientists, is that far larger proportions of middle- and upper-income Americans vote than do those who are poorer. In addition, middle- and upper-income Americans are far more likely to join and support INTEREST GROUPS than are lower-income citizens. Special interests overwhelmingly promote the interests of wealthier voters.

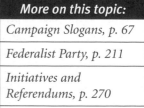

More on this topic:

Campaign Slogans, p. 67

Federalist Party, p. 211

Initiatives and Referendums, p. 270

Interest Group, p. 273

Party Identification by Voters, p. 377

What is clear is that pocketbook voting by poorer Americans has failed to produce a substantial redistribution of national income. Although the federal income tax is progressive, other federal taxes, including the Social Security payroll tax, are regressive. They proportionately take more from wage earners than from salaried executives and others who are far wealthier. When citizens vote their pocketbooks, the rich and not-so-rich often find that their interests are more in harmony than in conflict.

Political Action Committees

Political action committees (PACs) enable INTEREST GROUPS, politicians, and even some individuals to raise money and distribute it to candidates for elective office. Outright gifts to candidates from corporate or union treasuries are illegal, but contributions from PACs are not. This has made PACs popular with those hoping to influence the outcome of elections.

The rapid growth of PACs in both numbers and influence since the 1970s made them for a time one of the most controversial aspects of the CAMPAIGN FINANCE system. By the late 1990s, other controversies had erupted and efforts to curtail PACs were dropped.

Yet the concept of the "political action committee" has not been static, and there have been several developments over the past decade that have revived concerns remain about these organizations, which are not accountable to voters but can play a major role in steering the nation's electoral decisions.

This is especially true is relation to the rapid growth of a variant of PACs known as the "527" POLITICAL ORGANIZATIONS, so called because such groups are organized under Section 527 of the Internal Revenue Code and are regulated by the Internal Revenue Service rather than the Federal Election Commission (FEC), as are most PACs.

Traditional PACs involved in presidential and congressional elections mostly make direct donations to candidates and therefore are subject to strict limits set by federal campaign finance law for accepting and making campaign donations. But 527s, rather than donating to candidates, focus their efforts on "independent expenditure" campaigns that technically fall under the legal definition of issue advocacy, but in many cases are rather blatant efforts to persuade voters to support a candidate or oppose his or her rival.

Moreover, 527s, because they do not donate directly to candidates, are free to accept large SOFT MONEY donations from groups and wealthy individuals. As an example of the law of unintended consequences, their receipts skyrocketed in the years following the implementation of a ban on soft money contributions directly to national political party organizations, a key provision of the

House Speaker Nancy Pelosi of California listens as she is introduced at the EMILY's List luncheon in Washington, D.C., on March 6, 2007. EMILY's List, an acronym for "Early Money Is Like Yeast," is a political network that helps elect pro-choice Democratic women candidates to office.

Source: Images/Charles Dharapak

Bipartisan Campaign Reform Act (BCRA) of 2002 (see CAMPAIGN FINANCE) that went into effect with the 2003–2004 election cycle.

Legislation requiring that these groups—nicknamed "stealth PACs"—register with the Internal Revenue Service and disclose most of their receipts and expenditures was enacted in 2000. Many critics complained that the FEC was slow to respond to their concerns about outright electioneering by these tax-exempt groups. The commission did, however, show signs of more energetic supervision in early 2007, when it levied a negotiated $750,000 fine against Progress for America, a Republican-allied group that ran ads during the 2004 campaign deemed by the commission as clearly aimed at advocating the reelection of President George W. Bush.

Yet that did not forestall the next big development in expansion—and political reach—of political action committees. The Supreme Court—which over decades has upheld the basic federal legislation governing campaign finance but has shown leanings toward less rather than stricter regulation on free-speech grounds—opened wide a new and potential torrential outlet for political spending with its January 2010 decision in the case of *Citizens United v. Federal Election Commission*, a decision that paved the way for the rapid growth of what were labeled as SuperPACs.

These organizations were spawned by a ruling, approved by a 5-4 vote, that struck down a major provision in the 2002 BCRA legislation: a ban on "electioneering communications," or broadcast ads aimed at influencing the outcomes of elections, by groups associated with corporate entities (including labor unions) within sixty days of a general election and within thirty days of a primary. The decision essentially equated the free speech rights of corporations with those of individuals.

With corporate interests free to invest money in independent expenditure political ads right up through the day of an election, SuperPACs sprung up to channel such donations and attempt to maximize their impact. While traditional PACs had generally been involved in promoting the political agenda of one company or union or industry or interest group, many SuperPACs (following a path blazed by many "527" organizations before them) were ostensibly aimed at pursuing broader goals in support of one political party or ideology.

The SuperPAC that raised by far the most money during the 2010 midterm election cycle, which saw the Republican Party make major gains nationally, was American Crossroads, a Republican support group whose principals included two consultants who were among the leading figures in national GOP politics over a couple of decades: Karl Rove, the former White House political director under President George W. Bush, and Ed Gillespie, a former chairman of the Republican National Committee. The leading SuperPAC on the Democratic side was America's Family First Action Fund, whose stated mission was "to help protect the Democratic majority in the U.S. House of Representatives."

By the beginning of the 2012 presidential election cycle, SuperPACs had spun off a controversial variation: fund-raising groups were set up by supporters of several of the contenders for the Republican presidential nomination—some of whom were either former aides to those candidates or otherwise clearly identified their longtime political allies. Each of these groups was created with only one political goal, which was the nomination and election as president of the PAC's favored candidate. This, in turn, spurred criticism from campaign finance reformers and others, who view these organizations as vehicles for the presidential candidates to evade the strict federal limits on individual and PAC donations directly to their campaign treasuries.

SuperPACs were not technically 527 organizations but like 527s were able to receive unlimited contributions for unlimited independent expenditure advertising campaigns, which were deemed legal by authorities as long as they were not conducted in coordination with the campaigns of individual candidates. And some ads by SuperPACs directly attacked candidates for public office by name, a contrast to most issue ads by 527s, which were carefully crafted to persuade voters to support or oppose a candidate without saying so expressly in order to pass the so-called "magic words" test spelled out in the 1976 Supreme Court decision in BUCKLEY V. VALEO,

Meanwhile, another kind of political action committee, the "leadership" PAC, had been stirring some controversy for several years. These groups initially were the province of party leaders who used them to raise money to try to get other members of their party elected—hence the name leadership PACs. But the concept grew to the point that many rank-and-file members of Congress, including some who were recently elected freshmen, established their own leadership PACs to raise money and make donations to candidates of their own party—and, in many cases, to cultivate support for their own ambitions to serve in their party's congressional leadership or procure a highly sought-after committee chairmanship.

Defining PACs

Organizations commonly thought of as PACs have typically fallen into two main categories: those that are connected to either a labor organization or incorporated entity and those that are not. The first category—the largest—includes the PACs of corporations, labor unions, trade and health associations, and membership organizations. The non-connected category includes the PACs of ideological and single-issue groups, as well as those leadership PACs created by established political figures.

Business PACs, such as those sponsored by the National Association of Realtors and the National Automobile Dealers Association, generally favor Republican candidates. Labor PACs, such as those of the American Federation of State, County and Municipal Employees and the United Auto Workers, give primarily to Democrats. Among the single-issue or ideological PACs, the National Rifle Association's PAC gives more to the Republicans.

The single biggest PAC for many years, in terms of contributions expenditures, was EMILY's List (deriving its name from an acronym for the saying "Early Money Is Like Yeast, It Makes Dough Rise"), which gives only to Democratic women candidates who support abortion rights. In 2010, EMILY's LIST remained a potent force, with more than $33 million in expenditures, but ranked third behind two other organizations aligned with the Democratic Party: ActBlue, which raises money (mainly online) to support the campaigns of Democratic candidates, and the Service Employees International Union.

TOP TEN PACS BY TOTAL EXPENDITURES, 2009–2010 ELECTION CYCLE

PAC	(millions)
1. ActBlue	$60.4
2. Service Employees International Union	$54.0
3. EMILY's List	$33.0
4. MoveOn.org	$29.0
5. American Crossroads	$25.8
6. American Federation of State, County and Municipal Employees	$19.5
7. American Federation of Teachers	$19.1
8. National Association of Realtors	$16.0
9. Teamsters Union	$15.2
10. National Rifle Association	$14.0

Source: Center for Responsive Politics.

Note: Figures have been rounded.

PACs made nearly $473 million in contributions during the 2009–2010 election cycle, according to the Center for Responsive Politics. Business-related PACs gave the most money by far: $333.7 million cumulatively.

After the Republican takeover of Congress in 1994, GOP House and Senate candidates received the larger share of PAC contributions for the first time since the FEC began keeping such records in 1978. This tilt continued throughout the next dozen years, during which the Republicans maintained an unbroken hold on the House and were out of the Senate majority for just a year and a half.

But PACs, especially on the dominant business side, have hedged their bets to some extent, as they want to maintain influence regardless of the party in power. This was especially evident in 2006, a swing year in which widespread voter dissatisfaction with President Bush and the Republican-controlled Congress boosted the Democrats' chances of taking over both chambers (which they did).

Despite the Republicans' loss of thirty House seats that year, their candidates' share of total PAC contributions to contenders of the two major parties stayed stable at 55 percent, a slight 1 percentage-point uptick over the previous midterm elections in 2002, in which the Republicans made a net gain of six seats. But Democratic Senate candidates closed the gap noticeably in 2006, when they gained six seats and took narrow control of the chamber. Democrats took in 44 percent of the two-party PAC donations that year, compared with just 33 percent in 2002, a campaign year in which Republicans gained two seats to reclaim their own narrow majority.

This bet-hedging tendency was again clear during the 2010 midterm election, when businesses split their donations almost down the middle to Democrats, who then held majorities in both chambers of Congress, and Republicans, whose party was generating a major rebound that would restore it to control of the U.S. House and enable the GOP to cut deeply into the Democrats' Senate majorities.

Until the recent development of SuperPACs dedicated to the election of a particular candidate for president, PACs had little involvement in presidential elections other than the personal PACs presidential candidates used for their primary campaigns,. They provided only a small share of funds needed by candidates seeking their party's presidential nomination, and they continued to be barred from contributing to general election campaigns that accept PUBLIC FINANCING. Under federal law, most PACs are permitted to contribute $5,000 per candidate, per election (primary, runoff, special, and general elections are counted as separate elections). There is no limit on the total amount they can give to all candidates, though they are limited to $15,000 in donations to a single political party organization per year. They also can spend as much as they want to help candidates—for example, with heavy television advertising—so long as they operate independently of the candidates' campaigns. PACs must report their receipts and expenditures to the FEC at certain intervals in each two-year election cycle, with most filing monthly reports.

PACs sometimes increase their clout by pulling together a number of checks from individual donors or other PACs and passing them along to candidates. EMILY's List was among the earliest organizations to perfect this practice, known as BUNDLING, but its success has spawned many imitators.

Many states also limit contributions by PACs to candidates for state or local office. There is no uniformity to the limitations, and amounts vary widely from state to state.

Although PACs date back to the 1940s, their significance in political campaigns began with the passage in 1971 and 1974 of laws to reform campaign financing. The laws, along with FEC and Supreme Court rulings, allowed PACs to become a major factor in the financing of congressional elections. In 1974 only about 600 PACs were registered, and PACs gave about $12.5 million to House and Senate candidates. By 2000 more than 3,800 PACs were registered with the FEC, and $245 million in PAC money went to congressional candidates.

Nearly $75 million of all PAC contributions in 1999–2000 came from the fifty largest PACs. The largest single contributor was the Realtors Political Action Committee, which gave $3.4 million.

PAC contributions are especially important in House races. House candidates in 2000 received just over two-fifths of their campaign funds from PACs, whereas PAC money accounted for less than one-fifth of Senate candidates' receipts.

Perhaps the most salient characteristic that determines PAC giving is INCUMBENCY. Current congressional members are in a position to support PAC interests when legislation is drafted as well as when it comes to a vote. They are also able to vigorously court PAC donations on the national fund-raising circuit. This is particularly true for committee chairmen or chairwomen and party leaders, who have more power than other members to see that legislation is considered and to push for its passage.

In 2006 House incumbents of both parties combined received nearly $250 million or 84 percent of all federal PAC donations, compared with about $49 million or 16 percent for all other candidates, including challengers and open-seat candidates. The incumbent bias was even more astounding in Senate races. Of the total PAC contributions of about $71 million, $68 million or 96 percent went to incumbents.

Many people have criticized the role played by PACs, arguing that they allow well-financed interest groups to gain too much political influence. By accepting contributions from PACs, critics say, members of Congress become dependent on them and reluctant to vote against the interests of a PAC out of fear of either losing the PAC's contributions or of having the PAC help finance their political opponents. PACs' bias toward incumbents has also triggered charges that they are helping to squelch competition and turnover in Congress, although PAC advocates counter by pointing to the big political swings that put the Republicans in charge of Congress in the 1994 elections and did the same for the Democrats in 2006. PACs' tendency to favor incumbents also did little to break the Republicans' momentum during their 2010 election comeback.

Defenders argue that PACs provide a legitimate means by which citizens can join together to support candidates. PACs encourage people to participate in politics, they say, and offer the most efficient method for channeling campaign contributions. PAC officials say their groups are seeking not to buy votes but to gain access to members of Congress, so that their views are heard on legislative decisions affecting them.

Proposals to curb the influence of PACs have been debated by Congress a number of times, but the question of what, if anything, to do about them proved to be a particularly divisive one between the parties and the chambers. Democrats were more dependent on PAC contributions than were Republicans, and House members relied on them more than senators. Some called for banning PAC contributions altogether, some would have reduced the amount a PAC could contribute to a candidate, and others would have imposed an overall limit on the amount of PAC money a candidate could accept. Some members of the House called for weakening PACs by providing public funds for congressional campaigns, as the federal government has done for presidential campaigns since 1976.

But no proposal passed. Legislation that included public financing and limits on PACs was vetoed by President George H. W. Bush in 1992, and attempts in the next few Congresses never even got that far. By the late 1990s, the issue was off the table, overshadowed by growing controversy over campaign

More on this topic:
Bundling, p. 39
Campaign Finance, p. 53
"527" Political Organizations, p. 199
Interest Group, p. 273
Public Financing of Campaigns, p. 496
Soft Money, p. 592

money and tactics that fell outside the reach of federal campaign finance law. PAC contributions—limited by law and well-disclosed—began to pale in significance compared with unregulated soft money and the type of POLITICAL ADVERTISING called issue advocacy that were flooding the system.

Political Advertising

Election time in America is hard to miss. Yard signs suddenly blossom on front lawns. Political posters become familiar sights (and sometimes eyesores) on fences and utility poles. Mailboxes bulge with candidates' fliers and parties' appeals for money. Cars and lapels become vehicles for bumper stickers and CAMPAIGN BUTTONS. Especially in local races, these traditional artifacts of electioneering are still very much in evidence when the time comes for candidates to try to sell themselves to the voters.

But since the dawn of the electronic age during the twentieth century—and especially since television became the dominant platform for mass communication—the term *political advertising* became virtually synonymous with just one thing: political television commercials.

Spending on TV spots has long dwarfed other expenses of campaigns for most major offices. It continued to do so through the 2008 presidential campaign year, in which past TV ad spending records were obliterated, even as candidates became more sophisticated in their use of Internet-based New Media channels as campaign communications tools.

The emergence of online fund-raising as a major factor in campaigns helped victorious 2008 Democratic nominee Barack Obama raise a total of $770 million for his bid, almost three times more than the previous record set by President George W. Bush, the Republican who won re-election in 2004. Two other contenders—Republican nominee John McCain, a senator of Arizona, and Hillary Rodham Clinton, the New York senator who staged an extended battle with Obama for the Democratic nomination—also exceeded Bush's previous presidential fund-raising record.

These huge fund-raising hauls, combined with millions more pulled in by other candidates who had initially crowded into both major parties' nominating contests, were reflected in stunning amounts of money poured into television advertising. Calculations by the consulting firm TNS Media Intelligence/Campaign Media Analysis Group found that about $240 million was spent in total on TV ads just in the primary campaign—an amount that was more than Bush spent on his entire presidential campaign in 2004—and by November, the candidates' TV ad total had grown to more than $700 million.

The national major-party organizations layered in millions more on independent expenditures, which clearly advocated for the election of one candidate and the defeat of another but under law could not be coordinated with that candidate's campaign.

Piling on were INTEREST GROUPS operating through their POLITICAL ACTION COMMITTEES and an increasingly active and controversial sector, "527" POLITICAL ORGANIZATIONS (funded largely by unlimited SOFT MONEY contributions), which ran hundreds of millions of dollars of ads billed as issue advocacy, but which in many cases were thinly veiled efforts to persuade voters to think favorably about one candidate and unfavorably about the other.

The 2010 midterm election campaign ushered in the development of yet another major factor in outside political spending: SuperPACs, similar in concept to the "527" organizations, that were spawned by the January 2010 Supreme Court ruling in the case of *Citizens United v. Federal Election Commission*. The decision, approved on a 5-4 vote, struck down a provision of the 2002 CAMPAIGN FINANCE law revision known as the Bipartisan Campaign Reform Act (BCRA), which barred "electioneering communications"—a euphemism that mainly applied to TV ads—by corporate entities (including labor unions) within the last few weeks before a primary or general election. The decision essentially established as a matter of law that corporations and unions have the same free-speech rights under the First Amendment as do individuals.

The rapid upward spiral in TV ad spending appeared to have two major sources. One of these was positive for those seeking to use television ads to communicate campaign messages; the other was not.

On the upside for campaigns was the growing availability of campaign money, one of the unintended consequences of the enactment of BCRA in 2002.

The provisions in the law that cut off soft money contributions (which tended to be collected in larger amounts from fewer sources) to national party organizations were decried by critics, who viewed the measure as likely to starve the parties of needed resources. Yet the parties proved highly adaptable and succeeded at substituting larger numbers of smaller, regulated HARD MONEY donations for the prohibited soft money. Meanwhile, large soft money donors who still wanted to influence the outcomes of elections found a warm welcome from the 527 organizations.

Yet campaign practitioners contended that the vast amount being poured into political advertising, especially on television, was needed to track down target audiences that have become increasingly segmented and diffuse. Just a generation earlier, candidates looking to reach a mass audience could focus their advertising dollars on the three major television networks, ABC, CBS, and NBC, or their local affiliates. Today upstart networks such as Fox and dozens of cable and satellite providers have sluiced away large portions of the traditional networks' audience, greatly complicating the task of campaign media buyers.

The multiplicity of channels, the ease with which viewers can use their remote controls to avoid TV ads if they choose to do so, and the growing amounts of time that millions of Americans now spend on their computers and away from their televisions have added elements to long-standing questions about the efficacy of political advertising. Despite all the money and energy devoted to political ads on television, observers are divided on whether such ads have any significant effect on election outcomes. Too few studies have been made, they say, to provide any definitive answers.

Many campaigns have responded to technological change, as well as the growing expense of campaigning, by adding a new wrinkle to their media strategies: the production of video ads that are intended mainly, and in some cases exclusively, for posting online. Some of these ads are aimed at getting a "free ride" from the news media, especially when the content is hard-hitting and spurs some sort of controversy.

There is some agreement, however, that TV spots might be influential for lower political offices where the candidates and their positions on issues are not well known and for primaries, when candidates from the same party are vying for a nomination.

"Ads have their strongest impact with little-known candidates and electoral settings of low visibility, and when journalistic coverage reinforces the ad message," wrote political scientist Darrell M. West in *Air Wars: Television Advertising in Election Campaigns, 1952–1996.*

West, formerly a political scientist at Brown University in Providence, Rhode Island, and more recently the head of governance studies at the Brookings Institution in Washington, D.C., found that commercials influence how voters learn about candidates and what they identify as priorities. Timing and content of ads, and decisions on when and where to attack, help to determine viewers' response to the ads.

Each election cycle almost always includes examples of ads run in high-profile campaigns that made a difference to justify the continued heavy expenditures. It would be hard to find any political observer who doubts that ads attacking Democratic presidential

> **"Ads have their strongest impact with little-known candidates and electoral settings of low visibility, and when journalistic coverage reinforces the ad message."**
>
> **—Political scientist Darrell M. West** in Air Wars: Television Advertising in Election Campaigns, 1952–1996

nominee John Kerry's personal actions during the Vietnam War era, run in 2004 by a 527 group known as the Swift Boat Veterans for Truth, did significant damage to his image and contributed to his defeat by President Bush.

Ads versus Reportage

Political scientists speak of political ads as *unmediated messages* because candidates pay for them and dictate what they say, thus avoiding what has long been referred to as the "media filter." The newspaper or station carrying the ads does not edit or censor them, except to avoid libel or bad taste. *Mediated messages,* by contrast, originate with the news media. The press, print or electronic, acts as intermediary. It generates its own MEDIA COVERAGE of the candidate and the campaign (and, in some cases, of the ads run in those campaigns). If the candidate's message happens to be passed on in the news story or broadcast, it is the reporter's or commentator's version of that message—which may or may not match what the candidate intended.

Political ads lack the credibility or persuasiveness of news stories. Most people realize the paid ads are self-serving and therefore, as the saying goes, they let them go in one ear and out the other. And in the era of remote controls and devices that allow viewers to record programs and skip commercials, many viewers don't even give political ads a chance to penetrate their consciousness.

In the words of political scientist Doris Graber, "Commercials are perceiver-determined. People see in them pretty much what they want to see—attractive images for their favorite candidate and unattractive ones for the opponent."

Because a favorable news story is worth more than several paid commercials, POLITICAL CONSULTANTS go to great lengths to attract press attention that will show their candidate in the best possible light. A few candidates, however, prefer to bypass the press. Billionaire businessman H. Ross Perot, for example, hired and fired several political consultants for his independent campaign for president in 1992 and his Reform Party bid in 1996 before deciding to manage his own campaigns.

> **"Commercials are perceiver-determined. People see in them pretty much what they want to see—attractive images for their favorite candidate and unattractive ones for the opponent."**
>
> **—Political scientist Doris Graber**

In 1992 Perot's talk show appearances, along with his info-mercials, videos, and books, provided one of the least-mediated campaigns in modern history. Perot never hesitated to express his disdain for the working press. Rather than talk to voters through the print and broadcast reports, he set up his own information system. He used it again in 1996, when he was excluded from the presidential DEBATES between Democratic incumbent Bill Clinton and Republican challenger Bob Dole.

Computer technology provided an even newer and more direct way to reach the voters than talk shows. From 1996 and continuing and escalating into the 2012 election cycle, the two major parties, presidential candidates, and most candidates for other offices built increasingly sophisticated websites on the Internet from which online users could obtain schedules, speech texts, video messages, and other handouts from the various campaigns, and which beginning in 2004 emerged as major campaign fund-raising vehicles. The websites have since become a staple of the political parties' public relations apparatus. (See Reference Material, Political and Election-Related Websites, p. 700.)

The theory that television ads can outweigh press coverage received a boost after publication of Joe McGinniss's *The Selling of the President 1968,* which suggested that Republican nominee Richard M. Nixon in effect "bought" the election with slick and expensive advertising. Political scientists, however, have not uncovered persuasive evidence that paid media advertising has a significant effect on voter choice in presidential elections. In a study of the 1988 presidential campaign, media scholar Michael Robinson compared the George H. W. Bush campaign's week-by-week paid media buys with the candidate's standing in the POLLS and found no significant correlations.

In elections that receive little press attention, paid media can make a difference. Challengers for House seats, for example, can use them to build name recognition and compete with the generally more visible and familiar congressional INCUMBENTS. As challengers' expenditures increase, their share of the vote also goes up.

Statewide Races

The cost of political advertising on television is particularly high for candidates in states where large numbers of their voters are clustered in or near expensive metropolitan TV markets.

California, a state more populous than many countries (with more than 37 million people), has the second largest media market (Los Angeles), the sixth (San Francisco-Oakland-San Jose), the twentieth (Sacramento-Stockton-Modesto), and the twenty-eighth (San Diego). Candidates in competitive statewide races in California can now regularly expect to have to raise and spend tens of millions of dollars, which made the state's decision to move its 2008 presidential primary to early February a daunting one for all but the best-funded candidates.

New Jersey is the eleventh most-populous state, but the expense of running statewide there can reach epic proportions as well. Although New Jersey has no media markets of its own, it is enveloped in two massive metropolitan areas, those of New York City (the nation's largest media market) and Philadelphia (the fourth largest). The expense of New Jersey campaigns has recently given big advantages to wealthy candidates capable of self-financing their campaigns, such as longtime Democratic senator Frank R. Lautenberg, the founder of a leading national check-processing company. Democrat Jon Corzine, former chief executive officer of the Goldman Sachs investment company, spent lavishly of his own resources in winning races for the Senate in 2000 and for governor in 2005, though his money advantage failed to insulate him from a downturn in voter support when he lost his 2009 reelection bid to Republican Chris Christie.

Free Air Time

To level the political advertising playing field, advocates have sought legislation or regulatory action requiring broadcasters to provide free or low-cost air time for candidates. President Clinton tried unsuccessfully to persuade the Federal Communications Commission (FCC) to make such a ruling to benefit candidates who observe spending limits voluntarily. In his 1998 State of the Union address, Clinton called media advertising the "real reason for the explosion in campaign costs."

Broadcasters opposed the idea. They were already required by the FCC's EQUAL TIME RULE to provide rebuttal time to persons maligned on programs or commercials other than news programs. No such requirement could be made of print media because of press freedom rights, but the broadcast spectrum is a public resource that the government regulates through its licensing authority.

Political consultants say TV commercials are expensive because they require technological know-how. Time buying is a specialty, and the buyers have little incentive to reduce costs. "Mrs. Jones and her teenage kids can't go down to the congressman's corner headquarters and volunteer to make his TV spots," said veteran consultant Doug Bailey.

"Too many consultants, both Democratic and Republican, hire inexperienced 'buyers' to spend millions of dollars," Jan Ziska Crawford, a board member of the American Association of Political Consultants, told Congress in 1996. "Strategic time-buying includes knowing the law and maximizing every dollar raised. Given that most consultants are paid on a percentage basis, there is no incentive to keep media expenditures down."

According to Victor Kamber, president of the Kamber Group, a Washington, D.C., public relations firm, "Even if Congress passes new laws limiting advertising expenses, consultants will find loopholes in them." Makers of political spots, for example, base their fees on what a candidate spends for air time, not on their creative or production costs. If new laws required networks to provide free air time, the consultants would simply begin charging for creating and producing the candidates' ads.

> **"Even if Congress passes new laws limiting advertising expenses, consultants will find loopholes in them."**
>
> **—Victor Kamber,** president of the Kamber Group, a Washington public relations firm

"Running for political office has never been as costly as it was in 2002," Paul Taylor, president of the Alliance for Better Campaigns, said at the time. "And the biggest reason is that we continue to allow broadcasters to auction off the right to political speech before elections, using public air the American people have given them for free."

At the state level, some officials already enjoy free air time as a perquisite of incumbency. For example, Maryland governor Parris N. Glendening, a Democrat, and Robert L. Ehrlich Jr., his Republican successor, taped at state expense several public service and tourism spots featuring their names and pictures. Some TV stations ran them free at the state's request. As in other states, these governors also got free publicity from their names and likenesses appearing in state publications and their names appearing on highway signs. The opposing parties in each case complained to no avail that the public relations spots amounted to a covert form of taxpayer-funded political advertising.

Issue Advocacy

In the 1996 elections, issue ads gained prominence as a controversial means of circumventing CAMPAIGN FINANCE restrictions in efforts to elect or defeat political candidates. Interest groups argued that the ads in question did not violate disclosure laws or contribution limits because they did not name any particular candidate, thereby following the letter of the law as established in the 1976 Supreme Court decision in *BUCKLEY V. VALEO*, which established the so-called magic words test: issue advocacy ads are not tacit campaign contributions, and are thus deemed legal, as long as they do not expressly advocate that viewers vote for or against a specific candidate. But opponents countered that it was possible to frame an ad to target a candidate whose stand on an issue—abortion or gun control, for example—is well known, without actually using the person's name.

In October 1997 the Supreme Court declined to clarify whether government restrictions on issue ads violate free speech rights. It rejected a Federal Election Commission (FEC) request for a review of conflicting lower court decisions on issue ads that indirectly advocate election or defeat of particular candidates.

The Court gave no reason for not considering *Federal Election Commission v. Maine Right to Life,* in which a lower court had struck down the FEC's 1995 rule on issue ads as too vague. The FEC said the resulting confusion "threatens significantly to impair the effectiveness of the nation's election laws."

In more recent campaigns, many campaign advertising entities, and especially 527 groups and the newer SuperPAC variant, have grown more brazen, clearly naming—and most often criticizing—a targeted candidate. Although these ads avoid the magic words, their intentions to get people to vote for or against a certain candidate are virtually unmistakable. As a result, the FEC has faced increased pressure to regulate these kinds of activities.

A related controversy concerned so-called soft money, unlimited contributions to the political parties, ostensibly for party-building activities but widely used to assist candidates. Proponents of campaign reform feared that elimination of soft money for the parties would divert more interest group money to issue ads, where it would be even more unregulated.

The Clinton administration said that unless the FEC is allowed to regulate issue ads, the door would be opened "for corporations, unions, and others . . . to influence federal elections by spending large amounts of money in independent advertisements that unambiguously attack clearly identified candidates."

The campaign finance law enacted in 2002 did, in fact, seek to restrict this type of advertising by corporations and unions by barring it within the closing weeks of a political campaign for federal office. Yet the admonition laid out by the Clinton White House proved true, as issue advocacy advertising, in both volume and cost, expanded greatly in the 2003–2004 and 2005–2006 election cycles, the first two after enactment of the law. The 2010 Supreme Court ruling that revoked corporate advertising restrictions foreshadowed yet another torrent of money for issue advertising during the 2012 campaign.

Paid advertising seems to be most effective in campaigns for and against ballot propositions—lawmaking by popular INITIATIVES AND REFERENDUMS, which is permitted in some states (most notably in California). Especially where the public is unfamiliar with the pros and cons of an issue, ads can help to educate voters and crystallize public opinion. According to *Air Wars* author Darrell West,

> What started as a trickle of issue advocacy has become a torrent on every conceivable topic. In the last few years, groups interested in health care, tort reform, term limits, and a balanced budget have blanketed the airwaves with commercials promoting their point of view. Once the exception more than the rule, television ads have become the latest form of political volleyball on controversial issues.

The lack of disclosure rules for issue advocacy campaigns, West states, "takes us back to the secrecy and deception of the pre-Watergate system for contesting American elections."

Political Consultants

The business, and some would say art, of political consulting is hardly a new one. Mark Hanna, an Ohio industrialist in the late nineteenth century, is regarded as the father of the modern campaign for his role as manager of Ohio Republican William McKinley's successful 1896 bid for president of the United States. Hanna helped design the tactics and strategy that enabled McKinley to win an easy victory, including his decision to spend the campaign on his front porch in Canton, Ohio, to provide a mainstream counterpoint to the frantic travels of Democratic nominee William Jennings Bryan, a populist regarded by many voters (and portrayed by the McKinley camp) as an economic radical.

Hamilton Jordan, right, is credited with devising Jimmy Carter's winning campaign strategy in the 1976 election.

Source: White House.

Yet the rise of vastly expensive, media-oriented, and highly targeted campaigns has over the past few decades ballooned political consulting into a huge industry. A study by the nonpartisan watchdog group Center for Public Integrity found that a combined total of more than $1.9 billion had gone to political consultants in federal, state, and local races in the 2003–2004 election cycle.

This phenomenon has earned some national consultants headlines and even a degree of fame—from Roger Ailes, Republican Richard M. Nixon's ad man in 1968; to Hamilton Jordan, who helped lay out the strategy that turned Democrat Jimmy Carter from longshot to winner in the 1976 election; to political pros such as Michael Deaver and Richard Wirthlin, who were closely associated with Republican Ronald Reagan in the early 1980s; to Lee Atwater, the tough political in-fighter who fashioned Republican George H.W. Bush's 1988 win; to James Carville, the wry and blunt Cajun who helped Democrat Bill Clinton to a 1992 presidential victory with the rallying cry of "It's the economy, stupid!" Barack Obama's winning campaign for president in 2008, just four years after he moved from the Illinois state Senate to the U.S. Senate, turned Chicago consultants David Axelrod and David Plouffe, his chief campaign strategists, into nationally known figures.

No political consultant, though, has risen to greater heights, and experienced the risks that come with it, than Karl Rove, known almost universally in political circles as the political guru to Republican George W. Bush, son of the former president Bush.

Rove, a Texas political consultant and longtime Bush family associate, played a key role in designing the campaign strategy that enabled Bush to win his narrow—and controversial— victory over Democrat Al Gore in the 2000 campaign. Bush then brought Rove into the White House as his chief political adviser, a position in which he was frequently consulted about the political impact of the policies the administration was pursuing and in which he used the clout of the White House to help Republican strategists recruit top candidates for the GOP's successful effort to take control of the Senate in the 2002 campaign and expand it in the 2004 elections. His role in Bush's successful 2004 reelection campaign over Democrat John Kerry spurred the president to call Rove "The Architect."

But the more prominent Rove became, the more he stood out as a political lightning rod as the Bush administration ran into serious second-term problems, including the unexpectedly protracted, expensive, and deadly war in Iraq; government failures in coping with the damage wrought in 2005 by Hurricane Katrina in New Orleans and elsewhere on the Gulf Coast; and Bush's stymied pursuit of an initiative to add private savings accounts to the Social Security program.

Rove was initially given and then stripped of a policy-making role to go with his political role. Meanwhile, Rove became deeply embroiled, and later appeared to narrowly avoid prosecution, in a scandal involving the leaking in 2003 of the name of a CIA operative whose husband had contradicted a key administration claim about Iraq's alleged weapons of mass destruction. In early 2007 he was involved in another controversy over the firings of several U.S. attorneys that some claimed had political overtones. Failures to recruit high-profile Senate candidates in 2006, when the Republicans lost six seats and control of the chamber to the Democrats, were laid by some Republicans at Rove's feet, and a comeback to the heights he had previously reached appeared unlikely after a 2008 cycle in Bush's unpopularity contributed significantly to Obama's capture of the White House and the Democratic Party's expansion of its majorities in Congress.

Yet Rove proved his resilience in 2010 when he emerged as a high-profile adviser to American Crossroads, a conservative political advocacy group formed under Section 527 of the tax code, which spent millions of dollars on advertising to help boost Republican candidates in their party's big comeback in that year's midterm elections, in which the GOP regained control of the U.S. House and cut deeply into the Democrats' majority in the Senate.

Karl Rove, right, with Ohio senator Mike DeWine, played a key role in designing both of George W. Bush's successful presidential campaigns.
Source: CQ Photo/Scott J. Ferrell

Yet his fame and notoriety is an example to the rule: The obvious fact is that few political consultants will or even seek to rise to the levels reached by Rove. Plenty of rewards are to be had, and money to be made, being big fish in smaller ponds.

Around the country, thousands of professional consultants market expertise in CAMPAIGN FINANCE and management, direct mail, POLITICAL ADVERTISING, and public relations to the more than 50,000 political campaigns that occur each election cycle; increasingly over the past few cycles, many consulting firms have sought associates talented at using the tools of New Media, such as e-mail, text messaging, blogging and social networking. Of the greater mass of consultants, 1,100 are big enough players to belong to the American Association of Political Consultants, a Washington, D.C., trade association that, among other activities, holds an annual awards show for best achievements in political advertising and other consulting activities.

Given the number and influence of paid consultants, it is only a slight exaggeration to say that they wage more political battles in modern-day America than do candidates themselves. Gone are the days when faceless advisers stood discreetly behind candidates and whispered folksy suggestions.

But consultants—who rose to influence along with television—are also blamed by critics for many of the political system's problems, including voter apathy. There are common complaints that the professionalization of politics encourages NEGATIVE CAMPAIGNING, escalates campaign costs, reduces debate on the issues to sound bites, distorts the findings of PUBLIC OPINION polling, and even reduces once-eager campaign volunteers to spectators. Consultants respond that responsibility for their decisions must be borne by the candidates, and that they are paid, first and foremost, to win.

"The most significant change in consultants is their indispensability," said Larry J. Sabato, a University of Virginia government professor and author of *The Rise of Political Consultants,* published in 1981. "Back in the 1950s, they were rare, except at the presidential level. Then in the '70s you got consultants for senators and governors, and in the '80s, consultants in House races. Now you have them for ballot referendums, and every race for state legislature and city council."

The influence of consultants on politics is evident in the frequent use by the press of phrases that began as insider-speak: "sound bites," "spin doctors," "theme of the day," and "photo opportunity."

Campaign consultants have their own organization, and consulting has even become an academic program. At American University in Washington, DC, the Campaign Management Institute offers a two-week course taught by strategists and professors imparting insight into CAMPAIGN STRATEGIES, scheduling, theme, and message. George Washington University, also in Washington, offers advanced degrees at its Graduate School of Political Management.

> ## "The most significant change in consultants is their indispensability."
>
> —Larry J. Sabato, a University of Virginia government professor and author of *The Rise of Political Consultants* (1981)

Birth of an Industry

The first political consultants, according to the American Association of Political Consultants, were Aristotle, Plato, and other philosophers of ancient Greece and Rome. Quintus Cicero wrote a "Handbook of Electioneering" for Romans in 63 B.C. The more modern historical model for a political strategy paper was *The Prince*, written in 1532 by Italian philosopher Niccolo Machiavelli.

In the United States, political campaigns traditionally have been noteworthy for their domination by party machines and volunteers. When William Henry Harrison and John Tyler won the White House in 1840, their "Tippecanoe and Tyler, Too" campaign was run by handlers, who relied on volunteers lured by free whiskey to pack their rallies. (Tippecanoe was a reference to a frontier battle in which U.S. troops led by Harrison defeated American Indian warriors.)

Credit for bringing Abraham Lincoln to the national stage in 1860 went to Republican political clubs called the Wide Awakes. "After the campaign opened," wrote one biographer, "there was scarcely a county or village in the North without its organized and drilled association of Wide Awakes . . . to spread the fame of, and solicit votes for, the Republican presidential candidate."

During the next century, the national parties gained supremacy, developing powerful machines in cities such as Chicago, New York City, Boston, and Albany, among other places. Only occasionally did ad hoc entrepreneurs become national players. In 1940, for example, the presidential candidacy of Indiana businessman Wendell L. Willkie was primarily the fruit of a draft movement set in motion by a petition circulated in *Fortune* magazine by a young New York lawyer.

The first consulting business in the United States is thought to be the firm established in the 1930s in California by a husband-and-wife team of advertising professionals, Clem Whitaker and Leone Baxter. For two decades their firm presided over some seventy-five major campaigns, among them state ballot INITIATIVES AND REFERENDUMS and the gubernatorial campaigns of Republican Earl Warren.

In the late 1930s and 1940s, George Gallup and Elmo Roper set up shops as full-time analysts of electoral trends. Their elite fraternity was joined by regional poll takers, such as Mervin Field in California, who formed a group that began to meet annually at Gallup's New Jersey farm.

By the 1950s the presidential campaigns of Dwight D. Eisenhower and Adlai E. Stevenson were employing advisers from advertising firms and ghostwriters. But these early consultants toiled mostly outside the public eye.

Not until the 1960s were the internal workings of a political campaign unveiled to the public in all their moral complexity. Journalist Theodore H. White, in the first of what became the quadrennial series *The Making of the President*, documented the 1960 presidential race between John F. Kennedy and Richard M. Nixon with more behind-the-scenes detail than ever before, such as Kennedy's voice lessons and Nixon's decision not to wear TV makeup during the first presidential DEBATE.

The 1968 election was a turning point for political consulting. Nixon—seeking to reinvent his image as the exiled loser of the 1960 race and the bitter also-ran in the 1962 race for governor of

California in which he told a post-election news conference that "you don't have Nixon to kick around anymore"—brought in a team of advisers not from politics but from the news media and Madison Avenue. Luminaries such as CBS News executive Frank Shakespeare and TV producer Roger Ailes (who much later became the longtime head of Fox News Channel) persuaded Nixon that television—far from being a cheap gimmick—was the key to winning elections.

Nixon's opponent, Vice President Hubert H. Humphrey, hired Springfield, Massachusetts, consultant Joe Napolitan, who had helped Kennedy to win crucial primaries in 1960. A specialist in survey techniques, Napolitan made dramatic recommendations that Humphrey could not agree to, such as breaking with retiring president Lyndon B. Johnson's efforts to continue the Vietnam War; and he pleaded unsuccessfully with Humphrey to debate Nixon on TV.

Following Nixon's narrow victory, the new political handlers, now subject to increased public scrutiny, were saddled with a negative image. It was Napolitan who spotted the need for a professional organization to counter the criticism and develop bipartisan industry guidelines. He teamed with Republican strategists F. Clifton White and Stuart Spencer and several Democrats, among them consultants Robert Squier and Matt Reese and pollster Bill Hamilton, to form both the American Association of Political Consultants and the International Association of Political Consultants.

With some 300 firms plying the trade by the 1970s, more consultants came to prominence. Hal Evry, a Republican public relations man who also worked for presidential candidate George Wallace, gained a reputation as the "enfant terrible" of consulting for openly defending campaign gimmicks and unrestrained spending. "The more money a candidate spends, the more likely he is to win," Evry once said.

Jimmy Carter's campaigns were guided by two men who became household names: media adviser Gerald Rafshoon (satirized by Garry Trudeau for manipulative "Rafshoonery" in the comic strip "Doonesbury") and pollster Patrick Caddell, who had polled for leaders of the Florida legislature while a high school senior in 1968. Caddell is credited with providing overarching themes for Carter. His polling during the 1980 campaign showed that attacks from the detail-oriented Carter against Ronald Reagan's perceived ignorance on the issues would backfire.

The Reagan camp's pollster, Richard Wirthlin, gave consultancy the "hierarchical values map," which divided polling data on issues into color-coded charts. In 1984 his research showed that Democratic candidate Walter F. Mondale would win if the main issues were the proposed Equal Rights Amendment to the Constitution, abortion, poverty, and fairness. Reagan would win if the top issues were working to build "a better America and preserve world peace" and "make U.S./world a better place for future generations."

After losing the election, Mondale declared bitterly that "American politics is losing its substance. . . . It's losing the depth that tough problems require to be discussed, and more and more it is that twenty-second [sound bite] snippet."

> **"The more money a candidate spends, the more likely he is to win."**
>
> **—Republican public relations consultant Hal Evry**

> **"American politics is losing its substance. . . . It's losing the depth that tough problems require to be discussed, and more and more it is that twenty-second [sound bite] snippet."**
>
> **—Democratic presidential candidate Walter F. Mondale,** after losing the 1984 election

Effect on the Electoral Process

The consultants' newfound role as unelected power brokers or "preselectors" of candidates is widely viewed as a mixed blessing. One problem, said Sabato, is that consultants make candidates "too responsive to public opinion" rather than encouraging them to lead. "They rely on negative campaigning that drives down turnout, and they produce homogenized campaigns, like Holiday Inns and McDonald's, where a campaign in Idaho is like one in Pennsylvania, with the same consultant, the same slogans."

Consultants also are criticized by advocates of campaign finance reform, who see them as driving up the cost of campaigns. "Consultants certainly benefit from unrestricted spending," said Paul Hendrie, a former managing editor at the Center for Responsive Politics. "They push the prevalent theory that large blocks of TV ads" are the way to campaign, and in "states with major media markets, the high costs of campaigning will make candidates there less receptive to spending caps."

> **"I like having a manager who runs my campaigns, and if I don't have someone who is clearly in charge, I have problems."**
>
> **—Michael S. Dukakis,** 1988 Democratic presidential candidate and former Massachusetts governor

Consultants defend their freedom to spend a candidate's money in ways they think will win elections. They go to great lengths to market their expertise in the highly technical area of campaign finance disclosure law and ad buying. But they also admit they are one of the reasons that politicians have to chase money constantly.

Opinion polling methods increasingly are being slanted by pollsters to gain an advantage for a candidate or to provide backing for a preconceived notion. Some pollsters are viewed as advocates rather than dispassionate takers of the public pulse.

Among them is conservative pollster Frank Luntz, who gained fame for "test-driving" the legislative planks under consideration for the House Republicans' "Contract with America" in 1994. Luntz announced at the time that each of the contract's ten items had about 70 percent popular support, but the *Miami Herald* later reported that Luntz had not actually polled on the contract's provisions but had merely conducted focus groups, which primarily had been asked for their reaction to highly charged assertions. For example, according to the newspaper, the groups were asked if "we should stop excessive legal claims, frivolous lawsuits, and overzealous lawyers." That became a less incendiary contract plank calling for " 'loser pays' laws, reasonable limits on punitive damages, and reform of product liability laws to stem the tide of litigation." An industry group, the American Association for Public Opinion Research, later censured Luntz (a nonmember) for refusing to disclose the full wording of his poll or focus group questions.

Finally, there is the ever-present issue of consultants who shield their candidate from unscripted contact with the news media. Dan Balz, then a *Washington Post* reporter who covered the 1996 presidential campaign, found it astonishing a month before the election that GOP nominee Bob Dole had not appeared on NBC's *Meet the Press* since December 1995, when previously he had been the show's most frequent guest. A Dole spokesperson denied that the candidate had been inaccessible. Accessibility also became an issue in Democrat Al Gore's 2000 campaign for president.

A point in the consultants' favor is that candidates clearly value them. "I like having a manager who runs my campaigns, and if I don't have someone who is clearly in charge, I have problems," said 1988 Democratic presidential nominee and former Massachusetts governor Michael S. Dukakis. "You have to have someone for advice on things like media, and we had an in-house polling operation that was as accurate as any you could hire. I never felt hemmed in or frustrated by handlers."

On the contrary, Dukakis's chief regret about his unsuccessful campaign was the failure to respond to the Bush campaign's attacks on unforeseen issues such as prison furloughs, which the Republicans dramatized with TV spots based on the case of Willie Horton, a Massachusetts prisoner who raped a woman while on furlough. "That issue was as phony as a $3 bill, but obviously we did not handle it right because of our inexperience, which is partly my fault," Dukakis said.

A similar failure afflicted another Massachusetts Democrat, Sen. John Kerry, in his 2004 campaign against George W. Bush. Kerry came under fierce attack from an outside group called the Swift Boat Veterans for Truth, which aimed both to degrade his reputation as a Vietnam War hero and to portray as inappropriate his antiwar activism after returning from Vietnam. Kerry initially treated the group's ads as farfetched and unbelievable but was forced to respond belatedly when it became clear that the ads were damaging his campaign. The Swift Boat group's strategy was developed by Chris LaCivita, a Republican political consultant.

Celebrity Consultants

"I had star quality, and I had people interested in meeting me as much as meeting the candidate," Republican strategist Ed Rollins told an interviewer in explaining why he boasted, untruthfully, he later said, of spending money to suppress black voter turnout in the 1993 New Jersey governor's race. Rollins angered many in the political world with his 1996 tell-all memoir, *Bare Knuckles and Back Rooms: My Life in American Politics.* In the book, Rollins heaped scorn on some candidates whose campaigns he had mentored. He branded Ross Perot, the billionaire third-party candidate for president in 1992 and 1996, as "an extremely dangerous demagogue who would have been a disaster in the White House." He called California businessman Michael Huffington, who ran unsuccessfully for a Senate seat in 1994, and his then-wife, Arianna, "two of the most unprincipled political creatures I'd ever encountered."

In their 1994 campaign memoir, *All's Fair: Love, War, and Running for President,* Clinton strategist James Carville and his wife, Mary Matalin, a Republican and former political director to President George H. W. Bush, wrote that MEDIA COVERAGE of their interparty romance became a factor in the 1992 election. Matalin recalled resentfully that her political enemy and future husband used the news media to "look like a good guy, saying nice things about me, but it was really a backhanded way to keep the [romance] story alive and keep the [Bush] campaign off our game and off our message."

Consultants generally work exclusively for either Democrats or Republicans, but a few have worked for candidates of different parties. For example, several well-known consultants—Rollins, Luntz, and former Carter operative Hamilton Jordan—worked for Perot's presidential effort in 1992. And when Luntz left, disgusted (and unpaid), Democrats tried to recruit him.

A notable example of crossover consultants is Dick Morris. After working with Democrat Clinton when he was Arkansas governor in the 1980s, Morris signed on with prominent Republicans such as Sen. Jesse Helms of North Carolina, Sen. Trent Lott of Mississippi, and Gov. Pete Wilson of California. Indeed, in 1991 Morris worked simultaneously (in separate contests) for Mississippi Republican gubernatorial candidate Pete Johnson and Democratic lieutenant governor Brad Dye.

Morris was widely credited with crafting Clinton's successful centrist strategy in 1996. In its September 2 cover story, *Time* magazine called Morris "the most influential private citizen in America." A week later, Morris again made the magazine's cover, this time after a SCANDAL involving a prostitute forced him to resign. In the weeks thereafter, commentators continued their debates over whether Morris, Rasputin-like, had been too influential in moving a liberal-leaning Clinton to the political center. Morris eventually rebounded from his scandal by shifting far to the right and working exclusively to advance Republican candidates and causes.

In the rival campaign of Republican Bob Dole, the consultants made their presence felt after Dole raised eyebrows with some unscripted comments. For example, he expressed uncertainty about the dangers of tobacco and refused an invitation to address the NAACP. "I've taken my vow of silence," the former Senate majority leader said with a grimace as he followed his handlers' command to avoid taking questions from reporters.

It appeared to Doug Bailey, who helped run President Gerald R. Ford's 1976 campaign, that Dole had too many consultants, with no one of them in charge of the others. Bailey, then publisher of *Hotline,* an online political news service, said that Dole had "every consultant known to man tied up in some way to his campaign."

Consultancy's Future

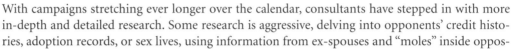

With campaigns stretching ever longer over the calendar, consultants have stepped in with more in-depth and detailed research. Some research is aggressive, delving into opponents' credit histories, adoption records, or sex lives, using information from ex-spouses and "moles" inside opposing campaigns. There are now dozens of firms specializing in opposition research, a number that grew 200 percent in the 1990s, according to Sabato.

Many observers say it is no coincidence that the consulting field exploded in the same period that the country saw a loosening of PARTY IDENTIFICATION, an electorate made passive through television, and a drastic decline in VOTER TURNOUT. The percentage of eligible voters who participate fell from 63 percent in 1960 to 49 percent in 1996. Yet voter turnout made a modest rebound in the first decade of the twenty-first century, and the industry of political consulting is more robust than ever.

Critics decry the strategists' encouragement of candidates to speak in CAMPAIGN SLOGANS and sound bites, which television news shows reduced from an average of forty-three seconds in 1960 to about eight seconds by 1996, according to the Free TV for Straight Talk Coalition, a group advocating free air time for candidates. (See EQUAL TIME AND REBUTTAL RULES.)

Critics also note that campaigns now devote most of their budgets to thirty-second TV spots. "Voters are fed up with TV politics," two former leaders of both major parties, Republican Frank J. Fahrenkopf Jr. and Democrat Charles T. Manatt, wrote in 1996. "The media, too, are critical of the system they helped create. And we, as former chairmen of the Republican and Democratic parties, can attest that politicians themselves don't like the current situation."

Consultants argue that they are merely stepping into a gap opened by the decline in party loyalty, the increase in party PRIMARIES, and technological changes in communication that includes the "24/7" news cycle (for twenty-four

> **"Voters are fed up with TV politics. The media, too, are critical of the system they helped create. And we, as former chairmen of the Republican and Democratic parties, can attest that politicians themselves don't like the current situation."**
>
> **— Republican Frank J. Fahrenkopf Jr. and Democrat Charles T. Manatt,** writing in 1996

More on this topic:

Campaign Finance, p. 53
Campaign Strategies, p. 70
Media Coverage of Campaigns, p. 313
Negative Campaigning, p. 365
Party Identification by Voters, p. 377
Political Advertising, p. 394
Public Opinion, p. 502
Voter Turnout, p. 656

hours a day, seven days a week) fueled by cable television and the Internet. One reason for the consultants' prominence, said Washington public relations executive Victor Kamber, "is that we live in an age of news."

Paul Taylor, a former *Washington Post* political reporter who launched the Free TV for Straight Talk Coalition, was reluctant to blame consultants for the deterioration of political debate, that is, until he headed the Alliance for Better Campaigns. For consultants, he said, "all the rewards are in thirty-second attack ads. More often than not, it works, and if I were in the consultants' shoes, I would want to win the election. That's the political marketplace."

Political Culture in America

The term *political culture* refers to people's fundamental beliefs and assumptions about how government and politics should operate. Among such beliefs, five are deeply rooted in the American psyche: popular sovereignty, an obligation of political participation, individual rights, individualism, and equality.

Even though Americans as a whole believe deeply in individual rights and individualism, it is unrealistic to expect that their political thinking would be uniform—and it is not. Within even the five fundamental beliefs there are shadings and gradations. Some people hold such beliefs and assumptions more deeply than others. And some, as is their right, do not hold them at all.

Political culture also varies from group to group. Racial, ethnic, and religious backgrounds can affect people's attitudes toward political parties, candidates, and issues. A city with a large population of northern European ancestry may have political leanings that are different from those in a city with a large Asian population. Socioeconomic status also causes variations in political culture and behavior.

A combination of core political beliefs and different backgrounds influences people's ELECTORAL BEHAVIOR and their expectations and evaluations of politicians and policies. They also impose limits on the number of alternatives that policy makers can seriously consider. A policy that violates a basic value—such as the right to own private property—does not have a realistic chance of being adopted.

Fundamental Beliefs

The Declaration of Independence proclaims that governments derive "their just powers from the consent of the governed." And the preamble to the Constitution begins, "We the People of the United States." Embedded in these words is the belief that the people, not some hereditary monarch, are the source of government power.

Abraham Lincoln's phrase in the Gettysburg Address about the nation having a "government of the people, by the people, and for the people" captures Americans' fundamental belief in

Popular sovereignty is one of several beliefs rooted in the American psyche. It is expressed here in a poster from a government-sponsored campaign during World War II.

Source: National Archives and Records Administration

popular sovereignty. The primacy of this belief is reflected in the importance we attach to periodic free elections and the role of PUBLIC OPINION in policy making.

Americans nevertheless have some reservations about DEMOCRACY. Many fear that voters may be misled by demagogues—leaders who play on voters' prejudices, fears, and baser emotions. And the value attached to strong presidential leadership is further proof that people believe they may not always be capable of choosing the best policies by themselves.

As for the widespread belief in individual rights, the Declaration of Independence proclaims that it is "self-evident, that all men are . . . endowed by their Creator with certain unalienable Rights, that among these are Life, Liberty and the pursuit of Happiness." *Liberty* is the right to make one's own decisions and live one's life freely without undue government restraints. The people's basic right to liberty constitutes a limitation on the power of the majority over individuals and groups.

Also well-ingrained in American thinking is the belief in the fundamental right to hold private property. The commitment to private property and individual economic initiative has been so strong in the United States that socialism has made little headway, unlike in some other Western democracies. The largest share of votes ever gained by a SOCIALIST candidate for president was the 6 percent (900,369 votes) won by Eugene V. Debs in 1912. No socialist presidential candidate has ever carried a single state.

> **"We hold these truths to be self-evident, that all men are created equal, that they are endowed by their Creator with certain unalienable Rights, that among these are Life, Liberty and the pursuit of Happiness."**
>
> —Declaration of Independence, July 4, 1776

Individualism is deeply embedded in the American culture. When asked in 1992 to assess the relative importance of various characteristics for getting ahead in life, Americans gave clear priority to three: ambition, hard work, and education. It was what "I do" that mattered— not family background, race, religion, or other factors extraneous to personal effort and commitment.

Recognizing the pervasiveness of individualism, the United States has been more reluctant than most Western nations to institute national social welfare programs. Moreover, it spends a lower share of its national income on these programs than most industrialized nations.

Equal Opportunity

Even before asserting that people have "unalienable rights," the Declaration of Independence states that "all men are created equal." In American thinking, equality and individual rights are closely linked—if all people are equal, they must have the same rights.

Equality has several dimensions. In the Declaration of Independence, Thomas Jefferson was referring to political equality. To provide for this kind of equality, the Constitution and statutes contain provisions ensuring that all citizens of legal age have the RIGHT TO VOTE, and the Fourteenth Amendment requires the states to grant all people the "equal protection of the laws."

Many Americans also care about equality of opportunity—that is, they want to help those who are disadvantaged through race, gender, ethnicity, disability, or poverty to compete more effectively. This concern is manifested in the government's expanded role in providing the poor with money, food, housing, education, health care, and legal services.

But despite a commitment to equality of opportunity, most Americans do not believe that everyone should be equally well off. Rather, everyone should have a relatively equal chance to become better off than his or her neighbors. Many, if not most, Americans are quite prepared in fact to accept large disparities in the economic status of their fellow citizens.

A commitment to equality also implies racial equality, although the Constitution did not provide it until ratification of the Civil War amendments. The goal of racial equality still has not been met, and this failing is a source of continuing frustration, particularly for minority groups. There have been some accomplishments—for example, the barriers intended to prevent racial minorities from exercising their voting rights have been largely eliminated since the 1960s, leading to increased BLACK SUFFRAGE and the election of black officials. Overt discrimination based on government statutes and rules, such as requiring segregated schools, restaurants, and theaters, is no longer tolerated, but minorities have not yet achieved full social and economic equality in America. Moreover, there is no consensus on how to deal with the plight of racial minorities.

One government-sponsored remedy, affirmative action programs, has stirred deep emotions in both its proponents and opponents. These programs seek to ensure that minorities (and women) are fairly considered for employment and college admission. In their most controversial form, they use procedures that give minorities a greater chance of being hired or admitted to educational institutions than their credentials alone would give them. Proponents see these programs as a way to compensate for past acts of discrimination and to give minorities a chance to live the American dream. Opponents, however, see affirmative action programs as reverse discrimination and as violations of society's commitment to rewarding people on the basis of merit.

Demographics: Distribution of Wealth

American politics, besides being affected by the country's unique political culture, is no less shaped by prevailing socioeconomic conditions such as the distribution of wealth within society; the ethnic, racial, and religious composition of the population; and changes in lifestyles ranging from how Americans earn a living to where they live.

The prevailing distribution of wealth and income provides one of American society's most important characteristics: the vast majority of Americans are not poor. However, by 2010 census data showed a significant and climbing increase in the number and percentage of Americans in poverty and a continuing stagnation in income among most groups, other than the very wealthy.

According to CENSUS data, in 2000 the median household income—the point that separates the upper 50 percent of families from the lower 50 percent—was $42,148. In the same year, 11.3 percent of Americans, or 31.1 million people, had incomes that fell below the official government poverty level. But in September 2010 census officials found that the median household income was $49,445, down 2.3 percent from the previous year. Census officials also reported that the national poverty rate reached 15.1 percent in 2010. The bureau said 46.2 million persons were under the poverty line, which was defined as an annual income of $22,314 for a family of four. These data help to identify and explain the basic forces influencing American politics. First, a substantial proportion of people (including 18.5 percent of all children under age eighteen in 2009) are living in poverty; they are not living the American dream. As a result, there is continuing pressure on the government to develop programs to enable the less fortunate to improve their circumstances. Second, a wide gap exists between the living standards of the average white person and those of the average African American or Hispanic. American Indians and Alaska Natives suffer from particularly high poverty rates: more than one in four has earnings below the poverty line, meaning they cannot fully afford such necessities as food and shelter. Third, the poor are a distinct minority in the United States: they cannot rely on the traditional weapon of the underprivileged—superior numbers—to achieve their political goals. Instead, they must make alliances with and gain the support of the nonpoor. Indeed, government programs to assist the needy must be supported by large segments of the middle class and by interests that are not poor.

National Origin

Although most of the American population was born in the United States (87.6 percent in 2009), the nation, except for Native Americans, descended from immigrants. Until the late 1800s, immigrants came primarily from northern and western Europe, with the largest percentage from Great Britain and Ireland.

The wave of "new immigration" in the late nineteenth and early twentieth centuries was quite different, however. It was dominated by former inhabitants of eastern and southern Europe—Italians, Poles, Czechs, Slavs, Greeks, and Russian Jews. Their ethnicity tended to set them apart from native-born Americans and constituted a source of psychological identification. But as the descendants of immigrants from eastern and southern Europe have become assimilated into American life and better off economically, their voting patterns have become less distinct and their traditional support of Democratic candidates is no longer assured.

Immigration at the end of the twentieth century reached new heights. A 2000 Census Bureau report estimated the foreign-born population in the United States at a record 31.1 million. Some 13.2 million immigrants arrived during the 1990s, easily breaking the former record set in the first decade of the twentieth century, when 8.8 million immigrants resettled here.

The latest wave of immigration is dramatically changing the ethnic and racial composition of the nation. Primarily from Latin America and Asia, these new immigrants are concentrated largely in states such as California, Florida, New York, Texas, and Arizona. But their gradual migration to other areas of the country, some of them quite unused to absorbing major influxes of immigrants, turned immigration into a controversial political issue by the end of the first decade of the twenty-first century. Exacerbating resentments in some quarters was the significant rise in illegal immigration.

Local community groups stage a protest outside the White House in May 1997, demanding full restoration of benefit cuts to legal immigrants.

Source: CQ Photo/Douglas Graham

The influx of Asian and Latin American immigrants is transforming American politics. Hispanic or Latino voters, for example, are critical in states with large numbers of electoral votes. In the 2010 census, more than half of the Hispanic population lives in California, Texas, and Florida. As the Hispanic American population has increased, so too has its representation in Congress, although their numbers are far below their share of the entire national population. (See Reference Material, table, page 726)

About 62 percent of the 50.5 million Hispanic or Latino Americans who lived in the United States in 2010 are of Mexican origin, according to the Census Bureau.

Because of high immigration and birth rates, the number of Hispanic Americans is increasing rapidly. Between 2000 and 2010 their numbers grew by 43 percent, about four times larger than total U.S. population growth in the decade. By the end of the 2000s decade, they made up more than 16 percent of the population and exceeded African Americans as the nation's largest minority constituency. As BILINGUAL VOTERS, their heavy concentrations in some areas require that ballots and other election materials be in both English and Spanish.

The political orientations of Hispanics vary widely. Many Hispanics live below the poverty level, and those of Mexican and Puerto Rican heritage tend to be heavily Democratic in their voting patterns. Cuban Americans, however, who are better off economically and ardent anticommunists, tend to be Republicans.

Even a number of typically Democratic-leaning Hispanics may be open to outreach from Republicans, in part because many members of this group hold conservative values on social issues. Race is another feature of American society. African Americans, most of whom are descendants of African slaves, constituted 12.3 percent of the U.S. population in the 2010 census. Unlike Europeans, for whom ethnicity has declining political relevance, African Americans are highly conscious of their ethnicity. They have done less well economically than European immigrants; in 2010, according to census figures, 27.4 percent lived below the poverty level.

African Americans tend to be concentrated in inner-city neighborhoods and poor rural areas, and many feel the continuing effects of racial discrimination. Government policies that combat poverty and deal with civil rights issues are high on the list of political concerns for African Americans, who are a critical element of the Democratic Party's electoral coalition. Asian Americans, who constituted 4.8 percent of the population in 2010, also lean toward the Democrats but by a smaller margin than Hispanics or African Americans.

Other Demographic Factors

Age variations also determine the issues government must confront. The U.S. population, on the whole, is aging, which puts heavy pressure on the government to provide the elderly with services, particularly pensions and health care. These pressures can only be expected to intensify. In the 2010 census, 13 percent of the population was sixty-five years or older, up by 15 percent from ten years earlier. Americans in this age bracket total 40.3 million individuals.

Religion, too, can affect voting patterns. Protestants are predominantly Republican; Catholics have traditionally been strongly Democratic, although conservative social values of many Catholic voters have shifted many into the Republican camp; and Jews have been overwhelmingly Democratic. In recent elections, Protestant evangelists have become increasingly active in politics and have tended to support Republican candidates for president.

Place of residence is yet another factor in America's political equation. For a large part of its history, the United States was a predominantly rural nation with most of its citizens living on farms and in small towns. But the urbanization that began by the late nineteenth century continued apace, followed by the vast growth of suburbs ringing the cities, making modern America a mainly metropolitan nation.

One analysis found that 220 of the 435 congressional districts were predominantly suburban, whereas another ninety were mainly urban. Just sixty-one districts were predominantly rural, with the remaining sixty-four defined as mixed. Residents of large cities tend to support Democrats; rural and small-town voters are more conservative. A key battleground has become the suburbs, where candidates fight for the support of new constituencies such as the so-called soccer moms.

These and many other factors determine the U.S. political culture, which in turn helps to chart the course of American politics. Stripped to its basics, politics is the pursuit and exercise of power as well as the process through which society expresses and manages its conflicts. But American politics does not play itself out in a vacuum. It is affected on a daily basis by the legal structure imposed by the Constitution, society's cultural values and socioeconomic characteristics, and the government's past policy decisions.

More on this topic:
Bilingual Voters, p. 26
Black Suffrage, p. 28
Democracy, p. 148
Electoral Behavior, p. 184
Public Opinion, p. 502
Right to Vote, p. 549

Political Party Development

Political parties are organizations that seek to gain control of government to further their social, economic, or ideological goals. The United States has usually had a TWO-PARTY SYSTEM, dominated since 1860 by the DEMOCRATIC and REPUBLICAN parties. Yet more than eighty political parties have formed since the 1790s, and THIRD PARTIES have occasionally had a decisive impact on presidential elections. For example, in 1912 the PROGRESSIVE–BULL MOOSE PARTY of former president Theodore Roosevelt siphoned enough Republican votes from incumbent William Howard Taft to enable Democrat Woodrow Wilson to win the election.

The United States did not start out with a two-party system—or any parties at all. Initially there were no formal parties, and in the early 1820s the nation had in effect only one party. The founders did not anticipate parties—which they derisively called factions—and this central aspect of American politics was unplanned and had no formal constitutional or legal status. Indeed, having seen the ill effects of overzealous parties in monarchical England and (beginning in 1789) revolutionary France, the founders hoped to avoid similar pitfalls in the fledgling nation. Accordingly, in Federalist No. 10, James Madison bragged that one of the Constitution's great virtues was that it would head off "the mischiefs of faction." In 1789

> **"If I could not go to heaven but with a party, I would not go there at all."**
>
> **—Thomas Jefferson,** 1789

Thomas Jefferson declared: "If I could not go to heaven but with a party, I would not go there at all." Similarly, in his farewell address in 1796, George Washington warned that in elective popular governments the dangers of excess in the "spirit of party" demanded "a uniform vigilance to prevent its bursting into a flame."

By the time Washington issued his warning, he was the titular head of the FEDERALIST PARTY, which faded after 1800 and, except for some local officeholders, was dead by 1821. Meanwhile, since 1794 Madison and Jefferson had been the leaders of another party, variously called the DEMOCRATIC-REPUBLICANS, the Jeffersonian Democrats, and the Jeffersonian Republicans, but today understood as the kernel of what became the modern Democratic Party.

Political Issues and the Emergence of Parties

The debate over ratification of the Constitution led to the organization of factions but not parties. Future Democratic-Republicans and Federalists, such as Madison and Alexander Hamilton, worked together for ratification, just as future Democratic-Republicans and Federalists, such as James Monroe and Samuel Chase, worked against ratification of the Constitution. Ratification brought about a new national government, where parties were unknown. Presidential electors unanimously elected Washington as the first president, and nearly half of them supported Adams, who was easily elected vice president. Washington's cabinet included future leaders of the nation's first two parties:

John Jay was a leader of the Federalist Party, one of the first two major political parties in the United States. The Federalists favored a centralized government and the creation of a national bank.

Source: Library of Congress

the future Federalist leader Alexander Hamilton and the future leader of the Democratic-Republicans, Thomas Jefferson.

By the end of Washington's administration, two parties were fully engaged in politics. The parties differed over the nature of public policy and the interpretation of the Constitution. The Federalists, led by Hamilton, John Adams, and John Jay, favored a national government vigorously involved in economic development. Key to the Federalist program was the establishment of a national bank, federal funding at face value of all state and national bonds issued during the Revolution, and a flexible interpretation of the Constitution. The Federalists also wanted to strengthen diplomatic and commercial ties with England.

Jefferson's followers, called Democratic-Republicans at this time, opposed funding the war debts at par because many of the original bondholders had sold their bonds at depreciated values to speculators. Their hostility to commerce and business also led them to oppose the establishment of a national bank. Unsuccessful on these issues, the Democratic-Republicans were nonetheless able to thwart Hamilton's plan to use high tariffs to stimulate commerce and manufacturing in the new country. Jefferson and his followers wanted a strict interpretation of the Constitution, favored states' rights over national power, and in foreign policy supported France in its wars with England.

On issues involving race, slavery, and foreign policy, the parties also differed. The Federalists favored giving full diplomatic recognition to Haiti, a black republic in the Caribbean, and refused to seek the return of slaves who had escaped with the British at the end of the Revolution. Jefferson, by contrast, unsuccessfully demanded the return of the slaves but was successful as president in blocking any diplomatic ties to Haiti.

Presidents, Parties, and Policies, 1800–1860

By the time of Jefferson's election in 1800, ending twelve years of Federalist control, the party concept was entrenched in U.S. politics. Despite his previous denunciation of parties, Jefferson justified his own party leadership as a necessary opposition to the "Monocrats of our country." Jefferson's election by the House, after a tie ELECTORAL COLLEGE vote between him and Aaron Burr, led to adoption of the Twelfth Amendment to the Constitution in 1804. That amendment, which required electors to vote separately for president and vice president, further buried the likelihood of "partyless" U.S. elections.

Federalists nearly won the presidency in 1800 and 1812, but the party quickly withered after the War of 1812, when many party leaders opposed the war and flirted with secession, most notably at the Hartford Convention of 1814–1815. Federalists made a brief comeback in 1819–1820 during the debates over allowing slavery in Missouri on its admission to the Union, but the party was effectively dead by the end of 1820, when James Monroe ran unopposed for reelection.

Andrew Jackson inherited the mantle of Jefferson and his party, while his opponents migrated to the newly formed Whig Party.

Source: Library of Congress

A system with only one party was less stable than a system with two or more parties. In 1824 four candidates competed for the presidency, with no one getting a majority of the popular or the electoral vote. The House of Representatives chose John Quincy Adams, who ran second in both categories. Andrew Jackson, who had led in popular and electoral votes, immediately began his campaign for the presidency, and he won in 1828. In 1832 the ANTI-MASONIC PARTY—the name of which represented a major societal schism of the time that was long ago lost to history—made its brief appearance, winning seven electoral votes, while Jackson was easily reelected. Jackson inherited the mantle of Jefferson and his party, while his political and personal opponents, such as Daniel Webster, Henry Clay, and John Quincy Adams, migrated in the 1830s to the newly formed WHIG PARTY. In 1836 four Whigs, representing different regions of the country, competed for the presidency against Jackson's heir, Martin Van Buren.

The Whigs won the presidency in 1840 and 1848; Democrats won in 1836, 1844, 1852, and 1856. The Whigs favored a national bank, federal support for internal improvements, national bankruptcy laws, protective tariffs, and a relatively humane policy toward American Indians. The Democrats disagreed with all these positions. Whigs opposed territorial acquisition, especially by force, whereas Democrats annexed Texas and eventually pushed the United States into a war with Mexico to gain new territory in the Southwest, advocating that it was the "manifest destiny" of the United States to control the continent.

The Jacksonian Democrats pushed for universal adult white male suffrage throughout the country, but at the same time worked to take the vote away from free blacks and to strengthen slavery at the national and local levels. Jackson's presidency is remembered most for his veto of the rechartering of the Second Bank of the United States; his successful opposition to internal improvements; and his policy of Native American removal, which pushed almost all Native Americans in the east into the Indian Territory (present-day Oklahoma). On an important issue that seemed to transcend party politics, Jackson vigorously opposed extreme states' rights ideology when South Carolina attempted to nullify a federal tariff. However, following the nullification crisis, the Democrats became increasingly solicitous of states' rights and southern demands for protections for slavery. Jackson and his fellow Democrats also accepted the South Carolinians' critique of the tariff, even as they rejected the Carolinians' nullification response.

The nation had two major parties in the 1840s, but third parties influenced some elections. In 1844, the antislavery LIBERTY PARTY won enough votes in New York to cost the Whigs the state and the presidential election, assuming all the Liberty voters would have supported the Whigs. The Whig candidate, Henry Clay, opposed expansion and was more moderate on slavery than his opponent, but it seems unlikely that the committed abolitionists who voted for the Liberty Party would otherwise have voted for the slave-owning Clay as the lesser of two evils. In 1848, however, the FREE SOIL candidate, former president Martin Van Buren, won more than 290,000 votes, many of which would have otherwise gone to the Democratic candidate, Lewis Cass of Michigan. As a result, the Whig candidate, Gen. Zachary Taylor, won the election. Equally significant, Free Soilers won state and local races, and in Ohio they held the balance of power in the state legislature and were able to elect an antislavery Democrat, Salmon P. Chase, to the U.S. Senate.

Yet the victorious Whigs of 1848 managed to carry only four states in 1852, and the party disappeared two years later. The 1856 election saw two new parties emerge: the KNOW NOTHING (AMERICAN) PARTY and the Republican Party.

The Know Nothing, or American, Party was a single-issue party, opposed to immigration in general and Catholic immigration in particular. The Know Nothings won a number of governorships and dominated a few state legislatures, including Massachusetts, in this period. In 1856 the Speaker of the House of Representatives, Nathaniel Banks, was a Know Nothing.

The Republican Party adopted many Whig policies but opposed the extension of slavery into the western territories. Many Republican leaders were former Whigs, including Abraham Lincoln and his future secretary of state, William H. Seward. Others came from the antislavery wing of the Democratic Party, among them Hannibal Hamlin, who would be Lincoln's first vice president, and future secretary of the Treasury Salmon P. Chase. By 1858 many Know Nothings had also joined this party. In 1856, the Republican candidate, John C. Fremont, and the Know Nothing candidate, Millard Fillmore, together won about 400,000 more POPULAR VOTES than Democrat James Buchanan, but Buchanan had the plurality of popular votes and, more important, carried nineteen states to win the election. Buchanan was the first "sectional" president since 1824, as fourteen of the states he carried were in the South. This election underscored the reality that the Democrats had become the party of slavery and the South.

The proslavery southerners who controlled the Democratic Party insisted on fidelity to their program to expand slavery into the territories. This arrangement unraveled in 1860, as the Democrats split into two parties—regular Democrats nominating Stephen A. Douglas of Illinois and SOUTHERN DEMOCRATS nominating John C. Breckinridge of Kentucky. The Republican candidate, Abraham Lincoln, carried every northern state. Moderates in the North and the South supported the CONSTITUTIONAL UNION PARTY, which hoped to hold the Union together by not discussing any of the key issues. The two Democratic parties and the Constitutional Unionists combined for more popular votes than Lincoln (who was not even on the ballot in many southern states), but Lincoln carried eighteen states and easily won a majority of the Electoral College.

Parties in U.S. Politics since 1860

Lincoln's victory set the stage for Republican dominance in national politics for the next half-century. During this period the Republicans stood at various times for preservation of the Union, homestead laws to facilitate western settlement, federal support for a transcontinental railroad, protective tariffs, abolition of slavery, guarantees of African Americans' civil rights, and the suppression of Mormon polygamists in the West. Democrats favored lower tariffs; opposed emancipation and civil rights; and championed white immigrants (but not immigrants from Asia), labor unions, and (at the end of the century) small farmers in the South and West. In international affairs, the late nineteenth-century Republicans favored expansion, ultimately leading to war with Spain and the acquisition of an overseas empire, while Democrats opposed these trends, with Grover Cleveland (the only Democratic president in this period) refusing to annex Hawaii.

From 1868 to 1908 various third parties—including the LIBERAL REPUBLICAN, GREENBACK, PROHIBITION, Equal Rights, Anti-Monopoly, Workers, SOCIALIST LABOR, SOCIALIST, United Christian, and POPULIST Parties—ran candidates. With the exception of the Populists in 1892, however, none ever won any electoral votes. Some of these parties did, however, elect candidates to state and local offices and to Congress. James B. Weaver, for example, ran successfully for Congress on the Greenback ticket in 1878, 1884, and 1886; ran for president on the Greenback ticket in 1880; and ran for president on the Populist ticket in 1892.

In 1912 a third party determined the outcome of the presidential race. The Republicans split as former president Theodore Roosevelt tried, and failed, to gain renomination after a term out of the White House. Roosevelt thought that his successor, William Howard Taft, had abandoned the progressive goals of the party. Running on the PROGRESSIVE ("Bull Moose") ticket, Roosevelt carried six states and won about half a million more popular votes than Taft. Together they outpolled Wilson, but Wilson carried forty states and won the election. The Socialist candidate, Eugene V. Debs, won nearly a million votes in the 1912 election, and although he carried no states, Socialists won various local elections and sent some party members to Congress. Victor Berger of Milwaukee, for example, served in Congress as a Socialist from 1911 to 1913 and from 1923 to 1929. He was also elected in 1918, but in that year Congress refused to allow him to take his seat because of his opposition to World War I.

Between the 1910s and the 1940s, Democrats became increasingly internationalist, while Republicans opposed American entrance into the League of Nations after World War I and were isolationist in the 1930s as the world moved toward a second world war. Democratic support came from labor, white southerners, and most northern urban immigrant groups. By the 1930s, African Americans began to leave the Republican Party, forced out by "lily white" Republicans in the South and welcomed into the emerging New Deal coalition. The Republicans by this time had become the party of conservative business interests, white Protestants (outside the South), small town and rural northerners, and owners of small businesses.

Various third parties ran presidential candidates in the 1920s and 1930s, but only Robert M. La Follette, running as the PROGRESSIVE PARTY candidate in 1924, won any electoral votes. In 1948, though, J. Strom Thurmond, candidate of the southern STATES' RIGHTS DEMOCRATIC PARTY "Dixiecrats," who abandoned the Democratic Party to protest President Harry S. Truman's support for civil rights and racial equality, took four Deep South states. Some other Democrats supported former vice president Henry A. Wallace, running on the Progressive ticket that year. Despite these defections, Truman won. At the state and local levels, third parties were sometimes successful, and various candidates running on Socialist, Communist, or various other tickets sporadically held office. For example, Wisconsin elected Progressives Robert M. La Follette Jr. to the Senate in 1934 and 1940 and Merlin Hull to the House from 1934 to 1944. Benjamin J. Davis, running as a Communist, served on the New York City Council as the "Communist Councilman from Harlem," while Vito Marcantonio, who had served one term in Congress as a Republican (1935–1937), served six terms in Congress (1939–1951) running on the ticket of the American Labor Party, which had COMMUNIST PARTY support. INDEPENDENTS also had some success; Henry F. Reams of Ohio, for example, served two full terms in the House (1951–1955).

By the 1960s Republicans and Democrats had swapped places on the issue of African Americans' civil rights since a hundred years earlier. In 1964 large numbers of white southerners left the Democratic Party over President Lyndon Johnson's support for civil rights. Since then the Democratic constituency has generally been composed of urban, northern, and far western liberals; Catholics and Jews; African Americans, Hispanics, Asian Americans, and ethnic minorities; blue-collar workers; and the underprivileged. Republicans are viewed as conservatives, southerners, white Protestants, and the affluent.

Third parties continued to run presidential candidates and in some places candidates for Congress and state and local offices. In the 1960s, John V. Lindsay, a former Republican representative, was elected mayor of New York City on the Liberal Party line, and in 1970 James L. Buckley won a U.S. Senate seat from New York, running on the Conservative Party line. But third-party candidates have also been spoilers, as in 1980 when incumbent Republican senator Jacob Javits of New York lost his party's nomination and ran as a Liberal Party candidate, dividing the votes of moderates, liberals, and Democrats and thus allowing for the election of conservative Republican Alfonse D'Amato.

George C. Wallace, running in 1968 as the presidential candidate of the segregationist AMERICAN INDEPENDENT PARTY, captured five states in the South. Most of his supporters voted Republican in subsequent elections. In 1980, former U.S. representative John Anderson ran on the NATIONAL UNITY PARTY ticket and carried more than five million popular votes, but he did not affect the election of Ronald Reagan. In 1992 Ross Perot ran as an independent and won almost twenty million votes. He may have cost the incumbent, George H. W. Bush, a few states. Perot influenced policy in the 1990s by highlighting the importance of the national debt. When he ran again in 1996, however, he had no effect on the election. In 2000 Ralph Nader, running on the GREEN PARTY ticket, won votes in two crucial Electoral College states that exceeded the victory margins of Texas governor George W. Bush over Vice President Al Gore, leading Democrats to accuse Nader of playing the spoiler in the race.

Party Systems

Historians and political scientists often use the concept "party systems" to refer to eras that more or less hang together in terms of major-party alignment. The first, from 1789 to approximately 1824, marked the emergence of a two-party system and lasted from Washington's presidency through the end of the "Virginia Dynasty." The second, from 1828 through 1854, marked the years from Jackson's elections through the demise of the Whig Party. The third, from 1856 through 1896, marked the emergence of the Republican Party and its rise to dominance. The 1896 election marked a transition to a period that featured the Progressive era and persisted through World War I and the 1920s. The election of Franklin D. Roosevelt in 1932 marked another great electoral REALIGNMENT, although the Democrats occasionally lost the presidency or one or both chambers of Congress in the years that followed.

In the thirty-six-year period from 1933 through 1969, Democrats held the White House for all but eight years. The exceptions were Dwight D. Eisenhower's two terms (1953–1961). But the perception that the Democrats as a national party had adopted a sharply liberal agenda beginning in the 1960s caused a weakening of their long-dominant coalition, with the realignment of the Democratic "Solid South" to a mainly Republican orientation having a major impact on subsequent presidential elections. Between 1969 and 2011, Republicans held the White House for twenty-eight of the forty-two years. The only Democratic presidents during that era were Jimmy Carter, Bill Clinton, and—beginning in 2009—Barack Obama. Democrats were able to maintain their dominance in Congress well past the point at which their grip on the White House slipped. In fact, the Democrats ended a two-year Republican hold on the U.S. House in the 1954 elections and managed to keep their majority until the 1994 elections. The Republicans had slightly more success in the Senate but still held majorities for only ten years between 1933 and 1995.

The rise of a conservative and aggressively partisan generation of Republican leaders enabled the party to maintain its hold on the House for the next twelve years and in the Senate for all but a year and a half of that period. A downturn in the Republican Party's fortunes in 2006, spurred largely by the unpopular war in Iraq launched by President George W. Bush, enabled the Democrats to win back both chambers in that year's elections.

Democrats won the White House in 2008 and improved their congressional margins, dominating the House and getting a nearly filibuster-proof Senate majority. Their ascendency fell apart just two years later, over a raft of issues but rooted most importantly in national economic woes and high unemployment that accompanied a deep recession that began late in 2007. In the 2010 MIDTERM ELECTIONS Republicans had a net gain of sixty-three House seats and commanding control of the chamber. The GOP also gained six Senate seats, which although short of a majority gave the party sufficient votes to block Democratic initiatives in the 112th Congress that began in 2011.

Internal Party Politics

Although all presidents since 1852 have been either Democrats or Republicans, their parties have sometimes borrowed ideas from third parties that quickly faded from the U.S. political scene. For example, the Democrats under Andrew Jackson in 1832 followed the example of the Anti-Masons in holding a NATIONAL PARTY CONVENTION to nominate their presidential candidate. Previously, party CAUCUSES in Congress, called King Caucus, chose their nominees in secret meetings. The 1824 election of John Quincy Adams, nominated by the Massachusetts legislature, spelled the end of King Caucus. The House decided the election when none of the four candidates, all Democratic-Republicans, was able to win the required electoral vote majority. The 1828 election, won by Jackson, marked a transition to the as-yet-unborn convention system.

National nominating conventions have remained a staple of the political party system, but they have been more show than substance in the modern age of primaries and television. With the presumptive nominee known well in advance, the convention nomination is a formality, although the convention still has the duty of approving a party PLATFORM, or statement of principles.

The Democratic convention of 1952, which chose Adlai Stevenson to oppose Republican Dwight D. Eisenhower, was the most recent to require more than one ballot to select a nominee. Multiple ballots were common earlier, particularly at Democratic conventions because of the party's rule requiring a TWO-THIRDS majority for nomination. Democrats dropped the rule, never used by Republicans, in 1936.

The PRIMARY system was a creation of the Progressive era of the early twentieth century. Progressive governor Robert M. La Follette of Wisconsin pushed through a state primary law in 1905, but few other states followed suit until after 1968. Primary elections and caucuses became the de facto presidential nominating mechanisms after the tumultuous 1968 Democratic convention, won by Hubert H. Humphrey without entering any primaries. As the Democrats strengthened their primary rules in the 1970s and 1980s, primaries proliferated in both parties, and they came earlier and earlier in the election year, a practice known as FRONT-LOADING. As a result, the parties' nominations, which at one time were decided at the conventions and which, even more recently, were seldom wrapped up until the final primaries in June, have been clinched by dominant front-running candidates before the end of the winter. The rare exception occurred in 2008 when the eventual Democratic nominee, Barack Obama, battled his principal opponent, New York Sen. Hillary Rodham Clinton, the former first lady during Bill Clinton's presidency, from January to early June in nearly all the primary and caucus states.

Federal and state CAMPAIGN FINANCE reforms enacted since the 1970s have both helped and hindered political parties. Beginning in 1976, presidential candidates became eligible for PUBLIC FINANCING of their campaigns, which reduced their reliance on money from party coffers. However, the legislation allowed so-called SOFT MONEY, contributions given directly to the parties, ostensibly for party building but often diverted to indirect support for the party's candidate. The reform legislation also permitted INTEREST GROUPS and candidates to form POLITICAL ACTION COMMITTEES (PACs) to raise and spend money for campaigns. This further reduced candidates' dependence on the political parties, with the result that more and more campaigns are CANDIDATE-CENTERED rather than party-centered. In 2002 Congress revised the federal campaign finance laws to ban some types of soft money and restrict corporate and union uses of issue advertising that indirectly support or attack candidates.

Third Parties

Although the United States has always had a two-party system, third parties have frequently played an important role in the political order. No third-party candidate has ever been elected to the presidency, but many have been elected to other federal, state, and local offices. The votes third parties have garnered have also been a crucial factor in the outcome of elections. Moreover, the issues spotlighted by minor parties have often ended up being co-opted into the platforms of the major parties.

As the original party system of Hamiltonian Federalists and Jeffersonian Democratic-Republicans broke down, and the NATIONAL REPUBLICAN PARTY developed and transformed itself into the Whig Party, there also arose the Anti-Masonic Party, which ran William Wirt for president in 1832, gaining almost 8 percent of the popular vote. Nonetheless, they achieved some state and local offices, particularly in New York State, where the party originated.

In 1844 the Liberty Party, which opposed slavery, won 2.3 percent of the popular vote, and it may have affected the outcome of the election. In 1848, however, the less radical Free Soil Party, which was dedicated to stopping the spread of slavery in the territories, played the role of spoiler. Running former president Martin Van Buren, the party won enough votes, mostly from Democrats, to enable the Whig candidate, Zachary Taylor, to defeat the Democrat, Lewis Cass. It ran John P. Hale for president in 1852, obtaining 5 percent of the popular

Eugene V. Debs was the Socialist candidate in five presidential elections. Debs secured nearly one million votes in the 1920 election.
Source: Library of Congress

vote. The demise of the Free Soil Party was caused primarily by the rise of the Republican Party, which took up its stance in opposition to slavery in the territories.

In the 1850s the Know Nothing, or American, Party reaped large votes in Pennsylvania and New York and even briefly gained control over the Massachusetts government. The party's main goals were excluding Catholics from public office, enacting restrictive immigration laws, and establishing literacy tests for voting.

Parties such as the Greenback Party (1874–1884) and the Prohibition Party, which started in 1869 and has continued ever since, never attracted many votes on the national level, but their success rested in persuading one of the major parties to take up their cause. Eventually the Republican Party embraced Prohibition in the late nineteenth and early twentieth centuries, while the Democratic Party espoused the expansion of the money supply, albeit with the free coinage of silver rather than by printing greenbacks.

The Populist, or People's, Party, which represented the interests of farmers and labor, arose in the South and West in the 1880s. Because it spoke for a perennial debtor class, the party tended to favor the free coinage of silver and backed free trade and the regulation of the railroads. The Populist platform would eventually be adopted by the Democratic Party under its 1896 presidential candidate, William Jennings Bryan.

The Socialist Party came to prominence in the Progressive era, with members winning state and local offices and serving in Congress. In 1900 and 1904 it ran Eugene V. Debs for president, winning 3 percent of the vote in 1904 against the Republican incumbent Theodore Roosevelt and Alton B. Parker, the Democrat. Debs would run again in 1908, 1912, and 1920, and in this last election (campaigning from a federal penitentiary, where he was imprisoned for opposition to World War I) he tallied 915,490 votes (3.4 percent). Later, Norman Thomas would serve as the Socialist Party standard bearer in several elections, with his largest vote in 1932 when he won 884,649 votes (2.2 percent). Before World War I, socialist Victor Berger served as mayor of Milwaukee, and he served as a member of the House of Representatives from 1911 to 1913 and from 1923 to 1929.

Although they lack the long-term ideological impact of the third parties described above, some minor parties have served as vehicles for the candidacies of certain individuals. The Progressive (or Bull Moose) Party became a vehicle for Theodore Roosevelt's attempt to recapture the White

House in 1912, running against Democrat Woodrow Wilson and Republican William Howard Taft. In that race, all three candidates were Progressives to an extent. When Taft's people prevented Roosevelt delegates from some states from being seated at the Republican convention, Roosevelt bolted the party and ran as a Progressive. The result was a split of the Republican vote and a victory for Wilson.

In 1924 the Progressive Party ran Robert M. La Follette for president, capturing 16.6 percent of the vote. In 1948, using the Progressive Party label, Henry A. Wallace, Franklin Roosevelt's former vice president and secretary of agriculture, scored 2.4 percent of the vote in a four-way race that saw President Truman reelected. Wallace ran to the left of Truman on both domestic and foreign affairs, where he pushed for greater cooperation with the Soviet Union. The 1948 election also saw the emergence of another third party, the States' Rights Democratic (or Dixiecrat) Party. The Dixiecrats ran J. Strom Thurmond, the governor of South Carolina, for president, opposing the Democratic Party's adoption of a civil rights plank in its 1948 platform. Thurmond won 2.4 percent of the vote.

In the close 1968 presidential race between Richard Nixon and Hubert H. Humphrey, George C. Wallace, the governor of Alabama, captured 13.5 percent of the popular vote and forty-six electoral votes. He ran on the American Independent ticket, pushing a conservative and somewhat racist agenda. In 1980 John B. Anderson ran on an independent line against Ronald Reagan and Jimmy Carter and received 6.6 percent of the popular vote but no electoral votes. In 1992 Ross Perot ran for president as an independent, receiving 18.9 percent of the popular vote but no electoral votes. In 1996 he ran again under the REFORM PARTY banner. This party has run candidates for state and local offices across the country, and in 1998 Jesse Ventura was elected governor of Minnesota on the Reform Party line. In 2000 the Reform Party seemed destined for oblivion as it split down the middle over the contested nomination of Patrick J. Buchanan for president. In the election, consumer advocate Ralph Nader of the Green Party was the only third-party candidate to receive more than 1.0 percent of the vote. He received 2.7 percent, followed by Buchanan with 0.4 percent.

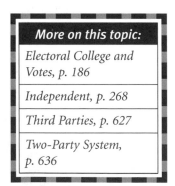

More on this topic:

Electoral College and Votes, p. 186

Independent, p. 268

Third Parties, p. 627

Two-Party System, p. 636

Today the LIBERTARIAN PARTY and to a lesser extent the Green Party offer fairly consistent ideologies through their small third-party movements.

Political Party System *See* TWO-PARTY SYSTEM.

Political Socialization of the Public

Political socialization—the acquisition of facts about and values related to politics—is a lifelong process. Among its agents are the family, schools, peers, the mass media, and leaders.

The influence of the family is profound. It is the family that first interprets the world for a child and, presumably, acquaints him or her with certain moral, religious, social, economic, and political values. If parents are interested in politics, this interest tends to be passed on to their children.

Parents often impart to their children a political attitude, called PARTY IDENTIFICATION, that is important in understanding ELECTORAL BEHAVIOR. Party identification is a feeling of attachment to and sympathy for a political party. As early as the third grade children frequently think of themselves as Democrats or Republicans.

Family influence on party identification is greatest when both parents identify with the same party. When the father and mother have different party preferences, mothers are likely to have a greater influence than fathers (reflecting the traditional tendency of mothers to spend more time with children than fathers). The maternal influence is especially strong on the daughters of college-educated, politically active mothers. Parents' influence on party identification is strengthened when it is reinforced, or at least not contradicted, by the messages received from other participants in the child's environment, such as friends or neighbors.

Parental influence on party identification decreases as children get older and are subjected to other, outside influences. In the 1960s and 1970s, millions of members of the "baby boom" generation adopted liberal values (and sometimes lifestyles) in rebelling to the social and political conservatism exhibited by many of their parents. But some of the children of the baby boomers who held to their liberal values showed their independence by adopting conservative views. Children are more likely to change from partisans to INDEPENDENTS, however, than they are to go through a conversion process and affiliate with the other party. When the conversion does occur, it typically can be attributed to economic issues.

Political learning occurs in the schools as well. Schools usually do not make a conscious effort to promote a preference for a political party or a specific viewpoint on issues. Rather, they tend to present children with the facts about their country and its political system and, in the process, foster patriotism and support for the institutions of government. The picture presented of American government in the early grades is beneficent and positive, with the president often viewed as a benevolent leader. Although the high schools continue the process of political education through American history and civics courses, such courses have been found to have only a modest influence on students' political interest, tolerance for differing opinions, trust in government, or inclination to participate in politics.

Adolescents' desire to conform—as seen in their clothing and hairstyles, as well as their musical tastes—is strong evidence of the power of peer pressure on young people's attitudes and behavior. This influence is more limited, however, in the realm of political attitudes. One of the factors contributing to the modest influence that peers have on adolescent political attitudes is the relatively low salience of politics to most adolescents' lives. Politics, except among youth who become active in campaigns or causes quite early in life, has little to do with their day-to-day concerns or their status in the peer group.

Politics is apt to take on greater relevance at the college level, where peer pressures can affect students' political attitudes. In his classic study of peer group influence, Theodore Newcombe examined the political attitudes of women attending Bennington College, an exclusive liberal arts college in Vermont, in the 1930s. These students' political attitudes were affected significantly by Bennington's liberal POLITICAL CULTURE.

Indeed, during their years at Bennington, many of the women students became a great deal more liberal in their IDEOLOGY than their generally well-to-do and conservative parents. Twenty-five years later in a follow-up study Newcombe found that Bennington alumnae retained the liberalism of their college days because it was reinforced by their spouses and adult peers.

The mass media—television, newspapers, magazines, and radio—are another influential agent of political socialization. Teachers, especially, rely heavily on the media for the information and values they transmit to their students. Outside the classroom, children's direct exposure to the media is extensive. When asked to identify sources of information on which they base their attitudes, high school students mention the mass media more often than families, teachers, friends, or personal experiences.

Yet skepticism about the mainstream media has increasingly turned young people to the Internet as a source for information of all kinds, and many get a good deal of their political information from popular pseudo-news shows such as the Comedy Channel's *The Daily Show with Jon Stewart* and Stephen Colbert's *The Colbert Report,* which present distinctly liberal viewpoints.

Adult Socialization

The shaping of basic political beliefs, values, and attitudes does not stop with graduation from high school or college. But the influences that were the most prominent in youth—parents, school, childhood peers—recede and are replaced by daily events and experiences, the mass media, political leaders, and new peer groups such as coworkers, neighbors, friends, and fellow church and club members.

As people grow older their politically relevant experiences abound. They encounter the Internal Revenue Service, military recruiting, government-influenced mortgage rates, Social Security and Medicare, and economic setbacks. The impressions gained from these experiences and interactions with peers continue to shape people's political attitudes. The daily hardships of the Great Depression of the 1930s, for example, caused people to change their views about the role of government. Unlike in earlier times, they now expected the government to manage the economy and provide social services.

Personal experiences, however, are quite limited compared with the range of politically relevant experiences that the mass media provide. Throughout adulthood, as in childhood, people consume the media in huge doses.

As a result, much of what the average person learns about politics is absorbed from the media's factual news programs as well as its fictional sitcoms, soap operas, and late night talk show comedians. Viewers may well conclude that most politicians are buffoons, crooks, or lechers because that is how most are depicted on such programs.

MEDIA COVERAGE OF CAMPAIGNS is a major force in shaping people's perceptions of reality. For example, the public's perception that the economy was in desperate straits during the 1992 presidential election campaign was a major factor in Democrat Bill Clinton's defeat of President George H. W. Bush, the Republican incumbent. Objective economic data indicated, however, that the economy was beginning to grow in late 1991 and more robustly in 1992. Yet content analysis showed that news coverage of the economy by ABC, CBS, and NBC was overwhelmingly (96 percent) negative and pessimistic in the July-September quarter of 1992.

PUBLIC OPINION analyst Everett Carll Ladd concluded that this almost uninterrupted stream of negative press reports and commentary on the nation's economy was the "most important political event of the 1992 campaign." He stressed, however, that this kind of reporting was not caused by some media plot to elect Clinton but rather by the coming together of three elements: journalists feeling closer to the stands of Democrats than those of Republicans; a sense that after twelve years the Republicans and their economic policies had become an old, tired news story; and the fact that "the economy in shambles" was an inherently more interesting story than "some problems, but also many economic strengths."

People's attitudes are affected as well by the actions and statements of political leaders, particularly the president. One of the most dramatic changes in public opinion began in the early 1970s when President Richard M. Nixon, a conservative Republican whose entire public career had been built on staunch anticommunism, began the process of normalizing diplomatic relations with the communist government of the People's Republic of China. Virtually overnight, American opinion changed from that of overwhelming opposition to that of heightened tolerance toward and interest in the communist government on mainland China. The actions of successive presidents to strengthen diplomatic, economic, and cultural ties with China continued to garner widespread public support until June 1989, when the communist government brutally repressed pro-democracy demonstrations.

Presidential leadership of public opinion is most effective when the president is riding a crest of popularity. During times of declining popular support, the president finds it difficult to sway the public.

The Effect of Social Backgrounds

No two Americans have identical political socialization experiences. People with similar social backgrounds, however, are apt to share some political opinions, which are likely to differ from the views of people with different backgrounds. Differences in education, income or class, ethnicity, race, religion, region, and gender can produce distinctive political orientations.

Education increases people's interest in and understanding of politics and affects the political attitudes that they develop. College graduates profess greater support for civil liberties and have more tolerant racial attitudes than people who attended but did not graduate from college. The better-educated also are more likely to support environmental protection measures, space research, and affirmative action hiring programs for women and minorities. They are less likely to back conservative social policy agenda items such as permitting prayer in the public schools or banning abortion.

Income and social class affect people's views on a range of issues. Those in the higher-income bracket are somewhat more supportive of racial and sexual equality, tolerant of diverse views, internationalist in foreign affairs, and conservative on social welfare issues. The higher education level characteristic of the well-to-do appears to be a major factor in their liberalism on noneconomic issues; income affects their views on social welfare issues.

In contrast to the situations found in many Western nations, class-based differences do not greatly divide American society. Many sociologists believe that for a sizable number of people near the bottom of the income scale, the belief in America as a land of opportunity where anyone can aspire to be rich trumps resentment of the wealthy. As a result, many politicians—usually Democrats—who used economic populist themes have recently found themselves falling short among their targeted audiences of less-affluent people.

Ethnicity and Race

America is frequently called a nation of immigrants, and with each new wave of immigration the mix of nationalities becomes more varied. Most of the earliest settlers came from England, Scotland, and Wales, followed by those from Ireland, Germany, and Scandinavia. During the late nineteenth and early twentieth centuries, immigrants from eastern and southern Europe—Poles, Italians, and Russians—predominated.

The cultural and religious differences between Americans with east and south European backgrounds and those of English heritage have often been a basis for political division within the United States. For example, the immigrants from eastern and southern Europe provided essential support for the New Deal Democratic coalition forged by President Franklin D. Roosevelt in the 1930s, and those of British heritage traditionally have constituted an important base of Republican voting strength.

Although differences in voting patterns among voters of European heritage are still detectable, the differences are diminishing as older immigrant groups become assimilated into American society. Public opinion surveys show modest differences in thinking, however, among European ethnic groups on issues of government responsibility for health care, improved living standards for the poor, and a more equitable distribution of income. For example, persons with British ancestry are less likely to support government social welfare programs than those with southern and eastern European roots.

The current tide of immigrants from Spanish-speaking (Hispanic) countries in this hemisphere—particularly Mexico and Central America—and from Asia is showing distinctive political attitudes and partisan preferences as well. Reflecting the relatively less well-off economic positions of these "new ethnics," Mexican Americans, for example, are more highly supportive of extending government services and of the Democratic Party than are the "old ethnics" from eastern and southern Europe. The political attitudes of Mexican Americans also differ from those of another Hispanic group, the Cuban Americans, who, with their fierce anticommunist stance and generally higher standard of living, are predominantly Republican.

In 2001 Hispanics (13 percent) surpassed African Americans (12.7 percent) as the country's largest racial minority, with other nonwhites (Asians and Native Americans) making up approximately 3 percent. African Americans and Asians are expanding segments of the population. According to numerous surveys conducted by the National Opinion Research Center, African Americans and other racial minorities tend to have some political attitudes in common. But in contrast to older European ethnics and Hispanics, African Americans are more likely to believe that government should assume a larger responsibility for solving the country's problems, helping the poor, reducing income differences between rich and poor, and providing health care. Asian Americans, in contrast, tend toward more conservative political positions.

Religious Background

America is a predominantly Protestant nation. According to a survey taken by the Pew Research Center for the People and the Press in 2005, 56 percent profess a Protestant religious preference, followed by Catholic (23 percent), Jewish (2 percent), other religions (6 percent), and no religious preference (11 percent). Some of the differences in attitudes and partisan preferences found among people of various faiths can be traced to historic causes. Most Catholic immigrants, for example, arrived in the United States at a time when Protestants and Republicans dominated the nation's political and economic life. This fact, as well as the discrimination to which Catholics were once subjected, has left traces of liberal and pro-Democratic sentiment among Catholics. The 1928 election also helped to forge an electoral bond between Catholics and the Democratic Party, as New York governor Al Smith became the first Catholic presidential nominee of a major party.

The unique history of Jews as a persecuted minority also has influenced their political views. Centuries of anti-Semitism have tended to drive them in a liberal direction, especially on civil liberties issues.

Doctrinal differences among religions have political relevance as well. The Catholic Church has taken a strong stand against abortion and birth control, and the emphasis Protestants place on individual responsibility for one's economic and spiritual well-being may predispose them toward conservative positions on economic issues. Fundamentalist Protestants tend to show a particularly conservative orientation. They overwhelmingly favor prayer in public schools and oppose abortion.

One of the most striking recent developments in religion and politics is the close relationship between frequency of church attendance and partisan choice. According to 1992 election data, among whites Republicans fare much better with the "churched" portion of the electorate than with the "less churched" and "unchurched." African Americans, including regular churchgoers, however, are overwhelmingly Democratic, a legacy of the party's strong shift to advocacy of civil rights in the 1960s as well as its ongoing progressive views on economic issues. Jewish voters, who tend to support progressive policies, are also strongly Democratic.

Regional Divisions

Regional differences of opinion have been sources of conflict periodically since the earliest days of the American political system. The Civil War was the most dramatic of such instances, and that war and its aftermath left their marks on American politics for more than a century. After the war, small-town, white Protestant, middle-class conservatives, who might otherwise have been Republicans, created a one-party Democratic stronghold in the South.

But as Civil War memories faded, northerners migrated to the South, and the region's per-capita income disadvantages began to diminish after World War II. The partisanship of whites changed, and some of the distinctiveness of southern attitudes receded. Southerners, however, continue to hold more conservative views on most issues than people from other regions. They are more likely to consider themselves conservatives, to trust the Republicans to deal with the country's most important problems, to oppose abortion, to favor prayer in the public schools, to oppose homosexual relations, and to support defense expenditures.

Liberalism on social issues tends to be bicoastal, with the Northeast and the Pacific Coast standing out as being the most supportive of women's rights, the right to an abortion, and other issues on the social agenda. The East is also more liberal on economic issues. On civil rights the South is more conservative than the rest of the nation.

Although the unique histories and cultures of the states have an impact on the political outlooks of their residents, powerful forces in American society are undermining these regional influences. For example, the mobility of Americans (approximately 20 percent move each year) is diluting the homogeneity of regional populations. Also diminishing the uniqueness of regional influences are the national media, which have made their way into living rooms across the country, as well as the growing ubiquity of the Internet.

The Gender Gap

Men and women, even those who share common racial, social class, ethnic, and religious backgrounds, do not have the same attitudes about some issues. The most frequently noted difference in attitude has been toward the Democratic Party: in the 1980s and through the early years of the twenty-first century, a higher proportion of women than men supported Democratic candidates. As a result, the term *gender gap* entered the political vocabulary.

Women are less apt than men to support military expenditures and the use of force in international affairs and are more apt to support gun control and social welfare spending. Not all issues, however, are gender-sensitive. On the questions of increased spending for education and family leave legislation, the views of men and women are much the same.

Women are more likely to support the Democratic Party and oppose the use of force in international relations than men are.

Source: AP Images/Lisa Nipp

From Socialization to Participation

Once adulthood is reached and political attitudes are largely formed, the next step for the politically active is to put those beliefs to work through political participation. Men and women with higher social and economic status—whether measured by level of education, income, occupation, or government benefits received—participate more actively in politics than do those with lower social and economic status.

Education is the single most important socioeconomic characteristic determining political participation. Better educated people are more likely to understand how the political process works, to be aware of how the machinations of government might affect their lives, to move in social environments in which politics is discussed, and to be subjected to social pressures to participate. In addition, education helps people to acquire the skills necessary to participate.

Age affects participation as well. Young people are less likely to vote and engage in election-related activities than are middle-aged and older citizens, but they are more likely than their elders to take part in unconventional forms of political participation such as protest demonstrations.

In the past, significant differences in political participation were related to gender and race, with women and blacks lagging behind men and whites. Today, however, the differences between men and women have diminished. And the gap between white and black participation rates has been narrowed as African Americans' RIGHT TO VOTE has been protected, black educational attainment and economic mobility have been enhanced, and black political awareness has increased with accompanying increases in BLACK SUFFRAGE. Black participation rates are now similar to those of whites, when differences between the races in educational attainment and socioeconomic status are taken into consideration.

Among the attitudes related to participation are a sense of civic duty (a feeling of obligation to participate), an interest in politics, a sense of political efficacy (a feeling of personal political effectiveness), and a sense of party identification. Although these attitudes are indicators of whether a person is predisposed to participate in politics, they do not, aside from party identification, indicate which issues or candidates will receive that person's attention. Short-term influences—such as the salient issues of the day and the qualities of particular candidates—also help determine whether a person's political socialization will manifest itself in political participation, and in what form.

More on this topic:
Electoral Behavior, p. 184
Ideology, p. 259
Media Coverage of Campaigns, p. 313
Party Identification by Voters, p. 377
Public Opinion, p. 502

Poll Taxes

The poll tax, a fee required for voting, once was commonplace in the United States. Its use waned in the nineteenth century as more people became property owners and therefore could be assessed real estate taxes.

But in the South after the Civil War, the reigning DEMOCRATIC PARTY seized upon the poll tax as a device to deter voting by blacks who were flocking to the party of Lincoln and building Republican strength. Later, as the trend to primaries took hold, the poll tax along with GRANDFATHER CLAUSES, LITERACY TESTS, and the WHITE PRIMARY proved effective in limiting voting by poor blacks and whites in the Democrats' SOUTHERN PRIMARIES, the most significant elections in the region because of the long-term weakness of the Republican Party.

The fee generally ranged from $1 to $2, but in Alabama, Georgia, Mississippi, and Virginia before 1945 the poll tax was cumulative. A new voter in Georgia could face up to $47 in fees. For impoverished sharecroppers, black or white, even a dollar or two was a hardship.

Various regulations as to the time and manner of payment of the tax also substantially reduced the number of voters. In Mississippi, for example, a person wanting to vote in the Democratic primary (usually held in August) had to pay the poll tax on or before the first day of the two preceding Februarys—long before most voters had even begun to think about the election.

After years of controversy about it, many states dropped the poll tax. But it lingered in much of the South until it was effectively barred by ratification of the Twenty-fourth Amendment to the Constitution in January 1964. The amendment simply stated that the "right of citizens of the United States to vote in any primary or other election [for federal office] . . . shall not be denied or abridged by the United States or any other State by reason of failure to pay any poll tax or other tax."

In its decision in the 1966 case of *Harper v. State Board of Elections,* the Supreme Court reversed an earlier decision and ruled that poll taxes were unconstitutional for state and local elections as well. Striking down Virginia's $1.50 poll tax, the Court said, "Wealth, like race, creed, or color is not germane to one's ability to participate intelligently in the electoral process."

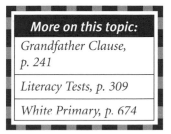

More on this topic:

Grandfather Clause, p. 241

Literacy Tests, p. 309

White Primary, p. 674

Polling

Polls of PUBLIC OPINION are a big part of modern-day American politics. Candidates and their POLITICAL CONSULTANTS rely on them to identify popular issues, test voter reaction to the candidates' image and programs, and help plan CAMPAIGN STRATEGIES.

Polling companies sell the results of their work to clients—newspapers, corporations, and interest groups—that need information on the public's thinking. The Gallup, Roper, Harris, and Yankelovich organizations were for many years the nation's dominant polling operations.

But major newspapers, news magazines, and television networks also do extensive polling, often in partnership, and have become as familiar to readers and viewers as names such as Gallup. The results have become a staple of MEDIA COVERAGE OF CAMPAIGNS as well as an important tool in MEDIA USE BY CAMPAIGNS—too much, say some critics, who portray the media as obsessed with the horse-race aspects of elections, such as who is winning and what strategies the candidates are following, at the expense of serious discussions of issues.

Far less controversial is the kind of ongoing survey research conducted by academic institutions, such as the Center for Political Studies (CPS) at the University of Michigan, which aims to develop a database for theoretical explanations of political behavior. Political scientists use these sources in their work and rely heavily on the CPS studies of ELECTORAL BEHAVIOR. A CPS adjunct, the NATIONAL ELECTION STUDIES, today a joint project of the University of Michigan and Stanford University, surveys the electorate in connection with every presidential and MIDTERM ELECTION.

Techniques and Ratings

Scientific methods of public opinion polling are a relatively recent development, dating only to the early twentieth century. Before scientific polling, it was almost impossible to measure public sentiment reliably.

In the Fish Room (now called the Roosevelt Room), across from the Oval Office, President Lyndon Johnson sets up charts displaying his private polls before the 1964 election.
Source: Library of Congress

George Gallup was the founder of modern polling. His surveys helped his mother-in-law win election as Iowa secretary of state in 1932. Gallup wrote a doctoral thesis on sampling techniques, and in 1935, with Elmo Roper and Archibald Crossley, he founded the independent Gallup poll, the leader in scientific polling for decades and still one of the major polling organizations.

Since 1945, the Gallup Organization has asked members of the public monthly—and sometimes more often—whether they approve or disapprove of the president's handling of the job. An increasing number of other polling firms do similar polls—more than a dozen in early 2007, according to a compilation on The Polling Report's website. Gallup's historical records are often cited as the baseline for gauging how the public rates presidential performance.

Franklin D. Roosevelt was the first president to take polling data routinely into account when weighing decisions about his administration's policies and actions. With war looming in Europe in the late 1930s, Roosevelt sought advice from Gallup on how to frame his rhetoric concerning U.S. involvement in what became World War II.

It was about that time that the term *pollster* came into existence, according to *New York Times* language columnist William Safire. The word first appeared in *Time* magazine in a 1939 article quoting Gallup's findings that 43 percent of voters favored FDR's running for an unprecedented third term.

After Roosevelt's death in his fourth term, the polls seriously misjudged President Harry S. Truman's chances of defeating Republican Thomas E. Dewey in 1948. The pollsters' error was forever memorialized by the famous picture of a smiling Truman holding up the headline "Dewey Defeats Truman."

By the 1960s public opinion polling was an accepted White House tool. Lyndon B. Johnson was the first president to have a staff pollster. He hired Albert Cantril, who provided LBJ with polling data from every state. Johnson used the polls to defend both his escalation of the Vietnam War and his decision in 1968 not to seek reelection in the face of mounting opposition to the war. Before the Vietnam War took its toll on his popularity, Johnson had one of the highest approval ratings in Gallup poll history—80 percent in January 1964. He won in a LANDSLIDE that year, but by the end of his term his ratings were in the 40 percent range.

The public's view of a president, measured by personal and job approval ratings in opinion polls, can change sharply and sometimes over relatively short periods of time. This was the experience of both George H. W. Bush, who was elected in 1988, and his son George W. Bush, who won elections in 2000 and 2004.

The elder Bush saw his job approval ratings soar to record heights in early 1991 following the quick victory of a U.S.-led military operation to end Iraq's occupation of Kuwait, only to see them plummet to as low as 30 percent because of public dissatisfaction with his handling of the economy. He lost his bid for reelection in 1992 to Democrat Bill Clinton.

The younger Bush's assertive response to the September 11, 2001, terrorist attacks, including the quick military overthrow of the radical Taliban government of Afghanistan, which had harbored al-Qaeda terrorists, was initially highly popular, enabling him to top 90 percent in some polls and break his father's record. But his decision to lead a much smaller U.S.-dominated coalition to invade Iraq and overthrow dictator Saddam Hussein grew unpopular as the war became longer, deadlier, and more expensive than predicted and failed to produce the stockpiles of weapons of mass destruction Iraq allegedly was harboring. This was the key reason for the roller-coaster drop in his job approval ratings, which slipped to the mediocre range by his narrow 2004 reelection victory over Democrat John Kerry, and then spiraled to the low 30s and (in a few polls) the high 20s in a 2006 midterm election campaign that saw his Republican Party lose control of both chambers of Congress.

Bush, however, did not hit the rock-bottom figure of 23 percent job approval in Gallup polls experienced in the early 1950s by Harry S. Truman, who, burdened by an intractable war in Korea and public weariness with a long run of Democratic control of the White House, chose not to seek reelection in 1952, or by Republican Richard M. Nixon just prior to his August 1974 resignation following the Watergate scandal. The only other president to score in the twenties was Jimmy Carter, who dipped to 29 percent at several crisis points in a presidency that ran from 1977 to 1981. Bush's successor, Barack Obama, dropped below 50 percent by his third year in office and in some polls closer to 40 percent.

Although the senior Bush was the first president to appoint a pollster (Robert M. Teeter) as his reelection campaign manager, Bush campaigned against "those crazy pollsters" in the same 1992 campaign. He accused the poll takers of trying to make him a loser to Clinton before he actually was.

Pollsters for presidential candidates tend to specialize in one party or the other. For example, Richard Wirthlin and Teeter polled for Republicans Ronald Reagan and Bush, respectively. Patrick Caddell polled for Democrats George S. McGovern, Jimmy Carter, Gary Hart, and Joseph R. Biden Jr.; Peter Hart is a well-recognized veteran on the Democratic polling scene. During Clinton's first year in the White House, pollster Stanley Greenberg was paid $1,986,410 by the DEMOCRATIC NATIONAL COMMITTEE to conduct frequent focus groups and polls for the president's use; Greenberg as of early 2007 remained a leading public opinion researcher for the Democratic side.

As president in early 1998, Clinton achieved a remarkable ratings feat. Despite a sensational SCANDAL involving his alleged (later admitted) affair with a young female White House intern, Clinton received approval scores ranging as high as 79 percent for his job as president. His job approval rating remained high a year later, even after the House impeached him for perjury and obstruction of justice in connection with the extramarital affair.

Polling Methods

Surveys conducted for partisan candidates or political parties, known familiarly as "own" polls, are not inherently wrong or misleading. But, not surprisingly, they are approached by political observers with some degree of caution, especially since such polls usually see the light of day only when the results present in a positive light the candidate for whom the poll was conducted.

Independent polls, however, are seldom challenged as being purposely biased. Skepticism about the results usually centers on the sophisticated, computerized sampling techniques that draw broad conclusions from surveys of small cross sections of the public.

Pollsters typically interview only 1,000 to 2,000 people in a national survey. But even such a small group of respondents can accurately reflect the nation's views if the people who are interviewed constitute a representative sample of the population whose opinion is being sought. To create such a sample, pollsters use a probability procedure in which every person in the population being surveyed has the same chance of being chosen for an interview.

To reach the people in the population sample, most polling organizations today use telephones instead of in-person interviews. Telephone polls are economical and do not significantly distort survey results. However, creating an accurate sample has become increasingly difficult. The rising use of cellular phones has spurred a number of people to abandon traditional "land-line" phones, for which pollsters are able to obtain databases of numbers to be called randomly to develop a representative sample of voters throughout a jurisdiction or the nation as a whole. Many people, already besieged by unsolicited calls from telemarketers, charities, and political candidates, simply hang up on pollsters or screen their calls using caller ID. Willingness to participate in polls has been affected negatively by the cynicism about politics voiced by many Americans. (See zzz.)

As a result, the accuracy of polls depends highly on the quality of the "weighting" performed by the survey researchers, as the responses are adjusted to offset any possible oversampling of particular demographic, regional, or partisan groups. This weighting is performed using statistical analysis based on past electoral performance but—especially in partisan "swing" years—may not perfectly reflect changes in the mood of the electorate.

As the polling industry adapts to changes in technology, new controversies arise about techniques. One of the current disputes concerns fully automated polling, in which a phone message asks respondents to answer to a series of prerecorded questions by punching numbers on their phone keypads. Some critics contend that this system requires respondents to give less thought to their answers than would be required in traditional live interviews conducted by polling company employees.

The ability of EXIT POLLS conducted on ELECTION DAY to collect vast amounts of data about the opinions and demographics of people who voted has made them a valuable tool since they became commonly used in the 1980s—not only for media outlets hungry to determine election results but also for researchers examining opinion trends over time. Problems in the accuracy of exit polls that became glaring on the election nights of 2000 and 2002, and which spurred an overhaul in how the polls are conducted, interrupted some of that continuity.

Responsible polling organizations take great care to determine that they have a representative sample of the population they are studying. Preelection polls pose special problems because not all those eligible will actually vote. So a poll that reports the preferences of all eligible voters presents a potentially inaccurate prediction. To deal with this problem, polling organizations try to determine which people are most likely to vote.

Most polling organizations rely on random digit dialing to overcome the problems associated with unlisted telephone numbers—30 percent or more in some areas. Random digit dialing typically involves using a computer random-number generator or table of random numbers to select the last four digits of the phone numbers to be called after the area codes and exchanges (the first three digits of a seven-digit phone number) in the survey area have been identified.

Survey interviews can last from a few minutes to as long as an hour, depending on the amount of information being sought. Most questions are close-ended—that is, the respondent chooses from a predetermined set of possible answers, thereby enhancing the comparability of the responses. A small number of questions may be open-ended, with respondents allowed to answer questions in their own words. Open-ended questions may elicit subtle distinctions in people's opinions, but they substantially complicate interpretation and analysis of interview data.

A 1992 New York Times/CBS poll asked respondents: "Are we spending too much, too little, or about the right amount on assistance to the poor?" Only 13 percent said we were spending too much. But when "welfare" was substituted for "assistance to the poor," 44 percent said we were spending too much.

Particular care must be taken that the wording of questions does not bias or influence respondents' answers, which would affect the poll's results. For example, a 1992 *New York Times*/CBS poll asked respondents: "Are we spending too much, too little, or about the right amount on assistance to the poor?" Only 13 percent said we were spending too much. But when "welfare" was substituted for "assistance to the poor," 44 percent said we were spending too much.

A classic example of a nonrepresentative sample that resulted in a distorted picture of public opinion was the 1936 *Literary Digest* poll that predicted Kansas governor Alfred Landon would defeat President Franklin Roosevelt in the presidential election. The sample had been selected from phone books and automobile registrations, overlooking the fact that in the depths of the Great Depression people with telephones and cars were only a fraction of the electorate and certainly not a cross section of American voters.

Polling Accuracy

As polling techniques have improved, so has the accuracy of polls. The Gallup poll, for example, had an average deviation from the actual winning vote in the ten presidential elections from 1960 through 1996 of only 2.0 percentage points. The Polling Report showed fourteen polls, mostly by independent organizations, just before the 2004 election in which President George W. Bush defeated Democratic challenger John Kerry by 2.7 percentage points in the national popular vote. Eight polls showed Bush leading by margins of between 1 and 3 points.

Polls can be correct and still vary widely. In August 1992, for example, polls by ten organizations showed Clinton leading in the presidential race by a high of 19 percentage points (ABC/ *Washington Post*) to a low of 5 points (Lou Harris). The polls had a margin of error of 3 to 5 points for each candidate.

Inaccurate polls might stem from a sampling error—the degree to which the sample can be expected to vary from the total population being studied. National surveys typically have a sampling error of about 4 percent. This means that if 55 percent of the respondents prefer the Republican candidate, the actual value is likely to be in the range of 51 percent to 59 percent (55 percent plus or minus 4 percent).

Inaccurate poll results also might stem from a faulty questionnaire, sloppy interview procedures, and mistakes in interpreting and analyzing survey responses. An analytical error, for example, occurred in the Gallup poll's final estimate of the 1992 presidential vote because of the unprecedented independent candidacy of Ross Perot, who received equal status with the major party nominees in the presidential DEBATES and had a record advertising budget. Based on the past performance of independent candidates, the Gallup Organization decided to allocate none of the undecided voters to Perot. As a result, Gallup underestimated Perot's vote by 6 percentage points.

It is hazardous to predict on the basis of polls what the public's opinions or behavior will be at some time in the future; the public's views can change dramatically and quickly. A poll is only a snapshot of opinions at the time it was taken, and its validity cannot be extended into time.

More on this topic:
Electoral Behavior, p. 184
Exit Polls, p. 196
Media Coverage of Campaigns, p. 313
Media Use by Campaigns, p. 324
National Election Studies, p. 346
Public Opinion, p. 502
Push Poll, p. 507

Popular Vote

The popular vote—the vote of the people—was less prevalent in early American elections than it is today. Then, as now, the president and vice president were elected by the ELECTORAL COLLEGE rather than by direct popular vote. State legislatures chose the electors in most cases, although in the first presidential election (1789) electors in four states were selected by popular vote. South Carolina was the last state to switch to popular vote in choosing electors, in 1868. Colorado, however, used legislative appointment in 1876, the year it became a state. (See DIRECT ELECTION.)

The House of Representatives, as the "people's branch," has always been elected by popular (direct) voting, but direct election of Senate members did not become universal until ratification of the Seventeenth Amendment to the Constitution in 1913. Previously, most senators were sent to Washington by state legislatures as the Constitution specified, although as early as 1912 twenty-nine states had some type of direct election. Popular direct election of governors in some states predates the 1789 election because the states existed earlier under the Articles of Confederation. Thirteen of them became the original states under the Constitution when they ratified it, beginning with Delaware on December 7, 1787.

Wider Participation

As the RIGHT TO VOTE was gradually extended to more and more people through state actions and constitutional amendments, the popular vote grew in significance for all elections. By 1972 virtually all law-abiding American citizens over age eighteen had the FRANCHISE. (See BLACK SUFFRAGE; WOMEN'S SUFFRAGE; YOUTH SUFFRAGE.)

How many people exercised the franchise, however, was difficult to determine until the latter half of the twentieth century. Reliable popular vote returns for presidential and congressional elections before 1824 are not available; and many of those for later years did not come into existence until after 1962, when a small army of social scientists, supported by grants from the Social Science Research Council and the National Science Foundation, began scouring the nation for old newspapers, state archives, historical society records, and anything else that could help reconstruct the vote tallies of early federal and state elections.

The result was the Historical Elections Returns File of the Inter-university Consortium for Political and Social Research (ICPSR) at the University of Michigan, Ann Arbor. The historical file was the basis for the *Guide to U.S. Elections,* published in 1975 by Congressional Quarterly and CQ Press and updated with a series of new editions beginning in 1985, most recently in a sixth edition in 2010. The ICPSR, part of the Institute for Social Research, disseminates the in-depth voting studies of a newer institute affiliate, the NATIONAL ELECTION STUDIES.

There is no one "official" set of election results outside of those maintained in each state. But the increasing availability of election data on the Internet provides more comprehensive and greater access to voting information for researchers, students, political analysts and activists, and the general public than existed ever before.

Compilation of reliable popular vote returns for elections after 1824 became feasible because by then the TWO-PARTY SYSTEM was beginning to develop and more states were choosing presidential electors by popular election. Scholars' efforts to compile earlier returns have been thwarted by a lack of records.

As it happened, the 1824 election marked a historic milestone in the role of the popular vote in presidential elections. When none of the four major candidates, all from different factions of the Democratic-Republican Party, received a majority of the electoral vote, the election had to be decided by the House of Representatives for only the second time in history. Although Andrew Jackson led in the popular vote with 41.3 percent, the House elected John Quincy Adams, who had run second with 30.9 percent.

As a result, Adams became the first "minority president," one who gained the office without a majority of the popular vote. Through 2004, there have been seventeen other minority presidents. (See table, "Minority" Presidents, page 180.)

Fourteen of the nation's eighteen minority presidents outpolled their opponents at the ballot box but received less than 50 percent of the vote. The other four, however, lost the popular vote yet still won the electoral contest. In addition to John Quincy Adams, the others were Rutherford B. Hayes, who ran behind Samuel Tilden in their 1876 CONTESTED ELECTION; Benjamin Harrison, who garnered fewer popular votes in 1888 than Grover Cleveland; and George W. Bush, who trailed Democrat Al Gore by roughly 540,000 votes in 2000.

Voting Trends

The popular vote is useful for measuring ebbs and flows in voter participation and preference in the United States. The figures show, for example, that each major liberalization of election laws resulted in a sharp increase in the number of people voting. From 1824 to 1856, a period in which states gradually relaxed property and taxpaying qualifications, voter participation in presidential elections increased from 3.8 percent to 16.7 percent of the total population. In 1920, after the Nineteenth Amendment gave women the franchise, voter participation increased to 25.1 percent.

Between 1932 and 1976, both the voting-age population and the number of voters in presidential elections almost doubled. Except for the 1948 presidential election, when just a little over half of the voting-age population was estimated to have gone to the polls, the turnout in the postwar years through 1968 was approximately 60 percent, according to Census Bureau surveys. This relatively high percentage was due partly to passage of the VOTING RIGHTS ACT and CIVIL RIGHTS ACTS protecting African Americans' voting privilege.

Despite a steady increase in the number of persons voting in the 1970s, voter turnout declined as a percentage of eligible voters, defined in the historical records as U.S. citizens of voting age.

Missouri governor Frederick Gardner signs the resolution ratifying the Nineteenth Amendment in 1919. Following ratification of the "Anthony Amendment," voter participation increased by 25.1 percent in 1920.
Source: Library of Congress

Turnout reached a modern peak of 62.8 percent in the 1960 presidential election. It declined steadily over the next decade, falling to 61.9 percent in 1964, 60.9 percent in 1968, 55.2 percent in 1972, and 52.8 percent in 1980. Voting in the congressional MIDTERM ELECTION, always lower than in presidential election years, also declined during this period, dropping from 45.4 percent in 1962 to 34.9 percent in 1978.

The decline in presidential voting generally continued from the 1980s on, except for upticks to 53.3 percent in 1984 and 55.1 percent in 1992. The 1992 election was the first in which more than 100 million Americans voted for president. The total vote was 104,425,014.

After participation in 1996 fell to 49.0 percent (the lowest mark since 1924), the turnout increased somewhat in 2000 to 51.3 percent. A record 105,405,100 Americans voted.

Turnout took an even bigger leap forward in 2004, to 56.7 percent, when the race George W. Bush won over Democrat John Kerry drew 122,295,345 voters. As a result of the closeness of the race—Bush won by 50.7 percent to Kerry's 48.3 percent—both candidates shattered the previous record for most votes received by a presidential candidate. Four years later, Barack Obama, a Democrat, won with 52.9 percent, while the turnout rate increased slightly, to 56.8 percent.

> **More on this topic:**
>
> Direct Election, p. 161
>
> Electoral College and Votes, p. 186
>
> Franchise, p. 215
>
> National Election Studies, p. 346
>
> Right to Vote, p. 549
>
> Two-Party System, p. 636

The turnout rate using the voting age population was challenged by some scholars after 2000, who contended that a different measure—the voting eligible population—was more accurate. This measure excluded people old enough to vote but who were not U.S. citizens, such as immigrants and others—prison inmates, for example—ineligible to cast a ballot. By this measure, the turnout rates are higher: 61.6 percent in 2008 and 60.1 percent in 2004.

Among the reasons for the voter turnout increase were the steady rise over recent decades of the U.S. population, which was over 300 million late in the 2000s decade; the general rise of partisan divisions and the particular polarization over Bush and his confrontationally conservative approach; and stepped-up VOTER TURNOUT efforts by the major party organizations and the interest groups affiliated with them. (See table, Growing Franchise in the United States, 1930–2010, page 658.)

Populist (People's) Party (1891–1908, 1984–)

The People's Party, also called the Populist Party, was organized at a convention in Cincinnati, Ohio, in May 1891 and climaxed several decades of farm protest against deteriorating economic conditions. Chronically depressed commodity prices, caused by overproduction and world competition, had spurred the politicization of farmers.

Most of the Populist leaders came from the defunct GREENBACK movement and southern and midwestern farm cooperative associations. The Populists tended to blame their problems on the most visible causes, primarily the high railroad rates and shrinking currency supply, but the platform they adopted at their first national nominating convention in 1892 was far-reaching. Besides advocating the government ownership of railroads and the free coinage of silver, the Populists proposed institution of a graduated income tax and the DIRECT ELECTION of senators. Yet even though the Populists proposed labor reforms, such as reducing the working day to eight hours, the party never gained appreciable support among industrial workers.

The Populists ran James B. Weaver, the former Greenback presidential candidate, as their presidential nominee in 1892. Weaver received 1,024,280 votes (8.5 percent of the popular vote) and carried five states in the Midwest and West. Increasingly tied to the silver issue, the party showed growing strength in the 1894 congressional races, especially west of the Mississippi River. Party congressional candidates polled nearly 1.5 million votes, and after the election the Populists had six senators and seven representatives in Congress.

The DEMOCRATIC PARTY surprised Populist leaders in 1896 by writing a free silver PLATFORM and nominating a candidate who was a strong advocate of that view, William Jennings Bryan. The Populists were faced with the dilemma of either endorsing Bryan and losing their party identity or running a separate ticket and splitting the free silver vote. The Populist convention endorsed Bryan but ran a separate candidate for vice president, Thomas E. Watson.

After this initial fusion, most Populists remained within the Democratic Party. The Populist Party remained in existence, running presidential candidates until 1908, but never received more than 0.8 percent of the POPULAR VOTE. The party did not expand its voter appeal beyond an agrarian reform movement, but many of its proposals, particularly in the areas of government and electoral reform, were espoused by progressive politicians in the early twentieth century and enacted into law.

After being absent from the political scene for nearly three-quarters of a century, the Populist Party revived in early 1984 to place former Olympic pole vaulter Bob Richards as a candidate on the presidential ballot in fourteen states. But the new, staunchly conservative version of the Populist Party was a polar ideological opposite of the old progressive People's Party. Backers of the new party advocated eliminating the Federal Reserve System, repealing the federal income tax, and protecting U.S. industry from imports. Richards received 66,336 votes nationally in 1984. In 1988 the Populists nominated David Duke—a former leader of the Ku Klux Klan, who received 47,047 votes nationwide.

In 1992 the Populist Party nominated former Green Beret commander James "Bo" Gritz for president and Cyril Minett for vice president. On the ballot as the America First Party in eighteen states, the Populists received 107,014 votes or 0.1 percent nationwide. Gritz performed especially well in the West, where he received 3.8 percent of the vote in Utah and 2.1 percent in Idaho.

The 1996 America First candidate, Ralph Forbes of Arkansas, received 932 votes. No America First or Populist presidential candidate appeared on the ballot of any state in 2000 or later.

> **More on this topic:**
>
> Greenback Party, p. 243

Postconvention Bounce

As a gigantic campaign rally that showcases the candidate in a favorable light, the NATIONAL PARTY CONVENTION often gives a "postconvention bounce" to the nominee's PUBLIC OPINION rating.

Occasionally the bounce is enough to leapfrog the lagging nominee's popularity over that of the preconvention leader. More often, however, the candidate who led in the final Gallup poll before the convention is the one who wins the presidential election. (See POLLING.)

The problem that a candidate faces is maintaining any momentum he or she might have built during the convention, when the visage and message dominate the national political scene for a week. This is especially problematic for the candidate of the party that does not currently hold the

The Democratic National Convention in July 2004 failed to deliver much momentum for candidate John Kerry. After the Republican National Convention in September, President Bush enjoyed a significant lead in the polls.

Source: CQ Photo/Scott J. Ferrell

White House. By a long-standing tradition, the "out" party holds its convention first, with the "in" party going second with the opportunity to respond to what transpired in the earlier convention.

That tradition was especially a factor in 2004, when President George W. Bush defended the White House for the Republicans against Democratic nominee John Kerry. In a clever scheduling stratagem, the Republicans slated their convention in New York City for August 30 through September 2, just after the end of the heavily televised Summer Olympic Games. To avoid conflicting with the sports spectacle, the Democrats held their convention in Boston from July 26 to 29.

Kerry, despite what most media observers described as a largely successful convention, had a negligible postconvention bounce, if any, that left him no better than even with Bush in most polls. But the five-week gap between the Democratic and Republican conventions turned into a political chasm. Kerry's decision to take a vacation in August instead of sustaining his campaign efforts robbed him of any momentum he might have had. His failure to respond aggressively to fiercely negative ads, mostly run by Republican Party organizations and allied outside groups, hurt him. And the Republicans had more than a month to plan a convention that responded scathingly to everything Kerry and the Democrats had claimed in Boston, while glorifying Bush.

The disparity enabled Bush to break away to a lead of double-digit percentages in some polls in September. Kerry's steadier campaign down the stretch and Bush's own waning job approval ratings made the race close at the end, but the Democrat's postconvention stumbles were never overcome completely.

From 1948 to 2000, ten of the fourteen preconvention FRONT-RUNNERS went on to win. In the first exception, President Harry S. Truman came from behind to defeat Republican governor Thomas E. Dewey of New York by 5 percentage points. Dewey had been 11 percentage points ahead before the 1948 party conventions.

Dewey's election had been so expected that beforehand *Life* magazine captioned his picture "the next president," and on ELECTION DAY the *Chicago Daily Tribune* rushed into print with a "Dewey Defeats Truman" headline. Truman gleefully held up the front page the next day for a famous news photograph.

In 1988, Vice President George H. W. Bush rebounded from a six-point ratings deficit to an eight-point victory over Democratic governor Michael S. Dukakis of Massachusetts.

As president in 1992, Bush was the preconvention poll leader by five points. But Democratic governor Bill Clinton of Arkansas, who had been in third place behind Bush and independent Ross Perot of Texas, rebounded to win in November by six points over Bush and twenty-one points over Perot.

In 2000, Texas governor George W. Bush led Vice President Al Gore in preconvention polls, with a Gallup poll showing him up by 11 percent just before the conventions. Gore's postconvention bounce left him roughly even to Bush in the polls, and the two remained locked in a close contest with Bush eventually winning the election but trailing in the popular vote. (See ELECTORAL ANOMALIES.)

In 2008, Democrat Barack Obama received little bounce after his party's convention, but his opponent, Arizona Sen. John McCain did. Fueled to some extent by the unexpected selection of Alaska Gov. Sarah Palin, who was quickly endorsed by conservative GOP voters, McCain briefly held a lead over Obama as the campaign began in September. But the bounce did not last and in November McCain lost to Obama by more than seven percentage points.

Precinct *See* DISTRICTS, WARDS, AND PRECINCTS.

President, Nominating and Electing

The election of a U.S. president is always costly, often rancorous, sometimes messy, seldom boring. The system is perhaps more complicated than it needs to be, but it has worked with few major repairs for more than 200 years, generally satisfying the citizenry and meeting the nation's changing needs.

The election occurs every four years and permits the peaceful transfer of power or continuation of the status quo for four more years, no matter how bitter or divisive the campaign that preceded it. Indeed, the American electoral system differs from those of other nations and, for all its flaws, is the envy of many other countries. (See INTERNATIONAL AND U.S. ELECTIONS COMPARED.)

That does not mean, though, that the process is static. NATIONAL PARTY CONVENTIONS, which played the decisive role in choosing presidential nominees from early in the nineteenth century until past the midpoint of the twentieth, have been supplanted more recently by a proliferation of primaries and party caucuses in which rank-and-file voters make the decisions for the parties. Long a deliberative process that took months in the presidential election year to unfold, the presidential nominating process has been accelerated greatly by the trend of scheduling primaries and caucuses earlier in the year, a practice known as FRONT-LOADING. The wide-open 2008 contests in both parties to succeed term-limited Republican incumbent George W. Bush spurred twenty or more Democrats and Republicans combined to launch or explore candidacies by the earliest part of 2007.

As the nation and the electorate have grown and technology has evolved, presidential elections have become more expensive, jumping from a then-stunning estimated $700 million in 1996 to widespread predictions of a $2 billion campaign in 2008. This escalation has occurred despite the myriad CAMPAIGN FINANCE reforms enacted since the 1970s to avoid corruption and reduce the influence of special interests. The proven ability of top-tier candidates to raise huge amounts of money has since 2000 spurred an increasing number of them to opt out of the PUBLIC FINANCING system—at least for the nominating campaigns. Created under a 1974 campaign finance law, the system guarantees tens of millions of dollars in public funds but comes with spending limitations not faced by candidates who raise their money on their own.

On the positive side, presidential nominations have become more open and representative of the voters at large. Party bosses no longer dictate the choice of nominees.

As televised spectaculars, the conventions remain important to the parties' public relations efforts during the intense weeks before the November election. Although ratings have dropped in recent years, the millions who watch the conventions on television are too big an audience for the parties to ignore, and they do not. With expert advice, they have streamlined the proceedings to showcase their nominees in prime time as the countdown to ELECTION DAY begins.

The confident nostrum that anyone in the United States can grow up to be president has been true in theory rather than practice. Through the 2004 election, all presidents were white, non-Hispanic men. All but one—Democrat John F. Kennedy, a Roman Catholic elected in 1960—were Protestants. Though thirty-five is the minimum age to serve as president, Kennedy (at forty-three) was the youngest at his election. Republican Ronald Reagan, elected in 1984 for a second four-year term at age seventy-three, was the eldest.

But the erosion of barriers and prejudices was broken in 2008 when Democrats nominated and voters elected an African American, Barack Obama, as president. Moreover, his principal opponent for the nomination was a woman, Hillary Rodham Clinton, then a New York senator and formerly first lady during Bill Clinton's two terms in the White House. Although Obama, at forty-seven when elected, reinforced the image of youth in candidates, the Republicans that year selected Arizona senator John McCain, who turned seventy-two in August 2008, two months before the election. In addition, other GOP candidates challenged past stereotypes. One was Mitt Romney, a Mormon, and Rudolph Giuliani, who had been married three times. In the middle of 2011 as the 2012 election campaign was under way, Romney was again one of the leading GOP candidates.

With President George W. Bush's second term drawing to a close, more than twenty Democrats and Republicans chose to announce their candidacies or form exploratory committees by the beginning of 2007. Here, Bush leaves the White House in October 2006 on a campaign trip in advance of the midterm elections.

Source: AP Images/Ron Edmonds

In these final campaign stages, today's nominees usually keep intact the organizations they built to help them survive the primaries. These increasingly professional organizations are made up of the candidate, his or her family, a hand-picked candidate for VICE PRESIDENT (also known as the RUNNING MATE), POLLING and POLITICAL CONSULTANTS, MEDIA COVERAGE and MEDIA USE consultants, fundraisers, issue advisers, schedulers, advance persons, and others. CAMPAIGN STRATEGIES must be managed carefully if a candidate is to move successfully through the primary season, the nominating conventions, and the general election campaign.

Who Runs for President

Candidates for president and vice president must meet the same few constitutional requirements. They must be at least thirty-five years old and natural-born citizens who have "been 14 years a Resident within the United States." (See PRESIDENT, QUALIFICATIONS; VICE PRESIDENT.)

Another requirement, one that affects few people, is that the candidate must *not* have been elected president twice before. The Twenty-second Amendment, ratified in 1951, limits presidents to two four-year terms. A vice president who succeeds to the presidency and serves more than two years of the predecessor's unexpired term may be elected president only once. Franklin D. Roosevelt, whose breaking of the two-term tradition prompted the term limitation, is the only president who served more than eight years. He died in 1945, less than three months into his fourth term.

There are politically ambitious people who view themselves from a very early age as someday occupying the White House and, so the old joke goes, see the president of the United States staring back at them whenever they look in the mirror.

Yet the decision to seek the presidency is a difficult one. The candidates must make complicated calculations about financial and time requirements. They must sort out the tangle of party and state rules and the makeup of the electorate in each state. They must assess their own ability to attract endorsements, recruit a competent staff, and develop an "image" suitable for media presentation. They must also consider the effect a campaign will have on their families, the psychological demands of the office, and possible revelations about their personal lives that might hinder a campaign.

By early March 2007, with the first voting on the nomination still months away in January 2008, at least five Democrats had taken themselves out of the running—including Massachusetts senator John Kerry, the party's 2004 presidential nominee; and retiring Republican senator Bill Frist of Tennessee, the former Senate majority leader. Former Iowa Democratic governor Tom Vilsack, who entered the race in November 2006, dropped out by February, citing insufficient campaign funds.

The 1996 election provided another example of such considerations. Polls showed that the popularity of retired general Colin L. Powell, who had been the first African American to head the Joint Chiefs of Staff, would have been a strong contender for the Republican presidential nomination. He declined to seek it, however, saying he had promised his wife he would not run for public office (though he later would serve as secretary of state under President George W. Bush).

There are several stages in an election, especially a presidential election. The first, for any office, is the exploratory stage. Since 1976, when Jimmy Carter won the presidency after a two-year campaign, candidates have tended to announce their intentions well ahead of the election, in part to have time to build a strong public profile and in part because early fund-raising can be crucial to a campaign.

Before announcing, candidates routinely establish an exploratory committee to help test the waters for a campaign. The exploratory advisers identify likely opponents and consider funding prospects and other preliminary factors, and if conditions appear favorable, the committee may form the nucleus of the candidate's campaign organization.

The Primary and Caucus Schedule

If a candidate decides to seek a major-party nomination, the next step is to enter the primaries and caucuses in which DEMOCRATIC and REPUBLICAN party members select DELEGATES to their national conventions. The states and the parties have a wide variety of rules for BALLOT ACCESS qualifications and allocation of delegates. Candidates must follow legal requirements to qualify for state contests, and they also have to adapt their campaign strategies to each state's particular circumstances.

The complexity can be daunting. Colorado representative Patricia Schroeder cited the complexity of state rules as a major factor in her decision not to seek the Democratic presidential nomination in 1988. Independent Ross Perot made it a condition of his 1992 candidacy that his supporters obtain enough signatures to get his name on the ballot in all fifty states. They succeeded.

For many presidential election cycles, the IOWA CAUCUS and the NEW HAMPSHIRE PRIMARY are the first delegate-selection events, giving two of the nation's least-populous states extraordinary influence over the selection process. Critics, however, complained that the system is unrepresentative because both states are largely rural, with mainly white, Anglo-Saxon, Protestant populations that lack the diversity of the Democratic Party electorate and the country as a whole.

In 1992 Democrat Bill Clinton became the first candidate since 1952 to win the presidency without winning the New Hampshire primary. Traditionally, the Iowa caucus and the New Hampshire primary have been the first delegate-selection events.
Source: William J. Clinton Presidential Library

Fierce resistance to change from Iowa and New Hampshire officials, who threatened to oppose presidential candidates who supported threats to their primacy, led to reluctance among national party officials to tamper with the process. Under continued pressure from other states, however, the DEMOCRATIC NATIONAL COMMITTEE decided to introduce two new very early events to provide more variety in the 2008 campaign: caucuses in Nevada in between the Iowa and New Hampshire events and a primary in South Carolina after the New Hampshire vote.

But the biggest threat to the traditional role of Iowa and New Hampshire came from the front-loading of the primary and caucus schedule, practiced by states competing with each other for more influence over the choices of party nominees. Moves by some of the nation's most populous states, including California, New York, Florida, and Illinois, to push their primaries up to just days after New Hampshire's appeared likely to cause some, if not most, candidates to shift resources to those states. In 2008 two states—Michigan and Florida—even moved their primaries into January in violation of party rules. Both states were threatened with loss of delegate seats at the conventions but the controversy was resolved before the parties met and delegates were seated.

PUBLIC FINANCING is available for primary campaigns, but only if the candidate raises $5,000 in matchable contributions from individuals (POLITICAL ACTION COMMITTEE contributions do not qualify) in each of twenty states. The federal government will match up to $250 of each individual contribution, even if that contribution was larger (up to the legal limit of $2,300 per candidate per election in place for the 2007–2008 election cycle).

The front-loading phenomenon has tended to speed up the winnowing effect on the fields of candidates as those who do not perform as well as expected typically withdraw. Even though convention delegates are typically meted out on the basis of PROPORTIONAL REPRESENTATION, at least to candidates meeting a threshold that in most states is 15 percent of the total vote, the candidates who emerge from the earliest contests as each party's FRONT-RUNNER almost always gain unstoppable momentum. Party nominations usually not settled until the latest primaries in June if not at the summer conventions are now most often wrapped up by early March.

The Presidential Nomination

The primary season culminates in the two national party conventions. These events usually were held in late July or August, but one or both parties have held off until later in the summer in several recent election years. The 1996 Democratic convention in Chicago was held in late August; the 2004 Republican convention in New York City carried over to the first days of September. For 2008, the parties took the unusual action of scheduling their conventions back to back, with the Democrats meeting in Denver during the last week in August and the Republicans in St. Paul, Minnesota, in the first week of September.

At these conventions, attended by thousands of delegates and even more guests and reporters, the presidential and vice presidential nominees are formally selected and a party PLATFORM, setting out the party's goals for the next four years, is approved. In recent elections, the convention also has become an important occasion for showcasing party unity after the sometimes divisive primary battles.

The first national convention was held in 1831, and for more than a century afterward state party leaders had the ultimate say in deciding who the presidential nominee would be. As direct primaries took hold in the twentieth century, this influence began to wane. Then in the 1970s and 1980s the Democrats initiated a series of PRESIDENTIAL SELECTION REFORMS that opened the nominating process. The reforms were expected to result in more open conventions, but instead they led to even more primaries.

Before the widespread use of primaries, the conventions were more competitive and frenetic than they are today. All the candidates still in the race had substantial campaign operations at the conventions. Campaign managers and strategists kept in close contact with state delegations. Candidates deployed floor leaders and "whips" to direct voting on the convention floor and to deal with any problems that arose among state delegations. In addition, "floaters" wandered the crowded floor in search of any signs of trouble. Floor leaders, whips, and floaters often wore specially colored clothing or caps so that they could be spotted easily on the convention floor.

This spectacle, however, has become a rarity at the conventions, leading a number of critics to brand them as nothing more than intricately staged "infomercials" for the parties and their candidates, with delegates relegated to the role of extras. It has been decades since either major party took more than one ballot to nominate a president.

Nominating speeches mark the beginning of the formal selection process. These remarks are usually followed by a series of short seconding speeches, and all of the speeches are accompanied by floor demonstrations staged by delegates supporting the candidate. For many years, a good deal of convention time was taken up by the nomination of FAVORITE SONS, candidates nominated by their own state's delegation in hopes of gaining leverage over the

In selecting Lyndon B. Johnson of Texas as his running mate, Democratic presidential candidate John F. Kennedy of Massachusetts broke with the tradition of geographically balancing the party ticket with an easterner and a midwesterner. Here they are campaigning in Austin, Texas, September 1960.

Source: LBJ Library Photo by Frank Muto

ultimate presidential nominating decision and perhaps the choice of the vice presidential candidates. Such nominations were seldom taken seriously, and since 1972 both parties have instituted rules that have effectively stopped them.

In recent years, the balloting for the presidential nominee has been anticlimactic. More attention focuses on whom the presidential nominee will select as a running mate. Even then, much of the suspense has been removed because the leading presidential candidates may have named their running mates before the convention begins.

With the young, politically moderate, all-southern ticket of Bill Clinton and Al Gore in 1992 an obvious exception, the choice of the vice presidential candidate often has been motivated by an effort to balance the ticket geographically. For years, a balanced ticket was one that boasted an easterner and a midwesterner. More recently, the balance has shifted so that the split is more often between a northerner and a southerner. Some examples: Democrats John F. Kennedy of Massachusetts and Lyndon B. Johnson of Texas in 1960, Johnson and Hubert H. Humphrey of Minnesota in 1964, Jimmy Carter of Georgia and Walter F. Mondale of Minnesota in 1976, Al Gore of Tennessee and Joseph I. Lieberman of Connecticut in 2000, and John Kerry of Massachusetts and John Edwards of North Carolina in 2004.

In 2008, the Democratic nominee and eventual winner, Barack Obama of Illinois, selected long-time Delaware senator Joe Biden as his running mate. This selection was seen as a move by Obama to shore up his foreign policy credentials, which some critics thought were thin. Biden, a senator since 1973, had served on and as chairman of both the Senate Foreign Relations Committee and the Judiciary Committee.

Obama's opponent, Arizona senator John McCain, took a different route and selected little-known Alaska governor Sarah Palin, who quickly became a rallying point for the most conservative parts of the Republican Party.

The method for nominating the vice presidential candidate mirrors the procedure for presidential nominations. The climax of the convention then occurs with the two nominees' acceptance speeches and their first appearance together, with their families, on the podium, accompanied by raucous music, thunderous cheering from the delegates, and the familiar balloon drops.

General Election Campaign

The traditional opening of the presidential election campaign is Labor Day, just two months before the general election on the first Tuesday after the first Monday in November. In reality, the campaigns are well under way months earlier, especially since the candidates almost always are settled by early in the year.

The campaign organization for the general election is usually an extension of the nomination organization, and it is separate from the national and state party organizations. Nominees typically have the prerogative of naming their party's national committee chairpersons to help coordinate the campaign.

President Richard Nixon makes a campaign stop while running for reelection in 1972. Though he made stops in every state during his 1960 campaign, Nixon lost that election to John F. Kennedy.

Source: National Archives and Records Administration/Richard Nixon Library

From the mid-1970s, following the fund-raising excesses of President Richard M. Nixon's 1972 reelection campaign that contributed to his downfall in the Watergate scandal, through the 1996 election, both major party candidates in each election subscribed to the public financing system, under which taxpayer dollars were transferred to the nominees' campaigns by the FEDERAL ELECTION COMMISSION (FEC). In 1996, the Clinton and Dole campaigns each received $61.8 million from the FEC. Neither party, however, lived within that income. Both raised millions of dollars in unlimited SOFT MONEY for party activities that indirectly supported the nominees' campaigns.

But the formidable fund-raising machine built by George W. Bush in the run-up to the 2000 campaign persuaded him and his advisers to take the political risk of forgoing public funds for the primaries to build a much bigger campaign treasury of his own. Bush's success at this strategy soon made it the virtual rule for front-running candidates rather than the exception. In the run-up to the 2008 campaign, some leading candidates suggested they might eschew public financing for the general election as well. Obama did not take the public funding but McCain did, $84.1 million.

Even in the years when public financing was in full force, it fell far short of providing the full picture. The national parties ran their own full-scale campaign efforts on their candidates' behalf, and their heavy reliance on large unlimited soft money contributions caused controversy that ultimately produced the Bipartisan Campaign Reform Act (BCRA) of 2002, which barred soft money donations to national party committees. Even the enactment of BCRA did little to limit the growth of well-funded outside political action committees that cumulatively spent hundreds of millions of dollars in "independent expenditures" seeking to influence the outcomes of the elections.

INCUMBENCY gives a president running for reelection inherent advantages that may tilt the balance in his favor. The incumbent already has the stature of the presidency and is able to influence MEDIA COVERAGE with official presidential actions and to use pork-barrel politics—the practice of directing government spending in a way that benefits specific constituencies—to lure voters. The president also benefits from the public's reluctance to reject a tested national leader for an unknown quantity.

In times of economic or foreign policy difficulties, however, the president's prominence can have negative effects on the campaign. Jimmy Carter's bid for a second term was plagued by both a sagging economy and the continued holding of U.S. citizens as hostages in Iran. In 1992, after achieving record-high approval ratings for success in the Gulf War, George H. W. Bush saw his reelection hopes dashed by an economic recession and the Democrats' emphasis on "it's the economy, stupid."

Postconvention strategies shift according to circumstances, but one element that usually remains intact is the decision about where to campaign. The winner-take-all ELECTORAL COLLEGE system, in which the leading vote-getter in a state wins all that state's electoral votes, encourages nominees to win as many populous states as possible rather than to build up strength in states where they are weak. Nominees generally spend most of their time in closely contested states, and just enough time in "likely win" states to ensure victory. Appearances in unfavorable states are usually symbolic efforts to show that the candidate is not conceding anything.

Competing in all regions of the country can be difficult. Richard Nixon in 1960 fulfilled his vow to make at least one campaign appearance in every state but lost the election. He might have won if he had spent more time in closely contested states such as Illinois and Missouri, and less time in states in which either Kennedy or he was heavily favored. In 1984, Democrat Walter F. Mondale and his running mate, Geraldine Ferraro, missed the opportunity to increase their support in northeastern states when they campaigned in the solidly Republican South and West.

In 2008, Obama ran an unusual national campaign in which he aggressively challenged in normally Republican states, such as Virginia, North Carolina, and Florida, all of which he won. He also campaigned in other normally Republican states, which required McCain's campaign to spend time and money defending areas that should have been GOP wins without much effort.

The ideological tone of the presidential campaign usually moderates once the parties have determined their nominees. To win the nomination, Democrats must appeal to the more liberal sections of their party and Republicans to the more conservative sections of theirs. But during the general election campaign, the nominees must try not only to unify their parties but also to attract independents and voters from the other party. The candidates usually can depend on the support of the most ideological members of their own party, so they are able to shift their sights in the fall.

The exceptions come when a third-party candidate appeals to the conservative or liberal elements of one or both parties or when a major-party nominee has suffered a bruising nomination battle and must persuade the backers of the defeated candidates to go to the polls. (See THIRD PARTIES.)

Whether to highlight specific issue stances or adopt a "fuzzy" ideological stance is a major question in every campaign. Campaign consultants often advise against being too specific. Mondale's attempt to be frank in 1984 by saying that taxes would have to be raised to address the federal deficit whether he or President Reagan were elected shows both the opportunity and the risk of adopting a specific position. For a while, the statement put Reagan, who presided over historic budget deficits, on the defensive. But Mondale's strategy backfired when Reagan regained the offensive and charged Democrats with fiscal and taxing irresponsibility.

Campaign debates between the presidential and the vice presidential candidates have been a mainstay of the fall election campaign since 1976. Although political pundits are quick to declare a winner at the end of each debate, most debates have not fundamentally changed the voters' perceptions of the candidates.

All of the campaign hoopla culminates on election day, when Americans go to the polls. Though turnout had lagged for many years, an uptick occurred in the early part of the twenty-first century, with more than 122 million voters participating in the 2004 presidential election and 131.3 million four years later.

Although ballots are tallied electronically in most parts of the United States, the major television networks have developed ways to make their own counts of the election in all states and report the results as soon as they come in. In 1980 the three broadcast networks declared Ronald Reagan the winner before the polls had closed on the West Coast. President Carter then publicly conceded defeat. This spurred complaints that the premature announcement discouraged westerners from voting and may have affected the races for members of Congress and state and local officials. Since then, the networks have refrained from announcing a winner until all the polls have closed.

Electoral College

Even though the winner has declared victory and the loser conceded defeat, at least two more steps must be taken before a president-elect is officially declared. The first occurs on the first Monday after the second Wednesday in December. That is the day on which electors are scheduled to meet in their respective state capitals to cast their votes for president (though after each election, several states usually have their electors meet on a different date without any penalty or repercussion).

Each state has as many electors as it has members of Congress (the District of Columbia, which has no full congressional representatives, was granted three electoral votes by the Twenty-third Amendment ratified in 1961). Typically, slates of electors are pledged before the popular election to each of the presidential nominees. The presidential nominee who wins the state wins that state's electors. There have been several instances in which "faithless electors" did not vote for their party's nominee. In none of these cases, however, did the faithless electors change the outcome.

The second step occurs when the electors' ballots are opened and counted before a joint session of Congress in early January. The candidate who wins a majority of the vote is declared the president-elect and is inaugurated three weeks later on January 20.

In the rare event that no presidential candidate receives a majority of the Electoral College vote—something that has not happened since the 1876 election—the election is thrown into the House of Representatives. If no vice presidential candidate receives a majority of the Electoral College vote, the Senate is called upon to make the selection.

Term of Office

A president's term begins with inauguration at noon on January 20 following the November election (by tradition, the inauguration is delayed until the next day if January 20 falls on a Sunday). Until the Twentieth Amendment was ratified in 1933, presidents were not inaugurated until March 4, leaving a four-month hiatus between the election and the inauguration. The briefer interval established by the so-called lame-duck amendment shortened the period in which the nation had, in effect, two presidents—the outgoing president and an incoming president-elect. Yet the amendment allowed time for an orderly transition between the old and the new administrations.

The Twentieth Amendment took effect in 1933 after President Franklin Roosevelt and Vice President John Nance Garner had been sworn in. In 1937, at the beginning of their second terms, they became the first president and vice president inaugurated on January 20.

Whether by tradition, TERM LIMITS, or voter action, turnover of administrations is characteristic of the U.S. presidential election system. Of the forty-two men from George Washington through George W. Bush, only twenty have served more than four years. Of those, only Franklin Roosevelt served more than two full terms, for a total of slightly more than twelve years. As of mid-2011, twelve presidents served one full term, ten served less than a full term, twelve served two full terms, and seven served for more than four years but less than eight years. Barack Obama is not included in these numbers.

Grover Cleveland is the only president ever elected to two nonconsecutive terms. Cleveland won the elections of 1884 and 1892.

Source: Library of Congress

Bush was the forty-third president because one man, Grover Cleveland, is counted twice. Cleveland, elected in 1884, defeated in 1888, and elected again in 1892, is the only president who served two nonconsecutive terms. Obama is the forty-fourth president.

There have been two father-son combinations among those forty-three presidents: John Adams (1797–1801) and John Quincy Adams (1825–1829) and George H. W. Bush (1989–1993) and George W. Bush (2001–2009). The proximity of the latter pair's presidencies led some observers to distinguish them by their rankings in the order of presidents: Bush 41 and Bush 43.

The Constitution as originally written in 1787 contained no limit on reelection of presidents. George Washington stepped down from the presidency voluntarily after two terms, saying in his farewell address that he had done so not as a matter of principle but because he longed for "the shade of retirement."

Thomas Jefferson was the first president to argue that no president should serve more than two terms. "If some termination to the services of the Chief Magistrate be not fixed by the Constitution, or supplied by practice, his office . . . will in fact become for life, and history shows how easily that degenerates into an inheritance," Jefferson wrote to the Vermont state legislature in 1807, declining its request that he run for a third term.

Jefferson's defense of a two-term limit took root quickly. Indeed, the WHIG PARTY and many Democrats soon argued for a one-term limit. Andrew Jackson was the last president until Abraham Lincoln to be elected to two terms, and even Jackson said he would prefer a constitutional amendment barring more than one six-year presidential term.

Of the first thirty presidents—Washington to Herbert Hoover—seventeen served one term or less (not including Cleveland's separate terms), though five of them died while in office. The issue of a third term arose only occasionally, and only one president, Franklin D. Roosevelt, actually pursued one.

As early as 1937, Roosevelt announced that he did not plan to seek a third term in 1940. But as his second term wore on, he became increasingly frustrated by congressional resistance to his policies and programs. In 1939 World War II broke out in Europe, and there was little hope that the United States would be able to remain aloof from the fray. Waiting until the Democratic convention in July 1940, Roosevelt finally signaled his willingness to be renominated. The delegates overwhelmingly approved.

Polls showed that the public was deeply divided over the propriety of Roosevelt's candidacy. Republicans took up the CAMPAIGN SLOGAN "no third term" on behalf of their nominee, Wendell L. Willkie. Roosevelt won the election, but his POPULAR VOTE margin was 5 million, compared with 11 million in 1936.

In 1944, with the United States and its allies nearing victory in the war, Roosevelt won his fourth term, this time by 3 million votes. He was ill at the time and died less than three months after the inauguration.

In a move led by Republicans who had been on the wrong end of Roosevelt's unprecedented success, the Twenty-second Amendment, ratified in 1951, barred presidents from being elected to more than two terms. A president who moved up from vice president to fill a vacancy could run for president twice, but only once if the unexpired term was more than two years. Some Republicans came to regret this amendment, though, when it prevented popular president Ronald Reagan from seeking a third term, if he had so desired, in 1988.

President, Qualifications

To be the president or VICE PRESIDENT of the United States, a person must meet only the few qualifications set forth in the Constitution. The occupant of either office must be at least thirty-five years old, be a native-born U.S. citizen, and have lived in the United States for fourteen years.

As a practical matter, however, the constitutional qualifications in Article II, section 1, have proven to be the least of what it takes to be elected to the nation's highest offices. The voters are the ultimate judges, and they typically measure presidential candidates and RUNNING MATES by their political skills, speaking ability, moral character, leadership qualities, physical appearance, and other yardsticks not found in any law or constitutional provision.

At first the framers of the Constitution did not think it necessary to spell out qualifications for the presidency. They assumed that Congress would select the president, and that anyone it chose would at least meet the minimal age, citizenship, and residency requirements for service in the House of Representatives or the Senate.

But as the DELEGATES settled on the idea of having an ELECTORAL COLLEGE elect the president and vice president, the need to specify the qualifications became apparent. The states would choose the electors, and there was no guarantee that so diverse a group would be mindful of the basic standards that the delegates thought the electors should apply. Accordingly, the Constitutional Convention's Committee on Postponed Matters proposed the presidential qualifications, and the convention unanimously approved them on September 7, 1787. The qualifications specified were basically like those for representatives and senators, but with a higher minimum age and longer residency in the United States. (See HOUSE OF REPRESENTATIVES, QUALIFICATIONS; SENATE, QUALIFICATIONS.)

The framers had a reason for each of the presidential qualifications. Age was thought to ensure maturity and a record of personal and political accomplishment on which the electors could base their evaluations of the presidential candidates.

The fourteen-year residency requirement excluded British sympathizers who had fled to the country during the Revolution. And the exclusion of persons who were not born in America or were not citizens when the Constitution was adopted ensured that there would be no move to invite a foreign monarch to accept the presidency, as some feared might happen.

No separate qualifications for the vice presidency were listed in the original Constitution. Under the convention's system of selection, the vice president would be the candidate with the second-highest number of votes in the Electoral College. The delegates assumed, therefore, that the vice president would meet the specifications to be president.

The original system proved unworkable, however, and the Twelfth Amendment (1804) established the current practice of separate electoral voting for president and vice president. The amendment also specified that the vice president have the same qualifications as the chief executive.

For the most part, the age, citizenship, and residency requirements for the presidency have not seriously limited the voters' choices of qualified candidates. Few persons are likely to have the stature and political support needed for a credible run for the White House before they are in their mid-thirties.

Of the three restrictions, native-born citizenship is one that may have precluded the candidacy of otherwise highly qualified persons. For example, former secretary of state Henry A. Kissinger, who was born in Germany, was frequently mentioned as a U.S. citizen whose foreign birth ruled out a potentially strong candidacy. There was never any indication, however, that Kissinger would have run if he could.

In the early years of the twenty-first century, two states elected popular governors who some believed might be potentially strong presidential candidates, were they not enjoined from running because of their foreign birth: California Republican Arnold Schwarzenegger, a native of Austria, and Michigan Democrat Jennifer A. Granholm, who was born in Canada.

All of the early presidents were born as British subjects in the colonial period, but they qualified for the office because they were U.S. citizens in 1788 when the Constitution was ratified. Martin Van Buren, born in 1782, was the first president born after the United States declared its independence from Britain in 1776.

Age Factor

Most presidents have been considerably older than the minimum age of thirty-five, but two have taken office in their early forties. Theodore Roosevelt was the youngest, at forty-two when he succeeded the assassinated William McKinley in 1901. John F. Kennedy was the youngest when elected—forty-three in 1960; his assassination in November 1963, at age forty-six, also gave Kennedy the shortest lifespan of any president.

Through the 2008 election, Republican Ronald Reagan was the oldest president—sixty-nine when he was inaugurated in 1981 and seventy-seven when he left office in 1989. The next oldest, Dwight D. Eisenhower, was seventy when he was succeeded in 1961 by the much younger Kennedy. Had Bob Dole been elected in 1996, he would have exceeded Reagan's record; he was seventy-three when he won the Republican nomination for president. John McCain, the 2008 Republican presidential nominee, was seventy-two when his Democratic opponent was inaugurated in 2009. Bill Clinton was the first president born in the "baby boom" era, after World War II. Born in August 1946, he was forty-six when elected in 1992 and served to age fifty-four in January

Dwight D. Eisenhower was the second-oldest president, behind Ronald Reagan. Eisenhower was seventy when he was succeeded by the much younger John F. Kennedy.

Source: Library of Congress

CLOSER LOOK

The Twelfth Amendment, which requires that the president and vice president be residents of different states, received a rare public airing in 2000. George W. Bush, then governor of Texas, selected Dick Cheney, a former secretary of defense, to be his vice presidential running mate. Though born in Nebraska and raised in Wyoming, which he represented in the House from 1979 to 1989, Cheney at the time of Bush's decision was also a resident of Texas, where he was chief executive officer of Halliburton Corporation. But Cheney resigned his position and relocated to Wyoming. Legal challenges by Democratic activists that the Bush-Cheney ticket violated the Twelfth Amendment were unsuccessful.

2001. Republican George W. Bush—son of Clinton's predecessor as president, George H. W. Bush—was born in July 1946 and was fifty-four when he won the first of two presidential terms in 2000. Barack Obama, born in 1961, was forty-seven on taking office.

Geography

The Constitution as amended does impose somewhat of a geographic restriction on the president. The Twelfth Amendment requires the electors to "vote by ballot for President and Vice-President, one of whom, at least, shall not be an inhabitant of the same state with themselves." This language, similar to the wording it replaced, has the effect of preventing the election of a president and vice president from the same state.

Almost all of the forty-three men who have served as president—including Grover Cleveland, the only president to serve two nonconsecutive terms—have been elected from the Northeast (fifteen), the Midwest (twelve), and the South (fourteen). Several were born in one region but resided in another when elected. They include Herbert Hoover and Ronald Reagan, the only two presidents from the West (California). Hoover was born in Iowa, Reagan in Illinois. Richard Nixon, the only president born in California, was elected in 1968 and 1972 from New York, where he had moved to pursue a law practice after losing a 1962 bid for governor of California.

By birthplace, Virginia leads as the home of presidents (eight), followed closely by Ohio (seven). Of the thirteen presidents since Hoover, nine were born west of the Mississippi River and one—Obama—also outside the continental United States. He was born in Hawaii.

Three presidents have been elected from Texas, all since 1964. The only one who was Texas-born and raised was Democrat Lyndon B. Johnson, who had moved up from vice president upon the assassination of Kennedy a year earlier and was elected to a single full term in 1964. George H. W. Bush, vice president for eight years under Reagan and a native of Massachusetts, won a single full term in 1988. The younger Bush, born in Connecticut but raised in Texas, won in 2000 and 2004.

Backgrounds

In theory, anyone who meets the constitutional criteria can become president, and in fact several did rise from humble beginnings to attain the highest office. But as a practical matter, a person who becomes president must have demonstrated leadership qualities and political skills—not the least of which is the ability to win enough primaries and caucuses nationally to lock up the nomination of a major political party.

All presidents through the 2008 election were white males and, with one exception (the Catholic Kennedy), were Protestant. Most have been lawyers, generally from a large industrial state. Military or public service has been the usual path to the White House. Twenty presidents were governors of states or territories, including four of the past six (Democrats Jimmy Carter of Georgia and Clinton of Arkansas, and Republicans Reagan of California and George W. Bush of Texas). Twenty-five presidents served in either or both chambers of Congress. Fourteen were vice presidents and attained the presidency through death of the predecessor or election in their own right.

The only president to serve more than two terms was Franklin D. Roosevelt. He was elected to a fourth four-year term but died in office after being president for twelve years, thirty-nine days.

The Twenty-second Amendment, ratified in 1951, limited future presidents to two terms, consecutive or nonconsecutive. The amendment exempted Harry S.

Before he became president, Rutherford B. Hayes served as governor of Ohio. Twenty presidents were previously governors of states or territories, including four of the last six presidents.

Source: Library of Congress

Truman, elected in 1948 after serving out the remainder of FDR's term, but he declined to seek a second full term in 1952.

Although George Washington began the two-term tradition, Thomas Jefferson formalized it in 1807 with a letter explaining his rejection of a third term. Reflecting his view that the original Constitution should have had a term limit, Jefferson wrote that if the omission is not fixed by amendment or practice the office of presidency "will, in fact, become for life, and history shows how easily that degenerates into an inheritance."

In addition to the constitutional qualifications, presidents must meet a number of unwritten, informal requirements. Americans demand that their chief executive meet standards of political and managerial expertise as well as moral and social standing. Sometimes, however, the voters are willing to soften those demands if the candidate has compensating appeal. Voters regularly list foreign policy expertise as an important consideration, yet the only international experience several recent presidents have had was their efforts as governors to attract foreign trade to their states.

Divorce formerly was an unwritten bar to the presidency, but Ronald Reagan broke that barrier with his 1980 election. He was divorced and remarried at the time.

Failure to meet moral standards has been troublesome for recent would-be presidents. In 1987, former Colorado senator Gary Hart's front-runner status collapsed within a week after the appearance of newspaper reports alleging that he had committed adultery. Soon after, media reports that Sen. Joseph R. Biden Jr. of Delaware had plagiarized a law school paper and parts of campaign speeches led to his early exit from the campaign. But Bill Clinton overcame questions about his character to win the presidency in 1992 and reelection in 1996. (See SCANDALS.)

Oath of Office

Besides citizenship, age, and residency, the same section of the Constitution (Article II, section 1) sets one other requirement for the president. He or she must take an oath of office, pledging to uphold the law.

The section reads:

Before he enter on the Execution of his Office, he shall take the following Oath or Affirmation— "I do solemnly swear (or affirm) that I will faithfully execute the Office of President of the United States, and will to the best of my Ability, preserve, protect and defend the Constitution of the United States."

The words "so help me God" do not appear in the Constitution, but they have traditionally ended the oath. It is not clear which president began this practice; some scholars claim that George Washington was the first, while others say that Chester A. Arthur set the precedent in 1881.

Only Franklin Pierce in 1853 chose to affirm the oath rather than swear it. Believing that it was God's punishment that he and his wife survived a train wreck just weeks before his inauguration that took the life of their eleven-year-old son, Pierce declined to place his hand on a Bible.

Presidential Draft

Genuine drafts of unwilling presidential nominees are rare. They are rarer still—even nonexistent— in the era of hard-fought, expensive PRESIDENTIAL PRIMARIES that eliminate any candidate who is the least bit equivocal about wanting the nomination.

Before primaries replaced NATIONAL PARTY CONVENTIONS as the venue in which nominations are really won, presidential drafts were difficult but not impossible. In several instances, conventions deadlocked over the choice of nominee and turned to alternative candidates.

In 1884 Gen. William Tecumseh Sherman refused to be drafted as the Republicans' presidential nominee, stating, "I will not accept if nominated, and will not serve if elected."

Source: Library of Congress

Most of these, however, were not considered genuine drafts but rather involved known political figures who did not have to be heavily persuaded. In 1880, for example, the Republicans nominated Ohio representative James A. Garfield on the thirty-sixth ballot after the convention deadlocked over other candidates, including former president Ulysses S. Grant. Garfield protested against being considered, after remaining silent earlier, but his official humility only served to make him more attractive to the delegates whose votes he needed to win. Garfield won the presidency that November but was assassinated the following year by a crazed job seeker.

Often cited as the first bona fide draft was that of New York governor Horatio Seymour, chosen by the Democrats in 1868 after protracted balloting. Despite his having made clear earlier that he did not want the nomination, the tide turned toward Seymour on the twenty-second ballot. He rushed to the platform shouting, "Your candidate I cannot be!" Hustled off to a private club, Seymour responded to his nomination with tears streaming down his cheeks saying, "Pity me! Pity me!"

Since then there have been two other drafts of balky candidates: the Republicans' selection of Supreme Court justice Charles Evans Hughes to oppose Democratic incumbent Woodrow Wilson in 1916 and the Democrats' selection of Illinois governor Adlai E. Stevenson in 1952 to oppose Republican Dwight D. Eisenhower. Both Hughes and Stevenson lost the general election.

Stevenson's reluctant acceptance brought to mind Seymour's plea for consolation. Quoting Jesus, Stevenson said he asked the Almighty Father "to let this cup pass from me.... So, if this cup may not pass from me except I drink it, Thy will be done." Stevenson, of his own volition, ran for and secured the Democratic nomination in 1956, but he again lost to Eisenhower.

The most famous statement of presidential nonavailability came from Civil War general William Tecumseh Sherman, who wired the GOP convention in 1884: "I will not accept if nominated, and will not serve if elected." The passage of time has since amended those words to the cryptic: "If nominated I will not accept; if elected I will not serve"—in what has become known as a "Shermanesque" statement.

> **More on this topic:**
>
> *National Party Conventions, p. 347*
>
> *Presidential Primaries, p. 468*

Presidential Elections Chronology

The American system of presidential selection has evolved over the years with little guidance from the nation's founders. The Constitution contained no provisions for organizing political parties, for nominating candidates, or for campaigning for office. Furthermore, the original provision for balloting by the ELECTORAL COLLEGE was flawed and had to be superseded by the Twelfth Amendment in 1804. Following are brief descriptions of elections that proved to be pivotal in the evolution of presidential selection.

Election of 1789

In 1789, there was no formal nomination of candidates. It had been obvious since the close of the Constitutional Convention that George Washington—commander of the American forces in the Revolutionary War—would be president, even though he was not eager to serve. The only real question was who his vice president would be. Most Federalist leaders ultimately decided to support John Adams of Massachusetts.

Federalist leader Alexander Hamilton disliked Adams and so plotted to siphon votes away from him. He feared that Adams could become president because, under the Constitution as originally written, each member of the Electoral College was to vote for two persons, with no distinction between votes for president or vice president. Hamilton's strategy worked. When the electoral votes were counted, Washington had been elected president unanimously, with all

There was no formal nomination of candidates in 1789 because at the close of the Constitutional Convention it was obvious that George Washington, the Revolutionary War hero, would be elected president.

Source: Library of Congress

sixty-nine votes. As the next-highest vote getter, Adams became vice president with thirty-four electoral votes; the others were divided among several candidates.

The First Contest: 1796

Washington won a second term in 1792 but chose not to run again in 1796. With Washington out of the race, the United States witnessed its first partisan contest for president. Once again the defects of the Electoral College system were evident. It was still possible for the two top candidates to receive the same number of votes, which would throw the election into the House of Representatives. And again it was also possible that the candidate for vice president—through fluke or machination—could end up with the most votes and be elected president.

The two presidential candidates were Federalist John Adams and Democratic-Republican Thomas Jefferson of Virginia. Hamilton once again sought to thwart Adams's ambitions by urging northern electors to divide their votes between Adams and his RUNNING MATE, Thomas Pinckney of South Carolina. Because Adams was unpopular in the South, Hamilton expected that Pinckney would win more votes there and, with northern electors divided, would win the election.

Hamilton's plot backfired, however, when eighteen northern electors voted not for Pinckney but for other Federalist candidates. As a result, Adams was elected president with seventy-one electoral votes, and Thomas Jefferson was named vice president with sixty-eight votes. Pinckney came in third. Neither the Federalists nor the Democratic-Republicans seemed unduly concerned that the president and vice president were of opposing parties. Both sides felt that they had prevented the opposition from gaining total victory.

The Jefferson-Burr Contest: 1800

The election of 1800 was notable for two reasons. It was the first in which both parties used congressional caucuses to nominate candidates for their tickets, and it was the first presidential election to be decided in the House of Representatives.

The Federalists named Adams and Maj. Gen. Charles Cotesworth Pinckney, older brother of Thomas Pinckney, to their ticket. Jefferson and Aaron Burr of New York were the nominees of the DEMOCRATIC-REPUBLICAN PARTY. Hamilton again sought to use the defect of the Electoral College system to defeat Adams and give Pinckney the presidency. But when the votes were counted, it turned out that Jefferson and Burr were tied for first place. The election was thrown into the Federalist-controlled House of Representatives.

Some Federalists felt that Burr was the lesser of two evils and plotted to elect him president instead of Jefferson. Hamilton helped to squelch that idea, but thirty-six ballots were taken before Jefferson received a majority. The crisis—which could have fatally wounded the new nation by calling into question the legitimacy of the president—was over.

The near disaster led to the ratification of the Twelfth Amendment to the Constitution in June 1804. It called for electors to vote for president and vice president on separate ballots, thus eliminating the possibility of a tie between the principal candidate and his running mate.

The Death of King Caucus: 1824

With Jefferson's election, the FEDERALIST PARTY began to fade away, leaving only one party. That meant that nomination by the Democratic-Republican caucus, or King Caucus as it was known, was tantamount to election. But with the young nation's politics complicated by philosophical and regional differences, the one-party system could not endure.

In 1824 the Democratic-Republicans were still the only party, but several candidates within it were seeking the presidential nomination: Secretary of State John Quincy Adams, son of former president John Adams; Sen. Andrew Jackson of Tennessee; Secretary of War John C. Calhoun of South Carolina; House Speaker Henry Clay of Kentucky; and Secretary of the Treasury William H. Crawford of Georgia.

Crawford was the early leader, and it was assumed that he would win the nomination if a congressional caucus were held. For that reason, supporters of the other candidates refused to attend a caucus. When it was finally convened, only sixty-six members of Congress were present, virtually all of them Crawford supporters. Although Crawford was suffering from the debilitating effects of a stroke, he won the nomination. The other candidates immediately criticized the caucus as being unrepresentative of the party and refused to abide by its results.

That incident put an end to the CAUCUS as a mechanism for naming presidential nominees. But it did not end the drama of the 1824 election. Calhoun dropped his race to join forces with Crawford, but Adams, Clay, and Jackson all continued to campaign. When none of the four received a majority of the electoral votes, the names of the top three candidates—Jackson, Adams, and Crawford—were placed before the House. Clay, who came in fourth, helped tip the balance when he announced that he would support Adams. Adams narrowly won the House election, even though Jackson had won the most popular votes and the most electoral votes. Rumor had it that Adams had promised to name Clay secretary of state, as in fact he did. The events of 1824 kindled the flame of popular democracy and set the stage for a rematch between Adams and Jackson in 1828.

The 1824 election has another distinction: the tenth presidential election in U.S. history, it is the first for which reliable popular vote data are available.

Jackson's Rise: 1828

Between the first election in 1789 and the tenth in 1824, Virginia had earned the nickname "cradle of the presidency." Except for the four-year tenures of John Adams (1797–1801) and John Quincy Adams (1825–1829), Virginia was the home of all the presidents during those formative years: Washington (1789–1797), Jefferson (1801–1809), James Madison (1809–1817), and James Monroe (1817–1825). The hold of this so-called Virginia dynasty on U.S. politics was loosened in 1828 when Tennessean Andrew Jackson—who had broad appeal among farmers and common laborers, especially in the West—won an easy victory. As the nation expanded economically and geographically, Jackson's appeal for democratic processes to replace elite maneuverings was bound to receive a sympathetic hearing.

It was during the Jackson era that the Democratic-Republican Party became known simply as the DEMOCRATIC PARTY. Under the tutelage of Vice President Martin Van Buren of New York, Jackson developed a strong national Democratic Party based on patronage. Strict party organization soon became a prerequisite for competition in national politics.

The Fateful Election of 1860

Jackson, who maintained the tradition of retiring after two terms rather than running for a third term in 1836, would be the nation's last unifying figure for many years. The rapid growth in both population and physical size of the United States as the nation's frontier pushed inexorably to the Pacific Ocean and the Rio Grande created new constituencies and tensions between industrial and agricultural regions, whose values and economies clashed most prominently over the issue of slavery as the nation headed toward civil war between the North and the South.

In the midst of this instability, the nation would have eight consecutive one-term presidents, including Whigs William Henry Harrison (1841) and Zachary Taylor (1849–1850), both of whom died in office. The others were Democrat Martin Van Buren (1837–1841), Whig John Tyler (Harrison's vice president and successor, 1841–1845), Democrat James K. Polk (1845–1849), Whig

After Illinois Republican Abraham Lincoln won the 1860 presidential election, seven southern states seceded from the Union and formed the Confederate States of America.

Source: Library of Congress

Millard Fillmore (Taylor's vice president and successor, 1850–1853), Democrat Franklin Pierce (1853–1857) and Democrat James Buchanan (1857–1861).

The regional differences that had torn the nation apart for decades reached their peak in 1860. Four major candidates sought the presidency. None could compete seriously throughout the nation, and it was probable that a candidate from the North would win because that region had the most electoral votes.

The two northern candidates were Abraham Lincoln, a former U.S. representative from Illinois, and Stephen Douglas, a Democrat who had defeated Lincoln in Illinois's 1858 election for the U.S. Senate. Southern Democrats who had defected from the party nominated Vice President John Breckinridge of Kentucky as their candidate for president. The CONSTITUTIONAL UNION PARTY—which developed as an attempt, although an unsuccessful one, to ameliorate the nation's geographic divisions by essentially setting aside its most contentious issues—nominated John Bell of Tennessee.

Lincoln was the consensus compromise choice of the REPUBLICAN PARTY, which had developed in the 1850s out of disgruntled elements from several parties. Above all else, the Republicans stood against the extension of slavery into new territories. By accepting slavery where it already existed but warning against nationalization of the system, the Republicans divided the Democrats and picked up support from an array of otherwise contentious factions—abolitionists, moderate abolitionists, and whites who feared for their position in the economy.

Lincoln took a plurality of 40 percent of the POPULAR VOTE, but easily won the election with 180 electoral votes. Although Douglas came in second with the electorate, winning 29.5 percent, he won only 12 electoral votes; Breckinridge received 72, and Bell, 39.

Southerners had vowed to secede from the Union if Lincoln won the presidency. After the election, South Carolina seceded, and Mississippi, Florida, Alabama, Georgia, Louisiana, and Texas followed suit. In February 1861, they formed the Confederate States of America. After a protracted standoff between Union soldiers who held Fort Sumter in the harbor off Charleston, South Carolina, and the Confederate soldiers who controlled the state, the Confederates fired on the fort and started the Civil War. Virginia, Arkansas, North Carolina, and Tennessee then joined the Confederacy.

It took four years of brutal fighting before the conflict ended with the surrender by the Confederacy in April 1865. Days later while attending the theater in Washington, D.C., Lincoln was assassinated by John Wilkes Booth, an actor and Confederate sympathizer.

The vice president who moved up to succeed Lincoln, Democrat Andrew Johnson of Tennessee, was regarded by the Radical Republicans who controlled Congress as too sympathetic to the South. The House ultimately impeached him for abuse of authority, and he barely avoided conviction in a Senate trial.

Republicans maintained control of the White House in 1868, with Gen. Ulysses S. Grant, who had led the Union forces and accepted Confederate general Robert E. Lee's surrender, as their nominee. Grant was reelected in 1872, even though his party had been tainted by corruption scandals.

The Compromise of 1876

Little more than ten years after the Civil War ended, disputed election results in the contest between Republican Rutherford B. Hayes and Democrat Samuel J. Tilden created a constitutional crisis and raised fears that another civil war was imminent. Hayes, the three-time governor of Ohio, lost the popular vote and had a questionable hold on the electoral vote, but he managed to win the presidency when the election was settled by a special commission created by Congress. (Hayes won 4.0 million votes to Tilden's 4.3 million.)

The problem arose when the vote tallies in Florida, South Carolina, and Louisiana were called into question. There was good reason to be suspicious of any vote count in these and other southern states. Although the Republicans controlled the balloting places under the postwar policy known as Reconstruction and mounted vigorous drives to get newly enfranchised blacks to the polls, the Democrats used physical intimidation and bribery to keep blacks away.

When state election board recounts and investigations did not settle the issue, Congress appointed a commission composed of five senators, five representatives, and five Supreme Court justices; eight commission members were Republican, seven Democratic. The crisis was resolved after weeks of bargaining that gave the Republicans the presidency in exchange for a pledge to pull federal troops out of the states of the former Confederacy and to commit federal money to making internal improvements in the South.

The compromise did more than settle the partisan dispute between Hayes and Tilden; it also established a rigid alignment of political interests that would dominate U.S. politics for the next half century. Although Democrats won occasional victories, the Republican, eastern, conservative, business-oriented establishment held sway over the system until Franklin Roosevelt's election in 1932. At the same time, southern politics was left in the hands of many of the same figures who led or, later, honored the Confederacy. Within months, southern states were erecting a powerful edifice of racial discrimination and barriers to black voting rights that would last until the 1960s.

The Lone Man of the House: 1880

In 1880, Ohio Republican and representative James A. Garfield became the only president to be elected while serving in the House of Representatives. A compromise candidate, Garfield, who had supported harsh Reconstruction policies, won the electoral vote despite losing every state in the South. He was the second president to be assassinated; shot by Charles Guiteau, a frustrated federal job seeker, in July 1881, he died in September. Vice President Chester A. Arthur succeeded him, but he was not nominated by the Republican Party in the 1884 election, which was won by New York Democrat Grover Cleveland. Cleveland lost to Indiana Republican Benjamin Harrison in 1888 but won a rematch in 1892, making him the only president elected to nonconsecutive terms.

The Rise of Progressivism: 1900

Ohio Republican William McKinley was elected president in 1896, succeeding Cleveland. McKinley was renominated in 1900 and replaced little-remembered Garret A. Hobart as his vice presidential running mate with New York's Theodore Roosevelt—a change that would have major historical consequences. The McKinley-Roosevelt ticket was elected in 1900 over a Democratic ticket headed by Nebraska Democrat William Jennings Bryan, who had also lost to McKinley in 1896. But McKinley was shot by leftist political extremist Leon Czolgosz in Buffalo, New York, in September 1901 and died a week later. Forty-two-year-old Roosevelt, still the youngest man to become president, took the nation in a sharply different direction associated with the era's Progressive movement, cracking down on business monopolies, taking an early lead on environmental conservation, and making mainly symbolic attempts to address the unequal status of blacks in post-Reconstruction America.

President William McKinley replaced his original vice presidential running mate with Theodore Roosevelt. This choice would have a major impact on history: When McKinley was assassinated less than eight months into his second term, Roosevelt rose to the presidency.
Source: Library of Congress

Although a number of pro-business Republicans expressed discomfort with Roosevelt's agenda, his stances and ebullient personality earned him a landslide election victory in 1904. Roosevelt stepped aside in 1908 and strongly endorsed his vice president, William Howard Taft of Ohio, who easily defeated Democrat William Jennings Bryan. But conservative Taft turned against Roosevelt's progressivism, alienating the former president.

The Republicans Self-Destruct: 1912

The Republican rift between progressives and conservatives culminated in a battle for the Republican Party nomination in 1912 that pitted the INCUMBENT Taft against popular former president Roosevelt. The feud between the two presidents enabled the 1912 Democratic nominee, New Jersey governor Woodrow Wilson, to win on a platform of a more liberal economic agenda and internationalist foreign policy.

Although Roosevelt challenged Taft in the Republican primaries—the first instance of a popular campaign for the nomination—Wilson plotted and plodded his way to the Democratic nomination. He won the nomination on the forty-sixth ballot. Wilson then took to the hustings, urging Americans to seek a moral awakening and to approve a program of liberal reforms.

Wilson's CAMPAIGNING alone might not have been enough to win him the presidency. The margin of victory was provided when Roosevelt bolted the Republican Party to run his own third-party campaign. (See PROGRESSIVE PARTY—BULL MOOSE.) Wilson won the election with a 41.8 percent plurality of the popular vote but 435 electoral votes. Roosevelt finished second, with 27.4 percent—the best popular vote performance by a non-major party candidate—but he won no electoral votes. The incumbent, Taft, brought up the rear with 23.2 percent and eight electoral votes.

Roosevelt returned to the Republican fold, reuniting his party in time for the 1916 election, but he declined to run again. As World War I raged in Europe, Wilson defeated Republican Charles Evans Hughes, albeit in a much closer race. Although he had run on the slogan "He kept us out of war," Wilson subsequently accused Germany of attacks on American interests and obtained a congressional declaration of war in April 1917. The United States and the Allies declared victory in November 1918, but the aftermath of the Great War—including Wilson's strenuous but failed drive to secure congressional approval of U.S. participation in Wilson's League of Nations (an exertion that contributed to Wilson's suffering a debilitating stroke in October 1919)—set the stage for a Republican revival.

The Roaring Republicans: 1920s

Though 1920 Republican nominee and Ohio senator Warren G. Harding was derided by critics as a tool of party bosses, a popular backlash against the incumbent Democratic presidential administration gave him a landslide victory: he is one of only four presidents to break 60 percent of the popular vote. A series of corruption scandals involving the president's associates appeared likely to cause trouble for the Republicans in the 1924 election, but Harding's sudden death in August 1923 put stolid New Englander Calvin Coolidge in the White House.

Benefiting greatly from an unprecedented economic boom, the Republicans reclaimed their political dominance. The party's presidential nominees, Coolidge in 1924 and former commerce secretary Herbert C. Hoover of Iowa in 1928, won easily. Hoover defeated Democrat Alfred E. Smith, the New York governor and the first Roman Catholic nominated for president by a major party, with 444 electoral votes to Smith's 87.

Dawn of the New Deal: 1932

After three years of Hoover's leadership following the stock market crash of 1929, Democrat Franklin D. Roosevelt won the presidency in 1932 and oversaw the greatest shift in political alignments in U.S. history.

Roosevelt, who won the Democratic nomination on the fourth ballot, was the first candidate to appear before the convention that nominated him. In his acceptance speech, he made passing reference to a "new deal" that his administration would offer Americans. After an active fall campaign, in which he largely managed to keep the effects of the polio that afflicted him hidden from the public, Roosevelt won 57.4 percent of the vote, forty-two of the forty-eight states, and 472 of 531 electoral votes.

The Democratic coalition that began to form during that election brought together a disparate group of interests. Until the New Deal, the party's base in the North had consisted of laborers and the poor, immigrants and Catholics; in the South, the Democrats were the party of white supremacy and agricultural interests. In 1932 blacks moved en masse to the Democratic Party from their traditional position in the "Party of Lincoln," partly because of Hoover's failure, but also because of the inclusive rhetoric of the New Deal. Jews, who had traditionally voted Republican, turned to the Democrats as they became the more liberal party.

Political scientist Samuel Beer has argued that with the New Deal, the Democratic Party was able to combine its traditional concern for local, individual interests with a national vision. By bringing "locked out" groups into the system, the Democrats contributed both to the building of the nation and to individual freedoms.

The political genius of the New Deal was not just that it offered something to everyone, but also that it created a situation in which everyone's interest lay in growth. The potentially divisive competition over restricted and unequally distributed resources was avoided with a general acceptance of growth as the common goal. When there was growth, everyone could get a little more. That public philosophy remained part of American political discourse.

Roosevelt's 1932 election gave the Democrats dominance of most aspects of American politics for more than a half-century. Roosevelt's coalition and leadership were so strong that he became the only president to win more than two elections. Roosevelt's four electoral triumphs caused Republicans to fume about his "imperial" presidency. After his death, they succeeded in passing a presidential TERM LIMIT. Ratified in 1951, the Twenty-second Amendment to the Constitution limited future presidents to two terms.

In his second run for the White House, Roosevelt won 60.8 percent of the popular vote and increased the number of Democrats in both the House and the Senate. His percentages dropped in the next two elections—to 54.7 percent in 1940 and 53.4 percent in 1944—but in neither election did his Republican challenger receive more than ninety-nine electoral votes.

Harry S. Truman, elected vice president on Roosevelt's ticket in 1944, succeeded to the presidency when Roosevelt died less than two months after his fourth inauguration. Lacking his

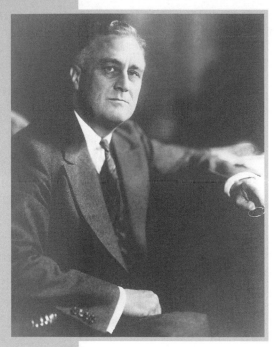

Franklin D. Roosevelt was the first candidate to appear before the convention that nominated him and the only president to be elected four times.

Source: National Archives and Records Administration

predecessor's charisma and dealing with a variety of postwar domestic and international problems, Truman had a much tougher time of it in 1948. He ran against not only Republican Thomas E. Dewey, who had lost to Roosevelt in 1944, but also two candidates backed by the left and right wings of his own party. The Dixiecrats, under the leadership of South Carolina's governor, J. Strom Thurmond, left the Democratic convention to form the STATES' RIGHTS DEMOCRATIC PARTY, based in the South, which ran on the core principle of segregationism to bar blacks from obtaining full civil rights in the South. Henry Wallace, the vice president during Roosevelt's third term, was the candidate of the Democratic left, campaigning under the Progressive Party banner against Truman's Marshall Plan program for reconstructing Europe, military buildup, and confrontational stance toward the Soviet Union as the Cold War began. Truman nonetheless squeaked by with 49.5 percent of the vote to Dewey's 45.1 percent and a 303–198 edge in the Electoral College. Each of the breakaway Democrats won 2.4 percent, with Thurmond carrying four southern states and 39 electoral votes.

Truman's political fortunes worsened after the 1948 election: with U.S.-led United Nations forces bogged down in a protracted fight with a North Korean army backed by Communist China, Truman belatedly decided against seeking a second full term. In 1952, for the first time in twenty-four years, neither party had an incumbent president as its nominee.

Eisenhower's Victory: 1952

In World War II hero Dwight D. Eisenhower, the general who commanded the Allied forces that defeated Nazi Germany, the Republicans were able to recruit a candidate with universal appeal who was coveted by both parties. Eisenhower, who had just left the presidency of Columbia University to take charge of the forces of the recently founded North Atlantic Treaty Organization, won the Republican nomination on the first convention ballot. He selected as his running mate Sen. Richard Nixon of California, a young conservative who had won national recognition for his role as an anticommunist crusader on the controversial House Committee on Un-American Activities.

The eventual Democratic nominee was Adlai E. Stevenson, governor of Illinois and the grandson of Grover Cleveland's second vice president. Stevenson's campaign was an eloquent call to arms for liberals and reformers. Years later, Democrats would recall how the campaign inspired the generation that would take the reins of power under John F. Kennedy in the early 1960s. But Stevenson did not stand a chance against the popular Eisenhower.

The campaign's biggest controversy developed when newspaper reports alleged that Nixon had used a "secret fund" provided by California millionaires to pay for travel and other expenses. Nixon admitted the existence of the fund but maintained that he had used the money solely for travel and that his family had not accepted personal gifts.

Eisenhower refused to back his running mate, and Nixon decided to confront his accusers with a television speech in what was the most dramatic early use of the new medium as a political device, even though campaign aides told him he would be dropped from the ticket if public reaction was not favorable. The speech was remarkable. Nixon denied that he had accepted gifts, such as a mink coat for his wife, Pat, saying that she wore a "Republican cloth coat." Nixon acknowledged receiving a dog named Checkers from a Texas admirer: "And you know, the kids love that dog, and I just want to say this right now, that regardless of what they say about it, we're going to keep it." Known through the remainder of Nixon's long and controversial career in public life as the "Checkers speech," his folksy message and appeal for telegrams created a wave of sympathy, which Eisenhower rewarded with a pledge of support.

Eisenhower swept into office in a personal victory, since surveys showed that the nation still favored the programs of the New Deal but wanted to put the cronyism of the Truman years and the Korean War behind it. Ike won 442 electoral votes and 55.1 percent of the popular vote.

The 1956 election was nearly a repeat of the 1952 match. Despite his age and a severe heart attack, Eisenhower once again trounced Stevenson, this time winning 457 electoral votes and 57.4 percent of the popular vote. The most significant development in the campaign was the emergence of a charismatic young Massachusetts senator named John F. Kennedy, who was considered by the Democratic convention as a vice presidential contender.

Kennedy and the Politics of Change: 1960

The periodic national desire for change took its toll on the Republicans in 1960, when forty-three-year-old Kennedy became the youngest person elected president. Kennedy defeated Nixon in one of the tightest elections in history.

The presidential election took shape in the 1958 midterm election. The Democrats made impressive gains in Congress, which gave them 64 of 98 Senate seats and 283 of 435 House seats. A recession and the election of several younger and more liberal Democrats to Congress created the first major shift toward liberalism since the administration of Franklin D. Roosevelt.

Running against senior party leaders such as Sens. Lyndon B. Johnson of Texas, Hubert H. Humphrey of Minnesota, and Stuart Symington of Missouri, Kennedy seemed more likely to win the vice presidential nomination. Well-financed and backed by a skilled campaign staff headed by his younger brother Robert, Kennedy used the primaries to allay fears both that he was too conservative and that his Catholic religion would affect his loyalty to the nation. With primary victories over Humphrey in the crucial states of Wisconsin and West Virginia, Kennedy was able to win the nomination on the first ballot. His surprise choice of Johnson for a running mate raised doubts even among Kennedy supporters, but the selection of the southerner was a classic ticket-balancing CAMPAIGN STRATEGY.

Nixon, as Eisenhower's vice president, was considered the Republicans' heir apparent and was the overwhelming choice for the Republican nomination; he selected United Nations ambassador Henry Cabot Lodge, who had lost his Senate seat in Massachusetts to Kennedy in 1952, as his running mate.

Nixon's campaign stressed the need for experience in a dangerous world and tried to portray Kennedy as an inexperienced upstart. Kennedy's campaign was based on a promise to "get the nation moving again" after eight years of calm Republican rule. The high point of the campaign came on September 26, 1960, when the candidates debated on national television before 70 million viewers. It was the first general presidential DEBATE in the nation's history and the last until 1976.

Kennedy was well rested and tan. Nixon was tired from two solid weeks of campaigning. His "five o'clock shadow" reinforced the political cartoonists' image of him as darkly sinister. Polls found that Nixon had "won" the debate in the minds of radio listeners but that Kennedy had captured the TV audience. "It was the picture image that had done it," wrote historian Theodore H. White, "and in 1960 it was television that had won the nation away from sound to images, and that was that."

The candidates held three more debates, but none of them had the effect of the first, which had neutralized Nixon's incumbency advantage. Nor was Nixon greatly helped by President Eisenhower, who did not campaign for his vice president until late in the race.

The election results were so close that Nixon did not concede his defeat until the afternoon of the day following the election. Just 115,000 votes separated Kennedy from Nixon in the popular vote tally. A shift of 11,000 to 13,000 votes in just five or six states would have given him the electoral vote triumph, but despite widespread allegations of voting irregularities, Nixon chose not to dispute the outcome. Kennedy won 303 electoral votes to Nixon's 219. (Democratic senator Harry F. Byrd of Virginia attracted 15 electoral votes.)

Johnson and the Great Society: 1964

Kennedy's youthful charisma and the glamour of his wife Jacqueline left an indelible image on American culture. And while Kennedy had some notable achievements during his abbreviated presidency, including his successful and peaceful resolution of a standoff with the Soviet Union during the Cuban Missile Crisis of 1962, he is perhaps best remembered for a clarion call to public service that inspired millions of Americans, including many members of the young post–World War II "baby boom" generation.

Kennedy's presidency was cut short by his assassination in Dallas, Texas, on November 22, 1963. His death was blamed on a disgruntled former Marine Corps marksman named Lee Harvey Oswald, who was himself gunned down two days later while in police custody. The confluence of these events spurred dozens of conspiracy theories, some of which were still in circulation more than four decades later.

Lyndon Johnson, Kennedy's vice president who took the oath of office on Air Force One as it prepared to leave Dallas, faced no serious opposition for the 1964 Democratic nomination. The Republicans, however, were bitterly divided between the conservatives, led by Sen. Barry Goldwater of Arizona, and the liberal wing of the party, led by New York governor Nelson A. Rockefeller. Goldwater had lined up most of the delegate support he needed even before the primaries began, and key primary victories, including his defeat of Rockefeller in California, ensured that he would receive the nomination.

There was never a real contest between the two presidential nominees in the fall campaign. Johnson's LANDSLIDE was the largest in U.S. history. He won 61 percent of the popular vote to Goldwater's 38 percent and 486 Electoral College votes to Goldwater's 52.

CLOSER LOOK

Legend has it that when President Lyndon B. Johnson signed the Civil Rights Act of 1964, he said of his Democratic Party, "We have lost the South for a generation."

Yet underlying those numbers were hints of a breakdown of the longstanding Democratic coalition and a Republican resurgence in the South, a region where for a century most white residents had regarded "Republican" as a curse word because of the party's association with Abraham Lincoln, the Civil War, and the Reconstruction era.

While Johnson dominated most of the country, including many states that rarely voted Democratic for president, he lost five states in the Democrats' "Solid South" along with Goldwater's home state of Arizona. Whether caused by backlash against Johnson's championship of the Civil Rights Act of 1964, an aversion to federal intrusion on states' rights, or opposition to a liberal trend in the national Democratic Party, the South in 1964 began a seismic shift that ultimately would turn it into a Republican presidential stronghold.

The Breakup of Consensus: 1968

A long period of uncertainty in U.S. politics began after Johnson's landslide victory in 1964. There was rising opposition to the Vietnam War, combined with a conservative reaction to

Johnson's "Great Society" domestic economic programs and to the race-related riots in many of the nation's cities. These issues seriously divided the nation and the Democratic Party. After Sen. Eugene McCarthy of Minnesota ran surprisingly well against Johnson on an antiwar platform in the New Hampshire primary, the beleaguered president withdrew from the campaign. Vice President Hubert H. Humphrey became the administration's candidate, relying on his strength with the party establishment and eschewing the primaries that at that time played a secondary role in the nominating process. New York senator Robert F. Kennedy, brother of the late president, entered the race as an antiwar candidate and had just gained momentum by defeating McCarthy in the California primary when he was assassinated in a Los Angeles hotel the night of his victory.

The Democratic convention in Chicago was marred by skirmishes on the convention floor and bloody confrontations between police and antiwar and civil rights demonstrators outside. Democrats nominated Humphrey on the strength of endorsements from state party organizations. The nomination of a candidate who had not entered a single primary led to major changes in the way Democrats selected their delegates and ultimately to the proliferation of presidential primaries.

The Republicans united behind Richard Nixon, who made a comeback after losing the 1960 race for president and the 1962 election for governor of California. The former vice president's fall campaign was well-financed and well-organized, and the Republican candidate capitalized on the national discontent.

Alabama governor George C. Wallace also made use of national sentiment, mounting one of the strongest third-party campaigns in U.S. history. Wallace ran as an antiestablishment conservative, railing at desegregation, crime, taxes, opponents of the Vietnam War, social programs, and "pointy head" bureaucrats. Wallace's campaign stirred fears that neither major party candidate would receive a majority of the Electoral College votes and that the election would be thrown into the House of Representatives, then controlled by the Democrats.

The election was one of the closest in U.S. history. Nixon attracted 31.8 million votes, to Humphrey's 31.3 million and Wallace's 9.9 million. But Nixon won 301 electoral votes, a clear majority. Humphrey picked up 191. Wallace won 46; he was the last third-party candidate to win electoral votes through the 2004 election.

Although Nixon undertook some policy initiatives that look rather progressive in retrospect, including establishment of the Environmental Protection Agency, he was reviled by Democrats, especially as his gradual de-escalation of the U.S. involvement in Vietnam lasted through his first term as president. His vice president, former Maryland governor Spiro T. Agnew, also drew criticism for his harsh rhetoric against antiwar protesters and other political opponents.

Nixon and Agnew were nominated for reelection in 1972 with barely a peep out of other Republicans. On the Democratic side, though, twelve serious contenders announced their candidacies. Sen. George S. McGovern of South Dakota led the pack at the end of a grueling primary season and was nominated at the convention.

Under the best of circumstances, the liberal Democrat would have been an underdog in the race against Nixon. But McGovern was badly damaged when his choice for vice president, Thomas F. Eagleton of Missouri, withdrew from the ticket after it was revealed that he had been treated previously for nervous exhaustion. McGovern replaced Eagleton with R. Sargent Shriver of Maryland, a brother-in-law of the late President Kennedy, but he never overcame the appearance of confusion that surrounded the Eagleton affair.

Nixon won all but Massachusetts and the DISTRICT OF COLUMBIA in the fall election, gaining 520 electoral votes to 17 for McGovern.

Effects of the Watergate Affair: 1976

Revelations that people associated with Nixon's campaign committee had been arrested for breaking into Democratic headquarters in the Watergate Hotel in June 1972 had little effect on that year's election. Eventually, the investigation of the burglary and the subsequent cover-up by Nixon and his aides drove the president from office in August 1974.

Nixon's resignation was prefaced in October 1973 by that of his vice president, which was forced by an unrelated scandal. Agnew stepped down after pleading no contest to charges that he had accepted bribes while he was governor of Maryland and vice president. Nixon named House minority leader Gerald R. Ford, a longtime Republican Party stalwart from Michigan, to become vice president under the Twenty-fifth Amendment. When Nixon resigned, Ford became the first president in U.S. history who had never run in a presidential election.

Although he started out with the support of the American public, Ford soon ignited a firestorm of criticism when he granted Nixon a full pardon for any crimes he might have committed as president. Combined with nagging economic problems and a stubborn, but losing, primary campaign waged by former California governor Ronald Reagan, the pardon left Ford and the Republican Party vulnerable in the 1976 election.

The Democrats appeared headed for a long and bitter nomination struggle for the third time in a row. But former Georgia governor Jimmy Carter, whose support as measured by national polls was extremely low when the campaign began, executed a brilliant campaign strategy by appealing to voters' desire for a Washington outsider in the wake of Watergate. Carter was nominated on the first ballot at the Democratic convention and went on to defeat Ford by a slim margin, winning 297 electoral votes to Ford's 240.

The 1976 election was notable in two ways. For the first time, the presidential campaigns were partially financed with public funds. And for the first time since 1960, the presidential nominees took part in televised debates. (See CAMPAIGN FINANCE; DEBATES.)

The Reagan Revolution: 1980

Carter's presidency was troubled by inflation and unemployment, his own inability to work with a Democratic Congress, an energy crisis, and the prolonged crisis that began in November 1979 when Islamic radicals, with support from the theocratic government of Iran, held fifty-two employees of the U.S. Embassy in Tehran as hostages. He nonetheless managed to win renomination on the first ballot, putting down a serious challenge from Massachusetts senator Edward M. Kennedy, brother of the late John and Robert Kennedy. But the Democratic ticket garnered little enthusiasm from the rank and file.

The Republicans united early behind Reagan, a conservative whose nomination would mark a sharp shift to the right in Republican and national politics. By the time of the convention, Reagan was the consensus candidate, and he improved party unity by adding George H. W. Bush of Texas, his only serious primary challenger, to the fall ticket. Rep. John B. Anderson of Illinois, a moderate who dropped out of the Republican race, ran an INDEPENDENT campaign.

Although polls before election day predicted a close race, Reagan won all but six states and took the White House in an electoral landslide, 489 electoral votes to 49. The Republicans also gained control over the Senate for the first time in twenty-six years.

The extraordinarily popular former movie actor was able to parlay his claims of an electoral mandate into wide-ranging changes in tax, budget, and military policies. Although Reagan's popularity fell during a recession early in his first term, he recovered, and there was no serious challenge to his renomination in 1984.

Jimmy Carter's vice president, Walter F. Mondale of Minnesota, was the early FRONT-RUNNER for the Democratic nomination and won it on the first ballot. Mondale named Rep. Geraldine Ferraro of New York as his running mate, the first woman ever to receive a major party nomination for national office. Ferraro's nomination was probably a drag on the ticket, not because of her gender but because of her lack of government experience and a controversy that surrounded her husband's finances. The Mondale-Ferraro campaign never caught fire, and Reagan rolled to an easy victory, winning 525 electoral votes to Mondale's 13.

The Election of 1988

In 1988, for the first time since 1968, the incumbent president was not a candidate, since Reagan was completing his second and final term. With no major figure and no single overriding issue, the campaign was a tumultuous affair. As fourteen candidates struggled to make themselves known to the voters during the parties' nominating contests, the campaign lurched from one symbolic issue to the next.

Massachusetts governor Michael S. Dukakis won the Democratic nomination, but only after a long and initially shaky primary season. His only competitor at the end was civil rights leader Jesse Jackson, who attracted support from blacks and from farmers and blue-collar workers disgruntled with the economy. When Dukakis passed over Jackson to choose Texas senator Lloyd M. Bentsen Jr. for vice president, Jackson complained both publicly and privately. But he eventually embraced Bentsen for the sake of party unity.

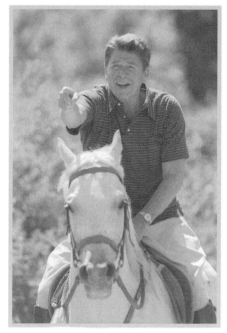

Ronald Reagan easily won the 1980 presidential election against Jimmy Carter, whose presidency was plagued with troubles. Reagan won all but six states, with an electoral landslide of 489 votes to Carter's 49.

Source: Ronald Reagan Library

Vice President Bush was an early favorite on the Republican side, and he overcame a loss in the Iowa caucus to win the nomination. He was hurt by his controversial choice of Dan Quayle, a youthful senator from Indiana, as his running mate, but benefited from Dukakis's inability to pull together his own inconsistent and confusing campaign strategy. Using a campaign strategy notable for its negative tone, the Bush-Quayle ticket won handily, capturing 54 percent of the vote to the Democrats' 46 percent. The 1988 elections had one of the lowest VOTER TURNOUT rates in modern times—barely 50 percent of all eligible citizens voted for president.

Clinton Victory: 1992

Democratic Arkansas governor Bill Clinton broke what seemed like a Republican lock on the White House when he defeated incumbent president George Bush in 1992. Republicans had won five of the six previous presidential elections, and for a while it did not seem as if 1992 would be any different.

Just a year before the campaign began, Bush seemed poised for one of the smoothest reelections in White House history. After he led the nation to victory in the brief 1991 Persian Gulf War, which ended Iraq's occupation of Kuwait, Bush's popularity soared. But in the months that followed, the economy went into what even the president called a "free fall." So, too, did Bush's popularity. And not much the White House did before or during the campaign helped revitalize either the economy or the president's political standing.

Forty-six-year-old Clinton and his running mate and fellow member of the so-called baby boom generation, forty-four-year-old Sen. Al Gore of Tennessee, called for generational change.

The widespread desire for change in government also benefited independent candidate Ross Perot, a Texas billionaire who spoke bluntly of the need to reduce the federal budget deficit. Perot won 19 percent of the popular vote, the most won by an independent candidate in presidential election history and the biggest share since 1912, when Theodore Roosevelt ran under the Progressive Party banner. But Perot won no electoral votes.

Clinton claimed the presidency, carrying thirty-two states and the District of Columbia to win 370 of 538 electoral votes and outscoring Bush by about 6 percentage points: 43 percent to 37 percent. Clinton won with the smallest popular vote plurality since 1912, when Democrat Woodrow Wilson defeated Republican president William Howard Taft and past president Theodore Roosevelt, a former Republican who ran as a Progressive.

Clinton was only the second Democrat to gain the White House in the nearly three decades since Lyndon Johnson's lopsided victory in 1964. Clinton's win was especially important to the Democratic Party, which had made dismal showings in the three national elections since Carter was in office in the late 1970s.

Divided Government Retained: 1996

The election of 1996 was significant in several ways. Clinton became the first Democrat elected to a second full term since Franklin Roosevelt in 1936. But unlike Roosevelt, whose party controlled Congress throughout his twelve-year tenure, Clinton would mainly preside over a divided government.

After a lackluster first two years in which he failed to deliver his promised health care reform, Clinton was an easy target for House Republicans led by Newt Gingrich of Georgia. Campaigning on a ten-point document of conservative policies known as the "Contract with America," the GOP won control of the House in the 1994 MIDTERM ELECTIONS—ending forty consecutive years of Democratic rule—and elected Gingrich as Speaker. The Democrats also lost control of the Senate, and Bob Dole of Kansas became the majority leader.

As the first Democratic president since Truman forced to deal with a Congress entirely controlled by the opposition party, Clinton faced an uphill fight to govern, and his chances of reelection looked slim. But after a series of budget battles that closed down the government briefly in late 1995 and early 1996, Gingrich became the lightning rod for public apprehension about Congress's intent. Congressional Democrats played on fears that the Republicans would end Social Security and Medicare, both targeted for "reform" in the Contract with America, and undo some health, safety, and environmental protections to lessen the burden of regulation on the economy.

By late 1996, with the economy healthy, Clinton's approval ratings had improved, and he enjoyed a strong lead in the polls over his Republican challenger, Dole. At seventy-three, Dole faced doubts about his age as well as his reputation for having an acerbic tongue. For his part, Gingrich kept a low profile during the campaign.

Meanwhile, Ross Perot had converted his independent candidacy into a new political organization, the REFORM PARTY. Although he had financed his 1992 campaign from his own deep pockets, Perot accepted federal campaign funding, which limited his personal spending and donations from outside sources. Perot and running mate Pat Choate, an economist, won only 8.5 percent of the popular vote and no electoral votes. Many political analysts thought the Reform Party had potential to grow into a force, but Perot soon abandoned it, and the new third party failed to take root. In 2000, with conservative commentator Pat Buchanan as its nominee, the Reform Party received a minuscule share of the national vote and did not even field a presidential nominee in 2004.

Although Clinton's 1996 reelection was no surprise in light of the polls, his coattails proved weaker than expected. For what was believed to be the first time, the electorate consciously voted for divided government, keeping the White House in Democratic hands and Congress in Republican hands as a check on one another.

The "status quo election," as it came to be called, gave the Clinton-Gore team 379 electoral votes to 159 for Dole and his running mate, former House member Jack Kemp of New York. The election was also dubbed the "whatever" election because of voter apathy. The voter turnout was the lowest in seventy-two years. Only 48.8 percent of the voting age population participated, depriving Clinton of any kind of mandate. Clinton fell short of his personal goal of winning more than 50 percent of the popular vote. He thus became a "minority president" for the second time, raising his 1992 vote total of 43 percent to 49 percent in 1996.

Election of 2000: Bitter to the End

Partisanship was at fever pitch even before the elections of November 2000. Since the "Republican Revolution" of 1994 had swept that party into control of both houses of Congress, relations between Congress and the Democratic administration of Bill Clinton had been rancorous. Relations between congressional Democrats and Republicans were no warmer.

Congressional Republicans objected not only to Clinton's priorities and programs—the normal fodder of partisan debate—but to what they viewed as his moral (and legal) lapses. An independent counsel probe into a financial scandal in Arkansas known as Whitewater, which began in January 1994 under Robert Fiske Jr., had continued under Kenneth Starr well into Clinton's second term. Starr, acting on longstanding rumors of personal misconduct by Clinton, ultimately investigated allegations that Clinton had maintained a sexual relationship with White House intern Monica Lewinsky and lied about it under oath in an unrelated sexual harassment lawsuit. Clinton's ensuing impeachment by the House of Representatives in December 1998 and acquittal in the Senate in 1999, largely along party lines, further poisoned relations.

Political observers had expected a close race and were proven correct. Texas governor George W. Bush, the Republican nominee, and Vice President Gore, the Democratic nominee, ran neck-and-neck. Gore, stigmatized to some degree by Clinton's impeachment and plagued by criticism over what many saw as a wooden campaign style, won twenty states and the District of Columbia for 267 electoral votes to Bush's twenty-nine states and 246 electoral votes in the election night count. But the outcome in one decisive state, Florida, remained undecided.

The final result took four weeks to determine. Accusations of ballot irregularities were rife, including complaints from residents in a Democratic-leaning south Florida county that a confusing ballot design had resulted in their ballots registering support for Reform Party candidate Patrick Buchanan when they had intended to vote for Gore. The Democrats demanded a partial recount of punch-card ballots that focused on whether incompletely dislodged paper "chads" indicated an intent to vote for Gore.

The election was not decided until the Supreme Court on December 12, by a 5–4 vote in BUSH V. GORE, overruled a state court order and halted the recount process. (See Chronology of 2000 Recount in Florida, pp. 44–45). Bush, who had been certified by Florida officials as the winner by 537 votes, claimed the state's 25 electoral votes for a national total of 271—just one more than the

Almost from the start, George W. Bush was the front-runner for the 2000 Republican presidential nomination.

Source: White House.

absolute majority needed for victory. Gore had received 537,179 more popular votes than Bush, making Bush just the fourth president ever, and the first since Benjamin Harrison in 1888, to win the electoral vote while losing the popular vote. The other two instances were when Andrew Jackson lost to John Quincy Adams in 1824 and Samuel J. Tilden to Rutherford B. Hayes in 1876.

The tumult focused new attention on proposals to abolish or reform the Electoral College system. It brought to light the need to modernize the problem-prone voting systems still in use in many states besides Florida. It also exposed serious flaws in the technology that broadcast media rely on to project election results before all the polls have closed. On election night 2000, the networks seesawed between Gore and Bush as the projected winner.

First Election after September 11: 2004

Bush entered the White House at a time of economic prosperity and relative peace around the world. He spent the early months of his presidency focused on domestic affairs, including his successful push for tax cuts and the implementation of an education policy reform package he labeled "No Child Left Behind."

That focus shifted drastically with the attacks of September 11, 2001, which caused one of the highest death tolls of any attack on American soil. The al-Qaeda network, led by Osama bin Laden and sheltered by the radical Islamic Taliban regime of Afghanistan, dispatched followers to the United States, where nineteen of them hijacked passenger aircraft and turned the planes into missiles. Two airplanes crashed into the twin towers of New York City's World Trade Center, causing them to collapse; another smashed into the Pentagon outside Washington, D.C., creating extensive damage; and a fourth crashed into an open field in Pennsylvania only because of heroic efforts by passengers to prevent their captors from completing an attack on the nation's capital.

The September 11 attacks changed the nature of Bush's presidency and the nation's politics. Bush's deployment of U.S. troops to aid domestic Afghan forces in quickly toppling the Taliban regime and forcing al-Qaeda from its sanctuary sent his job approval ratings to record heights. In fall 2002 Bush and other administration officials—including Vice President Richard Cheney, a former defense secretary and foreign policy hard-liner—argued that Iraq's repeated failures to comply with United Nations orders to allow weapons inspections posed a threat to national security that required a military response. Based on intelligence that Iraqi dictator Saddam Hussein had stockpiled weapons of mass destruction and had ties to al-Qaeda, allegations that later would prove to be flawed, Congress in October 2002 authorized the president to use military force against Iraq.

A U.S.-led coalition of nations launched an invasion in March 2003, and the quick fall of Hussein's regime at first appeared to justify the Bush administration's initial estimation that the war would be short with low U.S. costs and casualties. But an unpredicted insurgent backlash against the American presence, a spasm of violence among Iraq's sectarian groups, the failure to find the alleged weapons of mass destruction, and embarrassing scandals involving the abuse of Iraqi detainees by U.S. troops caused a sharp downturn in public support for the war.

Bush's approval ratings sagged to mediocre levels during his 2004 campaign, but voters supported his tough post–September 11 stance in the war against terrorism. He was also helped by the stumbles of his Democratic opponent, Massachusetts senator John Kerry, who came across to many people as a wealthy aristocrat, failed to connect well with voters, and responded ineffectively to attacks on his reputation as a Vietnam War hero that were launched by an outside group of Republican sympathizers known as the Swift Boat Veterans for Truth.

Bush won with a modest 50.7 percent of the vote and a 2.4 percentage-point margin over Kerry. This nonetheless made him the first majority presidential winner since his father in 1988, and he quickly declared a mandate for his policy agenda.

The next two years would prove difficult for the president, however. Bush's central domestic policy item, a controversial plan to alter the Social Security system by adding a program of personal savings accounts, failed to gain consideration in the Republican-controlled Congress. The situation in Iraq deteriorated, as the death toll among Americans and Iraqis mounted. And Bush incurred severe political damage after his administration responded ineffectively to Hurricane Katrina in 2005, which ravaged New Orleans and other Gulf Coast communities. Bush's plummeting job approval ratings, combined with a series of corruption scandals that tainted congressional Republicans, contributed greatly to a Democratic takeover of both the Senate and the House in the 2006 elections.

A Year of Firsts: 2008

When the 2008 votes were tallied, America had elected Barack Obama, an Illinois senator, as the first African American president, an outcome that most observers thought inconceivable a quarter century earlier. But even before the votes for president were counted in November 2008, that election already had become renowned.

Although Obama's election made 2008 "one for the books," in the words of many political commentators, by the time the primaries and caucuses ended and candidates were anointed at the conventions, the "firsts" of the 2008 cycle had become an impressive list.

- Most remarkable of all was Obama's capturing the nomination of a major political party.
- The 2008 race was the first since 1928 that no incumbent president or vice president sought the nomination, and was the first since 1952 that neither the incumbent president nor vice president was running on the final ticket.
- The presidential race started earlier than any other in history, when Democrat Tom Vilsack, who was stepping down as Iowa's governors after two terms, became the first candidate of either party to formally announce that he was seeking the presidential nomination. Vilsack's announcement came on November 2006—two full years before the election. Vilsack remained in the race for fewer than four months, withdrawing in February 2007 for lack of funding.
- The initial front-runner in the Democratic contest was Sen. Hillary Rodham Clinton, the first woman in American history to run a competitive race for the nomination. That Democrats were choosing between a woman and an African American male was a matchup that virtually no one could have imagined in previous national elections.
- For the first time ever, both candidates had been born outside the continental United States, Obama in Hawaii on Aug. 4, 1961, to a white woman from Kansas and a black man from Kenya, and his opponent, Sen. John McCain, an Arizona Republican, at a U.S. naval base in the Panama Canal Zone on Aug. 29, 1936.

- Two sitting members of the U.S. Senate were the major party candidates, the first time this had ever occurred. It also was the first time since 1960 that a sitting senator was elected. That year Sen. John F. Kennedy, D-Mass., defeated incumbent vice president Richard M. Nixon.
- For only the second time in U.S. history, a woman was selected to run on a major party ticket as the vice presidential candidate. McCain selected Gov. Sarah Palin of Alaska. In 1984, Geraldine A. Ferraro was the Democratic vice presidential candidate, but she was on the losing ticket headed by former senator and vice president Walter Mondale.

Presidential Primaries

 CLOSER LOOK

GROWTH OF PRESIDENTIAL PRIMARIES: MORE AND MORE, EARLIER AND EARLIER

In recent decades, there have been more and more states holding primaries earlier and earlier in the presidential election year. The result is that a nominating system that once featured primaries sprinkled across the spring is now front-loaded with the bulk of the primaries held during the winter months of February and March. In 2004 for the first time New Hampshire held its first-in-the-nation primary in January.

In 2008, South Carolina also held party-sanctioned primaries in January. In addition, two states—Michigan and Florida—moved their primaries into January, in violation of party rules prohibiting any state other than New Hampshire and South Carolina from voting before February 1. Both states faced party sanctions that threatened to eliminate or reduce their delegate representations at the national conventions, although the controversy was resolved before the parties met.

One state, New Mexico, split its primary activity. Democrats held an event in February technically called a caucus but with characteristics that resembled a regular primary; it is included in the February total. New Mexico Republicans held a regular primary in June, which is included in the total for that month. However, the total, forty-one, counts the two New Mexico votes as a single vote.

Following is a list of primaries held in each month of every nominating season from 1968 through 2008. Primaries included are those in the fifty states and the District of Columbia in which at least one of the parties permitted a direct vote for presidential candidates, or there was an aggregated statewide vote for delegates. Primaries in the U.S. territories, such as Puerto Rico, are not included.

	1968	1972	1976	1980	1984	1988	1992	1996	2000	2004	2008
January	0	0	0	0	0	0	0	0	0	2	4
February	0	0	1	1	1	2	2	5	7	9	22[1]
March	1	3	5	9	8	20	15	24	20	14	5
April	3	3	2	4	3	3	5	1	2	1	1
May	7	11	13	13	11	7	10	8	9	7	7
June	4	4	6	9	7	5	7	4	5	5	3[2]
Total	15	21	27	36	30	37	39	42	43	38	41

[1] Total includes a New Mexico Democratic presidential primary on February 5. This event was officially a caucus but had attributes of a regular primary. It was run by the Democratic Party in the state and was open exclusively to registered Democrats, who could vote by mail or in person at the more than 150 caucus sites between noon and 7 p.m. The results were used to assign pledged delegates to the candidates.

[2] Total includes New Mexico Republicans who held a direct primary on June 3.

The remarkable shift in the method used by the major parties to select presidential nominees—from one dominated by party insiders and centered on the NATIONAL PARTY CONVENTIONS to one ruled mainly by primaries in which rank-and-file voters choose the nominees for the parties—did not occur until the implementation of sweeping PRESIDENTIAL SELECTION REFORMS beginning in the early 1970s.

Woodrow Wilson—who six decades earlier was the first president elected in the era of presidential primaries—might be called a visionary for recognizing the potential of these contests to give voters a more direct role in choosing candidates for the nation's highest office. Elected in 1912, the first year that a substantial number of states (thirteen) held primaries, Wilson promptly asked Congress to establish a system of primary elections throughout the country. At these primaries, the voters of several parties would choose their nominees for the presidency without the intervention of nominating conventions. Wilson proposed keeping the conventions as a means to declare the results of the primaries and adopt the parties' PLATFORMS.

Although Congress never enacted a national primary law, the U.S. political system, in a patchwork, state-by-state fashion, ultimately in effect adopted a version of Wilson's idea. From just fourteen states holding primaries in 1968, the number had leapt to forty-one in 2008 (with virtually all the other states holding party CAUCUSES that to at least some degree were open to public participation). Every major-party nominee since 1976 has gone to the convention with the nomination in his pocket, having won at least a plurality in the party's primaries. Following that established pattern, most states in 2000, 2004, and 2008 held presidential primaries, and the conventions simply gave pro forma ratification to party platforms and formalized the nominations.

Wilson himself owed his election in part to the inequities of the old nominating convention system. Then the governor of New Jersey, he had entered primaries in twelve states and won only five of them. Nevertheless, he won the Democratic nomination for president on the forty-sixth ballot. On the Republican side in the same election, former president Theodore Roosevelt won nine of twelve primaries but lost the nomination to President William Howard Taft in a bruising convention fight. Roosevelt then formed his own PROGRESSIVE–BULL MOOSE PARTY to challenge both Taft and Wilson. The GOP split helped to ensure Wilson's election.

The Progressive fervor had spurred the spread of primaries, which originated with a Florida law in 1901. But after Wilson's election that spirit began to die out. Not until after World War II, when widespread pressures for change touched both parties but especially the Democrats, was there a rapid growth in presidential primaries.

That growth was steady, except for a brief period in the 1980s when some states reverted to the caucus method of DELEGATE selection.

Although Woodrow Wilson favored the primary system, he owed his election in 1912 to the nominating convention, where he outmaneuvered many other candidates.

Source: Library of Congress.

Impact of Progressives

In the early twentieth century, Progressives, Populists, and reformers in general objected to the links between political bosses and big business. They advocated returning the government to the people.

Part of this "return to the people" was a turn away from boss-dominated conventions. It was only a matter of time before the primary idea spread from state and local elections to presidential contests. Because there was no provision for a nationwide primary, state primaries were initiated to choose delegates to the national party conventions (delegate-selection primaries) and to register voters' preferences on their parties' eventual presidential nominees (preference primaries). (See PRIMARY TYPES.)

Florida's 1901 primary gave party officials an option of holding a party primary to choose any party candidate for public office, as well as delegates to the national conventions. There was no provision, however, for placing names of presidential candidates on the ballot—either in the form of a preference vote or with information indicating the preference of the candidates for convention delegates.

Wisconsin's Progressive Republican politician, Gov. Robert M. La Follette, gave a major boost to the presidential primary following the 1904 Republican National Convention. There the credentials of La Follette's Progressive delegation had been rejected and a regular Republican delegation from Wisconsin seated. Angered, La Follette returned to his home state and began pushing for a presidential primary law. The result was a 1905 Wisconsin law mandating the DIRECT ELECTION of national convention delegates but making no provision for indicating the delegates' presidential preference.

In 1906 Pennsylvania followed Wisconsin with a statute providing that candidates for delegate could have their names printed on the official ballot beside the name of the presidential candidate the delegate would support at the national convention. However, no member of either party exercised this option in the 1908 primary.

The next step in presidential primaries—the preferential vote for president—took place in Oregon. In 1910, Sen. Jonathan Bourne, a Progressive Republican colleague of La Follette (by then a U.S. senator), sponsored a referendum to establish a presidential preference primary, with delegates legally bound to support the winner of the preference primary. By 1912, with Oregon in the lead, twelve states had enacted presidential primary laws that provided for direct election of delegates, a preferential vote, or both. The number had expanded to twenty-six states by 1916.

Primaries and Conventions

As the 1912 election showed, victories in the presidential primaries did not ensure a candidate's nomination. One of former president Theodore Roosevelt's nine victories included a defeat of Taft in Ohio, the president's home state. Roosevelt lost to Taft by a narrow margin in Massachusetts and to La Follette in North Dakota and Wisconsin. Despite this impressive string of primary victories, the convention rejected Roosevelt in favor of Taft.

Taft supporters dominated the REPUBLICAN NATIONAL COMMITTEE, which ran the convention, and the convention's credentials committee, which ruled on contested delegates. Moreover, Taft was backed by many state organizations, especially in the South, where most delegates were chosen by caucuses or conventions dominated by party leaders.

On the Democratic side, the convention more closely reflected the results of the primaries. Gov. Wilson of New Jersey and House Speaker Champ Clark of Missouri were closely matched in total primary votes, with Wilson only 29,632 votes ahead of Clark. Wilson emerged with the nomination after a long struggle with Clark at the convention.

Likewise, in 1916, Democratic primary results foreshadowed the winner of the nomination, although Wilson, the incumbent, had no major opposition for renomination. But once again, Republican presidential primaries had little impact on the nominating process at the convention. The eventual nominee, a Supreme Court justice, Charles Evans Hughes, had won only two primaries.

In 1920, presidential primaries did not play a major role in determining the winner of either party's nomination. Democrat James M. Cox, the eventual nominee, ran in only one primary, his home state of Ohio. Most of the Democratic primaries featured FAVORITE-SON candidates or WRITE-IN VOTES. And at the convention, Democrats took forty-four ballots to make their choice.

Similarly, the main entrants in the Republican presidential primaries that year failed to capture their party's nomination. Sen. Warren G. Harding of Ohio, the compromise choice, won the primary in his home state but lost badly in Indiana and garnered only a handful of votes elsewhere. The three primary leaders—Sen. Hiram Johnson of California, Gen. Leonard Wood of New Hampshire, and Gov. Frank O. Lowden of Illinois—lost out in the end.

After the first wave of enthusiasm for presidential primaries in the early years of the century, interest waned. By 1935 eight states had repealed their presidential primary laws. The diminution of reform zeal during the 1920s and the preoccupation of the country with the Great Depression in the 1930s and war in the 1940s appeared to have been leading factors in the decline. Also, party leaders were ambivalent about primaries; the cost of conducting them was relatively high, both for the candidates and the states. Many presidential candidates ignored the primaries, and voter participation often was low.

But after World War II, interest picked up again. Some politicians with presidential ambitions, knowing the party leadership was lukewarm about their candidacies, entered the primaries to try to generate a BANDWAGON EFFECT.

In 1948 Harold Stassen, Republican governor of Minnesota from 1939 to 1943, entered presidential primaries in opposition to the Republican organization and made some headway before losing in Oregon to Gov. Thomas E. Dewey of New York.

New Hampshire, which for many years had held the presidential election year's first primary, but only to select unpledged delegates to the national convention, placed candidates' names on the ballot for the first time in 1952 and had an immediate impact. Tennessee senator Estes Kefauver, riding a wave of public recognition as head of the Senate Organized Crime Investigating Committee, challenged Democratic Party leaders and upset President Harry S. Truman in New Hampshire. Truman, who had not campaigned in New Hampshire, soon announced he would not seek reelection but asserted that he had come to that decision before the primary. Kefauver, though he won other primaries that year, ultimately faded in competition and lost the nomination to Illinois governor Adlai E. Stevenson.

The struggle between former general Dwight D. Eisenhower and Republican senator Robert Taft for the Republican Party nomination that year also stimulated interest in the primaries.

With the growing demand for political reform in the 1960s and early 1970s, the presidential primaries became more attractive as a path to the nomination. John F. Kennedy, then a relatively obscure U.S. senator from Massachusetts, helped to popularize that route with his successful uphill fight for the Democratic nomination in 1960. Kennedy used the primaries to prove to party leaders that he, a Roman Catholic, could be elected. An unbroken string of Kennedy victories persuaded his chief rival in the primaries, Sen. Hubert H. Humphrey of Minnesota, to withdraw.

Republicans Barry M. Goldwater of Arizona in 1964 and former vice president Richard Nixon in 1968 and Democrat George S. McGovern of South Dakota in 1972—all party presidential nominees—were able to use the primaries to show their vote-getting and organizational abilities. Having failed to win the presidency in 1960 and the California governorship in 1962, Nixon needed a strong primary showing to overcome his "loser" image among GOP leaders. McGovern, too liberal for the Democratic establishment, won the nomination through the primaries.

Democratic Rules Changes

Despite the progressive reforms, party leaders until 1968 remained in firm control of the nominating process. With only a handful of the fifteen to twenty primaries regularly contested, candidates could count on a short primary season. They began with the NEW HAMPSHIRE PRIMARY in March and then tested their appeal during the spring in Wisconsin, Nebraska, and Oregon, culminating in an often hotly contested June primary in California before resuming their courtship of party leaders.

But in 1968, the Democrats began tinkering with the nominating rules, resulting in presidential nominating campaigns that were predictable only in their unpredictability. The reforms were launched in an effort to reduce the alienation of liberals and minorities from the Democratic nominating system and to allow the people to choose their own leaders. The Republicans seldom made any changes in their rules. (See PRESIDENTIAL SELECTION REFORMS.)

The Democrats' era of grassroots control produced presidential candidates such as Senator McGovern, a liberal from South Dakota who lost in a LANDSLIDE to Nixon in 1972, and former Georgia governor Jimmy Carter, who beat incumbent president Gerald R. Ford in 1976.

Aided by the support of superdelegates, Walter Mondale, seen here with running mate Geraldine Ferraro, won the 1984 Democratic presidential nomination.

Source: Minnesota Historical Society

With a then record high of thirty-six primaries held in 1980, the opportunity for mass participation in the nominating process was greater than ever before. President Carter and former California governor Ronald Reagan, the Republican nominee, were the clear winners of the long primary season. Carter amassed a plurality of nearly 2.7 million votes over his major rival, Sen. Edward M. Kennedy of Massachusetts. With no opposition in the late primary contests, Reagan emerged as a more one-sided choice of GOP primary voters. He finished nearly 4.6 million votes ahead of George H. W. Bush, who eventually withdrew and ended up as Reagan's vice presidential RUNNING MATE.

Disheartened by Carter's massive loss to Reagan in 1980, the Democrats revised their nominating rules for the 1984 election. The party created the so-called SUPERDELEGATES; that is, delegate seats were reserved for party leaders who were not formally committed to any presidential candidate. This reform had two main goals. First, Democratic leaders wanted to ensure that the party's elected and appointed officials would participate at the convention. Second, they wanted to ensure that these uncommitted party leaders could play a major role in selecting the presidential nominee if no candidate was a clear FRONT-RUNNER.

While the reforms of the 1970s had been designed to give more influence to grassroots activists and less to party regulars, the 1980s revisions were intended to bring about a deliberative process in which experienced party leaders could help select a consensus Democratic nominee with a strong chance to win the presidency and then govern effectively.

The Democrats' new rules had some expected, as well as unexpected, results. For the first time since 1968, the number of primaries in 1984 declined and the number of caucuses increased. The Democrats held only twenty-five primaries in 1984. Yet, like McGovern in 1972 and Carter in 1976, Colorado senator Gary Hart used the primaries to pull ahead (temporarily) of former vice president Walter F. Mondale, an early front-runner whose strongest ties were to the party leadership and its traditional core elements. In 1984 the presence of superdelegates was important because about four out of five backed Mondale.

Some critics regarded the seating of superdelegates as undemocratic, and there were calls for reducing their numbers. Instead, by adding seventy-five superdelegate seats, the DEMOCRATIC NATIONAL COMMITTEE (DNC) increased their numbers from 14 percent of the delegates in 1984 to 15 percent for 1988. Moreover, another 150 new superdelegate seats were set aside for party leaders. All members of the DNC are guaranteed superdelegate seats, as are all Democratic governors and about 80 percent of the Democrats in Congress.

Still more seats were added to the various superdelegate categories in 1992, bringing the total to 772 or 18 percent of the 4,288 delegates to the Democratic convention in New York City. Having won 51.8 percent of the Democratic primary vote, Arkansas governor Bill Clinton went to the convention with the nomination virtually ensured. He was nominated by acclamation after receiving 3,372 votes on the first ballot. In 2000, both Texas governor George W. Bush and Vice President Al Gore clinched their respective nominations months before the conventions. Bush came within seven votes of winning the nomination unanimously at the Republican convention. Vice President Al Gore, the only candidate whose name was placed in nomination at the Democratic convention, was declared the unanimous winner. That year, the Democrats had 802 superdelegates, which amounted to 18.4 percent of all delegates. (See DELEGATES.)

The Republican Party does not guarantee delegate seats to its leaders, nor has the party created superdelegates. Its rules, however, permit less rigid pledging of delegates and generally have led to substantial participation by Republican leaders, despite the absence of such guarantees.

Regional Primaries and Super Tuesday

Problems of presidential primaries included the length of the primary season (nearly twice as long as the general election campaign), the expense, the physical strain on the candidates, and the variations and complexities of state laws. Several states in 1974 and 1975 discussed the feasibility of creating regional primaries, to reduce the candidates' expense and strain of travel and permit their concentration on regional issues. The idea achieved some limited success in 1976 when states in the West and South decided to organize regional primaries. Both groups, however, chose May 25 to hold their primaries, which defeated one of the main purposes of the plan by forcing candidates to shuttle across the country to cover both areas. The western states participating were Idaho, Nevada, and Oregon; the southern states were Arkansas, Kentucky, and Tennessee.

Attempts also were made in New England to construct a regional primary. But New Hampshire did not want to take part and could not because its law requires the state to hold its primary at least one week before any other state. Hesitancy by the other New England state legislatures defeated the idea.

In 1988 the southern states' goal of a regional primary finally was realized. Fourteen states below the Mason-Dixon line—Alabama, Arkansas, Florida, Georgia, Kentucky, Louisiana, Maryland, Mississippi, Missouri, North Carolina, Oklahoma, Tennessee, Texas, and Virginia—held primaries on what came to be known as SUPER TUESDAY. Two northern states, Massachusetts and Rhode Island, also held their primaries that day (March 8).

Although changes initiated by Democrats had created the surge of primaries, Republicans for the most part went along. By 1988 both parties were allocating the vast majority of their delegates among their candidates in primaries.

George H. W. Bush's win in the 1988 New Hampshire primary proved to be the turning point in his campaign, and because most Republican primaries were then the winner-take-all kind, Bush had the Republican nomination all but locked up after Super Tuesday. He went over the top with the Pennsylvania primary, April 26. In contrast, the Democratic candidates were awarded delegates based on the proportion of votes cast for them in each primary. Democrat Michael S. Dukakis won enough delegates by June 7 to become his party's nominee.

"March Madness"

By 1992, Super Tuesday had become part of a general rush among states to hold their primaries as early as possible and thus help to determine the ultimate nominees. Dubbed "March Madness," the early clustering or FRONT-LOADING of primaries was viewed with dismay by some political analysts. They said it could lead to nominees being locked in before most voters knew what was happening—a prediction that was not far off the mark—resulting in less informed and deliberative voting in the general election.

As winners in the eight Super Tuesday primaries on March 10, Republican incumbent Bush and Democratic challenger Clinton were already well on their way to nomination. Bush had half the delegates he needed for renomination, and with 707 delegates, Clinton held a commanding lead over his nearest rival, former senator Paul Tsongas of Massachusetts. In all, roughly half the states held their primaries before the end of March 1992.

In the wide-open Republican race in 1996, front-runner Bob Dole lost to conservative columnist Patrick J. Buchanan in the February 20 New Hampshire primary, but through victories in subsequent primaries Dole had the GOP nomination clinched by March 26. Only thirteen primaries were held after that date. Clinton faced no opposition.

The 1996 election saw the misnamed JUNIOR TUESDAY week surpassing Super Tuesday in the number of participating states. Fourteen states and Puerto Rico held Republican primaries or caucuses March 2 through March 9, compared with seven primaries on Super Tuesday, March 12.

The Republican contest followed a similar pattern in 2000. Front-runner George W. Bush lost the New Hampshire primary to Sen. John McCain of Arizona, but then Bush clinched the nomination in March. He routed McCain on March 7, when sixteen states from coast to coast held primaries and caucuses in the biggest event of the campaign season. On the Democratic side, Gore narrowly edged Bill Bradley in New Hampshire and then knocked him out of the race by winning every contest on March 7.

The next presidential campaign was similar. With Bush running as the incumbent, the interest in primaries declined from forty-three contests in 2000 to thirty-eight in 2004, with slightly more than a third (37 percent) held in March. The Democratic contest included ten principal candidates who drew more than 50,000 votes, but was essentially between two senators: John Kerry of Massachusetts, the winner with 61 percent of the vote, and John Edwards of North Carolina with 19 percent.

The 2008 campaign was different. The number of primaries increased, to forty-one, more states tried to increase their influence by holding earlier primaries (two in violation of party rules), and the Democratic race carried into early summer.

Front-loading increased again. Thirty-three states held primaries before April 1, compared with twenty-five four years earlier and ten in 1980. In 1968 only one primary was held before April (although only fifteen were held during the entire primary season). Most of the 2008 contests, twenty-two, came in February. Two states—Michigan and Florida—were so eager to boost their influence in the nomination game that they moved their primaries into January, in violation of party rules that allowed only New Hampshire and South Carolina to vote before February 1. As a result, both states faced party sanctions that threatened to eliminate or reduce their delegate representations at the national conventions, although the controversy was defused before the parties met and delegates from those states were seated.

In spite of the increasing front-loading, the 2008 Democratic contest between Barack Obama and Hillary Rodham Clinton lasted through the spring before being definitively settled in June. However, Obama's nationwide campaign to focus on smaller caucus and primary states as well as the large battleground states netted him enough delegates by the end of March to all but guarantee the nomination even though Clinton outpolled him by almost 294,000 primary votes by the last contest in early June.

On the Republican side, Sen. John McCain of Arizona wrapped up the nomination in March after losing in the Iowa caucuses but winning handily in the New Hampshire primary.

Approaches to Reform

In an effort to alleviate March Madness and reverse the bunching of primaries in the early months of presidential election years, the 1996 Republican National Convention approved rules changes that would reward states holding later primaries, beginning in 2000. States holding primaries after March 15 would receive 10 percent more delegates, with an additional 5 percent increase for each month of delay until May 15.

Despite losing the New Hampshire primary to Patrick Buchanan, Bob Dole secured the 1996 Republican presidential nomination by March 26.

Source: CQ Photo/Scott J. Ferrell

The effort proved ineffective, as would subsequent plans by both parties to provide bonus delegates to states willing to eschew the front-loading frenzy. Given the virtual negation of the conventions as decision-making venues, it had become more important to the states to be first, or at least early, in hopes of gaining candidate visits and media attention to their primaries, than it was to hold out—likely until after the choices of the nominees had already been set in stone—in order to obtain a few more delegate slots.

Through the run-up to the 2008 presidential nominating campaign, the last serious effort at putting the brakes on front-loading came from the Republican Party prior to the 2000 convention. Republican National Committee officials had impaneled a party commission to consider changing the primary schedule. After an extensive round of meetings, the commission was prepared to offer a plan to the convention that would have grouped states into four blocks spread out over several weeks of the spring of the presidential election year.

Plans to bring the matter to the convention floor were quashed by George W. Bush's campaign organization. Bush was to be nominated at the convention, and his campaign planners did not want debate on the primary schedule change to interfere with their intricately planned time line for the convention's events.

For their part, Democrats gave up on efforts to push back the primary calendar. Instead, they approved rules changes to move up the Iowa and New Hampshire contests to January in 2004, with other contests following soon after in February.

Since 1911 hundreds of bills have been introduced in Congress to reform the presidential primary system. Most of them appeared after the 1912, 1952, and 1968 nominating campaigns. These three campaigns produced the feeling among many voters that the will of the electorate, as expressed in the primaries, had been thwarted by national conventions. But since 1911, the only legislation of this type enacted by Congress concerned the presidential primary in the DISTRICT OF COLUMBIA.

Various other suggestions for changing the primary system have been made. One would establish a direct national primary. But a Democratic study commission as well as several academic groups rejected the idea. The consensus was that such a process would strip the party leadership of any role in the nominating process, enable presidential candidates to run factional or regional campaigns, and increase the primacy of media "image" over serious discussion of the issues.

Presidential Selection Reforms

The presidential nominating process in the early years of the twenty-first century is the product of numerous changes that date back to the late 1960s, almost all of them originating with the DEMOCRATIC PARTY. Whereas average voters once had little say in the choice of the major parties' presidential nominees—decisions that long were largely controlled by party "bosses"—now they play the dominant role.

The instrument for this influence is the PRESIDENTIAL PRIMARY, and the Democratic reforms dealt with the primary or CAUCUS election of DELEGATES to the NATIONAL PARTY CONVENTION.

Whereas the Democrats made their delegate-selection changes by amending the rules, the Republicans and the third parties have adopted many of the same reforms, though less formally. In some cases the Republicans had never followed the restrictive rules that the Democrats' changes affected; or the other parties had no choice but to follow the Democrats' lead because state legislatures voted the changes into law.

Ironically, the reforms that were intended to open the nominating conventions to more women and minorities resulted in all delegates having less to do. Though a rainbow of diversity, the delegates in recent conventions have played little substantial role in party policy-making—and virtually no role in choosing the presidential and vice presidential nominees.

That is because the primary-driven nominating process has invariably produced a front-runner in each party early in the presidential election calendar, and the mounting expense of running viable national campaigns has tended to quickly cull the candidate fields. The primaries and caucuses have predetermined the identity of the presidential nominees prior to the conventions dating back to the early 1970s.

The changes helped to transform both parties' conventions into archaic events where nominations were declared—and usually approved by acclamation—rather than fought out on the floor. The Democrats so overcompensated in reducing the power of political bosses that they had to find a new way to give party leaders at least a face-saving role in the nominating process, and they did so by creating the SUPERDELEGATE position, which guaranteed certain elected and party officials seats at the Democratic National Convention.

Moreover, the reforms that aimed to open the process to more participation and make the nominating campaigns more competitive have been thwarted to a significant extent by the "front-loading" of the primary and caucus calendar, with most states moving their contests up as early in the presidential election year as the rules of the major parties would allow (and in some cases earlier, despite the threat of party penalties) in pursuit of greater influence over who would receive the nominations.

Despite numerous proposals to reform the process, there has been little fundamental change, in part because of resistance from the states that have held the first presidential voting events for many years: Iowa, which has long kicked off the process with its precinct caucuses, and New Hampshire, to which candidates have long been drawn for its first-in-the-nation primary.

A pair of plans to overhaul the calendar and encourage a more deliberate process were drawn up by Republican Party task forces, one in 2000 and another in 2008, but both were tabled at the party's national convention by officials who did not want the issue to alienate voters in any state that might be key to the party's hopes of winning the election.

The GOP did, however, draw up some limited reforms in advance of the 2012 elections. Responding to criticism of a 2008 campaign that began with Iowa and New Hampshire events in early January and had its biggest day ("Super Tuesday") on February 5, the Republican rules bar any primary or caucus from being held in January, and limit February events to the states of Iowa, New Hampshire, Nevada, and South Carolina, with the Super Tuesday cluster of primaries set for no earlier than March 6. The Democratic Party, which at the time the schedule was set expected that incumbent President Barack Obama would have no serious opposition for the 2012 nomination, concurred in these changes.

The Republicans also altered their rules for primaries that allocate all of a state's delegates to the candidate who wins the state's primary (even if that candidate wins less than a majority of all votes). For 2012, the GOP mandated that states must hold their primaries on or after April 1 if they want the contests to be winner-take-all; states that hold contests prior to that date must allocate delegates in proportion to the vote percentages that all candidates received. This rule does not pertain to the Democrats, who have long required proportional allocation of delegates by all states.

But it was not clear as of late summer 2011 whether all states would stick to the new rules. Officials in Florida, the nation's third most-populous state and an important source of delegate votes, said they planned to hold their primary on January 31, which would violate the rules.

There is precedent for this kind of intraparty tension. Florida and Michigan broke the rules set by both parties for the 2008 nominating contests by scheduling their primaries in January. The Republican Party penalized the states by taking away half their delegates. The Democrats took a harder line initially by threatening to not seat any delegates from either state, though ultimately a compromise was reached that cut both states' delegations by half.

The Democrats' overhaul of the nominating system can be traced in part to the tumultuous political climate of 1968, when protests against the Vietnam War were reaching a peak and civil rights champion Rev. Martin Luther King Jr. and charismatic New York senator Robert F. Kennedy—brother of slain president John F. Kennedy—were assassinated. There were race riots in major cities, student uprisings throughout the country, and bitter confrontations between demonstrators and police.

North Vietnam's offensive against South Vietnam during the early 1968 Tet, or New Year's, holiday period brought massive U.S. casualties and provoked renewed backlash against the war. A leading opponent of the war, Sen. Eugene J. McCarthy of Minnesota, challenged

The assassination of Robert F. Kennedy, shown here appearing before a platform committee in 1964, led to major changes in the Democratic Party's nomination system in 1968.

Source: Library of Congress.

President Lyndon B. Johnson in the New Hampshire primary and campaigned against his Vietnam policies. Although Johnson won, his 50 percent to 42 percent margin was stunningly narrow and exposed Johnson's political vulnerability. Two weeks afterward, the president, who had won a historic landslide victory just four years earlier, withdrew his candidacy for reelection.

Johnson's heir apparent, Vice President Hubert H. Humphrey, delayed his formal entry into the race to avoid primary contests with McCarthy and Kennedy, who won the June 5 California primary but was shot and mortally wounded after making his victory speech. With the backing of party regulars, Humphrey assumed correctly that he would be nominated at the Democratic National Convention. But Humphrey's nomination was won at a price. The sizable number of delegates who opposed his nomination, many of whom had labored on the campaign trail for McCarthy or Kennedy, felt shut out, and they let their bitterness be known.

Before the convention, McCarthy supporters had formed the ad hoc Commission on the Democratic Selection of Presidential Nominees, chaired by Iowa governor Harold E. Hughes. The Hughes Commission report, issued just before the convention began, told of unfair representation of McCarthy during the delegate-selection process. Nearly one-third of the convention delegates already had been chosen before McCarthy announced his candidacy. In short, the Hughes Commission report concluded that the Democratic Party's delegate-selection process displayed "considerably less fidelity to basic democratic principles than a nation which claims to govern itself can safely tolerate."

Supporters of McCarthy and Sen. George S. McGovern of South Dakota—another opponent of the war who received a small amount of delegate support for president as a stand-in for Kennedy—won one significant reform early in the convention: rejection of the UNIT RULE, which allowed the leaders of a state delegation that was split among candidates to cast all of its votes for the candidate favored by the delegation's majority. Although Humphrey stood to gain from retention of the unit rule, he had long favored more open and democratic conventions, and his supporters helped to defeat the rule. About ten BORDER and southern states—notably Texas—were still using the unit rule in 1968. Texas governor John Connally, a Humphrey supporter who later would switch to the Republican Party, fought a vigorous losing battle to keep the rule.

After the 1968 convention, many elements of the Democratic Party were determined to change the rules of the game. The report of the convention's Credentials Committee echoed that sentiment. The report alleged unfair and exclusionary practices in the delegate-selection process and proposed the establishment of a committee to examine the problem and offer recommendations. As a result, in February 1969 the party established the Commission on Party Structure and Delegate Selection, chaired by Sen. McGovern and, later, by Rep. Donald M. Fraser of Minnesota. (The commission came to be known as the McGovern-Fraser Commission.) Its report, issued a little more than a year later, set forth eighteen detailed "guidelines" for the state delegate-selection processes.

The commission's guidelines were designed to counteract rules and practices that either inhibited access to the process or diluted the influence of those who had access. They condemned discrimination because of race, color, creed, sex, or age and required that affirmative steps be taken to give delegate representation to minorities, women, and young people in proportion to their population in each state. The guidelines further required that restrictive fees (defined as those exceeding $10) and petition requirements for delegate

> **The Democratic Party's delegate-selection process displays "considerably less fidelity to basic democratic principles than a nation which claims to govern itself can safely tolerate."**
>
> —Conclusion of the Hughes Commission report, 1968
> McGovern-Fraser Commission

candidates be eliminated, and they "urged" elimination of undue restrictions on voter registration (such as literacy tests, lengthy residency requirements, and untimely registration periods).

The guidelines banned the unit rule and "proxy voting" (which allowed votes to be cast for someone who was absent) at every level of the delegate-selection process; set minimum quorum provisions for party committees; and disallowed ex officio delegates (who were automatically appointed because of their public or party position). In addition, the guidelines limited the influence of party committees in the selection of delegates, required written rules for governing the process, demanded adequate public notice of all meetings pertaining to delegate selection, and called for a standardized formula for apportioning delegates among states.

Stressing that most of its guidelines were mandatory, the McGovern-Fraser Commission finished its work early. By the time the 1972 Democratic National Convention met to nominate McGovern, who had prevailed in that year's primaries, the commission was able to claim that virtually all the states were in at least substantial compliance with the guidelines, that only 1.1 percent of the convention delegates were still elected by state party committees, and that the percentages of black, female, and young delegates had increased three to four times over their percentages in 1968.

The guidelines' effects were considerable. On the one hand, compliance substantially democratized the system by opening avenues for citizen participation. On the other hand, it greatly reduced the power of party leaders, prompting some observers to say that the reforms had "dismantled" the party.

Party regulars were particularly rankled at the 1972 convention, when a delegation from Illinois dominated by McGovern supporters was seated instead of an establishment delegation headed by Chicago mayor Richard J. Daley. Many liberal activists still had a bitter view of Daley because of his police force's violent actions in attempting to contain antiwar protests at the chaotic 1968 convention in Chicago. But many old-school party leaders viewed the exclusion of Daley and his party regulars as a gratuitous insult, and essentially stood aside as McGovern's trouble-plagued campaign reeled into a landslide defeat at the hands of Republican incumbent Richard M. Nixon.

Yet delegate-selection systems had been fundamentally and permanently altered. For example, "party caucuses" and "delegate primaries" were abolished in favor of "participatory conventions" and "candidate primaries."

In the party caucus system, low-level party officials chose delegates, who in turn chose national convention delegates. In the participatory convention, selection of the intermediary delegates was not limited to party officers but was open to any party member. In the delegate-primary system, members voted for delegates to the national convention (rather than for presidential candidates, whose names did not appear on the ballot). The candidate primary required that the names of presidential candidates, instead of just the names of their potential delegates, be listed on the ballot.

The McGovern-Fraser guidelines also urged a move toward the PROPORTIONAL REPRESENTATION—or what they called fair representation—commonly found in European electoral systems but unusual in the United States. Under proportional representation, delegates were assigned in proportion to the percentage of the total that each candidate received. (The usual alternative was a WINNER-TAKE-ALL system, in which the candidate who won a plurality of the POPULAR VOTE received all of the delegate votes in the electoral district.) Furthermore, the guidelines were interpreted as requiring mandatory "quotas" for the representation of minority groups in proportion to their share of the population.

Although states were in substantial compliance with the guidelines by the 1972 Democratic convention, the reforms met with considerable resistance. More than 40 percent of the convention's membership and more than half of the states challenged some aspect of the guidelines. But complete compliance was achieved because a state's delegation at the convention could not be seated unless the state had followed the guidelines.

Criticism of the reforms increased after the Democratic Party's debacle in the 1972 election. Some observers argued that the new rules contributed to McGovern's overwhelming loss to Nixon, in part by empowering members of the liberal activist wing of the party at the expense of its more centrist and conservative factions. They argued that a demographically balanced slate of delegates was not necessarily representative of the party's constituency.

Mikulski Commission

The 1972 Democratic convention called for the establishment of another delegate-selection commission. The call was largely in response to the controversy over some of the McGovern-Fraser reforms. By the time it was appointed, the new Commission on Delegate Selection and Party Structure (chaired by Baltimore city councilwoman Barbara Mikulski, who would go on to serve long tenures in the U.S. House and Senate) was facing a Democratic Party split even worse than in 1968, between those who wanted a return to traditional procedures and those advocating further reforms. The commission responded by trying, at least rhetorically, to appease both sides.

With the strongest reaction against the McGovern-Fraser Commission being over quotas, the Mikulski Commission sought to placate critics by making it clear that quotas were not required, although they were permitted. (The McGovern-Fraser Commission had not originally intended for them to be mandatory.) The Mikulski Commission dictated, however, that "affirmative action programs" be adopted to expand the participation of women and minority groups in party affairs.

As further concessions to the critics of McGovern-Fraser, the Mikulski Commission allowed party regulars to appoint up to 25 percent (instead of 10 percent) of a state's delegation; partly removed the ban on proxy voting and eased quorum requirements; extended convention privileges (not including voting rights) to public officials and party regulars (although it retained the ban on ex officio delegates); and loosened the formula for apportioning delegates within states.

Nevertheless, reform advocates won a major victory in the Mikulski Commission's decision to require proportional representation of all candidates receiving at least 10 percent of the vote (later changed to "from 10 to 15 percent," to be decided by individual state parties)—something that McGovern-Fraser had "urged" but not required. In short, the Mikulski Commission advanced, to the extent that it could, the goals of the McGovern-Fraser Commission. In loosening earlier requirements, it tried to make them more palatable to party members who objected to the reforms.

Sen. Barbara Mikulski of Maryland headed the Mikulski Commission, which reformed the Democratic Party's delegate-selection process. Here, she attends a rally on Capitol Hill in 1998.
Source: CQ Photo/Scott J. Ferrell.

In the wake of the Democratic Party's reforms, the number of presidential primaries mushroomed. Between 1968 and 1976 they nearly doubled (increasing from seventeen to thirty). Most state party leaders felt that the adoption of a presidential primary was the easiest way to conform to the rules and thereby prevent a challenge to their delegates at the next national convention. Party regulars also feared that reformed caucuses would bring activists into wide-ranging party decision making—a consequence that they felt was worse than turning to a primary system.

> ## "We achieved the opposite of what we intended."
>
> —*Political scientist Austin Ranney,* writing on the McGovern-Fraser Commission

Members of the McGovern-Fraser Commission had not intended for there to be such an increase in primaries. Political scientist Austin Ranney, a member of the commission, later wrote, "We hoped to prevent any such development [a national primary or more state primaries] by reforming the delegate-selection rules so that the party's nonprimary processes would be open and fair, participation in them would greatly increase, and consequently the demand for more primaries would fade away. . . ." Instead, he said, "we achieved the opposite of what we intended."

Winograd Commission

Whatever its cause, the proliferation of presidential primaries was disturbing to party regulars because primary elections tend to weaken the role of state political parties in selecting candidates. The result was the party's formation in 1975 of the Commission on the Role and Future of Presidential Primaries (later changed to the Commission on Presidential Nomination and Party Structure), headed by Michigan Democratic chairman Morley Winograd.

Despite its original purpose, the Winograd Commission ultimately skirted the question of primaries. With the election of Jimmy Carter in 1976, the commission was recast to reflect at least partially the interests of President Carter (which included protecting the incumbent). When it produced its final report, the commission stated that it could not reach a consensus on primaries, and it offered no recommendations in that area.

A number of the commission's recommendations seemed to favor Carter's expectations. First, the nominating season was shortened to three months, from the second Tuesday in March to the second Tuesday in June (although exemptions to go earlier were given later to several states, including Iowa and New Hampshire). This change tended to favor the incumbent president because it diminished the effect of early primaries and caucuses, which give long-shot candidates more time to gain name recognition and money.

Second, the Winograd Commission proposed that filing deadlines for a candidate to enter a primary or a caucus be at least fifty-five days before the selection of delegates. This, too, favored an incumbent by discouraging last-minute challengers. The DEMOCRATIC NATIONAL COMMITTEE (DNC) later amended the proposal and allowed deadlines to fall within a more flexible thirty- to ninety-day range, according to each state.

Third, the commission proposed that the THRESHOLD for a candidate to be eligible for a proportional share of delegates be based on an increasing scale of 15 percent to 25 percent as the nominating season progressed. Although it was argued that this system would give a fair chance to long shots in the early phase of the campaign, the proposal made it extremely difficult for a candidate to wage a successful challenge to a FRONT-RUNNER or incumbent over the entire course of the season. Again, the DNC overruled the proposal and set a threshold range of 15 percent to 20 percent.

Finally, the commission proposed the "bound-delegate" rule, which required that a delegate who was elected on behalf of a particular candidate be bound to vote for that candidate at the national convention. This became a major point of contention at the 1980 Democratic convention when Sen. Edward M. Kennedy of Massachusetts—hoping to upset the renomination of Carter—forced a floor fight over the rule. Kennedy's argument was that the bound-delegate rule prevented delegates from taking into account events since their selection (such as the entry of a new candidate into the field).

Other proposals of the Winograd Commission included a ban on open primaries (meaning that a registered Republican could no longer vote in a Democratic primary); a suggestion that state party committees be able to appoint an additional 10 percent of the delegates to the national convention; continued support of affirmative action programs to represent women and minorities; and a rejection of the idea that state delegations should be equally divided between men and women because such a recommendation too closely resembled quotas. The Democratic National Committee later overturned this last point in its call to the 1980 convention.

Finally, the commission eliminated so-called loophole primaries, which had served to undermine proportional representation. In such primaries, citizens voted directly for individual delegates in each district (instead of having the delegates distributed in proportion to the statewide vote tallies of the presidential candidates). Because such primaries generally produced winner-take-all results, they were a loophole to the proportional representation requirement of the party rules. (See PRIMARY TYPES.)

Hunt Commission

In June 1982 the DNC adopted rules changes recommended by yet another party group, the Commission on Presidential Nomination, chaired by North Carolina governor James B. Hunt Jr. The Hunt Commission, as it came to be known, suggested revisions to increase the power of party regulars and give the convention more freedom to act. It was the fourth time in twelve years that the Democrats had rewritten their party rules in an attempt to repair their nominating system without repudiating earlier reforms.

One major Hunt Commission change was the creation of the new superdelegate category—party and elected officials who would go to the 1984 convention uncommitted and would cast about 14 percent of the ballots. The DNC also adopted a commission proposal to allow a presidential candidate to replace any disloyal delegate with a more faithful one.

Another significant revision relaxed proportional representation at the convention and ended the ban on the loophole primary—winner take all by district. Proportional representation of delegates was blamed by some Democrats for the protracted 1980 primary fight between Carter and Kennedy. Because candidates needed only about 20 percent of the vote in most places to qualify for a share of the delegates, Kennedy was able to remain in contention until he lost the nomination at the convention.

The Hunt Commission raised the threshold for receiving proportional representation to 20 percent in caucus states and to 25 percent in primary states, and states were allowed to give "bonus delegates" to the primary winner to better reflect that candidate's strength (the "winner-take-more" option).

In addition, the Hunt Commission repealed the bound-delegate rule that had caused controversy between Carter and Kennedy forces at the 1980 convention. This action returned delegates to the pre–Winograd Commission "good conscience" standard. Finally, the Hunt Commission retained the affirmative action rule; maintained the policy that delegations be equally divided between men and women (the "equal division" rule); continued to allow candidates to approve their delegates; and reaffirmed the Winograd Commission's shortening of the nominating season to three months. (The commission gave specific exemptions—notably to Iowa and New Hampshire—but with strict limits as to how much earlier than the other states they could be.)

Fairness Commission

The most recent of the long series of major reform efforts within the Democratic Party, the Fairness Commission, was headed by Donald L. Fowler, the party chairman in South Carolina (who would later chair the DNC). Its report, adopted by the DNC in March 1986, provided an opportunity for some states (such as Wisconsin and Montana) to hold open primaries. The rule, however, was worded tightly so that states that traditionally had restricted participation to Democrats could not move to open systems.

The Fairness Commission also eased the mechanism for loophole primaries, but it lowered the threshold for "fair" (proportional) representation to 15 percent. In addition, it further increased the number of delegate slots reserved for unpledged superdelegates, giving them about 16 percent of the votes.

In 1988, two years after the commission finished its work, African American civil rights activist Jesse Jackson won primaries in ten states plus the District of Columbia, Puerto Rico, and the Virgin Islands. At the Democratic National Convention, however, Jackson won only two states (South Carolina and Mississippi), the District of Columbia, and the Virgin Islands because of the votes of superdelegates. As a concession to Jackson, the convention's Rules Com-

Former Democratic National Committee chairman Donald L. Fowler headed the Fairness Commission, the most recent push for Democratic election reform.

Source: CQ Photo/Douglas Graham.

mittee recommended that the number of superdelegates be reduced in the future. Instead, the Democrats added more superdelegates, raising the total to about 18 percent of the delegates to the 1992 and 1996 conventions.

After 1986 the Democratic Party continued to adjust its presidential nominating process without the equivalent of a Fairness Commission. In 1990 the DNC banned winner-reward systems, which gave extra delegates to the winner of a primary or caucus. Fifteen states had used some form of winner-reward system in 1988. The Democrats required all states in 1992 and 1996 to divide their publicly elected delegates proportionally among candidates who drew at least 15 percent of the primary or caucus vote.

Rules Changes in the Republican Party

Although the proliferation of primaries that accompanied the Democratic Party reforms also affected the Republicans, they did not experience the same kind of internal pressures to reform. Whereas liberal insurgents within the Democratic Party found the party's rules to be a barrier to their participation, prompting them to push for reform in 1968, the Republicans faced no such problem. To a large degree, this was because the Republicans were a smaller, more ideologically cohesive party than the Democrats. The Republicans also had far fewer minority or feminist members, which meant there was less internal demand for equal representation.

To the extent that ideological factions did exist within the Republican Party, they did not find the rules problematic. Indeed, conservative insurgents had been quite successful in 1964. In short, a grassroots movement promoting specific policy goals was apparently more feasible among the Republicans than among the Democrats. It was the failure of a similar "amateur" movement against party "professionals" within the Democratic ranks that helped to spawn that party's reform.

The two parties also differed in their structures. Republican rules were strictly codified and could be changed only with the national convention's approval. In contrast, the Democrats' rules were loose and uncodified. Changes did not have to be approved by the national convention, making revision easy and inviting reform.

Finally, the Republicans already had achieved several reforms sought by Democrats. Use of the unit rule at the Republican national conventions had been banned since the mid-nineteenth century. A similar ban on proxy voting at the national conventions had long been in force.

Clearly the Democrats' reforms went beyond the GOP's existing rules. Nevertheless, rank-and-file Republicans were not overly eager to keep up the pace. The Democrats were more amenable to the centralization of national party control, and a number of the Democrats' further-reaching efforts—such as quotas or strictly enforced affirmative action programs—were discouraged by the conservative ideology of the Republican Party.

Nonetheless, the Republicans did institute some reforms in the post-1968 era, often along the same lines as the Democrats. At the same time, Republicans wanted to avoid "McGovernizing" their party through what they perceived as the debilitating aspects of the Democrats' early reforms. The Republican National Convention amended its rules in 1976 so that a subcommittee of the REPUBLICAN NATIONAL COMMITTEE (RNC) would undertake all future rules review—an effort to prevent "runaway" commissions.

Finally, the Democratic Party reforms often prompted changes in state laws that also affected the Republicans. As a result, Republicans had to accommodate those changes—whatever their own rules may have been. More recently, they have tried to anticipate Democratic rules changes that would affect them.

In 1968 the Republican convention called for the establishment of a committee to consider party rules changes. All sixteen members of the Committee on Delegates and Organization (DO Committee, chaired by Rosemary Ginn of Missouri) came from the RNC. Unlike the recommendations of the McGovern-Fraser Commission, the DO Committee's recommendations were not binding. Indeed, the report contained no enforcement or compliance mechanism, which reflected the states' rights orientation of the Republican Party.

Among the DO Committee's recommendations were proposals to ban ex officio delegates, to eliminate proxy voting in meetings on delegate selection, and to "attempt" to have an equal number of men and women in each state's delegation to the national convention. The 1972 convention later approved these recommendations but rejected a DO Committee proposal that delegations try to include people under the age of twenty-five in proportion to their population in each state. Nevertheless, the convention strengthened the rule to end discrimination and increase participation. It also established a new reform committee under Rule 29 of its bylaws.

The Rule 29 Committee was chaired by Rep. William A. Steiger of Wisconsin. Its fifty-eight members included not only members of the RNC but also state party leaders, governors, members of Congress, young people, and other representatives of the Republican Party. Among its recommendations was a proposal that state parties be required to take "positive action" to broaden participation and, most important, that state action be reviewed by the RNC. Although no sanctions were attached to the review procedure, and quotas were not a part of the recommendation, the RNC objected to the proposal on the grounds that it interfered with the states' rights outlook of the party. The 1976 national convention rejected the establishment of any compliance procedures.

Since 1976 subcommittees of the RNC have undertaken all rules reviews. The first significant change resulting from such a review was approved by the 1996 Republican National Convention. Designed to reduce the FRONT-LOADING of primaries in early March, the change aimed to award bonus delegates to states holding primaries between March 15 and May 15. But the change failed to sway states to push back their primary dates. (See DELEGATES; PRESIDENTIAL PRIMARIES.)

Other efforts to prevent accelerated front-loading of primary and caucus events in each presidential election year proved ineffective. Neither incentives (in the form of bonus delegates) nor the threat of sanctions (such as delegate reductions for states that challenged the schedule structure established by the party committees) slowed the process, as states competed for attention and influence in the presidential candidate nominating process.

More on this topic:
Caucus, p. 89
Delegates, p. 142
Front-Loading, p. 219
Front-Runner, p. 222
National Party Conventions, p. 347
Presidential Primaries, p. 468
Proportional Representation, p. 493
Superdelegate, p. 617
Unit Rule, p. 642
Winner Take All, p. 675

Primary Types

The use of primary elections to select party nominees for political office began more than a century ago, as a facet of Progressive Era political reform. But it was not until the 1960s and 1970s that a populist backlash against party machines and bosses made primaries the dominant means for nominating general election candidates.

Most states today do use primary elections to narrow candidate fields and choose the party nominees who will compete in the general election for congressional, state, and local offices. They also use primaries to allow voters to participate in the presidential nominating process.

The PRESIDENTIAL PRIMARIES fall into two basic categories: the *preference* primary, in which voters vote directly for the person they want to see nominated for president; and the *delegate-selection* primary, in which the voters elect DELEGATES to the NATIONAL PARTY CONVENTIONS. Today, most states rely on preference primaries for president, with convention delegates allocated largely according to the vote percentage each candidate received in the primary.

Within the two basic types, a wide and often confusing array of variations makes it difficult to categorize primaries. How they operate may differ somewhat from state to state and from party to party within the same

Sen. Edward M. Kennedy of Massachusetts was incumbent Jimmy Carter's major rival in the 1980 Democratic presidential primary.
Source: CQ Photo/Douglas Graham.

state. Because primaries are partisan events, state legislatures and election boards conform their primary laws and ballots largely to the wishes of the major political parties. PRESIDENTIAL SELECTION REFORMS within the DEMOCRATIC PARTY have been particularly influential in shaping the U.S. primary election system.

With the available options for presidential primaries, a state may

- Combine the preference and delegate-selection primaries by electing delegates pledged or favorable to a candidate named on the ballot. Under this system, state party organizations may run unpledged slates of delegates but rarely do. The simplest form of presidential primary and the easiest for voters to comprehend, this system has emerged as by far the dominant one and is in use in most states. The preference vote usually is binding on the delegates, who are elected in the primary itself or chosen outside of it by a CAUCUS process, by a state committee, or by the candidates who have qualified to win delegates

- Have a preference vote but choose delegates at state party conventions. Votes of this type that do not affect the allocation of delegates are known as BEAUTY CONTEST primaries. Once highly common, to give guidance to state party leaders about voters' candidate preferences and to give voters a sense that they had a say in a process then dominated by party insiders, these preference primaries are nearly an anachronism. By 2004, when only the Democrats had a competitive nominating process—President George W. Bush was UNOPPOSED in the Republican Party—the only state that held a beauty contest primary was Idaho.

- Have an advisory preference vote and a separate delegate-selection vote in which delegates may be listed three ways: pledged to a candidate, favorable to a candidate, or unpledged. Like the beauty contest primary, this inherently confusing system has become rare to nonexistent.

- Have a mandatory preference vote with a separate delegate-selection vote. In these cases, the delegates are required to reflect the preference primary vote. In primaries run under this system, candidates for delegate will often publicly declare their candidate preference in hopes that voters supporting that candidate will also vote to send them to the convention.

For those primaries in which the preference vote is binding, state laws may vary as to how many ballots at the national convention are binding on the affected delegates. In recent years, however, this issue has been moot. Not since the 1952 Democratic convention, when Adlai Stevenson was nominated on the third ballot, has either party taken more than one ballot to nominate a presidential candidate.

National Democratic Party rules in effect only in 1980 required delegates to be bound for one ballot unless released by the candidate they were elected to support. Before the rule was repealed later that year, it enabled Sen. Edward M. Kennedy of Massachusetts to sustain a losing primary challenge to President Jimmy Carter until the national convention—but then prevented Kennedy from overcoming Carter's hold on more than enough delegates to win at the convention.

Until 1980 the REPUBLICAN PARTY required delegates bound to a specific candidate by state law to vote for that candidate at the convention regardless of their personal presidential preferences. That rule was repealed at the July 1980 GOP convention.

Delegates from primary states are allocated to candidates in various ways. Most of the methods are based on the preference vote—PROPORTIONAL REPRESENTATION, statewide WINNER TAKE ALL (in which the candidate winning the most votes statewide wins all the delegates), congressional district and statewide winner take all (in which the high vote-getter in a district wins that district's delegates and the high vote-getter statewide wins all the AT-LARGE delegates), or some combination of the three. Most primary states use proportional representation, at least for Democratic primaries because it is mandatory. But on the Republican side, several states—including California, the most-populous state and biggest single source of delegates—still maintain winner take all by district or statewide.

Still another method is the selection of individual delegates in a loophole, or DIRECT ELECTION, primary. Then the preference vote is nonbinding. Among states choosing delegates this way are Illinois and Pennsylvania.

In the proportional representation system, the qualifying threshold for candidates to win delegates can vary. After a decade of intensive debate, Democratic leaders voted to require proportional representation in all primary and caucus states in 1980. This requirement was made optional in 1984 and 1988, with qualifying thresholds of 20 percent and 15 percent, respectively. For 1992, 1996, 2000, 2004, and 2008, the Democrats again made proportional allocation mandatory, with candidates awarded delegates if they received at least 15 percent of the vote; the same rules were applied for the 2012 nominating campaign.

Along with winner-take-all systems, the Democrats also banned winner-reward systems that gave extra delegates to primary or caucus victors.

In addition, the Democrats instituted a new class of unpledged SUPERDELEGATES, who go to the convention by virtue of the elective or party offices they hold. The concept of superdelegates is controversial in some quarters, with critics arguing that it potentially could allow party insiders to tip the nomination to their own favored candidates, overriding the will of primary voters. Yet superdelegates have tended to be swayed strongly by primary voter sentiment: For instance, in the 2008 race for the Democratic nomination, New York senator (and former first lady) Hillary Rodham Clinton was regarded as the favorite of the party establishment, but most superdelegates rallied behind Barack Obama, then a senator of Illinois, when he established a clear delegate lead over Clinton during the primary and caucus campaign.

The Republicans permit winner-take-all primaries and allow states to set their own proportional representation thresholds, which in many states were lower than what the Democrats specified. In Massachusetts, for example, a GOP candidate in 1996 had to receive only 2.703 percent of the vote to win a delegate.

There are even differences among states in how candidates are placed on the presidential primary ballot. In several states, presidential primary candidates are placed on the ballot by the secretary of state or a special nominating committee, who typically select those candidates who have announced they are running, are staging active campaigns and raising money (though they occasionally face complaints from little-known candidates who have been omitted). Elsewhere, candidates must take the initiative to get on the ballot. The filing requirements range from sending a letter of candidacy to election officials—the case in Puerto Rico, a U.S. commonwealth that participates in the presidential nominating process but whose residents are ineligible to vote in the general election—to filing petitions signed by a specified number of registered voters and paying a filing fee, the case in Alabama and other states.

On many primary ballots, voters have the opportunity to mark a line labeled "uncommitted" if they choose not to vote for any of the candidates.

Primaries may be *open, closed,* or *modified.* In an open primary, any registered voter may participate but must select in which party's primary he or she will vote; in other words, a voter could not participate in both the Democratic and Republican primary contests. Closed primaries are restricted to voters registered as members of the political party holding the election. In recent election cycles, states were divided about equally between open or closed primaries. In a few states, one or both parties held modified closed primaries that were open, for example, to INDEPENDENTS or voters who expressed no party preference during VOTER REGISTRATION.

About a dozen states nominate candidates in party caucuses rather than primaries.

Some states do not register voters by party affiliation and therefore have open primaries. CROSSOVER VOTING may occur in such states as voters take advantage of the opportunity to help nominate the opposing party's weakest candidates. Election officials take precautions to prevent voters from voting in both the Democratic and Republican primaries. If both parties' candidates are on the same ballot, the ballot is void if marked for both primaries.

The Supreme Court in December 1997 rejected Louisiana's unique open primary system, in which a congressional candidate is elected if he or she receives a majority of votes in the primary, but only on grounds that the primary was held before the national election day. By unanimous vote in *Foster v. Love* the Court upheld a lower court's ruling that the system "thwarts the congressional purpose of establishing a uniform day to prevent earlier elections from influencing later voters." But there were no successful legal challenges in the decade after Louisiana officials shifted the congressional primary to coincide with election day, with a runoff in December if no candidate in a race won outright with a majority in the primary.

Louisiana briefly converted to a conventional party primary system for congressional elections, with all contests decided on the November election day beginning in 2008, under a law enacted in 2006. But the state law was changed again, and the 2012 congressional primary will go back to being held to coincide with the national election day with a runoff, if necessary, on the first Saturday in December. Meanwhile, state-level elections, including for governor, are held in odd-numbered years under a different system. The 2011 primary election for governor was scheduled for the second to last Saturday in October, with a runoff that would have been held four weeks later if no candidate took a majority of the primary vote. That became a moot point, though, as Republican incumbent Bobby Jindal—whose popularity put off potentially strong challengers—won outright with 66 percent of the vote in the October balloting.

Another type of open primary won approval of California voters on an INITIATIVE (Proposition 198) in 1996. The highly controversial measure, opposed by the major political parties, permitted voters to pick and choose between the parties, office by office, on a single ballot. Known as the *jungle* type because of its wide open, few-holds-barred structure, the primary was patterned after one long used in Washington State. *Blanket* and jungle primaries are similar. Proposition 198 did not affect the 1996 California primary, at which it was approved by voters of both parties. The new law took effect in 1998. In 2000, the multiballot California primary was open to all registered voters, but only registered Democrats and Republicans could vote in the delegate-selection portion of each party's primary.

The system, however, was ruled unconstitutional in 2000 by the Supreme Court, which accepted the arguments waged by the two major parties that it abrogated the parties' right to limit participation in their primaries and thus have some control over who was nominated to run on the parties' lines. A state court in Washington deemed its longer-standing blanket primary system unconstitutional in 2003.

Yet both of these West Coast states revived the open primary concept with a unique wrinkle called "top two." Under this system, all candidates regardless of party are listed on a single primary ballot and all voters, regardless of party registration status, can participate. The top two vote-getters in the primary, again regardless of party affiliation, move on to the general election—meaning that in voting districts that strongly favor one party, it is possible for the general election to be a matchup between two candidates affiliated with that party.

Since the 1970s, states in different parts of the country have scheduled their presidential primaries on the same date to have more influence on the nominating process. These *regional* primaries have become known informally by names such as SUPER TUESDAY, originally a group of mostly southern primaries, but later expanded to have more national reach. (See PRESIDENTIAL PRIMARIES.)

For much of the first half of the twentieth century, SOUTHERN PRIMARIES held greater importance in U.S. elections than they do today. Because the Democratic Party dominated the South as the states began to adopt the primary system, a plurality victory in the party's primary for governor or senator was tantamount to election. Consequently, most southern states adopted the runoff system to make the election more competitive and representative. If no candidate received a majority or specified percentage in the primary, the two top vote-getters were matched again in the runoff a few weeks later. As the Republican Party gained strength in the South after World War II, some GOP governors and senators were elected and the runoff became less important.

Also in the South, African Americans were excluded from so-called WHITE PRIMARIES in some states and counties. The Democratic Party in these areas designated itself as a private organization to circumvent the Fifteenth Amendment's prohibition against states' denying the right to vote because of race or color. In 1944 the Supreme Court declared white primaries illegal.

The POLL TAX, LITERACY TESTS, and complex VOTER REGISTRATION laws were also used to keep the southern Democratic primaries essentially whites-only affairs.

When Theodore Roosevelt remarked to a reporter during the 1912 GOP convention, "I'm feeling like a bull moose," his vigorous campaign suddenly had a symbol. Roosevelt lost the GOP nomination and formed the Progressive Party.
Source: Library of Congress.

Progressive Party–Bull Moose (1912)

A split in Republican ranks, spurred by the bitter personal and ideological dispute between President William Howard Taft (1909–1913) and his predecessor, Theodore Roosevelt (1901–1909), resulted in the withdrawal of the Roosevelt faction from the REPUBLICAN PARTY after its June 1912 convention. Roosevelt then launched the Progressive Party two months later as the vehicle for his third-party campaign for president—one of the strongest such efforts in American history but one that left Roosevelt the runner-up to Democrat Woodrow Wilson.

The new outfit was known popularly as the Bull Moose Party, a name resulting from Roosevelt's assertion early in the campaign that he felt as fit as a bull moose. While the Taft-Roosevelt split was the immediate reason for the new party, the Bull Moosers were an outgrowth of the progressive movement, which was a powerful force in both major parties in the early years of the twentieth century.

In 1908, Roosevelt had handpicked Taft, a prominent Ohio Republican, as his successor. But his disillusionment with Taft's conservative philosophy came quickly, and, with the support of progressive Republicans, Roosevelt challenged the incumbent for the 1912 Republican presidential nomination. Roosevelt outpolled Taft in the handful of presidential primaries then held. But most delegates were chosen by party leaders at the time, and Taft won the nomination with nearly solid support in the South and among party conservatives, providing the narrow majority of DELEGATES that enabled him to win the bulk of the important credentials challenges.

Although few Republican politicians followed Roosevelt to the Bull Moose fold, the new party demonstrated a popular base at its convention in Chicago in August 1912. Thousands of delegates, basically middle- and upper-class reformers from small towns and cities, attended the convention that launched the party and nominated Roosevelt for president and California governor Hiram Johnson for vice president. Roosevelt appeared in person to deliver his "Confession of Faith," a speech detailing his nationalistic philosophy and progressive reform ideas. The Bull Moose platform reflected the crucial tenets of the Progressive movement, calling for more extensive government antitrust action and for labor, social, government, and electoral reform.

In October 1912 Roosevelt was wounded in an assassination attempt while campaigning in Milwaukee, Wisconsin, but he finished the campaign. In the general election, Roosevelt received more than 4 million votes (27.4 percent of the POPULAR VOTE) and carried six states. His percentage of the vote was the highest ever received by a THIRD-PARTY candidate in American history, but his candidacy split the Republican vote and enabled Wilson to win the election—the first Democratic win for president since Grover Cleveland was elected twenty years earlier. The Progressive Party had minimal success at the state and local levels, winning thirteen House seats but electing no senators or governors.

The party's close identification with Roosevelt quickly became its undoing. Returning to his partisan roots, Roosevelt declined the Progressive nomination in 1916 and endorsed the Republican candidate, Charles Evans Hughes. With the defection of its leader, the decline of the Progressive movement, and the lack of an effective party organization, the Bull Moose Party ceased to exist.

> ## "It takes more than that to kill a bull moose."
>
> **—Theodore Roosevelt,** immediately after surviving an assassination attempt in Milwaukee, Wisconsin, on October, 14, 1912

More on this topic:
Republican Party, p. 541
Third Parties, p. 627

Progressive Party (1924)

Robert M. La Follette (right) gives his son Bob advice before the Progressive Party's 1924 convention in Cleveland.

Source: Library of Congress.

Like the PROGRESSIVE–BULL MOOSE PARTY of Theodore Roosevelt a decade earlier, the Progressive Party that emerged in the mid-1920s was a reform effort led by a Republican. Wisconsin senator Robert M. La Follette led the new Progressive Party, a separate entity from the Bull Moosers. Unlike the middle- and upper-class Roosevelt party of the previous decade, the La Follette party had its greatest appeal among farmers and organized labor.

The La Follette Progressive Party grew out of the Conference for Progressive Political Action (CPPA), a COALITION formed in 1922 of railway union leaders and a remnant of the Bull Moose effort. The SOCIALIST PARTY joined the coalition the following year. Throughout 1923, the Socialists and labor unions argued, though, over whether their coalition should form a THIRD PARTY, with the Socialists in favor and the labor unions against it. They finally agreed to run an independent presidential candidate, La Follette, in the 1924 election but not to field candidates at the state and local levels. La Follette was given the power to choose his vice presidential RUNNING MATE and selected Montana senator Burton K. Wheeler, a Democrat.

Opposition to corporate monopolies was the major feature of the La Follette campaign, although the party advocated various other reforms, particularly aimed at farmers and workers, which had been proposed earlier by either the Populist Party of the 1890s or Bull Moosers. But the Progressive Party itself was a major issue in the 1924 campaign, as the Republicans attacked the alleged radicalism of the party.

Although La Follette had its endorsement, the American Federation of Labor (AFL) provided minimal support. The basic strength of the Progressives, like that of the Populists in the 1890s, derived from agrarian voters west of the Mississippi River. La Follette received 4,832,532 votes (16.6 percent of the POPULAR VOTE) but carried just one state, his native Wisconsin. When La Follette died in 1925, the party collapsed as a national force. It was revived by La Follette's sons on a statewide level in Wisconsin in the mid-1930s.

> **More on this topic:**
>
> *Running Mate, p. 553*
>
> *Third Party, p. 627*

Progressive Party (1948)

The iteration of the Progressive Party that emerged after World War II was founded by the strongly liberal Henry A. Wallace, vice president during Democrat Franklin D. Roosevelt's third term (1941–1945). The party resulted from the dissatisfaction of liberal elements in the DEMOCRATIC PARTY with the leadership of President Harry S. Truman, particularly in the realm of foreign policy.

Truman, formerly a senator from Missouri, had replaced Wallace on the Democratic ticket when Roosevelt ran successfully for a fourth term in 1944. Roosevelt died in April 1945, and Truman succeeded him.

The Democratic Party essentially split in three in 1948. Truman was nominated for a full term by the Democrats; liberals alienated by Truman's policy of using U.S. military power to contain the influence of the communist Soviet Union fostered Wallace's Progressive Party effort; while conservative southern elements, in a reaction to the early shifting of the Democratic Party toward a position of favoring civil rights advances for blacks, withdrew to form the segregationist STATES' RIGHTS DEMOCRATIC PARTY, which nominated South Carolina governor Strom Thurmond for president.

Despite these impediments and poor poll numbers, Truman stunned political experts by winning reelection over Republican Thomas Dewey, with Thurmond and Wallace running well behind.

Wallace was secretary of agriculture before he served as vice president and was secretary of commerce afterward under President Franklin Roosevelt. He was considered one

Henry A. Wallace, considered one of the most liberal idealists in the administration of Franklin Roosevelt, founded the Progressive Party because of dissatisfaction with the Democratic Party. Here, Wallace (right) appears with President Roosevelt (left) and Harry S. Truman in 1944.

Source: Harry S. Truman Library and Museum.

of the most liberal idealists in the Roosevelt administration. Fired from the Truman cabinet in 1946 after breaking with administration policy and publicly advocating peaceful coexistence with the Soviet Union, Wallace began to consider the idea of a liberal THIRD-PARTY candidacy. Supported by the American Labor Party, the Progressive Citizens of America, and other progressive organizations in California and Illinois, Wallace announced his candidacy in December 1947.

The Progressive Party was launched formally the following July at a convention in Philadelphia, which ratified the selection of Wallace for president and Sen. Glen H. Taylor, D-Idaho, as his vice presidential running mate. The party adopted a platform that emphasized foreign policy—opposing the Cold War anticommunism of the Truman administration and specifically urging abandonment of the Truman Doctrine of containment and the Marshall Plan that provided massive U.S. aid to rebuild noncommunist Europe. On domestic issues, the Progressives stressed humanitarian concerns and equal rights for both sexes and all races.

Particularly active in the party were members of groups—women, youth, blacks, Jews, Hispanics—who felt excluded or underrepresented in the political process. But the openness of the Progressives brought Wallace a damaging endorsement from the COMMUNIST PARTY, which had direct ties to the Soviet-directed international communist movement and favored the overthrow of the American government and capitalist system.

Professing that the two parties could work together, Wallace accepted the endorsement while characterizing his philosophy as "progressive capitalism." But at a time of rising anticommunist agitation across the nation, this tacit alliance gave Wallace's critics ammunition to portray the Progressive Party as a left-wing front.

More on this topic:

*Communist Party U.S.A.,
p. 110*

Democratic Party, p. 155

*States' Rights Democratic
Party, p. 612*

Third Parties, p. 627

In 1948, the Progressives appeared on the presidential ballot in forty-five states, but the Communist endorsement helped keep the party on the defensive the entire campaign. In the November election, Wallace received only 1,157,326 votes (2.4 percent of the national popular vote), with nearly half of those votes from the state of New York; he failed to carry a single state. The Progressives had poor results in the congressional races, failing to elect one representative or senator.

The Progressive Party's opposition to the Korean War in 1950 drove many moderate elements out of the party, including Wallace. The party ran a national ticket in 1952 but received only 140,023 votes nationwide, or 0.2 percent of the national popular vote. The party crumbled completely after the election.

Prohibition Party (1869–)

The Prohibition Party, founded in 1869, has existed longer than any third party in American history. In the late nineteenth and early twentieth centuries, it played a key role in agitating for the enactment of laws prohibiting the manufacture and sale of intoxicating liquor, which succeeded first in a number of states and then in the ultimate failed national experiment at prohibition instituted by the ratification of the Eighteenth Amendment to the Constitution in 1919.

The party also was in the forefront of the fight for WOMEN'S SUFFRAGE: The prohibition movement received much of its motivation from women who regarded alcohol consumption by men as a threat to family life. And the Prohibition Party survived the repeal of Prohibition by the Twenty-first Amendment ratified in 1933 to maintain the support of tens of thousands of American voters for years after.

Yet the party, though still technically in existence, has lost most of its relevance as the consumption of alcoholic beverages has become an accepted fact of life and a huge industry in the United States. Even though the party broadened its platform to a range of social conservative views—including, according to its website, opposition to abortion, commercial gambling, the "homosexual agenda," and commercial pornography—its support base has gone from minor to minuscule.

As late as 1948, the Prohibition presidential nominee pulled down 103,900 votes nationally. When Earl F. Dodge in 1988 ran the second of his six consecutive contests as the party's presidential candidate, he collected 8,004 votes. By 2000 Dodge—a marketer of CAMPAIGN BUTTONS—was on the ballot only in his home state of Colorado and received just 208 votes.

Efforts to wrest the 2004 nomination from Dodge resulted in a split of what little was left of the party. Both factions were on the ballot only in Colorado, with dissident leader Gene Amondson taking 1,944 votes on the Concerns of People line and Dodge receiving 140 votes on the Prohibition line. In 2008, the party was on the ballot in three states—Colorado, Florida, and Louisiana—and received 653 votes.

The party's more recent performance contrasts sharply with the party's beginnings. Its organizing convention in Chicago in September 1869 attracted approximately 500 delegates from twenty states. For the first time in U.S. politics, women had equal status with men as delegates. By a narrow majority the convention decided to form an independent party, and three years later the new party put forth its first national ticket.

For all but one election between 1884 and 1916, the party's presidential candidate received at least 1.0 percent of the popular vote. The party's best showing came in 1892, when its presidential nominee, John Bidwell, received 270,770 votes (2.2 percent of the popular vote) in the election won by Democrat Grover Cleveland.

The temperance movement succeeded in gaining prohibition legislation in numerous states in the late nineteenth and early twentieth centuries, and its efforts were capped in 1919 by passage of national prohibition legislation (the Eighteenth Amendment to the U.S. Constitution, repealed fourteen years later by the Twenty-first Amendment). The achievements of the temperance movement were due as much to independent organizations, such as the Women's Christian Temperance Union (WCTU) and the Anti-Saloon League, as to the Prohibition Party, which had limited success at the polls. These organizations allowed active Democrats and Republicans to remain in their parties while working for prohibition.

Prohibition turned out to be one of the least successful and most disruptive efforts at social engineering in the nation's history. The void in legal alcohol sales was filled by bootleggers smuggling legitimate products into the United States and by peddlers of cheap and sometimes poisonous homemade booze. The black market for alcohol spurred a huge upsurge in organized crime, epitomized by the ring headed by brutal Chicago mobster Al Capone.

With virtually no likelihood that it would be revived, the central focus of the Prohibition Party had been rendered moot.

More on this topic:

Campaign Buttons, p. 52

Women's Suffrage, p. 678

Proportional Representation

Democratic theorists have for a long time argued that the WINNER-TAKE-ALL system of elections used in the United States and in other democracies fails to satisfy the requirements of the NATURE OF REPRESENTATION. They contend that in a single-member constituency system persons who did not vote for the winner are not truly represented.

To these theorists, notably John Stuart Mill, each vote in a DEMOCRACY should result in an equal share in the legislature; each voter, so to speak, should have a representative fully and honestly speaking for him or her. But in the U.S. electoral system, the majority and the minority are not legislatively represented in any proportion that reflects their actual strength in the DISTRICT. Small minorities are not represented in any way, giving rise to a question: If 50.1 percent of voters elect a representative, are the other 49.9 percent of voters really represented by that person?

> ***If 50.1 percent of voters elect a representative, are the other 49.9 percent of voters really represented by that person?***

Proportional representation would make the legislature an exact mirror of the voting strength of the multiple interests within the electorate. To do this requires a multiple-member constituency system. Instead of one representative serving a congressional district, there might be eight or fifteen, or any likely number arising from a system that encourages more than two parties. What is of paramount importance to the advocates of proportional representation is that the legislature be, in essence, a photographic "snapshot" of the electorate—providing a "mathematically exact representation of the various segments of opinion among the electorate," as one political analyst writes.

MULTIMEMBER DISTRICTS are still found in some cities and states, and they once existed as congressional districts in some states until Congress abolished them in 1842. African American and other minority groups have argued that multiple-member districts, instead of guaranteeing their representation, actually deny it by submerging them into the district majority. The Supreme Court has agreed that a multimember district may be unconstitutional if it discriminates against a minority, and the 1965 VOTING RIGHTS ACT contained protection against such districting. (See RACIAL REDISTRICTING; REAPPORTIONMENT AND REDISTRICTING.)

John Stuart Mill (1806–1873), an English philosopher, economist, political theorist, journalist, and member of Parliament, believed that the United States was a false democracy in which the numerical majority ruled despotically.
Source: Library of Congress.

Complex Formulas

Two basic forms of proportional representation exist: the predominant "party list" system, in which political parties are awarded seats in the legislature in proportion to the number of votes cast for their differing party rosters (or "lists") on the ballot; and the single transferable vote system, used in some American cities, in which voters cast ballots for individual candidates instead of party lists.

In the single transferable vote system, where voters choose individual candidates, the question becomes one of determining how candidates rank in terms of voter preference, then using a quota to determine, say, the three winners out of five candidates.

It is obvious that whatever formula determines the winners of seats in proportional representation electoral systems, the systems themselves encourage the formation of multiple parties to faithfully represent the varied interests and concerns of the electorate as a whole and of its absolutely essential component, the individual voter. In the American TWO-PARTY SYSTEM, the

DEMOCRATIC and REPUBLICAN parties attempt to draw these varied interests, with varying degrees of success, into mass party organizations with competing wings, for example "moderate Republicans" and "liberal Democrats." The mass party organizations vie with one another for legislative success, and the factions within them contend for control of the party's agenda and ideology.

Reforms of the U.S. presidential system have centered on the question of proportional representation, particularly in the selection of DELEGATES to the NATIONAL PARTY CONVENTIONS. The Democratic Party has banned all types of winner-take-all PRIMARIES, but the Republican Party still permits them in some states.

Delegates are allocated to Democratic presidential candidates in proportion to their percentage of the total vote, provided they meet a THRESHOLD of at least 15 percent statewide and in each district.

Proportional representation has not been universally popular among Democratic leaders, and the party has attempted to blunt it by the appointment of so-called SUPERDELEGATES, elected and party officials who go to the conventions in addition to those elected in the primaries and CAUCUSES. Democrats in some states also have used loophole primaries, electing delegates directly in each district, to get around the ban on winner-take-all delegate selection. (See PRIMARY TYPES.)

Critics' Arguments

Proportional representation has its fair share of critics. Some cite the example of what happened in Germany's Weimar Republic between 1919 and 1930. Proportional representation was adopted at the end of World War I to maintain a political balance between the parties that still existed after the dissolution of the German Empire.

In the 1919 election, the first in which proportional representation was employed, some six major parties polled nearly a million votes; the Social Democrats on the left won about a third of that total. In union with the two major parties of the center, a strong majority was achieved. Eleven years later, in the sixth election governed by proportional representation, ten parties polled more than a million votes and six others made respectable showings. The result was that no party emerged dominant or even in a position to exert effective leadership as the head of a stable majority coalition.

Such fractionalization was also evident in New York City in 1936, when proportional representation was adopted for city council elections. It was at first hoped that the new system would make it possible for reform groups to realistically contest elections against entrenched political machines. The result, one writer noted wryly, was the election to the council of, besides Democrats and Republicans, "Fusionists, American Laborites, Liberals, Communists, and, of course, Independents." By the end of ten years, when proportional representation "had given a lion's roar to irresponsible fleas," the system was abolished, with many agreeing with the assessment of one political observer that proportional representation, in most of America, was, at best, "a fad." Another called it the "choice between democracy and anarchy."

Many critics of proportional representation argue that it encourages splinter groups, thus overrepresenting minorities at the expense of majorities. In Israel, for example, extremely small parties of ultra-Orthodox Jews, some adopting extremist positions not at all in accord with predominant national sentiment or secular needs, form the balance of power between the two major parties, Likud and Labor, and are able to make political demands and exert political leverage far in excess of their actual strength in numbers.

Critics also note that proportional representation offers voters, by and large, a complicated formula to master, one that is susceptible to manipulation by the parties contesting the election. They note that the system tends to reduce the personal contact between voters and their elected representative because the party machinery dictates the order of candidates, sometimes offering only mediocre candidates and therefore ignoring the vital question of quality of representation, opting instead only for quantity.

The most serious charges are that proportional representation, by basically weakening reasonably stable prodemocratic forces in Italy and Germany and fractionalizing the political process in the years after World War I, made possible the rise of the fascist dictatorships in both nations. As one political analyst noted of this period, "So preoccupied are the adherents [of proportional representation] with the technique of representation—which is only one part of the structure of popular government—that they continue to agitate for a device which not only fails to improve representation but even destroys popular government itself."

Public Financing of Campaigns

The system of taxpayer funding for qualified presidential candidates' campaigns—with limitations on how much candidates can spend—has been in existence since the mid-1970s and had a brief heyday in the years immediately after its inception. But in recent years, the viability of the program has been eroded by a decline in public enthusiasm, which coincided with a growing public skepticism about government and politics, and by the decisions by major presidential candidates beginning in 2000 to opt out of the public financing system and its strings attached—namely, strict spending limitations that are much lower than the amounts candidates can now raise and spend on their own.

Candidates increasingly concluded that the amount of money they were allowed to spend on their campaigns under the public funding process was insufficient to meet their needs in communicating with a national electorate. Republican George W. Bush, who set up a vast fund-raising network well in advance of his 2000 presidential bid, set a precedent when he bypassed public funding as he raised $95.5 million for use during the primaries and caucuses that led to his nomination. He was joined that year by the largely self-financed campaign of magazine publisher Steve Forbes, who raised $48.1 million, mostly from his own accounts.

By 2004 three major candidates eschewed public funding for the primaries, with numbers that underscored how rapidly campaign spending was escalating. Bush took in $269.6 million mainly to run ads during the primary season, even though he was unopposed for the Republican nomination in his bid for a second term. Massachusetts senator John Kerry, who went on to win the Democratic nomination, took in $234.6 million. And Democratic contender Howard Dean, who had a meteoric rise but faded quickly, raised $51.1 million outside the public financing system.

But the biggest step away from the public financing system came in 2008, when Democrat Barack Obama, then a senator of Illinois, became the first major party nominee to eschew public money and spending restrictions for what would be a successful general election campaign. The candidate's charismatic campaign persona, the historic drama of his bid to become the nation's first African American president, and his campaign organization's aggressive and innovative use of New Media as a fund-raising tool combined to enable Obama to obliterate all previous spending records. He ended up amassing nearly $779 million in contributions, almost three times more than the previous record Bush had set just four years earlier.

It also was twice as much as the total money raised by Obama's Republican opponent, Arizona senator John McCain, who brought in $384 million (which, in itself, also greatly exceeded Bush's 2004 haul).

McCain had also opted out of the public financing system during the primary campaign, as did three of the unsuccessful candidates for the Republican nomination—former Massachusetts governor Mitt Romney, former New York City mayor Rudolph Giuliani, and Rep. Ron Paul of Texas—and Obama's top rival for the Democratic nomination, New York senator Hillary Rodham Clinton.

But McCain's fund-raising total lagged well behind Obama's, and the reputation as a political "maverick" that McCain sought to project was based heavily on his coauthorship of a 2002 law, the Bipartisan Campaign Reform Act, that again revamped the nation's campaign finance laws, primarily by banning unlimited "soft money" contributions to the national political parties.

McCain decided to accept public financing for the general election campaign, which limited his spending to the $84 million in taxpayer funds that he received, although he did receive backup from the hundreds of millions of dollars in independent expenditures on his behalf by Republican Party organizations and outside interests allied with the GOP.

Even when the program was at the height of public acceptance, campaign finance reform advocates failed in efforts to expand it to cover congressional elections. There are fourteen states that provide direct public financing to candidates with spending limitations, but some of these plans—many of them bearing the "Clean Elections" label—have faced serious legal challenges in recent years.

For example, the Supreme Court, in the 2006 case of *Randall v. Sorrell*, ruled on a 6-3 vote that tight limits on financial donations to candidates amounted to an unconstitutional abridgement of citizens' right to free speech. In a June 2011 decision that was seen as having potential impact on many states' public financing programs, the Supreme Court, by a 5-4 vote, overturned Arizona's public campaign financing law. The majority determined that the law—which entitled candidates participating in public financing to receive additional funds if candidates who raised their own money exceeded spending thresholds—was again an unconstitutional restriction on the First Amendment rights of the privately funded candidates.

Nonetheless, public financing programs maintain fervent support among many political reformers, and public money is still seen as a lifeline by some

Magazine publisher Steve Forbes, shown here waving from his campaign bus in December 1999, opted out of the public financing system, raising $48.1 million, largely from his own accounts.
Source: AP Images/Matt York.

long shot candidates who lack the fund-raising infrastructure to compete financially with the better-established contenders. So it is notable that there was little discussion of doing away with the public financing system altogether—especially since it had proven so easy to circumvent anyway.

Roots of the System

Sen. Richard Durbin introduced a congressional campaign public financing bill in March 2007 calling for the first public financing system for congressional candidates.

Source: CQ Photo/Scott J. Ferrell.

The public financing program—enacted as a provision in a law enacted in 1971 but not implemented until the 1976 election—was spurred initially by the rapid escalation of the costs of campaigning, and by the increasing amount of money taken in from individuals and interest groups by candidates (especially incumbents). (See PRESIDENT, NOMINATING AND ELECTING.)

Congress's action to provide funding grew out of concerns raised by the 1968 election, in which the Republican Nixon outspent Democrat Hubert H. Humphrey by a ratio of two to one.

Support for the nascent system was magnified by the financial irregularities in President Richard M. Nixon's 1972 reelection campaign that were exposed during the Watergate scandal, which eventually drove Nixon from office on August 9, 1974.

Passage of the funding legislation, the Revenue Act of 1971, did not come easily. It followed a long and partisan struggle between congressional Democrats and the Nixon administration.

The act did not affect the 1972 election, but it created the Presidential Election Campaign Fund for future nomination and general election campaigns. In every presidential election from 1976 through 2004, all major party nominees accepted the federal funding at least for the general elections, and the spending cap that went with it.

The amount that candidates receive during the nominating process is determined by a per-voter spending formula. A candidate qualifies for matching federal funds by raising at least $100,000 in twenty or more states, with at least $5,000 from each state in individual contributions of $250 or less. Candidates receiving federal funds may not accept private contributions for their general election campaigns, and they must pledge not to spend more than $50,000 from personal funds on their campaigns. They are limited to spending $200,000 in each state, with an adjustment for inflation.

Presidential candidates of minor parties receive funding based on their parties' vote in the general election as a percentage of the major parties' average vote. Major parties are defined as those that received 25 percent or more of the vote in the previous election. Minor or THIRD PARTIES are those receiving between 5 percent and 25 percent. A nominee of a new party (defined as one that is neither a major party nor a minor party) can obtain partial funding retroactively if he or she receives 5 percent or more of the vote.

No provision was made for INDEPENDENT candidates, but in 1980 a ruling by the FEDERAL ELECTION COMMISSION (FEC) enabled John Anderson, then a U.S. representative from Illinois, to receive partial funding after his independent candidacy drew 6.6 percent of the presidential vote. The commission ruled that Anderson qualified under the provision for new-party retroactive funding, which is based on the ratio of the candidate's POPULAR VOTE to the average popular vote of the two major party candidates. Twelve years later, Texas billionaire Ross Perot financed his own campaign, but his 18.9 percent of the vote qualified his new REFORM PARTY to receive funding at about half the level of the major parties for his repeat try for the presidency in 1996.

Under the Revenue Act, the federal campaign money is raised through a "checkoff" option on income tax forms. Taxpayers can designate that $3 (originally $1) of their tax payment be put into the presidential campaign fund. Couples filing joint returns can designate $6 (originally $2) to go into the fund. Congress raised the checkoff in 1993 because the campaign fund was facing a shortage.

In pushing for creation of the fund, the Democrats, long the debt-ridden party, contended it was needed to control the amount of influence that the wealthy could exert in a presidential campaign. Republicans, looking forward to a bountiful presidential election in 1972 with one of their own seeking reelection, opposed the measure. The legislation passed, but with the 1972 election exempted. Nixon signed it into law.

Controversy over the system continued. In 2000 Democratic presidential nominee Al Gore called for public financing of campaigns to be extended to House and Senate races as a way of reducing influence by monied interests. But many Republicans, such as Kentucky's Mitch McConnell, objected strenuously. They contended it would force taxpayers to support attack ads and other campaign tactics that they found offensive.

Perhaps the biggest problem for supporters of public financing is that the public is largely ambivalent about it. A number of polls over the years have turned up a conundrum: Although most respondents said they supported public financing in principle, even many supporters did not want their tax money used to finance candidates, especially those with whom they sharply disagreed on issues. As with most political process questions, public financing was nowhere near as cogent, even to many supporters, as kitchen-table issues such as the economy, taxes, social concerns such as abortion, and national security.

The clearest sign that public support for public financing had waned in the early years of the twenty-first century came from the decline in participation in the tax checkoff program. The share of taxpayers using the checkoff for the presidential campaign fund—29 percent at its height in 1981—had shrunk to 9 percent by 2004, and then to just more than 7 percent in 2010, even though the checkoff came at no additional cost to individual taxpayers.

Despite the public's lukewarm attitude toward the checkoff, the two parties tacitly accepted its role in the electoral process. Part of their acceptance stemmed from the loopholes that significantly offset the HARD MONEY restrictions in federal CAMPAIGN FINANCE laws. The restrictions include contribution limits for all federal candidates and spending limits for presidential candidates who accept public funding.

> *I remain firmly opposed on principle to the tax checkoff device for financing presidential campaigns out of the public treasury which is also included in this act.*
>
> **—President Richard M. Nixon,** speaking at the signing of the Revenue Act of 1971 on December 10, 1971

One loophole allows groups or individuals to make unlimited "independent expenditures" on behalf of favorite candidates. Another permits the BUNDLING of numerous small contributions into one big one that otherwise would be prohibited. From 1979 until the practice was barred by the Bipartisan Campaign Reform Act of 2002, the national parties were allowed to receive unregulated SOFT MONEY that indirectly benefited their nominees' campaigns. In 1996 millions of dollars in soft money contributions were at the heart of a campaign finance SCANDAL centering on the DEMOCRATIC NATIONAL COMMITTEE and President Bill Clinton's reelection campaign. Both parties, however, were found to have misused soft money and were required to return some of it.

Even the ban on national parties' receipt of soft money hardly removed its presence from political campaigns. Outside political organizations—mainly "527" POLITICAL ORGANIZATIONS at first, and then a rising new variant called SuperPACs beginning in 2010—remained eligible to take in soft money, which they used on independent expenditure campaigns that were identified as issue advocacy but often were quite obvious attempts to persuade voters to support one candidate or oppose another.

In sum, the tax checkoff has not ended private influence. But the expansion of public financing into the nomination process has allowed numerous candidates to compete, at least in the early campaign stages.

The "Watergate" Election

The last completely privately financed presidential election was the 1972 race. Although spending on broadcast ads fell, overall campaign costs soared. President Nixon's campaign organization spent $61.4 million, while the Democratic campaign of George S. McGovern spent $21.2 million.

The Committee for the Reelection of the President (or CREEP, as it became known) relied mostly on large contributions, many of them solicited and received before April 7, 1972, the date when disclosure of such gifts would begin under the Federal Election Campaign Act (FECA).

Despite its heavy spending, the Nixon campaign had money left over after he was reelected, leading to reckless attempts to cover up the crime that gave the Watergate scandal its name: the burglary of the Democratic national headquarters in the Watergate hotel-office complex, in which operatives of Nixon's White House and campaign were involved. Congressional investigations into the cover-up, including payment of "hush money" to the perpetrators, resulted in Nixon's resignation in 1974 to avoid his almost certain impeachment by the House.

Post-Watergate Finance Laws

In the wake of Nixon's resignation, Congress passed the sweeping campaign finance legislation that still governs presidential and congressional elections. Gerald R. Ford, who succeeded to the presidency, reluctantly signed into law the Federal Election Campaign Act Amendments in October 1974. The amendments established limits for contributions to federal candidates and their POLITICAL ACTION COMMITTEES (PACs). (See table, Expenditure Limits for Publicly Funded Candidates, p. 501.)

States also became involved in campaign finance reform. By the time Nixon left office, some seventeen states had imposed contribution limitations. New Jersey's limit of $600, which was eligible for state matching funds, was the lowest in the nation.

The federal law was most important for presidential politics. Technically just an amendment to the 1971 law, the post-Watergate statute superseded some of the previous law's provisions and expanded others. The FECA amendments contained the following provisions relating to public financing of presidential elections:

- National spending limits of $10 million for presidential primary candidates and $20 million for major-party nominees' general election campaigns. Spending in the nominating process also would be limited in each state to $200,000 or sixteen cents times the state's voting-age population, whichever is greater. These sums have since been increased through inflation-adjustments.
- Extension of public funding to presidential primaries, with matching grants for candidates who qualify. The requirements were intended to demonstrate that the candidate has broad national support. Contributions from individuals of up to $250 are matched dollar for dollar. The FECA amendments also established the formulas for amounts awarded to the parties for their conventions. The amounts rise with inflation. In 2008 each NATIONAL PARTY CONVENTION received $16.8 million.

EXPENDITURE LIMITS FOR PUBLICLY FUNDED CANDIDATES

| | | General Election | |
	Primary Candidates	Major-Party Nominees	Minor or New Party Nominees
National spending limit	$10 mil. + COLA[1]	$20 mil. + COLA	$20 mil. + COLA
State spending limit	The greater of $200,000 + COLA or 16¢ × state VAP[2]	None	None
Exempt fund-raising limit	20% of national limit	Not applicable	20% of national limit
Maximum public funds candidate may receive	50% of national limit	Same as national limit	Percentage of national limit based on candidate's popular vote
National party spending limit for candidate[3]	Not applicable	2¢ × VAP of U.S. + COLA	2¢ × VAP of U.S. + COLA
Limit on spending from candidate's personal funds	$50,000	$50,000	$50,000

Source: Federal Election Commission.

Note: Legal and accounting expenses incurred solely to ensure the campaign's compliance with the law are exempt from all expenditure limits.

1. Spending limits are increased by the cost-of-living adjustment (COLA), which the Department of Labor calculates annually using 1974 as the base year.

2. VAP is the Voting Age Population, which the Department of Commerce calculates annually.

3. The national committee of a political party may make special, limited expenditures, called coordinated party expenditures, on behalf of its presidential nominee, even if the nominee does not accept public funds. Coordinated party expenditures are not considered contributions and do not count against a publicly funded campaign's candidate expenditure limit.

Court Cases and Constitutional Issues

The 1974 FECA amendments faced an important federal court challenge, BUCKLEY V. VALEO, soon after they took effect. The Supreme Court's final 1976 ruling reduced congressional authority over campaign activity.

The Court approved disclosure requirements and limitations on how much individuals and organizations could contribute to national candidates. The Court also approved the federal financing of presidential nominating campaigns and general election campaigns. But one of the most controversial elements of the reform—limits on independent expenditures on behalf of candidates—was overturned. The Court agreed with the plaintiffs' First Amendment argument that restrictions on spending amounted to abridgment of free speech. The Court ruled, however, that campaign organizations could be required to honor spending limits if they accepted federal money. The Court stated,

> A restriction on the amount of money a person or group can spend on political communi-cation during a campaign necessarily reduces the quantity of expression by restricting the number of issues discussed, the depth of their exploration, and the size of the audience reached. This is because every means of communicating ideas in today's mass society requires the expenditure of money.

Only Justice Byron White rejected the reasoning. White noted the "many expensive campaign activities that are not themselves communicative or remotely related to speech."

Public Opinion

American public opinion can be steadfast, as it was in support of the U.S. efforts in World War II when victory in that conflict was not certain. It can also be fickle, something experienced the hard way by Republicans George H.W. Bush and George W. Bush, the father and son who served as president in recent years and enjoyed both strong popularity and wither-ing unpopularity during their ten-ures. Policy makers must respect public opinion, but too much fealty to it can freeze those who are elected to lead and can produce gridlock. It can provide an accurate portrait of where most Americans stand on vital issues of defense, foreign pol-icy, and economics, but it can also magnify issues that sound good to average citizens—such as campaign finance reform—but about which few are very passionate.

The one thing that is certain is that virtually none of those involved

Former Reagan press secretary James Brady gives Bill Clinton's gun-control record a poignant thumbs-up while on stage August 26, 1996, at the Democratic National Convention in front of a video image of his wife, Sarah Brady.

Source: AP Images.

in the political arena, whether as a participant or an observer, ignores public opinion—nor would it be a good idea.

The use of scientific POLLING to determine the public's opinion of candidates and issues has deep implications for politics and elections in the United States. Political campaigns keep a close watch on public opinion for guidance on how to proceed or whether to stay in the race at all.

Candidates who stay and win will, as officeholders, keep abreast of trends in public opinion, both as a tool for formulating government policy and as a guide to prepare for the next election. Few INCUMBENTS or serious candidates ignore the polls in the highly competitive realm of modern politics.

Polling can help determine both the direction and the depth of public opinion. The direction is simply whether people view an issue, an action, or a performance favorably or unfavorably. Surveys can provide information on the yes-no dimension: how people align themselves on issues such as the death penalty, affirmative action, abortion, tax increases for Medicare and Social Security, or military intervention in Iraq.

A related and critical aspect of public opinion is the distribution, or extent, of agreement or consensus on an issue, with opinions clustering on one side or the other of the yes-no dimension. Some issues evoke high levels of agreement, such as keeping drugs illegal. Others are highly divisive, such as U.S. military involvement in Iraq, abortion, and gay marriage. When a high level of consensus exists, government policy makers usually find it wise to follow public opinion.

For example, when crime became a key concern in 1993 and the Gallup poll showed that 88 percent of the public was in favor of imposing a waiting period for the purchase of a handgun, Congress finally overcame its long-standing reluctance to offend the pro-gun lobby. By wide margins both chambers enacted the long-delayed Brady bill. Named for former presidential press secretary James Brady, who was permanently disabled by a handgun bullet during the 1981 attempt to assassinate Ronald Reagan, the legislation required a five-day waiting period for the purchase of a handgun.

When opinions divide and the public's feelings are strong, outcomes are less certain. In the first days of his presidency, Bill Clinton proposed to implement a campaign pledge to lift the ban on homosexuals in the military. He created a firestorm of controversy that revealed a deeply divided public. Stands were adamantly taken—87 percent of those opposed to Clinton's policy felt strongly about the issue, as did 63 percent of those who supported it. The public's emphatic response and the opposition of senior military personnel and influential

senators such as Sam Nunn, the Georgia Democrat who chaired the Armed Services Committee, forced Clinton to back down. He settled for a revised "don't ask, don't tell" policy under which homosexual conduct would still be prohibited, but recruits would no longer be asked if they were gay.

Importance and Stability

People differ in the extent to which they find an issue salient or important. National Rifle Association (NRA) members, for example, consider opposition to gun control extremely salient. In the same way, retired people care more about cost-of-living adjustments to Social Security

Issues that involve moral questions, such as abortion, are likely to generate the most impassioned opinions. Those who feel strongly are more likely to act on their sentiments and participate in the political process than are those whose views are weakly held.

benefits than do working parents, who find tax deductions for child care expenses more important than do retirees.

For the public as a whole, the saliency of issues changes over time. At the beginning of the Reagan administration in 1981, the Gallup poll reported that 72 percent of Americans believed inflation to be the most important problem facing the nation. But by 1988, when the inflation rate was
down to 4.1 percent from 13.5 percent, only 2 percent of the people gave it such importance. Similarly, Americans became highly concerned about national security after the September 11, 2001,
terrorist attacks, even though that had not registered in polls as a leading concern in the past few
years. When a CBS News poll asked Americans in early 2003 what they thought President George
W. Bush's should focus on, three of the top five priorities had to do with protecting the country.

The intensity of public opinion can vary as well: people may feel strongly about some issues
and not so strongly about others. Political process issues, such as campaign finance reform,
lobbying reform, and shifting responsibility for redistricting from state legislatures to a nonpartisan or bipartisan commission, tend to be examples of the latter. When asked if they favor
"good government" notions, resounding majorities of respondents will say yes. But when
asked what issues will drive their voting decisions in the next election, these issues—barring a
scandal of historic consequence, such as Watergate—typically are among the lowest-ranking
priorities.

Issues that involve moral questions, such as abortion, are likely to generate the most impassioned opinions. Those who feel strongly are more likely to act on their sentiments and participate
in the political process than are those whose views are weakly held.

The effect of public opinion is influenced by the strength of commitment people give to a
cause, with the result that small but energetic minorities often have an influence well out of proportion to their numbers. Understanding the intensity with which people hold and act on their
opinions helps to explain why policy positions opposed by a majority of the people can become
public policy.

For example, polls show that at least two-thirds of the public support tougher gun control
legislation. But deeply committed opponents, led by the NRA, have blocked new bills (except the
Brady bill) that would strengthen gun control laws and have even succeeded in weakening previously passed laws. The NRA efforts have included advertising campaigns, campaign contributions,
and aggressive lobbying, with NRA members deluging members of Congress with mail against
gun control. By contrast, people favoring tougher gun laws have generally not felt strongly enough
about the issue to act on their convictions.

Another example of different intensity levels is on the issue of whether the United States
should continue to isolate Cuba and its communist regime long dominated by 1950s revolutionary leader Fidel Castro. Though Castro drew the enmity of a broad spectrum of Americans
as he aligned with the Soviet Union during the Cold War era, that antipathy has weakened
greatly in recent years. Many Americans became perplexed about the United States' continued
treatment of Cuba as a pariah while maintaining vibrant economic and diplomatic relationships with China, by far the world's biggest remaining communist power, and Vietnam, where
just a few decades ago communist forces defied U.S. military power in an ugly war that was
very damaging to Americans' self-image. An Associated Press-Ipsos poll conducted January
30–February 1, 2007, showed that 62 percent of adult respondents nationwide believed the
United States should establish diplomatic relations with Cuba; only 30 percent said the country should not.

Yet that was a casually held position for many of the majority who favored easing the hard line against Cuba. Not so for a faction of the nearly one-third who said no: Cuban Americans, many of them either refugees or relatives of refugees from Castro's tyranny, who are vocally adamant that Cuba should continue to be regarded as an enemy state until communism falls there. Mainly concentrated and politically powerful in Florida—a key battleground state in presidential elections—the Cuban Americans maintain clout far out of proportion to the size of their constituencies and their impact on overall public opinion.

Public opinion can be contradictory on separate aspects of the same issue. A prime example can be found in the White House sex SCANDAL that rocked the nation in early 1998. Although President Clinton's acknowledged relationship with Monica S. Lewinsky, a young intern, involved morality—normally a hot-button issue—polls showed the public considered that less important than allegations that Clinton may have lied under oath about the relationship and urged Lewinsky to do the same. Moreover, the public regarded both issues as less important than the president's job performance, and his approval ratings actually rose to a high of 79 percent.

Another dimension of public opinion is its stability. The public can change its mind, occasionally with amazing rapidity. For example, President George H.W. Bush's public approval ratings resembled a roller-coaster ride. His rating dropped 23 points in the fall of 1990 from 76 percent to 53 percent after he reneged on his "Read my lips, no new taxes" campaign pledge and negotiated a budget compromise with congressional Democrats. In the aftermath of victory in the 1991 Persian Gulf War, Bush rebounded to a then-record 89 percent approval rating, which then fell precipitously to 30 percent by August 1992 as the public's anxiety over the economy grew.

A little more than a decade later, Republican George W. Bush faced the wrong kind of "like father, like son" situation. Elected in 2000 to succeed Clinton—who had defeated the elder Bush in the 1992 election—the younger Bush saw his approval ratings soar above 90 percent after he deployed U.S. troops to help indigenous Afghan forces overthrow the radical Islamic Taliban government that had sheltered the al-Qaeda terrorist operation that masterminded the September 11, 2001, attacks on the United States. But another, far less popular military venture, the war in Iraq, sent George W. Bush's ratings into a free-fall after his 2004 reelection victory. His approval ratings reached a low point of 25 percent in 2008 and were between 25 percent and 30 percent throughout all of 2008, his last year in office, according to Gallup poll surveys. His second term average, Gallup said, was 37 percent compared with 62 percent in his first four years in office.

Although these examples suggest a high level of volatility in public opinion, studies show that American opinion on many issues exhibits substantial stability and that change in public attitudes tends to occur gradually. Since 1972 the public has overwhelmingly supported a woman's right to have an abortion when there is a strong chance of a serious birth defect or when the pregnancy stems from rape. At the same time, most Americans have consistently opposed permitting abortions sought, for example, when a married woman does not want any more children.

Another aspect of the stability dimension is that a public once divided on an issue can over time achieve a high level of agreement. In 1942 only 30 percent of whites said that they thought white and black students should go to the same schools. Yet by 1984, 90 percent of whites said that they accepted integrated schools.

Analysis of these data, however, showed that whites were not monolithic in their racial attitudes. Differences stemmed from people's diverse social backgrounds and life experiences. An exploration of public opinion, therefore, must consider POLITICAL SOCIALIZATION—the learning process through which people acquire political attitudes.

Effect on Policy

Public opinion has its most obvious impact on government decision making through elections. In the United States, elections are usually held to vote for candidates for public office and not for specific policies, except in those states that permit voters to enact laws through INITIATIVES AND REFERENDUMS.

Clear electoral MANDATES from the voters are rare because candidates take stands on scores of issues and therefore collect voters for different and even conflicting reasons; elections are seldom dominated or decided by just one or two issues. Moreover, the candidates' positions are not always clear, nor are their positions necessarily in opposition to each other.

But even if it is hard to discern a clear policy mandate from the voters on ELECTION DAY, a verdict on the past performances of incumbent officeholders is frequently rendered. Indeed, the public can affect the general direction of government policy by changing the people and parties in control of government institutions.

In the 1992 election, for example, the public gave a negative verdict on President George H. W. Bush's handling of the economy and on divided party control of the government. But in rejecting Bush and replacing him with Clinton, the public did not necessarily signal its approval of Clinton's policy proposals. It did, however, indicate that it was prepared to give him a chance to solve the nation's problems, and Clinton's Democratic administration had a policy agenda of government activism that was markedly different from that of its Republican predecessor.

Similarly, the Republicans picked up seats in Congress in the 2002 MIDTERM ELECTION, partly because voters approved of Bush's handling of terrorism. But polls indicated public unease over Bush's handling of the economy and opposition to Republican efforts to pare back environmental regulations.

Public opinion can determine not only who governs but also the context within which political leaders must act. Periodic swings in Americans' IDEOLOGY—changes in their policy mood—provide the setting for and affect government policy making.

The liberal winds that began blowing during the latter 1950s provided the basis for the government activism that characterized the Kennedy-Johnson era of the 1960s. But these breezes died down in the mid-1970s as Americans became more conservative in their general disposition toward government's role in society. Indeed, this conservative policy mood was already in place before Ronald Reagan, the most conservative president since Herbert Hoover, took office and initiated policies designed to restrict the role of government.

Public opinion has its greatest impact on policy when people have clear preferences and feel strongly about an issue. A study by political scientist Alan Monroe found that on issues particularly important to the public, government policy and public opinion were in agreement more than two-thirds of the time. Research also has demonstrated that government policy moves in the direction of a change in public opinion 87 percent of the time when the shift is substantial and not temporary.

One of the most striking examples of the effect of public opinion on national policy was the congressional pay raise controversy of 1989. Overwhelming and vehement public opposition caused a reluctant Congress to reject the 50 percent salary increase proposed by a bipartisan, blue-ribbon commission and endorsed by Presidents Reagan and Bush.

Naturally, there are times when public opinion and government policy are not consistent. Such inconsistencies may stem from the influence of well-organized and energetic INTEREST GROUPS. For example, a popular majority favored tougher air pollution laws throughout the 1980s, yet Congress was unable to enact such legislation. This inaction reflected the ability of automakers, utilities, several unions, and influential legislators to mobilize opposition to clean air bills.

Similarly, activists pressing the issue of global warming for many years had trouble gaining the public's attention in the face of a countercampaign, heavily financed by business interests and conservative political groups, aimed at portraying concerns about global warming as overblown. In one of the most ironic twists of public opinion in recent years, former vice president Al Gore—mocked by many as a boring policy wonk in his close and controversial presidential loss to George W. Bush in 2000—revived his career as a public figure when his Oscar-winning 2006 documentary about his crusade against global warming, *An Inconvenient Truth*, raised the relevance of and public concerns about the dangers of climate change.

Inconsistencies between public opinion and government policy also occur when the public cares little about an issue. Polls have shown repeatedly, for example, that Americans favor abolishing the ELECTORAL COLLEGE system for electing the president, but this issue is not high on their list of concerns. As a result, the likelihood of Congress's proposing a constitutional amendment to abolish the Electoral College seems remote.

Public opinion influences public policy in the United States only through a complicated and often indirect process. It takes more than a majority of the public registering its approval or disapproval in a poll to affect policy. People's policy preferences are translated into government policy only when individuals act on opinions—that is, when they actually participate in politics. (See CITIZENSHIP AND VOTING.)

Push Poll

The controversial practice known as push polling is a type of NEGATIVE CAMPAIGNING. It traces its roots to Richard M. Nixon's first run for Congress in the late 1940s, when Nixon campaign workers made anonymous calls telling voters that Nixon's opponents were communists. In more recent times, push polling was used in the 1994 Florida gubernatorial race, to the embarrassment of the winner, Democrat Lawton Chiles.

In the 1996 election, President Bill Clinton's campaign pledged not to use push polling. The campaign of Bob Dole, that year's Republican presidential nominee, paid more than $1 million to New York City–based Campaign Tel Ltd. to do push polling during the primaries and declined to make such a promise concerning the general election.

In a February 1996 appearance on CNN'S *Larry King* show, a group of Republican campaign managers in Des Moines for the IOWA CAUCUS acknowledged that some of their contractors had phoned households under the guise of conducting an opinion poll and then planted negative information about an opposing candidate.

During the 2000 primaries, Republican front-runner George W. Bush pledged to fire anyone in his campaign who used push polling. The issue came up in the wake of allegations that his top rival, Sen. John McCain of Arizona, was being targeted in some push polls.

Modern push polling is made possible by computer technology that permits rapid dialing to thousands of households, then efficiently routes only the answered calls to a campaign employee ready to read from a script. Phone banks can cover entire areas at a third of the cost of such operations just a few years ago.

Push polling is not easily detectable. If a caller asked a voter if he would still vote for a candidate knowing, for example, that the candidate cheated on his taxes, no one would know about it unless the call recipient complained to the authorities or the press.

The National Council on Public Polls and the national and international political consultants associations have condemned "this abuse of legitimate public polling" as thinly disguised telemarketing.

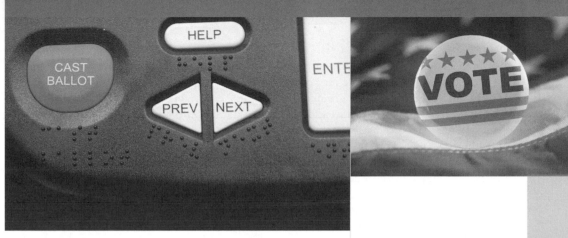

Racial Redistricting

Racial and ethnic considerations have long been a factor in the drawing of legislative and congressional DISTRICTS in the United States, which happens every ten years in the REAPPORTIONMENT AND REDISTRICTING processes that follow each CENSUS. After the 1990 census, several states, acting under pressure from the federal government, created a number of new congressional districts that included majority African American or Hispanic populations. In a series of legal challenges, the Supreme Court later forced the redrawing of some of the districts by ruling that racially motivated redistricting could, in some circumstances, violate constitutional rights of nonminority voters.

Historically, the pattern of racially and ethnically identifiable neighborhoods in many urban centers made it possible for lawmakers to draw district lines in a way likely to result in the election of candidates of a particular race or ethnic background—Irish Americans or Italian Americans, for example, from predominantly Irish or Italian districts. Very few blacks, however, were elected to Congress, even from states such as those in the South where they constituted a sizable proportion of the population. Likewise, Hispanic Americans had only a few representatives in Congress, despite the rapid growth in their numbers in the 1980s and 1990s and after 2000.

To remedy the underrepresentation of these two minority groups in Congress, the Justice Department decreed that states with histories of minority voting rights violations were required under the VOTING RIGHTS ACT to create so-called MINORITY-MAJORITY DISTRICTS—districts where African American or Hispanic populations were in the majority. The Voting Rights Act, as amended in 1982, prohibited election practices that had a disproportionate impact on minority group voting rights.

The newly drawn minority-majority districts resulted in the election of a larger number of African American and Hispanic members to the House of Representatives in the 1992 election. The elections cheered minority groups and traditional civil rights organizations. But some of the districts were sharply criticized as a form of racial GERRYMANDERING because of their irregular shapes. White voters challenged them in court as a violation of their rights under the Fourteenth Amendment's Equal Protection Clause. (See Reference Material, pages 725–726.)

The focal point of this dispute over racial redistricting, and the subject of the most protracted redistricting litigation of the decade, was the remap enacted in North Carolina following the 1990 census. African Americans made up about 20 percent of the population, but despite increased BLACK SUFFRAGE the state had sent no blacks to Congress since the post–Civil War Reconstruction era. When the state gained a new House seat after the 1990 census, the state legislature initially created one black-majority district, but then yielded to Justice Department pressure to create a second. One of the new congressional districts, the First, was relatively compact, but the second black-majority district, the Twelfth, wound 160 miles through the center of the state to link black neighborhoods in four urban areas. Both districts elected black representatives, each one a Democrat.

The ensuing legal fight over the map exposed a division within the Republican Party over how to approach racial redistricting. Many of the new minority-majority districts had been drawn with the support and sometimes active participation of Republican officials, who saw the new districts as offering them the opportunity to show their concern for the interests of minority voters—most of whom had long favored the Democratic Party—while also concentrating many minority voters into a small number of districts, thereby removing them from surrounding districts that would become more likely to vote Republican.

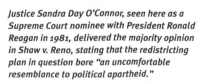

Justice Sandra Day O'Connor, seen here as a Supreme Court nominee with President Ronald Reagan in 1981, delivered the majority opinion in Shaw v. Reno, stating that the redistricting plan in question bore "an uncomfortable resemblance to political apartheid."

Source: National Archives and Records Administration.

This strategy was not universally hailed, though, as was evident when the North Carolina REPUBLICAN PARTY joined with a group of white voters to challenge the state's district map in court. Their suits contended that the plan set up a "racially discriminatory process" and deprived white voters of the right to vote "in a color-blind election." The Justice Department, under Republican president George H. W. Bush, joined the state in defending the plan. They argued that the minority-majority districts were necessary to comply with the Voting Rights Act and to remedy past discrimination against black voters. The suits were dismissed by a three-judge federal district court but reinstated by the Supreme Court in a 5–4 decision, *SHAW V. RENO* (1993).

In her opinion for the Court, Justice Sandra Day O'Connor acknowledged that racial considerations could not be excluded from the redistricting process. But she said that in "some exceptional cases" a plan could be "so highly irregular that, on its face, it rationally cannot be understood as anything other than an effort to segregate voters on the basis of race." A district that ignores geographical and political boundaries to concentrate members of a particular race, she said, "bears an uncomfortable resemblance to political apartheid" and risks perpetuating "the very patterns of racial bloc voting that minority-majority districting is sometimes said to counteract."

The dissenting justices sharply questioned the logic of the opinion. Justice Byron White argued that white voters had not been harmed by the redistricting because whites constituted 79 percent of the state's population and constituted majorities in ten of the twelve congressional districts. Justice John Paul Stevens called it "perverse" to permit redistricting plans drawn to provide adequate representation of other groups—mentioning rural voters, union members, Hasidic Jews, Polish Americans, and Republicans—but not for blacks.

The ruling returned the case to the lower court to determine whether the redistricting plan met the "strict scrutiny" test used in other racial challenges: that is, whether it was narrowly tailored to serve a compelling government interest. As the case continued, challenges to racially drawn redistricting plans were proceeding in other states, including Georgia and Texas. The Supreme Court used those cases over the next few years to refine its position on racial redistricting.

In its next ruling, the Court in 1995 struck down a Georgia plan that had created three black-majority districts, including one that stretched from the Atlanta suburbs across half the state to the coastal cities of Augusta and Savannah. The 5–4 vote in *Miller v. Johnson* was the same as in the North Carolina case, but the Court laid down a different rule for judging the use of race in redistricting plans.

Writing for the majority, Justice Anthony M. Kennedy said that the earlier decision had not limited challenges to plans with irregularly shaped districts. Instead, he said, redistricting plans were subject to challenge if race was "the predominant factor motivating the legislature's decision to place a significant number of voters within or without a particular district." Racial motivation could be shown, he said, by evidence that the legislature "subordinated" traditional districting principles such as "compactness," "contiguity," or "respect for political subdivisions or communities" to racial considerations.

Applying that test, Kennedy said the Georgia plan was racially motivated and could be upheld only if it satisfied the strict scrutiny test. And he said that the state could not justify the plan on grounds that it was necessary to comply with the Voting Rights Act because the Justice Department had incorrectly interpreted the law to require the maximum number of black-majority districts. Writing for the four dissenters, Justice Ruth Bader Ginsburg warned that the ruling would entangle the federal judiciary in what she called the "highly political business" of legislative districting and leave state legislators uncertain how to comply.

The decision was also criticized outside the Court. President Bill Clinton called the ruling "a setback in the struggle to ensure that all Americans participate fully in the electoral process." One civil rights leader said the decision could "resegregate our political institutions." But a black House Republican praised the ruling. "We have black districts, red districts, brown districts, yellow districts," said Rep. Gary Franks of Connecticut. "We should have only American districts."

> **"Hence, a legislature may, by placing reliable Democratic precincts within a district without regard to race, end up with a district containing more heavily African American precincts, but the reasons would be political rather than racial."**
>
> **—Supreme Court Justice Stephen Breyer**, writing for the majority in *Hunt v. Cromartie*

The criticism did not sway the Court's majority. A year later the same five-justice majority rejected the North Carolina redistricting plan after it had been upheld by a lower court. The suit in *Shaw v. Hunt* challenged the same congressional districts the Court had struck down in *Shaw v. Reno*. The Court also found that Texas had improperly used racial considerations in the drawing of three congressional districts—predominantly black districts in Houston and Dallas and a predominantly Hispanic district in Houston (*Bush v. Vera*). In both cases, the majority rejected arguments by the two states, the Justice Department, and civil rights groups that the plans could be justified on grounds of complying with the Voting Rights Act or remedying past discrimination. In the Texas case, the Court also discounted evidence that some of the irregularity of the districts resulted from changes aimed at benefiting incumbent lawmakers in adjoining districts.

Civil rights groups again complained that the rulings would make it harder for African American or Hispanic candidates to be elected to Congress. But their warnings were tempered by election results in Georgia in November 1996. The two African Americans elected in 1992 from newly drawn black-majority districts won reelection even though their districts had been redrawn and no longer had a majority of black voters. Critics of racial redistricting said the results indicated that racial bloc voting was lessening and would continue to decline in importance if the Supreme Court's stance against racial line-drawing stood.

The Court, however, took a more accepting view in 2001 when Justice O'Connor joined the bloc defending minority-majority districts. The case, *Hunt v. Cromartie,* marked the fourth time that the justices looked at the disputed North Carolina district, which was now drawn in such a way as to be seventy-one miles long and 47 percent African American. On a 5–4 vote, the justices overruled a trial court that had rejected the district because it favored one race over another.

Writing the majority opinion, Justice Stephen Breyer said the white voters bringing the suit had to prove that the reason for drawing such an oddly shaped district was unexplainable except for motives having to do with race. Breyer, however, noted that the state legislature had the right to create congressional districts based on political decisions—that is, to draw a district based on voting behavior that would enable a Democrat to be elected. In this case, it happened that the district also included many black voters, who tended to vote Democratic more reliably than did many white voters.

"Hence, a legislature may, by placing reliable Democratic precincts within a district without regard to race, end up with a district containing more heavily African American precincts, but the reasons would be political rather than racial," he wrote.

Justice Clarence Thomas, the Court's only black member, wrote a mild dissent. He said he might have reached the same conclusion as Breyer had he been the trial judge in the case, but he thought the lower court's ruling was not clearly erroneous and therefore should not be overruled. "In light of the direct evidence of racial motive and the inferences that may be drawn from the circumstantial evidence, I am satisfied that the District Court's finding was permissible, even if not compelled by the record," he wrote.

Litigation over congressional minority-majority districts was largely quelled over the next decade, however. In part, this was because few new minority-majority districts were drawn following the 2000 census, and the ones that were carried forward were mainly drawn based on the design of districts that had either faced no legal challenges or ultimately passed muster with the courts.

The most significant Supreme Court decision on this issue following the 2000 census came in the case of *Georgia v. Ashcroft* (2003), which dealt with a state legislative redistricting plan in Georgia. Although the state legislature had reduced the black

 CLOSER LOOK

The U.S. judiciary has shed much of its traditional reluctance to become involved in the intensely political issue of legislative redistricting, but only in cases of alleged racial or ethnic discrimination or population inequality among districts within a state. Although the courts have left open the possibility of ruling that a highly partisan redistricting plan, or gerrymander, could someday be struck down on grounds that it violates the civil rights of voters, they have declined to do so as of the end of their 2011 term.

During the 1990s, which saw a surge in the drawing of minority-majority districts, several legal cases presented a different aspect of racial redistricting: complaints by white voters that the political community had gone too far to accommodate minority voting interests, creating a form of reverse discrimination. These voters alleged that certain districts drawn to include large minority populations were in fact illegal "racial gerrymanders" that violated the Constitution's equal protection clause.

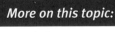

More on this topic:
Black Suffrage, p. 28
Franchise, p. 215
Minority-Majority District, p. 338
Shaw v. Reno, p. 586
Voting Rights Act, p. 663

population percentages in some of the state's black-majority state senate districts, the Court ruled that this did not constitute retrogression of minority voting rights.

In 2006 the Supreme Court ruled in *League of United Latin American Citizens v. Perry* that the voting rights of Hispanics had been violated in the drawing of Texas's Twenty-third District during the state's redistricting in 2003. This was the only case after the 2000 census in which a congressional district's lines were ruled unconstitutional by the Supreme Court on racial or ethnic grounds.

Radical Republicans *See* BLACK SUFFRAGE.

Realignments and Dealignments

The American electorate is not static. From time to time it regroups in response to certain conditions or crises in a phenomenon known as *realignment*. At other points it fragments in what is sometimes called *dealignment*.

Both phenomena concern how the voters ally themselves with a political party, the duration and strength of their allegiance, and—in the case of dealignment—whether parties matter much to the majority of the voters at a particular time.

In the latter portion of the twentieth century and the early part of the twenty-first century, the clearest case for a political realignment was in the South.

The agrarian populism established by Democratic Party founders such as Virginia's Thomas Jefferson and Tennessee's Andrew Jackson in the nation's formative years suited most southern voters, as did the party's support or at least tolerance for the maintenance of the institution of slavery. For about a century, the association of the Republican Party with Abraham Lincoln, the Union victory in the Civil War, and the postwar Reconstruction period made the GOP taboo in most of the region, and the "Solid South" became the foundation of the Democratic voting base for decades.

But with the rise of Franklin D. Roosevelt's New Deal programs in the 1930s, the Democratic Party became more urban, northern, racially and ethnically diverse, and liberal. The sharp shift of the party to leadership in the black civil rights effort in the 1960s, coupled with its increasingly liberal perspectives on social issues and foreign policy, spurred a

CLOSER LOOK

This chart illustrates how far the formerly "Solid South" and once-Republican New England have shifted from their traditions since 1932. The figures show the number of the eleven states of the Confederacy and the six New England states that Republican presidential nominees carried in each election since 1932. The national winner in each of those years is provided in the last column.

Year	South	New England	Election Winner (Party)
1932	0	4	Franklin D. Roosevelt (D)
1936	0	2	Franklin D. Roosevelt (D)
1940	0	2	Franklin D. Roosevelt (D)
1944	0	2	Franklin D. Roosevelt (D)
1948	0	4	Harry S. Truman (D)
1952	4	6	Dwight D. Eisenhower (R)
1956	5	6	Dwight D. Eisenhower (R)
1960	3	3	John F. Kennedy (D)
1964	5	0	Lyndon B. Johnson (D)
1968	5	2	Richard M. Nixon (R)
1972	11	5	Richard M. Nixon (R)
1976	1	4	Jimmy Carter (D)
1980	10	5	Ronald Reagan (R)
1984	11	6	Ronald Reagan (R)
1988	11	4	George Bush (R)
1992	7	0	Bill Clinton (D)
1996	7	0	Bill Clinton (D)
2000	11	1	George W. Bush (R)
2004	11	0	George W. Bush (R)
2008	8	0	Barack Obama (D)

mass movement of conservative, white southerners to the increasingly conservative national Republican Party. By the early 1990s, the South had become majority Republican and the building block for the party's electoral vote strategy in presidential elections.

Less noticed but also profound was a counter-realignment in New England, the long-time bastion of "Yankee Republicanism," where many New Englanders harbored a mind-your-own-business libertarianism. That attitude and the region's lack of a conservative religious contingent comparable to the South's led to a backlash against the GOP's shift toward social conservatism. Combined with the burgeoning liberalism of urban centers such as Boston, these sentiments turned New England into one of the nation's most reliably Democratic-voting regions. The defeats of two House Republicans from Connecticut and two more from New Hampshire during the 2006 elections left Connecticut representative Christopher Shays as the only Republican among the twenty-two House members from the region. He too was gone after the 2008 election, but Republicans made a modest comeback in 2010, picking up the two New Hampshire seats.

Party Systems and Realignment

Political scientist V. O. Key Jr. developed the basic theory of realignment in 1955 as the after-effect of "critical" elections "in which new and durable groupings are formed." More recently Lawrence G. McMichael and Richard J. Trilling defined realignment as "a significant and durable change in the distribution of party support over relevant groups within the electorate."

In his 1970 examination of critical elections, political scientist Walter Dean Burnham observed that realignments "recur with rather remarkable regularity approximately once in a generation, or every thirty to thirty-eight years." They tend to happen, he said, when "politics as usual" is inadequate to deal with serious problems in society or the economy.

There is general agreement among political historians that the United States has had five *party systems* in its history, each one characterized by its unique alignment of voters, the combination of parties, and the degree of competition among them. Except for the first alignment, each party system began with a realignment.

The five party systems and their approximate time periods are as follows:

A growing rift between urban (and mainly northern) workers and the Democratic Party propelled Republican William McKinley into the White House in 1897.

Source: Library of Congress.

- First, 1789–1824. Despite the founders' reservations about factionalism, two parties quickly emerged during the nation's first decade. The FEDERALISTS led by Alexander Hamilton and John Adams favored a strong national government and drew support mostly from business interests. Thomas Jefferson's DEMOCRATIC-REPUBLICANS opposed centralization of government and were supported by farmers and the less affluent. After the Jeffersonians' victory in 1800, the Federalists went into decline, setting the stage for the first realignment.

- Second, 1828–1854. Jefferson's party had evolved into the Democrats, who elected populist Andrew Jackson in 1828 and were opposed by the anti-Jackson WHIGS. Although the Democrats were the dominant party, the Whigs gave strong opposition throughout this period until division over the slavery issue took its toll of both parties. The Democrats survived, but the Whigs did not, electing their last president, Zachary Taylor, in 1848.

- Third, 1856–1896. This party system resulted from the first of three realignments that political historians classify as "major." With the Whigs dissolved, the REPUBLICAN PARTY emerged from the so-called Civil War realignment as the second major party. It elected its first president, former Whig Abraham Lincoln, in 1860. This realignment was the last to bring forth a new party. Both of the subsequent major realignments were characterized by shifts in power between the two major parties. Throughout the third partisan system the Republicans dominated the Democrats, who were weakened by their split into northern and southern factions.

- Fourth, 1896–1932. The second major realignment began with the watershed election of Republican William McKinley over William Jennings Bryan, a Populist nominated by the Democrats following the depression of 1893. By now Civil War animosities had faded, and economic issues dominated voter choices between the two parties. The agrarian South became solidly Democratic. The Republicans became the party of the industrialized North. The GOP continued to dominate, although a split in its ranks allowed a Democrat, Woodrow Wilson, to be elected president in 1912 and 1916.

- Fifth, 1932–present. The third major realignment produced a party system that still existed when the twenty-first century began, in the opinion of most political scientists. It began with the New Deal election of Franklin D. Roosevelt in the Great Depression year of 1932 and led to a long period of DEMOCRATIC PARTY dominance. Despite some setbacks, such as the elections of Republican Dwight D. Eisenhower in the 1950s, the New Deal COALITION of southern whites, union members, Catholics, African Americans, and Jews basically held together long after World War II. By the twenty-first century the Roosevelt coalition was diminished as southern whites turned in large numbers to the Republican Party, union strength declined, and more voters—disillusioned with both parties—became independents. Nevertheless, the basic political alignment dating from the Great Depression years had not collapsed.

By Burnham's rule of thumb that realignments take place every thirty to thirty-eight years, the United States was due for realignment in the 1960s or 1970s. Many election analysts agreed, however, that it did not happen, even in the 1980s with the Republican victories of Ronald Reagan and George H. W. Bush, the 1990s with the GOP takeover of Congress, or after 2000 and the election of George W. Bush and Republican congresses from 2000 to 2006.

And yet some writers argue that another kind of realignment was under way in the decades from the 1960s into the next century that was different from the earlier ones, in that it was not due to one epic election outcome or a single major historical event (such as the Civil War or Great Depression) that predicated it. In fact, the emergence of the Republican Party as both the nation's conservative party and the party of the South—a fact that would shape elections from the 1980s through the early twenty-first century—began with a huge electoral setback. Democratic president Lyndon B. Johnson persuaded most of the nation's voters that the 1964 Republican nominee, Arizona senator Barry Goldwater, was a right-wing extremist. But the Democrats' adoption of the black civil rights movement and its general shift toward liberalism spurred voters in five southern states to back Goldwater in a huge breakthrough for a party that had long been widely loathed in the region.

Republican growth in the South was gradual. In fact, the support of most southern states for 1976 Democratic presidential nominee Jimmy Carter, a former Georgia governor, enabled his narrow win over Republican incumbent Gerald R. Ford of Michigan. But Carter's troubled term and the challenge he faced in 1980 from Republican conservative Ronald Reagan, who heavily targeted the South, spurred a more permanent shift. By the time the Republican Party won control of Congress in 1994 and established dominance over the legislative branch that would last a dozen years, the faces of the party were largely southern, represented by lawmakers such as Georgia's Newt Gingrich, Texas's Tom DeLay, and the father and son from Texas who won the White House, George H. W. Bush and George W. Bush.

The southernization of the Republican Party had an opposite and nearly equal reaction in other, more centrist-to-liberal parts of the country. Along with the seismic shift of New England politics, populous states of the North, Midwest, and West—including California, New York, and Illinois—shifted with increasing dependability into the Democratic column.

By the end of the twentieth century, a pattern developed in presidential elections: the Republicans added their new southern clout to their traditional bastions in the rural farm states of the Midwest and Great Plains and the conservative-leaning states of the Mountain West, while the Democrats held sway in the Northeast, most of the Great Lakes region, and the Far West. The habit of television networks, adopted by much of the print media, of using blue to depict Democratic victories and red to show Republican wins led to a perception that the nation was divided into "red" and "blue" states.

Yet the permanence of these partisan alignments is subject to some doubt. From the time of the decline of the great party machines in the later twentieth century, the electorate generally split into thirds, with roughly equal numbers describing themselves as Republicans, Democrats, and independents. The heavily self-financed presidential campaign of businessman H. Ross Perot in 1992, which netted 19 percent of the popular vote, seemed to illustrate the potential of a strong outsider to galvanize loosely affiliated voters. And the fact that most states—even many that leaned strongly to one dominant party—were willing on occasion to break stride and support a minority-party candidate for a key office suggested that many states were more "purple," a combination of red and blue, than one single primary color.

> **"In order for the system to realign, it would have to dealign, and such a process was clearly taking place."**
>
> **—Political scientist Martin P. Wattenberg** in 1991

In fact, it appeared more likely to some respected political analysts in the 1990s that the United States was in a prolonged period of dealignment, which in itself could be significant. "In order for the system to realign, it would have to dealign, and such a process was clearly taking place," political scientist Martin P. Wattenberg wrote in 1991.

A concurring view was published in 1998 by political scientists William H. Flanigan and Nancy H. Zingale in *Political Behavior of the American Electorate*. Acknowledging that there has been a lot of voter movement and electoral volatility since the 1960s, Flanigan and Zingale characterize much of that movement as a "sorting out process" in which "a sizable number of voters have found neither political party a congenial place to be" and instead have avoided party identification and become independents. As a result, they conclude, neither party can claim to be the new majority party. "In this situation, we find it more useful to consider the current situation as a continuation of a period of dealignment."

Existing Alignments

Within the existing party system American voters align themselves with political parties in differing proportions according to age, religion, sex, socioeconomic status, ethnic or racial background, and other demographic characteristics. As coalitions rather than monoliths, both major parties draw considerable support from every subdivision of U.S. society.

A study of the Democratic and Republican coalitions by political scientist John R. Petrocik indicates that the composition of both changed from the 1950s to 1992. The Republican Party became more southern and white, while the Democratic Party became less southern and more black and Hispanic.

In 1992, African Americans accounted for 22 percent of Democratic supporters, up from 9 percent in the 1950s. Hispanic adherents increased from 1 percent to 11 percent. In the same period, northern union households favoring Democrats dropped from 22 percent to 12 percent and white southern Democrats fell from 31 percent to 19 percent.

Among components of Republican support, Catholics rose from 10 percent to 15 percent, while white Protestants fell from 51 percent to 38 percent. White southerners increased from 15 percent of the GOP base to 23 percent.

EXIT POLLS and other studies show that since 1980 there has been a "gender gap," with women voting Democratic more than men.

Reapportionment and Redistricting

Reapportionment and *redistricting* are related terms that pertain to the distribution of the 435 seats in Congress and other legislative bodies, including state legislatures, county boards and city councils, and the demographic and political landscape of each district. Both processes help to determine the partisan and geographic makeup of such bodies, and whether racial or ethnic minorities will receive fair representation. The terms are not synonymous, however.

Reapportionment is the redistribution of the numbers of seats allocated to individual units of government to reflect shifts in population as indicated by the national CENSUS, which is conducted every ten years in the spring of the year ending in "0." And reapportionment has its most universal—and politically important—impact on Congress: States that have had population gains over the previous decade that significantly exceed the average for the nation as a whole can gain one or more seats in the House, at the expense of states that have either lost population and or have grown significantly more slowly than the national average.

There are state legislatures and county or city legislative DISTRICTS in which reapportionment pertains, almost always in cases in which there are multimember districts. In these circumstances, the number of members assigned to individual districts is affected by population trends over the previous decade. Most states and localities have single-member districts, however, and reapportionment is not a factor in these places.

Redistricting, though, takes place at almost every level of government as districts within states and localities adjust lines to ensure nearly equal population as required by the one person, one vote Supreme Court rulings of the 1960s.

The necessity of redrawing the lines to balance the numbers of residents also gives politicians in most places the opportunity to shape the partisan voter preference of each district, a tactic that dates to the nation's beginnings—the term "gerrymandering" to describe political redistricting was coined in the early 1800s—and has been enhanced in very recent times by computer technology that enables very detailed analyses of local demographics and voting behavior.

Most U.S. House members represent a specific district within a state, although seven states with sparse populations—Alaska, Delaware, Montana, North Dakota, South Dakota, Vermont, and Wyoming—have only one House member apiece. Each of those states is, in effect, a single at-large congressional district. (See HOUSE OF REPRESENTATIVES, ELECTING.)

Redistricting usually occurs in the two years following reapportionment, although there are exceptions. Maine, which has long had just two districts that require only modest changes to bring their populations into balance, defers its redistricting until the third year of the redistricting cycle.

GOVERNORS and state legislators normally control the mapping process, for CONGRESSIONAL DISTRICTS as well as for state election districts. A handful of states have turned the redistricting process over to government agencies or panels that either are nonpartisan or have memberships relatively balanced between the two major parties. In addition, in almost every decade some states have called upon the state and federal judicial systems to assume responsibility for redistricting when elected officials have failed to agree on and implement a plan on their own.

Counties or cities that have home rule—full or limited independence from the state legislature—may be empowered to draw their own DISTRICT, WARD, AND PRECINCT boundaries.

No matter which body does the redistricting, the process may not be over when that body finishes its work. Affected persons or groups often file legal challenges to the maps. The courts sometimes order a second round of redistricting in the middle of a decade, and on occasion they even draw new district maps on their own.

Reapportionment and redistricting have been subjects of debate throughout U.S. history because the Constitution did not specify how they should be done. The framers decreed that House seats would be divided among the states on the basis of population, and that House members would be elected by the people. Beyond that, the Constitution gave little guidance on these subjects, leaving Congress, the courts, and state governments to wrestle with them.

As a result, the processes of reapportionment and redistricting are constantly evolving. The 1990s saw the proliferation of MINORITY-MAJORITY DISTRICTS—created under the auspices of the federal VOTING RIGHTS ACT, first enacted in the 1960s in response to the civil rights movement—to expand the numbers of African Americans, Hispanics, and other minorities in Congress and other legislative bodies. The first decade of the new century produced aggressively partisan Republican majorities in Texas and Georgia who broke historical precedent with their enactment of MID-DECADE REDISTRICTING plans to replace already implemented congressional maps in their states. And in all states, the advances in technology have allowed political participants, with increasing exactitude, to use redistricting to advance their partisan or demographic goals.

In contrast to the House, the Senate never undergoes reapportionment or redistricting. The Constitution gave each state two Senate seats, and senators are always chosen on a statewide basis. Moreover, the two-senator minimum cannot be changed other than by amending the Constitution. Article V states "that no State, without its Consent, shall be deprived of its equal Suffrage in the Senate."

State senators, however, are elected from smaller districts. Up until the latter part of the twentieth century, it was still common for state legislatures to have MULTIMEMBER DISTRICTS that were apportioned according to population, much like congressional districts. But complaints from a number of voters that the system was confusing, and concerns among policy makers that multi-member districts could complicate efforts to meet the requirements of the Voting Rights Act and the Supreme Court's population equality rulings prompted a number of states to convert to single-member districts, leaving just a small handful with multimember districts more than a decade into the twenty-first century.

After many decades of debate, the Supreme Court settled the basic goal of reapportionment and redistricting with rulings in the 1960s. The current guiding principle is one person, one vote, which requires that each citizen have approximately the same representation. For Congress, this means that the 435 congressional districts should be as close to equal in population as possible.

Many other questions about reapportionment and redistricting have yet to be settled. Most important, the courts have not decided definitively whether the Constitution permits GERRYMAN-DERING, the drawing of district boundaries to favor one party or group.

Reapportionment of the U.S. House

Apart from determining the number of seats and the amount of political strength that each state has in Congress, reapportionment plays two important roles in the U.S. political process.

One is that it also determines how many votes each state has in the Electoral College that decides the outcome of presidential elections. This is because that figure is based on the total number of a state's House seats plus the state's two senators (for example, California, by far the nation's most populous state, has fifty-three House seats and therefore has fifty-five electoral votes). (See Reference Material table, page 719.)

The other is that the shifts in House seats among the states provide a convenient guide to overall population trends among the nation's regions. In the nineteenth century, when most agriculture was performed by hand rather than machine, the influx of laborers to farm states such as Iowa and Nebraska boosted the size of their congressional delegations. The industrial revolution from the late nineteenth through mid-twentieth century drew millions of people from rural areas and from foreign countries into the states of the Northeast and upper Midwest, inflating the sizes of their congressional delegations.

And in the most recent era that dates for more than a half-century in the aftermath of World War II, which ended in 1945, population growth and congressional seats have shifted to the South and West from the Northeast and Midwest, because of factors that include the rise of a service-oriented economy, the decline of domestic manufacturing, and even the arrival of nearly universal air conditioning in the nation's hotter regions.

As a result of the 1980 census, seventeen House seats shifted from the Northeast and Midwest to the Sun Belt. The state that benefited most was Florida, which picked up four seats, followed by Texas with three and California with two. New York, on the other hand, lost five seats—the sharpest drop in House representation for any state since 1840. Illinois, Ohio, and Pennsylvania lost two seats each.

The 1990 census showed that the trend had continued. California picked up seven seats, reflecting a dramatic westward population shift, while Florida gained another four seats and Texas gained three. New York once again was the big loser, dropping three seats. Illinois, Ohio, and Pennsylvania again lost two seats each, as did Michigan. The trend continued, albeit less dramatically, following the 2000 census. Ten states, mostly in the Northeast and Midwest, lost a total of twelve seats that went to fast-growing states in the South and West. Texas picked up two districts for a total of thirty-two, allowing it to displace New York as the nation's second largest congressional delegation.

Many political observers predicted that the 1980 reapportionment would alter the ideological makeup of the House. Most of the states that lost seats tended to favor liberal Democrats, while the states that gained seats were more likely to favor Republicans or conservative Democrats. Because of Democratic successes in the state redistricting battles that followed reapportionment, however, the effects were less significant than expected.

Similarly, Republicans were disappointed in their hopes to substantially reduce the Democrats' majorities in Congress in the 1992 election, the first to reflect reapportionment following the 1990 census. The Republicans did not have to wait long, however, to see their hopes realized. They gained control of the House in 1994 and retained it in 1996 and, with smaller margins, in 1998. In both elections they also won and held majorities in the Senate.

The 2000 reapportionment initially appeared to marginally reinforce the Republicans' majority in the House. In the 2002 elections, Republicans picked up a net gain of six seats. In the 2004 elections, the Republicans netted a three-seat gain nationally that was abetted by a net gain of five seats under a strongly Republican-oriented mid-decade redistricting plan enacted in Texas.

A sharp decline in public support for the Republican Party in general and the Republican-controlled Congress in particular enabled Democrats to overcome what seemed to be the Republicans' advantage and make a net gain of thirty House seats in the 2006 midterm elections, giving them control of the House for the first time in a dozen years, and the Democrats expanded their margins with additional gains in the 2008 elections. But voter dissatisfaction stemming largely from the aftermath of a deep economic recession, which began in 2007 and reached crisis proportions in late 2008, spurred a backlash that fueled major gains for the Republicans in 2010, when they recaptured control of the House. The regional trend in reapportionment continued following the 2010 census. Texas, now the nation's second-most populous states, gained an additional four seats for a total of thirty-six for a decade beginning with the Congress to be chosen in the 2012 elections. Florida, the fourth most-populous state, gained two seats for a total of twenty-seven. The six states that gained one seat apiece were all in the South or West: Arizona, Georgia, Nevada, South Carolina, Utah, and Washington.

Meanwhile, New York—which led the nation in population from 1810 until it was passed by California in the 1970 census and barely retained the third position ahead of Florida in 2010—lost two seats for a total of twenty-seven (from a high point of forty-five in the 1930s and 1940s), while Ohio also lost two seats to fall to sixteen (its peak was twenty-four seats in the 1930s and then again in the 1960s). Of the states that lost one seat, almost all—Illinois, Iowa, Massachusetts, Michigan, Missouri, New Jersey, and Pennsylvania—are in the Northeast and Midwest. The one exception was Louisiana, where economic problems atypical of most southern states were dramatically exacerbated by population dislocations caused by Hurricane Katrina in 2005.

The seat distribution under reapportionment is arrived at according to a complex mathematical formula. It has not been easy to pick the best formula for the distribution. Congress has tried different methods over the years, but none, including the one currently in use, has worked perfectly. Many experts believe it is impossible to devise a method of allocating House seats that does not give some states more or less representation than they deserve.

The cause of the difficulty is simple: no state can have a fraction of a representative. Each state must have a whole number of House members, from a constitutional minimum of one to as many as the fifty-three that California has held since the 2000 census. There is some variation in the amount of representation states receive based on their populations.

The framers settled the distribution question for the first Congress by specifically listing the number of seats each of the thirteen original states would have. This was necessary because at that time there were no accurate statistics on the populations of the states. The Constitution directed that after the first census in 1790 each congressional district should have at least 30,000 residents. (If that ratio were still in effect, the House today would have about 9,300 members. After the 2010 reapportionment, the average population of a congressional district was 709,760.)

The Constitution made an exception for small states, which were guaranteed at least one representative no matter what their population. In a compromise between the slave-owning South and the rest of the country, the Constitution provided that each slave would be counted as three-fifths of a person.

At first Congress followed the Constitution in basing representation on an ideal population size of a congressional district. As a result, the total number of House members at any time varied widely. In 1832, for example, the standard size of a congressional district was set at 47,700 people, producing a House of 240 members. None of the different allocation methods used in those days could solve the problem of fractional representation, so congressional districts varied widely in population. The early reapportionment methods also failed to deal with the rapid growth in the nation's population. No matter what method was used, there seemed to be unanticipated effects that went against common sense.

Finally, around 1850, Congress settled on a method that seemed to solve many reapportionment problems—expanding the membership. The size of the House was supposed to be fixed by the most recent apportionment law at 233 members, but Congress regularly voted to add more members as new states entered the Union. The addition of members allowed the House to side-step the difficult task of cutting back on the representation of existing states to accommodate the new states.

By the beginning of the twentieth century, however, the process threatened to make the House too large to be a workable legislative body. In 1911 Congress fixed the size of the House at 435, where it has remained except for a brief period (1959–1963) when the admission of Alaska and Hawaii raised the total temporarily to 437.

The decision to freeze the size of the House set the stage for the reapportionment battles of the 1920s. The 1920 census was a landmark event in the nation's history because it showed that for the first time there were more Americans living in cities than in rural areas. States with large cities therefore were entitled to many more representatives, while rural states faced sharp cutbacks in their House representation.

The House of Representatives in session circa 1920. The House became the scene of pitched battles after the 1920 census revealed that, for the first time, more Americans lived in cities than in rural areas. Rural representatives managed to block reapportionment in the House throughout the decade.

Source: Library of Congress.

Arguing that people who lived on farms and in small towns were the heart and soul of America, rural representatives fought hard to prevent their loss of power. They managed to block reapportionment throughout the 1920s. Redistribution of House seats did not take place until after the 1930 census. That reapportionment led to drastic shifts in power, with California nearly doubling its House delegation, from eleven to twenty, while twenty-one other states lost a total of twenty-seven seats.

The current method of reapportionment, called "the method of equal proportions," was adopted after the 1940 census. It was initially to become effective after the 1950 census, but it was made retroactive to January 1941 to save a Democratic seat Arkansas would have lost to Michigan under a different formula that otherwise yielded identical results for the rest of the country. The equal proportions method allocates House seats according to a complicated mathematical formula designed to minimize population variation among districts. Its adoption put an end to most controversy over reapportionment until the early 1990s, when Massachusetts and Montana mounted legal challenges. Both succeeded in the lower federal courts, but the Supreme Court rejected their arguments in 1992.

Massachusetts argued that it deserved another seat because the census had counted overseas military personnel inaccurately. Montana, which had lost one of its two seats in the 1990 reapportionment, challenged the reapportionment formula on grounds that it was unfair to less populous states. The Supreme Court refused to support either claim.

Montana does provide a clear-cut example of the imperfect way in which the reapportionment system deals with the rounding of fractions. The 2010 reapportionment again assigned one seat to Montana even though its population of nearly 1 million people, by far the largest among single-district states, was almost a third larger than the nationwide average for the size of congressional districts, and was 75 percent larger than the population of Wyoming, the least-populous state with 568,000 residents.

Another conflict arose in the 2000 reapportionment, in which North Carolina gained the last of the 435 seats at the expense of Utah, which was next in line to receive the seat. Utah officials argued that the Census Bureau's counting techniques accorded an excessive number of military personnel to North Carolina, which has several major bases, while not giving Utah enough credit for members of the Mormon Church who were temporarily living outside the state while on religious missions. Utah sued to block the designation of that final seat to North Carolina, but its claim was rejected by the courts.

That case did have an effect on the 2010 reapportionment that, ironically, worked to North Carolina's disadvantage. The long U.S. military engagements in Iraq and Afghanistan that had transpired since the 2000 census had shifted many U.S. service members overseas from bases in North Carolina, where they would otherwise have accrued to that state's population total. And the Census Bureau also determined that military personnel serving overseas would be accorded to

CLOSER LOOK

The apportionment of House seats in the years since World War II underscores the overriding national demographic shift of that era: the rapid growth in population and political clout among states in the South and West at the expense of the slower-growing states of the Northeast and Midwest.

This chart lists the ten most populous states according to the 2010 census and compares the House seats allocated to those states in the 1950 reapportionment to the reapportionment in 2010.

State	1950 House seats	2010 House seats	Change in seats	Percentage change
California	30	53	+23	+77
Texas	22	36	+14	+64
New York	43	27	−16	−37
Florida	8	27	+19	+137
Illinois	25	18	−7	−28
Pennsylvania	30	18	−12	−40
Ohio	23	16	−7	−30
Michigan	18	14	−4	−22
Georgia	10	14	+4	+40
North Carolina	12	13	+1	+8

the states they personally regarded as home rather than automatically assigning them to their previous bases in North Carolina. These events contributed to the fact that North Carolina fell just short of gaining an additional seat following the 2010 census.

Redistricting

The early years of debate over redistricting were dominated by the question of whether there needed to be congressional districts within states at all. The Constitution does not say so, and several states favored the multimember-district system of AT-LARGE elections in which all the voters in the state chose all the state's House members. Use of the system declined because it did not encourage the close ties between representatives and citizens that developed when a member of Congress represented a specific area.

Congress banned at-large House elections in 1842, except in one-member states, although the ban sometimes was violated until the 1960s. The 1842 law also established the basic principle that House districts should be contiguous—that is, a single, connected area rather than several separate areas scattered across a state.

Redistricting has become a subject of intense debate in recent decades as a result of Supreme Court decisions in the 1960s, major population shifts within states, and the development of computer-based technology. The national REPUBLICAN and DEMOCRATIC parties devote immense resources to the effort to persuade state legislatures and the courts to approve redistricting plans favorable to their own candidates.

Some political scientists believe that redistricting is the single most important factor determining partisan control of the House. They argue that the former dominance of the Democratic Party, which controlled the House continuously from 1955 to 1995, was a result of Democratic control of the redistricting process. Republicans claimed that Democratic-dominated state legislatures devised district plans that gave the advantage to Democratic House candidates.

But in 1994, besides gaining control of Congress, the Republicans gained near-parity with the Democrats in control of state legislatures for the first time since 1968. More than half the states had divided control, with a governor of one party and at least one chamber controlled by the other party. After the 2000 elections the legislatures that would handle redistricting were split closely between the two parties. Republicans controlled both chambers in seventeen states, the Democrats controlled both chambers in sixteen states, and the two parties had divided control in another sixteen states (including four states in which one party had a majority in one chamber and the two parties were divided evenly in the second chamber). The last state, Nebraska, used a nonpartisan process.

The Republicans' surge during the 2010 elections was particularly well-timed as it pertained to redistricting, though. Among the forty-three states with more than one congressional district, Republicans held complete control of the redistricting process in eighteen. Democrats controlled the process in six states, while control of the process was split between the parties in thirteen states. In the six other states, redistricting was to be conducted by bipartisan commissions. Those states are Arizona, California, Hawaii, Idaho, New Jersey, and Washington.

Supreme Court Action

For a hundred years redistricting questions received little attention. State legislatures had to draw new congressional district lines when the state gained or lost House seats because of reapportionment, and occasionally there was a heated dispute over a single House district. But the legislatures usually ignored the population shifts within their states and rarely acted to change their own election district lines. As a result, cities did not gain additional representation in the state legislatures as their populations grew. Partisan fights over district lines were rare, however, and there was little pressure for major alterations in the shape of most districts.

Rural areas were vastly overrepresented, while cities did not have nearly so much representation as their populations warranted—a condition known as *malapportionment.* In every state the most populous state legislative district had more than twice as many people as the least populous district. The population balance was not usually so lopsided in congressional districts, but wide differences between rural and urban representation remained. For example, in Texas one urban congressional district had four times as many people in 1960 as one lightly populated rural district. (Such districts in ancient England were known as *rotten boroughs.*)

The state legislatures, dominated by members from rural areas, refused or neglected to change the existing districts, especially those for their own seats. Frustrated urban dwellers turned to the courts, arguing that the legislatures were denying them fair representation.

The situation changed radically when the Supreme Court began to consider redistricting issues in the 1960s, after refusing for decades to become involved in the matter. By the time the Court began to act, there was clear evidence that something was wrong with the way legislative districts were drawn. In its historic decision in BAKER V. CARR (1962), the Court ruled that the districts used in the Tennessee legislature were unconstitutional because they violated the principle of ONE PERSON, ONE VOTE.

In 1964 the Court extended the one-person, one-vote doctrine to the U.S. House in the case of *Wesberry v. Sanders,* which concerned congressional districts in Georgia. That decision stated that congressional districts should be as nearly equal in population "as is practicable."

Since then, the Court has continued to tighten the requirement that congressional districts should have equal populations. In *Kirkpatrick v. Preisler* (1969) the Court struck down Missouri's plan, even though the largest district had a population only 3.1 percent larger than that of the smallest district. Any population difference, "no matter how small," the Court declared, was unacceptable in all but a few cases. The Court set an even more rigorous standard in *Karcher v. Daggett* (1983). In that case the Court overturned New Jersey's congressional map because the difference between the most populated and the least populated districts was 0.69 percent.

A federal court ruling during the redistricting cycle that followed the 2000 census struck down and required an adjustment of the congressional district map enacted in Pennsylvania because of a population disparity of just nineteen people between the most and least populous districts in the state—or an average of one person across the state's nineteen districts.

Although the one-person, one-vote principle is now widely accepted in American politics, some political experts criticize the Court's strict standard of population equality. For one thing, the census figures for district populations are not entirely accurate, and they usually are out of date soon after the census has been taken. The 1990 census was especially controversial because studies showed that certain urban and minority populations were seriously undercounted.

For the 2000 census, the Clinton administration proposed using modern sampling techniques—commonly used in POLLING—to correct the undercount problem. Republicans in Congress objected, fearing that sampling would give more House representation to areas that usually elect Democrats. Contending that the Constitution requires an actual head count rather than a projection, several GOP House members filed suit against the sampling plan and won a 5–4 Supreme Court ruling in January 1999. The Court barred use of sampling figures for reapportionment but not for redistricting within states.

Whether voluntarily drawn by a legislature or ordered by a court, strict equality of redistricting can produce strangely contorted districts. Those drawn to ensure equal population often cross traditional political boundaries, such as cities, counties, or regions, that help voters develop a sense of identification with and interest in their congressional district. Also, critics have pointed out that the Supreme Court's standard can be satisfied by a districting plan that is a grossly unfair case of political GERRYMANDERING, so long as each district has the same number of people.

RACIAL REDISTRICTING is another potential form of gerrymandering. By dividing up African Americans or other minority voters among several districts, a legislature might be able to ensure that members of a minority group make up no more than half the voters in a district and so prevent election of a minority representative. Conversely, drawing a district to take in several black neighborhoods, to ensure that the minority has a population majority, may be unfair to the nonminority voters who happen to live within the boundaries.

When BLACK SUFFRAGE became a reality throughout the nation in the 1960s, civil rights groups feared that African Americans might be subjected to racial gerrymandering by white-dominated legislatures. To prevent this, Congress added provisions to the 1965 VOTING RIGHTS ACT barring redistricting plans that dilute the voting strength of blacks.

The law required states with histories of racial discrimination to submit their redistricting plans to the U.S. Justice Department to ensure that African American voters were being treated fairly. Other minorities, including Hispanics, Asian Americans, and Native Americans, were later included in the law's protection. The department and the courts have required changes in redistricting plans in several states to ensure that minority candidates have a chance of being elected. The department required seven full states and parts of nine others to submit their redistricting plans for approval after the 2010 census.

In a ruling on districts in North Carolina, *Thornburg v. Gingles* (1986), the Supreme Court said gerrymandering that deliberately diluted minority voting strength was illegal. The burden of proof shifted from minorities, who had been required to show that lines were being drawn to dilute their voting strength, to lawmakers, who had to show that they had done all they could to maximize minority voting strength.

In the 1990s, in a series of decisions beginning with *Shaw v. Reno* (1993), a North Carolina case, the Court cast doubt on the legitimacy of irregularly shaped congressional districts having minority majorities or others where race appeared to have been the "predominant factor" in drawing the district lines. Although in some cases the intent of such gerrymandering may have been benevolent—to ensure election of an African American or Hispanic representative—the Court said in *Shaw*, it bore "an uncomfortable resemblance to political apartheid."

The Court later invalidated some MINORITY-MAJORITY DISTRICTS, and lower federal courts followed suit. In 2001, the Court in *Hunt v. Cromartie* approved a largely minority district, contending that it had been drawn to favor Democratic, rather than black, voters.

More on this topic:
Baker v. Carr, p. 12
Census, p. 92
Congressional District, p. 111
Gerrymander, p. 226
House of Representatives, Electing, p. 250
Mid-decade Redistricting, p. 330
Minority-Majority District, p. 338
Voting Rights Act, p. 663

The controversies over racial redistricting faded in the early twenty-first century. There were no major court rulings following the 2000 census in which redistricting plans were overruled on grounds that they provided unfair benefits to minorities. In fact, the Court's ruling in the 2006 case *League of United Latin American Citizens v. Perry* required the redrawing of a congressional district in Texas on grounds that it diluted the voting rights of Hispanics.

Recall *See* REMOVAL FROM OFFICE.

Recount

Most elections produce decisive results. In the relatively few that do not, the apparent loser may demand a recount, officially creating a CONTESTED ELECTION.

The election recount in the presidential election of 2000 had a major impact on U.S. politics and underscored the complexity of recounting votes. Many counties in Florida, a state key to the electoral fortunes of both Vice President Al Gore and Texas governor George W. Bush, that year used a punch-card voting system. Voters had to use a stylus to punch tiny paper rectangles, known as "chads," from their ballots corresponding to their preferred candidates. Some voters did not press firmly enough with the stylus to fully detach the chads. Because the vote was so close—the initial tally showed Gore trailing by fewer than 2,000 votes out of almost six million cast—these "undervotes" had the potential to determine the winner of the state's twenty-five electoral votes and, therefore, who would be the next president.

The close vote and punch card controversy sparked a series of high-profile court battles over how to interpret ballots in which the chad was not fully detached. During the recount, election officials in some counties sought to divine the voters' intent from the condition of the chad.

Protesters assemble in December 2000 as the U.S. Supreme Court hears arguments for and against the hand recount of ballots cast in Florida in the presidential election. On December 12, the Court voted 5–4 to halt the recount.

Source: AP Images/Steve Helber.

The lack of consistent, statewide guidelines for doing so ultimately doomed Gore's request for a manual recount in four counties. The Florida Supreme Court ordered a recount of undervotes but was overturned on appeal by the U.S. Supreme Court (See *BUSH V. GORE*) five weeks after ELECTION DAY. The Court held that the absence of uniform guidelines based in state law rendered the recount a violation of the equal protection of all Florida voters.

Four decades earlier, a hard-fought presidential contest almost ended with a recount. After his narrow 1960 loss to Democrat John F. Kennedy, Vice President Richard M. Nixon considered asking for a recount, which would have been the only general recount of a presidential election. Nixon ultimately decided against it for fear of inciting a constitutional crisis. Republicans in 2000 cited Nixon as a role model as they contended that Gore should concede the presidential election to Bush.

Though the Bush-Gore clash was of a higher order of magnitude than virtually any other recount controversy the United States has seen, it had something in common with most others: the candidate who led in the initial vote count ultimately was declared the official winner.

In fact, the poor track record of successful challenges can sometimes deter recounts. The consistent failures of past recounts to reverse the outcomes in statewide races in Virginia played a role in Republican senator George Allen's decision not to contest his defeat by Democrat Jim Webb in 2006, even though Webb's victory margin was fewer than 9,000 votes of more than 2.3 million cast and clinched the Democrats' takeover of the Senate in that year's elections.

But there are enough examples of reversed outcomes that candidates who narrowly trail in the initial vote count may be tempted to pursue recounts. One recent recount success was in the 2004 race for governor in the state of Washington. After an initial canvass showed Republican Dino Rossi with a razor-thin lead over Democrat Christine Gregoire, 573 uncounted absentee ballots turned up in King County—which includes Seattle and is the state's premier Democratic Party stronghold. The inclusion of these votes in a protracted recount process helped Gregoire claim a victory by 129 votes out of about 2.75 million cast.

A similar, long drawn-out contest occurred in 2008 for a Senate seat in Minnesota. The winner, Democrat Al Franken, had to wait until July 2009 to claim his seat. Franken challenged the incumbent, Republican Norm Coleman, but appeared to lose in the November voting. However, Coleman's official margin of victory was just 215 votes out of 2.9 million cast. A statewide hand recount of ballots in 2009 gave Franken a lead of 312 votes. Coleman disputed the outcome in legal action, contending that some ballots were improperly excluded in the recount. His challenge eventually reached the Minnesota Supreme Court, which on June 30, 2009, ruled unanimously, 5–0, that Franken had won by that margin. Coleman quickly conceded and Franken took office July 7, almost eight months after the election.

Recount procedures vary by state, often by county, and sometimes by voting precincts within counties. Close elections in several states automatically trigger a recounting of the regular and ABSENTEE ballots, a process that can take many weeks in a large state. Unlike VOTING MACHINE ballots that can be tallied quickly, ballots that are marked in other ways can be difficult to retally. Absentee ballots must be verified as genuine and counted one by one.

Not everyone can initiate a recount. In most cases where they are not automatic, recounts can be requested only by the defeated candidate; in some states, the protesting candidate must cover the government's costs to conduct the recount, with reimbursement given only if the outcome of the election is reversed. State officials or the courts may order a recount if there is a possibility that ELECTION FRAUD corrupted the results.

Because states share the conduct of presidential and congressional elections with the federal government, state policies vary concerning jurisdiction over federal elections. Some states assert their authority over them, others prefer minimal involvement. For its part, the federal government generally leaves all the procedural aspects of elections to the states—VOTER REGISTRATION, preparation of the ballot, operation of the polling places, counting of the votes, and recounts if necessary. In the VOTING RIGHTS ACT of 1965, however, the federal government asserted its power to supervise elections in states where discrimination against minority voters is indicated. (See STATE AND FEDERAL ELECTION RESPONSIBILITIES.)

Federal authorities do not recount the POPULAR VOTE, even in disputes over congressional races. The states do the recounting and certify the winner to the House or the Senate. If the certified result is still in dispute, the affected body may investigate under its constitutional power to judge the qualifications of its own members. (See HOUSE OF REPRESENTATIVES, QUALIFICATIONS; SENATE, QUALIFICATIONS.)

Recount Logistics

Eligibility for review of a House regular or SPECIAL ELECTION is determined by the Federal Contested Elections Act of 1969, which limits challenges to candidates listed on the official state ballot or certified as WRITE-IN candidates. The Senate has no comparable legislation.

Only once in its history has the Senate been unable to resolve an election dispute. That was in New Hampshire's exceedingly close 1974 contest between Republican Louis C. Wyman and Democrat John A. Durkin. Even then, the Senate did not try to recount the New Hampshire votes. After two unsuccessful recounts by the state, the Senate called for a new election, which Durkin won.

State laws prohibit frivolous recounts. The challenger must have grounds, such as evidence of errors, irregularities, or fraud. The original count also must be close enough for a recount to change the result.

Errors may include voting machine malfunctions, the same precinct's vote counted twice, the wrong total read off a machine, or computer breakdown. Irregularities may include polls closed early, invalid signatures on absentee ballot envelopes, or poll officials entering booths with voters to give unwanted assistance.

Evidence of fraud may include unusually high or low VOTER TURNOUT in a precinct, illegal noncitizen votes, or voting in the names of deceased persons.

Redistricting *See* REAPPORTIONMENT AND REDISTRICTING.

Referendums *See* INITIATIVES AND REFERENDUMS.

Reform Party (1995–)

The Reform Party emerged almost full grown from independent Ross Perot's self-financed presidential candidacy of 1992. Running largely on a PLATFORM of eliminating the federal budget and appealing to disenchanted voters with his folksy, if sometimes quirky, style, the Texas billionaire that year drew the highest vote share of any INDEPENDENT or THIRD-PARTY candidate since Theodore Roosevelt in 1912: 19,741,657 votes or 18.9 percent of the nationwide vote. In the wake of that showing, he affiliated himself with United We Stand America, which promoted itself as a nonpartisan educational organization (not a political party) and stressed a balanced budget, government reform, and health care reform. In the fall of 1995 Perot created the Reform Party and prepared to run as its presidential candidate the following year.

Reform Party candidate Pat Buchanan applauds Ezola Foster, his running mate in the 2000 presidential election.

Source: AP Images/Stephan Savoia.

The Texan won the party's nomination in an unusual two-stage procedure over Richard D. Lamm, a former Democratic governor of Colorado. The nominating process began with a preliminary vote after nominating speeches at a convention in Long Beach, California, followed by a mail and electronic vote with the winner announced a week later in Valley Forge, Pennsylvania. Ballots had been sent to 1.3 million voters who were registered party members or signers of its BALLOT ACCESS petitions.

Maintaining the same populist themes of fiscal responsibility, protection of American jobs, and political reform in Washington, Perot again was on the ballot in all states. He chose as his running mate Pat Choate, a native Texan and economist who had coached Perot in his unsuccessful fight against the North American Free Trade Agreement (NAFTA) in 1993. The Reform Party also had congressional candidates in ten states.

Although Perot in 1992 had spurned public funding to avoid federal campaign spending limits, the Reform Party effort of 1996 qualified for federal funding and went along with the limitations that acceptance of the money entailed. By garnering more than 5 percent of the 1992 presidential vote, Perot qualified in 1996 for some $30 million, less than half the amount he spent from his own pocket four years earlier.

Locked out of the presidential DEBATES, Perot spent much of his campaign money on television "infomercials" espousing the party's principles. Even with the restricted budget, Perot again placed third in the national election after the two major-party candidates. However, his 8,085,285 votes (8.4 percent of the national total) came to less than half of his 1992 achievement. Perot had his best showing in Maine, where he received 14.2 percent of the vote. He won no electoral votes.

At a postelection convention in Nashville in early 1997, the Reform Party began the task of building a permanent political party to rival the two major parties. Unresolved at the start of the convention was the future role of Perot, with many party members arguing that the party needed to emerge from what Lamm termed Perot's "dominating shadow." Denying that Reform had become "the party of personality," Perot nevertheless declined to rule out another try for the presidency in 2000. The Nashville convention ended with Perot supporters still firmly in control of the Reform Party.

In 1998 the Reform Party appeared to make its big breakthrough: Jesse Ventura, a former professional wrestler and local official running as a political outsider, was elected governor of Minnesota on the Reform Party ticket. Ventura, however, left the party in February 2000, contending that bureaucratic inertia had prevented the party from growing.

By that point, though, Perot appeared to have lost interest and disappeared from the political scene, leaving a vacuum which two very opposite outside factions rushed to fill. One backed conservative television commentator Patrick Buchanan, who had staged an unsuccessful challenge to President George H. W. Bush in the 1992 Republican primaries, stirred controversy in a speech at that year's Republican Party convention by declaring that the nation was in the midst of a "culture war," and ran a failed bid for the 1996 Republican presidential nomination. The other faction was led by John Hagelin, the founder of the NATURAL LAW PARTY, which subscribed to the transcendental meditation philosophy of the Maharishi Mahesh Yogi.

At the party's August 10–13, 2000, nominating convention in Long Beach, California, the factions split and held rival proceedings, each nominating its preferred candidate.

Hanging in the balance was $12,613,452 in federal campaign funds, owed to the Reform Party's official candidate based on the party's showing in 1996. The FEDERAL ELECTION COMMISSION recognized Buchanan as the rightful claimant to the funds and ordered the Treasury Department to release the funds to the Buchanan campaign on September 14, 2000.

Nonetheless, Buchanan won just 448,868 votes, 0.42 percent of all ballots cast, in the general election that was won by Republican George W. Bush. The only splash he made was when the count in Palm Beach County, Florida, showed Buchanan receiving a vote that was proportionately much larger than he received elsewhere. County officials that year used a poorly designed and confusing "butterfly ballot," and voters may have cast their ballots for Buchanan by mistake.

More on this topic:

Third Parties, p. 627

United We Stand America, p. 642

Complaints from a number of liberal voters that they had unintentionally voted for Buchanan became an issue in the dispute between Bush and Democratic nominee Al Gore over the vote RECOUNT in the crucial state of Florida. (See *BUSH V. GORE.*)

By 2004 the Reform Party had become so disorganized that it failed to nominate a candidate for president, although the party affiliates in some states gave their ballot lines to a candidate who was a polar opposite to 2000 nominee Buchanan: liberal activist Ralph Nader, who was running in 2004 as an independent after making an impact as the Green Party nominee in 2000.

In 2006 the party's website listed only three candidates nationally, but their showing indicated that some voters were searching for an alternative to the Democratic and Republican parties. Reform nominee Earl Eidness took 11 percent of the vote in the race in Colorado's Fourth Congressional District, where Republican incumbent Marilyn Musgrave defeated Democrat Angie Paccione by 46 percent to 43 percent. In Florida, Max Linn, the Reform candidate for governor, took 92,595 votes, or 2 percent of the total, in the race in which Republican Charlie Crist defeated Democrat Jim Davis by 52 percent to 45 percent. In 2008 a Reform Party ticket was on the ballot only in Mississippi where its candidate, Ted Weill, got 481 votes.

Registration Laws *See* VOTER REGISTRATION.

Removal from Office

Recall and impeachment are processes that allow the people, directly or through their representatives, to remove from office an official who has broken the law or in some other way has presented grounds for dismissal.

Several states allow voters to petition for a recall election that, if successful, will remove the targeted official from office. Recall applies only to state and local officials and depends on the legalities in the particular state. There is no provision in federal law for recall of federal officeholders.

At the federal level, impeachment is the means for the removal from office of the president, vice president, federal judges, and other politically appointed officials. Impeachment by the House of Representatives (or a state legislative body in those states that allow such procedures against their executive branch officials) is equivalent to an indictment in the judicial system; if one or more articles of impeachment are approved by the House, a trial is held in the Senate in which the impeached official is either convicted (the penalties for which can include expulsion from office) or acquitted.

Both impeachment and recall are used sparingly. But their mere availability serves as a powerful check on elected and appointed officials.

Impeachment

On December 19, 1998, the U.S. House voted for only the second time in its history to impeach a president. The House approved two articles of impeachment against President Bill Clinton, charging perjury and obstruction of justice in the investigation of his admitted extramarital affair with White House intern Monica S. Lewinsky.

Voting mostly along party lines, the Republican-controlled House approved the perjury charge 228–206 and the obstruction of justice charge 221–212. After a five-week trial, however, the Senate acquitted Clinton on February 12, 1999. The House members serving as managers (a role equivalent to prosecuting attorneys) failed to obtain the two-thirds majority required for approval of either article to win a conviction. The Senate vote was 45–55 on perjury and 50–50 on obstruction. Five Republicans joined the forty-five Senate Democrats to defeat the perjury article.

Clinton was only the third president subjected to a formal impeachment inquiry and the only president besides Andrew Johnson to be impeached by the House and tried by the Senate. Johnson, the first, was tried in 1868 but not convicted. The second president targeted by an impeachment inquiry was Richard M. Nixon, who resigned August 9, 1974, to avoid almost certain impeachment in connection with the Watergate burglary and cover-up SCANDAL.

Of the sixteen officials impeached before Clinton, only seven—all federal judges—had been convicted and removed from office for the constitutional offenses (Article II, section 4) of "Treason, Bribery, or other High Crimes and Misdemeanors."

One of the impeached and convicted judges, Democrat Alcee L. Hastings of Florida, was elected to the House in 1992 after his criminal conviction was overturned in the courts and built a long career there. But that he was impeached at all turned out to be a lasting impediment; criticisms from Republican colleagues and some outside groups kept the Democratic leadership from appointing him to the chairmanship of the Homeland Security Committee after the 2006 elections gave the Democrats control of Congress.

Members of Congress at other time times failed to win support for a proposed impeachment. Such was the case in 1970, when then Rep. (and later President) Gerald R. Ford proposed impeaching Supreme Court Justice William O. Douglas, a liberal icon, for alleged conflicts of interest. The House never took up the matter, but Ford coined a much-quoted phrase, telling his colleagues that "an impeachable offense is whatever a majority of the House of Representatives considers it to be at a given moment in history."

Impeachment is a two-stage process in which the House of Representatives makes the formal charge, like a grand jury, and the Senate in closed session decides the accused's guilt or innocence, much as a regular jury would. The Senate may also disqualify the convicted official from holding future federal office, but it has done so in only two of the seven judge convictions. The House inserted such a provision in the articles against Clinton, saying his conduct warrants "disqualification to hold and enjoy any office of honor, trust or profit under the United States."

Under Article I of the Constitution, the House has the sole authority to impeach and the Senate alone tries all impeachments, with a two-thirds majority vote required for conviction. If the president or vice president is being tried, the chief justice of the United States presides.

Johnson, the first impeached president, was tried in 1868 on charges of violating the Tenure of Office Act by removing Secretary of War Edwin M. Stanton—who had been appointed by and served under his predecessor, Abraham Lincoln—without the assent of Congress, then controlled by the Radical Republicans bent on punishing the South for the Civil War. Johnson frequently clashed with Congress as he tried to carry out the "malice toward none" policy voiced by Lincoln before his 1865 assassination.

In the Senate trial, Johnson escaped conviction by a single vote—that of Edmund Gibson Ross of Kansas. Ross, a freshman, sided at the last minute with six other Republicans and twelve

"I . . . am . . . bulletproof."

—*Political impressionist Darrell Hammond* of NBC's *Saturday Night Live* television show in a comic impersonation of Bill Clinton following the president's acquittal in his 1999 Senate impeachment trial. Hammond also had his Clinton character warn his opponents, "Next time, you best bring kryptonite [a reference to the only substance that can weaken the powers of the fictional hero Superman]."

"An impeachable offense is whatever a majority of the House of Representatives considers it to be at a given moment in history."

—*Rep. Gerald R. Ford* in 1970 discussing the matter of the proposed impeachment of Supreme Court Justice William O. Douglas

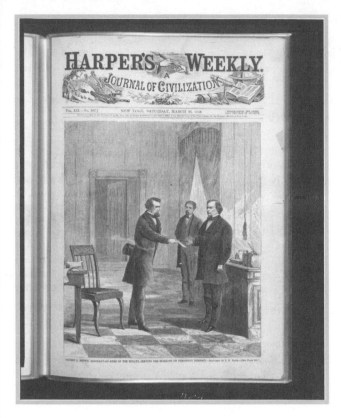

A sketch from Harper's Weekly depicts George T. Brown, sergeant-at-arms, serving impeachment summons on President Andrew Johnson in the White House.

Source: Library of Congress.

Democrats to make the vote 35–19, one short of the 36 needed to convict Johnson. Ross's vote is often cited as an example of political courage.

Besides Johnson and Clinton, only one other elected federal official had been impeached and tried. He was Sen. William Blount of Tennessee, impeached by the House in 1797 for having conspired to launch a military expedition to conquer Spanish territory for Great Britain. The Senate dismissed the impeachment charges because it already had expelled Blount.

Impeachment charges are presented to the House by its Judiciary Committee as "articles of impeachment." If approved by the full House, the articles go to the Senate for trial, with House-appointed managers serving as prosecutors.

In Nixon's case, the Judiciary Committee, July 27–30, 1974, approved three articles charging obstruction of justice, abuse of power, and contempt of Congress. Two other proposed articles were rejected. On August 5, Nixon by order of the Supreme Court released transcripts of subpoenaed tapes, including the "smoking gun" tape of June 23, 1972, that made clear Nixon knowingly participated in the cover-up of White House involvement in the burglary of DEMOCRATIC NATIONAL COMMITTEE headquarters in the Watergate Hotel complex. Faced with the new evidence and almost total loss of support in Congress, Nixon resigned.

In the case of Clinton, the House Judiciary Committee, after reviewing the report of independent counsel Kenneth W. Starr, concluded that the president may have committed fifteen possibly impeachable offenses, including obstruction of justice, lying under oath about his relationship with Lewinsky, and witness tampering. By a 258–176 vote October 8, the House directed the committee to investigate whether grounds for impeachment existed.

A problem in impeachment cases other than those for bribery or treason is the definition of "high crimes and misdemeanors." Generally, it has come to mean whatever the prosecution wanted it to mean. Because it involved engaging in and concealing private acts, the Clinton case presented a particularly difficult question of impeachability. But to some four hundred historians and presidential scholars the "current charges against him depart from what the Framers saw as grounds for impeachment." They signed an open letter to Congress saying that impeachment would undermine the presidency and leave it "permanently disfigured."

Recall

The example of the recall process most recognized by American voters is the petition and election process that resulted in the removal of California governor Gray Davis from office in October 2003.

Davis, a former state controller and lieutenant governor, was an early beneficiary of a Democratic voting trend in the nation's most populous state that began in earnest in the mid-1990s; he won his 1998 election easily over Republican Dan Lungren, who was then the state attorney general. After taking office, Davis struggled to maintain public support because of his rather colorless personality, his implementation of unpopular tax increases, and a state energy crisis (that was in large part the result of

President Richard Nixon bids farewell to his cabinet and members of the White House staff shortly after announcing his resignation.

Source: National Archives and Records Administration

market manipulation by some energy companies, including Enron, but still caused major political problems for Davis).

Davis managed to win reelection in November 2002 by 5 percentage points over conservative and politically inexperienced Republican Bill Simon. However, whether it was a case of political "buyer's remorse" or—as Democrats and some other critics of the recall campaign said—an effort by Republicans to get a "do-over" after failing to nominate a viable challenger in 2002, a recall petition drive launched in early 2003 gained immediate momentum and achieved its goal of placing a recall election on the state ballot for October 7, 2003.

When they went to the polls October 7, California voters had to vote on two matters. On the issue of whether to remove Davis from office, there was a simple yes or no question, with 55 percent of the voters in favor of recalling Davis. On the second question to determine who should replace Davis should he be recalled, voters were confronted with a daunting list of 135 candidates who had filed to run (though few ran visible and active campaigns). The list included Gary Coleman, a one-time child television star; Leo Gallagher, a comedian best known for smashing watermelons with a mallet as part of his stage act; and two people with well-known associations with the pornography industry, *Hustler* magazine publisher Larry Flynt and actress Mary Carey.

Emerging as the clear victor, with 49 percent of the vote, was Republican Arnold Schwarzenegger, an action film icon making his political debut. Schwarzenegger outran such established political figures as Democratic lieutenant governor Cruz Bustamante and Republican state senator Tom McClintock.

Schwarzenegger initially alienated some voters in the generally Democratic-leaning state by adopting a conservative posture. The failure of several ballot initiatives that he promoted in 2005 spurred him to change tacks, however. He began governing more as a moderate and reaching out to Democrats on issues such as infrastructure spending, education, and the environment. As a result, he won a full term by an overwhelming margin in November 2006.

However, recall elections are not sure bets even when they involve highly charged controversies that receive substantial media coverage. This was true in Wisconsin in 2011 when eight recall elections aimed at state legislators failed to change the balance of power in the Republican-controlled senate. The recalls grew out of the GOP's unexpected 2010 victory in Wisconsin when voters elected a Republican governor and turned over control of both legislative houses to the party. Facing significant budget shortfalls, the governor, Scott Walker, proposed spending cuts to Medicaid, state education aid, and other areas and sought other GOP-favored initiatives including requiring voters to show photo identification before being given a ballot. Most controversial of all, however, Walker proposed and won approval to curtail collective bargaining rights for many state employees. The bargaining rights issue was a red flag for not only Wisconsin public employees but organized labor nationwide, who saw it as an assault on all collective bargaining.

The controversy, which tied up the Wisconsin legislature for months in the winter, led to recall efforts aimed at eight legislators who supported Walker's proposals. These were held in July and August 2011 but did not unseat enough legislators to turn over control of the senate—where the recalls were focused—to Democrats. Rather, on August 8, the most important of the voting days, two GOP members were replaced but four others retained their seats. This meant the state senate stayed in GOP hands by one vote. The outcome was interpreted by Walker and neutral observers as voter endorsement for the budget cuts and bargaining rights changes approved earlier. Moreover, it was also seen as a setback for unions and Democrats nationwide who had hoped to use Wisconsin as a warning to other GOP-controlled states—of which there were a number after the 2010 elections—that programs such as Walker advanced did not have public support. Wisconsin's recall laws dated from 1926.

The recall procedure for removing state and local officials gained favor during the Progressive Era of the early 1900s as an antidote to political corruption and irresponsibility. It originated in Switzerland (where it is applicable to the entire legislature, not just an individual official) and was adopted by Los Angeles in 1903. From there it spread quickly to other cities, usually those using the commission form of government in which three to nine commissioners carry out both legislative and executive duties.

Oregon was the first state to adopt recall, in 1908, and California followed suit in 1911. By 2011 nineteen states, mostly in the West and Midwest, allowed recall of state officers, according to the National Conference of State Legislatures (NCSL). In addition, many state constitutions permitted it for municipal officers as well. The states are Arkansas, Arizona, California, Colorado, Georgia, Idaho, Illinois, Kansas, Louisiana, Michigan, Minnesota, Montana, Nevada, New Jersey, North Dakota, Oregon, Rhode Island, Washington, and Wisconsin. Two of those states—Illinois and Rhode Island—limited recalls to elected executive branch officials, such as the governor, but excluded legislators.

In Kansas, one of the first adopters, appointed as well as elected officers are covered by recall. Many of the adopting states had large numbers of elective officers who were immune to removal by a governor and were, in essence, beyond the control of the electorate during their term of office. A number of the states exempted judges from recall.

Laws governing recall usually provide that if a specified number of voters sign a petition, a SPECIAL ELECTION such as the one in California in 2003 must be held to decide whether the targeted official should continue to serve or immediately vacate the office. The number of signers required is normally a percentage of those who voted for the particular office in the previous election. This tends to average about 25 percent of the original electorate. The states all have different rules affecting the gathering of petition signatures and deciding upon their legitimacy; these variances can sometimes influence the recall effort, depending on the partisanship of those judging whether the petition satisfies the criteria.

In some jurisdictions, the question of vacating the office is decided in one election and another is then held to decide upon a replacement. In others, because of cost considerations, the elections are combined and the official whose conduct is under fire may register as a candidate. The vote to remove the current official can be either by simple majority or a higher percentage, such as an ABSOLUTE MAJORITY.

After the initial burst of enthusiasm, recall's popularity waned, and its end results have been inconclusive. The NCSL in August 2011 listed just twenty-three recall elections for legislators since 1913, with thirteen of them successful through 2008. Two more were recalled in the August 2011 Wisconsin vote, and three more recall elections were scheduled that year—two in Wisconsin on August 16 and in Arizona on November 8.

In January 1988 a recall movement against Republican governor Evan Mecham of Arizona obtained enough signatures to require a vote on his removal. But before the special election could be held, the state legislature impeached and convicted Mecham, which removed him from office. Mecham was convicted of obstructing investigation of a death threat and lending official funds to his auto dealership.

The impeachment process has been used more frequently than recall to remove governors from office. Mecham was the fifth governor in the twentieth century to be removed through impeachment and conviction.

In 1997, a petition drive to recall Wisconsin's two Democratic senators, Herb Kohl and Russell H. Feingold, fell about forty thousand short of the number required for a recall election. Abortion opponents launched the drive in protest against the senators' votes against a ban on so-called partial-birth abortions.

Although the U.S. Constitution does not provide for recall of senators, Wisconsin officials said if the signature quota had been met they would have scheduled a special election even if the results were only advisory. In the 1998 MIDTERM ELECTION Feingold won reelection with 51 percent of the vote and again in 2004 with 55 percent, but he was defeated in 2010 by a margin of 52 percent for his GOP opponent to 47 percent. Kohl was not up for reelection but later announced he would retire at the end of his current term in January 2013.

As in the Wisconsin case, recall need not be for illegal actions. In 1983 Michigan voters, angry over a tax increase, changed party control of the state senate from Democratic to Republican by recalling two members.

Critics say that recall usually is too cumbersome to be applied at the statewide level. Prior to the California upheaval in 2003, it had been successfully used only once to remove a governor—in 1921 in North Dakota when Republican Lynn J. Frazier was swept out of office. (See GOVERNOR.) Recall is used most often at the local level of government where petition gathering is relatively manageable.

Political theorists believe, however, that the very existence of recall restrains elected officials who fear its application. For the voters, it reinforces the comforting notion of representative-as-agent, in which the elected representative does the voters' bidding and must be periodically answerable to them if he or she fails this trust. (See NATURE OF REPRESENTATION.)

Republican Government

Although today the terms are almost interchangeable, *republican* government was not the same as DEMOCRACY to the founders of the United States. Made up almost entirely of members of the new nation's elite, they equated democracy with mob rule. What they were creating, they believed and intended, was a representative democracy or republican form of government.

In a democracy, they feared, a faction or party could become a tyrannical majority. But a "well-constructed Union" formed along republican lines, James Madison wrote in *The Federalist,* would tend to "break and control the violence of faction."

Besides ensuring a government of wise and patriotic citizens, the founders hoped, their Constitution would separate executive, legislative, and judicial powers sufficiently to prevent any one branch from assuming excessive control. Another of those checks and balances was the federal system, with powers shared between the national government and the states.

The powers of the national government were to be those spelled out or implied in the Constitution. By contrast, the states were to exercise *reserved powers*—that is, those not specifically prohibited to the states and those not granted to the national government. As an example of prohibited activities, the Constitution bars the states from coining money or entering into treaties or alliances with foreign countries.

Reflecting the split that preceded adoption of the Constitution in 1789, the first American political parties divided largely over the issue of national versus state government authority. The Federalists—a loose coalition of merchants, shippers, financiers, and other business interests—favored the strong central government established by the Constitution. The opposition (at first called ANTI-FEDERALISTS or Jeffersonians and later known as DEMOCRATIC-REPUBLICANS) were farmers and frontiersmen intent on preserving the sovereignty of the states.

> "The Constitution, in all its provisions, looks to an indestructible Union, composed of indestructible States. When, therefore, Texas became one of the United States, she entered into an indissoluble relation. All the obligations of perpetual union, and all the guaranties of republican government in the Union, attached at once to the State. The act which consummated her admission into the Union was something more than a compact; it was the incorporation of a new member into the political body. And it was final."
>
> —U.S. Supreme Court in *Texas v. White*, 1868

Federal Supremacy

In a system in which powers are divided between the federal government and the states, it is inevitable that conflicts will arise. To deal with them, Article VI contains a federal supremacy clause, which makes the Constitution and the laws and treaties passed under it the "supreme Law of the Land." This provision means that all state laws, executive orders, and judicial decisions must conform to the Constitution, treaties, and laws of the United States, or they are invalid.

Such conflicts arose almost immediately after the Constitution was put into effect. They aligned the Federalists, who advocated a strong national government capable of encouraging commercial development and exercising discipline over the states, against the Anti-Federalist advocates of states' rights. In one of its most important early decisions, *McCulloch v. Maryland* (1819), the Supreme Court came down strongly on the side of those who favored a broad interpretation of constitutional grants to the national government.

The *McCulloch* case arose over the refusal of the cashier of the United States Bank branch in Baltimore to pay a tax that the state of Maryland had levied on the bank. Maryland argued that Congress had no right to create the bank because the Constitution makes no mention of such a power in Article I.

In writing the Supreme Court's opinion, Chief Justice John Marshall, an ardent Federalist, rejected Maryland's call for a strict and literal interpretation of the grant of powers to Congress. He noted that it was entirely reasonable for Congress to decide that it was "necessary and proper" to create a national bank to carry out Congress's *delegated powers* to impose taxes, borrow money, and care for U.S. property. Marshall thereby established in

McCulloch the doctrine of *implied powers,* which means the national government may exercise powers that can be reasonably implied from its delegated powers.

In later years the Supreme Court used this precedent to provide the legal justification for sweeping extensions of the national government's powers. By virtue of the implied powers doctrine, the national government has been empowered to support public schools, welfare programs, farm prices, public housing, community development, crime control, and unemployment compensation; regulate working conditions and collective bargaining; fix a minimum wage; ban discrimination in housing, places of public accommodation, and employment; and even affect highway speed limits and the legal drinking age.

The Constitution gives a special role to the states in the government system by guaranteeing each state equal representation in the Senate, permitting electors chosen by each state (the ELECTORAL COLLEGE) to elect the president, and requiring that three-fourths of the states ratify all constitutional amendments. The permanent bond of the states to the Union was settled once and for all by the Civil War (1861–1865). As the Supreme Court declared in a post–Civil War case, *Texas v. White* (1868), the United States is "an indestructible Union composed of indestructible states."

When powers are not granted exclusively to the national government by the Constitution, the states may exercise those powers concurrently, provided there is no conflict with federal law. Among the states' *concurrent powers* are the powers to levy taxes, borrow money, and establish courts.

But there is no specific listing of states' reserved powers in the Constitution. In practical terms, this has meant that the states have the major responsibility for government activities such as public education, local government, intrastate highway transportation, protection of public health and safety, and family relations.

In today's politics, liberals, who mainly align with the Democratic Party, tend to favor stronger powers for the federal government, while conservatives, who mainly align with the Republicans, are more supportive of states' rights. Activists on both sides tend to be flexible when the occasion suits their views on an issue. Many conservatives, for example, seek to overturn the Supreme Court's 1973 *Roe v. Wade* ruling that legalized abortion so that individual states might have more latitude to ban the procedure, but favor federal preemption to bar states and cities from enacting laws that would allow individuals injured by gun violence (or their survivors) to sue gun manufacturers for financial damages. Liberals, conversely, favor federal preemption to keep abortion legal nationwide but prefer a states' rights position on gun lawsuits.

A similar divide was seen in the latter years of the 2000s decade over immigration policy. Although few persons denied it was a national and therefore federal matter, some states—particularly on the southwestern borders with Mexico—sought to enact their own policies to tamp down a growing Hispanic population that included sizeable numbers of illegal immigrants. Federal officials pushed back against these efforts, arguing that immigration was solely a federal matter that preempted state action.

More on this topic:
Anti-Federalists, p. 9
Democracy, p. 148
Democratic-Republican Party, p. 160
Electoral College and Votes, p. 186
Judicial System, p. 291

Role of the Courts

The national-state relationship of American federalism is constantly evolving, largely because of the JUDICIAL SYSTEM and its unending interpretation of the Constitution and the validity of laws passed by Congress or the state legislatures. Indeed, the frequency with which the Supreme Court has ruled on such laws, going back to *McCulloch v. Maryland,* points up an important feature of the Constitution-mandated federal system.

The courts' vehicle for their jurisdiction in the national-state relationship is their power of judicial review—an authority not mentioned in the Constitution but one asserted by Chief Justice Marshall in *Marbury v. Madison* in 1803, sixteen years before *McCulloch.*

Federalism has enlarged judicial power and influence because a system that divides power among governments requires an umpire able to resolve disputes. In the United States the courts often perform this function, making decisions that affect generations of Americans.

Republican Main Street Partnership

The political upsurge in 1994 that gave the REPUBLICAN PARTY its first House majority in forty years and its first Senate majority in eight brought Republican lawmakers of all political stripes to power. But the aggressively ideological tone of the conservatives who led and dominated the "Republican revolution" further marginalized the once-powerful but diminished moderate wing of the party. Moderate Republicans publicly expressed concern that an approach that was firing up the party's base in strongly conservative regions such as the South was losing voters in other parts of the United States.

Just as the centrist DEMOCRATIC LEADERSHIP COUNCIL emerged following a 1984 landslide presidential defeat that some blamed on the Democratic Party's strongly liberal image, the centrist Republican Main Street Partnership (RMSP) was founded in 1998 in part as a reaction to the defeat of Republican challenger Bob Dole by President Bill Clinton in 1996. Some attributed Senator Dole's loss to the confrontational approach taken toward the Clinton administration by newly empowered congressional leaders such as Newt Gingrich of Georgia and Tom DeLay of Texas.

> *" . . . to promote thoughtful leadership in the Republican Party, and to partner with individuals, organizations and institutions that share centrist values."*
>
> —Republican Main Street Partnership mission statement

The RMSP's mission is "to promote thoughtful leadership in the Republican Party, and to partner with individuals, organizations and institutions that share centrist values." The group's mission statement says, "The Partnership is comprised of party members and public officials who are fiscally conservative deficit hawks." Playing on the longtime Republican nickname of the Grand Old Party, or GOP, the statement continues, "The Partnership is working to Grow Our Party through a pragmatic approach to governing that reaches out to a broad base of Americans who share the Republican ideals of fiscal responsibility and limited government."

As the RMSP neared its tenth anniversary, conservatives dominated the leadership ranks in the Republican administration of President George W. Bush, who was narrowly elected in 2000 and by a wider margin in 2004 with support from a solid bloc of Southern states, and in both chambers of Congress. The group played more of a role in providing a platform for moderates and less ideological conservatives to trumpet their views than in enabling these Republicans to bargain for a greater say in shaping the party's legislative and political agenda.

The RMSP in mid-2011 counted among its members four Republican senators and fifty-one Republican representatives in the House. While the membership included moderate Republican lawmakers such as Sen. Susan Collins and Sen. Olympia J. Snowe, both of Maine, it also included a number of

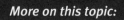

More on this topic:

Club for Growth, p. 106

Democratic Leadership Council, p. 151

more conservative members whose differences with most of their congressional Republican colleagues were more a matter of attitude than voting record.

Moderate and center-right Republicans face a challenge as many represent states or districts that have some Republican heritage but generally lean Democratic, partly as a reaction to the increasing conservatism of the national Republican Party. As a result, these Republicans made up a disproportionate number of the GOP incumbents defeated in the 2006 election that put the Democrats in control of the House and the Senate. One such defeated Republican, former six-term New Hampshire representative Charles Bass, took over as president and CEO of the RMSP following the 2006 elections.

The RMSP and moderates in general have also engaged in rhetorical battles with conservatives who believe the party's success is not in moving to the center, but in boldly advocating conservative principles and sticking to them. One conservative group is the CLUB FOR GROWTH, founded in 1999, which has become known for controversially labeling moderates as RINOs (Republicans in Name Only) and seeking their defeats in Republican primaries.

Longtime Pennsylvania senator Arlen Specter was one of the more moderate members of the Republican Main Street Partnership during his tenure in office. He later left the GOP and was defeated for reelection in a primary when running as a Democrat.

Source: CQ Photo/Scott J. Ferrell.

Republican National Committee

For all but twelve of the years 1969–2009, the Republican National Committee (RNC) enjoyed the advantage of having a Republican in the White House. One of those presidents was George H. W. Bush, whose 1989–1993 tenure made him the only former national party chairman to hold the nation's highest office.

Although national party involvement in presidential politics is weaker than it used to be, because of the rise of CANDIDATE-CENTERED CAMPAIGNS, the interests of the national committees and the White House remain inextricably linked. And being the "in" party lends prestige and strength to the national committee allied with the president—provided voters perceive that the party is on the right track.

Thus, the RNC was able to share in former chairman Bush's glory in 1988 when the two-term vice president continued the party's hold on the White House begun eight years earlier by Ronald Reagan. The committee rode the down slope with Bush as economic problems and a broken "no new taxes" pledge led to his defeat in 1992 at the hands of Democrat Bill Clinton.

Bush's son, George W. Bush, emerged from the governorship of Texas to win two presidential elections, in 2000 and 2004, and the RNC's experience was much the same. The national committee benefited as Bush's job approval rating rose to stratospheric heights in the wake of his assertive response to the September 11, 2001, al-Qaeda attacks. But by the 2006 midterm elections, the president's job approval ratings had plunged in response to the war in Iraq and the administration's

Timing is everything in terms of the reputations of national party committee chairs. Those who find themselves in the unenviable position of chairing a party that has grown unpopular among voters—because of policy decisions, troubles in the economy, scandals, or other factors—often end up sharing the blame if the party is punished at the polls, as was the case with the Republican National Committee (RNC) chairman Ken Mehlman following the 2006 campaign that cost the GOP control of the Senate and the House.

But when a party has a boom year, the chair gets to share in the glory. For example, during the 1994 campaign, Mississippi Republican Haley Barbour—a longtime Republican activist who had been a high-level aide in the administration of President Ronald Reagan—presided over the RNC's effort as the GOP gained control of both chambers of Congress. Barbour first leveraged his reputation as party chairman as a high-powered Washington lobbyist, then returned home and won the 2003 gubernatorial race in Mississippi.

response to Hurricane Katrina. In addition, the RNC faced setbacks stemming from corruption scandals involving members of Congress. Ken Mehlman, the RNC chairman at the time, was a Bush ally and a protégé of longtime Bush political adviser Karl Rove. Mehlman stayed "on message" promoting the administration's position with dogged intensity throughout the 2006 campaign, but neither Mehlman nor the well-funded RNC as a whole could prevent the Republicans that year from losing control of both congressional chambers to the Democrats.

Exercising the traditional authority of presidents of either party to select their national party's chair, after the 2006 election Bush employed a device more often used by the Democrats. Rather than have one person acting as both chief executive officer and party spokesperson, Bush split the job in two, although party rules do not explicitly authorize a dual chairmanship. He appointed longtime party operative Mike Duncan to run the committee as chairman and Florida senator Mel Martinez to be the public face of the party as general chairman. The 165-member committee signed off on the move.

Another chairman who had a short tenure was Michael Steele, an African American from Maryland and the only black ever to hold the GOP post. He took over in 2009 but lasted just two years in the face of continuing GOP losses at the polls and questions about his fund-raising efforts. (See Reference Material, National Party Chairs, 1848–2011, page 702.)

In general, besides their differing fortunes in presidential elections, the RNC and its counterpart, the DEMOCRATIC NATIONAL COMMITTEE (DNC), are dissimilar. The RNC is smaller, less bound by complex rules, and has been less active in PRESIDENTIAL SELECTION REFORMS. Its members serve two-year terms versus four years for DNC members.

In both parties, the NATIONAL PARTY CONVENTION is the supreme governing body, with the national committee and chair conducting party business between conventions. Like the DNC, the RNC is responsible for issuing the *Call,* which announces the particulars of the party's quadrennial convention. Unlike the DNC, the RNC cannot change party rules. Changes proposed by the Standing Committee on Rules must be approved by the GOP convention. Other RNC committees include finance and the convention *Call,* site, and arrangements committees.

A major responsibility of the national committees is the filling of vacancies on the presidential ticket after the nominating conventions. Both the DNC and RNC have had to make substitutions for vice presidential nominees. (See RUNNING MATE; VICE PRESIDENT.)

Besides a chair and cochair, the RNC elects a secretary and treasurer. Four regional caucuses each elect a man and a woman as vice chairs. These twelve officials also are members of the RNC's twenty-eight-member Executive Committee, which handles a number of executive and administrative functions for the organization.

The national committee and its sizable staff are headquartered at 310 First Street, S.E., on Capitol Hill in Washington, D.C.

GOP rules call for the cochair to be the opposite sex of the chair. Sharon Day, of Florida, held the post as of mid-2011.

Both parties have had only one chairwoman. Jean Westwood of Utah served as DNC chair in 1972, and Mary Louise Smith of Iowa was the RNC chair from 1974 to 1977.

Vacancies in the national chair occur occasionally when the president gives the incumbent another assignment. Richard M. Nixon, for example, tapped Rogers C. B. Morton to head the Interior Department in 1971, and two years later he sent the elder George Bush to the People's Republic of China as U.S. liaison.

As national chairmen during the second Nixon administration, 1973–1974, Kansas senator Bob Dole and Bush were burdened with the party's worst public relations crisis, Watergate, which ultimately drove Nixon from office in August 1974. Throughout the emergency, first Dole and then Bush were forced on a daily basis to fend off questions about the break-in at DNC headquarters in the Watergate Office Building on June 17, 1972, and the later discovery of White House tapes that ultimately exposed the "smoking gun" tape proving Nixon's knowledge of the burglary and the conspiracy to cover it up.

The abuses of Watergate, made possible in part by excessive contributions to Nixon's reelection campaign and uncontrolled use of the money, led to PUBLIC FINANCING of presidential campaigns and limits on individual and POLITICAL ACTION COMMITTEE (PAC) contributions to candidates for federal office. The reforms, however, did not bar unlimited SOFT MONEY contributions by corporations and other groups to political parties. It was the pursuit of soft money that raised questions about the DNC's fund-raising success in 1996. But the Republicans actually raised $18.9 million more in soft money ($141.2 million) than the Democrats' $122.3 million.

More on this topic:
Campaign Finance, p. 53
Democratic National Committee, p. 152
Hard Money, p. 245
National Party Conventions, p. 347
Political Action Committees, p. 389
Presidential Selection Reforms, p. 476
Public Financing of Campaigns, p. 496
Soft Money, p. 592

Not until 2002 was legislation, the Bipartisan Campaign Reform Act, enacted to bar national party organizations from accepting soft money contributions. The bill passed over the objections of critics who said the parties would be fatally weakened if that restriction became law. That turned out not to be the case, as both parties' national committees—but more so the RNC—successfully shifted their fund-raising efforts to amassing huge numbers of smaller, regulated HARD MONEY donations.

Republican National Convention *See* NATIONAL PARTY CONVENTIONS.

Republican Party (1854–)

The Republican Party over the past few decades, especially since the 1960s, has undergone a transformation mirroring that of the Democratic Party. Born out of the antislavery movement and first risen to power during the Civil War era, the Republicans built their base with a coalition of pro-business factions and conservative rural voters, with strong support in the Northeast and Midwest; for more than a century, the party of Abraham Lincoln was anathema in the South.

Though the overtone of what quickly became known as the Grand Old Party—the source of the familiar acronym "GOP"—was conservative, especially on economic issues such as taxation, government spending, and regulation of business, the party lacked the hard-line southern conservative element. As a result, the Republican Party for many years had substantial and influential moderate and even liberal wings that influenced its platforms.

But in the mid-twentieth century the GOP developed a different demeanor, ideological bearing, and regional makeup, driven by the rise of a fervent and often relentless conservative movement within its ranks.

The nation was not ready for the staunchly conservative views voiced by 1964 Republican presidential nominee Barry Goldwater, handing a crushing landslide victory to Democratic incumbent Lyndon B. Johnson. But Goldwater, by expressing sympathy with the states' rights stand taken by many southerners to justify their support for continued racial segregation and opposition to civil rights laws newly championed by the Democrats, planted the seeds for a vast political realignment.

Soon Republican strategists were trumpeting a "southern strategy" aimed at using dissent in the region toward the growing liberalism of the national Democratic Party to build a GOP base. The rise of Ronald Reagan, another staunch conservative, converted the South into a Republican stronghold in presidential politics by the 1980s. Congress followed suit with a Republican takeover of the House and Senate in 1994; the party's big gains gave the GOP majorities in the South.

However, the rise of southern dominance in the party coupled with a growing partnership with religious conservatives spurred a sharp swing to the right on social issues, and the change did not come without a price. Areas of the North and Far West where Republicans formerly won at least as often as they lost developed increasingly strong Democratic leanings.

California, the most populous state, gave its ELECTORAL COLLEGE votes to the Democratic presidential candidate in every election from 1992 through 2008, and the Democrats gained dominance in the congressional delegation and state legislature. New York, not long ago home to a vibrant liberal Republican wing identified with longtime governor and short-time vice president Nelson A. Rockefeller, became noncompetitive for Republicans beginning with the 1992 presidential election and continuing through the 2008 election, when the state's voters preferred the Democratic nominee by at least 15 percentage points for the fifth consecutive election. (It was 27 percentage points in 2008.) Illinois—the "Land of Lincoln"—was reliably Democratic by the early years of the twenty-first century.

Perhaps most telling was the counter-realignment in New England, the historic home of the "Yankee Republicanism" that produced the only two states (Maine and Vermont) that voted against Franklin D. Roosevelt's election to a second term in 1936. In 2008, for the second national election cycle in a row, every New England state favored Democrats, John Kerry of Massachusetts in 2004 and Barack Obama in 2008. Starting with the 1992 presidential contest and going through 2008, every New England state, with one exception, voted for the Democratic candidate. The one exception was in 2000 when historically conservative New Hampshire voted Republican. A national Democratic upsurge in 2006 left Connecticut moderate Christopher Shays as the only remaining Republican among the twenty-two House members in the six-state region, and he lost in 2008. However, the GOP made a modest comeback in 2010 when it picked up two New England seats, both in New Hampshire. Also, in Massachusetts in 2010 a Republican unexpectedly picked up a Senate seat in a special election to fill a vacant seat previously held by Democrat Ted Kennedy, who had died.

The 2006 elections, in which the Democrats broke a dozen years of Republican dominance in Congress, led to a split in the Republican ranks between those who contended that the party needed to tone down ideology to increase its appeal to moderate swing voters and those who said the party had failed because it had strayed from its conservative principles. The party's 2008 presidential nominee, Arizona senator John McCain, brought to the ticket long-standing and solid conservative credentials but also a well-polished maverick reputation that arose from his occasional and often controversial straying from established Republican orthodoxy. But McCain picked Gov. Sarah Palin of Alaska as his running mate, greatly pleasing the most staunch GOP conservatives.

The Rapid Rise of the Republican Party

Born in 1854 in the upper Midwest, the Republican Party grew out of the antislavery forces' bitter dissatisfaction with the Kansas-Nebraska Act. The act overturned earlier legislation (the Missouri Compromise of 1820 and the Compromise of 1850), limiting the extension of slavery into the territories, and instituted the concept of popular sovereignty, by which each territory decided its position on slavery.

While historians generally credit residents of Ripon, Wisconsin, with holding the party's first organizational meeting in March 1854 and citizens of Jackson, Michigan, with running the party's first electoral ticket in July 1854, the birth of the party was nearly simultaneous in many communities throughout the northern states. The volatile slavery issue was the catalyst that created the party, but the political vacuum caused by the decline of the WHIG PARTY and the failure of the KNOW-NOTHING and FREE SOIL parties to gain a stable national following allowed the Republicans to grow with dramatic rapidity.

The constituency of the new party was limited to the northern states because opposition to slavery was the basic issue of the Republicans. But the party did attract diverse elements in the political spectrum—former Whigs, Know-Nothings, Free Soilers, and dissident Democrats.

In its first year the party took the name Republican. Horace Greeley is credited with initiating the name in a June 1854 issue of his newspaper, the *New York Tribune*. In pushing the name, he referred to the Jeffersonian Republicans of the early nineteenth century and Henry Clay's NATIONAL REPUBLICAN PARTY of the 1830s, an early rival of the Democrats.

The Republicans ran candidates throughout the North in 1854 and, in combination with other candidates opposed to the Kansas-Nebraska Act, won a majority in the House of Representatives. Two years later the

The Lincoln-Hamlin ticket won a decisive Electoral College victory in 1860 despite receiving no Electoral College votes in the South, even though Lincoln was no abolitionist. In fact, Lincoln had won the nomination in part due to his moderation on the question of abolition.

Source: Library of Congress.

Republicans suffered much of the political blame for the Great Depression. President Herbert Hoover's inability to reverse the economic collapse led to his defeat in the 1932 election. This March 1933 magazine cover depicted a smiling Franklin D. Roosevelt en route to his inauguration accompanied by a glum outgoing President Hoover; the cover was not published because of the February 1933 assassination attempt on Roosevelt.

Source: The Granger Collection, New York.

Republicans ran their first national ticket. Although their presidential candidate, John C. Fremont, did not win, he polled one-third of the vote in a three-man race and carried eleven states. The Republicans were established as a major party.

Although founded on the slavery question, the Republican Party was far from a one-issue party. It presented a nationalistic platform with appeal to business and commercial interests as well as rural antislavery elements. The Republicans proposed legislation for homesteading (free land), the construction of a transcontinental railroad, and the institution of a protective tariff.

Firmly established by the late 1850s, the Republican Party benefited from the increasing sectional factionalism in the DEMOCRATIC PARTY over the slavery issue. In 1858 the party won control of the House of Representatives. Two years later, with Abraham Lincoln as its candidate, the Republicans won the White House and retained control of the House. Lincoln, benefiting from a sectional split in the Democratic Party, won an unusual four-way race and captured the presidency with 39.9 percent of the POPULAR VOTE.

Lincoln was a wartime president, and his success in preserving the Union helped the party for generations. After the Civil War, the Republicans projected a patriotic image, which, coupled with the party's belief in national expansion and limited federal involvement in the free enterprise system, helped make it the dominant party over the next three-quarters of a century. In the seventy-two years between 1860 and 1932, the Republicans occupied the White House for fifty-six years, and they controlled the Senate for sixty years and the House for fifty. Regionally, they were weak only in the South, where their support was basically limited to the small number of black voters.

Congressional leaders exercised the dominant power during this period of Republican hegemony. Presidents had little success in challenging the authority wielded by the GOP's congressional leadership.

Just as the party vaulted to power on the divisive slavery issue, its history was altered by a traumatic event—the Great Depression, which began in 1929. As the INCUMBENT party during the economic collapse, the Republicans suffered the political blame, and their fall from power was rapid. In 1928 the Republican presidential candidate (Herbert Hoover) carried forty states; in 1936, during Franklin D. Roosevelt's New Deal days, the Republican standard-bearer (Alfred M. Landon) won just two states. In 1928 the party held a clear majority of seats in both the House and Senate, 267 and 56, respectively; eight years later the party's numbers had shrunk dramatically, with the Republicans holding only 89 seats in the House and 17 in the Senate.

The party eventually made a comeback from this low point but remained the minority party in Congress for most of the next six decades. Between 1932 and 1994 the Republicans won seven of sixteen presidential elections but controlled both chambers of Congress for just four years.

While the Republicans struggled to find the formula for a new majority, the party's basic conservatism made it increasingly appealing, especially in presidential races, to segments of the electorate that previously were firm parts of the Democratic coalition—notably blue-collar workers and the once-Democratic South. The party was able to attract a winning combination when it ran presidential candidates with a moderate conservative image, such as Dwight D. Eisenhower in 1952 and 1956 and Richard M. Nixon in 1968 and 1972. The GOP enjoyed less success at the state and local levels where Democratic majorities, established during the New Deal, remained largely intact.

The Republican difficulties in establishing a new majority were compounded after the 1972 election by the Watergate SCANDAL, which brought down the Nixon administration. Gerald R. Ford, the center-right Republican who became president after Nixon resigned August 9, 1974, faced down another conservative bid to take the party's reins when he beat Ronald Reagan in the 1976 primaries, but he lost the general election to former Georgia governor Jimmy Carter, giving the Democrats control of the White House as well as Congress.

Republican fortunes improved dramatically in 1980 when Reagan, a former Cali-

Dwight D. Eisenhower's moderate conservative image helped him win the 1952 and 1956 presidential elections.
Source: National Archives and Records Administration.

fornia governor, won a LANDSLIDE electoral vote victory over Carter. Republicans also took control of the Senate for the first time in twenty-eight years and made substantial gains in the House. Although a resurgence of Democratic political strength in the 1982 MIDTERM ELECTION swept more Democrats into the House, the Republicans retained control of the Senate.

In a Gallup poll taken shortly before the 1984 national elections, 28 percent of the respondents identified themselves as Republicans. Although Republicans remained the minority party (42 percent of respondents identified themselves as Democrats), the party clearly was recovering from the lows it had experienced during the Watergate era. Not since the Eisenhower presidency had more voters called themselves Republicans. The party enjoyed a second landslide victory for Reagan, gaining even more strength and making Reagan one of the most popular presidents of the twentieth century.

In the 1986 election, the Democrats regained control of the Senate—despite a nationwide campaign by Reagan to promote Republican senatorial candidates—giving the Democrats full control of Congress and the GOP a sizable obstacle in policy making. A few weeks later the Iran-contra scandal broke. An independent counsel was appointed, and congressional investigations, including months of public hearings, lasted for almost all of 1987.

The setback to the party, if any, did not keep Reagan's VICE PRESIDENT, George H. W. Bush, from winning comfortably in 1988—53.4 percent of the vote and 426 electoral votes. Whereas he had challenged Reagan in the 1980 primaries as the candidate of the "mainstream" Republican establishment, in 1988 he ran on a conservative agenda that included a pledge of "no new taxes." Bush became the first sitting vice president to win the White House since Martin Van Buren in 1836. Bush also was the first candidate since John F. Kennedy to win the presidential election while his party lost seats in the House. His inability to carry others into office may have been partly because of his message, which was essentially a call to "stay the course." Despite his victory, the party never fully accepted Bush, and some rebelled openly when he reneged on the tax pledge in a deficit reduction compromise with the Democratic-controlled Congress.

In seeking a second term in 1992, Bush was burdened with an economy slowly recovering from the recession of 1990–1991. Bush took only 37.4 percent of the nationwide vote and received 168 electoral votes. Although Bill Clinton won the White House for the Democrats after twelve years of GOP presidents, the Republicans posted victories elsewhere, gaining ten seats in the House in 1992 and one Senate seat and two gubernatorial seats in 1993.

In 1994 the Democratic setbacks turned into a rout, with the GOP taking control of both houses of Congress. Grateful House Republicans elected as Speaker Newt Gingrich of Georgia, who had engineered their victory with a ten-point "Contract with America" setting forth conservative goals for the GOP Congress. For the next two years the Republican Congress tried to dismantle decades-old social programs, with repercussions for both parties in the following presidential election.

Despite an energetic campaign by former Senate majority leader Bob Dole of Kansas, Clinton stayed far ahead in the pre-election polls. The president appeared to benefit from a PUBLIC OPIN-ION backlash against the Republican Congress for its attacks on cherished Democratic programs. Although Dole narrowed the expected margin of defeat, Dole lost to Clinton with 39.2 million votes or 40.7 percent of the total. He won 159 electoral votes.

Despite the voters' reservations about Congress, and Gingrich in particular, in the 1996 elections, the GOP kept control of Congress while losing nine seats in the House but gaining two in the Senate. Under a cloud of ethics controversies for which he was later reprimanded, Gingrich in 1997 nevertheless became the first Republican Speaker reelected since 1929.

The president's party almost always suffers losses in the midterm election, especially in the sixth year of an administration. With President Clinton under a cloud of scandal that threatened to end with his impeachment, the GOP expected to make even larger gains than normal. In November 1998, however, the voters did not behave as expected, and the Republicans found their already slim majority in the House whittled to 223–211 (with 1 independent). Their margin in the Senate was unchanged at 55–45. Gingrich resigned not only the speakership but also his House seat in the wake of the poor showing.

The twenty-first century dawned with the nation split almost evenly between a Republican Party that leaned to the right and a Democratic Party that leaned to the left. This divide was underscored by the close and controversial 2000 presidential election, in which Texas governor George W. Bush—son of the former president—defeated Democratic vice president Al Gore, becoming only the fourth candidate in American history to lose the popular vote but win the electoral vote. As a result of the elections, Republicans controlled the White House and both houses of Congress simultaneously for the first time since 1953–1955. Bush, however, could not claim much of an electoral mandate because he lost the popular vote to Gore (see ELECTORAL ANOMALIES).

Moreover, the Republicans lost seats in both chambers of Congress in 2000—especially in the Senate, where Democrats drew even and were prevented from taking control only by the tie-breaking vote of Vice President Dick Cheney. Six months into Bush's term, the Republicans lost Senate control when veteran Republican James Jeffords left the party to become an INDEPENDENT. He caucused with the Democrats, giving them a 51–49 advantage.

But the political landscape changed dramatically with the terrorist attacks of September 11, 2001. Bush's popularity soared to a record 90 percent during the battle against terrorism overseas, especially in Afghanistan. Partly because of Bush's high popularity ratings and his party's perceived strength in protecting national security, Republicans picked up seats in the House and Senate in the 2002 elections, firmly taking control of both chambers. This marked the first time since 1934 that a president's party picked up seats in both chambers in a midterm election.

The 2004 elections underscored the Republicans' solidifying strength in the South and maintained single-party control of the federal government. Bush won reelection, this time with a narrow majority of the popular vote, defeating Democratic Massachusetts senator John Kerry by a margin of 2.4 percentage points. A four-seat net gain gave the GOP fifty-five Senate seats, seemingly a formidable majority for the Democrats to overcome. A controversial mid-decade redistricting plan enacted in Texas netted the Republicans six House seats in the state, though their national net gain was a modest three seats.

Bush quickly claimed a mandate for his policy agenda, and some Republicans boasted that they were on the verge of establishing a permanent majority in Congress. But those statements were quickly disproven. The rapid drop in popularity of the war in Iraq that Bush had launched in 2003 and several major domestic policy failures, along with a series of embarrassing scandals involving Republican members of Congress, set the stage for the Democrats' surprisingly strong comeback in the 2006 midterm elections.

When Democrats regained control of both houses of Congress in 2006, it was the beginning of a four-year roller coaster in Washington that remained unsettled as the nation headed into a national election in 2012. In 2008 Democrats advanced further, winning the presidency with Barack Obama defeating John McCain, and increasing their House majority to 257 to 178. In the Senate Democrats had 57 seats plus 2 independents who caucused with them. That gave Democrats a 59-to-41 Senate margin, which was just one vote away from having enough votes to break a Republican filibuster.

With these margins, the Democrats in 2009 embarked on an aggressive and controversial legislative program that included health care reform, tighter financial regulation, and economic stimulus actions to counteract the deep recession that began in late 2007.

It set the stage for a resounding Republican comeback in 2010. Economic troubles, and high unemployment at about 10 percent, in combination with sharp and continuing attacks on Democratic legislation by increasingly conservative elements within or sympathetic to the Republican Party, especially the new Tea Party movement, allowed the GOP to pick up a net of sixty-three House seats and control of the chamber. They also picked up six Senate seats, not enough for control but ample to block Democratic initiatives.

More on this topic:
Democratic Party, p. 155
Free Soil Party, p. 217
Know-Nothing (American) Party, p. 297
Whig Party, p. 671

Residency Requirements *See* ABSENTEE VOTING; HOUSE OF REPRESENTATIVES, QUALIFICATIONS.

Retrospective Voting

In the process known as *retrospective voting*, voters make decisions about the future based on judgments of the past. A candidate with a record in office is likely to be evaluated on that as to his or her chances of success in another term or a higher office. For an INCUMBENT, retrospection by the voters usually means reelection, but it can also mean rejection.

In 1980, voters issued a negative verdict on the performance of President Jimmy Carter, a Democrat, replacing him with Republican Ronald Reagan because of economic problems and

Economic problems and foreign policy setbacks plagued the country during Jimmy Carter's term in office. Above, cars wait for gas during the 1979 energy crisis. Ronald Reagan's overwhelming win over Carter in 1980 is a prime example of retrospective voting.

Source: Library of Congress.

foreign policy setbacks that included a prolonged crisis over the taking of U.S. hostages by Islamic radicals in Iran and the Soviet Union's invasion of Afghanistan. Republican George Bush lost the 1992 election to Democrat Bill Clinton after one term mainly because of public unhappiness with the economy.

By contrast, President Ronald Reagan won a LANDSLIDE reelection victory for the Republicans in 1984 because his performance was judged favorably on the whole. Clinton, after a rough first two years in office that culminated in the Democratic Party losing control of both chambers of Congress in the 1994 midterm elections, benefited from a timely economic boom and coasted to reelection in 1996.

But Clinton's victory was not just a retrospective affirmation of his record by voters; he also won because voters found him more appealing than his Republican opponent, Bob Dole, another known entity in U.S. politics. The same could be said about Republican George W. Bush's reelection in 2004. Bush, the son of the former president who was unseated by Clinton, had mediocre job approval ratings in polls as election day neared in 2004, largely because of growing public dissatisfaction with the war in Iraq that Bush had launched in March 2003. Yet enough voters found Bush preferable to his opponent, Sen. John Kerry, either on the basis of the president's record or his personality, to carry him to reelection.

Retrospective voting is not a phenomenon that affects only presidential races. It can also play a factor in big "swing" years in congressional politics, when voters grow so dissatisfied with the actions of the party in control that they remove it from power. This occurred in 1994, when the Republicans ended a long period of Democratic dominance in Congress, and in 2006, when Democrats wrested control of both chambers back from the Republican majority. The phenomenon then occurred again four years later, in 2010, when Republicans gained a net of sixty-three House seats and control of the chamber; they also gained six Senate seats, fewer than needed to be the majority but enough to block Democratic initiatives they opposed. In both cases, election analysts said the GOP gains reflected continued voter dissatisfaction with a slow recovery from the recession that began in late 2007 and anger over some of the most controversial actions by Democrats, both in Congress and the White House of Barack Obama.

Voters are notoriously skeptical of campaign promises. For them, past performance is a more credible indicator of prospective performance. An experienced politician is likely to be kept on the job if he or she has a record of accomplishment and an IDEOLOGY acceptable to the general public. But if the public feels an incumbent has stumbled in significant ways, it might be inclined to give someone else a chance.

An example of the former is the 1964 Democratic landslide that extended Lyndon B. Johnson's White House stay, one year after the assassination of John F. Kennedy had elevated him from the office of vice president. The landslide greatly strengthened Democratic majorities in the House and Senate and enabled the president to gain congressional approval for a wide range of social welfare legislation, including Medicare, Medicaid, and the War on Poverty. Many of Johnson's "Great Society" programs had been on Kennedy's agenda, but in his brief presidency Kennedy had been unable to push them through. With his mandate and mastery of legislative arm-twisting honed as a former Senate majority leader, Johnson gained enactment of much of the Kennedy-Johnson program.

Similarly, Reagan's election in 1980 resulted in a reordering of government priorities as the share of funds allocated to the military was increased, the rate of growth in domestic social spending was restricted, income tax rates were reduced, the budget deficit was allowed to grow, deregulation of the economy began, and the Supreme Court became more conservative as a result of three Reagan appointees.

President Carter had advocated some of the same policies, but in light of the Iran hostage crisis, high inflation, and other problems of Carter's administration, the voters felt that Reagan offered better prospects of managing the economy and lifting the national morale. Yet the voting was more retrospective than prospective. It was a rejection of Carter rather than an endorsement of Reagan and his somewhat radical "supply-side economics."

As in these cases, elections often serve as a referendum on the past and enable the voters to make educated guesses about the goals and policies of the candidates who are saying "it's time for a change."

Right to Vote

The U.S. Constitution never explicitly mentions the right of a citizen to vote, but it does contain implicit indications that Americans could elect their leaders. Article I, section 2, states that members of the House of Representatives "will be chosen . . . by the People of the Several States."

In the early days of the country, the states exercised complete sway over the question of voter qualifications in all elections. These qualifications were highly restrictive, reflecting the collective faith of the nation's first leaders that only the most virtuous and enlightened among them should lead the new nation. The states enfranchised only men with property and excluded all women, Native Americans, indentured servants, and slaves.

Since then the FRANCHISE has been expanded by class, race, sex, and age. In the 1824 presidential election, the first for which reliable statistics are available, only 3.8 percent of the population was allowed to vote, but by 1856, after states had relaxed taxpaying and property-owning qualifications, voter participation reached nearly 17 percent. By 1920, after women won the franchise, the figure rose to 25.1 percent. The national legal voting age was reduced to eighteen in 1971, and eligibility barriers such as poll taxes were removed in the 1960s, so that by the early twenty-first century more than 200 million people, or a bit more than two-thirds of the U.S. population, were eligible to vote, according to a study released in 2006 by the United States Election Project at Virginia's George Mason University.

The history of American elections has been a story of strenuous efforts by various groups to tear down legal barriers to voting and to expand the size of the electorate. Another side to the story is the dogged fight by

The women's suffrage movement existed for more than seventy years before the Nineteenth Amendment was ratified in 1920.

Source: Library of Congress.

opponents to keep these groups from voting at all or, later, to render their votes meaningless. Of the seventeen new amendments added to the Constitution since the passage of the Bill of Rights, nine concern the way citizens participate in elections. The Supreme Court has frequently addressed the topic, and some of the nation's legendary legislative battles have been fought over the regulation of elections. Voting rights, in short, have been a continual source of contention in U.S. politics for both the nation as a whole and for the individual states.

Three constitutional amendments—the Fifteenth, Nineteenth, and Twenty-sixth—broadened the suffrage. Two others—the Twenty-third and Twenty-fourth—have changed some of the rules for voting in presidential and other federal elections.

The Fifteenth Amendment

Before the Civil War, only nine states allowed African Americans to vote: the nine northernmost states of New England and the Upper Midwest that had the fewest blacks. After the war ended, the eleven states of the Confederacy were forced by the Reconstruction Act of 1867 (passed by the Republican-controlled Congress) to extend the suffrage to blacks as a condition for readmission to the Union. These new participants were indispensable to the POPULAR VOTE plurality of Ulysses S. Grant, the 1868 Republican candidate for president.

But fearing that southern blacks might lose their franchise to white politicians in these states, and eager for the votes of blacks in those northern and BORDER STATES that did not have universal male suffrage, the Republicans pushed the Fifteenth Amendment through a LAME-DUCK session of Congress in 1869. It provided that neither the United States nor any individual state could deprive a citizen of the right to vote "on account of race, color, or previous condition of servitude." The amendment was ratified a year later by a combination of New England, upper midwestern, and black-controlled southern legislatures.

While the amendment secured the Republicans' short-term goal of safeguarding the voting rights of northern blacks, it produced a virulent reaction in the southern states, one that would bedevil the nation for another century. After federal troops left the region in 1876, white politicians found a host of extra-constitutional ways to keep blacks from voting. The Fifteenth Amendment, seemingly so clear and unambiguous, was virtually ignored. In 1940, for example, only about 3 percent of the five million southern blacks of voting age were registered to vote. Of the amendment's effect in the South, one historian noted, "Ninety-five years after its passage, most southern blacks still could not vote."

The methods employed in the South ranged from outright violence and intimidation to legal subterfuges such as POLL TAXES, LITERACY TESTS (from which illiterate whites were exempted by the so-called GRANDFATHER CLAUSE if their ancestors had been eligible to vote before 1867), and WHITE PRIMARIES (political parties, posing as "private" organizations, could exclude blacks from membership and participation).

Black voters in New England, the Upper Midwest, and the former Confederate states helped put Ulysses S. Grant in the White House even before the Fifteenth Amendment was passed.

Source: Library of Congress.

Although the Supreme Court eventually declared both the grandfather clause (in 1915) and the white primary (in 1944) unconstitutional, VOTER REGISTRATION among eligible southern blacks remained well below 30 percent as late as 1960. Not until passage of the VOTING RIGHTS ACT in 1965 was the Fifteenth Amendment effectively implemented in the South. The act suspended literacy tests—they were permanently banned in 1970—and authorized the federal government to take over the registration process in any county in which less than 50 percent of the voting-age population was registered or had voted in the most recent presidential election. Since 1960, the registration rate for southern blacks has soared.

Blacks, grateful to the party of Abraham Lincoln for freeing the slaves, voted Republican until the Great Depression of the 1930s, when Franklin D. Roosevelt and the Democrats won about two-thirds of their votes with New Deal social and economic programs. The civil rights laws sponsored by the DEMOCRATIC PARTY and the Great Society social programs of the 1960s made African American voters into a monolithic Democratic constituency. In 2004, for example, despite increasing Republican efforts to reach out to more conservative-minded African American voters, exit polling showed 88 percent of the black vote going to Democratic presidential challenger John Kerry and only 11 percent to President George W. Bush. The results were even more dramatic in 2008 when Barack Obama, an African American, running at the Democratic nominee for president, got 95 percent of the black vote according to exit polls on election day. (See BLACK SUFFRAGE.)

"The right of citizens of the United States to vote shall not be denied or abridged by the United States or by any State on account of race, color, or previous condition of servitude."

—**Fifteenth Amendment,**
section 1, ratified in 1870

The Nineteenth Amendment

Securing the vote was a primary goal of the women's movement from the moment of its birth at the first women's rights convention in Seneca Falls, New York, in 1848. In 1890, women were granted full suffrage by Wyoming, and by 1919 women had the franchise in fifteen states and the right to vote in presidential elections in fourteen others. In time, the only significant opposition to granting women the vote came from the liquor industry, which feared that women would support Prohibition. But even without national WOMEN'S SUFFRAGE, Prohibition, in the form of the Eighteenth Amendment, became the law of the land in 1919. With liquor's opposition greatly reduced, the Nineteenth Amendment passed easily through both chambers of Congress in the spring of 1919 and was ratified by the required number of states by the summer of 1920, in time for the fall elections of that year.

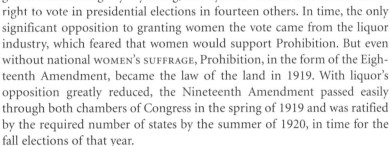

"The right of citizens of the United States to vote shall not be denied or abridged by the United States or by any State on account of sex."

—**Nineteenth Amendment,**
ratified in 1920

For more than fifty years after ratification of the amendment, women and men usually voted very much alike with the only "gender gap" being that fewer women than men went to the polls. By the 1980s, however, disparity in voter turnout had closed and a new one—significant differences between the sexes' views on certain issues and candidates—had developed. Women tend to be more concerned about and have more liberal views than men on issues such as social welfare, public policies concerning families, and policies about war and peace. Women also tend to favor the Democratic Party in most elections, while men tend to favor the Republicans.

The Twenty-sixth Amendment

The Fourteenth Amendment, ratified in 1868, established twenty-one as the highest minimum age that a state could require for a voter's eligibility. By 1970 only four states had exercised their right to establish a lower voting age.

Political pressure to reduce the voting age by constitutional amendment rose during the late 1960s, spurred on by an unusually large number of young people in the population (the post–World War II "baby boom" generation) and the Vietnam War, a highly controversial conflict that

conscripted hundreds of thousands of eighteen-to-twenty-year-olds into the military. Congress, bowing to the cry of "old enough to fight, old enough to vote," passed a law in 1970 to lower the voting age in all elections to eighteen. The Supreme Court ruled in OREGON V. MITCHELL (1970) that the law was constitutional in its application to federal elections but not to state elections. The decision, which would have required states to establish two sets of voting procedures for state and federal elections, threatened to throw the 1972 election into turmoil.

Responding quickly to the Court, Congress passed the Twenty-sixth Amendment in early 1971. As had the Nineteenth Amendment, it followed the form of the Fifteenth Amendment: the right to vote for citizens who are eighteen years of age or older shall not be denied or abridged by the United States or any state "on account of age." Ratification by the required number of states took only 107 days, less than half the usual time needed.

> **"The right of citizens of the United States, who are eighteen years of age or older, to vote shall not be denied or abridged by the United States or by any State on account of age."**
>
> **—Twenty-sixth Amendment,** section 1, ratified in 1971

As female voters had some fifty years earlier, young voters registered and voted at a much lower rate than other segments of the population—barely one-third of eighteen- to twenty-year-olds have voted in recent elections as compared with two-thirds of those aged forty-five and older. These results upset the pre-amendment forecasts of many political experts, who believed that masses of young people would turn out in the 1972 election and move the political system dramatically to the left.

But enhanced efforts to boost youth voting and the growing concerns over homeland security following the September 11, 2001, al-Qaeda attacks on the United States and the war in Iraq initiated what appeared to be a significant uptick in voting participation and political activism among this demographic group in the 2004 presidential election and the 2006 midterm election. Young voters' participation still lags significantly behind that of older age groups, but the gap has diminished.

Other Suffrage Amendments

The Twenty-third Amendment, ratified in 1961, gave the presidential vote to a special group of voters—eligible residents of the DISTRICT OF COLUMBIA, the nation's capital. The amendment gave the district three electoral votes in the ELECTORAL COLLEGE. Since the 1964 election, Washington has never given less than 75 percent of its vote to the Democratic candidate for president: in 2004, Sen. John Kerry received 89 percent to President George W. Bush's 9 percent. This lopsided Democratic advantage was largely a reflection of the voting tendencies of the black-majority population in the District; the capital also included such strongly Democratic-leaning constituencies as Hispanics, Jews, and gays. In 2008 Barack Obama won 92.5 percent of the District's vote.

> **"The right of citizens of the United States to vote in any primary or other election for President or Vice President . . . or for Senator or Representative in Congress, shall not be denied or abridged by the United States or any State by reason of failure to pay any poll tax or other tax."**
>
> **—Twenty-fourth Amendment,** section 1, ratified 1964

The Twenty-fourth Amendment, ratified in 1964 at the height of the nation's civil rights movement, abolished the poll tax, once used as a tool to disenfranchise blacks and poor whites, in federal elections. At the time of ratification, only five states still levied the tax. In 1966, the Supreme Court extended the ban on poll taxes to state and local elections under the Fourteenth Amendment's "equal protection" provision.

While an individual American's right to vote has been secured, the Supreme Court has come to recognize that, in the words of a legal scholar, "citizens were politically effective only as members of groups." Group voting rights underlay the ONE-PERSON, ONE-VOTE issue of legislative REAPPORTIONMENT AND REDISTRICTING. In the mid-1960s several cases reached the Court involving subjects such as MULTIMEMBER legislative districts, AT-LARGE voting, and redistricting plans, issues that the Court saw as fragmenting minority voting strength and reducing the likelihood of black office-holding. Later the question expanded beyond blacks to Latinos, Native Americans, and Asian Americans; even the use of an English-only BALLOT form was considered by the Court to be a disenfranchising device. In *Thornburg v. Gingles* (1986) the Court, ruling in a case involving the 1982 amendment to the VOTING RIGHTS ACT of 1965, came close to "equating proportionate electoral success with minority inclusion in the political process," according to a legal analyst.

In a true DEMOCRACY, each vote cast should have importance. But the "meaning of a meaningful ballot has radically altered over time," this analyst concludes, and the Court's rulings on cases involving minority votes are part of a continuing political process that shows no signs of ending.

More on this topic:
Black Suffrage, p. 28
District of Columbia, p. 163
Franchise, p. 215
Literacy Tests, p. 309
One Person, One Vote, p. 373
Poll Taxes, p. 426
Voting Rights Act, p. 663
White Primary, p. 674
Women's Suffrage, p. 678

Running Mate

The wait for a presidential nominee to announce the name of a running mate has lost much of its suspense in recent years. Sometimes the person chosen was a rival in the PRIMARIES and CAUCUSES where the top spot on the ticket was won. And the nominee may disclose the name early to gain maximum benefit from the announcement.

But even a little suspense is more than there originally was in the completion of a presidential team. During the country's first years, the runner-up for the presidency automatically became the VICE PRESIDENT.

That system did not last long. In 1800 Thomas Jefferson and Aaron Burr, though running together on the Democratic-Republican Party ticket, found themselves in a tie for electoral votes. Neither man's supporters were willing to settle for the lesser office. The deadlock went to the House of Representatives, where Jefferson needed thirty-six ballots to clinch the presidency, making Burr his vice president.

The unintended misfire of the Constitution's original method of presidential selection led to the Twelfth Amendment to the U.S. Constitution, ratified in 1804, providing for separate ELECTORAL COLLEGE balloting for presidents and vice presidents. With the emergence of political parties by

Aaron Burr became Thomas Jefferson's vice president by decision of the House of Representatives after the two candidates found themselves in a tie for electoral votes. The Twelfth Amendment was ratified soon thereafter, ushering in a new system of balloting for presidents and vice presidents.
Source: Library of Congress.

1800, candidates ran as teams. Once NATIONAL PARTY CONVENTIONS began in 1831, DELEGATES, with the guidance of party bosses, began to do the choosing.

It was only in 1940 that presidential nominees began regularly handpicking their running mates. That year Democratic incumbent Franklin D. Roosevelt—the only president ever to run for a third and later a fourth term—rejected his two-term vice president, John Nance Garner, with whom he had a falling out. After failing to persuade Secretary of State Cordell Hull to run in Garner's place, Roosevelt forced Secretary of Agriculture Henry A. Wallace on a reluctant Democratic convention by threatening to refuse his own nomination if Wallace were rejected.

The only exception to the practice Roosevelt established came in 1956, when Democrat Adlai E. Stevenson left the choice up to the convention, which chose Sen. Estes Kefauver of Tennessee.

In an otherwise unique situation that in one way resembled Roosevelt's dropping Garner, President Gerald R. Ford found a new running mate in his unsuccessful 1976 election against Jimmy Carter. Neither Ford nor his vice president, Nelson A. Rockefeller, had been elected by POPULAR VOTE. Both were elected by Congress under the Twenty-fifth Amendment—Ford as vice president when Spiro T. Agnew resigned in 1973 and Rockefeller as vice president in 1974 after Ford became president following Richard M. Nixon's resignation. To appease the party's right wing, with whom he had been unpopular, moderate Republican Rockefeller did not seek the vice presidency in 1976. Ford then chose a new partner, Sen. Bob Dole of Kansas, for the race to succeed himself in the presidency to which he had not been nationally elected.

Nixon himself survived an effort to drop him from the ticket as Dwight D. Eisenhower's running mate in 1952. After it was disclosed that a wealthy California couple had supplemented Nixon's Senate pay, he went on television with an emotional defense of his actions. In what came to be known as his "Checkers speech," he vowed to keep a gift cocker spaniel by that name and referred to his wife's "respectable Republican cloth coat" as evidence of their modest life style. The appeal worked. Thousands of viewers telegraphed their support, and Eisenhower kept Nixon as his running mate for two terms.

Nominations Refused

Occasionally the person chosen as a running mate declines the candidacy. If the refusal comes during the nominating convention, the presidential nominee makes another choice, subject to the convention's approval.

In the preconvention era, there were two occasions when the party's congressional caucus ("King Caucus") made substitutions after the nominees declined. In 1812 the DEMOCRATIC-REPUBLICAN caucus selected Elbridge Gerry of Massachusetts after John Langdon of New Hampshire rejected the nomination. In the 1824 election that marked the end of King Caucus, John C. Calhoun of South Carolina accepted the vice presidential nomination after Albert Gallatin of Pennsylvania declined. Calhoun became John Quincy Adams's vice president in only the second election decided by the House of Representatives. (See ELECTORAL COLLEGE AND VOTES.)

During the convention era, two nominees declined in time to be replaced by vote of the delegates. Silas Wright of New York turned down the Democratic nomination in 1844, and George M. Dallas of Pennsylvania, who accepted, became vice president to James K. Polk. Frank O. Lowden of Illinois refused the Republican nomination in 1924, and it went to Charles G. Dawes, also of Illinois, who became vice president under Calvin Coolidge.

If the vice presidential nominee withdraws after the convention, the vacancy is filled by the party's national committee. This happened in 1860 when Benjamin Fitzpatrick of Alabama refused the Democratic nomination and the DEMOCRATIC NATIONAL COMMITTEE (DNC) replaced him with Gov. Herschel V. Johnson of Georgia as Stephen A. Douglas's running mate.

In 1912, Vice President James S. Sherman of New York died the week before ELECTION DAY, and the REPUBLICAN NATIONAL COMMITTEE (RNC) nominated Columbia University president Nicholas Murray Butler as President William Howard Taft's running mate. It was too late to put Butler's name on the state ballots, but he received Sherman's eight electoral votes. Taft lost to Democrat Woodrow Wilson.

In 1972 Sen. Thomas F. Eagleton of Missouri withdrew as running mate to Sen. George S. McGovern of South Dakota after it was disclosed that Eagleton had been treated in the past for depression. The DNC gave the nomination to McGovern's substitute choice, R. Sargent Shriver of Maryland; the Democratic ticket lost in a landslide as Republican incumbent Nixon won a second term.

Currently, as in the Ford and Rockefeller cases, vacancies in the vice presidency itself are filled under procedures of the Twenty-fifth Amendment, ratified in 1967. (See VICE PRESIDENT.)

A Once-Maligned Office

If the selection of a running mate often seemed like something of an afterthought, it could be because until recently the position was not especially coveted. John Adams, the first man to hold the job, once complained, "My country has in its wisdom contrived for me the most insignificant office that ever the intention of man contrived or his imagination conceived."

More than a century later, Thomas R. Marshall, Woodrow Wilson's vice president, expressed a similarly dismal view: "Once there were two brothers. One ran away to sea; the other was elected Vice President. And nothing was ever heard of either of them again." Still later, Vice President Garner gave the office its most memorable put-down. It was, he said, "not worth a bucket of warm spit." (He actually used the vulgar term for another bodily fluid, but editors thought it unfit for family newspapers.)

Writing in *Atlantic* in 1974, historian Arthur Schlesinger Jr. suggested the office be done away with. "It is a doomed office," he commented. "The Vice President has only one serious thing to do: that is, to wait around for the President to die." But there is a reasonable chance that whoever fills the position will get a chance to move up, either by succession or election. As of 2011, fourteen presidents had held the second-ranking post, seven of them in the twentieth century.

Also, since the 1970s the vice presidency has evolved dramatically from the somnolent office it once was; during this period five vice presidents enjoyed responsibility their predecessors did not. President Ford gave Vice President Rockefeller considerable authority in domestic policy coordination. Walter F. Mondale and George H. W. Bush helped to set policy for their respective presidents, Jimmy Carter and Ronald Reagan. Bill Clinton placed Al Gore in charge of a "reinventing government" task force and gave him broad responsibilities over environmental issues.

Barack Obama, who won the 2008 election, selected long-time senator Joseph R. Biden Jr. as his running mate and relied heavily on him in his first three years in office, especially in negotiating with Congress on complex issues including health care reform and, in 2011, budget and tax issues. Although vice presidents have been given broader and serious responsibilities in recent decades, their principal purpose remains being ready to take over the presidency if necessary. As historian Arthur Schlesinger Jr. once cryptically put it: "The Vice President has only one serious thing to do: that is, to wait around for the President to die."

Elected in 2000, President George W. Bush granted his vice president, Dick Cheney, perhaps the most sweeping powers of all. A former chief of staff to President Gerald Ford, House member from Wyoming, defense secretary under the first President Bush, and CEO of the energy services company Halliburton, Cheney gained unprecedented influence as an adviser to Bush, especially on matters related to foreign policy, national security, and energy issues.

Factors in Selection

Whoever is selected as a running mate is scrutinized not so much as a policy maker, but for how well the choice balances (or unbalances) the ticket. One important factor is geography, which Clinton of Arkansas used unconventionally in choosing Gore of neighboring Tennessee to form the first successful all-southern ticket in 164 years.

The 2004 Democratic nominee, Massachusetts senator John Kerry, made a more traditional choice by selecting John Edwards. Then a senator from North Carolina, Edwards provided the ticket with some geographic balance; he also had drawn notice as a contender for the Democratic presidential nomination before ceding to Kerry.

John Kerry's choice of John Edwards as running mate provided the 2004 Democratic ticket with important geographic balance.
Source: CQ Photo/Scott J. Ferrell.

Other traditional factors weighed by nominees are religion and ethnicity. In 2000, Gore selected Sen. Joe Lieberman of Connecticut, the first Jewish vice presidential candidate of a major party. Race, gender, and age also play a role. In 1984, for example, the Democrats chose Rep. Geraldine A. Ferraro of New York to be their vice presidential candidate, the first woman to receive a major-party nomination.

Although no African American has so far been selected by either party, many Democrats thought that Jesse L. Jackson deserved second place on the ticket in 1988. Jackson had received 29 percent of the primary vote to 43 percent for Michael Dukakis. Instead, the fifty-four-year-old Dukakis chose Sen. Lloyd Bentsen of Texas, then sixty-seven, balancing the Democratic ticket by age as well as geographically and philosophically.

George H. W. Bush selected Sen. Dan Quayle of Indiana, a choice that proved extremely controversial, even among Republicans. Quayle, born in 1947, had served two terms in the House of Representatives before his election to the Senate in 1980. The brevity of his experience in politics and his avoidance of Vietnam War duty by serving in the Indiana National Guard fostered doubts that he was qualified to serve as president should that become necessary. However, Quayle was young and good looking, and the two swept to victory in November.

For his 1992 running mate, Clinton, in another unbalancing act, selected someone in his own age group (forty-six versus forty-four for Gore) rather than an elder statesperson such as Bentsen, who became secretary of the Treasury in the first Clinton administration. In 1996 Clinton and Gore became the first Democratic running mates to win reelection since Roosevelt and Garner in 1936. (Although FDR was reelected in 1940 and 1944, it was with two different vice presidents. He abandoned Wallace in 1944 in favor of Harry S. Truman.)

In many respects, Bush's selection of Cheney in 2000 was also unconventional. Cheney, as was Bush, was a conservative with ties to the oil industry, and he came from Wyoming, a state with little impact on the Electoral College. But Bush, who had no national experience, was looking for a Washington veteran. Cheney performed well on the campaign trail, projecting a solid and thoughtful presence.

In 2008 Obama selected Biden, a Senate colleague who had been in the chamber since 1973 and had much legislative experience including chairmanships of the prestigious Judiciary and Foreign Relations committees. From the small state of Delaware, Biden was not an obvious choice to deliver meaningful electoral votes. But the selection was widely seen as a need by Obama to shore up his thin foreign policy and congressional experience.

The Twelfth Amendment prohibits any one state from monopolizing the presidency and vice presidency. In roundabout fashion, the amendment requires the electors to "vote by ballot for President and Vice President, one of whom, at least, shall not be an inhabitant of the same state with themselves." No matter what state has the winning president or vice president, the electors there must vote for an outsider for one of the two offices. As a result of that amendment, Cheney in 2000 was obliged to change his official residency from Texas, where he was working at the time Bush selected him, to Wyoming, where he had spent much of his life. (See VICE PRESIDENT.)

More on this topic:

Caucus, p. 89

Electoral College and Votes, p. 186

National Party Conventions, p. 347

Primary Types, p. 485

Vice President, p. 644

Runoff and Preference Primary

Developed to ensure election by majority rather than PLURALITY, the primary runoff matches the two top finishers a few weeks after the first PRIMARY. Though used in South Dakota's elections as well as in the BORDER STATES and in city and county elections throughout the country, runoffs had their greatest impact for years as an integral part of the SOUTHERN PRIMARY system.

In the early decades of the twentieth century, white conservatives dominated the Democratic Party in the South, and the Democratic Party dominated the REPUBLICAN PARTY in the region; the GOP posed only token opposition to the Democrats in most of the South. As a result, most serious candidates ran in the Democratic primary, sometimes in such large numbers that a very small plurality could win the nomination for a fringe candidate who otherwise would have been out of the running.

Beginning in the 1930s most of the southern states adopted the runoff system. With only two candidates in the runoff, one was bound to get a majority vote (more than 50 percent). Of the eleven states of the old Confederacy, only Tennessee never adopted the runoff system.

But in the mid-to-late twentieth century, the national Democratic Party became more liberal and the Republicans first gained a foothold in the South, then rose to political dominance in the region.

With the emergence of the Republican Party as a power in the South, the Democratic runoff primary has lost much of its significance. For both major parties, however, the runoff helps to ensure

PREFERENCE AND RUNOFF PRIMARIES

State	Preferential Primary	Runoff Primary Adopted
Alabama	Until 1931	1931
Arkansas	—	1939[a]
Florida	Until 1929	1929
Georgia	—	1917[b]
Louisiana[c]	Until 1922	1922
Mississippi	—	1902
North Carolina	—	1915
South Carolina	—	1915
Tennessee[d]	—	—
Texas	—	1918
Virginia[e]	—	—

Sources: Alexander Heard and Donald S. Strong, *Southern Primaries and Elections* (1950; reprint, Salem, N.H.: Ayers, 1970); V. O. Key Jr., *Southern Politics in State and Nation* (New York: Alfred A. Knopf, 1949); Virginia secretary of state; updated by author.

a. Arkansas adopted the runoff in 1933, abandoned it in 1935, and reinstituted it in 1939.

b. Runoff held under county unit system.

c. Louisiana used the runoff "for a time prior to 1916," according to political scientist V. O. Key Jr.; in 1975 Louisiana adopted an initial nonpartisan primary followed by a general election runoff. After the Supreme Court invalidated the state's runoff system in 1997, Louisiana made the federal election day a primary for House and Senate candidates, with a runoff held later in any race where no candidate received a majority vote. Effective with the 2008 election, Louisiana established the separate party primaries used for federal elections in the rest of the country.

d. Tennessee has never used the preferential or runoff primary. Candidates are nominated by winning a plurality.

e. Virginia adopted the runoff primary in 1969 and repealed it in 1971.

that in the final election the opposing nominees were the choices of most of the party members in the DISTRICT or other constituency.

Since the civil rights laws of the 1960s assured blacks of participation in the southern primaries, African American leaders disagree on whether the still-existing runoffs in states around the region help or hurt their candidates. Some, notably the Rev. Jesse L. Jackson, long argued that a black candidate was almost certain to lose the runoff if the opponent was white. The issue has been tempered by the creation of numerous black-majority districts designed to enhance the prospects for increased black representation in the U.S. House and state legislatures. In these districts, runoffs have benefited blacks, by reducing the possibility that several black candidates could split the African American vote and allow a white candidate to win with a plurality vote.

Some African American leaders, including Rev. Jesse L. Jackson, argue that runoff primaries hurt black candidates, who they believe are almost certain to lose a runoff against a white opponent. Black-majority districts have been designed in recent years to enhance the prospects for increased black representation in federal and state government.

Source: CQ Photo/ Scott J. Ferrell.

Black advocates of maintaining runoff elections can point to the 2006 congressional elections in the state of Tennessee, which does not have runoffs. Several black candidates and one strong white candidate, liberal state senator Steve Cohen, entered the Democratic primary for an open House seat in the black-majority, Memphis-based Ninth District. Cohen took 31 percent of the vote, 6 percentage points more than the nearest African American candidate, winning the Democratic nomination that was tantamount to victory in the overwhelmingly Democratic district.

Preference Primaries

Three southern states—Alabama, Florida, and Louisiana—tried to avoid the effort and expense of runoff elections by experimenting with a preferential system of primary voting. All three later switched to the runoff system—Alabama after the election of 1930, Florida after the election of 1928, and Louisiana (whose system was similar to Alabama's) after the election of 1920. Louisiana modified its system yet again in 1975, this time to a two-step process: an initial nonpartisan primary followed by a general election runoff between the two top finishers (if the leading candidate in the first round of voting did not receive a majority of the vote). In 2008 it established the separate party primaries used for federal elections in the rest of the country.

Under the preferential system, voters, instead of simply marking an X opposite one candidate's name, write the digits *1* or *2*, beside the names of two candidates. This indicates the "preference" order voters give each of the candidates, the number one indicating their first choice, the number two their second choice. To determine the winner, without a runoff, second-choice votes are added to the first-choice votes and the candidate with the highest combined total wins.

Another variant of the primary system was Georgia's county unit system. Each county in the state was apportioned a certain number of unit votes. The candidate who received the largest number of popular votes in the county was awarded all the county's unit votes, even if he or she won only a plurality and not a majority. A candidate had to have a majority of the state's county unit votes to win the primary; otherwise a runoff became necessary. The runoff also was held on the basis of the county unit system.

For example, as of 1946, there were 410 county unit votes. The eight most populous counties had six unit votes each, the next thirty most populous counties had four each, and the remaining 121 counties had two each. The system was weighted toward rural and sparsely populated areas, because every county, no matter how small, had at least two unit votes.

The county unit system sometimes produced winners who received less than a majority of popular votes. Although no senators were ever elected through the county unit system without also attaining a majority of the popular vote, political scientist V. O. Key found that in two of sixteen gubernatorial races between 1915 and 1948 the winner of a majority of county units received less than a majority of the popular votes. In a third case, that of 1946, the winner of the county unit vote, Eugene Talmadge, actually received fewer popular votes than his chief opponent, James V. Carmichael.

The county unit system fell before the Supreme Court's one person, one vote doctrine. In the 1963 case *Gray v. Sanders*, the court declared the Georgia county unit system unconstitutional because of the disparity in representation between the urban and rural areas. (See RUNOFF AND PREFERENCE PRIMARIES.)

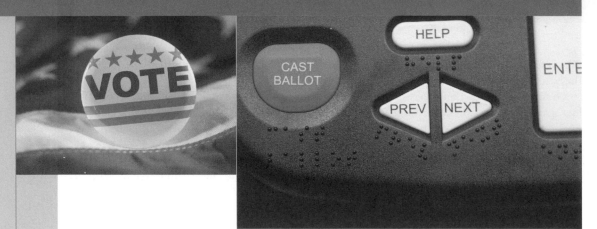

S

Safe Seat *See* INCUMBENCY.

Scandals

Political scandals have affected many an American election. Some have led to the withdrawal or defeat of candidates; others have led to the removal of officials after they have been elected. Some of the scandals are sweeping and shake many American people's faith in government, such as the Watergate affair that forced Richard M. Nixon in 1974 to become the only president to resign the office and the House impeachment and Senate acquittal in the late 1990s of Bill Clinton, who was accused of lying to a grand jury amid a scandal involving sexual misbehavior.

Sometimes scandals involve lesser-known individuals but occur amid other scandals, creating an overall sense of corruption in government that leads votes to exact major changes at the polls. This happened in 1994, when Republicans took advantage of Democratic scandals to win control of both chambers of Congress, and in 2006, when the Democrats turned the tables by accusing the Republican majorities of creating a "culture of corruption." In the years between the Democratic charges of 2006 and mid-2011, there continued a steady stream of controversies and scandals that engulfed some members of Congress—a few prominent individuals and more numerous back-benchers—that led to resignations and election defeats, but there was no broad scandal that captured continuing public attention. Overall, the scandals of this period—other than ruining a few political careers—contributed mainly to the public's dim and declining opinion of Congress.

A few of the more significant scandals involving elected officials or their administrations are listed here. Omitted are presidents' extramarital affairs that were rumored—such as those of Woodrow Wilson, Warren G. Harding, Franklin D. Roosevelt, and John F. Kennedy—but not confirmed or publicly exposed until after their deaths.

1802

President Thomas Jefferson is publicly accused of being the father of several children of a slave, Sally Hemings. During Jefferson's second term, six years after the accusations surfaced, Hemings has another son, Eston. For almost two hundred years, historians debate inconclusively about whether Jefferson fathered Hemings's children. On November 5, 1998, genetics researchers in Massachusetts publish DNA findings that they say strongly indicate Jefferson was Eston's father. Other experts, however, say the study merely shows that Jefferson, among other male members of his family, could have been the father.

This 1859 illustration in Harper's Weekly depicts Rep. Daniel Sickles shooting Phillip Barton Key, son of "Star-Spangled Banner" author Francis Scott Key. Sickles's wife had publicly confessed her affair with Key.

Source: Library of Congress

1831

The so-called petticoat wars of Andrew Jackson's administration end with the resignation of Secretary of War John Eaton. Wives of other cabinet members had refused to accept Eaton's wife, Peggy, because of her allegedly promiscuous past. Eaton's resignation enabled Jackson to shake up his cabinet and halt the two-year disruption. In 1832, Jackson rewards his former secretary of state Martin Van Buren, who resigned along with Eaton, by making him his second-term RUNNING MATE in place of Vice President John C. Calhoun. Van Buren wins the presidency four years later.

1859

Rep. Daniel Sickles, New York Democrat, shoots and kills Phillip Barton Key, son of "Star-Spangled Banner" author Francis Scott Key, on Washington's Lafayette Square. Sickles's wife, Teresa, had publicly confessed her affair with Key. Sickles later pleads temporary insanity and is acquitted of murder.

1873

The House censures Rep. Oakes Ames, Massachusetts Republican, and Rep. James Brooks, New York Democrat, for corruption in connection with the Crédit Mobilier scandal. Crédit Mobilier, the construction arm of Union Pacific Railroad, was suspected of using underhanded means to complete the last link of the transcontinental railroad in 1869. To head off a congressional inquiry, Ames, a shareholder, arranged to sell $33 million of the company's stock at low prices to members and executive branch officials. House Speaker James G. Blaine, Maine Republican, and Rep. James A. Garfield, Ohio Republican, are among those implicated but not disciplined. The scandal has political repercussions in 1872 as Schuyler Colfax loses renomination as Ulysses S. Grant's vice president. Garfield is elected president in 1880 but is shot the

*Captioned "Another Voice for Cleveland,"
this 1884 cartoon played on Grover
Cleveland's admission that he had fathered an
illegitimate son.*

Source: Library of Congress

following July and dies two months later. Blaine is nominated for president in 1884 but loses the election.

1875

The breakup of the Whiskey Ring during the Grant administration leads to the conviction of 110 officials. The ring was a conspiracy of revenue officials to defraud the government of excise taxes on liquor and distilled spirits. It included the collector of internal revenue in St. Louis, Gen. John A. McDonald, along with Treasury officials and Grant's private secretary, Gen. Orville E. Babcock. Grant's support helps to acquit Babcock, but Treasury Secretary Benjamin A. Bristow's efforts to break up the ring lead to his being eased from the cabinet. Bristow loses the 1876 GOP presidential nomination to Rutherford B. Hayes.

1884

Grover Cleveland wins election as president after admitting that he fathered a child out of wedlock. He supports the child financially. Elected again in 1892 (after being defeated in 1888), he becomes the only president to serve nonconsecutive terms.

1922–1923

Senate investigation of the Teapot Dome, Wyoming, oil-leasing scandal exposes corruption in the administration of President Warren G. Harding. Interior Secretary Albert B. Fall, convicted of bribery, becomes the first cabinet member sent to prison. The political repercussions of the scandal are never fully measured, as Harding dies in office in August 1923.

1947

Rep. James Michael Curley, Democrat and former governor of Massachusetts, enters jail June 26 on a mail fraud conviction. President Harry S. Truman commutes the sentence November 26.

1954

The Senate "condemns" (censures) Sen. Joseph R. McCarthy, Wisconsin Republican, on December 1 for actions that "tended to bring the Senate into dishonor and dispute." The resolution cites McCarthy, an outspoken and controversial anticommunist crusader, for reckless statements in connection with the Senate's investigation of the controversial Army-McCarthy hearings held earlier in the year. McCarthy loses his chairmanships when the Democrats take over the Senate in 1955. He dies in office in 1957.

1958

Sherman Adams, former governor of New Hampshire, resigns as President Dwight D. Eisenhower's chief of staff amid accusations that he interceded with federal regulators in behalf of Bernard Goldfine, a Boston industrialist who had given Adams expensive gifts.

1964

Walter W. Jenkins, special assistant to and longtime associate of President Lyndon B. Johnson, resigns October 14 following his arrest for soliciting sex at the Washington, D.C., YMCA. The White House says Jenkins was hospitalized for "extreme fatigue."

1967–1970

The House's attempt to exclude flamboyant Rep. Adam Clayton Powell Jr., New York Democrat, results in a landmark Supreme Court case, *Powell v. McCormack.* Powell, an African American, blames the House action on racism. The Court rules in 1969 that Powell met the constitutional qualifications for House membership. Powell regains his seat but rarely attends sessions. He fails to gain renomination in 1970. (See HOUSE OF REPRESENTATIVES, QUALIFICATIONS.)

1967

The Senate censures Thomas J. Dodd, Connecticut Democrat, on June 23 for spending campaign contributions for personal purposes. Dodd does not seek his party's renomination in 1970.

1969

A young woman, Mary Jo Kopechne, dies when a car driven by Sen. Edward M. Kennedy, Massachusetts Democrat, plunges off a narrow bridge on Chappaquiddick Island after midnight on July 19. Kennedy swims to safety but does not report the accident until nine hours later. Kennedy—brother of the late president John F. Kennedy and New York senator Robert F. Kennedy, and considered a strong potential contender for the presidency in his own right—pleads guilty to leaving the scene of an accident and receives a suspended jail sentence. The incident leaves many unanswered questions about Kennedy's behavior and his activities with Kopechne, a former secretary and campaign worker for Robert Kennedy, who was assassinated the previous year while running for president.

1972–1974

A June 17, 1972, break-in at Democratic National Committee headquarters in Washington's Watergate Hotel escalates into the greatest presidential scandal in American history, ultimately driving President Richard M. Nixon from office on August 9, 1974. Nixon and top officials of his administration are implicated in the cover-up of the burglary, which was committed by persons with ties to the White House or Nixon's 1972 reelection committee. A Supreme Court decision requires Nixon to relinquish secretly recorded audio tapes that prove he was aware of the cover-up. Among those jailed is Nixon's first attorney general, John N. Mitchell. Vice President Gerald R. Ford becomes president and pardons Nixon for any crimes he may have committed.

Vice President Spiro Agnew, seen here campaigning in 1972, resigned from his post in 1973 to avoid trial for tax evasion.

Source: National Archives and Records Administration/ Richard Nixon Library

1973

Spiro T. Agnew resigns as vice president October 10 to avoid trial on tax evasion charges dating to his time as governor of Maryland. Congress approves Nixon's nomination of Gerald Ford to fill the vacancy.

1974

House Ways and Means Committee chairman Wilbur D. Mills, Arkansas Democrat, is stopped in his car the night of October 9 with Anabell Battistella, an Argentine stripper also known as Fanne Foxe. Police rescue the woman after she jumps into the nearby Potomac River Tidal Basin. Mills is reelected despite the incident but later admits to alcoholism and relinquishes his chairmanship. He does not seek reelection in 1976.

1976

Ohio Democrat Wayne L. Hays resigns as chairman of the House Administration Committee amid publicity about his relations with Elizabeth Ray, a former committee clerk. Ray says Hays gave her the job in exchange for sexual favors. Hays denies the charge but admits having a "personal relation ship" with Ray. He does not seek reelection but later wins a seat in the Ohio legislature.

Donald W. Riegle Jr., formerly a Republican, is elected to the Senate in Michigan as a Democrat. During the campaign it is disclosed that Riegle had an affair with a younger woman in 1969. He later divorced to marry a different younger woman.

1977–1978

The House reprimands three California Democrats in connection with a South Korean lobbying scandal. John J. McFall, Edward R. Roybal, and Charles H. Wilson are disciplined in October 1978 for failing to report campaign or personal gifts from lobbyist Tongsun Park. The scandal is branded "Korea-gate," the first of many scandals to which the suffix, borrowed from the Watergate scandal, would be attached by the media and political pundits.

McFall resigns, and Wilson is censured on another matter after losing his 1980 primary race. Roybal serves until his retirement in 1993.

1977

Maryland governor Marvin Mandel, a Democrat, is convicted of federal mail fraud and racketeering charges and serves time in prison. In 1979 his conviction is overturned, and he is allowed to return to office for a few days before the newly elected governor is sworn in.

1979

For the first time since 1921 (when a member was censured for inserting indecent material in the *Congressional Record*) the House approves a censure resolution. Rep. Charles C. Diggs Jr., Michigan Democrat, is publicly chastised July 31 for diverting funds designated for the hiring of office employees to his own use. Diggs resigns in June 1980 after the Supreme Court refuses to overturn his 1978 conviction on related criminal charges.

In the Senate, Georgia Democrat Herman E. Talmadge is "denounced" (censured) October 11, 1979, for abuses in the collecting, reporting, and handling of expense vouchers and campaign contributions. Talmadge is denied reelection by Georgia voters in 1980.

1980

FBI agents posing as Arab sheiks ensnare seven members of Congress in a sting operation that becomes known as Abscam. The seven, including Sen. Harrison A. Williams Jr., a New Jersey Democrat, are later convicted for their apparent willingness to accept false bribes from the "sheiks." All leave Congress, some involuntarily. Rep. Michael J. "Ozzie" Myers, Pennsylvania Democrat, becomes the first House member expelled for corruption. Williams resigns to avoid expulsion from the Senate.

One of the targeted officials, Rep. John W. Jenrette Jr., South Carolina Democrat, is further embarrassed when his wife, Rita, tells the press that he and she once had sex on the Capitol steps. Rita poses for *Playboy,* and Jenrette enters an alcoholism program. He resigns December 10.

Rep. Robert E. Bauman, Maryland Republican, pleads innocent October 3 to sexually soliciting a teenage boy. The charge is dropped as Bauman agrees to counseling for alcoholism. Bauman is defeated for reelection.

Also in 1980, the House censures Charles Wilson, who had been reprimanded in 1978 in connection with the South Korean lobbying scandal. Wilson is censured for financial misconduct a week after losing his bid for renomination in California.

1981

Jon C. Hinson, a Mississippi Republican, resigns from the House April 13 after being arrested in a Capitol Hill men's room on a misdemeanor charge of attempted sodomy. He receives a suspended sentence.

1982

Fred W. Richmond, a New York Democrat, resigns from the House after pleading guilty to marijuana possession and other charges.

1983

The House on July 20 censures Gerry E. Studds, a Massachusetts Democrat, and Daniel B. Crane, an Illinois Republican, for having sexual relations with House pages, Studds with a male and Crane with a female. Crane loses reelection, but Studds wins several more terms.

1984

Rep. George V. Hansen, an Idaho Republican, is the first member of Congress convicted for noncompliance with financial disclosure laws. He is reprimanded by the House July 31 and is defeated for reelection in November.

1987

House and Senate committees in the Democratic-controlled Congress jointly investigate the so-called Iran-contra affair concerning undercover U.S. arms sales to Iran and the diversion of the proceeds to anticommunist "contra" guerrillas in Nicaragua by operatives of the Republican administration of President Ronald Reagan. The committees conclude that Reagan allowed a "cabal of zealots" to take over significant aspects of U.S. foreign policy. Congress had prohibited arms sales to Iran, which held U.S. embassy personnel hostage from late 1979 to early 1981 during the administration of Democrat Jimmy Carter, as well as continued aid to the contras, which opponents characterized as an unwarranted U.S. intervention in a brutal civil war. Several high-ranking officials are convicted in the affair, but others, including former defense secretary Caspar Weinberger, are pardoned by Reagan's Republican successor, George Bush.

Two leading candidates for the 1988 Democratic presidential nomination, former senator Gary Hart of Colorado and Sen. Joseph R. Biden Jr. of Delaware, drop out amidst widely differing scandals. Hart is the first to go, following reports that a young model named Donna Rice spent the night at his townhouse while his wife was away. Hart withdraws on May 8, reenters the race in December, but quits for good after the SUPER TUESDAY primaries in spring 1988.

Biden's fledgling campaign is undermined by a video showing that he plagiarized a speech by British Labor Party leader Neil Kinnock. Biden drops out in September. The man who assembled the video, John Sasso, resigns as manager of the rival campaign by Massachusetts governor Michael S. Dukakis, who goes on to win the Democratic nomination but loses the election to Bush.

The House on December 18 reprimands Austin J. Murphy, Pennsylvania Democrat, for financial misconduct and allowing another member to vote for him on the House floor. Murphy is reelected to three more terms.

1988

The Arizona Senate convicts Republican governor Evan Mecham and removes him from office April 4. A recall movement against Mecham obtained sufficient signatures in January, but his removal obviates the need for a recall election. Mecham is convicted of obstructing investigation of a death threat and lending official funds to his automobile dealership. (See REMOVAL FROM OFFICE.)

1989

The Senate rejects President George H. W. Bush's nomination of former senator John G. Tower, a Texas Republican, as secretary of defense. Hearings before the Armed Services Committee, which Tower formerly headed, focus on his reputation as a "womanizer" and heavy drinker. The committee recommends rejection of the appointment, the first of a cabinet nominee since 1959. Bush replaces Tower with Rep. Dick Cheney of Wyoming, who would go on to become the two-term vice president under Bush's son, George W. Bush.

Jim Wright, a Texas Democrat, resigns as Speaker of the House amid ethics questions about his profits from a book deal. It is the first time a Speaker has been forced by scandal to leave the office at midterm. His chief accuser, Georgia Republican Newt Gingrich, is himself rebuked by the House in January 1997 for misleading ethics investigators.

1990

Washington, D.C., mayor Marion S. Barry Jr. is videotaped using crack cocaine in a hotel where he had been lured by a former girlfriend. Convicted of cocaine possession, Barry serves six months in prison. Returned to office in 1994, Barry declines to seek another term in 1998 but remains a fixture for many years on the city council. (See DISTRICT OF COLUMBIA.)

The Senate denounces Dave Durenberger, Minnesota Republican, on July 25 for "unequivocally unethical" conduct in connection with a book deal and acceptance of Senate reimbursement for rent on a Minnesota condominium. Durenberger did not seek reelection in 1994.

Barney Frank, a Massachusetts Democrat, is reprimanded by the House on July 26 for improperly using his office to help a male prostitute. Frank, who acknowledged his homosexuality in 1987, is reelected to several more terms.

Donald E. "Bud" Lukens, Ohio Republican, resigns from the House October 24 facing accusations of sexual advances to a congressional elevator operator. He had been convicted in May 1989 of having sex with a sixteen-year-old Ohio girl.

1991

A scandal concerning practices at the House bank erupts in September when the General Accounting Office reports that members had cashed thousands of bad checks without penalty. The bank covered the checks that were "floated" before salaries were deposited. Although nearly all of the money was repaid by the individual House members, public indignation over their abusing the bank's privileges for what amounted to no-interest loans leads to the defeat of many of the "check-kiters," whose names are made public in April 1992.

The Senate Ethics Committee, acting in the name of the full Senate, reprimands Alan Cranston, California Democrat, on November 20 for his role in the so-called Keating Five affair. The punishment is the harshest handed out to the five senators investigated for possible intervention with federal regulators to save a savings and loan headed by Charles H. Keating Jr., a major contributor to political campaigns and causes. The other four senators are Democrats Dennis DeConcini of Arizona, John Glenn of Ohio, and Donald Riegle of Michigan and Republican John McCain of Arizona. The committee rebukes the four for poor judgment but says that only Cranston's actions were "substantially linked" to his fund-raising. Cranston, ill with prostate cancer, already had announced his decision to retire from the Senate. McCain rebounds from the scandal by adopting the mantle of a reformer and becomes a leading advocate for overhauling the nation's campaign finance system.

Also in 1991, an old sex scandal is revived against Sen. Charles S. Robb, a Virginia Democrat and son-in-law of the late president Lyndon B. Johnson. Former beauty queen Tanquil "Tai" Collins alleges that she and Robb had a love affair in 1983 when she was twenty and he was forty-four. Robb again denies the allegations, but Collins repeats them in a *Playboy* article and photo spread. Robb remains in office but is defeated in 2000.

1991–1992

An investigation of thefts from the House Post Office leads to exposure of lax procedures that allow members, whose franking privileges allow them to send official mail without postage, to exchange stamp vouchers for cash. By late 1992 the House postmaster resigns, and several clerks plead guilty to various charges. A grand jury subpoenas records of Ways and Means Committee chairman Dan Rostenkowski, a veteran House Democrat from Illinois and one of the major purchasers of stamps. Rostenkowski loses his seat in 1994 as the Republicans obtain their first House majority since 1954.

1992

Sen. Brock Adams, Washington Democrat, decides against seeking reelection after the *Seattle Times* reports finding eight women (none identified by name) claiming sexual abuse or harassment by Adams. In 1987, a woman family friend filed suit against Adams, claiming he drugged and fondled her while his wife was away. The case was closed with each side accusing the other of initiating settlement.

1992–1996

Scandals dog the administration of President Bill Clinton even before it begins. In February 1992, an Arkansas state employee, Gennifer Flowers, goes public with her story that she was Clinton's lover for twelve years. On television she plays tapes of intimate conversations with Clinton, then the governor. Flowers loses her state job but cashes in on the celebrity with her exposé in the tabloid *Star* and an article and photo spread in *Penthouse.*

Clinton and his wife, Hillary, appear on CBS's *60 Minutes,* where he acknowledges "problems in our marriage" but does not confirm Flowers's allegations. He goes on to win the Democratic nomination and defeat President George Bush.

Other scandals of Clinton's first term include the firing of the White House travel office staff, possible misuse of limited burial plots in Arlington National Cemetery, and the Whitewater realty development in Arkansas.

1994

In February 1994, former Arkansas state employee Paula Corbin Jones alleges that Clinton exposed himself to her in a Little Rock hotel while he was governor. She files a sexual harassment suit. In August, Kenneth W. Starr is named independent counsel to investigate the Whitewater matter, which also involves Mrs. Clinton and her former law firm.

1995

Sen. Bob Packwood, an Oregon Republican, resigns October 1, facing expulsion after a three-year Senate investigation of complaints by female staffers that Packwood sexually harassed them. Oregon conducts the special election to replace Packwood entirely by mail; it is won by Democrat Ron Wyden. (See ABSENTEE VOTING.)

1996

Clinton campaign strategist Dick Morris resigns following reports of his relationship with prostitute Sherry Rowlands. The story breaks during the Democratic National Convention in Chicago.

The news media disclose that Republican presidential nominee Bob Dole had an affair with Phyllis Wells, an employee in his Kansas City senatorial office, while he was still married to his first wife, also named Phyllis. The affair apparently was a factor in Dole's December 1970 decision to end his twenty-three-year marriage. Although the scandal is disclosed before the November election, it apparently is not the cause of Dole's loss to President Bill Clinton. Dole married Elizabeth Hanford in December 1975.

1997

Newt Gingrich, whose efforts to pursue conservative Republican priorities helped his party in 1994 end forty years of Democratic control of the House, becomes the first sitting House Speaker sanctioned for ethics violations. The House reprimands him January 21 and fines him $300,000 after he admits misleading the ethics (Standards of Official Conduct) committee about the relationship between a college course he taught and GOPAC, a POLITICAL ACTION COMMITTEE he headed until 1995. The fine is for the ethics committee's costs in sorting out Gingrich's conflicting statements. In April, Gingrich announces he will pay the fine with a loan from 1996 Republican presidential nominee Bob Dole, but in 1998 Gingrich says he will not need Dole's money.

Rep. Jay Kim, a California Republican, pleads guilty in August to federal charges of accepting $250,000 in illegal foreign and corporate campaign contributions in 1992. His wife and fundraiser, June Kim, also pleads guilty. In March 1998 Kim is sentenced to one year of probation and two months of home detention, which allows him to continue his House duties. Kim, the first Korean American elected to Congress, loses his 1998 reelection primary.

Arizona's Republican governor, J. Fife Symington, resigns after his September 3 bank fraud convictions for false statements to obtain loans for his failing real estate empire. One of the seven convictions is later dropped. In February 1998 he is sentenced to two and a half years in prison. Symington was among the 140 individuals who received a presidential pardon on Bill Clinton's last day as president.

1998: Clinton Impeachment

Independent counsel Kenneth Starr, whose investigation had extended beyond the Whitewater case, obtains tapes in which a former White House intern, Monica S. Lewinsky, claims to have had sexual relations with Clinton several times between November 15, 1995, and March 29, 1997. Starr receives court permission to expand his intervention in the Paula Jones case to cover the Lewinsky allegations. Clinton is deposed January 17 in the Jones case and gives secret testimony about his relationship with Lewinsky. On January 21 the media break the news of the Lewinsky tapes and Starr's investigation of her allegations. In a press conference that produces a frequently used sound bite, Clinton flatly denies sexual relations with "that woman, Ms. Lewinsky."

He later admits to an "inappropriate relationship" with Lewinsky but continues to deny a sexual relationship until the night of August 17, after he testified before a federal grand jury. Having admitted to the grand jury that he lied, Clinton appears on television to apologize to his family and to the American people. His relationship with Lewinsky, he says, "was not appropriate. In fact, it was wrong." In his grand jury testimony, later made public, he also acknowledges having sex with Gennifer Flowers, although he never admits to the extensive relationship claimed by Flowers.

Starr sends his voluminous report to Congress September 9—the contents of which include explicit descriptions of Clinton's sexual behavior that are widely reported by the media—and the House votes October 8 to begin a formal impeachment inquiry against Clinton. He joins Andrew Johnson (who was impeached but not convicted) and Richard Nixon (who resigned before impeachment) as one of only three presidents subjected to this indignity.

On November 13, the Paula Jones sexual harassment suit is settled with Clinton agreeing to pay her $850,000 with no admissions or apologies.

The Clinton-Lewinsky affair turns into something of a Pandora's Box, bringing forth disclosure of extramarital affairs by Republican members of Congress, including one committed years earlier by Henry J. Hyde, the Illinois Republican who as chairman presides over the House Judiciary Committee's impeachment inquiry. Hyde denies his past infidelity is relevant to Clinton's situation, as the case against the president centers on his lying under oath.

Also confessing marital infidelity is Rep. Robert L. Livingston, a Louisiana Republican and the FRONT-RUNNER to become

President Bill Clinton's relationship with White House intern Monica Lewinsky was only one of several extramarital affairs that made news in the 1990s.
Source: AP Images/Roberto Borea

Speaker following Gingrich's resignation after the GOP's poor showing in the 1998 House elections. As the House prepares to vote on Clinton's impeachment, Livingston declines to run for Speaker and announces he will shortly resign his seat.

On December 19 the House votes to impeach Clinton on charges of perjury and obstruction of justice in connection with the Starr investigation. Chairman Hyde delivers the articles of impeachment to the Senate for trial, which begins in January 1999.

1998: Other Scandals

Citing adverse publicity about him and other family members, Rep. Joseph F. Kennedy II, a Democrat and son of the late Sen. Robert F. Kennedy, announces August 28 that he will not run for governor of Massachusetts or for reelection to the House. He had received bad publicity because of the annulment of his marriage, and his brother, Michael, was in the news for having sex with a teenage babysitter. Michael later dies in a skiing accident.

In Georgia, the Republican gubernatorial campaign of front-runner Mike Bowers is set back by news reports that Bowers had a ten-year adulterous affair with a former employee. Bowers loses the July 21 primary to Guy Millner.

Veteran state senator Tommy Burks is found dead October 19 in Monterey, Tennessee, an apparent murder victim. His controversial Republican opponent, Putnam County tax assessor

Byron Looper, is charged with the close-range shooting. Looper is already under indictment for theft and misuse of county property.

Former Louisiana governor Edwin Edwards, a Democrat both loved and loathed for his roguish ways, is indicted November 6 by a federal grand jury on racketeering and conspiracy charges stemming from the awarding of riverboat casino licenses. Edwards, who was acquitted of other racketeering charges in the 1980s, was famed for boasting that he could be convicted only if police caught him "with a dead woman or a live boy."

Former Rhode Island governor Edward D. DiPrete, Republican, pleads guilty December 11 to bribery and racketeering charges for steering contracts to political donors. His one-year minimum-security prison sentence permits him to work weekdays at the family insurance business.

Clinton's first agriculture secretary, former House member Mike Espy, Mississippi Democrat, is acquitted by a federal district court jury December 2 on thirty corruption counts. Espy had been charged with accepting gratuities from agricultural producers. Nine others were convicted in the investigation.

Oklahoma's Republican governor Frank A. Keating is accused of hypocrisy for calling for President Clinton's resignation while refusing to criticize publicly Lt. Gov. Mary Fallin for her relationship with Greg Allen, one of her security guards. Allen resigns in early December for admitted "unprofessional conduct" with Fallin but asks for his job back. Fallin and Allen deny any sexual relationship. Keating's double standard is said to hurt his presidential ambitions. Fallin serves a total of twelve years as lieutenant governor and is elected to the U.S. House of Representatives in 2006 and the state's governor in 2010 with 60.4 percent of the vote.

1999: Clinton Trial

On January 7, the Senate opens the impeachment trial of President Clinton. With Chief Justice William H. Rehnquist presiding, House managers (prosecutors) lay out the House's case against Clinton, followed by rebuttal from the president's defense team. No witnesses are called, but the Senate—and the public—see excerpts of videotaped testimony by Lewinsky, White House aide Sidney Blumenthal, and lawyer and Clinton friend Vernon Jordan. Henry Hyde, chairman of the House managers, concedes that Lewinsky's testimony "wasn't harmful, but it wasn't helpful."

On February 12, the Senate, which has a 55–45 Republican majority, acquits Clinton, voting 45–55 on perjury and 50–50 on obstruction of justice. Five Republicans join the forty-five Senate Democrats in defeating the latter article. They and others say Clinton's offenses did not rise to the level of "high crimes and misdemeanors" required for conviction and removal from office. Neither article receives a majority vote, let alone the two-thirds vote required for an impeachment conviction.

2001

President Clinton's acquittal in the Senate does not deter independent counsel Robert W. Ray, successor to Kenneth Starr, from pursing a criminal investigation of the charges that had formed the basis of impeachment. On his next-to-last day in office, Clinton enters into a plea agreement with Ray. He admits to having made false statements under oath and agrees to a $25,000 fine and a five-year suspension of his Arkansas law license.

Allegations of scandal follow Clinton into retirement. On his last day in office, he pardons 140 individuals and commutes the sentences of 36 more. Among the recipients are his brother Roger; a fugitive financier, Marc Rich, whose ex-wife donated $1.5 million to the Democratic Party, the Clinton presidential library fund, and the Senate campaign fund of Hillary Rodham Clinton; and clients of attorney Hugh Rodham, brother of the first lady. Congressional and federal investigators look into the pardons and the process through which they were granted.

The former president and first lady are accused of converting to personal use gifts that had been intended for the permanent collection of the White House, including furniture and rugs. Of the $190,000 worth of gifts taken—a number that in itself raised eyebrows—gifts valued at $28,000 appear on a National Park Service gift registry. On February 7, the Clintons return the $28,000 in property that is in question.

2002: Traficant Beamed Out

Following his conviction on a variety of corruption charges—accepting bribes, racketeering, and misusing his staff to perform personal services—Rep. James A. Traficant Jr., a Democrat from Ohio, is expelled from the House, ending his flamboyant and controversial congressional career. First elected to the House in 1984, Traficant had developed a persona as the voice of the working class, proposing "America First" legislation requiring federal agencies to give preference to domestic-made goods. He peppered his House floor speeches with outrage over governmental actions, using a signature line borrowed from *Star Trek*: "beam me up." Although sentenced to federal prison, he runs for his old House seat in 2002 as an independent but finishes third of three candidates with 15 percent of the vote.

2004–2005: DeLay Reprimanded and Indicted

House majority leader Tom DeLay, a Republican from Texas, is reprimanded by the House Ethics Committee in 2004 for offering support for a retiring colleague's son to succeed him in return for his vote, for sponsoring a fund-raiser hosted by an energy company at a time when the House is considering energy legislation, and for using the Federal Aviation Administration to track the plane used by Texas Democrats who had left Austin to stall a mid-decade congressional redistricting.

On September 28, 2005, DeLay is indicted on charges of violating Texas campaign finance law in Travis County, which includes the state capital of Austin; he is accused of conspiring to launder illegal business contributions to state legislative candidates in 2002 to abet the Republican Party's efforts to take over the statehouse. DeLay is forced to relinquish his position as majority leader.

2005–2006: A "Culture of Corruption"?

On November 28, California representative Randy "Duke" Cunningham pleads guilty in federal court to accepting $2.4 million in bribes from defense contractors in exchange for legislative favors and becomes the first of four Republican House members who will be forced to resign their seats because of corruption scandals before the 2006 general elections.

Lobbyist Jack Abramoff, a longtime Republican activist and associate of DeLay, stands accused of taking millions of dollars from American Indian tribes who hired him to represent their interests in Congress, lavishing much of the money on himself and his personal associates, and attempting to buy influence in Congress by showering members with gifts, trips, and sizable campaign donations.

DeLay shows signs of damage from his indictment and ties to Abramoff, turning in a mediocre showing in his March Texas Republican primary. A month later, he withdraws his reelection bid, and he resigns in June.

Rep. Bob Ney, an Ohio Republican, is fingered for taking illegal gratuities from Abramoff by former aides who are

Rep. Bob Ney, R-Ohio, was the first member of Congress to be convicted as part of the wide-ranging Jack Abramoff lobbying scandal.

Source: CQ Photo/Scott J. Ferrell

facing criminal charges themselves. Ney denies wrongdoing and wins renomination in the May primary, but renounces his nomination in August and subsequently pleads guilty to corruption charges. He exacerbates the political problems for his party by staying in office several weeks after his conviction, resigning just days before the November elections.

The reliably Republican district of Rep. Don Sherwood of Pennsylvania suddenly becomes highly vulnerable following revelations that Sherwood had a lengthy extramarital affair with a much younger woman, who makes highly publicized allegations in June 2005 that Sherwood physically abused her. Sherwood, while denying the abuse charges, admits to the affair and in November 2005 settles out of court a lawsuit filed by the woman.

Rep. William J. Jefferson, Democrat from Louisiana, is the target of a widely reported federal investigation into bribery allegations; the FBI in May 2006 conducts a controversial raid on his Capitol Hill office. But federal authorities do not indict Jefferson during the 2006 election year, and he is reelected in a runoff election in December. Six months later, in June 2007, Jefferson is indicted on sixteen counts, including soliciting bribes, racketeering, money laundering, obstruction of justice, wire fraud, conspiracy, and violations of the Foreign Corrupt Practices Act. He loses his reelection bid in 2008 and, in November 2009, is convicted on eleven of the sixteen counts and is sentenced to prison for thirteen years.

In late September 2006, House Republicans are rocked by revelations that Rep. Mark Foley of Florida had sent sexually suggestive electronic communications to underage boys who had participated in the congressional page program. The scandal forces Foley to resign his seat immediately and quit a House race in which he had been heavily favored.

In November, the Democrats capture the seats vacated by DeLay, Ney, and Foley, as well as Sherwood's seat, and oust Republican incumbents who received major campaign funding from Abramoff and his associates, including Montana senator Conrad Burns and Representatives J. D. Hayworth of Arizona and Richard Pombo of California.

2007–2011: Scandals Personal and Financial

Sen. Ted Stevens, R-Alaska, is convicted in October 2008 on seven felony counts of lying on his Senate financial disclosure forms by omitting sizable gifts he received from Alaska business interests. The conviction is overturned in 2009 because of prosecutorial misconduct in the case, but Stevens loses his 2008 reelection bid.

House Speaker Dennis Hastert emerges after testifying before the House Ethics Committee investigating the Mark Foley page scandal.

Source: CQ Photo/Scott J. Ferrell

Sen. John Ensign, R-Nev., May 3, 2011, resigns his seat over an extramarital affair. The previous June, Ensign admitted he had an affair with Cynthia Hampton, his former campaign treasurer and the wife of Doug Hampton, who was Ensign's administrative assistant.

Sen. Larry E. Craig, R-Idaho, does not run for reelection in 2008 amid a growing controversy in which the Senate Select Ethics Committee in February admonished him for bringing discredit on the Senate through his action in 2007 in an airport restroom, his attempt to withdraw a guilty plea, and his unapproved use of campaign funds. Craig was arrested in a bathroom at the Minneapolis-St. Paul International Airport by a police officer investigating reports that the restroom had become a rendezvous point for men seeking gay sex.

Rep. Charles B. Rangel, D-N.Y., chairman of the powerful House Ways and Means Committee, steps down from his position in 2010 after the House votes 333–79 to censure him for violating chamber rules including seeking donations for an education center bearing his name, inaccurate reports of income, failure to pay taxes, and use of a rent-controlled apartment for office space.

Three House members resign in 2011 over personal misconduct controversies: Anthony Weiner, D-N.Y., David Wu, D-Ore., and Christopher Lee, R-N.Y. resign following revelations of online sexual contact with women, even though all three are married.

Second Midterm Elections ("The Six-Year Itch")

The idea that the second midterm congressional election of a two-term presidency—the one that occurs six years after the president's first victory—will be an electoral disaster for the party in the White House has become so ingrained that leaders of the victimized party feel free to blame their plight on the phenomenon.

That is what New York representative Thomas M. Reynolds, who as chairman of the National Republican Congressional Committee had headed the national Republican Party's House campaign effort in 2006, told reporters the day after the Democrats picked up thirty seats and gained a majority in the chamber after twelve years of GOP control. "The election really was a matter of history repeating itself," Reynolds said. "Second-term midterm elections are the toughest for the president's party, and last night was no different."

If Republican Theodore Roosevelt (1906) and Democrat Harry S. Truman (1950), who succeeded predecessors who died in office less than a year in a term, are included, there have been eight "second midterm" elections since the beginning of the twentieth century: Roosevelt (1906), Democrat Woodrow Wilson (1918), Democrat Franklin D. Roosevelt (1938), Truman (1950), Republican Dwight D. Eisenhower (1958), Republican Ronald Reagan (1986), Democrat Bill Clinton (1998), and Republican George W. Bush (2006).

Many historians would add two others: the 1966 election, which likely would have been the second midterm for Democrat John F. Kennedy had he not been assassinated in 1963 and succeeded by Lyndon B. Johnson, and the 1974 election, which would have been Republican Richard M. Nixon's second midterm had he not been forced to resign in August of that year because of his involvement in the Watergate scandal and turned the White House over to Gerald R. Ford.

Except for the anomaly of 1998, when the Democrats gained five House seats despite serious scandals plaguing Clinton, the president's party in each of these cases lost seats in the House—usually by the dozen—and often lost seats in the Senate as well.

Yet it is not at all clear that this long-running trend is a historical inevitability—a matter of voter weariness with the incumbent administration that cannot be avoided—or if it is just a coincidence that is more the result of a second-term president or his partisan allies in Congress making mistakes or getting involved in controversies that were not unavoidable.

The Republicans' 2006 setback, which also included a six-seat net gain by the Democrats in the Senate that enabled them to take over that chamber as well, came amid what a number of observers called a "perfect storm" of political problems, many of them self-inflicted, that severely damaged the Republican Party's cause.

Problems included the war in Iraq, which Bush had launched in 2003; the Bush administration's faltering response to the devastation wrought along the Gulf Coast in 2005 by Hurricane Katrina; the

> **"The election really was a matter of history repeating itself. Second-term midterm elections are the toughest for the president's party, and last night was no different."**
>
> **—National Republican Congressional Committee chairman Thomas M. Reynolds,** speaking to reporters the day after the 2006 midterm election

The following are brief descriptions of the circumstances surrounding second midterm elections since the beginning of the twentieth century through 2006, along with the partisan outcomes of those elections. The list includes Theodore Roosevelt and Harry S. Truman, who became president less than a year into the term of a predecessor who died in office; Lyndon B. Johnson, whose 1966 midterm election is regarded by some historians as the second midterm of the Democratic presidency begun by John F. Kennedy in 1960; and Richard M. Nixon, for whom the 1974 elections would have been the second midterm if he had not resigned that August.

1906

President: Theodore Roosevelt, Republican

Tenure: Moved up from vice president upon the September 1901 death of President William McKinley, won reelection in 1904; did not seek reelection in 1908.

Second midterm circumstances: Unrest among industrial workers spurred Democratic gains, particularly in New Jersey and Pennsylvania.

Election outcome for Republicans: –28 seats in the House, +3 in the Senate.

1918

President: Woodrow Wilson, Democrat

Tenure: Elected in 1912 and 1916; did not seek reelection in 1920.

Second midterm circumstances: The United States was in the midst of World War I, for which Wilson in April 1917 had obtained a congressional declaration of war against Germany after campaigning for reelection in 1916 on the slogan, "He kept us out of war." Ironically, the armistice ending the war came just days after election day.

Election outcome for Democrats: –19 in the House, –6 in the Senate; Republicans gained control of both chambers.

1938

President: Franklin D. Roosevelt, Democrat

Tenure: Elected 1932, 1936, 1940, and 1944; died in office, April 1945.

Second midterm circumstances: Enormously popular during his first term for his handling of the Great Depression, Roosevelt stirred controversy by trying to pressure into retirement Supreme Court justices who struck down some of his New Deal economic policies; also had to deal with a new economic downturn.

Election outcome for Democrats: –71 in the House, –6 in the Senate; Republican gains did not come close to wiping out the GOP's enormous losses in the 1930–1934 elections.

1950

President: Harry S. Truman, Democrat

Tenure: Succeeded Roosevelt in 1945, elected in 1948; did not seek reelection in 1952.

Second midterm circumstances: The invasion of U.S.-backed South Korea by communist North Korea embroiled the United States in another war less than five years after World War II ended.

Election outcome for Democrats: –29 in the House, –6 in the Senate.

1958

President: Dwight D. Eisenhower, Republican

Tenure: Elected in 1952 and 1956; first president prevented from running for a third term under the Twenty-second Amendment.

Second midterm circumstances: The nation's economy had gone into a recession; the Soviet Union's launch of the first space satellite caused Cold War concerns.

Election outcome for Republicans: –47 in the House, –13 in the Senate.

1966

President: Lyndon B. Johnson, Democrat

Tenure: Succeeded John F. Kennedy in November 1963, elected 1964; did not seek reelection in 1968.

Second midterm circumstances: After winning a historic landslide in 1964, Johnson escalated the U.S. military commitment to the Vietnam War, fueling the social ferment that marked the decade and in turn spurring a conservative backlash.

Election outcome for Democrats: –47 in the House, –3 in the Senate.

1974

President: Richard M. Nixon, Republican

Tenure: Elected in 1968 and 1972; resigned in August 1974 and was replaced by Vice President Gerald R. Ford.

Second midterm circumstances: Nixon's involvement in covering up White House connections to a break-in at Democratic National Committee headquarters, which occurred during the 1972 campaign that gave him a landslide victory, forced his resignation and spurred a voter backlash that was exacerbated when Ford pardoned Nixon for any crime he might have committed.

Election outcome for Republicans: –43 in the House, –3 in the Senate.

1986

President: Ronald Reagan, Republican

Tenure: Elected 1980 and 1984.

Second midterm circumstances: Some issues worked against Reagan and his fellow Republicans, including the collapse of a proposed nuclear arms reduction deal with the Soviet Union and problems in the domestic farm economy. But the Republicans' electoral problems, especially in the Senate, appeared related to some weak incumbents who had been elected on Reagan's "coattails" in 1980.

Election outcome for Republicans: –5 in the House, –8 in the Senate.

1998

President: Bill Clinton, Democrat

Tenure: Elected 1992 and 1996.

Second midterm circumstances: A sex scandal involving an extramarital relationship between Clinton and then–White House intern Monica Lewinsky, which the president denied before publicly confessing in August 1998, appeared to set the Democrats on a course with disaster. But a strong economy helped keep Clinton's job approval ratings high even as his personal approval ratings plummeted, and the Republicans' pursuit of articles of impeachment against Clinton for lying under oath about his affair alienated many voters.

Election outcome for Democrats: +5 in the House, no gain/loss in the Senate, in a glaring exception to the six-year itch.

2006

President: George W. Bush, Republican

Tenure: Elected 2000 and 2004.

Second midterm circumstances: The president and his party were plagued by the downward spiral in support for the war in Iraq that Bush had launched in March 2003, and their problems were made considerably worse by the flawed federal response in 2005 to Hurricane Katrina, an unproductive record for the Republican-controlled 109th Congress, and a series of scandals involving Republican members of Congress.

Election outcome for Republicans: –30 in the House, –6 in the Senate; Democrats took control of both chambers.

unwillingness of the Republicans who controlled both chambers of Congress to either compromise with their Democratic counterparts or find a way to pass legislation on their own dealing with a number of issues of importance to voters; and a series of embarrassing political and personal corruption scandals involving Republican members of Congress.

While some leaders of the losing party fall back on the "six-year itch" paradox, others worry that doing so can lead to a sense of complacency that may hinder the party's ability to rebound in subsequent elections.

In the wake of the 2006 elections, Republican National Committee chairman Ken Mehlman took a very different tack than Reynolds: "If we simply say there were historical problems we could not overcome, and that we did not have a chance to win, then we have a real problem."

Senate, Electing

For more than half of its first two centuries of existence, the United States chose senators indirectly, by vote of members of the state legislatures. Since 1914, however, the people have filled Senate seats by DIRECT ELECTION.

The change came about through the Seventeenth Amendment to the Constitution, ratified in 1913 following years of dissatisfaction with the original method of Senate elections. The amendment left the president and vice president as the only indirectly elected officials of the federal government, chosen by the ELECTORAL COLLEGE rather than direct POPULAR VOTE.

Senators serve six-year terms, and one-third of them come up for election every other year. Members of the House of Representatives serve two-year terms, and all must stand for election every even-numbered year. They have always been elected by direct vote of the people. (See HOUSE OF REPRESENTATIVES, ELECTING.)

The original, indirect method of Senate elections arose from a fundamental disagreement about the nature of Congress, which was settled by the so-called Great Compromise at the Constitutional Convention in 1787. Delegates from the small states wanted equal representation in Congress, while the larger states argued for a legislature based on population, where their strength would prevail.

As a compromise, the framers split the basis for representation between the two legislative chambers—population for the House and equal representation for the Senate, with two senators for each state regardless of its size. House members were to be representatives of the people, elected by the voters. Senators were to be, in effect, ambassadors representing the sovereign states to the federal government. As such, the framers felt, senators should be chosen by the states through their legislatures, rather than directly by the voters.

The argument was that legislatures would be able to give more sober and reflective thought to the kind of persons needed to represent the states' interests. The delegates to the Constitutional Convention also thought the state legislatures,

In November 1913, Blair Lee, D-Md., became the first U.S. senator to be popularly elected.

Source: Senate Historical Office

and therefore the states, would take a greater interest in the fledgling national government if they were involved in its operations this way. The delegates already were familiar with the procedure: they themselves had been chosen by the state legislatures, as had members of the Continental Congress (the Congress under the Articles of Confederation).

Before settling on the legislatures, however, delegates to the Constitutional Convention considered and abandoned several alternatives. One was that senators be elected by the House. Another was that they be nominated by the state legislatures and appointed by the president. The delegates discarded both ideas as making the Senate too dependent on another part of the federal government. They also turned down a system of senatorial electors, similar to presidential electors. And they rejected direct election as too radical and inconvenient.

Another problem was the length of the senatorial term. In settling on staggered six-year terms, the framers tried to balance the belief that relatively frequent elections were necessary to promote good behavior against the need for steadiness and continuity in government.

In the early decades of legislative appointment, the notion of senators being ambassadors was deeply entrenched. Some state legislatures even told senators how to vote. Occasionally the affected senators balked and resigned rather than vote against their consciences.

For example, in 1836 future president John Tyler, then a U.S. senator from Virginia, was instructed to vote in favor of expunging the Senate's censure of President Andrew Jackson for removing federal deposits from the Bank of the United States. Tyler, a bitter opponent of Jackson, had voted for the censure, and he resigned rather than comply. In another instance, Sen. Hugh Lawson White of Tennessee, a Whig, resigned in 1840 after his state legislature told him to vote for an economic measure supported by the Democratic Van Buren administration.

Legislative appointment, however, also produced some titans who were looked to for guidance in national affairs. The 1858 Illinois race between Abraham Lincoln and Democratic senator Stephen A. Douglas, for example, remains the most famous Senate election of all time. Lincoln, a member of the then-new Republican Party, engaged Douglas in seven nationally publicized DEBATES on the issues of slavery, states' rights, and the admission to the Union of pro-slavery territories. Although the Illinois legislature reelected Douglas, the debates paved the way for Lincoln's election as president in 1860.

Flawed System

Methods used by the legislatures to elect senators sometimes caused problems, particularly the requirement in most states that the candidates had to win majorities in both chambers of the legislature. Because the two chambers often disagreed, the system produced many deadlocks. Frequently, all other legislative business halted as members struggled to agree on a candidate. Sometimes the legislature was simply unable to elect anyone, leaving the state without full representation in the Senate.

Although the Constitution (Article I, section 4) empowered Congress to make or change state rules for electing senators, the national legislature took a hands-off approach for many years. Not until 1866 did Congress step in with a Senate election law. It required the two houses of a state legislature first to vote separately on candidates. If no candidate received a majority in both houses, then members of both chambers were to meet together and vote jointly, until one candidate received a majority of all votes.

Unfortunately, the 1866 law did little to correct the election problems. Deadlocks and election abuses continued to occur as political factions fought for control of each state's two Senate seats. The stakes were high because senators customarily controlled much of the federal patronage—government jobs and contracts—available in the state.

This cover story from Cosmopolitan magazine, dated April 1906, linked many senators to large corporations and political machines and provided another reason for passage of the Seventeenth Amendment.

Source: Senate Historical Office

A dispute in Delaware at the end of the nineteenth century illustrates how bitter and prolonged the fights over Senate elections could be. Divisions in the Delaware legislature were so fierce that no Senate candidate was elected for four years. Senate terms are staggered, and the state had only one senator for part of that time. For two years, from 1901 to 1903, Delaware was left entirely without representation in the Senate.

The system also encouraged corruption. Because of the importance of Senate seats, and the relatively small numbers of state legislators who controlled them, candidates frequently were tempted to use bribery and intimidation to win. Controversies over alleged ELECTION FRAUD often had to be resolved by the Senate, which, like the House, is the judge of its own members under the Constitution (Article I, section 5).

One of the most sensational cases concerned the election of William Lorimer, Republican, who won on the ninety-ninth ballot taken by the Illinois legislature in 1909. A year after he had taken his seat, the Senate cleared Lorimer of charges that he had won election by bribery. But new evidence prompted another investigation, and in 1912 the Senate invalidated Lorimer's election and excluded him from the chamber.

Towering over all criticisms of legislative elections of senators, however, was the complaint that they did not reflect the will of the people. For more than a century, the American political system had gradually tended to give voters more power. By the early years of the twentieth century, the Senate was the most conspicuous case in which the people had no direct say in choosing those who would govern them.

As pressure mounted to change the system, the House voted five times between 1893 and 1902 for a constitutional amendment to provide for Senate elections by popular vote. But each time the Senate refused to act. All the incumbent senators had been elected by the legislatures, and most were adamantly opposed to direct election.

Frustrated, reformers began implementing various formulas for preselecting Senate candidates, trying to reduce the legislative balloting to something approaching a mere formality. In some cases, party conventions endorsed nominees for the Senate, allowing the voters at least to know who the members of the legislature were likely to support.

Southern states, then known as the Solid South because of their strong allegiance to the DEMOCRATIC PARTY, adopted the party primary to choose Senate nominees. The SOUTHERN PRIMARY, as it came to be known, was the only election that mattered in that region. Even in the South, however, state legislators could not be legally bound to support anyone because the Constitution gave them the unfettered power of electing to the Senate the candidate of their choice.

Oregon, which had a strong tradition of political reform, made the most determined efforts to guarantee the popular choice of senators. Under a nonbinding 1901 law, Oregon voters expressed their preference for senator in popular ballots. While the election results had no legal force, the law required that the popular returns be formally announced to the state legislature before it elected a senator. At first the law did not work—the legislature did not elect the winner of the informal popular vote in 1902—but the reformers increased their pressure. They demanded that candidates for the legislature sign a pledge to vote for the winner of the popular vote. By 1908 the plan was successful. Oregon's Republican legislature elected to the U.S. Senate a Democrat, George Chamberlain, the winner of the popular contest. Several other states—including Colorado, Kansas, Minnesota, Montana, Nevada, and Oklahoma—adopted Oregon's plan. By 1910 nearly half the senators elected by the legislatures already had been "selected" by popular vote.

The Seventeenth Amendment

The state reform plans put more pressure on the Senate to agree to a constitutional amendment for direct elections. Proponents began pushing for a convention to propose this amendment and perhaps others. (Article V of the Constitution provides two methods of proposing amendments—passage by two-thirds of both houses of Congress or through the calling of a special convention if requested by the legislatures of two-thirds of the states. An amendment proposed by either method must be ratified by three-fourths of the states.)

Conservatives began to fear an unprecedented amending convention more than they did popular election of senators. They worried that it might be dominated by liberals and progressives who would propose numerous amendments and change the very nature of the government. Consequently, conservatives' opposition to popular election of senators diminished.

At the same time, progressives of both parties made strong gains in the midterm elections of 1910. Some successful Senate candidates had pledged to work for adoption of a constitutional amendment providing for popular election. In this atmosphere, the Senate debated and finally passed the amendment on June 12, 1911, by a vote of 64–24. The House concurred in the Senate version on May 13, 1912, by a vote of 238–39. Ratification of the Seventeenth Amendment was completed by the requisite number of states on April 8, 1913, and was proclaimed a part of the Constitution by Secretary of State William Jennings Bryan on May 31, 1913.

The first popularly elected senator was Blair Lee, Maryland Democrat, in November 1913. He was elected for the three years remaining in the term of a senator who had died.

No wholesale changeover in membership occurred when the Seventeenth Amendment became effective. Every one of the twenty-three senators seeking reelection to full terms in November 1914 was successful. All had been elected by state legislatures in their previous terms.

The transition to direct elections, however, did not eliminate Senate election disputes. One of the most bitterly fought took place in New Hampshire in 1974 between Republican Louis C. Wyman and Democrat John A. Durkin. It was the closest election in Senate history. Wyman had won by two votes, but Durkin appealed and ultimately won after the Democratic Senate called for a new election. (See CONTESTED ELECTIONS; zzz.)

Special Elections

Unlike House vacancies, which require the holding of a special election, Senate vacancies usually are filled by temporary appointment by the GOVERNOR. The Constitution grants this authority in Article I, section 3, paragraph 2, which, before it was amended, stated, "If Vacancies happen by Resignation, or otherwise, during the Recess of the Legislature of any State, the Executive thereof may make temporary Appointments until the next Meeting of the Legislature, which shall then fill such Vacancies."

The Seventeenth Amendment revised the governors' authority to fill vacancies. In such cases, the amendment says, "the executive authority of such State shall issue writs of election to fill such vacancies: *Provided,* That the legislature of any State may empower the executive thereof to make temporary appointments until the people fill the vacancies by election as the legislature may direct."

Some states, however, have held special elections shortly after vacancies occurred. But more often, Senate special elections held under this provision have usually taken place in November of even-numbered years, coincident with other federal or state elections.

That is what occurred in Missouri following one of the most unusual ELECTORAL ANOMALIES in U.S. history. In 2000 Democratic governor Mel Carnahan was killed in a plane crash during his campaign to unseat Republican senator John Ashcroft. Carnahan was elected posthumously that November, in part because the interim governor, Democrat Roger Wilson, publicly pledged to appoint the governor's widow, Jean Carnahan, as the interim senator to fill the vacancy that would automatically occur with his election. Jean Carnahan held the seat for less than two years, however. Under state law, a special election was held in November 2002, and Carnahan lost by a 1 percentage-point margin to Republican Jim Talent.

Timing also is important in determining whether special elections are held. In January 2006 New Jersey Democrat Bob Menendez was appointed by Democratic governor Jon Corzine to fill the Senate seat Corzine had vacated after his election as governor the previous November. Since Corzine's seat was up for election in November 2006, no special election was held; Menendez served out the remaining months of Corzine's term and won a full term in his own right in that year's general election.

When Sen. John Corzine, above, won the 2005 New Jersey gubernatorial election, he appointed Rep. Bob Menendez to fill his seat in the Senate and carry out the remaining months of the term, therefore bypassing the need for a special election.

Source: CQ Photo/Scott J. Ferrell

In the case of New Hampshire's Wyman-Durkin contest, the governor appointed former senator Norris H. Cotton to serve until the special election was held to resolve the disputed election. Cotton, whose retirement created the vacancy in the first place, served more than a month in 1975 until Durkin was sworn in.

Massachusetts held a special election in 2010 that turned out to be unexpectedly important. The incumbent, Sen. Edward M. Kennedy, Democrat, had died in 2009. In a staunchly Democratic state, nearly all observers expected a Democrat to win the seat in a special election the following January. Instead, it was won—convincingly, 52 percent to 47 percent—by a Republican, Scott Brown, previously a little-known state senator. The GOP victory deprived Senate Democrats of their sixty-vote margin that allowed them to break Republican filibusters. Brown's victory was seen by election experts as a consequence of a poorly run campaign by the Democrats who fielded a weak candidate, did not take his challenge seriously until too late, and faced a more volatile political environment than they anticipated.

Senate's Three Classes

To bring one-third of the Senate up for election every two years, rather than all at the same time, the founders divided the Senate into three classes or groups of members. A member's class depends on the year in which he or she is elected. Article I, section 3, paragraph 2, of the Constitution states, "Immediately after they shall be assembled in Consequence of the first Election, they shall be divided as equally as may be into three Classes. The Seats of the Senators of the first Class shall be vacated at the Expiration of the second Year, of the second Class at the Expiration of the fourth Year, and of the third Class at the Expiration of the sixth Year, so that one-third may be chosen every Second year."

Therefore, senators belonging to class one began their regular terms in the years 1789, 1791, 1797, 1803, and so on, continuing through to their next election in 2012. Senators belonging to class two began their regular terms in 1789, 1793, 1799, 1805, and so on, continuing through 2008. And senators belonging to class three began their regular terms in 1789, 1795, 1801, 1807, and so on, continuing through to 2010.

Sessions and Terms

In the fall of 1788, the expiring Continental Congress established a schedule for the incoming government under the new Constitution. The Congress decided that the new government was to commence on the first Wednesday in March 1789—March 4. Even though the House did not achieve a quorum until April 1 and the Senate April 6, and President Washington was not inaugurated until April 30, the terms of the Senate, House, and president were still considered to have begun March 4. The term of the First Congress continued through March 3, 1791. Because congressional and presidential terms were fixed at exactly two, four, and six years, March 4 became the official date of transition from one administration to another every four years and from one Congress to another every two years.

"Long" and "Short" Sessions

The Constitution did not mandate a regular congressional session to begin March 4. Instead, Article I, section 4, paragraph 2, called for at least one congressional session every year, to convene on the first Monday in December unless Congress by law set a different day. Consequently, except when called by the president for special sessions, or when Congress itself set a different day, Congress convened in regular session each December, until the Twentieth Amendment took effect in late 1933.

The original December date resulted in a long and short session. The first (long) session would meet in December of an odd-numbered year and continue into the next year, usually adjourning some time in the summer. The second (short) session began in December of an even-numbered year and continued through March 3 of the next year, when its term ran out. It also became customary for the Senate to meet in brief special session on March 4 or March 5, especially in years when a new president was inaugurated, to act on presidential nominations.

To illustrate with an example of a typical Congress, the Twenty-ninth (1845–1847): President James K. Polk, Democrat, was inaugurated on March 4, 1845. The Senate met in special session from March 4 to March 20 to confirm Polk's cabinet and other appointments. Then the first regular session convened December 1, 1845, working until August 10, 1846, when it adjourned. The second, a short session, lasted from December 7, 1846, through March 3, 1847. Because it was not clear whether terms of members of Congress ended at midnight March 3 or noon March 4, the custom evolved of extending the legislative day of March 3, in odd-numbered years, to noon March 4.

CLOSER LOOK

Historically, governors often appointed themselves to fill Senate seats that had become vacant because of the deaths, resignations, or expulsions of incumbents. That practice came to a halt in the late 1970s because of what came to be known as the "Minnesota jinx." In December 1976, Minnesota Democrat Wendell R. Anderson resigned as governor so his Democratic successor, Rudy Perpich, could, as prearranged, appoint Anderson to fill the vacancy created by Sen. Walter F. Mondale's election as vice president. The move caused such a serious voter backlash that the Republicans swept the state's major elections in 1978: They ousted Anderson in his bid for a full term, won a special election necessitated by the January death of Democratic senator Hubert H. Humphrey, and unseated Perpich in his bid for a full term as governor. In the years since, governors in several states have had opportunities to effectively appoint themselves to the Senate, but they have not done so.

The Twentieth Amendment

Like House members, senators were affected by ratification of the Twentieth Amendment, the so-called Lame-Duck Amendment, in 1933. The amendment moved up the beginning of congressional sessions to January 3, though this could be altered if Congress passed legislation to do so. (For example, the 110th Congress, elected in 2006, convened on January 4, 2007.) It also changed the date of presidential inaugurations from March 4 to January 20. (See PRESIDENT, NOMINATING AND ELECTING; VICE PRESIDENT.)

The short session had encouraged filibusters and other delaying tactics by members determined to block legislation that would die upon the automatic adjournment of Congress on March 3. Moreover, the Congresses that met in short session always included a substantial number of lame-duck members who had been defeated at the polls, yet were able quite often to determine the legislative outcome of the session.

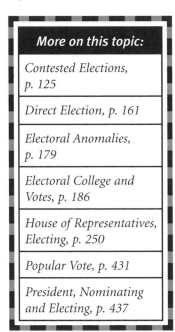

More on this topic:

Dissatisfaction with the short session began to mount after 1900. During the Wilson administration (1913–1921), each of four such sessions ended with a Senate filibuster and the loss of important bills, including several funding bills. Sen. George W. Norris, Nebraska Republican, became the leading advocate of a constitutional amendment to abolish the short session by starting the terms of Congress and the president in January instead of March.

The Senate approved the Norris amendment five times during the 1920s, only to see it blocked in the House each time. It was finally approved by both chambers in 1932 and became the Twentieth Amendment upon ratification by the thirty-sixth state in 1933. The amendment provided that the terms of senators and representatives would begin and end at noon on the third day of January of the year following the election. It provided also that Congress should meet annually on January 3 "unless they shall by law appoint a different day."

The second session of the Seventy-third Congress was the first to convene on the new date, January 3, 1934. The amendment was intended to permit Congress to extend its first session for as long as necessary and to complete the work of its second session before the next election, thus avoiding legislation by a lame-duck body.

Senate, Qualifications

The United States Senate is often called the nation's most exclusive club. Yet under the Constitution, Senate membership is open to most adult Americans. To be a senator, according to Article I, section 3, a person need only be at least thirty years old, a U.S. citizen for nine years, and an inhabitant of the state from which he or she is elected.

The Senate is also referred to erroneously as the "upper body," even though the House of Representatives has equal power and requires similar qualifications for election. (See HOUSE OF REPRESENTATIVES, ELECTING; HOUSE OF REPRESENTATIVES, QUALIFICATIONS.)

One reason for the Senate's greater prestige is its smaller size. Out of a nation of more than 300 million, only 100 men and women can be senators, compared with 435 representatives. And a state's two senators each represent the entire state, where all but the least populated states are carved into two or more DISTRICTS, each represented by a House member.

The consequences of the Senate's compact size and individuals' greater opportunities to affect legislation are the intense competition and high costs of statewide campaigning for each seat. In the television age the competition is expressed by heavy spending for advertising to reach the maximum number of voters. (See CAMPAIGN FINANCE; MEDIA USE BY CAMPAIGNS.)

Not so long ago, multimillion-dollar Senate campaigns were the province only of the largest states with the most expensive media markets, such as California or New York. But the explosion of campaign spending over the past few decades has made seven- and eight-figure Senate campaigns the rule rather than the exception. In 2006, as competition for control of the Senate was fierce, the two major-party candidates spent $43.4 million on the Pennsylvania race in which Democrat Bob Casey unseated Republican incumbent Rick Santorum. Additional spending by the parties' national campaign committees brought the total to $46.5 million. Spending in Missouri, where the population is about half that of Pennsylvania, topped out at $47.2 million as Democrat Claire McCaskill defeated Republican incumbent Jim Talent. Amounts were even higher four years later. The most expensive Senate campaign was run by Republican Linda McMahon in Connecticut who spent over $50 million in her losing bid for an open seat; moreover, she lost by 12 percentage points. In the House, Republican Michelle Bachmann spent $11.7 million in her successful campaign to win reelection.

Sen. Hiram R. Revels, Republican of Mississippi, was the first black senator, serving 1870–1871. The Fifteenth Amendment gave former slaves the right to vote in national elections.

Source: Library of Congress

Senate Characteristics

By quirks of history, both the Senate and House have had members who did not meet the constitutional minimum age requirements. The youngest senator was John H. Eaton, Tennessee Republican, who was twenty-eight years, four months, and twenty-nine days in 1818 when he was sworn in. The other underage senators were Henry Clay of Kentucky (no party), twenty-nine years, eight months, when he first entered the Senate in 1806, and Armistead Mason, Virginia Republican, twenty-eight years, five months, and eighteen days in 1816. Because no one challenged their election, all three were duly sworn in.

A West Virginian, Democrat Rush D. Holt, was underage when elected at twenty-nine in 1934, but he did not claim his seat until his thirtieth birthday in June 1935. The Senate later rejected an effort to invalidate Holt's election.

Two of the Democrats' most senior senators serving in the 110th Congress that began in January 2007 both pushed the minimum age limit when they started their career. Edward M. Kennedy of Massachusetts turned thirty less than eight months before his November 1962 election. Joseph R. Biden Jr. of Delaware was still twenty-nine when first elected in November 1972 but turned thirty a couple of weeks later, well in advance of his swearing-in the following January. The oldest senator

On June 12, 2006, Sen. Robert C. Byrd of West Virginia surpassed Strom Thurmond's tenure record and became the longest-serving senator in U.S. history.

Source: CQ Photo / Scott J. Ferrell

in history is the late J. Strom Thurmond, South Carolina Republican, who was born December 5, 1902, and retired one month after his one-hundredth birthday. Thurmond surpassed Theodore Francis Green, Rhode Island Democrat, born October 2, 1867. Green was ninety-three and seven months old when he retired in 1961, and he lived another five years.

At the time of his retirement, Thurmond also held the record as the longest-serving senator. But his tenure of forty-seven years and five months was surpassed on June 12, 2006, by West Virginia Democrat Robert C. Byrd, who was elected that November, just before his eighty-ninth birthday, to a record ninth Senate term. Byrd died in office on June 28, 2010. He was ninety-two years old and had served in Congress for fifty-seven years and 176 days.

The continued presence of Byrd and several other elder statesmen pegged the average age of senators at the onset of the 110th Congress (2007–2009) at 61.7 years, setting a new record by roughly eighteen months. Four years later, at the beginning of the 112th Congress in 2011, the average age had risen slightly to 62.2 years.

The first black senator was Hiram R. Revels, Mississippi Republican, who was chosen by the state's Reconstruction-era state legislature and served in 1870 and 1871. After the Civil War, the Fifteenth Amendment, ratified in 1870, gave former slaves the right to vote in national elections. The POLL TAX, WHITE PRIMARIES, and similar impediments to BLACK SUFFRAGE continued, however, until passage of the VOTING RIGHTS ACT OF 1965 and subsequent amendments.

Since adoption of the Fifteenth Amendment, scores of African Americans have served in the House, but only five have been senators. Blanche K. Bruce, like Revels, was a post–Civil War Mississippi Republican chosen by the state legislature to serve from 1875 to 1881. The first popular election of a black senator did not occur until 1966, when Massachusetts Republican Edward W. Brooke won his first of two terms. The only two elected subsequent to Brooke were both Illinois Democrats: Carol Moseley-Braun, who won her seat in 1992 but was defeated for reelection in 1998, and Barack Obama, who successfully ran for president in 2008.

The first female senator, Rebecca L. Felton, Georgia Democrat, was also the oldest new senator and served the shortest term. At age eighty-seven she was appointed October 1, 1922, to fill a vacancy, but she was not sworn in until November 21, 1922. She was replaced the following day by Walter F. George, who had been elected to fill the seat.

Although the Constitution did not bar women from Congress, their election was a rarity until the Nineteenth Amendment made WOMEN'S SUFFRAGE universal in 1920. The first elected female senator was Hattie W. Caraway, an Arkansas Democrat, who was first appointed in 1931 to replace her late husband—a familiar route for most of the early women to serve in Congress. She won a 1932 special election to fill out the remainder of his unexpired term, and then was reelected later that year and in 1938 before losing the 1944 Democratic primary.

The first woman to serve in both chambers of Congress was Margaret Chase Smith, a Maine Republican who served in the House from 1940 to 1949 (she also succeeded her late husband) and then in the Senate for twenty-four years (1949–1973). Maryland Democrat Barbara A. Mikulski equaled that record when her fourth term ended in January 2011; with her easy reelection in 2010 she became the longest serving woman in that chamber. Eight women have served in both chambers. In addition to Smith and Mikulski, the other six were Democrats Barbara Boxer of California, Blanche Lincoln of Arkansas, Debbie Stabenow of Michigan, Maria Cantwell of Washington, and Kristen Gillibrand of New York and Republican Olympia J. Snowe of Maine. Of these six, all were members of the 112th Congress (2011–2013) except for Lincoln who lost her reelection bid in 2010.

Qualification Disputes

Since the founding of the nation there have been six formal efforts to disqualify senators-elect on the constitutional requirements of age, citizenship, or residence. Only two of those resulted in exclusion from the Senate, both on grounds of citizenship.

In the first case, in 1793, the Senate excluded Geneva-born Albert Gallatin of Pennsylvania, who had been a citizen less than the required nine years. He argued unsuccessfully that he in effect became a citizen when he took part in the Revolution. Gallatin later served six years in the House and was Treasury secretary from 1801 to 1814. In 1812 he was nominated for the vice presidency but declined. (See RUNNING MATE.)

In the other case, the Senate voided the election of Ireland native James Shields of Illinois after he was seated briefly in 1849 before he reached the ninth year of his naturalized citizenship. He was then elected to the vacancy created by his disqualification and served until 1855. He later was a senator from Minnesota (1858–1859) and Missouri (January-March 1879), making him the only senator to serve three states.

A third citizenship case concerned the first black senator, Hiram Revels. The Senate admitted him, however, ruling that the Fourteenth Amendment, ratified two years before his election, had made him a citizen retroactively.

The unsuccessful disqualification effort against Rush Holt in 1935 was the only one based on age.

Two senators challenged on grounds of nonresidence—Stanley Griswold of Ohio in 1809 and Adelbert Ames of Mississippi in 1870—won their cases and were admitted.

Charges of nonresidence are more common, however, in senatorial campaigns than in Senate floor challenges. In 1988, for example, Sen. Frank Lautenberg, Democrat, fended off a celebrity challenge from former army general and Heisman Trophy winner Pete Dawkins, in part by questioning Dawkins's claim to New Jersey residence.

Charges of "carpetbagging," however, are not always effective. Two of the most famous people elected as senator by New York voters had shallow roots in the state: Democrat Robert F. Kennedy, who was elected in 1964 and served until he was assassinated while running for the Democratic presidential nomination in 1968, and Democrat Hillary Rodham Clinton, the wife of former president Bill Clinton (1993–2001), who won Senate elections in 2000 and 2006. She resigned from the Senate in 2009 to become secretary of state in Barack Obama's administration.

The Supreme Court has struck down efforts by INTEREST GROUPS, and Congress itself, to add to the Senate and House qualifications set forth in the Constitution. The one additional qualification still in effect is in the Fourteenth Amendment,

More on this topic:

Black Suffrage, p. 28

Campaign Finance, p. 53

House of Representatives, Electing, p. 250

House of Representatives, Qualifications, p. 256

Media Use by Campaigns, p. 324

Voting Rights Act, p. 663

ratified in 1868, which excludes from Congress anyone who "has engaged in rebellion against the United States or given aid or comfort to its enemies."

The only senator-elect excluded as one of the Civil War cases was Philip F. Thomas, Maryland Democrat, in 1867. He was charged with aiding the enemy because he gave his son $100 as he left to fight for the Confederacy. Although the Fourteenth Amendment had not yet been ratified, the Senate excluded Thomas on grounds of noncitizenship.

Efforts of almost half the states to impose TERM LIMITS on members of Congress have been nullified by the Supreme Court. In his opinion in *U.S. Term Limits v. Thornton* (1995), Justice John Paul Stevens explained that it was unconstitutional for individual states to change the qualifications for election to Congress.

Seventeenth Amendment *See* SENATE, ELECTING.

Shaw v. Reno

The Supreme Court's 1993 decision in *Shaw v. Reno* established the right of white voters to challenge CONGRESSIONAL DISTRICTS drawn to include a black-majority population. The ruling, which raised questions about a number of so-called MINORITY-MAJORITY DISTRICTS around the country, was hailed by advocates of "color-blind" districting but criticized by minority groups and traditional civil rights organizations.

The case involved a RACIAL REDISTRICTING plan approved by the North Carolina legislature after the state gained one new congressional seat through REAPPORTIONMENT following the 1990 CENSUS. Under pressure from the U.S. Justice Department, the legislature created two districts with African American majorities. One relatively compact district lay in the state's Piedmont region. The other—the Twelfth District—connected mainly black neighborhoods in four urban areas by means of a snakelike, 160-mile-long corridor across the center of the state.

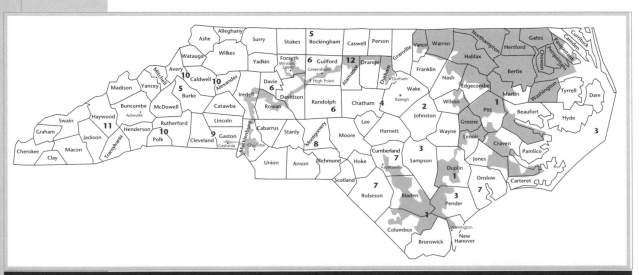

The irregular shapes of North Carolina's First and Twelfth congressional districts were challenged in Shaw v. Reno.
Source: CQ Press

Both districts elected black representatives in the 1992 election: Eva Clayton in the First and Melvin Watt in the Twelfth, both Democrats. White voters then challenged the plan. They claimed it set up a "racially discriminatory voting process" and deprived them of the right to vote in "a color-blind" election.

A three-judge federal district court, in a split decision, rejected the white voters' suit. But by a 5–4 vote, the Supreme Court reinstated the suit, ruling that white voters could challenge racially drawn districts under the Equal Protection Clause of the Fourteenth Amendment if the districts were "highly irregular" and "lacked sufficient justification."

Writing for the majority, Justice Sandra Day O'Connor said that in some cases a redistricting plan could be "so highly irregular that, on its face, it rationally cannot be understood as anything other than an effort to segregate voters on the basis of race." The Court's four most conservative members joined in the opinion: Chief Justice William H. Rehnquist and Justices Antonin Scalia, Anthony M. Kennedy, and Clarence Thomas.

In a dissenting opinion, Justice Byron R. White contended that the white voters had suffered no legal injury. "Though they might be dissatisfied at the prospect of casting a vote for a losing candidate, surely they cannot complain of discriminatory treatment." Justices Harry A. Blackmun and John Paul Stevens joined White's dissent; Justice David H. Souter dissented separately.

The decision returned the case to the three-judge court to determine whether the state had sufficient justification for the districting plan. O'Connor said the panel should weigh whether the plan met the "strict scrutiny" test used in other racial challenges: whether it was narrowly tailored to meet a compelling government interest.

In its second ruling, the three-judge court again upheld the districting scheme. The panel held the state had a compelling interest in overcoming past racial discrimination and in creating separate black-majority districts with rural and urban populations. But the Supreme Court disagreed. In its second ruling in the case, *Shaw v. Hunt* (1996), the Court by a 5–4 vote said the state could not justify the plan on grounds of overcoming past discrimination or complying with the federal VOTING RIGHTS ACT.

Continued litigation resulted in the Twelfth District being redrawn twice prior to the 1998 election. A final round of lawsuits was not decided until the Supreme Court narrowly ruled in favor of the state of North Carolina in the case of *Hunt v. Cromartie*. The justices, in a 5–4 decision, said the district could be construed as having been drawn for political purposes (to enable the election of a Democratic candidate) rather than for racial purposes. Because legislators had the right to create congressional districts for political means, the district passed constitutional muster. However, the Court's ruling came in April 2001, more than five months after the final election of the decade in which that district map would be used.

Based on the 2000 census, a new district map was drafted prior to the 2002 elections. Although it again included a Twelfth District that meandered from Greensboro to Charlotte, its relative racial balance— 45 percent black, 45 percent white, and 7 percent Hispanic—appeared to protect it from attack in the courts. This time, there was no litigation seeking to overturn the district's lines. Its overwhelmingly Democratic-voting residents continued to elect Watt through the 2010 contest.

More on this topic:

Congressional District, p. 111

Racial Redistricting, p. 509

Reapportionment and Redistricting, p. 517

Single-Issue Voting

MORE SECURITY FOR THE AMERICAN FAMILY

WHEN AN INSURED WORKER DIES, LEAVING DEPENDENT CHILDREN AND A WIDOW, BOTH MOTHER AND CHILDREN RECEIVE MONTHLY BENEFITS UNTIL THE LATTER REACH 18.

FOR INFORMATION WRITE OR CALL AT THE NEAREST FIELD OFFICE OF THE
SOCIAL SECURITY BOARD

Voters concerned about the future of Social Security may base their voting decisions solely on a candidate's stand on that issue.

Source: SSA History Archives

Some people feel so strongly about an issue that they base their voting decisions solely on candidates' stands on that issue. This way of making electoral choices is called *single-issue voting*. In contrast, PARTY IDENTIFICATION has waned somewhat among modern voters, making political affiliation less of a factor in how they vote. (See ISSUE VOTING.)

Issues that arouse voters' passions are apt to be volatile subjects that do not lend themselves to compromise, middle-of-the-road solutions. Before the Civil War, the abolition of slavery was one such issue. During the first decade of the twenty-first century, "hot button" issues included abortion, gay rights, gun control, and the war in Iraq that began in March 2003. People are usually for or against issues such as these, with little in between.

Voters for whom one issue is decisive typically use that issue as the compass that determines their partisan and candidate choices—if there is a clear-cut distinction between the parties on that issue. For many years, voters whose strongest priority was support for abortion rights were overwhelmingly inclined to favor the Democrats, a party that as a whole stood for that view, while voters motivated by opposition to abortion leaned strongly to the Republican Party. During the 2006 midterm congressional elections, for example, voters strongly opposed to the war in Iraq also leaned Democratic, while those supporting President George W. Bush's decision to launch the war and maintain the U.S. troop commitment to try to stabilize the strife-torn Iraqi society stuck with the Republicans.

Single-issue voting took on a different coloration in 2010 when a group that came to be called the TEA PARTY, although it was more of a movement than a traditional political party, coalesced around opposition to government—particularly federal—spending, tax increases, and large deficits. Persons who found a home in this political view brought an energy to the 2010 elections that sent into Congress—especially the House—dozens of like-minded legislators. That, in turn, led in 2011 to a drawn-out and deeply bitter confrontation between the White House, under Democrat Barack Obama and his allies, and House Republicans. It played out in legislation in the summer to increase the nation's debt limit—normally a routine action—so that the government could continue borrowing to pay bills for expenses Congress had approved. Democrats were open to cutting government spending so long as there also was at least some additional tax revenue. House Republicans refused, which led the nation to within hours of defaulting on debt payments, the first time ever the U.S. government defaulted. A last minute compromise, which increased the limit and set up a special congressional committee with unusual power to force Congress to vote on a plan for government austerity and perhaps tax increases, prevented a default. But it left Americans, and the world, looking at the once omnipotent United States as a nation politically deadlocked and barely able to act even in the face of the most serious consequences of not acting.

Single-issue voting has benefited from CAMPAIGN FINANCE laws that exempt controversial issue-advocacy POLITICAL ADVERTISING from limits on contributions to candidates. So long as the issue ad does not name the candidate and is run independently, it does not count as a contribution.

But public opinion research has found consistently that most voters are not single-issue voters, but instead make their decisions based on a range of concerns that include the candidates' positions on economic, foreign, and military policy and social issues such as health care, education, and Social Security.

Single-Member Districts

Most legislators in the United States, including members of the House of Representatives, are elected from single-member DISTRICTS by PLURALITY vote. For the seven states currently entitled by population to only one representative—Alaska, Delaware, Montana, North Dakota, South Dakota, Vermont, and Wyoming—the entire state is the district and the candidates for the seat run AT-LARGE.

In the early nineteenth century, some states elected U.S. representatives from MULTIMEMBER DISTRICTS. Congress banned the practice in 1842, however, when it decreed that no district could elect more than one representative. Some multimember districts or wards are still used in state and local elections. (See DISTRICTS, WARDS, AND PRECINCTS.)

The WINNER-TAKE-ALL characteristic of congressional and other single-member elections stands in contrast to PROPORTIONAL REPRESENTATION, in which parties receive a share of the seats based on their share of the vote. Winner take all favors the TWO-PARTY SYSTEM because THIRD PARTIES have little realistic chance of sharing in the political power, and the major parties have little to gain by forming COALITIONS with weaker parties.

Racial and ethnic minorities generally prefer single-member districts over multimember districts covering a wider geographical area. A compact district that is predominantly African American has a better chance of electing a black representative than does a predominantly white district where candidates must run at large for two or more seats. The Supreme Court has frowned, however, on efforts to ensure minority representation by creating MINORITY-MAJORITY DISTRICTS through artificially contorted district lines. (See CUMULATIVE VOTING; RACIAL REDISTRICTING.)

Socialist Labor Party (1874–)

The Socialist Labor Party, the first national socialist party in the United States, ranks second only to the PROHIBITION PARTY among third parties in longevity. Formed in 1874 by elements of the Socialist International in New York, it was first known as the Social Democratic Workingmen's Party. In 1877 the group adopted the name Socialist Labor Party. Throughout the 1880s, the party worked in concert with other left-wing third parties, including the Greenbacks.

The Socialist Labor Party ran national tickets in every presidential election from 1892 through 1976, but without making a major impact on the overall contest. The party collected its highest proportion of the national vote in 1896, when its candidate received 36,356 votes (0.3 percent of the popular vote).

Led by the autocratic Daniel DeLeon (1852–1914), a former Columbia University law lecturer, the Socialist Labor Party became increasingly militant and made its best showing in local races in 1898. But DeLeon's insistence on rigid party discipline and his opposition to the organized labor movement created a feeling of alienation among many members. Moderate elements bolted from the party, joining the SOCIALIST PARTY of Eugene V. Debs, which formed in 1901 and for the next four decades maintained one of the largest followings of any U.S. alternative or third party.

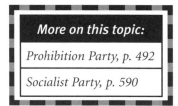

More on this topic:

Prohibition Party, p. 492

Socialist Party, p. 590

The Socialist Labor Party continued as a small, tightly organized far-left group bound to DeLeon's uncompromising belief in revolution. As late as 1976 the party advocated direct worker action to take over control of production and claimed five thousand members nationwide. However, it has not been active in presidential politics in the years since.

Socialist Party (1901–)

The Socialist Party was established officially in July 1901 at a convention in Indianapolis, Indiana, which joined together former American Railway Union president Eugene V. Debs's Social Democratic Party with a moderate faction of the SOCIALIST LABOR PARTY. The two groups had begun discussions a year before and in the 1900 presidential campaign jointly supported a ticket headed by Debs that received 86,935 votes (0.6 percent of the popular vote).

The 1901 unity convention identified the new Socialist Party with the working class and described the party's goal as "collective ownership . . . of the means of production and distribution." The party grew rapidly in the early twentieth century, reaching a peak membership of approximately 118,000 in 1912. That year also proved to be the party's best at the polls. Debs, a presidential candidate five times between 1900 and 1920, received 900,369 votes (6.0 percent of the popular vote). The Socialists elected 1,200 candidates to local offices, including 79 mayors.

With the outbreak of World War I, the party became a vehicle for antiwar protest. In 1917 pacifist Socialists converted a number of mayoral elections into referendums on the war, winning 34 percent of the vote in Chicago, more than 25 percent in Buffalo, and 22 percent in New York City.

The following year Debs was convicted of sedition for making an antiwar speech and was sentenced to a term in the Atlanta federal penitentiary, from which he ran for president in 1920 and received 915,490 votes (3.4 percent of the popular vote).

Although the party advocated collective ownership and criticized what it viewed as the flaws and unfairness of capitalism, its members for the most part eschewed the international communism embodied by the Soviet Union following the Bolshevik Revolution of 1917. In 1924 they made their strongest alliance with the political mainstream, endorsing Wisconsin senator Robert M. La Follette's presidential candidacy on the Progressive Party ticket, an unsuccessful attempt to establish a farm-labor coalition. In 1928 the Socialists resumed running a presidential ticket. With the death of Debs in 1926, the party selected Norman Thomas, a former minister and social worker, to be the party's standard-bearer for the next six elections.

The Great Depression brought a brief surge for the Socialists in 1932, with Thomas polling 884,649 votes (2.2 percent of the popular vote). But 1932 proved to be only a temporary revival for the Socialists. Roosevelt's New Deal program, which established a greater role for the federal government in shaping the nation's economy and dealing with problems such as poverty, stole the Socialists' thunder, and they failed to attract even one-half of 1 percent of the vote in any succeeding presidential election.

In the early 1970s, a schism in the party ranks between those who opposed U.S. military intervention in Vietnam and others who saw it as a necessary effort to bar the advance of communist totalitarianism essentially ended the old Socialist Party. A faction of the party, however, has carried on since then under the banner of the Socialist Party USA, which according to its website stands "to establish a radical democracy that places people's lives under their own control—a non-racist, classless, feminist, socialist society in which people cooperate at work, at home, and in the community."

In 1976 the party ran its first presidential ticket in two decades. The candidates received 6,038 votes, 0.01 percent of the popular vote. The party's national vote totals have since ranged from a low of 3,057 in 1992 to a high of 10,837 in 2004. In 2008, its candidates received 6,538 votes.

THE SOWER. Cartoon made for the Socialist Party.

0004698   EUGENE DEBS (1855–1926).
Credit: The Granger Collection, New York

The Socialists have been among the most persistent and successful vote getters of America's third parties. Eugene Debs was the Socialist candidate in five of the first six presidential elections in the twentieth century.

Source: Library of Congress

More on this topic:

Progressive Party,
p. 491

Socialist Labor Party,
p. 590

Socialist Workers Party (1938–)

The Socialist Workers Party was formed in 1938 by followers of the Russian revolutionary Leon Trotsky. Originally a faction within the U.S. COMMUNIST PARTY, the Trotskyites were expelled in 1936 on instructions from Soviet leader Joseph Stalin. A brief Trotskyite coalition with the SOCIALIST PARTY ended in 1938 when the dissidents decided to organize independently as the Socialist Workers Party.

More on this topic:

Communist Party U.S.A., p. 110

Socialist Party, p. 590

Through its youth arm, the Young Socialist Alliance, the Socialist Workers Party was active in the anti–Vietnam War movement and contributed activists to civil rights protests.

Since 1948 the party has run a presidential candidate, but its entries have never received more than 0.1 percent of the popular vote.

Soft Money

Concerns about the escalating costs of political campaigns led to efforts beginning in the mid-1990s to overhaul the Federal Election Campaign Act of 1971 and its amendments, a mission that culminated in the enactment of the Bipartisan Campaign Reform Act (BCRA) of 2002. The biggest change invoked by BCRA was a prohibition on unlimited contributions by individuals and groups, known as *soft money,* to national party committees for use in campaigns for federal offices. Such funds had greatly escalated since a federal law was passed in 1979 permitting such fund-raising.

For reform-minded individuals and groups whose priority was to regulate the flow of money to campaigns for president and Congress more strictly—and to create greater distance between the parties and big campaign donors—the soft money ban was the right thing to do in and of itself. But those who hoped that BCRA regulations would reduce the importance of money in politics were quickly disappointed.

Despite predictions from some BCRA opponents that the parties would wither without access to the soft money on which they had come to depend, both the Republicans and Democrats proved highly adept at replacing the fewer but larger soft money contributions with smaller and much more numerous regulated HARD MONEY donations. This was greatly abetted by the increasingly sophisticated use of the Internet as a conduit for campaign fund-raising, with instant contributions paid for by credit card on candidate websites supplemented by electronic communications to known or potential donors.

Meanwhile, soft money donors did not simply fade away; rather, they found new ways to influence election outcomes. One of the biggest consequences of BCRA, and one not intended by its advocates, was a rapid expansion of "527" POLITICAL ORGANIZATIONS, so called because they are organized under Section 527 of the Internal Revenue Code, are overseen by the Internal Revenue Service, and are subject to less stringent regulation than are POLITICAL ACTION COMMITTEES, which make direct hard money donations to candidates and parties and are regulated by the FEDERAL ELECTION COMMISSION (FEC).

In 2002, the last year in which soft money donations could be made to national party

In efforts to raise soft money for the Democratic National Committee, the Clinton administration invited donors to spend the night in the Lincoln bedroom.

Source: White House

committees, 527 groups spent $229.5 million. By 2004, 527s reported spending a cumulative $595.5 million; much of that money went into negative advertising by Democratic-oriented groups (such as America Coming Together, the Media Fund, and MoveOn.org), which attacked President George W. Bush, and Republican-oriented groups, such as the Swift Boat Veterans for Truth, which raised questions about Democratic challenger John Kerry's reputation as a Vietnam War hero.

Spending levels by 527s have remained in the hundreds of millions of dollars in each election cycle since. The names and ideological leanings of the top spending groups have varied, though.

In 2008, a year in which Democrat Barack Obama was elected president and his party made significant electoral gains across the nation, the biggest spending 527 was allied with the Democrats—a PAC set up by the Service Employees International Union—as were two of the next three: America Votes, a broad alliance of labor unions and other progressive groups, and the feminist organization EMILY's List. The one Republican-allied exception was American Solutions Winning the Future, a PAC established by former U.S. House Speaker Newt Gingrich.

In 2010, a strong comeback year for the Republicans, those same four groups again were atop the spending list for 527 organizations. But this time, the Gingrich-led American Solutions group topped the list by a wide margin.

The most significant development in campaign finance that year, though, came in a Supreme Court ruling that opened a wide new avenue for outside groups to raise unlimited contributions, and dealt a further blow to the goals of those who advocated the ban on soft money contributions to the national political parties.

The January 2010 ruling in the case OF *CITIZENS UNITED V. FEDERAL ELECTION COMMISSION*, approved by a 5–4 vote, struck down the other biggest provision in BCRA: a ban on "electioneering communications," or broadcast ads aimed at influencing the outcomes of elections, by groups associated with corporate entities (including labor unions) within sixty days of a general election and within thirty days of a primary. The decision, which essentially equated the free speech rights of corporations with those of individuals, led almost immediately to the rise of so-called SuperPACs.

SuperPACs were not technically 527 organizations but like 527s were able to receive unlimited contributions for unlimited independent expenditure advertising campaigns. Moreover, some ads by SuperPACs directly attacked candidates for public office by name, a contrast to most issue ads by 527s, which were carefully crafted to persuade voters to support or oppose a candidate without saying so expressly in order to pass the so-called "magic words" test spelled out in the Supreme Court's 1976 *BUCKLEY V. VALEO* decision.

A caution flag had been raised by 527 groups in March 2007, when the FEC announced it had reached a settlement on a $750,000 fine—the third largest levy in its history—against the Progress for America Voter Fund, on grounds that the 527 group in 2004 had raised excessive contributions for ads that, according to the FEC, did expressly call for the election of Bush and the defeat of Kerry.

1996: The Turning Point

Though the parties had been allowed to employ soft money in federal campaigns since 1979, its use first became a major point of public discussion in the aftermath of the 1996 presidential campaign.

Aggressive pursuit of soft money, particularly by President Bill Clinton's 1996 reelection campaign, prompted congressional investigations and calls for further reforms of the campaign finance system.

Growth in Soft Money

In millions of dollars

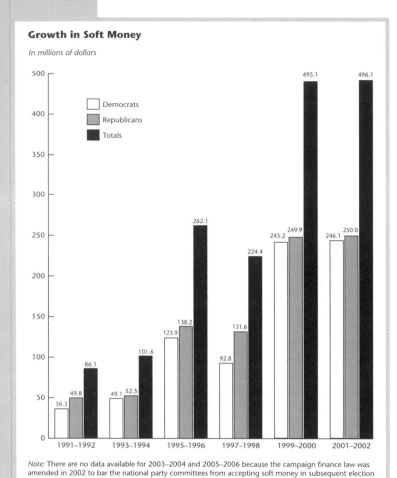

Legend:
- Democrats
- Republicans
- Totals

Year	Democrats	Republicans	Totals
1991–1992	36.3	49.8	86.1
1993–1994	49.1	52.5	101.6
1995–1996	123.9	138.2	262.1
1997–1998	92.8	131.6	224.4
1999–2000	245.2	249.9	495.1
2001–2002	246.1	250.0	496.1

Note: There are no data available for 2003–2004 and 2005–2006 because the campaign finance law was amended in 2002 to bar the national party committees from accepting soft money in subsequent election cycles.

Source: Federal Election Commission.

Democratic and Republican party committees reported raising a total of $263.5 million in soft money for the 1995–1996 election cycle, according to the FEC. The figures were up substantially for both parties since the 1992 presidential election. Republican committees raised $141.2 million and spent $149.7 million. Democratic committees raised $122.3 million and spent $117.5 million.

Despite the Republicans' higher totals, the Democrats' soft money tactics drew more MEDIA COVERAGE and were the primary focus of hearings by the Republican-controlled 105th Congress (1997–1999). The FEC itself came under fire for not doing more to police the soft money situation before it got out of control.

The Clinton White House was criticized for overzealous solicitation of soft money contributions to the DEMOCRATIC NATIONAL COMMITTEE (DNC). Supposedly to be used for party-building activities, some of the money reportedly was converted to hard money for the reelection of Clinton and Vice President Al Gore. Under the 1974 Federal Election Campaign Act (FECA) as amended, the Clinton-Gore general election campaign was restricted to spending the $61.8 million it received in PUBLIC FINANCING under FECA. (The Republican ticket of Robert J. Dole and Jack F. Kemp received the same amount, with the same limitations.)

Following disclosure of the sources, the DNC returned several millions of dollars in contributions. Some came from Chinese and other foreign nationals who are barred from contributing to U.S. elections. Other donors were guests at White House coffees or overnight stays in the historic Lincoln Bedroom or other guest rooms.

Reformers viewed soft money as a backdoor entrance for corporations and unions that had long been prohibited from giving money to political candidates. Corporate and labor POLITICAL ACTION COMMITTEES, as well as other PACs and individuals, are permitted to donate money but are limited in the amounts they can give to candidates for federal office.

The 1979 soft money law, however, allowed donations of $100,000 or more to the parties, which were permitted to spend without limit for voter registration, turnout drives, and other activities to benefit the party rather than specific federal candidates. A portion of the "nonfederal money," as it is technically known, was transferred by the national committees to their state and local committees. Some goes to help candidates in nonfederal races.

But the parties, just as many 527 groups have continued to do, deployed significant sums of soft money on advertising worded to meet the "magic words" test but which sent a clear message that voters should support or oppose a particular candidate.

Sophisticated Voting

Also known as strategic voting, *sophisticated voting* can take several forms. For example, a partisan voter whose highest priority is to see his or her party win (or the other party lose) might pass over a primary candidate with whom the voter agrees more closely on issues and support a contender who is perceived as more "electable." In states that allow crossover voting in primaries, a Democrat might take a Republican ballot, or vice versa, and vote for an underdog candidate considered a weak opponent for the general election.

Sincere voters, on the other hand, do not take into consideration the strategic consequences of their ballots. They simply vote for the candidates who are their first choice for the elective office at stake.

Almost every election cycle produces one or more interesting examples of sophisticated voting. Polling in early 2007, during the extremely early onset of the 2008 presidential campaign, showed an interesting result: former New York City mayor Rudolph Giuliani, who held conservative views on some issues but was decidedly more liberal than the Republican Party norm on volatile social issues such as abortion and gay rights, led in presidential preference surveys of Republican voters. He even drew substantial support from social conservatives who for many years had demanded that the Republicans only nominate candidates who opposed abortion.

The strong image Giuliani had projected leading his city through the aftermath of the September 11, 2001, terrorist attacks earned him respect among many of these Republican voters. But a major reason for the early support he received in polls was that a sharp downturn in President George W. Bush's second-term job approval ratings threatened the GOP's continued hold on the White House in 2008. This may—at least early on—have had some voters normally driven by ideology eyeing the potential electability of the more moderate Giuliani.

Moreover, the more visceral the Republican respondents' dislike for early Democratic nomination front-runner Hillary Rodham Clinton, the New York senator and wife of former president Bill Clinton, the more likely they were to countenance supporting Giuliani.

Another example occurred in California during the controversial recall election of 2003, in which voters turned Democratic incumbent Gray Davis out of office. For many years, the conservatives who dominated the ranks of the state's Republican Party preferred staunchly conservative nominees for key races, even though such candidates were becoming increasingly less viable in general elections because the state was undergoing a strong Democratic

In an act of sophisticated voting, Republican voters afraid of losing the White House in 2008 may have preferred Rudolph Giuliani for his electability, despite his relatively liberal positions on social issues such as abortion and gay marriage. Polls in fall 2007 showed him among the leading Republican candidates.

Source: CQ Photo/Scott J. Ferrell

trend. Yet the opportunity to win in 2003 made even many conservative Republican activists abandon ideological purity for pragmatism, and they rallied behind the ultimately successful candidacy of movie star Arnold Schwarzenegger, who held relatively liberal views on social issues, over conservative stalwart Tom McClintock, a veteran of the state legislature.

Sophisticated voting does not always provide the desired result, though, as illustrated by the 2006 Senate race in Rhode Island. Lincoln Chafee, the most liberal Republican in the Senate, faced a serious primary challenge from conservative Steve Laffey. Although Laffey portrayed himself as a truer Republican than Chafee, national Republican strategists believed only a moderate such as Chafee could win a statewide race in strongly Democratic-leaning Rhode Island.

The party poured vast resources into the state to try to persuade Republicans to support Chafee as more electable and to draw in independents, who were eligible to vote in the Republican primary under the state's election system. But Chafee, after fending off Laffey in the primary, was pummeled by Democrats who claimed the Republican Party wanted him to win only because his election was crucial to their continued control of the Senate and conservative agenda. Chafee lost the general election to Democrat Sheldon Whitehouse, and the Democrats narrowly gained control of the Senate.

Sore Loser Laws

Election laws in all but a few states prevent candidates who have run and lost in party primaries from coming back in the general election campaign and running as independent or third-party candidates. These *sore loser laws* can take the form of outright statutory prohibitions, provisions that require non–major-party candidates to file to run for the general election prior to the date on which the primary is held, or other limitations. As of 2011 only three states—Connecticut, Iowa, and New York—did not have a sore loser law.

Although they are rarely the cause for much public discussion during a campaign, sore loser laws—or the lack thereof—made the news in a pair of controversy-tinged congressional elections in 2006 and one spectacular contest in 2010.

The biggest newsmaker involved Democratic senator Joseph I. Lieberman's campaign for reelection in Connecticut, which has no sore loser law but makes it difficult for a primary loser to switch to an independent or third-party candidacy. A candidate wishing to do so must file sufficient petition signatures and meet other ballot qualifications by the close of business on the day after the primary, which occurred on August 8 in 2006.

Lieberman, who in 2000 had been the Democratic nominee for vice president on the narrowly unsuccessful ticket headed by Al Gore, had in more recent years stirred a backlash among many Democratic voters, particularly liberal activists, with his outspoken defense of President George W. Bush's decision to commit U.S. troops to war in Iraq. By midsummer 2006, it had become clear that Lieberman was at serious risk of losing the primary to Ned Lamont, a wealthy businessman and antiwar activist who was little known to voters when he entered the contest.

Because the one-day separation between the primary and the independent candidate filing deadline made it impossible for him to wait for the primary outcome, Lieberman announced well in advance that he would run as an independent if he lost the primary. That move further alienated some Democrats and may have contributed to his narrow primary defeat by Lamont, but it enabled him to comfortably meet the filing requirements to run on a third-party line. Running as the nominee of "Connecticut for Lieberman" and benefiting from widespread support from Republican voters who opposed the liberal Lamont but were turned off by the weak Republican nominee, Lieberman won reelection with 50 percent of the vote and a 10-point margin over Lamont.

Lieberman had said he would continue to caucus with the Democrats in the Senate, and he provided Democratic leaders with the crucial fifty-first vote they needed to take control of the Senate following their six-seat gain in the 2006 elections. But Lieberman soon thereafter declared himself an independent.

The other 2006 case in which a sore loser law came into play was the contest in Ohio's Eighteenth Congressional District. After long denying wrongdoing in the scandal involving influence peddling by lobbyist Jack Abramoff, Republican representative Bob Ney in August 2006 renounced the GOP nomination he had won in May, quit the race, and announced he would soon resign his seat. At the recommendation of Ney and others, the state Republican Party backed state senator Joy Padgett to replace Ney on the ballot.

Democrats initially protested that Padgett's nomination would violate the state's sore loser law, as she had run for and lost the Republican nomination for lieutenant governor in the May primary. But state officials ruled that the bid for the other office was not relevant to the congressional race. Nonetheless, the damage done to Republican interests in the district by Ney, who pleaded guilty to corruption charges in the midst of the campaign, and by Padgett's image as an ally of Ney enabled Democrat Zack Space to win a landslide victory for the seat that November.

The 2010 contest was in Alaska where the incumbent Republican senator, Lisa Murkowski, lost her primary race to a little known conservative challenger who had won strong support from TEA PARTY activists. Election experts concluded, after the voting, that Murkowski never took her challenger seriously, and as a result did not get deeply involved in the primary race.

The defeat left Murkowski with no good options because the state's sore loser law blocked her from running on another ticket or as an independent. Her only choice was to wage a write-in campaign, which she did. Against all odds and predictions, she won, the first time a senator had been elected as a write-in since J. Strom Thurmond was successful in 1954.

Sore loser laws have been challenged, unsuccessfully, on constitution grounds and as contributing to ever more polarized political parties. Because these laws are integral to primary contests, they have the potential to filter out candidates with moderate political stances that might appeal to the wider public in a general election contest. Rather, primaries—especially in the latter period of the 1990s and after 2000—often became vehicles for the most dedicated, and often most liberal or most conservative, elements in a party. This was the dynamic that was seen in the Lieberman, Ney, and Murkowski cases. Although Lieberman and Murkowski managed to finesse the problem, the increasingly polarized political environment by 2011 reinforced the ability of the most extreme advocates of both parties to place significant roadblocks to centrist candidates in general elections and later when serving in office.

Although sore loser laws have been challenged as an unconstitutional denial of BALLOT ACCESS, the U.S. Supreme Court has upheld them as a fair and reasonable way to limit the length of election battles while still giving the voters a sufficient choice of candidates. In a 1974 case, *Storer v. Brown*, the Court upheld the California sore loser law as being in harmony with the state's goal of having political parties use primaries to settle their internal differences and limit the ballot to primary winners and qualified independents. Besides giving the people "understandable choices," the Court said, this system should give the general election winner "sufficient support to govern effectively."

The Court also upheld a related "disaffiliation" law that prevented California candidates from running as independents if they had been registered with a party less than a year before the primary. Both actions strengthened the parties' role in winnowing out candidates and avoiding the dangers of what the Court called "unrestrained factionalism."

Until 1959, California had permitted cross-filing of candidates in other parties' primaries, which some saw as a dilution of the parties' distinctive identities. Repeal of cross-filing, the Court said, made the primary "not merely a warm-up for the general election, but an integral part of the entire election process."

Presidential candidate John B. Anderson encountered sore loser laws in several states in 1980 when he sought to run as an independent in the general election after losing several early primaries to the eventual Republican nominee, Ronald Reagan. Anderson ultimately was able to get on the ballot in every state, largely because he had tried to remove his name from the primary ballot in some states before the primary was held.

At first, however, the early filing deadlines in some states threatened to keep Anderson off the November ballot. Anderson brought suit in one such state, challenging Ohio's early deadline as an unconstitutional restriction on independent candidates. He won in federal district court and received 5.9 percent of Ohio's vote on ELECTION DAY. The state appealed, however, and in 1982 the Supreme Court in *Anderson et al. v. Celebrezze* overturned a federal appeals court that had reversed the district court action. The Supreme Court ruled that early filing deadlines for independents put them at a disadvantage and deny a choice to voters not satisfied with the candidates put forth by existing political parties.

> Sore loser laws give the people "understandable choices" and give the general election winner "sufficient support to govern effectively."
>
> —U.S. Supreme Court in *Storer v. Brown* (1974)

Although the *Anderson* ruling seemed to contradict the Court's earlier decision in *Storer,* the Court said Ohio's early deadline approach was more burdensome to independents than California's sore loser approach.

In January 1998, Ohio's supreme court ruled that the state's sore loser law applied even to a nonpartisan election for the Ohio board of education. Persons who had run in a partisan primary the previous May were ineligible to run in November for a seat on the board, the court said. It upheld the sore loser law as preventing "intraparty conflicts, voter confusion, and candidacies prompted by short-range goals."

Southern Democrats (1860)

National divisions over the slavery issue, building for a generation, reached a political climax in 1860 and produced a sectional split in the DEMOCRATIC PARTY. Throughout the mid-nineteenth century, the Democrats had remained unified by supporting the various pieces of compromise legislation that both protected slavery in the southern states and endorsed the policy of popular sovereignty in the territories. But in 1860, Southern Democrats wanted the Democratic convention (meeting in Charleston, South Carolina) to insert a PLATFORM plank specifically protecting slavery in the territories. When their plank was defeated, delegates from most of the southern states walked out.

The Charleston convention stalemated over a presidential choice and, after recessing for six weeks, reconvened in Baltimore, where Illinois senator Stephen A. Douglas was nominated. Most of the southern delegates, plus those from California and Oregon, bolted the convention and nominated their own ticket in a rump convention held after Douglas's selection. John C. Breckinridge of Kentucky, the incumbent vice president elected on the 1856 ticket headed by Democrat James Buchanan, was chosen for president, and Joseph Lane, a states' rights advocate from Oregon, was selected as his vice presidential RUNNING MATE. A platform was adopted that recognized the right of slavery to exist in the territories.

After the formation of the two sectional tickets, two separate Democratic national committees operated in Washington, D.C., to oversee their campaigns.

The split produced an election outcome that would have monumental historical significance—the victory of Republican Abraham Lincoln. Although the combined Douglas and Breckinridge votes amounted to a majority of the ballots cast, Lincoln outran each individual Democrat with a plurality of the popular vote and, more important, a majority of the electoral votes. That gave the recently founded Republican Party a victory in only its second presidential election, just two years after Douglas was selected by the Illinois legislature over Lincoln for a seat in the U.S. Senate after a series of famous debates.

The Breckinridge ticket received 848,019 votes (18.1 percent of the POPULAR VOTE) in 1860 and carried nine southern and BORDER STATES.

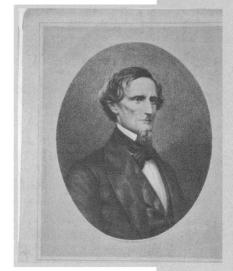

Jefferson Davis, president of the Confederate States of America.

Source: Library of Congress

During the Civil War that soon ensued, the Southern Democrats provided much of the leadership for the Confederate states' government, including its president, Jefferson Davis. At the end of the conflict, the Southern Democrats made no attempt to continue as a separate sectional entity and rejoined the national Democratic Party.

More on this topic:

Border States, p. 34

Democratic Party, p. 155

Platform, p. 383

Republican Party, p. 541

Southern Primary

Throughout much of the time after the PRIMARY came into widespread use in the early twentieth century, the DEMOCRATIC PARTY primaries were the only elections that counted in the South. Most conservative white voters, who dominated the region's politics, maintained a fierce antipathy toward the Republican Party because of its association with Abraham Lincoln, the Civil War, and the postwar Reconstruction era. As a result, the Democratic Party so dominated the region that to win its nomination was in effect to win the election.

That changed dramatically in recent years as the REPUBLICAN PARTY, which in the latter part of the twentieth century established itself firmly as the nation's more conservative party, gained strength in the South and indeed came to dominate the area much as the Democrats once did. By the end of the century, Republicans outnumbered Democrats in southern governorships and congressional delegations, and in presidential politics the South usually voted solidly Republican.

Nevertheless, the southern primary holds a special place in U.S. political history and deserves separate discussion in any examination of primaries and how they work. Also, because they were so lopsided politically, the southern primaries spawned a regional addition to the nominating process: the RUNOFF PRIMARY.

In a 1949 study of politics in the region, political scientist V. O. Key Jr. concluded, "In fact, the Democratic primary is no nominating method at all. The primary is the election." The area of his study comprised the eleven states—all members of the Civil War Confederacy—traditionally known

> *"In fact, the Democratic primary is no nominating method at all. The primary is the election."*
>
> —*Political scientist V. O. Key Jr.*

as the Old South: Alabama, Arkansas, Florida, Georgia, Louisiana, Mississippi, North Carolina, South Carolina, Tennessee, Texas, and Virginia.

Through World War II and the postwar years, the Democratic primary predominated in the South. Of the 114 gubernatorial elections held there between 1919 and 1948, the Democratic nominee won 113 times. The exception was Tennessee's election of a Republican governor in the Harding presidential LANDSLIDE of 1920. In the same period, the Democratic nominee won 131 of 132 southern Senate elections, the only exception being a SPECIAL ELECTION in Arkansas in 1937 when the Democratic nominee lost to an independent Democrat.

The first popularly elected Republican U.S. senator from the South, John G. Tower of Texas, won a special election in 1961. Thereafter, Republicans gradually won Senate seats in all southern states except Louisiana, where they broke through only with GOP nominee David Vitter's victory in 2004. Likewise, Republicans picked up governorships slowly after 1949, their first victories in the South coming in Arkansas and Florida in 1966.

As recently as 1994 Republicans were still a distinct minority in southern state and congressional offices. They were outnumbered eight to three in governorships, twelve to ten in Senate seats, and seventy-seven to forty-eight in U.S. House seats. The Democratic primaries continued to be the deciding election in most southern states.

The Democrats' numerical strength in the South, however, did not ensure a liberal Congress. Although elected under the Democratic label, southern House and Senate members tended to vote more like conservative Republicans. They often sided with Republicans to form the so-called conservative COALITION on crucial floor votes in Congress. When it came together as a majority of Republicans and a majority of southern Democrats, the conservative coalition often had a high success rate against northern Democrats.

The Republican takeover of Congress in 1994 dramatically increased the coalition's victory rate to a near-perfect 98.9 percent while at the same time diminishing the coalition's importance. On many of the coalition votes, the southern Democrats' support was superfluous because the majority Republicans would have won anyway. Some political scientists dismissed the usefulness of continuing to analyze the coalition's performance. "It's a concept designed to measure a phenomenon that's no longer there," said one. *Congressional Quarterly*, a nonpartisan authority on Congress, long published a definitive annual study of the conservative coalition but abandoned it by the turn of the twenty-first century.

The region's political tide continued to advance in the 2004 elections, when the Republican Party won four seats in the South that Democratic incumbents had left open, boosting the GOP to control of twenty-two of the twenty-six Senate seats.

By 2011, Republicans held 72 percent of the House seats in the South and 77 percent of the Senate seats. They also held all but three of the governorships.

At the presidential level, the South has long since ceased to be a Democratic bastion. Republican nominee Richard M. Nixon carried each of the eleven states of the Old South with at least 65 percent of the vote in 1972. In 1984 and 1988, Ronald Reagan and George H. W. Bush did almost as well, carrying every southern state with at least 58 percent (Reagan) or 54 percent (Bush) of the vote. In 1992, Democrat Bill Clinton won despite the South, losing seven of the eleven states to Bush. He did better in 1996, again losing seven states but trading a loss in Georgia for a win in Florida, for a net gain of twelve southern state electoral votes. But Republican George W. Bush restored the Republicans' presidential lock on the South, carrying all the region's states in 2000 (including his very close and controversial victory in Florida) and again in 2004, most—including Florida—by comfortable margins.

Barack Obama improved on his party's southern performance in 2008, winning Florida, North Carolina, and Virginia.

Runoff Primaries

By 1920 all southern states were choosing their Democratic gubernatorial and senatorial nominees through the primary process. But many legislators found the system flawed because it frequently allowed a candidate in a multicandidate race to win a plurality of the popular vote—and therefore the Democratic nomination that ensured election—even if his vote amounted to only a fraction of the total vote in the primary.

Consequently, most southern states adopted the runoff primary—a second election following the first primary, usually by two to four weeks—that matched only the top two contenders from the first primary. The runoff election ensured a majority nomination. Mississippi was the first to adopt the runoff system, in 1902, followed by North Carolina and South Carolina in 1915, Georgia in 1917 (using a county unit system), Texas in 1918, Louisiana in 1922, Florida in 1929, Alabama in 1931, and Arkansas in 1933. (Arkansas dropped the runoff in 1935 and re-established it in 1939.) Tennessee never adopted the runoff system. Virginia adopted it in 1969 and repealed it two years later. (With some exceptions, Virginia since 1977 has nominated candidates at state conventions rather than primaries.) Florida, which maintained its system of runoff elections for more than seventy years, eliminated them on a temporary basis as of the 2002 elections and then barred them permanently in 2005.

Under Georgia's county unit system, each county was apportioned a certain number of unit votes. The candidate who received the largest number of a county's popular votes was awarded all of its unit votes, even if he won only a plurality. A candidate had to have a majority of the state's county unit votes to win the primary, otherwise a runoff became necessary. The runoff also was held on the basis of the county unit system.

The system was heavily weighted toward sparsely populated rural areas because every county, no matter how small, had at least two unit votes. It sometimes produced winners who received less than a majority of popular votes, even in the runoff. In 1963, the county unit system fell before the Supreme Court's ONE-PERSON, ONE-VOTE doctrine. In *Gray v. Sanders,* the Court declared the system unconstitutional because of the disparity in representation between urban and rural areas.

Runoffs are not always obligatory. In most states, if the second-place primary finisher declines a runoff, the first-place candidate is then the nominee.

After using the runoff for fifty-three years, Louisiana modified its system again in 1975. The new law allowed voters to participate in an open primary in which all candidates, regardless of party, ran on a single ballot. If no candidate received a majority of all votes cast in the open primary, a runoff election would be held between the top two finishers, again regardless of party affiliation. This system was maintained through the 2007 elections. A law enacted in 2006, however, ordered the reinstatement as of 2008 of a more orthodox primary system, under which the parties would hold their own primaries to nominate candidates for a general election.

In 1984, Jesse L. Jackson, then a contender for the Democratic presidential nomination, tried unsuccessfully to abolish runoffs, which he claimed hurt black candidates' chances of election. The Democratic National Convention, however, defeated his proposal, 2,500.8 to 1,253.2.

Forty years earlier, the Supreme Court struck down another PRIMARY TYPE, the so-called WHITE PRIMARY from which blacks were excluded under the Democrats' guise that they were a private organization not subject to the Fifteenth Amendment's protection of the RIGHT TO VOTE. Until LITERACY TESTS and POLL TAXES were struck down, they too were widely used in the South to deter voting by blacks.

Preferential Primaries

Before switching to the runoff system, Alabama, Florida, and Louisiana experimented for several years with a preferential system of primary voting. Under this system a voter indicates his first and second choices by writing the number one or two beside two candidates' names. To determine the winner, without a runoff, second-choice votes are added to the first-choice votes, and the candidate with the highest combined total wins.

The preference system, however, faded out by 1931. Apparently it was too confusing for voters; most did not bother to cast second-choice votes. In Alabama's 1920 Democratic primary for the Senate, for example, there were 130,814 first-choice votes but only 34,768 second-choice votes.

Special Elections

Vacancies in congressional seats or governorships often create the need for special elections. House vacancies, especially, must be filled as soon as possible to maintain the affected state's full representation based on population. (See HOUSE OF REPRESENTATIVES, ELECTING.)

Special elections are not always required, however, for Senate or governorship vacancies. The GOVERNOR may be empowered to appoint an interim senator to fill the unexpired term. Or, if a governor dies, the LIEUTENANT GOVERNOR may take over the job.

But when special elections for senator or governor are held in the South, the runoff system may complicate matters. There may not be time to go through the lengthy runoff primary process. The primary filing deadline may have passed, or it may be a year when no regular primary is scheduled. In such cases, the state committee sometimes selected the party nominee without holding a primary.

In the heyday of the Democratic southern primary, this process led to some unexpected results. In Arkansas in 1937, for example, a bypassed House member, John E. Miller, won as an independent Democrat after the state committee nominated Gov. Carl E. Bailey for a vacant Senate seat.

In another case, in 1954, former governor J. Strom Thurmond became a write-in candidate for the Senate after South Carolina Democratic leaders chose another candidate to succeed a renominated senator who had died. Thurmond, who later switched to the Republicans, became until 2010 the only senator ever elected by WRITE-IN VOTE. In 2010 Alaska incumbent senator Lisa Murkowski, a Republican, unexpectedly lost in the primary to a lightly considered challenger. Barred by SORE LOSER LAWS from running as an independent candidate, Murkowski waged a write-in campaign and won to retain her seat.

To avoid the pitfalls of no-primary party nominations, Texas adopted an unusual method of filling congressional vacancies. All candidates, regardless of party, compete in a free-for-all special primary like the system used by Louisiana for its primary election. (Similar "jungle" primaries have been adopted in other states.) If no one receives a majority, a special runoff election is held between the top two candidates. The Texas system was used in 1961 when Lyndon B. Johnson left the Senate to become vice president. In the first contest, Republican John Tower and Democrat William Blakley finished first and second without a majority. Tower defeated Blakley in the second election.

The system was used again in 1993 after Sen. Lloyd Bentsen resigned to become Treasury secretary. In the

Republican Kay Bailey Hutchison became Texas's first female senator after winning both the special primary and the special runoff election held to fill the seat of Lloyd Bentsen, who had been appointed secretary of the Treasury.

Source: CQ Photo/Scott J. Ferrell

special runoff election, Republican Kay Bailey Hutchison became Texas's first woman senator by defeating the interim incumbent, Democrat Bob Krueger, who had run a close second to Hutchison in the special primary.

The "Solid South" Meltdown

For decades the term "solid South" meant solidly Democratic and solidly white. Today it means strongly Republican-leaning in ideology and less solidly white in voting participation.

With the abolition of poll taxes, literacy tests, and other bars to voting by blacks, the racial mixture of VOTER TURNOUT in southern elections is not much different from that in the rest of the country. African Americans in the South, however, still tend to be loyal to the Democratic Party, which pushed the civil rights reforms of the 1960s and later mandated more DELEGATE slots for women and minorities at its own national conventions.

Conservative reaction to the Democrats' antiwar and equal rights policies helped to transform the South into a Republican stronghold. After the 2000 elections, the country was as closely divided as at any time in more than four decades. While no party owned the map nationally, the Republicans had a solid lock on the South, where congressional GOP candidates outpolled their Democratic opponents by 12 percentage points. In the 2006 U.S. House elections, which Democrats dominated, Republican candidates still outpolled Democratic candidates by 8 percentage points. By 2011 the GOP held about three-quarters of House and Senate seats in southern states. (See above) Whatever the geographic polarization meant nationally, in the South it signified the dethroning of the Democratic primary.

Special Elections

A special election, known in British usage as a *by-election*, is an election held at a different time from the regular election, usually to fill a vacancy.

In Congress, a special election is required to fill a House seat vacated because of the death, resignation, or expulsion of the incumbent representative. That is because the Constitution mandates an election to fill any House seat, barring the appointment of an interim member. Some states empower the governor to make an interim appointment when a Senate vacancy occurs, although special elections are not uncommon in such cases. (See HOUSE OF REPRESENTATIVES, ELECTING; SENATE, ELECTING.) There is a variety of approaches to filling vacant House seats among the states, as illustrated by three instances in the 2006 national campaign.

In California's Fiftieth District, Republican Randy "Duke" Cunningham resigned in December 2005, having pleaded guilty to bribery charges. Republican governor Arnold Schwarzenegger scheduled a special election primary for the following April, with the special general election to coincide with the regularly scheduled June primaries for the November elections. Republican Brian P. Bilbray won the special election in June and was nominated the same day for the November election, which he also won.

In New Jersey's Thirteenth District, Democratic representative Bob Menendez had vacated his House seat in January 2006 after he was appointed to fill a vacant Senate seat. Under New Jersey law, the House seat went unoccupied until a special election that was held simultaneously with the November 2006 general election. Democrat Albio Sires won both the special election for the final weeks of Menendez's unexpired term and the general election for a full term; Menendez, on the same day, was elected to a full term in the Senate.

Finally, Republican representative Tom DeLay, formerly the House majority leader, resigned his seat in Texas's Twenty-second District in June after a series of ethics controversies. Republican

Albio Sires won a New Jersey special election in November 2006 that permitted him to serve the remaining weeks of an unexpired House term. On the same day he also won the general election for a full term in the House, representing the same district.

Source: CQ Photo/Scott J. Ferrell

governor Rick Perry at first decided not to schedule a special election to fill the vacancy. But Republicans learned that a legal technicality barred the party from replacing DeLay on the November general election ballot, forcing the GOP's candidate, Shelley Sekula-Gibbs, to run a nearly impossible write-in campaign. In hopes of boosting her visibility, Perry belatedly scheduled a special election to coincide with the November general election. Though Sekula-Gibbs won the short-term election, she lost the general election for a full term to Democrat Nick Lampson, who declined to run in the special election.

In the case of U.S. Senate vacancies, special elections are not universally required, though they often occur. A notable one occurred in January 2010 in normally Democratic Massachusetts when Republican Scott Brown, a state senator, won a special election to fill the seat of Democratic senator Edward M. Kennedy, who had died the previous year. The victory, other than being unexpected in that state, was important because it denied Senate Democrats the sixtieth vote they had enjoyed to hold off GOP filibusters against their legislative initiatives.

The first step to filling a Senate vacancy almost always is the interim appointment of a replacement, made by the governor of the state with the vacant seat. If the vacancy occurs in the same election cycle as the regularly scheduled election for that seat, the governor will usually forgo scheduling a special election. If the vacancy occurs earlier in the elected senator's term, however, a special election will usually be held to fill the remainder of the unexpired term. Many states require the scheduling of a special election to coincide with the next regularly scheduled congressional general elections.

Special elections are never held for president or VICE PRESIDENT. Succession to the presidency is provided for in the Twenty-fifth Amendment to the Constitution, ratified in 1967. If the president dies, resigns, or is removed from office, the vice president becomes president. If the president is unable to serve, the vice president becomes acting president. If there is no vice president, the president names a replacement subject to confirmation by Congress.

In most states the LIEUTENANT GOVERNOR becomes the governor if the office becomes vacant; in the few states that do not have the office of lieutenant governor, the successor to the vacated governor's seat is designated by law. For example, when New Jersey Democratic governor James E. McGreevey resigned in 2004 because of a personal scandal, he was replaced on an interim basis by state senate president Richard J. Codey, also a Democrat. Laws vary from state to state for the holding of special elections to fill vacancies in state or local offices.

Spending Limits *See* CAMPAIGN FINANCE; PUBLIC FINANCING OF CAMPAIGNS.

Split- and Straight-Ticket Voting

Voting for candidates of different political parties on the same ballot is known as *split-ticket voting*. Voting for candidates of only one party is called *straight-ticket voting*.

Except in a PRIMARY, where all the candidates are of the same party, the BALLOT TYPES used in most states permit either split- or straight-ticket voting. A few states, however, prohibit straight-ticket voting, and their ballots are designed accordingly.

The "party-column" ballot used in some states facilitates straight-ticket voting because each party's candidates for various offices are arranged vertically under the party label. Marking a single block or pulling a single lever on the VOTING MACHINE casts votes for all of a party's candidates for all offices. The party-column ballot also encourages a COATTAILS effect. A strong candidate at the top may draw a vote for the whole ticket.

The "office-group" ballot is more conducive to split-ticket voting. Candidates are identified by party, and their names are arranged alphabetically under the office being sought, requiring the voter to pick and choose individually.

Even though it takes more effort than straight-ticket voting, split-ticket voting is more prevalent than in the past. Reasons include a decline in PARTY IDENTIFICATION and increases in the number of INDEPENDENT voters and CANDIDATE CENTERED CAMPAIGNS.

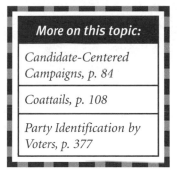

> **More on this topic:**
>
> Candidate-Centered Campaigns, p. 84
>
> Coattails, p. 108
>
> Party Identification by Voters, p. 377

Stalking Horse

A stalking horse is a candidate running as a decoy for another, perhaps stronger, candidate. The term comes from the hunting trick of hiding behind a horse to get in close for a shot at the prey.

In the age of the PRESIDENTIAL PRIMARY and PUBLIC OPINION POLLING, the stalking-horse strategy is rare. Those institutions now perform one of the stalker's main functions: testing voter reaction to the candidate relative to the one for whom he is fronting. And presidential nominations are now won in the primaries, not at the NATIONAL PARTY CONVENTION where the nomination is formalized. In the preprimary era of BROKERED CONVENTIONS, a stalking horse might have had some usefulness as a way to deadlock the convention.

The last presidential nominees to avoid full participation in the primaries were Republican Richard M. Nixon and Democrat Hubert H. Humphrey in 1968. Nixon entered few primaries, and Humphrey, none. Four years later Humphrey entered some primaries but was outpolled by George S. McGovern, whom some observers regarded as a stalking horse for Edward M. Kennedy. But McGovern received the Democratic nomination himself and waged an ill-fated attempt to unseat Nixon. In 1976, many Humphrey backers thought that California governor Edmund G. "Jerry" Brown Jr. was a stalking horse for Kennedy, but Brown insisted he was running on his own, and Kennedy in fact never entered the race. That year, Humphrey dropped out after Jimmy Carter won the important NEW HAMPSHIRE PRIMARY.

In these cases, as in earlier elections, the candidates accused of being stalking horses did not admit to being such, if that is what they were.

> **More on this topic:**
>
> Brokered Convention, p. 36

State and Federal Election Responsibilities

Democratic senator George McGovern, seen here on the television program Face the Nation, was thought by many—incorrectly—to be a stalking horse for Edward Kennedy in the 1972 presidential election.

Source: AP Photo/Jeff Robbins

Operation of the American election system is a dual responsibility shared by the federal and state governments. In some ways the states have the larger share of the burden because of their broad constitutional authority to regulate elections.

Even for federal elections, states do most of the work and make many of the major decisions. They or their subdivisions are in charge of VOTER REGISTRATION, operating the polling stations, counting the votes, and certifying the results. Within limits prescribed by the Constitution or acts of Congress, the states decide the qualifications for voting in the general election and participation in political party events such as PRIMARIES or CAUCUSES.

The federal government, on the other hand, plays mainly a monitoring role. It regulates CAMPAIGN FINANCE in federal elections and some aspects of state and local fundraising. It watches for illegal denial of the constitutional RIGHT TO VOTE, through racial discrimination or other means. It sets the times for federal elections, and it determines the winner in cases of CONTESTED ELECTIONS for the presidency and House and Senate seats.

Article I, section 4, of the U.S. Constitution authorizes the states to set the "Times, Places and Manner of holding Elections for Senators and Representatives," but the same section empowers Congress to make laws superseding such regulations. Under that authority or through constitutional amendments, the national government has overridden state laws by setting a uniform federal ELECTION DAY (the first Tuesday after the first Monday in November of even-numbered years), extending the FRANCHISE to women and eighteen-year-olds, protecting BLACK SUFFRAGE, and requiring easier voter registration.

At the same time, states on their own initiative have acted in recent years to give voters more candidate choices through easier BALLOT ACCESS, to make voting more convenient by extended ABSENTEE VOTING or postal elections. States also have opened primaries and caucuses to voters excluded from such events by rules limiting participation to party members.

The federal and state responsibilities for elections overlap each other a good deal, making it difficult to label any one area as exclusively "national" or "state." Often the federal and state governments work in concert to improve the nation's voting processes: this is exemplified by the Help America Vote Act, enacted in 2002 in the wake of the voting controversies during the 2000 presidential election contests. Among the law's provisions was the authorization of federal grants to states to phase out use of punch-card ballots, the source of delays in the final vote count in Florida that decided the 2000 election in favor of Republican George W. Bush.

Regulation of Parties

Except in the area of campaign finance, there is little regulation of political parties at the national level. Party regulation is largely a state function that varies considerably from state to state.

Introduction of the state-provided, secret Australian BALLOT TYPE in the late nineteenth century brought widespread changes in public policy toward parties, which until then had distributed their own ballots. The government ballots designated candidates by party labels, giving a justification for regulating what had been considered private organizations.

At first, however, regulation did not extend to the then-new mechanism of party primaries for the nomination of candidates. Under a 1921 Supreme Court ruling, primaries were internal affairs not subject to government interference. After the Court reversed itself in *United States v. Classic* (1941), more and more states required primary nominations, with significant effects for partisan politics.

Over the years, the Democratic and Republican national committees grew in staff size and influence, resulting in top-down changes in state laws on primaries. PRESIDENTIAL SELECTION REFORMS in the Democratic Party, particularly, affected state rules for the selection of delegates to the NATIONAL PARTY CONVENTIONS.

State regulations define party membership and eligibility to vote in *closed* primaries—those in which only party members can vote. According to the Center for the Study of the American Electorate at the American University in Washington, D.C., twenty-eight states plus the District of Columbia register voters by political party affiliation, in effect maintaining the parties' membership rolls.

States also determine ballot access, which may ensure a place on the general election ballot for major-party candidates but may require that new or THIRD PARTIES obtain large numbers of valid voters' signatures on petitions to be listed on the ballot.

Some state regulations help preserve the U.S. TWO-PARTY SYSTEM. For example, some states have SORE LOSER LAWS that prevent defeated primary candidates from running in the general election under another label. Some also permit prenomination PARTY ENDORSEMENTS of selected candidates, which tilt the primary or caucus playing field toward favorites of the party establishment. In a 1989 case, *Eu v. San Francisco Democratic Committee,* the Supreme Court invalidated California's attempt to prohibit parties from endorsing or opposing primary candidates.

Voter Registration

Registration of voters is the most important of the states' responsibilities in the regulation of elections. Maintenance of clean voting rolls free of fictitious or duplicate names, noncitizens, nonresidents, deceased persons, and persons under age eighteen is essential to the prevention of ELECTION FRAUD and loss of confidence in the electoral process.

Requirements for registration vary from state to state. Most states have a registration deadline well in advance of the election, but a few permit election day registration at the polls. One state, North Dakota, does not require prior registration for voting.

Although the states have wide discretion in setting the terms for voting, the federal government has imposed mandatory guidelines that affect some aspects of voter registration. The VOTING RIGHTS ACT of 1965 and its extensions, for example, barred LITERACY TESTS for voting and required federal clearance of election law changes in states where registration levels were below 50 percent. It also provided for federal monitors at the polls in low-registration states.

An Ohio citizen fills out her voter registration form at a county fair. State authorities are responsible for registering voters.

Source: AP Images/Jay LaPrete

The 1993 MOTOR VOTER ACT required states to provide voter registration forms and assistance at vehicle or driver registries, welfare bureaus, and other state offices serving large segments of the public.

Various constitutional amendments that originated in Congress also have limited states' rights in determining eligibility to vote. For example, the Fifteenth Amendment (1870) provided voting rights for all races, the Nineteenth Amendment (1920) gave the vote to women, the Twenty-fourth Amendment (1964) abolished POLL TAXES, and the Twenty-sixth Amendment (1971) lowered the voting age to eighteen.

Campaign Finance

Federal regulation of elections is confined mostly to the fund-raising aspect of candidates' campaigns in federal elections. The Bipartisan Campaign Reform Act (BCRA) of 2002, which superseded the Federal Elections Campaign Act of 1971 and its extensions, requires disclosure of contributions to presidential, House, and Senate campaigns. The law also limits contributions from individuals and POLITICAL ACTION COMMITTEES and sets spending limits for presidential campaigns that receive PUBLIC FINANCING. Spending for House and Senate campaigns is not limited in amounts but must be reported.

The law requires certain types of expenditures by state and local party committees to be reported to the FEDERAL ELECTION COMMISSION. The federal law takes precedence over state campaign finance laws regarding contributions from foreign nationals, who are barred from making gifts or expenditures in any U.S. election—federal, state, or local. The federal law also takes precedence over any state law affecting the financing of federal election campaigns.

One of the major changes was a ban on using unlimited and loosely regulated "soft money" contributions in campaigns for federal office. But the law allowed state parties to accept soft money contributions of up to $10,000 to cover the cost of voter registration and get-out-the-vote efforts, and states were allowed the authority to determine whether such contributions were to come only from individuals or from entities such as corporations and unions as well.

Ballots and Voting Methods

The states determine the types of ballots used and the methods by which the voters indicate their choices. The two most common types are the *party-column ballot* and the *office-group ballot*. In the former, all the candidates of one party are listed in the same column or row. This type discourages SPLIT-TICKET VOTING because a voter can vote a straight party ticket by pulling a single lever or marking a single block. The office-group ballot, used in more than half the states, lists candidates by the office being sought, which makes split-ticket voting easier.

Most states use VOTING MACHINES rather than paper ballots, or a combination of the two in which a computer "reads" the ballot fed into it and keeps a running tally of the votes. States may choose from a number of different systems, but those used in federal elections must meet standards set by the Federal Election Commission. States have increasingly adopted different forms of electronic voting technology, a trend accelerated by the problems with punch-card ballots in 2000.

Apportionment and Districting

The dual federal/state nature of U.S. elections also extends to the important task of apportioning seats in the House of Representatives and seats in state legislatures that are distributed on a population basis.

The CENSUS taken every ten years by the federal Census Bureau identifies population shifts among and within states, and the House of Representatives then reallocates its 435 seats on the basis of that information.

The legislatures then redraw the CONGRESSIONAL DISTRICT and state legislative district boundaries to make them as nearly equal as possible under the Supreme Court's ONE PERSON, ONE VOTE mandatory guidelines. Frequently there are partisan battles over redistricting, sometimes because of conflicting federal and state interests, and a few of these require court settlement. (See REAPPORTIONMENT AND REDISTRICTING.)

Another function of the Census Bureau is to estimate the size of the voting age population for each election, to help in measuring the VOTER TURNOUT as a percentage of those eligible to vote. Because voter registration rules differ from state to state, the Census Bureau does not try to calculate the national total of registered voters.

> **More on this topic:**
>
> *Campaign Finance, p. 53*
>
> *Motor Voter Act, p. 340*
>
> *Primary Types, p. 485*
>
> *Reapportionment and Redistricting, p. 517*
>
> *Voter Registration, p. 653*
>
> *Voting Rights Act, p. 663*

State Legislatures

The fifty state legislatures make up a fundamental building block of American DEMOCRACY, representing their constituencies on issues and concerns that range from local to national. If, as it has often been said, the states are the "laboratories of democracy," then the state legislatures are the places where policy ideas and proposals are first put to the test.

State legislatures deal with POCKETBOOK issues such as taxation, the allocation of state aid to schools, the building of public works, master plans and regional zoning questions, and the regulation of businesses. They also influence the overall future political design of the U.S. Congress and provide a political proving ground for many of future members of Congress.

Although the legislatures, with their long histories and established traditions, all face common problems of governance, they exhibit a wide range of differing characteristics. Among these differences is what the state legislative bodies call themselves. In Massachusetts and New Hampshire, for example, they call themselves the General Court. In other states they are the general assembly or the legislative assembly or, simply, the legislature.

In all but Nebraska, which has a UNICAMERAL legislature, there are so-called upper houses (always called senates) and lower houses, which go under varying titles including house of representatives, house of delegates, and assembly.

Most state legislatures are required to meet annually, though Texas has sessions scheduled only every other year. The pressure of state business often requires the Texas governor to call special sessions, however, and it is rare for an "off-year" to go by without the legislature meeting at some point.

Some states have established limits on the length of any legislative session. For example, Alabama restricts its annual session to thirty legislative days (days in which legislative business is transacted), which must all occur within 105 calendar days; in Virginia, the sessions last forty legislative days that must occur in January and February of odd years (when the state holds its legislative elections), and sixty days in even years. Other states stipulate that their legislatures conclude their business by a specific date.

Still others, mostly the larger states, have much longer sessions, presumably because of the complexity and continuing nature of their tasks. California, New York, and Pennsylvania, for example, convene year-round, with recesses and end-of-session adjournment dates set on an annual basis by the legislatures' leaders.

In terms of partisan politics, the distribution of the 7,382 state legislative seats tends to reflect trends in the overall electorate. Beginning with Franklin D. Roosevelt's first of four presidential election victories in 1932, the Democrats dominated congressional elections in most years and did the same in most state legislatures. The Republicans' big congressional surge in the 1994 elections, which gave the party control of the Senate and its first House majority in forty years, also produced big GOP gains in state legislatures.

States are often called the "laboratories of democracy."

The Republicans continued to make incremental gains until they emerged with a narrow majority of all seats after the 2002 elections, the first time that had happened in fifty years. The Democrats, however, made a small comeback in 2004 and then a much bigger one—which pushed them back into an overall majority—in 2006, an election year in which voter dissatisfaction with President George W. Bush and the Republican-controlled Congress also gave Democrats control of the U.S. Senate and House.

The 2010 elections gave Republicans a significant boost. Before election day that year, Democrats controlled both legislative chambers in twenty-seven states and Republicans were in the majority in fourteen, with eight states split. After the election, Democrats controlled both houses in just sixteen states while Republicans took full control in twenty-five. Eight state legislatures remained split. (One state, Nebraska, has a nonpartisan, unicameral legislature.) Moreover, Republican control at the state level was significantly enhanced by GOP gubernatorial victories in 2010. After the 2008 elections there were twenty-nine Democratic governors and twenty-one Republican. After the 2010 vote the number was almost exactly reversed: twenty-nine Republican governors and twenty Democrats, with one independent.

Party control of state legislatures is important to the federal government because state legislatures in most states are responsible for redrawing congressional and state legislative district lines after each national CENSUS, which occurs every ten years.

After the census is concluded, the national party organizations devote immense resources to persuading the state legislatures to approve congressional districting plans favorable to their interests. In the past, Democratic-dominated state legislatures have devised district plans that gave advantages to Democratic House candidates, making it difficult for Republicans to win.

Republican advances in the 1990s, however, particularly in the legislatures of the South and other "Sun Belt" states, helped the party—at least temporarily—reverse the situation.

It is possible, however, for one party to completely dominate the redistricting process and implement a one-sided partisan plan only if it controls both chambers of a legislature. If control is split, with the Democrats running one chamber and the Republicans the other, there are two possible outcomes: a compromise, usually an "incumbent protection" plan that ensures that each party will retain its current seats, or a stalemate that forces the legislature to cede its redistricting responsibility to another body (usually a state or federal court).

Texas experienced both sides of this equation during some unusually aggressive partisan maneuvering following the 2000 census. Prior to the 2002 elections, a state court panel had to draw the congressional district map because the legislature—a Republican-controlled senate and Democratic-controlled house—failed to agree on a plan. But the Republicans in 2002 won control of the state house as well and—in a highly unorthodox maneuver—performed a mid-decade redistricting prior to the 2004 elections, skewing the map heavily in favor of their party.

Legislators in most states also are empowered to redraw the districts for the state legislature itself. Many members, not surprisingly, put a high priority on protecting their own political interests. This kind of "self-interested" action has spurred calls from political reformers to turn at least state legislative redistricting over to commissions or other bipartisan or nonpartisan agencies.

Turnover rates for legislators vary greatly from state to state. In 2002, turnover was only 9 percent in the Pennsylvania house and 3 percent in the Massachusetts senate. The same year, turnover was 55 percent in the Arizona house and 35 percent in the New Hampshire house. In many of the larger states, the legislatures are populated by professional politicians whose primary business is government; in many of the smaller states with shorter legislative sessions, so-called citizen legislators serve and then return to their homes and businesses once the legislature's work is done.

Enactment of TERM LIMITS in twenty states between 1990 and 1995, with limits on service ranging from six to twelve years for house and senate members. As of 2011, term limits were in effect in fifteen states.

The first states to feel the impact of term limits were Maine and California, where many incumbents chose not to run for reelection or resigned their seats. In 1998, for example, nearly 25 percent of California's assembly members and senators were ineligible to run for reelection. Half the members of the 100-seat Arkansas house and sixty-seven of Michigan's 110 house members were ineligible to run. Michigan also illustrated the dramatic impact of term limits. In the three elections from 2006 through 2010, the entire house membership and 92 percent of the senate turned over due to limits.

Advocates of term limits contend that rotating members in and out with some frequency will encourage the election of more "citizen legislators," who they contend are more closely in touch with the views and concerns of the people and will prevent legislatures from being dominated by long-entrenched members. Opponents decry the loss of veteran members' expertise, warn that unelected staff members (who face no term limits) could gain inordinate power, and say term limits abrogate the right of voters to choose the representatives they prefer. Because the first of the term-limit laws took effect only in the late 1990s, it will likely take some time to settle the debate.

The states have no standard set of qualifications for candidates. Most require a period of residency, however. Age requirements vary widely, from eighteen in some states for candidates to both chambers, to thirty for some state senates. Most states have lower age limits for house candidates than for those running for seats in the upper house.

Many states set two-year terms for both chambers, with some preferring two-year terms for the lower house and four-year terms for the upper house. A handful elect members of both the lower and upper chambers to four-year terms. Some also require that half the senate membership stand for reelection every two years.

The legislatures themselves set their number of seats, and all seats are apportioned on the basis of population. In many states, the houses are twice as large as the senates, with senate districts equaling two house districts. The size of the bodies varies widely among the states. As might be expected, some of the less populous have the smallest

J. Strom Thurmond of South Carolina was the presidential candidate of the States' Rights Democratic Party in 1948. The party, also known as the Dixiecrats, broke away from the Democratic Party in a dispute over the Democrats' civil rights platform.

Source: CQ Photo

houses. As of 2011, Alaska, for example, had forty members; Delaware, forty-one; and Nevada, forty-two. But New Hampshire, a small state, has 400 members, far more than the next largest legislative chamber, the Pennsylvania house, with 203. Alaska, Delaware, and Nevada also have the smallest senate memberships.

Legislators in populous states have year-round staff serving them and their constituents at the capitol and at their district offices. As government's role in everyday life expands, state legislators have increasingly been called upon to intervene on behalf of constituents with state agencies, including welfare bureaus, motor vehicle agencies, and boards charged with determining unemployment and disability compensation.

Yet several studies have shown that constituents in many states are poorly informed about what their state legislators do, are not very interested in the legislature's business, and are somewhat cynical about how it does it. It is not uncommon for a voter not to know the name of his or her state senator or representative.

Compensation for state legislators spans a wide range. New Hampshire's 400 representatives are paid $200 for their two-year term, and as of 2007 California's legislators make about $113,000 annually. The larger states also reward the leadership positions in both houses (president of the senate, Speaker of the house) with extra pay and allowances.

More on this topic:

Reapportionment and Redistricting, p. 517

Unicameral, p. 640

States' Rights Democratic Party (1948)

The States' Rights Democratic Party was a conservative southern faction that bolted from the Democratic Party in 1948. The immediate reason for the new party, popularly known as the Dixiecrats, was dissatisfaction with President Harry S. Truman's proposed program to provide greater civil rights protections for the nation's black population. But the Dixiecrat effort to maintain a segregated way of life was also an attempt to demonstrate the political power of the twentieth-century southern Democrats and to reestablish their importance in the DEMOCRATIC PARTY.

The Mississippi Democratic Party's state executive committee met in Jackson in May 1948 to lay the groundwork for the Dixiecrat secession. The meeting called for a bolt by southern delegates if the Democratic National Convention endorsed Truman's civil rights program, which was nowhere as sweeping as the historic laws that would be enacted during the 1960s but was considered a break from the past in the late 1940s.

When the convention did approve a civil rights plank, the entire Mississippi delegation and half the Alabama delegation left the convention. Gov. Fielding L. Wright of Mississippi invited all anti-Truman delegates to meet in Birmingham three days after the close of the Democratic convention to select a states' rights ticket.

Most southern Democrats with something at stake—national prominence, seniority in Congress, patronage privileges—shunned the new Dixiecrat Party. The party's leaders came from the ranks of southern governors and other state and local officials. The Birmingham convention chose two governors to lead the party: J. Strom Thurmond of South Carolina for president and Fielding Wright of Mississippi for vice president.

Other than the presidential ticket, the Dixiecrats did not run candidates for any office. Rather than try to develop an independent party organization, the Dixiecrats, whenever possible, used existing Democratic Party apparatus.

The party was on the ballot in only one state outside the South and in the Novem-

As Republican National Committee chairman, in 1996 Haley Barbour approved rules changes to relieve congestion by giving bonus delegates to states that delay their primaries.
Source: CQ Photo/Scott J. Ferrell

ber election received 1,157,326 votes (2.4 percent of the popular vote), failing in its basic objective to prevent the reelection of Truman. Nonetheless, the Thurmond ticket carried four Deep South states where it ran under the Democratic Party label.

After the election the party ceased to exist almost as abruptly as it had begun, with most of its members returning, at least for a time, to the Democratic Party. In a statement upon reentering the Democratic fold, Thurmond characterized the Dixiecrat episode as "a fight within our family."

That perspective changed, with politically historic consequences, after the Democratic-controlled Congress, at the urging of President Lyndon B. Johnson, enacted a series of sweeping civil rights measures beginning with the Civil Rights Act of 1964. That same year, Thurmond quit the Democratic Party and joined the Republicans, giving southern legitimacy to a party largely shunned for a century in the region as the legacy of Abraham Lincoln. That action put Thurmond in the vanguard of a massive shift of conservative white voters to the Republican Party, ending the region's longstanding heritage as the Democrats' "Solid South."

Mostly forgotten to history by the early years of the twenty-first century, the defunct party flared to attention in December 2002, as Thurmond—about to retire from the Senate after more than forty-eight years of service—celebrated his one-hundredth birthday. At an event, Mississippi Republican Trent Lott, then the Senate majority leader, toasted Thurmond with the proclamation that if the nation had elected him president, "we wouldn't be in the mess we are today." Though Thurmond had years earlier abandoned segregationism and hired African American aides, Lott's comments were widely seen as an endorsement of the States' Rights Democratic Party's white supremacist platform.

After several attempts at public apology, Lott stepped down from his leadership post and was replaced by Tennessee Republican Bill Frist. But Frist's retirement and the Republicans' loss of their Senate majority in the 2006 election gave Lott an opportunity for a comeback, and he won the position of minority whip for the 110th Congress. Lott resigned his Senate seat in December 2007, halfway through the congressional session.

Straight-Ticket Voting *See* SPLIT- AND STRAIGHT-TICKET VOTING.

Straw Vote

One of the early types of preelection polls, the straw vote, got its name from the farmers' trick of throwing a handful of straw in the air to see which way the wind was blowing. For more than a century, newspaper and magazine straw polls were the leading predictors of major elections.

The first published presidential poll was in the *Harrisburg Pennsylvanian* on July 24, 1824. The publication's straw vote among people in Wilmington and Newark, Delaware, showed a preference for Andrew Jackson over John Quincy Adams. Jackson did win the popular vote but lost to Adams in the second presidential election decided by the U.S. House. (See PRESIDENT, NOMINATING AND ELECTING.)

In 1866 the *Cleveland Leader* reported that a straw vote taken on a train showed passengers favoring Congress over President Andrew Johnson in their conflicting views on Reconstruction. Two years later the conflict peaked when Johnson became the first president to be impeached.

By 1896 straw polling had become fairly scientific. For the presidential election that year, the *Chicago Tribune* polled railroad and factory workers and found 80 percent supporting Republican William McKinley over Democrat William Jennings Bryan, who had been expected to win the labor vote.

Another Chicago paper, the *Record,* conducted an even more scientific poll. It mailed ballots to all 300,000 registered voters in the city and, based on the responses, predicted McKinley would win in Chicago with 57.95 percent of the vote—matching almost exactly the actual vote of 57.91 percent.

Basically there were three ways to conduct a straw vote: by printing a ballot in the newspaper; mailing ballots to all registered voters or to a random sample of them, such as every twelfth voter; or sending canvassers into communities to have residents fill out ballots then and there. Of the three methods, the first was the least reliable because it was subject to ballot stuffing: people could buy extra papers and "vote" many times. Mailed ballots were safer but they could be counterfeited, and sometimes were. Personal canvassing was the most reliable method.

Newspapers became quite skilled in taking straw votes. Polls by the *Cincinnati Enquirer,* for example, mirrored actual results in presidential elections from 1908 to 1928.

The most famous straw poll, however, was by a magazine, the *Literary Digest,* and it did not end well.

The *Digest* began presidential polling in 1924 and gained a reputation for uncanny accuracy by correctly predicting that election and the next two, including Franklin D. Roosevelt's unexpected defeat of incumbent Herbert Hoover in 1932. But the *Digest* poll was a massive undertaking, requiring millions of ballot mailings. Even more problematic, the mailing list was derived mostly from telephone directories and motor vehicle registrations, which were unrepresentative of the U.S. population in the Great Depression year of 1936 because only the wealthier households had phones or cars. The *Digest* suffered a major embarrassment that year with its erroneous prediction that Kansas Republican governor Alfred M. Landon would unseat Roosevelt.

In the same election, a newcomer, George Gallup, gained credibility at the *Digest*'s expense with his prediction that Roosevelt would win a second term. Although Gallup underestimated Roosevelt's 60.8 percent vote—the biggest presidential LANDSLIDE up to that time—his methodology worked and his reputation was established.

The *Digest*'s wrong call was the beginning of the end for straw polls and the magazine itself. Not long after 1936 the *Literary Digest* went out of business.

Straw polls sometimes impact presidential aspirants seeking to become their party's nominee. Iowa Republicans have held a straw poll of potential candidates since 1979, in years when there is a contest, such as 2011. The poll often pushes aside weak candidates as occurred in August 2011 when former Minnesota governor Tim Pawlenty dropped out of the presidential race less than three months after entering it following a poor finish in an Iowa GOP straw poll. (See CAMPAIGN STRATEGIES.)

Succession *See* LIEUTENANT GOVERNOR; VICE PRESIDENT.

Suffrage *See* BLACK SUFFRAGE; RIGHT TO VOTE; WOMEN'S SUFFRAGE; YOUTH SUFFRAGE.

Super Tuesday

What began as basically a regional PRIMARY in the South came to fruition in 1988 after years of discussion. The same-day primary early in the nominating season quickly gained the unofficial name *Super Tuesday*.

Southern advocates of the idea hoped to draw some attention away from the first-in-the-nation NEW HAMPSHIRE PRIMARY by scheduling simultaneous primaries a few weeks after New Hampshire's. The main goal of the sponsors was to bring forth moderate presidential candidates of national stature who were from the South or were at least acceptable to southern voters.

The 1988 Super Tuesday, however, proved more helpful to liberal Democrats Michael Dukakis and Jesse Jackson than to any moderate or conservative southerners. The one southern Republican who had emerged as a contender, TV evangelist Pat Robertson, saw his candidacy collapse after a poor showing in Super Tuesday Republican primaries. Vice President George H. W. Bush, a Connecticut Yankee transplanted to Texas, did well on Super Tuesday and eventually won election as Ronald Reagan's successor.

Super Tuesday fell on March 8 in 1988, when fourteen southern or BORDER STATES held their presidential primaries. However, the northern states of Massachusetts and Rhode Island also held Super Tuesday primaries, and victories there boosted Dukakis's campaign for the Democratic nomination, which he ultimately won.

The high percentage of black voters among the Democrats who turned out for the southern primaries on Super Tuesday largely benefited Jackson, who outpolled Dukakis in eight of the fourteen southern and border state primaries. Although Al Gore of Tennessee and Richard Gephardt of Missouri won their own states, only Gore's overall Super Tuesday performances was impressive.

In 1992, with incumbent president Bush expected to overcome television commentator Patrick J. Buchanan's challenge to his renomination by the Republicans, the Democratic primaries provided most of the Super Tuesday suspense. Only eight states held primaries on March 10, and they again included Massachusetts and Rhode Island.

Having lost the New Hampshire primary to former senator Paul Tsongas of Massachusetts, Bill Clinton of Arkansas needed a big win on Super Tuesday. He got it, with victories in five of the eight contests, losing Massachusetts, Rhode Island, and Texas to Tsongas. Former California governor Jerry Brown, the runner-up to Clinton in the total 1992 Democratic primary vote, won none of the Super Tuesday primaries that year.

In 1996, Republican contests dominated the primaries scene because President Clinton faced only token opposition for renomination by the Democrats. Front-runner Bob Dole and several other GOP stalwarts competed for the party's nomination to oppose Clinton.

Super Tuesday was somewhat upstaged, however, by a newcomer: JUNIOR TUESDAY Week, thirteen primaries or caucuses held March 2–9, mostly in the Northeast. Four of the original 1988 Super Tuesday states—Georgia, Maryland, Massachusetts, and Rhode Island—moved their 1996 primaries up to Junior Tuesday Week. With all but one (New Hampshire) of the six New England states participating, Junior Tuesday, March 5, became largely a regional primary.

Six other of the original participants—Florida, Louisiana, Mississippi, Oklahoma, Tennessee, and Texas—stayed with Super Tuesday, March 12. They were joined by Oregon. The two remaining original participants—Missouri and Virginia—did not hold presidential primaries.

Although Dole lost the February 20 New Hampshire primary to Buchanan, he quickly regained front-runner status with a sweep of all the Junior Tuesday Week contests. Two of Dole's rivals, former Tennessee governor Lamar Alexander and Sen. Richard G. Lugar of Indiana, dropped out.

The following week, Dole repeated his success, taking all of the southern-oriented Super Tuesday contests. With Dole appearing unstoppable, one of his last remaining rivals, publishing magnate Malcolm S. "Steve" Forbes Jr., withdrew. By March 26, after victories in the Midwest and California, Dole had clinched the Republican nomination. Buchanan nevertheless stayed in the race.

Both Super Tuesday and Junior Tuesday were part of a phenomenon known as FRONT-LOAD-ING or "March Madness"—the rush among states to hold their primaries as early as possible and help to determine the ultimate nominees.

Some political analysts and party leaders viewed the trend with dismay. They said it could lead to nominees' being locked in before most voters knew what was happening, resulting in less-informed and less-deliberative voting in the general election.

Under Barbour's leadership, the 1996 GOP convention approved rules changes to relieve the congestion by giving bonus delegates to states that delay their primaries, beginning in 2000. But California, the most populous state, did not find the bonus enticing. It moved up its 2000 primary to March 7, the same as New York and several New England states, and one week before Super Tuesday.

Front-loading continued to accelerate in 2004, when the Democrats staged a crowded contest to choose the challenger to President George W. Bush, who was virtually unopposed on the

Republican side. There was a Super Tuesday on March 2, which included nominating events in ten states across the nation—California, New York, Ohio, Georgia, Massachusetts, Maryland, Minnesota, Connecticut, Rhode Island, and Vermont. But several states had leapfrogged Super Tuesday to join the traditional campaign kickoff events, the Iowa caucuses and New Hampshire primary, in the earliest part of the schedule. By Super Tuesday, Massachusetts senator John Kerry had already developed strong momentum with a series of early victories, and his near-sweep on Super Tuesday effectively clinched his nomination.

In 2008 this broad virtual national primary occurred on February 5, a month earlier, when sixteen states held primaries. Six more states held primaries later that month, making February the key month in the 2008 presidential primary season.

> **More on this topic:**
>
> *Border States, p. 34*
>
> *Front-Loading, p. 219*
>
> *New Hampshire Primary, p. 369*
>
> *Primary Types, p. 485*
>
> *Voter Turnout, p. 656*

Superdelegate

Also known as an automatic delegate, a superdelegate is an elected or appointed official who attends the Democratic NATIONAL PARTY CONVENTION as a formally unpledged DELEGATE by virtue of a leadership position. The Republican Party does not use superdelegates.

PRESIDENTIAL SELECTION REFORMS in the Democratic Party after the 1968 election, when Hubert H. Humphrey won the party's nomination without entering any PRIMARY contests, almost totally excluded party leaders from meaningful participation at the conventions of 1972, 1976, and 1980, years that produced lopsided general election defeats for the Democrats. Some in the party felt that the reforms, which shifted delegate selection entirely to the primary and CAUCUS system, had gone too far. They lobbied for bringing the leadership back into the nominating process.

In response, the Hunt Commission, one of several Democratic rules revision committees in the 1970s and 1980s, proposed creation of the superdelegate category in 1984. But the party insiders who automatically receive or are picked for the superdelegate slots quickly showed that they would tend to support the leading candidate of the party establishment, who was usually the front-running candidate in the primaries and caucuses as well, with results that would not necessarily turn out any better at the polls.

At the 1984 party convention, 568 superdelegates cast about 14 percent of the ballots. They voted overwhelmingly for Walter F. Mondale, a former Minnesota senator and the one-term vice president under Jimmy Carter, to oppose Republican president Ronald Reagan, who had easily defeated the Carter-Mondale ticket in 1980. Without his 450 superdelegate votes, Mondale would have fallen short of the convention majority that gave him the nomination on the first ballot over Colorado senator Gary Hart and civil rights activist Jesse L. Jackson. Mondale went on to lose in a historic landslide to Reagan, carrying only his home state of Minnesota and the District of Columbia.

In 1988 Jackson, who emerged as the strongest competitor to the front-running candidate, Massachusetts governor Michael S. Dukakis, complained that superdelegate votes at the convention cost him some of the states he had won in primaries. Although Dukakis won the nomination, the convention Rules Committee recommended fewer superdelegates in the future.

Instead, after Dukakis lost the election that November to Republican George H.W. Bush, Reagan's two-term vice president, the party added more superdelegates, raising the proportion of superdelegates to about 16 percent of the delegate total in 1988 and 18 percent in 1992 and 1996—campaigns in which Democratic nominee Bill Clinton went on to win his two White House terms. The superdelegates included 80 percent of the Democratic members of Congress, all Democratic governors, Democratic National Committee members, and state party chairs and vice chairs.

> **More on this topic:**
>
> *Delegates, p. 142*
>
> *National Party Conventions, p. 347*
>
> *Primary Types, p. 485*

The proportion remained fairly constant through the 2000 convention that nominated two-term vice president Al Gore and the 2004 convention that picked Massachusetts senator John Kerry, both of whom lost to Republican George W. Bush. The 802 superdelegates at the 2004 convention in Boston amounted to 18.6 percent of the total 4,322 delegates. In 2008 about 20 percent of the 4,440 attending were superdelegates when the convention by acclamation nominated Barack Obama for president.

Republicans traditionally have selected party leaders as nominating convention delegates, making it unnecessary for them to have a counterpart to the Democrats' superdelegate category.

Swing District *See* CONGRESSIONAL DISTRICT.

Swing Voter *See* REALIGNMENTS AND DEALIGNMENTS.

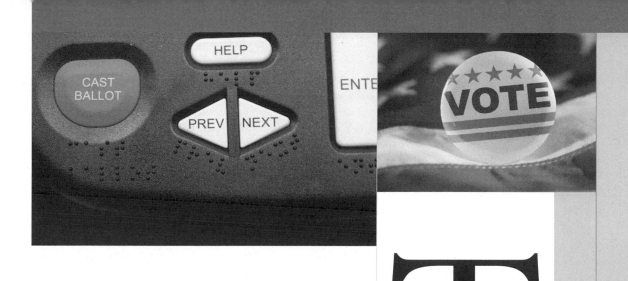

Tea Party

The Tea Party, a loosely organized movement dedicated to advocating a strongly ideological approach to political conservatism, emerged on the American political scene just months after Barack Obama won the 2008 election to succeed Republican George W. Bush as president and his Democratic Party expanded its majorities in both chambers of Congress. The link between these events was not accidental and contributed to a stark contrast between widely differing views of the purpose of governmental activity.

The movement that became known as the Tea Party was not a political party in the historical sense of organized groups of individuals, such as Democrats or Republicans and the many third parties of American history, that sought to gain control of governmental institutions. Rather, the movement was a composite of a widely dispersed collection of small groups without a single clear leadership or structure.

Many of the activists who came to the fore as leading Tea Party spokespersons described it as an organic and spontaneous protest movement against a variety of perceived intrusions on individual liberty, ranging from high taxes and spending to governmental restrictions on personal conduct and property rights to regulations on business activities, which many Tea Party subscribers believed were hurting American job opportunities. The Tea Party arose as a backlash against this picture of "big government" that its members identified with Obama and the Democratic Party.

That did not mean that the Tea Party was apolitical and not mainly associated with the interests of one national political party, the Republicans. In fact, the energy and enthusiasm that the movement generated among the Republican Party's strongly conservative voter base helped the GOP rebound from its own big setbacks in the 2006 and 2008 election cycles. The candidates for election in 2010 who either emerged from the nascent Tea Party movement or chose to associate themselves with it nearly all ran on the Republican Party line, and a number of the newly elected Republicans who helped their party reclaim control of the House and cut deeply into the Democrats' Senate majority were so-called "Tea Party candidates." Overall, Tea Party activists succeeded in nationalizing the 2010 elections by making it a referendum on the president and his Democratic allies in Congress even though Obama was not on any ballot.

Nevertheless, the Tea Party was different from just another party faction in that many of its adherents, though fueled by outrage at the Democratic Party, also were angry with members of the Republican Party establishment who they believed had been insufficiently faithful to conservative principles, especially on matters related to public spending and the size of government. The Tea Party tomented serious primary challenges not only against some of the already greatly diminished group of moderate Republicans in Congress and other offices, but also against some incumbents who had long been viewed as GOP stalwarts but who those in the Tea Party accused of being "big government conservatives."

This approach turned out to have mixed results at the polls in 2010. For example, in Utah, a state with strongly conservative and Republican voting tendencies, the Republican Party denied renomination to three-term Sen. Robert F. Bennett and instead chose lawyer Mike Lee, a candidate with close ties to the Tea Party who went on to an easy victory. But in Democratic-leaning Delaware, the nomination of Tea Party favorite Christine O'Donnell over longtime Rep. Michael N. Castle, one of the most moderate Republicans in Congress, proved disastrous for the party's hopes of defeating Democrat Chris Coons in the race for the Senate seat that had long been held by Democrat Joseph R. Biden Jr. until he was elected as vice president on Obama's 2008 ticket. In Nevada, a Tea Party favorite, Sharron Angle, won the nomination to challenge incumbent Sen. Harry Reid in a race observers thought the GOP could win. But she too went down to defeat. The name of the movement came from the American Revolutionary period event known as the Boston Tea Party in which colonials in 1773, protesting a British tax on tea, dumped boxes of British tea from ships in Boston harbor. By most accounts, the modern Tea Party got its start in early 2009, in Washington and New York states, when small groups of individuals gathered—often in private homes—to protest among themselves about the state of political affairs in the nation, although at that early time the name "Tea Party" had not yet attached to the movement. The movement began to galvanize and gain political momentum following a series of rallies that were timed to coincide with the April 15, 2009, deadline for most Americans to file their 2008 income tax returns.

As word of these events spread, similar groupings formed nationwide, but without overarching organization or formal links that continued even as the movement gained greater notoriety through 2010 and into 2011. Moreover, no single political leader emerged as a principal spokesperson, consistent with the view of most local Tea Party groups that it was not a political party in the traditional sense. Nevertheless, a few prominent Republicans, most notably Sarah Palin, the GOP vice presidential nominee in 2008, and—later—Texas governor Rick Perry, were often noted enthusiastically by many Tea Party supporters.

By summer of 2011, with the Tea Party's influence looming increasingly large in the Republican Party's early sorting out of candidates to be the 2012 presidential nominee, the movement had become one of most intensely studied—and commented on—phenomena since the 1992 emergence of billionaire H. Ross Perot as an independent candidate for president. Perot, whose folksy idiosyncrasies attracted a following in a year when voters were also highly dissatisfied with the nation's political establishment, won almost 20 percent of the national vote although no electoral votes.

These examinations of the Tea Party, including journalists' shoe-leather reporting, sophisticated polling by news organizations and established research organizations, and academic papers from political scientists, showed an increasingly clear portrait of the movement: like-minded individuals of shared political outlook, deeply conservative, and largely aligned with the Republican Party, thereby driving the GOP's political orientation.

The portrait was succinctly described by researchers at the Gallup Organization who—following three separate national polls in the first half of 2010—concluded there was a "significant overlap" between Tea Party advocates and individuals who identify themselves as conservative Republicans. The Gallup researchers said the Tea Party "is more a rebranding of core Republicanism than a new or distinct entity on the American political scene."

This conclusion was shared by numerous others who looked closely at the Tea Party. Academic papers written late in 2011 by several political scientists said the movement sat comfortably within existing ideological trends in the nation that had been shaping political debate for some years. Rather than reflecting a spontaneous and unique development, the Tea Party gave a handy label to a part of the Republican Party that had long shared similar and exceptionally conservative views.

Polling data reinforced this conclusion. Gallup Organization polls from early 2010 showed 62 percent of Tea Party supporters also were conservative Republicans, compared with 29 percent of all Americans. By contrast, just 17 percent of moderate to liberal Republicans were Tea Party supporters, compared with 15 percent of all Americans. Overall, Gallup found, about 80 percent of Tea Party supporters were Republicans, compared with 44 percent of all national adults.

Although polling results from different organizations varied in detail, they all painted roughly the same demographic, social, and political picture of the movement's supporters: older, white, married, very conservative, and often deeply religious. Polling by CBS News and the *New York Times* in 2010 showed that three-quarters of Tea Party supporters were over age forty-five and nearly 30 percent over sixty-five. About 59 percent were male and about 89 percent white. More were found in the South than other regions (more than a third) and were more likely to have a college education (37 percent compared with a quarter of the overall population). In addition, the CBS/*Times* poll showed them relatively well off economically, with 35 percent having annual income of $50,000 or more and one in five more than $100,000. The national median income in 2010—the exact midpoint of the income range—was $49,445.

Some polling data also supported the belief that racial resentment was present in the attitude of staunch Tea Party advocates, reinforced by the election of Obama, the first African American president, and growing concern about immigration. The data prompted one scholar, Gary Jacobson of the University of California, San Diego, to observe that although many Tea Party views on issues were not "intrinsically racist," nevertheless "it is clear that the movement is more appealing to people who are unsympathetic to blacks and who prefer a harder line on illegal immigration than it is to other Americans."

The issues that gave rise to the Tea Party's prominence in 2009 and later were well-known political, economic, and social conflicts that had confounded both political parties in the 2000s and earlier. One was health care, represented by the legislation Obama and congressional allies enacted in 2010 that was one of the most controversial issues throughout the 2009–2010 election cycle. Another was government spending and debt, which included federal taxation (although in some surveys a substantial number of Tea Party advocates said they thought their tax bills were fair). Other important issues driving the Tea Party view included unemployment and the tenuous recovery from the deep recession that started in 2007, and various social issues including abortion and same-sex marriage. An overarching theme that polls showed motivated Tea Party anger was

Former Alaska governor Sarah Palin speaks at a tax day Tea Party rally on April 16, 2011, in Madison, Wisconsin. (AP Photo/Morry Gash)

Source: AP Images/Morry Gash

the perceived extensive role of the federal government in the daily life of everyday Americans.

Surveys and interviews by news reporters showed a repeated use of the word "anger" to describe Tea Party attitudes toward much of the political establishment. (A *New York Times* correspondent who wrote a book about her reporting on the Tea Party called it *Boiling Mad: Inside Tea Party America*.) The CBS/*Times* poll reported that 53 percent of supporters said they were angry about developments in Washington and the conduct of politicians. Much of that was directed toward Obama. At the time of the poll in 2010, 88 percent disapproved of his job performance.

Term Limits

The president, the GOVERNOR in most states, and executive officials in many local governments are limited to a fixed number of terms in office—most commonly, two four-year terms. The limits, most of which were enacted in the twentieth century, reflected a widespread popular concern with allowing a single individual to gain too much power in office over time, or to stay in office past the point at which he or she is politically effective.

A wave of public dissatisfaction with the governments in Washington, D.C., and in some state capitals sparked a strong movement in the 1990s to impose term limits on STATE LEGISLATORS and members of Congress. Republican leaders adopted the term limit issue in 1994 and included a pledge to pursue legislation capping congressional terms in their "Contract with America" campaign platform in their successful effort to end forty consecutive years of Democratic control in the U.S. House.

"Along the way, I was able to figure out that it was a mistake, and it was tantamount to unilateral disarmament. So I won't repeat that mistake. . . . I won't be announcing my departure before I get there."

—Rep. Bob Inglis (R-S.C.), during his successful 2004 campaign to return to the U.S. House. Inglis pledged to serve no more than three terms when he first won a House seat in 1992 and stuck to his promise in 1998, when he left to stage an unsuccessful bid for the Senate.

Voters in twenty-three states approved ballot measures to impose such limits, but that turned out to be the movement's peak. The Supreme Court in 1995 invalidated the congressional term limits by ruling that they could be enacted only by an amendment to the U.S. Constitution. And as the Republicans settled into the House majority, the efforts to limit members' service lost momentum.

Many states enacted term limits for state legislators, most during the period of ferment in the 1990s, but several states subsequently dropped their limits. For example, the Utah legislature revoked the state's term limits for legislators by law in 2003. Court rulings invalidated state legislative term limits in Massachusetts, Wyoming, and the state of Washington. According to the National Conference of State Legislatures, fifteen of the fifty states had state legislative term limits in effect as of mid-2011. Advocates said the idea of term limits—or "rotation in office"—had historical precedents in ancient Greece and Rome, the Renaissance city-states of Florence and Venice, and at least three of the American colonies. The Articles of Confederation included a provision limiting delegates to the Continental Congress to three years in office over a six-year period.

An early draft of the Constitution also included a tenure limitation for members of what was to become the House of Representatives, but the provision was dropped without dissent or debate. Alexander Hamilton also persuaded the delegates to the Constitutional Convention not to require rotation for the presidency. Anti-Federalists complained about the lack of a rotation provision in their unsuccessful effort to prevent ratification of the Constitution.

Despite the lack of mandatory tenure restrictions, voluntary retirement from federal office was common through the nineteenth century. George Washington unintentionally established a precedent by voluntarily stepping down from the presidency after completing his second four-year term; Franklin D. Roosevelt in the 1940s was the only president in history to seek a third and then fourth term. Turnover in Congress was high through the 1800s, above 40 percent for the House in most years.

Longer congressional careers became more common in the twentieth century. The national government had only limited impact on day-to-day life in the country before 1900. But the rise of the federal administrative state and the emergence of the United States as a major military and diplomatic power made Washington a much more important place for Congress and president alike. Vast improvements in transportation also facilitated congressional careerism by making it much easier for members to maintain both a family life and direct contact with their constituents back home.

> ## CLOSER LOOK ◉
>
> These fifteen states had limited state legislators to the following maximum tenures as of mid-2011, according to the National Conference on State Legislatures:
>
> Six years in the state house or assembly, eight years in the state senate:
> Arkansas, California, Michigan
>
> Eight years in the unicameral legislature:
> Nebraska (the only state with just one legislative chamber)
>
> Eight years in the statehouse or assembly, eight years in the state senate:
> Arizona, Colorado, Florida, Maine, Missouri, Montana, Ohio, South Dakota
>
> Twelve years in the statehouse or assembly, twelve years in the state senate:
> Louisiana, Nevada, Oklahoma

Presidents' Two-Term Limit

Congress had always been discontented with the Constitution's failure to restrict the number of presidential terms. From 1789 to 1947, 270 resolutions to limit the president's tenure had been introduced in the House and Senate, sixty of them since 1928. But the Roosevelt years added a partisan dimension to this long-standing concern.

Roosevelt's decision to seek a third term in the White House in 1940 was controversial despite his personal popularity. He won reelection that year and then again in 1944 but died in April 1945 only a few months into his fourth term.

After his death, Republicans in Congress began advocating a constitutional amendment to limit the president to two four-year terms. In 1947, the Republican-controlled Congress approved the proposal by substantial majorities: 285–121 in the House and 59–23 in the Senate. All of the votes against the amendment in each chamber came from Democrats. After three years and eleven months, the requisite three-fourths of the states had ratified the amendment, and it was added as the Twenty-second Amendment on February 27, 1951. (Only the Twenty-seventh Amendment, concerning congressional pay raises, took longer to ratify.)

Because so few presidents have served even two full terms since the Twenty-second Amendment was enacted, its effects on the modern presidency are difficult to measure. As the incumbent, Roosevelt's successor, Harry S. Truman, was exempt from the amendment but declined to seek a second full term in 1952.

John Kennedy was assassinated in the third year of the one term to which he was elected in 1960. His successor, Lyndon B. Johnson, was eligible to run for two full terms on his own. But Johnson's political unpopularity in 1968, largely over his Vietnam War policy, led him to abandon his attempt to win a second full term.

Richard M. Nixon was elected to a second full term in 1972, but his role in the Watergate SCANDAL forced him to resign less than two years later. Gerald R. Ford served more than half of Nixon's second term, which limited Ford to only one elected term as president. But Ford failed to win even that. The candidate who defeated him in 1976, Jimmy Carter, was defeated in turn by Ronald Reagan in 1980; he served two full terms.

As this campaign button reflects, Franklin Roosevelt's decision to seek an unprecedented third term in office was controversial. It led to the passage of the Twenty-second Amendment, which limited presidents to two four-year terms.

Source: Courtesy of Christopher Schardt

Reagan's successor, George H. W. Bush, served one term but lost in 1992 to Bill Clinton. A third term for Clinton, even if allowed, would have been an unlikely prospect; his second term was marred by his impeachment by the Republican-controlled U.S. House for lying under oath about a sex scandal, and he remained politically tainted even though he was acquitted in a 1999 Senate trial.

His successor, George W. Bush, also won twice, in 2000 and 2004, but his prospects for a third term would likely have been grim as well. His plunging job approval ratings, caused largely by the growing unpopularity of the war in Iraq, contributed to the Republicans' loss of their majorities in both chambers of Congress in the 2006 midterm elections.

Other presidents have proposed that the holder of the office be limited to a single term of six years. Advocates, including Andrew Jackson in the early nineteenth century and Johnson and Carter in the second half of the twentieth century, claimed that a single six-year term would free the president from the political pressures of reelection and grant the administration more time to accomplish its long-term goals. Opponents noted that under a six-year term an unpopular president would serve two more years than under the current system, and a popular president, two fewer years. Another argument was that the president would in effect be a LAME DUCK for the full six years, rather than only in the second term as is now the case.

CLOSER LOOK

As of 2011, two popular two-term Republican presidents have felt the pinch of the presidential term limit. After leaving office, Dwight D. Eisenhower backed a change to three terms. Ronald Reagan, reelected in a 1984 landslide, had a large contingent of loyalists who bemoaned the fact that he could not run for a third term in 1988. Reagan himself, during his second term, campaigned for repeal of the limit, although in a way that would not have applied to him: he argued that the voters should be able to extend a future president's tenure for as long as they liked. But no serious move was made to lift the term limit then or has been made since.

Proposed Congressional Limits

During debate on the Twenty-second Amendment, one senator offered an alternative to limit both the president and members of Congress to a single six-year term. It failed, 82–1. But support for term limits for members of Congress began to emerge after ratification of the amendment. President Truman endorsed twelve-year limits for lawmakers in 1951. Public opinion polls found increasing support for the idea: a plurality of 49 percent favored the idea in a 1964 survey; polls in 1977 and 1981 found 59 percent majorities in support.

Congress finally gave the idea official attention in the late 1970s. Lawmakers from both major parties introduced a flurry of constitutional amendments aimed at increasing congressional effectiveness either by limiting tenure, increasing House terms to four years, or both. A Senate judiciary subcommittee held hearings on the term-limit issue in 1978, but no further action was taken.

Republicans took up the issue in the 1980s, in part out of frustration with the Democrats' dominance of Congress since the 1950s. The Republican Party platform in 1988 called for limiting congressional terms. A year later, two Republican political consultants created a national term-limits group. Two more national groups were formed in 1990. In the same year, voters in three states—California, Colorado, and Oklahoma—approved measures to limit the tenure of state lawmakers. The Colorado measure also included a provision to limit members of the state's congressional delegation to twelve years in office.

The Colorado proposal became the model for congressional term limit measures in other states. Supporters campaigned for the proposals by contending that long-term members of Congress lost touch with constituents and abused their positions by approving dubious "pork-barrel" spending to benefit their states or districts. They also argued that term limits would make congressional elections more competitive, noting that the reelection rate of members of Congress since the end of World War II had been high—above 90 percent for House members. Opponents responded that the proposals would restrict voter choice, deprive Congress of its most experienced and knowledgeable members, and weaken Congress vis-à-vis the president.

Through 1994, term limit supporters won approval of measures to restrict congressional tenure in twenty-two states; state legislators were also term-limited in all but two of those states. All but one of the congressional term limit measures were contained in ballot INITIATIVES approved by voters; most were approved by substantial majorities of more than 60 percent. The earlier measures imposed twelve-year limits on members of the House or the Senate; later measures tightened the tenure restriction for House members to six years.

The term limits issue also appeared to influence the outcome of several individual races for Congress in November 1994. Republican candidates for the House included congressional term limits as part of their ten-point "Contract with America."

Republicans recaptured control of both houses of Congress in the election, for the first time since the 1952 election. GOP candidates also defeated a number of prominent, long-serving Democrats, including the Speaker of the House, Thomas R. Foley of the state of Washington, who had been a vocal opponent of his own state's congressional term limits.

Rep. Helen Chenoweth-Hage of Idaho, here with Sen. Larry Craig, left Congress in 2000 when her eight-year self-imposed term limit came to an end.

Despite the popular support for term limits, the Democratic-controlled Congress refused to act on the issue prior to the 1994 election. A House judiciary subcommittee held hearings in 1993 and 1994, but proposals for a constitutional amendment on the issue were not brought to a vote. In addition, members of Congress and citizens' groups opposed to congressional term limits filed suits against the measures in two of the states: Washington and Arkansas. They contended that the states had no power to add to the qualifications for serving in Congress established in Article I of the Constitution: a minimum age, U.S. citizenship, and state residency for a specified period of time. (See HOUSE OF REPRESENTATIVES, QUALIFICATIONS; SENATE, QUALIFICATIONS.)

The Supreme Court ruled on the issue in 1995 in the Arkansas case, *U.S. Term Limits Inc. v. Thornton.* In a 5–4 decision on May 22, the Court held that the states indeed had no power to change the qualifications for serving in Congress. "Allowing individual States to adopt their own qualifications for congressional service would be inconsistent with the framers' vision of a uniform National Legislature representing the people of the United States," Justice John Paul Stevens wrote for the majority.

Writing for the four dissenters, Justice Clarence Thomas responded: "Nothing in the Constitution deprives the people of each State of the power to prescribe eligibility requirements for the candidates who seek to represent them in Congress."

The ruling was the year's second blow to the term-limits movement. In March, the House

Thomas R. Foley, Democrat of Washington, was the first sitting Speaker of the House to lose a reelection bid in 134 years.

Source: CQ Photo/Michael Jenkins

had brought four separate term-limit constitutional amendments to a vote, but each one fell well short of the two-thirds majority required for approval. After the Supreme Court ruling, supporters vowed to continue their efforts to elect members of Congress committed to voting for term limits. But at a news conference on the day of the ruling, Foley said he believed the term limit issue was dead.

Several congressional incumbents and successful candidates, most of them Republicans, took self-imposed term limit pledges during this period. While a few stuck to these pledges, most gradually retracted them, saying that their self-removal from Congress would amount to "unilateral disarmament" for their districts in a legislative process driven heavily by members' seniority. Some said they had learned only after they became lawmakers how much time and seniority was necessary to make an impact in Congress. And although voters in national polls had expressed strong generic support for term limits, the issue turned out to

 CLOSER LOOK

The decline in political salience of the congressional term limits issue after a peak in the early 1990s can be seen in the case of Republican George Nethercutt of Washington's Fifth Congressional District, who took a three-term-and-out pledge prior to his election in 1994. One of the reasons Nethercutt upset the incumbent, House Speaker Tom Foley, in the 1994 GOP upsurge was that voters decided Foley had served too long after thirty years in office. But in 2000, Nethercutt broke his pledge and ran for a fourth term. "I made a mistake when I chose to set a limit on my service," he said in 1999. "The work I've done will not be finished by the end of this term." Despite outrage from former allies in the term limits movement and the label of "Weasel King" thrust on him by Doonesbury cartoonist Garry Trudeau, Nethercutt easily won reelection—an experience shared by other members who backed away from term limit pledges. After winning again in 2002, Nethercutt in 2004 lost a challenge to Democratic senator Patty Murray; the term limit flap played little role in the outcome.

More on this topic:

House of Representatives, Qualifications, p. 256
Initiatives and Referendums, p. 270
Scandals, p. 560
Senate, Qualifications, p. 582
State Legislatures, p. 609

be a low priority in their actual voting behavior as incumbents who backed off on a term limit continued to be reelected.

The limits on state lawmakers, however, remained on the books in most states that had imposed them and began to force the retirement of veteran legislators in many states. Supporters claimed the term-limit measures were resulting in increased electoral competition, but opponents disagreed and instead claimed the measures were weakening state legislatures.

Terms of Office *See* ELECTION CYCLE IN AMERICA.

Third Parties

The TWO-PARTY SYSTEM is one of the most prominent features of the political process in the United States. Since the 1850s, American elections have been defined by the competition between the Democratic Party and the Republican Party.

Yet the two parties—even though they each encompass a range of ideological viewpoints—at times engender opposition from political activists and average voters who contend their views are not represented by the Democrats and the Republicans. This sentiment has spawned the development of numerous alternative parties, generically known as *third parties* because they exist outside the boundaries of the two major parties.

In the early years of the United States, new parties emerged and had a major impact on the political system. The Republican Party was born as an antislavery third party in the 1850s, as an alternative to the Democratic Party, home to the most fervent defenders of the southern institution of slavery, and the Whig Party, a coalition of proslavery and antislavery forces that was doomed to failure.

But most third parties, even those that have developed a long-standing presence on ballots across the country, have developed relatively tiny followings, have elected few members to public offices, and are seen mainly as potential "spoilers" that can take enough votes from major-party candidates to deny them victory in very close elections. Some early twenty-first-century examples are the Libertarian Party, which takes personal liberty positions on social and national security associated with liberal activists but government spending and regulation positions that reflect the views of hard-line conservatives; the Constitution Party, which holds to a strictly conservative agenda; and the Green Party, which has a strongly liberal agenda.

The most ballyhooed true third-party candidacy in recent years, liberal activist Ralph Nader's bid as the Green Party nominee in the 2000 presidential election, is illustrative. Nader received just 2.7 percent of the national popular vote, but the numbers of votes he won in a pair of states, Florida and New Hampshire, exceeded the victory margin of Republican George W. Bush over Democrat Al Gore. Had Gore won either of those states, he would have been the victor in the Electoral College rather than Bush. It is

Sen. Joseph Lieberman of Connecticut appears at a news conference with Sen. Susan Collins of Maine. Despite losing the Democratic primary in his state, Lieberman won the 2006 Senate election on an independent ticket.

Source: CQ Photo/Scott J. Ferrel

not clear, though, whether all or most of the Nader voters would have backed Gore had Nader not been in the contest, and Nader has adamantly denied being a spoiler, contending that he also took votes from Bush.

By 2010 a new quasi-organization emerged, known as the TEA PARTY. However, it was not a true political party, in the traditional sense they have existed in the United States, with a formal structure, acknowledged leaders, a platform addressing a variety of issues, and candidates running under its name. Rather, the Tea Party was an amorphous movement closely linked to the most conservative elements in the Republican Party. Its energy and the outspoken opinions of its most vocal advocates gave it outsized influence in the 2010 voting and helped bring a net gain of sixty-three new Republicans to the House, allowing the GOP to regain control of the chamber.

For the most part third parties, lacking the name recognition, financial resources, and media attention enjoyed by the Democrats and the Republicans, have faced a losing cause.

No INDEPENDENT or third-party candidate has ever won the presidency; even George Washington, elected to two terms by near acclamation as the nation's first president, was associated with the Federalist Party. Only twice since 1832 have third parties or independents won more than 20 percent of the POPULAR VOTE in presidential elections. Eight times they have won 10 percent or more, most recently in 1992.

The most successful alternative parties were short-lived institutions built around a single issue or the personality of an individual with which the party or movement was identified. In 1912 former Republican president Theodore Roosevelt, running on the PROGRESSIVE—Bull Moose—Party line, became the only third-party candidate to date to finish ahead of a major-party candidate. He came in second, behind Democrat Woodrow Wilson and ahead of Republican incumbent William Howard Taft.

A pair of parties in the mid-twentieth century represented a backlash of conservative southern whites against the movement for black civil rights: the States' Rights Democratic Party, which nominated J. Strom Thurmond of South Carolina in 1948, and the American Independent Party, which was the vehicle for Alabama's George Wallace in 1968. Both won southern electoral votes in those elections but quickly faded as the principal figures in both parties rejoined major-party politics.

Similarly, billionaire H. Ross Perot's quirky personality and criticisms of politics as usual played a major role in the unusual success of his independent candidacy in the 1992 presidential election. Perot tried to leverage that support by running in the 1996 election as the nominee of the newly formed Reform Party, but he did less than half as well as in 1992 and soon abandoned the effort.

Yet despite the odds, third-party and independent candidates do on occasion win elections, and sometimes for high offices below the presidential level. Vermont has been especially fertile ground for this in recent years. In 2006, Bernard Sanders, who won eight terms in the House as an independent, was elected to the Senate to succeed retiring incumbent James M. Jeffords, who had

STORMING THE CASTLE

This 1860 cartoon shows two of the top vote-winning third-party candidates, Southern Democrat John C. Breckinridge and Constitutional Union candidate John Bell. Bell warns Stephen Douglas of Abraham Lincoln's approach, while James Buchanan tries, without success, to help Breckinridge enter the White House.

Source: Library of Congress

quit the Republican Party in 2001 to become an independent but never ran for office on a third-party line.

One of the most unusual third-party success stories also occurred during the 2006 Senate campaign. Connecticut senator Joseph I. Lieberman, who just six years earlier was the Democratic vice presidential nominee on the ticket with Gore, had angered many Democratic activists with his outspoken support of U.S. military intervention in Iraq. Ned Lamont, a wealthy political newcomer opposed to the war, rode this dissatisfaction within the Democratic base to defeat Lieberman in the party's August 2006 primary.

But state law allowed Lieberman to run as an independent, despite his primary defeat, and he defeated Lamont and a little-known Republican candidate in November. After the election, Lieberman changed his party label in the Senate to independent, though his decision to continue to align with the Democrats for organization allowed the party to claim a 51–49 majority and take control of the chamber in the 110th Congress.

Advocates of alternatives to the two major parties complain that BALLOT ACCESS and CAMPAIGN FINANCE laws, the ELECTORAL COLLEGE system, as well as tradition and mainstream party loyalties, all make it difficult for third parties to organize and survive.

Third parties do exert influence by publicizing important issues or options that the major parties have ignored. Because the major parties do not want to lose support to third parties, they may adopt positions they otherwise might not have taken.

Often, however, the third-party PLATFORM has been too radical for the political temper of the day. Such platforms have in some cases been denounced as impractical, dangerous, destructive of

TOP VOTE-WINNING THIRD PARTIES, 1832–2011

Party	Election Year	Popular Vote Candidate	Popular Vote (percentage)	Number of Electoral Votes
Anti-Masonic	1832	William Wirt	7.8	7
Free Soil	1848	Martin Van Buren	10.1	0
American ("Know Nothing")	1856	Millard Fillmore	21.5	8
Southern Democrats	1860	John C. Breckinridge	18.1	72
Constitutional Union	1860	John Bell	12.6	39
Populist	1892	James B. Weaver	8.5	22
Socialist	1912	Eugene V. Debs	6.0	0
Progressive (Bull Moose)	1912	Theodore Roosevelt	27.4	88
Progressive	1924	Robert M. La Follette	16.6	13
American Independent	1968	George C. Wallace	13.5	46
Independent	1980	John B. Anderson	6.6	0
Independent	1992	Ross Perot	18.9	0
Reform Party	1996	Ross Perot	8.4	0

Source: Michael Nelson, ed., *Guide to the Presidency,* 4th ed. (Washington, D.C.: CQ Press, 2007), 324; Daniel A. Mazmanian, *Third Parties in Presidential Elections* (Washington, D.C.: Brookings, 1974), 4–5; various sources.

Note: These parties (or independents) received more than 5.6 percent of the popular vote, the average third-party vote historically cast for president. No third party received 5.6 percent of the vote in 2000, 2004, or 2008.

moral virtues, and even traitorous. The advocates have been more anticstablishment and more far-reaching in their proposed solutions to problems than the major parties have dared to be.

Some observers view third parties as a threat to the stability of the democratic system in the United States. Others see them as a vital element in expressing minority sentiments and as a testing ground for new ideas and policies. Many of the ideas originally viewed as extreme—WOMEN'S SUFFRAGE, for example—eventually have gained acceptance and been adopted into law.

Types of Third Parties

Political scientist James Q. Wilson has identified four types of third parties: ideological, one-issue, economic protest, and factional.

Ideological parties, according to Wilson, have a "comprehensive view of American society and government that is radically different from that of the established parties." They can be found at both ends of the political spectrum and include such entities as the SOCIALIST and the LIBERTARIAN parties. Although ideological parties appeal to a narrow base of support, they have proved to be the most enduring type of third party, largely because of the ideological commitment of their members.

One-issue parties may grow out of dissatisfaction with the major parties' stance on a particular issue, such as slavery, states' rights, currency, opposition to immigration, abortion, and even hostility to lawyers. Once the issue ceases to be of importance, the basis for the party's existence disappears.

Because most issues provoke either intense feelings for a relatively short period of time—or, if they persist, eventually are addressed adequately by the major parties—one-issue parties tend to be short-lived. An exception is the PROHIBITION PARTY, which has run a presidential candidate in each election since its founding in 1869—though with minimal impact in recent years, including 2008, when its presidential nominee Gene Amondson received just 653 votes nationwide. It is the longest-running third party in U.S. history. Although primarily dedicated to banning the sale of liquor, the party was closely linked to the early feminist movement. Indeed, it was the first party to endorse women's suffrage.

Economic protest parties evolve in opposition to depressed economic conditions. A sour economy, for example, prompted formation of the PEOPLE'S PARTY, better known as the Populists. In 1891 the Populists nominated presidential and vice presidential candidates at a national convention in Cincinnati. Calling for free coinage of silver (the country was then on a gold standard), the party won 8.5 percent of the popular vote in the 1892 presidential election.

Four years later, however, the Democrats embraced many of the Populists' issues and nominated William Jennings Bryan on a free-silver platform. Populists continued to run in presidential elections through 1908 but with no appreciable accumulation of support.

Perot's REFORM PARTY, which grew out of his 1992 movement entitled UNITED WE STAND AMERICA, was another example of an economic protest party. The party received 18.9 percent of the total vote in 1992 from voters who were disgruntled over an economy that had slipped into recession in the early 1990s and was marked by large federal budget deficits. But by 1996, with the economy healthy, Perot's message had lost much of its appeal, and he mustered only 8.4 percent of the vote against President Clinton and challenger Bob Dole.

Factional parties evolve from a split in one of the major parties. According to Wilson, they usually form to protest "the identity and philosophy of the major party's presidential candidate." In the twentieth century, factional parties drew more votes than any other type of third party.

> **Factional parties usually form to protest "the identity and philosophy of the major party's presidential candidate."**
>
> **—Political scientist James Q. Wilson**

The most successful was Theodore Roosevelt's Progressive Party. In November 1912 Roosevelt won 27.4 percent of the popular vote to Taft's 23.2 percent, but both men lost to Wilson. When Roosevelt later defected from the Progressives, the party disintegrated.

In 1924, Sen. Robert M. La Follette of Wisconsin split off from the Republican Party and revived the Progressive Party label. The liberal La Follette went on to receive 16.6 percent of the popular vote. But when he died in 1925, the party again collapsed.

Another party formed briefly under the Progressive banner in 1948, this time splitting off from the liberal wing of the Democratic Party. But the third party with more impact that year was the STATES' RIGHTS DEMOCRATIC PARTY, formed by southerners who walked out of the Democratic convention in opposition to President Harry S. Truman's civil rights program. Led by Thurmond, then the governor of South Carolina and later a senator for more than forty-eight years, the party won four southern states and thirty-nine electoral votes.

Civil rights was again the issue in 1968, when Wallace, a former governor of Alabama who would later return to that office, bolted from the Democratic Party to form the American Independent Party. Wallace was supported by many whites, especially blue-collar workers who were fed up with civil rights activism, Vietnam War protests, urban riots, and what they saw as the liberal ideology of the Democratic Party. Wallace won 13.5 percent of the popular vote and forty-six electoral votes.

Running again in May 1972, this time for the Democratic nomination, Wallace was shot by would-be assassin Arthur Bremer while campaigning in Laurel, Maryland. Wallace was paralyzed from the waist down. He lost the nomination and never returned to presidential politics.

In 1980, Illinois representative John B. Anderson formed the NATIONAL UNITY PARTY as the vehicle for his independent candidacy after he lost the Republican nomination to Ronald Reagan. Anderson, a GOP moderate who criticized both the conservative agenda laid out by Reagan and the liberalism of the Democratic Party, received a good deal of attention but only 6.6 percent of the popular vote and no electoral votes.

As of the 2008 election, Wallace was the last third-party candidate to receive any electoral votes. Since 1968, only five independent or minor candidates, including Anderson in 1980 and Perot in 1992 and 1996, have received even 1 percent of the popular vote for president. The others are John G. Schmitz of the AMERICAN PARTY, with 1.4 percent in 1972, and Edward Clark, a Libertarian, with 1.1 percent in 1980.

Obstacles to Success

Third parties face considerable legal, political, and cultural barriers. Often voters do not cast their ballots for third parties because of their allegiance to a major party. Indeed, loyal members tend to work within their party to promote change. They leave the party only as a last resort.

Some voters disillusioned with their party simply do not vote. When third parties prosper, voter participation nationwide usually declines. People with weak PARTY IDENTIFICATION, such as new voters, are more likely to vote for third-party candidates.

The fact that third parties have little chance of winning further diminishes their support. People often feel that a vote for a third party is a wasted vote. Some also have the sense that third parties are somehow illegitimate, a belief that the major parties try to encourage.

The legal barriers facing third parties may seem daunting. To appear on the election ballots in the fifty states and the District of Columbia, third parties must pass a series of hurdles, including petition requirements, filing deadlines, and fees. The requirements vary greatly from state to state.

Forty states prohibit FUSIONISM, under which candidates may run for office under several different party names. The practice, allowed in New York and nine other states, permits voters to vote

THIRD PARTIES USUALLY FADE RAPIDLY

Most third-party movements are like shooting stars, shining brightly in one election and then quickly disappearing. Since 1832, eleven third parties—plus independents John B. Anderson in 1980 and Ross Perot in 1992—have drawn at least 5 percent of the popular vote in a presidential election.

As of 2008, none of the third parties or independents were able to maintain their foothold in the electoral process. Four had disappeared by the next election, six others drew a smaller vote total, and three endorsed one of the major parties. The Reform Party, which first received 8.5 percent of the vote in 1996 with Perot atop the ticket, confirmed this pattern in 2000 when its

candidate Pat Buchanan received 0.4 percent. Perot had received his highest popular vote percentage (18.9 percent) in 1992 when he first ran for president as an independent.

Each of these significant third parties, except the Socialists in 1912, made its best showing in its first election. (The Socialists, led by Eugene V. Debs, first ran in 1900, winning just 0.62 percent of the vote.) The following chart lists each party's presidential candidate and the percentage of the vote the party received in its most successful race and in the following election. A dash (–) indicates that the party had disappeared.

Party (candidate)	Year	Percentage of vote	Next election
Anti-Masonic (William Wirt)	1832	7.8	endorsed Whig
Free Soil (Martin Van Buren)	1848	10.1	4.9%
Whig-American (Millard Fillmore)	1856	21.5	–
Southern Democrats (John C. Breckinridge)	1860	18.1	–
Constitutional Union (John Bell)	1860	12.6	–
Populist (James B. Weaver)	1892	8.5	endorsed Democrat
Progressive (Bull Moose) (Theodore Roosevelt)	1912	27.4	0.2%
Socialist (Eugene V. Debs)	1912	6.0	3.2%
Progressive (Robert M. La Follette)	1924	16.6	–
American Independent (George C. Wallace)	1968	13.5	1.4%
John B. Anderson	1980	6.6	endorsed Democrat
Ross Perot	1992	18.9	created Reform Party
Reform Party (Ross Perot)	1996	8.4	0.4%

Source: *Guide to U.S. Elections*, 6th ed. (Washington, D.C.: CQ Press, 2010), 503.

for the candidate under the party label most compatible with their own views. The Supreme Court, however, ruled in a Minnesota case, *McKenna v. Twin Cities Area New Party,* in April 1997 that states have a right to bar the multiple listings. Fusion advocates had argued that the prohibition violated their First Amendment rights.

Federal campaign finance laws, including the 1974 Federal Election Campaign Act and its successor, the 2002 Bipartisan Campaign Reform Act, also have been barriers to third-party presidential candidates. The act allows major-party candidates to receive PUBLIC FINANCING during the campaign. But third parties are allowed public funds only after the election is over and only if they appear on the ballot in at least ten states and receive at least 5 percent of the popular vote nationwide.

In 1996 Perot qualified for public funds on the strength of his showing four years earlier. He had rejected the federal grants in 1992, thereby avoiding spending limits; instead, he financed his campaign with a reported $72.9 million of his own money.

Receiving public funds only after the campaign is ended puts third-party candidates at a significant disadvantage. The money is not available when it is most needed, and valuable time must be spent on fund-raising rather than on other campaign activities. Fund-raising itself is more difficult because third parties do not have the organizational structure or expertise of the major parties.

Third parties are also at a disadvantage because their party organizations are weaker than those of the major parties and their candidates are usually less experienced in politics and less known to the public. Third-party candidates receive less free MEDIA COVERAGE than the major-party candidates. In 1996 the commission in charge of presidential DEBATES barred Perot from participation in the Clinton-Dole forums, a valuable source of publicity for the major candidates; Ralph Nader was similarly barred in 2000 and 2004.

In sum, the POLITICAL CULTURE in the United States is not particularly conducive to third parties. The American political tradition of moderation, consensus, and compromise does not lead to the formation of vigorous and persistent third-party movements.

> ### More on this topic:
>
> Ballot Access, p. 13
>
> Campaign Finance, p. 53
>
> Electoral College and Votes, p. 186
>
> Independent, p. 268
>
> Party Identification by Voters, p. 377
>
> Two-Party System, p. 636

CLOSER LOOK

New York has long presented a comfortable environment for the existence of third, or alternative, parties as one of the few states that allows and even encourages fusionism. Fusionism, which credits candidates with the sum of all votes they receive in an election even if they run on more than one party line, became important because politics in the state and many of its localities, including New York City, were once dominated by major-party "machines" that brooked little internal dissent and limited opportunity for political advancement to those most closely associated with party leaders, known as "bosses."

The Conservative Party, the longest-running and most successful of New York's third parties, emerged in the mid-1960s in reaction to the rise of the Republican Party's then-potent liberal wing, identified with Gov. Nelson A. Rockefeller, while the Liberal Party, which folded in 2003 after nearly sixty years of influence, represented activists who felt the Democratic Party in the state was too centrist. These parties have had occasional successes in their own right. For example, James Buckley, brother of conservative journalist William F. Buckley, a Conservative Party cofounder, defeated the major parties' Senate nominees in 1970 on the Conservative line; John V. Lindsay, a liberal Republican, was elected mayor of New York City in 1965, but was reelected four years later on the Liberal line. The parties generally have played an auxiliary role under New York's fusionist system, however, with the Conservatives generally endorsing Republican Party nominees and the Liberals (and the party's ideological successor, the Working Families Party) generally siding with Democratic nominees.

Threshold Rules

In presidential nominating politics the Democratic Party employs a *threshold rule* to determine which PRIMARY candidates are entitled to any delegates to the NATIONAL PARTY CONVENTION. A candidate must get at least a certain percentage of the primary vote to receive a share of that state's delegates. Since 1988 the threshold has been 15 percent.

The Democrats have banned WINNER-TAKE-ALL primaries in which the plurality winner gains all of the state's delegates. The Democrats award delegates by a form of PROPORTIONAL REPRESENTATION, with candidates who meet the threshold receiving the share of delegates that is the same as his or her share of the primary POPULAR VOTE.

The Republicans allow winner-take-all primaries, an option exercised by a few states at least through the 2008 election. But most states have established proportional division of their Republican convention delegates with thresholds that candidates must meet to qualify.

In true proportional representation, there would be no threshold. Any candidate who received 1 percent of the vote would receive 1 percent of the delegates. The Democrats, and Republicans where applicable, imposed a threshold to keep the delegations from splintering into too many small factions.

After banning winner-take-all systems as of the 1976 contest, the Democrats continued on and off to accept some state rules that allowed candidates to receive more than their proportionate share of the delegates. These "bonus" or "winner-take-more" plans were prohibited in 1980, allowed again in 1984 and 1988, and then banned in 1992 and in subsequent elections.

In 1976, the Winograd Commission, one of several panels the Democrats appointed to study their rules, recommended a 15 percent threshold rule that would increase to 25 percent later in the primary season. The DEMOCRATIC NATIONAL COMMITTEE reduced the higher percentage from 25 percent to 20 percent. (See PRESIDENTIAL SELECTION REFORMS.)

In 1984 the Hunt Commission raised the threshold to 20 percent in CAUCUS states and 25 percent in primary states. After one of that year's major candidates, Jesse L. Jackson, argued that the 20 percent threshold was too high, the Fairness Commission lowered it for the 1988 primaries to 15 percent, where it has remained since.

Turnout *See* VOTER TURNOUT.

Twelfth Amendment *See* PRESIDENT, NOMINATING AND ELECTING; VICE PRESIDENT.

Twentieth (Lame-Duck) Amendment *See* PRESIDENT, NOMINATING AND ELECTING; SENATE, ELECTING; VICE PRESIDENT.

Twenty-Fifth Amendment *See* PRESIDENT, NOMINATING AND ELECTING; VICE PRESIDENT.

Twenty-Fourth Amendment *See* RIGHT TO VOTE.

Twenty-Second Amendment *See* PRESIDENT,

NOMINATING AND ELECTING.

Twenty-Sixth Amendment

The Twenty-sixth Amendment, ratified in 1971, established a uniform national voting age of eighteen for federal, state, and local elections. The amendment was proposed and ratified after the Supreme Court upheld Congress's power to lower the voting age for federal elections but blocked it from establishing the same voting age for state and local balloting.

Before 1970 all but four states set the minimum voting age at twenty-one; the exceptions were Georgia and Kentucky (eighteen), Alaska (nineteen), and Hawaii (twenty).

The drive to lower the voting age to eighteen gained momentum during the Vietnam War. Proponents raised the battle cry, "Old enough to fight, old enough to vote!" They argued that it was unfair to draft young men for military service but deny them the RIGHT TO VOTE. Also, the post–World War II "baby boom" meant that the eighteen- to twenty-year-old population was unusually large in the 1960s and into the 1970s.

By 1970, there was a broad consensus in Congress in favor of allowing citizens as young as eighteen to vote. But supporters differed on whether the change could be accomplished by statute or required a constitutional amendment.

Congress eventually inserted a statutory provision setting a uniform voting age of eighteen for federal, state, and local elections into an omnibus extension of the VOTING RIGHTS ACT in 1970. President Richard Nixon signed the measure into law but expressed doubts about the constitutionality of the voting-age change.

The push to lower the voting age to eighteen gained momentum from the youth activism during the 1960s, particularly on college campuses, in opposition to the Vietnam War. Many Democrats hoped that a new cohort of young voters would boost their party's prospects in the 1972 presidential contest and beyond. But the record speed with which the Twenty-sixth Amendment to lower the voting age raced through state legislatures—whether controlled by Democrats or Republicans—should have suggested otherwise. Despite the prominence of the liberal "student movement," the political preferences of voters aged eighteen to twenty reflected the nation's regional, demographic, and socioeconomic differences. While young liberals helped South Dakota senator George McGovern, a staunch foe of the Vietnam War, earn the 1972 Democratic presidential nomination, they could not keep him from losing to Republican incumbent Richard M. Nixon in a landslide that November.

Several states immediately challenged the law. In *OREGON V. MITCHELL*, the Supreme Court on December 21, 1970, upheld all of the law except the provision lowering the voting age for state and local elections. Justice Hugo L. Black wrote the pivotal opinion in the 5–4 decision on the voting age change. He said that the Constitution gave Congress supervisory power over the conduct of presidential and congressional elections. But he said the Fourteenth Amendment gave Congress authority to override state voting standards only to combat discrimination based on race, not on age.

Supporters of the lower voting age immediately said they would seek a constitutional amendment to achieve their goal. They were joined by state election officials, who said the Court's ruling would impose a costly administrative burden of maintaining separate voting lists for federal and state elections.

> ### More on this topic:
>
> *Oregon v. Mitchell, p. 375*
>
> *Voting Rights Act, p. 663*
>
> *Youth Suffrage, p. 687*

The amendment, only thirty-six words long, provided that the right to vote of citizens at least eighteen years of age could not be "denied or abridged by the United States or any state on account of age." Congress completed action on the amendment on March 23, 1971, and submitted it to the states for approval. Ratification by the needed thirty-eight states was completed by June 30—a record time for approval of a constitutional amendment.

The newly enfranchised young voters, however, showed little enthusiasm for the privilege of voting. Only 48.3 percent of eighteen- to twenty-year-olds turned out to vote in 1972, the first presidential election in which they were eligible to vote in all states. Youth turnout declined steadily over the next quarter-century, a trend that both partisan strategists and independent voter participation organizations have strived to reverse, with limited success into the early years of the twenty-first century.

Twenty-Third Amendment SEE DISTRICT OF COLUMBIA.

Two-Party System

The phrase "two-party system" accurately describes the overall pattern of electoral competition in the United States. But it also masks a great deal of variation in the nature and extent of interparty competition.

Most statewide elections—contests for a state's ELECTORAL COLLEGE votes and for the Senate and governorships—tend to be confrontations between the DEMOCRATS and the REPUBLICANS. A large proportion of congressional (House) districts, however, are safe havens for one party. About 15 percent of House seats on average are uncontested by one of the major parties in each election

---

HOW THE PARTIES GOT THEIR NAMES

Understanding of political party development in the United States is complicated by considerable confusion surrounding the names of the parties. Contemporary Democrats trace their partisan ancestry back to Thomas Jefferson. In Jefferson's day, however, the party went by two different names, either Republican or Democratic-Republican. By 1830 the dominant wing of a divided Democratic-Republican Party, led by President Andrew Jackson, abandoned the *Republican* portion of their label, leaving *Democratic* standing alone ever since.

A quarter-century later, in 1854, antislavery sympathizers forming a new party appropriated the name *Republican*. Today's Republicans are their descendants.

The term *democrat* comes from the Greek word *democratia*, a combination of *demos,* meaning "common people," and the suffix *kratia,* denoting "strength, power." Thus democratia means "power of the people," or "the people rule."

The term *republican* derives from the Latin phrase *res publica.* It literally means "public thing," or "public affair," and it connotes a government in which citizens participate. Both party names suggest the Democrats' and Republicans' common belief in popular government, conducted by representatives of the people and accountable to them.

Gilded Age political cartoonist Thomas Nast endowed the two major political parties with enduring symbols: the Democratic donkey and the Republican elephant. The association of the Democrats with the donkey actually dates back to the 1830s when Andrew Jackson was characterized by his opponents as a jackass. In the 1870s, Nast resurrected this image in a series of compelling political cartoons appearing in *Harper's Weekly.* The donkey aptly symbolized the rowdy, outrageous, tough, durable Democrats. Nast portrayed the Republican Party as an elephant. His initial employment of this symbol lampooned the foolishness of the Republican vote. Nast and other cartoonists later likened the elephant's size and strength advantages over other animals to the GOP's domination of the post–Civil War political landscape. The symbol came to suggest such elephant-like attributes as cleverness, majesty, ponderousness, and unwieldiness.

In an age when literacy rates were much lower than today, and when information about specific party candidates and their policies was in short supply for the mass public, these party symbols came to serve as valuable cues to prospective voters, providing them with an easy way to distinguish candidates of one party from those of another. For modern electorates, these traditional symbols have diminished significance, but they endure as part of the popular culture.

Source: Michael Nelson, ed., *Guide to the Presidency,* 4th ed. (Washington, D.C.: CQ Press, 2007), 874.

cycle, with the percentage typically lowest after redistricting and highest toward the end of the decade. Only eight incumbents were unopposed in 1992, but the number of uncontested races soared to ninety-five in 1998. Moreover, only a few dozen seats tend to be truly competitive. In 2000, 81.1 percent of House incumbents seeking reelection, and 69.0 percent of Senate incumbents, won with at least 60 percent of the major-party vote. Moreover in that year 97.8 percent of incumbents seeking reelection won.

However, these numbers can change significantly in volatile election years. One such year was the midterm voting in 2010 when Republicans made a dramatic comeback—especially in the House—after four years in which Democrats were prevalent. GOP candidates picked up a net of sixty-three House seats and six Senate seats, although the latter gain was insufficient to get the party control of the chamber. The Republican gains brought down the reelection rate for House incumbents to 86.3 percent. In the previous election, in 2008, the reelection rate was 94.3 percent, and it had not dropped below 90 percent since 1992.

Comparative state studies have shown that socioeconomic diversity within a state's population contributes to two-party competition. A socially diverse population provides a basis for differences over government policy and allows both parties to build up support among selected groups.

The changeover of the South from a one-party Democratic region to one characterized by increased interparty competition and much stronger Republican showings in both national and statewide elections illustrates what happens when a society becomes more diverse. Until the 1950s the southern electorate was relatively homogeneous, sharing common ethnic, religious, and economic characteristics. It was overwhelmingly white, Anglo Saxon, and Protestant. The economy of the South was primarily agrarian, and its people tended to live in rural areas and small towns.

Such homogeneity, therefore, offered little basis for the development of two parties. Real two-party competition did not come to the region until industrialization, unionization, urbanization, the immigration of northerners, and increased BLACK SUFFRAGE created divisions within southern society that enabled the Republicans to gain a basis of support.

Origins

The two major parties have dominated American politics and Congress since the mid–nineteenth century. Scholars have posed various theories for the dualistic national politics of a country as diverse as the United States. Some trace the origins of the national two-party system to early conflicts between Federalists (advocates of a strong central government) and Anti-Federalists, who took the opposite view. This difference continued in subsequent divisions: North versus South, East versus West, agricultural versus financial and industrial interests, and rural versus urban areas.

Constitutional, political, and legal arrangements are other bases of the two-party system. Plurality elections in single-member districts, for example, encouraged the creation and maintenance of two major parties. Under the WINNER-TAKE-ALL principle, the person who wins the most votes in a state or district is elected to the Senate, House, or other elective

Sen. John McCain of Arizona talks to reporters in September 2006. Some people hoped McCain would break with the Republican Party and run a third-party candidacy in 2004.

Source: CQ Photo/Scott J. Ferrell

office. This principle discourages the formation of THIRD PARTIES. In addition, many states have laws that make it difficult to create new parties. Nonetheless, voters' disillusionment with both major parties and growing independent-mindedness has occasionally led some scholars to suggest that conditions are ripe for the formation of another major party—though such predictions have thus far proved flawed.

For example, in 1996—a year marked by the reelection of Democrat Bill Clinton as president— voters in 110 of 435 congressional districts, or 25.5 percent, split their tickets, voting for the presidential candidate of one party and the House candidate of another party. Some observers viewed this as a sign that voters were becoming unmoored from their traditional party allegiances. Yet such split-ticket voting was a much smaller factor in the 2000 and 2004 elections, both won by Republican George W. Bush, and in the 2008 election won by Democrat Barack Obama.

BALLOT ACCESS and CAMPAIGN FINANCE laws, the ELECTORAL COLLEGE system, as well as tradition and mainstream party loyalties make it difficult for third parties to organize and survive— and threaten the primacy of the two major parties.

As a result, even political figures with populist appeal that gives them potential as third-party candidates tend to pursue their political goals within the boundaries of the two major parties. The best example from the early years of the twenty-first century was Republican senator John McCain of Arizona. Though McCain was mainly a reliable conservative vote, he voiced his differences on a few prominent issues, including campaign finance reform, some environmental matters, and some social issues. The former Vietnam prisoner of war developed a stalwart image as a "straight talker" that was burnished when he emerged as a serious but unsuccessful challenger to George W. Bush, then the governor of Texas and the front-runner for the 2000 Republican presidential nomination.

Some advocates of shaking up the political system in Washington placed their hopes on McCain breaking with the Republican Party and running a third-party candidacy for president in 2004. But despite lingering hard feelings about some negative campaigning waged against him by Bush and his allies in 2000, McCain instead endorsed the president in 2004 and made a speech at that year's Republican National Convention hailing Bush's leadership on controversial foreign policy matters in the wake of the September 11, 2001, terrorist attacks. In 2008, McCain stayed with the GOP to become that party's presidential nominee, although he lost the race to Obama.

Two-Thirds Rule

Candidates for the DEMOCRATIC presidential or vice presidential nomination faced an especially high hurdle during the party's first century. Unlike other major parties, the Democrats used a controversial rule that required a two-thirds majority vote of the NATIONAL PARTY CONVENTION to obtain either nomination.

The party adopted the rule at its first convention, in 1832 and followed it until 1936. During those 104 years, the rule denied the presidential nomination to two candidates—Martin Van Buren in 1844 and James Beauchamp "Champ" Clark in 1912—who received majorities on early ballots but never achieved the two-thirds vote required for nomination.

Van Buren had won one four-year term as president in 1836 but was defeated for reelection in 1840 by the Whig ticket headed by William Henry Harrison. Seeking a comeback in 1844, he won 146 of the 266 convention votes, or a 54.9 percent majority, on the first ballot. His total fell below a simple majority on succeeding roll calls, however, and on the ninth ballot the nomination went to former Tennessee governor James K. Polk. Polk thus became the first DARK-HORSE presidential candidate.

Ironically, Van Buren had benefited twice from the two-thirds rule since its inception. At the 1832 convention, President Andrew Jackson wanted the rule adopted because it ensured the nomination of Van Buren in place of Vice President John C. Calhoun of South Carolina, who had clashed with Jackson on several issues, notably Calhoun's support of southern states' rights to nullify federal laws they deemed unconstitutional. After being dumped from the ticket, Calhoun returned to South Carolina to continue his fight against Jackson as a U.S. senator. He was the first vice president to resign.

Jackson decided to retire after two terms as president and did not run again in 1836. Van Buren, the incumbent vice president, was Jackson's choice to succeed him. Again the two-thirds rule favored Van Buren, who won the nomination and the election. His defeat for reelection in 1840 made him the first INCUMBENT president denied a second term after first completing a full term as vice president. Republican George H.W. Bush in 1992 became the second such person when he lost to Democrat Bill Clinton.

In 1912, Missouri representative Champ Clark, the House Speaker, entered the Democratic convention with more support than any other candidate, though he was well short of the necessary two-thirds vote. He received a bare 50.8 percent majority on the tenth ballot with 556 of the 1,094 convention votes. He received even smaller majorities through the sixteenth ballot. The nomination ultimately went on the forty-sixth ballot to New Jersey governor Woodrow Wilson, who went on to win the general elections in that November and in 1916.

The REPUBLICAN PARTY never adopted the two-thirds rule. In contrast to the typical GOP convention, Democratic conventions often were characterized by turbulence and multiballot contests over nominations. In 1924, it took Wall Street lawyer John W. Davis 103 roll calls to win the Democratic nomination.

Vice President John C. Calhoun, celebrated in the South for his eloquent advocacy of slavery and states' rights, was ousted from the ticket at the instigation of ardent nationalist Andrew Jackson.

Source: Library of Congress

With the assistance of Clark's son, Sen. Joel Bennett Clark of Missouri, President Franklin D. Roosevelt won repeal of the two-thirds rule at the 1936 convention.

Southern delegations had long fought repeal because the rule gave the South a virtual veto over the selection of national ticket nominees. The issue was settled with a compromise that promised larger southern delegations at future Democratic conventions, with seats allocated on the basis of the party's voting strength in a state rather than solely by population.

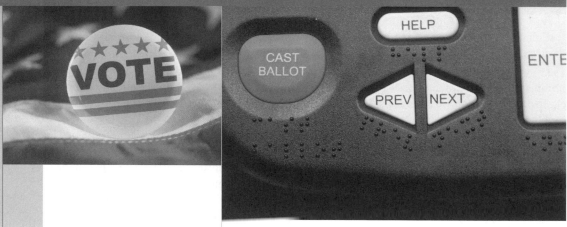

U

Unicameral

Sen. George W. Norris of Nebraska was a driving force in transforming Nebraska's state legislature into the only unicameral legislature in the United States.

Source: Library of Congress

A unicameral legislature is a single-chamber governing body. Only one state, Nebraska, has a unicameral legislature, but city, county, and town councils typically consist of a single body.

Under the Articles of Confederation adopted in 1777, the United States had a unicameral Congress and a weak central government. But the Virginia Plan, as modified by the so-called Great Compromise (the Connecticut Plan) at the Constitutional Convention in 1787, gave the nation a bicameral Congress, with members of the House of Representatives elected by POPULAR VOTE and members of the Senate elected by state legislatures (until popular election of senators was instituted in 1913). The two-chamber Congress was better suited to the concept of federalism, with the national government sharing powers with the states, and its adoption helped to ensure ratification of the Constitution in 1788.

Since then some states have tried to argue that their legislatures, like Congress, ought to be able to have one chamber (like the U.S. Senate) that is not subject to the Supreme Court's ONE-PERSON, ONE-VOTE standard of equal representation. But the Court ruled in *Reynolds v. Sims* (1964) that both chambers of a state legislature must be apportioned on the basis of population. The Court rejected the "federal analogy" on grounds that the states are not "sovereign" and were not exempted by the Constitution from equal representation as the U.S. Senate was. (Each state has two senators, regardless of population.)

Three of the original thirteen states had unicameral legislatures, but all three converted to bicameralism: Georgia in 1789, Pennsylvania in 1790, and Vermont in 1836.

Nebraska changed to a unicameral legislature in 1934, largely at the instigation of a Republican senator, George W. Norris. Norris was also the author of the so-called LAME-DUCK (Twentieth) Amendment to the U.S. Constitution. The Nebraska legislature has forty-nine members, called "senators," chosen on a nonpartisan basis from districts apportioned according to population.

Several states, most recently California, have considered conversion to unicameralism. In 1996, the California Constitutional Revision Commission, after a year of hearings, recommended that the state have a single-body legislature of 121 members and a TERM LIMIT of three four-year terms. The recommendations, however, were not among the propositions put before the California voters in November 1996 or June 1998. A two-thirds vote of each chamber of the state legislature was required for placement on the ballot.

Union Party (1936)

Advocating more radical economic measures in light of the Great Depression, several early supporters of President Franklin D. Roosevelt broke with him and ran their own ticket in 1936 under the Union Party label. Largely an outgrowth of the Rev. Charles E. Coughlin's National Union for Social Justice, the new party also had the support of Francis E. Townsend, leader of a movement for government-supported old-age pensions, and Gerald L. K. Smith, self-appointed heir of Louisiana senator Huey P. Long's "share-the-wealth" program.

Father Coughlin was the keystone of the Union Party and was instrumental in choosing its presidential ticket in June 1936—Rep. William Lemke, Republican of North Dakota, for president, and Thomas O'Brien, a Massachusetts railroad union lawyer, for vice president. The new party did not hold a convention. The party's platform reportedly was written by Coughlin, Lemke, and O'Brien and was similar to the program espoused by Coughlin's National Union. Among the features of the Union Party platform were proposals for banking and currency reform, a guaranteed income for workers, restrictions on wealth, and an isolationist foreign policy.

Lacking organization and finances during the campaign, the party further suffered from the increasingly violent and often anti-Semitic tone of the oratory of both Coughlin and Smith.

Father Charles E. Coughlin of the Union Party delivers one of his notorious radio addresses. His violent, anti-Semitic oratory contributed to the party's demise.

Source: AP Images

The Union Party failed miserably in its primary goal of defeating Roosevelt. Roosevelt won a LANDSLIDE victory, and the Lemke ticket received only 892,267 votes (2 percent of the POPULAR VOTE). The party standard-bearers were unable to carry a single state, and the Union Party's candidates for the House and Senate all were defeated. The party continued on a local level until it was finally dissolved in 1939.

Unit Rule

The so-called unit rule was one of two controversial nominating rules used for years by the DEMOCRATIC PARTY but never embraced by the Republicans. The other was the TWO-THIRDS RULE, which required a two-thirds majority for nomination as president or vice president.

The unit rule enabled a NATIONAL PARTY CONVENTION delegation to cast all of its votes as the majority wished, regardless of minority objections. The rule prevailed from the earliest Democratic conventions until the turbulent 1968 Chicago convention rejected it. The party subsequently prohibited the unit rule in all phases of party activity. (See PRESIDENTIAL SELECTION REFORMS.)

Not all states followed the unit rule. It was most popular in the South, which until the mid-twentieth century tended to be heavily Democratic.

Along with the two-thirds rule, which the party dropped in 1936, the unit rule enhanced the power of the South in choosing party nominees. Although at the time they were less populous than some of the northern industrial states, southern states could deliver—or withhold—crucial blocs of convention votes.

By the time of the 1968 convention, only about a fifth of the states, mostly BORDER and southern states, still used the unit rule. They made up the core of opposition to the motion to abolish the rule, which won 1,351.25 votes to 1,209.

In effect, the unit rule created WINNER-TAKE-ALL possibilities, especially in CAUCUS states. With the rule eliminated, it still remained possible for caucus and PRIMARY winners in certain states to take all of the delegates by a simple majority victory. The Democratic Party, however, later banned all types of winner-take-all contests.

United We Stand America (Independent Ross Perot) (founded 1992)

The presidential campaign of Texas billionaire Ross Perot in 1992 drew the highest vote share of any INDEPENDENT or THIRD-PARTY candidate in eighty years. Yet despite the broad appeal of Perot's populist economic rhetoric, harsh critique of the nation's political establishment, and eccentric personal manner, he lacked overwhelming strength in any particular state or region and thus ended up winning no electoral votes in the election in which Democrat Bill Clinton unseated Republican incumbent George Bush.

Relying heavily on his wealth and on grassroots volunteer efforts to get his name on the ballot in all fifty states and the District of Columbia, Perot received 19,741,657 votes or 18.9 percent of the nationwide vote. He drew a respectable 10 percent to 30 percent in popular voting in states across the nation. He ran best in the West, New England, the Plains states, around his Dallas base, in economically distressed parts of the northern industrial states known as the Rust Belt, and in high-growth districts on Florida's coasts.

Perot, who announced the possibility of his candidacy in February 1992, ran his early unofficial campaign mainly on one issue—eliminating the federal deficit. He had the luxury of funding his entire campaign, which included buying huge amounts of television time.

Drawing on the disenchantment of voters, Perot and his folksy, no-nonsense approach to government reform struck a populist chord. But he also demonstrated his quirkiness by withdrawing from the presidential race in mid-July and then reversing himself and reentering in October. He chose as his RUNNING MATE retired admiral James B. Stockdale, who as a Navy flier had been a prisoner of war during much of the Vietnam conflict.

United We Stand America (UWSA), formed from the ashes of Perot's candidacy, did not bill itself as an official political party. Promoting itself instead as a nonpartisan educational organization, UWSA called for a balanced budget, government reform, and health care reform. While the group's leaders did not endorse candidates or offer them financial assistance, the leaders attempted to influence elections and hold incumbents accountable through election forums and voter guides ranking candidates on selected issues.

Ross Perot, right, stands with Newt Gingrich at the United We Stand America National Conference in 1995. After running in the 1992 election as an independent, Perot formed United We Stand America as a nonpartisan political organization promoting reforms in health care and government.

Source: AP Images/Tim Sharp

Yet it was Perot himself, rather than UWSA, who commanded considerable attention on Capitol Hill after the 1992 election. From marshaling grassroots support on congressional reform to unsuccessfully opposing the North American Free Trade Agreement (NAFTA), Perot remained highly visible on the political scene. Democrats and Republicans were unable to co-opt his following as they had those of major third-party movements in the past. And Perot continued to use his supporters' anger with government and the political process to sustain himself as an independent political force, albeit for a short period.

In the fall of 1995, Perot created a full-fledged political party, the REFORM PARTY, and ran as its nominee in a campaign financed with federal funds. But after receiving far fewer votes in the 1996 election, in which Clinton was reelected over Republican challenger Bob Dole, Perot abandoned active participation in the political process. The Reform Party, subject to internal schisms and takeover attempts by outside political forces, failed to establish itself as an ongoing factor in presidential politics.

U.S. Labor Party *See* LAROUCHE MOVEMENT.

U.S. Taxpayers Party *See* CONSTITUTION PARTY (U.S. TAXPAYERS PARTY).

V

Vacancy in Office *See* SPECIFIC OFFICE.

Vice President

Alben Barkley, Harry Truman's vice president, was popularly known as the "veep," a nickname for the vice president that is still used today.

The office of vice president of the United States, as established by the nation's founders in the Constitution, is a perplexing conundrum. On the one hand, the vice president bears the weight of great responsibility, standing "a heartbeat away from the presidency." The vice president must be prepared to take on the role of president officially if the incumbent dies, resigns, or is removed from office—something that has happened nine times in the nation's history—or on an interim basis under the Twenty-fifth Amendment to the Constitution, if the president is temporarily incapacitated or otherwise unable to carry out the duties of the office.

Yet neither the Constitution nor laws spell out the day-to-day responsibilities of the vice presidency. It has thus been up to the president to determine whether the second-in-command has any substantial duties or just bides time.

Through much of the nation's history, vice presidents were given little to do. Many holders of the office had so little responsibility that they have been largely forgotten to history. One of them was Indiana Democrat Thomas R. Marshall, the two-term vice president under President Woodrow Wilson (1913–21), who is best known for this quote: "What this country needs is a really good five-cent cigar." He is credited as the source of the joke in which a mother sends one son off to sea and the other to be vice president—and neither is ever heard from again.

No vice president was more outspoken about how useless he felt in the job than was Texas Democrat John Nance Garner, who gave up true political clout as Speaker of the House to become vice president during the first two terms of Franklin D. Roosevelt's presidency (1933–41). Garner said resigning as Speaker to become vice president was the worst mistake he had ever made; he is known for saying the vice presidency was not worth "a bucket of warm spit." Reporters supposedly changed the last word to "spit" to make it suitable for print.

But the level of responsibility associated with the office has changed greatly in recent years. Republican Dan Quayle, the Indiana senator chosen by George H. W. Bush as his 1988 and 1992 running mate, was widely derided by partisan opponents as undistinguished and was not regarded as a member of the president's inner circle, but he was put in charge of the administration's "competitiveness" agenda aimed at carrying out conservatives' longstanding goal of relieving the business sector of the allegedly burdensome costs of regulation. Democrat Al Gore, the Tennessee senator elected in 1992 and 1996 as vice president on the ticket with Bill Clinton, headed a "Reinventing Government" initiative to reorganize the federal bureaucracy. Gore was also the administration's leading voice on his trademark issue, environmental protection.

The trend reached what might be its climax with the two-term tenure (elected in 2000 and 2004) of George W. Bush's vice president, Republican Dick Cheney, a former Wyoming congressman and secretary of defense under the first President Bush.

CLOSER LOOK

Nine vice presidents have succeeded to the presidency because their predecessors did not complete their terms:

- John Tyler, Whig (April 6, 1841): Succeeded William Henry Harrison, whose death of natural causes only a month after his inauguration made him the first president to die in office and the shortest-tenured president. Tyler served out the term, which ended in March 1845, but did not seek election in his own right in 1844.
- Millard Fillmore, Whig (July 10, 1850): Succeeded Zachary Taylor, who was elected president in 1848 and died in office of natural causes. Fillmore was denied the party's nomination in 1852 and served out the term, which ended in March 1853.
- Andrew Johnson, Democrat (April 15, 1865): Succeeded Republican Abraham Lincoln, who was inaugurated to a second term in March 1865 and died a day after being shot on April 14 by assassin John Wilkes Booth. Johnson's unpopularity among the Republicans led to his impeachment by the House, though he was acquitted in 1868 by the Senate. Johnson did not run for president that year and retired in March 1869.
- Chester A. Arthur, Republican (September 20, 1881): Succeeded James A. Garfield, who was shot by assassin Charles Guiteau in July and died September 19, less than a year after his 1880 election as president. Arthur was not nominated in 1884 and retired when the term expired in March 1885.
- Theodore Roosevelt, Republican (September 14, 1901): Succeeded William McKinley, who was elected to a second term in November 1900 and died the following September 14, a week after he was shot by assassin Leon Czolgosz. Roosevelt became a popular president and was easily elected to his own term in 1904. He declined to run again in 1908 and retired at the end of his term in March 1909.
- Calvin Coolidge, Republican (August 3, 1923): Coolidge succeeded Warren G. Harding, who died a day earlier of natural causes. Elected vice president in 1920, Coolidge won a presidential term in his own right in 1924. He retired in March 1929.
- Harry S. Truman, Democrat (April 12, 1945): Truman succeeded Franklin D. Roosevelt, who died of natural causes less than three months after he was sworn in to an unprecedented fourth term. Truman won election in his own right in 1948, declined to seek reelection in 1952, and retired in January 1953.
- Lyndon B. Johnson, Democrat (November 22, 1963): Succeeded John F. Kennedy, who was shot to death on that day by assassin Lee Harvey Oswald. Johnson easily won a full term of his own in 1964, but the unpopularity of his Vietnam War policies led him to not seek reelection in 1968. He retired in January 1969.
- Gerald R. Ford, Republican (August 9, 1974): Succeeded Richard M. Nixon, whose involvement in the Watergate scandal forced him to become the only president in U.S. history to resign. Ford, who had himself been appointed by Nixon to replace resigned Vice President Spiro T. Agnew in late 1973, ran for president in 1976 but lost to Democrat Jimmy Carter. Ford's term ended in January 1977.

Five vice presidents have been elected president without first succeeding to the office because of the death or resignation of their predecessors:

- John Adams, Federalist (1796): Succeeded George Washington, under whom he served as vice president for two terms. Adams served one term and was defeated by his Democratic-Republican vice president, Thomas Jefferson, when he ran for reelection in 1800.
- Thomas Jefferson, Democratic-Republican (1800): Defeated his predecessor, John Adams. Jefferson served two full terms.
- Martin Van Buren, Democrat (1836): Succeeded Democrat Andrew Jackson, who retired. Van Buren served one term and was defeated by Whig William Henry Harrison in 1840.
- Richard Nixon, Republican (1968): Nixon is the only vice president to lose a bid for the presidency immediately after completing his vice presidential tenure and then come back to win the White House later. Nixon, who served two terms as vice president under Republican Dwight D. Eisenhower, lost the 1960 election to Democrat John F. Kennedy but defeated Democrat Hubert H. Humphrey in 1968. Nixon was elected to a second term in 1972 and resigned in 1974 because of his role in the Watergate scandal.
- George H. W. Bush, Republican (1988): Succeeded Republican Ronald Reagan, under whom he served two terms as vice president. Bush served one term, was defeated in his 1992 reelection bid by Democrat Bill Clinton, and retired in January 1993.

Cheney's enormous influence in White House affairs, especially on such controversial matters as the response to the September 11, 2001, al-Qaeda attacks and the war in Iraq, led many observers to describe Cheney as the most powerful vice president in history—and led many of the administration's critics to suggest that Cheney, not Bush, was in charge, an implication strongly denied by all parties in the administration.

Although he did not suffer from the extreme boredom claimed by some predecessors, Cheney showed that being an inside player and highly visible vice president can have its downside, too. A Harris poll taken in early February 2007 showed that only 29 percent of those interviewed thought Cheney was doing an excellent or good job as vice president, while 67 percent said he was doing a fair or poor job.

Bush's successor, Democrat Barack Obama, selected a long-time legislator, Sen. Joseph R. Biden Jr. of Delaware, to bolster the young president's influence in Congress and his foreign policy credentials, which some observers thought were thin. Biden, a thirty-year Senate veteran, had been involved in dozens of legislative issues and served as chairman of both the Judiciary and Foreign Relations committee.

Electing the Vice President

The vice president is the electoral twin of the PRESIDENT. Paired on the same ticket, both must meet the same few constitutional requirements: be at least thirty-five years old, a natural-born U.S. citizen, and have lived in the United States for the previous fourteen years.

Those qualifications, spelled out in Article II, section 1, clause 5, of the Constitution, were originally intended for presidents and did not mention vice presidents. The framers stipulated that the vice president would be the runner-up in the presidential contest and therefore would have the necessary qualifications to hold either office. For the first three elections, the ELECTORAL COLLEGE worked as planned, with each elector casting two votes for president and the second-highest vote getter becoming vice president.

But in the fourth presidential election, 1800, the system backfired. Thomas Jefferson and Aaron Burr, running together against other candidates, drew the same number of electoral votes. The tie threw the election to the House of Representatives, which chose Jefferson. Burr became his vice president.

By the time of the fifth election, 1804, Congress and the states had adopted the Twelfth Amendment, which required separate ballots for president and vice president, with electors casting only one vote for each office. That procedure is in effect today.

Under this system, it is possible for the president and vice president to receive different electoral vote totals, even though as a pair they received the same popular vote. There have been nine instances of *faithless electors* who refused to give their vote to the candidate who won their state, the most recent in 1988. West Virginia elector Margaret Leach voted for the defeated Democratic candidates in reverse order. Instead of each receiving 112 electoral votes nationally, Massachusetts governor Michael S. Dukakis wound up with 111 for president and 1 for vice president and his RUNNING MATE, Texas senator Lloyd Bentsen, received the reverse.

If no vice presidential candidate receives a majority of electoral votes, the Senate elects the vice president under terms of the Twelfth Amendment. The choice is limited to the two contenders who received the most electoral votes. Two-thirds of the Senate must be present for the vote, but a simple majority of the total Senate membership is enough for election.

The Senate has chosen a vice president only once, in 1837, when Martin Van Buren's running mate, Richard M. Johnson of Kentucky, received only 147 electoral votes—one fewer than a majority. Twenty-three Virginia electors who supported Van Buren, a Democrat, boycotted Johnson because he was known to have had a series of sexual relationships with female black slaves. The remaining electoral votes were split among three candidates, with Francis Granger, a Whig from New York, having the next highest total. Required to choose between Johnson and Granger, the Senate voted along party lines, electing Johnson on a 33–16 vote. If the Whigs had controlled the Senate, it is conceivable that the president would have been from one party, his vice president from another.

The Twelfth Amendment specified that the vice president must meet the same qualifications as the president. And, by requiring the electors to vote for at least one candidate not from their own state, the amendment retained the Constitution's requirement that the president and vice president be from different states. Rarely, however, has this deprived a presidential candidate of the first choice of a running mate. Candidates usually try to strengthen the

The youngest vice president was John C. Breckinridge, who was thirty-six when he took office with Democrat James Buchanan following their election in 1856. Breckinridge served one term as vice president. With Buchanan retiring, Breckinridge was the presidential nominee of the Southern Democrats in 1860, but he lost to Republican Abraham Lincoln.

The oldest was Harry S. Truman's vice president, Alben W. Barkley (1949–1953), who was seventy-five when he left office. Barkley was popularly known as the "veep," which is still a nickname for the vice president. Barkley hoped to be the Democratic Party's presidential candidate in 1952, but his age was an obstacle. The party instead nominated Illinois governor Adlai E. Stevenson, who lost that November to Republican Dwight D. Eisenhower.

Republican Dan Quayle, who served one term (1989–1993) with George Bush, was born in 1947, making him the first "baby boomer" vice president.

Like the presidents, most vice presidents have prepared for the office with long public service careers. Thirty-three vice presidents—including recent vice presidents Dick Cheney (Republican, 2001–2009), Al Gore (Democrat, 1993–2001), and Joseph R. Biden Jr. (1973–)—have served in the U.S. Congress.

The longest-serving president, Franklin D. Roosevelt, had three vice presidents: John Nance Garner (1933–1941), Henry A. Wallace (1941–1945), and Harry S. Truman, who served less than three months before he succeeded to the presidency upon Roosevelt's death. Garner was the first vice president sworn in under the terms of the Twentieth Amendment, the so-called Lame-Duck Amendment, ratified in 1933. Previously, presidential inaugurations took place on March 4. Roosevelt and Garner were sworn in January 20, 1937, at the start of their second terms.

ticket by choosing a popular figure from another part of the country, as well as someone from a different age group or who brings another special quality to the vice presidential candidacy.

Walter F. Mondale in 1984 tried to balance the Democratic ticket by sex. He chose as running mate Rep. Geraldine A. Ferraro of New York, making her the only woman to receive a major-party nomination for vice president through the end of the twentieth century. The Mondale-Ferraro ticket lost in a landslide, though, to the incumbent Republican ticket of Ronald Reagan and George H. W. Bush. In 2008, Republicans selected their first female vice presidential candidate, Alaska governor Sarah Palin, to run with Sen. John McCain of Arizona. Their ticket, like the 1984 Democratic nominees, lost by a substantial electoral vote margin.

Oath and Duties

Like the president, the vice president is required to take an oath of office. Unlike the president's, however, the vice president's oath is not spelled out in the Constitution. It is prescribed by Congress in the *United States Code* and is the same oath required of all federal officers except the president:

"I, ..., do solemnly swear (or affirm) that I will support and defend the Constitution of the United States against all enemies, foreign and domestic; that I will bear true faith and allegiance to the same; that I take this obligation freely, without any mental reservation; and that I will well and faithfully discharge the duties of the office on which I am about to enter, so help me God."

> **"I, ..., do solemnly swear (or affirm) that I will support and defend the Constitution of the United States against all enemies, foreign and domestic; that I will bear true faith and allegiance to the same; that I take this obligation freely, without any mental reservation; and that I will well and faithfully discharge the duties of the office on which I am about to enter, so help me God."**
>
> —Oath taken by the vice president and all federal officers other than the president

Besides being the standby president, the vice president has the duty under the Constitution to preside over the Senate and to vote there as a tie-breaker. In practice, the Senate president pro tempore (usually the majority party senator with the longest service) or, more frequently, a junior senator preside over the day-to-day sessions in the absence of the vice president.

The position of president of the Senate put Cheney in a crucial position just after his election as vice president in 2000. In the 2000 election, despite the Republican presidential victory, the Democrats scored a net gain of four Senate seats, to break even at 50–50. But the fact that Cheney would provide the Republicans with the tie-breaking vote after his inauguration in January forced Democrats to concede majority control to the GOP.

Although recent vice presidents have cast tie-breaking votes, when the Senate was smaller than it is today (because there were fewer states), ties were much more common. The first vice president, John Adams, decided twenty-nine votes. By contrast, Lyndon Johnson and Dan Quayle cast no deciding votes.

Only two vice presidents have resigned the office. John C. Calhoun, Andrew Jackson's first vice president, resigned in 1832 to become a member, from South Carolina, of the Senate he had presided over as vice president. Spiro T. Agnew, Richard M. Nixon's first vice president, resigned in 1973 after pleading no contest to federal charges that he evaded income taxes while he was GOVERNOR of Maryland.

In the past, vice presidents had little to do other than act as Senate president and stand in for the president at ceremonial and diplomatic functions. One early exception was Republican Charles G. Dawes. In 1925, the year he took office with Calvin Coolidge, Dawes was awarded the Nobel Peace Prize for helping Germany recover after World War I.

As the trend toward more responsibility, discussed above, picked up momentum, Democratic president Lyndon B. Johnson used his vice president, Hubert H. Humphrey (1965–69), a former senator from Minnesota, as a goodwill ambassador on Capitol Hill. Democratic

Charles G. Dawes was one of the most accomplished vice presidents: lawyer, businessman, financier, brigadier general, director of the Bureau of the Budget, chairman of the Allied Reparations Commission, and winner of the Nobel Peace Prize.

Source: Library of Congress

president Jimmy Carter sent Vice President Walter Mondale (1977–81) abroad on numerous missions and relied on him as a general adviser. Rep. Gerald R. Ford of Michigan and former New York governor Nelson A. Rockefeller, the only two appointed vice presidents, accepted the job with the understanding that they would be more than figureheads. Ford became vice president on Nixon's selection and congressional approval following Agnew's resignation. Ford became president when Nixon resigned, and he selected Rockefeller to become the vice president.

> ## "You die, I fly."
> —*Vice President George H. W. Bush,* who attended so many funerals of foreign dignitaries that he coined this slogan

The vice president also has two statutory roles: member of the National Security Council and member of the Smithsonian Institution's Board of Regents.

But attending funerals of foreign dignitaries remains a part of the vice president's job. George H. W. Bush, during his time as Reagan's vice president, went to so many he coined a slogan: "You die, I fly."

Succession

Ever since William Henry Harrison became the first president to die in office in 1841, it has been clear that the vice president becomes the new president in such cases. The Constitution was vague on that point, but Vice President John Tyler set that precedent by refusing to become merely the "acting president." He claimed the full powers of the office for the balance of Harrison's term.

But periodically concern arose about what would happen if the president were disabled, or if there were a vacancy in the vice presidency. Most such questions were answered with ratification of the Twenty-fifth Amendment to the Constitution. Approved by the House and Senate in 1965, the amendment took effect February 10, 1967, after ratification by thirty-eight states.

Congressional consideration of the problem had been prompted by President Dwight D. Eisenhower's heart attack in 1955. The ambiguity of the language of the disability clause (Article II, section 1, clause 6) of the Constitution had provoked occasional debate ever since the Constitutional Convention of 1787. But it never had been decided how far the term *disability* extended or who would be the judge of it. (The original wording also included the term *inability*.) Clause 6 provided that Congress should decide who was to succeed to the presidency if both the president and the vice president died, resigned, or became disabled.

Congress has enacted succession laws three times. By the act of March 1, 1792, it provided for succession (after the vice president) of the president pro tempore of the Senate, then of the House Speaker; if those offices were vacant, states were to send electors to Washington to choose a new president. That law stood until passage of the Presidential Succession Act of January 19, 1886, which changed the line of succession to run from the vice president to the secretary of state, secretary of the Treasury, and so on through the cabinet in order of rank. Sixty-one years later, the Presidential Succession Act of July 18, 1947, (still in force) placed the Speaker of the House and the president pro tempore of the Senate ahead of cabinet officers in succession after the vice president. (See box, Order of Presidential Succession.)

Before ratification of the Twenty-fifth Amendment, no procedures had been laid down to govern situations arising in the event of presidential incapacity or of a vacancy in the office of vice president. Two presidents had serious disabilities. James A. Garfield was shot in 1881 and confined to his bed until he died two and a half months later; Woodrow Wilson suffered a stroke in 1919 and was incapacitated for several months. In each case the vice president did not assume any duties of the presidency for fear he would appear to be usurping the powers of that office.

ORDER OF PRESIDENTIAL SUCCESSION

Vice President	Secretary of Commerce
Speaker of the House of Representatives	Secretary of Labor
President Pro Tempore of the Senate	Secretary of Health and Human Services
Secretary of State	Secretary of Housing and Urban Development
Secretary of the Treasury	Secretary of Transportation
Secretary of Defense	Secretary of Energy
Attorney General	Secretary of Education
Secretary of the Interior	Secretary of Veterans Affairs
Secretary of Agriculture	Secretary of Homeland Security

Note: Succession Act of 1947, as modified following the creation of new departments. Any successor to the presidency must meet the qualifications for the office established by the Constitution.

Presidential Disability, Vice Presidential Vacancy

The United States has been without a vice president eighteen times for a total of forty years through mid-2011, after the elected vice president succeeded to the presidency, died, or resigned. In 1912 William Howard Taft's vice president, James S. Sherman, died a week before ELECTION DAY. Taft and Sherman's hastily named replacement were defeated. In several other instances, vice presidential nominees have withdrawn and been replaced. (See RUNNING MATE.)

The Twenty-fifth Amendment established procedures that clarified what happens if the president is disabled or if there is a vacancy in the vice presidency. The amendment provided that the vice president should become acting president if (1) the president informed Congress that he was unable to perform his duties, or (2) if the vice president and a majority of the cabinet, or another body designated by Congress, found the president to be incapacitated. In either case, the vice president would be acting president until the president could resume his duties or informed Congress that his disability had ended.

Congress was given twenty-one days to resolve any dispute among the president, vice president, and cabinet over the president's disability; a two-thirds vote of both chambers was required to overrule the president's declaration that he was no longer incapacitated.

If the vice presidency became vacant by death, succession to the presidency, or resignation, the president was to nominate a vice president, and the nomination was to be confirmed by a majority vote of both chambers of Congress. Within only eight years, that provision of the Twenty-fifth Amendment was put to use.

In 1973 when Vice President Agnew resigned, President Nixon nominated Rep. Gerald Ford, R-Mich., the House minority leader, as the new vice president. Both chambers of Congress confirmed Ford, and he was sworn in December 6, 1973. Upon Nixon's resignation August 9, 1974, Ford succeeded to the presidency, becoming the

Gerald R. Ford, seen here with wife Betty, is the only president in American history who was elected neither to the presidency nor to the vice presidency.

Source: Gerald R. Ford Library

first president in American history who was elected neither to the presidency nor to the vice presidency. Ford chose as his new vice president Nelson A. Rockefeller, who was sworn in December 19, 1974.

With both the president and vice president holding office through appointment rather than election, members of Congress and the public expressed concern about the power of a president to appoint, in effect, his own successor. Accordingly, Sen. John O. Pastore, Democrat of Rhode Island, introduced a proposed constitutional amendment February 3, 1975, to provide for a special national election for president if more than one year remained in a presidential term. Hearings were held before the Senate Judiciary Subcommittee on Constitutional Amendments, but no action was taken.

The Amendment in Operation

Situations of presidential disability have rarely arisen since the Twenty-fifth Amendment was adopted; the two most prominent occurred during the Reagan administration. The first happened when Reagan was shot on March 30, 1981. Although Reagan needed surgery, Vice President Bush was not named acting president. White House aides discouraged any such action for fear that it would make Reagan appear weak or confuse the nation.

Within the White House itself, however, there was brief uncertainty about who is in charge when the president temporarily is unable to function. Soon after news of the shooting became known, the Reagan cabinet gathered in the White House, ready to invoke the amendment's procedures, if necessary. Bush was airborne, returning to Washington from Texas.

At a televised press briefing that afternoon, Secretary of State Alexander M. Haig Jr. confirmed that Reagan was in surgery and under anesthesia. It was clear that he temporarily was unable to make presidential decisions should a national emergency require them.

Trying to reassure the country, Haig stated that he was in control in the White House pending the return of Vice President Bush, with whom he was in contact. This assertion was followed by a question from the press about who was making administration decisions. Haig responded, "Constitutionally, gentlemen, you have the president, the vice president, and the secretary of state in that order, and should the president decide he wants to transfer the helm to the vice president, he will do so. He has not done that." Actually, Haig was referring to succession before the 1947 act—the next in succession after Bush was the Democratic House Speaker, Thomas P. "Tip" O'Neill of Massachusetts.

Criticism of the administration's failure to act after Reagan was shot shaped its response to the second instance of presidential disability, Reagan's cancer surgery on July 13, 1985. This time Reagan did relinquish his powers and duties to Bush before undergoing anesthesia.

Curiously, however, he did not explicitly invoke the Twenty-fifth Amendment, saying instead that he was not convinced that the amendment was meant to apply to "such brief and temporary periods of incapacity." Still, a precedent was established that the Twenty-fifth Amendment would work as intended in future administrations. This precedent was followed in May 1991 when President Bush said he would turn power over to Vice President Quayle if his irregular heartbeat required electroshock therapy. It did not.

On June 29, 2002, and on July 21, 2007, President George W. Bush transferred power to Vice President Dick Cheney while he underwent colonoscopy procedures. In each case, Cheney was acting president for about two hours.

> **More on this topic:**
>
> *Electoral College and Votes, p. 186*
>
> *President, Nominating and Electing, p. 437*
>
> *Running Mate, p. 553*

Voter Apathy *See* ZZZ.

Voting: Early and Absentee *See* ABSENTEE VOTING.

Voter Identification

The most contentious disputes about access to the polling booth by 2011 involved voter identification requirements. The battle over tightened ID requirements typically, but not always, split neatly along partisan lines, with Democrats accusing Republican of imposing requirements to keep thousands of voters from the polls, particularly in constituencies in urban areas and among low income persons and minorities who often vote Democratic but who more than more middle-class citizens may not have photo IDs. Republicans responded that tighter standards were needed to prevent voter fraud. Opposition to strict ID requirements also came from antipoverty advocacy groups and student organizations.

By August 2011, thirty states required voters to show identification before being allowed to vote. But the requirements ranged from some type of ID, such as a utility bill or bank statement that does not have to include a photo, to a government-issued photo, such as a driver's license.

Sixteen states by mid-2011 required a photo. Eight of them were "strict photo" states that required a photo image for a person to vote. A ninth state, Rhode Island, in 2011 passed legislation establishing a photo requirement beginning in 2014. A person who could not provide a photo was allowed to cast a provisional ballot that would be counted if he or she returned within several days with a photo ID. Eight other states required a photo ID but allowed voters to cast ballots if certain other standards were met. Those criteria varied by state but typically involved showing personal information such as a birth certificate or signing an affidavit swearing to the identity claimed.

Nationwide, voter ID legislation was on the agenda in more states than it was not in 2011. As a measure of the growing momentum for stricter ID requirements, seven states enacted some type of legislation—more than passed in all states from 2006 through 2010. Three of the 2011 states acting imposed first-time requirements while four others tightened existing laws. Only three states—Oregon, Vermont, and Wyoming—that did not have an ID requirement did not consider the issue during their 2011 legislative sessions.

A number of states specified that ID requirements would not take effect until 2012 or, as with Rhode Island, later. Although voter ID was the hottest election issue by mid-2011, not all states adopted strict new rules. In Colorado, senate Democrats blocked a proposed voter photo ID law and Democratic governors vetoed strict photo ID bills in Minnesota, Missouri, Montana, New Hampshire, and North Carolina. In Ohio, a strict photo ID law was moving quickly through the GOP-controlled legislature when the effort stalled after the Republican secretary of state, who previously was a state senator and state house Speaker, said he "would rather have no bill than one with a rigid photo identification provision that does little to protect against fraud and excludes legally registered voters' ballots from counting." But in one unexpected case, Rhode Island—a solidly Democratic state with a governor who had previously been a moderate Republican before running as an independent—overwhelmingly approved its new voter ID law.

The issue was engaged early in Indiana, which had approved photo ID legislation. That law proved to be less of an issue than originally feared as voter turnout increased after 2004. Critics of the identification card requirements, however, said the increased turnout was not a full measure because it did not account for voters who may have stayed away from the polls because they lacked a picture identification card.

A challenge to the Indiana law, *Crawford v. Marion County Election Board,* rose to the Supreme Court, which decided in April 2008 in favor of Indiana. The justices turned aside arguments that the Indiana law made it difficult for the poor and members of minority groups. In October 2008 the Court also ruled on another voting case, *Brunner v. Ohio Republican Party,* that had direct bearing on the ability to challenge voters' eligibility. The state Republican Party had sued the state secretary of state, Democrat Jennifer Brunner, to compel her to provide local officials with information about any mismatching data that could make it more difficult for a given voter to cast a ballot. The Supreme Court overturned a lower court ruling that had sided with the state Republicans. Ohio had been a vigorously contested state in 2004, with the Republican Bush narrowly winning its electoral votes; it was a battleground again in 2008, but this time the Democrat Obama won.

Typically, ID requirements allow a voter to cast a provisional ballot that will be counted if he or she could provide proof that they were eligible to vote. But this, too, raised concerns in political circles and especially among voting officials, who predicted that the paperwork and expense of handling a significant increase in provisional ballots will cost taxpayers substantial amounts of money. Florida, which had a photo ID law, in 2011 passed major election-reform legislation that—in addition to cutting early voting—set a new set of requirements under which many voters were expected to ask for provisional ballots.

Another provision of the Florida legislation required third-party organization such as the League of Women Voters that sign up new voters to register with the state, file regular reports, and turn in completed registrations within forty-eight hours or face penalties of $50 for each late form. The league's president said her organization would stop its registration efforts, and added that the law was "designed . . . to suppress voter registration and to entrap groups and individuals."

In December 2011, the U.S. Justice Department rejected a voter ID law enacted earlier in the year by South Carolina's legislature. The department said it discriminated against minority voters who are 20 percent more likely than white voters to lack a state-issued photo ID, according to Justice lawyers. South Carolina, like most other southern states, is required by the 1965 Voting Rights Act to get federal "preclearance" for voting law changes. A number of other challenges to voter ID laws were pending in early 2012 in both federal courts and under the 1965 law through the Justice Department. In March 2012 the department blocked a Texas voter ID law, also under the 1965 law.

Voter Registration

To guard against abuses of the American electoral system, states employ a number of devices designed to restrict voting within their jurisdictions to persons legally entitled to do so. Chief among these protections is the voter registration process.

The need for such a system is a reflection of America's growth in population and diversity. The Census Bureau reported that there were about 142 million registered voters in 2004, or about 66 percent of the voting-age population. An exact number, however, is impossible to determine because each state controls its registration lists and critics say many jurisdictions are less than aggressive in keeping the rolls up to date by purging names of individuals who should no longer be included, such as those who have moved to another location or are deceased.

When the United States was primarily a rural nation, its scattered communities were small and most people knew each other. Voting was a relatively simple matter: a voter simply had to show up at the polls, be recognized by the election judges, and cast his ballot. If he were challenged, he

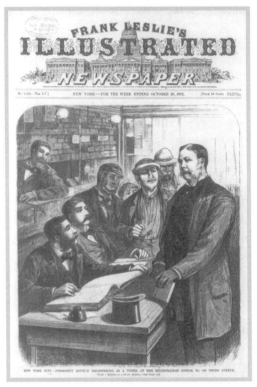

This newspaper illustration depicts President Chester Arthur registering to vote in New York City in 1882.

Source: Library of Congress

could either sign or mark an affidavit that swore to his qualifications or produce other voters who were recognized from the area to attest to his standing. (At that time, WOMEN'S SUFFRAGE had not come into existence, so all voters were men.)

But toward the end of the nineteenth century, the country had ceased to be rural in nature. The growth of cities and their concentrations of people made the simple system of voter recognition and approval, while still workable in some places, impractical and highly susceptible to fraudulent voting practices.

In the urban areas, practices such as "repeating" (casting ballots at multiple polling places) and "voting the graveyard" (using the names of dead people to cast ballots) became commonplace. As the FRANCHISE grew, sheer numbers of voters outweighed the ability of election judges to know who was eligible to vote and who was not. States began to turn to systems of registering voters, and by the beginning of the twentieth century all the states had a type of registration in place and working. When women gained the RIGHT TO VOTE, more names were added to the burgeoning rolls.

Fraud Protection

The overriding purpose of the registration systems, whatever their particularities, is to ensure that votes are cast only by eligible voters. To thwart the ELECTION DAY schemes of the unscrupulous, all the systems provided a register, prepared in advance, of all voters in a given DISTRICT eligible to vote in that election. This roster, while not a complete protection against ELECTION FRAUD or corrupt election judges, offers some assurance that, in almost every situation, eligibility questions have been answered and that a voter duly listed on the rolls can vote when he or she reaches the polls. With passage of the VOTING RIGHTS ACT of 1965, virtually all bars to voting eligibility disappeared. (See BLACK SUFFRAGE.)

The states employ a variety of registration systems, but all follow one of two basic approaches. The first is the *periodic* system, in which the existing voting rolls are cast aside at certain stipulated periods and new lists are drawn up, requiring voters to reregister. The second is the *permanent* system, under which the same list of voters is used indefinitely, with legally specified types of updates regarding additions and deletions of voters' names. Because the permanent system offers states some savings in time and money, and also because it appears to be more immune to fraudulent practices, it is the preferred choice.

In the United States, the burden of registering to vote rests primarily with the individual voter. Except in North Dakota, which has no formal registration system, registration is a prerequisite to voting, and the citizen of voting age must take the initiative of getting on the rolls. This policy is in contrast to that in most other Western democracies, where registration is virtually automatic. (See INTERNATIONAL AND U.S. ELECTIONS COMPARED.) American voters as a rule must go to a designated office to register or to obtain a registration form that can be mailed in. The federal MOTOR VOTER ACT of 1993, however, now requires all states to provide mail-in voter registration forms in government offices such as motor vehicle bureaus and public assistance agencies. The Motor Voter Act is said to have added 10 million new voters to the rolls. The increase, however, was not reflected in VOTER TURNOUT in 1996, the first presidential election after the act became effective.

Overall, the motor-voter law has had neither the negative results that critics feared nor the positive impact that supporters hoped. One year after the law was enacted, Republicans won control of both houses of Congress; they retained control of the House until January 2007 and held the Senate for most of that same period. Democrats retained full control until 2011 when Republicans in the 2010 elections gained sixty-three House seats and control of the chamber. Although they picked up Senate seats they did not get a majority. For the 2008 election, according to the Census Bureau's survey for that year, 22 percent of registered voters obtained their registration at a government registration office or while getting a driver's license or identification card at a motor vehicle department. Another 14 percent mailed a registration form to a local election office while 6 percent reported registering in some other way including at the polls on election day. In 2008, eight states allowed election-day registration (Idaho, Iowa, Maine, Minnesota, Montana, New Hampshire, Wisconsin, and Wyoming). Three others (Alaska, Connecticut, and Rhode Island) allowed it for voters wishing to vote for president, and North Carolina offered it during its early voting period but not on election day. Of the remaining states, most required registration twenty to thirty days before an election but others set the deadline at fifteen or fewer days before the polls opened, according to the National Association of Secretaries of State.

The Motor Voter Act is also credited with helping to keep the voting rolls up to date. Voters who fail to respond to election board mailings can be placed on an inactive list and removed from the rolls if they do not vote during a specified period. The requirements for keeping accurate and current voting lists indirectly affect political candidates as well. The registration indicates whether a candidate meets the residency requirements for the office being sought, and there have been numerous instances of candidates being kept off the ballot for being registered in the wrong area.

Forms and Procedures

Registration forms common in most states are simple and straightforward. An applicant is asked to check off whether the registration is a new one or represents a change of address or name. The applicant then fills in his or her name, address, date of birth, mailing address (if different from residence), a home telephone (optional), and information about the person's previous voter registration, including the county name, if it is in a different voting area.

The potential voter is also asked to "swear or affirm" that he or she is a U.S. citizen, that the address provided is correct, that he or she will be eighteen years of age on or before the next election, and is not on parole, probation, or serving a sentence for any indictable offense under federal or state law. This affidavit form also asks if the signer understands that making a false or fraudulent registration may subject him or her to a fine and/or imprisonment.

Once the form is completed, signed, and received by election officials, the new voter is registered on the election rolls of the appropriate voting precinct. The registration office may then, if the voter is re-registering at a new address, inform the voter's previous voting district that his or her name should be removed from those rolls.

The closing date for registration before an election varies from state to state. Some allow registration up to election day, but on average registration must take place twenty-eight days prior to the election.

Most states register voters according to party affiliation, largely to prevent "party raiding" by limiting closed PRIMARY and CAUCUS elections to party members. Usually the state requires changes in party registration to be made well in advance of the primary or caucus date.

In separate 1997 cases, the Supreme Court made two rulings on how long someone switching parties must wait before voting in another party's closed primary. The Court upheld New York's eight- to eleven-month waiting period, but struck down Illinois's twenty-three-month waiting period as excessive. (See CROSSOVER VOTING.)

Voter registration lists are a public record, and copies are available to candidates and others, usually for a fee. Some states, however, have passed legislation creating secret voting lists to protect women from abusive partners. Such laws allow the abuse victims to be put on the secret list and vote by mail if they receive a court restraining or "no contact" order against the partner trying to locate them. Civil libertarians have opposed the laws, however, arguing that voter registrations are "the quintessential public record" and should be kept that way.

> **More on this topic:**
>
> Election Day, p. 173
>
> Motor Voter Act, p. 340
>
> Right to Vote, p. 549
>
> Voting Rights Act, p. 663

Voter Turnout

Voting participation by Americans is lower than in most democratic nations. Much was made after President Bill Clinton's relatively easy 1996 reelection victory of the fact that just 49 percent of the nation's voting-age population (the standard measure of turnout for many years) had actually cast votes. Participation in midterm congressional elections might be as low as a third of the voting-age population. Voting in local elections can often amount to a tiny fraction of the electorate.

In the 2004 presidential elections, 60.3 percent of eligible voters cast ballots.
Source: CQ Photo/Scott J. Ferrell

Many political activists and analysts describe low voter turnout as a critical problem for the nation, a sign of a dangerous disconnect between Americans and their governing institutions. Nonprofit, nonpartisan groups alone spend millions of dollars on voter education and awareness drives to urge people to exercise their patriotic duty and preserve their self-interest by participating in the processes of democratic self-governance. And that is in addition to candidates' and partisans' exertions targeted at persuading people sympathetic to their causes to get out and vote.

There is a sizable faction among political scientists and others, however, that disagrees about the statistical dimensions of voter turnout and how big a problem it is. Some researchers have determined that using voting-age population as the baseline for measuring turnout provides an inaccurate and unnecessarily dire view of voting participation, because it includes millions of U.S. residents, such as noncitizens and most felons, who are not eligible to vote.

George Mason University political science professor Michael P. McDonald, who heads the United States Election Project, is prominent among those who believe that turnout should be measured as a percentage of the voting-eligible population, which excludes those who could not vote even if they wanted to. His calculations for the 2010 midterm elections showed that turnout was 40.9 percent of the voting-eligible population, compared with 36.8 percent of the voting-age population. The comparable figures for the 2008 presidential election were 61.6 percent of voting-eligible versus 56.8 percent of the voting-age population.

The other reason commonly cited for the decline in turnout rates from the higher levels seen until the 1960s is the lowering of the voting age from twenty-one to eighteen with the ratification of the TWENTY-SIXTH AMENDMENT in 1971. Though an upsurge in youth political activism, largely surrounding the Vietnam War, had spurred expectations of a big surge of young voters, those in the eighteen- to twenty-one-year-old group established immediately that they would vote at much lower rates than people in older age brackets. This has not changed over the many elections since. (See YOUTH SUFFRAGE.)

Nonetheless, maximizing voter turnout will continue to be viewed by most Americans as an important goal.

For candidates and political parties, boosting participation among supportive constituencies can be the difference between winning and losing. For example, Republicans in election years in the 1990s and into the 2000s tried to increase turnout among religious conservatives, who generally support the party's positions on social issues such as abortion and stem cell research. Democrats have been putting an increased emphasis on groups that, according to opinion polling, tend to support the party's issue positions but whose participation lags behind that of the nation as a whole, such as young voters and Hispanics.

Relatively few Americans exercise their cherished RIGHT TO VOTE. Fewer than half (49.0 percent) of the voting-age population actually cast ballots in 1996—the lowest rate for a presidential election year since 1924. Turnout tends to be even lower in MIDTERM ELECTIONS, when the U.S. House and one-third of the Senate are up for election. In 1998, for example, turnout was 36.0 percent.

Scholars, journalists, and voting analysts have for years lamented what appeared to be a declining rate of voter turnout in elections, which they feared showed a national lack of interest in politics and in deciding which party would control governmental powers. Not everyone agrees.

Declining turnout analyses have traditionally used actual vote counts compared to the voting-age population (VAP), persons eighteen years and older. But the VAP number increasingly came under scrutiny as one of its components—immigrants of age but not U.S. citizens and therefore not eligible to vote—grew rapidly in the 1990s and after 2000. Scholars began to look at a turnout rate that showed votes cast in terms of the voter eligible population (VEP). To get a VEP, analysts removed from the VAP persons of legal age who are not eligible to vote because they are not citizens. Increasingly, the largest group was immigrants, but included others in prison, on probation, or mentally incapacitated. With this approach the turnout rate is higher than calculations using VAP.[1]

The figures in the table below were prepared by Professor Michael P. McDonald of George Mason University. He estimates that the average midterm turnout rate from 1974 to 2002 was 39.4 percent. His calculations include votes for House and Senate seats and for governor depending on which drew the highest number of votes.

Presidential election years		Congressional election years	
2008	61.6	2010	40.9
2004	60.1	2006	40.4
2000	54.2	2002	39.5
1996	51.7	1998	38.1
1992	58.1	1994	41.1
1988	52.8	1990	38.4
1984	55.2	1986	38.1
1980	54.2	1982	42.1

1. Another often quoted measure of turnout came from Census Bureau surveys that asked a representative sample of Americans if they had voted. The bureau's numbers showed a higher turnout rate than analyses using actual votes cast and either VAP or VEP. SOURCE: United States Elections Project, George Mason University, http://elections.gmu.edu.

GROWING FRANCHISE IN THE UNITED STATES, 1930–2010

Year	Estimated Voting-Age Population	Vote Cast for Presidential Electors		Vote Cast for U.S. Representatives	
		Number	Percent of Voting-Age Population	Number	Percent of Voting-Age Population
1930	73,623,000	—	—	24,777,000	33.7
1932	75,768,000	39,758,759	52.5	37,657,000	49.7
1934	77,997,000	—	—	32,256,000	41.4
1936	80,174,000	45,654,763	56.9	42,886,000	53.5
1938	82,354,000	—	—	36,236,000	44.0
1940	84,728,000	49,900,418	58.9	46,951,000	55.4
1942	86,465,000	—	—	28,074,000	32.5
1944	85,654,000	47,976,670	56.0	45,103,000	52.7
1946	92,659,000	—	—	34,398,000	37.1
1948	95,573,000	48,793,826	51.1	45,933,000	48.1
1950	98,134,000	—	—	40,342,000	41.1
1952	99,929,000	61,550,918	61.6	57,571,000	57.6
1954	102,075,000	—	—	42,580,000	41.7
1956	104,515,000	62,026,908	59.3	58,426,000	55.9
1958	106,447,000	—	—	45,818,000	43.0
1960	109,672,000	68,838,219	62.8	64,133,000	58.5
1962	112,952,000	—	—	51,267,000	45.4
1964	114,090,000	70,644,592	61.9	65,895,000	57.8
1966	116,638,000	—	—	52,908,000	45.4
1968	120,285,000	73,211,875	60.9	66,288,000	55.1
1970	124,498,000	—	—	54,173,000	43.5
1972	140,777,000	77,718,554	55.2	71,430,000	50.7
1974	146,338,000	—	—	52,495,000	35.9
1976	152,308,000	81,555,889	53.5	74,422,000	48.9
1978	158,369,000	—	—	55,332,000	34.9
1980	163,945,000	86,515,221	52.8	77,995,000	47.6
1982	169,643,000	—	—	64,514,000	38.0
1984	173,995,000	92,652,842	53.3	83,231,000	47.8
1986	177,922,000	—	—	59,619,000	33.5
1988	181,956,000	91,594,809	50.3	81,786,000	44.9
1990	185,812,000	—	—	61,513,000	33.1
1992	189,524,000	104,425,014	55.1	96,239,000	50.8
1994	193,650,000	—	—	69,770,000	36.0
1996	196,511,000	96,277,223	49.0	92,272,000	47.0
1998	200,515,000	—	—	65,896,772	32.9
2000	205,814,000	105,396,627	51.2	97,226,000	48.2
2002	214,557,000	—	—	73,449,133	34.2
2004	215,694,000	122,295,345	56.7	111,910,944	51.9
2006	220,603,000	—	—	80,136,543	36.3
2008	230,917,000	131,235,000	56.8	120,622,955	52.2
2010	234,564,071	—	—	86,536,289	36.8

Sources: Bureau of the Census, Statistical Abstract of the United States, 1996 (Washington, D.C.: U.S. Government Printing Office, 1996); Federal Election Commission, Federal Elections 96 (Washington, D.C.: Federal Election Commission, 2000); Rhodes Cook, America Votes 23–28 (Washington, D.C.: Congressional Quarterly/Sage Publications, 1999–2010).

Many other countries have higher voter participation rates, and some are much higher. Turnout in recent national elections has topped 90 percent in countries such as Australia (94.3 percent) and Angola (91.2 percent). Direct comparison is difficult, however, because of varied methods of registration and calculation. Some countries, for example, have national registration and voter turnout is based on those figures. In the United States, with no national registration, turnout is calculated on the size of the voting-age population, not on the number of registered voters.

Part of the problem with developing a "cure" for voter turnout is that voters behave differently from state to state. According to the United States Election Project, 76.8 percent of eligible voters turned out in Minnesota in 2004. Turnout also topped 70 percent in Alaska, Maine, New Hampshire, and Wisconsin. At the other end of the scale was South Carolina with 52.7 percent.

One of the major factors that influence voter turnout is the competitiveness of elections. In 2004, three of the states with the greatest turnout also produced presidential race outcomes that were among the closest in the nation, with Democrat John Kerry edging Republican incumbent George W. Bush in Minnesota, New Hampshire, and Wisconsin. A recent uptick in overall turnout also may be attributable to intense partisan competition: national turnout for the fiercely contested Bush-Kerry election was a record 122,295,345 vot-

Music artist Sean "P. Diddy" Combs waits in line to vote Tuesday, November 2, 2004, in New York City. Combs spearheaded the "Vote or Die" campaign aimed at drawing youth and minority voters to the polls.

Source: AP Images/Gregory Bull

ers. The strong and ultimately successful effort by Democrats to gain control of the U.S. House and Senate in the 2006 midterm election contributed to voter-eligible turnout topping 40 percent that year.

A second factor is VOTER REGISTRATION requirements, which differ significantly by state. North Dakota has no voter registration; in 2008 eight states allowed election-day registration. A few others allowed it in certain circumstances such as casting a ballot for president. Most states require registration about a month before the election. (See also Voter Identification, p. 652, and Voter Registration, p. 653.)

The third factor affecting voter turnout is the composition of a state's electorate. Associated with high levels of turnout are a high income, a high-status occupation, educational achievement, and being middle-aged, Jewish or Catholic, and white.

Although efforts to boost turnout have typically been the province of parties, other politically oriented organizations, and "good government" groups, public officials have at times acted to try to effect higher participation through changes in law. Early in his first term as president, Bill Clinton signed into law the National Voter Registration Act of 1993. Better known as the MOTOR VOTER ACT, it enables eligible citizens to register as voters when they apply for or renew their driver's licenses. Although the act has added millions of eligible voters to the states' rolls, the law itself had not translated into a corresponding increase in voter participation through the 2008 presidential election.

Congress has also considered a uniform polls closing time for presidential elections. The earlier closing of polls in the East is considered a deterrent to voting in the West because of the television networks' success in FORECASTING ELECTION RESULTS. In 1980, for example, the networks projected

Australian prime minister John Howard votes in his country's legislative elections in 2004. Voting in Australia is mandatory by law, which accounts for its high turnout rate.

Source: AP Images/Mark Baker

Ronald Reagan's defeat of President Jimmy Carter shortly after eastern polls closed. Carter immediately conceded defeat, removing a major incentive for western voters to go to their still-open polls. The networks have since promised not to project winners in a given state until the polls have closed there. But that did not solve the problem of premature naming of presidential election winners.

Neither Congress nor the individual states have seriously considered making voting compulsory by fining nonvoters. Alien as it may seem to the American concept of DEMOCRACY, compulsory or mandatory voting is the law in several democracies including Australia, which helps account for that nation's exceptionally high turnout rate. (See INTERNATIONAL AND U.S. ELECTIONS COMPARED.)

To encourage voter participation, some states, notably Oregon, have decided to hold their elections entirely by mail. Postal voting, formerly limited to ABSENTEE VOTING, has both its champions and its detractors and is too new to assess as a cure for nonvoting.

Nonvoting is not primarily a matter of cumbersome voter registration holding down turnout. Rather, it is caused by personal attitudes—a lack of interest, a distrust of government, a low sense of civic duty, a feeling that elections are not important or that an individual's vote will not matter, and weak attachments to a political party. (See PARTY IDENTIFICATION BY VOTERS.)

To date, however, there is no convincing evidence that the low U.S. turnout rates are distorting the public's policy and candidate preferences. In general, public opinion research has shown rather consistently that nonvoters have candidate preferences much like those of voters.

Voter turnout rates provide only a limited perspective on the electoral and more general political participation within a society. There is more to political participation than casting a ballot, and Americans tend to have higher rates of nonvoting participation in politics than do the citizens of most democracies. Nor do turnout rates reflect the amount of electing—frequency of elections, the range of offices, and type of electoral decisions—that can take place in a country.

Therefore, although Americans have a turnout rate below that of most other democracies, they do not necessarily do less voting than other citizens; in fact, they probably do more.

Rather than indicating perceived alienation from government, Americans' relatively low rates of turnout may even reflect general satisfaction with the political order and a belief that the next election will not bring major and threatening changes because both the Republican and Democratic parties usually espouse essentially middle-of-the-road policies. The validity of this belief was being tested, but not fully disproved, by 2010 as both parties became more identified by their core voters, with liberal-leaning individuals associated with Democrats and staunch conservatives with Republicans. Although there was evidence to show these trends in both parties, the GOP had become by 2011 a more prominent example because of its identification with exceptionally conservative candidates maneuvering for the 2012 presidential nomination and strong support from the conservative movement that came to be called the TEA PARTY.

Although nonvoting in America is perhaps less worrisome than it might appear at first glance, reasons for concern still exist. With the educated, more well-to-do, and influential having the highest turnout rates, universal suffrage does not provide the kind of counterweight to power and wealth once envisioned by the advocates of universal suffrage. A high incidence of nonvoting also can threaten the legitimacy of democratic government—there is the danger that people will withdraw their support from the government as the principle of government by the consent of the governed is called into question.

Voting Machines

For many years, there were essentially two methods for voting at polling places: the paper ballot, which voters marked and placed in a ballot box, and the mechanical voting booth, in which voters closed a curtain and registered their preferences by pushing levers.

The relatively recent advent of the electronic age has produced a series of computerized voting machines, each billed as more efficient, easier to use, and more effective at rapidly counting votes than the one before. But each technological innovation has brought with it a new set of complications and controversies, leaving election officials searching for the right solution through the early years of the twenty-first century.

The search for reliable technology began in earnest following the close and controversial 2000 presidential election that discredited paper punch-card ballots, which in their day had been widely viewed as a great innovation. With the outcome of the extremely close vote in Florida

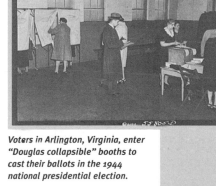

Voters in Arlington, Virginia, enter "Douglas collapsible" booths to cast their ballots in the 1944 national presidential election.
Source: Library of Congress

set to determine the winner of the contest between Republican George W. Bush and Democrat Al Gore, voters across the nation watched as Florida election officials gazed at individual paper ballots, trying to determine whether a voter had attempted but failed to completely dislodge the tiny paper rectangle known as a "chad" that would enable his or her intended vote to be counted.

Controversy also arose over a poorly designed "butterfly ballot" used that year in Florida's Palm Beach County. The confusing layout and close proximity of the punch marks for different candidates led a number of voters to complain later that they had accidentally cast their ballots for the wrong candidate.

In response to these problems that threatened the integrity of the American election system and citizens' confidence that their votes would be counted accurately, Congress passed the Help America Vote Act of 2002, known by its acronym HAVA.

A Diebold Election Systems electronic voting machine is tested for touch-screen sensitivity.
Source: AP Images/Rogelio Solis

HAVA provided grants to states to voluntarily retire their paper-based punch-card and lever-machine voting systems and replace them with more reliable systems. In their haste to replace their machines, however, many states made expensive investments in electronic touch-screen devices that were new to the market and had not been thoroughly tested in actual elections. Moreover, some critics worried that the machines could be programmed by manufacturers or technicians or taken over by outside "hackers" to produce a desired partisan result.

Predictions of election-day disasters in 2006—of massive computer breakdowns or outright fraud—proved greatly exaggerated, leading manufacturers of electronic voting machines and many public officials to declare vindication. But across the nation there were thousands of reports of problems and glitches, many of them caused by unfamiliarity with the new technology among voters and poll workers (most of whom were volunteers and many of whom were elderly).

Two years later in the national elections of 2008, the nation experienced a drop in the use of electronic voting equipment, according to a study by Election Data Services, a political consulting firm in Washington, D.C. The percentage of registered voters using electronic voting equipment declined from 37.3 percent in 2006 to 32.6 percent in 2008. However, the use of optically scanned paper ballots continued to grow. In total, EDS said, 60 percent of the nation's counties in 2008 used optical scan systems, covering about 56 percent of registered voters. In 2000, only about 30 percent of registered voters used optical scan systems.

The biggest voting controversy in 2006 centered on touch-screen voting machines. Florida officials declared Republican Vern Buchanan the winner by 369 votes over Democrat Christine Jennings in an open-seat race in the state's Thirteenth Congressional District. But Jennings sued and called for a revote, citing a disproportionate number of "undervotes"—ballots on which votes were cast in other contests but not in the House race—in the district's most populous county. Jennings's camp argued that a programming problem caused the machines not to count votes that had been cast in the House race; other critics said poor design of the electronic ballots had caused many voters to overlook the House contest. Jennings's efforts were unsuccessful, but the Government Accountability Office was prompted to investigate the matter in 2007 as she and Buchanan prepared for a rematch in the 2008 election. Buchanan won that contest by more than 66,000 votes and retained the seat in the 2010 elections.

This and other such disputes spawned an effort by some members of Congress and political activists to call on states to institute a "paper trail"—a hard copy record of each vote cast—to ensure the integrity of the vote counts and enhance the ability of officials to conduct recounts if necessary. Election officials in some locations, including Florida, discussed using a hybrid option: optical scan technology, with voters filling in boxes to indicate their choices on computer-readable paper ballots analogous to the forms used in standardized educational testing. But many states and localities decried the cost of such a requirement, with some saying they might have to scrap expensive new voting machines because they lacked a paper-trail capability.

Jacob A. Myers, a safe maker in Rochester, New York, created a voting machine for public use to "protect mechanically the voter from rascaldom, and make the process of casting the ballot perfectly plain, simple and secret."

The progress and problems of mechanical voting machines began well more than a century ago. Although Thomas A. Edison invented the voting machine and received his first patent for it in 1869, it was twenty-three years later that a similar machine was first used, at a Lockport, New York, town meeting on April 15, 1892. The creator was Jacob H. Myers, a Rochester safe maker, who built the machine to "protect mechanically the voter from rascaldom, and make the process of casting the ballot perfectly plain, simple and secret."

Unlike the Edison device, which was meant for recording and counting votes in Congress, Myers's machine was intended for public use. As Myers continued to develop his machine, his company expanded to become the Automatic Voting Machine Co. of Jamestown, New York.

Voting Rights Act

Passage of the Voting Rights Act of 1965 authorized direct federal action to help African Americans register and vote. Earlier BLACK SUFFRAGE legislation required affected groups or individuals to seek court action to obtain the rights being protected.

Other than the Fourteenth Amendment to the Constitution, which guaranteed equal protection of the laws, perhaps no single document matched the Voting Rights Act in righting the wrongs of discrimination against the descendants of slaves. Within months of the act's passage, a million southern black voters had been added to the rolls. And within a few years, black elected officials numbered in the thousands, mostly in the South.

President Lyndon B. Johnson pushed through the bill over the strenuous states' rights opposition of southern delegations in Congress. He signed it into law on August 6, 1965.

The act suspended the use of LITERACY TESTS and similar devices that had been used to keep African Americans from voting. It authorized the U.S. attorney general to supervise elections in states and their political subdivisions where voting registration had fallen below 50 percent or where the VOTER TURNOUT was below that level in the 1964 presidential election.

Initially, the act brought the federal machinery to bear in seven states, mostly in the South—Alabama, Georgia, Louisiana, Mississippi, South Carolina, and Virginia; the seventh was Alaska. Parts of Arizona, Idaho, and North Carolina were included, and other states were later brought under the act's provisions. By 1989 it covered all or parts of sixteen states.

While most major provisions of the Voting Rights Act are permanent law, some parts were set to expire after a set period. But Congress has approved repeated extensions of almost all of these provisions and has even expanded some of them. With the federal Voting Rights Act amendments enacted in 1982 set to expire in 2007, another twenty-five-year extension of the nonpermanent provisions was cleared by the Republican-controlled Congress in 2006 and signed into law by President George W. Bush that July. The reauthorization was named after Fannie Lou Hamer, Rosa Parks, and Coretta Scott King, three southern women who were giants in the civil rights movement in the 1960s.

The 2006 measure was enacted over the objections of some lawmakers and officials from states covered by the section 5 "preclearance" provisions, which require them to get approval from the U.S. Justice Department or the federal district court in Washington, D.C., for any changes to their election procedures and district maps. The affected states argued unsuccessfully that the preclearance provisions were unnecessarily time-consuming and expensive, given the removal of strictures against minority voting, the vast increase in black voter registration and participation, and the sizable roster of black elected officials in their states.

Congress also rejected efforts by some members, mostly conservative Republicans, to remove the provisions of the Voting Rights

Rep. John Lewis of Georgia embraces Jesse Jackson in July 2006 after the Senate cleared a twenty-five-year extension of expiring provisions of the 1965 Voting Rights Act.

Source: CQ Photo/Scott J. Ferrell

Act that require officials from states and localities with sizable non-English-speaking populations to provide voters with election-related materials in their primary languages. The opponents argued unsuccessfully that these BILINGUAL voting requirements hindered the assimilation of non-English-speakers into mainstream American society and encouraged the establishment of "language enclaves."

Pressure for Enactment

Impetus for the Voting Rights Act came from events in Selma, Alabama, on March 7, 1965, when state and local election officials interfered with African American demonstrations against discriminatory voting practices. Led by the Reverend Martin Luther King Jr., civil rights activists set out to march from Selma to the capital at Montgomery. They hoped to dramatize their drive to register voters in Dallas County, where only 2.1 percent of the eligible black voters were on the rolls.

Six blocks into the fifty-mile march, the civil rights demonstrators were confronted by police and white protesters. When the marchers tried to retreat, they were clubbed and tear-gassed as national news media televised the scene.

Ten days later, on March 17, President Johnson went before Congress to deliver a tough new voting rights bill. Adopting a slightly altered version of the slogan of the civil rights movement, Johnson vowed, "We will overcome."

Johnson and his predecessor, John F. Kennedy, both Democrats, had been under pressure from black leaders since the 1960 election. Kennedy's narrow victory over Republican Richard M. Nixon had been achieved with crucial help from black voters, who were growing impatient for help in return. The 1963 assassinations of Mississippi civil rights leader Medgar Evers and Kennedy himself added impetus to the black leaders' efforts.

The Kennedy and Johnson administrations had won passage of CIVIL RIGHTS ACTS banning discrimination in areas of public accommodation such as hotels, restaurants, and theaters. The new laws also brought minorities somewhat closer to realization of their RIGHT TO VOTE. For example, a 1960 law authorized the appointment of federal officials to monitor elections. And the 1964 Civil Rights Act eased procedures for federal authorities to look into voting rights cases. Also, the Twenty-fourth Amendment (1964) banned the use of POLL TAXES in federal elections.

But civil rights leaders criticized the 1960 law as too cumbersome to be effective. Its complicated procedures for registering black voters required the attorney general to first win a civil suit for deprivation of civil rights. Other steps then had to follow before a black voter could apply for a court order that would require state officials to let the applicant vote. Thurgood Marshall, then an official of the National Association for the Advancement of Colored People (NAACP) and later the first African American on the Supreme Court, called the law "a fraud."

Against this background, Congress went to work on Johnson's voting rights proposal. An expected Senate filibuster never materialized. Instead, southern opponents tried to weaken the bill with a series of amendments, most of which were defeated by margins of 2 to 1 or 3 to 1.

One of the most controversial provisions was a flat ban on poll taxes, which were still permissible in state and local elections despite the Twenty-fourth Amendment. To win the bill's passage over adamant southern opposition to the poll tax ban, the floor managers dropped

African Americans came to the United States "in darkness and they came in chains. And today we strike away the last major shackle of those fierce, ancient bonds."

—**President Lyndon B. Johnson,** signing the Voting Rights Act of 1965 the outright ban. The bill as finally enacted merely called for the attorney general to seek court action against enforcement of poll tax laws.

In 1966, however, the Supreme Court ruled that poll taxes were unconstitutional in state and local elections as well as federal elections.

Congress completed action on the Voting Rights Act on August 3, 1965. President Johnson signed it into law three days later in a nationally televised ceremony under the Capitol dome. African Americans, he said, came to the United States "in darkness and they came in chains. And today we strike away the last major shackle of those fierce, ancient bonds."

Implementation of the Act

The day after Johnson signed the Voting Rights Act, the Justice Department sued to eliminate Mississippi's poll tax. It took similar action three days later against Alabama, Texas, and Virginia. On August 10, the department suspended literacy tests and similar voter qualification devices in Alaska and the six southern states where registration was below the 50 percent "trigger." The affected states and counties were required to obtain federal approval (preclearance) before changing their voting laws or procedures.

President Johnson announced that in the first nineteen days under the new law, examiners had registered 27,385 blacks in three southern states. In one day alone in Selma, 381 blacks had been put on the rolls—more than all the black registrants there in the previous sixty years. By November the number would rise to nearly eight thousand.

President Lyndon Johnson presented a new voting rights proposal to Congress after state and local police interfered with marchers in Selma, Alabama, in March 1965 as they demonstrated against voter discrimination.

Source: Library of Congress

In March 1966, the Supreme Court upheld the Voting Rights Act in *South Carolina v. Katzenbach.* (Nicholas deB. Katzenbach was the U.S. attorney general.) The Court said Congress had acted within its powers under the Fifteenth Amendment (1870), which authorized the enactment of "appropriate legislation" to enforce the right to vote.

Several times in the following two decades Congress amended the Voting Rights Act to extend the section 5 enforcement authority (1970, 1975, 1982), cover voters who primarily speak Spanish or other languages besides English (1975), and overturn a 1980 Court decision that required proof of discriminatory intent (1982). The 1975 amendments required bilingual ballots in jurisdictions where more than 5 percent of the population was non-English-speaking.

In late 2011, for the first time in two decades, the Justice Department rejected a southern-state election-law change when it ruled that a South Carolina voter ID requirement was discriminatory. (See VOTER IDENTIFICATION.)

Supreme Court Decisions

As the Voting Rights Act continued to revolutionize southern politics, resulting in larger numbers of elected African American officials, states and individuals filed more challenges to the act's legality. After the 1990 CENSUS, some of the challenges dealt with the problems of RACIAL REDISTRICTING.

In 1969, in *Allen v. Virginia Board of Elections,* the Supreme Court upheld the government's enforcement authority under section 5, which required renewal by Congress five years after passage of the act. The case concerned two proposed changes in local election procedures, from districtwide elections to AT-LARGE elections, and from elected to appointed county superintendents of education. The Court consolidated the Virginia case with one from Mississippi. Officials of both states had contended that electoral decisions were not covered by the Voting Rights Act.

Five years later in a Texas case, *White v. Regester,* the Court again considered at-large elections, which minority voters said diluted their strength by submerging them into the larger majority pool of voters. The Court said such MULTIMEMBER DISTRICTS were not automatically unconstitutional under the Fourteenth Amendment, but that they could be in violation if they were used "invidiously to cancel out or minimize the voting strength of racial groups."

Two years after *White,* in 1975, the Court further refined its views on enforcement in *Beer v. United States.* The issue was whether a New Orleans REAPPORTIONMENT plan providing for two black-majority districts, where there had been none, was acceptable even though a differently drawn map could have provided the chance for election of more black city council members. The Court ruled that an electoral plan from a jurisdiction covered by the Voting Rights Act was acceptable under the law, provided there was "no retrogression in the position of racial minorities with respect to their effective exercise of the electoral franchise."

In 1980 the Court handed voting rights activists another setback by ruling in *Mobile v. Bolden* that intent to discriminate had to be shown for there to have been a violation of section 2 of the act. Unlike section 5, which Congress had to renew after taking into account registration improvements in the covered jurisdictions, section 2 was permanent and covered the entire nation.

Civil rights lawyers took their complaints to Capitol Hill in 1982 when section 5 was due for renewal. Under a House-Senate compromise, section 2 was revised to overturn the *Mobile* decision.

The compromise retained House wording that an election procedure could violate the act if it "results in the denial or abridgment" of the right to vote. But Senate language was added based on the 1973 *White v. Regester* decision, which required a court to look at the "totality of the circumstances" before determining whether a violation existed. The compromise also stipulated that minority groups did not have a "right" to PROPORTIONAL REPRESENTATION and that lack of such representation was only one circumstance a court could consider in a voting rights case.

Four years later, in *Thornburg v. Gingles* (pronounced "jingles"), the Supreme Court upheld the revised section 2 and set out the criteria needed to prove a violation existed under the provision. The essential elements were whether a MINORITY-MAJORITY DISTRICT could be created, whether minority voters tended to vote for particular candidates, and whether white-bloc voting usually defeated minority-preferred candidates. The Court rejected the argument that once one or more black candidates have been elected from a challenged district, the district is immune from challenges under the Voting Rights Act.

Barely five months after the *Gingles* decision, Mike Espy became the first black elected to Congress from Mississippi since Reconstruction, bringing to four the total number of African American House members from southern states.

More on this topic:
Bilingual Voters, p. 26
Black Suffrage, p. 28
Civil Rights Acts, p. 102
Literacy Tests, p. 309
Minority-Majority District, p. 338
Poll Taxes, p. 426
Racial Redistricting, p. 509
Right to Vote, p. 549
Voter Identification, p. 652
Voter Turnout, p. 656

When the 112th Congress, elected in 2010, began work in January 2011, there were forty-two blacks in Congress, all of them in the House; the Senate had no blacks. South Carolina's James E. Clyburn was serving as assistant Democratic leader, the third-ranking position in his party's leadership, making him the highest-ranking African American official in the history of the U.S. Congress.

Though they were long allied with the Republican Party because of its historical ties to Abraham Lincoln and its effort to end slavery, blacks shifted their support to the Democratic Party, beginning with the social programs of Franklin D. Roosevelt's New Deal during the 1930s and then overwhelmingly with the national Democratic leadership's adoption of the civil rights cause in the 1960s. All of the black members in the 110th Congress were Democrats, and black voters often gave 90 percent or higher support to Democratic candidates for president and Congress.

Cumulative Voting

The 1993 Supreme Court decision in SHAW V. RENO focused new attention on the concept of CUMULATIVE VOTING as an alternative to the existing WINNER-TAKE-ALL system of congressional elections. Under cumulative voting, voters in, for example, a five-member at-large district would each have five votes. They could cast all five votes for one candidate, or they could divide up their votes among the candidates.

In *Shaw* the Court reinstated a challenge to two oddly shaped North Carolina CONGRESSIONAL DISTRICTS drawn to have a black majority in each district. Both districts elected African Americans in 1992, the state's first black members of Congress in ninety years.

North Carolina had drawn the districts under pressure from the Justice Department as enforcer of the Voting Rights Act. The Court said, however, that it appeared the state had engaged in racial GERRYMANDERING.

A better way to ensure minority rights, some voting rights advocates believe, would have been for the state to create three large districts with multiple representatives elected under the cumulative voting system. Federal law, however, requires single-member congressional districts with representatives elected under the winner-take-all method. The only at-large voting for U.S. representatives takes place in states entitled to only one House seat.

Cumulative voting requires multimember districts. Although it is currently barred for federal elections, cumulative voting has been tried for local elections, and some political scientists view it as worth examining in the continuing search for effective minority voting participation at the state and national levels.

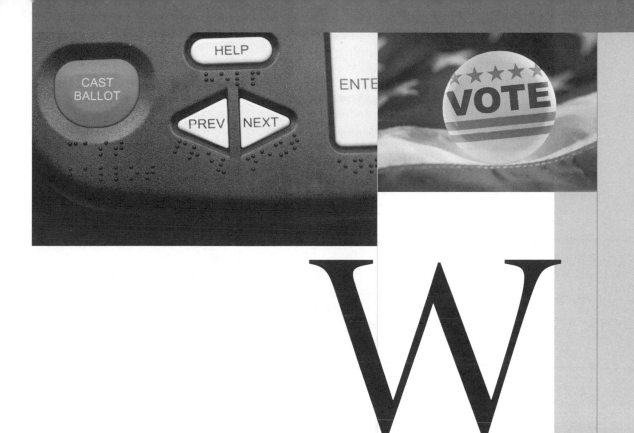

W

Ward *See* DISTRICTS, WARDS, AND PRECINCTS.

Watershed Elections

Five presidential contests stand out as "watershed elections" or crucial turning points in American political history. They are the elections of 1800, 1828, 1860, 1896, and 1932. Each led to a long-lasting shift in party power and a fundamental change in national policy.

In 1800 Thomas Jefferson of the DEMOCRATIC-REPUBLICAN PARTY defeated INCUMBENT President John Adams of the FEDERALIST PARTY with 53 percent of the vote. This was the first time in the modern world that an incumbent national executive was removed from office by a peaceful revolution at the ballot box. Jefferson's ascension to office confirmed the success of the fledging American political system, and it also set the stage for the TWO-PARTY SYSTEM.

With the effective demise of Adams's Federalist Party by 1816, the Democratic-Republican Party evolved into an amorphous organization that incorporated virtually all political viewpoints. The inherent instability of a one-party system became apparent in 1824 when four candidates competed for the presidency, with no one getting a majority of the popular or electoral vote. As a result, the election was thrown into the House of Representatives, which chose John Quincy Adams—even though Andrew Jackson had won more popular and electoral votes. (See ELECTORAL ANOMALIES.)

Four years later, Jackson and Adams squared off directly in what historians now view as the nation's second watershed election. Jackson crushed Adams with 68 percent of the vote, which led to the emergence of the new DEMOCRATIC PARTY with Jackson as its leader. The party, which dominated politics until 1860, abandoned the nationalism of earlier presidents, and it took staunchly proslavery stands. The rival Democratic-Republican Party coalesced into the WHIG PARTY, which disintegrated in the 1850s as antislavery advocates in the North formed the new REPUBLICAN PARTY.

The Republicans came of age in 1860, which was the third watershed election. Republican candidate Abraham Lincoln won a majority of the ELECTORAL COLLEGE in a highly fractured, four-way contest, even though he received just 39.8 percent of the vote and no support at all in the South. Eleven southern states seceded from the nation in protest of the Republicans' antislavery platform. Lincoln's party lost seats in the 1862 MIDTERM ELECTIONS, but the party firmly established itself in 1864, thanks to military victories over the secessionist states. Lincoln won reelection in 1864—the first reelected president since Jackson. Republicans, favoring a strong national government and federal protections for the recently emancipated slaves, dominated politics for the next two decades.

The fourth watershed election occurred in 1896, when Democrats nominated the radical midwestern populist William Jennings Bryan. The Democratic platform stressed agrarian reform, and Republicans responded with a well-organized, $4 million campaign that appealed to industry leaders, urban workers, and some new immigrant groups. The Republican candidate, William McKinley, won the election, setting the stage for Republican dominance for most of the next thirty-six years. During most of that time, Republicans generally sided with business leaders in public policy matters.

The collapse of the American economy following the stock market crash of 1929 led to the most successful political alignment in American history. In 1932, running against President Herbert Hoover's failure to come to terms with the Great Depression on either a policy or a psychological level, Democrat Franklin D. Roosevelt carried forty-two states, and Democrats swept to overwhelming majorities in both the House and Senate. The Democrats would hold the White House for twenty-eight of the next thirty-six years, and control one or both chambers of Congress for nearly all of the subsequent six decades. The "Roosevelt coalition" of urban workers, midwestern and southern farmers, Catholics, Jews, eastern and southern European immigrants and their children, Asian Americans, southern whites, northern blacks, and intellectuals seemed invincible until the Vietnam War and the conflicts over desegregation tore it apart.

With the narrow victory of Richard M. Nixon in 1968, the Democrats began losing their once solid majority in the South. Still, the parties seemed closely divided, with the Republicans generally controlling the White House and the Democrats generally controlling Congress. Nixon's LANDSLIDE win in 1972, with the overwhelming support of the once Democratic South, appeared to presage a possible Republican REALIGNMENT. Similarly, the Ronald Reagan landslide of 1980 stirred predictions of Republican dominance because a key Democratic constituency, northern blue-collar workers, turned to the Republicans. In both cases, however, the Democrats were able to storm back with electoral victories in Congress just two years later.

Similarly, when Bill Clinton ended twelve years of Republican control of the White House in 1992, it briefly appeared that another electoral alignment might be taking place. Clinton appealed to moderate voters, and he attempted to offset the loss of southern whites by bringing women and new economy "techies" into the Democratic coalition. In 1994, however, the Republicans capitalized on voter discontent with Clinton by taking majorities in both chambers of Congress.

By winning the White House in the close election of 2000, Republicans found themselves in control of both the executive and legislative branches of government for the first time since 1953–1955. After temporarily losing control of the Senate, they picked up Senate seats in the 2002 election, giving them firm control over the federal government. The Republicans retained control of the federal government after the 2004 election, in which the party again won the presidential election and also increased their majorities in Congress. But any Republican plans for a lasting realignment were dashed in the 2006 midterm election, when the Democrats won control of Congress.

Any hopes of a Republican realignment were further quashed in 2008 when Democrat Barack Obama won the presidency with a comfortable popular vote and an overwhelming Electoral College majority. With Democrats firmly in control of Congress by then, new talk arouse about a continuing dominant Democratic future. That, too, proved illusory just two years later when voter discontent over a variety of issues, most prominently the continued effects of the deep recession that begin in late 2007, allowed Republicans in 2010 to win a net of sixty-three House seats and regain control of the chamber. They also picked up six Senate seats, although that was insufficient to put them in control.

Whig Party (1834–1856)

Organized in 1834 during the administration of President Andrew Jackson, the Whig Party was an amalgam of forces opposed to Jackson administration policies.

Even the name "Whig" was symbolic of the intense anti-Jackson feeling among the party's adherents. The name was taken from the earlier British Whig Party, founded in the seventeenth century in opposition to the tyranny of the Stuart monarchs. Likewise, the term was popular during the American Revolution, as the colonists fought against what they considered the despotism of King George III. The new Whig Party was opposed to "King Andrew," its characterization of Jackson, a Democrat, and his strong executive actions.

Among those who joined the COALITION early were southerners who were enraged over Jackson's stand against states' rights in a dispute with South Carolina officials who held that states had the right to nullify federal laws with which they disagreed. Then came businessmen, merchants, and conservatives, shocked by and fearful of Jackson's efforts to abolish the Bank of the United States. This group, basically a remnant of the NATIONAL REPUBLICAN PARTY that had a brief existence in the 1820s, espoused the American Plan proposed by Kentucky statesman Henry Clay. The plan, a program of federal action to aid the economy and tie together the sections of the country, included tariff protection for business, a national bank, public works, and distribution to the states of money received for the sale of public lands. The Clay plan became the basis for the Whigs' nationalistic economic program.

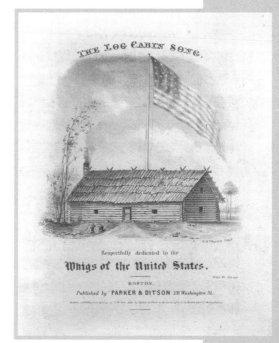

An 1840 sheet music cover to "The Log Cabin Song," dedicated to the Whig Party.

Source: Library of Congress

Another influential group joining the Whig coalition was the Anti-Masons, an egalitarian movement strong in parts of New England, New York, and Pennsylvania.

Throughout its life, the Whig Party was plagued by factionalism and disunity. In the 1836 presidential election, the first in which the Whigs took part, the party had no national presidential candidate. Rather, three different candidates ran in different parts of the country—Gen. William Henry Harrison, Hugh L. White, and Daniel Webster—each hoping to carry Whig electors in states where they were popular. Then the Whig electors, if a majority, could combine in the ELECTORAL

COLLEGE on one candidate or, if that proved impossible, throw the election into the House. But Martin Van Buren, the incumbent VICE PRESIDENT and the Democratic presidential nominee, won a majority of the electors.

Befitting their lack of unity, the Whigs adopted no platform in 1840 but did manage to settle on a single nominee—Harrison, a military hero and 1836 contender—for the presidency. His campaign, emphasizing an apocryphal log cabin and hard cider home life in Ohio that belied his landed upbringing in Virginia, resulted in a LANDSLIDE victory.

Harrison ended up being the shortest-tenured president in U.S. history, dying only a month after taking office (April 4, 1841). Though the new president, John Tyler of Virginia, had been elected on the Whig ticket with Harrison, he proceeded to veto most elements of the Whig economic program, including the tariff and reestablishment of the national bank.

Given Tyler's well-known states' rights position—ignored by the Whigs in 1840 when they nominated him for vice president to capitalize on his southern appeal—the vetoes were inevitable. Members of the cabinet resigned in outrage, and for the rest of his term Tyler remained a president without a party.

Because the Whigs controlled the presidency and both houses of Congress just for Tyler's first two years in office, his vetoes spoiled the only chance the Whigs ever had of implementing their program.

The Whigs won the White House for the second and last time in 1848 by running another military hero, Gen. Zachary Taylor. Like Harrison, Taylor was a nonideological candidate, and he too died in office of natural causes, in 1850. He was succeeded by Vice President Millard Fillmore of New York.

The development of the slavery question in the 1840s and its intensification in the 1850s proved to be the death knell for the Whig Party. A party containing antislavery New Englanders and southern plantation owners was simply unable to bridge the gap between them. The Compromise of 1850, forged by Clay, only briefly allayed the controversy over extension of slavery into the western territories. It involved the future of southwestern areas acquired from Mexico during the Mexican-American war of 1846–1848, including how much of the territory could become slaveholding states. Many southern Whigs gravitated toward the Democrats, whom they believed more responsive to their interests. In the North, new parties specifically dedicated to opposing the expansion of slavery (FREE SOILERS, Anti-Nebraskans, REPUBLICANS) attracted Whig voters.

> **More on this topic:**
>
> *Coalition, p. 107*
>
> *Electoral College and Votes, p. 186*
>
> *Landslide, p. 301*

The last Whig national convention, in 1856, adopted a PLATFORM but endorsed former president Millard Fillmore, already the nominee of the KNOW-NOTHING (AMERICAN) PARTY, which mainly embodied nativist and anti-immigrant sentiment among a segment of the U.S. electorate. The Whig platform deplored sectional strife and called for compromise to save the Union. But it was a futile campaign, with Fillmore carrying only Maryland and winning just 21.5 percent of the national vote.

In that same year, the recently founded REPUBLICAN PARTY made its first appearance in presidential politics. By 1860 many antislavery voters who had been part of the Whig coalition aligned with the Republicans, helping that party's nominee, Abraham Lincoln, win the presidency.

Whistle Stop

In the language of elections, the phrase *whistle stop* means to campaign by making brief appearances in many small communities. It originated with President Harry S. Truman's nationwide campaign by train in 1948.

Railroaders had long used the word *whistle stop* to mean a town too small for a regularly scheduled stop. To let passengers off, the conductor would have to pull the steam whistle cord to signal the engineer to stop.

Writer and former House member Ken Hechler, a West Virginia Democrat, recalled in his book *Working with Truman: A Personal Memoir of the White House Years,* that in Butte, Montana, Truman made one of his usual attacks on the Republican Congress. He particularly targeted one of its leaders, Sen. Robert A. Taft of Ohio, who had urged people to fight inflation by eating less. "I guess he would let you starve, I don't know," Truman said.

Reported by the press, the remark stung Taft into responding with a speech castigating Truman for "blackguarding Congress at every whistle station in the West." Truman and the Democrats struck back, accusing Taft of insulting Truman's campaign stops by implying they were backward, rural communities. In Los Angeles, Truman joked that the city was the biggest whistle stop he had made. He changed Taft's "whistle station" to "whistle stop" and the phrase stuck.

President Harry S. Truman popularized the whistle stop during the 1948 campaign.

Source: National Archives and Records Administration

Truman went on to score an upset victory over New York governor Thomas A. Dewey, a Republican who according to the POLLS was almost certain to win.

Truman did not invent campaigning by train, however. In 1896 Democrat William Jennings Bryan traveled 18,000 miles and made 600 speeches while his opponent, Republican William McKinley, campaigned from his front porch in Canton, Ohio. McKinley won the election, though.

Tactics such as whistle-stop tours could be an effective means of communicating with voters even as late as 1948, before mass communication truly transformed the nature of campaigning. From inner-city wards to small rural communities, candidate visits, rallies, and parades were a form of entertainment as well as civic engagement.

The rise of the age of television, which was occurring even as Truman was campaigning, offered Americans other diversions and candidates a faster and more effective means of communicating with mass audiences. Since air transportation became the norm for presidential candidates, the whistle-stop tour has been supplanted by an exhausting travel schedule in which the candidates' stops often are no more than news conferences or small rallies at airports, held to provide footage for local television news stations rather than to engage individual voters.

In modern campaigning, most ground-transportation excursions are aimed at invoking a sense of nostalgia, political populism, or both. In 1992 buses replaced trains as the transportation mode of choice by Bill Clinton and his running mate, Al Gore. After the Democrats' NATIONAL PARTY

CONVENTION, the candidates took off on an intercity bus version of Truman's whistle-stop tour. Boosted more by media attention to the tour than by its impact on the campaign trail, the Clinton-Gore ticket gained in the polls. Ultimately, the Democrats defeated the Republican ticket of President George H. W. Bush and Vice President Dan Quayle.

In the elections of 1996 and 2000, neither trains nor buses figured prominently in the campaigns of most major-party candidates. Both parties' standard-bearers used jet aircraft for their travels to meet the voters in person, and they relied on televised POLITICAL ADVERTISING and the newer electronic medium of the Internet to present their views to voters in their own homes. One exception was the 2000 presidential campaign of Sen. John McCain, R-Ariz., who would frequently speak with members of the press aboard a campaign bus dubbed "Straight Talk Express." McCain revived the "Straight Talk Express" bus tours for his 2008 White House campaign.

> **More on this topic:**
>
> *National Party Conventions, p. 347*

White Primary

The issue of race is closely connected with the history of the SOUTHERN PRIMARY, an institution that existed from the post–Civil War era of the late nineteenth century until undone by the civil rights era of the mid-twentieth century. Conservative white southerners, many of whom declared racial superiority over blacks, then made up a large and vital part of the national Democratic Party coalition. They instituted a number of exclusionary devices that were used to keep blacks from voting in the DEMOCRATIC PARTY's primary— which in effect was the election, because the party then had no real opposition in the South from the REPUBLICANS, the reviled party of Abraham Lincoln.

In 1944, Thurgood Marshall represented the plaintiff in *Smith v. Allwright*, in which the Supreme Court declared white primaries unconstitutional. Marshall went on to become the first African American to serve on the Supreme Court.

Source: Library of Congress

Among those devices was the so-called white primary, in which the party designated itself a private association or club, open only to whites. (See PRIMARY TYPES.)

After primaries came into general use for nominating party candidates, it was not clear that Congress had the authority to regulate primaries as it did regular elections. The Supreme Court added to the confusion in a 1921 ruling, *Newberry v. United States,* which implied Congress lacked such power.

The doubt created by the Court encouraged the eleven states of the old Confederacy to exclude blacks from the primaries. The states or counties holding white primaries defended the practice as constitutional because the Fifteenth Amendment, ratified in 1870, prohibited only *states,* not private associations, from denying the RIGHT TO VOTE to persons on account of race or color.

Five times after the *Newberry* decision, the issue of white primaries came before the Supreme Court in cases from Texas and Louisiana. In two Texas cases in 1927 and 1932, the Court agreed with a black man, Dr. L. A. Nixon, that he had been wrongfully excluded from the Democratic primary by the legislature or the party as a delegate of the state. But in 1935, in *Grovey v. Townsend*, the Court upheld the right of the Texas Democratic Party, acting on its own as a private association, to close its primaries to nonmembers.

In 1941, however, the Supreme Court discarded the *Newberry* restriction on federal regulation of primaries. It declared in *United States v. Classic*, a Louisiana case unrelated to racial discrimination, that Congress has the power to regulate primaries as it does other elections. Three years later, in *Smith v. Allwright*, the Court declared the white primary unconstitutional, holding that a primary was an integral part of the election machinery for choosing state and federal officials.

Lonnie E. Smith, a black man who sued after Texas officials barred him from the primary, was represented by attorneys from the National Association for the Advancement of Colored People, including Thurgood Marshall, who later became the first African American on the Supreme Court.

Winner Take All

Most elections, whether of government officials or officers of private clubs, are decided on the winner-take-all system. It is the simplest kind of election to conduct and the easiest to understand: the person who receives the most votes wins the office being sought.

Members of Congress, governors, other state constitutional officers, and most state legislators are elected under the winner-take-all rule. They run either statewide or in SINGLE-MEMBER DISTRICTS (the whole state in those states that, because of their small population, have only one AT-LARGE House seat) and win if they receive at least a PLURALITY of the vote.

A more complicated system, PROPORTIONAL REPRESENTATION, is more likely to give fair representation to the various racial, ethnic, and other demographic or political groups within a state or district. Under proportional representation, seats are distributed among candidates in proportion to their share of the POPULAR VOTE. To do this, however, requires the use of MULTIMEMBER DISTRICTS or a similar form of multiple representation in the geographical area covered by the election. Then if a ten-member district is 40 percent African American, for example, the black community has a reasonable chance of winning four of the ten seats if it puts up a full complement of candidates.

A few states had multimember CONGRESSIONAL DISTRICTS until Congress abolished them in 1842. Some state legislative districts or city council wards still elect multiple members.

In PRESIDENTIAL PRIMARIES, delegates to the NATIONAL PARTY CONVENTIONS usually are awarded on the basis of proportional representation rather than winner-take-all. In many cases a candidate must meet a THRESHOLD RULE, such as 15 percent of the vote, before winning any delegates. Some Republican primaries use winner take all, but the Democratic Party does not allow them.

Presidential elections—in which the victor must win an ABSOLUTE MAJORITY of the 538 votes in the ELECTORAL COLLEGE—are essentially won or lost on a winner-take-all basis. In all but two states, the winner of the statewide popular vote receives all of the state's electoral votes.

The exceptions are Nebraska, which has five electoral votes, and Maine, which has four. In both states, the statewide winner is automatically accorded two electoral votes, but the remaining votes are allotted to the winner in each of the states'

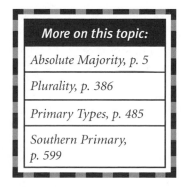

More on this topic:

Absolute Majority, p. 5

Plurality, p. 386

Primary Types, p. 485

Southern Primary, p. 599

congressional districts. Though it is possible for the loser of the statewide vote to nonetheless finish ahead in an individual district and thus earn an electoral vote, this never happened until 2008 when Democratic presidential nominee Barack Obama won enough votes in one congressional district in Nebraska to gain an electoral vote even while losing the state to his opponent, Sen. John McCain.

Women in Politics

The date of January 4, 2007, is one of the most significant in the history of women in American politics. On that day, the 110th Congress, with its Democratic majorities in the Senate and House, was sworn in—and on that day, on a party line vote, the House elected Democrat Nancy Pelosi of California as the first woman to hold the office of Speaker of the House.

As Pelosi accepted the position, becoming the highest ranking female officeholder to date in the United States, she was observed by seventy other female House members—forty-nine Democrats and twenty-one Republicans—plus three female Democratic delegates, from the District of Columbia, Guam, and the U.S. Virgin Islands.

The significance of the moment was hailed by Republicans as well as Democrats. Rep. John A. Boehner of Ohio, chosen by fellow Republicans as the minority leader, introduced Pelosi as the new Speaker, saying, "In a few moments, I'll have the high privilege of handing the gavel of the House of Representatives to a woman for the first time in American history. Whether you're a Republican, a Democrat, or an independent, this is a cause for celebration."

Nineteen days later, President George W. Bush, appearing in the House chamber to deliver his annual State of the Union address, pronounced, "Tonight, I have a high privilege and distinct honor of my own—as the first president to begin the State of the Union message with these words: Madam Speaker."

> "In a few moments, I'll have the high privilege of handing the gavel of the House of Representatives to a woman for the first time in American history. Whether you're a Republican, a Democrat, or an independent, this is a cause for celebration."
>
> —Republican minority leader John A. Boehner of Ohio, introducing Democrat Nancy Pelosi of California as the Speaker of the House

Sixteen women were elected to the Senate in 2006, eleven Democrats and five Republicans. Democrats Amy Klobuchar of Minnesota and Claire McCaskill of Missouri were newly elected in 2006, replacing men who had held the seats. And at that time, New York Democratic senator Hillary Rodham Clinton was the FRONT-RUNNER for the 2008 Democratic presidential nomination, the first woman to hold that status in a major party. Even though she eventually lost the nomination to Barack Obama, she garnered more than 18 million votes in various primaries. Although this was more than Obama won, he prevailed in gathering the all-important delegate total because Democrats use a system that awards delegates in proportion to a candidate's primary votes.

Despite these advances and the longtime feminist slogan that "a woman's place is in the House . . . and in the Senate," women are still a long way from parity. Although women make up slightly more than half of the U.S. population, the seventy-two women in the House at the beginning of the 112th Congress in January 2011 amounted to just 16.5 percent of the total membership of 435 and closely matched women's 17 percent share of the Senate. One reason for the disparity may be that many voters view past political experience favorably in choosing among candidates, and that experience continues to be an asset enjoyed by more male than female candidates.

But Pelosi's progression to the leadership of the U.S. House suggests how much has changed since the women's rights movement, which gained momentum in the 1960s, forced the issue of increased representation for women. It is not just important that she achieved her high position, but also how she did so. Although Pelosi has strongly advocated the policy goals of the liberal feminist movement, the former public relations executive and mother of five spent much of that movement's formative years as a San Francisco homemaker.

Pelosi is the daughter of Thomas D'Alesandro Jr., a former Maryland congressman and former mayor of Baltimore, and sister of Thomas D'Alesandro III, also a former Baltimore mayor. She did not storm the congressional barricade as a women's rights activist; rather, Pelosi entered politics as a campaign fund-raiser, won a House special election in 1987, and then worked her way up the leadership ranks of what long was known as an "old boys' club." Her election by House Democrats as minority leader after the 2002 midterm campaign made her ascension to Speaker a given when Democrats won control of the House in 2006.

Women have succeeded in U.S. politics over a short period of time. Although a few western states granted women the vote in the late 1800s—starting with Wyoming upon its admission to the Union in 1890—women won the universal RIGHT TO VOTE through ratification of the Nineteenth Amendment in 1920, 144 years after the Declaration of Independence and fol-

Rep. Nancy Pelosi of California brandishes the gavel as she is installed as House Speaker on January 4, 2007, the opening day of the 110th Congress. The position made her the highest-ranking woman to date in the U.S. government.
Source: AP Images/Susan Walsh

lowing decades of agitation by the WOMEN'S SUFFRAGE movement. More than fifty years after that, women began to make material gains in elections for major public offices.

Following the 1966 elections, for example, there was just one woman in the Senate and eleven women in the House. The elections in 1986 advanced the number of female senators to two and the women in the House to twenty-three. By the time Pelosi took the gavel after elections twenty years later, the number of women in the House had more than tripled and the number of female senators had increased eightfold.

According to the Center for American Women in Politics, a collection of historical data on the topic located at New Jersey's Rutgers University, women have continued to increase in number in most national and state elective offices. In 2011, 16.8 percent of members of Congress were female, up from just 4 percent thirty years earlier. In state legislatures, women constituted 23.7 percent of all members. Although this number was down slightly from the high point of 24.5 percent in 2010, it was nearly double the 12 percent recorded thirty years earlier. In statewide elective offices in 2011, 22.1 percent were women. This number was a decline from the high of 27.6 percent a decade earlier, a declining trend seen throughout the 2000s decade. However, the 2011 number was about double thirty years earlier.

Milestones for Women in U.S. Politics

| 1894 | With women still barred from voting in most of the nation, three women are elected to the Colorado House of Representatives and become the first female state lawmakers. |

1894 — With women still barred from voting in most of the nation, three women are elected to the Colorado House of Representatives and become the first female state lawmakers.

1916 — Montana Republican Jeannette Rankin becomes the first woman elected to the U.S. House of Representatives. Although Rankin did not seek reelection in 1918, she returned for one more term after being elected in 1940. An isolationist on foreign policy, Rankin votes against U.S. entry into both world wars. She is the only member of Congress to do so.

1920 — The long battle for women's suffrage concludes with ratification of the Nineteenth Amendment to the Constitution: "The right of citizens in the United States to vote shall not be denied or abridged by the United States or by any State on account of sex."

1922 — Rebecca L. Felton becomes the first female senator after being appointed in October by the governor of Georgia, following the death of Democratic incumbent Thomas E. Watson. Felton serves only one day in November before giving way to Democrat Walter George, the winner of a special election to fill out Watson's unexpired term.

1925 — Wyoming Democrat Nellie Tayloe Ross becomes the first female governor after winning a special election to replace the interim successor to her late husband, Gov. William B. Ross. She serves the two years of his unexpired term but loses the 1926 election to Republican Frank C. Emerson by a 2 percentage-point margin.

1931 — Arkansas Democrat Hattie W. Caraway becomes the first woman to actually serve as a lawmaker in the U.S. Senate when the state's governor appoints her to fill out the unexpired term of her late husband, Thaddeus H. Caraway. She subsequently becomes the first woman elected to the Senate, easily winning contests in 1932 and 1938. She loses the 1944 Democratic primary to Democrat J. William Fulbright, coming in fourth of four candidates.

1964 — Maine Republican Margaret Chase Smith, in the midst of a four-term Senate tenure that began with her election in 1948, becomes the first woman to have her name placed in nomination for president at a major-party convention; she receives 27 of the 1,308 delegate votes in the balloting won by Arizona senator Barry Goldwater. She is the first woman to serve in both the House (1940–49) and the Senate (1949–73).

1964 — Hawaii Democrat Patsy T. Mink, a Japanese American, becomes the first nonwhite woman elected to the U.S. House. She serves twelve years, leaves her seat open for a 1976 Senate primary bid that failed, then returns after her 1990 election. Her House career ends with her death in 2002.

1968 — New York Democrat Shirley Chisholm becomes the first African American woman elected to Congress, beginning a fourteen-year tenure.

1972 — Chisholm becomes the first woman to campaign actively for a major party's presidential nomination. She receives 151.95 of the 3,016 delegate votes in convention balloting that is won by South Dakota senator George McGovern.

1974 — Connecticut Democrat Ella Grasso is the first woman elected as governor without succeeding her husband. She is reelected in 1978, but serious health problems force her to resign on the last day of 1980.

1984 — New York representative Geraldine A. Ferraro is selected by Democratic presidential nominee Walter F. Mondale to be his vice presidential running mate, making her the first (and, through

	2004, only) woman nominated to a major party's national ticket. Mondale loses in a landslide to Republican incumbent Ronald Reagan.
1986	Nebraska's Kay Orr becomes the first Republican woman elected as governor. She narrowly loses a 1990 reelection bid to Democrat Ben Nelson.
1989	Florida Republican Ileana Ros-Lehtinen, a Cuban American, becomes the first Hispanic woman elected to the U.S. House, winning a special election and beginning a long tenure that extends past her victory in the 2012 election.
1992	Illinois Democrat Carol Moseley-Braun becomes the first African American woman elected to the Senate, and only the second black senatorial candidate ever to win popular election. She serves one term before losing her 1998 reelection bid to Republican Peter G. Fitzgerald.
2000	Democrat Hillary Rodham Clinton, wife of retiring two-term president Bill Clinton, becomes both the first first lady to seek and win public office and the first female senator from New York. Clinton is easily reelected in 2006 and enters a bid for the 2008 Democratic presidential nomination as the front-runner in early polls.
2002	California representative Nancy Pelosi is chosen by her Democratic House colleagues as minority leader, making her the first woman to head her party in either chamber of Congress.
2007	The Democrats' takeover of the House in the 2006 elections promotes Pelosi to the position of Speaker of the House, making her the highest-ranking woman in the history of the U.S. government.
2008	New York senator Hillary Rodham Clinton begins the 2008 race for the Democratic presidential nominee as the front-runner. However, fellow senator Barack Obama enters the race and through a cleverly orchestrated national campaign in all states assembles enough delegates to best Clinton even though she garners almost 18 million primary votes, 294,000 more than Obama. After Obama wins the presidency, Clinton becomes his secretary of state. On the Republican ticket Alaska governor Sarah Palin is selected as the female vice presidential candidate, the first time for the GOP to select a woman for this role.

Women's Suffrage

Full voting rights were not extended to all American women until 1920, when the Nineteenth Amendment to the Constitution won ratification from the states. That year, for the first time, women in every state had the right to participate in the November election. The amendment states: "The right of citizens of the United States to vote shall not be denied or abridged by the United States or by any State on account of sex."

Almost one hundred years elapsed between the time the fight for women's suffrage began in earnest, before the Civil War, and the Nineteenth Amendment won approval. Pioneer suffragists were women active in the antislavery movement who were struck by the similarity between their lot, under law, and that of slaves.

Ironically, male former slaves or descendants of slaves gained the RIGHT TO VOTE long before women did, although southern states thwarted that right well into the twentieth century with a variety of devices such as LITERACY TESTS, POLL TAXES, and the WHITE PRIMARY. The Fifteenth

Amendment to the Constitution, ratified in 1870, made it illegal to deny the vote "on account of race, color, or previous condition of servitude." At that time, the amendment affected only men. (See BLACK SUFFRAGE.)

"The right of citizens of the United States to vote shall not be denied or abridged by the United States or by any State on account of sex."

—Nineteenth Amendment, ratified in 1920

History of the Movement

Before the Civil War, three significant events in women's suffrage took place at about the same time. One was the 1848 Women's Rights Convention called by Lucretia Mott and Elizabeth Cady Stanton at Seneca Falls, New York, Stanton's hometown. The two women persuaded the convention to take the highly controversial step of including a call for the vote in its declaration of principles. This act marked the unofficial start of the women's suffrage movement.

The second major event was the first national suffrage convention, organized at Worcester, Massachusetts, in 1850 by Lucy Stone, who later founded the American Woman Suffrage Association. Two years later Stanton and Susan B. Anthony jointly organized another convention, this one at Syracuse, New York. Both women, like Lucy Stone, were veterans of the effort to abolish slavery. Anthony had vowed to "ignore all laws to help the slave, [and] ignore it all to protect an enslaved woman."

Also prominent in both the abolition and suffrage causes were Victoria Claflin Woodhull and Sojourner Truth. Woodhull, a spiritualist and preacher, ran for president in 1872, before women could vote. Her RUNNING MATE was African American leader Frederick Douglass. Truth, a former slave born Isabella, was known for her "Aren't I a Woman?" speech to a mid-1800s women's convention. (Scholars later determined that this famous phrase was never uttered by her.) She later fell out with Mott, Stanton, and other white suffragists because she thought black men should have the vote before women.

This illustrated program cover, published by the National American Women's Suffrage Association in 1913, depicts decorated women marching toward the U.S. Capitol.

Source: Library of Congress

After the Civil War, Anthony and others contended that the Fourteenth Amendment (1868), which forbade states to "abridge the privileges or immunities of citizens of the United States," had given women equal rights, including voting rights. The amendment set penalties for any state that denied the vote to its adult male inhabitants, without reference to race. Undeterred by the fact that the amendment specified *male* inhabitants, the militant women seized upon its broader recognition of equality. They also contended that the Fifteenth Amendment's use of the word *race* was not meant to exclude women but was instead meant to suggest a type of forbidden discrimination. The combined effect of the Fourteenth and Fifteenth Amendments undergirded the demand for women's suffrage.

In St. Louis, suffragists Francis and Virginia Minor were among those who argued that the Fourteenth Amendment and the Fifteenth Amendment implied a national citizenship that included voting rights. They encouraged test cases, and Virginia Minor's own denial of registration reached the Supreme Court. In *Minor v. Happersett* (1875) the Court dismissed the national citizenship theory and declared that the Constitution conferred no suffrage rights. Women's suffrage would have to come from the states or a constitutional amendment.

In 1872, Anthony and fifteen other women were arrested for "voting without a lawful right to vote" in Rochester, New York, after registering under the Fourteenth Amendment's guarantee of protection of citizens' privileges and immunities. Anthony never paid the $100 fine. She and her followers then pressed Congress for a constitutional amendment granting the FRANCHISE to women, but the Senate rejected the proposal 34–16 in 1887.

The suffragists were more successful in some states. By the end of the nineteenth century, four western states had extended the franchise to women, beginning with Wyoming in 1890, followed by Colorado in 1893 and Utah and Idaho in 1896. Then, as the PROGRESSIVE movement gained influence, additional states gave women the vote: Washington in 1910; California in 1911; Arizona, Kansas, and Oregon in 1912; Montana and Nevada in 1914; New York in 1917; and Michigan, South Dakota, and Oklahoma in 1918.

Arguments for and against the vote included extravagant claims. Some said women's enfranchisement would end corruption in American politics; others cautioned that it would lead to free love. Those in favor of keeping the status quo argued that women had virtual representation in government through the votes of husbands, fathers, and other men in their lives.

Activist suffragettes (as women suffragists were sometimes called) did not accept that rationale. By 1914 some advocates, led by Alice Paul, president of the National Women's Party, were using more militant tactics. They opposed every Democratic candidate in the eleven states where women could vote, regardless of the candidate's position on women's suffrage. They reasoned that the majority party should be held responsible for the failure of Congress to endorse a constitutional amendment. More than half of the forty-three Democrats running in those races were defeated.

> "We hold these truths to be self-evident: that all men and women are created equal; that they are endowed by their Creator with certain inalienable rights; that among these are life, liberty, and the pursuit of happiness; that to secure these rights governments are instituted, deriving their just powers from the consent of the governed. Whenever any form of Government becomes destructive of these ends, it is the right of those who suffer from it to refuse allegiance to it, and to insist upon the institution of a new government. ... Prudence, indeed, will dictate that governments long established should not be changed for light and transient causes. ... But when a long train of abuses and usurpations, pursuing invariably the same object, evinces a design to reduce them under absolute despotism, it is their duty to throw off such government, and to provide new guards for their future security. Such has been the patient sufferance of the women under this government, and such is now the necessity which constrains them to demand the equal station to which they are entitled."
>
> —From the Declaration of Sentiments, which was closely modeled on the Declaration of Independence and issued at the Women's Rights Convention held at Seneca Falls, New York, July 19 and 20, 1848

Many suffragists saw President Woodrow Wilson as a major obstacle to their movement, even though he favored women's suffrage. Wilson preferred to let the states handle voting qualifications and was opposed to the idea of a constitutional amendment. Women responded by demonstrating in Washington, D.C., and thousands were arrested and jailed.

In January 1918 Wilson finally announced his support for the proposed amendment. The House agreed the next day. Only after a new Congress met in 1919, however, did the Senate join the House in mustering the two-thirds majority required to send the amendment to the states for ratification. The amendment took effect in August 1920, when three-fourths of the states had consented to ratification.

After the Nineteenth Amendment took effect, VOTER TURNOUT rose significantly. The amendment added women in thirty-three states to those in the fifteen states that had already granted the vote to women. The total vote for president in 1916, when Wilson won reelection, was 18.5 million. Four years later, when Republican Warren G. Harding defeated Democrat James M. Cox, the turnout was 26.8 million.

Harding was the first president elected after all American women became eligible to vote. The last president elected entirely by men—before any state had enfranchised women—was Benjamin Harrison, a Republican, in 1888.

Aftermath

In 1921 a marble statue honoring suffragists Anthony, Stanton, and Mott was dedicated in the Rotunda of the U.S. Capitol. Congress had grudgingly accepted the gift at the insistence of Alice Paul.

The day after its dedication, the statue was moved to the Crypt area below the main floor level. Irreverently nicknamed "Three Ladies in a Bathtub," the statue has been viewed by millions of Capitol visitors.

Women's rights advocates protested the location, however, and raised private funds to have it moved in 1997 to the Rotunda area. Some African American women leaders tried unsuccessfully to stop the move because the statue did not depict Sojourner Truth.

The sculptor, Adelaide Johnson, left an uncarved background to the statue to symbolize the unfinished fight for women's rights. She died in 1955 at age 108.

"When the women of the country come in and sit with you, though there may be but very few in the next few years, I pledge you that you will get ability, you will get integrity of purpose, you will get exalted patriotism, and you will get unstinted usefulness."

—*Georgia Democrat Rebecca Latimer Felton,* following her swearing-in at age eighty-seven to a one-day appointed tenure in November 1922 that made her the first woman to serve in the U.S. Senate

By 2011, ninety-one years after the Nineteenth Amendment was ratified, women are represented in the Capitol not only by a statue but also by statutes they have helped to enact. By the first decade of the twenty-first century, more than 200 women had served as senators and representatives.

Women as voters are far from a monolithic constituency. Their partisan preferences over the years have followed regional, demographic, and socioeconomic patterns similar to those of men. Yet at least since the shift of the Republican Party to a more conservative stance during the presidency of Ronald Reagan in the 1980s, a "gender gap" has intermittently emerged in voters' preferences. Public opinion polls tend to show that women have stronger concerns about issues involving children, education, health care, and retirement security and favor less militaristic solutions to international problems—positions more closely identified with the Democratic Party than the Republican Party. Polling on election day by media outlets has shown women, in most but not all years, have favored Democratic candidates by modest margins.

The gender gap varies in size, however, and at times seems to disappear. For instance, concerns over national and homeland security in the wake of the September 11, 2001, attacks led women to vote for President George W. Bush on the Republican ticket in 2004 at about the same rate as men. But as the war in Iraq became prolonged and unpopular, many polls showed job approval ratings for Bush dropping more sharply among women than among men.

The League of Women Voters, successor in 1920 to the National American Woman Suffrage Association (formed in 1890 by a merger of Stone's American Woman Suffrage Association and

Stanton and Anthony's National Woman Suffrage Association), sponsored televised presidential DEBATES in 1976–1984. Since 1988 the sponsor has been the Commission on Presidential Debates.

Sixty-two years after ratification of the Nineteenth Amendment, the proposed Equal Rights Amendment (ERA) died because it fell three states short of the thirty-eight needed for ratification. In spirit, if not in potential application, the ERA was related to the women's suffrage movement. Alice Paul had proposed an early version of it. The failed amendment, as sent to the states by Congress in 1972, said in part, "Equality of rights under the law shall not be abridged or denied by the United States or by any state on account of sex." But the amendment was strongly opposed by many conservatives who viewed the ERA as either unnecessary—on grounds that women already had sufficient protections under the law—or as an instrument for creating special rights for women.

More on this topic:

Black Suffrage, p. 28

Literacy Tests, p. 309

Poll Taxes, p. 426

Right to Vote, p. 549

Workers World Party (1959–)

With the Hungarian citizen revolt and other developments in Eastern Europe providing some impetus, the Workers World Party in 1959 split off from the SOCIALIST WORKERS PARTY. The party theoretically supports worker uprisings in all parts of the world. Yet it backed the communist governments that put down rebellions in Hungary during the 1950s, Czechoslovakia in the 1960s, and Poland in the 1980s.

Workers World is an activist revolutionary group that, up until 1980, concentrated its efforts on specific issues, such as the antiwar and civil rights demonstrations during the 1960s and 1970s. The party has an active youth organization, Youth Against War and Fascism.

Workers World Party presidential candidate Monica Morehead attends a third-party presidential debate in October 1996. Morehead and her supporters disrupted the debate with complaints that she had not been formally invited to participate.

Source: AP Images/Joe Marquette

In 1980 party leaders saw an opportunity, created by the weakness of the U.S. economy and the related high unemployment, to interest voters in its revolutionary ideas. That year it placed Deirdre Griswold, the editor of the party's newspaper and one of its founding members, on the presidential ballot in ten states. Together with her RUNNING MATE Larry Holmes, a twenty-seven-year-old black activist, Griswold received 13,300 votes. In 1984, Holmes ran as the presidential candidate, getting on the ballot in eight states and receiving 15,329 votes. In 1988 Holmes ran with Gloria La Riva, and they garnered 7,846 votes. La Riva ran as the presidential candidate in 1992 and was on the ballot only in New Mexico, where she received 181 votes.

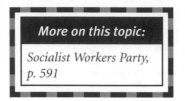

More on this topic:

Socialist Workers Party, p. 591

The Workers World Party improved its support base in 1996, though it remained a sliver of the national electorate. Its candidate, Monica Moorehead of New Jersey, was on the ballot in twelve states and received 29,082 votes.

Even that lift was temporary. Moorehead, as the party's 2000 nominee, received a total of fewer than 5,000 votes from four states. The party hit low ebb in 2004 when presidential nominee John Parker of California received just 1,646 votes, most of those from the state of Washington. The party did not appear on any ballot in 2008.

Write-In Vote

Voters who opt to write in the name of a candidate usually do so because they are not satisfied with any of the official candidates who qualified for the ballot. On rarer occasions, an unusually strong candidate will attract support with a write-in candidacy occasioned because of BALLOT ACCESS problems or because the candidate entered the contest too late to qualify for the ballot.

Only an exceptionally strong candidate can win by write-in votes or even make a serious impact on the outcome of the race. An impressive demonstration of voter sentiment occurred in Minnesota's 1952 Republican PRESIDENTIAL PRIMARY when more than 100,000 voters wrote in Dwight D. Eisenhower's name. That showing of strength gave Eisenhower a commanding lead in his contest with Sen. Robert A. Taft of Ohio for the GOP nomination. Two years later, Strom Thurmond, the former governor of South Carolina, received 143,442 write-in votes in the state's DEMOCRATIC PARTY primary for U.S. senator, defeating the PARTY-ENDORSED candidate. At that time, a Democratic SOUTHERN PRIMARY victory virtually ensured election. Thurmond, who switched to the REPUBLICAN PARTY in 1964, was—until 2010—the only U.S. senator in the history of popular election (instituted nationally in 1913 by the Seventeenth Amendment to the Constitution) to owe his election to write-in votes.

But in 2010, in Alaska, an even more astounding write-in campaign allowed Republican incumbent senator Lisa Murkowski to retain her seat after losing the GOP primary to a largely unknown challenger, Jeff Miller, a former U.S. magistrate judge. Miller was a favorite of TEA PARTY activists who influenced many contests nationwide that year and significantly helped Republicans recapture control of the House of Representatives. Murkowski was believed to never have taken Miller's challenge seriously until too late in the campaign to reverse the movement that led to her defeat. Miller was aided by the typically low voter turnout that often characterizes midterm elections, especially party primaries. The two candidates together polled under 110,000 votes, compared with more than 258,000 cast in the fall election that Murkowski won. Blocked from running as an independent by SORE LOSER LAWS, she decided to wage a high-risk write-in campaign. Murkowski beat Miller by more than 10,000 votes.

Gregory Giroux, senior reporter for *Congressional Quarterly*'s CQPolitics.com, in August 2006 conducted an analysis of past elections. He identified only three House members in the post–World War II era who were elected on write-in votes: Dale Alford of Arkansas in 1958, Joe Skeen of New Mexico in 1980, and Ron Packard of California in 1982.

Giroux's analysis was written in the midst of the 2006 campaign season in which two contests showed that it is possible to win as a write-in candidate—but it is certainly not likely.

The 2006 write-in victory occurred in the Democratic primary in Ohio's Sixth Congressional District. With popular Democratic incumbent Ted Strickland leaving the seat open for what would be his successful run for governor, Democratic officials banked on a strong campaign by state lawmaker Charlie Wilson to enable them to hold the vulnerable "swing" district. The campaign initially looked like it was headed toward disaster: Wilson's organization failed to meet the minimal threshold of valid petition signatures required to qualify the candidate for the May primary ballot. But Wilson staged an intense and successful effort to persuade Democratic primary voters to write his name in rather than vote for one of the two little-known candidates whose names appeared on the ballot. The grass-roots network Wilson built to accomplish this gave him such momentum that he ended up cruising to an easy victory in November, when his name appeared on the general election ballot.

The more usual scenario, of a write-in campaign ending in defeat, was exposed in the general election in Texas's Twenty-second Congressional District. Republican representative Tom DeLay, one of the top power-brokers in Washington during the ascendancy of a House Republican majority that began with the 1994 elections, had become the target of numerous ethics controversies. Failing in the polls, DeLay decided to renounce the nomination for reelection that he had won in the March 2006 primary and resign from Congress that June.

DeLay intended to change his official residence to his apartment in the Virginia suburbs of Washington, D.C., to disqualify himself from running; the Constitution requires members of Congress to live in the states they represent. Had he been allowed to do this, the Republicans could have replaced him on the ballot with another candidate, under Texas law. But the Democrats sued, arguing that DeLay's change of address was a partisan ruse, and a federal court ruled that the Republicans could not prove beyond doubt that DeLay would not reestablish Texas residency before the November election and thus be eligible to run for election.

As a result, the Republicans could not put the name of their replacement candidate, Houston City Councilwoman Shelley Sekula-Gibbs, on the ballot on the Republican line, which remained blank. Instead, Sekula-Gibbs waged a write-in campaign against Democrat Nick Lampson, a former House member seeking a comeback. But the campaign required a massive voter-education effort and dedication from voters, who had to enter Sekula-Gibbs's eighteen-letter name on the touch-screen voting machines. The effort fell short, with Lampson winning by 52 percent to 42 percent.

Perhaps more than any other aspect of elections, write-in voting has held an uncertain place in the constitutional guarantee of the RIGHT TO VOTE. This ambiguity reflects the perceived inefficiency of counting write-in votes when elections are conducted with printed ballots or VOTING MACHINES.

The U.S. Constitution leaves to each state the administration of its own elections and also gives each state the dominant role in conducting federal elections within its borders. Additionally, the Supreme Court has taken into account the need for substantial state regulation of the electoral process so that elections may be held in a fair and orderly way. (See STATE AND FEDERAL ELECTION RESPONSIBILITIES.)

At the same time, however, the Court in numerous instances has upheld voters' rights and invalidated some state regulations as too restrictive. Many observers therefore were surprised when the Court ruled 6–3 in a Hawaii case June 8, 1992, that states may prohibit write-in voting altogether, rejecting arguments that such action violates citizens' rights to free speech and political association. The Court made it clear, however, that a state is free to provide for write-in voting and that the Court's decision should not be read to discourage such voting.

In the colonial period and in the early decades of the United States, all voting by ballots was, in a sense, write-in voting. Preprinted ballots were not yet in use, and voters wrote on their ballots the name of their choice for public office. Actually, during that time most elections, especially in the South, were decided by voice vote.

Secret Ballot

In the face of widespread voting corruption, the Australian ballot—dating from South Australia in the mid-nineteenth century—was introduced in the United States in the 1880s; this was an official ballot printed at public expense, and carrying the names of all legitimately nominated candidates. The

Washington, D.C., mayor Anthony A. Williams celebrates an election victory in November 2002.

Source: AP Images/Lawrence Jackson

In September 2002, Washington, D.C., mayor Anthony A. Williams waged a successful write-in campaign after he was denied ballot access for the Democratic Party primary because his nominating petitions contained many invalid signatures, some of them forgeries or fraudulent in other ways. He won the primary with 61,848 votes—more than any other candidate in either party's primary, some of them also write-ins—and easily won reelection in November. His campaign was fined $277,700 for its preprimary signature infractions. Among the "5,465 obvious forgeries" noted by city officials were the names of actor Kelsey Grammer, singer Billy Joel, and United Nations secretary-general Kofi Annan.

Australian ballot filled the need for an absolutely secret and indistinguishable ballot. Its size, shape, and color gave no indication of what candidates or political parties the user voted for. Previously, parties printed and distributed their own ballots, making SPLIT-TICKET or THIRD-PARTY voting difficult if not impossible. (See BALLOT TYPES.)

By about 1910 most of the states had adopted the Australian system. About that time, too, voting machines were beginning to be used, and in the computer age they play an ever-larger role in elections.

Generally, after the Australian ballot came into use, states made a blank line on the paper ballots available for write-in votes. Then too, manufacturers of voting machines typically included a device that made write-in votes possible, if seldom easy.

Because the Australian ballot tended to diminish the rights of citizens to vote for persons not listed on the printed ballots, many state courts took actions in the late nineteenth century upholding write-in voting. State courts also played a significant role in asserting the option of write-in voting when automated voting became the rule in heavily populated areas.

Balancing Test

The Supreme Court has provided the states with considerable leeway in their conduct of elections. In an Ohio case, *Anderson v. Celebrezze,* the Court in 1983 established a so-called balancing test for reviewing election rules. The balancing test requires that any court must first determine whether, and to what extent, an election law injures a voter's First Amendment rights. Next, the court must decide whether the state's interests are sufficient to justify the burden imposed on the voter's First Amendment rights.

In the case brought by INDEPENDENT presidential candidate John B. Anderson in 1980, the Court found in Anderson's favor, overturning a lower federal court that had upheld Ohio's early filing deadline for independent candidates. Despite such deadlines and various SORE LOSER LAWS, Anderson had managed to appear on the ballot in every state in 1980 as an opponent to President Jimmy Carter and his successful Republican challenger, Ronald Reagan.

The Supreme Court used its balancing test in deciding the 1992 Hawaii write-in case, *Burdick v. Takushi.* The state's prohibition of write-in voting was permissible, the majority said, because the ban imposed only a "very limited burden" on voters' rights.

Hawaii in 1992 was one of three states (the others were Oklahoma and Nevada) that banned write-in voting. Thirty-six other states restricted write-ins in a significant way. In the *Washington Post* April 14, 1991, before the *Burdick* decision, political reporter David Broder wrote, "Hawaii is virtually a one-party state. . . . The ruling Democrats have rigged the laws so that where there is no opponent the office does not even appear on the general election ballot." Indeed, Alan Burdick, the Honolulu voter who challenged his state's write-in ban, did not want to vote for a Democratic candidate unopposed in his local legislative district.

More on this topic:
Ballot Types, p. 17
Right to Vote, p. 549
State and Federal Election Responsibilities, p. 606
Voting Machines, p. 661

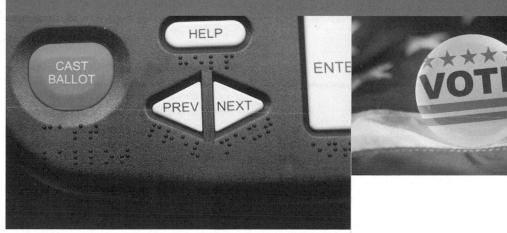

Y

Yellow Dog Democrat *See* BLUE DOG DEMOCRAT; BRASS COLLAR DEMOCRAT.

Youth Suffrage

Actor John Cusack spoke in October 2004 at a "Youth to the Booth" student rally at New Mexico State University. The rally was held to motivate young people to vote for John Kerry in the 2004 presidential election.

Source: AP Images/Norm Dettlaff

The most recent constitutional change affecting the RIGHT TO VOTE was the lowering of the voting age to eighteen. The TWENTY-SIXTH AMENDMENT made the change in 1971.

Lowering the voting age had long been debated, but the proposition gained momentum in the 1960s because of three overlapping factors: the huge post–World War II "baby boom" generation, generally defined by demographers as Americans born between 1946 and 1964, began to reach adulthood; there was an upsurge in youth student activism, especially on college campuses, spurred largely by the unpopularity of the U.S. military intervention in Vietnam; and the fact that

◉ **CLOSER LOOK**

There are dozens of organizations working to elevate the numbers of young Americans engaged in the political process. Groups with a high national profile and that are nonpartisan in nature include Rock the Vote, which leverages the resources of the music and entertainment industries to attract youth participation; Youthvote.org; and Generation Engage, which in 2010 became part of Mobilize.org., a related youth organization. Mobilize.org describes itself as a nonpartisan organization to help young persons born between 1976 and 1999—often referred to as millennials—to "create and implement solutions to social problems" and "to create long-term, sustainable and community-based solutions to the challenges facing our generation." It was founded in 2000 on the University of California's Berkeley campus in reaction to proposed tuition hikes.

Numerous interest groups with ostensibly nonpartisan youth voting efforts are focused on specific issues, such as minority concerns, economic opportunity, or the environment. On the partisan side, both major parties and some third, or alternative, parties have divisions that encourage support and participation by young voters; the major-party committees also provide material and logistical support to their college affiliates, the College Democrats and the College Republicans.

It remains to be seen, though, whether youth political engagement will continue to grow, or if it is a phenomenon tied largely to the rise of certain issues such as the war in Iraq, ferment over social issues such as abortion and gay rights, and rising higher education costs, that could prove ephemeral.

many thousands of Americans between the ages of eighteen and twenty-one had been sent to fight in Vietnam yet did not have the right to vote on the leaders making decisions about the war.

The idea of changing the voting age to eighteen emerged during an earlier war. Before World War II, no state permitted voting by persons under twenty-one. Led by Georgia's wartime lowering of the voting age in 1943, after a drive marked by the CAMPAIGN SLOGAN "Fight at Eighteen, Vote at Eighteen," several states passed the more liberal requirement.

Also in the early 1940s, Sen. Arthur Vandenberg, a Republican from Michigan, and Rep. Jennings Randolph, a Democrat from West Virginia, introduced measures to lower the voting age to eighteen, but Congress did not act on them. President Dwight D. Eisenhower, a Republican and former general who had led the Allied forces in Europe during World War II, pro-

posed a constitutional amendment in 1954, but it failed to receive the two-thirds vote in the Senate necessary for advancement.

Sixteen years later, in the midst of the Vietnam War, Congress included an age provision in the 1970 amendments to the 1965 VOTING RIGHTS ACT. The amendments set a minimum voting age of eighteen for all federal, state, and local elections. But later in 1970, by a 5–4 vote in *OREGON V. MITCHELL*, the Supreme Court declared the age requirement unconstitutional for state and local elections. Although it upheld most other sections of the act, including the lower voting age in federal elections, the Court said Congress exceeded its authority in attempting to over-rule state constitutions that set the voting age between nineteen and twenty-one.

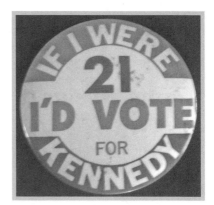

This campaign button predates the Twenty-sixth Amendment.

Source: Courtesy of Christopher Schardt

"The right of citizens of the United States, who are eighteen years of age or older, to vote shall not be denied or abridged by the United States or by any State on account of age."

—Twenty-sixth Amendment to the Constitution, section 1, ratified 1971

Congress and the states promptly moved to correct the situation, which would have required election officials in some states to maintain two sets of VOTER REGISTRATION rolls—one for presidential and congressional elections, and the other for state and local elections. Ratification of the Twenty-sixth Amendment in 1971 took only 107 days—less than half the time needed to ratify any other amendment.

The amendment states: "The right of citizens of the United States, who are eighteen years of age or older, to vote shall not be denied or abridged by the United States or by any State on account of age."

Test Case Sought

Although the Constitution leaves presidents out of the procedure for passing amendments, presidents can use the "bully pulpit" of their office to try to influence their approval or defeat by Congress or the states. In the case of the Twenty-sixth Amendment, President Richard M. Nixon urged Congress in 1970 to work on such an amendment in case the Supreme Court invalidated Congress's action lowering the voting age in state elections to eighteen—which it ultimately did in *Oregon v. Mitchell.* At Nixon's direction, Attorney General John N. Mitchell helped to bring about the suit in which he was named, resulting in a speedy determination that Congress alone could not lower the vote age for all elections.

Before the amendment was ratified, only four states permitted voting under age twenty-one. Besides Georgia, they were Kentucky, which also set the minimum at eighteen; Hawaii, twenty; and Alaska, nineteen. Voters in three states—New Jersey, Ohio, and Oregon—had recently rejected lower voting ages. Fifteen other states planned to hold referendums on the issue in the 1970 elections.

The Twenty-sixth Amendment was the fourth amendment to enlarge the electorate since the Constitution was adopted in 1789. The others were the Fifteenth, which gave the vote to former slaves and their descendants (1870); the Nineteenth, which enfranchised women (1920); and the Twenty-third, which permitted Washington, D.C., residents to vote for president (1961). (See BLACK SUFFRAGE; DISTRICT OF COLUMBIA; WOMEN'S SUFFRAGE.)

Some 11 million young Americans gained the right to vote because of the Twenty-sixth Amendment. Another 14 million became eligible to vote for president for the first time in 1972 because in the 1968 election they had been under twenty-one, the minimum voting age then in effect in most states.

Appeals to Young Voters

The prevalence of young Americans in liberal political movements of the 1960s and early 1970s, especially in opposition to the Vietnam War, spurred hopes among Democratic strategists that the Twenty-sixth Amendment would be a boon to their party's hopes in the 1972 presidential election and beyond. But Republicans such as Nixon and Republican-controlled state legislatures also advocated the amendment, signaling that young voters were much more diverse and politically divided than suggested by the popular culture of the time.

In the 1972 election, both Nixon and his Democratic opponent, Sen. George S. McGovern of South Dakota, courted the youth vote. An estimated 7.5 million of the newly eligible young voters were students, and McGovern's anti–Vietnam War stance was popular on campuses. The McGovern campaign concentrated its efforts on the student segment of the young voters.

The Nixon campaign aimed its appeal at the larger nonstudent group of young voters, numbering about 17.5 million. They included workers, housewives, soldiers, and job seekers.

According to a profile by the Commerce Department, a typical young first-time voter in 1972 was white, single, living in a family, not going to school. He or she was a high school graduate, a jobholder, and lived in a metropolitan area.

A Gallup POLL before the November 1972 election indicated that college students were almost evenly divided between Nixon and McGovern, who ran a stumbling campaign and was effectively branded by Nixon's reelection operation as too liberal on a range of issues, including national defense. Earlier polls had shown McGovern leading Nixon among young voters by a substantial margin. On that basis McGovern's organization initially predicted a 10-million-vote victory, which never happened.

Nixon was reelected with 60.7 percent of the POPULAR VOTE, a LANDSLIDE second only to Lyndon B. Johnson's 61.1 percent in 1964. McGovern and his RUNNING MATE, R. Sargent Shriver, won only Massachusetts and the District of Columbia.

In his reelection statement Nixon attributed his victory partly to the youth vote. He said: "We have accomplished what was thought to be impossible . . . we won a majority of the votes of young Americans."

> **"We have accomplished what was thought to be impossible . . . we won a majority of the votes of young Americans."**
>
> **—President Richard Nixon,** after winning reelection in 1972

Nixon's jubilation was short-lived, however. Less than two years later, facing impeachment, he resigned from office for his role in the Watergate SCANDAL stemming from a burglary before the 1972 election at the DEMOCRATIC NATIONAL COMMITTEE headquarters that had been orchestrated by members of his administration and campaign team and then covered up.

New voters eighteen to twenty years old showed no great enthusiasm for going to the polls in 1972 or later, at least until well into the 2000s decade. Their VOTER TURNOUT rate in the 1972 election was 48.3 percent, compared with 55.2 percent for the population as a whole. But periodic surveys by the Census Bureau found a noticeable increase in the voting rate of this group in 2004 and 2008. In both presidential elections, the bureau's survey found 41 percent of this age group went to the polls, up from just 28 percent in 2000 and 31.2 percent in 1996. Guide to US Elections shows that number as 31 percent; so, 31.2 is most likely the more exact number; go with it. The 2004 uptick was attributed at least in part to the unpopularity of the Bush administration, especially its war in Iraq. The 2008 number was likewise seen as a reflection on President Bush but also enthusiasm for the Democratic presidential candidate, Barack Obama. Exit polls on election day in 2008 supported this belief. They showed that voters eighteen to twenty-one favored Obama 66 percent to 32 percent for his opponent, Sen. John McCain.

This apparent increase in political engagement accompanied the rise of the Internet and various social media such as Facebook and Twitter as tools for political organizing and information. In addition, partisan and nonpartisan groups have stepped up their efforts to attract young voters, who have frequently complained that such groups do not address their unique concerns and perspectives. Although in the past many candidates had essentially written off the youth vote because of its low turnout rates, a number of contenders stepped up their efforts to target this constituency after 2000.

However, continued low turnout rates of youth in the midterm congressional elections showed that this age bracket was less motivated than older voters to participate in the political process. In 2006, for example, census surveys showed a turnout rate for eighteen to twenty-one year olds of just 17 percent compared to 22 percent for those twenty-one to twenty-four and 28 percent of persons twenty-five to thirty-four years old.

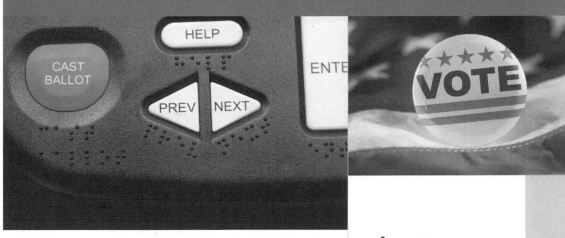

ZZZ

Facebook. MySpace. YouTube. Twitter. A myriad of other Internet sites catering to esoteric interests from puppies to quantum physics. Casinos and other gambling venues as one of the nation's growth industries. Poker tournaments and twenty-hour sports channels on television. Cable and satellite television, now available in high definition. Digital cameras. Cell phones that fit in the palm of your hand—and contain digital cameras and allow Internet access. Notebook-sized electronic pads that allow online connections and substitute for laptop computers. E-readers that allow full books to be downloaded and read without a person ever touching paper. Personal digital assistants. High-powered video game systems. Tiny music players that store massive digital libraries.

These are just a few of the diversions that have, in recent years, captured the American public's attention to a degree far greater than politics and government. To many Americans, a population seldom prone throughout the nation's history to give rapt daily attention to politics, politics is one big snore—or ZZZ, the cartoon symbol of sleep. Veteran political reporters Jack Germond and Jules Witcover even titled their chronicle of the 1992 presidential election *Wake Me When It's Over*.

Further, many voters feel that their vote does not count, despite the sharply conflicting evidence that a few votes' difference could have changed the outcomes of scores of close U.S. elections, notably the 1976 race between Gerald R. Ford and Jimmy Carter and the 2000 contest between George W. Bush and Al Gore, the POPULAR VOTE winner. A few thousand votes in certain states could have changed the result of the 1976 race, and the 2000 race hinged on the outcome of the tally in Florida, where Bush was certified as the winner by just 537 votes.

The sense of civic duty that once drove a stronger interest in the political sphere—and was briefly invigorated just a couple of generations ago by President John F. Kennedy's clarion call to public service—has surely not disappeared from American society. After all, more than 131 million people took the time to vote in the 2008 presidential election, the largest number in U.S. history.

"Let every nation know, whether it wishes us well or ill, that we shall pay any price, bear any burden, meet any hardship, support any friend, oppose any foe, in order to assure the survival and the success of liberty. . . . And so, my fellow Americans: ask not what your country can do for you—ask what you can do for your country."

—President John F. Kennedy in his inaugural address on January 20, 1961

But the days in which Americans viewed politics as a form of entertainment are long gone. Before there was pervasive mass communication, torchlight parades, stem-winder speeches, and WHISTLE-STOP train tours brought color to citizens' lives in tightly packed cities and isolated rural towns alike. Such events do not belong to the distant past alone: the ability of a visiting president to draw throngs of the curious and the star-struck persuaded President Kennedy to visit Dallas on November 22, 1963, and travel a well-publicized motorcade route in an open convertible.

The gruesome murder of Kennedy that day is said by some historians and sociologists to have ended the age of American innocence. Then there were the subsequent assassinations of the president's brother, Sen. Robert F. Kennedy, and civil rights icon the Rev. Martin Luther King Jr.; the menacing of President Gerald R. Ford and the shooting of presidential contender George Wallace and President Ronald Reagan by would-be assassins; the dangers inferred by the bombing in Oklahoma City in 1995 and the attacks on September 11, 2001. All of these events forced the nation's political leaders into tighter and tighter security bubbles, creating ever more distance between them and the citizens they govern.

Some commentators argue that the pervasive national sense of optimism, present for much of U.S. history, has been eroded by the events noted above as well as costly and controversial wars in Vietnam, Iraq, and Afghanistan. Others contend that the vibrancy of the nation's political discourse is not waning, but flourishing. And there is some evidence that they may be right.

Although much has been made of the fact that only 49 percent of the voting-age population—and far less of the population eighteen to twenty years old—turned out for the 1996 presidential election, some experts believe that the voter turnout situation is hardly dire. They point to the use of voting-age population as a benchmark as distorting because that figure includes millions of noncitizens (many of them recent immigrants) and felons who are not permitted to vote. These analysts' statistics show that calculating voter turnout as a percentage of the voting-*eligible* population results in participation rates at or at least near their historic norms.

Such statistical analysis also shows that voting among the youngest Americans, while still lagging behind the general population, has seen an uptick over recent elections, spurred by response to international terrorism, the war in Iraq, and concerns about the nation's energy supply and the environment.

Politically oriented sites have flourished on the Internet. The "mainstream media" and alternative sources offer news sites, while hosts of blogs offer town-hall-style bipartisan discussion groups, rallying centers for political partisans, highly partisan perspectives that sometimes are intended mainly to irritate and outrage readers. Politicians have proven nimble in using this still fairly new technology, using their own sites, blogs, and even social networking sites such as Facebook to grow and energize their support bases and raise money.

In the early twenty-first century, two of the most popular programs on cable television are political satires on Comedy Central: *The Daily Show with Jon Stewart* and its spin-off, *The Colbert Report*. The shows have mainly youthful and liberal-leaning audiences. Many of their viewers have said that they learn most of what they know about current affairs from watching these shows, which are clearly advertised as "fake news." It is not clear whether this says more about the audience or the ability of traditional journalists to reach these viewers. Nonetheless, with no obligation to maintain objectivity, these programs cut to the quick in a fashion that resonates, at least with like-minded Americans.

Another late night comedian, *The Tonight Show*'s Jay Leno, has a long-running feature called "Jaywalking," in which he reveals the lack of knowledge some Americans have of politics and government. Leno interviews men and women on the street, many of whom are attractive and engaging but appear to be entirely clueless of what is going on in the world around them.

Many Americans receive their political news through popular "fake news" programs such as The Daily Show with Jon Stewart. In turn, many politicians have decided to make appearances on these shows, with the hopes of reaching new audiences.

Source: AP Images/Jason DeCrow

But it appears there is reason for hope that the "ZZZ" represents more of a nap than a coma in the body politic. Technological improvements might allow political parties and candidates for office to campaign in ways that capture greater public interest. At the beginning of the twenty-first century, the nation was grappling with substantial issues that demanded greater public participation in politics and elections: the war in Iraq and Afghanistan, global climate change, large federal budget deficits, illegal immigration, and a looming crisis in financing Social Security and Medicare benefits for future generations. The close 2000, 2004, and 2008 presidential elections, which revealed sharp differences between the nominees of the two major political parties, amply demonstrated that elections do indeed have consequences.

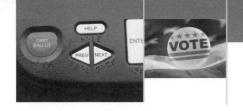

Reference Material

CHANGES IN DEMOCRATS' NOMINATING RULES

Between 1972 and 1992, Democrats tinkered with their nominating rules every four years, producing a system that, if not better than before, was always different. In 1996 the party left its rules unchanged for the first time in twenty years. The Democrats also did not make any significant rule changes in 2000, 2004, or 2008. As they prepared for the 2008 presidential nomination process, though, the Democrats adopted rule changes that addressed the primary and caucus calendar.

Responding to longstanding complaints about the primacy of the "first in the nation" Iowa caucuses and New Hampshire primary and concerns about those states' relative lack of demographic diversity, the Democrats officially moved the dates of two other events up near the start of the process.

They also attempted to persuade states not to join in the "front-loading," or early scheduling of nominating events, but it quickly became clear that this effort would not be successful. Many states, including such major population centers as California, New York, Florida, Illinois, and New Jersey, moved their primaries up so that they would be held much earlier than in the past. Two states, Michigan and Florida, even moved their primaries into January in violation of party rules.

The following chart shows the ebb and flow of the Democratic Party's rules changes, with a "✓" indicating the years these major rules were in effect.

	1972	1976	1980	1984	1988	1992–2004	2008
Timing: Restrict all or most delegate-selection events to a three-month period (the "window").			✓	✓	✓	✓	✓
Move up Nevada caucuses and South Carolina primary to provide regional and demographic balance to traditional kickoff events, the Iowa caucuses and New Hampshire primary.							✓
Provide bonus delegates to states that do not join in "front loading" of the primary and caucus schedule.							✓
Conditions of Participation: Restrict participation in delegate-selection events to Democrats.		✓	✓	✓	✓	✓	✓
Proportional Representation: Ban all types of winner-take-all contests.				✓		✓	✓
Ban all types of winner-reward contests (where winner receives extra delegates).						✓	✓
Delegate Loyalty: Give candidates the right to approve delegates identifying with their candidacy.		✓	✓	✓	✓	✓	✓
Bind delegates to vote for their original presidential preference at convention on first ballot.				✓			
Party and Elected Officials: Expand each delegation to include pledged party and elected officials.			✓	✓	✓	✓	✓
Further expand each delegation to include uncommitted party and elected officials ("superdelegates").					✓	✓	✓
Demographic Representation: Encourage participation and representation of minorities and traditionally underrepresented groups (affirmative action).			✓	✓	✓	✓	✓
Require delegations to be equally divided between men and women.			✓	✓	✓	✓	✓

DEMOCRATIC PARTY'S REFORM COMMISSIONS ON PRESIDENTIAL SELECTION

Known as	Formal name	Years in operation	Chair	Size	Mandating body
McGovern-Fraser Commission	Commission on Party Structure and Delegate Selection	1969–1972	Sen. George McGovern (S.D.), 1969–1970; Rep. Donald M. Fraser (Minn.), 1971–1972a	28	1968 national convention
Mikulski Commission	Commission on Delegate Selection and Party Structure	1972–1973	Barbara A. Mikulski, Baltimore city councilwoman	81	1972 national convention
Winograd Commission	Commission on Presidential Nomination and Party Structure	1975–1976 1976–1980b	Morley Winograd, former chairman of Michigan Democratic Party	58	1976 national Convention
Hunt Commission	Commission on Presidential Nomination	1980–1982	Gov. James B. Hunt Jr. of North Carolina	70	1980 national convention
Fairness Commission	Fairness Commission	1984–1986	Donald Fowler, chairman of South Carolina Democratic Party	53	1984 national convention

Source: William J. Crotty, Party Reform (New York: Longman, 1983), 40–43. Updated by the author.

Notes: a. Fraser assumed chair January 7, 1971. b. The original Winograd Commission was not authorized by the national convention. It was created by the national chairman, Robert Strauss. The post-1976 committee membership was expanded.

REPUBLICAN PARTY'S REFORM COMMITTEES ON PRESIDENTIAL SELECTION

Known as	Formal name	Years in operation	Chair	Size	Mandating body
DO Committee	Committee on Delegates and Organization	1969–1971	Rosemary Ginn, member, Republican National Committee, from Missouri	16	1968 national convention
Rule 29 Committee	Rule 29 Committee	1973–1975	Rep. William A. Steiger (Wis.)	57	1972 national convention

Major recommendations	Distinctive features	Principal report
"Quotas"; rules for opening delegate selection to 1972 national convention	First, most ambitious, and most important of reform groups. Completely rewrote rules for presidential selection; made them mandatory for state parties and state practices; changed power distribution within Democratic Party; set model other reform commissions attempted to follow.	Mandate for Change (1970)
Modified McGovern-Fraser rules; revised quotas; provided for proportional representation of presidential candidates' strength; increased role of party regulars in delegate selection	Commission had a stormy, if brief, life. Its principal recommendations were intended to placate regulars and modify most controversial aspects of McGovern-Fraser rules. Its major achievement, however, was in not seriously revising the McGovern-Fraser provisions. With the work of this commission, the assumption underlying the reforms became generally accepted within the party.	Democrats All (1973)
10% "add-on" delegates for party officials; steps to close system at top	Vehicle of party regulars and Carter administration to tighten system, increase role of party regulars, and adopt rules expected to help Carter's renomination. Developed complicated procedures that are heavily dependent on national party interpretation.	Openness, Participation and Party Building: Reforms for a Stronger Democratic Party (1978)
25% quota for party officials	Expanded role of party and elected officials in national conventions.	Report of the Commission on Presidential Nomination (1982)
Loosened restrictions on "open primaries"; lowered the threshold for "fair representation" to 15%; increased number of "superdelegates"	Tried to satisfy both wings of the party by simultaneously increasing the power of party leaders (by increasing the number of superdelegates) and by lowering the threshold for fair representation.	No formal report

Major recommendations	Distinctive features	Principal report
Proposals for increasing participation in delegate selection process.	The committee's recommendations were not binding; designed "to implement the Republican Party's Open Door policy."	No formal report
Implement "positive action" to open delegate selection process; institute RNC review of such action	Most ambitious reform effort by the Republican Party. The committee's major recommendations, however, were rejected by the RNC and by the 1976 national convention.	No formal report

POLITICAL AND ELECTION WEBSITES

Thousands of Internet sites provide information about elections and politics. They are operated by candidates, political parties, interest groups, think tanks, trade associations, labor unions, businesses, government agencies, news organizations, polling firms, universities, and individuals.

These sites can have very short lives. Many spring up just before a particular election and then disappear once the ballots are counted. The sites listed below, however, have proven themselves to be stable sources of ongoing election information—at least as of mid-2011.

American National Election Studies
http://www.electionstudies.org

ANES conducts questionnaires and public opinion polls to determine why Americans vote as they do on election day. This website offers a rich collection of data on voting, public opinion, and political participation.

Ballot Access News
http://www.ballot-access.org

The full text of the newsletter *Ballot Access News* from early 1994 to the present is available at this site. The newsletter publishes news about efforts around the country to overturn laws that restrict ballot access by candidates. It is run by Richard Winger who has been one of the most tireless advocates of broader ballot access. The site also contains extensive information on minor parties nationwide.

Ballot Watch
http://www.iandrinstitute.org/ballotwatch.htm

A database at Ballot Watch has details about initiatives and referendums that are moving toward qualification on state ballots or that have already qualified in states around the country. You can search the database by subject, status, state, and type of measure.

Census: Voting and Registration Data
http://www.census.gov/population/www/socdemo/voting.html

The U.S. Census Bureau operates this site, which has data about registration and voting by various demographic and socioeconomic groups. Data are available from 1964 to the present.

Center for Public Integrity
http://www.iwatchnews.org

Investigative reports and databases on lobbying firms and political spending are among the features on this site. CPI emphasizes government transparency and investigative journalism.

CQRollCall
http://rollcall.com/politics

This website resulting from the merger of Congressional Quarterly, long-time publisher of the CQ Weekly magazine, and Capitol Hill newspaper Rollcall examines congressional activity including elections and election maps, candidate lists and ratings, and other detailed overage of Washington political news.

CQMoneyLine
http://moneyline.cq.com

This site, from CQRollCall, presents data on campaign finance and lobbying from the 1979–1980 election cycle to the present. It also includes quick links to information on contribution limits and filings calendars. Most information is free, although some sections of the site are limited to subscribers.

Electionline.org
http://wwwelectionline.org

This site is produced by the Pew Center on the States' Election Initiatives. A nonpartisan, non-advocacy site, Electionline.org provides current news and analysis on election reform.

Electoral College Home Page
http://www.archives.gov/federalregister/electoralcollege/

Background information about how the Electoral College operates is available at this site. It also has results for popular votes and Electoral College votes in presidential elections from 1789 to the present and provisions of the U.S. Constitution and federal law pertaining to presidential elections.

Federal Election Commission
http://www.fec.gov

This site's main feature is a database of campaign finance reports filed from May 1996 to the present by House and presidential candidates, political action committees, and political party committees. The site also includes Senate reports, which are first filed with the Senate public records office. Another valuable resource is the *Combined Federal/State Disclosure and Election Directory,* which provides detailed information about every federal and state office that collects campaign finance data or regulates election spending. For each office, the publication lists the types of data that are available and complete contact information, including a link to the office's website.

Federal Election Reform Network
http://www.tcf.org/elections

This site is the home of the National Commission on Federal Election Reform, organized in the wake of the 2000 presidential election by the Miller Center of Public Affairs at the University of Virginia and the Century Foundation. Available on the site is the full text of the bipartisan commission's 114-page final report, issued July 31, 2001. Many of the commission's recommendations were incorporated in the Help America Vote Act signed by President George W. Bush on October 29, 2002.

The Hill
http://www.thehill.com

The Hill is a newspaper focused on congressional activity. It publishes daily when Congress is in session, focusing on business, lobbying, campaigns, and legislative activity.

International Foundation for Election Systems

http://www.ifes.org/

One of this site's highlights is its collection of links to websites operated by election commissions and other election-related organizations in countries around the world. It also provides a worldwide election calendar, links to news about current elections, and a newsletter titled *Elections Today*.

The New York Times: Politics

http://www.nytimes.com/pages/politics/index.html

Political stories from the current day's issue of the *New York Times* are available through this site. It also offers breaking Washington news stories from the Associated Press, archived *Times* stories about specific political topics, results from political polls, and political cartoons by a variety of artists.

Opensecrets.org

http://www.opensecrets.org

Both raw data about money in politics and reports that analyze all the numbers are available at this site. It is operated by the Center for Responsive Politics, a nonprofit research group. Numerous databases provide detailed campaign finance data for federal candidates and information about contributions by political action committees. The site also has lists of the top federal contributors by industry, profiles of every political action committee registered with the Federal Election Commission, data about soft money contributions, links to sources of state campaign finance data, reports with titles such as *Influence Inc.: The Bottom Line on Washington Lobbyists* and *The Politics of Sugar,* and much more.

The Pew Research Center for the People & the Press

http://www.peoplepress.org

The Pew site presents the results of polls regarding the press, politics, and public policy issues conducted from 1995 to the present. The polls measure public attitudes about topics such as China policy, Congress, the economy, elections, and the Internet's impact in elections.

Political Resources on the Net

http://www.politicalresources.net

Links to more than 24,000 election and politics-related websites around the world are presented at this site. The links lead to sites operated by political parties, organizations, governments, media outlets, and others. You can browse the links by region or country, and you also can search the whole site.

Political Science Resources: United States Politics

http://www.lib.umich.edu/govdocs/polisci.html

This site of the University of Michigan Documents Center offers links to hundreds of websites about politics and elections. The listings are divided into more than two dozen categories, including campaign finance, cybercitizenry, elections, foreign policy, lobbying groups, news sources, political parties, primaries, public opinion, public policy issues, statistics, and think tanks, among others.

Politico

http://politico.com

POLITICO.com is a multiplatform news source that reports on events in Congress, lobbying in Washington, and election campaigns. The site maintains a sizeable reporting staff in Washington and also is published in print form.

Politics1

http://www.politics1.com

Politics1 provides a huge set of annotated links to websites operated by candidates, political parties, election offices, and election news sources in states across the country. It also has links to sites for presidential candidates, the two major parties, third parties, and political news sources.

PoliticsOnline

http://www.politicsonline.com

This site's highlight is its large collection of links to news stories about how the Internet is being used in elections and politics around the world.

Project Vote Smart

http://www.votesmart.org

The Project Vote Smart site provides biographies of thousands of candidates and elected officials in offices ranging from state legislator to president, voting records for members of Congress, detailed campaign finance data for members of Congress, the texts of ballot initiatives from states around the country, links to thousands of other political websites, and lots more.

U.S. Election Atlas

http://www.uselectionatlas.org

This site features maps detailing the results of recent presidential, senatorial, and gubernatorial elections by state. It also includes polling information and predictions for upcoming elections. Note to users: the site reverses the use of blue and red colors often employed by news organizations to designate Republicans and Democrats.

Voter Information

http://vote411.org/

This League of Women Voters site has links to information about state and local candidates around the country, details about how to register to vote, voter registration contact numbers for every state, and links to other election sites.

Washingtonpost.com: Politics

http://www.washingtonpost.com/politics

The latest political news from the *Washington Post* and the Associated Press highlights this page. It also has archived stories about dozens of political issues, such as gun control and health care, election coverage, and more.

Yahoo! News: Politics

http://news.yahoo.com/politics

Hundreds of news stories about politics and elections are available through this Yahoo! page. Sources include the Associated Press, Reuters, and other news organizations.

NATIONAL PARTY CHAIRS, 1848–2011

Name	State	Years of Service	Name	State	Years of Service
Democratic Party			**Republican Party** (Continued)		
B. F. Hallett	Massachusetts	1848–52	Marshall Jewell	Connecticut	1880–83
Robert McLane	Maryland	1852–56	D. M. Sabin	Minnesota	1883–84
David A. Smalley	Virginia	1856–60	B. F. Jones	Pennsylvania	1884–88
August Belmont	New York	1860–72	Matthew S. Quay	Pennsylvania	1888–91
Augustus Schell	New York	1872–76	James S. Clarkson	Iowa	1891–92
Abram S. Hewitt	New York	1876–77	Thomas H. Carter	Montana	1892–96
William H. Barnum	Connecticut	1877–89	Mark A. Hanna	Ohio	1896–1904
Calvin S. Brice	Ohio	1889–92	Henry C. Payne	Wisconsin	1904
William F. Harrity	Pennsylvania	1892–96	George B. Cortelyou	New York	1904–07
James K. Jones	Arkansas	1896–1904	Harry S. New	Indiana	1907–08
Thomas Taggart	Indiana	1904–08	Frank H. Hitchcock	Massachusetts	1908–09
Norman E. Mack	New York	1908–12	John F. Hill	Maine	1909–12
William F. McCombs	New York	1912–16	Victor Rosewater	Nebraska	1912
Vance C. McCormick	Pennsylvania	1916–19	Charles D. Hilles	New York	1912–16
Homer S. Cummings	Connecticut	1919–20	William R. Willcox	New York	1916–18
George White	Ohio	1920–21	Will Hays	Indiana	1918–21
Cordell Hull	Tennessee	1921–24	John T. Adams	Iowa	1921–24
Clem Shaver	West Virginia	1924–28	William M. Butler	Massachusetts	1924–28
John J. Raskob	Maryland	1928–32	Hubert Work	Colorado	1928–29
James A. Farley	New York	1932–40	Claudius H. Huston	Tennessee	1929–30
Edward J. Flynn	New York	1940–43	Simeon D. Fess	Ohio	1930–32
Frank C. Walker	Pennsylvania	1943–44	Everett Sanders	Indiana	1932–34
Robert E. Hannegan	Missouri	1944–47	Henry P. Fletcher	Pennsylvania	1934–36
J. Howard McGrath	Rhode Island	1947–49	John Hamilton	Kansas	1936–40
William M. Boyle Jr.	Missouri	1949–51	Joseph W. Martin Jr.	Massachusetts	1940–42
Frank E. McKinney	Indiana	1951–52	Harrison E. Spangler	Iowa	1942–44
Stephen A. Mitchell	Illinois	1952–54	Herbert Brownell Jr.	New York	1944–46
Paul M. Butler	Indiana	1955–60	B. Carroll Reece	Tennessee	1946–48
Henry M. Jackson	Washington	1960–61	Hugh D. Scott Jr.	Pennsylvania	1948–49
John M. Bailey	Connecticut	1961–68	Guy George Gabrielson	New Jersey	1949–52
Lawrence F. O'Brien	Massachusetts	1968–69	Arthur E. Summerfield	Michigan	1952–53
Fred Harris	Oklahoma	1969–70	C. Wesley Roberts	Kansas	1953
Lawrence F. O'Brien	Massachusetts	1970–72	Leonard W. Hall	New York	1953–57
Jean Westwood	Utah	1972	H. Meade Alcorn Jr.	Connecticut	1957–59
Robert Strauss	Texas	1972–77	Thruston B. Morton	Kentucky	1959–61
Kenneth Curtis	Maine	1977–78	William E. Miller	New York	1961–64
John White	Texas	1978–81	Dean Burch	Arizona	1964–65
Charles Manatt	California	1981–85	Ray C. Bliss	Ohio	1965–69
Paul Kirk	Massachusetts	1985–89	Rogers C. B. Morton	Maryland	1969–71
Ronald H. Brown	Washington, D.C.	1989–93	Robert Dole	Kansas	1971–73
David Wilhelm	Illinois	1993–94	George H. W. Bush	Texas	1973–74
Christopher Dodd (general chair)	Connecticut	1994–97	Mary Louise Smith	Iowa	1974–77
			William Brock	Tennessee	1977–81
Donald Fowler	South Carolina	1994–97	Richard Richards	Utah	1981–83
Roy Romer (general chair)	Colorado	1997–99	Paul Laxalt (general chair)	Nevada	1983–86
Steven Grossman	Massachusetts	1997–99	Frank Fahrenkopf Jr.	Nevada	1983–89
Ed Rendell (general chair)	Pennsylvania	1999–2001	Lee Atwater	South Carolina	1989–91
Joe Andrew	Indiana	1999–2001	Clayton Yeutter	Nebraska	1991–92
Terence McAuliffe	New York	2001–2005	Rich Bond	New York	1992–93
Howard Dean	Vermont	2005–2009	Haley Barbour	Mississippi	1993–97
Timothy M. Kaine	Virginia	2009-11	Jim Nicholson	Colorado	1997–2001
Debbie Wasserman Schultz	Florida	2011-	James Gilmore	Virginia	2001–2002
Republican Party			Marc Racicot	Montana	2002–2003
Edwin D. Morgan	New York	1856–64	Ed Gillespie	Virginia	2003–2005
Henry J. Raymond	New York	1864–66	Ken Mehlman	Washington, D.C.	2005–2007
Marcus L. Ward	New Jersey	1866–68	Mike Duncan	Kentucky	2007–2009
William Claflin	Massachusetts	1868–72	Mel Martinez (general chairman)	Florida	2007–2009
Edwin D. Morgan	New York	1872–76			
Zachariah Chandler	Michigan	1876–79	Michael S. Steele	Maryland	2009–2011
J. Donald Cameron	Pennsylvania	1879–80	Reince Priebus	Wisconsin	2011–

Sources: Hugh A. Bone, *Party Committees and National Politics* (Seattle: University of Washington, 1958), 241–243; *The President, the Public, and the Parties*, 2nd ed. (Washington, D.C.: CQ Press, 1997), 21; Republican and Democratic websites.

Major Platform Fights

1860 Democratic. A minority report on the slavery plank, stating that the decision on allowing slavery in the territories should be left to the Supreme Court, was approved, 165 to 138. The majority report (favored by the South) declared that no government—local, state, or federal—could outlaw slavery in the territories. The acceptance of the minority report precipitated a walkout by several dozen southern delegates and the eventual sectional split in the party.

1896 Democratic. The monetary plank of the platform committee, favoring free and unlimited coinage of silver at a ratio of 16 to 1 with gold, was accepted by the convention, which defeated a proposed gold plank, 626 to 303. During debate, William Jennings Bryan made his famous "Cross of Gold" speech supporting the platform committee plank, bringing him to the attention of the convention and resulting in his nomination for president.

1908 Republican. A minority report, proposing a substitute platform, was presented by Sen. Robert M. La Follette of Wisconsin. Minority proposals included increased antitrust activities, enactment of a law requiring publication of campaign expenditures, and popular election of senators. All the proposed planks were defeated by wide margins; the closest vote, on direct election of senators, was 114 for, 866 against.

1924 Democratic. A minority plank was presented that condemned the activities of the Ku Klux Klan, then enjoying a resurgence in the South and some states in the Midwest. The plank was defeated 542 7/20 to 543 3/20, the closest vote in Democratic convention history.

1932 Republican. A minority plank favoring repeal of the Eighteenth Amendment (Prohibition) in favor of a state-option arrangement was defeated, 460 2/9 to 690 19/36.

1948 Democratic. An amendment to the platform, strengthening the civil rights plank by guaranteeing full and equal political participation, equal employment opportunity, personal security and equal treatment in the military service, was accepted, 651 1/2 to 582 1/2.

1964 Republican. An amendment offered by Sen. Hugh Scott of Pennsylvania to strengthen the civil rights plank by including voting guarantees in state as well as in federal elections and by eliminating job bias was defeated, 409 to 897.

1968 Democratic. A minority report on Vietnam called for cessation of the bombing of North Vietnam, halting of offensive and search-and-destroy missions by American combat units, a negotiated withdrawal of American troops, and establishment of a coalition government in South Vietnam. It was defeated, 1,041 1/4 to 1,567 3/4.

1972 Democratic. By a vote of 1,852.86 to 999.34, the convention rejected a minority report proposing a government guaranteed annual income of $6,500 for a family of four. By a vote of 1,101.37 to 1,572.80, a women's rights plank supporting abortion rights was defeated.

1980 Democratic. The platform battle, one of the longest in party history, pitted President Jimmy Carter against his persistent rival, Sen. Edward M. Kennedy of Massachusetts. Stretching over seventeen hours, the debate focused on Kennedy's economics plank, which finally was defeated by a voice vote. Yet Carter was forced to concede on so many specific points, including Kennedy's $12 billion antirecession jobs programs, that the final document bore little resemblance to the draft initially drawn up by Carter's operatives.

1992 Democratic. A tax fairness plank offered by former senator Paul E. Tsongas of Massachusetts was defeated by a vote of 953 to 2,287. The plank called for a delay in any middle-class tax cut and tax credit for families with children until the deficit was under control.

Democratic Conventions, 1832–2008

Years	City	Dates	Presidential Nominee	Vice Presidential Nominee	No. of Presidential Ballots
1832	Baltimore	May 21–23	Andrew Jackson	Martin Van Buren	1
1835	Baltimore	May 20–23	Martin Van Buren	Richard M. Johnson	1
1840	Baltimore	May 5–6	Martin Van Buren	—[1]	1
1844	Baltimore	May 27–29	James K. Polk	George M. Dallas	9
1848	Baltimore	May 22–25	Lewis Cass	William O. Butler	4
1852	Baltimore	June 1–5	Franklin Pierce	William R. King	49
1856	Cincinnati	June 2–6	James Buchanan	John C. Breckinridge	17
1860	Charleston	April 23–May 3	Deadlocked		57
	Baltimore	June 18–23	Stephen A. Douglas	Benjamin Fitzpatrick/Herschel V. Johnson[2]	2
1864	Chicago	Aug. 29–31	George B. McClellan	George H. Pendleton	1
1868	New York	July 4–9	Horatio Seymour	Francis P. Blair	22
1872	Baltimore	July 9–10	Horace Greeley	Benjamin G. Brown	1
1876	St. Louis	June 27–29	Samuel J. Tilden	Thomas A. Hendricks	2
1880	Cincinnati	June 22–24	Winfield S. Hancock	William H. English	2
1884	Chicago	July 8–11	Grover Cleveland	Thomas A. Hendricks	2
1888	St. Louis	June 5–7	Grover Cleveland	Allen G. Thurman	1
1892	Chicago	June 21–23	Grover Cleveland	Adlai E. Stevenson	1
1896	Chicago	July 7–11	William J. Bryan	Arthur Sewall	5
1900	Kansas City	July 4–6	William J. Bryan	Adlai E. Stevenson	1
1904	St. Louis	July 6–9	Alton S. Parker	Henry G. Davis	1
1908	Denver	July 7–10	William J. Bryan	John W. Kern	1
1912	Baltimore	June 25–July 2	Woodrow Wilson	Thomas R. Marshall	46
1916	St. Louis	June 14–16	Woodrow Wilson	Thomas R. Marshall	1
1920	San Francisco	June 28–July 6	James M. Cox	Franklin D. Roosevelt	44
1924	New York	June 24–July 9	John W. Davis	Charles W. Bryan	103
1928	Houston	June 26–29	Alfred E. Smith	Joseph T. Robinson	1
1932	Chicago	June 27–July 2	Franklin D. Roosevelt	John N. Garner	4
1936	Philadelphia	June 23–27	Franklin D. Roosevelt	John N. Garner	Acclamation
1940	Chicago	July 15–18	Franklin D. Roosevelt	Henry A. Wallace	1
1944	Chicago	July 19–21	Franklin D. Roosevelt	Harry S. Truman	1
1948	Philadelphia	July 12–14	Harry S. Truman	Alben W. Barkley	1
1952	Chicago	July 21–26	Adlai E. Stevenson	John J. Sparkman	3
1956	Chicago	Aug. 13–17	Adlai E. Stevenson	Estes Kefauver	1
1960	Los Angeles	July 11–15	John F. Kennedy	Lyndon B. Johnson	1
1964	Atlantic City	Aug. 24–27	Lyndon B. Johnson	Hubert H. Humphrey	Acclamation
1968	Chicago	Aug. 26–29	Hubert H. Humphrey	Edmund S. Muskie	1
1972	Miami Beach	July 10–13	George McGovern	Thomas F. Eagleton/R. Sargent Shriver[3]	1
1976	New York	July 12–15	Jimmy Carter	Walter F. Mondale	1
1980	New York	Aug. 11–14	Jimmy Carter	Walter F. Mondale	1
1984	San Francisco	July 16–19	Walter F. Mondale	Geraldine A. Ferraro	1
1988	Atlanta	July 18–21	Michael S. Dukakis	Lloyd Bentsen	1
1992	New York	July 13–16	Bill Clinton	Albert Gore Jr.	1
1996	Chicago	Aug. 26–29	Bill Clinton	Albert Gore Jr.	1
2000	Los Angeles	Aug. 14–17	Al Gore	Joseph Lieberman	1
2004	Boston	July 26–29	John Kerry	John Edwards	1
2008	Denver	Aug. 25–28	Barack Obama	Joseph R. Biden Jr.	Acclamation

Notes

1. The 1840 Democratic convention did not nominate a candidate for vice president.

2. The 1860 Democratic convention nominated Benjamin Fitzpatrick, who declined the nomination shortly after the convention adjourned. On June 25 the Democratic National Committee selected Herschel V. Johnson as the party's candidate for vice president.

3. The 1972 Democratic convention nominated Thomas F. Eagleton, who withdrew from the ticket on July 31. On August 8 the Democratic National Committee selected R. Sargent Shriver as the party's candidate for vice president.

REPUBLICAN CONVENTIONS, 1856–2008

Years	City	Dates	Presidential Nominee	Vice Presidential Nominee	No. of Pres. Ballots
1856	Philadelphia	June 17–19	John C. Fremont	William L. Dayton	2
1860	Chicago	May 16–18	Abraham Lincoln	Hannibal Hamlin	3
1864	Baltimore	June 7–8	Abraham Lincoln	Andrew Johnson	1
1868	Chicago	May 20–21	Ulysses S. Grant	Schuyler Colfax	1
1872	Philadelphia	June 5–6	Ulysses S. Grant	Henry Wilson	1
1876	Cincinnati	June 14–16	Rutherford B. Hayes	William A. Wheeler	7
1880	Chicago	June 2–8	James A. Garfield	Chester A. Arthur	36
1884	Chicago	June 3–6	James G. Blaine	John A. Logan	4
1888	Chicago	June 19–25	Benjamin Harrison	Levi P. Morton	8
1892	Minneapolis	June 7–10	Benjamin Harrison	Whitelaw Reid	1
1896	St. Louis	June 16–18	William McKinley	Garret A. Hobart	1
1900	Philadelphia	June 19–21	William McKinley	Theodore Roosevelt	1
1904	Chicago	June 21–23	Theodore Roosevelt	Charles W. Fairbanks	1
1908	Chicago	June 16–19	William II. Taft	James S. Sherman	1
1912	Chicago	June 18–22	William H. Taft	James S. Sherman/Nicholas Murray Butler[1]	1
1916	Chicago	June 7–10	Charles E. Hughes	Charles W. Fairbanks	3
1920	Chicago	June 8–12	Warren G. Harding	Calvin Coolidge	10
1924	Cleveland	June 10–12	Calvin Coolidge	Charles G. Dawes	1
1928	Kansas City	June 12–15	Herbert Hoover	Charles Curtis	1
1932	Chicago	June 14–16	Herbert Hoover	Charles Curtis	1
1936	Cleveland	June 9–12	Alfred M. Landon	Frank Knox	1
1940	Philadelphia	June 24–28	Wendell L. Willkie	Charles L. McNary	6
1944	Chicago	June 26–28	Thomas E. Dewey	John W. Bricker	1
1948	Philadelphia	June 21–25	Thomas E. Dewey	Earl Warren	3
1952	Chicago	July 7–11	Dwight D. Eisenhower	Richard M. Nixon	1
1956	San Francisco	Aug. 20–23	Dwight D. Eisenhower	Richard M. Nixon	1
1960	Chicago	July 25–28	Richard M. Nixon	Henry Cabot Lodge	1
1964	San Francisco	July 13–16	Barry Goldwater	William E. Miller	1
1968	Miami Beach	Aug. 5–8	Richard M. Nixon	Spiro T. Agnew	1
1972	Miami Beach	Aug. 21–23	Richard M. Nixon	Spiro T. Agnew	1
1976	Kansas City	Aug. 16–19	Gerald R. Ford	Robert Dole	1
1980	Detroit	July 14–17	Ronald Reagan	George H. W Bush	1
1984	Dallas	Aug. 20–23	Ronald Reagan	George H. W Bush	1
1988	New Orleans	Aug. 15–18	George H. W Bush	Dan Quayle	1
1992	Houston	Aug. 17–20	George H. W Bush	Dan Quayle	1
1996	San Diego	Aug. 12–15	Robert Dole	Jack Kemp	1
2000	Philadelphia	July 31–Aug. 3	George W. Bush	Richard B. Cheney	1
2004	New York City	Aug. 30–Sept. 2	George W. Bush	Richard B. Cheney	1
2008	St. Paul	Sept. 1-4	John McCain	Sarah Palin	1

Note

1. The 1912 Republican convention nominated James S. Sherman, who died on October 30. The Republican National Committee subsequently selected Nicholas Murray Butler to receive the Republican electoral votes for vice president.

Chief Officers and Keynote Speakers at Democratic National Conventions, 1832–2008

Year	Chair National Committee	Temporary Chair	Permanent Chair	Keynote Speaker
1832		Robert Lucas, Ohio	Robert Lucas, Ohio	
1836		Andrew Stevenson, Va.	Andrew Stevenson, Va.	
1840		Isaac Hill, N.H.	William Carroll, Tenn.	
1844		Hendrick B. Wright, Pa.	Hendrick B. Wright, Pa.	
1848	Benjamin Hallet, Mass.	J.S. Bryce, La.	Andrew Stevenson, Va.	
1852	Robert M. McLane, Md.	Gen. Romulus M. Saunders, N.C.	John W. Davis, Ind.	
1856	David A. Smalley, Vt.	Samuel Medary, Ohio	John E. Ward, Ga.	
1860	August Belmont, N.Y.	Francis B. Flournoy, Ark.	Caleb Cushing, Mass.	
1864	August Belmont, N.Y.	William Bigler, Pa.	Horatio Seymour, N.Y.	
1868	August Belmont, N.Y.	Henry L. Palmer, Wis.	Horatio Seymour, N.Y.	
1872	Augustus Schell, N.Y.	Thomas Jefferson Randolph, Va.	James R. Doolittle, Wis.	
1876	Abram Stevens Hewitt, N.Y.	Henry M. Watterson, Ky.	John A. McClernand, Ill.	
1880	William H. Barnum, Conn.	George Hoadly, Ohio	John W. Stevenson, Ky.	
1884	William H. Barnum, Conn.	Richard B. Hubbard, Texas	William F. Vilas, Wis.	
1888	William H. Barnum, Conn.	Stephen M. White, Calif.	Patrick A. Collins, Mass.	
1892	William F. Harrity, Penn.	William C. Owens, Ky.	William L. Wilson, W.Va.	
1896	James K. Jones, Ark.	John W. Daniel, Va.	Stephen M. White, Calif.	
1900	James K. Jones, Ark.	Charles S. Thomas, Colo.	James D. Richardson, Tenn.	
1904	Thomas Taggart, Ind.	John Sharp Williams, Miss.	Champ Clark, Mo.	
1908	Norman E. Mack, N.Y.	Theodore A. Bell, Calif.	Henry D. Clayton, Ala.	
1912	William F. McCombs, N.Y.	Alton B. Parker, N.Y.	Ollie M. James, Ky.	
1916	Vance C. McCormick, Pa.	Martin H. Glynn, N.Y.	Ollie M. James, Ky.	
1920	George H. White, Ohio	Homer S. Cummings, Conn.	Joseph T. Robinson, Ark.	
1924	Clem Shaver, W.Va.	Pat Harrison, Miss.	Thomas J. Walsh, Mont.	
1928	John J. Raskob, Md.	Claude G. Bowers, Ind.	Joseph T. Robinson, Ark.	
1932	James A. Farley, N.Y.	Alben W. Barkley, Ky.	Thomas J. Walsh, Mont.	
1936	James A. Farley, N.Y.	Alben W. Barkley, Ky.	Joseph T. Robinson, Ark.	Alben W. Barkley, Ky.
1940	Edward J. Flynn, N.Y.	William B. Bankhead, Ala.	Alben W. Barkley, Ky.	William B. Bankhead, Ala.
1944	Robert E. Hannegan, Mo.	Robert S. Kerr, Okla.	Samuel D. Jackson, Ind.	Robert S. Kerr, Okla.
1948	J. Howard McGrath, R.I.	Alben W. Barkley, Ky.	Sam Rayburn, Texas	Alben W. Barkley, Ky.
1952	Stephen A. Mitchell, Ill.	Paul A. Dever, Mass.	Sam Rayburn, Texas	Paul A. Dever, Mass.
1956	Paul M. Butler, Ind.	Frank G. Clement, Tenn.	Sam Rayburn, Texas	Frank Clement, Tenn.
1960	Henry Jackson, Wash.	Frank Church, Idaho	LeRoy Collins, Fla.	Frank Church, Idaho
1964	John M. Bailey, Conn.	John O. Pastore, R.I.	John W. McCormack, Mass.	John O. Pastore, R.I.
1968	Lawrence F. O'Brien, Mass.	Daniel K. Inouye, Hawaii	Carl B. Albert, Okla.	Daniel K. Inouye, Hawaii
1972[1]	Lawrence F. O'Brien, Mass.		Lawrence F. O'Brien, Mass.	Reubin Askew, Fla.
1976	Robert S. Strauss, Texas		Lindy Boggs, La.	John Glenn, Ohio Barbara C. Jordan, Texas
1980	John C. White, Texas		Thomas P. O'Neill Jr., Mass.	Morris K. Udall, Ariz.
1984	Charles T. Manatt, Calif.		Martha Layne Collins, Ky.	Mario M. Cuomo, N.Y.
1988	Paul G. Kirk Jr., Mass.		Jim Wright, Texas	Ann W. Richards, Texas
1992	Ronald H. Brown, D.C.		Ann W. Richards, Texas	Bill Bradley, N.J. Zell Miller, Ga. Barbara C. Jordan, Texas
1996	Donald Fowler, S.C.		Thomas A. Daschle, S.D. Richard A. Gephardt, Mo.	Evan Bayh, Ind.
2000	Joe Andrew, Ind.		Barbara Boxer, Calif. Dianne Feinstein, Calif.	Harold E. Ford Jr., Tenn.
2004	Terence McAuliffe, N.Y.		Bill Richardson, N.M.	Barack Obama, Ill.
2008	Howard Dean, Vt.		Nancy Pelosi, Calif.	Mark Warner, Va.

Note

1. A rule change eliminated the position of temporary chair.

CHIEF OFFICERS AND KEYNOTE SPEAKERS AT REPUBLICAN NATIONAL CONVENTIONS, 1856–2008

Year	Chair National Committee	Temporary Chair	Permanent Chair	Keynote Speaker
1856	Edwin D. Morgan, N.Y.	Robert Emmet, N.Y.	Henry S. Lane, Ind.	
1860	Edwin D. Morgan, N.Y.	David Wilmot, Pa.	George Ashmun, Mass.	
1864	Edwin D. Morgan, N.Y.	Robert J. Breckinridge, Ky.	William Dennison, Ohio	
1868	Marcus L. Ward, N.J.	Carl Schurz, Mo.	Joseph R. Hawley, Conn.	
1872	William Claflin, Mass.	Morton McMichael, Pa.	Thomas Settle, N.C.	
1876	Edwin D. Morgan, N.Y.	Theodore M. Pomeroy, N.Y.	Edward McPherson, Pa.	
1880	J. Donald Cameron, Pa.	George F. Hoar, Mass.	George F. Hoar, Mass.	
1884	Dwight M. Sabin, Minn.	John R. Lynch, Miss.	John B. Henderson, Mo.	
1888	B.F. Jones, Pa.	John M. Thurston, Neb.	Morris M. Estee, Calif.	
1892	James S. Clarkson, Iowa	J. Sloat Fassett, N.Y.	William McKinley Jr., Ohio	
1896	Thomas H. Carter, Mont.	Charles W. Fairbanks, Ind.	John M. Thurston, Neb.	
1900	Marcus A. Hanna, Ohio	Edward O. Wolcott, Colo.	Henry Cabot Lodge, Mass.	
1904	Henry C. Payne, Wis.	Elihu Root, N.Y.	Joseph G. Cannon, Ill.	
1908	Harry S. New, Ind.	Julius C. Burrows, Mich.	Henry Cabot Lodge, Mass.	
1912	Victor Rosewater, Neb.	Elihu Root, N.Y.	Elihu Root, N.Y.	
1916	Charles D. Hilles, N.Y.	Warren G. Harding, Ohio	Warren G. Harding, Ohio	
1920	Will H. Hays, Ind.	Henry Cabot Lodge, Mass.	Henry Cabot Lodge, Mass.	Henry Cabot Lodge, Mass.
1924	John T. Adams, Iowa	Theodore E. Burton, Ohio	Frank W. Mortdell, Wyo.	
1928	William M. Butler, Mass.	Simeon D. Fess, Ohio	George H. Moses, N.H.	
1932	Simeon D. Fess, Ohio	L. J. Dickinson, Iowa	Bertrand H. Snell, N.Y.	
1936	Henry P. Fletcher, Pa.	Frederick Steiwer, Ore.	Bertrand H. Snell, N.Y.	Frederick Steiwer, Ore.
1940	John Hamilton, Kan.	Harold E. Stassen, Minn.	Joseph W. Martin Jr., Mass.	Harold E. Stassen, Minn.
1944	Harrison E. Spangler, Iowa	Earl Warren, Calif.	Joseph W. Martin Jr., Mass.	Earl Warren, Calif.
1948	Carroll Reece, Tenn.	Dwight H. Green, Ill.	Joseph W. Martin Jr., Mass.	Dwight H. Green, Ill.
1952	Guy George Gabrielson, N.J.	Walter S. Hallanan, W.Va.	Joseph W. Martin Jr., Mass.	Douglas MacArthur
1956	Leonard W. Hall, N.Y.	William F. Knowland, Calif.	Joseph W. Martin Jr., Mass.	Arthur B. Langlie, Wash.
1960	Thruston B. Morton. Ky.	Cecil H. Underwood, W.Va.	Charles A. Halleck, Ind.	Walter H. Judd, Minn.
1964	William E. Miller, N.Y.	Mark O. Hatfield, Ore.	Thruston B. Morton, Ky.	Mark O. Hatfield, Ore.
1968	Ray C. Bliss, Ohio	Edward W. Brooke, Mass.	Gerald R. Ford, Mich.	Daniel J. Evans, Wash.
1972	Robert Dole, Kan.	Ronald Reagan, Calif.	Gerald R. Ford, Mich.	Richard G. Lugar, Ind. Anne L. Armstrong, Texas
1976	Mary Louise Smith, Iowa	Robert Dole, Kan.	John J. Rhodes, Ariz.	Howard H. Baker Jr., Tenn.
1980	Bill Brock, Tenn.	Nancy Landon Kassebaum, Kan.	John J. Rhodes, Ariz.	Guy Vander Jagt, Mich.
1984	Frank J. Fahrenkopf Jr., Nev.	Howard H. Baker Jr., Tenn.	Robert H. Michel, Ill.	Katherine Ortega, N.M.
1988	Lee Atwater, S.C.	Elizabeth Hanford Dole, N.C.	Robert H. Michel, Ill.	Thomas H. Kean, N.J.
1992	Richard N. Bond, N.Y.	Kay Bailey Hutchison, Texas	Robert H. Michel, Ill.	Phil Gramm, Texas
1996	Haley Barbour, Miss.	Christine Todd Whitman, N.J. George W. Bush, Texas	Newt Gingrich, Ga.	Susan Molinari, N.Y.
2000	Jim Nicholson, Colo.	Trent Lott, Miss.	J. Dennis Hastert, Ill.	Colin Powell, D.C.
2004	Ed Gillespie, Va.	Linda Lingle, Hawaii	J. Dennis Hastert, Ill.	Zell Miller, Ga.
2008	Robert M. (Mike) Duncan, Ky.	Mitch McConnell, Ky	John Boehner, Ohio	Rudolph Giuliani, N.Y.

GENERAL ELECTION DEBATES, 1960–2008

Date	Location	Participants	Moderator	Sponsor
September 26, 1960	WBBM studio, Chicago, Illinois	Sen. John F. Kennedy and Vice President Richard M. Nixon	Howard K. Smith, CBS News	CBS
October 7, 1960	NBC studio, Washington, D.C.	Sen. John F. Kennedy and Vice President Richard M. Nixon	Frank McGee, NBC	NBC
October 13, 1960	Nixon in Hollywood, California, and Kennedy in New York City	Sen. John F. Kennedy and Vice President Richard M. Nixon	Bill Shadel, ABC	ABC
October 21, 1960	ABC studio, New York City	Sen. John F. Kennedy and Vice President Richard M. Nixon	Quincy Howe, ABC News	ABC
September 23, 1976	Walnut Theater, Philadelphia, Pennsylvania	Former governor Jimmy Carter and President Gerald R. Ford	Edwin Newman, NBC News	League of Women Voters
October 6, 1976	Palace of Fine Arts, San Francisco, California	Former governor Jimmy Carter and President Gerald R. Ford	Pauline Frederick, NPR	League of Women Voters
October 22, 1976	Phi Beta Kappa Hall, College of William and Mary, Williamsburg, Virginia	Former governor Jimmy Carter and President Gerald R. Ford	Barbara Walters, ABC News	League of Women Voters
September 21, 1980	Baltimore Convention Center, Baltimore, Maryland	Rep. John Anderson and former governor Ronald Reagan	Bill Moyers, PBS	League of Women Voters
October 28, 1980	Convention Center Music Hall, Cleveland, Ohio	President Jimmy Carter and former governor Ronald Reagan	Howard K. Smith, ABC News	League of Women Voters
October 7, 1984	Kentucky Center for Arts, Louisville, Kentucky	Former vice president Walter Mondale and President Ronald Reagan	Barbara Walters, ABC News	League of Women Voters
October 21, 1984	Music Hall, Kansas City, Missouri	Former vice president Walter Mondale and President Ronald Reagan	Edwin Newman, retired NBC News	League of Women Voters
September 25, 1988	Wait Chapel, Wake Forest University, Winston-Salem, North Carolina	Gov. Michael Dukakis and Vice President George Bush	Jim Lehrer, *McNeil-Lehrer News Hour*, PBS	Commission on Presidential Debates
October 13, 1988	Pauley Pavilion, University of California at Los Angeles, Los Angeles, California	Gov. Michael Dukakis and Vice President George Bush	Bernard Shaw, CNN	Commission on Presidential Debates
October 11, 1992	Washington University, St. Louis, Missouri	President George Bush, Gov. Bill Clinton, and independent candidate Ross Perot	Jim Lehrer, PBS	Commission on Presidential Debates
October 15, 1992	University of Richmond, Richmond, Virginia	President George Bush, Gov. Bill Clinton, and independent candidate Ross Perot	Carole Simpson, ABC News	Commission on Presidential Debates
October 19, 1992	Michigan State University, East Lansing, Michigan	President George Bush, Gov. Bill Clinton, and independent candidate Ross Perot	Jim Lehrer, PBS	Commission on Presidential Debates
October 6, 1996	Bushnell Theatre, Hartford, Connecticut	President Bill Clinton and Sen. Robert Dole	Jim Lehrer, PBS	Commission on Presidential Debates

GENERAL ELECTION DEBATES, 1960–2008 *(Continued)*

Date	Location	Participants	Moderator	Sponsor
October 16, 1996	Shiley Theatre at the University of San Diego, San Diego, California	President Bill Clinton and Sen. Robert Dole	Jim Lehrer, PBS	Commission on Presidential Debates
October 3, 2000	University of Massachusetts, Boston, Massachusetts	Vice President Al Gore and Gov. George W. Bush	Jim Lehrer, PBS	Commission on Presidential Debates
October 11, 2000	Wake Forest University, Winston-Salem, North Carolina	Vice President Al Gore and Gov. George W. Bush	Jim Lehrer, PBS	Commission on Presidential Debates
October 17, 2000	Washington University, St. Louis, Missouri	Vice President Al Gore and Gov. George W. Bush	Jim Lehrer, PBS	Commission on Presidential Debates
September 30, 2004	University of Miami, Coral Gables, Florida	President George W. Bush and Sen. John Kerry	Jim Lehrer, PBS	Commission on Presidential Debates
October 8, 2004	Washington University, St. Louis, Missouri	President George W. Bush and Sen. John Kerry	Charles Gibson, ABC News	Commission on Presidential Debates
October 13, 2004	Arizona State University, Tempe, Arizona	President George W. Bush and Sen. John Kerry	Bob Schieffer, CBS News	Commission on Presidential Debates
September 26, 2011	University of Mississippi, Oxford, Mississippi	Sen. Barack Obama and Sen. John McCain	Jim Lehrer, PBS	Commission on Presidential Debates
October 7, 2011	Belmont University, Nashville, Tennessee	Sen. Barack Obama and Sen. John McCain	Tom Brokaw, NBC	Commission on Presidential Debates
October 15, 2011	Hofstra University, Hempstead, New York	Sen. Barack Obama and Sen. John McCain	Bob Schieffer, CBS	Commission on Presidential Debates

Sources: Joel L. Swerdlow, *Presidential Debates: 1988 and Beyond* (Washington, D.C.: CQ Press, 1987); and the Commission on Presidential Debates.

U.S. Presidents and Vice Presidents

President and Political Party	Born	Died	Age at Inauguration	Native of	Elected from	Term of Service	Vice President
George Washington (F)	1732	1799	57	Va.	Va.	April 30, 1789–March 4, 1793	John Adams
George Washington (F)			61			March 4, 1793–March 4, 1797	John Adams
John Adams (F)	1735	1826	61	Mass.	Mass.	March 4, 1797–March 4, 1801	Thomas Jefferson
Thomas Jefferson (DR)	1743	1826	57	Va.	Va.	March 4, 1801–March 4, 1805	Aaron Burr
Thomas Jefferson (DR)			61			March 4, 1805–March 4, 1809	George Clinton
James Madison (DR)	1751	1836	57	Va.	Va.	March 4, 1809–March 4, 1813	George Clinton
James Madison (DR)			61			March 4, 1813–March 4, 1817	Elbridge Gerry
James Monroe (DR)	1758	1831	58	Va.	Va.	March 4, 1817–March 4, 1821	Daniel D. Tompkins
James Monroe (DR)			62			March 4, 1821–March 4, 1825	Daniel D. Tompkins
John Q. Adams (DR)	1767	1848	57	Mass.	Mass.	March 4, 1825–March 4, 1829	John C. Calhoun
Andrew Jackson (D)	1767	1845	61	S.C.	Tenn.	March 4, 1829–March 4, 1833	John C. Calhoun
Andrew Jackson (D)			65			March 4, 1833–March 4, 1837	Martin Van Buren
Martin Van Buren (D)	1782	1862	54	N.Y.	N.Y.	March 4, 1837–March 4, 1841	Richard M. Johnson
W. H. Harrison (W)	1773	1841	68	Va.	Ohio	March 4, 1841–April 4, 1841	John Tyler
John Tyler (W)	1790	1862	51	Va.	Va.	April 6, 1841–March 4, 1845	
James K. Polk (D)	1795	1849	49	N.C.	Tenn.	March 4, 1985–March 4, 1849	George M. Dallas
Zachary Taylor (W)	1784	1850	64	Va.	La.	March 4, 1849–July 9, 1850	Millard Fillmore
Millard Fillmore (W)	1800	1874	50	N.Y.	N.Y.	July 10, 1850–March 4, 1853	
Franklin Pierce (D)	1804	1869	48	N.H.	N.H.	March 4, 1853–March 4, 1857	William R. King
James Buchanan (D)	1791	1868	65	Pa.	Pa.	March 4, 1857–March 4, 1861	John C. Breckinridge
Abraham Lincoln (R)	1809	1865	52	Ky.	Ill.	March 4, 1861–March 4, 1865	Hannibal Hamlin
Abraham Lincoln (R)			56			March 4, 1865–April 15, 1865	Andrew Johnson
Andrew Johnson (R)	1808	1875	56	N.C.	Tenn.	April 15, 1865–March 4, 1869	
Ulysses S. Grant (R)	1822	1885	46	Ohio	Ill.	March 4, 1869–March 4, 1873	Schuyler Colfax
Ulysses S. Grant (R)			50			March 4, 1873–March 4, 1877	Henry Wilson
Rutherford B. Hayes (R)	1822	1893	54	Ohio	Ohio	March 4, 1877–March 4, 1881	William A. Wheeler
James A. Garfield (R)	1831	1881	49	Ohio	Ohio	March 4, 1881–Sept. 19, 1881	Chester A. Arthur
Chester A. Arthur (R)	1830	1886	50	Vt.	N.Y.	Sept. 20, 1881–March 4, 1885	
Grover Cleveland (D)	1837	1908	47	N.J.	N.Y.	March 4, 1885–March 4, 1889	Thomas A. Hendricks
Benjamin Harrison (R)	1833	1901	55	Ohio	Ind.	March 4, 1889–March 4, 1893	Levi P. Morton
Grover Cleveland (D)	1837	1908	55	N.J.	N.Y.	March 4, 1893–March 4, 1897	Adlai E. Stevenson
William McKinley (R)	1843	1901	54	Ohio	Ohio	March 4, 1897–March 4, 1901	Garret A. Hobart
William McKinley (R)			58			March 4, 1901–Sept. 14, 1901	Theodore Roosevelt
Theodore Roosevelt (R)	1858	1919	42	N.Y.	N.Y.	Sept. 14, 1901–March 4, 1905	
Theodore Roosevelt (R)			46			March 4, 1905–March 4, 1909	Charles W. Fairbanks
William H. Taft (R)	1857	1930	51	Ohio	Ohio	March 4, 1909–March 4, 1913	James S. Sherman
Woodrow Wilson (D)	1856	1924	56	Va.	N.J.	March 4, 1913–March 4, 1917	Thomas R. Marshall
Woodrow Wilson (D)			60			March 4, 1917–March 4, 1921	Thomas R. Marshall
Warren G. Harding (R)	1865	1923	55	Ohio	Ohio	March 4, 1921–Aug. 2, 1923	Calvin Coolidge

U.S. PRESIDENTS AND VICE PRESIDENTS *(Continued)*

President and Political Party	Born	Died	Age at Inauguration	Native of	Elected from	Term of Service	Vice President
Calvin Coolidge (R)	1872	1933	51	Vt.	Mass.	Aug. 3, 1923–March 4, 1925	
Calvin Coolidge (R)			52			March 4, 1925–March 4, 1929	Charles G. Dawes
Herbert Hoover (R)	1874	1964	54	Iowa	Calif.	March 4, 1929–March 4, 1933	Charles Curtis
Franklin D. Roosevelt (D)	1882	1945	51	N.Y.	N.Y.	March 4, 1933–Jan. 20, 1937	John N. Garner
Franklin D. Roosevelt (D)			55			Jan. 20, 1937–Jan. 20, 1941	John N. Garner
Franklin D. Roosevelt (D)			59			Jan. 20, 1941–Jan. 20, 1945	Henry A. Wallace
Franklin D. Roosevelt (D)			63			Jan. 20, 1945–April 12, 1945	Harry S. Truman
Harry S. Truman (D)	1884	1972	60	Mo.	Mo.	April 12, 1945–Jan. 20, 1949	
Harry S. Truman (D)			64			Jan. 20, 1949–Jan. 20, 1953	Alben W. Barkley
Dwight D. Eisenhower (R)	1890	1969	62	Texas	N.Y.	Jan. 20, 1953–Jan. 20, 1957	Richard Nixon
Dwight D. Eisenhower (R)			66		Pa.	Jan. 20, 1957–Jan. 20, 1961	Richard Nixon
John F. Kennedy (D)	1917	1963	43	Mass.	Mass.	Jan. 20, 1961–Nov. 22, 1963	Lyndon B. Johnson
Lyndon B. Johnson (D)	1908	1973	55	Texas	Texas	Nov. 22, 1963–Jan. 20, 1965	
Lyndon B. Johnson (D)			56			Jan. 20, 1965–Jan. 20, 1969	Hubert H. Humphrey
Richard Nixon (R)	1913	1994	56	Calif.	N.Y.	Jan. 20, 1969–Jan. 20, 1973	Spiro T. Agnew
Richard Nixon (R)			60		Calif.	Jan. 20, 1973–Aug, 9, 1974	Spiro T. Agnew / Gerald R. Ford
Gerald R. Ford (R)	1913	2006	61	Neb.	Mich.	Aug. 9, 1974–Jan. 20, 1977	Nelson A. Rockefeller
Jimmy Carter (D)	1924		52	Ga.	Ga.	Jan. 20, 1977–Jan. 20, 1981	Walter F. Mondale
Ronald Reagan (R)	1911	2004	69	Ill.	Calif.	Jan. 20, 1981–Jan. 20, 1985	George Bush
Ronald Reagan (R)			73			Jan. 20, 1985–Jan. 20, 1989	George Bush
George H. W. Bush (R)	1924		64	Mass.	Texas	Jan. 20, 1989–Jan. 20, 1993	Dan Quayle
Bill Clinton (D)	1946		46	Ark.	Ark.	Jan. 20, 1993–Jan. 20, 1997	Albert Gore Jr.
Bill Clinton (D)			50			Jan. 20, 1997–Jan. 20, 2001	Albert Gore Jr.
George W. Bush (R)	1946		54	Conn.	Texas	Jan. 20, 2001–Jan. 20, 2005	Richard B. Cheney
George W. Bush (R)			58			Jan. 20, 2005–Jan. 20, 2009	Richard B. Cheney
Barack Obama (D)	1961		47	Hawaii	Illinois	Jan. 20, 2009–	Joseph R. Biden Jr.

Note: D–Democrat; DR–Democratic-Republican; F–Federalist; R–Republican; W–Whig.

Summary of Presidential Elections, 1789–2008

Year	No. of states	Candidates	Party	Electoral vote	Popular vote
1789[a]	10	George Washington	Fed.	69	—[b]
		John Adams	Fed.	34	
1792[a]	15	George Washington	Fed.	132	—[b]
		John Adams	Fed.	77	
1796[a]	16	John Adams	Fed.	71	—[b]
		Thomas Jefferson	Dem.-Rep.	68	
1800[a]	16	Thomas Jefferson	Dem.-Rep.	73	—[b]
		Aaron Burr	Dem.-Rep.	73	
		John Adams	Fed.	65	
		Charles Cotes-Worth Pinckney	Fed.	64	
1804	17	Thomas Jefferson	Dem.-Rep.	162	—[b]
		George Clinton			
		Charles Cotes-Worth Pinckney	Fed.	64	
		Rufus King			
1808	17	James Madison	Dem.-Rep.	122	—[b]
		George Clinton			
		Charles Cotes-Worth Pinckney	Fed.	64	
		Rufus King			
1812	18	James Madison	Dem.-Rep.	128	—[b]
		Elbridge Gerry			
		George Clinton	Fed.	89	
		Jared Ingersoll			
1816	19	James Monroe	Dem.-Rep.	183	—[b]
		Daniel D. Tompkins			
		Rufus King	Fed.	34	
		John Howard			
1820	24	James Monroe	Dem.-Rep.	231[c]	—[b]
		Daniel D. Tompkins			
1824[d]	24	John Quincy Adams	Dem.-Rep.	99	113,122 (30.9%)
		John C. Calhoun			
		Andrew Jackson	Dem.-Rep.	84	151,271 (41.3%)
		Nathan Sanford			
1828	24	Andrew Jackson	Dem.-Rep.	178	642,553 (56.0%)
		John C. Calhoun			
		John Quincy Adams	Nat.-Rep.	83	500,897 (43.6%)
		Richard Rush			

SUMMARY OF PRESIDENTIAL ELECTIONS, 1789–2008 *(Continued)*

Year	No. of states	Candidates	Party	Electoral vote	Popular vote
1832[e]	24	Andrew Jackson *Martin Van Buren*	Dem.	219	701,780 (54.2%)
		Henry Clay *John Sergeant*	Nat.-Rep.	49	484,205 (37.4%)
1836[f]	26	Martin Van Buren *Richard M. Johnson*	Dem.	170	764,176 (50.8%)
		William Henry Harrison *Francis Granger*	Whig	73	550,816 (36.6%)
1840	26	William Henry Harrison *John Tyler*	Whig	234	1,275,390 (52.9%)
		Martin Van Buren *Richard M. Johnson*	Dem.	60	1,128,854 (46.8%)
1844	26	James K. Polk *George M. Dallas*	Dem.	170	1,339,494 (49.5%)
		Henry Clay *Theodore Frelinghuysen*	Whig	105	1,300,004 (48.1%)
1848	30	Zachary Taylor *Millard Fillmore*	Whig	163	1,361,393 (47.3%)
		Lewis Cass *William O. Butler*	Dem.	127	1,223,460 (42.5%)
1852	31	Franklin Pierce *William R. King*	Dem.	254	1,607,510 (50.8%)
		Winfield Scott *William A. Graham*	Whig	42	1,386,942 (43.9%)
1856[g]	31	James Buchanan *John C. Breckinridge*	Dem.	174	1,836,072 (45.3%)
		John C. Fremont *William L. Dayton*	Rep.	114	1,342,345 (33.1%)
1860[h]	33	Abraham Lincoln *Hannibal Hamlin*	Rep.	180	1,865,908 (39.8%)
		Stephen A. Douglas *Herschel V. Johnson*	Dem.	12	1,380,202 (29.5%)
1864[i]	36	Abraham Lincoln *Andrew Johnson*	Rep.	212	2,218,388 (55.0%)
		George B. McClellan *George H. Pendleton*	Dem.	21	1,812,807 (45.0%)
1868[j]	37	Ulysses S. Grant *Schuyler Colfax*	Rep.	214	3,013,650 (52.7%)
		Horatio Seymour *Francis P. Blair Jr.*	Dem.	80	2,708,744 (47.3%)

(Continued)

SUMMARY OF PRESIDENTIAL ELECTIONS, 1789–2008   *(Continued)*

Year	No. of states	Candidates	Party	Electoral vote	Popular vote
1872	37	Ulysses S. Grant *Henry Wilson*	Rep.	286	3,598,235 (55.6%)
		Horace Greeley *Benjamin Gratz Brown*	Dem.	—k	2,834,761 (43.8%)
1876	38	Rutherford B. Hayes *William A. Wheeler*	Rep.	185	4,034,311 (47.9%)
		Samuel J. Tilden *Thomas A. Hendricks*	Dem.	184	4,288,546 (51.0%)
1880	38	James A. Garfield *Chester A. Arthur*	Rep.	214	4,446,158 (48.3%)
		Winfield S. Hancock *William H. English*	Dem.	155	4,444,260 (48.2%)
1884	38	Grover Cleveland *Thomas A. Hendricks*	Dem.	219	4,874,621 (48.5%)
		James G. Blaine *John A. Logan*	Rep.	182	4,848,936 (48.2%)
1888	38	Benjamin Harrison *Levi P. Morton*	Rep.	233	5,443,892 (47.8%)
		Grover Cleveland *Allen G. Thurman*	Dem.	168	5,534,488 (48.6%)
1892[l]	44	Grover Cleveland *Adlai E. Stevenson*	Dem.	277	5,551,883 (46.1%)
		Benjamin Harrison *Whitelaw Reid*	Rep.	145	5,179,244 (43.0%)
1896	45	William McKinley *Garret A. Hobart*	Rep.	271	7,108,480 (51.0%)
		William J. Bryan *Arthur Sewall*	Dem.	176	6,511,495 (46.7%)
1900	45	William McKinley *Theodore Roosevelt*	Rep.	292	7,218,039 (51.7%)
		William J. Bryan *Adlai E. Stevenson*	Dem.	155	6,358,345 (45.5%)
1904	45	Theodore Roosevelt *Charles W. Fairbanks*	Rep.	336	7,626,593 (56.4%)
		Alton B. Parker *Henry G. Davis*	Dem.	140	5,028,898 (37.6%)
1908	46	William Howard Taft *James S. Sherman*	Rep.	321	7,676,258 (51.6%)
		William J. Bryan *John W. Kern*	Dem.	162	6,406,801 (43.0%)

SUMMARY OF PRESIDENTIAL ELECTIONS, 1789–2008   *(Continued)*

Year	No. of states	Candidates	Party	Electoral vote	Popular vote
1912[m]	48	Woodrow Wilson *Thomas R. Marshall*	Dem.	435	6,293,152 (41.8%)
		William Howard Taft *James S. Sherman*	Rep.	8	3,486,333 (23.2%)
1916	48	Woodrow Wilson *Thomas R. Marshall*	Dem.	277	9,126,300 (49.2%)
		Charles E. Hughes *Charles W. Fairbanks*	Rep.	254	8,546,789 (46.1%)
1920	48	Warren G. Harding *Calvin Coolidge*	Rep.	404	16,133,314 (60.3%)
		James M. Cox *Franklin D. Roosevelt*	Dem.	127	9,140,884 (34.2%)
1924[n]	48	Calvin Coolidge *Charles G. Dawes*	Rep.	382	15,717,553 (54.1%)
		John W. Davis *Charles W. Bryan*	Dem.	136	8,386,169 (28.8%)
1928	48	Herbert C. Hoover *Charles Curtis*	Rep.	444	21,411,991 (58.2%)
		Alfred E. Smith *Joseph T. Robinson*	Dem.	87	15,000,185 (40.8%)
1932	48	Franklin D. Roosevelt *John N. Garner*	Dem.	472	22,825,016 (57.4%)
		Herbert C. Hoover *Charles Curtis*	Rep.	59	15,758,397 (39.6%)
1936	48	Franklin D. Roosevelt *John N. Garner*	Dem.	523	27,747,636 (60.8%)
		Alfred M. Landon *Frank Knox*	Rep.	8	16,679,543 (36.5%)
1940	48	Franklin D. Roosevelt *Henry A. Wallace*	Dem.	449	27,263,448 (54.7%)
		Wendell L. Willkie *Charles L. McNary*	Rep.	82	22,336,260 (44.8%)
1944	48	Franklin D. Roosevelt *Harry S. Truman*	Dem.	432	25,611,936 (53.4%)
		Thomas E. Dewey *John W. Bricker*	Rep.	99	22,013,372 (45.9%)
1948[o]	48	Harry S. Truman *Alben W. Barkley*	Dem.	303	24,105,587 (49.5%)
		Thomas E. Dewey *Earl Warren*	Rep.	198	21,970,017 (45.1%)

(Continued)

SUMMARY OF PRESIDENTIAL ELECTIONS, 1789–2008 *(Continued)*

Year	No. of states	Candidates	Party	Electoral vote	Popular vote
1952	48	Dwight D. Eisenhower *Richard M. Nixon*	Rep.	442	33,936,137 (55.1%)
		Adlai E. Stevenson II *John J. Sparkman*	Dem.	89	27,314,649 (44.4%)
1956[p]	48	Dwight D. Eisenhower *Richard M. Nixon*	Rep.	457	35,585,245 (57.4%)
		Adlai E. Stevenson II *Estes Kefauver*	Dem.	73	26,030,172 (42.0%)
1960[q]	50	John F. Kennedy *Lyndon B. Johnson*	Dem.	303	34,221,344 (49.7%)
		Richard Nixon *Henry Cabot Lodge*	Rep.	219	34,106,671 (49.5%)
1964	50*	Lyndon B. Johnson *Hubert H. Humphrey*	Dem.	486	43,126,584 (61.1%)
		Barry Goldwater *William E. Miller*	Rep.	52	27,177,838 (38.5%)
1968[r]	50*	Richard Nixon *Spiro T. Agnew*	Rep.	301	31,785,148 (43.4%)
		Hubert H. Humphrey *Edmund S. Muskie*	Dem.	191	31,274,503 (42.7%)
1972[s]	50*	Richard Nixon *Spiro T. Agnew*	Rep.	520	47,170,179 (60.7%)
		George McGovern *Sargent Shriver*	Dem.	17	29,171,791 (37.5%)
1976[t]	50*	Jimmy Carter *Walter F. Mondale*	Dem.	297	40,830,763 (50.1%)
		Gerald R. Ford *Robert Dole*	Rep.	240	39,147,793 (48.0%)
1980	50*	Ronald Reagan *George Bush*	Rep.	489	43,904,153 (50.7%)
		Jimmy Carter *Walter F. Mondale*	Dem.	49	35,483,883 (41.0%)
1984	50*	Ronald Reagan *George Bush*	Rep.	525	54,455,074(58.8%)
		Walter F. Mondale *Geraldine Ferraro*	Dem.	13	37,577,137 (40.6%)
1988[u]	50*	George Bush *Dan Quayle*	Rep.	426	48,881,278 (53.4%)
		Michael S. Dukakis *Lloyd Bentsen*	Dem.	111	41,805,374 (45.6%)

SUMMARY OF PRESIDENTIAL ELECTIONS, 1789–2008 *(Continued)*

Year	No. of states	Candidates	Party	Electoral vote	Popular vote
1992	50*	Bill Clinton *Al Gore*	Dem.	370	44,908,233 (43.0%)
		George Bush *Dan Quayle*	Rep.	168	39,102,282 (37.4%)
1996	50*	Bill Clinton *Al Gore*	Dem.	379	47,402,357 (49.2%)
		Robert Dole *Jack Kemp*	Rep.	159	39,1987,755 (40.7%)
2000ᵛ	50*	George W. Bush *Richard B. Cheney*	Rep.	271	50,455,1256 (47.9%)
		Al Gore *Joseph I. Lieberman*	Dem.	266	50,992,335 (48.4%)
2004ʷ	50*	George W. Bush *Richard B. Cheney*	Rep.	286	62,040,610 (50.7%)
		John Kerry *John Edwards*	Dem.	251	59,028,439 (48.3%)
2008	50*	Barack Obama *Joseph R. Biden Jr.*	Dem.	365	69,498,516 (52.9%)
		John McCain *Sarah Palin*	Rep.	173	59,948,323 (45.7%)

Source: Harold W. Stanley and Richard G. Niemi, *Vital Statistics on American Politics*, 5th ed. (Washington, D.C.: CQ Press, 1995), Table 3-13; 1996 data, Richard M. Scammon, Alice V. McGillivray, and Rhodes Cook, *America Votes 22* through *28* (Washington, D.C.: CQ Press, 1998-2010).

Notes: In the elections of 1789, 1792, 1796, and 1800, each candidate ran for the office of president. The candidate with the second highest number of electoral votes became vice president. For elections after 1800, italic indicates vice-presidential candidates. Dem.-Rep.—Democratic-Republican; Fed.—Federalist; Nat.-Rep.—National-Republican; Dem.—Democratic; Rep.—Republican.

a. Elections of 1789–1800 were held under rules that did not allow separate voting for president and vice president.***

b. Popular vote returns are not shown before 1824 because consistent, reliable data are not available.

c. Monroe ran unopposed. One electoral vote was cast for John Adams and Richard Stockton, who were not candidates.

d. 1824: All four candidates represented Democratic-Republican factions. William H. Crawford received 41 electoral votes, and Henry Clay received 37 votes. Since no candidate received a majority, the election was decided (in Adams's favor) by the House of Representatives.

e. 1832: Two electoral votes were not cast.

f. 1836: Other Whig candidates receiving electoral votes were Hugh L. White, who received 26 votes, and Daniel Webster, who received 14 votes.

g. 1856: Millard Fillmore, Whig-American, received 8 electoral votes.

h. 1860: John C. Breckinridge, Southern Democrat, received 72 electoral votes. John Bell, Constitutional Union, received 39 electoral votes.

i. 1864: Eighty-one electoral votes were not cast.

j. 1868: Twenty-three electoral votes were not cast.

k. 1872: Horace Greeley, Democrat, died after the election. In the Electoral College, Democratic electoral votes went to Thomas Hendricks, 42 votes; Benjamin Gratz Brown, 18 votes; Charles J. Jenkins, 2 votes; and David Davis, 1 vote. Seventeen electoral votes were not cast.

l. 1892: James B. Weaver, People's Party, received 22 electoral votes.

m. 1912: Theodore Roosevelt, Progressive Party, received 86 electoral votes.

n. 1924: Robert M. La Follette, Progressive Party, received 13 electoral votes.

o. 1948: J. Strom Thurmond, States' Rights Party, received 39 electoral votes.

p. 1956: Walter B. Jones, Democrat, received 1 electoral vote.

q. 1960: Harry Flood Byrd, Democrat, received 15 electoral votes.

r. 1968: George C. Wallace, American Independent Party, received 46 electoral votes.

s. 1972: John Hospers, Libertarian Party, received 1 electoral vote.

t. 1976: Ronald Reagan, Republican, received 1 electoral vote.

u. 1988: Lloyd Bentsen, the Democratic vice-presidential nominee, received 1 electoral vote for president.

v. 2000: One District of Columbia elector withheld her vote for Gore.

w. 2004: One Minnesota elector cast an electoral vote for president for Democratic vice presidential nominee John Edwards rather than presidential nominee John Kerry.

*Fifty states plus the District of Columbia.

2008 POPULAR VOTE SUMMARY, PRESIDENTIAL

State	Electoral Vote Rep.	Dem.	Other	Total Vote	McCain Republican	Obama Democratic	Other Vote	Plurality		Percentage (%) Rep.	Dem.	Other
Alabama	9	0	0	2,099,819	1,266,546	813,479	19,794	453,067	R	60.3	38.7	0.9
Alaska	3	0	0	326,197	193,841	123,594	8,762	70,247	R	59.4	37.9	2.7
Arizona	10	0	0	2,293,475	1,230,111	1,034,707	28,657	195,404	R	53.6	45.1	1.3
Arkansas	6	0	0	1,086,617	638,017	422,310	26,290	215,707	R	58.7	38.9	2.4
California	0	55	0	13,561,900	5,011,781	8,274,473	275,646	3,262,692	D	37.0	61.0	2.0
Colorado	0	9	0	2,900,864	1,073,629	1,288,633	538,602	215,004	D	37.0	44.4	18.6
Connecticut	0	7	0	1,646,792	629,428	997,772	19,592	368,344	D	38.2	60.6	1.2
Delaware	0	3	0	412,412	152,374	255,459	4,579	103,085	D	37.0	61.9	1.1
Florida	0	27	0	8,390,744	4,045,624	4,282,074	63,046	236,450	D	48.2	51.0	0.8
Georgia	15	0	0	3,924,486	2,048,759	1,844,123	31,604	204,636	R	52.2	47.0	0.8
Hawaii	0	4	0	453,568	120,566	325,871	7,131	205,305	D	26.6	71.9	1.6
Idaho	4	0	0	655,032	403,012	236,440	15,580	166,572	R	61.5	36.1	2.4
Illinois	0	21	0	5,522,371	2,031,179	3,419,348	71,844	1,388,169	D	36.8	61.9	1.3
Indiana	0	11	0	2,751,054	1,345,648	1,374,039	31,367	28,391	D	48.9	50.0	1.1
Iowa	0	7	0	1,537,123	682,379	828,940	25,804	146,561	D	44.4	53.9	1.7
Kansas	6	0	0	1,235,872	699,655	514,765	21,452	184,890	R	56.6	41.7	1.7
Kentucky	8	0	0	1,826,620	1,048,462	751,985	26,173	296,477	R	57.4	41.2	1.4
Louisiana	9	0	0	1,960,761	1,148,275	782,989	29,497	365,286	R	58.6	39.9	1.5
Maine	0	4	0	731,163	295,273	421,923	13,967	126,650	D	40.4	57.7	1.9
Maryland	0	10	0	2,631,596	959,862	1,629,467	42,267	669,605	D	36.5	61.9	1.6
Massachusetts	0	12	0	3,080,985	1,108,854	1,904,097	68,034	795,243	D	36.0	61.8	2.2
Michigan	0	17	0	5,001,766	2,048,639	2,872,579	80,548	823,940	D	41.0	57.4	1.6
Minnesota	0	10	0	2,910,369	1,275,409	1,573,354	61,606	297,945	D	43.8	54.1	2.1
Mississippi	6	0	0	1,289,865	724,597	554,662	10,606	169,935	R	56.2	43.0	0.8
Missouri	11	0	0	2,913,334	1,439,923	1,436,176	37,235	3,747	R	49.4	49.3	1.3
Montana	3	0	0	490,302	242,763	231,667	15,872	11,096	R	49.5	47.3	3.2
Nebraska	4	1	0	801,281	452,979	333,319	14,983	119,660	R	56.5	41.6	1.9
Nevada	0	5	0	967,848	412,827	533,736	21,285	120,909	D	42.7	55.2	2.2
New Hampshire	0	4	0	710,970	316,534	384,826	9,610	68,292	D	44.5	54.1	1.4
New Jersey	0	15	0	3,868,237	1,613,207	2,215,422	39,608	602,215	D	41.7	57.3	1.0
New Mexico	0	5	0	830,158	346,832	472,422	10,904	125,590	D	41.8	56.9	1.3
New York	0	31	0	7,640,931	2,752,771	4,804,945	83,215	2,052,174	D	36.0	62.9	1.1
North Carolina	0	15	0	4,310,789	2,128,474	2,142,651	39,664	14,177	D	49.4	49.7	0.9
North Dakota	3	0	0	316,621	168,601	141,278	6,742	27,323	R	53.3	44.6	2.1
Ohio	0	20	0	5,708,350	2,677,820	2,940,044	90,486	262,224	D	46.9	51.5	1.6
Oklahoma	7	0	0	1,462,661	960,165	502,496	N/A	457,669	R	65.7	34.4	0.0
Oregon	0	7	0	1,827,864	738,475	1,037,291	52,098	298,816	D	40.4	56.8	2.9
Pennsylvania	0	21	0	5,995,137	2,655,885	3,276,363	62,889	620,478	D	44.3	54.7	1.1
Rhode Island	0	4	0	471,766	165,391	296,571	9,804	131,180	D	35.1	62.9	2.1
South Carolina	8	0	0	1,909,968	1,028,632	857,856	23,480	170,776	R	53.9	44.9	1.2
South Dakota	3	0	0	381,975	203,054	170,924	7,997	32,130	R	53.2	44.8	2.1
Tennessee	11	0	0	2,599,749	1,479,178	1,087,437	33,134	391,741	R	56.9	41.8	1.3
Texas	34	0	0	8,077,795	4,479,328	3,528,633	69,834	950,695	R	55.5	43.7	0.9
Utah	5	0	0	952,370	596,030	327,670	28,670	268,360	R	62.6	34.4	3.0
Vermont	0	3	0	325,046	98,974	219,262	6,810	120,288	D	30.5	67.5	2.1
Virginia	0	13	0	3,723,260	1,725,005	1,959,532	38,723	234,527	D	46.3	52.6	1.0
Washington	0	11	0	3,036,878	1,229,216	1,750,848	56,814	521,632	D	40.5	57.7	1.9
West Virginia	5	0	0	713,451	397,466	303,857	12,128	93,609	R	55.7	42.6	1.7
Wisconsin	0	10	0	2,983,417	1,262,393	1,677,211	43,813	414,818	D	42.3	56.2	1.5
Wyoming	3	0	0	254,658	164,958	82,868	6,832	82,090	R	64.8	32.5	2.7
District of Columbia	0	3	0	265,853	17,367	245,800	2,686	228,433	D	6.5	92.5	1.0
United States	173	365	0	131,772,120	59,936,168	69,488,188	2,347,764	9,552,020	D	45.5	52.7	1.8

"Presidential General Election, All States, 2008 Summary." In CQ Voting and Elections Collection (Web site) Washington, DC: CQ Press, 2003. http://library.cqpress.com/elections/avg2008-1us1.

DISTRIBUTION OF HOUSE SEATS AND ELECTORAL VOTES

State	1963–1973	1970 Census Changes	1973–1983	1980 Census Changes	1983–1993	1990 Census Changes	1993–2003	2000 Census Changes	2003–2013	2010 Census Changes	2013–2023	1952, 1956, 1960	1964, 1968	1972, 1976, 1980	1984, 1988	1992, 1996, 2000	2004, 2008	2012, 2016, 2020
Alabama	8	−1	7	—	7	—	7	—	7	–	7	11	10	9	9	9	9	9
Alaska	1	—	1	—	1	—	1	—	1	–	1	3	3	3	3	3	3	3
Arizona	3	+1	4	+1	5	+1	6	+2	8	+1	9	4	5	6	7	8	10	11
Arkansas	4	—	4	—	4	—	4	—	4	–	4	8	6	6	6	6	6	6
California	38	+5	43	+2	45	+7	52	+1	53	–	53	32	40	45	47	54	55	55
Colorado	4	+1	5	+1	6	—	6	+1	7	–	7	6	6	7	8	8	9	9
Connecticut	6	—	6	—	6	—	6	−1	5	–	5	8	8	8	8	8	7	7
Delaware	1	—	1	—	1	—	1	—	1	–	1	3	3	3	3	3	3	3
Dist. of Col.	—	—	—	—	—	—	—	—	—	–	—	—	3	3	3	3	3	3
Florida	12	+3	15	+4	19	+4	23	+2	25	+2	27	10	14	17	21	25	27	29
Georgia	10	—	10	—	10	+1	11	+2	13	+1	14	12	12	12	12	13	15	16
Hawaii	2	—	2	—	2	—	2	—	2	–	2	3	4	4	4	4	4	4
Idaho	2	—	2	—	2	—	2	—	2	–	2	4	4	4	4	4	4	4
Illinois	24	—	24	−2	22	−2	20	−1	19	−1	18	27	26	26	24	22	21	20
Indiana	11	—	11	−1	10	—	10	−1	9	–	9	13	13	13	12	12	11	11
Iowa	7	−1	6	—	6	−1	5	—	5	−1	4	10	9	8	8	7	7	6
Kansas	5	—	5	—	5	−1	4	—	4	–	4	8	7	7	7	6	6	6
Kentucky	7	—	7	—	7	−1	6	—	6	–	6	10	9	9	9	8	8	8
Louisiana	8	—	8	—	8	−1	7	—	7	−1	6	10	10	10	10	9	9	8
Maine	2	—	2	—	2	—	2	—	2	–	2	5	4	4	4	4	4	4
Maryland	8	—	8	—	8	—	8	—	8	–	8	9	10	10	10	10	10	10
Massachusetts	12	—	12	−1	11	−1	10	—	10	−1	9	16	14	14	13	12	12	11
Michigan	19	—	19	−1	18	−2	16	−1	15	−1	14	20	21	21	20	18	17	16
Minnesota	8	—	8	—	8	—	8	—	8	–	8	11	10	10	10	10	10	10
Mississippi	5	—	5	—	5	—	5	−1	4	–	4	8	7	7	7	7	6	6
Missouri	10	—	10	−1	9	—	9	—	9	−1	8	13	12	12	11	11	11	10
Montana	2	—	2	—	2	−1	1	—	1	–	1	4	4	4	4	3	3	3
Nebraska	3	—	3	—	3	—	3	—	3	–	3	6	5	5	5	5	5	5
Nevada	1	—	1	+1	2	—	2	+1	3	+1	4	3	3	3	4	4	5	6
New Hampshire	2	—	2	—	2	—	2	—	2	–	2	4	4	4	4	4	4	4
New Jersey	15	—	15	−1	14	−1	13	—	13	−1	12	16	17	17	16	15	15	15
New Mexico	2	—	2	+1	3	—	3	—	3	–	3	4	4	4	5	5	5	5
New York	41	−2	39	−5	34	−3	31	−2	29	−2	27	45	43	41	36	33	31	29
North Carolina	11	—	11	—	11	+1	12	+1	13	–	13	14	13	13	13	14	15	15
North Dakota	2	−1	1	—	1	—	1	—	1	–	1	4	4	3	3	3	3	3
Ohio	24	−1	23	−2	21	−2	19	−1	18	−2	16	25	26	25	23	21	20	18
Oklahoma	6	—	6	—	6	—	6	−1	5	–	5	8	8	8	8	8	7	7
Oregon	4	—	4	+1	5	—	5	—	5	–	5	6	6	6	7	7	7	7
Pennsylvania	27	−2	25	−2	23	−2	21	−2	19	−1	18	32	29	27	25	23	21	20
Rhode Island	2	—	2	—	2	—	2	—	2	–	2	4	4	4	4	4	4	4
South Carolina	6	—	6	—	6	—	6	—	6	+1	7	8	8	8	8	8	8	9
South Dakota	2	—	2	−1	1	—	1	—	1	–	1	4	4	4	3	3	3	3
Tennessee	9	−1	8	+1	9	—	9	—	9	–	9	11	11	10	11	11	11	11
Texas	23	+1	24	+3	27	+3	30	+2	32	+4	36	24	25	26	29	32	34	38
Utah	2	—	2	+1	3	—	3	—	3	+1	4	4	4	4	5	5	5	6
Vermont	1	—	1	—	1	—	1	—	1	–	1	3	3	3	3	3	3	3
Virginia	10	—	10	—	10	+1	11	—	11	–	11	12	12	12	12	13	13	13
Washington	7	—	7	+1	8	+1	9	—	9	+1	10	9	9	9	10	11	11	12
West Virginia	5	−1	4	—	4	−1	3	—	3	–	3	8	7	6	6	5	5	5
Wisconsin	10	−1	9	—	9	—	9	−1	8	–	8	12	12	11	11	11	10	10
Wyoming	1	—	1	—	1	—	1	—	1	–	1	3	3	3	3	3	3	3

Source: *Guide to U.S. Elections*, 6th ed. (Washington, D.C.: CQ Press, 2010) and U.S. Census Bureau http://2010.census.gov/2010census/data/apportionment-pop-text.php.
Note: Table is based on the censuses of 1950, 1960, 1970, 1980, 1990, 2000, and 2010.

Law for Counting Electoral Votes in Congress

Following is the complete text of Title 3, section 15, of the U.S. Code, enacted originally in 1887, governing the counting of electoral votes in Congress:

Congress shall be in session on the sixth day of January succeeding every meeting of the electors. The Senate and House of Representatives shall meet in the Hall of the House of Representatives at the hour of 1 o'clock in the afternoon on that day, and the President of the Senate shall be their presiding officer. Two tellers shall be previously appointed on the part of the Senate and two on the part of the House of Representatives, to whom shall be handed, as they are opened by the President of the Senate, all the certificates and papers purporting to be certificates of the electoral votes, which certificates and papers shall be opened, presented, and acted upon in the alphabetical order of the States, beginning with the letter A; and said tellers, having then read the same in the presence and hearing of the two Houses, shall make a list of the votes as they shall appear from the said certificates; and the votes having been ascertained and counted according to the rules in this subchapter provided, the result of the same shall be delivered to the President of the Senate, who shall thereupon announce the state of the vote, which announcement shall be deemed a sufficient declaration of the persons, if any, elected President and Vice President of the United States, and, together with a list of votes, be entered on the Journals of the two Houses. Upon such reading of any such certificate or paper, the President of the Senate shall call for objections, if any. Every objection shall be made in writing, and shall state clearly and concisely, and without argument, the ground thereof, and shall be signed by at least one Senator and one Member of the House of Representatives before the same shall be received. When all objections so made to any vote or paper from a State shall have been received and read, the Senate shall thereupon withdraw, and such objections shall be submitted to the Senate for its decision; and the Speaker of the House of Representatives shall, in like manner, submit such objections to the House of Representatives for its decision; and no electoral vote or votes from any State which shall have been regularly given by electors whose appointment has been lawfully certified to according to section 6* of this title from which but one return has been received shall be rejected, but the two Houses concurrently may reject the vote or votes when they agree that such vote or votes have not been so regularly given by electors whose appointment has been so certified. If more than one return or paper purporting to be a return from a State shall have been received by the President of the Senate, those votes, and those only, shall be counted which shall have been regularly given by the electors who are shown by the determination mentioned in section 5† of this title to have been appointed, if the determination in said section provided for shall have been made, or by such successors or substitutes, in case of a vacancy in the board of electors so ascertained, as have been appointed to fill such vacancy in the mode provided by the laws of the State; but in case there shall arise the question which of two or more of such State authorities determining what electors have been appointed, as mentioned in section 5 of this title, is the lawful tribunal of such State, the votes regularly given of those electors, and those only, of such State shall be counted whose title as electors the two Houses, acting separately, shall concurrently decide is supported by the decision of such State so authorized by its law; and in such case of more than one return or paper purporting to be a return from a State, if there shall have been no such determination of the question in the State aforesaid, then those votes, and those only, shall be counted which the two Houses shall concurrently decide were cast by lawful electors appointed in accordance with the laws of the State, unless the two Houses, acting separately, shall concurrently decide such votes not to be the lawful votes of the legally appointed electors of such State. But if the two Houses shall disagree in respect of the counting of such votes, then, and in that case, the votes of the electors whose appointment shall have been certified by the executive of the State, under the seal thereof, shall be counted. When the two Houses have voted, they shall immediately again meet, and the presiding officer shall then announce the decision of the questions submitted. No votes or papers from any other State shall be acted upon until the objections previously made to the votes or papers from any State shall have been finally disposed of.

NOTES:

*Section 6 provides for certification of votes by electors by state governors.

†Section 5 provides that if state law specifies a method for resolving disputes concerning the vote for presidential electors, Congress must respect any determination so made by a state.

Election Results: Congress and the Presidency, 1860–2010

| | | House | | | | | Senate | | | | | |
| | | Members elected | | | Gains/losses | | Members elected | | | Gains/losses | | |
Election year	Congress	Dem.	Rep.	Misc.	Dem.	Rep.	Dem.	Rep.	Misc.	Dem.	Rep.	President
1860	37th	42	106	28	−59	−7	11	31	7	−27	+5	Lincoln (R)
1862	38th	80	103		+38	−3	12	39		+1	+8	
1864	39th	46	145		−34	+42	10	42		−2	+3	Lincoln (R)
1866	40th	49	143		+3	−2	11	42		+1	0	Johnson (R)
1868	41st	73	170		+24	+27	11	61		0	+19	Grant (R)
1870	42nd	104	139		+31	−31	17	57		+6	−4	
1872	43rd	88	203		−16	+64	19	54		+2	−3	Grant (R)
1874	44th	181	107	3	+93	−96	29	46		+10	−8	
1876	45th	156	137		−25	+30	36	39	1	+7	−7	Hayes (R)
1878	46th	150	128	14	−6	−9	43	33		+7	−6	
1880	47th	130	152	11	−20	+24	37	37	2	−6	+4	Garfield (R)
1882	48th	200	119	6	+70	−33	36	40		−1	+3	Arthur (R)
1884	49th	182	140	2	−18	+21	34	41		−2	+2	Cleveland (D)
1886	50th	170	151	4	−12	+11	37	39		+3	−2	
1888	51st	156	173	1	−14	+22	37	47		0	+8	Harrison (R)
1890	52nd	231	88	14	+75	85	39	47	2	+2	0	
1892	53rd	220	126	8	−11	+38	44	38	3	+5	−9	Cleveland (D)
1894	54th	104	246	7	−116	+120	30	44	5	−5	+6	
1896	55th	134	206	16	+30	−40	34	46	10	−5	+2	McKinley (R)
1898	56th	163	185	9	+29	−21	26	53	11	−8	+7	
1900	57th	153	198	5	−10	+13	29	56	3	+3	+3	McKinley (R)
1902	58th	178	207		+25	+9	32	58		+3	+2	Roosevelt (R)
1904	59th	136	250		−42	+43	32	58		0	0	Roosevelt (R)
1906	60th	164	222		+28	−28	29	61		−3	−3	
1908	61st	172	219		+8	−3	32	59		+3	−2	Taft (R)
1910	62nd	228	162	1	+56	−57	42	49		+10	−10	
1912	63rd	290	127	18	+62	−35	51	44	1	19	−5	Wilson (D)
1914	64th	231	193	8	−59	+66	56	39	1	+5	−5	
1916	65th	210	216	9	−21	+23	53	42	1	−3	+3	Wilson (D)
1918	66th	191	237	7	−19	+21	47	48	1	−6	+6	
1920	67th	132	300	1	−59	+63	37	59		−10	+11	Harding (R)
1922	68th	207	225	3	+75	−75	43	51	2	+6	−8	Coolidge (R)
1924	69th	183	247	5	−24	+22	40	54	1	−3	+3	Coolidge (R)
1926	70th	195	237	3	+12	−10	47	48	1	+7	−6	
1928	71st	167	267	1	−28	+30	39	56	1	−8	+8	Hoover (R)
1930	72nd	220	214	1	+53	−53	47	48	1	+8	−8	
1932	73rd	313	117	5	+97	−101	59	36	1	+12	−12	Roosevelt (D)
1934	74th	322	103	10	+9	−14	69	25	2	+10	−11	
1936	75th	333	89	13	+11	−14	75	17	4	+6	−8	Roosevelt (D)
1938	76th	262	169	4	−71	+80	69	23	4	−6	+6	

(Continued)

ELECTION RESULTS: CONGRESS AND THE PRESIDENCY, 1860–2010 *(Continued)*

| | | House | | | | | Senate | | | | | |
| | | Members elected | | | Gains/losses | | Members elected | | | Gains/losses | | |
Election year	Congress	Dem.	Rep.	Misc.	Dem.	Rep.	Dem.	Rep.	Misc.	Dem.	Rep.	President
1940	77th	267	162	6	+5	−7	66	28	2	−3	+5	Roosevelt (D)
1942	78th	222	209	4	−45	+47	57	38	1	−9	+10	
1944	79th	243	190	2	+21	−19	57	38	1	0	0	Roosevelt (D)
1946	80th	188	246	1	−55	+56	45	51		−12	+13	Truman (D)
1948	81st	263	171	1	+75	−75	54	42		+9	−9	Truman (D)
1950	82nd	234	199	2	−29	+28	48	47	1	−6	15	
1952	83rd	213	221	1	−21	+22	47	48	1	−1	+1	Eisenhower (R)
1954	84th	232	203		+19	−18	48	47	1	+1	−1	
1956	85th	234	201		+2	−2	49	47		+1	0	Eisenhower (R)
1958	86th	283	154		+49	−47	64	34		+17	−13	
1960	87th	263	174		−20	+20	64	36		−2	+2	Kennedy (D)
1962	88th	258	176	1[1]	−4	+2	67	33		+4	−4	
1964	89th	295	140		+38	−38	68	32		+2	−2	Johnson (D)
1966	90th	248	187		−47	+47	64	36		−3	+3	
1968	91st	243	192		−4	+4	58	42		−5	+5	Nixon (R)
1970	92nd	255	180		+12	−12	55	45		−4	+2	
1972	93rd	243	192		−12	+12	57	43		+2	−2	Nixon (R)
1974	94th	291	144		+43	−43	61	38		+3	−3	
1976	95th	292	143		+1	−1	62	38		0	0	Carter (D)
1978	96th	277	158		−11	+11	59	41		−3	+3	
1980	97th	243	192		−33	+33	47	53		−12	+12	Reagan (R)
1982	98th	269	166		+26	−26	46	54		0	0	
1984	99th	253	182		−14	+14	47	53		+2	−2	Reagan (R)
1986	100th	258	177		+5	−5	55	45		+8	−8	
1988	101st	259	174		+2	−2	55	45		+1	−1	George. H. W. Bush (R)
1990	102nd	267	167	1	+9	−8	56	44		+1	−1	
1992	103rd	258	176	1	−9	+9	57	43		+1	−1	Clinton (D)
1994	104th	204	230	1	−52	+52	47	53		−8	+8[2]	
1996	105th	207	227	1	+3	−3	45	55		−2	+2	Clinton (D)
1998	106th	211	223	1	+5	−5	45	55		0	0	
2000	107th	212	221	2	+1	−2	50	50		+4	−4	G. W. Bush (R)
2002	108th	205	229	1	−6	+6	48	51	1	+2	−2	
2004	109th	202	232	1	−3	+3	44	55	1	−4	+4	G. W. Bush (R)
2006	110th	233	202		+30	−30	49	49	2	+5	−6[3]	
2008	111th	257	178		+24	−24	57	41	2	+8	−8	Barack Obama (D)
2010	112th	193	242		−63[4]	+63[4]	51	47	2	−6	+6	

Source: Adapted from *Guide to U.S. Elections*, 6th ed. (Washington, D.C.: CQ Press, 2010), 1748-1749; Richard Scammon, Alice McGillivray, and Rhodes Cook, *America Votes 28 and 29* (Washington, D.C.: CQ Press, 2010 and 2012).

NOTES: The seats totals reflect the makeup of the House and Senate at the start of each Congress. Special elections that shifted party ratios in between elections are not noted.

1. Vacancy—Rep. Clem Miller (D-Calif. 1959–62) died Oct. 6, 1962, but his name remained on the ballot and he received a plurality.

2. Sen. Richard Shelby (Ala.) switched from the Democratic Party to the Republican Party the day after the election, bringing the total Republican gain to nine.

3. Independents Joseph I. Lieberman of Connecticut and Bernard Sanders of Vermont voted for the Democratic Party leadership team, allowing Democrats to take control of the Senate in the 110th Congress.

4. Even though Republicans increased their total to 242 seats from 178 in the 2010 voting, the GOP is credited with a net gain of sixty-three because one of the two vacant seats going into the election was previously held by a Republican.

INCUMBENTS REELECTED, DEFEATED, OR RETIRED, 1946–2010

Chamber/ year	Retired[1]	Number seeking reelection	Defeated		Reelected	
			Primaries	General election	Total	Percentage of those seeking reelection
House						
1946	32	398	18	52	328	82.4
1948	29	400	15	68	317	79.3
1950	29	400	6	32	362	90.5
1952	42	389	9	26	354	91.0
1954	24	407	6	22	379	93.1
1956	21	411	6	16	389	94.6
1958	33	396	3	37	356	89.9
1960[2, 3]	27	405	6	25	375	92.6
1962[4]	24	402	12	22	368	91.5
1964	33	397	8	45	344	86.6
1966	23	411	8	41	362	88.1
1968[5]	24	408	4	9	395	96.8
1970[3]	30	401	10	12	379	94.5
1972[3, 6]	40	392	14	13	366	93.4
1974	43	391	8	40	343	87.7
1976	47	384	3	13	368	95.8
1978	49	382	5	19	358	93.7
1980[3]	34	398	6	31	361	90.7
1982	31	387	4	29	354	91.5
1984	22	411	3	16	392	95.4
1986	40	394	3	6	385	97.7
1988	23	409	1	6	402	98.3
1990	27	407	1	15	391	96.1
1992	65	368	19	24	325	88.3
1994[3]	48	387	4	34	349	90.2
1996	49	384	2	21	361	94.0
1998	33	402	1	6	395	98.3
2000	32	403	3	6	394	97.8
2002	35	398	8	8	382	96.0
2004	29	404	2	7	395	97.8
2006[7]	27	404	2	22	380	94.1
2008	32	403	4	19	380	94.3
2010	36	393	4	54	339	86.3
Senate						
1946	9	30	6	7	17	56.7
1948	8	25	2	8	15	60.0
1950	4	32	5	5	22	68.8
1952	4	31	2	9	20	64.5
1954	6	32	2	6	24	75.0
1956	6	29	0	4	25	86.2
1958	6	28	0	10	18	64.3
1960	4	29	0	1	28	96.6
1962	4	35	1	5	29	82.9
1964	2	33	1	4	28	84.8

(Continued)

INCUMBENTS REELECTED, DEFEATED, OR RETIRED, 1946–2010   *(Continued)*

Chamber/ year	Retired[1]	Number seeking reelection	Defeated Primaries	Defeated General election	Reelected Total	Reelected Percentage of those seeking reelection
1966	3	32	3	1	28	87.5
1968[3]	6	28	4	4	20	71.4
1970	4	31	1	6	24	77.4
1972	6	27	2	5	20	74.1
1974	7	27	2	2	23	85.2
1976	8	25	0	9	16	64.0
1978	10	25	3	7	15	60.0
1980[3]	5	29	4	9	16	55.2
1982	3	30	0	2	28	93.3
1984	4	29	0	3	26	89.7
1986	6	28	0	7	21	75.0
1988	6	27	0	4	23	85.2
1990	3	32	0	1	31	96.9
1992	7	28	1	4	23	82.1
1994	9	26	0	2	24	92.2
1996	13	21	1	1	19	90.5
1998	5	29	0	3	26	89.7
2000	5	29	0	6	23	79.3
2002	6	28	1	3	24	85.7
2004	8	26	0	1	25	96.2
2006[8]	4	29	1	6	23	79.3
2008	5	30	0	5	25	83.3
2010[9]	12	25	3	2	21	84.0

Source: Harold W. Stanley and Richard G. Niemi, *Vital Statistics on American Politics 2011-2012* (Washington, D.C.: CQ Press, 2011), 43-44.

Notes

1. Does not include persons who died or resigned before the election.

2. Harold B. McSween, D-La., lost the Democratic primary in 1960 and is counted as an incumbent defeated in the primary. However, his victorious primary opponent, Earl K. Long, died after winning the primary, and McSween was appointed to replace Long in the general election by the Eighth District Democratic Committee. McSween won the general election and is counted as an incumbent winning the general election.

3. In this year, an incumbent candidate lost the party primary and is counted as an incumbent defeated in the primary. The candidate then ran in the general election on a minor-party label or as a write-in candidate and lost again, but is not also counted as an incumbent defeated in the general election. House: 1960, Ludwig Teller, D-N.Y.; 1970, Philip Philbin, D-Mass.; 1972, Emanuel Celler, D-N.Y.; 1980, John Buchanan, R-Ala.; 1994, David A. Levy, R-N.Y. Senate: 1968, Ernest Gruening, D-Alaska; 1980, Jacob K. Javits, R-N.Y.

4. Clem Miller, D-Calif., was killed in a plane crash on October 7, 1962, but his name remained on the 1962 general election ballot. He won the election posthumously and is counted here as an incumbent winning the general election.

5. Adam Clayton Powell, D-N.Y., won a special election on April 11, 1967, but he was prevented from taking the oath of office and did not take his seat in Congress. Therefore, he is not counted here as an incumbent in the 1968 general election.

6. Bella Abzug, D-N.Y., lost the Democratic primary in 1972 and is counted as an incumbent defeated in the primary. However, her victorious primary opponent, William F. Ryan, died after winning the primary, and Abzug was appointed to replace him in the general election by the local party committee. Abzug won the general election and is counted as an incumbent winning the general election.

7. In 2006, three representatives withdrew from the general election after winning their primaries: Tom DeLay, R-Texas; Mark Foley, R-Fla.; and Bob Ney, R-Ohio. Because they did not run in the general election, they are not counted as incumbents seeking reelection.

8. Joseph I. Lieberman, D-Conn., lost the Democratic primary in 2006 and is counted as an incumbent defeated in the primary. He ran as an independent in the general election and won. He is counted as an incumbent winning the general election.

9. Lisa Murkowski, the incumbent Republican senator from Alaska, lost the GOP primary in 2010 and is counted as an incumbent defeated in the primary. She ran as a write-in candidate in the general election and won; she is counted as an incumbent winning the general election.

BLACKS IN CONGRESS, 41ST–112TH CONGRESSES, 1869–2011

Congress		House D	House R	Senate D	Senate R	Congress		House D	House R	Senate D	Senate R
41st	(1869)	—	2	—	1	83d	(1953)	2	—	—	—
42d	(1871)	—	5	—	—	84th	(1955)	3	—	—	—
43d	(1873)	—	7	—	—	85th	(1957)	3	—	—	—
44th	(1875)	—	7	—	1	86th	(1959)	3	—	—	—
45th	(1877)	—	3	—	1	87th	(1961)	3	—	—	—
46th	(1879)	—	—	—	1	88th	(1963)	4	—	—	—
47th	(1881)	—	2	—	—	89th	(1965)	5	—	—	—
48th	(1883)	—	2	—	—	90th	(1967)	5	—	—	1
49th	(1885)	—	2	—	—	91st	(1969)	9	—	—	1
50th	(1887)	—	—	—	—	92d	(1971)	13	—	—	1
51st	(1889)	—	3	—	—	93d	(1973)	16	—	—	1
52d	(1891)	—	1	—	—	94th	(1975)	16	—	—	1
53d	(1893)	—	1	—	—	95th	(1977)	15	—	—	1
54th	(1895)	—	1	—	—	96th	(1979)	15	—	—	—
55th	(1897)	—	1	—	—	97th	(1981)	17	—	—	—
56th	(1899)[a]	—	1	—	—	98th	(1983)	20	—	—	—
71st	(1929)	—	1	—	—	99th	(1985)	20	—	—	—
72d	(1931)	—	1	—	—	100th	(1987)	22	—	—	—
73d	(1933)	—	1	—	—	101st	(1989)	23	—	—	—
74th	(1935)	1	—	—	—	102d	(1991)	25	1	—	—
75th	(1937)	1	—	—	—	103d	(1993)	38	1	1	—
76th	(1939)	1	—	—	—	104th	(1995)	37	2	1	—
77th	(1941)	1	—	—	—	105th	(1997)	36	1	1	—
78th	(1943)	1	—	—	—	106th	(1999)	36	1	—	—
79th	(1945)	2	—	—	—	107th	(2001)	36	1	—	—
80th	(1947)	2	—	—	—	108th	(2003)	37	—	—	—
81st	(1949)	2	—	—	—	109th	(2005)	40	—	1	—
82d	(1951)	2	—	—	—	110th	(2007)	40	—	1	—
						111th	(2009)	39	–	1	–
						112th	(2011)	40	2	–	–

Sources: *Black Americans in Congress,* 1870–1977, H.Doc. 95258, 95th Cong., 1st sess., 1977; *Congressional Quarterly Almanac,* various years; *Guide to U.S. Elections,* 6th ed. (Washington, D.C.: CQ Press, 2010), 916. Note: Does not include nonvoting delegates. Figures represent seats held at the beginning of a Congress. Senate figures for the 111th Congress were as of Jan. 15, 2009. President-elect Barack Obama of Illinois resigned his seat in November 2008. African-American Roland W. Burris assumed the seat on Jan. 15, 2009.

a. After the Fifty-sixth Congress, there were no black members in either the House or Senate until the Seventy-first Congress.

HISPANIC AMERICANS IN CONGRESS, 45TH–112TH CONGRESSES, 1877–2011

		House		Senate				House		Senate	
Congress		D	R	D	R	Congress		D	R	D	R
45th	(1877)	—	1	—	—	78th	(1943)	1	—	1	—
46th	(1879)	—	1	—	—	79th	(1945)	1	—	1	—
47th	(1881)	—	1	—	—	80th	(1947)	1	—	1	—
48th	(1883)	—	—	—	—	81st	(1949)	1	—	1	—
49th	(1885)	—	—	—	—	82nd	(1951)	1	—	1	—
50th	(1887)	—	—	—	—	83nd	(1953)	1	—	1	—
51st	(1889)			—	—	84th	(1955)	1	—	1	—
52d	(1891)	—	—	—	—	85th	(1957)	1	—	1	—
53d	(1893)	—	—	—	—	86th	(1959)	1	—	1	—
54th	(1895)	—	—	—	—	87th	(1961)	2	—	1	—
55th	(1897)	—	—	—	—	88th	(1963)	3	—	1	—
56th	(1899)	—	—	—	—	89th	(1965)	3	—	1	—
57th	(1901)	—	—	—	—	90th	(1967)	3	—	1	—
58th	(1903)	—	—	—	—	91st	(1969)	3	1	1	—
59th	(1905)	—	—	—	—	9n2d	(1971)	4	1	1	—
60th	(1907)	—	—	—	—	93nd	(1973)	4	1	1	—
61st	(1909)	—	—	—	—	94th	(1975)	4	1	1	—
62d	(1911)	—	—	—	—	95th	(1977)	4	1	—	—
63d	(1913)	1	—	—	—	96th	(1979)	5	1	—	—
64th	(1915)	1	1	—	—	97th	(1981)	6	1	—	—
65th	(1917)	1	—	—	—	98th	(1983)	9	1	—	—
66th	(1919)	1	1	—	—	99th	(1985)	10	1	—	—
67th	(1921)	1	1	—	—	100th	(1987)	10	1	—	—
68th	(1923)	1	—	—	—	101st	(1989)	9	1	—	—
69th	(1925)	1	—	—	—	102nd	(1991)	10	1	—	—
70th	(1927)	1	—	—	1	103nd	(1993)	14	3	—	—
71st	(1929)	—	—	—	—	104th	(1995)	14	3	—	—
72d	(1931)	2	—	—	—	105th	(1997)	14	3	—	—
73d	(1933)	2	—	—	—	106th	(1999)	15	3	—	—
74th	(1935)	1	—	1	—	107th	(2001)	16	1	—	—
75th	(1937)	1	—	1	—	108th	(2003)	19	4	—	—
76th	(1939)	1	—	1	—	109th	(2005)	19	4	1	1
77th	(1941)	—	—	1	—	110th	(2007)	20	3	2	1
						111th	(2009)	22	3	2	1
						112th	(2011)	17	7	1	1

Sources: *Biographical Directory of the United States Congress 1774–1989*; *Congressional Quarterly Almanac*, various years; *CQ Weekly*, January 9, 1999, 62; various issues of *CQ Weekly*. Stanley, Harold W., and Richard G. Niemi. *Vital Statistics on American Politics, 2011–2012*. Washington, D.C.: CQ Press, 2011.

Note: Statistics do not include delegates or commissioners. Since the 17th Congress, there have been three Democrats and five Republicans who have served in the House of Representatives as delegates for territories that would later become states. In addition, Joseph Marion Hernandez (W-Fla.) served as a delegate to the U.S. House of Representatives during the 17th Congress. There have also been twenty-one Hispanic Americans who have served as delegates to the House of Representatives representing the territories of Puerto Rico, Guam, and the Virgin Islands since 1901.

WOMEN IN CONGRESS, 45TH—112TH CONGRESSES, 1877–2011

Congress		House		Senate	
		D	R	D	R
45th	(1877)	—	1	—	—
65th	(1917)	—	1	—	—
66th	(1919)	—	—	—	—
67th	(1921)	—	2	—	1
68th	(1923)	—	1	—	—
69th	(1925)	1	2	—	—
70th	(1927)	2	3	—	—
71st	(1929)	4	5	—	—
72d	(1931)	4	3	1	—
73d	(1933)	4	3	1	—
74th	(1935)	4	2	2	—
75th	(1937)	4	1	2	—
76th	(1939)	4	4	1	—
77th	(1941)	4	5	1	—
78th	(1943)	2	6	1	—
79th	(1945)	6	5	—	—
80th	(1947)	3	4	—	1
81st	(1949)	5	4	—	1
82d	(1951)	4	6	—	1
83d	(1953)	5	7	—	1b
84th	(1955)	10	7	—	1
85th	(1957)	9	6	—	1
86th	(1959)	9	8	—	1
87th	(1961)	11	7	1	1
88th	(1963)	6	6	1	1
89th	(1965)	7	4	1	1
90th	(1967)	5	5	—	1
91st	(1969)	6	4	—	1
92nd	(1971)	10	3	—	1
93nd	(1973)	14	2	1	—
94th	(1975)	14	5	—	—
95th	(1977)	13	5	—	—
96th	(1979)	11	5	1	1
97th	(1981)	10	9	—	2
98th	(1983)	13	9	—	2
99th	(1985)	13	9	—	2
100th	(1987)	12a	11	1	1
101st	(1989)	14	11	1	1
102nd	(1991)	19	9	1	1
103nd	(1993)	36	12	5	1
104th	(1995)	31	17	5	3b
105th	(1997)	35	16	6	3
106th	(1999)	39	17	6	3
107th	(2001)	41	18	10	3
108th	(2003)	38	21	9	5
109th	(2005)	43	25	9	5
110th	(2007)	50	21	11	5
111th	(2009)	57	17	13	4
112th	(2011)	48	24	12	5

Sources: *Women in Congress*, H. Rept. 941732, 94th Cong., 2nd sess., 1976; *Congressional Quarterly Almanac*, various years; *Congressional Quarterly Weekly Report*, November 10, 1984, 2921; November 8, 1986, 2863; November 12, 1988, 3294; November 10, 1990, 3836; November 7, 1992, Supplement, 8; November 12, 1994, Supplement, 10; January 4, 1997, 28; January 9, 1999, 62; various issues of *CQ Weekly*; Center for American Women in Politics, Rutgers University, New Brunswick, New Jersey. http://womenincongress.house.gov/historical-data/representatives-senators-by-congress.html?congress=112

Note: Includes only women who were sworn in as members and served more than one day. Statistics do not include delegates or commissioners.

a. Includes the late Sala Burton, who died after being sworn into the 100th Congress, and who was replaced by another Democratic woman, Nancy Pelosi.

b. Sheila Frahm (R-Kan.) was appointed to fill the vacancy left by Sen. Robert Dole (R-Kan.) bringing the total to four Republican female senators. Frahm ran for the open Senate seat but lost in the Kansas Republican primary.

SENATE VOTES CAST BY VICE PRESIDENTS

Following is a list of the number of votes cast by each vice president through September 24, 2011.

Period	Vice President	Votes Cast	Period	Vice President	Votes Cast
1789–1797	John Adams	29	1901	Theodore Roosevelt	0
1797–1801	Thomas Jefferson	3	1905–1909	Charles W. Fairbanks	0
1801–1805	Aaron Burr	3	1909–1912	James S. Sherman	4
1805–1812	George Clinton	12	1913–1921	Thomas R. Marshall	8
1813–1814	Elbridge Gerry	6	1921–1923	Calvin Coolidge	0
1817–1825	Daniel D. Tompkins	3	1925–1929	Charles G. Dawes	2
1825–1832	John C. Calhoun	28	1929–1933	Charles Curtis	3
1833–1837	Martin Van Buren	4	1933–1941	John N. Garner	3
1837–1841	Richard M. Johnson	17	1941–1945	Henry A. Wallace	4
1841	John Tyler	0	1945	Harry S. Truman	1
1845–1849	George M. Dallas	19	1949–1953	Alben W. Barkley	8
1849–1850	Millard Fillmore	3	1953–1961	Richard M. Nixon	8
1853	William R. King	0	1961–1963	Lyndon B. Johnson	0
1857–1861	John C. Breckinridge	9	1965–1969	Hubert H. Humphrey	4
1861–1865	Hannibal Hamlin	7	1969–1973	Spiro T. Agnew	2
1865	Andrew Johnson	0	1973–1974	Gerald R. Ford	0
1869–1873	Schuyler Colfax	17	1974–1977	Nelson A. Rockefeller	0
1873–1875	Henry Wilson	1	1977–1981	Walter F. Mondale	1
1877–1881	William A. Wheeler	6	1981–1989	George Bush	7
1881	Chester A. Arthur	3	1989–1993	Dan Quayle	0
1885	Thomas A. Hendricks	0	1993–2001	Al Gore	4
1889–1893	Levi P. Morton	4	2001–2009	Richard B. Cheney	8
1893–1897	Adlai E. Stevenson	2	2009–	Joseph R. Biden Jr.	0
1897–1899	Garret A. Hobart	1			Total 244

Source: Senate Historical Office.

STATE GOVERNMENT

State	Governor	Name of Lawmaking Body	Total House	Dem.	Rep.	Other	Total Senate	Dem.	Rep.	Other
Alabama	Robert Bentley (R)	Legislature	105	40	65		35	12	22	1
Alaska	Sean Parnell (R)	Legislature	40	18	22		20	10	10	
Arizona	Jan Brewer (R)	Legislature	60	20	40		30	9	21	
Arkansas	Mike Beebe (D)	General Assembly	100	55	44		35	25	15	
California	Jerry Brown (D)	Legislature	80	52	28		40	25	15	
Colorado	John Hickenlooper (D)	General Assembly	65	32	33		35	20	15	
Connecticut	Dan Malloy (D)	General Assembly	151	100	51		36	22	14	
Delaware	Jack Markell (D)	General Assembly	41	26	15		21	14	7	
Florida	Rick Scott (R)	Legislature	120	39	81		40	12	28	
Georgia	Nathan Deal (R)	General Assembly	180	63	115	1, 1v	56	20	36	
Hawaii	Neal Abercombie (D)	Legislature	51	43	8		25	24	1	
Idaho	C.L. "Butch" Otter (R)	Legislature	70	13	57		35	7	28	
Illinois	Pat Quinn (D)	General Assembly	118	64	54		59	35	24	
Indiana	Mitch Daniels (R)	General Assembly	100	40	60		50	13	37	
Iowa	Terry Branstad (R)	General Assembly	100	40	60		50	26	14	
Kansas	Sam Brownback (R)	Legislature	125	33	92		40	8	32	
Kentucky	Steve Beshear (D)	General Assembly	100	59	41		38	15	22	1
Louisiana	Bobby Jindal (R)	Legislature	105	45	58	2	39	15	24	
Maine	Paul LePage (R)	Legislature	151	72	78	1	35	14	20	1
Maryland	Martin O'Malley (D)	General Assembly	141	98	43		47	35	12	
Massachusetts	Deval Patrick (D)	General Court	160	126	32	2v	40	35	4	1v
Michigan	Rick Snyder (R)	Legislature	110	46	62	2v	38	12	26	
Minnesota	Mark Dayton (R)	Legislature	134	62	72		67	30	37	
Mississippi	Phil Bryant (R)	Legislature	122	58	64		52	21	31	
Missouri	Jay Nixon (D)	General Assembly	163	56	106	1	34	8	26	
Montana	Brian Schweitzer (D)	Legislative Assembly	100	32	68		50	22	28	
Nebraska	Dave Heineman (R)	Legislature	n/a	n/a	n/a	n/a	49	n/a	n/a	49
Nevada	Brian Sandoval (R)	Legislature	42	26	16		21	11	10	
New Hampshire	John Lynch (D)	General Court	400	104	294	2v	24	5	19	
New Jersey	Christ Christie (R)	Legislature	80	48	30	2v	40	24	16	
New Mexico	Susana Martinez (R)	Legislature	70	36	33	1	42	27	15	
New York	Andrew Cuomo (D)	Legislature	150	99	51		62	30	32	
North Carolina	Beverly Perdue (D)	General Assembly	120	52	67	1	50	19	31	
North Dakota	Jack Dalrymple (R)	Legislative Assembly	94	25	69		47	12	35	
Ohio	John Kasich (R)	General Assembly	99	40	59		33	10	23	
Oklahoma	Mary Fallin (R)	Legislature	101	31	69	1v	48	15	31	2v
Oregon	John Kitzhaber (D)	Legislative Assembly	60	30	30		30	16	14	
Pennsylvania	Tom Corbett (R)	General Assembly	203	91	112		50	20	30	
Rhode Island	Lincoln Chafee (I)	General Assembly	75	65	10		38	29	8	1
South Carolina	Nikki Haley (R)	General Assembly	124	48	75	1v	46	19	27	
South Dakota	Dennis Daugaard (R)	Legislature	70	19	50	1	35	5	30	

(Continued)

STATE GOVERNMENT *(Continued)*

State	Governor	Name of Lawmaking Body	Total House	Dem.	Rep.	Other	Total Senate	Dem.	Rep.	Other
Tennessee	Bill Haslam (R)	General Assembly	99	34	64	1	33	13	20	
Texas	Rick Perry (R)	Legislature	150	49	101		31	12	19	
Utah	Gary Herbert (R)	Legislature	75	17	58		29	7	22	
Vermont	Peter Shumlin (D)	General Assembly	150	95	48	8	30	22	8	
Virginia	Robert F. McDonnell (R)	General Assembly	100	32	67	1	40	20	20	
Washington	Christine Gregoire (D)	Legislature	98	56	42		49	27	22	
West Virginia	Earl Ray Tomblin (D)	Legislature	100	65	35		34	28	6	
Wisconsin	Scott Walker (R)	Legislature	99	39	59	1	33	16	17	
Wyoming	Matthew Mead (R)	Legislature	60	10	50		30	4	26	

As of January 12, 2012. Nebraska has a unicameral legislature with members elected on a nonpartisan basis. V indicates a vacancy.

Sources: National Council of State Legislatures.

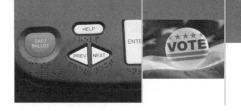

Selected Bibliography

Abramson, Paul R., John H. Aldrich, and David W. Rohde. *Change and Continuity in the 2008 and 2010 Elections.* Washington, D.C.: CQ Press, 2011.

———.Change and Continuity in the 1996 and 1998 Elections. Washington, D.C.: CQ Press, 1999.

———. Change and Continuity in the 2004 and 2006 Elections. Washington, D.C.: CQ Press, 2007.

Alexander, Herbert E. *Financing Politics: Money, Elections, and Political Reform,* 4th ed. Washington, D.C.: CQ Press, 1992.

Almanac of American Politics. Washington, D.C.: National Journal, 1972.

Asher, Herbert. *Polling and the Public: What Every Citizen Should Know,* 8th ed. Washington, D.C.: CQ Press, 2011.

Baker, Richard A. *The Senate of the United States: A Bicentennial History.* Malamar, Fla.: Krieger Publishing, 1988.

Bendavid, Naftali. *The Thumpin': How Rahm Emanuel and the Democrats Learned to Be Ruthless and Ended the Republican Revolution.* New York: Doubleday, 2007.

Benjamin, Gerald, and Michael J. Malbin. *Limiting Legislative Terms.* Washington, D.C.: CQ Press, 1992.

Bennett, Robert W. *Taming the Electoral College.* Stanford, Calif.: Stanford Law and Politics, 2006.

Bogdanor, Vernon, ed. *The Blackwell Encyclopedia of Political Science.* Cambridge, Mass.: Blackwell Publishers, 1991.

Boller, Paul F. Jr. *Presidential Campaigns,* rev. ed. New York: Oxford University Press, 1996.

Book of the States. Lexington, Ky.: Council of State Governments, 1935–.

Broder, David S. *Democracy Derailed: Initiative Campaigns and the Power of Money.* New York: Harcourt, 2000.

Bruni, Frank. *Ambling into History: The Unlikely Odyssey of George W. Bush.* New York: HarperCollins, 2002.

Campbell, Angus, Philip E. Converse, Warren E. Miller, and Donald E. Stokes. *The American Voter.* New York: Wiley, 1960.

Cappella, Joseph A., and Kathleen Hall Jamieson. *The Spiral of Cynicism: The Press and the Public Good.* New York: Oxford University Press, 1997.

Cigler, Allan J., and Burdett A. Loomis. *Interest Group Politics,* 8th ed. Washington, D.C.: CQ Press, 2011.

Cohen, Marty. *The Party Decides: Presidential Nominations before and after Reform.* Chicago: Chicago University Press, 2008.

Congress and the Nation, vols. 1–12 1945–2008. Washington, D.C.: Congressional Quarterly, 1969–2010.

Congressional Quarterly Almanac, yearly editions. Washington, D.C.: Congressional Quarterly.

Cook, Rhodes. *The Presidential Nominating Process: A Place for Us?* Lanham, Md.: Rowman and Littlefield, 2004.

Currie, James T. *The United States House of Representatives.* Malabar, Fla.: Krieger Publishing, 1988.

Davidson, Roger H., Walter J. Oleszek, and Frances E. Lee. *Congress and Its Members.* 13th ed. Washington, D.C.: CQ Press, 2011.

Edsall, Thomas Byrne. *The New Politics of Inequality.* New York: W. W. Norton, 1984.

Fenno, Richard F. *Home Style: House Members in Their Districts.* Boston: Little, Brown, 1978.

Fensenthal, Dan. *Topics in Social Choice: Sophisticated Voting, Efficacy and Proportional Representation.* New York: Praeger, 1990.

Finkelman, Paul, and Peter Wallenstein, eds. *Encyclopedia of American Political History.* Washington, D.C.: CQ Press, 2001.

Flanigan, William H., and Nancy H. Zingale. *Political Behavior of the American Electorate,* 12th ed. Washington, D.C.: CQ Press, 2011.

Gillespie, J. David. *Politics at the Periphery: Third Parties in Two-Party America.* Columbia: University of South Carolina Press, 1993.

Graber, Doris A. *Mass Media and American Politics,* 8th ed. Washington, D.C.: CQ Press, 2009.

Graber, Doris A. *Media Power in Politics,* 6th ed. Washington, D.C., 2010.

Graber, Doris A., Denis McQuail, and Pippa Norris, eds. *The Politics of News, The News of Politics,* 2nd ed. Washington, D.C.: CQ Press, 2007.

Graham, Gene. *One Man, One Vote: Baker v. Carr and the American Levellers.* Boston: Atlantic Monthly Press, 1972.

Guber, Susan. *How to Win Your 1st Election.* Boca Raton, Fla.: St. Lucie Press, 1997.

Guide to U.S. Elections, 6th ed. Washington, D.C.: CQ Press, 2010.

Havel, James T. *U.S. Presidential Candidates and the Elections: A Biographical and Historical Guide,* 2 vols. New York: Macmillan Library Reference USA, 1996.

Herrnson, Paul S. *Congressional Elections: Campaigning at Home and in Washington,* 6th ed. Washington, D.C.: CQ Press, 2011.

Jacobson, Gary C. *The Politics of Congressional Elections,* 7th ed. New York: Pearson/Longman, 2009.

Jamieson, Kathleen Hall. *Packaging the Presidency,* 3rd ed. New York: Oxford University Press, 1996.

Kernell, Samuel, Gary C. Jacobson, Thad Kousser, and Rene B. Van Vechten. *The Logic of American Politics,* 5th ed. Washington, D.C.: CQ Press, 2011.

King, Anthony Stephen. *Running Scared: Why America's Politicians Campaign Too Much and Govern Too Little.* New York: Free Press, 1997.

Kruschke, Earl R. *Encyclopedia of Third Parties in the United States.* Santa Barbara, Calif.: ABCCLIO, 1991.

Kurian, George T. *World Encyclopedia of Parliaments and Legislatures.* Washington, D.C.: CQ Press, 1997.

Lewis, Charles, and the Center for Public Integrity. *The Buying of the President 2004.* New York: Perennial, 2004.

Lipset, Seymour Martin. *Political Man: The Social Bases of Politics,* expanded ed. Baltimore: Johns Hopkins University Press, 1981.

Maddex, Robert L., Jr. *Illustrated Dictionary of Constitutional Concepts.* Washington, D.C.: CQ Press, 1996.

———. *Constitutions of the World,* 3rd ed. Washington, D.C.: CQ Press, 2007.

Maisel, L. Sandy. *American Political Parties and Elections: A Very Short Introduction.* New York: Oxford University Press, 2007.

McGillivray, Alice V., Richard M. Scammon, and Rhodes Cook. *America at the Polls, 1920–1956* and *1960–2004: A Handbook of American Presidential Election Statistics,* 2 vols. Washington, D.C.: CQ Press, 2005.

Mintz, Morton, and Jerry S. Cohen. *America, Inc.: Who Owns and Operates the United States.* New York: Dial Press, 1971.

Moore, David W. *The Super Pollsters: How They Measure and Manipulate Public Opinion in America.* New York: Four Walls Eight Windows, 1992.

Moore, John L. *Speaking of Washington: Facts, Firsts, and Folklore.* Washington, D.C.: CQ Press, 1993.

National Party Conventions, 1831–2008. Washington, D.C.: CQ Press, 2009

Nelson, Michael. *The Elections of 2008.* Washington, D.C.: CQ Press, 2009.

———. *The Elections of 2004.* Washington, D.C.: CQ Press, 2005.

Oleszek, Walter J. *Congressional Procedures and the Policy Process,* 8th ed. Washington, D.C.: CQ Press, 2010.

Percy, Herma. *Will Your Vote Count? Fixing America's Broken Electoral System*. Westport, Conn.: Praeger, 2009.

Plano, Jack C., and Milton Greenberg. *The American Political Dictionary*, 8th ed. New York: Holt, Rinehart and Winston, 1989.

Politics in America 2012. Washington, D.C.: CQ Press, 2011.

Ragsdale, Lyn. *Vital Statistics on the Presidency*, 3rd ed. Washington, D.C.: CQ Press, 2008.

Rapoport, Ronald B., and Walter J. Stone. *Three's a Crowd: The Dynamic of Third Parties, Ross Perot, and the Republican Revolution*. Ann Arbor: University of Michigan Press, 2005.

Rose, Richard. *International Encyclopedia of Elections*. Washington, D.C.: CQ Press, 2000.

Rosenstone, Steven J., Roy L. Behr, and Edward H. Lazarus. *Third Parties in America: Citizen Response to Major Party Failure*, rev. ed. Princeton, N.J.: Princeton University Press, 1995.

Sabato, Larry. *Goodbye to Goodtime Charlie: The American Governorship Transformed*, 2nd ed. Washington, D.C.: CQ Press, 1983.

———. *The Sixth Year Itch: The Rise and Fall of the George W. Bush Presidency*. New York: Longman, 2007.

Safire, William. *Safire's New Political Dictionary: The Definitive Guide to the New Language of Politics*. New York: Random House, 1993.

Scammon, Richard M. *America Votes: A Handbook of Contemporary Election Statistics*. Vols. 1 and 2. New York: Macmillan, 1956–1958. *American Votes*. Vols. 3–5. Pittsburgh: University of Pittsburgh, 1959–1964. *American Votes*. Vols. 6–11. Washington, D.C.: CQ Press, 1966–1975.

Scammon, Richard M., and Alice V. McGillivray. *America Votes*. Vols. 12–21. Washington, D.C.: CQ Press, 1977–1995.

Scammon, Richard M., Alice V. McGillivray, and Rhodes Cook. *America Votes*. Vols. 22–28. Washington, D.C.: CQ Press, 1996–2011.

Shafritz, Jay M. *The Dorsey Dictionary of American Government and Politics*. Chicago: Dorsey Press, 1988.

Smith, Kevin B. *State and Local Government, 2007–2008*. Washington, D.C.: CQ Press, 2007.

Southwick, Leslie H. *Presidential Also-Rans and Running Mates, 1788–1980*. Jefferson, N.C.: McFarland, 1984.

Stanley, Harold W., and Richard G. Niemi. *Vital Statistics on American Politics, 2011-2012*. Washington, D.C.: CQ Press, 2011.

Zelden, Charles L. *The Supreme Court and Elections*. Washington, D.C.: CQ Press, 2009.

Zernike, Kate. *Boiling Mad: Inside Tea Party America*. New York: Times Books, 2010.

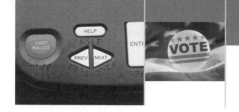

Index

Note to index: Page numbers in italics indicate illustrations and photos. Page numbers in bold indicate complete articles on the subject.

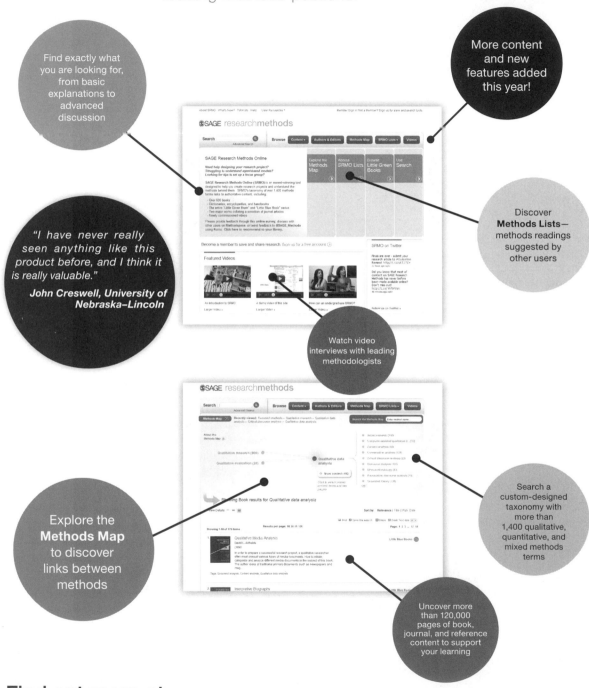

SSAGE research**methods**

The essential online tool for researchers from the world's leading methods publisher

Find exactly what you are looking for, from basic explanations to advanced discussion

More content and new features added this year!

"I have never really seen anything like this product before, and I think it is really valuable."

John Creswell, University of Nebraska–Lincoln

Discover **Methods Lists—** methods readings suggested by other users

Watch video interviews with leading methodologists

Explore the **Methods Map** to discover links between methods

Search a custom-designed taxonomy with more than 1,400 qualitative, quantitative, and mixed methods terms

Uncover more than 120,000 pages of book, journal, and reference content to support your learning

Find out more at
www.sageresearchmethods.com